A Guide to Reviewing
History of the United States
Volume 2   Civil War to the Present

HISTORY OF THE UNITED STATES (Volume Two) provides an in-depth examination of American history from the Civil War to the present together with a review of the nation's beginnings. The textbook's clear organization and vivid narrative help students develop a strong understanding of American history and their place in it.

The following list of features is a brief guide to **HISTORY OF THE UNITED STATES (Volume Two).** Page references indicate an example of each feature.

★ Each of the 27 **Chapters** opens with a representative photograph or piece of art (page 2) and a caption that creates interest in the broad themes of the chapter. Each chapter is divided into clearly numbered **Sections** (page 3), which break the narrative into manageable lessons.

★ The **Section Focus** (page 3) introduces the essential information covered in each section. This includes:

  ☆ **Key Terms:** A list of important terms presented in the section.
  ☆ **Main Idea:** A concise statement of the main idea of the section.
  ☆ **Objectives:** Pre-reading questions regarding the content of the section.

★ **Section Reviews** (page 7) and **Chapter Reviews** (page 30) test students' learning and reinforce key concepts.

★ **Skill Development** is enhanced through the use of **Critical Thinking** questions, which accompany every map and chart and appear in every Section and Chapter Review. The Skill Review section (pages 825–839) helps students develop basic study skills and critical thinking skills.

★ The **Civics Handbook** (pages 685–718) contains information on the American system of government and our role in it—information students will need to exercise the rights and responsibilities of an American citizen.

★ A wide variety of **Special Features** enrich the text and strengthen historical connections. The **Geographic Perspective** (page 74) reinforces the link between geography and history. **Historians' Corner** (page 81) draws students into the interpretations of key issues in American history. **American Mosaic** (page 82) provides a multicultural perspective on American History. **American Literature** (pages 769–824) provides readings from outstanding fiction of each period covered.

★ The **Reference Section** (pages 840–891) contains an Atlas, a Gazetteer, an extensive Glossary, and an Index. **Primary Sources** (pages 719–765) include the complete texts of the Declaration of Independence, the Constitution and other **Historical Documents.**

★ The **Teacher's Annotated Edition** offers creative suggestions for classroom activities, provides useful background information, and guides the teacher in implementing the many support materials offered with **HISTORY OF THE UNITED STATES (Volume Two).** The convenient format includes the teaching commentary "wrapped around" reproduced student pages, as well as teacher planning pages inserted before each chapter.

History of The United States

Volume 2   Civil War to the Present

Thomas V. DiBacco   **Lorna C. Mason**   **Christian G. Appy**

HOUGHTON MIFFLIN COMPANY ▪ BOSTON

Atlanta   Dallas   Geneva, Illinois   Palo Alto   Princeton   Toronto

★ CONTENTS ★

Chapter Planner material, to assist teachers in lesson preparation, is found on the pages immediately preceding a given chapter. To find the Chapter Planner pages for Chapter 1, for example, see pages 1A-1B.

Printed in the U.S.A.

Student's Edition ISBN: 0-395-58290–3
Teacher's Edition–TX ISBN: 0-395-58292–X
Teacher's Edition–Nat. ISBN: 0-395-58291–1

CDEFGHIJ-VH-99876543

Emphasizing both the broad themes of our history as a nation and the richness of our heritage as a people, **History of the United States** tells the absorbing story of our nation's past . . . and present.

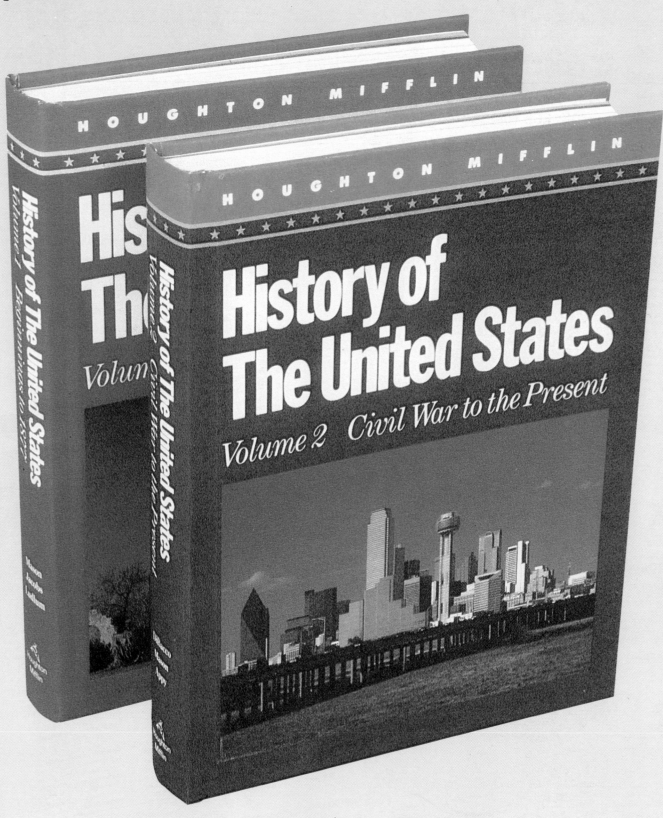

History of the United States tells the *whole* story, integrating multicultural perspectives and geographic, constitutional, religious, and economic themes. And it presents both sides—or all sides—of the story, engaging students in historical, ethical, and political controversies that have changed the course of history.

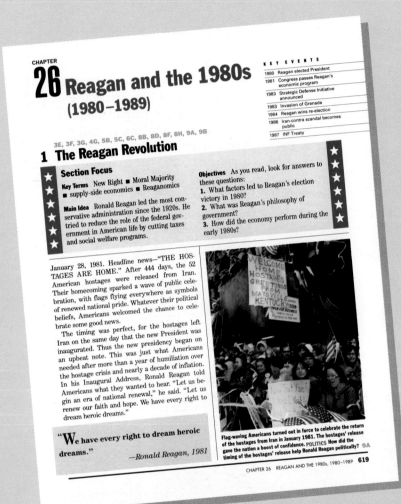

The **Section Focus** previews the main idea for each section, enabling students to grasp recurring themes in the study of American history.

Geographic Perspective pages in each unit highlight geographic themes to help students appreciate the connection between geography and historic events.

Compelling, well-told narrative, vivid in detail, brings to life for students the people, events, and ideas that have shaped the present.

Historians' Corner draws students into the interpretation of controversial events by comparing and contrasting the views of leading historians.

American Literature excerpts for each chapter enrich the study of history by exposing students to outstanding works of fiction both *of* and *about* the period.

Civics Handbook contains information on the American system of government and our role in it—information students will need to exercise the rights and responsibilities of an American citizen.

American Mosaic introduces students to people of all cultural and ethnic backgrounds who made their mark on this nation.

HISTORIANS' CORNER

Perspectives on Pluralism

Many historians agree that since the 1960s, Americans have become more conscious of their distinctive racial, cultural, and ethnic backgrounds. This awareness, along with increased immigration, has raised new questions about diversity and equality, and about ethnic and racial patterns in American history. These excerpts present some of these points of view about our pluralistic society.

Ronald Takaki

Study of the history of citizenship and suffrage disclosed a racial and exclusionist pattern. For 162 years the Naturalization Law, while allowing various European or "white" ethnic groups to enter the United States and acquire citizenship, specifically denied citizenship to other groups on a racial basis. . . .

But what happened to nonwhite citizens? Did they have "equal" rights, particularly the right of suffrage? Citizenship did not necessarily carry this right, for states determined the requirements for voting. A review of this history reveals a basic political inequality between white citizens and nonwhite citizens. . . .

This difference . . . may . . . be seen in the experiences of Native Americans. While the Treaty of Guadalupe-Hidalgo had offered United States citizenship to Mexicans living within its acquired territories, the 1849 Constitution of California granted the right of suffrage only to every "white" male citizen of the United States and only to every "white" male citizen of Mexico who had elected

A color line, in short, had been drawn for the granting of suffrage to American citizens in California. Native Americans were also proscribed politically in other states.

From Ronald Takaki, "Reflections on Racial Patterns in America: An Historical Perspective" from *Ethnicity and Public Policy*, edited by Winston A. Van Horne and Thomas V. Tonnesson. Copyright © 1982 by the Board of Regents, University of Wisconsin System. Reprinted by permission of the University of Wisconsin System Ethnic Studies Coordinating Committee.

John Hope Franklin

It has become fashionable in the past three or four decades for various hyphenated Americans [white ethnic groups, such as Irish-Americans] to emphasize the distinctive aspects of their respective cultures—as though these groups have been so successfully and securely assimilated that they can afford to look back to their origins and pay homage to their languages, histories, and the special features of their culture. This new way of looking at themselves and their past has become a luxury no less important than their expensive homes and automobiles.

These same decades witnessed a

Americans, black Americans, Puerto Ricans, and Mexican Americans. It was as though this was *not* the land of room enough and that the assimilation of the others had been accomplished at their expense. These cries of anguish and these demands for attention to their problems serve as a reminder that the very term *assimilability* is one that suggests there are problems that lie outside its scope. These are the problems of those who have not been assimilated.

From John Hope Franklin, "The Land of Room Enough." Reprinted by permission of *Daedalus*, Journal of the American Academy of Arts and Sciences, Spring, 1981, Cambridge, Massachusetts.

Critical Thinking

1. According to both these historians, what groups have received unequal treatment in American society?

2. What assumptions about the acceptance of new groups into American society does Takaki challenge?

3. What contradictory American attitudes does Takaki identify?

4. What factors, do you think,

UNIT 9: American Mosaic

★ A Multicultural Perspective ★

The population of the United States is now more diverse than ever. African Americans, Hispanic Americans, Asian Americans, and Arab Americans are among the many increasingly visible cultural groups that make up a nation of immigrants.

Philip Habib (right), the son of Lebanese grocery-store owners, grew up in Brooklyn, New York. After joining the Army in World War II, he began a long diplomatic career. Habib's greatest success came when he helped President Carter negotiate the Camp David Accords between Egypt and Israel in 1977.

A native of India, **Ved Mehta** (right) became blind from meningitis when he was three years old. He attended a school for blind children in Bombay, but in 1947 war came and Mehta's family lost their home and had to flee for their lives. Mehta traveled to the Arkansas School for the Blind in Little Rock and later attended college in California. In 1957 he published an autobiography and later joined the *New Yorker* magazine as a writer. Since then, Mehta has published many works which tell of his experiences of loss of sight, of family and country, and of the new home he found in the United States.

In 1986 **Ben Nighthorse Campbell** (left) of the North Cheyenne tribe became the eighth Native American to serve in Congress. As a representative from Colorado, Campbell worked to keep scarce water resources available. Campbell's varied interests include horse breeding and judo, for which he won an Olympic gold medal in 1964.

Cuban-born **Roberto Goizueta** (left) came to the United States in 1950 at age eighteen. After receiving a degree in chemical engineering, he went to work for the Coca Cola corporation. For the next 26 years, Goizueta climbed Coke's corporate ladder and in 1980 became the company's chairman and chief executive. Goizueta's bilingualism and Hispanic background proved to be an asset in a company that does two-thirds of its business outside the United States.

Patrick Flores (right) grew up in a family of nine children who worked alongside their parents as migrant farm laborers in South Texas. When the family settled in Pearland, Flores became involved in a fight led by a Hispanic priest to integrate the town's schools. This experience helped convince Flores to become a priest and fight for social justice. In 1970 he became the first Mexican American bishop, and was later named Archbishop of San Antonio.

Maya Ying Lin (right), a Chinese American architecture student, gained national attention after she won a contest to design a memorial to veterans of the Vietnam War. Despite controversy over the design, the Vietnam Memorial is now considered one of the most moving monuments in the nation. Lin later designed a highly regarded memorial to the civil rights movement which stands in front of the Southern Poverty Law Center in Montgomery, Alabama.

Marva Collins (left) became America's best-known teacher in the early 1980s for her work with some of the nation's least privileged students. Collins founded her own school, where she worked with children from Chicago's inner city. Chiefly through her own forceful personality, she improved their reading skills and interested them in classics of literature. According to Collins, "When I see children who are going to fail, when I see a sixteen-year-old kid who can't read . . . those things make me unhappy. I'm not really in this life to buy a lot of things for myself. I ask the children, 'If you died, what would you like the newspapers to say?'"

Luis Valdez (left) changed schools often as his family moved around California in search of farm work. One thing that remained constant was Valdez's love of theater. In the 1960s, he began writing plays whose themes included civil rights issues. Valdez organized a theater group called El Teatro Campesino that performed on college campuses and helped the cause of Cesar Chavez and the United Farm Workers. Valdez later directed *La Bamba*, a 1987 film about Mexican American rock star Ritchie Valens.

The diversity of her influences is one factor that has helped propel singer **Linda Ronstadt** (above) to the top of the music world. Her records include songs from the worlds of folk, country, rock, and gospel music. Ronstadt, who is of Mexican and German descent, grew up in a musical household. Her mother played the ukulele and her father sang Mexican folk songs. Later in her career, she returned to her roots and recorded a highly successful album of songs in Spanish, *Canciones de mi Padre* (Songs of My Father).

In the years between 1980 and 1990 almost half of all legal immigrants to the United States—45 percent—came from Asia. Latin American immigrants made up 35 percent, Europeans and Canadians were 14 percent, and Africans and others were 4 percent of the flood of 5.7 million immigrants who arrived in the decade.

History of the United States infuses the teaching of American history with excitement, flexibility, and purpose. The *Teacher's Annotated Edition* is rich with creative instructional strategies for engaging students of all abilities and learning styles, providing full teacher support just where you want it.

Chapter Planner pages, at the beginning of each chapter, present an easy-to-use guide to all supplementary teaching aids for each section, plus recommended bibliography and audiovisual materials. Essential Elements included to help teachers plan and organize their course.

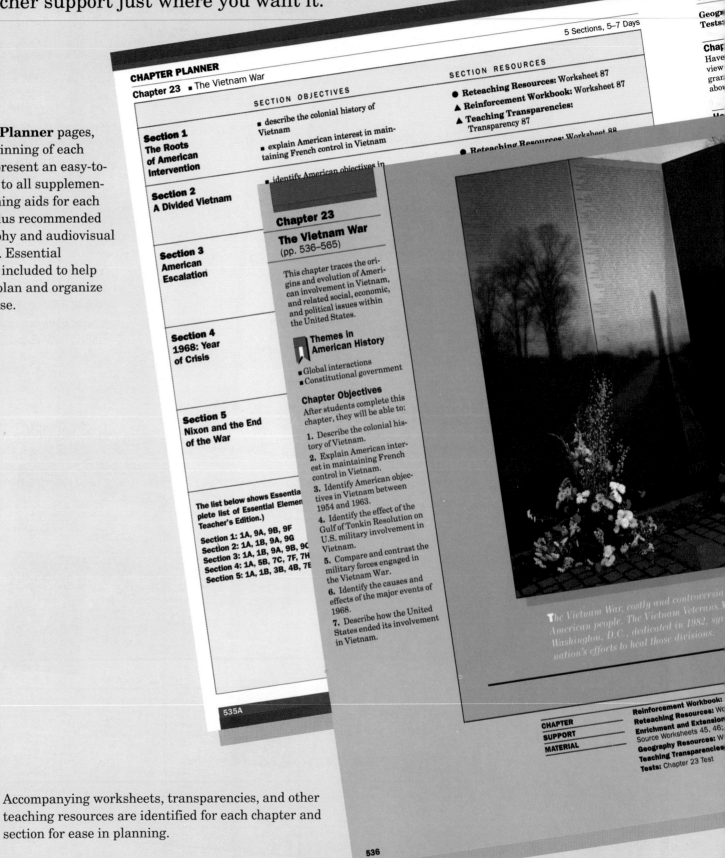

5 Sections, 5–7 Days

CHAPTER PLANNER
Chapter 23 ■ The Vietnam War

SECTION OBJECTIVES

SECTION RESOURCES

Section 1
The Roots of American Intervention

■ describe the colonial history of Vietnam
■ explain American interest in maintaining French control in Vietnam

Section 2
A Divided Vietnam

■ identify American objectives in

Section 3
American Escalation

Section 4
1968: Year of Crisis

Section 5
Nixon and the End of the War

● **Reteaching Resources:** Worksheet 87
▲ **Reinforcement Workbook:** Worksheet 87
▲ **Teaching Transparencies:** Transparency 87
● **Reteaching Resources:** Worksheet 88

The list below shows Essentia plete list of Essential Elemen Teacher's Edition.)

Section 1: 1A, 9A, 9B, 9F
Section 2: 1A, 1B, 9A, 9G
Section 3: 1A, 1B, 9A, 9B, 9C
Section 4: 1A, 5B, 7C, 7F, 7H
Section 5: 1A, 1B, 3B, 4B, 7E

535A

Chapter 23

The Vietnam War
(pp. 536–565)

This chapter traces the origins and evolution of American involvement in Vietnam, and related social, economic, and political issues within the United States.

Themes in American History

■ Global interactions
■ Constitutional government

Chapter Objectives
After students complete this chapter, they will be able to:

1. Describe the colonial history of Vietnam.
2. Explain American interest in maintaining French control in Vietnam.
3. Identify American objectives in Vietnam between 1954 and 1963.
4. Identify the effect of the Gulf of Tonkin Resolution on U.S. military involvement in Vietnam.
5. Compare and contrast the military forces engaged in the Vietnam War.
6. Identify the causes and effects of the major events of 1968.
7. Describe how the United States ended its involvement in Vietnam.

The Vietnam War, costly and controversia American people. The Vietnam Veterans Washington, D.C., dedicated in 1982, sy nation's efforts to heal those divisions.

CHAPTER SUPPORT MATERIAL

Reinforcement Workbook: Wo
Reteaching Resources: Worksh
Enrichment and Extension
Source Worksheets 45, 46;
Geography Resources: W
Teaching Transparencies:
Tests: Chapter 23 Test

536

Accompanying worksheets, transparencies, and other teaching resources are identified for each chapter and section for ease in planning.

RESOURCES

Resources: Worksheets 45, 46
...er 23 Test

...oject
...ts compile an oral history of Vietnam based on inter-
...eterans, former protesters, Southeast Asian immi-
...others involved in some way, and draw conclusions
...ar experience.

Literature

Beckham, Barry. *Runner Mack.* Howard University Press, 1984. A black baseball player, drafted into the Army, becomes involved in a plot to bomb the White House and take over the United States.

Caputo, Philip. *A Rumor of War.* Ballantine, 1986. A marine's experiences in Vietnam.

Kovic, Ron. *Born on the Fourth of July.* Pocket Books, 1984. An account of how a patriotic marine slowly becomes an antiwar activist.

Mason, Bobbie Ann. *In Country.* Harper and Row, 1985. A

CHAPTER

23 The Vietnam War

(1945–1975)

KEY EVENTS	
1954	French defeated at Dienbienphu
1954	Geneva Conference divides Vietnam
1964	Gulf of Tonkin Resolution
1968	Tet Offensive
1973	Peace agreement ends American involvement
1975	South Vietnam falls to Communists

1 The Roots of American Intervention

Section Focus

Key Terms Vietnam War ■ Vietminh

Main Idea Vietnam, which had fought for-eign domination for centuries, struggled for independence from France after World War II. The United States supported France in this conflict.

Objectives As you read, look for answers to these questions:
1. Which countries had controlled Vietnam in the past? Why?
2. What was Ho Chi Minh's vision of Vietnam?
3. What was the outcome of the struggle for independence from France?

The Eastern world, it is explodin'
Violence flarin', bullets loadin'
You're old enough to kill but not for votin'
You don't believe in war but what's that
    gun you're totin'...
And you tell me over and over and over
    again, my friend,
You don't believe we're on the eve of
    destruction.

"Eve of Destruction" was pop music's top hit of August 1965. It expressed young people's concern about the state of the world, especially the war in Vietnam and racism at home. Like the civil rights movement, the Vietnam War shook the nation to its core.

Ever since the end of World War II, American Presidents had tried to stop the rise of communism in Southeast Asia. This effort grew to major proportions in the 1960s. Eventually the United States sent 3 million soldiers to Vietnam, losing nearly 60,000 of them. It dropped three times more bomb tonnage on Vietnam than all sides had

used in World War II. American taxpayers paid $150 billion to fight the Vietnam War. Yet this enormous display of military power did not bring victory. Moreover, the war had other, dreadful costs—a divided public opinion at home, a loss of respect for elected leaders, and a tarnished image abroad.

The painful truth was that it was the United States' longest war and its first defeat. Through-out the war, the determination of their Vietnam-ese foes amazed American leaders. How, they wondered, could a country without helicopter gun-ships and jet bombers fight for so long against the most powerful nation in the world?

Had they paid more attention to Vietnamese history and geography, American policymakers might have been less surprised. For centuries the Vietnamese had struggled against foreign invaders—the Chinese, the French, and the Japa-nese. Many Vietnamese viewed the United States as yet another foreign power seeking to control their nation. They would make great sacrifices to win independence.

CHAPTER 23 THE VIETNAM WAR, 1945–1975 **537**

SUPPORTING THE SECTION

Reinforcement Workbook: Worksheet 87
Reteaching Resources: Worksheet 87
Teaching Transparencies: Transparency 87

Background In addition to Vietnam's struggle to be free of foreign domination, there were armed conflicts between regional factions. These helped forge the warrior mentality and skills of the Vietnamese.

...ts 87–91
...87–91
...es: Primary
...Worksheet 9
...45, 46
...encies 87–91

SECTION 1

The Roots of American Intervention

(pp. 537–540)

Section Objectives

■ describe the colonial histo-ry of Vietnam
■ explain American interest in maintaining French con-trol in Vietnam

Introducing the Section

Connecting with Past Learnings
What was the attitude in the country toward communism in the 1950s? How was it ex-pressed? (There was a great fear of Communist subver-sion which led to McCarthy-ism.) As students work through the lesson, ask them to note how this climate in-fluenced foreign policy deci-sions in regard to Vietnam.

Key Terms
Write each key term on a file card and give the file cards to volunteers. The volunteers should lead a class discus-sion on the definitions of the terms, until students agree on a definition they feel is most accurate. Student lead-ers should then write that definition on the back of the file card, creating a set of flash cards on Vietnam War terms. **LEP**

Focus
Have students create a time-line of Vietnamese history up until 1954. Ask them to use colors or symbols to show when different powers ruled the country. (About the year 1 to the 900s, Chinese rule; 900s to 1500s, Vietnamese rule; 1500s to 1940, arrival of European missionaries and French control; 1940–1945, Japanese control; 1941, Ho Chi Minh launches guerrilla

537

History of the United States supports *your* American history curriculum and your student needs. A wide variety of supplementary resources provides practice, reinforcement, and enrichment—and motivation.

Teacher's Resource Files

Convenient storage for *all* your supplementary materials. Contain loose-leaf blackline masters organized in chapter file folders. Worksheets for each chapter include:

- *Reinforcement Resources* to provide skill practice—both basic study skills and critical thinking skills.
- *Reteaching Resources* to redirect students through the main points of the section material.
- *Enrichment Resources* offer Primary Source Worksheets and Historians' Worksheets to enrich and extend the course for average and above-average students.

Also provided:

- *Civics Resources* in blackline format to help students become more involved in the governmental process.

The *Teacher's Resource Files* also contain *Geography Resources, Tests,* and *Teacher's Management and Planning Guide,* which are described on the following pages.

File folders help organize and store your teaching materials.

Geography Resources: Using Geographic Themes These worksheets are a valuable resource for strengthening map and geography skills and for teaching the five geographic themes.

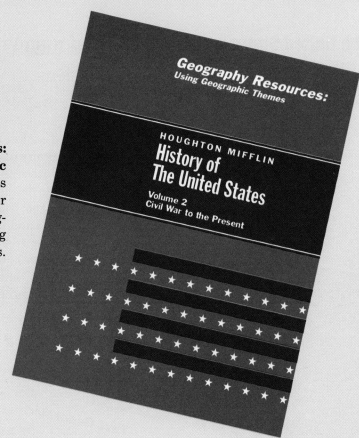

Tests A comprehensive and flexible testing package. Three versions of chapter tests, plus a quiz for each section, provide a variety of testing options.

Teaching Transparencies Colorful overhead transparencies present graphic organizers, timelines, maps, fine art—the types of visuals you can use every day. One per section.

History of the United States offers an array of unique teaching aids that recognize that your class preparation time may be in short supply.

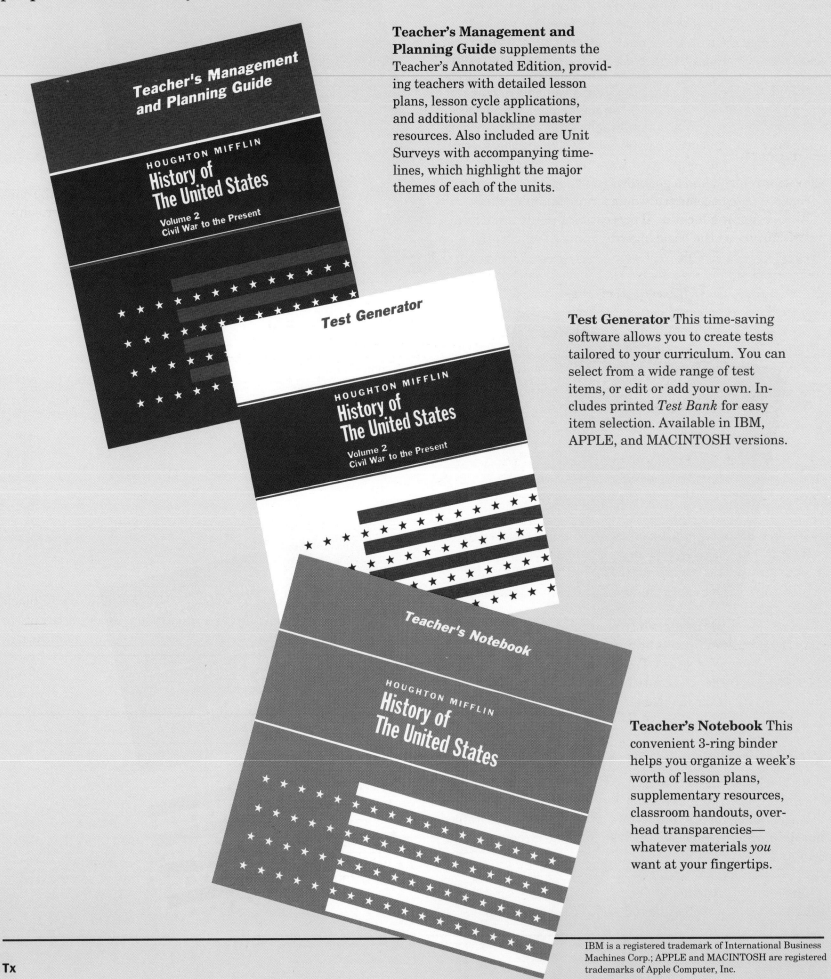

Teacher's Management and Planning Guide supplements the Teacher's Annotated Edition, providing teachers with detailed lesson plans, lesson cycle applications, and additional blackline master resources. Also included are Unit Surveys with accompanying time-lines, which highlight the major themes of each of the units.

Test Generator This time-saving software allows you to create tests tailored to your curriculum. You can select from a wide range of test items, or edit or add your own. Includes printed *Test Bank* for easy item selection. Available in IBM, APPLE, and MACINTOSH versions.

Teacher's Notebook This convenient 3-ring binder helps you organize a week's worth of lesson plans, supplementary resources, classroom handouts, over-head transparencies— whatever materials *you* want at your fingertips.

The Multicultural Challenge

Bartley L. McSwine

Bartley L. McSwine is Coordinator of Secondary Education at Chicago State University and Associate Professor in the Department of Curriculum and Instruction. He formerly served as Professor of Multicultural Methods at the University of North Texas.

Multicultural education can be defined on several levels. It is simultaneously an organic educational process, a movement for social reform, and a goal toward which a society must strive if it is to become truly democratic and pluralistic.

As an organic educational process, multicultural education views culture as the basic ingredient out of which all human society evolves. Empirical research shows that culture determines not only *what* we learn, but also *how* we learn. In other words, culture literally structures how we view our world. Our languages, eating habits, religious practices, and even thoughts are in some respects all unique to our cultural group. Multicultural education recognizes and attempts to utilize the unique cultural characteristics of each ethnic group.

Multicultural education is also a growing movement for social reform. The number of immigrants coming to this country is rising, as is the number of large city school systems made up primarily of minority group and immigrant children. Cities such as Dallas and Los Angeles, which even two decades ago had predominantly white public school systems, now serve mostly minority populations. One American in four currently defines himself or herself as Hispanic or nonwhite. By the year 2020 the number of United States residents who are Hispanic or nonwhite will have more than doubled, while the white population will have increased very little, if at all.

The increase in the nonwhite population has led to demands that more cultures and cultural values be made part of the educational process. Traditional curricula have ignored the histories and contributions of minority groups, to the detriment of the children. A growing chorus of voices is calling for inclusion of these elements.

Strategies for Multicultural Teaching

Secondary classroom teachers may want to consider the following broad strategies for the addition of ethnic content into their classroom syllabus or lesson plans. James Banks has defined four levels at which such integration may be attempted.

The Contributions Approach. Level 1, the contributions approach, involves including ethnic heroes and various aspects of their cultures in the curriculum. Individuals such as Harriet Tubman, Sitting Bull, and Cesar Chavez would be discussed along with mainstream heroes such as Abraham Lincoln, Thomas Edison, and Albert Einstein. Elements unique to each individual's cultural background—food, clothing, dance, and music, for example—would also be discussed. Banks cautions, however, that this approach leaves the basic goals and structure of the mainstream curriculum unchanged.

The Ethnic Additive Approach. Level 2, the ethnic additive approach, involves including new concepts, themes, and perspectives in the curriculum—again without changing its basic goals or structure. This is often accomplished through the addition of a book, a unit, or a course to the curriculum. Thus, for example, a book such as Toni Morrison's *Beloved* or a unit on American Indian literature may be added to a twentieth-century English class.

The Transformation Approach. Level 3, the transformation approach, alters the curriculum's basic goals and structure through the perspectives that are presented to students. It enables students to view concepts and issues from several ethnic points of view. The mainstream Anglo perspective then becomes only one perspective among many. It is neither desirable nor possible to examine every concept and issue from the point of view of every ethnic group. Rather, the goal is to enable students to view concepts and issues from more than one point of view. In studying the American Civil War, for example, students might explore the points of view of black as well as white soldiers.

The Social Action Approach. Level 4, the social action approach, attempts to make students active participants in the educational process. For example, in covering the American Civil War, students might be encouraged to look at the moral or ethical aspects of the war. Case studies on all-black regiments or on the roles of women would enable students to explore these groups' status in society as well as historical or changing attitudes, beliefs, or values. Role-playing by students might also be useful. The teacher should keep in mind, however, that at level 4 the primary goal is to have students develop skills that ensure high cognitive and affective functioning.

In summary, the multicultural challenge is the challenge of taking American education beyond a monocultural focus to the incorporation of all the ethnic and racial groups that make up the American cultural mosaic. It is the challenge of making every classroom a model of cultural pluralism, in which every child is cherished for his or her unique ability to contribute to the development of a truly democratic society.

What Educational Research Says to Classroom History Teachers

C. Frederick Risinger

C. Frederick Risinger's nearly 30 years in education have been almost evenly divided between 14 years as a classroom teacher, department head, and coach in suburban Chicago and 16 years working with a variety of projects at Indiana University's Social Studies Development Center.

Is there a best way to teach social studies? Probably not, but educational research has identified several classroom strategies and ways of dealing with students that seem to lead to improved achievement on tests and heightened interest in social studies classes.

In the past decade the Educational Resources Information Center (ERIC) system, a federally funded database, has collected data from more than 150 research studies to develop the following set of suggestions. Some were narrowly focused and included only two or three classes in the same or nearby schools. Others were meta-research—reviews of 100 or more similar studies. I have arbitrarily divided them into four categories: (1) teacher perceptions and behavior, (2) cooperative learning, (3) homework, and (4) effective use of textbooks.

Teacher Perceptions and Behavior

Perhaps the most important point to make is that *teachers really do make a difference*. In an article summarizing education in the 1980s, Diane Ravitch contends that the primary lesson learned during the "decade of educational reform" was that changing the way schools operate and improving instruction can make a difference in test scores, graduation rates, and student attitudes toward schooling and society. A review of research conducted with a group of outstanding teachers supports that view.

A national search identified history teachers considered "the best" at promoting critical analysis and higher order thinking skills. These teachers worked with all ability levels of students and used somewhat different strategies. But their views of history and its purpose in society were passed along to their students. At the beginning of the study (the beginning of a year-long course in U.S. history), the students had only a vague idea of history. At the end of the course, the students had developed ideas about history that were very close to those of the teacher. In his conclusion, the researcher suggested that teacher conceptions may be a major determinant of the transmitted curriculum, playing a significant role in content selection, emphasis, questions raised, and pedagogy employed.

Another significant factor is the teacher's perceptions of the students. Several studies reveal that teacher expectations play a determining role in evaluation. In an intensive review of research related to ability groupings in social studies and science classes, both students and teachers accepted their placement in ability groups and reacted accordingly. Teachers expected less of students placed on "low ability" groups, and the students gave them what they wanted. No research has ever supported the idea that homogeneous grouping by ability improves student achievement.

Hundreds of studies have tried to identify the factors that make a "good" or effective teacher. Research conducted in the United States and England agree on several points. Among the most frequently cited characteristic by students and administrators is "well organized." Students in England said that, in addition to being well-organized, a good teacher was one who:

(1) could clearly explain assignments and lessons;
(2) showed personal interest in students without calling too much attention to them;
(3) used a variety of instructional techniques; and
(4) made the students feel like the class was a unified group working toward a goal.

Students also preferred a teacher who could achieve a balance between being in control of the class and being "mean" and intimidating.

While the evidence clearly shows that a variety of instructional strategies is preferred, studies suggest that many secondary teachers tend to use the least effective strategies all too often. In a study of 20,000 classrooms, one researcher ranked fifteen teaching strategies as to frequency of use and effectiveness in teaching. Small group learning ranked tenth in frequency of use, yet is first in student achievement. Lecture ranked fifth in frequency of use (second among social studies teachers). But lecture is fifteenth—dead last—in student achievement and comprehension.

The most frequently used strategy among social studies teachers is class recitation—where the teacher directs questions to individual students or the entire class and waits for a response. Several studies point out that this activity can be improved by following some simple guidelines.

First, reading assignments should be accompanied by questions to guide student reading. However, the questions should not all be of the factual recall variety. Of more than 61,000 questions studied in teacher guides, textbooks, and student handouts, more than 95 percent were devoted to factual recall.

Second, questions asked in class should include those which call for interpretation and opinion. A study of elementary and secondary social studies teachers indicated that when teachers began to ask higher order questions, the change was dramatic and immediate. Student answers were longer and more thoughtful. Their responses had a higher conceptual load and were much more likely to generate discussions by other students.

Cooperative Learning

There is a clear consensus on what seems to be the most effective way to teach any subject—small cooperative group work.

A review of six cooperative learning studies suggests that the technique fosters better student achievement than individualistic methods. It also increases cross-ethnic friendships, improves students' self esteem, and leads to more positive attitudes toward other students and the school.

Teachers like cooperative learning too. A study of teachers revealed that they considered cooperation more conducive to student productivity than individual competitive work. The same study showed that students enjoyed cooperative work more and were more productive.

Teachers who use cooperative learning employ a variety of grading techniques. Of course, tests are still administered to individual students. Some teachers will give a group grade knowing that some students may have contributed more to the effort than others. But as one teacher said in a workshop, "If they learn more this way than by themselves, I've achieved my goal." Another effective grading technique is to assign a point total to the group and allow them to divide the points as they see fit. (For more on cooperative learning, see p. Txiv.)

Homework

There is no doubt that homework improves student achievement. However, *homework can be even more effective if a few guidelines are followed.*

High school students in Oregon in four subject areas including U.S. history were much more likely to spend more time on their homework if they felt it was going to be evaluated in a timely fashion. When teachers prepare written instructions and discuss homework assignments with the class, the students are much more likely to complete the assignment. Also, students need to see that the homework is an integral part of the course. Assignments that require students to think are more interesting and cause students to learn more in and out of school. Such activities include explaining what is seen or read in class, comparing, relating, experimenting with ideas, and analyzing principles.

Finally, it appears that asking students to write essay responses to higher order questions is the best type of homework to assign. Secondary history students were tested and assigned to groups. One group of students read textbook material and then wrote analytical essays. Another group answered "short answer" questions. A third group did not write at all. All three groups participated in a teacher-led class discussion about the material in the text. Several learning measures, including sections of a standardized test, were used to compare achievement. Students who wrote outperformed the group that did not write. Students assigned the analytical essays scored higher than those who wrote short answers to questions.

Effective Use of Textbooks

The evidence is clear that *there are techniques that make the textbook a more effective learning tool.* Many of the latest research studies on the use of textbooks focus on "pre-reading" or preparing students to obtain the most knowledge and understanding from an assignment.

In a New Jersey study, one group of secondary students was merely assigned a textbook chapter to read. A second group was given a brief summary of the chapter by the teacher. Then, with their textbooks open, the students were told to look at headings, pictures, maps, and diagrams. The teacher pronounced and defined new vocabulary terms that would appear in the reading and noted names of people and places in the chapter. Additionally, the teacher briefly described how the new chapter fit within the course framework. As you might expect, there was a significant positive difference in favor of the pre-reading group on an achievement test. The teacher spent no more than five minutes each day, yet the difference in achievement was tremendous. While this might appear to be a "common sense" research finding, other studies have found that many teachers simply assign the page numbers to be read by the next day. Today's textbooks are filled with pictures, maps, tables, and other graphics. Significant information is included in the captions to these features and in special features apart from the regular text. Yet, many students simply pass over these items and concentrate only on the reading. By encouraging students to read all parts of the textbook, teachers can help students get the most from it.

Using New Approaches to Teaching History

Elizabeth F. Russell

Elizabeth F. Russell, a professional writer and editor, is a former teacher at the middle and high school levels.

What is good history teaching? Good teaching brings history alive. Words on the page become real people, real problems, real events, and students want to know more about them. To make this happen, teachers need to use a wide range of methods and materials.

Variety is the essence of good teaching because students learn in many different ways. Some learn more by listening, some by looking, some by moving. As you increase the number of ways in which students take in information, you become more likely to engage all students in the process of learning.

The following suggestions will help you broaden and deepen your students' understanding of the complex fabric of American history.

Cooperative Learning

What is this latest buzzword? Cooperative learning is an old teaching method with a significant new twist. Under the old method, small groups of students were supposed to work together on a project. In practice, the most able student often did most of the work, and the others coasted. In cooperative learning situations, small groups of students also work together, but the success of the group depends on the contributions of all students. Students are grouped heterogeneously. Each group member has a different role to play and is individually accountable.

Cooperative learning is not a substitute for good teaching; nor is it a panacea for all of the problems found in the classroom. But it does offer decided benefits. Research has shown that small group learning produces high levels of student achievement. Through heterogeneous grouping, more able students help less able ones. Cooperative learning forces students to think critically and to be creative. It promotes communication among different ethnic groups within a class, and it builds participation skills, interpersonal skills, and self-esteem. It is also an excellent way to develop language skills for students learning English.

Successful cooperative learning depends on careful structuring and preparation by the teacher. Groups should be no larger than five students. At first you may want to assign students to groups, balancing achievement levels, gender, and language within each cluster. Make clear your expectations for group behavior: everyone speaks in turn, everyone listens, everyone contributes to the final product. Assign a role to each group member, such as recorder, moderator, checker, presenter, and vary the assignments so that all students will perform each role. After the first cooperative learning sessions, have students evaluate their performance and determine how to improve the way they function as a group.

As students become more familiar with cooperative learning, assign them to groups randomly so that they will have the chance to work with everyone else in the class. You can divide them into groups by having them draw assignments from a "fish bowl," handing out color cards as they enter the room, counting off, sitting by birth months, etc.

Define clearly what you want the small groups to accomplish, and specify a time limit. While students are working, circulate about the classroom to observe their interactions and help keep them on track, but do not oversee every step. Part of the value of cooperative learning for students is developing problem-solving skills. To this end, the teacher becomes a facilitator.

The kinds of tasks students can do in small groups vary greatly. One of the simplest is completing a worksheet. Each student in the group does a geography worksheet, for example, but only one is graded for the group. To get the best possible grade, group members need to share information and help each other complete the worksheet accurately. The group will receive a lower grade if some students do not complete their worksheets.

You will find an enormous range of ideas for cooperative learning in the *Teacher's Annotated Edition*.

Cooperative Learning is an activity heading under "Developing the Lesson" in the *Teacher's Annotated Edition*. A cooperative learning strategy is always identified for each section of the text. Activities include discussion questions, art projects, mock trials, role playing, and many kinds of writing.

In each activity, it is of crucial importance that each student contribute to the group's output. Success should be the product of positive interdependence. There are numerous ways to structure individual participation. Here are a few suggestions:

- Have students conduct brainstorming activities as a "round robin." Students write all their ideas on a single sheet of paper, with each student initialing his or her work.
- Have students record skits, interviews, and debates on audio- or videotape.
- Interview activities can be conducted in pairs, with students asking each other questions and reporting to the group. From this data pool, the group can put together its presentation for the class.
- Display art projects such as posters or short writing projects such as telegrams as collages of the work of all members of a group.

- For investigation projects, have students become experts on various topics by using the jigsaw technique. Assign students to groups using color/number cards: each color group has numbered cards. All groups are to report on the same subject, for example battles of the Civil War. Each numbered member of a group has a different subtopic assignment; all like numbers in the class have the same assignment, such as naval battles. Like numbers meet together to research their subject. Then color groups come together. Each member contributes his or her area of expertise to produce the group report.

Introduce cooperative learning into your classroom gradually. As you become more comfortable with it, vary the assignments. As students develop good group participation skills, you may want to encourage some competition among small groups.

Limited English Proficiency

More and more students throughout the United States speak a language other than English as their primary language. The rising numbers of students of limited English proficiency (LEP) present teachers with one of their biggest and most important challenges.

How do you teach a content-rich subject like United States history to LEP students? The principles of good teaching for LEP students are just that—principles of good teaching, appropriate for all students.

- Focus on the human story being told. History is about people, and good teaching brings their stories to life.
- Connect with students' own experiences and prior knowledge. For example, recent newcomers will be eager to read first-person accounts of earlier immigrants.
- Preteach the essential vocabulary, explaining very carefully any terms that might prove especially difficult, such as examples of idiomatic usage.

- Use visual aids and props wherever possible to establish context. Refer to maps, photos, and graphs in the textbook frequently. Also use gestures and facial expressions as cues to meaning.
- Connect with other curriculum areas. For example, have students use math to calculate the cost of food for a week for a family during the Great Depression. Examining the details of everyday life is an excellent way to bring history alive.
- Provide varied opportunities to practice English. Encourage students to retell events in their own words. Use role playing. Have students practice oral reading in pairs or small groups.

The **History of the United States** program has several features to help teachers of LEP students.

- **Key Terms** is a brief teaching strategy that is part of "Introducing the Section" in each section of the *Teacher's Annotated Edition.* These suggestions have been developed specifically for students who need further language development. Most are appropriate for LEP students and are identified by an LEP symbol.
- **Cooperative Learning** activities that are well suited for LEP students are identified in the *Teacher's Annotated Edition* with the LEP symbol. Small groups are an excellent place for LEP students to practice their English language skills.
- **Teaching Transparencies** provide valuable visual aids in the form of diagrams, timelines, photographs, fine art, and flow charts.

While bringing LEP students into the flow of a United States history course is a challenge to the teacher, it also presents excellent opportunities to develop democratic values among students and to foster respect for the multicultural nature of American society.

The following chart provides content (Essential Elements) for a study of the second part of a two-year study of United States history. The chart shows the chapters in the textbook where you will find content related to each Element. In addition, the chart provides examples of ways in which the Essential Elements can be further broken down specifically to meet local district objectives.

Essential Elements	Chapters	Specific Content Objectives
1. Emergence of the United States as a world power. The student shall be provided opportunities to:		
1A. describe the causes and effects of United States involvement in foreign affairs, international conflicts, and international cooperative efforts (political, humanitarian, economic, and military);	1, 11–13, 17–21, 23–27	• Spanish-American War • World War I • isolationism and the American refusal to join the League of Nations • World War II • American participation in the United Nations • Truman Doctrine, the Marshall Plan, and the cold war • involvement in Korea, Vietnam • Peace Corps and aid to developing nations • superpower arms control and disarmament efforts
1B. analyze the foreign policies of the United States and their impact; and	1, 11–13, 17–21, 23–27	• imperialism in Asia and Latin America • isolationism following World War I • containment of communism following World War II • détente with Communist powers
1C. describe overseas expansion of trade.	11, 27	• Open Door Policy toward China • opening of trade with Japan • trade and investment in Latin America • Marshall Plan and the growth of trade with Western Europe • trade with Pacific Rim nations
2. Geographic influences on the historical development of the United States. The student shall be provided opportunities to:		
2A. understand the causes and effects of urbanization;	1, 4, 6–8, 14, 22	• industrial expansion after the Civil War • rise of big business • availability of jobs in cities • migration from rural areas and foreign nations • overcrowded tenement housing • growth of city services • emergence of political machines
2B. describe the national government land and environmental policies and their historical significance;	3, 5–6, 10, 21, 24, 26–27	• Homestead Act • Dawes Act • Forest Reserve Act • National Reclamation Act • Antiquities Act • National Park Service Act • Clean Air Act • Water Quality Improvement Act • creation of the Environmental Protection Agency
2C. examine the uses, abuses, and preservation of natural resources and the physical environment;	4, 5, 8, 10, 13, 15, 21, 24–27	• oil exploration and drilling in Pennsylvania, Texas, Alaska • mining and lumbering in the West • creation of national parks and forests • construction of hydroelectric power stations • pollution of rivers, lakes, oceans, and the air • nuclear waste and accidents • energy crises and attempts at energy conservation • threat of global warming, deforestation, and acid rain
2D. describe the influences of physical features and the distribution of natural resources on population movements and patterns of settlement; and	1–6, 13, 20, 27	• lure of territory in the West for settlement, farming, and ranching • gold rushes and the settlement of California and Alaska • western mineral and lumber resources as a spur to settlement and economic development • climate and the migration to the sunbelt
2E. explain the importance of selected historic sites.	2, 9, 12, 18, 25	• Civil War sites • sites related to westward expansion • sites related to international affairs • sites related to industrial growth • sites related to the contemporary United States

Essential Elements	Chapters	Specific Content Objectives
3. Economic development and growth of the United States. The student shall be provided opportunities to:		
3A. analyze the impact of new developments in science and technology on business, labor, industry, agriculture, transportation, communications, and the environment;	1–7, 12–14, 18, 20, 27	• steel and the expansion of railroads • dynamo and the generation of electricity • telegraph and telephone • advances in agriculture: dry farming, steel plows • automobiles • nuclear technology: atomic power and atomic waste • television • space technology • genetic engineering • industrial pollution: air, land, and water
3B. explain the impact of various wars;	1, 2, 4, 13–14, 16–19, 23, 27	• Civil War: spurred industrial growth • World War I: increased economic opportunities for women and minorities during the war; inflation following the war; United States as creditor nation and world economic power • World War II: economic expansion during the war (end of the Great Depression); increased economic opportunities for women and minorities during the war; inflation, higher spending, and wage strikes following the war; United States as world's dominant economic power • Vietnam War: increased national debt and mounting inflation following the war
3C. explain the development and importance of new business structures and labor organizations;	1, 3–6, 8–10, 14, 16, 20	• evolution of corporations and conglomerates • introduction of vertical and horizontal integration • impact of pools and trusts on the market • emergence of unions for skilled and unskilled workers • labor laws such as eight-hour day, limits on child labor, and workmen's compensation
3D. identify notable business, industrial, and labor leaders;	4, 7–9, 13–14, 17, 19	• founders of such industries as steel and oil • heads of corporations • union organizers and leaders
3E. understand the impact of business cycles, panics, depressions and recessions, and deflation and inflation;	8, 14–16, 19–21, 24–27	• rise and fall of prices • changing levels of employment • effects of economic booms such as the 1920s and the 1950s • human cost of economic downturns such as the Great Depression
3F. analyze the changing relationship of government and the economy; and	1, 2, 4, 7–10, 13–16, 18–21, 24–26	• Sixteenth Amendment allowing Congress to levy an income tax • increased federal regulation of the economy during World War I and World War II • less government involvement in the economy during the 1920s and 1950s • New Deal and Great Society legislation increasing the economic role and power of the federal government • less government involvement in the economy under Reagan
3G. understand the development of the United States banking system.	1, 4, 10, 15–16, 26	• National Banking Act • Federal Reserve Act • Failure of banks during the Great Depression • Emergency Banking Bill • Savings and Loan crisis
4. Social and cultural developments of the United States. The student shall be provided opportunities to:		
4A. describe the long-term social impact of the Civil War and Reconstruction;	3, 4, 22	• efforts to deny African Americans their rights • southern planter class's loss of economic and political power • rise in sharecropping • growth of new industries in the South
4B. explain the causes for and impact of immigration, past and present;	1, 4–6, 11, 14, 23, 27	• causes for immigration before 1880: poverty, overcrowding, famine, and the lure of available land • causes for immigration after 1880: religious persecution, relaxed emigration laws, improved steamship service, positive reports from earlier immigrants, and the search for economic opportunity • causes for recent immigration: more liberal United States immigration laws, war, political persecution, poverty, and the search for economic opportunity • effects of immigration: rise of urban political machines, broadening of American cultural life, greater national ethnic diversity, expanded labor supply, rise in anti-immigrant sentiment
4C. recognize the contributions of ethnic, racial, cultural, and religious groups and individuals, both men and women, to the growth and development of the United States;	1–7, 9–11, 14–16, 18–22, 24–27	• contributions in reform movements • contributions in government service • contributions to economic growth • contributions to American culture

Essential Elements	Chapters	Specific Content Objectives
4D. identify reform movements, leaders, issues, and results (e.g., the struggle for equal rights, temperance, housing, and education);	1–4, 6–7, 9–10, 14, 16–17, 19, 21–22, 25, 27	• Jane Addams and the settlement house movement • emergence of the Social Gospel • muckrakers and progressivism • temperance movement • suffragist movement • reforms in government • increased government regulation of business • W.E.B. Du Bois and the NAACP • Franklin Roosevelt and the New Deal • John L. Lewis, Cesar Chavez, and workers' rights • John F. Kennedy and the New Frontier • Lyndon Johnson and the Great Society • civil rights movement • women's rights movement
4E. analyze the impact of science and technology on social and cultural developments;	2, 4, 6, 8, 12, 18, 20–21, 27	• improvements in daily life • advances in medicine • automation • pollution
4F. describe developments in art, music, literature, drama, and other culturally related activities; and	5–7, 9–11, 13–14, 16, 20, 24, 26	• frontier paintings and literature • Ash Can School and realistic artwork characterizing urban life • Impressionism • emergence of mass entertainment • jazz music and the age of the flapper • Harlem Renaissance • Lost Generation writers • emergence of rock 'n' roll • rise of a counterculture in the 1960s
4G. analyze religious leaders, groups, movements, and issues from the post-Civil War era to the present.	1, 7, 14, 20, 22, 25–26	• Russell H. Conwell and the Gospel of Wealth • Social Gospel • evolution theory versus creationism (Scopes monkey trial) • revivalists of the 1920s • televangelists • African American churches and the civil rights movement • fundamentalist churches and conservativism in the 1980s

5. Political development of the United States. The student shall be provided opportunities to:

Essential Elements	Chapters	Specific Content Objectives
5A. describe the long-term political effects of the Civil War and Reconstruction (e.g., the one-party South, Jim Crowism, and disenfranchisement of Blacks);	3, 22	• Democratic Party control of southern politics • Jim Crow laws • rise of the Ku Klux Klan • efforts to keep African Americans from voting
5B. describe major political campaigns, elections, issues, leaders, and results;	2, 3, 7–10, 13–16, 19–21, 23–27	• campaigns and issues from the Reconstruction era • campaigns and issues from the Gilded Age • campaigns and issues from the Progressive era • campaigns and issues from the 1920s • Franklin Roosevelt and the New Deal • campaigns and issues from the postwar era
5C. understand major political reform movements, leaders, issues, and results (e.g., changing political alignments, minor political parties, special interest groups, and the Progressive movement);	2, 7–10, 14, 24–26	• Mugwumps and civil service reform • fight for workers' rights • Populists • Progressive movement • New Deal • postwar movements for expanded rights and opportunities by African Americans, American Indians, Hispanic Americans, women • Ronald Reagan and the growth of conservatism
5D. evaluate constitutional developments reflected by amendments and court decisions;	1, 3–4, 8–10, 13, 21–22, 24, 27	• protection of individual liberties (in the Bill of Rights and subsequent amendments and decisions) • expansion of the authority of the federal government (in such areas as taxation and desegregation) • expansion of the rights of women and minority groups
5E. analyze major historic documents relating to the development of the United States; and	1–3, 10, 13, 16–17, 19–22, 27	• Mayflower Compact • Declaration of Independence • Articles of Confederation • United States Constitution • Monroe Doctrine • Emancipation Proclamation • Gettysburg Address • Truman Doctrine
5F. analyze growth and development of the three branches of federal government.	3, 16, 24	• executive branch • legislative branch • judicial branch

6. Respect for self and others. The student shall be provided opportunities to:

6A. respect beliefs of other individuals, groups, and cultures;	3, 5, 12, 16, 18–19, 21–22, 25–27
6B. recognize how societal values affect individual beliefs and values; and	1, 4, 6, 9, 18–19, 20–22
6C. recognize that some things are valued more in some groups and cultures than in others.	5, 6, 16, 20–21, 25–27

7. Democratic beliefs and personal responsibility. The student shall be provided opportunities to:

7A. recognize that individuals must accept the consequences of their decisions and actions;	1–3, 18–20, 24–25
7B. support the principles that underlie the United States Constitution (including the Bill of Rights and all other amendments) and the Declaration of Independence;	1–3, 6, 13, 18–19, 21–25
7C. judge self-interest and public interest when making political decisions;	6, 7, 23, 25, 27
7D. value open-mindedness, tolerance of different opinions, and civic participation and compromise as important aspects of democratic behavior;	1–3, 9, 17, 20, 25, 27
7E. respect the laws of one's society and work responsibly to change laws one judges to be unjust;	1, 8–10, 19, 22, 25–27
7F. understand the importance of individual participation in civic affairs;	2, 7, 9, 13, 21–23, 25–27
7G. recognize the necessity of balancing legal rights with civic responsibilities;	7, 9–10, 13, 18, 21–22
7H. acknowledge that participation and decision making in civic affairs requires knowledge, time, and personal effort;	8, 9, 21–23, 26–27
7I. support the democratic processes of the republican form of government;	1, 2, 9, 17, 22, 24–25, 27
7J. support the basic civic values of American society (e.g., justice, responsibility, political and religious freedom, diversity, privacy, private property rights, voluntary exchange, and respect for the law); and	1–2, 6–7, 10, 13–14, 16–22, 24–25, 27
7K. support the rules and laws of the school, community, state, and nation.	20, 22, 25, 27

8. Support for the American economic system. The student shall be provided opportunities to:

8A. recognize the contributions of the American economic system to the standard of living of Americans;	4, 6–8, 14, 20, 26
8B. support the role of profit in the American economic system;	1, 4, 7, 9–10, 20, 26
8C. acknowledge the right of individuals to acquire, responsibly use, and dispose of property;	1, 4–6, 14, 20, 27
8D. support the freedom of consumers to choose how to spend their income;	1, 4, 6–7, 14, 24, 26
8E. recognize that citizens can influence economic decisions made by government through legal political activities;	8, 19, 20, 25–26
8F. support economic competition as it affects the quantity and quality of goods and services;	4, 10, 14, 16, 24, 26–27
8G. acknowledge the role of government in regulating competition of both producers and consumers;	4, 9, 10, 20, 24, 27
8H. recognize that economic self-interest may also serve the economic interest of others; and	1, 3–4, 7, 14–15, 26
8I. compare the control and treatment of public and private property.	3, 5, 16, 20, 24

9. Application of social studies skills. The student shall be provided opportunities to:

9A. analyze, synthesize, and evaluate information;	1–5, 7–14, 16–27
9B. interpret visual materials (e.g., charts, graphs, pictures, maps);	1–10, 12–14, 16–20, 23–27
9C. distinguish fact from opinion;	2–3, 23
9D. sequence historical data;	1–27
9E. perceive cause/effect relationships;	1–2, 4–5, 9, 13–24, 26
9F. use problem-solving skills; and	5, 7–8, 17–18, 23–24
9G. apply decision-making skills.	5, 8, 11, 23, 26

Audiovisual and Software Sources

AES	American Eagle Software, Inc. P.O. Box 46080 Lincolnwood, IL 60646	**ELEC**	Electronic Arts 1820 Gateway Drive San Mateo, CA 94404	**MIND**	Mindscape, Inc. 3444 Dundee Road Northbrook, IL 60062
AIMS	Aims Media 6901 Woodley Avenue Van Nuys, CA 91406	**FFH**	Films for the Humanities P.O. Box 2053 Princeton, NJ 08540	**MVP**	MVP Software 1035 Dallas S.E. Grand Rapids, MI 49507
ALT	Altana Films 340 East 34th Street New York, NY 10016	**FI**	Films Incorporated Video 5547 N. Ravenswood Avenue Chicago, IL 60640	**NATGEO**	National Geographic Society Educational Services 17th & M Streets, N.W. Washington, DC 20036
AMBR	Ambrose Video Publishing 381 Park Avenue South Suite 1601 New York, NY 10016	**FL**	Filmmakers Library 124 East 40th Street New York, NY 10016	**NAVC**	National Audiovisual Center 8700 Edgeworth Drive Capitol Heights, MD 20743
BLFG	Bullfrog Films, Inc. Oley, PA 19547	**FOCUS**	Focus Media 839 Stewart Avenue Garden City, NY 11530	**NCSC**	National Collegiate Software Duke University Press 6697 College Station Durham, NC 27708
BNCHMK	Benchmark Films, Inc. 145 Scarborough Road Briarcliff Manor, NY 10510	**FRF**	First Run Features/Icarus 200 Park Avenue South Suite 1319 New York, NY 10003	**OCS**	Orange Cherry Software P.O. Box 390 Pound Ridge, NY 10576
BRI	Bright Ideas, Inc. 87A Ocean Street South Portland, ME 04106	**GA**	Guidance Associates Communications Park Box 3000 Mt Kisco, NY 10549	**ONEWEST**	Onewest Media P.O. Box 5766 559 Onate Place Santa Fe, NM 87501
BRIT	Britannica Software 345 Fourth Street San Francisco, CA 94107	**GEM**	Gemstar P.O. Box 050228 Staten Island, NY 10305	**PBS**	PBS 1320 Braddock Place Alexandria, VA 22314
CCS	Cross Cultural Software 5385 Elrose Avenue San Jose, CA 95124	**GMP**	Green Mountain Post Films P.O. Box 229 Turners Falls, MA 01376	**PHOENIX**	Phoenix Films/BFA Films & Video 468 Park Avenue South New York, NY 10016
CDF	Cambridge Documentary Films P.O. Box 385 Cambridge, MA 02139	**HS**	Hartley Software c/o Michaels Associates 5171 Greensburg Road Murrysville, PA 15668	**PYR**	Pyramid Films & Video P.O. Box 1048 Santa Monica, CA 90406
CF	Churchill Films 12210 Nebraska Avenue Los Angeles, CA 90025	**INTELI**	Intelimation, Inc. 2040 Alameda Padre Serra Santa Barbara, 93103	**QUEUE**	Queue 338 Commerce Drive Fairfield, CT 06430
CG	Cinema Guild 1697 Broadway Suite 802 New York, NY 10019	**KAW**	Kaw Valley Films P.O. Box 3900 Shawnee, KS 66203	**SIERRA**	Sierra On-Line, Inc. Sierra On-Line Building Coarsegold, CA 93614
CINEMA 70	Cinema 70 7 Davis Road Port Washington, NY 11050	**LAND**	Landmark Films 3450 Slade Run Drive Falls Church, VA 22042	**SS**	Scholastic Software 730 Broadway New York, NY 10003
COR/MTI	Coronet/MTI Film & Video 108 Wilmot Road Deerfield, IL 60015	**LCA**	Learning Corporation of America 108 Wilmot Road Deerfield, IL 60015	**SVE**	Society For Visual Education, Inc. Dept. BP 1345 Diversey Pkwy. Chicago, IL 60614
CUE	CUE SoftSwap P.O. Box 271704 Concord, CA 94527	**LUCERNE**	Lucerne Media, Inc. 37 Ground Pine Road Morris Plains, NJ 07950	**TS**	Tom Snyder Productions Educational Software 90 Sherman Street Cambridge, MA 02140
DCL	Direct Cinema Limited P.O. Box 69589 Los Angeles, CA 90069	**MECC**	MECC 3490 Lexington Avenue North St. Paul, MN 55126	**UNI**	Unison World, Inc. 1321 Harbor Bay Parkway Alameda, CA 94501
DUART	DU-ART Film Labs, Inc. 245 West 55th Street New York, NY 10019	**MER**	Merit Software 157 Chambers Street New York, NY 10007	**WB**	World Book, Inc. Merchandise Mart Plaza, #13 Chicago, IL 60654
EDACT	Educational Activities, Inc. P.O. Box 392 Freeport, NY 11520	**MG**	Media Guild 11722 Sorrento Valley Road Suite E San Diego, CA 92121	**WOMBAT**	Wombat Film & Video 250 West 57th Street New York, NY 10019
EBEC	Encyclopaedia Britannica Educational Corp. 310 S. Michigan Avenue Chicago, IL 60604	**MICRO**	Micro Ed, Inc. P.O. Box 24750 Edina, MN 55424	**WORD**	Word Associates, Inc. 3226 Robincrest Drive Northbrook, IL 60062

History of The United States

Volume 2   Civil War to the Present

THE AUTHORS

Thomas V. DiBacco is a Professor of Business History at the American University, Washington, D.C., where he has taught since 1965. Dr. DiBacco received his B.A. from Rollins College in Florida and his Ph.D. in American History from The American University. He is the author of several books, including *Made in the U.S.A.: The History of American Business*. Dr. DiBacco writes regularly for many newspapers and serves as a frequent radio and television commentator and lecturer.

Lorna C. Mason is a professional editor and writer. Born in Colorado and raised in Kansas, she has spent most of her adult life in California. Mrs. Mason holds a M.A. in history from the University of California, Berkeley, and has taught history at both the secondary and junior college levels in California. She is the author of several social studies textbooks, both basal and supplementary. Mrs. Mason is the editor and publisher of *Voice of the Plains*, commentaries of rancher John Cogswell.

Christian G. Appy is Assistant Professor of History at the Massachusetts Institute of Technology. Born in Atlanta, Dr. Appy received his B.A. from Amherst College and his Ph.D. from Harvard. His dissertation, a study of American soldiers in the Vietnam War, was named outstanding dissertation of the year by the American Studies Association. Dr. Appy taught history and literature at Harvard for nine years. He is currently at work on an interdisciplinary study of American society, 1945–1975.

★ ★ ★ ★ ★ ★ ★ ★ ★ ★ ★ ★ ★ ★ ★ ★ ★

History of The United States

Volume 2 _Civil War to the Present_

Thomas V. DiBacco

Lorna C. Mason

Christian G. Appy

HOUGHTON MIFFLIN COMPANY ■ BOSTON

Atlanta Dallas Geneva, Illinois Palo Alto Princeton Toronto

SPECIAL CURRICULUM ADVISERS

Larry Bybee
Secondary Social Studies Supervisor
Northside Independent School District
San Antonio, Texas

David Depew
Social Studies Consultant
Ector Independent School District
Odessa, Texas

Douglas E. Miller
Social Studies Department Chair
Fremont Union High School
Sunnyvale, California

Gail Riley
Social Studies Consultant
Hurst-Euless-Bedford School District
Bedford, Texas

SPECIAL MULTICULTURAL ADVISER

Bartley L. McSwine
Coordinator of Secondary Education
Chicago State University

CONSULTANTS AND TEACHER REVIEWERS

George Allan
Ehret High School
Marrero, Louisiana

Robert Barnshaw
Washington Township High School
Sewell, New Jersey

Jayne Beatty
Blue Springs High School
Blue Springs, Missouri

Bonnie Anne Briggs
Gates Chili Senior High School
Rochester, New York

Wanda J. Calloway
Lakeland High School
Lakeland, Florida

Ralph Clement
Bullard High School
Fresno, California

Jean Craven
Albuquerque School District
Albuquerque, New Mexico

Jean Evans
Chamberlain High School
Tampa, Florida

Ray Foley
Salesianum School
Wilmington, Delaware

Bernell Helm
Elyria City Schools
Elyria, Ohio

Eliseo C. Hernandez
Bowie Junior High
Odessa, Texas

Lannah Hughes
Green Run High School
Virginia Beach, Virginia

William Jones
Jacksonville Senior High School
Jacksonville, Arkansas

Ann Kashiwa
Mariner High School
Everett, Washington

Kevin Kelly
Lake Braddock High School
Burke, Virginia

Paul Kinzer
Lapeer East Senior High School
Lapeer, Michigan

Bill Koscher
Ludlow High School
Ludlow, Massachusetts

Katherine Lai
San Francisco USD
San Francisco, California

Ann Nunn
Higgens High School
Marrero, Louisiana

Clint Peterson
Bridgeport Schools
Bridgeport, Connecticut

Ed Smith
Classical High School
Providence, Rhode Island

Richard Terry
Linton High School
Schenectady, New York

Robert Van Amburgh
City School District of Albany
Albany, New York

Marilyn Washington
Jordan High School
Los Angeles, California

John Wolff
Hopewell Valley School District Central High School
Pennington, New Jersey

★ C O N T E N T S ★

Poster promoting Theodore Roosevelt as the person who can lead America to prosperity

Broadway in New York City

U.S. propaganda poster from
World War II

Winston Churchill, Franklin Roosevelt, and
Joseph Stalin at the Yalta Conference in 1945

Outpost in South Vietnam of the U.S. Special Forces (the Green Berets)

Reference Section

CIVICS HANDBOOK   685

AMERICAN LITERATURE   769

SKILL REVIEW   825

Study Skills

Critical Thinking Skills

SPECIAL FEATURES

The Geographic Perspective

Historians' Corner

Cause and Effect

CAUSE AND EFFECT: THE CIVIL RIGHTS MOVEMENT

Causes

- Black urbanization
- Religious faith
- Demand for constitutional rights
- Greater media coverage of protests
- Success of African independence movements

The Civil Rights Movement (1954–1968)

Effects

- Elimination of legal segregation
- Civil Rights Acts of 1964 and 1968
- Voting Rights Act of 1965
- Creation of affirmative action programs
- Example for other minority groups

Historical Documents

The Presidents

FEDERAL SURPLUS OR DEFICIT, 1960–1990

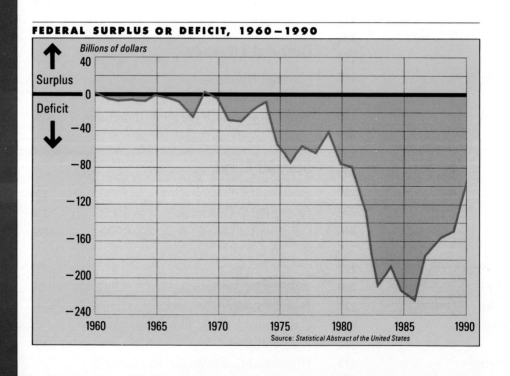

Source: Statistical Abstract of the United States

MAPS

THE VIETNAM WAR, 1957–1973

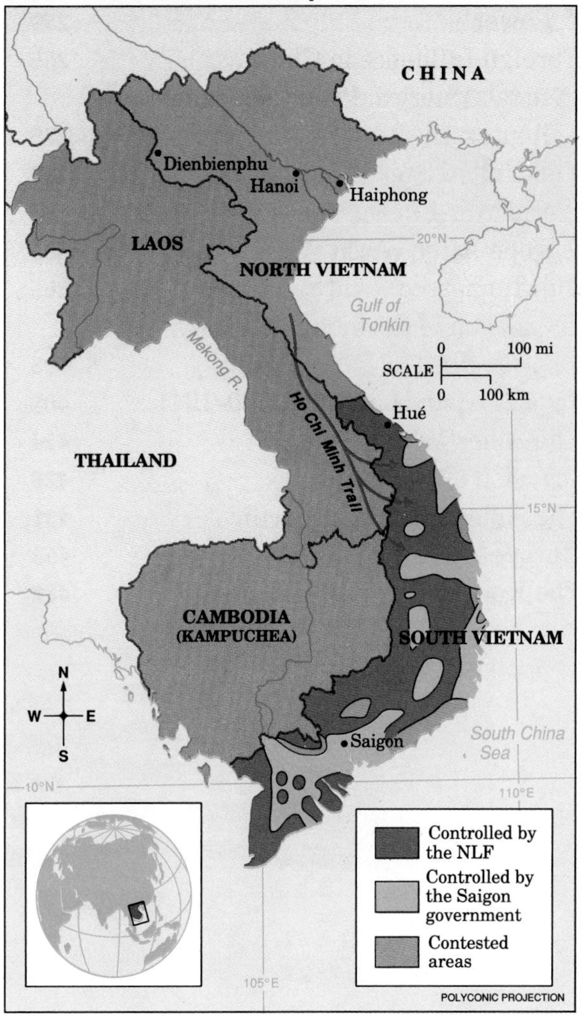

CHINA

Dienbienphu
Hanoi
Haiphong

LAOS

NORTH VIETNAM

Gulf of
Tonkin

20°N

SCALE
0   100 mi
0   100 km

Hué

THAILAND

Ho Chi Minh Trail

Mekong R.

15°N

CAMBODIA
(KAMPUCHEA)

SOUTH VIETNAM

N
W   E
S

South China
Sea

Saigon

10°N

110°E

Controlled by
the NLF

Controlled by
the Saigon
government

Contested
areas

105°E

POLYCONIC PROJECTION

Dear Student:

If you are like most people your age, you are primarily concerned with the present and with the future. That is as it should be. Then why study history?

We study the past to better know the present. The historian is not like an antique collector who may love something just because it's old. Instead, the historian looks at life today and asks *Why are we the way we are?* To find answers the historian considers, among other things, how individuals, ideas, religion, geography, technology, and economics have interacted to shape our nation and our national character.

One generation of historians may interpret the past in a completely different way from the next generation. This can happen because new information may emerge. Time, too, allows us a new perspective on more recent events, such as the Vietnam War. Present-day concerns also affect how we view the past. Today, as never before, we are aware that America is a multicultural nation. This increased awareness affects how we write history.

History textbooks, too, change to reflect the concerns of the present. This textbook, in particular, has been designed and written with you in mind—you who will live more of your life in the twenty-first century than in the twentieth century. Our journey into American history begins with the Civil War. In that great and bloody struggle are the roots of much of our twentieth-century history: the advance of democracy, the quest for social justice, the expansion of cities and industries, technological change, and the growth of the federal government.

The Authors

The Goals of This Book

History of the United States (Volume 2) was designed with three goals in mind:

1. To provide coverage of American history from earliest times to the present, with special emphasis on the period from Reconstruction through the twentieth century.

2. To identify the major themes in American history and explain their importance at each stage in the development of the United States.

3. To convey a sense of the breadth of experiences and influences that have shaped the United States.

Comprehensive Coverage

The structure of this book reflects the first of those three goals. The book is divided into nine units. The first unit sets the stage by describing the path to American independence, the early years of the new nation, the Civil War era, and Reconstruction. Unit Two recounts how the United States grew into a powerful industrial nation by 1900. Units Three through Six describe the tumultuous decades in the first half of the twentieth century. During those years the United States experienced war and peace, prosperity and depression, conservatism and reform. Finally, Units Seven through Nine detail the events of the postwar era, the time of the United States' greatest wealth, power, and influence.

Themes in American History

To accomplish the second of the book's goals, the authors have identified seven Themes in American History. They are explained below.

Global Interactions From its earliest days as a colonial outpost, the United States has been a part of events in the rest of the world. The outside world has influenced the United States in its people, its ideals, and its form of government. As it has grown into a global superpower, this nation has played an increasingly important role abroad.

Constitutional Government Ours is a government of limited powers. These powers are derived from the consent of the governed and are divided among the branches of government. This form of government has been in place for two centuries. During that time, the size and power of the federal government have increased substantially.

Expanding Democracy Over the course of American history, as the concept of liberty has expanded, so too have the rights enjoyed by Americans. Groups that once suffered unfair treatment eventually received equal protection under the laws. These gains, however, came about only after much struggle, controversy, and hardship.

Economic Development Despite periods of stagnation and the continuing problem of poverty, the United States has had enormous economic success. One result was the building of the world's most powerful economy. Another was the belief in this nation as a land of opportunity for all.

Pluralistic Society Millions of people from nations around the world have come to live in the United States. That these many cultures have coexisted in a stable, democratic society is one of the United States' greatest triumphs. Yet racial and ethnic intolerance have posed roadblocks to the achievement of full equality.

American Culture The American people's diverse heritage, combined with the legal guarantee of free expression, have produced a rich and dynamic culture.

Geography The United States has benefited enormously from its natural resources. Chief among these is the land itself—the frontier, whose conquest played such a key role in our history. Natural abundance speeded industrial growth, encouraged immigration, and in a host of other ways contributed to American prosperity. It also encouraged the rapid exploitation of natural resources, which led—in turn—to concerns about the environment.

These Themes in American History, which reappear throughout the book, are reviewed following Chapter 27. There, an essay and a timeline chart the progression of each theme through American history.

Breadth of Influences

The third of the book's goals is to convey a sense of the breadth of American history. A history of the United States must include Presidents and senators, battles and treaties, laws and court decisions. To give a complete picture of this nation,

however, it must do more. It must explain the many effects of geography and the importance of economic factors. It must show how Americans lived—what their homes were like, what they did for recreation, how religion influenced their lives. It must demonstrate that public policy in a free society emerges from open discussion and compromise, and that controversy is a part of this process.

Finally, it must pull all these facts together into one story. Many of the people and events described in this book were separated by thousands of miles and hundreds of years. Yet all played a part in building the nation of which you are a citizen. What does it mean to be an American in the 1990s? The answer to that question lies not only in the present and future, but also in the past.

How This Book Helps You Learn

This book has been designed to make learning about American history easier and more enjoyable. Its many features are described below.

Units, Chapters, and Sections

History of the United States (Volume 2) is divided into 9 units and 27 chapters. Each unit, with two or more chapters, covers a specific time period and deals with a major development in

American history. The first page of each unit lists the chapters in the unit as well as the Themes in American History contained in that unit.

Each chapter opens with a picture reflecting the period of American history described in that chapter. Next to the chapter title is a list of Key Events—some of the important events in that chapter. These events are repeated at the end of each chapter in a timeline such as the one below.

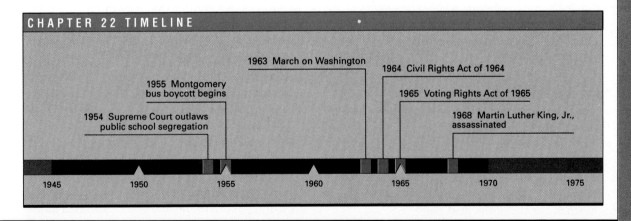

CHAPTER 22 TIMELINE

1963 March on Washington

1955 Montgomery bus boycott begins

1964 Civil Rights Act of 1964

1965 Voting Rights Act of 1965

1954 Supreme Court outlaws public school segregation

1968 Martin Luther King, Jr., assassinated

1945 1950 1955 1960 1965 1970 1975

Each chapter is divided into three or more sections. At the beginning of a section, in a box like the one below, you will find a list of Key Terms found in the section. Key Terms, printed blue in the text, are either vocabulary words or important terms in American history. They are all defined in the text. You will also find the Main Idea, a brief preview of the section, and two or three Objectives. The Objectives are questions covering the material in the section; you should keep these questions in mind as you read.

At the end of each section is a Section Review. You will be asked to review the Key Terms and important people and places in the section. There will be questions covering the Section Objectives, and a Critical Thinking question that asks you to reflect on what you have learned.

At the end of each chapter is a Chapter Review. It begins with a summary of the chapter, followed by a variety of exercises, including a map exercise, critical thinking questions, and writing assignments.

3 The Rise of Big Business

Section Focus

Key Terms corporation ■ dividend ■ economies of scale ■ limited liability ■ vertical integration ■ horizontal integration ■ promotion ■ patent war ■ installment plan

Main Idea Seeking greater efficiency and profits, many American businesses grew to enormous sizes in the late 1800s.

Objectives As you read, look for answers to these questions:
1. What were the features and advantages of corporations?
2. How did different companies learn to prosper in the marketplace?

Pictures

The illustrations in this book have been carefully chosen to broaden your understanding of people, places, and events. Illustrations include paintings, drawings, and photographs.

Maps and Charts

Numerous maps and charts appear throughout the book. Maps are an essential part of any history book, for they show where the events being described took place. Charts are a useful tool because they squeeze a lot of information into a small space.

Special Features

A number of special features have been carefully woven into the text of *History of the United States (Volume 2).*

■ **Cause and Effect**, located in each unit, shows the causes and effects of an important development in American history. An example is shown at the top of the next page.

■ **The Geographic Perspective**, located in each unit, explains in detail how geography influenced one of the events covered in that unit.

■ **American Mosaic: A Multicultural Perspective**, located at the end of each unit, profiles significant individuals from a variety of backgrounds.

■ **Historians' Corner**, also located at the end of each unit, compares and contrasts historians' views of issues in American history.

■ **The Presidents** gives for each American President a portrait and an outline of his life and accomplishments in office.

■ **Cultural Literacy** shows how our language has been influenced by historical events.

■ **Special Maps** present the continental United States as it appeared at three points in its history: 1790, 1900, and 1990. Each map by itself conveys the diversity of this nation. Viewed together, they hint at the incredible changes the United States has undergone over the course of its history.

Causes
◆ Dissatisfaction with liberal policies
◆ Revival of evangelical Christianity
◆ Reagan as spearhead of conservatism

**The Conservative 1980s
(1980–1990)**

Effects
◆ Republican control of the presidency
◆ Cuts in taxes and government spending
◆ More conservative Supreme Court

■ **Social History: Famous Firsts** lists new developments taking place in American society during a given period.

■ **Biography**, located in every chapter, presents biographical sketches of important Americans from all walks of life. One example follows.

BIOGRAPHY

JEANE KIRKPATRICK (1926–) held several important positions in the Democratic Party, but grew critical of President Carter's foreign policy emphasis on human rights. Kirkpatrick argued that the United States should support all governments that fought communism even if they were repressive dictatorships. Under President Reagan, Kirkpatrick served as U.S. ambassador to the United Nations, becoming the first woman to do so.

Primary Sources

History of the United States (Volume 2) is rich in primary sources. Throughout the text you will find firsthand accounts of the people and events of American history. They give you a true sense of history in the making. Some of these accounts have themselves become part of our nation's heritage, as have statements by the makers of American history. Many of these statements are shown in special boxes like the one below.

"**T**he buck stops here."
                          —Harry Truman

Reference Section

Materials at the end of the book provide helpful learning aids and reference sources. The Government and Citizenship section includes a Voter's Handbook, extended excerpts from important Historical Documents, and the complete text of the Declaration of Independence and the Constitution. American Literature presents excerpts from a variety of literary works, one for each chapter. Other useful learning tools and reference sources include a Skill Review, lists of the Presidents, the states, and important dates in American history, atlas maps, a gazetteer, a glossary defining Key Terms, and an index.

Geography and American History

History is far more than an account of what happened in the past. It also tells where, when, how, and why these events occurred. Finding the answers to such questions is impossible without geographic literacy. Once we understand the importance of geography in history, and once we know how to use geography in exploring history, the study of history becomes more meaningful. We begin to see that history is not a mass of random, unrelated events. Rather, it contains patterns and meanings that help explain the present as well as the past.

The first step in studying American history, therefore, is to study American geography. North America contains a wide variety of geographic features. In western North America, several major mountain chains run north and south. Between the mountains are high plateaus, deep canyons, and fertile valleys. At the center of the continent is a huge grassland, as well as the five Great Lakes. Down the eastern side of the continent runs a chain of forested mountains. A broad coastal plain edges the coasts of the Atlantic Ocean and the Gulf of Mexico.

Over the course of American history, people settled the coastal plain, crossed mountains, and moved westward. Explorers sailed the lakes and rivers. Pioneers turned the prairies into farmland. Miners found gold in the western mountains. An abundance of natural resources, combined with a generally temperate climate, helped the United States prosper. Thus, much of the story of American history has also been a story about geography.

WHAT IS GEOGRAPHY?

Each nation's history and culture have been affected in important ways by its geography. Geography includes landscapes and **landforms** such as mountains, hills, deserts, rivers, lakes, and oceans. It also includes climate—long-term weather patterns—as well as plants, animals, and natural resources such as gold, oil, timber, and soil. Because people change their physical environment (and are changed by it), humans are also an important part of geography.

PEOPLE AND GEOGRAPHY

Throughout history, geographical factors have influenced where people settled, what crops they grew, what clothes they wore, and many other features of their cultures. People in rugged mountain country, for example, developed cultures quite different from those that settled in tropical forests or on flat, windblown plains.

Much of human history also involves people's interactions with their geographic environment. Since earliest times, people have hunted animals, farmed the land, stored water for irrigation, cut down forests, mined mineral resources, and built roads and communities. Geography—good land or valuable resources—has often been the reason behind wars of conquest or mass migrations.

THE AMERICAS

Geographical influence has been especially strong in the history of the Americas, for two reasons. First, North and South America cover a huge area and have a great variety of climates, landforms, and natural resources. Of the five largest nations in the world, three are in the Americas—Canada, the United States, and Brazil. The "lower 48" states of the United States stretch about 2,500 miles from east to west. The island state of Hawaii is about 2,000 miles away, in the Pacific Ocean, while the largest state,

G1

Alaska, is at the northwestern tip of North America. Climates in the Americas range from steamy tropics to the icy Arctic.

Second, people came to the Americas from many other continents. The cultures they brought with them had already been shaped by the geography of their homelands. These older geographical influences blended into the American cultures that were developing.

LOCATING PLACES

How would geographers describe a place? They might mention weather, landscape, plants and animals, and other *physical* characteristics. Or they might include distinctive *human* characteristics such as language, religion, and art.

To pinpoint a place's location, geographers use a special method called the **grid system**. If you look at most of the maps in this book, you will see a system of intersecting lines that form a grid. The lines usually are numbered at the edge of the map. These imaginary lines on the earth's surface let you locate any place on earth accurately. Each place has an "address" on the grid, stated in degrees and minutes of latitude and longitude. (A degree, like an hour, contains 60 minutes. A full circle has 360 degrees.) This address is always the same, regardless of the kind of map used.

(a) Latitude. The lines of **latitude** are parallel circles that run horizontally around the earth. They are also called **parallels**. A place can be located in terms of its distance from the equator (0 degrees) in degrees of north (N) or south (S) latitude.

(b) Longitude. On a globe, the lines of **longitude** run the length of the earth between the North and South poles. They are also called **meridians**. The so-called **prime meridian,** which passes through Greenwich, England, is at 0 degrees. From this meridian, locations are stated in degrees of east (E) or west (W) longitude. The dividing line on the opposite side of the earth is the 180 degree meridian.

(c) Coordinates. Each place on earth, then, has a grid address made up of these two **coordinates**: degrees of N or S latitude and E or W

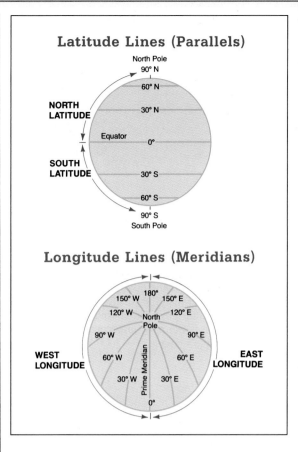

Latitude Lines (Parallels)

Longitude Lines (Meridians)

longitude. With this address, you can locate a place on any map. Even without a map, you can learn some things about a place just by knowing its coordinates.

The grid system is used to divide the earth into halves, or **hemispheres**. (*Hemisphere* means "half a sphere.") The north-south dividing line is the equator. A place's latitude—N or S—tells you whether it is in the Northern or Southern Hemisphere. Similarly, the longitude E or W can tell you whether a place is in the Eastern or Western Hemisphere. The prime meridian and the 180 degree meridian form the imaginary boundary between the east-west halves of the earth.

For practice, use the world map in the Atlas at the back of the book to find in which nations these grid locations lie: 40°N, 116°E; 34°N, 118°W; 34°S, 151°E; 1°S, 37°E. Which of these nations is closest to the equator? Which are in the Eastern Hemisphere? Now use a globe or atlas to find the cities with those coordinates.

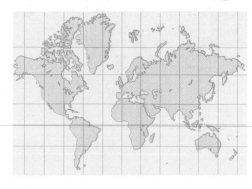

Mercator Projection. This projection shows direction accurately, but it distorts size, especially away from the equator. Landmasses near the North and South poles appear to be much larger than they really are. Sailors favor the Mercator projection because determining direction is the most important part of plotting a ship's course.

Polar Projection (equidistant). This projection is drawn from above either the North Pole or the South Pole. Size and shape are fairly true near the center of the map but become distorted the farther a landmass is from the pole. However, the distance from the pole to any point on the map is accurate. For this reason and because many of the shortest flying routes go over the pole, airplane pilots prefer this projection.

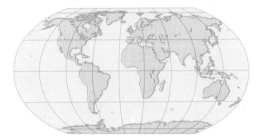

Robinson Projection. This projection shows accurately how the continents compare with each other in size. Because the oceans are not interrupted, their relative sizes are also shown clearly. There is some distortion of shape, however, near the edges of the map.

Goode's Interrupted Projection (equal-area). This projection cuts the world into sections. As a result, it shows sizes and shapes of continents better than other projections. Distances across water areas, however, are generally inaccurate.

MAP PROJECTIONS

A map is flat, like the page you are reading. The world, though, is round like a globe. These two facts pose a problem that mapmakers try to solve—how to show a round surface on a flat map. The solution is to make compromises in the way a map is drawn. The different approaches result in what are called **map projections**. Like the grid system, projections are mapmaking devices that help people get a better picture of what the earth is like.

Every map projection shows some features accurately and distorts others. Some show land areas and distances in correct proportions. Some show the shapes of continents accurately. Others show directions well. Maps usually are most accurate in the center and more distorted at the edges. Generally, the larger the area a map shows, the more distortions it will have.

Map projections often are named after the geographer or cartographer who invented them. A name can also give you information about what dimensions are most accurate in the projection or about how it was made. Each map in this book is labeled with the name of the projection it uses. You will find, among others, Lambert equal-area projections, the Albers conical equal-area projection, and the Robinson projection.

To read and interpret a map, you need to know something about the projection used in making it. On the facing page are examples of four commonly used projections. Use the information in the captions to compare them. If possible, also compare them with a globe.

One way to compare projections is to see how the lines of latitude and longitude appear. Look at the diagram of the Mercator projection. You can see that the latitude-longitude grid forms perfect squares. Since you know that the lines of longitude curve to meet at the poles, you can assume that the sizes of areas in the north and south "edges" of this map must be distorted.

The conical projection (see page G6) is accurate at middle latitudes. Because of this, it is often used to show the United States, which lies mainly in the middle latitudes.

BUILDING MAP SKILLS

Learning the grid system and understanding projections are two basic steps in learning to read maps. You will find that this ability is a useful skill both in and out of school. You need to read maps in studying geography, history, and some of the sciences. In everyday life you need to get information from street maps, highway maps, weather maps, and maps illustrating news stories on television and in magazines and newspapers. Airline pilots, ship captains, surveyors, builders, soldiers, and explorers are only a few of the people who must get accurate information from maps in order to do their jobs.

Before trying to read any map, you need to ask a few questions: What kind of map is it? What is its purpose? What special symbols and features does it use?

KINDS OF MAPS

Except for very specialized subjects, most maps can be classified broadly as either "physical" or "political." As its name suggests, a **physical map** emphasizes natural landforms and geographical features. It may use special colors and shadings to indicate elevation (height above sea level), precipitation, types of soil, types of plant life, or other physical features of the area shown. Dark and light shading may be used to show **relief**, the ruggedness of hills and mountains in an area.

A **political map** focuses on political divisions such as state and national borders. Because it shows fewer physical details, it can include more towns, cities, roads, and other human features. On this type of map, color is commonly used as a means of showing political boundaries or territorial possessions.

To compare physical and political maps of the same area, look at the two United States maps on pages 842–845 of the Atlas at the back of the book. Which one would you consult to find the capital of Virginia? Which one would you look at to learn more about the terrain of northern California?

SPECIAL-PURPOSE MAPS

In addition to showing physical or political characteristics, some maps have an additional special purpose. Often the title tells you what the map's purpose is or what specialized information it presents.

A book like this one commonly includes many **historical maps.** Such maps show a place as it appeared at a certain time in history. Historical maps may show the territories of ancient kingdoms, changes in political boundaries, routes followed by explorers and pioneers, or similar information.

The maps on page 462, for example, show how the boundary between North and South Korea shifted during the Korean War. The map on page 35 uses color to indicate divisions between the states and territories on the issue of slavery before the Civil War. Some historical maps, like the one on pages 846–847 of the Atlas, trace changes in territory over a period of time.

Kinds of Maps Answers
To find the capital of Virginia, check the political map ("Cities and States"). To learn more about the terrain of northern California, consult the physical map ("Physical Features").

Other special-purpose maps give specific information about places or regions. Such maps may show religions, languages, population density, rainfall, crops, or similar data. Be sure to read the title of map first to discover whether it is presenting specialized information.

MAP FEATURES AND SYMBOLS

No matter what their subject matter, maps use certain standard features and symbols to give as much information as possible in a small space. The **key,** or legend, tells you what symbols are used and what each one represents. For example, a dot usually represents a city; different sizes of dots may be used for city populations. A star symbol commonly means that a city is a state or national capital. On a road map, an airplane symbol points out the airport. In some maps in this book, an explosion symbol shows the site of a battle.

The key also gives you the meaning of colors and patterns used on the map. Textbook maps commonly use brighter colors for the areas that show the main subject of the map. The rest of the territory may be in a neutral color.

It is important to be sure of a map's direction, or **orientation**. Traditionally, north is at the top of a map, with east on the right and west on the left. This is not always true, however, particularly with certain types of map projections. Always check the directional symbol known as a **compass rose**. Its "N" arrow points to the North Pole.

Scale indicates how the size and distance on the map compare with reality. That is, one inch on a map may represent a certain number of miles (or kilometers) of real territory. With the map scale, you can find approximate distances and areas on the map. A map that includes a lot of territory—such as a world map—is said to be "large-scale." One that shows a fairly small area, such as a city street map, is "small-scale."

LOCATOR AND INSET MAPS

Two other features that sometimes appear on maps are locator maps and inset maps. In this book, **locator maps** are used to give you a larger context for a map. That is, they show you where the area of the map is located in relation to a larger area. For instance, the map on page 275 of proposed canal routes across Central America has a locator map showing you where that area is relative to North and South America.

Inset maps have the opposite purpose. They give a close-up view of one part of the larger map—perhaps a city or an area with complicated detail.

THE FIVE GEOGRAPHIC THEMES

One way that geographers think about their subject is in terms of major themes, or ideas that run through teaching and learning about geography. All these themes have been a part of this overview of geography and history. They are described in greater detail below.

As you continue to learn about geography—and to see how it applies to history, science, and many other parts of everyday life—try to become aware of these five geographic themes. When you visit a new place, for instance, look at it as a geographer might see it. Ask yourself questions: How can I describe this location? What characteristics make this place special? "Thinking geographically" can give you a new outlook on the world around you.

1. LOCATION

This theme can be expressed as "Where in the world are we?" You have already learned one way to answer this question—the coordinates of latitude and longitude on the grid system. These can give you the accurate, *absolute* location of any place on earth.

In ordinary speech, you are more likely to describe location in a different way. To the question, "Where is it?" people often answer in terms of something else: next door, down the hall, east of Sacramento, south of the Mason-Dixon line. Phrases like this point out *relative* location.

2. PLACE

Place and *location* mean about the same thing in ordinary speech, but these terms have special meanings in geography. The idea of "place" goes beyond the idea of where something is. It includes the special characteristics that make one place different from another. Physical characteristics of any place are its natural features, such as landscape, physical setting, plants and animals, and weather. Human characteristics include the things people have made, from buildings and pottery to language and philosophy.

3. INTERACTIONS

As soon as human beings appeared on earth, they began to change their surroundings. For millions of years, people have interacted with their natural environment. Sometimes they have changed it, leveling hills to build highways or plowing the prairies to plant wheat. Sometimes the environment has changed them, forcing them to invent ways of coping with extremes of hot or cold, natural disasters, floods, and other problems.

4. MOVEMENT

People in different places interact through travel, trade, and modern methods of transportation and communication. For much of the nineteenth century, the United States relied on its natural defenses of two great oceans to protect itself from potential enemies. Today, even if Americans wished to isolate themselves, this would probably be impossible. Computers, television, satellite hookups, and other almost instantaneous forms of communication have increased the movement of people and ideas from place to place.

5. REGIONS

Just as you cannot study an entire subject at once, geographers do not try to study the whole world. They break it into **regions**. A region can be as large as a continent or as small as a neighborhood or a building, but it has certain shared characteristics that set it apart. The simplest way to define a region is by one characteristic, such as political division, type of climate, language spoken, or belief in one religion. Geographers sometimes define regions by other, more complicated sets of features.

LAND REGIONS OF THE UNITED STATES

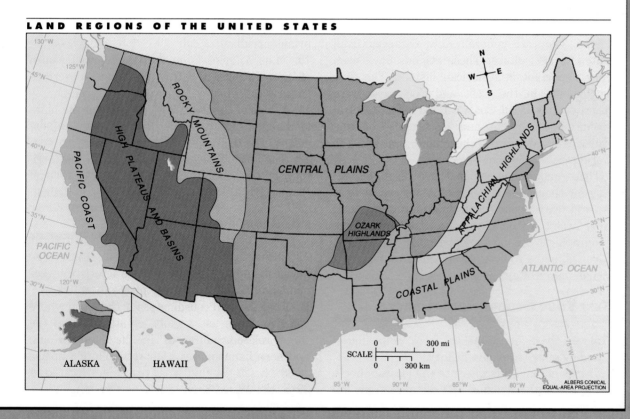

1. C   7. A
2. A   8. B
3. C   9. B
4. A   10. B
5. A   11. C
6. B   12. C

A. While answers may vary, students should be sure to distinguish between physical and human characteristics.

B. Answers will vary, with many of the coordinates falling in the Indian Ocean.

REGIONS OF THE UNITED STATES

The map called "Land Regions of the United States" (on the preceding page) is based on one method for defining regions—physical similarities in landscape and landforms.

Five of the regions shown on the map are highlands. Here the typical landforms are mountain chains, hills, and rugged plateaus.

The highland region in the eastern United States is the Appalachian Mountains and their foothills. (These foothills are sometimes called the piedmont.) A smaller highland region, the Ozark Highlands, is located to the west of the Appalachians. The western United States contains three different highland regions. The Rockies are part of a chain of mountains that begins in Alaska and runs the length of North and South America. Another mountain region is made up of several ranges that run parallel to the Pacific coast. Between the coastal mountains and the Rockies is a dry region of high plateaus, great rivers, and broad valleys. It is sometimes called the "High Plateaus and Basins."

The United States also contains two large lowland areas—the Coastal Plains and the Central Plains. They are generally low, flat areas well suited to agriculture. These regions have been very important in American history. The first settlements in the East and Southeast were made on the broad Coastal Plains. The Central Plains, once forests and grasslands, became America's agricultural heartland, one of the world's richest farming regions.

These geographic regions have been the setting for thousands of years of American history. As you learn about events in American history, refer back to this map to get a better idea of the geographical setting in which they took place. This will make your study of American history a richer, more rewarding experience.

TEST YOUR GEOGRAPHIC LITERACY

Answer these questions to check your understanding of geography in history.
1. Lines of longitude measure (A) location north or south of the equator, (B) distance from the North Pole, (C) distance east or west of the prime meridian.
2. "Parallels" is another term for (A) lines of latitude, (B) meridians, (C) lines of longitude.
3. North and South America are located in the (A) Northern Hemisphere, (B) Eastern Hemisphere, (C) Western Hemisphere.
4. Of the places with these coordinates, which one is nearest the prime meridian? (A) 42°N, 13°E (B) 37°N, 137°W (C) 4°N, 74°W
5. Generally, the most accurate portion of a map is the (A) area near the equator, (B) center of the map, (C) northern half of the map.
6. A map that shows shaded mountain ranges, deserts, and woodlands of the United States is a (A) historical map, (B) physical map, (C) political map.
7. To find what a dotted red line means on a map, you would look at the (A) key, (B) scale, (C) grid.
8. To find what city is about 300 miles northeast of Mobile, Alabama, you should use the (A) lines of longitude and latitude, (B) compass rose and scale, (C) scale and locator.
9. The "N" arrow on a compass rose points to (A) North America, (B) the North Pole, (C) the prime meridian.
10. "Los Angeles is on the Pacific coast, south of San Francisco." This statement describes (A) grid coordinates, (B) location, (C) place.
11. Which of the following is *not* one of the highland regions of the United States? (A) Appalachians (B) Ozarks (C) Central Plains
12. The largest geographical region in the territory of the United States is the (A) Coastal Plains, (B) Rocky Mountains, (C) Central Plains.

FOR MORE PRACTICE

A. Choose a place you know well. List three physical and three human characteristics that make it different from other places.
B. Find the grid coordinates for the place where you live. Then use a globe or atlas to find the three related addresses in the Eastern and Southern hemispheres. (For example, if you live at 38°N, 122°W, find what places are located at 38°S, 122°W, at 38°N, 122°E, and so on.)

Perhaps you have seen a TV news program where the anchor is handed a piece of paper on camera, glances at it, says, "This, just in . . ." and begins to read a late-breaking story. THIS JUST IN enables us to bring you some of the news stories breaking just as this book went to press.

Someone once said that journalism is the "first draft of history." This means that the big stories that daily journalism covers are eventually combined by the historian with many other sources—including archives, journals, diaries, and other materials often not available for many years after the event. The "first draft" is weighed, examined from different perspectives, related to other main developments, and in general given a lasting significance in a lasting medium—the book. THIS JUST IN cannot of course provide the judgments of history. But it can provide some of the facts that will eventually become part of the historian's material.

As we went to press, the following stories were breaking.

WAR IN THE PERSIAN GULF

(See pages 657–659 of your textbook for the background of this story.)

Despite frantic diplomatic efforts on the part of members of the Desert Shield alliance and on the part of Javier Pérez de Cuéllar, Secretary-General of the United Nations, the deadline for Saddam Hussein to comply with U.N. Resolution 678 came and went.

Days before the January 15, 1991, deadline, Iraqi Foreign Minister Tariq Aziz had refused to accept a final letter from President George Bush—a serious insult in diplomatic terms—and Hussein made a public statement that American GI's would "swim in their own blood."

Congress met to decide whether or not to give the President constitutional authority to commit the United States to war in the form of an attack on Iraqi military forces both in Kuwait and in Iraq itself.

Among the issues Congress debated were: Was there some other way short of war? Would the economic sanctions work, if given more time? How large, costly, or long could this war be? What were the goals of American policy? Were they goals the American people could support, and if so, for how long? Had the long-term effects of this war been properly calculated? What would actually happen if Hussein's aggression went unchecked? What would happen if Hussein's regime were totally destroyed? Could we afford the financial burden of a major war at a time when the Treasury was already living on huge amounts of borrowed money? How much actual support in terms of dollars and blood could we expect from our Arab, European, and Japanese allies? Was this declaration of war like the Gulf of Tonkin Resolution? Or was it a vote against the type of Munich-style appeasement that had strengthened Hitler and brought on World War II?

On January 12, 1991, Congress voted for war. The vote was fairly close: 52–47 in the Senate, 250–183 in the House. The questions that members of Congress asked themselves and the nation were good questions. But the answers to such questions, as always, were not to be found in the present moment. Such questions can only be answered by the passage of time, by the unfolding of actual events, and by the work of historians.

On January 16, 1991, armed forces of the Desert Shield coalition attacked along a broad front, beginning with massive aerial strikes on Iraqi airfields, missile sites, and other military targets. President Bush assured the nation and the world that the goals of the military action—now named Desert Storm—were limited. The goals were, he said, to restore Kuwait to its people and rulers, to uphold international law, and to defeat Iraq but not destroy it, so that Iraq could once again take its place in the "family of nations." Bush also stressed that Desert Storm forces would receive all the support necessary to achieve victory. U.S. forces would not be asked to fight "with one hand tied behind their back," he said.

In the first few days of the war, it appeared that Desert Storm forces had achieved almost complete surprise. There was almost no resistance from the Iraqi air force, and the massive, high-tech "smart" bombing seemed to have severely disrupted Iraqi communications and to have destroyed suspected Iraqi chemical and atomic weapons facilities. But then, Saddam Hussein, true to his promise, fired Soviet-made Scud missiles at several locations in Israel and Saudi Arabia. The U.S. immediately supplied Israel with Patriot anti-missile missiles, which had proven effective against the Scuds, and American crews to operate them.

The Scud missile launchings were a last-gasp effort by Hussein, however. On February 23, allied forces launched a brilliantly planned ground assault that liberated Kuwait in a matter of days. American soldiers returned home to heroes' welcomes. Inside Iraq,

civil war began to rage. Hussein clung to power by putting down rebellions in the south and north. Many Kurds, fearing for their lives, fled into Turkey, only to face harsh conditions in refugee camps. Allied soldiers were sent to help them return safely to Iraq.

SOVIET BALTIC CRISIS: END OF *GLASNOST*?
(See text pages 653–655 for the background of this story.)

In mid-January 1991, as the Gulf crisis unfolded, Soviet paratroopers killed and wounded civilians in a takeover of the Lithuanian capital of Vilnius, signaling a probable end to *glasnost* and the likelihood of more repression to follow.

In Latvia, Communist Party officials, many of whom had been swept from office in free elections, engineered a series of attacks by local police forces in an attempt to bring on direct Soviet intervention to restore order. Angered by criticism of the Lithuanian takeover in the Soviet press, President Mikhail Gorbachev asked for a suspension of freedom of the press in order to restore "objectivity." A shocked Soviet parliament gave him about half of what he asked for.

President Bush and members of the European Community expressed grave concern at these developments. At the same time, Western leaders hoped to retain Soviet support for the Desert Storm operation.

Observers inside and outside

the Soviet Union had long worried about a reversal of Soviet policies. In late 1990, for example, Soviet Foreign Minister Eduard Shevardnadze, a long-time friend and ally of Mikhail Gorbachev, stunned the world by resigning from the Soviet government and warning that Communist Party hard-liners were attempting to bring back the old dictatorship. Gorbachev, beset by rebellions in the Baltic and Asian Soviet republics, by democratic defiance of his policies in the central Russian republic, and by the prospect of acute food and energy shortages or even a complete economic collapse, has increasingly sought support from the traditional agents of repression in his country—the armed forces, the KGB, and the hard-line bureaucrats of the Party.

Some Europeans, including observers in the newly independent Eastern Bloc nations as well as in the recently unified Germany, wondered if the forces unleashed within the Soviet Union by *glasnost* and *perestroika* were strong enough to withstand a full-scale effort on the part of the central government to reinstate the old system. If they were not sufficiently strong, brutal repression of the old Stalinist sort was a possibility. If they were strong enough, actual civil war among the Soviet republics—where many thousands of nuclear weapons left over from the cold war were stockpiled—was also a possibility.

UNIT ONE

Beginnings Through Reconstruction

CHAPTERS IN THIS UNIT

1 A New Nation (Beginnings–1850)

2 The Civil War Era (1850–1865)

3 Rebuilding the South (1865–1900)

THEMES IN AMERICAN HISTORY

Global Interactions   European explorers and settlers reached and then began to colonize the Americas.

Constitutional Government   After winning independence, Americans established representative government, first under the Articles of Confederation and later under the Constitution.

American Culture   A spirit of reform, energized by a religious revival, led to movements for abolition and other causes during the 1830s and 1840s.

Geography   Victory over Mexico in 1848 gave the United States vast new western lands.

Pluralistic Society   The Civil War and the ending of slavery failed to eliminate the nation's racial divisions.

Unit One

Beginnings Through Reconstruction
(pp. 1–84)

This unit reviews the early history of America, noting American Indian civilizations and the effect of European colonization on them. It describes the development of colonial economies and the establishment of self-government in the English colonies of North America. The American Revolution, the Constitutional Convention, and the first decades of the republic are also covered.

The unit explains how increasing sectional differences and conflicts over states' rights led to the outbreak of the Civil War, and details the political philosophies of both the North and South, their military actions, and the economic and social impact of the war. The legacy of the Civil War is also described, with emphasis on the situation of southern blacks after the war, the struggle between the President and Congress over the reconstruction of the South, the constitutional and legal changes in the status of African Americans, and the return of the South to local control with the subsequent development of unique southern economic and cultural institutions.

1

Chapter 1 ■ A New Nation

4 Sections, 4–8 Days

	SECTION OBJECTIVES	SECTION RESOURCES
Section 1 **The Beginnings**	■ identify steps English colonists took to achieve self-government	● **Reteaching Resources:** Worksheet 1 ▲ **Reinforcement Workbook:** Worksheet 1 ▲ **Teaching Transparencies:** Transparency 1
Section 2 **Establishing a New Nation**	■ relate the events that led the colonists to declare their independence ■ explain why a Constitutional Convention had to be called	● **Reteaching Resources:** Worksheet 2 ▲ **Reinforcement Workbook:** Worksheet 2 ▲ **Teaching Transparencies:** Transparency 2
Section 3 **Launching a New Government**	■ describe the process of debate and compromise through which the Constitutional Convention worked out a new form of government ■ explain the causes and effects of the War of 1812	● **Reteaching Resources:** Worksheet 3 ▲ **Reinforcement Workbook:** Worksheet 3 ■ **Enrichment and Extension Resources:** Primary Source Worksheet 1 ▲ **Teaching Transparencies:** Transparency 3
Section 4 **Pulling Together, Pulling Apart**	■ discuss the changes brought about by industrialization ■ describe the ways in which Andrew Jackson's presidency reflected the changes occurring in the United States ■ describe the events that led to the Mexican War	● **Reteaching Resources:** Worksheet 4 ▲ **Reinforcement Workbook:** Worksheet 4 ■ **Enrichment and Extension Resources:** Primary Source Worksheet 2 ▲ **Teaching Transparencies:** Transparency 4

The list below shows Essential Elements relevant to this chapter. (The complete list of Essential Elements appears in the introductory pages of this Teacher's Edition.)

Section 1: 2D, 3C, 4B, 4C, 5E, 7B, 7J, 8C, 9B, 9E
Section 2: 1A, 3B, 4B, 4C, 5E, 6B, 7A, 7E, 7I, 8D, 8H, 9A
Section 3: 1A, 1B, 2D, 3F, 3G, 4C, 5D, 5E, 7B, 7D, 7I, 8B, 9B
Section 4: 1A, 1B, 2A, 2D, 3A, 3B, 4C, 4D, 4G, 7D, 9B, 9D

Section Resources are keyed for
student abilities:
● = Basic
▲ = Average
■ = Average/Advanced

CHAPTER RESOURCES

Geography Resources: Worksheets 1, 2
Tests: Chapter 1 Test

Chapter Project: American Culture

Have students prepare and develop a project illustrating changes in the way people lived in North America between 1500 and 1800. This project may take the form of an illustrated timeline, a series of maps, a diorama, or posters.

Homework Options

Each section contains activities labeled "Addressing Individual Needs." You may wish to choose from among these activities when assigning homework.

> **Provisions for Limited English Proficiency (LEP)**
> Several suggested activities may be particularly helpful for teachers of students with limited English proficiency. These activities have been marked throughout the Teacher's Annotated Edition with the symbol **LEP** .

BIBLIOGRAPHY AND AUDIOVISUAL AIDS

Teacher Bibliography

Bolton, Herbert E., ed. *Spanish Exploration in the Southwest, 1542–1706.* Barnes and Noble, 1963. Original narratives.

Cunliffe, Marcus. *The Nation Takes Shape: Seventeen Eighty-Nine–Eighteen Thirty-Seven.* University of Chicago Press, 1960.

Greene, Jack P. *American Colonies in the Eighteenth Century, 1689–1763.* Harlan Davidson, 1969.

Josephy, Alvin M., Jr. *Indian Heritage of America.* Knopf, 1968.

Morison, Samuel E., ed. *Sources and Documents Illustrating the American Revolution, 1764–1788, and the Formation of the Federal Constitution.* Oxford University Press, 1965.

Student Bibliography

Alderman, Clifford L. *Rum, Slaves and Molasses: The Story of New England's Triangular Trade.* Macmillan, 1972.

DePauw, Linda Grant. *Founding Mothers: Women of America in the Revolutionary Era.* Houghton Mifflin, 1975.

Franklin, Paula. *Indians of North America: Survey of Tribes That Inhabit the Continent.* McKay, 1979.

Smith, Barbara C. *After the Revolution: The Smithsonian History of Everyday Life in the 18th Century.* Pantheon, 1987.

Van Doren, Carl. *The Great Rehearsal: The Story of the Making and Ratifying of the Constitution of the U.S.* Greenwood, 1982.

Literature

Cooper, James Fenimore. *The Last of the Mohicans.* Macmillan, 1986.

Edmonds, Walter D. *Drums Along the Mohawk.* Little, Brown, 1936.

Forester, C.S. *The Captain from Connecticut.* Little, Brown, 1941. An adventure story of the naval battles in the War of 1812.

Franklin, Benjamin. *The Autobiography of Benjamin Franklin.* Yale University Press, 1964.

Melville, Herman. *Moby Dick.* McDougal-Littell, 1977.

Richter, Conrad. *The Awakening Land.* Knopf, 1966. Three novels which trace the settlement and growth of the Ohio Valley.

Sanders, Thomas E. and Walter W. Peek. *Literature of the American Indian.* Macmillan, 1973.

Films and Videotapes*

America Before the Europeans (The World: A Television History Series). 26 min. LAND. Early Americans from 300–1500. Includes the Maya, Aztec, and Inca civilizations.

Background of the American Revolutionary War. 23 min. MG. Traces the events leading to the American Revolution.

The Constitution: A History of Our Future. 21 min. COR/MTI. Historical data and background on the framing of the Constitution and its effect on our lives today.

The Golden Land (West of the Imagination Series). 52 min. FFH. Americans' westward surge during the mid-1800s. Covers the Texas Revolution, Mexican War, gold strikes, and the Oregon Trail.

New Found Land (America Series). 52 min. AMBR. Spanish, French, and English arrive in North America and introduce new ways of life.

A New Nation: The Struggle to Survive. 25 min. BNCHMK. Events between 1789 and 1815.

Filmstrips*

Europeans discover America (set of five). SVE. Titles include: *American Indians; Europeans Explore a New World; Spain Builds a Great Empire; Rise and Fall of New France;* and *English Colonies in America.* Also available in video.

Spirit of Independence (set of five). SVE. Titles include: *Life in Colonial Times; Patriots and Minutemen; The American Revolution; Free Americans Start a New Nation;* and *The Young Nation and Foreign Affairs.*

Computer Software*

Across the Plains (2 disks: Commodore/Amiga). MICRO. Interactive instructional program depicting journeys across the Great Plains to the West Coast.

Creating the U.S. Constitution (1 disk: Apple or IBM). EDACT. Interactive program that introduces the leaders, ideas, conflicts, and compromises of the Constitutional Convention.

The Santa Fe Trail (1 disk: Apple or IBM, Tandy 1000 or 2000). EDACT. As traders traveling the Santa Fe Trail between 1820 and 1829, students must make decisions concerning routes, interactions with Indians, how to survive random disasters, etc.

Washington's Decisions (1 disk: Apple or IBM). EDACT. Students are presented with choices faced by Washington and are challenged to duplicate his decisions.

*For a complete guide to audiovisual sources, see the introduction to this book (page Txx).

Themes in American History

- Global Interactions
- Constitutional Government
- American Culture

Chapter Objectives

After students complete this chapter, they will be able to:

1. Identify steps English colonists took to achieve self-government.

2. Relate the events that led the colonists to declare their independence.

3. Explain why a Constitutional Convention had to be called.

4. Describe the process of debate and compromise through which the Constitutional Convention worked out a new form of government.

5. Explain the causes and effects of the War of 1812.

6. Discuss the changes brought about by industrialization.

7. Describe the ways in which Andrew Jackson's presidency reflected the changes occurring in the United States.

8. Describe the events that led to the Mexican War.

The wisdom gained from the struggle for liberty and independence led Americans to a new plan of government—the Constitution of the United States. The Union forged by that Constitution would later be sorely tested by a terrible Civil War.

Chapter Opener Art
Replica of the Constitution of the United States.

CHAPTER SUPPORT MATERIAL	
Reinforcement Workbook: Worksheets 1–4	
Reteaching Resources: Worksheets 1–4	
Enrichment and Extension Resources: Primary Source Worksheets 1, 2	
Geography Resources: Worksheets 1, 2	
Teaching Transparencies: 1–4	
Tests: Chapter 1 Test	

1 A New Nation
(Beginnings–1850)

KEY EVENTS

1492	Columbus reaches America
1607	Jamestown established
1620	Pilgrims settle Plymouth
1775–1783	American Revolution
1788	Constitution ratified
1803	Louisiana Purchase
1812–1814	War of 1812
1846–1848	Mexican War

2D, 3C, 4B, 4C, 5E, 7B, 7J, 8C, 9B, 9E

1 The Beginnings

Section Focus

Key Terms Columbian exchange ■ mercantilism ■ House of Burgesses ■ Mayflower Compact ■ Great Migration ■ charter ■ Glorious Revolution

Main Idea European powers colonized the Americas in order to gain wealth from the new land and to convert new peoples to Christianity. The English colonies established ideas of self-government and liberty.

Objectives As you read, look for answers to these questions:
1. What effects did European colonization have on Native Americans?
2. How did English colonists establish a degree of self-government?
3. What distinguished the three regions within the English colonies?

In 1492 Christopher Columbus set out on his historic voyage across the Atlantic Ocean. His hope was to reach the Indies—the spice islands of Asia—by sailing west. Ferdinand and Isabella, the monarchs of Spain, financed the voyage. A new route to the Indies, they knew, would break the monopoly that Italian merchants had on trade with the Indies. Isabella also hoped that Columbus's expedition would lead to the conversion of new peoples to Christianity.

On October 12, 1492, Columbus landed on the Caribbean island of San Salvador. Certain that he was in the Indies, he called the natives "Indians." Columbus was not the first European in the Western Hemisphere. Norsemen, or Vikings, sailing from a settlement in Greenland, established at least one settlement on Newfoundland about A.D. 1000. Yet no previous voyage had the impact of the one taken in 1492. Columbus's voyage began a European conquest of the Americas that would bring massive change to both the Western and the Eastern hemispheres.

THE COLUMBIAN EXCHANGE 2D

With the arrival of Columbus, the Western Hemisphere became part of an Atlantic world. No longer a barrier, the Atlantic Ocean became a water highway linking Africa, the Americas, and Europe. People, animals, and plants moved between continents. This movement, called the Columbian exchange, caused profound changes on each continent.

Western Hemisphere foods such as potatoes, corn, tomatoes, and peppers helped feed the whole world. Likewise, such domesticated animals as the horse, cow, goat, and pig changed the Western Hemisphere. After the Spanish brought horses to North America, for instance, the Indians learned to tame and ride the animals. As a result, many left their farming ways and lived primarily by hunting buffalo.

The Columbian exchange resulted in massive population changes as Europeans invaded the Western Hemisphere. In the process, Europeans kidnapped thousands of Africans and brought

---

SUPPORTING THE SECTION

Reinforcement Workbook: Worksheet 1
Reteaching Resources: Worksheet 1
Teaching Transparencies: Transparency 1

Section 1

The Beginnings
pp. (3–7)

Section Objective
■ identify steps English colonists took to achieve self-government

Introducing the Section

Connecting with Past Learnings
Ask students to recall important events and trends related to the founding of the English colonies in North America. List their suggestions on the board. Then have the class rearrange the list in chronological order.

Key Terms
Write each key term on a slip of paper, put the terms in a bag, and ask volunteers to reach in the bag and choose one of the slips. Have the volunteers write the definition of their term on the board, and have the class identify the term. Follow this procedure for each term. **LEP**

Focus
On the board, create a chart with column headings *1500s* and *1600s,* and row headings *Americas, Africa,* and *Europe.* Have the class fill in the chart with the events and trends in those places during those centuries.

1500s
Americas introduction of European animals, Spanish exploration and colonization, conquest of Inca and Aztec empires, death of millions of Indians from European diseases.
Africa introduction of some American foods.
Europe introduction of American foods; Spain grows wealthier because of goods from the Americas.

Americas
English colonies founded, Dutch colony founded and then taken over by British, local governments set up.

Africa
interior kingdoms weakened while coastal kingdoms grow richer from slave trade.

Europe
Puritans leave England in the 1630s, the Glorious Revolution establishes Parliament's preeminence.

What major differences were emerging among the New England, Middle, and Southern colonies by the end of the 1600s?
(New Englanders were traders and shipbuilders; the Southern Colonies grew cash crops; the Middle Colonies were a blend of both.)

Developing the Lesson

After students have read the lesson, you may want to consider the following activities:

Geographic Themes: Place
Ask students to imagine landing on an inhabited planet "somewhere in space." Have them speculate on their possible interaction with the inhabitants of the planet. Encourage comparisons between such an imaginary situation and the arrival of Spanish explorers in the Americas.

Cultural Pluralism
Why were some of the English colonies in America more ethnically diverse than others?
(New York had been settled by the Dutch and welcomed Africans, Scandinavians, and Jews; the Puritans of Massachusetts were intolerant of those who disagreed with them and drove other groups out of the colony; southern colonies had African slaves.)

Which colony would you have preferred to live in? Why?

---

them to the Americas as slaves. In Africa, the slave trade weakened African kingdoms of the interior, for that was where most slaves came from. Some kingdoms on Africa's west coast became stronger and richer from their profits in the slave trade.

Native Americans were overwhelmed by the European invasion. Particularly devastating were the unseen invaders—the microbes of disease. For thousands of years the Indians had been isolated from the common diseases of the rest of the world. These included chicken pox, measles, smallpox, and the flu. As a result, an ordinary case of flu for a European became a ticket to death for an Indian. With mortality rates as high as 90 percent, the social and economic foundation of whole tribes was wiped out. The Indian population of North America dropped from about 10–12 million in 1500 to about half a million in 1900. It was a population catastrophe without precedent.

THE SPANISH CENTURY 3C
The first colonial power in North America was Spain. For more than a century, from 1492 to about 1600, Spain steadily extended its influence over the Americas. Its first colonies were in the Caribbean, on islands like Hispaniola and Cuba. Then, between 1519 and 1521 Hernan Cortés conquered the Aztecs of Mexico. Not long after, Francisco Pizarro conquered Peru for Spain. In both Mexico and Peru, the Spaniards found more wealth than they had ever dreamed of. In search of even more wealth, explorers such as Hernando de Soto and Francisco Coronado explored North America in the 1540s. De Soto came upon the Mississippi River in his exploration of the Southeast. Coronado reached the very heart of the continent, the plains of Kansas.

To deal with its colonies, Spain developed a new economic system called mercantilism. In this system all trade was regulated with the purpose of enriching the parent country. In practice, mercantilism meant that the precious goods and produce of the Americas were shipped to Spain. On their return, ships carried manufactured goods needed by the colonists.

The success of mercantilism depended on the production of crops and metals for export. A cheap, plentiful supply of labor was necessary to develop the new colonial economy. Spanish

An Aztec artist drew the meeting between conquistador Hernan Cortés and Montezuma, the Aztec emperor. The Aztecs gave the Spaniards many gifts, including precious objects of gold and turquoise. TECHNOLOGY What do you think impressed the artist most about the Spaniards? 9B

4   UNIT 1   BEGINNINGS THROUGH RECONSTRUCTION

Photo Caption Answer
Their armor and horses.

Background Spain transferred the precious goods of the Americas in large merchant ships called *galleons*. These were loaded at various Caribbean ports and then left Havana for Spain in a protected convoy once a year. The rich trade routes of the area led the Caribbean Sea to become known as the Spanish Main.

planters in the Caribbean were the first to bring African slaves to labor in the Americas.

Other European nations, meanwhile, were learning from Spanish success. Nations with ports on the north Atlantic—France, Holland, and England—began to challenge Spain's hold on North America. They sent out their own explorations and laid their own claims to chunks of North America. Sir Walter Raleigh thus named and claimed Virginia for England. Henry Hudson explored and claimed the Hudson River valley for Holland. The French explored and claimed the St. Lawrence River valley.

JAMESTOWN AND PLYMOUTH 5E, 7J

In 1607 the Virginia Company founded England's first successful colony at Jamestown. The company propped up the tiny colony for years by sending forth both new colonists and supplies. Jamestown finally achieved a firm footing when the settlers began to raise tobacco for export to England.

For more than a decade the colonists squirmed under the authority of a governor appointed by the company. Then in 1619 the Virginia Company allowed the settlers a measure of self-government by creating an elected assembly. This assembly, the House of Burgesses, became the first representative assembly in the colonies. It was a pattern that other English colonies would adopt.

The 1600s was a time of religious turmoil in Europe. Supporters of the Catholic Church battled those who had broken away from the Church. Those who broke with the Church were called Protestants because they protested Catholic practices. The Protestants themselves, however, were not united and were often intolerant of each other.

English authorities persecuted a Protestant group, the Separatists, that broke from the Church of England. The Separatists then fled to Holland. Although Holland was tolerant of their faith, the Separatists wanted to hold on to their English ways. To do so, they decided to establish a colony in America. The Separatists received permission to settle on the Virginia Company's land grant. Those who made the journey we call Pilgrims.

On the voyage the Pilgrims' ship the *Mayflower* was blown off course. The Pilgrims found themselves off Cape Cod, far north of the Virginia Com-

pany grant. Thus they were beyond established authority, in an area of no government. Before landing, therefore, the men signed an agreement, the Mayflower Compact. In the compact they consented to obey any laws agreed upon for the general good of the colony. The Pilgrims then went ashore at the place called Plymouth.

★ Historical Documents

For an excerpt from the *Mayflower Compact*, see page 719 of this book.

THE PURITAN EMIGRATION 2D, 4B

During the 1620s the population of colonial New England remained small, numbering only about 500. The population ballooned in the 1630s, however, because of people fleeing political, economic, and religious unrest in England.

The new immigrants to New England in the 1630s were Puritans. Similar to the Pilgrims, they disagreed with practices of the Church of England. Most Puritans were also members of England's rising middle class. Many of them were in the wool trade, and in the 1630s this trade faced hard and uncertain times. Thinking that England was going to rack and ruin, many Puritans decided to emigrate to America in order to better their lot and practice their faith. Thus in 1630 began the Great Migration.

About 20,000 Puritan emigrants settled in New England under the authority of the Massachusetts Bay Company. This company had a royal charter to settle land in New England. A charter is a written contract from a governmental authority.

The Puritans used the charter of the Massachusetts Bay Company as the basis for a new society. Leading this effort was John Winthrop. Massachusetts, Winthrop said, would be a society of justice and mercy. It would be a commonwealth, a community in which people worked together for the good of the whole. It would be a model for the world—"a city upon a hill."

The Puritans believed they had a covenant—solemn agreement—with God to build such a holy society. The Pilgrims' Mayflower Compact was but the first of a tradition of written covenants. When a group of Puritans left Massachusetts to

Local History
The United States is rich in place names that come from different ethnic cultures. Have students refer to an almanac or encyclopedia to find out the origins of your state name. Ask them to identify the origin of the name of your city or town. Discuss what your community's name says about the original settlers of your area.

Patterns in History
As the English colonies grew, the colonists began to import more manufactured goods from England than they exported to England in raw materials. *How might this trade deficit have hurt the American economy?* (Drained money out of the colonies; prevented them from developing local industry.)

Tell students that, starting in the 1970s, the United States has been running a trade deficit. Discuss the similarities and differences between the causes and effects of the colonial and present-day trade deficits.

Ⓒ Cooperative Learning

Divide the class into small groups whose task is to establish a colony far from home. Have different members of the group list the problems the colony will face, the economic activities of the colony, and the structure of the government. Have the group discuss these lists and then write a set of fundamental rules or laws which will be necessary for the common good. Then ask each group to report to the class the process it used to develop these laws—consensus, simple majority rule, agreement of highest percentage of the group, etc. **LEP**

This painting from 1613 shows how the scene might have looked when the Pilgrims left Europe for North America.
CULTURAL PLURALISM Why did the Pilgrims want to leave their homeland? 9E

establish Connecticut, they too wrote a compact, the Fundamental Orders of Connecticut. This compact was, in fact, a constitution—a document describing a framework of government.

Although seeking religious liberty for themselves, the Puritans were not tolerant of those who disagreed with them. Any who questioned Puritan ideas were driven from the colony.

EXPANSION OF THE ENGLISH COLONIES 4C
In the middle 1600s there were two clusters of English colonists in America: those of the Chesapeake Bay area and those of New England. The Chesapeake region included the colonies of Virginia and Maryland. There the principal economic activity centered on growing tobacco. For decades most immigrants into the Chesapeake region were English indentured servants. They worked as laborers, usually from four to seven years, until their boat passage had been paid for. As the supply of indentured servants dwindled in the 1660s, planters turned increasingly to African slaves.

Between the English settlements of New England and the Chesapeake was New Amsterdam, part of the Dutch colony of New Netherland. Though small, the population of New Netherland was more diverse than that of its neighboring English colonies. Eager to attract and keep settlers, the colony had welcomed a variety of people. From its founding in 1625 New Amsterdam had included Africans, Scandinavians, Puritans, and Jews.

In the 1660s the English king, Charles II, decided to enlarge England's American empire. The king's brother, the Duke of York, forced the Dutch to abandon New Netherland. New Netherland would in time be divided into the colonies of New York, New Jersey, Delaware, and Pennsylvania. In addition, the English established the colony of Carolina. It would eventually be divided into North Carolina and South Carolina. In 1732 Georgia, the thirteenth colony, was founded.

COLONIAL PROSPERITY 2D
Distinct regional characteristics developed among the colonies. The colonists of New England prospered through trade, shipbuilding, and fishing. Settlers in the Southern Colonies built an economy centered on the cash crops of tobacco, rice, and indigo. In this, they became increasingly dependent on slave labor. The Middle Colonies were a blend of both North and South. A rich agricultural region, the Middle Colonies raised wheat and other foodstuffs. Ports such as Philadelphia and New York City became important shipping and trading centers.

England did not forget the purpose of its colonies: to make England more powerful and more wealthy. English law encouraged the colonists to produce raw materials for England and to buy manufactured goods from England.

COLONIAL GOVERNMENT 5E, 7B
Representative government in England, meanwhile, was becoming stronger. The English had a long tradition of rights going back to the Magna Carta of 1215. The Magna Carta asserted the right

Rice Hope was the name of this 20,000-acre plantation near Charleston, South Carolina. In colonial times, rice was South Carolina's most important export. ECONOMICS What other crops were important in the colonial South? 8C

to trial by a jury of one's peers, no imprisonment without trial, and no taxation except by legal means. In later centuries Parliament acquired the power to make laws and to pass taxes. The rights of Englishmen also included common law—a tradition of customs and law based on previous court decisions.

During the 1600s the Crown and Parliament had battled for control. The kings had declared they had a God-given right to rule. On the other hand, Parliament was determined not to give up its traditional rights. In the Glorious Revolution of 1688 the issue was decided in favor of Parliament. Law had precedence over the whims of a king. To make this clear, Parliament passed a Bill of Rights that affirmed the traditional rights of the people.

By 1700 each colony was ruled by a governor, either elected or appointed. Assisting the governor was an appointed council of great power. It could make laws, carry them out, and act as judge and jury. The colonial assemblies could introduce both legislation and money bills.

In general, England let the colonies alone to manage their own affairs. The colonies thrived.

Their citizens gained valuable experience in self-government. Then both international and frontier rivalries forced a change in English policy. The result was the series of events known as the American Revolution.

SECTION REVIEW

1. KEY TERMS Columbian exchange, mercantilism, House of Burgesses, Mayflower Compact, Great Migration, charter, Glorious Revolution

2. PEOPLE AND PLACES Christopher Columbus, Jamestown, Plymouth, John Winthrop

3. COMPREHENSION What American foods spread to other continents as part of the Columbian exchange? What did Europeans bring to the Americas?

4. COMPREHENSION How was the economy of New England different from that of the Southern Colonies?

5. CRITICAL THINKING Why are the Fundamental Orders of Connecticut so important historically?

Burgesses—Colonial assembly of elected representatives established by the Virginia Company. *Mayflower Compact*—Document of self-government drawn up by the men on board the Mayflower. *Great Migration*—Emigration of Puritans from England to the Americas in the 1630s. *charter*—Written contract from a governmental authority. *Glorious Revolution*—1688 overthrow of the king by Parliament.

2. *Christopher Columbus*—Explorer who arrived in America in 1492. *Jamestown*—First successful English colony founded in Virginia in 1607. *Plymouth*—English colony founded by Separatists, also called Pilgrims, in New England. *John Winthrop*—Leader of the Puritan migration.

3. Corn, potatoes, peppers, tomatoes from the Americas. Horses, cows, goats, pigs from Europe, as well as diseases.

4. New England colonies prospered through trade, shipbuilding, and fishing. The Southern colonies economy centered on the cash crops tobacco, rice, and indigo, and was dependent on slave labor.

5. The Fundamental Orders was an early model of a constitution, a document describing a framework of government.

Closure

Ask one student to transform the Main Idea of the section into a question, and have other students answer that question. Then have students read Section 2 for the next class period, noting the causes and effects of the American Revolution.

Photo Caption Answer
Cash crops such as tobacco and indigo.

Background Rhode Island and Connecticut were totally self-governing, with the governors elected by the voters. In other colonies, government tended to split into two factions: the governor and his appointed council served the interests of England, while the assemblies represented the interests of the colonists who elected them.

Colonial Expressions

Introducing the Feature

Have students consider how the colonial experience affected the language of English-speaking colonists. *Why might a new environment require new words?* (Needed words to describe things that did not exist in Great Britain.) *How might the diversity of cultures that existed in the colonies have affected the language?* (Introduced foreign words, new concepts and expressions.)

Have students examine the pictures on these pages. *What aspects of British culture affected language in the colonies?* (British law, fashion, ways of making a living.)

Teaching the Expressions

Bigwigs: Point out to students that in British courts today, lawyers and judges still wear wigs and robes. *Is that custom followed in American courts?* (American judges often wear robes, but not ceremonial wigs.)

Bucks: The official name of U.S. currency, the *dollar,* comes from the German and Dutch *thaler.* Ask students to suggest other slang terms for money (dough, moolah, bread, a grand, etc.) and speculate on the origins of those slang terms.

Two bits: The smallest unit of currency in the United States is the one-cent coin. You may ask students to examine the coin. Point out that the term "one penny" does not appear on it. Explain that *penny* is strictly unofficial, an old English word that people continue to use.

Colonial Expressions

Many expressions that people use today come from customs and crafts that were familiar centuries ago. In colonial America, the strongest influence on both customs and language came from England. Some phrases crossed the oceans with the colonists and found a home in American speech.

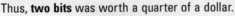

In the law courts of England and the American colonies, lawyers and judges wore wigs and robes. Lawyers' wigs were short and curly. The judge wore a large wig that came to his shoulders, making him a **bigwig**.

Fashionable gentlemen and ladies also wore wigs, known as "wool," on other formal occasions. If someone jokingly **"pulled the wool over your eyes,"** you couldn't see what was going on. At dances and balls, a special **powder room** was set aside so that servants could put fresh powder on people's formal white wigs.

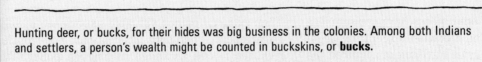

Hunting deer, or bucks, for their hides was big business in the colonies. Among both Indians and settlers, a person's wealth might be counted in buckskins, or **bucks.**

The Spanish silver *peso* was used widely in America in the 1600s and 1700s. For small amounts, people often cut the coin into "pieces of eight" or **bits** worth 12 1/2 cents each. Thus, **two bits** was worth a quarter of a dollar.

Blacksmiths, who made iron tools and horseshoes, had to heat the metal so it would be soft enough to bend. To work the metal, the smith had to **strike while the iron was hot.** If the blacksmith had **too many irons in the fire,** none would get hot enough to work well.

Background
The material on these pages was written by Mary Conway, a historical specialist at Colonial Williamsburg in Virginia.

In colonial times, printers set type by hand, picking each letter from a wooden case. Capital letters were in the **upper case,** small ones in the **lower case.** Beginners could easily mix up similar letters and so were told to **"mind your p's and q's."**

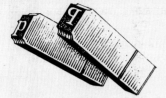

Apprentice sailors also had to be careful. Since there were more than a hundred different ropes for the sails and yards on a sailing ship, a sailor who didn't **know the ropes** could cause serious trouble.

Royal officials faced with an unruly crowd of colonists might **read them the riot act.** Under English law, once the Riot Act had been read aloud to a crowd or meeting, they had one hour in which to break up or they would be arrested.

In England and France, legal documents were tied with a pinkish-red tape or ribbon, then sealed with a blob of wax and stamped with an official seal. Dealing with the government meant getting through the **red tape.**

How did Americans get the name **Yankees**? People disagree. Some people think it came from nicknames given to Dutch sailors: *Janke* (little Jan) or *Jan Kees* (a sort of Dutch John Doe). Others think it came from the Indians' pronunciation of "Yengleesh" for *English.*

Mind your p's and q's: Besides the explanation of this phrase described here, there are several others. Some attribute it to hand-writing teachers warning against confusing the two letters. Other explanations refer to sailors' pea-jackets and pigtails, called queues, and to the pints and quarts purchased in a pub. Ask students if they can think of other possible explanations.

Riot Act: Refer students to the First Amendment of the Constitution on page 754. *Which provision of the amendment would make the Riot Act unconstitutional?* (The right of the people to assemble peaceably.) Point out that nearly all of the guarantees of civil liberties in the Bill of Rights can be traced back to restrictions found in British law.

Yankees: The Dutch influence extends to more than the national nickname. Have students identify the following Dutch words that came into English in colonial times: *stoop* (front steps); *sleigh* (large sled pulled by horses); *boss* (supervisor or employer); and *pit* (of a fruit). Many New York-area place names, such as Harlem and Brooklyn, are Dutch. Both the idea and name of Santa Claus (from *Sint Klass,* the Dutch name for Saint Nicholas) are Dutch. See the next Cultural Literacy feature, pages 146–147, for the influence of Dutch cooking.

2 Establishing a New Nation

Section Objectives

- relate the events that led the colonists to declare their independence
- explain why a Constitutional Convention had to be called

Introducing the Section

Connecting with Past Learnings

Review with the class the establishment of self-government in the English colonies in America. Have students list the compacts and governmental bodies that formed the basis of the American political tradition. (Magna Carta, House of Burgesses, Mayflower Compact, Fundamental Orders of Connecticut.) *What was the basic principle of the compacts?* (The idea of people creating and obeying laws for the common good.)

Key Terms

Have students create a timetable using as many of the key terms as possible. They should list the key term, the year or years it occurred, and a short description. **LEP**

Section Focus

Key Terms French and Indian War ■ Stamp Act ■ Declaration of Independence ■ republic ■ Articles of Confederation

Main Idea Increasing dissatisfaction with life under British rule led the American colonies to declare their independence. The resulting American Revolution led to the establishment of a republic.

Objectives As you read, look for answers to these questions:
1. What were the causes of tension between Britain and the colonies?
2. How did the Revolutionary War start? How did it end?
3. How did the new republic govern itself?

In 1700 England, France, and Spain each claimed hunks of the North American continent for themselves. England controlled the middle part of North America's east coast. Spain's empire reached from Mexico northward into New Mexico and Florida. (It would soon establish settlements in Texas and California.) New France included the St. Lawrence River valley, the Great Lakes region, and all the land drained by the Mississippi River.

FRONTIER HOSTILITIES 4B

The hostility between rival empires at times erupted into warfare. On the frontier shared by the English colonies and New France, warfare could be particularly ferocious. In general the Indians fought the wars, with French or English support.

By the 1750s, the expanding population of the English colonies was causing the balance of power between France and England to shift. In 1750 French colonists numbered about 60,000, compared with over one million in the English colonies. English colonists began to plan for the settlement of the Ohio Valley.

France became alarmed. An English presence along the Ohio River would threaten its control of the Mississippi Valley. The French and English battled for empire once again in the French and Indian War. This war became part of a larger, worldwide war known as the Seven Years' War (1756–1763). The turning point of the war came when British soldiers swarmed up steep cliffs to conquer the fortress of Quebec. Quebec was the head and heart of New France. When it fell, so did New France.

By the terms of the Treaty of Paris (1763), Britain took from France all its territory east of the Mississippi River except New Orleans. This vast territory included the St. Lawrence Valley and the Great Lakes as well as the Ohio Valley. France's territory west of the Mississippi River went to Spain.

NEW STRESSES IN THE EMPIRE 3B

As a result of the French and Indian War, Parliament took a long, hard look at its American colonies. Taxes in Britain had risen steeply to pay for the war. The British Parliament thought it reasonable to make the colonists pay part of the price of empire. After all, had British soldiers not driven the French from America?

It looked, too, as if the end of war meant new military commitments. Fearful that English colonists would swarm onto their lands, the Ohio Valley Indians under Chief Pontiac revolted against the British. It became clear that Britain would have a new responsibility: keeping peace on the frontier between Indians and colonists.

At the same time, colonial merchants had grown rich smuggling goods into America and avoiding customs duties. British officials decided to enforce the principle of mercantilism: that the proper role of the colonies was to enrich Britain.

SUPPORTING THE SECTION

Reinforcement Workbook: Worksheet 2
Reteaching Resources: Worksheet 2
Teaching Transparencies: Transparency 2

Background Most French settlers in North America were missionaries or fur traders. The French king's efforts to encourage farming settlements were unsuccessful, except for a string of farming communities along the St. Lawrence and Richelieu rivers.

This painting shows a group of Abenaki Indians and their French allies attacking the British frontier settlement at Deerfield, Massachusetts, in 1704. POLITICS Why did the French and English compete for allies among the Indian tribes? 3B

THE INFLUENCE OF THE ENLIGHTENMENT 7E

To stop smuggling, the government planned to use blank search warrants that allowed officials at any time and in any place to search for and confiscate smuggled goods. Boston merchants challenged the legality of blank search warrants. They wanted a separate search warrant for each place to be searched.

Speaking on behalf of the merchants, the lawyer James Otis attacked the government orders. According to the principles of English law, Otis said, "A man is as secure in his house as a prince in his castle." Otis also declared the blank search warrants to be against "the law of nature." Everyone knew what he meant. The law of nature, the English philosopher John Locke had written, was reason. Reason "teaches all mankind . . . that, being all equal and independent, no one ought to harm another in his life, health, liberty, or possessions." Laws and rules, Locke said, must conform to the law of nature.

John Locke was but one of the thinkers associated with the philosophical movement called the Enlightenment. Thinkers of the Enlightenment emphasized reason as the key to understanding nature, economics, and politics. Their ideas would greatly influence the founders of the United States.

TURMOIL AND PROTESTS 1A, 8D

To protect the frontier, Britain planned to leave 10,000 British soldiers in the American colonies. To help pay the cost, Parliament passed the Stamp Act in 1765.

By the terms of the Stamp Act, each piece of legal paper had to carry a stamp showing that a tax had been paid. The new law was Britain's first attempt to tax the colonists directly. Those caught disobeying the law were to be tried in special courts in which there was no trial by jury.

The colonists were outraged. Citizens organized themselves as Sons of Liberty. The Sons of Liberty burned the stamped paper. They tarred and feathered customs officials.

The collective roar of protest caused Parliament to cancel the Stamp Act within a year. Although

Focus
Review the events and battles leading up to and taking place during the Revolution by having students create a flow chart of British policy and American reaction. *How did each event trigger the one that followed?* (French and Indian War led the British to increase revenues. They raised taxes on colonists and enforced laws against smuggling. These new laws led colonists to boycott tea and store weapons. The British attempted to seize the weapons, and battled the Americans. The beginning of fighting led Americans to attempt to make peace, but the king declared them in rebellion. The Americans continued to fight and declared themselves independent. Victories in the north in the late 1770s and the south in the early 1780s led to independence. Free of British rule, Americans established a weak national government.)

Photo Caption Answer
Each country hoped to use their Indian allies against each other.

Background   The first poem written by an African American, Lucy Terry, described an Indian raid on Deerfield in 1746. Terry, a slave at that time, married a free man and was freed by her husband. As an old woman, she reportedly argued a land dispute before the Supreme Court—and won.

Developing the Lesson

After students have read the lesson, you may want to consider the following activities:

Impact of Geography

On a classroom map or the physical map of the United States at the back of the textbook, have students locate the four river valleys mentioned in the section. (Mississippi, St. Lawrence, Ohio, Hudson.) Why would control of these river valleys be important? (The St. Lawrence and Hudson provide outlets to the Atlantic Ocean, while the Ohio and Mississippi are transportation routes for the center of the continent.)

Why are river valleys, in general, important geographic features? (They are often fertile, have good transportation, and provide water for farming.) **LEP**

Constitutional Heritage

Discuss Britain's use of blank search warrants to stop American smugglers. Then have students read and explain the Fourth Amendment of the Constitution (page 754). Have students consider present-day situations where the need for a search warrant may conflict with law enforcement. (Police looking for drugs or arms.) *What are the drawbacks to the Fourth Amendment? What are its strengths?* (It may allow some criminals to go free, but it protects ordinary citizens from arbitrary harrassment.)

Ethics

The signers of the Declaration of Independence knew that Britain might label them traitors and that the punishment for treason was death. Ask students to discuss what values these men held that would allow them to take such risks.

This 1793 engraving is the earliest known picture of the Boston Tea Party. Colonists disguised as Mohawk Indians are destroying a cargo of British tea. ECONOMICS Who among the colonists probably most resented low-priced British tea? 8H

Parliament had backed down, it insisted it had the right to rule and tax the colonies. For the next seven years Parliament and the American colonies faced off over who held the power. In each of the confrontations the British backed down, and the Americans became dedicated more than ever to the cause of liberty.

In 1773 Parliament again inflamed American passions, but this time confrontation led to war. Parliament had voted to give the East India Company a monopoly on the American tea trade. American shippers and merchants were appalled. If Parliament could establish a monopoly on tea, what monopoly might it create next?

When the tea ships arrived in Boston, the Sons of Liberty, disguised as Indians and carrying hatchets, split open the chests of tea and pushed them into the harbor. A furious Parliament reacted to the Boston Tea Party by passing harsh laws the colonists called the Intolerable Acts. The port of Boston was closed until the tea had been paid for, and Massachusetts was placed under military rule.

In response to the Intolerable Acts, colonial representatives met in the First Continental Congress. While the Congress debated its course of action, New England militias began to store weapons and hold drills.

WAR BREAKS OUT 1A

The efforts of the British to seize militia supplies triggered the first battle of the American Revolution. At the Battle of Lexington and Concord, on April 19, 1775, the militias forced the British redcoats to retreat to Boston.

The Second Continental Congress met in May. The delegates appointed George Washington as commander-in-chief. Before he could reach Boston, however, Washington learned that still another battle had been fought. This was the Battle of Bunker Hill (actually fought at nearby Breed's Hill). This battle proved that the home-trained militias were a match for the British regulars.

Despite two bloody battles and the appointment of Washington as commander-in-chief of a Continental Army, Congress still hoped for peace. In

12 UNIT 1 BEGINNINGS THROUGH RECONSTRUCTION

Photo Caption Answer
American shippers, merchants, and tea dealers.

Background Other British actions which angered Americans were the Townshend Acts which placed duties on glass, paper, paint, lead, and tea; customs officials seizing John

Hancock's ship, *Liberty,* in Boston harbor; enforcing of the Quartering Act, which forced colonies to house and feed British troops; and the Boston Massacre in which five men were killed.

this the delegates reflected the thinking of most Americans. Parliament and the king's ministers might have made some bad decisions, their thinking went, but what about the king himself? They were loyal to King George III and believed that, like a good father, he would step in and settle the dispute.

They were wrong. The king declared the Americans to be rebels. He announced a blockade of American shipping and the plan to send 10,000 Hessian (German) mercenaries to fight in America.

THE DECLARATION OF INDEPENDENCE 5E, 7A

Despite the battles that had been fought, Americans were reluctant to declare a break from Britain. George Washington, for instance, still toasted the king's health each evening. In January 1776 a 46-page pamphlet jolted Americans from their uncertainty. *Common Sense* was written by a recently arrived immigrant, Thomas Paine. Paine argued that America had its own destiny. "Every thing that is right or reasonable pleads for separation," he said. As a result of *Common Sense*, an upsurge for independence rolled in on Congress "like a torrent."

On July 4, 1776, Congress adopted the Declaration of Independence. Written by Thomas Jefferson, the document explained why the colonies had the right to be independent. Its core idea is that people have rights that cannot be taken away. When a government disregards those rights, the people have a right to set up a new government.

5E

> ★ **Historical Documents**
>
> For the complete text of the *Declaration of Independence*, see pages 730–733 of this book.

This famous painting of Washington crossing the Delaware River to attack the British forces during the American Revolution dates from 1851. The artist has changed Washington's stance for dramatic effect. NATIONAL IDENTITY Why did artists tend to show Washington in heroic poses? 6B

Religion
Religious background played a role in influencing which side Americans chose in the Revolution. *How might the religious history of New England have led to the large number of Patriots there?* (The first settlers had been religious dissenters so they had a tradition of independent thought.)
Interested students may research other religious groups and report on their role in the Revolution.

Cause and Effect
Have students examine the chart on page 15 and write a brief paragraph explaining the links between the long-term causes and immediate causes of the American Revolution.

Civic Values
Discuss the idea of fundamental laws with students, asking them to suggest specific fundamental laws. (Possible answers include freedom of conscience, the right of people to participate in government, freedom from want or fear.) Have them explain their answers.

ⓒ Cooperative Learning

Divide the class into groups and have each group write a basic outline for a proposed state constitution of one of the original states. Groups should refer to the ideas of the Enlightenment and the principles behind state constitutions outlined in the section. **LEP**

Photo Caption Answer
Washington was the first great national hero, the man who led the country during war and peace.

Background   The committee appointed to draft the Declaration included Benjamin Franklin, John Adams, Roger Sherman, and Robert Livingston, as well as Jefferson. The Declaration contained a list of George III's misdeeds and concluded with the statement that the colonies were free and independent states. The signers were therefore committing treason—a grave crime.

THE REVOLUTIONARY WAR 7A

The Revolutionary War was more than a revolt; it was also a civil war that bitterly divided families and neighbors. About two-fifths of the Americans were active Patriots, about one-fifth were active Loyalists, and the remainder were neutral. Many Loyalists suffered harsh treatment at Patriot hands, and much of their property was seized. Both Patriots and Loyalists included Americans from all walks of life and from all the colonies.

Throughout the war George Washington continually faced the problem of how to hold the Continental Army together. His genius was that he succeeded in doing so against heavy odds.

The war had two distinct parts, the northern campaigns of 1775–1778 and the southern campaigns of 1778–1781. In the north the British strategy was to get control of the Hudson Valley. If they succeeded, they would cut off New England from the rest of the country. The British bungled their plan, with the result that the Americans were able to defeat the British army in October 1777 at the Battle of Saratoga (New York).

The American victory at Saratoga was crucial because it convinced France to come to the aid of the Americans. France had long wanted revenge on its old enemy, Britain, for its defeat in the Seven Years' War. It had not, however, wanted to join in a losing cause. Now it recognized America's independence and entered an alliance with the new nation. France also persuaded its ally, Spain, to join the American side. Spain and France donated more badly needed funds.

USA 15c

Gen. Bernardo de Gálvez
Battle of Mobile 1780

Bernardo de Gálvez, the Spanish governor of Louisiana, aided the Patriot cause by capturing several British forts in the South. This stamp, issued in 1983, honored him. HISTORY Why was France and Spain's help so important to the Americans? 4C

After their failure to secure the Hudson Valley, the British changed their strategy by trying to take the South. By 1781, however, American hit-and-run attacks had so weakened the British that the main army retreated to a base at Yorktown, Virginia. There they were trapped by the coordinated efforts of French and American forces in the Battle of Yorktown. The British surrendered, and the war was over.

By the Treaty of Paris (1783), Britain recognized the independence of the United States, with the Mississippi River as its western boundary. Britain held on to Canada.

ESTABLISHING A REPUBLIC 7I

One thing most Americans agreed on was that the new nation should be a **republic**. A republic is ruled by elected representatives of the people. Much of the American struggle with Britain had been over rights. Time and again Americans believed that Parliament had violated their traditional rights as Englishmen. Therefore, in setting up their governments, the people of the states were not willing to leave rights to tradition. They wanted them written down.

Between 1776 and 1784 each of the thirteen former colonies wrote down the rules by which each was to function as a republic. Never before in history had a people written down the rules and conditions under which they were to be governed.

Several important ideas underlay the state constitutions. One was the idea of compact, of people making an agreement for the good of the whole. Another was that a good government derives its authority from the consent of the governed. A third idea was that there were fundamental laws that differed from ordinary laws. Fundamental laws could not be changed by mere lawmakers.

In 1776 the Continental Congress had also appointed a committee to devise a plan for the national government. In 1781 that plan of government, called the **Articles of Confederation**, was accepted by the states. Under the Articles of Confederation the states held most of the power. The central government could not tax, regulate trade, or control coinage.

Congress under the Articles of Confederation passed laws describing how the western lands

Long-Term Causes
◆ Tighter British control over colonies
◆ Colonial protests against British policies
◆ Creation of colonial militias

Immediate Causes
◆ Fighting at Lexington and Concord
◆ Declaration of Independence

The American Revolution (1775–1783)

Effects
◆ United States independence
◆ Establishment of Confederation government
◆ Self-government for Americans

CHART SKILLS Colonial resistance to Britain's attempts to tighten its control led to the American Revolution. **CRITICAL THINKING** Could the Revolution have been avoided? Why or why not? 9A

would be governed and how new states could come into the Union. It had trouble, however, paying its debts, making trade agreements, or keeping economic stability. The states were quarreling, even placing duties on each other's produce. In Massachusetts the economic situation was so bad that a group of debt-ridden farmers, led by Daniel Shays, rose up in rebellion.

Something must be done, people said, so the central government could deal with problems facing the nation. A collapse of the national government could mean the end of those ideals that had fired the American Revolution. Responding to the national mood, Congress called for the states to send delegates to a convention to revise the Articles of Confederation. They would meet in Philadelphia in May of 1787.

SECTION REVIEW

1. KEY TERMS French and Indian War, Stamp Act, Declaration of Independence, republic, Articles of Confederation

2. PEOPLE AND PLACES Boston, John Locke, Lexington and Concord, George Washington, Thomas Paine, Thomas Jefferson, Saratoga, Yorktown

3. COMPREHENSION Why was American victory at the Battle of Saratoga so crucial?

4. COMPREHENSION Under the Articles of Confederation, how was power distributed between the federal and state governments?

5. CRITICAL THINKING Were the British justified in trying to make the colonists pay part of the price of the French and Indian War? Explain.

republic—Government of elected representatives. *Articles of Confederation*—1781 plan creating a national government giving the states most of the power.

2. *Boston*—Center of Patriot activity at the time of the American Revolution. *John Locke*—Enlightenment thinker. *Lexington and Concord*—Sites of the first battles of the Revolutionary War. *George Washington*—Commander-in-Chief of the Continental Army. *Thomas Paine*—Author of *Common Sense*. *Thomas Jefferson*—Author of the Declaration of Independence. *Saratoga*—American victory in 1777 over the British. *Yorktown*—Site of British surrender in 1781.

3. It persuaded France to aid the Americans.

4. The states held the power to tax, regulate trade, and control coinage; the central government had little power.

5. Students may suggest that Britain helped to drive the French from America, and thus the colonists should help share the burden. Others may say that the colonists should have the right to tax themselves, or at least have some say in how they were taxed.

Closure

Use the Section 2 information in the Chapter 1 Summary (p. 30) to synthesize the important elements covered in the section. Then have students read Section 3 for the next class, noting the conflicts which arose during the first decades of the nation's existence.

Cause and Effect Answers
Students who say yes may point to attempts to make peace that might have worked. Students who say no may say that feelings in the colonies were running too high for compromise.

Background Under the Articles of Confederation, each state had one vote. To create laws or make major decisions, nine of the thirteen states had to agree. Congress could wage war, make peace, and govern trade with Indian nations. The executive branch was a three-person committee, chosen by Congress.

3 Launching a New Government

Section Focus

Key Terms   Great Compromise ■ checks and balances ■ federalism ■ Bill of Rights ■ capitalism

Main Idea   Through debate and compromise, delegates to the Constitutional Convention devised a new form of government, which the states ratified. An early test of the republic was the War of 1812.

Objectives   As you read, look for answers to these questions:
1. What compromises marked the Constitutional Convention?
2. How did the political philosophies of Thomas Jefferson and Alexander Hamilton differ?
3. How did the War of 1812 lead to a new spirit of nationalism?

Section Objectives

■ describe the process of debate and compromise through which the Constitutional Convention worked out a new form of government

■ explain the causes and effects of the War of 1812

Introducing the Section

Connecting with Past Learnings
Ask students to identify the weaknesses of the Articles of Confederation. (Central government could not pay debts, resolve disputes between states, or tax.)

Key Terms
Play "Jeopardy" with the class by announcing each key term as if it were the answer to a question. Have students ask a question answered by the key term. Follow this procedure for all terms. **LEP**

Focus
Ask four volunteers to play the parts of Madison, Hamilton, Washington, and Jefferson. Each of these students may choose two advisers to help at a "press conference." The rest of the class should play reporters. Each student should ask at least one question of Madison, Hamilton, or Washington on their opinion on some aspect of the Constitution, their political philosophy, the Louisiana Purchase, maintaining neutrality, the War of 1812, or the Monroe Doctrine. The "reporters" should be prepared to answer their own questions.

Twelve states responded to the call to send delegates to the Philadelphia Convention, what we call the Constitutional Convention. Only feisty Rhode Island declined to participate.

THE CONSTITUTIONAL CONVENTION 7B
The 55 delegates who attended the Convention shared certain fundamental goals and values. They agreed that the purpose of government is to ensure the people's natural rights to life, liberty, and the pursuit of happiness. They also agreed that these natural rights could not exist without government. Government, therefore, was necessary to liberty.

The delegates also agreed that governments derive their just powers from the consent of the governed. Yet they were mindful that people in government might use their power to serve their own ends rather than the needs of the common people. They were also mindful that the common people had no monopoly on either truth or virtue. As James Madison would write, "If men were angels, no government would be necessary. If angels were to govern men, neither external nor internal controls on government would be necessary."

The Convention delegates met in secret. One of the first things they did was agree to scrap the Articles of Confederation and construct a new plan of government. This new plan came from Madison, who had studied the failures and successes of ancient republics. Madison proposed a national government with three branches: a legislative, a judiciary, and an executive. The legislative branch would have two houses. One house would be elected directly by the people, and the other house would be elected indirectly by the first house. Representation in each would be proportional to the number of free inhabitants of the states.

THE GREAT COMPROMISE 7D
The Convention nearly collapsed over the disagreements between large and small states. Small states feared they would lose all influence in a Congress based on population. They finally worked out the Great Compromise. The Great Compromise called for the *people* to be represented in the lower house, the House of Representatives, and for the *states* to be equally represented in the upper house, the Senate. A turning point in the Convention, the Great Compromise allowed the delegates to get on to other matters—and other compromises.

OTHER COMPROMISES 7D
The delegates also compromised over the issue of slavery. By this time many Americans, north and south, realized they could not talk of liberty and yet condone slavery. To many northern delegates, however, slavery looked like a dying institution not worth sacrificing for. It was better, they believed, to compromise and thus keep southern support for the Constitution. In the Three-Fifths Compromise, delegates agreed that for purposes of representation five slaves would count as three. They also agreed that the importation of slaves could not be banned before 1808.

SUPPORTING THE SECTION

Reinforcement Workbook: Worksheet 3
Reteaching Resources: Worksheet 3
Enrichment and Extension Resources: Primary Source Worksheet 1
Teaching Transparencies: Transparency 3

Background   All state constitutions provided for a legislature of elected representatives. The right to vote for representatives was generally limited to white males who owned property. Seven states allowed free blacks and Indians to vote if they met property requirements. New Jersey allowed women to vote until 1807.

THE SYSTEM OF CHECKS AND BALANCES

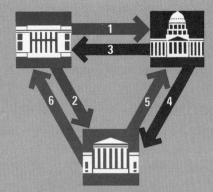

THE EXECUTIVE BRANCH
(The President)

1 Checks on Congress
- Can veto acts of Congress
- Can call special sessions of Congress
- Can suggest legislation and send messages to Congress

2 Checks on Court
- Appoints Supreme Court justices and other federal judges
- Can grant reprieves and pardons

THE JUDICIAL BRANCH
(The Supreme Court)

5 Checks on Congress
- Can declare acts of Congress unconstitutional

6 Checks on President
- Can declare executive acts unconstitutional
- Appointment for life makes judges free from executive control

THE LEGISLATIVE BRANCH
(Congress)

3 Checks on President
- Can impeach and remove the President
- Can override the President's veto by a two-thirds vote
- Controls appropriation of money
- Senate can refuse to confirm presidential appointments
- Senate can refuse to ratify treaties

4 Checks on Court
- Can impeach and remove federal judges
- Can refuse to confirm judicial appointments
- Establishes lower federal court
- Can propose constitutional amendments to overturn court decisions

CHART SKILLS The system of checks and balances was designed to prevent any one branch of government from becoming all-powerful. **CRITICAL THINKING** Does the system work? What might be some of its flaws? **9B**

We take for granted that the chief executive of the United States is the President. Yet this was an idea that emerged from the Convention only after heated debate. The Virginia Plan had only specified an executive branch. Nothing was said about whether the executive powers would be held by one person or by several, as in the Articles of Confederation.

As they entered the debate on the executive branch, the delegates worked to find a path between those holding opposite fears. Looking forward, the younger delegates feared an ineffective national government and thus wanted a strong executive. Looking backward, the older delegates feared a tyrannical executive such as they had experienced under the British royal governors. Their greatest fear was that a single executive would become a monarch.

In the end the delegates voted for a single executive, a President. The solution was a typical one for the Convention because it gave the office strong powers and at the same time checked those pow-

ers. For instance, the President would have the power to veto laws of the Congress, but Congress could override the veto with a two-thirds majority vote. This principle of checks and balances would be used in every part of the Constitution. **5E**

> ★ **Historical Documents**
>
> For the complete text of the Constitution of the United States, see pages 738–764 of this book.

FEDERALISM 3F, 7I

The Constitution created a federal form of government in which powers were distributed between the state and national governments. This is called federalism. Under the Constitution some powers would remain exclusively those of the federal (national) government. Only Congress had the power to make treaties, coin money, tax imports, and declare war. However, the Constitution also allowed for other powers to be shared by both the federal and state governments. For instance, both

The Declaration of Independence, the Articles of Confederation, and the Constitution were all signed in the Assembly Room of Philadelphia's Independence Hall. **CONSTITUTIONAL HERITAGE** Did the Constitution favor the states or the federal government? Explain. 5E

could tax, borrow money, regulate banks, build roads, and maintain courts. In case of conflict between national and state laws, the Constitution was to be the "supreme law of the land."

RATIFICATION OF THE CONSTITUTION 5D, 5E

To become law, the Constitution needed the ratification—approval—of three-fourths of the state legislatures. The process triggered a vigorous and sometimes bitter debate over the merits of the Constitution. In this debate the supporters of the Constitution became known as Federalists. Those who opposed the Constitution were Antifederalists.

Antifederalists criticized the Constitution on two main points: the lack of protection for the rights of the states and the lack of a bill of rights for individual citizens. Without such protections, they feared the new government could become a tyranny.

Alexander Hamilton, James Madison, and John Jay wrote a series of newspaper essays, *The Federalist*. The essays sought to explain federalism, to point out weaknesses in the Articles of Confederation, and to analyze the new Constitution and point out its benefits. The 85 essays, written quickly and under the pressure of newspaper deadlines, have become a classic of American political thought.

5E

> ★ **Historical Documents**
>
> For an excerpt from *The Federalist No. 10*, see page 719 of this book.

The necessary number of states finally approved the Constitution with the understanding that a bill of rights would be added to the document. Madison, a member of the first Congress, wrote the first ten amendments to the Constitution. These amendments form the Bill of Rights. The first nine amendments guarantee basic individual rights. They include freedom of religion, freedom of the press, the right to bear arms, the right to a jury trial, and the right not to testify against oneself. The Tenth Amendment guarantees to the states all powers not specifically assigned by the Constitution to the national government.

GROWING POLITICAL DIFFERENCES 3G, 8B

The new government took shape in the summer of 1789. George Washington had been elected the nation's first President. Two of the ablest men in America served under him. Alexander Hamilton was Secretary of Treasury, and Thomas Jefferson was Secretary of State. Each of these men had clear ideas about the nation's future, and each disagreed bitterly with the other.

Jefferson's vision was of a rural America of educated, self-employed citizen-farmers. In Jefferson's America the role of government would be kept at a minimum.

Hamilton wanted a strong central government that encouraged business and industry. One way to do this was to establish a banking system and stable currency. As the Secretary of Treasury, Hamilton was able to put the new nation on a firm financial footing.

Hamilton's ideas showed the strong influence of Adam Smith, a Scottish philosopher. Smith favored private enterprise over the existing practice of mercantilism. He thought the government should set as few limits as possible over business, trade, and manufacturing. Smith also favored the development of banking and paper money. Today Adam Smith's ideas go by the name of capitalism. Under this economic system (1) most businesses are privately owned and operated, and (2) competition and the free market primarily determine prices and production.

The differences in philosophy and temperament between Alexander Hamilton and Thomas Jefferson resulted in a split that was reflected in the nation at large. The growing split led to the establishment of political parties. Jefferson called his followers Republicans (no relation to the modern Republican Party). Hamilton's followers called themselves Federalists.

In his Farewell Address in 1796 Washington urged the nation to avoid party politics. Party politics, however, would become an enduring part of the American system of government. The nation paid more attention to Washington's advice on foreign policy. The United States should, he said, avoid permanent alliances with other nations. It was a principle the United States would follow for the next 150 years.

THE LOUISIANA PURCHASE 2D

British law had forbidden Americans to settle west of the Appalachians. With American independence, therefore, pioneers poured over the mountains in search of new farms and opportunities. By 1800 both Kentucky and Tennessee were states.

The pioneers in these states had only one practical way to get their produce to market. They shipped it downriver to the Spanish-held port of New Orleans. There it was loaded into oceangoing ships. The free navigation of the Mississippi and the right of deposit (warehousing) at New Orleans was, therefore, crucial to the economic well-being of westerners. Yet the right of deposit was not secure. Spain might end it at any time.

In 1801, Americans learned that Napoleon Bonaparte, the ruler of France, had strong-armed Spain into giving Louisiana back to France. Now President, Thomas Jefferson decided to try to buy New Orleans from France.

Napoleon at first ignored the Americans, because he hoped to send a French army up the Mississippi. But then, the winds of fate changed. The French army suffered a shocking defeat at the hands of former slaves in its colony of Haiti. Also, a war with Britain was draining the treasury. Napoleon decided to sell all of Louisiana to the United States for $15 million. The Louisiana Purchase included all the land between the Mississippi River and the crest of the Rocky Mountains. The purchase doubled the area of the United States.

To learn more about the new territory, Jefferson sent out the Lewis and Clark expedition in 1803. The expedition traveled to the headwaters of the Missouri River, crossed the Rockies, and eventually followed the Columbia River to the Pacific Ocean. It brought back valuable information about the people, the geography, the plants, and the animals of the West. Lewis and Clark's journey opened the way first for American fur traders and then for settlers.

RESENTMENTS LEAD TO WAR 1A

In 1803 France and Britain were at war. Each tried to strangle the other by blocking off food and supplies. Both countries thus seized American ships and cargoes. Britain even seized American sailors for its navy.

The Continental United States in 1790

Background

This illustrated map was drawn by cartographer Howard S. Friedman to show the cultural diversity, economic activities, and population centers in 1790 of the area that now makes up the contiguous United States. The activities and cultures shown are far from exhaustive, and have been chosen to give a flavor of the variety that existed. Though only thirteen eastern states existed in 1790, other state boundaries are shown for geographic reference. The projection, developed for this map by Mr. Friedman, is based on an oblique view of a polyconic projection. (Other illustrated maps are found in Chapters 9 and 27.)

Examining the Map for Content

Review the labeled symbols on the map with the class. Help students identify symbols that have not been labeled by calling attention to the ox-drawn Conestoga wagons and the Mississippi barge. *What do these symbols represent?* (Trans-Appalachian migration and settlement, and trade and travel on the Mississippi River.) Explain that ships symbolize trade with Europe and other coastal regions of the United States. *What areas are shown as centers of trade?* (The Northeast, mouth of the Mississippi River in the Gulf of Mexico, Pacific ports.)

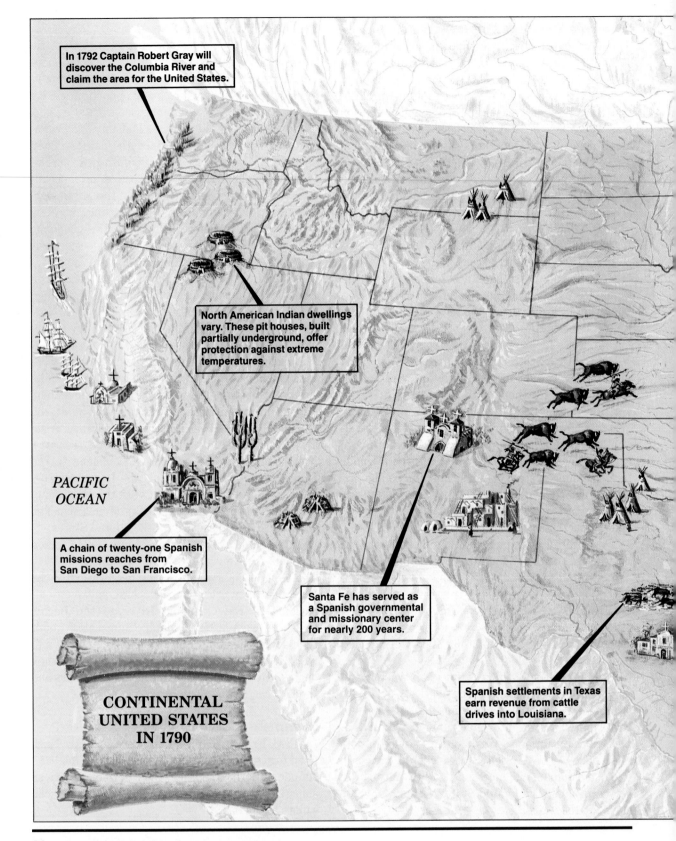

In 1792 Captain Robert Gray will discover the Columbia River and claim the area for the United States.

North American Indian dwellings vary. These pit houses, built partially underground, offer protection against extreme temperatures.

PACIFIC OCEAN

A chain of twenty-one Spanish missions reaches from San Diego to San Francisco.

Santa Fe has served as a Spanish governmental and missionary center for nearly 200 years.

Spanish settlements in Texas earn revenue from cattle drives into Louisiana.

CONTINENTAL UNITED STATES IN 1790

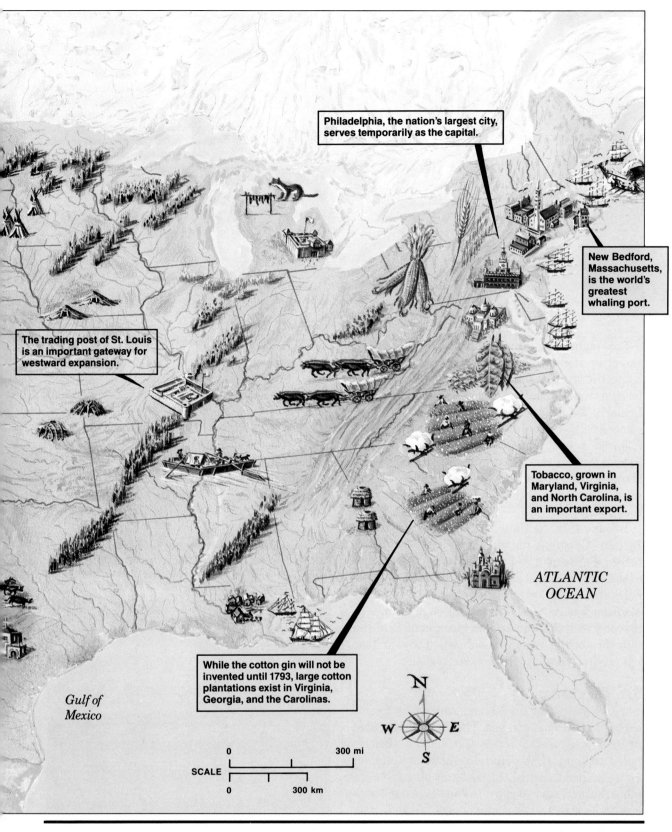

Philadelphia, the nation's largest city, serves temporarily as the capital.

New Bedford, Massachusetts, is the world's greatest whaling port.

The trading post of St. Louis is an important gateway for westward expansion.

Tobacco, grown in Maryland, Virginia, and North Carolina, is an important export.

While the cotton gin will not be invented until 1793, large cotton plantations exist in Virginia, Georgia, and the Carolinas.

Gulf of Mexico

ATLANTIC OCEAN

N
W E
S

SCALE

| 0 | | 300 mi |

| 0 | | 300 km |

Have students refer to the political map of the United States on pages 842–843 to find the symbols that show the cities of Boston, Massachusetts; New York City; Philadelphia, Pennsylvania; Baltimore, Maryland; St. Augustine, Florida; Detroit, Michigan; New Orleans, Louisiana; and San Antonio, Texas.

Have students identify the various Indian dwellings shown on the map. Ask them to locate examples of the nation's Spanish heritage. (Missions in Florida, Texas, and California.)

Connecting Geography and History

Have students compare this map with the one on pages 846–847, noting which areas were part of the United States in 1790 (the area east of the Mississippi River and north of Florida); which were claimed by Spain (Florida, New Orleans, and the area west of the Mississippi to California); and which were claimed by Great Britain (Canada and the Pacific Northwest).

Ask students to suggest trends, activities, and locations that were not included in the map. (Slavery in the South; Indian life in the Northwest; Alaska and Hawaii, etc.) Have them devise symbols and create their own maps of the United States in 1790, paying special attention to the region of the country where they live.

Assessment
You may wish to use the
Section 3 Review, page 23, to
see how well your students
understand the main points
of this lesson.

Section Review
Answers
1. *Great Compromise*—
Called for proportional
representation in House of
Representatives and equal
representation for each state
in Senate. *checks and
balances*—Government
structure that balances one
branch against another.
federalism—Form of government in which powers are
distributed between the
state and national governments. *Bill of Rights*—the
first ten amendments to the
Constitution. *capitalism*—
Economic system based on
private ownership and
competition.

The Thomas Gilcrease Institute of American History and Art, Tulsa, Oklahoma.

This painting shows Lewis and Clark, with their Indian guide Sacajawea and their servant York, standing at the Great Falls of the Missouri River in 1804. Lewis and Clark recorded their expedition in this notebook bound with elkskin. CULTURAL PLURALISM How could an Indian guide be helpful to such an expedition? 4C

For eight years the United States tried to assert its rights as a neutral country and get the respect it wanted. Jefferson's policy was to forbid foreign trade altogether. That was disastrous, particularly for a nation whose wealth was tied to commerce. Jefferson's successor, James Madison, followed a policy of forbidding trade just with France and Britain. Meanwhile, westerners were blaming Britain for the Indian troubles on the frontier and were urging war to drive Britain from the continent.

In June 1812 the United States declared war on Britain. Congress did not know that two days before, Parliament had voted to respect the rights of the United States as a neutral nation. The United States could have backed out of the war, but Madison was re-elected President on a promise to proceed with the war. In that election of 1812 the influence of the West was decisive. The war that followed was a war to meet western goals.

THE WAR OF 1812 1A

For two years the British and Americans fought each other on land and sea. The Americans failed in their attempts to invade Canada. The British failed to conquer the Hudson Valley and cut off New England. British hit-and-run attacks were more dramatic than deadly. In June 1814 a hit-and-run force attacked Washington D.C. The British

torched the city's public buildings, including the White House and Capitol.

From Washington, the British moved on to attack Fort McHenry at Baltimore. The most notable result of that attack was the writing of our national anthem. Held prisoner by the British, Francis Scott Key watched the all-night battle and then wrote "The Star-Spangled Banner."

This picture shows the actual flag that flew over Baltimore's Fort McHenry, inspiring Francis Scott Key to write the national anthem. NATIONAL IDENTITY What were some of the characteristics of American nationalism in the early 1800s? 1A

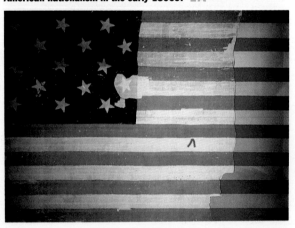

Photo Caption Answers
(Top) Indians lived in those areas and were familiar with the terrain. An Indian guide would also be able to serve as an interpreter and negotiator for other Indians that explorers would meet along the way. (Bottom) Pride in the country, belief in its uniqueness, and loyalty to the federal government.

BIOGRAPHY 4C

The last British effort in the war was the invasion of New Orleans. In December 1814 a fleet of ships carrying 7,500 troops approached Louisiana. Waiting for them was Andrew Jackson.

Lean and tough, Jackson was a self-made man of the frontier. Now, with an army of frontier militiamen he hastened to defend New Orleans. The ensuing battle was a great victory for Jackson. The battle, however, had not been necessary. Neither side at New Orleans knew that a peace treaty, the Treaty of Ghent, had been signed before they fought.

Because everything turned out well, it is easy to forget that the War of 1812 was a time of crisis. If the British offensive strategy had worked, the United States would probably have collapsed, either from conquest or internal dissension. New Englanders strongly opposed the war because their economy was dependent on trade with Britain. At the Hartford Convention in 1814, New England Federalists even talked of seceding from the United States. The war's quick end soon silenced such talk.

A SPIRIT OF NATIONALISM 1B, 7I

Americans had stood up to and fought a great power. As a consequence, the War of 1812 reinforced nationalism, the consciousness of nationhood. Nationalism had several aspects. People felt pride in the achievements of the nation as a whole. They believed that Americans were unique and did not have to look elsewhere for models. There was also a growing belief in the authority of the federal government over the state governments. The focus was on the nation as a whole.

The new nationalism was reinforced by the decisions of an old Federalist. John Marshall, Chief Justice of the United States, had been appointed by President John Adams. Under Marshall's leadership, the Supreme Court upheld federal authority and strengthened the federal judiciary. The first of these important landmark decisions was *Marbury v. Madison* (1803). It established the principle of judicial review—that is, that a law can be declared unconstitutional.

The United States also flexed its national muscle in international affairs when President James Monroe issued the Monroe Doctrine in 1823. It dealt with two issues. (1) Russia was moving into the Pacific Northwest. Monroe announced that the American continents were closed to further colonization. (2) Nations in Latin America had rebelled against Portugal and Spain. The new nations looked to the American republic as an example of national liberty and freedom. The Monroe Doctrine warned European powers not to try to reestablish their authority. In sum, Europe was told to stay away from the Western Hemisphere. **5E**

★ Historical Documents

For an excerpt from the Monroe Doctrine, see page 719 of this book.

SECTION REVIEW

1. KEY TERMS Great Compromise, checks and balances, federalism, Bill of Rights, capitalism

2. PEOPLE AND PLACES Philadelphia, James Madison, Alexander Hamilton, Adam Smith, New Orleans, Lewis and Clark, Andrew Jackson, John Marshall, James Monroe

3. COMPREHENSION What compromise did delegates to the Constitutional Convention make on the slavery issue?

4. COMPREHENSION What were the two main points of the Monroe Doctrine?

5. CRITICAL THINKING Why was the Louisiana Purchase so important to westerners?

2. *Philadelphia*—Site of Constitutional Convention. *James Madison*—Proposed the three branch system of government. *Alexander Hamilton*—Author of essays pointing out benefits of the Constitution. *Adam Smith*—Scottish philosopher and economist whose ideas of capitalism influenced Hamilton. *New Orleans*—Spanish-held port crucial to pioneer trade. *Lewis and Clark*—Leaders of 1803 expedition exploring land gained by the Louisiana Purchase. *Andrew Jackson*—Led American forces at the Battle of New Orleans. *John Marshall*—Supreme Court Chief Justice whose court upheld federal authority and strengthened the federal judiciary. *James Monroe*—Author of the Monroe Doctrine.

3. The Three-Fifths Compromise allowed that, for the purposes of representation, five slaves would count as three free people. It also prohibited banning importation of slaves before 1808.

4. American continents were closed to further colonization and Europe was to stay away from the Western Hemisphere.

5. It secured for them the free navigation of the Mississippi and gave them a port—New Orleans—from which they could ship their produce to market.

Closure

Remind students of the pre-reading objectives in the section opener. Pose one or all of these questions again. Then have students read Section 4 for the next class, noting the dramatic changes in American life in the mid-1800s.

Biography
For further reading consider: Wilson, Dorothy Clarke. *Queen Dolley*. Doubleday & Company, Inc., 1987.

Background Other important decisions by the Marshall Court were *United States v. Judge Peters* (1809) in which the Court determined that the authority of federal judges was greater than that of state legislatures; *McCulloch v. Maryland* (1819) which held that the federal government was a government of the people not the states and therefore had power over the states; *Dartmouth v. Woodward* (1819) defended the sanctity of contracts; and *Gibbons v. Ogden* (1824) established that the government had complete control over interstate commerce.

Section 4

Pulling Together, Pulling Apart
(pp. 24–29)

Section Objectives

- discuss the changes brought about by industrialization
- describe the ways in which Andrew Jackson's presidency reflected the changes occurring in the United States
- describe the events that led to the Mexican War

Introducing the Section

Connecting with Past Learnings
Remind students of the colonial economic system by asking them to define the term *mercantilism.* (Economic system used by European countries and their colonies in which all trade is regulated to enrich the parent country.) Have students contrast Alexander Hamilton's economic philosophy with mercantilism. (He agreed with the capitalist philosophy of Adam Smith which called for little government involvement and free enterprise.)

Key Terms
List the key terms for this section on the board. Ask students to write a sentence using each of the terms in context. Call on volunteers to read their sentences aloud, leaving out the key terms as they read. Then ask the rest of the class to supply the missing terms. **LEP**

4 Pulling Together, Pulling Apart

★ Section Focus

Key Terms Industrial Revolution
- Jacksonian democracy ■ spoils system
- abolitionist ■ Missouri Compromise
- doctrine of nullification ■ Mexican War

Main Idea The Industrial Revolution and a new democratic spirit led to economic strength and social reform but also created sectional differences.

Objectives As you read, look for answers to these questions:
1. How did the Industrial Revolution change life in the United States?
2. Why did Andrew Jackson's election mark a change in the democratic spirit of America?
3. How did Texas enter the Union?

The three decades between 1820 and 1850 were a time of rapid technological and social change in the United States. New forms of transportation linked states and regions of the country. Americans shared a national pride and a vision of the importance of all people, rich and poor. Despite this pulling together, however, there were forces pulling Americans apart.

THE INDUSTRIAL REVOLUTION 3B
In the American Revolution the United States won political independence from Britain. As a result of the War of 1812, the United States established its economic independence of Britain.

Economic independence for the United States meant becoming part of the Industrial Revolution. The Industrial Revolution marked the change from handmade goods to machine-made goods. But it was far more than a mere change in technology. The Industrial Revolution changed the way people used resources. It changed the way they worked and lived, thought and communicated.

The Industrial Revolution started in Britain. There, inventions that mechanized the spinning and weaving of cotton cloth profoundly changed the textile industry. The new machines multiplied the amount that a single worker could produce. The effect of these inventions was to transfer manufacturing operations into a factory where workers operated the machines that produced the goods.

The War of 1812 cut America's economic ties to Britain. Unable to make money in the import-

American entrepreneurs copied British spinning and weaving machines that were developed during the Industrial Revolution. This illustration shows one of those machines inside an American textile mill. **CULTURE** How did the new industrial technology affect traditional ways of life and work? 3A

export trade, investors turned to manufacturing. Following the examples of the early textile manufacturers, Americans began to produce paper, leather goods, finished ironware, and woodenware. Manufacturing centers developed where there was available water power to run the machines—in New England and near Philadelphia. As a consequence, the Northeast became a center of manufacturing.

SUPPORTING THE SECTION

Reinforcement Workbook: Worksheet 4
Reteaching Resources: Worksheet 4
Enrichment and Extension Resources: Primary Source Worksheet 2
Teaching Transparencies: Transparency 4

Photo Caption Answer
People moved from farms to be closer to factories. They worked, not with their families, but away from home. Also, they did not work for themselves, but for factory owners.

This illustration from 1832 shows mules towing barges through the Erie Canal. Construction of the canal gave the Great Lakes region a direct water route to the Atlantic Ocean. **ECONOMICS** What effect did the Erie Canal have on the development of New York City? Why? 2A, 2D

CHANGES IN TRANSPORTATION 2D

Rapid and dramatic changes in transportation began to link different sections of the country together. The most successful, and most famous, of the improvements of this period was the Erie Canal. Built by the state of New York, the canal connected the Hudson River with Lake Erie. The Erie Canal was a massive project on a scale never before seen in America.

The completion of the "big ditch" in 1825 had enormous consequences. It speeded up communication and transportation between East and West. It lowered the cost of freight between Buffalo and New York from $100 a ton to about $10 a ton. It opened up the Great Lakes region to settlement. The huge volume of trade through the canal caused New York City to become the nation's largest city.

In the same decades, the steam engine was revolutionizing transportation. In 1807 Robert Fulton's steamship *Clermont* had chugged from New York to Albany and back in 63 hours. By 1820, 60 steamboats were operating on the Mississippi and its tributaries. For decades the steamboat made possible speedy, two-way transportation on America's rivers and lakes. In the 1830s, inventors began to experiment with steam-powered locomotives. By the 1840s the railroad too was becoming a part of the transportation network.

THE COTTON KINGDOM 3A

In 1793 Eli Whitney invented the cotton gin, a machine that easily removed seeds from short-staple cotton, the cotton that grew in the southern uplands. The cotton gin drastically changed life in the South. (1) It made the uplands more valuable than the coastlands and thus triggered a vast migration westward. (2) The new textile mills were creating a great demand for cotton. Because cotton was such a valuable crop, the South soon evolved into a one-crop economy. Cotton became King. (3) Cotton culture needed a large work force.

THE AFRICAN AMERICANS 4G

Instead of dying out, the institution of slavery became more entrenched than ever. Between 1820 and 1850 the number of slaves in the United States more than doubled, from 1.5 million to 3.2 million.

By the early 1800s a distinct African American culture was also emerging. Music is an example. Most slave songs were adaptations of Christian hymns. The rhythms, however, were rooted in African traditions; the emotions reflected the slave experience.

The Second Great Awakening, a religious movement of the early 1800s, had brought Christianity on a large scale to slaves. (The First Great Awakening had taken place in colonial times.) Whites hoped that Christian teaching would make the

Photo Caption Answer
Shipping through the canal and the Hudson River helped make New York, located at the mouth of the Hudson, a financial center and the nation's largest city.

Background   The word *gin* is short for *engine*.

After students have read the lesson, you may want to consider the following activities:

Geographic Themes: Movement
Have students examine a classroom map or the political map of the United States at the back of the book. *What cities are located on Lake Erie?* (Toledo and Cleveland, Ohio, Buffalo, New York.) *How might the construction of the Erie Canal have led to the growth of these cities?* (It linked Lake Erie with the Hudson River, allowing the cities on the Erie access to the sea, improving trade possibilities.) **LEP**

Science and Technology
Help students construct a flow chart illustrating the connection between industrialization and cotton. (Mechanization of textile mills led to an increase in the demand for cotton. The invention of the cotton gin allowed cotton to be processed quickly and efficiently so that more cotton was cultivated.)

Participating in Government
Have students debate the spoils system, asking them to present arguments for and against a President choosing top government officials. (For—the President needs to work with people who will support and implement the administration's programs; against—the President could choose people on the basis of how much they helped in the election, not on their ability.)

The photograph (right) from 1862 is the earliest to show slaves on a plantation. These families worked in the cotton fields on Edisto Island, South Carolina. An engraving from 1861 (above) shows white buyers at a slave auction in Virginia. **ETHICS** Judging from the picture above, do you think the artist supported or opposed slavery? How can you tell? **9B**

slaves more accepting of their lot. White ministers, spreading their message of faith at outdoor camp meetings, often preached the importance of obedience. However, slaves heard something else in the Bible stories: they heard about enslavement of the Jews in Egypt and how Moses led the Jews to freedom. The story of Moses, told again and again by black preachers, offered the hope that a new Moses would come to lead them to freedom.

Thousands of individual slaves sought freedom by running away. On occasion there were outright slave rebellions. The most famous of these was led by Nat Turner in Southampton County, Virginia, in 1831. The short revolt triggered a fearsome reaction in the South. Virginians were so scared, the legislature considered abolishing slavery altogether. As did other southern states, Virginia decided instead to pass harsh laws restricting literacy, movement, and religion among African Americans, slave or free.

THE RISE OF THE COMMON MAN 7D

Andrew Jackson, the hero of New Orleans, was elected President in 1828 in a landslide. Jackson's election coincided with a new democratic spirit in America—Jacksonian democracy. The mass of people once had been content to let their "betters" make the decisions of government. Jackson's election signaled new thinking in the land. Americans no longer thought of themselves as having betters.

By 1828 more adult white males were eligible to vote than ever before. The constitutions of the new western states had provided for universal manhood suffrage, and the older states were lowering property qualifications for voting. In all but two states the people, rather than the legislatures, voted for presidential electors.

Once in office, Jackson launched a new era in politics. He started by replacing a number of government officeholders, many of them members of the upper classes. Jackson said that the duties of

Photo Caption Answers
Probably opposed slavery since the artist has portrayed the buyers as without sympathy for the lonely figures on the block.

Background Nat Turner had read the Bible closely. He dreamed of black and white angels fighting and took it as a sign to rise up against his enemies. Turner and his followers killed about 60 white men, women, and children.

BIOGRAPHY 4C
SEQUOYA (1770?–1843), was a Cherokee Indian after whom the giant redwood tree is named. Sequoya devised an alphabet with 85 characters, to represent each of the sounds in the Cherokee language. The system was easily mastered, and by 1828 there were many books and a newspaper written in Cherokee. Sequoya also helped keep peace between his people and the U.S. government.

public office were so simple that any man of intelligence could do the work. He also wanted to reward loyal supporters with jobs. This practice of giving government jobs to political backers is called the spoils system. Although subject to abuse, the spoils system did destroy the monopoly of the upper class over government jobs.

Jackson's election also changed the government's attitude toward eastern Indians. The previous President, John Quincy Adams, had tried to protect Indian rights against efforts of the states to take their land. In contrast, Jackson called for the Indians to be moved to public lands west of the Mississippi. The new policies caused thousands of Indians to die of hardship, sickness, and starvation as they headed west on the Trail of Tears.

AN AGE OF REFORM 4D

The time of the 1830s and 1840s was a time of reform in all areas of society. The nation, full of confidence in itself, had come to believe that democracy was its destiny and its strength. An important part of the energy of Jacksonian democracy was directed toward making the society better.

Much of the impulse toward reform, particularly among women, was rooted in the revivals of the Second Great Awakening. First organized in church groups, women then reached out to reform society. Reform movements sprouted throughout the country, but especially in New England and the Ohio Valley.

Of all the reformers, none were so dedicated as the abolitionists—those seeking to abolish slavery. The abolitionist movement began when William Lloyd Garrison published the first issue of the *Liberator* in Boston on January 1, 1831.

In the early 1800s many American Baptists, Methodists, and other Protestants participated in the Second Great Awakening. Traveling preachers turned frontier camp meetings into emotionally charged religious experiences, as shown in this watercolor from 1839. According to historian William G. McLoughlin, "women in particular were drawn to camp meetings. With the coming of religious institutions to a community, women found a place outside the home where they could gather, express their fears and hopes, and join in song and prayer with other women." RELIGION What impression does the painting give of the revival meeting? 4G

Patterns in History
Have students identify the reform movements of the 1830s and 1840s and compare them with reform movements today. *Do you think our era will be remembered as a period of reform? Explain your answer.*

Cultural Pluralism
Discuss Spanish and Mexican contributions in American heritage as a result of the Mexican War—particularly in California, Texas, and the Southwest. Have students create posters illustrating aspects of Spanish and Mexican heritage. LEP

C Cooperative Learning

Divide the class into small groups. Assign each group to cover the West, South, or North. Then have the groups create a newspaper front page which includes articles, advertisements, and/or features describing the changes affecting their regions in the first half of the 1800s. Be sure each student in the group writes at least one article or feature. LEP

Biography
For further reading consider: Foreman, Grant. *Sequoyah.* Civilization of the American Indian Series: No. 16. University of Oklahoma Press, 1984.

Photo Caption Answer
Students may suggest that the swooning congregants and the preacher's waving arm imply an emotional atmosphere.

Addressing Individual Needs

**Guided/
Independent Practice**
Have students complete **Reinforcement Workbook**
Worksheet 4, which guides
students in comparing points
of view.

Reteaching/Correctives
Working in pairs, have students create posters illustrating social, political, or
economic trends in the
United States in the early
1800s.
   Assign **Reteaching
Resources** Worksheet 4, in
which students complete a
timeline of important historical events.

Enrichment/Extension
Assign students **Enrich-
ment and Extension
Resources** Primary Source
Worksheet 2. This worksheet
guides students in interpret-
ing passages from Alexis de
Tocqueville's *Democracy in
America*.

Assessment
You may wish to use the
Section 4 Review, page 29, to
see how well your students
understand the main points
of this lesson.

Section Review Answers

1. *Industrial Revolution*—
The change from handmade
goods to machine-made
goods. *Jacksonian
Democracy*—A new demo-
cratic spirit in America.
spoils system—Practice of
giving government jobs to
political backers.
abolitionist—Reformer
seeking to abolish slavery.
Missouri Compromise—
Congressional compromise
which admitted Missouri as
a slave state and Maine as a
free state, outlawed slavery
in Louisiana Territory north
of the parallel 36° 30'.

Among those who agreed with Garrison were Sarah and Angelina Grimké. Raised on a South Carolina plantation, the Grimké sisters soon saw the contradictions between slavery and the Chris-tianity they were taught. Moving north, they joined the Quakers and became active members in Garrison's Anti-Slavery Society. They wrote appeals to southern women to act against slavery. They won thousands to the abolitionist cause.

Men, however, did not welcome women as aboli-tionists—or in any public role. In Massachusetts ministers spoke out against the women reformers. When abolitionists Lucretia Mott and Elizabeth Cady Stanton tried to attend an antislavery con-vention in London, they were denied admission. Mott, Stanton, and the Grimké sisters all came to the same conclusion: to be effective reformers they would have to establish a larger role for women in the society.

In 1848 the women's rights movement formally began when Mott and Stanton called for a meeting at Seneca Falls, New York. The gathering of about 100 men and women adopted a Declaration of Women's Rights. Among the rights they called for was the right to vote. It would be a long time in coming.

GROWING SECTIONAL DIFFERENCES 3A
The changing economics of the country—manufac-turing in the Northeast, cotton in the South, an expanding frontier in the West—created social and economic tensions among the sections. These ten-sions burst into the open when Missouri applied for statehood. At the time, the United States was evenly divided into 11 slave states and 11 free states. The admission of a new state would tilt the balance of power in Congress, something neither side wanted.

While the debate raged, Maine too applied for statehood. That opened the way for the Missouri Compromise of 1820. The compromise proposed that Missouri be admitted as a slave state, and Maine as a free state. The compromise also called for slavery to be excluded from the Louisiana Ter-ritory above 36°30' north latitude. The compro-mise would hold for three decades.

In the meantime sectional differences arose over other issues, including tariffs and states'

rights. The manufacturing interests of the North-east wanted tariffs to protect their industries. In contrast, the South depended on exporting cotton and importing manufactured goods. Southerners thus saw the tariff as a form of taxation forced on them by the North.

When Congress passed the highest tariff ever in 1828, Vice President John C. Calhoun proposed the doctrine of nullification. The doctrine said that a state could declare an act of the federal gov-ernment "null and void within the limits of the state." The nullification crisis passed, but only for a while. The politics, economics, and social system of the South increasingly isolated it from the rest of the country.

THE MEXICAN WAR 1B, 3B
Westward-moving Americans had always been a step ahead of their government. Restless, eager, adventurous, looking for new opportunities—Americans soon pushed beyond the borders of the United States. This westward thrust was three-pronged: into New Mexico, into Texas, and across the continent toward California and Oregon. With the exception of Oregon, it was a thrust into Mexi-can territory.

Mexico had granted Americans the right to set-tle in Texas, provided they became Catholics and pledged loyalty to Mexico. The number of Anglo-Americans quickly outnumbered the number of native-born *Tejanos*. Beginning to regret its hospi-tality, in 1830 Mexico prohibited immigration into Texas and the importation of slaves. Texans grum-bled, but when the Mexican leader Santa Anna assumed the powers of a dictator, they revolted. The Texans defeated Santa Anna's army and declared their independence in 1836.

Texas had hoped to join the Union at once, but this was not to be. Northerners objected to anoth-er slave state, and government leaders feared that annexation of Texas would lead to war with Mexico.

In 1844 James K. Polk was elected President on a platform that called for adding Texas, Oregon, and California to the United States. Polk's ideas reflected a feeling in the United States that it was the destiny of the nation to stretch from sea to sea. A newspaper called it manifest destiny.

Background   Of all the
women who attended the
Seneca Falls Convention in
1848, only one, nineteen-
year-old Charlotte Woodward,
lived until 1920 when she was
able to vote for the President
of the United States.

Background   In 1821 Moses
Austin received permission
from the Spanish government
to settle 300 families in
Texas. He died before colonization occurred, however, and
on his deathbed asked his
son, Stephen, to carry through
with his plan. The "Old Three
Hundred" settled into a
prosperous model colony.

Robert Onderdonk's painting of the Battle of the Alamo shows the Texans defending themselves against Santa Anna's army during their revolt against Mexico. In the center, with his rifle raised overhead, stands the famous frontier hunter and scout Davy Crockett. Crockett had moved from Tennessee to Texas in 1835. **HISTORY** Why might Texans have preferred not to remain an independent republic? **1A**

With Polk's election, Congress voted to annex Texas. As President, Polk arranged with the British to divide the jointly held Oregon Country. Then Polk tried to buy New Mexico and California. When Mexico rebuffed the offer, Polk engineered a war to settle the issue. The Mexican War (1846–1848) ended with the Treaty of Guadalupe Hidalgo. In it Mexico recognized the Texas annexation and ceded New Mexico, California, and the land between them to the United States.

Even before the peace treaty with Mexico was signed, gold was discovered in California. By 1849 tens of thousands of "forty-niners" were on their way to California by land and by sea. By 1850 California had a non-Indian population of 93,000 and was ready for statehood. One result of this population shift would be another crisis over slavery.

SECTION REVIEW

1. KEY TERMS Industrial Revolution, Jacksonian democracy, spoils system, abolitionist, Missouri Compromise, doctrine of nullification, Mexican War

2. PEOPLE AND PLACES Nat Turner, William Lloyd Garrison, Sarah and Angelina Grimké, Lucretia Mott, Elizabeth Cady Stanton, Texas, California

3. COMPREHENSION Why did the invention of the steam engine revolutionize transportation?

4. COMPREHENSION What factors led to the conflict between Texas and Mexico?

5. CRITICAL THINKING How might abuse of the spoils system lead to problems?

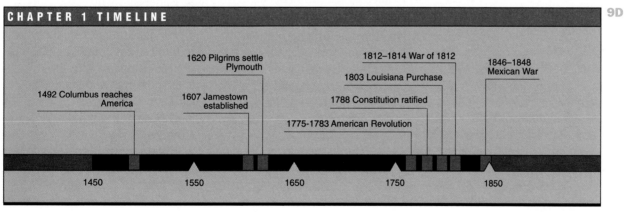

CHAPTER 1 TIMELINE   9D

- 1492 Columbus reaches America
- 1607 Jamestown established
- 1620 Pilgrims settle Plymouth
- 1775-1783 American Revolution
- 1788 Constitution ratified
- 1803 Louisiana Purchase
- 1812–1814 War of 1812
- 1846–1848 Mexican War

1450   1550   1650   1750   1850

---

doctrine of nullification—Allowed a state to declare an act of the federal government null and void within state limits. *Mexican War*—Resulted in the ceding of California, New Mexico, and the land between them to the United States.

2. *Nat Turner*—Leader of an 1831 slave rebellion in Virginia. *William Lloyd Garrison*—Founder of abolitionist movement. *Sarah and Angelina Grimké*—Southern abolitionists. *Lucretia Mott*—Abolitionist and co-founder of women's rights movement. *Elizabeth Cady Stanton*—Abolitionist and co-founder of women's rights movement. *Texas*—Area which gained independence from Mexico before being annexed by the United States. *California*—Obtained in treaty with Mexico, site of 1849 gold rush.

3. It powered railroads and made the steamboat possible, which allowed for speedy two-way transportation on rivers and lakes.

4. Growing numbers of American settlers in Texas, and resulting prohibition of further settlements.

5. It could encourage corruption and allow unqualified individuals to hold government offices.

Closure

Ask one student to transform the Main Idea of the section into a question and have other students answer that question. Then have students read Section 1 of Chapter 2 for the next class period, noting the growing tensions between regions of the country.

Photo Caption Answer
They would be more secure against any Mexican attempt to recapture Texas if they were being defended by the United States.

Chapter 1 REVIEW

CHAPTER 1 SUMMARY

SECTION 1: America was colonized by powerful European nations that expected to profit from the wealth of their colonies.

■ In what is called the Columbian exchange, people, animals, and plants moved between continents.

■ Spain established a new economic system called mercantilism to regulate trade with its colonies.

■ The English colonies established a measure of self-government.

■ Distinct regional characteristics developed in the English colonies.

SECTION 2: British attempts to exert control over the colonies led to protests and then to revolution.

■ After the French and Indian War, Britain tightened its grip on the colonies and tried to raise revenues from them in a variety of ways.

■ In July 1776 the American colonists took the momentous step of declaring their complete independence from Britain.

■ The Revolutionary War ended with the British surrender at Yorktown in 1781 and the Treaty of Paris (1783).

■ After independence, Americans established a republican government under the Articles of Confederation.

SECTION 3: A new Constitution was ratified, and the federal government was shaped and tested.

■ The Constitutional Convention, through debate and compromise, created a federal form of government.

■ Thomas Jefferson bought Louisiana for $15 million and sent Lewis and Clark to explore it.

■ The United States fought and won the War of 1812 with Britain, resulting in a new mood of nationalism.

■ James Monroe issued the Monroe Doctrine to protect the Americas from European interference.

SECTION 4: Great changes marked the first half of the nineteenth century.

■ The Industrial Revolution led to new methods of manufacture and transportation.

■ Andrew Jackson's election reflected a new democratic spirit in America.

■ Democratic reform movements of the 1830s and 1840s called for abolition of slavery and for women's rights.

■ Tensions among regions of the country, brought about by changing economic needs, created growing sectionalism.

■ The United States fought a war with Mexico to gain western territories, including Texas, New Mexico, and California.

KEY TERMS ●

Define the terms in each of the following pairs.

1. Columbian exchange; Great Migration
2. mercantilism; capitalism
3. Mayflower Compact; Articles of Confederation
4. Glorious Revolution; Industrial Revolution
5. Great Compromise; Missouri Compromise

PEOPLE TO IDENTIFY ●

Match each of the following people with the correct description.

Alexander Hamilton
Andrew Jackson
John Locke
James Monroe
Elizabeth Cady Stanton
Nat Turner
George Washington

1. Commander-in-chief of the Continental Army.
2. President who warned European powers to stay out of Latin America.
3. Federalist who established a national banking system.
4. Enlightenment thinker who influenced the founders of the United States.
5. Abolitionist and women's rights activist.
6. Leader of a slave revolt in Virginia.
7. President who started the so-called spoils system.

Reviewing the Facts
1. To break the monopoly of Italian merchants over trade with the Indies.
2. It was the first representative assembly in the English colonies.

3. The Southern colonies were dependent on slave labor to raise cash crops. The New England colonial economy was based on trade, shipbuilding, and fishing.
4. To pay the cost of maintaining British soldiers in the American colonies.

5. The American victory convinced France to come to the aid of the Americans.
6. They worried that the new government could become a tyranny unless it specifically protected the rights of states and citizens.

PLACES TO LOCATE ●

Match each of the letters on the map with the places that are listed below.

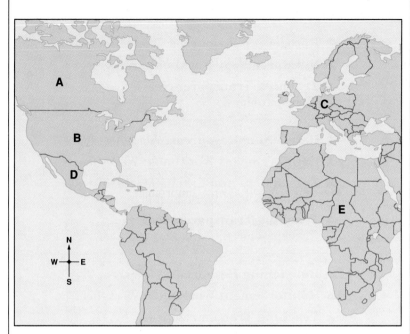

1. Africa
2. Canada
3. Europe
4. Mexico
5. United States

REVIEWING THE FACTS ▲

1. Why did Columbus want to find a westward route to the Indies?
2. What was the significance of the establishment of the House of Burgesses?
3. How did the economy of the Southern Colonies differ from that of New England?
4. Why did Parliament pass the Stamp Act?
5. Why was the Battle of Saratoga so important to American revolutionaries?
6. Why did states of the new American republic insist on writing down their rights?
7. How did delegates to the Constitutional Convention deal with the issue of slavery?
8. How did Jefferson's and Hamilton's political philosophies differ?
9. What effects did differences in regional economies have on the United States?
10. What was the cause of the Mexican War? What were its results?

CRITICAL THINKING SKILLS ▲

1. **DRAWING CONCLUSIONS** Why did slavery become central to the farming economy of the Southern Colonies but not to the Middle Colonies?

2. **WEIGHING BOTH SIDES OF AN ISSUE** What were the advantages and disadvantages to the American colonists of remaining part of the British Empire?

3. **MAKING JUDGMENTS** How does the principle of checks and balances serve to protect liberty in the United States?

WRITING ABOUT TOPICS IN AMERICAN HISTORY ■

1. **CONNECTING WITH LITERATURE** A selection from *The Ordways* by William Humphrey appears on pages 770–771. Read it and answer the questions. Then answer the following questions: What event or image from American history do you consider most important? Why?

2. **APPLYING THEMES: CONSTITUTIONAL GOVERNMENT** Research the elastic clause of the Constitution (the last clause in Article 1, Section 8). Write a paragraph to answer this question: How might the elastic clause have been a source of tension between nationalists and those who argued for states' rights?

10. Growing numbers of American settlers in Mexican territory, the belief in manifest destiny, the United States annexation of Texas led to war. As a result of its defeat, Mexico recognized the Texas annexation, and ceded New Mexico, California, and the land in between to the United States.

Critical Thinking Skills
1. Crops grown on southern plantations required a larger supply of labor than those grown on farms in the Middle Colonies.

2. An advantage was British military protection. Disadvantages included British taxes, restricted trade, and military rule.

3. Checks and balances limit the influence of any single person or group. If one power threatens the people's liberty, another power will check it.

Writing About Topics in American History
1. Possible answers include the Revolution, because it was the start of the nation; the writing of the Constitution, since we still live under those laws; or industrialization, since it made the United States a wealthy nation.

2. The "elastic clause" can be interpreted to give Congress implied power to do anything "necessary and proper." While nationalists would interpret this to give Congress many powers, powers that states' rights advocates believed belonged solely to the states.

7. They decided on the Three-Fifths Compromise, which said that, for representation purposes, five slaves would count as three free people and that the importing of slaves could not be banned before 1808.

8. Jefferson wanted the role of government kept to a minimum. Hamilton wanted a strong central government that encouraged business and industry.

9. The South supported slavery and low tariffs so that they could sell their cotton abroad. The northern states developed industry and supported high tariffs to protect these industries. Westerners wanted internal improvements in transportation and territorial expansion.

Chapter Review exercises are keyed for student abilities:
● = Basic
▲ = Average
■ = Average/Advanced

Chapter 2 ■ The Civil War Era

	SECTION OBJECTIVES	SECTION RESOURCES
Section 1 **The Roots** **of Conflict**	■ identify events of the 1850s that deepened divisions between the North and South	● **Reteaching Resources:** Worksheet 5 ▲ **Reinforcement Workbook:** Worksheet 5 ▲ **Teaching Transparencies:** Transparency 5
Section 2 **The Drums of War**	■ explain how the election of Abraham Lincoln led to the outbreak of the Civil War	● **Reteaching Resources:** Worksheet 6 ▲ **Reinforcement Workbook:** Worksheet 6 ■ **Enrichment and Extension Resources:** Primary Source Worksheet 3 ▲ **Teaching Transparencies:** Transparency 6
Section 3 **The Call to Arms**	■ describe the preparations and strategies of the North and South at the outbreak of the Civil War	● **Reteaching Resources:** Worksheet 7 ▲ **Reinforcement Workbook:** Worksheet 7 ▲ **Teaching Transparencies:** Transparency 7
Section 4 **The Agony of War**	■ describe the successes of each side during the first two years of the Civil War	● **Reteaching Resources:** Worksheet 8 ▲ **Reinforcement Workbook:** Worksheet 8 ▲ **Teaching Transparencies:** Transparency 8
Section 5 **The Union** **Victorious**	■ describe the events that led to the surrender of the Confederacy	● **Reteaching Resources:** Worksheet 9 ▲ **Reinforcement Workbook:** Worksheet 9 ■ **Enrichment and Extension Resources:** Primary Source Worksheet 4 ▲ **Teaching Transparencies:** Transparency 9

The list below shows Essential Elements relevant to this chapter. (The complete list of Essential Elements appears in the introductory pages of this Teacher's Edition.)

Section 1: 4C, 5B, 7D, 7F, 7I, 7J, 9A, 9B
Section 2: 5B, 7A, 7B, 7D, 9A, 9B, 9C
Section 3: 2D, 2E, 3B, 4C, 4E, 5B, 9A, 9B, 9E
Section 4: 2E, 3A, 3F, 5B, 9A, 9B
Section 5: 2E, 3B, 3F, 4C, 4D, 5B, 5C, 5E, 7B, 9A, 9B, 9C, 9D, 9E

> Section Resources are keyed for student abilities:
> ● = Basic
> ▲ = Average
> ■ = Average/Advanced

CHAPTER RESOURCES

Geography Resources: Worksheets 3, 4
Tests: Chapter 2 Test

Chapter Project: Constitutional Government

Have students create an illustrated report on the Civil War, on one of the following topics: a biography of Lincoln, military strategies of the war, or the changing role of women during the war.

Homework Options

Each section contains activities labeled "Addressing Individual Needs." You may wish to choose from among these activities when assigning homework.

> **Provisions for Limited English Proficiency (LEP)**
> Several suggested activities may be particularly helpful for teachers of students with limited English proficiency. These activities have been marked throughout the Teacher's Annotated Edition with the symbol **LEP** .

BIBLIOGRAPHY AND AUDIOVISUAL AIDS

Teacher Bibliography

Berlin, Ira; Joseph P. Reidy; and Leslie S. Rowland, eds. *Freedom, a Documentary History of Emancipation, 1861–1867: The Destruction of Slavery, No. 1.* Cambridge University Press, 1986.

Commager, Henry S., ed. *The Blue and Gray: The Story of the Civil War as Told by Participants.* 2 vols. NAL Penguin, 1973.

McPherson, James M. *Ordeal by Fire: The Civil War and Reconstruction.* Knopf, 1982.

Student Bibliography

Botkin, Benjamin. *Lay My Burden Down: A Folk History of Slavery.* University of Chicago Press, 1945.

Hunt, Irene. *Across Five Aprils.* Berkley-Pacer, 1987. Using her grandfather's boyhood as a model, the author tells the story of the Civil War through the eyes of a teenager with brothers in both armies.

Literature

Crane, Stephen. *The Red Badge of Courage: An Annotated Text with Critical Essays.* Norton, 1962.

Douglass, Frederick. *Narrative of the Life of Frederick Douglass, an American Slave, Written by Himself.* Harvard University Press, 1960.

Kemble, Frances A. *Journal of a Residence on a Georgian Plantation in 1838–1839.* Metro Books, 1969.

Mitchell, Margaret. *Gone with the Wind.* Avon, 1973.

Stowe, Harriet B. *Uncle Tom's Cabin.* Bantam, 1981.

Whitman, Walt. *Leaves of Grass.* NAL Penguin, 1971. One of the most famous poetry collections by an American poet.

Films and Videotapes*

Abraham Lincoln. 28 min. COR/MTI. Dramatization provides insight into Lincoln's philosophy, attitudes, and deepest concerns.

The Divided Union. 51 min (each). FI. Five-part series about the Civil War and its impact on American life and culture.

The Last Full Measure. 30 min. LUCERNE. Historical account illustrates the psychological impact and political significance of the Battle of Gettysburg.

Lincoln's Gettysburg Address. 15 min. AIMS. Highlights historical events of the Civil War from its beginning to the Battle of Gettysburg.

Computer Software*

Civil War (1 disk: Apple or IBM). HS. The goal of the northern army is to preserve the Union while the southern army strives for independence.

Lincoln's Decision (1 disk: Apple, IBM, Tandy 1000 or 2000, or TRS-80). EDACT. Presents key events in Lincoln's life and administration. At major turning points, students are presented with choices faced and are challenged to duplicate Lincoln's decisions.

---

*For a complete guide to audiovisual sources, see the introduction to this book (page Txx).

This chapter traces the development of the Civil War from its roots in underlying sectional differences in the 1850s to the victory of the North in 1865.

Themes in American History

- Constitutional government
- Pluralistic society
- Geography

Chapter Objectives

After students complete this chapter, they will be able to:

1. Identify events of the 1850s that deepened divisions between the North and South.

2. Explain how the election of Abraham Lincoln led to the outbreak of the Civil War.

3. Describe the preparations and strategies of the North and South at the outbreak of the Civil War.

4. Describe the successes of each side during the first two years of the Civil War.

5. Describe the events that led to the surrender of the Confederacy.

Chapter Opener Art
Winslow Homer, *Home Sweet Home,* c. 1863.

The Civil War era was a time of unparalleled agony for the American nation. Home, Sweet Home *was Winslow Homer's ironic title for his painting of a Union army encampment.*

CHAPTER SUPPORT MATERIAL	
Reinforcement Workbook: Worksheets 5–9	
Reteaching Resources: Worksheets 5–9	
Enrichment and Extension Resources: Primary Source Worksheets 3, 4	
Geography Resources: Worksheets 3, 4	
Teaching Transparencies: Transparencies 5–9	
Tests: Chapter 2 Test	

2 The Civil War Era
(1850–1865)

4C, 5B, 7D, 7F, 7I, 7J, 9A, 9B

1 The Roots of Conflict

★ Section Focus

Key Terms Compromise of 1850 ■ Kansas-Nebraska Act ■ Dred Scott case

Main Idea In the 1850s the issue of slavery and its extension to the western territories split North and South.

Objectives As you read, look for answers to these questions:
1. How did the issue of statehood for California revive sectional differences?
2. What events deepened the division between North and South?

The hoisting of the American flag over California in 1848 created a problem for the lawmakers in Washington, D.C. Congress could not agree on what kind of government California should have.

For the sake of unity, the major political parties had tried to ignore sectional divisions over slavery. But the admission of new states to the Union made this impossible. When Congress had to deal with the practical matter of how to govern California, it deadlocked over whether California would be a free or a slave state. In the end, Congress did not make the decision. California did.

CALIFORNIA CHOOSES 5B
The forty-niners themselves were the first to decide that California should be a free territory. Among those streaming into California during the gold rush of 1849 were a number of slaveholders from Texas. The Texans set the slaves to work on the Yuba River. Other miners working the river were indignant. They did not want to compete with slaves, whose masters could push them to the limit of human endurance. Racism too made them object. At a mass meeting the miners voted to outlaw slavery in the mines.

Meanwhile, General Bennet Riley, the acting military governor, had called for a constitutional convention. The convention, he hoped, might break the impasse in Congress over California. Of the 48 delegates to this convention, 8 were Mexican *Californios*. As a result of their influence, the new constitution was the first in the nation to allow a married woman to retain control over her own property. That had been the law in Mexican California. More important, however, for its impact on the nation, was the delegates' unanimous decision to exclude slavery from California.

THE COMPROMISE OF 1850 5B
With its new constitution in hand, California then requested admittance to the Union as a free state. The request set off nine months of heated debate in Congress. Southerners wanted to divide California into two states, one slave and one free. But antislavery forces would have none of it. They were determined not to admit any more slave states into the Union.

At last, Henry Clay of Kentucky proposed a compromise under which California would be admitted to the Union as a free state. In an angry debate on the Senate floor, southern members of Congress accused Clay of betraying the South.

CHAPTER 2   THE CIVIL WAR ERA, 1850–1865   **33**

Section Objective
■ identify events of the 1850s that deepened divisions between the North and South

Introducing the Section

Connecting with Past Learnings
Review the introduction and growth of slavery in the South. *Why did many white southerners feel slavery was essential?* (They needed a cheap source of labor to grow cotton.)

What effect did Nat Turner's revolt have on the South? (It scared them; southern states passed harsh laws restricting literacy, movement, and religion among African Americans.)

Key Terms
Write the key terms on the board and help students find them in their text and define them. Then discuss the event described by each term, asking the class to determine how that event moved the nation closer to war. **LEP**

SUPPORTING THE SECTION

Reinforcement Workbook: Worksheet 5
Reteaching Resources: Worksheet 5
Teaching Transparencies: Transparency 5

Have the class develop a timeline of the issues escalating the conflict between North and South during the 1850s. *What issue, more than any other, led to sectional arguments?* (Extension of slavery into territories.)

How did the 1850s mark a turning point in the nation's ability to deal with sectional differences? (Compromise became increasingly difficult, and both sides became more polarized; sometimes violence flared.)

Developing the Lesson

After students have read the lesson, you may want to consider the following activities:

Ethics

Helping slaves escape was illegal, but many northerners argued that they were acting upon a higher law. Discuss the conflict between being a law-abiding citizen and following laws which you believe to be immoral. Ask students to state if, and how, they would have supported the Underground Railroad had they been alive in the 1850s.

Connecting with Literature

Discuss with students why a work of fiction, *Uncle Tom's Cabin,* was so successful in raising abolitionist sentiment.

Religion

Remind students that Harriet Beecher Stowe was the daughter, sister, and wife of clergymen, and that her brother, Henry Ward Beecher, spoke out from the pulpit against slavery. Discuss with students why the clergy played a leading role in the abolitionist movement, and the role of religion in the debate over slavery.

Clay would not be moved: "I know my duty and coming from a slave state as I do, no power on earth shall ever make me vote for the extension of slavery over one foot of territory now free. Never. No, sir, NO."

> "**N**o power on earth shall ever make me vote for the extension of slavery over one foot of territory now free. Never. No, sir, NO."
>
> —*Henry Clay, 1850*

Despite the passions in Congress, most Americans wanted compromise. It was a time of growing prosperity in both North and South, and no one wanted disruption. Public pressure forced Congress to accept the Compromise of 1850. The compromise had several provisions: (1) California was admitted to the Union as a free state. (2) The territories of New Mexico and Utah were created without restrictions on slavery. (3) The slave trade was abolished in Washington, D.C. (4) Congress passed a stricter fugitive slave law. This new law made it easier for slave catchers to retake fugitives or even to kidnap free blacks. It also specified a heavy fine and imprisonment for anyone who helped the fugitives.

The compromise satisfied neither side. Southerners were so upset that California had been made a free state that four southern states threatened to secede. In the end they decided to give compromise a chance. Northerners, meanwhile, were unhappy with the fugitive slave law. Many were active supporters of the Underground Railroad. This informal network of guides and "safe houses" had helped several hundred slaves to escape to freedom each year. Despite their objections to the fugitive slave law, most northerners, too, decided to give compromise a chance.

UNCLE TOM'S CABIN 4C

The divisive effect of slavery on American society was especially apparent along the Ohio River. Many fugitive slaves heading north tried to cross

the river into the free states of Illinois, Indiana, and Ohio. In Cincinnati, Harriet Beecher Stowe, the wife of a clergyman, witnessed the agony as part of the population helped slaves escape and another part tried to recapture them.

When the fugitive slave law was passed in 1850, Harriet received a letter from her sister. "Hattie," the letter read, "if I could use a pen as you can, I would write something that will make this whole nation feel what an accursed thing slavery is." Harriet Beecher Stowe took up the challenge. In 1852 she published *Uncle Tom's Cabin*—a dramatic account of the sufferings of a beautiful young slave named Eliza and of her flight to freedom. The novel became an instant success, selling over 300,000 copies the first year. *Uncle Tom's Cabin* touched thousands who had not thought much about slavery one way or another. Stowe pointed out that slavery was not the South's problem; it was the nation's problem. All were responsible. She wrote:

> The people of the free states have defended, encouraged, and participated; and are more guilty for it, before God, than the South, in that they have *not* the apology of education or custom.

Biography
Stowe, like many other abolitionist leaders, was a New Englander. Several of her early novels were about Puritan New England. Discuss with students how Puritan traditions may have influenced abolitionists.

Background The largest figure in the California state seal is the Roman goddess Minerva, patron of wisdom. According to myth, Minerva was born full-grown from the forehead of her father, Jupiter. The state of California, too, was born full-grown—without going through an interim period as a territory.

The nation could only be saved, Stowe wrote, "by repentance, justice and mercy."

Uncle Tom's Cabin set off a tidal wave of abolitionist sentiment. Resentful and defensive, southerners repeated their argument that slavery was a positive good. Planters even talked of re-opening the African slave trade.

THE KANSAS-NEBRASKA ACT 71

In 1854 plans for a transcontinental railroad brought the slavery issue once more into the halls of Congress. Stephen Douglas, a senator from Illinois, wanted the railroad to run through Chicago. He knew, however, that a railroad heading west from Chicago would have to cross the unorganized territory of the Great Plains. He therefore proposed the Kansas-Nebraska Act.

The Kansas-Nebraska Act created two new territories, Kansas and Nebraska. Both territories lay north of the Missouri Compromise line, and by law should have been closed to slavery. To win southern support, however, Douglas proposed scrapping the Missouri Compromise in favor of the principle of popular sovereignty. That is, the people in each territory would themselves determine whether a territory was to be slave or free.

The Kansas-Nebraska Act passed with the solid backing of the South. Northerners, however, were divided over the law. Some saw it as a useful compromise, while others argued strongly against the extension of slavery on any terms. This group of antislavery northerners banded together and organized the Republican Party in the summer of 1854. (This is the same Republican Party that exists today.) The new party quickly gained vigorous public support. In the 1854 congressional elections, Republicans defeated 35 of the 42 northern Democrats who had voted for the Kansas-Nebraska Act.

MAP SKILLS 9A, 9B

These maps show the changing balance between slave and free states during the mid-1800s. Under the Compromise of 1850, which new territories were open to slavery? How did the Kansas-Nebraska Act overrule the Missouri Compromise? CRITICAL THINKING Why did antislavery northerners perceive the Kansas-Nebraska Act as such a threat?

SLAVE VERSUS FREE TERRITORY IN THE WEST

AFTER MISSOURI COMPROMISE — 1820

ME.
MO.
36°30'
LA.

Territory acquired as part of Louisiana Purchase

Missouri Compromise Line

AFTER COMPROMISE OF 1850

OREGON TERRITORY
MINNESOTA TERR.
UTAH TERRITORY
CALIF.
NEW MEXICO TERRITORY
36°30'

Territory acquired from Mexico and Texas

AFTER KANSAS-NEBRASKA ACT — 1854

NEBRASKA TERRITORY
KANSAS TERR.

Free states and territory closed to slavery

Slave states

Territory open to slavery

ALBERS CONICAL EQUAL-AREA PROJECTION

National Identity
Many northerners viewed western territories as the land of opportunity, where an individual or family could go to start a life with equal opportunity. *If slavery were permitted in the West, how would that image of the West be changed?* (Individuals could not compete with slave labor.) *Do we still view our country as a land of opportunity?*

Participating in Government
Have students discuss how the principle of popular sovereignty was supposed to work in Kansas. (The people who lived there would determine if it would be a slave or free state.) *Do you think that principle worked? Why or why not?* (It didn't work because violence erupted when emotions became too hot.)

Constitutional Heritage
Have students read the sections in the Constitution, as it read in 1850, that dealt with slavery: Article I, Section 2, Clause 3; Article IV, Section 2, Clause 3. Ask them to discuss how the Supreme Court interpreted those sections to decide the Dred Scott case. *How could Americans make sure the Constitution gave citizenship to blacks?* (Pass an amendment.)

Map Skills Answers
Utah and New Mexico. It opened territory north of 36°30' to slavery. Had the territories voted to permit slavery, free states would have been at a numerical disadvantage.

Cooperative Learning

Divide the class into small groups, assigning each group to examine either the Compromise of 1850, the Kansas-Nebraska Act, the Dred Scott case, the Lincoln-Douglas debates, or John Brown's attack on Harpers Ferry. Each group should determine the different points of view involved in the event and write a short paragraph describing these points of view. Then members of the group should decide with which point of view they agree. Have the groups present their synopses to the class and have the class vote on which point of view it would support in each case. **LEP**

Addressing Individual Needs

Guided/ Independent Practice

Have students complete **Reinforcement Workbook** Worksheet 5. This worksheet guides students in analyzing a political cartoon.

Reteaching/Correctives

Just as tensions grew between the British and the colonists before the American Revolution, the 1850s marked the rising conflict between North and South. Have the class create a cause-and-effect chart on the chalkboard, listing events that led to civil war. Have students use different colors for events favoring North or South.

Have students complete **Reteaching Resources** Worksheet 5, which guides them in relating the causes and effects of the historical events of the 1850s.

THE PRESIDENTS

Zachary Taylor

1849–1850
12th President, Whig

- Born November 24, 1784, in Virginia
- Married Margaret Smith in 1810; 6 children
- Major-general in army; won the Battle of Buena Vista
- Lived in Louisiana when elected President
- Vice President: Millard Fillmore
- Died July 9, 1850, in Washington, D.C.
- Key events while in office: California gold rush

Franklin Pierce

1853–1857
14th President, Democrat

- Born November 23, 1804, in New Hampshire
- Married Jane Appleton in 1834; 3 children
- Lawyer; representative and senator from New Hampshire; brigadier general in Mexican War
- Lived in New Hampshire when elected President
- Vice President: William King
- Died October 8, 1869, in New Hampshire
- Key events while in office: Gadsden Purchase; Kansas-Nebraska Act; Republican Party started

Millard Fillmore

1850–1853
13th President, Whig

- Born January 7, 1800, in New York
- Married Abigail Powers in 1826; 2 children
- Married Caroline McIntosh in 1858; no children
- Lawyer; representative from New York; Vice President under Taylor
- Lived in New York when elected Vice President
- Vice President: none
- Died March 8, 1874, in New York
- Key events while in office: Compromise of 1850; California became a state

James Buchanan

1857–1861
15th President, Democrat

- Born April 23, 1791, in Pennsylvania
- Never married
- Lawyer; representative and senator from Pennsylvania; ambassador to Russia; Secretary of State; ambassador to England
- Lived in Pennsylvania when elected President
- Vice President: John Breckinridge
- Died June 1, 1868, in Pennsylvania
- Key events while in office: *Dred Scott* decision; Panic of 1857; John Brown's raid on Harpers Ferry; Minnesota and Oregon became states

36 UNIT 1 BEGINNINGS THROUGH RECONSTRUCTION

The Presidents
Discuss with students the important events taking place during these presidencies and ask them how effective these Presidents were as leaders.

"BLEEDING KANSAS" 7F

Kansas became a battleground over slavery. Antislavery organizations paid the way for settlers to move to Kansas. Proslavery Missourians crossed the border to stuff ballot boxes during the territorial elections. "We had at least 7,000 men in the Territory on the day of the election, and one-third of them will remain there," bragged a Missouri senator. "Now let the southern men come on with their slaves."

Henry Ward Beecher, a New York clergyman and brother of Harriet Beecher Stowe, suggested that rifles might be "a greater moral agency" in Kansas than the Bible. Funds were raised to send "Beecher's Bibles," as the rifles were then called, to the antislavery settlers. Violence broke out. When proslavery ruffians sacked the free-state town of Lawrence, the abolitionist John Brown took revenge by killing five proslavery settlers. Several hundred settlers would die before peace was finally restored to "Bleeding Kansas."

THE DRED SCOTT DECISION 7J

In 1857 a landmark case in the slavery debate came before the Supreme Court. The case concerned a Missouri slave named Dred Scott, whose master took him to live in Illinois and then in Wisconsin Territory. Back in Missouri four years later, Scott sued for his freedom. He argued that his residence in a free territory had made him free.

In the Dred Scott case the Supreme Court delivered two important decisions. First, Chief Justice Roger Taney said that Dred Scott could not sue in the federal courts because he was not a citizen. The Constitution of the United States did not apply to blacks, Taney asserted. Second, the Court decreed that Congress had no right to forbid slavery in the territories. Territories were open to all settlers, slaveholding or free. Once a territory became a state, it alone could decide whether or not to ban slavery.

Predictably, southerners applauded the decision in the Dred Scott case. But Republicans were outraged. They decided their best course of action was to win control of the government and then, by appointing new judges, to change the makeup of the Supreme Court.

THE LINCOLN-DOUGLAS DEBATES 5B

In the 1858 congressional elections the Republicans once again campaigned against northern Democrats willing to compromise with the South. One of their targets was Stephen Douglas, the powerful and popular Illinois Democrat. To run against Douglas they chose Abraham Lincoln. Lincoln was a Springfield lawyer known for his wry wit and his forceful oratory. He was also an experienced politician who had served both in the Illinois legislature and in Congress. When he accepted the Republican nomination for senator, Lincoln outlined the nation's dilemma:

> A house divided against itself cannot stand. I believe this government cannot endure permanently half slave and half free. I do not expect the Union to be dissolved—I do not expect the house to fall—but I do expect it will cease to be divided. It will become all one thing or all the other.

> "**A** house divided against itself cannot stand."
>
> —*Abraham Lincoln, 1858*

When Douglas then accused Lincoln of urging a "war of the sections," Lincoln suggested a series of debates. Douglas accepted, and in seven Illinois towns the two men debated the issue of slavery. The debates attracted large crowds and were printed in national newspapers.

Douglas used the debates to defend the principle of popular sovereignty. The issue, as Douglas saw it, was not the morality of slavery but the protection of democracy. The people's will was all that mattered. But by means of a skillful question, Lincoln forced Douglas to admit that it was not quite so simple. Lincoln raised the issue of the Dred Scott decision. If the people's will is so important, he said, could the people of a territory exclude slavery entirely if they chose to do so? Douglas answered that a territorial legislature could exclude slavery by passing laws that were

Enrichment/Extension
Have students imagine they are reporters for an abolitionist newspaper. Their assignment is to interview a slave who has escaped from a plantation and is being transported north on the Underground Railroad. Have them list ten questions they would ask.

Assessment
You may wish to use the Section 1 Review, page 38, to see how well your students understand the main points in this lesson.

Section Review Answers
1. *Compromise of 1850*— Compromise determining admission of new states to the Union. *Kansas-Nebraska Act*—Allowed those territories to determine for themselves whether to be slave or free. *Dred Scott case*— Supreme Court case stating that blacks were not citizens, and that Congress could not forbid slavery in U.S. territories.

Background Kansas ultimately was admitted to the Union in 1861 as a free state.

2. *Henry Clay*—Kentucky senator who proposed Compromise of 1850. *Harriet Beecher Stowe*—Author of *Uncle Tom's Cabin. Kansas Territory*—Battleground over slavery in the mid-1850s. *Stephen Douglas*—Democratic senator who argued in favor of popular sovereignty. *Abraham Lincoln*—Republican nominee for senator from Illinois in 1858. *John Brown*—Abolitionist who led an attack on the U.S. arsenal at Harpers Ferry. *Harpers Ferry*—Site of U.S. arsenal in western Virginia.

3. California was admitted as one free state. Southerners had wanted California split into one slave and one free state while northerners objected to the fugitive slave laws.

4. Lincoln believed that the Union could not exist split into two parts, one slave and the other free, while Douglas believed that each state should be able to choose to be a slave state or a free state.

5. Compromise is possible only when both sides are willing to respect the other point of view and give in somewhat. By the late 1850s, hatred and distrust between North and South had progressed to a degree where compromise was no longer possible.

Closure

Call students' attention to the boxed beige quotation (p. 37). How does this quotation relate to the main idea of the section? Then have students read Section 2 for the next class period, noting the escalation of events from the election of Abraham Lincoln to the firing on Fort Sumter.

Abraham Lincoln argued against slavery in new territories while debating Stephen A. Douglas (standing behind Lincoln) in the 1858 Illinois Senate race. Although he lost the election, Lincoln's debating skills won him national fame. **POLITICS** Why are debates important in political contests? **7D**

"unfriendly" to slavery. In other words, they could refuse to hire law officers to catch runaway slaves. They could make it possible for slaves like Dred Scott to get away from their masters while within the boundaries of a free territory.

While Douglas won the election, the debates cost him southern support. Southerners never forgave Douglas for showing how popular sovereignty could work against slavery. By losing influence in the South, Douglas lost the possibility of one day becoming President. At the same time, the debates pushed the gaunt and savvy Abraham Lincoln forward into the national limelight.

JOHN BROWN'S ATTACK 5B

Sectional distrust was bad enough in 1859, but John Brown, the Kansas raider, made it worse. By some accounts, Brown had an unbalanced mind. He was consumed with the idea of starting a slave rebellion that would sweep through the South. On October 16, 1859, Brown and eighteen followers—

thirteen whites and five blacks—attacked the United States Arsenal at Harpers Ferry in western Virginia. Brown believed that they could use the arsenal as a rallying point and a supply station for a huge slave revolt. He was mistaken. After thirty-six hours of fighting, he and four survivors surrendered to Colonel Robert E. Lee of the United States Army. Within six weeks John Brown had been tried for murder and treason, found guilty, and hanged.

But that was not the end of it. Northerners began to idolize John Brown as a martyr to the antislavery cause. On the day he was hanged, bells tolled and guns fired in salute. Henry David Thoreau called Brown "a crucified hero." Newspapers applauded the nobility of his aims even though they condemned his means.

Southerners, stunned by Brown's attack, were even more horrified by the northern reaction to Brown's death. How, they asked, could southerners share the same government with people who regarded John Brown "as a martyr and Christian hero"? For many it was the last straw. "I have always been a fervid Union man," a North Carolinian wrote, "but I confess the endorsement of the Harpers Ferry outrage . . . has shaken my fidelity and . . . I am willing to take the chances of every possible evil that may arise from disunion, sooner than submit any longer to northern insolence."

SECTION REVIEW

1. KEY TERMS Compromise of 1850, Kansas-Nebraska Act, Dred Scott case

2. PEOPLE AND PLACES Henry Clay, Harriet Beecher Stowe, Kansas Territory, Stephen Douglas, Abraham Lincoln, John Brown, Harpers Ferry

3. COMPREHENSION How did the Compromise of 1850 settle the debate over California's admission to the Union? What were some complaints against the compromise?

4. COMPREHENSION How did Abraham Lincoln and Stephen Douglas differ over the issue of slavery?

5. CRITICAL THINKING Why was compromise between North and South no longer workable by the late 1850s?

Photo Caption Answer
They give voters an opportunity to see politicians speak spontaneously.

Background Slavery in the South helped the North grow in population, since many immigrants stayed in the North, unwilling to compete with slave labor.

2 The Drums of War

Section Focus

Key Term Confederate States of America

Main Idea Following the election of Abraham Lincoln as President, the states of the lower South seceded from the Union and formed their own government. The Civil War began when the South attacked Fort Sumter.

Objectives As you read, look for answers to these questions:
1. What part did the issue of slavery play in the election of 1860?
2. Why did Lincoln's election cause the southern states to secede?

As the election year of 1860 opened, the South was in an uproar. Thousands were joining military companies. Rumors of slave insurrections and abolitionist invaders abounded. Every Yankee was an enemy. Some northerners were tarred and feathered, and a few were lynched.

THE ELECTION OF 1860 5B

The widening chasm between North and South ripped apart the Democratic Party. At the party convention in Charleston, southern Democrats insisted that the platform call for the protection of slavery in the territories. But Stephen Douglas, who controlled a majority of the delegates, refused to abandon the principle of popular sovereignty. The convention then moved to Baltimore. Northern Democrats chose Douglas as their candidate. Southern Democrats, meeting in a convention hall across town, nominated John C. Breckinridge of Kentucky.

With the Democrats divided, the Republicans knew that they had a good chance at winning the

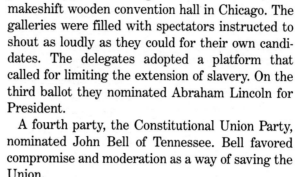

Lincoln supporters at the 1860 Republican convention wore ribbons like the one at right. A split between northern and southern Democrats helped Lincoln become President. Although 1.9 million people voted for Lincoln, his three opponents received 2.8 million votes. **POLITICS** Why might the election be described as an indirect vote on slavery? 9A

presidency. There was great excitement at their makeshift wooden convention hall in Chicago. The galleries were filled with spectators instructed to shout as loudly as they could for their own candidates. The delegates adopted a platform that called for limiting the extension of slavery. On the third ballot they nominated Abraham Lincoln for President.

A fourth party, the Constitutional Union Party, nominated John Bell of Tennessee. Bell favored compromise and moderation as a way of saving the Union.

The election of 1860 was really two different races, one in the North and one in the South. In the North the main contenders were Lincoln and Douglas. In the South they were Breckinridge and Bell. Lincoln and Breckinridge were on the extremes, the one against any extension of slavery, the other for protecting slavery in the territories. Douglas and Bell were moderates who hoped to save the Union through compromise.

The election results made it clear that the nation was no longer in a mood to compromise. Lincoln won with 60 percent of the northern vote and a majority of the electoral vote. Breckinridge carried most of the South. Douglas and Bell did well only in the border states—the states between North and South.

Mass hysteria swept through the South upon the Republican victory. Lincoln's election, southerners were certain, meant their ruin. They foresaw slave insurrections and dreaded the effect of northern majority rule. The vote for Lincoln had been, one southerner said, "a deliberate, cold-blooded insult and outrage" to southern honor.

SUPPORTING THE SECTION

Reinforcement Workbook: Worksheet 6
Reteaching Resources: Worksheet 6
Enrichment and Extension Resources: Primary Source Worksheet 3
Teaching Transparencies: Transparency 6

Photo Caption Answer
Slavery was the main campaign issue and the leading candidates represented positions for and against it.

Background Lincoln won with only 40 percent of the popular vote.

SECTION 2

The Drums of War
(pp. 39–42)

Section Objective

■ explain how the election of Abraham Lincoln led to the outbreak of the Civil War

Introducing the Section

Connecting with Past Learnings
Remind students that compromise had helped ease tensions caused by the slavery issue. *What compromises over slavery had been made before 1860?* (The Three-Fifths Compromise in 1787, the Missouri Compromise of 1820, and the Compromise of 1850.)

Key Term
Write the key term on the board and have students find the term in their texts and define it in their own words. Ask students to list the states which created the Confederacy. Explain that the word *confederate* means "joined in a league, alliance, or union." **LEP**

Focus

Have the class develop a flow chart showing how the events of 1860–1861 culminated in civil war. (Split in elections of 1860; victory of Lincoln; South secedes; compromise attempt fails; Fort Sumter.) Beneath each label have students interpret each event listed.

Could civil war have been avoided? If so, how? If not, why not? (Avoidable—should have been more attempts at compromise; unavoidable—events and emotions had gone too far to stop at that point.)

39

Developing the Lesson

Developing the Lesson

After students have read the section, you may want to consider the following activities:

Geographic Themes: Regions

Discuss the importance of geography in determining the Civil War. **How was the economy of the South affected by geography?** (Cotton grew well in warm, wet climate and broad, fertile coastal plains, and its success ensured the maintenance of an agrarian culture in the South.)

Point out that California extends farther south than many Confederate states. **Why was California a Union state?** (Its culture and economy made it part of the West, not the South.)

Patterns in History

A civil war is a war between factions or sections of a country. The word *civil* comes from the Latin *civis,* meaning "citizen." Have students think of other examples of civil wars that they have studied or that are occurring today.

Analyzing Controversial Issues

Why did the North see itself fighting for democracy? (Democracy only functions if majority rule is accepted; the South refused to follow decisions of the majority.) **Why did southerners see themselves as fighting for liberty?** (They feared that they would lose their freedom to have slaves, and did not see black people as deserving of the same rights as whites.)

What issues today polarize factions or sections of the country? (Possible responses include environmental issues, foreign policy, legality of abortion.) **Do you think any of these could cause a civil war?**

SECESSION AND CONFEDERACY 5B

Southern radicals saw no alternative but to secede from the Union. Lincoln had never claimed he would abolish slavery altogether; he had only said that it should not spread to the territories. But few in the South listened. They assumed that the new President planned to free the slaves.

South Carolina led the way, seceding from the Union on December 20, 1860. In its "Declaration of the Causes of Secession," the South Carolina legislature justified its action on the basis of states' rights. According to this argument, the states had voluntarily joined the Union and had therefore the right to leave the Union. With Lincoln's forthcoming inauguration, the declaration stated, "The slaveholding states will no longer have the power of self-government, or self-protection, and the federal government will have become their enemy. . . ."

During the next six weeks Mississippi, Florida, Alabama, Georgia, Louisiana, and Texas voted to secede from the Union. It was a revolution fed by passion and emotion. "You might as well attempt

to control a tornado as to attempt to stop them," a southerner observed. The seceding states established a new nation, the Confederate States of America, in February 1861. For president they chose Jefferson Davis of Mississippi, and for vice president, Alexander H. Stephens of Georgia. Secession, Jefferson Davis pointed out, was necessary to "renew such sacrifices as our fathers made to the holy cause of constitutional liberty."

But how could the Confederacy talk about liberty and hold 3.5 million black people in bondage? The Confederate constitution answered the question bluntly. "Our new government is founded . . . upon the great truth that the Negro is not equal to the white man," Stephens wrote. Liberty, in other words, was for white people only.

Jefferson Davis also spoke bluntly about the South's economic dependence on slaves. The South could not afford to give up property worth many millions of dollars. Nor could southern agriculture be expected to continue without slaves. Davis argued that slavery was "absolutely necessary to the wants of civilized man."

Yet only about one-fourth of the white families of the Confederacy owned slaves. What about the other three-fourths? Why should they be willing to fight the battles of the slaveholders? For many, the answer was simple: to protect hearth and homeland. As one Confederate soldier later told his Yankee captor, "I'm fighting because you're down here."

Representatives from the seceding states convened in Montgomery, Alabama, to form the Confederate States of America. They elected Jefferson Davis president. Davis's inauguration took place on the steps of Montgomery's capitol building in 1861. Because it lacked hard currency, the new Confederate government issued paper money, such as the treasury note below. NATIONAL IDENTITY How did the Confederate states justify their secession? 9A

Photo Caption Answer
They claimed that since they had joined the Union voluntarily, they could elect to leave it.

THE STATES CHOOSE SIDES

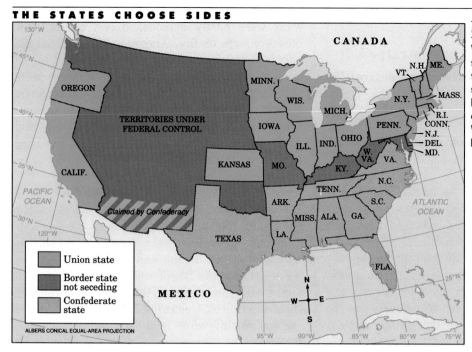

MAP SKILLS 9B

When the Civil War began, most southern states quickly joined the Confederacy. Which border states remained in the Union? How many states were there on each side? **CRITICAL THINKING** What special difficulties might border states have faced?

Map legend:
- Union state
- Border state not seceding
- Confederate state

ALBERS CONICAL EQUAL-AREA PROJECTION

THE NORTHERN RESPONSE 7B

The idea that states had the right to defy the national government was hardly new. It had been asserted in the Kentucky and Virginia Resolutions of 1798–1799 as well as by South Carolina during the nullification controversy of 1828–1832. Now, however, most northerners rejected the principle.

President Buchanan, although he sympathized with the southern cause, spoke for the majority. The Constitution of the United States, Buchanan said, was the supreme law of the land. If secession were permitted, the Union would become "a rope of sand." He warned that the 33 states could break up "into as many petty, jarring, and hostile republics." Abraham Lincoln, soon to take office, agreed with Buchanan. "The Union is older than any of the states," said Lincoln, "and, in fact, it created them as states."

> "**T**he Union is older than any of the states, and, in fact, it created them as states."
>
> —*Abraham Lincoln, 1861*

Secession also raised the issue of democracy and majority rule. From the South's point of view, majority rule was a threat to liberty. The unrestricted right of the majority to dictate to the minority was nothing less than tyranny, southerners said.

The North saw it differently. James Russell Lowell, a poet and essayist, complained that after being "defeated overwhelmingly before the people," southerners were now questioning "the right of the majority to govern." He added, "Their quarrel is not with the Republican Party, but with the theory of democracy."

THE FAILURE OF COMPROMISE 7D

As war threatened, Congress made one last attempt to reach a compromise. Senator John J. Crittenden of Kentucky proposed to restore the Missouri Compromise line of 36°30′ as the division between free and slave states and territories. Lincoln, however, would have none of it. From Springfield he wrote a friend, "The tug has to come, and better now than later." The Republicans refused to allow the extension of slavery, and the South would have no less. The compromise failed.

C **Cooperative Learning**

Divide the class into small groups. Assign half the groups the southern point of view, and the other half the northern point of view. Have each group create a newspaper front page reporting events described in the section. Students should take care with their headlines and illustrations. They should try to convey the emotions of the time. **LEP**

Addressing Individual Needs

Guided/ Independent Practice
Instruct students to complete **Reinforcement Workbook** Worksheet 6. This worksheet guides students in interpreting results of the election of 1860.

Reteaching/Correctives
Review the meaning of compromise and how it is achieved. Then, for each section heading, have students assume the roles of either northerners or southerners and explain why that event or issue moved that region closer to war and further from compromise.

Have students complete **Reteaching Resources** Worksheet 6, in which they decide whether statements about the coming of the war are true or false.

Enrichment/Extension
Have students complete **Enrichment and Extension Resources** Primary Source Worksheet 3. This worksheet examines the Confederate Constitution and compares it to the Constitution of the United States.

Assessment

You may wish to use the Section 2 Review, page 42, to see how well your students understand the main points in this lesson.

"**T**hough passion may have strained, it must not break our bonds of affection."

—*Abraham Lincoln, 1861*

As Lincoln's inauguration approached, the nation waited. What would he do? In his First Inaugural Address, Lincoln made public his position. He told the audience that he had no intention of interfering with slavery in the states where it already existed. But he also asserted that "the Union of these states is perpetual." No state, he said, could lawfully withdraw from the Union.

Lincoln announced that he would use the power of the federal government "to hold, occupy, and possess the property, and places belonging to the government, and to collect the duties and imposts." Yet Lincoln did not want to provoke war. "There will be no invasion," Lincoln said, "no using of force against, or among the people anywhere." Lincoln urged calmness. "We are not enemies, but friends," he concluded. "Though passion may have strained, it must not break our bonds of affection."

CRISIS AT FORT SUMTER 5B

Once in office, Lincoln faced a crucial decision: what to do about Fort Sumter in Charleston harbor and Fort Pickens in the harbor of Pensacola, Florida. Each needed supplies. In January 1861, President Buchanan had sent a ship carrying supplies and reinforcements to Fort Sumter, but it turned back when fired upon by South Carolina batteries. Now time was running out for Major Robert Anderson and his garrison at Fort Sumter. If Lincoln withdrew the garrison, he would be recognizing the Confederacy. If he supplied the garrison, he risked war. On April 4, 1861, Lincoln announced that he was sending relief expeditions to both Fort Sumter and Fort Pickens.

Lincoln's announcement meant he intended to fight if necessary. Confederate leaders decided to attack Fort Sumter before the supply ship arrived. At 4:30 A.M. on April 12, 1861, the shore guns opened fire on the island fort. For 33 hours the Confederates fired shells into the fort, until its walls were partly demolished and the officers' quarters were on fire. Anderson had kept his 128 men well under cover, firing only the lowest tier of guns at the Confederates. But the gunners were choking from the smoke, and the fire threatened to reach the fort's supplies of gunpowder. Anderson then lowered the Stars and Stripes and surrendered to the Confederates. No one had been killed, but the Civil War had begun.

COULD WAR HAVE BEEN AVOIDED? 7A, 9C

Historians have long debated the causes of the Civil War. Was slavery the cause of the war? Or economic differences? Or constitutional differences? Or even bungling leadership?

For decades the South and North had been different, and for decades they had compromised their differences. Compromise, however, no longer seemed possible after 1860 because of the intense disagreement over slavery and the deep distrust of one section toward the other.

Could the war have been avoided, or was it inevitable? Some historians claim that it could have been avoided with more skillful leadership. The historian Arthur Schlesinger, Jr., however, concluded that it was inevitable. "The unhappy fact is that man occasionally works himself into a log-jam; and that the log-jam must be burst by violence," Schlesinger has written. "Nothing exists in history to assure us that the great moral dilemmas can be resolved without pain."

SECTION REVIEW

1. KEY TERM Confederate States of America

2. PEOPLE AND PLACES John C. Breckinridge, John Bell, Jefferson Davis, John J. Crittenden, Fort Sumter

3. COMPREHENSION What did the election of 1860 reveal about the political sentiments of North and South?

4. COMPREHENSION Why did the election of Lincoln alarm the South?

5. CRITICAL THINKING Compare the South's reasons for leaving the Union with the American colonies' reasons for breaking with Britain.

Background Major Robert Anderson, defender of Fort Sumter, came from the slave state of Kentucky. Nevertheless he was determined to carry through with his duties to the Union. P. G. T. Beauregard, who led the firing on Fort Sumter, had been an artillery student under Anderson at West Point.

3 The Call to Arms

Section Focus

Key Terms antiseptic ▪ anesthetic

Main Idea By calling out the state militias, Lincoln forced the border states to choose sides. Both North and South prepared for war.

Objectives As you read, look for answers to these questions:
1. What were the strengths and weaknesses of each side?
2. How did geography affect each side's strategy for fighting the war?
3. What roles did women have in the war?

A week after Major Anderson surrendered at Fort Sumter, Mary Chesnut, wife of a Confederate officer, sat down to write in her diary. "I have been sitting idly today," she wrote, "looking out upon this beautiful lawn, wondering if this can be the same world I was in a few days ago."

Indeed, the battle at Fort Sumter had shattered the springtime calm. The four years of war that followed would destroy one America and witness the building of another. Few that spring of 1861, however, recognized how great a trauma the nation was about to face. Northerners and southerners alike were confident that the war would last only two or three months.

LINCOLN CALLS OUT THE MILITIA 5B

On April 15, 1861, President Lincoln called on the states to provide 75,000 militiamen for 90 days to put down the insurrection in the South. The call to arms was as exhilarating as a thunderstorm breaking the sultriness of a hot day. Northerners responded with energy, even gaiety, to Lincoln's command to muster Union forces. A young Illinois recruit wrote, "It is worth everything to live in this time." One woman wrote, "It seems as if we never were alive till now; never had a country till now." In Washington, D.C., an office worker named Clara Barton took a pistol, put up a target, and blazed away.

Throughout the North, volunteers hastened to sign up. The border states, however, responded with anger and defiance. The governor of Kentucky telegraphed, "Kentucky will furnish no troops for the wicked purpose of subduing her sister southern states." In the days that followed Lincoln's demand, Virginia, North Carolina, Ten-

nessee, and Arkansas voted to secede and join the Confederacy.

With Virginia on its side, the South had a much better chance for victory. Virginia was wealthy and populous. Just as important, it was also the home of Robert E. Lee. A brave and able leader, Lee had been Lincoln's choice for commander of the Union army. When Virginia seceded, Lee resigned from the United States Army and joined the Confederacy. He wrote, "Save in defense of my native state I have no desire ever again to draw my sword." He soon found himself the commanding general of the Confederate forces.

> "**S**ave in defense of my native state I have no desire ever again to draw my sword."
>
> —*Robert E. Lee, 1861*

In May 1861, the Confederate Congress voted to set up its capital in Richmond, Virginia. This was a gesture of defiance, since Richmond stood only 100 miles from Washington, D.C.

CHOOSING SIDES 7C

Both sides understood that the border states would play a key role in the war's outcome. From the Union's point of view, the most important of the border states was Maryland. If Maryland seceded, then Washington, D.C., would be cut off from the North. The Confederates might then capture the President and destroy the government. Determined to keep Maryland within the Union,

---

SUPPORTING THE SECTION

Reinforcement Workbook: Worksheet 7
Reteaching Resources: Worksheet 7
Teaching Transparencies: Transparency 7

Background Many generals on opposing sides had once been classmates together at West Point or fellow soldiers in the field and were often familiar with each other's weaknesses and favorite strategies.

SECTION 3

The Call to Arms
(pp. 43–47)

Section Objective
▪ describe the preparations and strategies of the North and South at the outbreak of the Civil War

Introducing the Section

Connecting with Past Learnings
Review the events leading to the firing on Fort Sumter. (Election of 1860, secession of southern states.) *Why did the surrender of Fort Sumter start the Civil War?* (The attack on a federal fort showed that the South was willing to fight to support its secession, and that the North would have to fight to prevent federal property from being taken over by the Confederacy.)

Key Terms
Have students find the key terms in the text and define them. Point out the prefixes *anti* and *an,* meaning "against" and "without," respectively. Have students suggest examples of anesthetic and antiseptic medications. **LEP**

Focus
Have the class create a balance sheet showing the strengths and weaknesses of the North and South as they prepared for war. Include available resources, composition of armies, and aid societies.

Which side had the advantage at the start of war? Have students explain their answers. (Those saying the North should cite population, industry, minerals, railroads, Lincoln as a leader; those saying the South should cite defensive strategy, army's experience, better generals.)

Civic Values
Discuss with students the excitement generated by the start of the war. *Why were people so optimistic at the outbreak of the war?* (The conflict had been building for a long time and they felt it would finally be resolved. Also, they thought the war would be over quickly.) Ask students to imagine how they might feel if they were alive in those days.

Global Awareness
Why might Britain have sympathized with the South? (Economic reasons, to continue to buy southern cotton; political reasons, to weaken the United States; social reasons, upper class English might have sympathized with the South's aristocracy.) *Why would some people in Europe sympathize with the North?* (They were against slavery.)

President Lincoln ordered the arrest of secessionist lawmakers in Baltimore. The remaining members of the Maryland legislature voted to stay neutral and to remain in the Union.

Federal troops helped a block of western counties break away from Virginia. These counties formed the state of West Virginia and returned to the Union. Delaware and Missouri also voted to side with the the Union. Kentucky declared itself neutral, but a Confederate invasion later prompted it to join the Union.

In the border states, war wrenched families apart. This tragedy reached even into the White House. Mary Lincoln, wife of the President, had four brothers and three brothers-in-law fighting for the South. Senator John Crittenden of Kentucky, who had labored so intently for a last-minute compromise, had one son who became a Confederate general and another who became a Union general.

ʃ 3B
STRENGTHS AND WEAKNESSES OF EACH SIDE
On the face of it, the Union had overwhelming advantages. It had a population of 22 million. The Confederacy had 9 million, of whom 3.5 million were slaves. The Union had most of the mineral deposits—iron, coal, copper, and other precious metals. A full 86 percent of the nation's manufacturing plants were located in the North. The North had 2.5 times the railroad mileage of the South. Almost every ship in the navy—90 of them—stayed with the Union. The war started just as the first phase of the Industrial Revolution was ending. For the North, the demands of the war hastened the development of a new phase of the Industrial Revolution. This phase would be characterized by steel production and the development of heavy industry.

Wealth alone, however, will not win a war. The Union's greatest asset would turn out to be Abraham Lincoln. Lincoln was able to convince the North that the survival of democracy and freedom depended on preserving the Union. "Every war has its political no less than its military side," one historian has written. "Lincoln's genius was the management of the political side."

The Confederacy began the war with better generals. One-third of the career officers in the

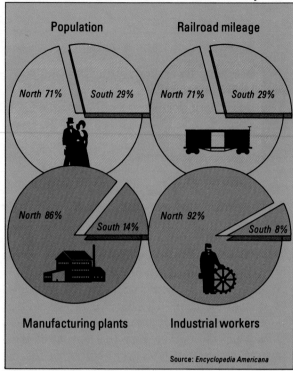

UNION AND CONFEDERATE RESOURCES, 1860

Population — North 71% | South 29%

Railroad mileage — North 71% | South 29%

Manufacturing plants — North 86% | South 14%

Industrial workers — North 92% | South 8%

Source: *Encyclopedia Americana*

GRAPH SKILLS 9B

These pie graphs show the overwhelming advantage the Union's greater population and industrialization gave it. What percentage of Americans lived in the North? CRITICAL THINKING How might the North's railways and factories have helped its armies?

United States Army resigned to join the Confederacy. These officers, most of whom had been trained at West Point, had experience fighting in the Mexican War. Foremost among them was Robert E. Lee.

The Confederacy had another advantage. It would be fighting a defensive war. "All we ask is to be let alone," Jefferson Davis said. An invading army is usually at a disadvantage. Invaders generally have less will to fight than soldiers defending their homes. Furthermore, maintaining the supply lines of an invading army takes great resources.

" **A**ll we ask is to be let alone."
—*Jefferson Davis, 1861*

Graph Skills Answers
71 percent. Manufacturing and transport of clothing and weapons, transport of troops.

Background In the North, regimental officers were often political appointees with little experience. In contrast, Confederate officers generally had military training and experience.

Although the Confederate soldiers never lost a battle for want of ammunition, other needs such as food and clothing were often in short supply. At times the southerners appeared to live only on spirit and courage. Well into the war a Union officer wrote, "How such men as the rebel troops can fight as they do; that, filthy, sick, hungry and miserable, they should prove such heroes in fight, is past explanation."

GEOGRAPHY AND STRATEGY 2D, 2E

The two sides entered the war with different war aims and thus different strategies. The North aimed at reuniting the country. At first, Lincoln hoped to bring the South to terms by economic suffocation. He thus immediately declared a blockade of its coast and made plans to seize Confederate strongholds along the Mississippi River.

The South, in contrast, aimed only at remaining independent. As historian James M. McPherson has pointed out, "The South could 'win' the war by not losing; the North could win only by winning." Thus the South would avoid large-scale battles even if this meant giving up territory. Southern leaders hoped that just as Britain finally gave up trying to subdue its rebellious American colonies, the North would soon tire of the war and accept southern independence.

The Confederate strategy also depended on King Cotton as a way to win foreign support. When the war broke out, southern planters withheld cotton from the world market. By doing so, they hoped to force France and Britain to aid the Confederate cause in order to keep European cotton mills running. But in 1861 Europe had a stockpile of cotton, and this southern strategy failed. By the next year southern planters were again selling cotton—if they could get it through the Union blockade. For the remainder of the war they would seek, but in vain, for European support of their cause.

Before long, both North and South moved away from their cautious strategies and looked for decisive victories on the battlefield. This happened for several reasons. Public opinion on both sides demanded action to win the war in one fell swoop. In addition, the North came to believe that only destruction of the southern armies could force a Confederate surrender. The South, meanwhile, looked to military conquests to wreck northern morale and impress neutral Europe.

Much of the fighting took place on two fronts along the Confederacy's northern border, which stretched from Virginia to Arkansas. The eastern front lay primarily east of the Appalachian Mountains, and the western front lay between the Mississippi River and the Appalachians. Fighting also took place at sea and along the 3,500 miles of Confederate coast.

On the eastern front, the Confederate armies blocked the major routes southward. They were encamped in the Shenandoah Valley of central Virginia and on Virginia's coastal uplands.

On the western front, the main access to the South was by river. Union forces were based at Cairo, Illinois, at the crucial junction of the Ohio and Mississippi rivers. Not far away were the mouths of the Tennessee and Cumberland rivers. These rivers led into one of the most productive regions of the Confederacy. Here grain was grown, mules and horses bred, and iron produced. Much of the war on the western front would focus on the struggle for control of this region.

THE TWO ARMIES 4E

In 1861 the Union was completely unprepared for war. The volunteer militias were enthusiastic but untrained. Many of them were city residents who had never ridden a horse or fired a gun. In contrast, the southern militias had begun organizing several months before Fort Sumter. The Confederate volunteers were used to outdoor life. They knew how to handle both horses and guns.

When the war started, there were no standards for uniforms. Companies and regiments came dressed as their women had outfitted them. This caused confusion on battlefields because troops were not always certain who was friend or foe. As the war progressed, textile mills on each side began to turn out uniforms—dark blue for the Union and gray for the Confederates.

The great slayer of each army was not bullets but the microbes of disease and infection. By the end of the war, roughly 140,000 Union soldiers had been killed in action or died of wounds, while more than 220,000 died of disease and other causes. Few

On a classroom map or the physical map of the United States at the back of the book, have students find the eastern and western fronts of the war. Discuss with the class the geographic significance of these areas. (Both were in relatively narrow areas between water and mountains and blocked the way to the flat, fertile land of the southern coastal plains.)

C **Cooperative Learning**

Divide the class into small groups. To each group, assign one of these roles: a northerner, a southerner, someone from a border state, a woman volunteer. Ask each group to write a letter to a friend or relative, describing the point of view of the assigned person at the start of the war. Each person in the group must contribute at least one idea to the letter. Have each group share its letter with the class. **LEP**

Instruct students to complete **Reinforcement Workbook** Worksheet 7. This worksheet guides students in interpreting varying points of view.

Reteaching/Correctives
What advantages did each side possess? (North: population, minerals, navy, manufacturing, railroads, Lincoln; South: generals, defensive war.) Assign individual students to represent advantages. Have the northern and southern advantages move to different sides of the room. *Which side had the overall advantage?* (North.)

Have students complete **Reteaching Resources** Worksheet 7, in which they review the main ideas of the section.

Enrichment/Extension
Have students research and write a short essay on the role in the Civil War of one of the following groups: blacks, women, immigrants.

Assessment
You may wish to use the Section 3 Review, page 47, to see how well your students understand the main points in this lesson.

Section Review Answers

1. *antiseptic*—Germ-killing drug. *anesthetic*—Pain-killer.

2. *Richmond*—City in Virginia, capital of Confederacy. *Baltimore*—City in Maryland, a border state. *Robert E. Lee*—Commanding general of the Confederate forces. *Elizabeth Blackwell*—Nation's first woman doctor.

3. Much greater population; most of the mineral deposits; almost all of the nation's manufacturing capacity; more than twice the South's railroad mileage; almost all

Mathew Brady used a new invention, the camera, to record hundreds of powerful scenes during the Civil War. This photograph shows a Union soldier from Pennsylvania whose family has joined him in camp. **HISTORY** What false impression might have led families to stay together in the early stages of the war? **9A**

doctors knew that cleanliness prevented infection, and antiseptics—germ-killing substances—were unknown. Anesthetics, or pain-killers, were also rare. Most soldiers endured amputations and other operations by "biting the bullet."

WOMEN IN THE WAR 4C

As men in the North and South enlisted in militias, the women too prepared for war. Few provisions had been made for the health and general welfare of the soldiers. Women volunteered to do what the governments would not or could not do.

Hundreds of thousands of women in the North and South organized aid societies. They raised funds for the war and produced bandages and clothing for the soldiers. Clara Barton, one such woman, labored as a one-person aid society throughout the war. (After the war, Barton founded the American Red Cross.) Thousands of other women went to the front. Many of these women, as in wars past, accompanied their husbands in order to cook and care for them. At least 600 Union soldiers were women who passed as men until illness or death revealed their disguise.

The women of the Soldiers' Aid Societies also formed the backbone of the Union's Sanitary Commission. The purpose of the Sanitary Commission

was to coordinate the efforts of the aid societies and to further the war effort in every respect. It was organized with the help of Elizabeth Blackwell, the nation's first woman doctor. Over the army's objections, the government allowed the Sanitary Commission to inspect and advise camps and hospitals.

The Sanitary Commission was so effective that it became a distinct advantage to the Union. Its national officers, paid agents, and inspectors were men. Supporting them were the women volunteers who raised money, sent supplies to the

BIOGRAPHY 4C

CLARA BARTON (1821–1912) was known as the "Angel of the Battlefield" for her nursing work with the wounded during the Civil War. After the war, she helped mark over 12,000 graves. In the Franco-Prussian War (1870–1871), Barton served with the International Red Cross and later established its American branch. She dedicated the American Red Cross to bringing relief in times of war and natural disaster.

Photo Caption Answer
They expected the war to end quickly.

Biography
Discuss the contrast between the activities of Clara Barton and other women who nursed the sick and wounded during the war and the traditional role of women.

camps, helped soldiers on leave, aided fugitive slaves, and recruited volunteer nurses.

The Civil War was the first war in which several thousand women served as nurses. Traditionalists on each side did not approve of women taking what had previously been considered a man's job. But in 1861 women had a new heroine. She was Florence Nightingale, who had earned fame caring for British soldiers several years earlier in the Crimean War. Altogether, some 3,000 women would serve as official Union army nurses. The Confederacy was slower to accept women nurses, but by 1862, they too were part of the Confederate army service.

of the naval ships; Abraham Lincoln, a brilliant leader.

4. The blockade would suffocate the South economically.

5. The war gave women the chance to work as nurses and doctors, and to organize in aid societies and the Sanitary Commission. Women's role outside the home grew, and women gained respect for their contributions.

Closure
Remind students of the pre-reading objectives in the section opener. Pose one or all of these questions again. Then have students read Section 4 for the next class period, noting how the first years of the war went for the North and South.

2E, 3A, 3F, 5B, 9A, 9B

4 The Agony of War

Section Focus

Key Terms Battle of Bull Run ■ Battle of Shiloh ■ Seven Days' Battle

Main Idea In the first two years of war, the Confederate army successfully held its line of defense on the eastern front. On the western front, however, the Union won significant victories.

Objectives As you read, look for answers to these questions:
1. What was the impact of the war's first major battle?
2. How did the Union triumph in the war at sea?
3. What was the impact of Union victories in the West?

On to Richmond! the northern papers cried. By capturing the Confederate capital, the Union hoped to crush the rebellion in a single, swift blow. But to win Richmond the Union army would first have to take Manassas Junction. This important railway center was only 30 miles south of Washington.

On July 18, 1861, Union troops began the march to Manassas. They were raw recruits, undisciplined and in poor physical condition, who had signed up for 90 days of service. It took them three days to reach the battle site.

On July 21 a bevy of sightseers and picnickers rode out from Washington to watch the battle. Among them were society women carrying ele-

gant gowns in trunks. They expected the day to end with a grand ball of celebration at Richmond.

THE BATTLE OF BULL RUN 2E

The two armies met at the stream called Bull Run, just north of Manassas Junction. The Union forces outnumbered the Confederates 30,000 to 20,000. By midday they had driven a Confederate flank back a mile. During a heavy Union barrage, a Confederate officer rallied his troops by pointing his sword to General Thomas J. Jackson. "There is Jackson standing like a stone wall! Rally behind the Virginians!" he is said to have cried. Thus Jackson, one of the Confederacy's most able generals, won the nickname of "Stonewall Jackson."

SECTION 4

The Agony of War
(pp. 47–52)

Section Objective
■ describe the successes of each side during the first two years of the Civil War

Introducing the Section

Connecting with Past Learnings
Help students to notice how expectations for the war changed. *At the war's outset, what were northern and southern attitudes regarding its length and outcome?* (Each side believed it would win quickly.)

Key Terms
List the key terms on the board. Have students supply the dates of each battle and which side won, and write them on the board. Then have volunteers explain how each battle got its name. **LEP**

SUPPORTING THE SECTION

Reinforcement Workbook: Worksheet 8
Reteaching Resources: Worksheet 8
Teaching Transparencies: Transparency 8

Civil War enthusiasts act out the Battle of Bull Run. The triumph of the Confederate army at Bull Run confirmed suspicions that the Union forces lacked training, and it shattered northern hopes for easy victory in the Civil War. CULTURE Why do many Americans remain fascinated by Civil War history? 9A

And like a stone wall, Jackson's brigade held fast against the Union assault.

With the arrival of fresh troops, the Confederates then rallied and launched a countercharge. Attacking the Union line, they let out a bloodcurdling scream. The scream, later known as the "rebel yell," demoralized the Union troops. "There is nothing like it on this side of the infernal region," a northern veteran later recalled. "The peculiar corkscrew sensation that it sends down your backbone under these circumstances can never be told. You have to feel it."

The Union troops—discouraged, tired, and hungry—broke ranks and scattered. For raw recruits they had fought well, but they had reached their limit.

The retreating soldiers became entangled with the sightseers and picnickers. Convinced that the rebels were right behind them, the whole crowd panicked. Supplies were abandoned, horses were cut loose from their traces, and soldiers began to run. Yet the Confederate army did not pursue its advantage. General Joseph Johnston later explained, "Our army was more disorganized by victory than that of the United States by defeat."

The Battle of Bull Run was a great shock to northerners. Confident of victory, they faced instead a sobering defeat. The day after the battle, Lincoln sent the 90-day militias home and called for a real army of 500,000 volunteers serving for three years. Three days later, he called for another 500,000. To command this army, Lincoln appointed George B. McClellan, who had won distinction fighting Confederate forces in West Virginia.

News of Bull Run electrified the South. "We have broken the backbone of invasion and utterly broken the spirit of the North," the *Richmond Examiner* rejoiced. But more reflective southerners saw that the South had won a battle, not the war. The victory "lulls us into a fool's paradise of conceit at our superior valor," Mary Chesnut wrote in her diary. She was right to be cautious. The war was far from over.

THE NAVAL WAR 3A

Although the great battles of the Civil War would take place on land, the ability of the Union navy to restrict southern shipping had a decisive effect on the outcome. The Union choked off southern shipping in two ways: by blockade and by seizing major harbors.

A number of southerners entered the lucrative business of blockade-running. From bases in the Caribbean the runners carried cargoes ranging from guns to hoop skirts. They used specially designed ships that were low in the water, fast, quiet, and painted gray. On the return voyage the blockade runners carried southern cotton.

In the first year of the war the Union blockade was practically useless—nine out of ten ships got through. But northern shipyards were soon busy turning out a fleet of new boats, including shore-hugging gunboats and deep-sea cruisers. For the crews, blockade patrol offered the chance of riches. Each cargo captured was divided between the ship's crew and the government.

Enforcing the blockade patrol became much easier as the Union captured most of the Confederacy's major harbors. By April 1862 the Union had control over every important Atlantic harbor except those of Charleston, South Carolina, and Wilmington, North Carolina. Steadily the blockade tightened. By 1865 only one runner out of every two managed to evade the Union patrols.

The war also hastened a revolutionary development in naval technology: the ironclad warship. In 1861 the Confederates took the captured Union frigate *Merrimack* and refitted it with iron sides. On a trial run in March 1862, the *Merrimack* (now renamed the *Virginia*) unexpectedly encountered a Union squadron at the mouth of Virginia's York River. The ironclad destroyed two wooden Union warships and ran one aground. At day's end the Confederates were exulting in their new weapon.

The next morning, however, the Confederate crew was amazed to see that a new craft had anchored nearby. The "tin can on a shingle" was the Union's own ironclad, the *Monitor*, which was on its way south from New York. In the first fight ever between ironclad warships, the *Virginia* and *Monitor* hammered away at each other for two hours before calling it a draw. Although both sides built ironclads for bay and river fighting, the new ships had little effect on the war's outcome. The real importance of the *Virginia* and *Monitor* is that they were the forerunners of future navies.

UNION VICTORIES IN THE WEST 3A

Union troops in the West spent most of 1861 preparing for war. In February 1862, however, General Ulysses S. Grant made a bold move to take Tennessee.

Using new ironclad gunboats, Grant's forces captured two Confederate river forts, Fort Henry on the Tennessee and Fort Donelson on the nearby Cumberland. The seizure of Fort Henry opened up a river highway into the heart of the South. Union gunboats could now travel on the river as far as northern Alabama. When the people of Nashville heard the forts were lost, they fled the city in panic. A week later, Union troops marched into Nashville. It was the first major Confederate city to be captured.

Meanwhile, Earl Van Dorn, commander of a Confederate army in Arkansas, planned an end run around Union troops by marching into Missouri and taking St. Louis. With 16,000 soldiers, including three Cherokee regiments from the Indian Territory, Van Dorn headed north. Between Van Dorn and St. Louis, however, stood a Union army of 11,000. On March 7, 1862, the two armies collided at Pea Ridge, near the Arkansas-Missouri border. The Confederates could not hold out against the well-drilled and well-supplied Union troops. They broke ranks, high-tailing it in all directions. It would take two weeks for Van Dorn to reassemble his army.

THE BATTLE OF SHILOH 2E

After Grant's river victories, Albert S. Johnston, Confederate commander on the western front, ordered a retreat to Corinth, Mississippi. Grant followed, and in early April his troops encamped at Pittsburg Landing on the Tennessee River. There he awaited reinforcements. Johnston, however, was not about to wait for Grant to take the offensive. Marching his troops north from Corinth, on April 6, 1862, Johnston surprised the Union forces at the Battle of Shiloh (SHY-lo), named after a meetinghouse near the battlefield.

Science and Technology
What technological innovation did Confederate forces introduce in the war? (Ironclad ships.) *What advantages did ironclads hold over wooden ships?* (Iron was a stronger material, and could not be damaged or burned as easily.) *Why was the South unable to win the naval war with this innovation?* (The North designed its own ironclads and the South lacked the resources to build many.)
Discuss the importance of another technological development to the Civil War—the telegraph. *How did the use of the telegraph change the way war was waged?* (Information on enemy whereabouts could be wired quickly; generals could confer with the President and among themselves.)

Impact of Geography
Explain to the class that northerners referred to battles by water locations while southerners referred to land locations. Ask students to give the southern name for the Battle of Bull Run (Manassas Junction). You may want them to note that the Battle of Antietam, discussed in the next section, was called Sharpsburg by the South.

Background   Rumors of the newly clad *Merrimack* had reached the North, and, in fear, Congress directed the Union to build ironclads. Ship designer John Ericsson, who earlier had developed the screw propeller, came up with a startling new ship that looked like a metal raft on which was a revolving turret with two large guns. He called it the *Monitor*.
You may wish to call attention to the American Mosaic profile of Ericsson on page 82.

History

Discuss the strategies of the North and South leading to the Seven Days' Battle. *How long did McClellan take between Bull Run and the offensive against Richmond?* (Eleven months.) *What evidence of Lee's greater ability to command can you find?* (Sent Stewart around Union army, which had psychological and military value; McClellan planned to attack, but Lee attacked first.)

Geographic Themes: Location

Direct students' attention to the map on this page showing the fighting in 1861 and 1862. *What was the strategic importance of Shiloh?* (Secured Tennessee River down to the Mississippi border.) *Why, after Shiloh, did Grant say that he "gave up all idea of saving the Union except by complete conquest"?* (Realized the stubbornness and valor of the South's forces; foresaw immense scale that the war would take.)

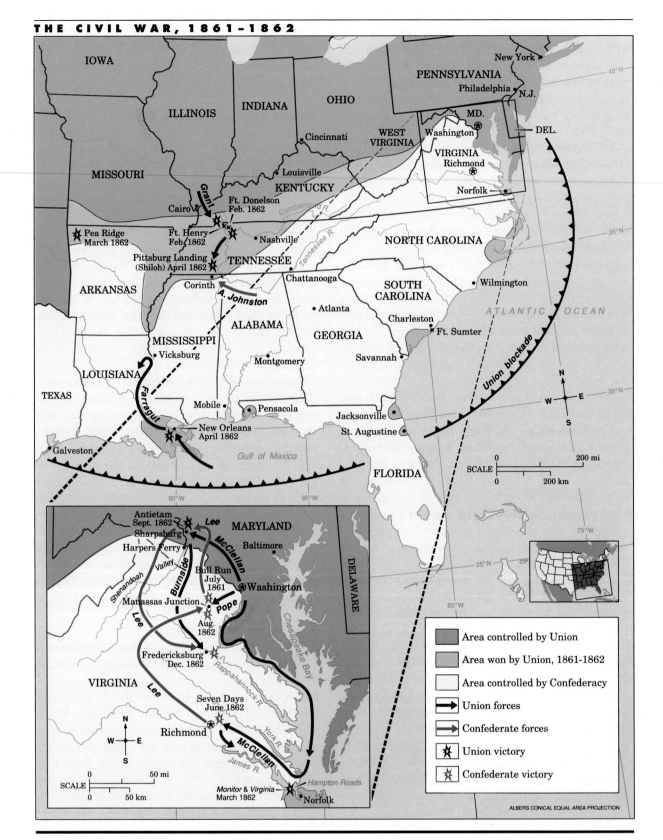

THE CIVIL WAR, 1861-1862

C Cooperative Learning

Divide the class into small groups. Have the groups look through the book, or other sources in the classroom, for photographs and pictures of the Civil War. Ask each member of the group to nominate one picture which best characterizes the war, and explain his or her choice to the group. Then have the group choose a picture and develop other reasons for the choice. Have each group present its picture to the class, allowing time for class members to comment. **LEP**

Map Skills Answers
To split the Confederacy in two. Deprived it of export revenues. Near the location of capitals at Washington and Richmond.

It was the fiercest fighting the Civil War had yet seen.

Commanders on each side were in the pitch of battle to encourage their troops, most of whom had never fired at another human being. One Union general, William Tecumseh Sherman, had three horses shot out from under him. General Johnston was killed, and the command of the Confederates passed to General Pierre Beauregard. By the end of the day, each side was confident that dawn would bring victory.

That night a terrible thunderstorm passed over the battlefield. Rain fell in torrents. Lightning periodically lit up the battlefield, where soldiers dead and dying lay in water and mud. During that awful night, Union boats ran upriver to deliver reinforcements to Grant's camp. With fresh troops, Grant made a surprise attack at dawn and forced the exhausted Confederates to retreat.

The cost of the Union victory was dreadful. Union casualties at Shiloh were 13,000—about one-fourth of the army. The Confederates lost 11,000 out of 41,000 soldiers. Describing the piles of mangled bodies, General Sherman wrote home, "The scenes on this field would have cured anybody of war." But there would be more such scenes—and worse—before the war was over.

> "The scenes on this field would have cured anybody of war."
> —*General Sherman on the Battle of Shiloh, 1862*

THE FALL OF NEW ORLEANS

The South was just absorbing the news of Shiloh, when more bad news arrived. On April 25, 1862, a Union squadron commanded by David Farragut

---

MAP SKILLS 9B

Farragut captured New Orleans in 1862 while Grant's troops pushed toward Mississippi. What did the two hope to accomplish? How did the Union blockade of southern ports affect the Confederacy? CRITICAL THINKING Why did much of the war's fighting take place in the Virginia-Maryland region (inset map)?

BIOGRAPHY

ROBERT E. LEE (1807–1870) was the son of "Light-Horse Harry" Lee, a Revolutionary War hero. Lee married Martha Washington's great-granddaughter, Mary Custis. He fought in the Mexican War and in 1859 led the capture of John Brown at Harpers Ferry. When the Civil War began, Lee's loyalties lay with his home state, Virginia, so he joined the Confederate army. His bold strategies rank him among history's greatest generals. After the war he became president of Washington and Lee University.

had taken New Orleans. To do so, Farragut's ships had run a gauntlet of cannon fire and then dodged burning rafts set adrift on the river. As Farragut's men landed, the city's residents stood on the docks and cursed the Yankee invaders.

In despair, Mary Chesnut wrote in her diary: "New Orleans gone—and with it the Confederacy. Are we not cut in two?" Indeed, after the victories of Grant and Farragut, only a 150-mile stretch of the Mississippi remained in Confederate hands. Standing guard over that section was the heavily armed Confederate fort at Vicksburg, Mississippi. Vicksburg, however, would hold out against the Union forces for another year. By mid-1862 the Union offensive had come to a halt in the West.

THE VICTORIOUS MEN IN GRAY 5B

After Bull Run the eastern front had remained fairly quiet. McClellan built up the new Army of the Potomac, preparing for the day when the North would try once again to capture Richmond. McClellan had more men than the Confederates, but he was slow to move—afraid, some said, of failure. In the spring of 1862 he finally began a cautious offensive. Transporting his troops to the York Peninsula between the York and James rivers, McClellan planned to attack Richmond by way of the peninsula.

Robert E. Lee now commanded the Army of Northern Virginia. To assess Union strength, he sent Jeb Stuart on a cavalry reconnaissance. With

---

Biography
Tell students that Lee has been described by the following: "Do your duty in all things. You cannot do more. You should never wish to do less." Ask them how his life reflects that quotation.

Addressing Individual Needs

Guided/ Independent Practice
Ask students to complete **Reinforcement Workbook** Worksheet 8, which has them interpret a photograph taken by Mathew Brady.

Reteaching/Correctives
Have the class form small groups and create timelines of the Civil War battles discussed in this section. Have students use blue or gray to denote which side was victorious in each battle. Ask students to explain the importance of each battle on the timeline.

Instruct students to complete **Reteaching Resources** Worksheet 8, which helps students work with a time-line of Confederate and Union battles during the first year of the war.

Enrichment/Extension
Have students research and write a short biography of one of the people mentioned in this section.

Assessment
You may wish to use the Section 4 Review, page 52, to see how well your students understand the main points in this lesson.

Section Review Answers
1. *Battle of Bull Run*—First major battle of the Civil War, victory for the South. *Battle of Shiloh*—Union victory in Tennessee, 1862. *Seven Days' Battle*—Confederate victory in northern Virginia, 1862.

2. *Manassas Junction*—Site of the Battle of Bull Run. *Stonewall Jackson*—Confederate general whose brigade held fast at the Battle of Bull Run. *George B. McClellan*—Appointed Union commander after Bull Run. *Ulysses S. Grant*—Union general who won victories in West. *Nashville*—First Confederate city to fall to the North.

David Farragut—Union officer who captured New Orleans.

3. Shocked the North into the reality of war and the need for a well-trained army instead of short-term militias. Made the South over-optimistic about eventual victory.

4. They came close to dividing the South in half and halted southern shipping on the Mississippi River.

5. The northern blockade was an attempt to keep the South from getting supplies and from exporting cotton which would have given the Confederacy the money to buy more supplies.

Closure

Remind students of the pre-reading objective in the section opener. Pose one or all of these questions again. Then have students read Section 5 for the next class period. Ask them to note how the North ultimately won the Civil War.

SECTION 5

The Union Victorious
(pp. 52–59)

Section Objective

■ describe the events that led to the surrender of the Confederacy

Introducing the Section

Connecting with Past Learnings
Help students see that southern strategy changed as the war progressed. *What was the Confederate strategy at the beginning of the war?* (Defensive strategy; let the North invade and be defeated, when the North tired, it would let the South go free.)

1,200 men, the dashing Stuart rode around the whole Union army in four days and reported its size and position to Lee. Lee attacked McClellan on June 26, 1862. The two armies clashed repeatedly for an entire week in what became known as the Seven Days' Battle. The Virginians suffered heavier losses, but it was McClellan's army that was forced to retreat.

In late August the Confederates won a second decisive victory at Bull Run, this time routing Union forces under General John Pope. With Washington in danger, Union troops withdrew from much of Virginia to protect the capital. By the end of the summer of 1862, Confederate troops once again stood on the banks of the Potomac.

SECTION REVIEW

1. KEY TERMS Battle of Bull Run, Battle of Shiloh, Seven Days' Battle

2. PEOPLE AND PLACES Manassas Junction, Stonewall Jackson, George B. McClellan, Ulysses S. Grant, Nashville, David Farragut

3. COMPREHENSION What was the effect of the Battle of Bull Run on the North?

4. COMPREHENSION Why were Union victories in the West strategically important?

5. CRITICAL THINKING Explain why the naval war between North and South was as much an economic contest as a military one. **3F**

2E, 3B, 3F, 4C, 4D, 5B, 5C, 5E, 7B, 7D, 9A, 9B, 9C, 9D, 9E

5 The Union Victorious

Section Focus

Key Terms Battle of Antietam ■ Emancipation Proclamation ■ Copperhead ■ Battle of Gettysburg ■ Battle of Vicksburg ■ total war

Main Idea Union forces stopped Lee's invasions of the North and invaded the South. In 1865 the Confederacy surrendered.

Objectives As you read, look for answers to these questions:
1. Why did Lee invade the North in 1862? In 1863?
2. Why did Lincoln free some of the slaves but not all of them?
3. How did the North force the Confederacy to surrender?

Riding a wave of Confederate victories, General Lee decided to invade the Union in the fall of 1862. It was a crucial time, for the fate of the Confederacy was at stake.

Lee had several motives for taking the war north. A significant victory in the enemy's territory would, he hoped, force Lincoln to negotiate peace. The invasion, too, would give northern Virginia a rest from war during the harvest season and at the same time let the hungry Confederates fill their stomachs with northern food. And, finally, Lee hoped the invasion would bring the diplomatic recognition the South so craved.

By now, both Britain and France were leaning

toward recognizing the Confederacy. They were impressed by Lee's military successes, and their textile mills were closing down for lack of cotton. The Confederates knew that diplomatic recognition would help ensure their survival. At the most, it would mean financial and military aid. At the very least, it would prompt the Europeans to try to convince Lincoln to leave the South alone.

THE BATTLE OF ANTIETAM 2E

Lee's drive into the North was stopped on September 17, 1862, at Antietam Creek near Sharpsburg, Maryland. The Battle of Antietam was the bloodiest single day of the war. The

SUPPORTING THE SECTION

Reinforcement Workbook: Worksheet 9

Reteaching Resources: Worksheet 9

Enrichment and Extension Resources: Primary Source Worksheet 4

Teaching Transparencies: Transparency 9

two armies fought all day, and at nightfall they held the same ground that they had held in the morning. The only difference was that 23,000 men were dead or wounded. Lee, who had lost one-fourth of his army, withdrew to Virginia. The ever-cautious McClellan declined to follow, missing a chance to finish off the Confederate army.

Although a military draw, Antietam was a political victory for the Union. It caused the British and French to delay any plans to recognize the Confederacy. It also marked a new stage in Lincoln's conduct of the war. After Antietam, Lincoln announced his intention to free all slaves in the rebelling states as of January 1, 1863. Accordingly, on New Year's Day he issued the Emancipation Proclamation.

THE EMANCIPATION PROCLAMATION 7B

The call for emancipation changed the character of the war. The old South was to be destroyed and, in Lincoln's words "replaced by new propositions and ideas." The abolitionists were ecstatic. "We shout for joy that we live to record this righteous decree," wrote Frederick Douglass. Abolitionists brought new energy and renewed dedication to the war effort.

BIOGRAPHY 4D

SOJOURNER TRUTH (1797?–1883) was born into slavery in New York but was freed in 1828. She became an evangelical preacher whose message was caring for others. Sojourner Truth spoke out for women's rights and the abolition of slavery. Born Isabella Baumfree, she took the name Sojourner Truth to reflect her life's work: to travel (or sojourn) and preach the truth.

Why, critics charged, did Lincoln free slaves in the rebellious South and not in the loyal border states? The reason lay in the Constitution. Freeing Confederate slaves weakened the South and was thus considered a military necessity. As commander-in-chief of Union forces, Lincoln had the authority to do this. But the Constitution did not give the President the power to free slaves within the Union. Lincoln did recommend, however, that Congress gradually abolish slavery throughout the land.

Some 200,000 black soldiers served in the Union forces, and 38,000 died during the war. Black soldiers suffered especially harsh treatment if captured. **PARTICIPATION** Why might blacks have been particularly motivated to fight in the Civil War? 4C

Key Terms
Group key terms into two columns—names of battles and other words. Have students find descriptions of the battles in their texts and explain the importance of each. Then have them find the other words in the text and define them in their own words.

Explain that *emancipation* means "freedom from bondage." Copperheads were so called because they wore lapel pins cut from copper pennies, and because of their snake-like attitudes. **LEP**

Focus
Some historians consider the American Civil War to be the first example of modern war in world history. Discuss with the class the ways this war was dramatically different from previous wars in American history. (Cities and civilians were targeted; the North fought for total victory; the government's power and bureaucracy grew.)

What changes, brought about by the war, moved the United States closer to the society it is today? (Increased the size of government; made it more of an industrial nation; ended slavery; gave women opportunities outside the home.)

Biography
Have students read Sojourner Truth's famous speech, "Aren't I a Woman," made at the Women's Rights Convention in Akron, Ohio, in 1851, and write a short essay on what it says about the life of women slaves.

Photo Caption Answer
They were fighting to help eliminate slavery.

After students have read the section, you may want to consider the following activities:

Cultural Pluralism
Have students read the Emancipation Proclamation on page 720 and discuss it as the first step toward abolishing slavery in the United States. *How did the Proclamation open the way toward black participation in the war?* (It declared that freedmen could join the armed services; black women also organized into aid societies.) *Do you agree with Frederick Douglass's argument in favor of blacks joining up?*

Ethics
How did Sherman justify his destruction of Georgia? (Said that people as well as armies must feel the hardness of war.) Have students suggest the reasons why armies wage total war. (Undermine civilian morale, to starve and frighten opponents into submission.) Discuss the ethics of total war, asking students under what circumstances they think total war is justified.

The Emancipation Proclamation also stated that freedmen willing to fight "will be received into the armed service of the United States." From the start of the Civil War African Americans had served in the navy, but they had been rejected by the army. As of 1863, however, free blacks in Louisiana, Kansas, and the South Carolina Sea Islands formed their own military regiments. Massachusetts later raised two black regiments.

Black troops were led by white officers and for most of the war were paid less than whites. Despite such unequal treatment, black leaders urged blacks to enlist. Once the black man had been a soldier and fought for his country, Douglass said, "there is no power on earth which can deny that he has earned the right to citizenship." By war's end about 200,000 black men had served in the Union army and navy. Black women, too, organized aid societies and worked behind the lines. Harriet Tubman, a famous "conductor" of the Underground Railroad, accompanied Union gunboats evacuating slaves to freedom.

5E

⭐ **Historical Documents**

For the text of the Emancipation Proclamation, see page 720 of this book.

THE ROAD TO GETTYSBURG 5C
President Lincoln's great frustration was finding a general who would take the offensive against Lee. Lincoln tried and then discarded one general after another. General McClellan was put to pasture after his failure to pursue Lee at Antietam. His successor, Ambrose Burnside, fared no better. He lost his job after Lee defeated him in December 1862 at Fredericksburg, Virginia. General "Fighting Joe" Hooker took on Lee the next spring at Chancellorsville. Although Hooker had 130,000 troops to Lee's 62,000, he too was defeated by the brilliant southern general.

By summer 1863 the Confederate army seemed invincible. Lee decided to head north once again, this time from the Shenandoah Valley into Pennsylvania.

Lee had two goals in heading north. First of all, he needed food and supplies for his army. His men were as thin and ragged as scarecrows, and horses were dying of starvation. Second, Lee hoped to force a peace settlement.

Time was running out for the Confederacy. The northern blockade was causing severe economic hardship. What had cost one dollar in 1861 now cost seven dollars. With the men gone, small-farm production dropped. Many of the men in gray deserted to help their families survive. "We are poor men and are willing to defend our country, but our families [come] first," a Mississippi soldier wrote the governor. Things were no better in the cities. Just a few months earlier a mob in Richmond had rioted, shouting for bread and breaking into stores.

Lee knew that northerners were growing tired of the war. For lack of volunteers, Congress had recently imposed a draft that was highly unpopular. More and more people were listening to the Copperheads—northern Democrats who called for peace and a compromise with the South. A successful invasion of the North, Lee figured, would encourage the "peace party" and thereby divide and weaken the enemy. Lee also hoped that an invasion would revive European interest in recognizing the Confederacy and helping end the war.

THE BATTLE OF GETTYSBURG 2E
In late June 1863, Lee's army crossed into the fertile farmlands of southern Pennsylvania. "You never saw such a land of plenty," a Confederate soldier wrote home. "We could live here mighty well for the next twelve months. . . . Of course we will have to fight here, and when it comes it will be the biggest on record." The soldier was right.

In a line parallel to Lee's, the Army of the Potomac marched north along the east side of the Blue Ridge Mountains. "We cannot help beating them, if we have the man," Lincoln said. But Lincoln was still not satisfied that he had the right general. Lee's army was already in Pennsylvania when Lincoln replaced General Hooker with General George Meade.

Meanwhile, morale had risen in the oft-defeated Army of the Potomac. The men knew that they would be fighting to protect their own soil. "They are more determined than I have ever before seen them," a Union doctor wrote.

Background Chancellorsville has been called a barren victory for the South. It was there that General Stonewall Jackson was mortally wounded, fired upon accidentally in the dusk by southern troops. When Lee heard about his death, he said, "I have lost my right arm."

Background McClellan ran as the presidential candidate for the Democrats in 1864 under a platform of making peace. Until the fall of Atlanta in September of that year, Lincoln was convinced that the Republicans could not win the election.

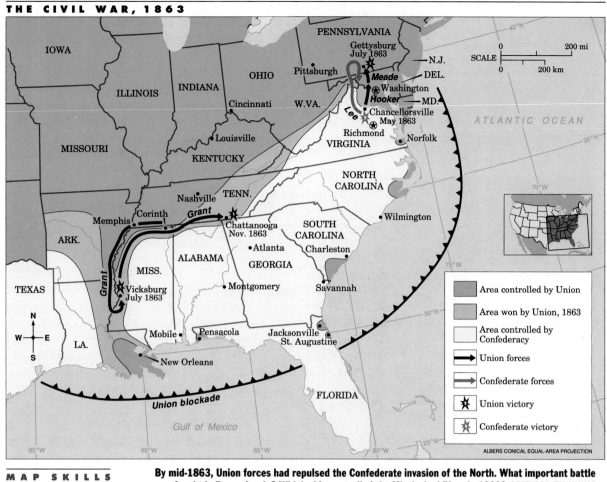

MAP SKILLS

By mid-1863, Union forces had repulsed the Confederate invasion of the North. What important battle was fought in Pennsylvania? Which side controlled the Mississippi River in 1863? **CRITICAL THINKING** Why was the Union able to control port cities on the southern coast? **9B**

Neither Meade nor Lee planned to fight at Gettysburg. It just happened. On July 1, 1863, Lee sent troops into the prosperous town of Gettysburg to get a supply of shoes. There the Confederates stumbled upon a Union cavalry force, and the Battle of Gettysburg was on.

The fighting lasted for three days in what would be the greatest single battle of the Civil War. The most famous, and most pivotal, moment of the battle was Pickett's Charge. For two days the armies had held their positions on opposite ridges. Then on the third day, Lee ordered George Pickett to lead a charge of 15,000 men in an assault on the Union center on Cemetery Ridge. Pickett's troops had to cross a wide-open field in order to reach the Union army. Within half an hour, intense Union gunfire had leveled half the rebels. Most of Pickett's men never even saw the enemy.

Pickett's Charge ended the Battle of Gettysburg. Lee's hopes of victory were dashed. "It's all my fault," he said, and ordered a retreat. Meade was amazed at his own success. "I did not believe the enemy could be whipped," he said.

What neither Lee nor Meade realized was that the Confederates lost the Battle of Gettysburg largely because new technology had made Lee's tactics obsolete. By 1863 rifles had replaced the old, inaccurate muskets that soldiers on both sides had carried at the beginning of the war. Rifling—the cutting of spiral grooves in a gun's bore—multiplied the gun's accuracy and range. Soldiers who were marching in close formation, as they did

Impact of Geography

Have students examine the map on page 57 and suggest reasons why Sherman led his army along the path it took. (The major cities of Atlanta and Savannah were in the path; headed toward an area of coastline already controlled by the Union.)

National Identity

Have students read the Gettysburg Address on page 721 and, working individually or in small groups, paraphrase it. Ask them to suggest reasons why it has become one of the most important documents in American history. (It was written at a time of great national crisis; it captures the spirit of American democracy.)

Cause and Effect

Have students examine the chart on page 58 and then chose a significant event of the war—Antietam or Gettysburg, for example—and create their own chart of the causes and effects of that event.

Map Skills Answers
Gettysburg. The Union. Naval superiority.

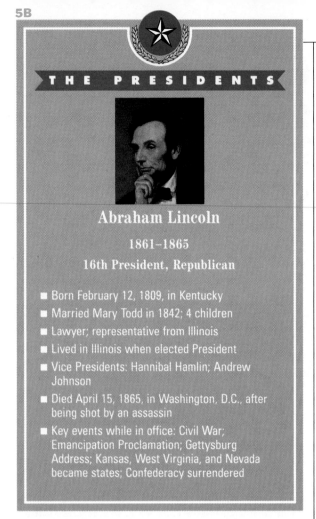

THE PRESIDENTS

Abraham Lincoln

1861–1865

16th President, Republican

- Born February 12, 1809, in Kentucky
- Married Mary Todd in 1842; 4 children
- Lawyer; representative from Illinois
- Lived in Illinois when elected President
- Vice Presidents: Hannibal Hamlin; Andrew Johnson
- Died April 15, 1865, in Washington, D.C., after being shot by an assassin
- Key events while in office: Civil War; Emancipation Proclamation; Gettysburg Address; Kansas, West Virginia, and Nevada became states; Confederacy surrendered

in Pickett's Charge, could be mowed down from a half mile away.

General Meade was so pleased with the Union victory that he did not pursue and finish off Lee's army. Lincoln was distraught. When would he find a general who was a match for Lee?

Then came news of the Battle of Vicksburg. On July 4, 1863, the day after Pickett's Charge, General Grant had taken Vicksburg after a three-month siege. The victory was even more important than Gettysburg, for it gave the Union complete control of the Mississippi. The Confederacy had been cut in half. "Grant is my man," exulted the President.

THE GETTYSBURG ADDRESS 7B

In November 1863, Lincoln journeyed to Gettysburg to dedicate the cemetery in which about 6,000 battle dead lay buried. The speech he gave that day was short, but powerful. He wanted to make it clear that the Union soldiers were fighting for the preservation of democracy. The nation, Lincoln said, was founded on "the proposition that all men are created equal." The "great task remaining" was "that this nation, under God, shall have a new birth of freedom—and that government of the people, by the people, for the people, shall not perish from the earth." No one has ever expressed better the spirit of democracy.

★ Historical Documents

For the text of the Gettysburg Address, see page 721 of this book.

GRANT TAKES COMMAND 5B

The battles of Gettysburg and Vicksburg marked the turning point of the war. From then on, it was all downhill for the Confederacy. Late in 1863 Grant broke a Confederate siege around Chattanooga, Tennessee. He thereby opened up another invasion route into the lower South.

Impressed with Grant's ability to get things done, Lincoln decided to give him command of all the Union armies. In the spring of 1864, Grant was in Washington. His strategy was to attack the Confederacy on all fronts. He planned to go into the field himself to pursue Lee. Admiral Farragut was to go after Mobile, one of the few remaining ports in Confederate hands. William Tecumseh Sherman, who had assumed command of Grant's old army, was to advance southeast from Chattanooga to Atlanta.

Sherman took Atlanta in September 1864. He then set out on a march to the sea, cutting a swath of destruction through Georgia. Leaving his supply trains behind, Sherman told his men to live off the land. He was the first American general to wage total war—a war designed to destroy not only enemy troops, but also enemy factories, fields, railroads, and livestock. A Georgia girl described the scene after Sherman had passed through:

> There was hardly a fence left standing all the way from Sparta to Gordon. The fields were trampled down and the road was

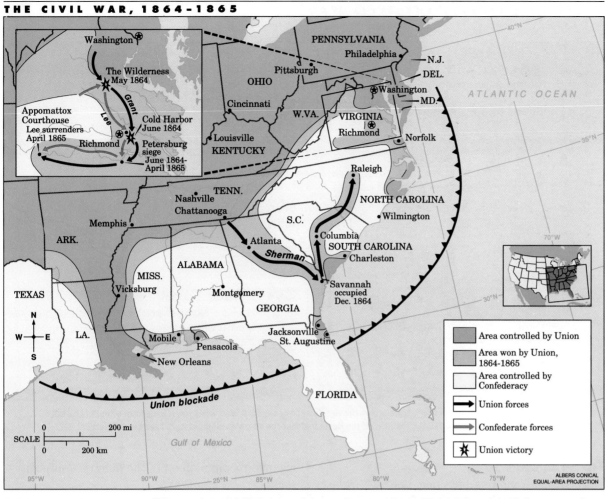

MAP SKILLS

9B

This map shows the final events of the war. Sherman advanced through Georgia in his famous march to the sea. Grant advanced on the Confederate capital at Richmond (inset). **CRITICAL THINKING** In what ways did the waging of total war represent an important change from previous military strategy?

lined with carcasses of horses, hogs, and cattle that the invaders, unable either to consume or to carry away with them, had wantonly shot down, to starve out the people and prevent them from making their crops. The stench in some places was unbearable.

Sherman himself was not apologetic. "We are not only fighting hostile armies, but a hostile people, and must make old and young, rich and poor, feel the hard hand of war," he said. In December 1864, Sherman's army reached the port city of Savannah. Behind him lay a corridor of devastation 60 miles wide and nearly 300 miles long.

BIOGRAPHY

ULYSSES S. GRANT (1822–1885), a native of Ohio, graduated from West Point and served in the Mexican War. Later, he was posted to the Oregon Territory where, depressed and lonely, he became an alcoholic and resigned his commission. Grant rejoined the army at age 39. His courage in battles against Confederate forces in the West led Lincoln to appoint him commander of the Union armies. He later became the eighteenth President.

CHAPTER 2   THE CIVIL WAR ERA, 1850–1865   **57**

Addressing Individual Needs

Guided/ Independent Practice
Instruct students to complete **Reinforcement Workbook** Worksheet 9, which asks students to analyze a poem written at the time of Lincoln's death.

Reteaching/Correctives
Divide the class into eight groups, assigning one subhead of Section 5 to each group. Have each group select the three most essential points made in the material under its assigned subhead. Then have students transcribe the subheads and these points onto poster paper and arrange the papers on a wall of the classroom.

Have students complete **Reteaching Resources** Worksheet 9, which asks them to read a map of important battles of the Civil War.

Enrichment/Extension
Have students complete **Enrichment and Extension Resources** Primary Source Worksheet 4, which includes anecdotes about Abraham Lincoln.

Map Skills Answer
War was no longer limited to the battlefront, civilians suffered as well as soldiers.

Biography
For six years before the war, Grant had been trying, unsuccessfully, to make a living as a civilian. By August 1861 Grant was a general and in charge of the Cairo camp. Discuss with students the abilities that made Grant a great soldier and less successful as a civilian.

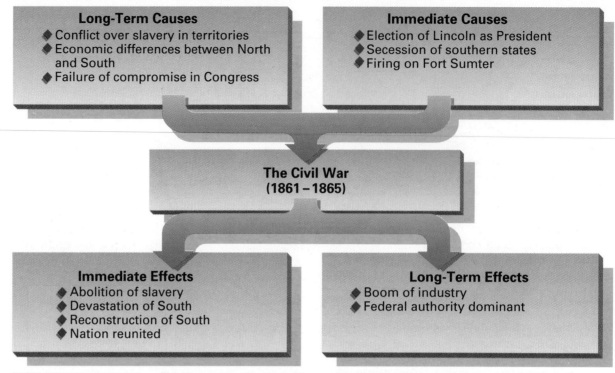

CAUSE AND EFFECT: THE CIVIL WAR

Long-Term Causes
- ◆ Conflict over slavery in territories
- ◆ Economic differences between North and South
- ◆ Failure of compromise in Congress

Immediate Causes
- ◆ Election of Lincoln as President
- ◆ Secession of southern states
- ◆ Firing on Fort Sumter

The Civil War (1861–1865)

Immediate Effects
- ◆ Abolition of slavery
- ◆ Devastation of South
- ◆ Reconstruction of South
- ◆ Nation reunited

Long-Term Effects
- ◆ Boom of industry
- ◆ Federal authority dominant

CHART SKILLS This chart summarizes the significance of the Civil War. What was a long-term effect of the war? **CRITICAL THINKING** If the North had lost the war, how might history have been different? **9E**

THE WAR ENDS 7D

Meanwhile, Grant was pursuing Lee in Virginia. In May and June of 1864, their forces clashed at the Wilderness and at Cold Harbor. Grant then laid siege to Petersburg, which controlled the rail lines to the Confederate capital of Richmond.

The noose was tightening around Lee's army. By the spring of 1865, Grant had an army twice the size of Lee's—120,000 to Lee's 55,000. In addition, Sherman was now moving north from Savannah. Lee decided to abandon Richmond and head for the mountains. But then he learned that Sheridan was ahead of him. Trapped, Lee made the decision to surrender.

On April 9, 1865, in the small Virginia town of Appomattox Courthouse, Lee and Grant arranged the terms of surrender. Operating under Lincoln's instructions, Grant was generous. The Confederate soldiers were to return to their homes, and those who owned horses or mules could keep them. When Lee left Appomattox, Grant ordered

his men to supply food to the hungry Confederate soldiers.

The final act of the Civil War tragedy was now played out. A few days after Appomattox, President and Mrs. Lincoln went to the theater to see a popular comedy. During the third act John Wilkes Booth, a Confederate sympathizer, shot Lincoln in the back of the head. Early the next morning, April 15, 1865, Lincoln died from the assassin's bullet. With Lincoln's last breath rose up a wail of grief from freedom-lovers the world over.

ASSESSING THE WAR 3B, 3F, 9C

The Civil War was the most wrenching experience this nation has ever endured. The Union was preserved and slavery abolished, but at a frightening cost. In four years 620,000 men had died—360,000 for the Union, 260,000 for the Confederacy. No other war in our history has caused such loss of life.

Throughout most of the war, the outcome was in doubt. Even today historians cannot with confidence say exactly why the North won and why the South lost. They do agree, however, that final Union victory reflected the far-sighted leadership of Abraham Lincoln. During the darkest hour in the history of the Union, he held firm to the principles of freedom and democracy. And as great leaders must, he bore the terrible burden of responsibility for the fate of his nation.

The consequences of the war were enormous. In fighting to defend the Union, people accepted that the nation itself was more important than the states that composed it. After 1865 people no longer said "the United States are," but instead, "the United States *is*."

Prior to the Civil War, the federal government was a relatively small body with limited responsibilities and powers. By placing staggering new demands on the government, the war gave rise to a vastly larger bureaucracy. This expanded government began to play an important role in the day-to-day life of its citizens in such areas as taxation, banking, and education. The growth in federal power would continue long after the guns of war had fallen silent.

The Civil War also stimulated the growth of industrial America. The war nurtured the early development of several great postwar enterprises—petroleum, steel, food processing, manufacturing, and finance. Such trends too would continue for decades after the end of the war.

These legacies of the Civil War—the growth of the federal government and industry—must have seemed especially bitter to southerners. For as historian David M. McPherson has written, the South had left the Union to protect itself from exactly these sorts of changes:

> The South fought to preserve its version of the republic of the founding fathers—a government of limited powers that protected the rights of property and whose constituency comprised an independent gentry and yeomanry [upper and middle class] of the white race undisturbed by large cities, heartless factories, restless free workers, and class conflict.

Change would probably have come to the South in any event. But the war speeded the changes southerners had fought to hold back. The challenge facing the South after 1865 would be to construct a new society to deal with the realities of postwar America.

SECTION REVIEW

1. KEY TERMS Battle of Antietam, Emancipation Proclamation, Copperhead, Battle of Gettysburg, Battle of Vicksburg, total war

2. PEOPLE AND PLACES Sharpsburg, Harriet Tubman, George Meade, Appomattox Courthouse

3. COMPREHENSION Why did the Emancipation Proclamation not apply to slaves in Union states?

4. COMPREHENSION What did Lee hope to gain when he invaded Pennsylvania?

5. CRITICAL THINKING Explain this statement: "The war aims of North and South ensured that the war would continue until one side won total victory." **9A**

9D

2. *Sharpsburg*—Site of the Battle of Antietam. *Harriet Tubman*—"Conductor" on the Underground Railroad. *George Meade*—Union commander at the Battle of Gettysburg. *Appomattox Courthouse*—Site of Lee's surrender to Grant, April 1865.

3. Because the Constitution did not give the President power to free slaves within the Union. Freeing slaves in the South could be considered a military step and constitutional under the President's powers as commander-in-chief.

4. Food and supplies for the Confederate army; a peace settlement with the invaded North; a victory might encourage Europeans to recognize the Confederacy.

5. The South was determined to leave the Union, and North was determined that it stay—there was no room for compromise.

Closure

Use the Section 5 information in the Chapter 2 Summary (p. 60) to synthesize the important elements covered in Section 2. Then have students read Section 1 of Chapter 3 for the next class period, noting the initial steps of reconstructing the South.

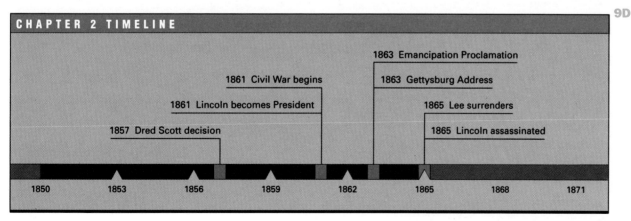

CHAPTER 2 TIMELINE

1863 Emancipation Proclamation

1861 Civil War begins

1863 Gettysburg Address

1861 Lincoln becomes President

1865 Lee surrenders

1857 Dred Scott decision

1865 Lincoln assassinated

1850 1853 1856 1859 1862 1865 1868 1871

CHAPTER 2 SUMMARY

SECTION 1: During the 1850s tensions over the extension of slavery into the territories divided North and South.

■ The Compromise of 1850, which led to the admission of California as a free state, reduced North-South tensions, but satisfied neither side.

■ The Kansas-Nebraska Act, which allowed the people of each territory to decide whether or not to legalize slavery, outraged antislavery northerners.

■ In its 1857 Dred Scott decision, the Supreme Court ruled that the Constitution did not apply to blacks, and that Congress had no right to forbid slavery in the territories.

SECTION 2: The election of Abraham Lincoln in 1860 led to the secession of the South. The Civil War began in April 1861 when the South attacked Fort Sumter.

■ The seceding states formed the Confederate States of America and chose Jefferson Davis as their president.

SECTION 3: Early in 1861, both sides prepared for war.

■ The North's advantages included more industry, greater wealth, and a larger population. The North also had the advantage of the inspired leadership of Abraham Lincoln.

■ The South's advantages included superior military leadership and the fact that it was fighting on its own soil.

SECTION 4: In the early years of the war, the South held its own in the East, but lost ground in the West.

■ The Union's naval blockade of the South hurt the ability of the Confederacy to fight.

■ Union victories in the West, including the Battle of Shiloh and the capture of Nashville and New Orleans, weakened the South.

SECTION 5: The turning point of the war came in July 1863, when Union forces blocked a Confederate offensive in the North and invaded the South.

■ The North won decisive victories at the battles of Gettysburg and Vicksburg.

■ The Confederates surrendered at Appomattox Courthouse, Virginia, in April 1865.

■ The war strengthened the authority of the federal government and encouraged industrial growth in the North.

KEY TERMS ●

Use the following terms to complete the sentences below.

Battle of Antietam
Battle of Vicksburg
Compromise of 1850
Copperhead
Dred Scott case
Emancipation Proclamation

1. Henry Clay introduced the _____ to settle the debate over the admission of California as a state.
2. In the _____ , the Supreme Court ruled that the Constitution did not apply to black people.
3. In 1862 the Union blocked the Confederate drive into the North at the _____ .
4. A _____ was a northerner who sympathized with the South during the Civil War.
5. The _____ gave the North control of the Mississippi.
6. In the _____ , Lincoln outlawed slavery in Confederate territory.

PEOPLE TO IDENTIFY ●

Identify the following people and tell why each was important.

1. John Brown
2. Henry Clay
3. Jefferson Davis
4. Stephen Douglas
5. Robert E. Lee
6. Harriet Beecher Stowe

Places to Locate ●

Match each of the letters on the map with the places that are listed below. Then explain the importance of each place.

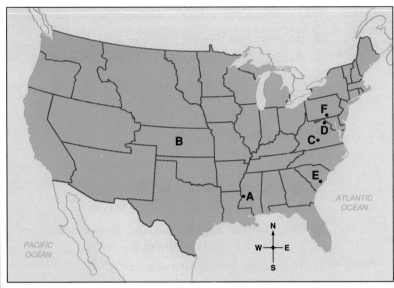

1. Kansas Territory
2. Harpers Ferry
3. Fort Sumter
4. Vicksburg
5. Gettysburg
6. Appomattox Courthouse

Reviewing the Facts ▲

1. What were the terms of the Compromise of 1850? Why did each side remain dissatisfied?
2. Why were antislavery northerners angered by the Kansas-Nebraska Act? The Dred Scott case?
3. Who were the candidates for President in 1860? What factors enabled Abraham Lincoln to win the election?
4. How did southerners justify their secession from the Union? How did the North respond?
5. What were the strengths and weaknesses of each side in the war?
6. How did each side's objectives influence its strategy in waging war? How did these strategies change over the course of the war?
7. Why did the North blockade southern ports? How effective was the blockade by the end of the war?
8. Where was the western front in the Civil War? Why was it important?
9. What battles marked the turning point in the war? Why were they significant?
10. What were the consequences of the Civil War?

Critical Thinking Skills ▲

1. Forming a Hypothesis Reread the quote from Harriet Beecher Stowe on page 34. Why did Stowe think that northerners bore some responsibility for slavery?

2. Stating Both Sides of an Issue Make the strongest possible case for each side in the debate over whether states had the right to secede.

3. Analyzing a Quotation Explain what Lincoln meant by this statement: "It is called the Army of the Potomac but it is only McClellan's bodyguard. . . . If McClellan is not using the army, I should like to borrow it for a while."

Writing About Topics in American History ■

1. Connecting with Literature A selection from *Jubilee* by Margaret Walker appears on pages 771–774. Read it and answer the questions. Then answer the following question: Why was it so important to Randall Ware to be a part of the war effort?

2. Applying Themes: Geography List some of the geographical advantages the South had in the Civil War. Then draw comparisons between those advantages and the advantages American soldiers enjoyed during the Revolutionary War.

8. The western front, between the Mississippi River and the Appalachian Mountains, controlled crucial Confederate shipping routes and important natural resources.

9. In the Battle of Gettysburg, the Union soundly defeated the South. The Battle of Vicksburg gave the Union total control of the Mississippi River.

10. The abolition of slavery and the preservation of the Union; the growth of industry and increased federal power.

Critical Thinking Skills
1. They did not have the excuse of having been raised to view slavery as acceptable.
2. Individual states formed the Union and if the Union does not suit them, the states have the right to return to their original arrangement. On the other hand, in signing the Constitution, each state promised to turn itself over to a larger entity—the Union.
3. Lincoln meant McClellan used his army too defensively and the Union needed the army to act.

Writing About Topics in American History
1. He saw a chance to contribute to the cause of freeing the slaves while at the same time working at a job he could be proud of.
2. The South was fighting a defensive war. This gave them a number of advantages: it was easier for the South to maintain its supply lines; Southern soldiers were more familiar with the terrain; and the Southerners were fighting to save their homes. The American rebels had these same advantages against the British.

6. Southern strategy was to resist the invading North. Northern strategy was to pressure the South into yielding. Both sides changed their strategies, aiming for decisive victories.

7. The North blockaded the South to prevent the Confederacy from selling cotton and buying supplies. The Northern blockade became very effective.

Chapter Review exercises are keyed for student abilities:
● = Basic
▲ = Average
■ = Average/Advanced

Chapter 3 ■ Rebuilding the South

	SECTION OBJECTIVES	SECTION RESOURCES
Section 1 **The Challenge of Emancipation**	■ describe the first steps taken in reconstructing the South	● **Reteaching Resources:** Worksheet 10 ▲ **Reinforcement Workbook:** Worksheet 10 ■ **Enrichment and Extension Resources:** Primary Source Worksheet 5; Historian Worksheet 1 ▲ **Teaching Transparencies:** Transparency 10
Section 2 **Congressional Reconstruction**	■ describe the congressional response to President Johnson's plans for reconstructing the South	● **Reteaching Resources:** Worksheet 11 ▲ **Reinforcement Workbook:** Worksheet 11 ■ **Enrichment and Extension Resources:** Primary Source Worksheet 6 ▲ **Teaching Transparencies:** Transparency 11
Section 3 **The Changing South**	■ explain the reasons for ending Reconstruction in the South ■ describe the important economic and political trends of the South after Reconstruction	● **Reteaching Resources:** Worksheet 12 ▲ **Reinforcement Workbook:** Worksheet 12 ▲ **Teaching Transparencies:** Transparency 12

The list below shows Essential Elements relevant to this chapter. (The complete list of Essential Elements appears in the introductory pages of this Teacher's Edition.)

Section 1: 3C, 4A, 5B, 5D, 5F, 5E, 6A, 7D, 9A, 9B
Section 2: 4A, 4D, 5A, 5B, 5D, 7A
Section 3: 2B, 2D, 3A, 3C, 4A, 4C, 5A, 5B, 5D, 7B, 8H, 8I, 9A, 9B, 9D

> Section Resources are keyed for student abilities:
> ● = Basic
> ▲ = Average
> ■ = Average/Advanced

Geography Resources: Worksheets 5, 6
Tests: Chapter 3 Test

Chapter Project: Pluralistic Society

Have students do research and write a report on one of the following topics: an evaluation of the record of Radical Reconstructionists, profiles of elected black officials, speculation on how Reconstruction would have differed if Lincoln had survived, or a discussion of Reconstruction as the precursor to the civil rights movement of the 1950s and 1960s.

Homework Options

Each section contains activities labeled "Addressing Individual Needs." You may wish to choose from among these activities when assigning homework.

Provisions for Limited English Proficiency (LEP)

Several suggested activities may be particularly helpful for teachers of students with limited English proficiency. These activities have been marked throughout the Teacher's Annotated Edition with the symbol **LEP** .

BIBLIOGRAPHY AND AUDIOVISUAL AIDS

Teacher Bibliography

Du Bois, W.E.B. *Black Reconstruction in America*. Russell & Russell, 1956.

Foner, Eric. *Reconstruction: America's Unfinished Revolution, 1863–1877*. Harper and Row, 1988.

Woodward, C. Vann. *Origins of the New South, 1877–1913*. Louisiana State University Press, 1971.

Student Bibliography

Buck, Paul H. *The Road to Reunion, 1865–1900*. Little, Brown, 1937.

Stampp, Kenneth M. *Era of Reconstruction: Eighteen Sixty-Five to Eighteen Seventy-Seven*. Random House, 1967.

Literature

Cable, George Washington. *Strong Hearts*. Irvington, 1986. Novel of life in Louisiana at the end of the 1800s by a southern regionalist.

Chopin, Kate. *The Awakening and Selected Stories*. Penguin, 1984.

Douglass, Frederick. *My Bondage & My Freedom*. Dover, 1969.

Du Bois, W. E. B. *The Autobiography of W. E. B. DuBois: A Soliloquy on Viewing My Life from the Last Decade of Its First Century*. UNIPUB/Kraus-Thomson Organization, 1976.

Glasgow, Ellen. *The Voice of the People*. Godshalk, W.L. ed. (Masterworks of Literatures Series). The New College and University Press, 1972. First of the author's series on Virginia society.

Films and Videotapes*

Civil War: Postwar Period. 20 min. COR/MTI. President Johnson and Congress battle over the political reorganization of the South, the Freedman's Bureau faces the problems of homeless and former slaves, and Congress passes the Fourteenth Amendment.

Civil War: The Promise of Reconstruction. 30 min. LCA. The Union's Post Royal experiment anticipated many developments of the Reconstruction Era that were to occur throughout the South.

Impeachment of Andrew Johnson. 25 min. FI. Andrew Johnson's impeachment raises questions on the nature of the American presidency, the system of checks and balances, and the boundaries of power.

Filmstrips*

Rebuilding the American Nation, 1865-1890 (set of 2). GA. Explores the influence of events that followed the Civil War, including emancipation, the transfer of wealth from the South to the North, and unprecedented technological progress.

Computer Software*

America's President Series: The Age of Growth—Presidents During the Late 19th and 20th Centuries (Apple with 48K; IBM with 64K). QUEUE. Each President is covered in a separate menu option and prominent Presidents have multiple selections on different phases of their lives and administrations. Presidents Hayes–Taft, 1877–1913.

*For a complete guide to audiovisual sources, see the introduction to this book (page Txx).

Rebuilding the South
(pp. 62–81)

This chapter discusses the South after the Civil War, from Reconstruction through the economic and political developments of the late 1800s.

 Themes in American History

■ Constitutional government
■ Pluralistic society

Chapter Objectives

After students complete this chapter, they will be able to:

1. Describe the first steps taken in reconstructing the South.

2. Describe the congressional response to President Johnson's plans for reconstructing the South.

3. Explain the reasons for ending Reconstruction in the South.

4. Describe the important economic and political trends of the South after Reconstruction.

Chapter Opener Art
Belle Grove plantation, Louisiana, built 1857.

Rebuilding a South devastated by war was a pressing task for the United States after 1865. Southern farms, towns and cities, roads and bridges, mills and factories had to be rebuilt or repaired.

CHAPTER SUPPORT MATERIAL	
Reinforcement Workbook: Worksheets 10–12	
Reteaching Resources: Worksheets 10–12	
Enrichment and Extension Resources: Primary Source Worksheets 5, 6; Historian Worksheet 1	
Geography Resources: Worksheets 5, 6	
Teaching Transparencies: Transparencies 10–12	
Tests: Chapter 3 Test	

3 Rebuilding the South
(1865–1900)

SECTION 1

The Challenge of Emancipation
(pp. 63–67)

3C, 4A, 5B, 5D, 5F, 5E, 6A, 7D, 9A, 9B

1 The Challenge of Emancipation

Section Focus

Key Terms   Reconstruction ■ amnesty
■ Thirteenth Amendment ■ black codes
■ Freedmen's Bureau

Main Idea   Emancipation forced Congress, the President, and the southern states to work out a plan for rebuilding the government and society of the South.

Objectives   As you read, look for answers to these questions:
1. What was the black response to emancipation?
2. What was the President's plan for re-building the South?
3. How did southern states seek to restore the old order?

When the Civil War ended in 1865, America had been transformed. The North was on the thresh-old of the modern industrial age. Business was booming in all the industries involved with the war effort. These included railroads, meat-packing plants, woolen mills, shoe-and-boot factories, and agriculture. The South, on the other hand, was in ruins. A South Carolina planter visiting Baltimore wrote that he found it "hard to bear . . . this exulting, abounding, overrunning wealth of the North in contrast with the utter desolation of the unfortunate South."

The Yankee invasion had wrecked the South. Its railroads were torn up, its barns and dwellings burned, its livestock destroyed. To ex-Confederate soldiers returning to their land and homes, the job of rebuilding the economy seemed overwhelming. But they faced an even greater challenge: to work out the meaning and consequences of emancipa-tion. The federal government played an active role in both tasks. Its plan to rebuild and re-establish the states of the former Confederacy is known as Reconstruction. Reconstruction took place dur-ing the years 1865–1877.

THE BLACK RESPONSE TO EMANCIPATION 4A
The day freedom came was an event former slaves could never forget. Decades later one freedman described the feeling:

> The end of the war, it come just like that—like you snap your fingers. . . . Soldiers, all of a sudden, was everywhere—coming in bunches, crossing and walking and riding. Everyone was a-singing. We was all walk-ing on golden clouds. Hallelujah! . . . Everybody went wild. We all felt like he-roes, and nobody had made us that way but ourselves. We was free. Just like that, we was free.

Blacks' first reaction to freedom was to escape white domination over their lives. They began to move—to return to homes they had been sold away from, to search for scattered family mem-bers, or just to experience the open road. "Right off colored folks started on the move," recalled a freedman. "They seemed to want to get closer to freedom, so they'd know what it was—like it was a place or a city."

SUPPORTING THE SECTION

Reinforcement Workbook: Worksheet 10
Reteaching Resources: Worksheet 10
Enrichment and Extension Resources: Primary Source Worksheet 5; Historian Worksheet 1
Teaching Transparencies: Transparency 10

Section Objective

■ describe the first steps taken in reconstructing the South

Introducing the Section

Connecting with Past Learnings
What did the Emancipation Proclamation of 1863 do?
(Freed slaves in rebelling states.) As students work through this section, have them note the directions that this freedom took, and the problems it generated in southern society.

Key Terms
Write the key terms on the board and have volunteers define the terms in their own words. Have students divide the terms into two lists, one with terms describing things most northerners would have supported, and the oth-er with terms describing things white southerners would have supported. **LEP**

Focus
On one side of the board, have students list the problems faced by the South after the Civil War. (Farms and railroads destroyed; destruction of the traditional economic system; unem-ployed and untrained black population.) On the other side, have students list the different solutions to these problems mentioned in the section. (Schools for black children; wage contracts and land grants to freed slaves; amnesty and restoration of property to former leaders of the Confederacy; Thirteenth Amendment; Freedmen's Bureau.)

How had Reconstruction progressed by the end of 1865? (Blacks were freed but their rights were beginning to be restricted; Johnson was ready to welcome southern states back into the Union, but Congress was unwilling to accept the old South back so readily.)

Developing the Lesson

After students have read the section, you may want to consider the following activities:

Cultural Pluralism

Discuss with students the emotions described by the freedmen quoted in the section. Have them write short journal entries describing the feelings of a southern black upon hearing that the Thirteenth Amendment had been ratified.

Have students suggest the difficulties blacks may have encountered in suddenly being free after centuries of slavery. (Learning to work for themselves; learning to work for wages; gaining an education; aspiring to citizenship.)

Religion

What cultural institutions did southern blacks turn to after emancipation? (Church, schools, family.) *How might religion have played an important role in strengthening the black community?* (Provided a unifying force; clergy served as community leaders.) Interested students may research and report on the role of religion in black history.

Winslow Homer's oil painting *Sunday Morning* depicts a black family reading from the Bible. Homer traveled to Petersburg, Virginia, to make the portrait in 1877. **CULTURAL PLURALISM** Which members of the family shown here were probably born into slavery? **6A, 9B**

Emancipation allowed families to reunite and strengthened family ties. Under slavery marriage had been an informal affair, but with freedom many couples went through marriage ceremonies.

Blacks also took steps to free their religion from white control. Throughout the South, blacks es-tablished their own churches. The church then became the central institution in the black community. It was a place for social events and political gatherings. Often it was also a school.

With emancipation, schools sprouted up everywhere in the South. Both adults and children flocked to these schools. Reading and writing, as many realized, paved the way to a new economic freedom. By 1870, African Americans had raised over $1 million toward their own education. However, it was not enough to meet the need. In the long run, northern aid societies, the federal Freedmen's Bureau, and state governments would pay most of the cost of education.

The teachers in these schools were both black and white. Ten percent of the South's black adults were literate, and a number of them chose to become teachers. Other teachers included free northern blacks like Charlotte Forten of Philadelphia. "My heart sings a song of thanksgiving," she wrote, "that even I am permitted to do something for a long-abused race." But the teachers in black schools were often targets of harassment by white Confederate die-hards. In some parts of the South, schools were burned and teachers beaten or killed.

This illustration shows a class at the Zion School for Colored Children, a freedmen's school in Charleston, South Carolina. A federal agency, the Freedmen's Bureau established schools for black Americans during Reconstruction. Some of these schools developed into leading black colleges, such as Howard University and Hampton Institute. **HISTORY** Why might some white southerners have tried to keep blacks from getting an education? **9A**

64 UNIT 1 BEGINNINGS THROUGH RECONSTRUCTION

Photo Caption Answers
(Top) The old woman at right and the woman holding the Bible. (Bottom) Uneducated people are more easily controlled and taken advantage of.

Issues of Land and Labor 3C

More than anything else, freed slaves hoped to own land. General Sherman had ordered that coastal South Carolina be divided into 40-acre parcels of land and given to freedmen. The rumor then spread among the freedmen all over the South that they would be given "40 acres and a mule." That was, most believed, no more than their right. As one Virginia freedman explained:

Didn't we clear the land, and raise the crops of corn, of cotton, of tobacco, of rice, of sugar, of everything? And then didn't them large cities in the North grow up on the cotton and the sugars and the rice that we made?

In fact, most freedmen never received land, and those who did often had to return it. In the early years of Reconstruction, many African Americans were without the means of earning a living. It was clear that the South needed a new system of labor. There were landowners with little cash and no laborers, and laborers without land.

The wage contract was a new experience for both planters and freedmen. Planters were reluctant to recognize that freedmen had the right to bargain over terms of work. On the other hand, many freedmen assumed that the wage was an extra—that the landowner still had the responsibility to clothe, house, and feed them.

A journal entry written by Henry William Ravenel, a South Carolina planter, described his reaction to the new system:

The new relation in which we now stand toward the Negroes, our former slaves, is a matter for grave and serious consideration, if we desire to act justly toward them. We are very apt to retain former feelings and wish to exact more service than what would be implied in a fair contract with a white worker. . . . The former relation has to be unlearnt by both parties.

Presidential Reconstruction 5B

The policies of the federal government played a pivotal role in the Reconstruction of the South. In the last year of the war, Lincoln had begun to consider how the South should be treated when peace came. In his Second Inaugural Address in March 1865, Lincoln declared:

With malice toward none; with charity for all; with firmness in the right, as God gives us to see the right, let us strive on to finish the work we are in; to bind up the nation's wounds . . . to do all which may achieve and cherish a just, and a lasting peace, among ourselves, and with all nations.

In a speech given during the last week of his life, Lincoln further explained his ideas on Reconstruction. From his point of view, the Confederate states had never left the Union. Therefore the task at hand was not to punish them, but "to restore the proper practical relations between these states and the Union." What this meant exactly, Lincoln did not make clear. His policies for "restoration" would be forthcoming, he said. Lincoln said he would prefer that the vote be given to all black soldiers, but he did not call for universal black suffrage. **5E**

★ **Historical Documents**

For an excerpt from Lincoln's Second Inaugural Address, see page 722 of this book.

At Lincoln's death, Vice President Andrew Johnson became President. Johnson had been put on the Republican ticket in 1864 to broaden its appeal to the border states. A self-made man from Tennessee, Johnson was a former slaveholder. As a backcountry politician, Johnson was suspicious of the planter aristocracy and had little sympathy for black people. Johnson was also stubborn to a fault and had none of the political intuition of his predecessor.

Johnson held that Reconstruction was the job of the President, not of the Congress. Johnson's policies, called Presidential Reconstruction, were based on what he believed to be Lincoln's intentions: charity toward the former Confederates and the establishment of new state governments.

To most southerners Johnson offered amnesty—official pardon—and the restoration of their property. This was granted on the condition they take

Constitutional Heritage
The Constitution made no mention of wholesale secession; whether postwar reconstruction was the domain of the executive or legislative branch was open to question. *On what grounds might Congress have claimed responsibility for Reconstruction?* (More representative of the people; had the power to admit states into the Union and to judge the qualifications of its members.)

History
Have students read Lincoln's Second Inaugural Address on page 722 and suggest what ideas he may have had for reconstructing the South.

Civic Values
Discuss the establishment of black codes in the South after the war. *What do these codes imply about prevailing southern attitudes toward blacks at that time?* (Believed they were inferior; wanted them to stay like slaves.) Have students explain why many northerners were angered by these practices. (They felt that the South was trying to re-establish the society northerners had fought the Civil War to change.)

C Cooperative Learning

Divide the class into groups representing either ex-Confederates, freed slaves, or Republican members of Congress. Ask each group to discuss its opinion of Presidential Reconstruction, listing its strong and weak points and presenting possible alternatives. Each member of the group should suggest at least one idea. **LEP**

Background The abolition of slavery freed an estimated four million people. In 1880, only about 15 percent of these former slaves, or their descendants, owned land.

Addressing Individual Needs

Guided/ Independent Practice
Instruct students to complete **Reinforcement Workbook** Worksheet 10. This worksheet guides students in analyzing white and black school enrollment figures between 1850 and 1900.

Reteaching/Correctives
Have students work in groups to dramatize the problems facing the South after the Civil War. Points of view to be represented include freed slaves, former slaveholders, President Johnson, and northerners. Have students scan the section for information pertaining to each point of view.

Have students complete **Reteaching Resources** Worksheet 10, in which they determine the main ideas of the section.

Enrichment/Extension
Have students complete **Enrichment and Extension Resources** Primary Source Worksheet 5, which guides students in understanding an ex-slave's experience in the postwar South. Also have them complete Historian Worksheet 1, which discusses the education of freedmen.

Assessment
You may wish to use the Section 1 Review, page 67, to see how well your students understand the main points in this lesson.

Section Review Answers
1. *Reconstruction*—Federal government's plan to rebuild and re-integrate former Confederate states. *amnesty*—Official pardon. *Thirteenth Amendment*—Abolished slavery in the United States. *black codes*—Laws intended to stop movement of freedmen and to return blacks to

an oath of allegiance to the Union. The great planters, high-ranking military officers, and ex-Confederate officials were excluded from this arrangement. Even these, however, were often able to win amnesty. Johnson was easily flattered when the once high-and-mighty humbly asked him for pardon.

Johnson also took steps to set up provisional governments that would write new constitutions for the states. These constitutions, he said, must recognize the abolition of slavery and reject the principle of nullification—the idea that states had the right to declare certain federal laws invalid. They would also have to cancel any state debts incurred during the time of the Confederacy.

REVIVING THE OLD SOUTH 4A, 5D

Congress was not in session when Johnson became President in April 1865. It did not reconvene until the following December. During these eight months the former Confederate states moved to

This photograph shows laborers on a South Carolina rice plantation. Rice production dropped sharply after emancipation because many freedmen refused to return to plantation work. ECONOMICS Why might the establishment of black codes be viewed as an attempt to save the plantation system? 9A

rebuild their governments and their society. The problem was, however, that the new forms looked suspiciously like the old ones. Much to the disappointment of black political leaders in the North and South, nothing was said about black suffrage. "This is a white man's government," said the provisional governor of South Carolina, "and intended for white men only. . . ." After all, the governor pointed out, the Supreme Court's Dred Scott decision had said blacks could not be citizens.

President Johnson's "soft" attitude encouraged southern leaders to believe that they could resist his reconstruction policies. Mississippi and Texas refused to ratify the Thirteenth Amendment abolishing slavery in the United States. Several states refused to reject the principle of nullification or to cancel Confederate debts.

Northerners were particularly distressed that southern states began to pass laws restricting the freedom of black people. The black codes were laws intended to stop the movement of freedmen and to return blacks to plantation labor. In effect, the black codes set up another form of black servitude.

In Mississippi, for instance, the black codes decreed that each person must have written proof of employment. Vagrants could be punished with forced labor on plantations. Contracts of employment were for one year, and a black person had no right to break such a contract. Upset that so many black women had withdrawn from field labor, Louisiana and Texas required that a labor contract include the whole family.

In South Carolina, blacks who chose to pursue any occupation other than farmer or servant were required to pay a heavy tax. Other codes declared that blacks working on plantations had to labor from sunup to sundown. They could not leave the plantation without permission. Using "insulting" language and preaching without a license were considered criminal offenses.

Even harder for many blacks to stomach were the apprenticeship laws. These laws allowed courts to assign black orphans to white masters. In fact, many of these "orphans" had parents and were required to work without pay well past the age of sixteen.

Photo Caption Answer
They restricted blacks' freedom of movement and choice of occupation, effectively tying them to plantation work.

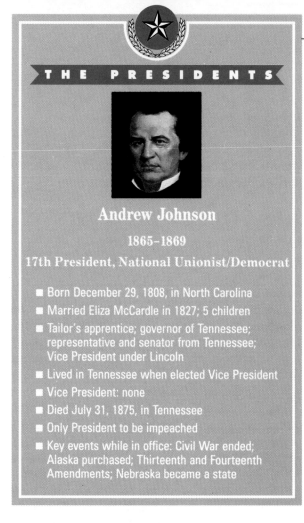
Andrew Johnson

1865–1869

17th President, National Unionist/Democrat

- Born December 29, 1808, in North Carolina
- Married Eliza McCardle in 1827; 5 children
- Tailor's apprentice; governor of Tennessee; representative and senator from Tennessee; Vice President under Lincoln
- Lived in Tennessee when elected Vice President
- Vice President: none
- Died July 31, 1875, in Tennessee
- Only President to be impeached
- Key events while in office: Civil War ended; Alaska purchased; Thirteenth and Fourteenth Amendments; Nebraska became a state

THE FREEDMEN'S BUREAU 7D

In 1865 the only institution that opposed restrictions against blacks was the Freedmen's Bureau. This federal agency had been established in the waning days of the war in order to distribute clothing, food, and fuel to the poor of the South. The bureau was also given the authority to manage abandoned and confiscated Confederate land. It divided this land into 40-acre plots, which were rented to freedmen until the land could be sold.

But Johnson's liberal grants of amnesty undermined the bureau's efforts to give freedmen their own land. Johnson arranged for pardoned Confederate landowners to have their land returned to them. All too often, therefore, freedmen were forced to give up their new farms, to give up their hopes of economic independence.

The Freedmen's Bureau did what it could to oversee labor contracts and to protect freedmen from exploitation. But, as one bureau agent wrote, the former masters "still have the ingrained feeling that the black people at large belong to the whites at large."

CONGRESS TAKES A STAND 5F

When Congress convened in December 1865, senators and representatives from the southern states were there to take their seats. President Johnson was ready to welcome them. But Congress was not willing to forget old differences quite so fast.

Under the Constitution, Congress has the right to judge the qualifications of its own members. Northern members of Congress were alarmed that so many of the new representatives had been Confederate officeholders only the year before. This list included 4 Confederate generals, 6 Confederate cabinet officers, and 58 Confederate congressmen, as well as the former vice president of the Confederacy. Northerners were also concerned about conditions in the southern states, particularly the black codes. Northerners asked: Had the Civil War been fought just to allow the South to return to its old ways?

Instead of admitting the southerners, Congress voted to establish the Joint Committee on Reconstruction. The Committee would investigate conditions in the South and decide whether the southern states were entitled to representation. Congress thus put the President on notice: Reconstruction was also Congress's responsibility.

SECTION REVIEW

1. KEY TERMS Reconstruction, amnesty, Thirteenth Amendment, black codes, Freedmen's Bureau

2. PEOPLE Andrew Johnson

3. COMPREHENSION How did the lives of southern blacks change after emancipation?

4. COMPREHENSION How did the South respond to President Johnson's reconstruction policies?

5. CRITICAL THINKING Do you think Lincoln would have approved of President Johnson's policies on Reconstruction? Why or why not?

CHAPTER 3 REBUILDING THE SOUTH, 1865–1900 **67**

plantation labor. *Freedmen's Bureau*—Federal agency established to help the southern poor and to manage abandoned and confiscated Confederate land.

2. *Andrew Johnson*—President who took office after Lincoln was assassinated.

3. They were freed from slavery, allowing them freedom of movement. Families could reunite and couples could marry. Blacks established their own churches. Schools to educate blacks were established.

4. Southern leaders believed they could resist President Johnson's reconstruction policies. Some states refused to ratify the Thirteenth Amendment, rejected the principle of nullification, and refused to repudiate the Confederate debt. Southern states also began passing black codes, restricting the freedom of black people.

5. To a great extent, Lincoln would probably have approved of Johnson's policies on Reconstruction. Johnson showed charity to the Confederates by making it easy to be accepted back into the Union. In addition, both Lincoln and Johnson viewed this as a job for the President, rather than Congress. On the other hand, Lincoln probably would have disapproved of Johnson's refusal to advocate some form of black suffrage.

Closure

Ask one student to transform the Main Idea of the section into a question, and have other students answer that question. Then have students read Section 2 for the next class period. Ask them to note how Congressional Reconstruction differed from Presidential Reconstruction.

The Presidents
Using Johnson as an example, have students discuss the problems faced by a Vice President who takes over the presidency.

Background The Joint Committee on Reconstruction held extensive hearings on the treatment of blacks in the South. Colonel George A. Custer, stationed in Texas, testified, "It is of weekly, if not of daily occurrence that freedmen are murdered." Such stories shocked and angered northerners.

Section Objective

- describe the congressional response to President Johnson's plans for reconstructing the South

Introducing the Section

Connecting with Past Learnings

Review with students the important points of Presidential Reconstruction. (Clemency towards the South; pardons granted; requirement that new governments recognize the abolition of slavery, reject nullification, and repudiate Confederate debt.) *Why was Congress unhappy with Presidential Reconstruction?* (Felt reconstruction policy was *its* job; felt President was too lenient; alarmed at South's resistance to new order.)

Key Terms

List the key terms on the board. Have students write a one-sentence definition for each term. Then have them check their definitions with the way the word is defined in context, modifying their definitions if necessary. **LEP**

4A, 4D, 5A, 5B, 5D, 7A

2 Congressional Reconstruction

Section Focus

Key Terms disenfranchisement ■ Fourteenth Amendment ■ scalawag ■ carpetbagger ■ Fifteenth Amendment

Main Idea Congress took over Reconstruction of the South from the President, imposing military rule on the South in an attempt to establish political equality for blacks. New amendments reflected the nation's commitment to political democracy.

Objectives As you read, look for answers to these questions:
1. Why did Congress become increasingly radical in its position toward the South?
2. How did Congressional Reconstruction affect politics in the South?
3. Why did Congress seek to limit the President's power?

As the year 1866 began, it was clear that the passions that had led to war remained strong. A newspaper in Jackson, Mississippi, told the new state government, "We must keep the ex-slave in a position of inferiority. We must pass such laws as will make him *feel* his inferiority." The *Chicago Tribune* fired back, "We tell the white men of Mississippi that the men of the North will convert the state of Mississippi into a frog pond before they will allow any such laws. . . ." The nation was in a feisty mood as Congress began to consider the problems of Reconstruction.

THE REPUBLICANS IN CONGRESS 4A, 5A

The Republican Party held an overwhelming majority in both houses of Congress. Most Republican congressmen were moderates who hoped to work with the President on Reconstruction. They were primarily concerned about the large number of ex-Confederates holding office and about the disregard of civil rights in the South.

Moderate Republicans wanted to protect the freedmen from abuse. At the same time they were reluctant to grant too much power to the federal government. Like most Americans in the Reconstruction era, they were suspicious of government interference in the lives of individuals or in the business of the states.

The Radical Republicans, however, had no such qualms. They had long urged the abolition of slavery. They now called for full and equal citizenship for the freedmen. They argued that a true republic should grant citizenship to all.

The Radical Republicans were a minority in Congress, but they would have increasing influence over reconstruction legislation. The Republican leaders in this fight were Representative Thaddeus Stevens of Pennsylvania and Senator Charles Sumner of Massachusetts.

The Radicals hoped that the federal government would foster a social, economic, and political revolution in the South. This revolution would destroy the old planter class and make the South into a place of small farms, free schools, respect for labor, and political equality. To achieve this goal, Radicals called for four new policies. (1) They wanted suffrage for all blacks. (2) They called for long-term disenfranchisement—exclusion from voting privileges—of ex-Confederates to allow time for a new political order to get established.

BIOGRAPHY 4D

CHARLES SUMNER (1811–1874), a senator and founder of the Republican Party, favored freeing the slaves and giving them the vote. After making an especially strong speech attacking slavery and its defenders, Sumner was beaten by an outraged congressman from South Carolina. It took Sumner more than three years to recover from his injuries.

68 UNIT 1 BEGINNINGS THROUGH RECONSTRUCTION

SUPPORTING THE SECTION

Reinforcement Workbook: Worksheet 11
Reteaching Resources: Worksheet 11
Enrichment and Extension Resources: Primary Source Worksheet 18
Teaching Transparencies: Transparency 11

Biography

Have students imagine they are speechwriters for Sumner and ask them to write a short speech, supporting the Fifteenth Amendment, to be delivered in the Senate.

(3) They demanded that the government confiscate land belonging to large planters and redistribute it to freedmen. (4) They wanted federally supported schools to prepare blacks for jobs and citizenship. In 1866, however, Congress was not prepared to accept most of these proposals.

THE CIVIL RIGHTS ACT 4A, 4D

Congress did move to modify President Johnson's reconstruction policy by passing two new bills in 1866. The first bill extended the life of the Freedmen's Bureau and expanded its powers. The Bureau could now enforce black civil rights and establish schools. Congress also passed a civil rights bill. This bill declared that all persons born in the United States (except Indians) were citizens. It said that all citizens were entitled to equal rights without regard to race.

Republicans were shocked when President Johnson vetoed both bills. Johnson explained that federal protection of black civil rights would lead "towards centralization" of the national government. In an example of outright racism, Johnson added that black citizenship would "operate against the white race."

Congress voted to pass the Civil Rights Act over Johnson's veto. It was the first time Congress had ever passed major legislation over a veto. Later, Congress also passed a new Freedmen's Bureau law over the President's veto. Congress had taken over Reconstruction.

THE FOURTEENTH AMENDMENT 4A, 5D

Republicans were not satisfied with protecting the equality of all citizens by legislation. They wanted that equality to be protected by the Constitution itself. To do this they proposed the Fourteenth Amendment, which declared that all native-born or naturalized persons were citizens and had the same rights as citizens. The amendment therefore nullified the Supreme Court's Dred Scott decision. It also prohibited states from depriving "any person of life, liberty, and property" without due process of law. All citizens were to be granted the "equal protection of the laws."

The Fourteenth Amendment stopped just short of calling for black suffrage. Instead, it declared that the congressional representation of each state would be reduced in proportion to the number of male citizens denied the vote. This meant that the southern states would have less power in Congress if they did not grant black men the vote.

Support for black suffrage was still a radical position in 1866. Northerners wanted blacks to be free from slavery. Equal voting rights, however, was another matter. Only six states in the North allowed blacks to vote. Just the year before, Connecticut, Wisconsin, and Minnesota had narrowly defeated constitutional amendments to give blacks the vote. Racism was no stranger to the North.

Feminists denounced the Fourteenth Amendment because it introduced the word *male* into the Constitution. Many women had long backed the abolitionist movement. Now, however, women began to ask why expanded suffrage was limited to men. Elizabeth Cady Stanton, a leader of the women's suffrage movement, urged Congress to extend the vote to women. But even Senator Sumner found this proposal too radical. Women's suffrage, he said, was "the great question of the future." Embittered, many white women withdrew from the movement for black rights.

The year 1866 was a congressional election year. Johnson took advantage of the campaign to condemn the Fourteenth Amendment. He argued that southerners were loyal Americans and that the real traitors were the Radical Republicans. The voters, however, rejected Johnson's appeal. They returned a 3 to 1 Republican majority in both houses of Congress.

RADICAL RECONSTRUCTION 4A, 5A

Encouraged by Johnson's support, each of the ex-Confederate states except Tennessee voted to reject the Fourteenth Amendment. By doing so, however, they incurred the wrath of Congress. Moderate Republicans now joined the Radicals to pass the tough Reconstruction Act of 1867. Thus began the part of Congressional Reconstruction known as Radical Reconstruction.

The Reconstruction Act of 1867 divided the former Confederacy into five military districts, each governed by an army commander. It disenfranchised much of the prewar planter class—about 10 to 15 percent of the white electorate. The law also explained the steps by which the states

Background The major general of each military district had almost dictatorial powers. His job was to protect the civil rights of *all* people, oversee the administration of justice, and maintain order.

Background Tennessee, having accepted the Fourteenth Amendment, was readmitted into the Union in 1866.

Ask students to describe Congressional Reconstruction from the point of view of southern whites, carpetbaggers, freed blacks, and Radical Republicans. (Southerners—loss of control of their states, anger at elevation of the status of blacks; carpetbaggers—increase of opportunities; freed blacks—chance to participate in government, economic possibilities increased; Radical Republicans—chance to remake the South and to exert congressional authority.)

How did this phase of Reconstruction change the South? (Went under military rule; all states admitted back into Union; Republican state governments; blacks voted, received rights as citizens, and served in the government.)

Developing the Lesson

After students have read the section, you may want to consider the following activities:

Analyzing Controversial Issues

Discuss the conflict between President Johnson and the Radical Republicans over increasing the role of the federal government. Students should note that the country had become more centralized during the Civil War, and that the South had traditionally been opposed to centralization. *What are possible dangers and benefits of centralization?* (Dangers—might overlook individual or states' rights; benefits—leads to greater efficiency, country unified on issues.)

Do you think the federal government is too powerful today? Not powerful enough? Explain your answer.

Discuss with students the enfranchisement of black Americans. *Why did Radical Republicans feel the Fifteenth Amendment was necessary?* (They wanted to make sure southern states would not be able to reverse black suffrage and that blacks would be able to vote in all states.)

Constitutional Heritage
Refer to the Constitution, found on pages 738–764. Have students find the sections that describe (a) impeachment processes in general; and (b) the impeachment of the President. (a—Article I, Section 2, Clause 5 and Section 3, Clauses 6 and 7; b—Article II, Section 4). Discuss whether Johnson's actions were worthy of impeachment. *How did Johnson's acquittal affect the American system of government?* (Preserved the strength and independence of the executive branch.)

C **Cooperative Learning**

Set up a mock impeachment trial in the classroom, with one group of students acting as the witnesses and lawyer for Johnson; one group acting as the witnesses and lawyer for the House of Representatives; and one group acting as the Senate. While the prosecution and defense are preparing their cases, have the group serving as the Senate determine the rules of procedure. Then have the groups present their cases. The group representing the Senate should decide the case and explain that decision. **LEP**

could re-enter the Union and be recognized by Congress. The states would have to: (1) write new constitutions that provided for universal manhood suffrage; (2) approve those constitutions by a majority of registered voters; and (3) ratify the Fourteenth Amendment.

A NEW ORDER IN THE SOUTH 5A, 4A

In 1867 Freedmen's Bureau agents under army protection began to register voters in the South. About 735,000 blacks and 635,000 whites were registered to vote in the ten unreconstructed states. The voters then chose delegates to the new constitutional conventions. Three-fourths of them were Republicans.

Of the Republican delegates to these conventions, 45 percent were southern white Unionists (sympathizers with the North). For the most part, these were whites who had little power in the South before the war. Living in sparsely settled areas, they were poor people who produced just enough to feed themselves. Many of them had lost faith in the Confederate cause long before the war's end. They were angry at the destruction of their farms and livestock, and they blamed the planter class for starting what they called "a rich man's war." When the war was over, they were eager to seize political power from the old ruling class. The planters called them scalawags—meaning "scoundrels"—for cooperating with Radical Reconstruction.

About 25 percent of the Republican delegates were white northerners who had settled in the South after the war. These included former Union soldiers as well as agents of the Freedmen's Bureau. They liked the South and saw it as a place of new economic opportunity. They were resented by many southerners, who referred to them as carpetbaggers after a kind of hand luggage. But, as one historian has pointed out:

> [They] brought not skimpy carpetbags but rather considerable capital, which they invested in the South. They also invested human capital—themselves—in a drive to modernize the region's social structure, revive its crippled economy, and democratize its politics.

African Americans made up about 30 percent of the Republican delegates. Of these, half had been free before the war. Most of the African American delegates were ministers, teachers, or artisans. Eighty percent were literate, and some had college educations. The best-educated man at the South Carolina convention may have been Francis Louis Cardozo. Born free in South Carolina, the son of a Jewish man and a black woman, Cardozo had been educated in Britain. He would become South Carolina's secretary of state and then its treasurer. Attending the Florida convention was Jonathan Gibbs, a northern black who had been educated at Dartmouth and Princeton. He would become Florida's secretary of state and later its superintendent of schools.

The delegates to the constitutional conventions wrote new, progressive constitutions that were based on those of northern states. The constitutions set up public school systems and granted universal manhood suffrage. By 1869, the voters had approved these constitutions. Within a year, all the former Confederate states had been admitted back into the Union. Fourteen black congressmen and two black senators would serve in Congress during the Reconstruction era.

THE IMPEACHMENT OF JOHNSON 7I

Although obeying the letter of the reconstruction laws, Andrew Johnson worked against them in spirit. For instance, he appointed military commanders with views particularly "soft" toward the ex-Confederates. Radical Republicans became more and more impatient with Johnson's interference. At last there was a showdown between the President and Congress.

To keep the President from sabotaging Congressional Reconstruction, Congress passed a law in 1867 forbidding the President to dismiss any official whose appointment had been approved by the Senate. The immediate intent of the law was to protect those Lincoln appointees who were sympathetic to Congressional Reconstruction.

In defiance of the law, which he considered unconstitutional, Johnson dismissed Secretary of War Edwin Stanton in February 1868. Three days later the House of Representatives voted to impeach the President.

Background In June 1868, Arkansas became the first of the remaining Confederate states to fulfill Congress's requirements and join the Union. Georgia, re-admitted in June 1870, was the last.

The conflict between Congress and the President went far beyond the issue of the 1867 law. Johnson's real offense in the eyes of most members of Congress was standing in the way of Congressional Reconstruction. They hoped that Johnson's conviction would solidify Congress's control over Reconstruction. More generally, they wanted to make Congress as powerful in the United States as Parliament was in Britain. A congressman asked, "May we not anticipate a time when the President will no more think of vetoing a bill passed by Congress than the British Crown thinks of doing?"

In cases of impeachment, the Senate acts as the jury, with a two-thirds vote needed for conviction. After a full trial, the Senate voted 35–19 for conviction. This was one vote short of the required two-thirds. Johnson was acquitted. By one vote, the tradition of a strong presidency and the separation of powers remained intact.

THE FIFTEENTH AMENDMENT 5A, 5D

One of the last trumpet calls of the Radical Republicans was the Fifteenth Amendment, which became law in 1870. This amendment took the Fourteenth Amendment (which had been ratified in 1868) one step further. It declared that the right to vote should not be denied "on account of race, color, or previous condition of servitude."

Congress had proposed this amendment to prevent southern states from reversing black suffrage. But leaders were also concerned about black suffrage in the rest of the country. Black men could not vote in sixteen states. "We have no moral right to impose an obligation on one part of the land which the rest will not accept," one Radical wrote. The Radical leadership was convincing. By endorsing the Fifteenth Amendment, the nation accepted the full consequences of emancipation and affirmed its commitment to democracy.

GRANT VERSUS THE KU KLUX KLAN 4A, 5A

In 1868 the nation elected Ulysses S. Grant as President. At the time, he was undoubtedly the most popular man in the North. In the South it was a different story. There, people had already launched an outright assault on Reconstruction.

Revolutions are likely to give rise to counterrevolutions. A counterrevolution started in the South with the election of 1868. Its source was primarily

This lithograph commemorates passage in May 1870 of the Fifteenth Amendment, which gave black men the right to vote. The text of the amendment appears at the far right above the picture of a black soldier. CULTURAL PLURALISM Why are Abraham Lincoln, Frederick Douglass, and John Brown pictured here? 9B

Photo Caption Answer
Lincoln issued the Emancipation Proclamation; Frederick Douglass was a famous abolitionist and journalist; John Brown's raid at Harpers Ferry was an attempt to start a slave revolt.

Background   In 1875 Johnson returned to Congress as a senator from Tennessee. Soon after Congress adjourned that year, he died and was buried with a copy of the Constitution.

Addressing Individual Needs

Guided/ Independent Practice
Have students complete **Reinforcement Workbook** Worksheet 11, in which they analyze a political cartoon on the Reconstruction Era.

Reteaching/Correctives
Have students form small groups to create cause-and-effect charts of Congressional Reconstruction. First have students scan the section for important events. Have them include such issues as the presidential veto of the civil rights bill, southern states' rejecting Fourteenth Amendment, and Grant's election as President.

Instruct students to complete **Reteaching Resources** Worksheet 11. This worksheet will help students relate causes and effects during Congressional Reconstruction.

Enrichment/Extension
Instruct students to complete **Enrichment and Extension Resources** Primary Source Worksheet 6, in which students examine a Radical Republican's speech to the House of Representatives in 1867.

Assessment
You may wish to use the Section 2 Review, page 72, to see how well your students understand the main points in this lesson.

Section Review Answers

1. *disenfranchisement*— Exclusion from voting privileges. *Fourteenth Amendment*—Declared that all native-born or naturalized persons were citizens. *scalawag*—Name used by planters to describe southern whites who cooperated with Radical Reconstruction. *carpetbagger*—Name used by some southerners for white northerners who settled in the South after the war. *Fifteenth Amendment*—Declared that the right to vote should not be denied on the basis of race.

2. *Thaddeus Stevens*—Republican who led the fight for Radical Reconstruction in the House of Representatives. *Charles Sumner*—Radical Republican leader in the Senate. *Edwin Stanton*—Secretary of War whose dismissal led to the impeachment of President Johnson. *Ulysses S. Grant*—President, 1869–1877.

3. Vetoed civil rights bill and bill extending the Freedmen's Bureau; encouraged southern states not to ratify Fourteenth Amendment; appointed military commanders who were sympathetic to the South; defied law forbidding the President to dismiss officials whose appointments had been approved by Congress.

4. It divided the former Confederacy into five military districts; disenfranchised much of the prewar planter class; required states to allow black men to vote and to approve new constitutions by a majority of registered voters. Some southern whites responded by organizing the Ku Klux Klan, which terrorized black people and their supporters.

5. Decreased; Radical Reconstruction made the federal government responsible for changing the South while the Fourteenth Amendment took powers that had belonged to states and made them the responsibility of the federal government.

Closure

Use the Section 2 information in the Chapter 3 Summary (p. 80) to synthesize the important elements covered in Section 2. Then have students read Section 3 for the next class period, noting how Radical Reconstruction ended.

the disenfranchised planter class and the ex-Confederate soldiers. A number of these men joined the Ku Klux Klan, a secret organization formed just after the war. The Klan's immediate goal was to control elections and to destroy the Republican Party in the South. Beyond that, however, the Klan aimed to keep African Americans in a subordinate role. It targeted blacks who owned their own land, any blacks who prospered, and teachers of black children. Such people were often harassed and even lynched by Klansmen who believed they had gotten "above their station." The Klan was known to have murdered freedmen just because they could read and write.

The Klan became the terrorist arm of the Democratic Party. The Democratic platform in 1868 had called the reconstruction policies "unconstitutional, revolutionary, and void." It demanded the abolition of the Freedmen's Bureau. The white-robed, gun-toting, horse-riding Klansmen attacked and murdered Republican leaders and Republican voters. Across the South, Klan raids killed thousands of African Americans—200 in Arkansas, for instance, and nearly 1,000 in Louisiana. The tactics worked. In every county where the Klan was active, Republicans stayed away from the polls.

At first, President Grant's policy toward the South was low-key and conciliatory. After all, he had campaigned on the slogan, "Let us have peace." By 1871, however, he could no longer ignore the reign of terror that swept the South before elections. In that year he asked Congress to pass a tough law against the Klan. Joseph Rainey, a black South Carolina congressman who received death threats from the Klan, spoke of the fear of retaliation:

> When myself and [my] colleagues shall leave these Halls and turn our footsteps toward our southern home we know not but that the assassin may await our coming. Be it as it may we have resolved to be loyal and firm, and if we perish, we perish! I earnestly hope the bill will pass.

The bill did pass. With the help of the cavalry, federal marshals arrested thousands of Klansmen, some of whom later stood trial for their crimes. As a result, the 1872 election was both fair and peace-

THE PRESIDENTS

Ulysses S. Grant
1869–1877
18th President, Republican

- Born April 27, 1822, in Ohio
- Married Julia Dent in 1848; 4 children
- Farmer; commander of all Union armies in Civil War
- Lived in Illinois when elected President
- Vice Presidents: Schuyler Colfax; Henry Wilson
- Died July 23, 1885, in New York
- Key events while in office: First transcontinental railroad completed; Fifteenth Amendment; Colorado became a state

ful. In the coming decades, however, southern elections would again be plagued by corruption and racial discrimination.

SECTION REVIEW

1. **KEY TERMS** disenfranchisement, Fourteenth Amendment, scalawag, carpetbagger, Fifteenth Amendment

2. **PEOPLE** Thaddeus Stevens, Charles Sumner, Edwin Stanton, Ulysses S. Grant

3. **COMPREHENSION** In what ways did the President try to interfere with Congressional Reconstruction?

4. **COMPREHENSION** How did Radical Reconstruction change the South?

5. **CRITICAL THINKING** Did Reconstruction increase or decrease states' power? Why did this occur?

The Presidents
Grant was one of several Presidents who had been war heroes with little or no political experience. Discuss the advantages and pitfalls of having a military leader serve as President.

Background In the presidential election of 1868, 450,000 of 500,000 enfranchised southern blacks voted for Grant. Grant's margin in the popular vote was only 300,000. Thus it could be said that black voters in the South gave Grant the popular vote in the election.

3 The Changing South

Section Focus

Key Terms coalition ■ Mississippi Plan ■ Compromise of 1877 ■ share tenantry ■ Jim Crow laws ■ solid South ■ *Plessy v. Ferguson*

Main Idea In the 1870s southern white Democrats began to force blacks out of politics. At the same time, land and labor practices led to the growth of rural poverty, while a "New South" was built on the foundation of industry and business.

Objectives As you read, look for answers to these questions:
1. What were the achievements and failures of the reconstruction legislatures?
2. How did Democrats get control of southern state governments?
3. What economic changes occurred in the South in the late 1800s?

In the 1870s most northerners grew tired of the reconstruction issue. In New York City, Horace Greeley's *Tribune* campaigned for reconciliation and the cooperation of the "better class" of southern whites. The old abolitionist fire began to die out. The southern Republicans who dominated the state legislatures became increasingly isolated, both from northern support and from the mainstream of the white South.

RECONSTRUCTION LEGISLATURES 5A

While more than 600 African Americans served in the reconstruction legislatures, the scalawags and carpetbaggers held most of the power. On some issues, black legislators joined with carpetbaggers in a loose coalition—combination of interests. Blacks and carpetbaggers teamed up to guarantee equal access to transportation and to such public places as restaurants and theaters. School integration, however, was another matter. School systems were unofficially segregated. Black leaders left the issue alone, feeling that white opposition to black education would grow if they stirred up the debate.

The reconstruction legislatures planned to forge a new order in the South. The new governments began rebuilding the South's public facilities, including roads, bridges, levees, and railroads. The new legislatures took a wider view of government's responsibility to the citizen. Thus they voted to build hospitals, orphanages, and schools. The legislatures also created commissions to at-

tract northern investment and sold bonds to raise funds for railroad construction.

Schools, hospitals, and roads all cost money. To pay for these improvements, the reconstruction legislatures turned to property taxes. Thus plantation owners, who held the least political power in the new system, were paying the greatest share of the cost. A number of southern Republicans hoped that the tax burden would force plantation owners to sell their land, which could then be

This print shows Frederick Douglass flanked by two of the first black senators, Blanche K. Bruce (left) and Hiram R. Revels (right), both of Mississippi. Reconstruction legislators hoped to transform the South economically and politically. HISTORY For what historical reason does John Brown appear in the print (bottom)? 9A

SECTION 3

The Changing South
(pp. 73–79)

Section Objectives
■ explain the reasons for ending Reconstruction in the South
■ describe the important economic and political trends of the South after Reconstruction

Introducing the Section

Connecting with Past Learnings
Review with students the effect of Reconstruction on southerners, asking them which groups supported and opposed Reconstruction and why. (Blacks—supported, gained rights and opportunities; scalawags—supported, gained economic opportunities; planters—opposed, lost power and money; small farmers—mostly opposed, lost control of their region.)

Key Terms
Have students write sentences using the key terms. Then ask volunteers to write one of their sentences on the board, leaving a blank space where the term was used. Have the class fill in the missing term. Continue this procedure until all the key terms have been used at least once. **LEP**

SUPPORTING THE SECTION

Reinforcement Workbook: Worksheet 12
Reteaching Resources: Worksheet 12
Teaching Transparencies: Transparency 12

Photo Caption Answer
Brown was considered a martyr to the cause of emancipation.

Help students synthesize information in the section by asking volunteers to deliver short presentations on the following topics: reconstruction legislatures, economic conditions in the South in the late 1800s, laws affecting black southerners, and the Democratic Party's recovery of the control of southern legislatures.

Was Reconstruction a success or failure? (Some of both; in the short term blacks were able to gain the vote and participate in government, although they were ultimately prohibited from voting; the South recovered economically from war, but slowly.)

Developing the Lesson

After students have read the section, you may want to consider the following activities:

Economics

Help students understand the difficulties of share tenantry by having the class create a balance sheet for a tenant farmer. Start by having them list the tenant's debits. (Rent on tools, housing, and land; seed; food and other purchases at the store; interest on debt.) Then list the credits. (Sale of the crop.)
How would bad weather or lower crop prices affect the tenant? (Lower the credit side and push him or her deeper into debt.)

In this cartoon from 1880, a "southern belle" stumbles barefoot on rough stones while President Grant lounges on a carpetbag full of guns. **ISSUES** What situation has the artist portrayed in this cartoon? Are the artist's symbols effective? Explain. **9B**

bought by poor whites and blacks. Many landowners did indeed have to give up their plantations. One-fifth of the entire state of Mississippi went on the auction block. Yet little of this land was redistributed. Wealthy northern investors bought some of it; other plantations were returned to their landowners after payment of debts.

The ambitious spending programs of the reconstruction legislatures created many opportunities for corruption. Plenty of money was going into public works. People were willing to pay bribes—railroads looking for funding, industries hoping for special privileges, towns wanting a new bridge or a railroad station. Louisiana's carpetbagger governor, Henry C. Warmoth, retired a rich man from taking railroad bribes. Officeholders were not bashful about lining their own pockets while they were in the service of the public.

DEMOCRATS TAKE OVER 5B

Southern Democrats complained bitterly about high taxation and about the corrupt and debt-ridden legislatures. But corruption was not limited to the former Confederate states. In

Washington, D.C., and in northern state and city governments, lawmakers and business interests were likewise making deals. Many legislators in both the North and South were for sale in the feverish business expansion that followed the war.

In Mississippi, white taxpayers overlooked the real accomplishments of the reconstruction legislatures. They were too distracted by a staggering tax increase of 1,300 percent in five years. Determined to win back the government from the Republicans, Mississippi Democrats developed a strategy. The Mississippi Plan called for forcing all whites into the Democratic Party and intimidating black voters. To do this, the Democrats used bullying, violence, and even murder. When they did, the federal government looked the other way.

Adopted throughout the South, the Mississippi Plan made it possible for the white propertied class to re-establish control over the state governments. The Mississippi Plan also prevented blacks and poor whites from joining forces in the struggle for a better life. Race, not class, became the dividing line in southern society.

THE END OF RECONSTRUCTION 5B

In 1876 a closely decided presidential election led to the end of Reconstruction. In that year the Democrats chose Samuel J. Tilden, governor of New York, to run for President. The Republicans nominated Rutherford B. Hayes, governor of Ohio. The race was so close that victory depended on the disputed returns from four states. Three of these states—South Carolina, Louisiana, and Florida—still had reconstruction governments, which were propped up by the military but in fact had no real power. The real power was now held by Democratic shadow governments. The three states, therefore, ended up submitting two different sets of electoral returns.

If Congress accepted the Republican count, Hayes would win. If it accepted the Democratic count, Tilden would win. When a congressional commission tried to decide the issue impartially, it split along party lines.

The dilemma was solved by an "understanding" negotiated between Hayes's supporters and the southern Democrats. Under the terms of the

Photo Caption Answers
Southern view of Reconstruction. Artist's symbols promote sympathy for the South and anger at the North.

Background By 1876, reconstruction legislatures had been rejected in all but three southern states—Florida, Louisiana, and South Carolina. In the election of 1876, these states voted Democratic at first, but the Republican machines

ordered recounts which invalidated many Democratic ballots.

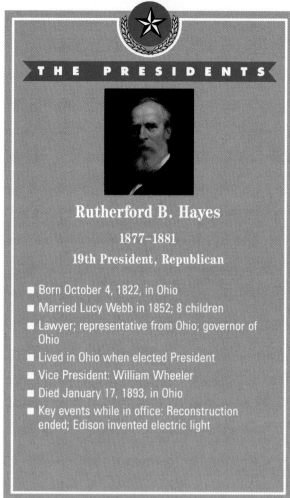

THE PRESIDENTS

Rutherford B. Hayes

1877–1881
19th President, Republican

- Born October 4, 1822, in Ohio
- Married Lucy Webb in 1852; 8 children
- Lawyer; representative from Ohio; governor of Ohio
- Lived in Ohio when elected President
- Vice President: William Wheeler
- Died January 17, 1893, in Ohio
- Key events while in office: Reconstruction ended; Edison invented electric light

Compromise of 1877, southern Democrats in the disputed states agreed to let the Republican votes for Hayes stand *if* he would remove the last federal troops from the South. Hayes agreed. As soon as he became President, he ended the military presence in the South. The last few reconstruction governments collapsed, and with them went black southerners' best hope for political equality.

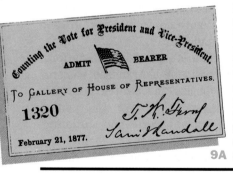

People with a ticket such as the one at left could watch politicians negotiate the outcome of the 1876 presidential election. The Compromise of 1877 broke the election deadlock. POLITICS Explain the compromise's effect on black southerners. 9A

THE DEVELOPMENT OF TENANT FARMING 4A

A major reason that African Americans could not hold on to political power was that they lacked economic power. Had they been given 40 acres of land and a mule, blacks would have been in a stronger position to defend their rights. But most depended on whites for their livelihood. They were vulnerable to the threat of dismissal or eviction if they made use of their vote.

By 1880, about 25 percent of African Americans in agriculture worked for wages. About 15 percent owned their own land. Almost 20 percent rented land. The remaining 40 percent engaged in some form of share tenantry. Under share tenantry, a farmer and his family worked a plot of land in exchange for part of the crop. The advantage of share tenantry for the landowner was that he did not have to pay cash wages. The advantage for black laborers was that they did not have to work under white supervision.

Sharecropping was the most common form of share tenantry for black people. A sharecropper was expected to provide labor only. The landowner provided tools, seed, and housing. In another form of share tenantry, farmers provided their own livestock and equipment and paid a percentage of the crop as rent. This was the more typical form for white tenants.

During Reconstruction, white tenantry increased throughout the South. The war had destroyed the homesteads and livestock of many upcountry whites. They were forced to trade their old independence for the more secure life of tenantry. Other white farmers had been driven into tenantry because they lost their land to taxes. By 1880, one-third of the white farmers in the deep South were tenants.

Tenants and landowners had opposite goals. Tenants wanted to grow food to support themselves. But landowners forced tenants to grow cash crops such as cotton. Tenants were required to buy food from the country store, which was often owned by the landlord. Most tenants got caught in a never-ending cycle of debt, in which this year's harvest went to pay last year's bill.

The landowners' insistence on growing cotton greatly harmed the southern economy. The repeated crops of cotton exhausted the soil and

Have students sum up by describing the cycle leading to rural poverty. (Landowners wanted sharecroppers to grow cash crops, which depleted the soil of nutrients; income went down and tenants fell into endless debt.)

Ask students to contrast industrial recovery in the South with its agricultural stagnation.

Geographic Themes: Regions
Have students consider the factors that characterized the South in the late 1800s. Ask them to choose the factors they feel were most important and create a visual or verbal presentation: for example, a photograph exhibit, short story, song, or poster.

Patterns in History
Freeing slaves was only the first step in a long process toward equality. *Why has the civil rights movement of the 1960s has been called the Second Reconstruction?* (Attempted to complete the work that Reconstruction ignored or that slid backwards after Reconstruction.) Ask students to evaluate our country's progress in establishing equality of opportunity between the races today.

Photo Caption Answer
The compromise returned political power to politicians who opposed civil rights for blacks.

The Presidents
Have students write a "letter to the editor" expressing their views on the way Hayes won the presidency.

Ethics
Discuss the establishment of
Jim Crow laws in the South.
*How might whites have justi-
fied such actions?* (Believed in
blacks' inferiority; wanted to
feel superior; afraid of black
power; feared economic competition from blacks.)
Have students think about
how they would have
responded to racism in the
South in the late 1800s. Ask
them what they might have
done had they lived in Union
County, Arkansas, in 1888.

**Analyzing Controversial
Issues**
Have students discuss the
doctrine of "separate but
equal." Start by asking them
to sum up the arguments
made by the Supreme Court
for that doctrine in the case
of *Plessy v. Ferguson* and
Harlan's arguments against
the doctrine. Then ask
students to state their
opinion of segregation.

Civic Values
Have students sum up
Booker T. Washington's and
W.E.B. Du Bois's views on
how black people could get
ahead. Ask them to state
with whom they agree and
why.

reduced the amount of land available for food
crops. As a result, the fertile South had to import
half its food. The higher cost of food was borne by
those who could least afford it—the tenant
farmers. These agricultural practices doomed the
deep South to decades of rural poverty.

THE GROWTH OF INDUSTRY 3C

The South's agricultural problems spurred calls
for a shift to new kinds of economic activities. One
of the most prominent voices was that of Henry
Grady, editor of the *Atlanta Constitution*. Grady
urged the South to embrace the spirit of enterprise and business. What the region needed, he
said, was "fewer stump-speakers and more stump-
pullers." He wanted a "New South"—one that was
more like the North, with large cities and
factories.

Buoyed by new leaders and by a nationwide
boom in business, the South developed new industries. It repaired its war-damaged railroads and
began an ambitious program of railroad expansion. In the 1880s the South reduced the 5-foot
gauge of its tracks to match that of the North,
which was 4 feet, 8½ inches. Thus, southern railroads were integrated into those of the rest of the
nation. The southern railroads were, however, controlled mostly by the northern bankers and industrialists who had helped to build them.

This photograph shows a worker using machinery to process
tobacco. Virginia tobacco had been exported to Europe since the
founding of Jamestown. After the invention of cigarette-rolling
machines in 1880, tobacco use spread rapidly. ECONOMICS How
was the South's economy transformed in the late 1800s? 3A

One of the most successful new businesses in
the South was the tobacco industry. James B.
Duke of Durham, North Carolina, bought the
rights to the first cigarette-making machine. By
the 1890s his American Tobacco Company held a
monopoly over tobacco manufacturing.

Southern textile mills also expanded. "Bring the
Cotton Mills to the Cotton," southern boosters declared. So many textile mills sprouted up in the
piedmont region that by 1900 the South was producing almost a quarter of the nation's cotton
cloth. A visiting northerner wrote:

> It is among the factory workers and the
> small farmers of Georgia that one finds
> the chief prosperity of the State. Here
> there is little or no debt; money circulates
> rapidly; improvements are seen.

There had been a marked change in the southern economy since the years of desperate poverty
that followed the war. Conditions in the South still
did not compare with those in the North, however.
There white women and children earned double
the wages of their counterparts in the South.

JIM CROW LAWS 4A, 5A, 5D

With the end of Reconstruction and the loss of
black political power, southern society became increasingly segregated. The integrated streetcars,
railroads, and theaters of the 1870s gave way in
the 1880s to Jim Crow laws. (Jim Crow was a
term commonly used to refer to African
Americans.) Jim Crow laws made segregation
official in a number of areas of southern life.

At the same time, some white Democrats revived efforts to keep blacks away from the polls.
The old planter class had tried to maintain power
by using the black vote or by controlling black
officeholders. The next generation of southerners
was more racist and more determined to prevent
blacks from voting at all.

Intimidation played a large role in this effort.
Jim Reeves, a black resident of Arkansas, remembered that in 1888 blacks and whites in Union
County "had an insurrection over the polls."
White people went around the county ordering
the blacks not to vote. Some blacks boldly declared that no one could keep them from voting.

Photo Caption Answer
It became more industrialized.

Background Jim Crow laws,
requiring separate public
facilities for blacks and
whites, were first developed in
the North in the early 1800s.
Laws varied from state to
state, but the most common
Jim Crow laws in the South
required separate public
schools, and separated
blacks and whites on public

transportation, hotels,
restaurants, and public
swimming pools and other
recreation services.

The Geographic Perspective: Florida Joins the "New South"

One Yankee who moved south after the Civil War was Harriet Beecher Stowe. Mrs. Stowe's book *Palmetto Leaves*, published in 1873, extolled the beauty of Florida and popularized the state as a retreat from the North's blustery winters.

Tourism was one of the forces that made Florida part of the "New South." This was a South less dependent on cotton farming, a South with a more diverse economy.

THE CHANGE TO ORANGES

The majority of Florida's prewar settlers had preferred the state's northern and central uplands to its coastal lowlands. The sparsely settled lowlands included vast areas of wetlands and sandy beaches.

After the war, Floridians went back to planting cotton on the uplands, but prices were low and times were hard. Then, in the 1870s, the central part of the state caught "orange fever." Orange groves began to replace cotton fields and grazing land throughout the uplands below the frost line. As the settlement line advanced south, so did the citrus groves.

THE IMPACT OF NORTHERN CAPITAL

Northern capital and technology were primarily responsible for the development of coastal Florida and its wetlands. In 1881 Hamilton Disston of Philadelphia purchased from the state 4 million acres of wetlands north and west of Lake

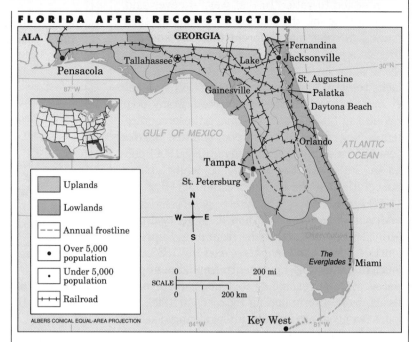

FLORIDA AFTER RECONSTRUCTION

- Uplands
- Lowlands
- Annual frostline
- Over 5,000 population
- Under 5,000 population
- Railroad

SCALE
0 — 200 mi
0 — 200 km

ALBERS CONICAL EQUAL-AREA PROJECTION

Okeechobee. Canals were dug to drain the wetlands. Disston then sold the reclaimed land to new settlers.

Two Yankee empire-builders, Henry B. Plant and Henry M. Flagler, developed Florida's railroad system and changed Florida forever. A Connecticut native, Plant had settled in the South before the war, making a business of buying out bankrupt railway lines. In 1884 he extended an existing rail line to the fishing village of Tampa on Florida's west coast. Tampa grew into an important shipping center for lumber, phosphate, and cattle bound for Cuba.

Meanwhile, millionaire Henry M. Flagler was developing Florida's east coast. While vacationing in Florida in 1883, Flagler had been shocked by the

narrow-gauge railway and inadequate hotels on the east coast. He proceeded to build a railroad down the east coast to link Florida with a rail route to New York. At the same time, Flagler constructed a string of elegant hotels to lure tourists.

Flagler's railroad opened new regions to agriculture, trade, and tourism. The railroad carried citrus fruit and vegetables north and brought tourists south. In 1896 the railroad reached Miami, which quickly became a boom town.

CRITICAL THINKING QUESTIONS

1. Why, do you think, did most of the capital for Florida's expansion come from the North?

2. Why were railroads crucial to Florida's economic growth?

The Geographic Perspective Answers
1. Because the South was still recovering from the devastation of the Civil War.
2. They connected Florida with the rest of the nation; they provided fast transportation for perishable crops; by opening new areas

to development, they encouraged trade, tourism, and population growth.

Geographic Themes
Geographic themes covered on this page:
___ Location
✓ Place
___ Interactions
✓ Movement
___ Regions

Cooperative Learning

Divide the class into small groups. Have each group create a time capsule of Reconstruction in the South. Students may include such items as newspaper reports, pictures of sharecroppers' cabins, or letters detailing conditions in the South. Each group member must be responsible for at least one item in the capsule. Have groups examine and comment on each other's capsules. **LEP**

Addressing Individual Needs

Guided/Independent Practice
Have students complete **Reinforcement Workbook** Worksheet 12, which asks students to compare and contrast the writings of Booker T. Washington and W.E.B. Du Bois.

Reteaching/Correctives
Have students construct posters illustrating four main ideas of the section. Have them begin by deciding what the main ideas are, and then make a sketch and final copy of the poster. Each main idea should be accompanied by an explanatory phrase or sentence.

Instruct students to complete **Reteaching Resources** Worksheet 12. This worksheet helps students remember the events discussed in this section by organizing them in the form of an outline.

Enrichment/Extension
Have students research the Jim Crow laws and their effects on the real lives of African Americans in the South. Have them list five types of public facility that might have been affected, and for each one, describe why "separate but equal" was so demeaning.

They were wrong. On the day before the election, white gangs shot a number of those blacks who had intended to vote. "In that way," Reeves said, "quite a few of the Negroes disbanded their homes and went into different counties and . . . different states." Those who stayed quit voting.

New state laws also made it more difficult for blacks to vote. They required voters to pay a poll tax or to prove that they could read. Many poor uneducated blacks could not meet these requirements. Neither could many poor whites, but for them the rules were often waived. By 1900, politics in the South had become so white and so Democratic that the region became known as the solid South.

African Americans who hoped for federal protection received little help from the Supreme Court. In the *Civil Rights Cases* in 1883, the Court ruled that the Fourteenth Amendment prevented state governments, but not private businesses, from discriminating by race. In 1896, the Court went even further in legalizing racism. In the landmark case *Plessy v. Ferguson*, the Supreme Court ruled that segregation was lawful as long as blacks and whites had access to equal facilities. This became known as the "separate but equal" doctrine. The Court offered this explanation: "If one race be inferior to the other socially, the Constitution of the United States cannot put them upon the same plane."

One member of the Supreme Court disagreed with the decision in *Plessy v. Ferguson*. Justice John Marshall Harlan wrote, "Our Constitution is colorblind, and neither knows nor tolerates classes among citizens. . . . The thin disguise of 'equal' accommodations . . . will not mislead anyone." Indeed, segregation had become a thin disguise for reducing blacks to the status of second-class citizens.

> "**O**ur Constitution is colorblind, and neither knows nor tolerates classes among citizens."
> —*Justice John Marshall Harlan, 1896*

SOCIAL HISTORY
Famous Firsts

1866	Three national soldiers' homes opened.
1870	First pension to a President's widow (Mary Lincoln) authorized (July 14).
	Joseph Hayne Rainey from South Carolina sworn in as first black representative in Congress (Dec. 12).
1872	Pinckney Pinchback serves as acting governor of Louisiana, from Dec. 11, 1872 to Jan. 14, 1873.
1875	First black senator to serve a full term, B.K. Bruce of Mississippi, begins service (March 4).
1877	H. O. Flipper is the first black man to graduate from West Point.

AFRICAN AMERICANS HELPING THEMSELVES 4C, 7B

These were bitter days for southern blacks. The high hopes of Reconstruction days had been dashed. American society no longer seemed inspired by those words of the Declaration of Independence: "All men are created equal."

Frozen out of politics and white institutions, blacks found nurture and hope in their own communities. Black schools and colleges were short of funds, but they continued to educate the new generation of free black persons. Black churches provided leadership and gave aid to the needy. Organizations like the National Negro Business League enabled black people to help each other.

The founder of the National Negro Business League was Booker T. Washington, a former slave. Washington became one of the most visible African American leaders of his day. In 1881 he established Tuskegee Institute, a vocational school for blacks in Tuskegee, Alabama. The school reflected Washington's view that blacks needed to learn a useful trade rather than demand social equality from the government. "It is at the bottom of life we must begin, and not at the top," he said. "The opportunity to earn a dollar in a factory just now is worth infinitely more than the opportunity to spend a dollar in an opera house."

Later generations of black people came to doubt the wisdom of Washington's advice. Blacks could

BOOKER T. WASHINGTON (1856–1915), founder of the Tuskegee Institute, was born a slave. After the Civil War, Washington became an educator and social reformer. His concern for poor and illiterate blacks led Washington to promote educational and economic advancement rather than political equality—a philosophy that angered some other African American leaders.

> "It is at the bottom of life we must begin, and not at the top."
> —*Booker T. Washington*

not make solid economic gains without political power, and winning this power would take years of dedicated struggle. Nevertheless, the Fourteenth and Fifteenth Amendments stood out as beacons of liberty and democracy. Perhaps it is for this reason that the African American historian W.E.B. Du Bois called Reconstruction "a glorious failure."

Writing in the 1930s, Du Bois presented one of the first major challenges to the traditional interpretations of Reconstruction. By this time historians had accepted the view that Reconstruction was a dismal chapter in American history. They described Reconstruction as a time in which a vengeful Congress, uneducated blacks, unscrupulous carpetbaggers, and self-seeking scalawags nearly ruined the South. Du Bois challenged this view by asserting that scholars had sacrificed objectivity to racial bias.

Not until the 1960s, however, did historians follow Du Bois's lead and reconsider Reconstruction. They pointed out, for instance, that corruption was not confined to reconstruction legislatures and could not be blamed on the freedmen. Corruption was a characteristic of the whole country in the postwar years. Historians today are focusing less on the politics and more on the social and economic aspects of Reconstruction. No matter their focus, however, they tend to agree that the Reconstruction years, 1865–1877, were a time in which America made one more advance toward its vision of liberty and justice for all.

SECTION REVIEW

1. KEY TERMS coalition, Mississippi Plan, Compromise of 1877, share tenantry, Jim Crow laws, solid South, *Plessy v. Ferguson*

2. PEOPLE Samuel J. Tilden, Rutherford B. Hayes, Henry Grady, Booker T. Washington, W.E.B. Du Bois

3. COMPREHENSION Why was corruption a problem for the reconstruction legislatures?

4. COMPREHENSION What led to the Democratic backlash in the South during the 1870s?

5. CRITICAL THINKING Why might the "New South" have offered black people new opportunities for advancement?

2. *Samuel J. Tilden*—Democratic Party presidential candidate, 1876. *Rutherford B. Hayes*—Republican President, 1877–1881. *Henry Grady*—Editor of Atlanta newspaper who favored the development of southern business and industry. *Booker T. Washington*—Black leader, founded the National Negro Business League and Tuskegee Institute. *W.E.B. Du Bois*— Black historian who challenged the accepted interpretation of Reconstruction as a shameful period.

3. Ambitious spending programs created opportunities for corruption. With lots of money going into public works, people were willing to pay bribes for special favors.

4. High taxes and corruption of Reconstruction legislatures; the Mississippi Plan forced whites into the Democratic Party and intimidated black voters.

5. Blacks could have been employed in building railroads and working in industry, escaping the sharecropper's cycle of debt.

Closure

Ask one student to transform the Main Idea of the section into two questions, and have other students answer those questions. Then have students read Section 1 of Chapter 4 for the next class period, noting the causes and effects of the expansion of industry in the United States.

9D

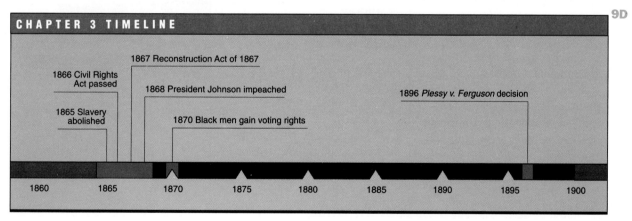

CHAPTER 3 TIMELINE

1867 Reconstruction Act of 1867

1866 Civil Rights Act passed

1868 President Johnson impeached

1865 Slavery abolished

1896 *Plessy v. Ferguson* decision

1870 Black men gain voting rights

1860 1865 1870 1875 1880 1885 1890 1895 1900

Biography
Ask students to present arguments in favor of Washington's view that education was important for black people to achieve success.

Chapter 3 Review Answers

Chapter 3 Review Answers

Key Terms
1. carpetbagger
2. share tenantry
3. scalawag
4. disenfranchisement
5. solid South
6. black codes

People to Identify
1. Black historian who reassessed the traditional view of the Reconstruction Era.
2. Editor who advocated the growth of southern enterprise.
3. Secretary of War whom President Johnson dismissed in defiance of the law.
4. Prominent Radical Republican during Reconstruction.
5. Democrat who lost to Hayes in the Compromise of 1877.
6. Founder of the National Negro Business League.

Places to Locate
1. C   4. D
2. A   5. F
3. E   6. B

Reviewing the Facts
1. He believed that the Union should not take a hard line.
2. They passed black codes and Jim Crow laws, ignored new laws, and subordinated the freedmen economically.
3. The Bureau was set up to provide poor southerners with clothing, food, and fuel. It also rented old Confederate land. Johnson's policy of granting amnesty to ex-Confederates worked against these efforts.
4. Moderate Republicans did not want to give the federal government more power. The moderates joined the radicals when Johnson encouraged the ex-Confederate states to reject the Fourteenth Amendment.

CHAPTER 3 SUMMARY

SECTION 1: After the Civil War, the economy and social structure of the South had to be rebuilt.

■ The Thirteenth Amendment abolished slavery. Though freedom allowed ex-slaves to build new lives, their economic future was uncertain because most were uneducated and did not own land.

■ Lincoln followed a generous policy of reconciliation with the South. Andrew Johnson tried to continue this policy, but white southerners resisted even minimal reform, leading to a more hard-line northern attitude toward Reconstruction.

SECTION 2: In 1867 Radical Republicans in Congress took over Reconstruction, imposing military rule on the South. Constitutional amendments were passed to extend political rights to African Americans.

■ The Fourteenth Amendment declared that all native-born or naturalized persons had full citizenship and could not be deprived of their rights without due process of law.

■ The Reconstruction Act of 1867 imposed military rule on the South, disenfranchised the planter class, and set strict requirements for the readmission of the ex-Confederate states to the Union.

■ The Fifteenth Amendment declared that the right to vote could not be denied on account of race, color, or previous condition of servitude.

■ Disenfranchised white southerners used violence to prevent freedmen from exercising their newly won rights.

SECTION 3: During the 1870s, white Democrats regained control of the South. Despite extreme rural poverty, the growth of southern industry led to the birth of the "New South."

■ Political corruption plagued the South as well as the North after the Civil War.

■ Share tenantry became common among blacks and poor whites throughout the South, trapping many of them in a vicious cycle of poverty.

KEY TERMS ●

Use the following terms to complete the sentences below.

black codes
carpetbagger
disenfranchisement
scalawag
share tenantry
solid South

1. A northerner who came to the South to live during Reconstruction was known as a
_____ .

2. Under _____, farm families worked the land in return for a share of the crop.

3. A _____ was a southerner who cooperated with Radical Reconstruction.

4. One of the goals of the Radical Republicans was the _____ of the planter class.

5. The term _____ refers to the white southerners' almost unanimous support of the Democratic Party after the period of Reconstruction.

6. Southern states passed laws known as _____ to keep freedmen from moving freely and to return them to plantation labor.

PEOPLE TO IDENTIFY ●

Identify the following people and tell why each was important.

1. W.E.B. Du Bois
2. Henry Grady
3. Edwin Stanton
4. Charles Sumner
5. Samuel Tilden
6. Booker T. Washington

5. The Thirteenth Amendment freed blacks, the Fourteenth Amendment declared that black people were American citizens, the Fifteenth Amendment gave black men the vote.

6. President Johnson violated a law protecting officials whose appointments had been approved by Congress. Johnson was acquitted when the Senate fell one vote short of the number needed for conviction.

PLACES TO LOCATE ●

Match each of the letters on the map with the places that are listed below.

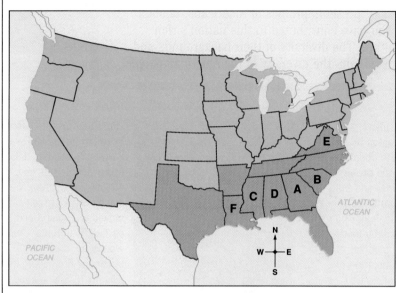

1. Mississippi
2. Georgia
3. Virginia
4. Alabama
5. Louisiana
6. South Carolina

REVIEWING THE FACTS ▲

1. What was the attitude of President Johnson toward the Reconstruction of the South?
2. How did white southerners try to restore the prewar order?
3. What was the Freedmen's Bureau? How did President Johnson undermine its authority?
4. Why did moderate Republicans at first oppose the goals of the Radicals? Why did they change their minds?
5. How did the the Thirteenth, Fourteenth, and Fifteenth Amendments affect black southerners?

6. Why was President Johnson impeached? What was the outcome of the trial?
7. How did the Ku Klux Klan intimidate black people? What were the group's aims?
8. What groups held office in the reconstruction legislatures? Why did many white southerners resent them?
9. What new economic developments characterized the postwar South?
10. How did Supreme Court decisions in the late 1800s affect African Americans?

CRITICAL THINKING SKILLS ▲

1. **PARAPHRASING** Reread the paragraphs under the heading "The Black Response to Emancipation" (pages 63–64). In your own words, state the main idea of this section.

2. **PREDICTING CONSEQUENCES** How, if at all, would the situation of black southerners have been different in the late 1800s if Radical Reconstruction had never occurred?

3. **MAKING JUDGMENTS** During Radical Reconstruction, could white southern landowners justly object to property taxes on the grounds that there should be "no taxation without representation"? Why or why not?

WRITING ABOUT TOPICS IN AMERICAN HISTORY ■

1. **CONNECTING WITH LITERATURE** A selection from *The Deliverance* by Ellen Glasgow appears on pages 774–776. Read it and answer the questions. Then answer the following questions: How did the effects of Reconstruction differ for different social classes in the South? Did some people benefit?

2. **APPLYING THEMES: EXPANDING DEMOCRACY** Imagine that you are (a) a newly freed slave, (b) a carpetbagger, or (c) a member of the old planter aristocracy. Write a letter to a relative outside the South describing your view of Radical Reconstruction.

10. The *Civil Rights Cases* made it legal for private businesses to discriminate on the basis of race. In *Plessy v. Ferguson* (1896), the Court ruled that segregation was lawful as long as blacks and whites had access to equal facilities.

Critical Thinking Skills
1. Black people responded to emancipation by exercising their new freedoms and trying to rid themselves of white domination.
2. Students might cite the gains made toward racial equality during Radical Reconstruction. They might also mention that blacks were set back by white backlash against Reconstruction.
3. White southerners had, by seceding from the Union, disenfranchised themselves. After the war, they eventually gained the right to vote.

Writing About Topics in American History
1. The planter class lost much of its power; African Americans gained power at first, but later lost much of it; poor whites stayed poor; some carpetbaggers and officeholders took bribes and otherwise made a fortune through corrupt practices.
2. Students should show an understanding of the way a freedman, a carpetbagger, or a plantation owner would view the dramatic changes in the South.

7. The Klan often harassed and murdered freedmen in order to subordinate black people and to keep them from voting.
8. White people resented the carpetbaggers, scalawags, and black people who held office because these

groups favored some racial integration and heavy property taxes.
9. Share tenantry and growing industry became the common economic system for the postwar South.

Chapter Review exercises are keyed for student abilities:
● = Basic
▲ = Average
■ = Average/Advanced

Introducing the Feature

Ask students to explain why periods of war provide women and minorities with opportunities to take new roles in society. *In what ways did women and minorities participate in the Civil War?* (Women participated indirectly as heads of households, farms, and businesses, and directly as nurses. Minorities participated as support personnel, soldiers, spies, and guides.)

Discuss with students how the rights of citizenship granted to African Americans during Reconstruction afforded former slaves and free blacks their first real opportunity to take an active role in determining the course of their lives.

Teaching Multiculturalism

Science and Technology

Have students find examples of how Americans of many backgrounds spurred the nation's growth and development with their confidence and inventiveness. *What incident might have prevented a less optimistic person than John Ericsson from developing new battleship technology for the U.S. Navy?* (The steam-powered ship that he designed for the navy exploded, killing two Cabinet members.) *What ship did Ericsson design for the Union navy?* (The ironclad *Monitor*.)

History

Have students imagine that the story of Rose Greenhow will be made into a Hollywood movie. Ask students to write a proposal for the movie. In addition to giving the movie a title and assigning the leading role to an appropriate actress, students should include an account of the main events in Greenhow's life and evaluate how her character related to the historical period in which she lived.

UNIT 1: American Mosaic

★ A Multicultural Perspective ★

"American Mosaic" presents profiles of Americans, famous and obscure, who have contributed to this nation's rich history and culture. The diversity of their backgrounds and national origins mirrors the diversity of the American people.

When Californians elected delegates to write the state constitution in 1849, the prominent landowner and politician **Mariano Vallejo** (left) was a logical choice. A wealthy landowner and supporter of American annexation of California, Vallejo had once stated, "Why should we shrink from incorporating ourselves with the happiest and freest nation in the world, destined soon to be the most wealthy and powerful?" Vallejo later served as a member of the first state senate of California.

The life of inventor **John Ericsson** (left), who was born in Sweden in 1803, had dramatic ups and downs. Fascinated by machinery, Ericsson moved to England and earned 30 patents—yet wound up in debtors' prison for not paying his bills. In 1839 he moved again, to the United States, where he designed the U.S. Navy's first steam-powered ship. Unfortunately, an explosion on that ship killed two Cabinet members. Nevertheless, in September 1861 it was Ericsson, now an American citizen, who answered Congress's call for a plan for a Union ironclad warship. Less than four months later Ericsson's ship, the *Monitor,* took to sea, just in time to confront the Confederate ironclad *Virginia* in a historic battle.

The Union forces in the Civil War included Hispanics. One, **J. Francisco Chaves** (left), a native of New Mexico, fought as a lieutenant colonel in the Union Army. Chaves later served as New Mexico's territorial representative to Congress.

When the Civil War began, **Rose Greenhow** (right), a proslavery hostess in the political circles of Washington, D.C., began to work as a spy. Learning of secret Union military plans, she sent the information south, thus helping the Confederates prepare for the first Battle of Bull Run. Union authorities soon learned of her activities and sent her to prison, but she was eventually released. A book she wrote in prison and her social charm made Greenhow a celebrity among the royal families of Europe whom she visited in 1863. On her return, her ship ran aground and Greenhow drowned clutching a bag heavy with gold earned from sales of her book.

"I am a Negro and proud of my race," declared the first African American to serve a full term in the Senate, **Blanche Kelso Bruce** (left). Born a slave, Bruce escaped to freedom during the Civil War. He started several schools to educate African American children before moving to Mississippi during Reconstruction, where he became a landowner and politician. Elected to the Senate in 1874, Bruce fought to protect the civil rights of Native Americans and Chinese immigrants, as well as African Americans. The end of Reconstruction brought an end to Bruce's congressional career. He later served twice as register of the Treasury, and his signature appeared on all U.S. bills issued from 1881 to 1885 and 1897 to 1898.

A famous Cherokee guide and trader, **Jesse Chisholm** (left) served as an interpreter in almost all of the peace conferences between the government and the various Southern Plains tribes from 1825 until his death in 1868. One of the most admired leaders in the Indian Territory, Chisholm first traveled the route that became famous during the days of the great cattle drives. The Chisholm Trail started south of San Antonio and wound through Oklahoma to Abilene, Kansas.

The Five Civilized Tribes (the Chickasaw, Choctaw, Cherokee, Creek, and Seminole Indians) supported the Confederacy during the Civil War. In fact, their casualties as a percentage of population were higher than those of any southern state.

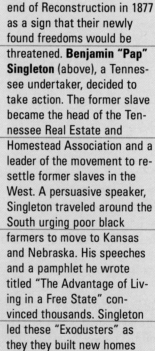

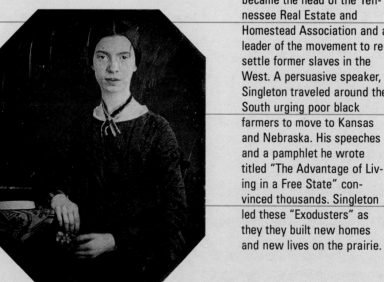

Emily Dickinson (right) was one of this nation's greatest poets. Born in Amherst, Massachusetts, in 1830, she lived in the same house all her life, never married, and saw few people besides her relatives. While the Civil War raged, Dickinson used her solitude to compose many of her best poems. One poem, written in 1864, reads:

> If I can stop one Heart from breaking
> I shall not live in vain
> If I can ease one Life the Aching
> Or cool one Pain
> Or help one fainting Robin
> Unto his Nest again
> I shall not live in Vain.

African Americans saw the end of Reconstruction in 1877 as a sign that their newly found freedoms would be threatened. **Benjamin "Pap" Singleton** (above), a Tennessee undertaker, decided to take action. The former slave became the head of the Tennessee Real Estate and Homestead Association and a leader of the movement to resettle former slaves in the West. A persuasive speaker, Singleton traveled around the South urging poor black farmers to move to Kansas and Nebraska. His speeches and a pamphlet he wrote titled "The Advantage of Living in a Free State" convinced thousands. Singleton led these "Exodusters" as they they built new homes and new lives on the prairie.

Interested students may wish to make a movie poster that illustrates scenes from the Rose Greenhow story.

Geographic Themes: Movement

What role did Jesse Chisholm play in the negotiations between the government and the Southern Plains tribes during the 1800s? (He served as an interpreter in most of the peace conferences.) *What use of the Chisholm Trail gave it a celebrated place in American history?* (Cattle drives.)

Civic Values

Who were the members of the Five Civilized Tribes? (The Chickasaw, Choctaw, Cherokee, Creek, and Seminole Indians.) *What evidence is there that the Tribes made a wholehearted commitment to the Confederate cause?* (Their high rate of casualties.)

Geographic Themes: Movement

Have students write a speech that Benjamin "Pap" Singleton might have given to a gathering of poor black farmers in the South at the end of the Reconstruction era. Students should present the arguments that Singleton might have made to persuade the farmers to join his "Exodusters" in their movement to resettle in Kansas and Nebraska.

Connecting with Literature

Remind students that while some Americans distinguished themselves through their public roles and heroic deeds, others made quiet and private contributions to the life of the nation. *How did Emily Dickinson enrich American culture?* (Through her poetry.) *What were the central themes in her work?* (Nature, love, God, and death.)

Historians' Corner

Vocabulary Preview

Be sure students understand the following terms:
renegade—Outlaw.
travesty—Parody.
innately—Possessing as an essential characteristic.
empirical—Capable of proof.

Analyzing Historical Issues

Samuel Eliot Morison judges Reconstruction a failure because it produced no long-term economic or political gains for blacks. Kenneth M. Stampp examines the constitutional impact of Reconstruction, praising its expansion of democracy through new amendments.

How would each historian answer this question: Did the Reconstruction Era mark a step forward or a step back for blacks, for the South, and for the nation as a whole? What might account for the difference in their answers?

Critical Thinking Answers

1. Morison says Radical Republicans were motivated by political and economic profit. Stampp says they were motivated by religious principles and abolitionist idealism.

2. Morison's account reflects the view of white Americans in the early 1900s that blacks were incapable of participating in government.

3. Stampp believes the most important accomplishments of Radical Reconstruction were the Fourteenth and Fifteenth Amendments, which embodied the principles on which the republic was founded. They failed, however, to improve the economic and social status of African Americans.

HISTORIANS' CORNER

Reconstruction—Radicals and Revisionists

For many years, traditional historians described the Republican plan for the post-Civil War South as a disastrous experiment. Reflecting widespread social prejudices, they focused more on southern politics than on black civil rights. By the 1960s, however, new social attitudes and an awareness of black history changed how history was written. Compare the attitudes in these accounts from 1927 and 1965.

Samuel Eliot Morison

In every reconstructed state government there was a Radical-Republican majority, composed of Negroes and their white leaders. These last were composed of two classes: the 'carpet-baggers'—Northerners who went South after the war, largely for the purposes of political profit—and the 'scalawags' or Southern white renegades. . . .

The resulting state administrations offered the most grotesque travesty of representative government that has ever existed in an English-speaking country. For a period varying from two to nine years the Southern States were governed by majorities composed of lately emancipated slaves, led by carpet-baggers and scalawags. A certain amount of good legislation was passed, especially in the field of education, but corruption was the outstanding feature. . . .

Something might be said for these governments if they had really done anything for the Negro; but the money voted for his schools and land was largely stolen by scalawags, his social and economic status was in no way improved, and his political equality ended with the restoration of white rule.

From Samuel Eliot Morison, *The Oxford History of the United States 1783-1927*, pp. 340-341. Reprinted by permission of Oxford University Press.

Kenneth M. Stampp

In the nineteenth century most white Americans, North and South, had reservations about the Negro's potentialities. . . . But some of the radical Republicans refused to believe that the Negroes were innately inferior and hoped passionately that they would confound their critics. The radicals then had little empirical evidence and no scientific evidence to support their belief—nothing, in fact, but faith. Their faith was derived mostly from their religion: all men, they said, are the sons of Adam and equal in the sight of God. . . . Here, surely, was a projection into the reconstruction era of the idealism of the abolitionist crusade and of the Civil War.

Radical idealism was in part responsible for two of the momentous enactments of the reconstruction years: the Fourteenth Amendment to the Federal Constitution which gave Negroes citizenship and promised them equal protection of the laws, and the Fifteenth Amendment which gave them the right to vote. The fact that these amendments could not have been adopted under any circumstances, or at any other time, before or since, may suggest the crucial importance of the reconstruction era in American history.

From Kenneth M. Stampp, *The Era of Reconstruction, 1865-1877*, pp. 12-13. Copyright © 1965 by Kenneth M. Stampp. Reprinted by permission of Alfred A. Knopf, Inc.

Critical Thinking

1. How are the motives of the Radical Republicans explained by Morison? By Stampp?

2. What does Morison's account reveal about general attitudes toward African Americans in the early 1900s?

3. How does Stampp's description support the idea that reconstruction was a "glorious failure"?

Samuel Eliot Morison (1887–1976) was a specialist in naval and early American history who won two Pulitzer Prizes. Morison was appointed historian of U.S. naval operations during World War II.

Kenneth M. Stampp (1912–   ) is a specialist in Civil War history who taught at the University of California–Berkeley.

The Nation Transformed

CHAPTERS IN THIS UNIT

THEMES IN AMERICAN HISTORY

 Economic Development   Following the Civil War the nation entered a period of industrial transformation and rapid growth.

 Geography   The nation's resources fueled economic growth and spurred westward migration.

 American Culture   The West became a symbol of freedom and opportunity for Americans. Growing cities, meanwhile, provided their residents new opportunities for work and leisure.

 Pluralistic Society   Millions of immigrants came to live and work in the United States' growing cities.

Unit Two

The Nation Transformed
(pp. 85–178)

This unit describes the dramatic economic and social changes of the late 1800s caused by a combination of new inventions and technology, abundant resources, the construction of railroads, the growth of factories, the development of modern management and marketing techniques, and the increasing involvement of government in the economy.

It discusses the transformation of the West during those years and the lasting influence of the American frontier through an examination of the destruction of American Indian life and culture, the effects of railroads and bad weather on the cattle industry, the role of government and technological advances in encouraging farming on the Great Plains and in California, and the influence of mining and lumbering on western patterns of settlement.

The unit also examines the geography of urban growth by detailing the development of city services, the impact of massive immigration, and the effect of city life on merchandising, education, and leisure activities. The influence of increased wealth and poverty on the self-image and philosophy of the nation is also discussed, as well as the corruption and passivity of local and federal government in the face of growing problems.

Chapter 4 ■ Emergence of Industrial America

4 Sections, 4–6 Days

	SECTION OBJECTIVES	SECTION RESOURCES
Section 1 **The Shaping of Modern America**	■ explain how industrial expansion changed the American way of life in the late 1800s	● **Reteaching Resources:** Worksheet 13 ▲ **Reinforcement Workbook:** Worksheet 13 ▲ **Teaching Transparencies:** Transparency 13
Section 2 **Industries and Inventions**	■ describe the inventions that transformed the American economy from an agricultural to an industrial one	● **Reteaching Resources:** Worksheet 14 ▲ **Reinforcement Workbook:** Worksheet 14 ▲ **Teaching Transparencies:** Transparency 14
Section 3 **The Rise of Big Business**	■ identify the ways in which American businesses grew and developed into giant corporations	● **Reteaching Resources:** Worksheet 15 ▲ **Reinforcement Workbook:** Worksheet 15 ■ **Enrichment and Extension Resources:** Primary Source Worksheet 7 ▲ **Teaching Transparencies:** Transparency 15
Section 4 **Government and Business**	■ describe the changes in the relationship between government and business in the late 1800s	● **Reteaching Resources:** Worksheet 16 ▲ **Reinforcement Workbook:** Worksheet 16 ■ **Enrichment and Extension Resources:** Primary Source Worksheet 8 ▲ **Teaching Transparencies:** Transparency 16

The list below shows Essential Elements relevant to this chapter. (The complete list of Essential Elements appears in the introductory pages of this Teacher's Edition.)

Section 1: 2A, 2C, 3A, 3B, 4A, 4B, 6B, 8A, 8B, 9B
Section 2: 2D, 3A, 4C, 4E, 9B
Section 3: 3A, 3C, 3D, 4E, 8A, 8B, 8C, 8D, 8H, 9A, 9B
Section 4: 2A, 3A, 3C, 3D, 3F, 3G, 4D, 4E, 5D, 8B, 8C, 8D, 8F, 8G, 9B, 9D, 9E

Section Resources are keyed for student abilities:
● = Basic
▲ = Average
■ = Average/Advanced

CHAPTER RESOURCES

Geography Resources: Worksheets 7, 8
Tests: Chapter 4 Test

Chapter Project: Economic Development

Have students focus on the emergence of industrial America by creating one of the following: an illustrated report on internal combustion engine or electricity, including diagrams and discussion of its impact on American society; a script of a talk show with representatives of business and industry, held in the late 1800s; a biography of a captain of industry discussed in the chapter.

Homework Options

Each section contains activities labeled "Addressing Individual Needs." You may wish to choose from among these activities when assigning homework.

> **Provisions for Limited English Proficiency (LEP)**
> Several suggested activities may be particularly helpful for teachers of students with limited English proficiency. These activities have been marked throughout the Teacher's Annotated Edition with the symbol **LEP** .

BIBLIOGRAPHY AND AUDIOVISUAL AIDS

Teacher Bibliography

American Heritage History of American Business and Industry. American Heritage, 1972.

Brooks, Thomas R. *Toil and Trouble: A History of American Labor.* Dell, 1986.

Cochran Thomas C., and William Miller. *Age of Enterprise: A Social History of Industrial America.* Harper and Row, 1968.

Nevins, Allan. *John D. Rockefeller: The Heroic Age of American Enterprise.* Kraus Reprint and Periodicals, 1940.

Student Bibliography

Cousins, Margaret. *The Story of Thomas Alva Edison.* Random House, 1981.

Fisher, Leonard Everett. *The Railroads.* Holiday, 1979.

Latham, Frank B. *The Transcontinental Railroad, 1862–1869: A Great Engineering Feat Links America Coast to Coast.* Watts, 1973.

Literature

Davis, Rebecca H. *Life in the Iron Mills and Other Stories.* Tillie Olsen, ed. Feminist Press, 1985.

Norris, Frank. *Octopus.* Airmont, 1968. Dramatic account of the railroad's power over California wheat farmers.

Poe, Edgar Allen. *Complete Tales and Poems.* Random House, 1975.

Films and Videotapes*

Inventors and America's Industrial Revolution. 14 min. CF. The period of America's rapid industrial growth is revealed through the contribution of important inventors from Eli Whitney through Thomas Edison.

Technology in America: Age of Invention. 18 min. COR/MTI. Illustrates the effects of inventions such as the telephone and electricity.

Technology in America: Age of Material Progress. 18 min. COR/MTI. How technological developments from 1850 to 1940 altered the American economy, fostering consumerism and an optimistic faith in material progress.

Computer Software*

Industrialism in America (1 disk: Apple II). FOCUS. Titles include: The Industrial Revolution comes to the U.S.; The Age of Big Business; and Industrial America. Introduces concepts and vocabulary.

*For a complete guide to audiovisual sources, see the introduction to this book (page Txx).

Chapter 4

Emergence of Industrial America
(pp. 86–109)

This chapter focuses on the phenomenal economic growth and rise in technology in the U.S. between 1865 and 1900, describing causes of industrial expansion, the development of corporations, and the government's relationship to big business.

Themes in American History

- Economic development
- American culture
- Geography

Chapter Objectives

After students complete this chapter, they will be able to:

1. Explain how industrial expansion changed the American way of life in the late 1800s.

2. Describe the inventions that transformed the American economy from an agricultural to an industrial one.

3. Identify the ways in which American businesses grew and developed into giant corporations.

4. Describe the changes in the relationship between government and business in the late 1800s.

Chapter Opener Art
John Ferguson Weir, *The Gun Foundry.*

After the Civil War, the nation's industrial transformation went into high gear. Huge mills such as this one turned out vast amounts of steel, a vital material in the industrial age.

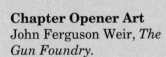

CHAPTER SUPPORT MATERIAL

Reinforcement Workbook: Worksheets 13–16
Reteaching Resources: Worksheets 13–16
Enrichment and Extension Resources: Primary Source Worksheets 7, 8
Geography Resources: Worksheets 7, 8
Teaching Transparencies: Transparencies 13–16
Tests: Chapter 4 Test

4 Emergence of Industrial America (1860–1900)

KEY EVENTS

1844	First telegraph message sent
c. 1850	Bessemer process discovered
1869	Transcontinental railroad completed
1876	Telephone invented
1887	Interstate Commerce Act
1890	Sherman Antitrust Act

2A, 2C, 3A, 3B, 4A, 4B, 6B, 8A, 8B, 9B

1 The Shaping of Modern America

★ Section Focus

Key Term productivity

Main Idea Between the Civil War and 1900, industry expanded, the West was settled, and cities grew. These developments helped shape modern American society.

Objectives As you read, look for answers to these questions:
1. Why were the developments of this period so important?
2. What factors contributed to America's industrial growth?

When we speak of the American Revolution, we usually mean the events that took place between 1776 and 1789. During those years the American colonies declared their independence from Britain, fought to earn that independence, and then created the constitutional form of government we enjoy today. But during the last four decades of the 1800s the United States experienced another kind of revolution. Unlike the American Revolution, this revolution was economic and social rather than political.

DAILY LIFE IN 1860 AND 1900 2A, 6B

To appreciate the changes in American society, let us compare daily life in 1860 and in 1900. In 1860 most Americans lived on farms or in small towns. A family that was neither poor nor rich had much in common with many other families. "Home" might be a wooden house shaded by trees. It probably had a wide front porch with a swing. The house was on a dirt street that was muddy in winter and dusty in summer.

The kitchen had a huge black stove that burned coal or wood. Food that did not spoil quickly was kept in the pantry, just off the kitchen. Milk, eggs, butter, fruits, and vegetables were stored in the cellar. There was no running water or indoor plumbing. A well supplied water for drinking and cooking; instead of a bathroom there was an outhouse in the back yard.

Running the household was thought of as "women's work," and it was a full-time job. Women spent a large part of the day preparing meals, since there were no frozen foods and few canned foods. They also did a lot of sewing, because few people bought ready-to-wear clothes. House cleaning and laundry were hard work, done without a vacuum, an electric iron, or a washer and dryer.

Children walked to and from school even if it was far away. They did homework in the evening. They also had chores—chopping wood, carrying out ashes from the stove, carrying water up to the bedrooms.

Now contrast that scene with 1900. The small town has become a city. It has new factories and expanding neighborhoods peopled by immigrants and ex-farmers. The house stands on a paved street that is lit at night by electric lights. The

---

SUPPORTING THE SECTION

Reinforcement Workbook: Worksheet 13
Reteaching Resources: Worksheet 13
Teaching Transparencies: Transparency 13

Background Another important component of women's work was caring for the ill; sicknesses were more dangerous and lengthy then, without the benefit of modern medicines.

SECTION 1

The Shaping of Modern America
(pp. 87–90)

Section Objective

■ explain how industrial expansion changed the American way of life in the late 1800s

Introducing the Section

Connecting with Past Learnings
Review with students the factors of industrialization that were already present in the United States by 1865. (Factories existed, interchangeable parts used, water wheels and steam engines sources of power, iron a basic material, wood and coal burned as fuels.)

Tell students to notice as they work through this lesson additional factors which accounted for the changes in industry between 1865 and 1900.

Key Term
Discuss the meaning of *productivity* with the class. To test their understanding of this economic concept, give them the example of ten workers in Factory A producing twenty widgets in an hour versus five workers in Factory B producing fifteen widgets an hour. **Which factory is more productive?** (Factory B.) Have students list ways that productivity is increased. **LEP**

Have students imagine they grew up in the 1860s. Have them describe the world in 1860, from the point of view of someone living in 1900.

Ask students to describe the four main causes of industrial expansion, relating their effects to the description in the text of American life in 1900. (1—natural resources supplied factories which produced consumer goods; 2—growing numbers of workers led to growth of cities; 3—increased supply of capital helped businesses grow and expand; 4—innovations brought new, helpful machines to consumers.)

Developing the Lesson

After students have read the section, you may want to consider the following activities:

Impact of Geography

Have students list the natural resources mentioned in the text and discuss the use of each. (Coal and oil—fuel; iron ore— steel; timber—construction; copper—electrical wiring and equipment; lead—building material; farmland and grassland—food.)

How was it possible to bring resources to manufacturing areas? (First waterways were used, then railroads.)

Economics

European investment offset the expense of industrialization in America. British and French investors, for example, supplied about one-third the cost of American railroads. Ask students to present arguments American corporations might have used to persuade European bankers to lend them money.

How was foreign investment beneficial to both Americans and Europeans? (Made industrial expansion possible for Americans; was profitable for Europeans.)

A photograph from around 1900 shows an American family of seven in their home. The son standing in back holds a violin while the daughter sitting in front plays a banjo. CULTURE What does the photograph tell you about the family's way of life? 9B

house too has electric lights, as well as a bathroom.

The woman of the family still spends much of her time at home, though one or two of her friends have taken jobs in offices. All members of the family now have some store-bought clothes. A hand-powered carpet sweeper is a big help in cleaning the house.

The young people still have homework and chores to do in the evening. But in their free time they ride bicycles and listen to phonograph records. They take the trolley car into the city, and maybe to school as well. The family has a telephone to keep in touch with friends and relatives.

Shopping has changed a great deal. Canned goods have cut down the time needed to prepare meals. Since the house now has an icebox, fresh foods can be stored longer. Ice, delivered daily, keeps the icebox cold. Butchers no longer sell meat from animals killed in their shops. Instead, they buy meat from a meat-packing company. At the corner grocery store, people can buy all sorts of household items, such as soap, that they see advertised in newspapers and magazines.

A SOCIETY TRANSFORMED 4A, 8A

The changes described above reflected deeper trends going on in the United States in the late 1800s. These trends were:

(1) The expansion of American industry. Between the Civil War and the end of the century, a whole range of industries in the United States enjoyed phenomenal growth.

(2) The settling of the West. By about 1890, a flood of new settlers had moved into previously unsettled lands west of the Mississippi River.

(3) The growth of cities. Throughout the late 1800s, countless towns gained area and population. Cities both young and old expanded, some of them reaching the one-million mark in population.

These three developments were all closely linked. The expanding West provided new sources of such raw materials as timber and iron ore. Industry also relied on the large supply of workers in the nation's growing cities. And both western settlers and urban workers provided ready markets for the products of industry.

Western settlement benefited from industrial expansion. The railroad, in particular, brought the

Photo Caption Answer
They have time for leisure activities such as music; portraits on the wall and the clothes suggest prosperity.

West closer to the settled East. Trains headed west with new settlers and with manufactured goods; they returned east with the products of western mines, ranches, and farms.

Cities needed the industries located in and around them. The presence of factories encouraged people to come live and work in the cities. These workers bought goods from city businesses, sent their children to city schools, and in many other ways helped the cities thrive. Some cities, such as Chicago, were located on travel routes to the West. Thus they enjoyed spectacular growth as a result of the massive migration westward.

Why did all these momentous changes occur during the late 1800s? Though their roots dated back well before the Civil War, that conflict gave a decisive boost to industry, western settlement, and urban growth. In the years before the war, conflicts between northern and southern leaders over national policy had almost paralyzed the federal government. Once the southern states seceded from the Union in 1861, northern leaders were able to pursue their plans for the nation.

As you will read in this chapter, Congress passed several laws during the war that aided the growth of business. Likewise, in Chapter 5 you will read of government efforts to encourage settlement of the West. And in Chapter 6 you will read about the great cities that profited from industrial growth during and after the Civil War.

Also in Chapter 6 you will read the story of the immigrants who arrived on American shores in record numbers beginning late in the 1800s. Coming from both Europe and Asia—from Italy, Russia, Japan, and many other countries—they helped power the momentous changes in American society. They mined the coal that fueled the steel mills of Pittsburgh. They plowed the fertile land of the Great Plains. They built New York City into one of the world's largest, most exciting cities.

The expansion of industry, the settling of the West, and the growth of cities transformed American society. Once rural, the nation became urban; once agricultural, the nation became industrial. In fact, the United States as we know it today took shape during these years. If the American Revolution was this nation's birth, the years 1860–1900 marked its coming of age.

New York has been America's most populous city since 1800. During the 1800s, waves of immigrants arrived in New York, first from such western European nations as Germany and Ireland and later from eastern Europe and Russia. CULTURE What in this 1890 picture would not have appeared in a similar picture from 1860? 4B

CAUSES OF INDUSTRIAL EXPANSION 2C, 3A, 3B

In Chapter 2 you read how the Civil War moved the Industrial Revolution into a new phase. Four factors boosted industrialization even further.

(1) Many natural resources. The United States had an abundance of timber and rich deposits of coal, oil, and iron ore. Each of these was critical as a source for making goods or as fuel for running industrial machines. In addition, copper was plentiful in Arizona, Montana, and the Lake Superior region. The upper Mississippi Valley yielded ample supplies of lead.

The nation's numerous rivers provided water power to run early factories. Although coal and oil would become the most important energy sources for industrialization, wood was for a long time the major fuel, especially for the railroad industry. Forests in both the East and West seemed unlimited. By the 1880s water, oil, and coal could be transformed into electricity, which was an even more effective power source.

A wealth of farmland and grasslands throughout the nation's midsection ensured ample food supplies for Americans. Farm surpluses were also sold abroad, which helped pay for imports of those goods Americans did not yet manufacture.

Photo Caption Answer
Telegraph and telephone lines, manufacturing, and retail businesses.

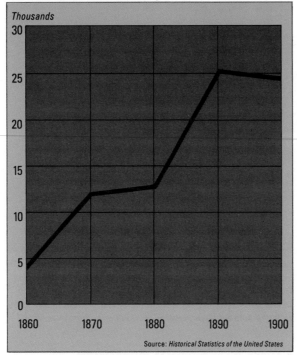

INVENTIONS PATENTED, 1860–1900

Thousands

Source: *Historical Statistics of the United States*

GRAPH SKILLS 3A, 8B, 9B

This graph shows the number of inventions patented in the years between 1860 and 1900. How many inventions were patented in 1870? In what decade did the greatest increase in the total number of patents take place? CRITICAL THINKING How did patents provide an incentive to inventors?

(2) *The growing number of workers.* The labor force grew steadily during the late 1800s as a result of a high birthrate and immigration. These workers not only kept the factories running but also bought the products of industry. This large consumer market helped maintain industrial expansion.

(3) *An increased supply of capital.* Building factories to make goods, transportation systems to move goods, and stores to sell goods—all these took huge amounts of capital. Some of this capital came from foreign investors. Some was raised by business partnerships called corporations (page 97). And some came from within the American soil. One silver deposit in Nevada, the Comstock Lode, produced over $300 million worth of the metal within twenty years of its discovery in 1859. California gold mines also supplied the nation with the world's most precious metal.

(4) *Innovations and inventions.* By ensuring people's rights to engage in business and to profit from it, the American free enterprise system encouraged innovation. The United States Patent Office, opened in 1790, operated on a simple first-come, first-served principle. Inventors only had to prove that their ideas were new and useful and pay less than $5 in fees. In return, they obtained exclusive rights to develop and sell their ideas as they saw fit. Little wonder that farm boys with a disposition to tinker, city folk who could fix any mechanical device, and women with a flair for finding shortcuts to housework paraded before the Patent Board with their products.

Between 1790 and 1860, the Board approved 36,000 patents. This number mushroomed to 640,000 in the period 1860–1900. People like Thomas Alva Edison (1847–1931), a brilliant self-taught inventor, thrived in a democracy where genius and not formal training counted.

These four factors, and the push provided by the Civil War, led to an explosion of economic growth during the late 1800s. Productivity—the rate of output of production—jumped by 12 times in 50 years. The number of factory workers increased by 10 times. So widespread was economic expansion that the nation's growth became self-sustaining. For example, steel produced in Pennsylvania was used to make ships and trains; these, in turn, carried iron ore from the Midwest to those same steel mills. Such progress made the United States a leading economic power by 1900.

SECTION REVIEW

1. **KEY TERM** productivity

2. **COMPREHENSION** List the three key trends going on in American society in the late 1800s.

3. **COMPREHENSION** Why was immigration important to the developments of this period?

4. **COMPREHENSION** What four factors led to the growth of the Industrial Revolution in the United States?

5. **CRITICAL THINKING** What aspect of the changes in American society from 1860 to 1900 seems most revolutionary to you? Why?

90 UNIT 2 THE NATION TRANSFORMED

Graph Skills Answers
About 12,500. 1880–1890.
They protected inventors' rights.

2 Industries and Inventions

Section Focus

Key Terms Bessemer process ■ standard gauge ■ dynamo

Main Idea Inventions revolutionized transportation, communication, and almost every other area of American life. They also helped power the growth of new industries.

Objectives As you read, look for answers to these questions:
1. What led to the growth of the steel industry?
2. How did the railroads become a central part of the American economy?
3. What new sources of power emerged?

A list of the inventions made in the second half of the 1800s would fill a catalog—which is fitting, since the mail-order catalog was one of those inventions. They include small household items like the coat hanger, chewing gum, the fountain pen, and the square-bottomed paper bag. Other inventions, however, radically changed American industry. The age of iron and steam, which had lasted from 1790 to 1860, gave way to an age of steel, oil, and electricity.

THE STEEL INDUSTRY 3A

Perhaps more than any other development, the coming of steel helped propel the United States into an unprecedented period of industrial growth. A stronger and less brittle metal than iron, steel had been around for centuries. Yet no one had found a way to make it cheaply and in large quantities. Impurities had to be removed from iron to make steel. Until the 1860s, this was done by heating pig iron, stirring it, and reheating it—a process that sometimes lasted a full day.

In the 1850s William Kelly, an American scientist, and Henry Bessemer, a British inventor, independently discovered a new way to make steel. They found that a blast of hot air directed at melted iron would reduce its impurities. This technique, eventually called the Bessemer process, meant that steel was now cheap enough to be mass-produced.

With the discovery of the Bessemer process, the American steel industry grew at a staggering rate. The amount of steel produced leaped by almost twenty times between 1876 and 1900. The industry originally centered in western Pennsylvania and Ohio, near vast supplies of coal needed to fire the steel furnaces. As the industry grew, companies began mining high-grade iron ore in Michigan and Minnesota. Cleveland and Detroit joined Pittsburgh as major steel producers. A large steel industry also developed in Birmingham, Alabama, which called itself the "Pittsburgh of the South."

Steel had almost endless uses. With steel, bridges could last for decades and huge skyscrapers could be built. Steel replaced iron in industrial machines. Even household objects like stoves and hammers could be improved with the use of steel.

THE BIRTH OF AMERICAN RAILROADS 3A

Perhaps the most important use of steel was in railroad rails. Iron rails were weak and brittle; they had to be replaced every few years to keep them from buckling under the weight of locomotives. Steel rails lasted far longer, allowing railroad companies to build bigger trains and lay more track. Without steel, the United States could never have become "an empire of rails."

The world's first commercial railroad began running in England in 1825. Not long afterward, enterprising business people were building railroads in the United States. Yet the existence of many small railroad companies created problems. Few railroad lines ran more than 50 miles. Those that headed into the wilderness usually led, as a popular saying claimed, from "nowhere to nothing." Furthermore, many lines only had a single track, creating a constant threat of collision.

An additional complication was the lack of a standard gauge, or common distance between the rails of a railroad track. Each railroad line often had its own cars with its own gauge. As a result,

---

SUPPORTING THE SECTION

Reinforcement Workbook: Worksheet 14
Reteaching Resources: Worksheet 14
Teaching Transparencies: Transparency 14

Background The Bessemer process was ultimately replaced by the open-hearth furnace, which reached higher temperatures and gave the worker more control in testing during production.

SECTION 2

Industries and Inventions
(pp. 91–96)

Section Objective
■ describe the inventions that transformed the American economy from an agricultural to an industrial one

Introducing the Section

Connecting with Past Learnings
To help students understand the importance of trains, have them consider the methods of transportation used before railroads. *What was the most important method of transportation?* (Water—rivers, lakes, and canals.) *What were the shortcomings of this mode of transportation?* (Limited mainly to existing bodies of water since canals could not cover long distances; limited in winter.)

Key Terms
Write the key terms on the board. Have students use the terms in a short paragraph about industrial expansion in the United States in the late 1800s. **LEP**

Focus
Have students create a chart by asking them to list the inventions and innovations mentioned in the section and write what the invention or innovation replaced and how it affected the U.S. economy. (Bessemer process speeded up steel-making, industry boomed; railroads replaced slower methods of transportation; dynamo made electricity an important power source; telegraph and telephone sped up communications.)

What general statement can be made about industrial innovations between 1865 and 1900? (Revolutionized industry, making the United States an economic power.)

Developing the Lesson

After students have read the section, you may want to consider the following activities:

Geographic Themes: Movement

On the board, write the years: *1820, 1870, 1900,* and *1990.* Ask students what method they would have used in each of those years to send a message or a package across the United States quickly. (1820—mail carried by horse or boat; 1870—telegraph for message, railroad for package; 1900—telephone or telegraph for message, railroad for package; 1990—telephone or fax machine for message, air express service for package.)

Ask the class to suggest ways the increase in the speed of communications has affected society and the economy.

the cars of one line would not fit on the tracks of another. Passengers and goods had to be unloaded each time they changed lines. A single trip between Chicago and Buffalo required at least five transfers.

Early train travel was hazardous as well as inconvenient. Smoke from a belching locomotive sometimes drifted into cars, blurring riders' vision and leaving them gasping for breath. Brakes failed, and engineers overshot their stations. As a Philadelphia businessman put it, travelers dreaded the thought "of being blown sky-high or knocked off the rails."

Despite these growing pains, railroad construction soared after the Civil War. High profits encouraged the building of new lines, even though track construction was difficult and costly. Federal and state governments smiled on railroads as carriers of troops, mail, and trade. They spurred construction through grants of money and public lands. With the American industrial economy booming, railroads seemed more necessary than ever. Demands grew louder for a railroad to cross the thousands of miles of prairie, desert, and mountains of the western United States.

THE FIRST TRANSCONTINENTAL RAILROAD 3A

Plans for a transcontinental railroad had begun before the Civil War, with North and South vying for the route. When the South seceded from the Union, the wartime Congress—now dominated entirely by northern representatives—decided on a line connecting Omaha, Nebraska, to Sacramento, California. Congress then awarded construction to two railroad companies, the Central Pacific and the Union Pacific. As an incentive, it gave the companies loans of money and grants of land for each mile of rail built.

From the start, construction of the railroad took on the air of a contest. From California, the Central Pacific pushed east; from Nebraska, the Union Pacific pushed west. Every mile crossed meant more money, more land, and more glory for the competing companies.

Starting in 1863, the two companies recruited armies of workers to put down the track. Many of the workers were recent immigrants from Asia and Europe. Charles Crocker, chief engineer for the Central Pacific, hired 7,000 Chinese immigrants, who toiled for $1 a day. The Union Pacific's Grenville Dodge relied heavily on Irish laborers.

This 1868 photograph shows Union Pacific railway workers building a bridge in Wyoming. Railway construction led to settlement of vast, previously unsettled areas of the Midwest, South, and West. GEOGRAPHY Which mountain ranges lay in the path of the railway as it pushed east from Sacramento, California? 2D

Photo Caption Answer
Sierra Nevada and Rocky Mountains.

Background Both the Union Pacific and Central Pacific companies were given 20 square miles of land along the track for each mile of track built. In total, railroad companies received about $300 million from local governments and $228 million from state governments.

Crews from the Central Pacific and Union Pacific railroads shake hands and celebrate the completion of the world's first transcontinental railway in 1869. The poster (above right) trumpets the news. The eastward and westward teams met in the Promontory Mountains of northern Utah. NATIONAL IDENTITY Besides making travel easier, how did the railway affect the way Americans viewed their nation? **3A**

Workers for both sides faced a heroic and grueling task. Progress was toughest in the high Sierra Nevada range. Laborers had to cut through mountains with little more than their bare hands. Some hung in baskets against sheer cliffs while they pecked holes in the rock and stuffed them with blasting powder. Others clawed underground, tunneling through granite so hard that it could barely be chipped. Through all this, the workers had to contend with blizzards that whipped up gigantic snow drifts and avalanches that buried everything in their paths. By some estimates, accidents claimed the lives of more than 1,200 workers.

On May 10, 1869, two locomotives rested nose to nose on a stretch of track in Promontory, Utah. Standing between them, Central Pacific President Leland Stanford of California drove a solid gold spike into the track, marking the completion of the nation's first transcontinental railroad. An iron road now connected the nation.

AN EMPIRE OF RAILS 3A, 4E

Meanwhile, railroad building in general increased. From 35,000 miles of track in 1865, the network expanded to 193,000 miles in 1900. Railroad service and safety gradually improved. In 1864 a former cabinetmaker named George Pullman invented a luxury sleeping car. Four years later he devised a separate dining car. In 1869 New York inventor George Westinghouse patented an automatic air brake that assured far greater safety aboard high-speed trains. By 1870 a standard gauge of 4 feet 8 1/2 inches had gone into wide use. And, in the 1880s, railroads began laying tracks of steel able to carry the heavy loads of industry.

Railroads had grown into the nation's leading business. They created a distribution system for what became a national marketplace. Shoes stitched in Boston wound up in shoe stores in St. Louis. Iron ore from around Lake Superior moved

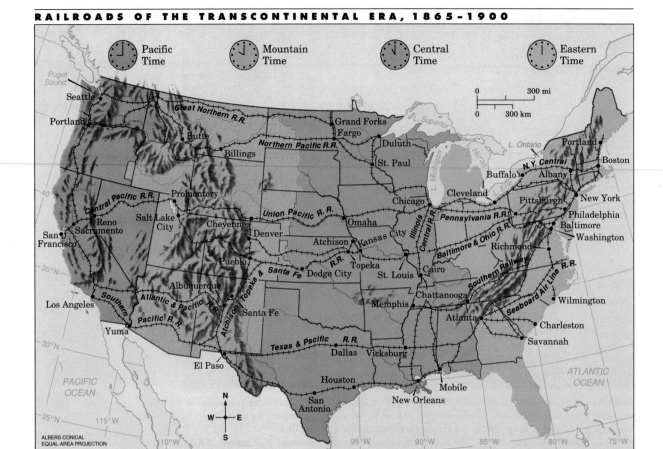

MAP SKILLS

3A, 9B

Railway lines stretched from coast to coast during the late 1800s. By 1900, the United States had almost 200,000 miles of track—about one-third of the world total. **CRITICAL THINKING** Why was the development of the railroad important to industrial growth?

Local History

The map on this page shows time zones as they existed in 1883. Have students refer to the map to determine the time zone their community was in at that time and whether it has changed since then. If possible, have them compare those zones with the ones that exist today.

Cooperative Learning

Divide the class into small groups. Ask each group to choose the invention or innovation mentioned in the section that they consider to be most important. When they have decided, have the members of the group write a memo justifying their choice. Have each group present its choice and justifications to the class. **LEP**

east to steel mills in Pennsylvania. New towns sprang up along the tracks, and at the intersections of major lines, towns grew into prosperous cities.

Railroads even affected American understanding of time itself. Before railroads, American communities had set the time of day according to the movement of the sun. The nation thus had more than 100 different time zones. New York City, for example, was ten minutes and two seconds ahead of Baltimore. This system, geared to the slower pace of life in pre-industrial America, made no sense in the railroad era. The many time zones made it difficult to coordinate the movements of trains from different parts of the country.

Railroad officials finally came up with a solution: Railroad Standard Time. This plan divided the na-

tion into four time zones with the same time used throughout each zone. Although the plan went into effect on November 18, 1883, many communities refused to accept it. Congress itself did not adopt the scheme until 1918.

ENERGY FROM OIL AND ELECTRICITY 3A, 4E

The railroads, like all industries, consumed energy. American industry needed cheap, reliable sources of energy to power its growth. Inventors answered the call by finding new ways to harness energy sources previously untapped.

Oil was one example. Until 1859, farmers saw oil merely as a nuisance. It leaked into their wells and streams, polluting the water. But in the early 1850s some scientists found that oil could be used as a fuel for lamps. In 1859 a railroad conductor

Map Skills Answer
It provided the means of bringing raw materials to factories and of distributing finished products.

named Edwin Drake drilled the first oil well, in Titusville, Pennsylvania. Lured by the prospect of quick profits, numerous entrepreneurs went to Pennsylvania, bought land, and went into the oil business.

Oil was a better source of light than either natural gas or whale oil. It was also a better lubricant for machinery than animal fat, which had a terrible odor after a few days. People did not realize the true importance of oil, however, until the internal combustion engine was developed in the late 1800s. This engine, which burns refined petroleum, would make possible the growth of the automobile industry in the early 1900s (Chapter 14).

Electricity was another form of energy not fully tapped until the 1800s. Though scientists had known for ages that electricity existed, it was not until 1831 that large-scale uses for electricity seemed possible. In that year an Englishman named Michael Faraday and an American named Joseph Henry, working independently, discovered the principle behind the dynamo, or electric generator. Using energy provided by steam, water, or some other source, the dynamo could produce electricity to run factories.

The coming of electric power spawned countless inventions. Several of these resulted from the

The great inventor Thomas Edison lost his hearing as a boy, but he claimed that deafness made concentration easier. Besides inventing the light bulb and the phonograph, Edison improved the typewriter, movie projector, and telephone. **TECHNOLOGY** In your own words, explain Edison's definition of genius as "one percent inspiration and ninety-nine percent perspiration." 4C

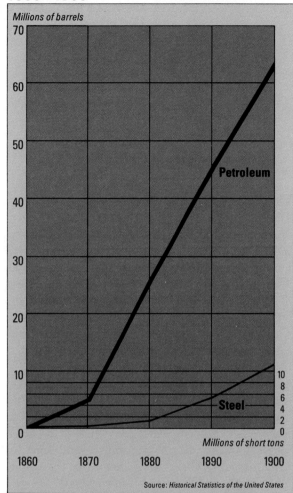

PETROLEUM AND STEEL PRODUCTION, 1860–1900

Source: *Historical Statistics of the United States*

GRAPH SKILLS

This graph illustrates the dramatic takeoff in petroleum and steel production during the late 1800s. About how many times greater was the level of petroleum production in 1890 than it was in 1870? **CRITICAL THINKING** Why was there a great demand for steel at the end of the 19th century? 3A, 9B

genius of Thomas Alva Edison. This self-educated tinkerer patented 1,093 items during his lifetime, an all-time record. He designed the country's first electric power plant, installed in New York in 1882. He also invented the phonograph, and in 1879 came his most famous invention, the electric light bulb. Largely through Edison's work, virtually every American would come to depend on electric power.

THE TELEGRAPH AND TELEPHONE 3A, 4E

The telegraph and telephone—two more inventions using electricity—revolutionized communication. The telegraph began as a scientific novelty. Fascinated by the mysteries of electricity, Samuel F. B. Morse, a portrait painter from New York, designed a machine that could send coded impulses over a copper wire. The code that Morse worked out was a system of dots and dashes representing letters that could be tapped out on a finger-key transmitter.

Morse applied for a patent in 1837. Then he set out to prove the usefulness of his device. With support from Congress, he built a telegraph line from Washington to Baltimore. On May 24, 1844, Morse hunched over a transmitter and sent his first message. Choosing a line from the Bible, Morse tapped: "What hath God wrought!"

"**W**hat hath God wrought!"
—*First telegraph message, Samuel F. B. Morse*

Incredibly, no one seemed much interested in Morse's invention at first. Only one person sent a message during its first four days of operation. A few enterprising business people, however, realized the telegraph's great potential. Investors could buy stocks more quickly. Railroads could keep customers informed of schedules. Merchants could order goods as soon as inventories fell low. Newspapers could get the latest news for the next edition.

Telegraph service expanded when several companies bought the rights to Morse's invention. Long-distance messages often had to be handled by three or four different companies, however. The result was slower, more costly service for customers. Eventually Western Union bought out all its competitors and established a monopoly over the American telegraph system.

Harnessing electricity to send coded messages was only the first step in the communications revolution. The next step was to make the wires speak. That step was taken by Alexander Graham Bell, a Scottish immigrant who moved to Boston in 1871. Like Morse, Bell was fascinated by the workings of electricity. Along with his assistant, Thomas A. Watson, Bell looked for a way to transmit the human voice over wire. On March 10, 1876, their device worked, and the telephone was born.

In 1877 Bell and his backers formed the Bell Telephone Company, which soon gained a monopoly over the telephone industry. Early telephones were somewhat crude. Conversations, said one reporter, sounded like a person talking with "his mouth full and his head in a barrel." Service improved, however, and the telephone's convenience brought in many new customers. By 1900 there were over a million telephones in use in the United States. People all across the nation could now benefit from the revolution in communication.

3A, 3C, 3D, 4E, 8A, 8B, 8C, 8D, 8H, 9A, 9B

3 The Rise of Big Business

Section Focus

Key Terms corporation ■ dividend ■ economies of scale ■ limited liability ■ vertical integration ■ horizontal integration ■ promotion ■ patent war ■ installment plan

Main Idea Seeking greater efficiency and profits, many American businesses grew to enormous sizes in the late 1800s.

Objectives As you read, look for answers to these questions:
1. What were the features and advantages of corporations?
2. How did different companies learn to prosper in the marketplace?

Before 1860, most American businesses were of two kinds. They were either proprietorships (owned by one person) or partnerships (owned by a small group of people). The Industrial Revolution changed all that. Newly invented machines could make products more efficiently than human hands. These new machines, however, cost a great deal of money. It was also costly to buy raw materials, move finished products to market, and sell these products. A new kind of business organization emerged to handle these tasks.

CORPORATIONS 3C, 8B, 8C

These new businesses were corporations. A corporation is created when a state government gives a group of people the right to sell shares of stock (certificates of ownership) in order to raise capital. They then use this capital to run their business. The stockholders, the true owners of the corporation, receive dividends—a portion of the profits.

A corporation has three distinct advantages over a proprietorship:

(1) By selling shares of stock, it can raise large amounts of capital. This capital can be used to expand production, resulting in bringing about economies of scale. That is, the more units of a product a company makes, the less it costs to make each unit.

(2) Stockholders enjoy limited liability. If the corporation goes into debt, each stockholder can lose only as much money as he or she invested in it. (In contrast, owners of proprietorships and partnerships are responsible for all the business's debts.) Limited liability thus encourages people to invest in corporations.

(3) Unlike other businesses, a corporation is not affected by the death or resignation of an owner. That person's shares of stock are simply bought up by someone else. This arrangement gives the corporation great stability. Banks, reassured by this stability, are more likely to lend money to corporations.

THE CASE OF STANDARD OIL 3C, 3D, 8C, 8H

A good way to understand the workings of a corporation is to look at a successful firm in the late 1800s, Standard Oil Company. John D. Rockefeller entered the oil business in 1862 in Cleveland, where he had already organized a small grocery firm. He became a member of a partnership formed to refine oil. The firm was moderately successful, but Rockefeller wanted more.

Rockefeller looked at the many steps involved in bringing oil from the well to market. Getting the oil out of the ground was only the first step. Drillers sold their oil to refiners, who made it into kerosene or lubricants. Then the refiners sold the product to transportation firms. They, in turn, sold it to other businesses, who then sold it directly to the consumers. All these steps took considerable time and money.

Rockefeller realized that he could cut costs and improve efficiency if he gained control of all processes of the oil industry—drilling, refining, transportation, and sales. Combining the steps involved in turning a raw material into a finished product is called vertical integration.

In 1870 Rockefeller organized the Standard Oil Company. To raise money for expansion, Standard Oil sold 10,000 shares of stock for $1 million. Us-

SUPPORTING THE SECTION

Reinforcement Workbook: Worksheet 15
Reteaching Resources: Worksheet 15
Enrichment and Extension Resources: Primary Source Worksheet 7
Teaching Transparencies: Transparency 15

SECTION 3

The Rise of Big Business
(pp. 97–102)

Section Objective

■ identify the ways in which American businesses grew and developed into giant corporations

Introducing the Section

Connecting with Past Learnings
Review economic concepts by asking: **What are the main characteristics of capitalism?** (Most businesses are privately owned; competition and the free market determine prices and production.)

Key Terms
Give the meaning of a key term as if it were the answer to a question. Then call on students to ask the appropriate question, using the key term. Follow this procedure for all terms. **LEP**

Focus

What caused corporations to develop at this time? (Industrial Revolution created a need for big businesses to raise capital for production.)

Discuss with students the business methods used by corporate heads mentioned in the section. Based on these, have students create a list of guidelines entitled "How to Succeed in Business." (Examples: incorporate your business; implement vertical integration; advertise.)

97

After students have read the section, you may want to consider the following activities:

Economics

Make sure students understand the concepts of *economies of scale, vertical integration,* and *horizontal integration.* (Economies of scale—companies pay lower prices on larger quantities of raw materials and spread the cost of equipment over a greater quantity of the product so the cost per item is lower; vertical integration— one corporation owns all the operations that are involved in producing and selling a product; horizontal integration— one corporation buys out its competitors in order to control production.)

To check their understanding, have students create a diagram illustrating how one of the concepts works.

Participating in Government

A corporation is a legal entity that can buy, sell, sue, and be sued as though it were a person. States charter most business corporations. *Why might the government want control over the establishment of corporations?* (Shareholders in corporations have special rights and states regulate corporations to be sure that those rights are not abused.)

Have several students write to the Corporate Division of your state's Secretary of State's office requesting information on the procedures needed to file for corporate status. Have other students write to the state Department of Revenue to find out how corporate income tax is determined. Have them share the responses with the class.

ing this capital, it bought more refineries in the Cleveland area, and even set up its own barrel-making business. Because it refined the most oil in Cleveland, Standard Oil was able to force railroads transporting its product to give it special rates. The corporation also set up an office in New York City, as well as warehouses and docks, for the purpose of selling its products abroad.

Using the profits from these efforts, Rockefeller was able to take still other risks. In order to get ahead of competitors by cutting its refining costs,

John D. Rockefeller, the son of a peddler, became one of the world's richest men by gaining control of the drilling, refining, and oil distribution industries. **ECONOMICS** How does this cartoon illustrate the principle of vertical integration? **9B**

Standard built its own system of pipelines. It thus took oil directly from the wells to the refineries without relying on railroads. Then it purchased several Pennsylvania drilling companies, thereby guaranteeing an adequate supply of oil at all times. It also bought out companies that used petroleum to make certain products. One firm, for instance, made petroleum jelly (called Vaseline).

Standard Oil was able to set up a corporate organization with various departments, each specializing in a certain area. Individual departments handled legal affairs, purchasing, foreign shipping and sales, oil inspection, and cost accounting. That last department kept track of every expense in the production process, giving Rockefeller and his managers precise information about costs and prices. Standard Oil's accountants worked these figures out to the thousandth of a cent.

Rockefeller's efforts paid off. Standard Oil's efficiency allowed it to cut prices. The company could even afford to sell oil temporarily for less than it cost to produce it. In this way, Rockefeller drove his competitors out of business. By 1900 the mighty Standard Oil Company had a monopoly on the nation's oil industry.

CAPTAINS OF INDUSTRY 3D

The example of John D. Rockefeller shows that the Industrial Revolution was a time of great people as well as huge corporations. In fact, it took the genius and dedication—and, on occasion, the ruthlessness—of a few individuals to create these mammoth industries. Some were talented inventors, such as Thomas Alva Edison. Others were merely lucky, such as Mr. Procter and Mr. Gamble, whose floating Ivory soap came from a defective batch of ingredients. As we can see in the stories of steel, cereals, and sewing machines, survival in the marketplace required a variety of skills.

ANDREW CARNEGIE'S WORLD OF STEEL 3C, 3D, 8C, 8H

Some large American corporations arose because there was a great demand for their product. A case in point was the United States Steel Corporation, formed in 1901 as the first corporation with stock totaling $1 billion.

The genius behind U. S. Steel—and the steel industry in general—was Andrew Carnegie. Young

Photo Caption Answer
Oil wells represent production, railroads represent distribution, and Rockefeller owns them all.

Background By 1892 Rockefeller's fortune had grown to more then $800 million. During his lifetime, Rockefeller donated some $550 million to higher education, cultural institutions, and charity.

Carnegie came to America from Scotland in 1848. He first worked as a railroad telegrapher, rising to the position of superintendent. He also invested in a firm that helped build the Brooklyn Bridge, the longest suspension bridge in the world when it was opened in 1883.

What really challenged Carnegie was the poor way in which the steel for his bridge company was developed. Each process, like that in the oil industry, was done separately. One firm smelted the iron (separated the metal from its ore). Another made it into slabs, which were sold to still another firm to be made into sheets. Still other firms molded the sheets into a consumer product, such as a clothes iron. The final cost to the consumer reflected all these add-on costs.

Carnegie set out to change the steel industry. He started with one steel firm and did his homework. He hired experts in chemistry to find the best and cheapest way of smelting iron. Then he did studies on the big furnaces in steel mills to arrive at the best way to run them. He hired an accountant to determine the exact expenses in making a ton of steel, and made certain that employees who did the most work would be promoted. Competitors thought Carnegie was crazy to spend so much time and money on research.

However, armed with precise figures about the making of steel, Carnegie had an advantage. He could produce steel more cheaply than his competitors and sell it for lower prices. Then, with his profits, Carnegie bought out competing steel firms. This process of expanding in one area of production is called **horizontal integration**. He also integrated the industry vertically by purchasing iron mines and even railroads, so he could transport the ore and finished products. The first ton of steel that Carnegie made cost him $56. By 1900 he had cut that figure to $11.50.

In 1901 Carnegie retired. He sold his steel company to a wealthy investment banker, J. P. Morgan. Morgan combined it with other steel companies to form the United States Steel Corporation, the world's largest steel manufacturer. Carnegie spent the rest of his life donating his great wealth to charity. His gifts, totaling $350 million, helped establish libraries, schools, and even an organization to bring about world peace.

This caricature from 1902 shows steel tycoon Andrew Carnegie carrying library buildings. Carnegie established over 2,500 libraries and several educational institutions. Carnegie's charitable gifts helped offset charges that his wealth came at the expense of steel workers whose unions Carnegie opposed. **CIVIC VALUES** How does building public libraries benefit society? **3D, 8C, 8H**

⌐ 3C, 8A, 8D

Kellogg, Post, and the Cereal Wars

Some large corporations arose even though there was no demand for their products. Their developers were convinced that the new products could be sold to every American. First, however, the products would need a great deal of advertising. Such was the case of the Kellogg Toasted Corn Flake Company, incorporated in 1906.

The Kellogg Company was born in Battle Creek, Michigan, home of the Seventh Day Adventists (a Christian denomination). The Adventists, who were convinced that many bodily ills were due to improper diet, ate mainly vegetables. Their Battle Creek Sanitarium not only practiced their dietary beliefs but cared for large numbers of outsiders who could not find traditional cures for their health problems. The superintendent of the sanitarium was Dr. John Harvey Kellogg. He hoped to find a vegetarian breakfast for his patients to re-

W. K. Kellogg developed Corn Flakes as a vegetarian health food and started a revolution in American eating habits.
ECONOMICS What strategies did Kellogg use to market Corn Flakes? 8B, 9A

place the typical American breakfast of pancakes, salted meats, bacon fat, molasses, and coffee.

In 1877 Dr. Kellogg came up with what he called Granola, the first cold cereal for breakfast. It consisted of wheat, oatmeal, and cornmeal that had been baked slowly for several hours. Kellogg's patients ate the product, but complained that it tasted too much like heavy, toasted bread crumbs. By 1895 Dr. Kellogg got a patent for a toasted flake cereal made of wheat called Granose. It was light and tasty. So Dr. Kellogg started production for his patients.

Entrepreneurs soon came to Battle Creek to set up their own cold cereal companies. One was C. W. Post, who came up with a best-seller called Postum, a cereal coffee. Post also made a product called Grape Nuts that was advertised as a health remedy for malaria and loose teeth. Soon, when Americans thought of cold cereal they thought of C. W. Post's new company.

Not to be outdone, Dr. Kellogg and his brother W. K. Kellogg came up with a flaked corn cereal to outsell Post's products. They called it Kellogg's Corn Flakes. W. K. Kellogg opened the Kellogg Company in 1906 and began mass-producing the new product. The cereal firms in Battle Creek rushed to make their own version of corn flakes, and by 1911 there were 108 different brands on the market. C. W. Post contributed his version, called Post Toasties, in 1911. A corn flake war was under way.

The Kellogg Company thought that advertising would provide the key to success for its product. The best way to market corn flakes, Kellogg decided, was for their taste, not health appeal. Too few Americans were interested in health food. One advertisement urged Americans to stop buying Kellogg's Corn Flakes because there weren't enough to go around. As he had expected, consumers responded by buying more.

The Kellogg Company used several kinds of promotions—gimmicks designed to increase sales. It put little trinkets in each box and drew games on the cardboard carton. The company sponsored contests for the prettiest cornflake-fed baby. Kellogg even gave its sales force a pep talk:

> When you call on your trade and they talk
> "Hard Times,"
> "Lower prices," and decided declines,
> But you talk and you smile, make the
> world look bright,
> And send in your orders every blamed
> night,
> Then you're a SALESMAN!
> By gad, you're a salesman.

The Kellogg Company and C. W. Post's firm have continued their lively competition up to the

100 UNIT 2 THE NATION TRANSFORMED

present day. Both companies took risks by making new products, used creative advertising and promotions, and adapted their products to keep pace with changing times. These tactics produced success for many other companies as well.

3A, 8C

Isaac Singer and the Sewing Machine

Some American corporations prospered by taking an old product, making a few improvements, and marketing it in an exciting way. Such was the case of the Singer Company, producer of the sewing machine. The sewing machine had been invented by a Frenchman named Barthélemy Thimonnier in 1830. An American inventor, Elias Howe, got a patent for his version of the sewing machine in 1846. Yet neither man was able to market the new product successfully. Some 200 firms arose to make and sell the new product, but most had little success.

Isaac Merritt Singer, an inventor who spent most of his time trying to become a great actor, came up with his own design for a sewing machine in 1851. The first models had copied the arm motion of a tailor by using a large, curved needle that moved in a circle. This curved needle often got out of sequence and broke down. Singer's model, in contrast, sported a straight up-and-down needle that moved through the material faster and without hitches.

Singer had to defend his product in numerous patent wars—legal battles over who owned the various patents for a given product, in this case the sewing machine. A court ruled that Singer's machine was merely a refinement of Howe's earlier invention. This meant that Singer and other manufacturers had to pay Howe a royalty for each machine they produced. Thus the only way that businesses could make a great deal of money was to sell a great many sewing machines.

One way to increase sales was to cover two markets with one model. Earlier sewing machine manufacturers had concentrated on selling their products for use in the home. However, sales of home models were disappointingly low, because the machines were small, expensive, and unreliable. Singer made a sturdy machine for use by clothing manufacturers, and then he marketed this same machine to housewives.

This poster was part of the Singer Company's advertising campaign for its home sewing machines. Isaac Merritt Singer was the first person to spend a million dollars a year on advertising. CULTURE What indications does the poster give concerning the role of women in the mid-1800s? 4E, 8C, 8D, 9B

The Singer Company originally relied on commission agents to sell its machines. These were not employees of the firm, but independent salespersons who received a percentage of their total sales. However, Singer soon realized that these agents simply wanted to sell the model, get the money, and forget about the customer. Many did not even know how the machines worked. Singer set up stores across the nation containing trained employees. A salesperson sold the product, a demonstrator showed how it worked, a mechanic repaired broken machines, and a manager oversaw the complete operation. The firm also started an installment plan, whereby consumers could buy a

Section Review Answers

1. *corporation*—Business organization owned by stockholding investors. *dividend*—Portion of corporate profits. *economies of scale*—The more units of a product a company makes, the less it costs to make each unit. *limited liability*—Stockholder in a corporation can lose only as much money as invested. *vertical integration*—Combining steps involved in turning a raw material into a finished product. *horizontal integration*—Expanding in one area of production. *promotion*—Gimmick to increase sales. *patent war*—Legal battle over who owns patents for a given product. *installment plan*—Plan in which consumer buys a product by paying small sums over time.

2. *John D. Rockefeller*—Organized the Standard Oil Company. *Andrew Carnegie*—Scottish immigrant who revolutionized steel industry. *J. P. Morgan*—Investment banker who formed U.S. Steel Corporation. *John Kellogg*—Developed breakfast cereal. *C. W. Post*—Kellogg's major competitor. *Isaac Singer*—Sewing machine manufacturer who used many techniques to increase sales.

3. Can raise large amounts of capital; stockholders enjoy limited liability; corporation not affected by death or resignation of owner.

4. Those figures allowed companies to figure out the most efficient and inexpensive way to make a product, which could then be sold at a lower price, increasing company sales.

5. Might have said that he was cutting costs which might mean lower prices for the consumer; also pushing out inefficient companies.

Closure

Ask one student to transform the Main Idea of the section into a question, and have other students answer that question. Then have students read Section 4 for the next class period, noting the problems the government faced in its attempts to regulate business in the late 1800s.

SECTION 4

Government and Business

(pp. 102–107)

Section Objective

■ describe the changes in the relationship between government and business in the late 1800s

Introducing the Section

Connecting with Past Learnings
Remind students that before the Civil War, tariffs were the most significant way that the government influenced business. *Why did northerners and southerners feel differently about tariffs?* (North favored

---

machine by paying a small sum of money over several months.

Dependable sales and service soon allowed the Singer Company to become the world's leading producer of sewing machines. In 1874 Singer built the largest factory in the world at Elizabethport, New Jersey, and eleven years later set up a factory in Scotland. The company also vertically integrated, buying iron mills, timber lands, and even transportation firms.

One major problem remained for Singer: resales. Its sewing machine lasted indefinitely, which meant that once a customer bought a model, there was no reason to purchase another. Singer responded by developing new models with more technological features and by encouraging customers to trade in their old models for new ones. The Singer Company spent so much money advertising its new models that the Singer name became known all across the country.

SECTION REVIEW

1. KEY TERMS corporation, dividend, economies of scale, limited liability, vertical integration, horizontal integration, promotion, patent war, installment plan

2. PEOPLE John D. Rockefeller, Andrew Carnegie, J. P. Morgan, John Kellogg, C. W. Post, Isaac Singer

3. COMPREHENSION What advantages did corporations offer over other kinds of businesses?

4. COMPREHENSION Why did both Rockefeller and Carnegie feel that it was important to have accurate figures on company costs?

5. CRITICAL THINKING Many people complained that it was unfair for any company to gain a monopoly over an industry. How might John D. Rockefeller have responded to this charge?

2A, 3A, 3C, 3D, 3F, 3G, 4D, 4E, 5D, 8B, 8C, 8D, 8F, 8G, 9B, 9D, 9E

4 Government and Business

Section Focus

Key Terms laissez faire ■ Morrill Tariff ■ National Banking Act ■ interstate commerce ■ Morrill Act ■ subsidy ■ pool ■ trust ■ Interstate Commerce Act ■ Sherman Antitrust Act

Main Idea Government at all levels spurred the growth of industry. As some corporations grew larger and more powerful, however, the federal government took steps toward regulating business.

Objectives As you read, look for answers to these questions:
1. How did government aid the growth of business?
2. What led to popular anger against big business?
3. What efforts were made to regulate business?

What was the proper role of government regarding the industries that were springing up across the nation? Should it try to help them grow? Should it lay down rules of operation for businesses? Until the 1880s, the most common answer

8B to these questions was laissez faire (LES–ay FAYR), a French phrase meaning "let people do as they choose." The theory of laissez faire stated that business would run most efficiently if govern-

ment kept out of economic affairs. As business prospered, the people as a whole would benefit.

In reality, during the middle of the 1800s the federal government took many steps to aid business. Most of these actions took place during the Civil War. Congress, faced with the urgent need to mobilize the nation's resources to conduct the war, passed several bills that had far-reaching effects on the nation's economy.

102 UNIT 2   THE NATION TRANSFORMED

SUPPORTING THE SECTION

Reinforcement Workbook: Worksheet 16
Reteaching Resources: Worksheet 16
Enrichment and Extension Resources: Primary Source Worksheet 8
Teaching Transparencies: Transparency 16

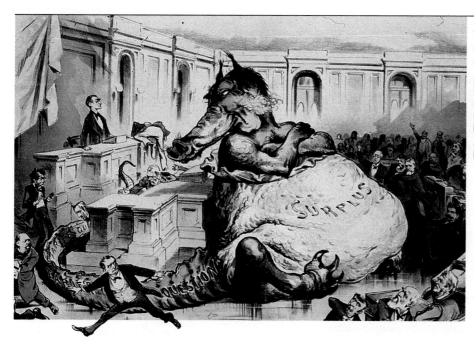

This cartoon shows congressmen fleeing in panic from an enormous dragon labeled *surplus*. The cartoon illustrates how tariffs—taxes on imported goods—gave the nation's treasury a surplus of $100 million by 1887. **ECONOMICS** Which Americans benefited most from high tariffs? **8B, 8G, 9B**

THE MORRILL TARIFF 3F

One way Congress helped business during the Civil War was through higher tariffs. In 1861 Congress passed the Morrill Tariff, which called for a sizable increase in tariff rates. The federal government raised tariff rates even higher as the war progressed. High tariffs brought in desperately needed revenue to help pay for the war. Even after 1865, tariff rates remained high because they were such a useful source of revenue.

In fact, tariffs brought the federal government so much money that it did not have to tax big business. After the Civil War, the federal treasury often had more money than it could spend. Although corporate wealth rose greatly in that period, there was no federal corporate income tax. Nor was there the need for an individual income tax. Corporations that made large profits could reinvest them, provide bigger dividends to the stockholders, or pay corporate heads higher salaries.

American businesses had their own reason for liking high tariffs. Tariffs were usually placed on goods, such as steel rails, which were cheaper to produce in Europe. Without foreign competition, the American companies making steel rails could make huge profits, charging prices far above their costs of production.

BANKING 3G

Another wartime measure, the National Banking Act of 1863, aided big business by creating a system of federally licensed banks. Previously, states had licensed all banks. Many state regulations, however, were lax. They did not require banks, for example, to keep adequate cash reserves on hand.

Most states also let their banks issue paper money called bank notes. In 1862, for example, about 1,500 state banks issued over 7,000 different notes. The value of these notes varied from time to time, depending on how many notes a specific bank issued. If an institution printed too many notes, their value dropped. The number of different notes, as well as their unstable value, made life miserable for companies trying to do business in several states.

The National Banking Act gave individuals the opportunity to set up banks chartered by the federal government rather than by the states. People who wanted to set up a bank had to deposit a certain amount of gold with the Comptroller of the Currency. (This requirement both strengthened the banks and boosted the federal government's gold reserves.) Banks also had to keep a certain amount of cash on hand for their customers.

Further, the act created a national currency, called National Bank Notes. The federal govern-

tariffs that raised the prices of European manufactured goods, making American goods—made mostly in the North—more competitive. Tariffs meant higher prices for southerners, who sold raw materials and had to buy manufactured goods.)

Key Terms
List the key terms on the board and ask students to define them. Have students identify the terms connected to acts of Congress and create a timeline from these terms, listing the date, term, and definition. **LEP**

Focus

What adjectives describe corporations in the late 1800s? (Strong, efficient, big.)

Ask students to list government actions which fostered the expansion of business. Write this list on one side of the board. Then have them list ways that states and the federal government tried to regulate business and put this list on the other half of the board.

Why did the government begin to regulate business? (Worried that corporations were too powerful.) *How effective were these attempts?* (Not very, because the Supreme Court declared many of the laws unconstitutional.)

Photo Caption Answer
Manufacturers with foreign competition.

Background   About half of the federal government's annual revenues in the 1880s came from customs receipts. Relying mostly on tariffs, the United States experienced budget surpluses throughout the decade.

After students have read the section, you may want to consider the following activities:

Analyzing Controversial Issues

Have students explain how tariffs reduce imports. (They raise prices of foreign goods above domestic goods so that consumers buy fewer imports.) *How might a foreign country respond to an increase in U.S. tariffs?* (Raise their own tariffs on U.S. goods.)

Have students debate the issue of protectionism in light of today's unfavorable balance of trade. *Should the United States raise tariffs to protect troubled businesses?*

Ethics

Discuss the business practices of Gould and Fisk, asking students if they feel that those men's behavior was acceptable. *Do you think that business leaders operate under a different set of moral standards than other people? Should they?*

Economics

Have students draw diagrams representing the structures of a corporation, a pool, and a trust. The diagrams should clearly show the different way each business organization functions.

Cause and Effect

Have students examine the chart on this page, and ask them to consider another heading on the chart, *Long-Term Effects*. Have them add entries under that new heading. (Possibilities include higher standard of living, becoming a major world power, depletion of natural resources.)

CAUSE AND EFFECT: INDUSTRIAL GROWTH

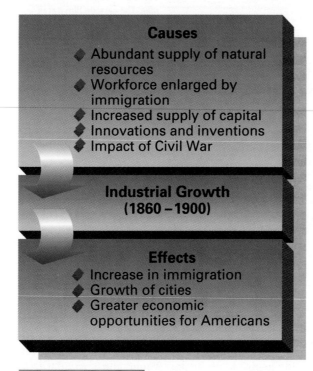

Causes
- Abundant supply of natural resources
- Workforce enlarged by immigration
- Increased supply of capital
- Innovations and inventions
- Impact of Civil War

Industrial Growth (1860–1900)

Effects
- Increase in immigration
- Growth of cities
- Greater economic opportunities for Americans

CHART SKILLS 2A, 9E

This chart summarizes important economic and social changes that occurred during the period of industrialization in the late nineteenth century. How did the Civil War contribute to industrial growth? CRITICAL THINKING Explain how industrial growth contributed to the growth of cities.

ment provided these notes to national banks in limited numbers so as to keep their value high. New taxes on the state banking notes eventually made it too expensive for the state banks to issue them at all.

The result was a much more stable banking system. A single national currency made it easy for firms to engage in interstate commerce—business across state lines. Corporations had higher confidence in national banks because they were regulated by the federal government and were less likely to fail. But not everyone was pleased with the federal government's stronger role in the banking system. Many in the West and South came to feel that eastern banks now had control over the nation's money supply.

EDUCATION 3A, 4E

The Morrill Act of 1862 also assisted big business in America, although not right away. It was designed to fix a major problem with public education in the nation. Most states had public elementary schools by the time of the Civil War, and many others were starting to set up public secondary schools. Higher education, however, was largely in the hands of private institutions. There were too few private colleges and universities to serve the needs of a growing population. These schools, in addition, emphasized the study of ancient civilizations and their languages. Such courses were inadequate for farmers and business persons, who needed practical training.

The Morrill Act gave each state federal land to be used to set up a public institution of higher education "for the benefit of Agriculture and the Mechanic Arts." These new public institutions, such as Michigan State University, were often the first ones in a state. Some used the term "A & M" (for "agriculture and mechanical" college) to signify their focus. These state institutions did offer the traditional courses. However, they also sponsored important research and provided instruction in business and agriculture. By opening up the

This photograph shows a class at Michigan State University, home to one of the nation's earliest agricultural programs. Government support for agricultural education helped prepare students for work as food scientists, veterinarians, farmers, and ranchers. SCIENCE What might these students have been studying? 9B

Chart Skills Answers
The war stimulated northern industries to supply the Union army's needs and it later forced the South to rely less on agriculture. Since industries were usually located in cities they attracted workers and capital to urban areas.

Photo Caption Answer
Students may suggest animal biology or veterinary science.

promise of higher education to a larger part of the population, these land-grant institutions helped make the American work force one of the best-educated in the world.

POSTAL REFORM 4D, 8D

The federal government even helped businesses get their products to customers. In the early nineteenth century, the United States mail system had left much to be desired. Yet by the mid-1800s, Congress actually began to reduce mail rates. The U.S. Post Office also began in 1863 to deliver mail directly to city homes rather than have customers come to post offices. Farmers, who often had to travel long distances to a post office, were provided with the same convenience in 1896. This was called Rural Free Delivery (RFD).

Corporations selling goods by mail, such as Montgomery Ward and Sears, Roebuck and Company, took full advantage of the lower rates and improved service. Huge catalogs describing these companies' products were mailed to customers across the nation. Big businesses also campaigned for a better system of sending packages to customers, who had to rely on private express companies charging high rates. Congress passed legislation in 1913 establishing an inexpensive parcel post system throughout the nation. Big corporations got bigger through an expanded mail service. Soon Sears, Roebuck was opening 27,000 letters per hour from customers and sending out orders within 24 hours. Within a week after an order was placed, customers received their products, absolutely delighted with such speedy service.

GOVERNMENT INCENTIVES TO BUSINESS 3F

Governments at the local, state, and federal level also used different kinds of subsidies—payments—to support business. Towns and cities offered corporations free factory sites and tax breaks to encourage them to move there. States likewise used various incentives to lure businesses away from other areas.

No industry benefited more from government help than the railroads. Railroads were so important to the economy that the federal government rewarded them for carrying the mail by paying

them far more than it cost to perform this service. States aided railroads with tax breaks and gifts of money. Both state and federal governments donated land as well—more than 150 million acres. Much of this land contained timber and other natural resources that the railroad companies were free to develop or sell.

IS BIGGER BETTER? 3C, 8F

The railroads, which had profited so handsomely from government handouts, were one of the first targets of rising public anger toward big business. Farmers, who depended on trains to transport their goods to market, were especially angry. In places served by only one railroad, railroad rates were often high. In addition, some railroad companies sometimes lowered the freight charges for large shippers, which put smaller firms at a disadvantage.

People also complained about the actions of railroad tycoons such as Jay Gould. In 1867 Gould found that Cornelius Vanderbilt, another fabulously wealthy railroad head, was buying up stock in Gould's Erie Railroad. Gould illegally flooded the stock market with thousands of shares of Erie stock. This made Vanderbilt's stock (and the stock of smaller investors) nearly worthless. Gould then bought back control of Erie, pocketing several million dollars in profit.

Two years later, Gould and a speculator named James Fisk tried to corner the gold market. They bought up vast amounts of gold, thereby driving up its price. When the federal government found

BIOGRAPHY 3D

JAY GOULD (1836–1892) was one of the most successful and notorious "robber barons." Through shrewd and often illegal stock acquisitions, bribery of politicians, and ruthless dealings with competitors, Gould became the leading railroad tycoon of the late 1800s. In 1869 Gould tried to corner the gold market and triggered the Black Friday financial panic. Many smaller investors suffered losses as a result of his manipulations.

Civic Values
Ask students to explain how monopolies, pools, and trusts contradict the free enterprise system. (They destroy competition, the means by which fair prices and wages are determined.) *What should the government do to encourage or ensure competition?* (Suggestions may range from nothing to imposition of guidelines or restraints against monopoly.)

Constitutional Heritage
Have students paraphrase the commerce clause in the Constitution—Article I, Section 8, Clause 3. (It gives Congress the power to regulate commerce among the states.) Explain to them that in an early case, *Gibbons v. Ogden* (1824), the Supreme Court defined commerce as the movement of services and people as well as goods.

Using this information, have students discuss the three questions in the last paragraph of the section.

C Cooperative Learning

Divide the class into groups. Establish three pairs in each group—representing business, Congress, and the Supreme Court. Have each group debate one of the following laws or cases: Interstate Commerce Act, Sherman Antitrust Act, *Santa Clara County v. Southern Pacific Railroad Company,* and *Chicago, Milwaukee, and St. Paul Railway Co. v. Minnesota.* **LEP**

Biography
Ask students if they think that Gould would be as successful in business today as he was 100 years ago. Have them consider in what ways business practices have changed in the last century.

SOCIAL HISTORY
Famous Firsts

1859	First commercial oil well, at Titusville, Pennsylvania.
1867	First elevated railroad opened to public, New York City (July 2).
1869	Central Pacific and Union Pacific railroads meet at Promontory, Utah (May 10).
1873	First illustrated daily newspaper, *New York Daily Graphic*.
1875	First electric dental drill patented.
1879	Frank Woolworth opens first Five and Ten Cents Store, Utica, N.Y.
1881	Lewis Latimer patents an improved incandescent light bulb.
1888	Tutti-Frutti Gum, first chewing gum sold from vending machines, on station platforms of the New York Elevated Railroad.
1889	First daily railroad service to West Coast without a change of trains (Nov. 17).

out, it quickly sold some of its gold in order to bring gold prices back down. But before this could happen, Gould and Fisk sold their gold at the higher price, earning some $11 million in the process. Average investors were not so lucky. The wild swings in the price of gold sparked a financial panic that ruined many people.

Beyond the actions of a few greedy individuals, there was a larger problem: declining competition. In order to raise their profits, many firms decided to join together to limit competition. A **pool** was an agreement among several firms to control their output and divide up the market. A **trust** was a group of companies whose stock was controlled by a central board of directors. Using their vast resources, pools and trusts could push their smaller rivals out of business.

Throughout the 1870s and 1880s, larger firms swallowed up smaller ones in many different industries—steel, oil, meat packing, and so on. By 1900 there were fewer companies in most business fields than there had been in 1865. These develop-

ments alarmed small businesses (which could not compete with the new giants) as well as consumers (who worried that prices would skyrocket as competition declined). The public at large grew uneasy at the arrogance of the leaders of these business giants. When told that his actions violated New York state laws, Cornelius Vanderbilt is said to have responded, "Law! What do I care about law? Hain't [Haven't] I got the power?"

> "**L**aw! What do I care about law?"
> —*Cornelius Vanderbilt*

CORPORATIONS AND THE COURTS 5D, 8B, 8C

Pressed by angry citizens, several state legislatures passed laws in the 1880s regulating the operations of big business. Yet in 1886, two Supreme Court decisions severely limited states' abilities to regulate corporations. In *Wabash, St. Louis and Pacific Railroad Company v. Illinois* the Court ruled that states could not regulate railroads moving across state lines. Such railroads, said the Court, were involved in interstate commerce. Only Congress could regulate them.

The other case—*Santa Clara County v. Southern Pacific Railroad Company*—concerned the Fourteenth Amendment (page 69). This amendment, ratified in 1868, declared that states could not "deprive any person of life, liberty, or property, without due process of law." Though the amendment had been designed to protect blacks from discrimination, the Supreme Court declared that it also protected corporations, since a corporation was legally a "person." This meant that states could not seize or harshly regulate corporate property.

In 1890 a third Supreme Court decision reinforced these limits on state powers. In *Chicago, Milwaukee & St. Paul Railway Co. v. Minnesota*, the Court ruled that state regulation of big businesses had to be "reasonable." That is, regulation could not be so severe that the corporation would be unable to earn a fair profit. The final determination of what was "reasonable," according to the Court, was to be left to judges.

106 UNIT 2 THE NATION TRANSFORMED

EARLY FEDERAL REGULATIONS 8G

While the Supreme Court was limiting the power of the states to regulate business, Congress was moving in the opposite direction. Responding to popular pressure, it passed two historic bills. The Interstate Commerce Act of 1887 established a commission whose goal was to make certain that railroads charged "reasonable and just" rates. This task proved nearly impossible. Sixteen times between 1887 and 1905 the railroad companies went to court to block the commission's rulings. The railroads won all but one of those cases. As a corporation lawyer explained to a railroad executive in 1892:

> The commission . . . can be made of great use to the railroads. It satisfies the popular clamor for a government supervision of railroads, at the same time that such supervision is almost entirely nominal [in name only]. . . .

Congress passed the Sherman Antitrust Act in 1890. Its aim was to prevent corporations from trying "to monopolize any part of trade or commerce among the several states." The penalty for violating the act was severe. Corporate officials could go to jail. A guilty corporation, in addition, would have to pay three times the amount of money lost by its competitors. In other words, suppose a competitor firm proved that it lost $100,000 in business because of illegal actions. Then the guilty corporation would have to pay $300,000 in damages. Monopolies could also be broken up entirely.

Like the Interstate Commerce Act, the Sherman Antitrust Act fell victim to legal haggling. One writer joked, "What looks like a stone wall to a layman, is a triumphal arch to a corporation lawyer." Corporations took advantage of every ambiguity in the Sherman Antitrust Act to avoid abiding by it.

Both these early efforts at government regulation were hamstrung by their lack of clarity. What constituted a monopoly or a trust? What was the definition of interstate commerce? Under what conditions was the violation of the law so serious as to justify breaking up the monopoly? Early in the twentieth century, a reform movement known as progressivism (Chapter 9) would provide more precise answers to these questions.

SECTION REVIEW

1. KEY TERMS laissez faire, Morrill Tariff, National Banking Act, interstate commerce, Morrill Act, subsidy, pool, trust, Interstate Commerce Act, Sherman Antitrust Act

2. PEOPLE Jay Gould, Cornelius Vanderbilt, James Fisk

3. COMPREHENSION Why did the decline in competition among businesses alarm people?

4. COMPREHENSION What were the shortcomings of the Interstate Commerce Act and the Sherman Antitrust Act?

5. CRITICAL THINKING Was the government being inconsistent in both supporting the rise of business and then trying to control its power? Explain.

9D

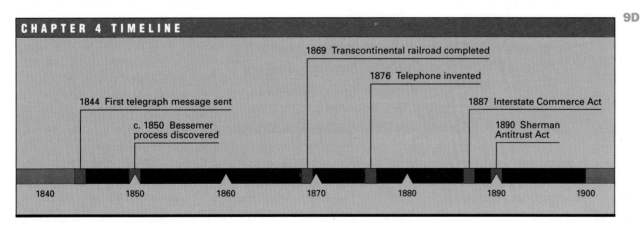

CHAPTER 4 TIMELINE

1844 First telegraph message sent
c. 1850 Bessemer process discovered
1869 Transcontinental railroad completed
1876 Telephone invented
1887 Interstate Commerce Act
1890 Sherman Antitrust Act

1840   1850   1860   1870   1880   1890   1900

National Banking Act—Created a system of federally licensed banks. *interstate commerce*—Business across state lines. *Morrill Act*—Gave states federal land for public institutions of higher learning. *subsidy*—Government payments to support business. *pool*—Agreement among several firms to control output and divide up their market. *trust*—Group of companies whose stock was controlled by a central board of directors. *Interstate Commerce Act*—Established commission to ensure that railroads charged reasonable rates. *Sherman Antitrust Act*—Aimed at keeping corporations from monopolizing trade.

2. *Jay Gould*—Railroad tycoon. *Cornelius Vanderbilt*—Wealthy head of railroads. *James Fisk*—Speculator who, with Gould, tried to corner the gold market.

3. Consumers worried that businesses would raise prices.

4. Both lacked clarity so that businesses were able to successfully defend themselves in court.

5. No; wholehearted support of business came earlier, when businesses were getting started; control came later, when some companies had grown so powerful they hurt small businesses and investors.

Closure

Call students' attention to the boxed beige quotation (p. 106). Ask how this quotation relates to the main idea of the section. Then have students read Section 1 of Chapter 5 for the next class period, noting the causes for conflicts between settlers and American Indians in the West.

Chapter 4 Review Answers

Key Terms
1. standard gauge
2. corporation
3. installment plan
4. Vertical integration
5. dividend

People to Identify
1. Inventor of the telephone.
2. Discovered how to make steel cheaply from iron.
3. Steel industry genius who devised horizontal integration.
4. Inventor of over a thousand patented devices.
5. Engineered the incorporation of U.S. Steel.
6. Inventor of the telegraph.
7. Organized and headed the Standard Oil Company.

Places to Locate
1. D   4. A
2. C   5. B
3. E

Reviewing the Facts
1. The expansion of industry, the settlement of the West, and the growth of cities. Industry depended on raw materials from the West, the West relied on industrial advances, and cities needed industries to supply jobs and goods.
2. The abundance of natural resources, the growing number of workers, a larger pool of capital, and new inventions.
3. The Bessemer process increased the rate of production, making steel cheap. Steel was used in building skyscrapers, machines, and railroads.
4. Railroads brought the West closer to the East, carried troops, mail, and trade, spurred the growth of cities, and increased opportunities to settle in the West.
5. The telegraph and telephone increased the pace of buying stocks, allowed merchants to order goods, and transmitted the latest news.

Chapter 4 REVIEW

CHAPTER 4 SUMMARY

SECTION 1: Following the Civil War, the United States underwent a social and economic revolution.

■ The Civil War spurred industrial development, which changed American life.

■ The growth of a national network of railroads fostered settlement of the frontier.

■ Industrialization was made possible by vast natural resources, a large labor force, the availability of capital, and government policies that favored innovation.

SECTION 2: Advances in energy, transportation, and communications transformed both industrial production and daily life in the late 1800s.

■ A national network of railroads revolutionized business and transportation.

■ The invention of the electric generator made electrical power available for factories and cities.

■ The telephone and telegraph speeded communications.

SECTION 3: Innovations in business led to the growth of huge industries.

■ Compared to private companies, corporations were more stable, could raise more money, and could produce more cheaply.

■ Such innovations as vertical and horizontal integration, sales promotions, professional sales forces, and installment buying fueled economic growth.

SECTION 4: The dominance of big business changed many people's attitudes toward the government's role in the economy.

■ Declining competition in many industries prompted public demands for government regulation of business practices.

■ The Supreme Court blocked early attempts to regulate business.

■ Through the Sherman Antitrust Act and Interstate Commerce Act, the federal government tried with little success to curb the power of large companies.

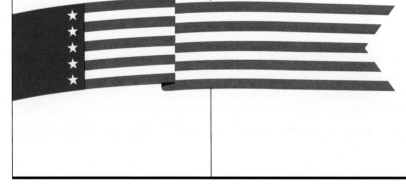

KEY TERMS ●

Use one of the following terms to complete each of the sentences below.

corporation
dividend
installment plan
standard gauge
vertical integration

1. A _____ makes it possible for the cars of one railroad line to use the tracks of another railroad line.
2. A _____ is created when a state legislature allows a group of people to sell stock to fund a business enterprise.
3. Buying something on the _____ means that it can be paid for over a number of months rather than all at once.
4. _____ is gaining control of all the steps involved in turning raw materials into a finished product.
5. Part of a corporation's profits are paid to each shareholder in the form of a _____ .

PEOPLE TO IDENTIFY ●

Identify the following people and tell why each was important.

1. Alexander Graham Bell
2. Henry Bessemer
3. Andrew Carnegie
4. Thomas Alva Edison
5. J. P. Morgan
6. Samuel F. B. Morse
7. John D. Rockefeller

---

6. A corporation can raise large amounts of capital; its stockholders enjoy limited liability; and it is not affected by death or resignation.

7. Vertical integration combines the steps involved in turning raw material into a finished product, cutting costs and promoting efficiency. Horizontal integration enables a company to produce a product more cheaply than competitors.

8. Laissez-faire capitalism states that government should keep out of economic affairs. The U.S. government aided business with higher tariffs, a system of federally licensed banks, an increased number of institutions of higher learning.

PLACES TO LOCATE ●

Match each of the letters on the map with the places that are listed below.

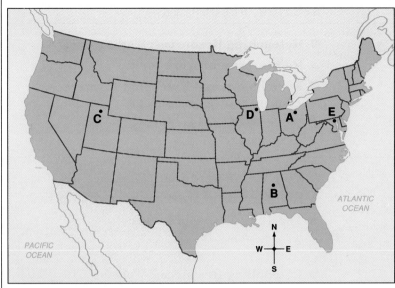

1. Chicago
2. Promontory, Utah
3. Baltimore
4. Cleveland
5. Birmingham

REVIEWING THE FACTS ▲

1. What three important trends shaped American life in the decades after the Civil War? What were three ways in which those trends were related?
2. What factors encouraged the growth of industry in the United States after 1860?
3. How did steel production change during the 1860s? Why was steel important to the industrialization of America?
4. How did the growth of vast railroad networks affect American life?
5. What inventions revolutionized communications in the 1800s? How did these inventions boost industry?

6. What are three advantages that corporations have over other forms of business organization?
7. How does vertical integration differ from horizontal integration? How does each increase an industry's efficiency?
8. What was the theory of laissez-faire capitalism? How did the United States government promote the growth of business?
9. What problems did monopolies create?
10. How did the Supreme Court limit the power of state legislatures to regulate big business?

CRITICAL THINKING SKILLS ▲

1. ANALYZING A QUOTATION
Read the following quotation: "What looks like a stone wall to a layman is a triumphal arch to a corporation lawyer." What do you think the author meant?

2. IDENTIFYING ADVANTAGES AND DISADVANTAGES How did industrialization and the growth of cities improve the quality of American life? How did they worsen it?

3. IDENTIFYING THE MAIN IDEA
In your own words, state the main idea of each of the passages under the first five headings of Section 4.

4. FORMING A HYPOTHESIS
Why did many Americans believe that prices would rise in industries that were dominated by a few companies? Explain how this might happen.

WRITING ABOUT TOPICS IN AMERICAN HISTORY ■

1. CONNECTING WITH LITERATURE
A selection from *1876* by Gore Vidal appears on pages 776–778. Read it and answer the questions. Then answer the following question: How was New York in 1876 more like the modern city than like the small town Schuyler remembered?

2. APPLYING THEMES: AMERICAN CULTURE The growth of railroads sparked the American imagination and spawned dozens of popular songs and poems. Find and read some of these songs and poems. Then write a report analyzing the themes in this folk literature.

Critical Thinking Skills
1. Answers should reflect that a lawyer could find loopholes in a law, allowing a corporation to avoid abiding by it.
2. Improvements were new conveniences within the home, improved transportation and communication, and greater opportunities for education and jobs. Overcrowding and pollution in the city lowered the quality of life.
3. The benefit of tariffs, the importance of a federal banking system, the improvement of the education system through the Morrill Act, the reform of postal service, and the incentive offered to business through government subsidies.
4. After pushing smaller companies out of business, larger ones could agree on a set price. With no competition, prices would most likely be higher.

Writing About Topics in American History
1. Students might point out that modern New York has a large foreign-born population, beggars on the streets, high crime rate, and elevated railways.
2. Students may discuss such themes as the struggle to build the railroad, freedom provided by railroad travel, the impact of railroads on surrounding towns, and others.

9. Monopolies decreased competition and raised prices.

10. By applying the Fourteenth Amendment to corporations, the Supreme Court kept states from closely regulating corporate properties.

Chapter Review exercises are keyed for student abilities:
● = Basic
▲ = Average
■ = Average/Advanced

Chapter 5 ▪ New Frontiers, New Resources 5 Sections, 5–7 Days

	SECTION OBJECTIVES	SECTION RESOURCES
Section 1 **The Conquest** **of the Indians**	▪ describe the response of American Indians to the settlement of the Great Plains	● **Reteaching Resources:** Worksheet 17 ▲ **Reinforcement Workbook:** Worksheet 17 ■ **Enrichment and Extension Resources:** Primary Source Worksheet 9 ▲ **Teaching Transparencies:** Transparency 17
Section 2 **The Cowboys and** **the Ranchers**	▪ describe the development of ranching on the Great Plains	● **Reteaching Resources:** Worksheet 18 ▲ **Reinforcement Workbook:** Worksheet 18 ▲ **Teaching Transparencies:** Transparency 18
Section 3 **Farming** **the Frontier**	▪ describe the role of the government and technology in the settlement of the Great Plains	● **Reteaching Resources:** Worksheet 19 ▲ **Reinforcement Workbook:** Worksheet 19 ■ **Enrichment and Extension Resources:** Primary Source Worksheet 10 ▲ **Teaching Transparencies:** Transparency 19
Section 4 **Mining and** **Lumbering**	▪ describe how mining and lumbering became major industries in the West	● **Reteaching Resources:** Worksheet 20 ▲ **Reinforcement Workbook:** Worksheet 20 ▲ **Teaching Transparencies:** Transparency 20
Section 5 **The Impact** **of the Frontier**	▪ explain the influence of the image of the western frontier on American culture	● **Reteaching Resources:** Worksheet 21 ▲ **Reinforcement Workbook:** Worksheet 21 ▲ **Teaching Transparencies:** Transparency 21

The list below shows Essential Elements relevant to this chapter. (The complete list of Essential Elements appears in the introductory pages of this Teacher's Edition.)

Section 1: 2B, 2D, 3A, 4C, 4F, 6C, 8I, 9A, 9B, 9G
Section 2: 3A, 3C, 9A, 9E
Section 3: 2C, 3A, 3C, 4B, 4C, 8C, 9A, 9B
Section 4: 2C, 2D, 3A, 4B, 4C, 9B
Section 5: 2B, 2C, 2D, 4F, 6A, 8I, 9D, 9F

> Section Resources are keyed for student abilities:
> ● = Basic
> ▲ = Average
> ■ = Average/Advanced

CHAPTER RESOURCES

Geography Resources: Worksheets 9, 10
Tests: Chapter 5 Test

Chapter Project: Geography

Have students create a scrapbook of westward migration told from the point of view of an Indian, a cowboy, a farming family, a miner, or a lumber tycoon. Encourage students to use drawings or copies of historical photographs in their scrapbooks. Explain that they can create newspaper clippings, letters, and other artifacts.

Homework Options

Each section contains activities labeled "Addressing Individual Needs." You may wish to choose from among these activities when assigning homework.

> **Provisions for Limited English Proficiency (LEP)**
> Several suggested activities may be particularly helpful for teachers of students with limited English proficiency. These activities have been marked throughout the Teacher's Annotated Edition with the symbol **LEP** .

BIBLIOGRAPHY AND AUDIOVISUAL AIDS

Teacher Bibliography

Billington, Ray. *Land of Savagery, Land of Promise: The European Image of the American Frontier in the Nineteenth Century.* University of Oklahoma Press, 1985.

Jackson, Helen Hunt. *A Century of Dishonor: A Sketch of the United States Government's Dealing with Some Indian Tribes.* Scholarly, 1972.

Pizer, Donald, ed. *Hamlin Garland's Early Work and Career.* Russell, 1969.

Student Bibliography

Freedman, Russell. *Cowboys of the Wild West.* Ticknor and Fields, 1985.

Jeffrey, Julie Roy. *Frontier Women: The Trans-Mississippi West 1840–1900.* Eric Foner, ed. Hill and Wang, 1979.

Literature

Brown, Dee. *Bury My Heart at Wounded Knee.* Washington Square Press, 1984. An impassioned account of American Indian history.

Cather Willa. *My Antonia.* Houghton Mifflin, 1988. A novel based on the author's experiences as a settler in Nebraska following the passage of the Homestead Act.

Custer, George Armstrong. *My Life on the Plains.* University of Nebraska Press, 1966.

Garland, Hamlin. *Main-Travelled Roads.* Folcroft, 1985. A collection of stories of life on the Plains.

Harte, Bret. *The Outcasts of Poker Flat.* Creative Education, 1980.

London, Jack. *The Call of the Wild.* Buccaneer Books, 1983.

Twain, Mark. *Roughing It.* Penguin, 1981.

Films and Videotapes*

Indians, Outlaws and Angie Debo (American Experience Series). 58 min. PBS. Historian Angie Debo came to Oklahoma in 1899 in a covered wagon. Decades later she reveals a conspiracy to rob the Indians of their oil-rich land.

Filmstrips*

Railroads West: 1870-1917 (set of 3). GA. Historical photographs and eyewitness accounts help illuminate this period of economic progress and social and moral change.

Computer Software*

The Indian Wars (2 or 3 disks: Apple or IBM). HS. The U.S. Army pushes westward while the Indians attempt to preserve their way of life.

*For a complete guide to audiovisual sources, see the introduction to this book (page Txx).

Chapter 5

New Frontiers, New Resources
(pp. 110–133)

This chapter describes the settlement of the West, its effect on American Indian culture, and the outcome of this settlement—the passing of the frontier in the United States.

Themes in American History

■ Economic development
■ American culture
■ Geography

Chapter Objectives

After students complete this chapter, they will be able to:

1. Describe the response of American Indians to the settlement of the Great Plains.

2. Describe the development of ranching on the Great Plains.

3. Describe the role of the government and technology in the settlement of the Great Plains.

4. Describe how mining and lumbering became major industries in the West.

5. Explain the influence of the image of the western frontier on American culture.

Chapter Opener Art
Edwin Deakin, *Wasatch Range from Immigrant Gap near Promontory, Utah.*

For centuries the land west of the Mississippi had been the home of Indian tribes. In the years following the Civil War, the arrival of ranchers, farmers, and miners brought sweeping changes to the Indians' ways of living.

CHAPTER SUPPORT MATERIAL

Reinforcement Workbook: Worksheets 17–21
Reteaching Resources: Worksheets 17–21
Enrichment and Extension Resources: Primary Source Worksheets 9, 10
Geography Resources: Worksheets 9, 10
Teaching Transparencies: Transparencies 17–21
Tests: Chapter 5 Test

5 New Frontiers, New Resources (1860–1900)

2B, 2D, 3A, 4C, 4F, 6C, 8I, 9A, 9B, 9G

1 The Conquest of the Indians

Section Focus

Key Terms Bureau of Indian Affairs ▪ assimilate ▪ Dawes Act

Main Idea The westward migration of white settlers cost the Plains Indians their lands and, ultimately, their way of life.

Objectives As you read, look for answers to these questions:
1. Why did fighting break out between settlers and Indians?
2. What was the outcome of the Indian wars?
3. How did the United States government treat the Indians?

We did not ask you white men to come here. The Great Spirit gave us this country as a home. You had yours. We did not interfere with you. . . . But you have come here; you are taking my land from me. . . . You say, why do you not become civilized? We do not want your civilization!

Chief Crazy Horse spoke for all the Indians of the Great Plains when he uttered these words. Although angered by the coming of the settlers, the Indians were nevertheless unable to halt the drive westward.

THE GEOGRAPHY OF THE FRONTIER 2D

At first, most Americans were content to let the Indians remain on the Great Plains forever. From the 100th meridian west to the Rocky Mountains, pioneers had noted, the annual rainfall gradually decreases. As a result, maps of the early 1800s called the plains the "Great American Desert." The idea that the West was an uninhabited wasteland was wrong, however. First, far from being barren, the region had many riches to offer. The fertile Plains soil could support both ranching and farming. Valuable minerals were buried in the mountains. Second, both the agricultural frontier and the mining frontier were inhabited by Indians. These conditions set the stage for the two great dramas of westward expansion—the destruction of the Indians and the development of the region's natural resources.

By the 1850s, pioneers passing through the Great Plains were reporting that much of the country was good for cattle ranching and farming. White settlers gradually began to move onto the Plains. Soon, this westward procession swelled into a flood. The Civil War played an important role. Needing food for its soldiers and raw materials for its factories, the North encouraged people to move west. The war's end brought another spurt of settlement, with thousands of ex-soldiers heading west. As industry continued to expand and cities continued to grow in the late 1800s, the country's appetite for the products of western mines, ranches, and farms reached new heights.

CHAPTER 5   NEW FRONTIERS, NEW RESOURCES, 1860–1900   **111**

SECTION 1

The Conquest of the Indians
(pp. 111–116)

Section Objective

▪ describe the response of American Indians to the settlement of the Great Plains

Introducing the Section

Connecting with Past Learnings
Review with students government actions relating to the Indians. *What was Andrew Jackson's policy toward Indians in the 1830's?* (Forced Indians in southeastern United States to move to Indian Territory.) *In general, what was government policy toward Indians?* (They were usually forced to move when white settlers wanted Indian lands.)

Key Terms
Have students find where the key terms are defined in context and ask individual students to define terms in their own words. Have students use *assimilate* in an original sentence. **LEP**

Focus

On the board, create a vertical timeline. On one side, have students enter important dates in western settlement. (1840s—American settlement of California and Oregon; 1858—gold in Colorado; 1869—completion of transcontinental railroad; 1875—gold rush in the Dakotas; 1889—opening of Oklahoma.) On the other side, ask students to list important dates in the history of the Plains Indians. (Early

But it was one thing to want what the West had to offer, and another thing to get at it. Here is where the railroad came in. The railroad carried settlers west, supplied them with products from the East, and transported western products back to eastern factories. The completion of the transcontinental railroad in 1869 marked the end of the West's isolation from the rest of the country. It also sealed the fate of the Indians.

CONFLICT ON THE PLAINS 81
Many Americans in the 1800s argued that development of the West required total defeat of the Indians. They asked how two cultures so different from each other could live side by side.

The Indians knew that they had to fight the settlers or lose their land. The Indians had good cause to view the Plains as their legal homeland. In the early 1800s the federal government had designated the Plains as "one big reservation" for Indians. However, after heavy settlement of Oregon and California started in the 1840s, people clamored for a new policy.

Federal officials eventually bowed to public pressure and switched to a policy of concentration. Under that policy, the tribes would allow settlers free passage through their territories and would confine their hunting to specific areas. In an 1851 treaty with the federal government, several Indian tribes agreed to these conditions.

The policy of concentration failed for two reasons. First, Plains Indians depended on the buffalo for food and most other essentials of life. Thus they wandered outside their assigned boundaries in pursuit of game. Second, the discovery of gold in Colorado in 1858 unleashed hordes of prospectors. These prospectors had little respect for Indian territorial rights.

The federal government tried to reach a new agreement with the Indians. Yet hopes for peace were dashed in 1864. After a few skirmishes between whites and Indians in Colorado, Chief Black Kettle of the Cheyenne had agreed to an armistice. Colonel John M. Chivington, head of Colorado's militia, knew nothing of the armistice. It was dawn on November 28, 1864. Chivington and 1,000 troops swept into the sleeping Cheyenne camp on the banks of the Sand Creek. Ignoring an

American flag and a white flag that Black Kettle raised as a sign of peace, the attackers massacred some 450 Indians. An eyewitness later recalled the Sand Creek Massacre:

> There seemed to be indiscriminate slaughter of men, women, and children. There were some 30 or 40 women collected in a hole for protection; they sent out a little girl about six years old with a white flag on a stick; she had not proceeded but a few steps when she was shot and killed. All the squaws in that hole were afterwards killed. . . .

Fighting also broke out between whites and the Sioux. In 1862–1863 the Sioux raided white settlements in Minnesota. That conflict ended when Little Crow, the Sioux leader, was killed. The government forced the Sioux to move westward to Montana. In 1865 the government began building a road through Sioux lands in Montana. Once again the Sioux went to war. In December 1866, a band of Sioux led by Red Cloud ambushed a convoy traveling along the new road. Captain W. J. Fetterman and all 82 soldiers in his party were wiped out.

The Sioux War ended in 1868. In that year a peace commission from Washington, D.C., replaced the concentration policy with a policy of reservations. These were small, sharply defined areas supervised by federal officials and closed off to non-Indian settlement.

While some Indians agreed to move to reservations, others refused. For another six years Indians battled army troops. The army ultimately defeated the Indians, and by 1874 a number of small reservations, usually on the poorest lands, dotted the Plains.

THE END OF THE INDIAN WARS 3A
In 1875 the lure of gold struck once again, this time in the Dakota Territory. Thousands of prospectors tramped across the territory to reach new finds in the Black Hills—lands sacred to the Sioux. Furious, the Sioux declared war.

The most famous battle of what was called the Second Sioux War took place on June 25, 1876. On that day, an arrogant and flamboyant general

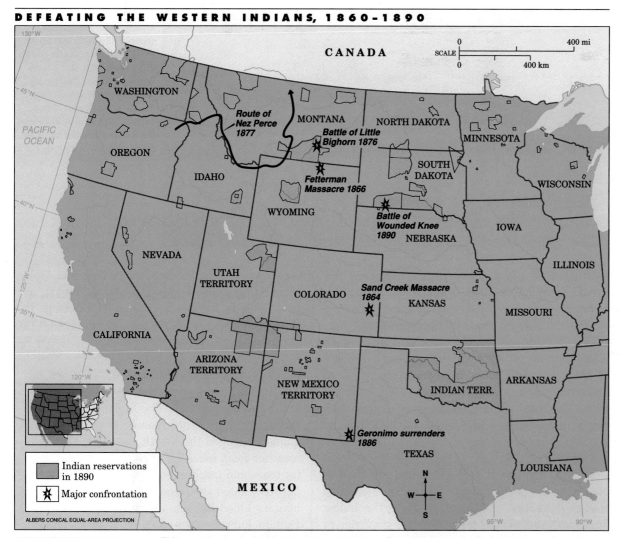

This map shows principal battles between Indians and the U.S. Army. In which states were the last major Indian wars fought? Which territory had the largest Indian reservations? **CRITICAL THINKING** What determined the location of Indian reservations?

Legend:
- Indian reservations in 1890
- ✹ Major confrontation

ALBERS CONICAL EQUAL-AREA PROJECTION

---

named George Armstrong Custer swooped down on a Sioux camp. The Sioux, led by Chief Sitting Bull, far outnumbered Custer's forces. With such outstanding warriors as Crazy Horse, the Sioux killed all 265 soldiers at the Battle of Little Bighorn—also called "Custer's Last Stand."

Little Bighorn was the last great Indian victory on the Plains. Though they fought bravely, the Indians could not match the army's technology. The telegraph gave the army speedy communication: troops could now be called out at the first sign of trouble. The railroad allowed the army to outrun even the swiftest horses. And with the six-shot

Colt revolver and other modern weapons, army soldiers held a huge advantage in firepower. The army also benefited from the courage and professionalism of its soldiers, including two highly decorated black units, the 9th and 10th Cavalry.

Still, the Indians did not give up easily. Fighting between Indians and the army went on for over a decade after the Battle of Little Bighorn, on the Plains and elsewhere. In 1877 the Nez Perce of Oregon went to war rather than give up their lands. Pursued by government troops, Chief Joseph led his people on a harrowing 1,500-mile trek across Oregon, Idaho, and Montana. They were

---

Discuss with students the U.S. response to Indian attacks. *Do you think the government treated Indians unfairly? Should anything be done today to compensate Indians for the loss of their land?*

Impact of Geography
Have students compare the map on this page with the map of mining towns on page 125. *What mining area was the Sand Creek Massacre near?* (Pikes Peak.) *What precious metal was being mined near where Geronimo surrendered?* (Silver.) Make sure that students note that while Indian reservations were often close to mining areas, they did not overlap.

Cultural Pluralism
How was the Plains Indians' way of life destroyed in the late 1800s? (Buffalo herds which had provided their food, shelter, and clothing were destroyed; reservation land was so poor that many Indians became dependent on the government and fell prey to illness, alcoholism, and despair.) *How did the Dawes Act attempt to help Indians?* (It aimed to speed the process of assimilation by weakening tribal ties.)

Ask students if they would have chosen to accept a plot of land and American citizenship or remained on a reservation and preserved tribal traditions. Discuss with them the tension between assimilation into a larger society and the preservation of a traditional culture.

Map Skills Answers
South Dakota, Wyoming, and Montana. Indian Territory. They were generally located on land that settlers considered undesirable.

A Sioux artist painted this scene of "Custer's Last Stand" at Little Bighorn. Custer and his 265 soldiers attacked a Sioux encampment of 7,000 people and were overwhelmed. Note the brands on the U.S. Army horses. **TECHNOLOGY** With what kinds of weapons did the Sioux fight? **9A**

captured just a few miles from the Canadian border. In New Mexico, the brilliant military leader Geronimo led the Apache in a fierce struggle against the government until his capture in 1886.

The last Indian "battle" of the century took place in 1890 at Wounded Knee, South Dakota. There a massacre happened as army troops were disarming Sioux warriors. The Sioux were no match for the soldiers, who came armed with newly developed machine guns. In the end some 200 Indian men, women, and children lay dead in the snow.

By 1890 thousands of Indians had perished in battles to keep their land. Thousands more had died of starvation and exposure. Even the Indian Territory had shrunk. The federal government bought part of this land from the Indians, and in 1889 opened it to settlement. At noon on April 22 a pistol shot signaled the opening of the territory, and some 50,000 settlers rushed in to stake their claims in present-day Oklahoma. As the century ended, Indian resistance throughout the West died down, and the government forced the surviving Indians onto reservations.

A WAY OF LIFE DESTROYED 6C

The Indians had lost more than a war. Their way of life had died as well. The Indians had relied on the buffalo herds that roamed the Plains. These animals supplied them with most of their needs—meat for food, hides for clothes and shelter, bones for tools, and much more. Yet railroad crews seeking food killed thousands of buffalo. Professional hunters killed millions of buffalo for their hides. Buffalo hunting even became a sport. Settlers would shoot buffalo from passing trains, leaving the carcasses to rot in the sun.

Seeing the Indians' dependence on the buffalo, settlers had realized early on that by destroying the buffalo herds they could weaken Indian resistance. As an army officer put it, "Every buffalo dead is an Indian gone." This relentless slaughter had its intended effect. By 1900 only a handful of buffalo survived, down from herds numbering 65 million, and the Indians had been defeated.

BIOGRAPHY 4C

CHIEF JOSEPH (1840–1904), of the Nez Perce tribe, decided to fight rather than let federal troops force his people from their ancestral home in Oregon. A brilliant military tactician who often won skirmishes with larger U.S. forces, Chief Joseph finally surrendered with the solemn words: "I am tired; my heart is sick and sad. . . . I will fight no more forever."

"**E**very buffalo dead is an Indian gone."

—*Army officer*

114 UNIT 2 THE NATION TRANSFORMED

This painting shows a railway train pausing to shoot at a herd of buffalo. Expanding railways and the settlers they carried soon drove the buffalo herds of the Great Plains to the edge of extinction.
ENVIRONMENT Why was it the policy of settlers and the army to destroy the buffalo? 2B, 6C

Assessment
You may wish to use the Section 1 Review, page 116, to see how well your students understand the main points in this lesson.

Section Review Answers

1. *Bureau of Indian Affairs*—Government agency charged with caring for Indians. *assimilate*—Absorb into a different culture. *Dawes Act*—Law which undercut tribal ties by parceling out reservation lands to individuals.

Western Indians had struggled to preserve their traditions, but defeat in the wars meant that the Indians were forced onto reservations. Often these reservations occupied poor land, unwanted by white settlers. The Indians were unable to hunt sufficient food or raise adequate crops on the land. They therefore became increasingly dependent on the federal government for food, clothing, and other necessities. Meanwhile, agents of the Bureau of Indian Affairs, the government agency charged with caring for the Indians, became notorious for their corruption. Even William W. Belknap, Secretary of War under President Grant, accepted bribes from traders at various Indian posts.

Reports of the harsh conditions faced by Indians began to appear in newspapers and books. Helen Hunt Jackson recorded the failures of government policy in her book *A Century of Dishonor* (1881). Sarah Winnemucca, a Paiute (PY-yoot), traveled across the country pleading for better treatment of the Indians. The message of such reformers began to sink in. In 1881 President Chester Arthur made the following observation:

> Though thousands of lives have been sacrificed and hundreds of millions of dollars expended in an attempt to solve the Indian problem, it has . . . seemed scarcely nearer a solution than it was half a century ago.

4C, 4F

BIOGRAPHY

HELEN HUNT JACKSON (1830–1885) was a crusader for Indian rights. Appalled by the treatment of the Indian people, Jackson wrote *A Century of Dishonor* (1881), the story of many broken treaties. Congress responded by appointing Jackson to investigate the living conditions of Indians in the California missions. She later wrote the novel *Ramona* (1884), about Indian life in California.

Photo Caption Answer
They knew that since Indians depended on buffalo, this policy would hasten the decline of the Indians as well.

Biography
Ask students to list modern-day Helen Hunt Jacksons—people who are crusading for political or social change—and compare their actions with Jackson's.

2. *Crazy Horse*—Sioux Indian chief. *Sand Creek*—Site of massacre of Cheyenne Indians, 1864. *George Armstrong Custer*—General who, along with 264 soldiers, was killed in battle with the Sioux. *Sitting Bull*—Chief who led Sioux at Battle of Little Bighorn. *Little Bighorn*—Site of "Custer's Last Stand." *Wounded Knee*—Site of massacre of Indians in 1890. *Helen Hunt Jackson*—Wrote book on the failures of government policy toward Indians.

3. The war was an outcome of a clash of cultures. Whites wanted to own the land and believed they had a right to it; Indians felt it was their land, and their cultural and physical survival depended on it.

4. Reservations were usually on poor land where Indians were unable to hunt enough food or raise sufficient crops. They often lacked the tools and training to succeed as farmers. They depended upon government agencies, which were often corrupt. These poor conditions led to illness, alcoholism, unemployment, and despair.

5. Arguments favoring assimilation should state that Indians would be able to survive only by learning white culture's ways. Arguments opposing assimilation should state that the Indian culture was and is worthy of respect. For Indians to maintain self-esteem, they would need to preserve as much of their culture as possible.

Closure

Call students' attention to the boxed beige quotation (p. 114). How does this quotation relate to the main idea of the section? Then have students read Section 2 for the next class period, noting how cattle raising became a big business in the Great Plains.

116

This photograph of the Sioux Indian reservation at Pine Ridge, South Dakota, shows a watering hole in the foreground and tepees in the background. Pine Ridge lies near the Badlands, and it contains the town of Wounded Knee. **HISTORY** What was the significance of the events at Wounded Knee in 1890? **2E**

THE DAWES ACT 6C, 8I

White Americans began to develop new ideas about the Indians. One general who had fought against them now declared, "They should be taught the English language, habits of work, the benefits of civilization, and the power of the white race." Reformers came to believe that if the Indians were to survive, they could not hold on to their ancient traditions. Instead, Indians would have to be assimilated—absorbed—into white culture.

To this end, the government tried to stamp out traditional tribal rituals, such as the Sun Dance of the Sioux. To replace the old rituals, the government funded white church organizations to open schools and bring Christianity to the Indians. New boarding schools opened to teach Indian children how to speak, dress, work, and think like whites.

The most significant attack on traditional Indian ways came in 1887, when Congress passed the Dawes Act. Reformers of the time hailed it as a "Magna Carta" for Indians. It aimed to speed the "Americanization" of the Indians by undercutting tribal ties. Reservation lands were broken into small plots of 80 and 160 acres and parceled out to families and individuals. Any remaining land was sold to white settlers. The profits were used for Indian schools. Indians who accepted the plots of land could, for the first time, become American citizens.

Under the plan, Indians received 47 million acres of land. Another 90 million acres were sold directly to settlers or land speculators. Many Indians found that they lacked the tools and the training to succeed as farmers. They sold their plots to whites for a fraction of their real value.

Some Indians refused to accept the government offer. They continued to live on reservations as legal dependents of the federal government. Conditions on the reservations remained harsh, with government-supplied food and clothing often of poor quality. Illness, alcoholism, unemployment, and despair soared.

By 1900 the number of Indians in the United States had dwindled to fewer than 250,000. Not until well into the twentieth century would the federal government recognize the importance of tribal ties to the Indian way of life. Indians would then come to demand recognition of their unique cultural heritage.

SECTION REVIEW

1. KEY TERMS Bureau of Indian Affairs, assimilate, Dawes Act

2. PEOPLE AND PLACES Crazy Horse, Sand Creek, George Armstrong Custer, Sitting Bull, Little Bighorn, Wounded Knee, Helen Hunt Jackson

3. COMPREHENSION Why did both whites and Indians see war as unavoidable?

4. COMPREHENSION What problems did Indians who lived on reservations face?

5. CRITICAL THINKING Present two opposing arguments—one claiming that assimilation was in the Indians' best interest, and another claiming that it was not. Which argument do you find more convincing? Why? **9G**

Photo Caption Answer
This last major battle between Indians and white settlers ended in a massacre of the Indians.

2 The Cowboys and the Ranchers

Section Focus

Key Terms railhead ■ long drive

Main Idea Cattle ranching became a big business in the Great Plains.

Objectives As you read, look for answers to these questions:
1. Why did the growth of railroads lead to the birth of cattle drives?
2. Why were cattle drives replaced by cattle ranching?

Long before the Indians had been conquered, cattle ranchers began to move onto the Plains. In time, cattle ranching became big business. Here is an 1880 description of a cattle drive:

> Once begun, it . . . made a picturesque sight. The leaders were flanked by cowboys on wiry Texas ponies, riding at ease in great saddles with high backs and pommels [hand grips]. At regular distances were other riders, and the progress of the cavalcade was not unlike that of an army on a march.

The cattle were destined for railroad towns such as Abilene or Dodge City. From there, the animals were loaded into freight cars and sent off to meet their fate in the packing houses of Chicago or Cincinnati. Packing houses still exist, but the cattle drives quickly vanished.

START OF THE CATTLE INDUSTRY 3C

The cattle industry had its roots in the Mexican territory of Texas during the 1700s. Here colorful cowboys called *vaqueros* (vah-KAYR-oz) rounded up the wild steers that roamed the grasslands of southern Texas. Later, as American settlers moved into Texas, tame and wild cattle mixed, producing hardy breeds such as the famous Texas longhorn. In rounding up the longhorns, American ranchers adopted some of the ways of the *vaqueros*. They learned to rope cattle from horseback and to mark steers for identification with branding irons. Names of equipment and clothing reflect their Mexican origins. "Lariat" comes from *la reata*, or rope. "Chaps" comes from *chaparreras*, or leather overpants.

To turn cattle ranching into a successful business, Americans needed a way to get western herds to markets in the East. The answer came

This painting from 1877 shows Mexican *vaqueros* in a horse corral. North American cowhands adopted *vaquero* techniques and equipment, notably lassos, sombrero hats, riding boots and spurs, and leather chaps. HISTORY Which European explorers introduced horses into the Americas? 3A

THOMAS GILCREASE INSTITUTE OF AMERICAN HISTORY AND ART, TULSA, OKLAHOMA.

SUPPORTING THE SECTION

Reinforcement Workbook: Worksheet 18
Reteaching Resources: Worksheet 18
Teaching Transparencies: Transparency 18

Photo Caption Answer
The Spanish.

SECTION 2

The Cowboys and the Ranchers
(pp. 117–119)

Section Objective
■ describe the development of ranching on the Great Plains

Introducing the Section

Connecting with Past Learnings
Why were Spanish influences strongest in California, Texas, and the Southwest? (These areas were colonized by Spain and were once part of Mexico.)

Key Terms
Write the key terms on the board and point out that both are made up of short words. Ask students to determine the smaller words in each term; based on the meanings of the smaller words, have them suggest a meaning for each compound word. **LEP**

Focus
Have the class develop a flow chart showing the growth of cattle ranching in the West, including its origin in Texas, cattle drives, expansion of railroads, and the influx of ranchers. Have students supply reasons for each development.
What factors led to ranching falling into fewer and fewer hands? (Lack of water, grazing land being settled, lower prices, cattle diseases, harsh weather.)

Developing the Lesson
After students have read the section, you may want to consider the following activities:

Geographic Themes: Movement
Why were railroads an improvement over driving cattle all the way to population centers?

(Big cities were too far from Texas, where the cattle were; cattle lost weight on drives and were worth less.) **What other means of cheap transportation was used to transport goods?** (Shipping on waterways.)

National Identity
Ask students to suggest adjectives that describe the popular image of cowboys. (Wild, free, rough, self-sufficient, etc.) Discuss with the class why cowboys have become an important national symbol.

Cooperative Learning

Divide the class into small groups. Have each group write the script for a videotape or an audiotape describing some part of the section, such as a cattle drive, the life of a cowboy, or problems faced by ranchers. You may wish to provide students with several songbooks containing cowboy songs. **LEP**

Addressing Individual Needs

Guided/ Independent Practice
Have students complete **Reinforcement Workbook** Worksheet 18. This worksheet guides students in analyzing an account of a stampede.

Reteaching/Correctives
List these causes on the board: cattle industry's roots in Texas; expansion of railroads; value of cattle drops because of hardship of long drive; beef prices fall because of overproduction. For each cause, have students scan the text to find an effect. Group students to create cause-and-effect charts.

Instruct students to work through **Reteaching Resources** Worksheet 18, which helps them view the development of ranching in terms of causes and effects.

MAJOR CATTLE TRAILS

[Map showing major cattle trails across the central United States, with legend for Railroad and Cattle trail. States shown include North Dakota, South Dakota, Minnesota, Wisconsin, Wyoming, Iowa, Nebraska, Colorado, Kansas, Missouri, Illinois, New Mexico Terr., Oklahoma, Arkansas, Texas, and Louisiana. Cities marked include Cheyenne, Denver, Pueblo, Dodge City, Ogallala, Omaha, Chicago, Abilene, Topeka, Kansas City, St. Louis, Wichita, San Antonio. Trails labeled: Goodnight-Loving Trail, Western Trail, Chisholm Trail, Shawnee Trail. Railroads include Union Pacific R.R., Kansas Pacific R.R., Atchison Topeka & Santa Fe R.R. Gulf of Mexico, Rio Grande, Red R., Missouri R. shown. Scale: 300 mi / 300 km. ALBERS CONICAL EQUAL-AREA PROJECTION]

MAP SKILLS 9E

Cattle were driven north from Texas and then loaded onto railroad cars headed to slaughterhouses in the Midwest. Where did the Chisholm and Shawnee trails originate? **CRITICAL THINKING** What problems might result from long-term use of the same trails?

through the expansion of the railroads and the ingenuity of Joseph McCoy, an Illinois livestock shipper. McCoy hit on a scheme whereby Texas ranchers would drive their herds to railheads, or shipping stations, along one of the new railroad lines.

Railroad officials scoffed at the idea at first. But McCoy persisted. In 1867 owners of the Hannibal and St. Joseph Railroad agreed to set up a railhead in the sleepy prairie town of Abilene, Kansas. McCoy's first shipment numbered 20 carloads of Texas longhorns. By the end of 1871, shipments peaked at more than 700,000 cattle.

Soon other railheads opened and the era of the long drive, the movement of cattle north from

Texas, began. "Cow towns" sprang up at key railheads in Oklahoma, Kansas, and Missouri—the prime shipping centers in the 1870s. During this decade, popular imagination turned the long drive into a romantic event. The rough-and-tumble ways of cowboys became legendary in the East and as far away as Europe.

Life along the trail had little of the glamour described in song and story, however. Cowboys, many of whom were blacks and Mexicans, rode for hours at a time, under a blazing sun and in steady downpours. Every waking moment they strained to hear the first stirrings of a stampede. Explained one cowboy:

> No one could tell what caused a stampede. . . . A burst of lightning, a crackling stick, a wolf's howl, little things in themselves, but in a moment every horned head was lifted, and the mass of hair and horns, with fierce, frightened eyes gleaming like thousands of emeralds, was off. . . . Lashing their ponies . . . the cowboys followed at breakneck speed, . . . [hoping] to turn the herd.

After pushing two to three thousand steers northward, the cowboys rode into a railroad town dusty and tired, their pockets full of hard-earned cash. Some headed straight for a hot bath and a good night's sleep. Others blew off steam with liquor and gambling. Keeping the peace fell to such well-known marshals as Wyatt Earp and Wild Bill Hickok.

RANCHING AS A BIG BUSINESS 3C
The era of the great cattle drives ended almost as quickly as it began. Economics was one factor: cattle lost so much weight in their 1,000-mile journey to the railheads that their value fell sharply. Another factor was a law passed in Kansas in 1884. Trying to prevent the spread of disease carried by Texas cattle, Kansas forbade Texas cattle to pass through Kansas except during the winter.

The solution to these problems, it seemed, was to move the railroads nearer the cattle or the cattle nearer the railroads. Both were done. New rail lines were built connecting Texas ranches with cities farther east. Also, many ranchers set up

118 UNIT 2 THE NATION TRANSFORMED

Map Skills Answers
San Antonio. Overgrazing and lack of food.

ranches farther north, nearer the existing rail-heads. To deal with this region's colder winters, ranchers bred Texas longhorns with eastern cattle to produce a strong, hardy breed.

The further expansion of the railroads, as well as the development of tough new breeds of cattle, produced a thriving business for cattle ranchers throughout the Plains. Their success lured many prospective cattle barons to the West. Land there was virtually free; the cattle and grass were for

Many cowboys and soldiers on the American frontier were black. This portrait shows a ranch hand named Nat Love who gained fame for horsemanship and skill on cattle drives. **PARTICIPATION** Why might large numbers of blacks have moved to the frontier in the middle and late 1800s? **9A**

the taking. Eastern city "dudes" and European investors bought shares in cattle companies and waited for the profits to roll in.

In reality, of course, getting rich proved difficult. Cattle needed water, but the best streams and water holes were controlled by the first ranchers to arrive on the Plains. With each passing year, more farmers and sheepherders arrived, fencing in land with barbed wire and sparking bloody fights with ranchers over land ownership. And even the best grasslands could be overgrazed, leaving little food to fatten herds for the winter months. Ranchers found themselves crowding their many steers onto trampled, heavily grazed grasslands. At the same time, the overproduction of beef had forced down prices.

Bad weather finally undermined the system altogether. A cold winter in 1885–1886 was followed by an unusually hot and dry summer. As winter again approached, ranchers rushed to sell their weakened herds. Beef prices plummeted. The winter of 1886–1887 proved even nastier than the one before. Tens of thousands of cattle froze or starved to death. Their prized herds destroyed, many ranchers gave up in despair.

As with other industries, such as steelmaking and oil refining, cattle ranching fell into the hands of a relatively few companies. They reduced the size of herds, fenced the cattle in, and grew hay for winter feeding. Instead of investing in extra cattle, they often bought mowing machines, hay rakes, and tractors. Lamented one veteran cowboy in 1905, "I tell you, times have changed."

SECTION REVIEW

1. KEY TERMS railhead, long drive

2. PEOPLE AND PLACES Joseph McCoy, Abilene

3. COMPREHENSION What problems brought an end to the great cattle drives?

4. COMPREHENSION How did a few large firms come to dominate the ranching industry?

5. CRITICAL THINKING What personal qualities do you associate with cowboys? In what way did the conditions in which they lived and worked bring out these qualities?

Photo Caption Answer
To escape the prejudice they had experienced in the East and South.

Background The cattle might have survived the winter of 1886–1887 had they been able to move ahead of the storms, as was their custom. Barbed wire fencing kept them from doing this, however, and after the winter thousands upon thousands of frozen cattle were found heaped along the fences.

Enrichment/Extension
Have students construct a hypothesis to explain why the great cattle drives came to an end. Then have them do research to find out what actually happened.

Assessment
You may wish to use the Section 2 Review, on this page, to see how well your students understand the main points in this lesson.

Section Review Answers
1. *railhead*—Shipping station along a railroad line. *long drive*—Movement of cattle north from Texas.
2. *Joseph McCoy*—Developed idea of driving Texas cattle to railheads. *Abilene*—Cow town in Kansas, first cattle railhead.
3. The cattle lost weight on the trail and their value dropped; to prevent the spread of disease, Kansas forbade Texas cattle to pass through except during winter.
4. Many cattle herds were destroyed during the harsh winter of 1886–1887. Prices dropped and big companies were able to buy out smaller ranchers who had been ruined.
5. Possible responses include hardworking, individualistic, strong, and quiet. They were often away from civilization for long periods of time; this would encourage silence and individualism. To participate in cattle drives they had to be strong and hardworking.

Closure
Ask one student to transform the Main Idea of the section into a question, and have other students answer that question. Then have students read Section 3 for the next class period, noting how technology aided in the settlement of the West.

Section Objective

■ describe the role of the government and technology in the settlement of the Great Plains

Introducing the Section

Connecting with Past Learnings

Have students consider how the Civil War dislocated Americans. *Why would soldiers of both the North and South want to move westward?* (Government made land available; North—move from crowded conditions; South—make new start after defeat and poverty.)

Key Terms

List the key terms on the board. For each term, have students write a question to which the term is the answer. Explain that *bonanza* is a Spanish word meaning "fair weather or prosperity." **LEP**

Focus

Set up a chart on the board, labeling horizontal rows *Plains, Bonanza Farms,* and *California.* Label vertical columns *Government Help* and *Technological Advances.* Have students fill in the chart with specific examples of technology and governmental action that led to the development of the Great Plains, California, and bonanza farms.

In what ways were farming, eastern manufacturing, and the cattle industry similar? (Greatly influenced by technology; absorbed new immigrants; small businesses that failed were bought up by larger companies, leading to a few companies.)

2C, 3A, 3C, 4B, 4C, 8C, 9A, 9B

3 Farming the Frontier

Section Focus

Key Terms Exoduster ■ Homestead Act ■ dry farming ■ sod ■ bonanza farm

Main Idea With help from the government and new technology, settlers worked hard to farm new lands.

Objectives As you read, look for answers to these questions:
1. How did the government encourage people to move west?
2. What technological advances improved life on the farm?
3. How did farming become a big business?

In her novel *My Ántonia* (1918), Willa Cather described a boy's wagon trip to a farming homestead on the Plains:

> I tried to go to sleep, but the jolting made me bite my tongue, and I soon began to ache all over. . . . Cautiously, I slipped from under the buffalo hide, got up on my knees and peered over the side of the wagon. There seemed to be nothing to see; no fences, no creeks or trees, no hills or fields. . . . There was nothing but land: not a country at all, but the material out of which countries are made. No, there was nothing but land. . . .

Farmers trailed behind the cattle ranchers onto the Plains. The farmers would transform the region from a seeming emptiness to a settled land. Their story was one of sweat, aching muscles, uncertainty, and, most of all, determination.

WHO WERE THE SETTLERS? 4B

What kind of people "pulled up stakes" and took their chances in the western territories? The settlers represented a cross-section of American society—honest business people and swindlers, former Civil War soldiers, land speculators and the sons and daughters of eastern farmers. And black Americans were attracted by the freedom of the West. A former slave, Benjamin "Pap" Singleton, led a migration of poor southern blacks in what was called the "Exodus of 1879." By the time winter winds began to howl that year, some 15,000 Exodusters had reached Kansas, claimed land, and built shelters. Still more blacks started farming in Nebraska and other nearby states.

Many settlers were immigrants from Europe, lured to the United States by American railroad companies. These companies, which had received vast tracts of land to build railroads, now looked to resell this land at a profit. They sent agents to Europe to recruit settlers. Company agents also greeted arriving immigrants at eastern ports with promises of cheap land and instant success.

ENCOURAGING SETTLEMENT 8C

Through grants of land and other programs, the federal government also aided western settlement. As early as the 1830s, people had called on the federal government to parcel out public lands

This painting by Harvey Dunn, entitled *The Homesteader's Wife,* portrays a pioneer woman of the South Dakota plains. NATIONAL IDENTITY What impression does the painting give of life on the plains and the pioneers who lived there?

SOUTH DAKOTA ART MUSEUM

SUPPORTING THE SECTION

Reinforcement Workbook: Worksheet 19
Reteaching Resources: Worksheet 19
Enrichment and Extension Resources: Primary Source Worksheet 10
Teaching Transparencies: Transparency 19

Photo Caption Answer
Difficult and frustrating life; determined, gritty pioneers.

A family in Custer County, Nebraska, poses before their sod house in 1886. Families such as this one were often called "sodbusters," and the sod they cut for their houses was known as "Nebraska marble." This house is built into a hillside for warmth in the winter, which has also allowed the family's cow to wander onto the roof. **CULTURE** Describe your impression of these family members and their lives.
9B

to private settlers. Southern states, fearing this would result in the creation of new nonslave states, blocked the idea. But the southern states left the Union in 1861. As the Civil War raged, the way was clear for a new land policy.

In 1862 Congress passed the Homestead Act. This measure offered 160 acres of land free to any American citizen who was a family head and over 21. The only conditions were that the settler live on the land for five years and make improvements to it. In the well-watered East, 160 acres was a sizable farm. Yet in the semi-arid West, it was barely enough to support a family. To prosper, a farmer needed at least twice that amount.

Despite these risks, the Homestead Act produced an explosion of settlement. Within a half century after its passage, all western territories had gained enough settlers—at least 60,000—to become states. Most western areas experienced enormous population growth:

	1870	1880	1890
Colorado	39,864	194,327	413,429
Kansas	364,399	996,096	1,428,108
Montana	20,595	39,159	142,924
Nebraska	122,993	452,402	1,062,656
Wyoming	9,118	20,789	62,555

The Timber Culture Act of 1873 further encouraged settlement. It gave settlers another 160 acres of free land if they agreed to plant trees on at least 40 acres. Four years later, the Desert Land Act gave settlers 640 acres of land at $1.25 an acre. The settler was required to irrigate the land within three years. For the settler interested in lumber and mining, there was the Timber and Stone Act of 1878. This law also provided land well below the market price.

All these acts were intended to help average citizens start new lives on the frontier. Yet some people took advantage of the government's generosity. Buying land from settlers or directly from the government, speculators made a killing by reselling the land at higher prices. The Federal Land Office did not have enough employees to make certain that the system worked properly.

The federal government encouraged settlement of the West in many ways besides land grants. It set up military posts throughout the West and provided soldiers to protect settlers and help build roads. The Department of Agriculture, created in 1862, searched the world for crops—such as Russian wheat—that would thrive in the conditions found on the Plains. Its scientists also taught farmers new techniques, such as dry farming, a **3A** practice designed to gain the most value from every rainfall. Farmers learned that by plowing and planting seeds deeply, and by stirring the topsoil after every rain, they could raise crops despite the lack of rain.

The Hatch Act of 1887 required the Department of Agriculture to set up Experiment Stations, 43 of which were in operation a year later. The stations, located in various parts of the country, worked to solve problems facing farmers. By 1891 they were sending out more than 300 instructive reports per year to about 350,000 farmers.

After students have read the section, you may want to consider the following activities:

Religion
Discuss with students the biblical connection of the term *Exodusters*. (*Exodus* originally referred to the Jews' fleeing from slavery in Egypt. That story is found in the second book of the Bible, entitled *Exodus*.) *In what ways were the Exodusters like the Jews in the Bible?* (They were fleeing from slavery to a new land that would be their own.) Ask students to consider why these pioneers went to a biblical source for their name.

Geographic Themes: Place
Have students create a graph of population growth based on the list on page 121. *Which of the five states were most populous in 1890?* (Kansas and Nebraska.) Have students locate the states on a physical map of the United States and suggest why the populations of Colorado, Montana, and Wyoming were far lower than those of Kansas and Nebraska. (Terrain was much more mountainous; Montana was farther north.) **LEP**

Environment
Have students examine the physical map of the United States at the back of the book. *Where did water for irrigation in California come from?* (Colorado River in the south; rivers flowing down from Sierra Nevada.) Discuss with students the ways that irrigation affects the environment.

Photo Caption Answer
Students may suggest that the family appears rugged, hardworking, and careworn.

Background The 60,000-resident requirement for statehood originated with the Northwest Ordinance of 1787.

LIFE ON THE FARM 2C

Despite this help, life on the farm was not for the faint-hearted. Because of the shortage of lumber on the Plains, pioneers there built houses with blocks of **sod**—thickly matted soil. These houses had dirt floors and mud-plastered walls. Even the roofs were usually made of sod. A thin layer of dust and bits of soil often covered everything in the house.

Pioneers fought a year-round battle against the elements. On icy winter days, as winds hurled snow against walls and doors, families huddled around fires indoors and prayed that their fuel

A pioneer woman of the Plains gathers buffalo chips in a homemade wheelbarrow. ENVIRONMENT What were the buffalo chips used for? Why? 9A

would last. Wood was so scarce that many pioneers burned "cow chips"—the dried droppings of cattle and buffalo. Others burned twisted bundles of hay. Summer brought the danger of prairie fires, which raced across the land on hot, dry winds. Sometimes, summer also brought armies of grasshoppers and locusts. These insects devoured everything in their path, from the crops in the field to the clothes on the pioneer's back.

Everyone in a Plains family worked, and worked hard. There were always chores to be done. Fences had to be strung, land plowed, seed planted, crops harvested, food preserved, animals cared for. Life was often lonely, as the nearest neighbor might be miles away. But loneliness was relieved by farmers' meetings, church dinners, and county fairs.

NEW TECHNOLOGY 3A

Farmers needed more than companionship to help them deal with the special farming conditions that existed on the Plains. New technology came to their rescue.

A semi-arid region that received less than twenty inches of rainfall in a good year, the Plains needed water for development as a farm and cattle area. Wells could be dug, but they often had to go several hundred feet deep. Yet because the Plains boasted ample wind, farmers could buy windmills to pump out the deep water for irrigation and drinking. American manufacturers succeeded in making the windmill smaller and more reliable.

The development of barbed wire from 1874 to 1890 also made Plains farming more feasible. The Great Plains had few trees. No farmer could raise crops or keep animals without timber to build fences. Barbed wire, however, could be stretched long distances between fence posts. It grew cheaper over the years, costing 90 percent less in 1897 than in 1874.

The Plains soil itself, though rich, was tough and difficult to plow. New, advanced plows eased this back-breaking work. In 1837 John Deere invented the first steel plow. Two decades later James Oliver patented an improved version of that plow, one strong enough to furrow the Plains soil. Then in 1880 came the lister. This double plow could move soil in two directions while an attachment planted the seed deeply. Lighter and more effective than earlier plows, these new plows could be pulled by horses as well as oxen.

LARGE-SCALE FARMING 3A, 3C

Inventors and manufacturers devised new and improved equipment for harvesting. These included the twine binder in the 1870s, the "combine" reaper-thresher in the 1880s, and more. As farmers bought up more and more machinery, the making of farm equipment became a major industry. John Deere, McCormick Reaper, and other companies joined the ranks of big business in the United States. Thanks to the use of heavy machinery, farmers on the Plains not only expanded production but also saved time.

Such time savings encouraged farmers to buy more land and grow more crops. By the late 1880s, farmers were producing more wheat than their markets could handle. Also, farmers throughout the world—in Australia, Canada, and South America—had entered into competition with the Americans. As a result, grain prices fell and many farmers went bankrupt. Gradually, large operators with capital to invest came to dominate the industry.

The most famous of the new bonanza farms— large farms financed by outside capital—stretched across the Red River Valley of Minnesota and the Dakotas. One farm, run by Oliver Dalrymple, measured almost 100,000 acres, several times the size of New York's Manhattan Island. Like the corporations of the East, bonanza farms could lower their costs through economies of scale. Railroads gave them special bulk shipping rates. Suppliers sold them seed and equipment at discounted prices. These practices earned bonanza farmers huge profits. In one year, for example, Dalrymple grew 25 bushels of wheat per acre and sold it for 90 cents a bushel, or $22.50 per acre. Since his investment costs were just $9.50 an acre, Dalrymple earned a profit of $13 an acre—a return of more than 100 percent.

Many small, independent farmers resented the new bonanza farms. They feared they would be overwhelmed by the large businesses, which could outproduce and undersell them. Small farmers also resented the special treatment that bonanza farms received from railroads and suppliers. Frustrated and angry, farmers would band together in a political movement to defend their interests (Chapter 8).

FARMING BEYOND THE PLAINS 3A

To the forty-niners, California's great Central Valley was but a plain to cross on the way to the gold fields of the Sierra foothills. This level valley is 400 miles long and 40 to 80 miles wide. Rivers carrying the Sierra's heavy snowmelt cross the valley's northern part on their way to San Francisco Bay.

By the 1860s Californians had begun to plow up the valley's fertile meadows and grasslands to raise wheat. For three decades, wheat was California's largest and most profitable crop, and the state was the second-largest wheat producer in the nation.

Other crops, too, did well in California's mild climate. A grape and wine industry began to flourish in the valleys near San Francisco Bay. By 1890 growers were raising grapes and raisins in the Central Valley near Fresno. In southern California growers began using irrigation to raise oranges. By the 1880s the first refrigerated railroad cars made it possible to ship fresh produce all across the nation. (The new Florida citrus industry also benefited from these cars.)

During these decades bitter and intense controversies hampered the efforts of Californians to harness river water for irrigation. The basic issue was, who controlled the water? Did miners have the right to wash millions of tons of earth into the rivers and thereby bury downriver farms in mud? Did a landowner have the right to divert water from a river and sell it to others?

In the 1880s, posters like this one lured thousands of people to California. The cross-country railroads carried hopeful farmers to fruit- and grain-producing land in the Central Valley, to the grape-growing valleys north of San Francisco, and to the citrus-growing region around Los Angeles. ECONOMICS What techniques does the poster use to attract settlers? 9B

3. Land grants; Homestead Act; Timber Culture Act; Desert Land Act; set up military posts; provided soldiers who helped build roads; Department of Agriculture found grains that thrived on Plains and taught farmers techniques such as dry farming; Experiment Stations worked to solve farmers' problems.

4. Smaller, portable, more reliable windmills; barbed wire; new, advanced plows.

5. Because of time-saving devices, farmers bought more land and grew more crops. When they produced more wheat than markets could handle, prices dropped and many went bankrupt.

Closure

The Section 3 information in the Chapter 5 Summary (p. 132) can be used to synthesize the important elements covered in Section 3. Then have students read Section 4 for the next class period, noting why mining and lumbering gained economic importance in the West.

SECTION 4

Mining and Lumbering
(pp. 124–127)

Section Objective

■ describe how mining and lumbering became major industries in the West

Introducing the Section

Connecting with Past Learnings

Review patterns of western settlement. *How might settlement by miners differ from settlement by farmers?* (Farmers moved consistently westward and remained in an area for a long time; miners

---

These issues were finally settled by government regulation. In 1887 the California legislature authorized the establishment of irrigation districts. These districts, formed by a majority of landowners in the area, had the power to take, store, and distribute water for the benefit of the district as a whole. In 1893 the federal government began to regulate how much debris could be put in a stream. With the establishment of government control over water use, California entered a new era marked by intensive irrigation and the transportation of water. The wheat fields gave way to new, more profitable crops made possible by irrigation.

2C, 2D, 3A, 4B, 4C, 9B

4 Mining and Lumbering

★ Section Focus

Key Terms placer mining ■ quartz mining ■ log drive

Main Idea Mining and lumbering became major industries in various parts of the West.

Objectives As you read, look for answers to these questions:
1. What types of minerals lured prospectors westward?
2. Where did the new lumber industry locate in the late 1800s?
3. What early efforts were made to tap the resources of Alaska?

"Gold!" That cry could stir people like none other. Often it made people abandon homes and loved ones and rush off to seek fame and fortune. A strike at Sutter's Mill in 1848 (map, page 125) set loose a wave of change across the land. In one California town, an observer wrote, "An American woman who had recently established a boardinghouse here pulled up stakes and was off before her lodgers had even time to pay their bills."

The West saw many gold and silver rushes in the second half of the nineteenth century. Miners by the thousands poured into the West in search of precious metals. Another natural resource of the region—its rich timber supply—would lure still other workers. Meanwhile, western resources would help speed the Industrial Revolution. The

gold and silver from western mines would provide capital to build industries.

PROSPECTORS AND BOOM TOWNS 2D

The dream of finding precious metals beckoned people from near and far. Margaret Frink was one of thousands eager to "strike it rich." All across the Plains, she and her husband worried that "there would only be a few barrels of gold left for us when we got to California."

Prospectors such as the Frinks needed little experience and almost no capital. 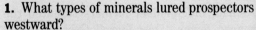Placer mining—mining the deposits of a stream bed—could be done with a shovel, a washpan, and a good pair of eyes. (Hydraulic mining, a kind of placer mining in which miners blasted hillsides with thousands of

---

1. KEY TERMS Exoduster, Homestead Act, dry farming, sod, bonanza farm

2. PLACE Red River Valley

3. COMPREHENSION How did the federal government encourage people to settle the Plains?

4. COMPREHENSION Name three of the technological advances that made farming on the Great Plains easier.

5. CRITICAL THINKING In what way were farmers victims of their own success?

SUPPORTING THE SECTION

Reinforcement Workbook: Worksheet 20
Reteaching Resources: Worksheet 20
Teaching Transparencies: Transparency 20

Background To control speculators and better market their produce, California citrus growers organized growers' cooperatives. The brand "Sunkist" represented the largest of these cooperatives.

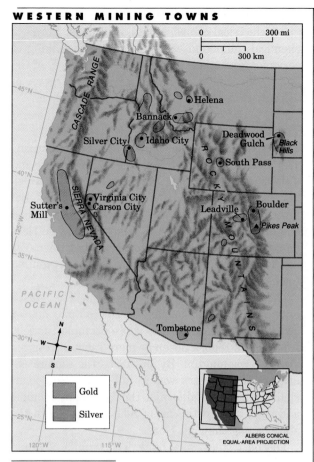

MAP SKILLS 2D, 9B

This map shows mining towns in the West. Which metal was found in Boulder, Colorado? Which of the cities on the map are now state capitals? (See Atlas map of the United States if necessary.) CRITICAL THINKING What connection might you make between the location of gold and silver mines and the location of mountain ranges?

gallons of water to wash gold-bearing soil and gravel into troughs, was more effective. It was also more expensive, however.)

Few of the early prospectors actually found much gold. Undaunted, they moved on to new sites. From California, many rushed to Colorado after the Pikes Peak gold strike of 1858–1859. Others headed for Nevada. Each prospector dreamed of the luck of Henry Comstock, whose claims in Nevada in 1859 ultimately brought forth hundreds of millions of dollars in gold and silver.

The fabulous Comstock Lode created the most colorful city in all the West—Virginia City, Ne-

vada. Here is how Mark Twain described the town in his book *Roughing It* (1872):

> The sidewalks swarmed with people. . . . Buggies frequently had to wait half an hour for an opportunity to cross the principal street. . . . There was a glad, almost fierce, intensity in every eye, that told of the money-getting schemes that were seething in every brain and the high hope that held sway in every heart.

Other mining towns sprang up as the search for gold spread—Bannack, Montana (1862); South Pass, Wyoming (1867); Juneau, Alaska (1880). The towns grew so fast that territorial governments had no time to create law and order, so the miners made their own. They met to set rules for claims and to settle disputes. Nevertheless, gunfights and lynchings often made justice quick and final.

The last mass effort of individual prospectors to strike it rich occurred in 1876, at Deadwood Gulch in the Black Hills of the Dakota Territory. Men and women with a taste for excitement roared into town, giving Deadwood Gulch a reputation for shootouts and sin. A hillside cemetery overlooking the town boasted as residents such well-known figures as Potato Creek Johnny and Calamity Jane.

The booming mining industry spawned new consumer businesses. Levi Strauss intended to sell California miners sturdy canvas for tents. Miners,

Levi Strauss, a German businessman, began making riveted blue jeans and jackets in 1874. Today the company is the world's largest clothing manufacturer. TECHNOLOGY Comment on the kind of plow the farmer is using. 3A

CHAPTER 5 NEW FRONTIERS, NEW RESOURCES, 1860–1900 **125**

moved relatively quickly from one mineral deposit to another.)

Key Terms
Have students find the key terms in their texts and define them. Have them compare placer mining to quartz mining, and log drives to cattle drives. LEP

Focus
Have the class create a profile of a "typical" miner of the late 1800s. Ask them to suggest adjectives describing the miner (restless, gambler, strong); the miner's equipment (washpan, shovel, pickax); and the miner's clothing (Levis). Ask students to find a photograph of such a miner, or to draw one.

Why did mining and lumber industries become, for the most part, big businesses? (Needed big machines and investments to remain competitive.)

Developing the Lesson
After students have read the section, you may want to consider the following activities:

Science and Technology
Have students draw a diagram, create a diorama, or design some other form of visual presentation of one of the mining or logging methods discussed in the section.

Environment
What role do forests play in maintaining the environment? (Prevent erosion, release oxygen, provide a habitat for wildlife.)

Ask students to explain the difference between lumber, a renewable resource, and minerals, which are nonrenewable. (People can plant more trees and log forever while minerals removed will not be replaced.) Have students suggest ways that loggers can harvest trees without causing permanent damage.

Map Skills Answers
Gold. Carson City, Nevada; Helena, Montana. The mines are mostly located in the foothills of mountain ranges.

Photo Caption Answer
Lightweight, horsedrawn, steel plow.

Background The biggest strike in the Comstock Lode was not made until 1878, when John W. Mackay and three partners dug into a mountain to find the Big Bonanza, a 54-foot wide seam of gold and silver.

however, were more interested in practical clothes that would last. Strauss came up with trousers riveted together at key points to withstand great stress. "Levi's" remained popular long after the mining frontier had ended. James Cash Penney set up what he called "Golden Rule Stores," meaning that they would treat customers as you would want other people to treat you. J. C. Penney stores later spread throughout the nation.

THE BUSINESS OF MINING 4B
Despite the wild stories of instant wealth, few individual miners prospered. Even Henry Comstock did not get rich from his famous discoveries. He sold one valuable claim on the Comstock Lode for $40. He received just $10,000 for his share of the richest claim, and died penniless.

There really was little a lone prospector like Comstock could do to exploit the riches he might uncover. Most gold and silver lay embedded in quartz rock beneath the surface. The only way to get at it was through quartz mining. This process involved blasting the rock from a mountainside and then crushing it to separate the gold from the surrounding rock. Such work required heavy machinery and many hired hands. Very few prospectors could afford either the equipment or the workers. Most sold out to a mining company.

The large mining companies hired hundreds of unskilled laborers. These included recent immigrants from the East as well as Mexican and Chinese laborers who had helped lay track for western railroads. For these laborers, the work was hard and the pay poor; most of the profits went to the mine owners.

OTHER RICHES FROM THE EARTH 2C
The mining companies saw value in other western mineral deposits. Minerals such as copper, lead, and borax were becoming increasingly important to the United States' growing industries. Once electric power came into use, copper became an essential metal for wiring. The Anaconda Copper Company, founded in 1881 in Montana, grew into one of the nation's largest mining concerns.

Large firms also mined lead in places like Idaho and Utah, and borax in Death Valley, California. Industry used lead to form strong alloys and to make electrical cables, paints, and pipes. Borax, a chemical compound, was needed in the making of ceramics and glass. Railroad freight cars of the late 1800s rolled eastward carrying cargoes of western ores often as valuable as gold or silver.

THE LUMBER INDUSTRY 2C, 2D, 3A
The West offered more than mineral resources. The Pacific region of Washington, Oregon, and California could exploit a living resource—the California redwoods, Douglas fir, and other trees. Before the Civil War the lumber industry had centered around the Great Lakes, but as settlers moved west, so did the loggers. Lumber towns, as rowdy and ramshackle as cow towns or mining towns, sprang up near the forests.

The loggers found plenty of work. The West's growing population needed boards to build houses as well as thick timbers to shore up mine tunnels. As early as 1865, a dozen or more sawmills buzzed away in Washington. By the 1880s the northwestern lumber industry was in full swing. Ships carried lumber to California, the Hawaiian Islands, and even around the tip of South America to the states along the East Coast.

The best trees were huge. The trunks of Douglas fir trees were 8 to 10 feet thick, and redwoods could have a diameter of 20 to 30 feet. The first limbs of either tree could be as high as 100 feet above the ground. Using special kinds of axes, loggers worked in pairs to fell the trees. Horses or oxen dragged the downed trees to a river. Then came the arduous log drive, by which the logs were floated downstream to a sawmill.

After 1880, new technology raised lumber production dramatically. One invention, the donkey engine, used a steam engine to power a giant pulley to move logs. Another new device used a small railroad engine to pull logs quickly and easily to sawmills. By 1900 Oregon's foresters were producing more than five times as much lumber as they had twenty years earlier.

Lumbering, like mining, required heavy investments in machinery and workers. Not surprisingly, a few large corporations came to dominate the industry. The Weyerhaeuser Company became a leading lumber and papermaking firm in the Northwest.

This photograph shows employees of the Weyerhaeuser Company floating logs down a northern tributary of the Mississippi River. Water transport of logs to sawmills was cheap, but slow. Massive log jams often resulted in clogged waterways and damaged riverbanks and streambeds. Frederick Weyerhaeuser, a German immigrant, began operations on the northern tributaries of the Mississippi and later purchased large areas of timberland in the Pacific Northwest. HISTORY Use your imagination to describe briefly what the life of a logger might have been like. 4C

ALASKA: THE LAST FRONTIER 2D

Mining and lumbering played important parts in the development of the nation's last frontier region: Alaska. Secretary of State William Seward bought Alaska from Russia in 1867. Though the United States paid less than two cents per acre for the huge region, skeptics laughed at the purchase. Regarding Alaska as a frigid wasteland, they called it "Icebergia" and "Seward's Folly." Seward was quick to point out that *Alaska* meant "great land" in the language of the Aleuts who lived there.

Alaska received little attention at first. For seventeen years, the federal government left Alaska's administration up to the army, the navy, or customs collectors. The discovery of gold put Alaska on the map. In 1880 two prospectors spied the glitter of yellow metal in a creek in southern Alaska. More miners soon rushed in. Juneau and nearby towns sprang up.

As in California, corporate mining followed close on the heels of lone prospectors. While prospectors searched in vain for rich new placer deposits, the Alaska Mill and Mining Company set up quartz mining operations near Juneau.

In 1896 an American named George Carmack and his two Indian brothers-in-law came upon another deposit of gold. Their find was in the Klondike, a region of Canada along the Alaskan border. Thus began the great Yukon and Alaska gold rushes. Tens of thousands of miners poured in, finding gold at Nome in 1899 and at Fairbanks in 1902. Alaska's white population multiplied nine times between 1890 and 1910.

Settlers soon learned that Alaska had much to offer besides gold. Fur-bearing animals like mink, fur seal, beaver, muskrat, and sable abounded. Fish were plentiful, and timber, copper, and coal seemed unlimited. Companies moved in to take advantage of these resources. Yet long after other parts of the West had been developed, Alaska continued to provide Americans with a glimpse of life on the frontier.

SECTION REVIEW

1. KEY TERMS placer mining, quartz mining, log drive

2. PEOPLE AND PLACES Henry Comstock, Virginia City, Deadwood Gulch, Levi Strauss, James Cash Penney, William Seward, Klondike

3. COMPREHENSION Why did large businesses usually benefit more from gold and silver mining than individual prospectors?

4. COMPREHENSION What economic opportunities in addition to mining existed in the Pacific states? In Alaska?

5. CRITICAL THINKING Some of the boom towns of the West later turned into ghost towns. Why might this have happened? 2D

Photo Caption Answer
Students may suggest a rugged outdoor life, hard work, reliance on fellow workers, lack of women and culture.

SECTION 5

Section Objective

■ explain the influence of the image of the western frontier on American culture

Introducing the Section

Connecting with Past Learnings

Have students consider the spread of non-Indian settlement in the United States. *In what general direction did the frontier move?* (Generally from the Atlantic coast west, though some settlers moved east from California and others north from Texas.)

Key Terms

List the key terms on the board. Have volunteers suggest definitions for each term. Discuss the definitions and agree on the most precise one for each term. **LEP**

Focus

On the board create a web, with "the passing of the frontier" in the center circle. Tell students to consider the end of the frontier as a cause and to surround this cause with the effects described in the section. Be sure that the Turner thesis, images of the West, and conservation are included.

How are images of the West and conservation related to the passing of the frontier? (Frontier became idealized, as in westerns; conservation became important, because empty space was no longer perceived as unlimited and resources had to be protected.)

128

2B, 2C, 2D, 4F, 6A, 8I, 9D, 9F

5 The Impact of the Frontier

Section Focus

Key Terms Turner thesis ■ dime novel ■ National Park Service ■ conservation

Main Idea Americans continued to be influenced by images of the western frontier long after it had vanished.

Objectives As you read, look for answers to these questions:
1. What influence did some historians believe the West had on American life?
2. In what ways did images of the West reach mass audiences?
3. What early efforts were made to protect America's natural beauty?

In 1890 the United States Census Director noted that it was no longer possible to draw a line of advancing settlement across a map of the West. "The unsettled area has been so broken into by isolated bodies of settlement that there can hardly be said to be a frontier line," he observed. In short, the frontier had vanished. Pioneer days, it seemed, were gone forever.

Americans had different reactions to the passing of the frontier. Some sought to change the West into something new and modern. Others hoped to make the Old West live on. The struggle between these conflicting ideas lives on today.

> "The advance of the frontier has meant . . . a steady growth of independence on American lines."
> —*Frederick Jackson Turner*

THE WEST AND THE AMERICAN CHARACTER 2D

Would the absence of a frontier pose a threat to America's unique qualities as a nation? Some people thought so. Frederick Jackson Turner, a young historian at the University of Wisconsin, published in 1893 what became known as the Turner thesis. Turner claimed that the frontier had distinguished the United States from Europe. It had, he said, molded the democratic American spirit. Turner contended:

> The advance of the frontier has meant a steady movement away from the influence

of Europe, a steady growth of independence on American lines. And to study this advance . . . is to study the really American part of our history.

As long as the West remained unsettled, Americans could always begin new lives in new lands. In a sense, the West had been a "gate of escape," a safety valve. Turner wrote:

> This perennial rebirth, this fluidity of American life, this expansion westward with its new opportunities, its continuous touch with the simplicity of primitive society, furnish the forces driving [the] American character.

The Turner thesis had a profound influence on American thought. Later historians, however, began to challenge Turner's argument. First, they said, the West had never been a safety valve for the East's many low-paid workers. These people could rarely afford the trip west or the tools needed to begin an independent life. Second, while some unhappy easterners did move west, the opposite also occurred. Many westerners moved east in search of better-paying jobs and security. These and other questions are still being debated today.

VISIONS OF THE WEST 4F

Most Americans, of course, did not think of the West as a safety valve. They saw it as a land of excitement and bravery. They learned about the West mainly through so-called dime novels, cheap and plentiful books from popular fiction writers after the Civil War. These books enthralled read-

---

SUPPORTING THE SECTION

Reinforcement Workbook: Worksheet 21
Reteaching Resources: Worksheet 21
Teaching Transparencies: Transparency 21

COURTESY OF THE BUFFALO BILL HISTORICAL CENTER, CODY, WYOMING.

Buffalo Bill Cody, posing at left with the great Sioux leader Sitting Bull, helped shape the romantic image of the American West. An ad for his Wild West Show pictures him soaring high above the newly built Statue of Liberty and Brooklyn Bridge. CULTURE Why did Cody, an Indian fighter, include Sitting Bull in his Wild West Show? 4F, 9F

ers who had never been west of the Mississippi (or even the Hudson!). Cowboys and Indians stormed across the pages in one thrilling episode after another.

In 1873 William F. Cody burst upon the American scene in a stage play called "Scouts of the Prairies." Known as Buffalo Bill, Cody was a former scout and buffalo hunter. He had also ridden for the Pony Express, carrying mail on the long journey from Missouri to California. Cody was most famous, though, as an Indian fighter, having killed Chief Yellow Hand in the Battle of Yellow Creek.

The public received Cody so warmly that he started his own "Wild West Show" and toured the country for the next 30 years. Cody's show featured real cowboys twirling lariats, busting broncos, and firing pistols. It also included Indians such as Sitting Bull, who had defeated General Custer in 1876.

Romantic notions of the West remained popular far into the twentieth century. Owen Wister's novel *The Virginian* (1902) set the standard for a literary genre known as the "Western." *The Virginian* told of the growing love between a rough cowboy and a pretty schoolteacher from Vermont. Later writers like Zane Grey and Louis L'Amour

carried on the tradition of the Western novel. Radio, movies, and television did their parts to recall "the thrilling days of yesteryear."

Some artists created vivid visual images of the West. The etchings and paintings of Thomas Moran and the photography of Edward S. Curtis excited the interest of Americans. Born in England, Moran came to America and joined survey crews mapping the West. At the same time, he painted western scenes, most notably of the

"Coming for the Bride," by famed photographer Edward S. Curtis, records the ceremonial costumes worn by Qagyuhe Indians of the Pacific Northwest. CULTURE Why are photographs of Indians from the late 1800s important? 6A

Grand Canyon and the Yellowstone area of Wyoming. His fellow surveyors called him "T. Yellowstone Moran."

Curtis, born in Wisconsin, made his reputation in the Pacific Northwest. His most famous work was a 20-volume study of American Indians, with 1,500 photographs. Curtis believed that unless he provided a photographic record of the many tribes, future Americans would know little about them.

CONSERVING THE LAND 2B, 8I

People like Moran and Curtis tried to preserve the West through art. Others struggled to preserve western lands themselves. Parts of the West contained wonders that dazzled the mind. One of the most stunning areas lay in what is now western Wyoming.

In 1807 a man named John Colter was roaming the Rockies. On a high plateau drained by the Yellowstone River, Colter gazed in awe at columns of steam and hot water erupting high into the air.

Colter had stumbled upon a natural marvel—a volcanic plateau seething with thermal pools and geysers.

Some 60 years later, a government expedition entered the area. It found that Yellowstone not only contained unique geological features but also teemed with wildlife. There were black bears and bison, birds and fish. Something had to be done to protect the natural beauty of the area, expedition leaders felt. They wanted to prevent the kind of commercial exploitation that had marred eastern landmarks like Niagara Falls.

Congress agreed. In 1872 Congress made Yellowstone the world's first national park. Other parks were later set up, and in 1916 Congress created the National Park Service to run these protected areas.

The establishment of national parks reflected a new mood in the United States. As Frederick Jackson Turner had pointed out, Americans had always been wasteful. Settlers could afford to ruin the lands around them because there was always

Thomas Moran painted magnificent landscapes such as *Grand Canyon of the Yellowstone* (1872), shown here. This painting, exhibited in Washington, D.C., impressed members of Congress and helped persuade them to establish a national park system. **ENVIRONMENT** Why did Americans consider national parks necessary? 2C, 8I

more land available on the frontier. But now the frontier was closed. Conservation—the preservation and wise use of the nation's natural resources—was necessary.

Conservationists had seen western mining companies tear down mountains with hydraulic mining. In the forests, lumber companies cleared huge areas of land in their search for timber. They took no steps to preserve young saplings. Neither did they protect wildlife or prevent forest fires. By the end of the 1800s, they had cut 800 million acres of forest land—80 percent of the nation's original forests.

The government, conservationists held, should protect the nation's resources for future generations. They won a key victory in 1891 when Congress passed the Forest Reserve Act. This measure authorized the President to protect timber areas on federally owned lands.

John Muir (MYUR), a Scottish immigrant, played a leading role in the conservation movement. He roamed the West, discovering new wonders and urging federal action to preserve them. In 1892 Muir founded the Sierra Club, an organization that helped keep the conservation movement going.

Many similar groups were formed in the twentieth century. Americans increasingly recognized that the nation's natural resources, in the West and elsewhere, could not be treated simply as fuel for American industry. An irreplaceable part of America's heritage, the land had to be used wisely, not squandered out of greed or carelessness. In one sense the Indians, who viewed themselves as caretakers of the earth, had prevailed.

SOCIAL HISTORY
Famous Firsts

1874	Barbed wire patented (Nov. 24).
	Mennonites from Russia introduce Turkey Red wheat to Kansas.
1877	Swift & Company ships meat from Chicago to New York in ten refrigerated cars, the beginning of year-round, long-distance shipments of beef.
1879	First American Indian school of prominence opened, at Carlisle, Pa. (Nov. 1).
1889	Agriculture Bureau made an executive department (Feb. 9).
1891	First national forest—Shoshone National Forest, Wyoming—established (March 30).

SECTION REVIEW

1. KEY TERMS Turner thesis, dime novel, National Park Service, conservation

2. PEOPLE AND PLACES Frederick Jackson Turner, William F. Cody, Owen Wister, Thomas Moran, Edward S. Curtis, Yellowstone Park, John Muir

3. COMPREHENSION What objections were raised against the Turner thesis?

4. COMPREHENSION What kinds of activities damaged the environment in western states?

5. CRITICAL THINKING Assume Frederick Jackson Turner's point of view. What aspects of American society today reflect the influence of the frontier?

9D

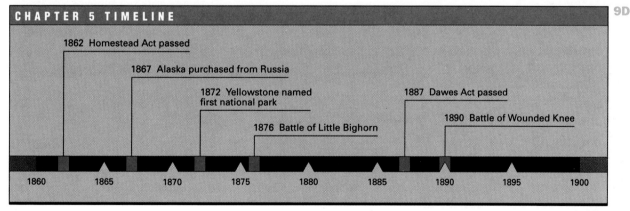

CHAPTER 5 TIMELINE

1862 Homestead Act passed

1867 Alaska purchased from Russia

1872 Yellowstone named first national park

1876 Battle of Little Bighorn

1887 Dawes Act passed

1890 Battle of Wounded Knee

1860   1865   1870   1875   1880   1885   1890   1895   1900

CHAPTER 5 NEW FRONTIERS, NEW RESOURCES, 1860–1900 **131**

Famous Firsts
Have students expand the list, entering important dates mentioned in the text, such as the creation of Yellowstone and the National Park Service.

Section Review Answers

1. *Turner thesis*—Idea that the frontier distinguished America from Europe and molded the country's democratic spirit. *dime novel*—Cheap, popular fiction. *National Park Service*—Federal agency created to administer national parks. *conservation*—Preservation and wise use of natural resources.

2. *Frederick Jackson Turner*—Historian who developed the Turner thesis. *William F. Cody*—Former scout who created a "Wild West Show." *Owen Wister*—Author of *The Virginian*. *Thomas Moran*— Artist who painted western landscapes. *Edward S. Curtis*—Photographed American Indians. *Yellowstone Park*—First national park. *John Muir*—Founder of the Sierra Club.

3. The West had never been a safety valve for low-paid eastern workers who could not afford to travel; many westerners moved east.

4. Mining companies tore down mountains; lumber companies cut down millions of acres of trees, with no thought of replanting, the destruction of wildlife habitats, or prevention of forest fires.

5. Possible responses include Americans' tendency to move frequently, optimism about new opportunities, a wasteful attitude toward resources.

Closure

Call students' attention to the boxed beige quotation (p. 128). How does this quotation relate to the main idea of the section? Then have students read Section 1 of Chapter 6 for the next class period, noting the major reasons for the growth of American cities.

131

Chapter 5 Review Answers

Key Terms
1. Dawes Act
2. railhead
3. conservation
4. assimilate
5. bonanza farm

People to Identify
1. Henry Comstock
2. William Seward
3. Sitting Bull
4. Helen Hunt Jackson
5. William F. Cody
6. Joseph McCoy

Places to Locate
1. D   4. E
2. F   5. C
3. A   6. B

Reviewing the Facts
1. The encroachment on established Indian lands by prospectors, ranchers, and other settlers escalated conflicts. Advanced technology, the destruction of the buffalo, and pressure from settlers led to the Indians' defeat.

2. The Dawes Act attempted to speed up Indian assimilation by parceling plots of land out to individuals. The Act failed because some Indians refused to leave the reservation while others lost their property.

3. The cattle drives were how ranchers got steers to railheads and to market. When bringing railroads to the cattle became more economical, efficient, and safe, the drives died out.

4. Land grants, incentive farming programs, and a military presence encouraged people to settle the West.

5. Technological advances like new lightweight windmills, barbed wire, and steel plows made Plains farming more practical.

Chapter 5 REVIEW

Chapter 5 Summary

Section 1: American settlers and soldiers defeated the Indians in the West after the Civil War.

■ Government policies, wars, and the destruction of the buffalo led to the defeat of the Plains Indians by 1890.

■ Indians were put on reservations, where living conditions were poor.

Section 2: The cattle industry thrived briefly on the Plains.

■ Once rails gave western ranchers access to markets, some people used the cheap land and livestock to get rich.

■ New settlement, barbed wire, overgrazing, and bad weather ended the cattle boom.

Section 3: Farmers brought the Great Plains under cultivation.

■ Through the Homestead Act, the federal government made land available to new settlers.

■ Settlers used new farming techniques and new technology to increase output.

■ Large businesses came to dominate the farming industry.

Section 4: Gold, silver, industrial minerals, and timber brought new wealth.

■ Gold strikes led to a frenzy of prospecting in the West.

■ In the Northwest, new technology led to a lumber boom.

■ Gold, fur, fish, and minerals brought new settlers and economic growth to Alaska.

Section 5: The West lived on in the American imagination long after the frontier had been closed.

■ Historian Frederick Jackson Turner linked frontier attitudes to the American character.

■ Artists and writers captured the natural beauty and historical drama of the West.

■ Conservationists called for the protection of the West's natural resources.

Key Terms ●

Use the following terms to complete the sentences below.

**assimilate
bonanza farm
conservation
Dawes Act
railhead**

1. The _____ was an attempt to solve the "Indian problem" by encouraging Indians to adopt white culture.
2. A shipping station for cattle was known as a _____ .
3. Concerned about environmental damage caused by certain mining and lumbering techniques, John Muir and others urged _____ .
4. To adopt the language and customs of another people is to _____ .
5. Like a large corporation, a _____ could lower its costs through economies of scale.

People to Identify ●

Match each of the following people with the correct description.

**William F. Cody
Henry Comstock
Helen Hunt Jackson
Joseph McCoy
William Seward
Sitting Bull**

1. The person whose discovery of gold and silver in 1859 led to the growth of Virginia City, Nevada.
2. The Secretary of State who endured ridicule for his purchase of Alaska from Russia in 1867.
3. Indian leader whose warriors massacred U.S. soldiers at the Battle of Little Bighorn.
4. Author of *A Century of Dishonor*, an indictment of America's Indian policy.
5. Indian fighter, scout, and buffalo hunter who toured the country for 30 years with his "Wild West Show."
6. The Illinois livestock shipper who devised a plan by which Texas ranchers would drive their herds to railheads.

6. Productive mining required heavy machinery and many hired hands, an expense only a corporation could afford.

7. Copper, lead, and borax were important minerals mined in the West.

8. The donkey engine, a machine that moved logs more efficiently, created a lumber boom after 1880.

PLACES TO LOCATE ●

Match each of the letters on the map with the places that are listed below.

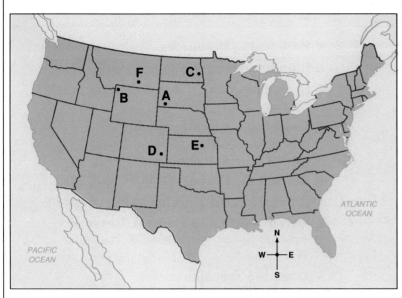

1. Sand Creek
2. Little Bighorn
3. Wounded Knee
4. Abilene
5. Red River Valley
6. Yellowstone Park

REVIEWING THE FACTS ▲

1. What caused conflict between Indians and white settlers on the Great Plains? What factors led to the Indians' final defeat?
2. What was the Dawes Act? Why did the Dawes Act fail to achieve its goals?
3. What was the goal of cattle drives? For what reasons did they die out?
4. What steps did the United States government take to encourage people to settle the West?
5. What technological advances made Plains farming more practical?

6. Why was mining more profitable for corporations than for most prospectors?
7. What minerals were mined in the West?
8. What new advances in technology created a lumber boom after 1880?
9. According to Frederick Jackson Turner, what were some of the qualities that frontier life encouraged?
10. What concerns led to the establishment of the National Park Service?

CRITICAL THINKING SKILLS ▲

1. **PARAPHRASING** In your own words, state the Turner thesis.

2. **MAKING JUDGMENTS** What elements of western life made stories about the West so appealing to easterners and Europeans?

3. **FORMING A HYPOTHESIS** Why were frontier towns often raucous and violent?

4. **INFERRING** What did Turner fear would happen to the United States when the frontier was no longer open?

5. **STATING BOTH SIDES OF AN ISSUE** Make the best case you can to support each of the following statements: (a) White settlers had no right to settle on Indian lands. (b) White settlers were justified in taking Indian lands.

WRITING ABOUT TOPICS IN AMERICAN HISTORY ■

1. **CONNECTING WITH LITERATURE** A selection from *Black Elk Speaks* by John G. Neihardt appears on pages 778–780. Read it and answer the questions. Then answer the following question: Why did Black Elk have a special feeling for the country in the Black Hills?

2. **APPLYING THEMES: AMERICAN CULTURE** Find out more about one of the legendary westerners you have read about in this chapter. Write a biographical sketch to share with the class. How do the real facts of the person's life compare with what you imagined before you started your research?

9. Frontier life encouraged independence and pursuit of new opportunities.

10. Concern over growing commercial exploitation led to the establishment of the Park Service.

Critical Thinking Skills
1. Turner believed the opportunities and challenges of frontier life created a uniquely American lifestyle.

2. Students should note that the romanticized image of living in the raw and rugged wilderness, with its wild animals, Indians, and untapped natural resources was appealing to those people in the settled parts of the world.

3. Students should consider the type of people that settled the West, where they came from and what they were after, as well as the conditions they operated under.

4. There would no longer be an escape valve for overcrowding in the East, nor the sense of limitless opportunities.

5. (a) Students should recognize the Indian point of view and the effect settlement had on the Indian culture. (b) Students should also note the importance of the natural resources for the United States and the western tradition of taming and harvesting the land.

Writing About Topics in American History
1. The Black Hills were his home when he was young. Having been forced out of them as a youth, he looks back at them romantically.
2. Students should clarify the differences between the reality of someone's life and the romantic version oftentimes popularized.

Chapter Review exercises are keyed for student abilities:
● = Basic
▲ = Average
■ = Average/Advanced

Chapter 6 ▪ Urban American Society   3 Sections, 3–5 Days

	SECTION OBJECTIVES	SECTION RESOURCES
Section 1 **The Rise of** **American Cities**	▪ describe the growth of American cities and the new technologies that made large cities feasible	● **Reteaching Resources:** Worksheet 22 ▲ **Reinforcement Workbook:** Worksheet 22 ■ **Enrichment and Extension Resources:** Primary Source Worksheet 11 ▲ **Teaching Transparencies:** Transparency 22
Section 2 **The New** **Americans**	▪ identify the reasons for the upsurge in immigration in the late 1800s ▪ describe the responses of city politicians and nativists to the new immigrants	● **Reteaching Resources:** Worksheet 23 ▲ **Reinforcement Workbook:** Worksheet 23 ■ **Enrichment and Extension Resources:** Primary Source Worksheet 12; Historian Worksheet 2 ▲ **Teaching Transparencies:** Transparency 23
Section 3 **City Life** **and Leisure**	▪ explain how an increase in the number of products, information, and entertainment changed American lifestyles ▪ describe how artistic styles reflected the urban age	● **Reteaching Resources:** Worksheet 24 ▲ **Reinforcement Workbook:** Worksheet 24 ▲ **Teaching Transparencies:** Transparency 24

The list below shows Essential Elements relevant to this chapter. (The complete list of Essential Elements appears in the introductory pages of this Teacher's Edition.)

Section 1: 2A, 2B, 2D, 3A, 4F, 4E, 8A, 8C, 9B
Section 2: 4B, 4F, 6B, 6C, 7C, 9B
Section 3: 3A, 3C, 4C, 4D, 4E, 4F, 6B, 6C, 7B, 7J, 8A, 8D, 9B, 9D

Section Resources are keyed for
student abilities:
● = Basic
▲ = Average
■ = Average/Advanced

CHAPTER RESOURCES

Geography Resources: Worksheets 11, 12
Tests: Chapter 6 Test

Chapter Project: American Culture

Have students create a cartoon strip, write a short story, or build a model describing some aspect of change in American cities between 1865 and 1900. Areas of focus might be immigration, lifestyle and leisure in cities, or reasons for the growth of cities.

Homework Options

Each section contains activities labeled "Addressing Individual Needs." You may wish to choose from among these activities when assigning homework.

Provisions for Limited English Proficiency (LEP)

Several suggested activities may be particularly helpful for teachers of students with limited English proficiency. These activities have been marked throughout the Teacher's Annotated Edition with the symbol **LEP** .

BIBLIOGRAPHY AND AUDIOVISUAL AIDS

Teacher Bibliography

Glaab, Charles N., and Theodore A. Brown. *A History of Urban America.* Macmillan, 1983.

Handlin, Oscar. *The Uprooted.* Little, Brown, 1973. A classic study of the American immigrant experience.

Student Bibliography

Asimov, Isaac. *The Golden Door: The United States from 1865 to 1918.* Houghton Mifflin, 1977.

Jones, Maldwyn A. *American Immigration.* University of Chicago Press, 1960.

McKelvey, Blake. *Urbanization of America, 1860–1915.* Rutgers University Press, 1963.

Literature

Antin, Mary. *The Promised Land: The Autobiography of a Russian Immigrant.* Princeton University Press, 1985.

Crane, Stephen. *Maggie: A Girl of the Streets.* Norton, 1980. Novel based on Crane's observations of the New York City slums.

Norris, Frank. *The Pit: A Story of Chicago.* Bentley, 1971. The second of Norris's series on the production and distribution of wheat.

O'Connor, Edwin. *The Last Hurrah.* Little, Brown, 1985.

Films and Videotapes*

Chinese Gold: The Chinese of Monterey Bay. 40 min. ONEWEST. Immigration experience of Chinese Americans from the 1850s to the present.

Dreams of Distant Shores. 28 min. CINEMA 70. Immigration to America between 1890 and 1915 from the immigrants' point of view.

Journey to Freedom: The Immigrant Experience. 13 min. AIMS. History of American immigration over the past century, revealed through newsreel footage, vintage photos, and artwork.

Filmstrips*

The Coming of Modern Times (set of 3). GA. Titles include: The New American Woman, 1848–1920; Material and Social Progress, 1870–1917; and The Road to War, 1870–1917.

Computer Software*

Immigration (Decisions, Decisions Series) (1 disk: Apple). TS. Overview of the history of immigration in the U.S. since the 1840s, including immigration from China and southern and eastern Europe; and the growth of cities at the turn of the century.

Urbanization (Decisions, Decisions Series) (1 disk: Apple). TS. The growth of cities throughout the history of the U.S. and the critical issues surrounding the process of urbanization.

*For a complete guide to audiovisual sources, see the introduction to this book (page Txx).

Chapter 6

Urban American Society
(pp. 134–157)

This chapter examines technological and geographic factors that contributed to the growth of American cities, the new wave of immigrants who flocked to these urban centers after 1880, and changing lifestyles and new artistic movements that emerged at the close of the century as a result of increased prosperity.

Themes in American History

■ Economic development
■ Pluralistic society
■ American culture

Chapter Objectives

After students complete this chapter, they will be able to:

1. Describe the growth of American cities and the new technologies which made large cities feasible.

2. Identify the reasons for the upsurge in immigration in the late 1800s.

3. Describe the responses of city politicians and nativists to the new immigrants.

4. Explain how an increase in the number of products, information, and entertainment changed American lifestyles.

5. Describe how artistic styles reflected the urban age.

Chapter Opener Art
George Wesley Bellows, *New York,* 1911.

While some Americans moved west, others—including millions of European immigrants—flocked to the city. This scene of New York City shows the rising American urban center in all its bustle and excitement.

CHAPTER SUPPORT MATERIAL

Reinforcement Workbook: Worksheets 22–24
Reteaching Resources: Worksheets 22–24
Enrichment and Extension Resources: Primary Source Worksheets 11, 12; Historian Worksheet 2
Geography Resources: Worksheets 11, 12
Teaching Transparencies: Transparencies 22–24
Tests: Chapter 6 Test

6 Urban American Society
(1865–1900)

2A, 2B, 2D, 3A, 4F, 4E, 8A, 8C, 9B

1 The Rise of American Cities

Section Focus

Key Term mass transit

Main Idea American cities mushroomed in area and population in the late nineteenth century.

Objectives As you read, look for answers to these questions:
1. What accounts for the growth of American cities?
2. What new technology made large cities feasible?
3. What were the patterns of urban growth?

On July 4, 1776, only one American in twenty lived in a city. A century later that figure had jumped to one in three. By 1920, the Census Bureau noted that more than half of all Americans were living in cities.

The decades following the Civil War witnessed a tremendous expansion of American cities. This was the era of industrialization, western settlement, and heavy immigration. All these forces nurtured the explosive growth of cities, which became the economic and cultural centers of the nation.

2A, 8A

THE GEOGRAPHY OF URBAN GROWTH

Even the largest cities began life as small towns. Yet while some towns grew only modestly, or vanished altogether, others enjoyed spectacular growth. Geography played a large role in determining which towns succeeded, and which failed. For example, New York, Philadelphia, Baltimore, Boston, and New Orleans were the five biggest American cities in 1820. All were ocean ports. Their economies depended on trade with Europe.

Since water provided the best means of transporting goods, and since many of the United States' manufactured goods came from abroad, these ports thrived.

After the Civil War, cities with ties to industry benefited most. Some were located close to sources of raw materials. Pittsburgh's growth was fueled by the iron and steel industry located near the coal deposits of Pennsylvania. The flour mills of Minneapolis handled the products of the Midwest's thousands of acres of wheat. Omaha's meat-packing plants stood just a few miles from cattle ranches.

The products of industry had to be transported to consumers. Cities located on major transportation lines thus benefited from industrial growth. Pittsburgh and Minneapolis, for example, were river ports. Omaha was an important railroad center, one of many cities aided by the building of new railroad lines. Thanks to the railroad, even cities lacking water transportation could thrive. The largest cities, such as New York City and Chicago, combined manufacturing, railroads, and shipping.

SECTION 1

The Rise of American Cities
(pp. 135–139)

Section Objective

■ describe the growth of American cities and the new technologies which made large cities feasible

Introducing the Section

Connecting with Past Learnings

Help students understand the economic reasons behind the growth of cities by reviewing the Industrial Revolution. *What four factors led to the expansion of industry after 1860?* (Abundance of natural resources; a growing number of workers; growth of the supply of capital; major innovations and inventions.)

Key Term

Write the key term for this section on the board. Have students find the word in the text and state its meaning. *What kinds of mass transit were there in the late 1800s?* (Trolley cars, subways, cable cars.) *How did mass transit help make large cities possible?* (People could live farther away from work, so cities spread out and suburbs developed.) **LEP**

Focus

What factors brought people to cities in the late 1800s? (Industrialization creating jobs, farmers moving to town, immigrants entering the United States.)

SUPPORTING THE SECTION

Reinforcement Workbook: Worksheet 22
Reteaching Resources: Worksheet 22
Enrichment and Extension Resources: Primary Source Worksheet 11
Teaching Transparencies: Transparency 22

Write the following topic heads on the board: *Architecture, Transit, Services, Jobs.* Ask students to name all the things they associate with cities under each heading. (Examples: architecture—skyscrapers, apartment buildings; services—trash pick-up, local library branches, etc.) *Which of these things characterized cities at the end of the last century?*

Developing the Lesson

After students have read the section, you may want to consider the following activities:

Geographic Themes: Regions

On a classroom map or the political map of the United States at the back of the book, have students locate the five largest U.S. cities in 1820, which were mentioned in the section. (New York, Philadelphia, Baltimore, Boston, and New Orleans.) Then have them find the five largest cities in 1900: New York, Chicago, Philadelphia, St. Louis, and Boston.

Where were most of the big cities in both 1820 and 1900? (Northeast.) *What region, not represented in the 1820 list of top cities, contained two of the country's largest cities in 1900?* (The Midwest.) *What region, represented in the 1820 list, no longer had one of the five largest cities in 1900?* (South.) Ask students to suggest reasons for these regional differences. (Northeast—received more immigrants, site of the first factories, with capital to invest; Midwest—transportation and industrial centers near resources; South—recovering from the Civil War, and largely agricultural.)

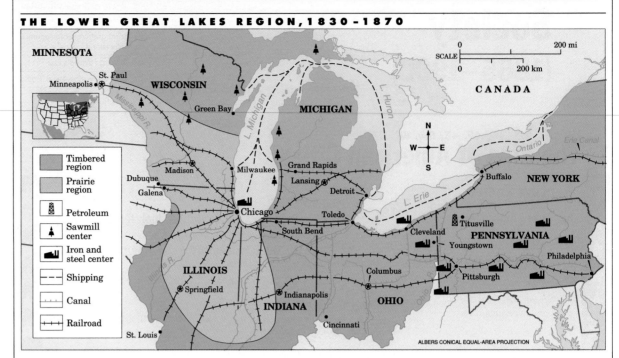

The Geographic Perspective: The Growth of Chicago

THE LOWER GREAT LAKES REGION, 1830–1870

Legend:
- Timbered region
- Prairie region
- Petroleum
- Sawmill center
- Iron and steel center
- Shipping
- Canal
- Railroad

ALBERS CONICAL EQUAL-AREA PROJECTION

In 1833 Chicago was a town of 43 houses on the muddy shores of Lake Michigan. Fifteen years later Chicago's population was 30,000. By 1880 half a million people lived there.

Chicago's phenomenal growth was no accident. The city boomed as a result of its unique location in the American heartland. There, at the southern tip of Lake Michigan, prairie, lake, and river meet. This location made Chicago a natural transportation center linking eastern cities, northern forests, and western prairies.

The completion of the Erie Canal in 1825 had first thrown open the Great Lakes region to settlement. Yankees and immigrants alike were lured westward by new economic opportunities. Improved transportation routes eased the settlers' trek to the Great Lakes.

In the 1830s and 1840s, canals were built to connect Great Lake ports with the Ohio and Mississippi rivers. By such routes, cargo could travel by water between New Orleans and the Great Lakes. By 1848 Chicago was at the center of this north-south water route.

Then came the railroad, turning Chicago from just another city into the Midwest's greatest city. Chicago's first rail line was built in 1848. Within a decade Chicago had become the center of a railroad network that fanned out in all directions.

Railroad lines coming from the west carried corn, wheat, hogs, and cattle. Chicago mills and packing houses processed these products and then shipped east such goods as flour, bacon, and leather.

Chicago also traded huge quantities of lumber that came by train or ship from forests in Michigan and Wisconsin. Much of this lumber was then moved westward by train to prairie settlers for fences and farmhouses. Later, the city also became a center for iron and steel works. Manufacturing, such as farm equipment, became a big business in the area.

2A, 2B

CRITICAL THINKING QUESTIONS

1. How could goods made in Cleveland reach St. Louis?
2. By what means might Michigan lumber reach a farm in Illinois?

The Geographic Perspective Answers

1. Water—by ship to Chicago, then by canal and river to St. Louis; or by canal to the Ohio River and to St. Louis. Land—first by railroad, to Chicago and then to St. Louis.

2. By ship or railroad to Chicago and then by rail to Illinois.

Geographic Themes
Geographic themes covered on this page:
- ✔ Location
- ___ Place
- ___ Interactions
- ✔ Movement
- ✔ Regions

HOW CITIES GREW 2A, 3A

City growth required more than a good location near raw materials and transportation routes. City residents needed places to live and ways to get to work. Technological breakthroughs in the mid-1800s revolutionized housing and transportation, making rapid urban growth possible.

One of the most important advances was the Bessemer process (page 91). It made steel cheap and plentiful enough for wide-scale use in buildings. A skeleton of steel beams could support the enormous weight of tall buildings. Since the walls of the building did not have to bear much of the weight, they could be built hundreds of feet high. Chicago boasted the world's first metal frame skyscraper, the ten-story Home Insurance Building designed by William Le Baron Jenney and completed in 1885. Skyscrapers soon appeared in other cities.

The problem of getting up and down these buildings had already been solved by a Vermont-born inventor named Elisha Otis. In 1857 he installed the world's first passenger elevator in a New York City department store. By 1889 the first electric-powered elevator was in service.

Before the 1870s, getting around in the city meant either walking or riding a horse-drawn carriage. To meet the needs of their growing populations, cities searched for an efficient, reliable system of **mass transit**—a way to transport large numbers of people. In 1870 New York experimented with an elevated railway line, but found the trains too noisy and dirty for crowded areas. Three years later, San Franciscans were given their first chance to ride cable cars—carriages connected to underground wires. In 1887 Richmond, Virginia, installed the first system of trolley cars with overhead wires, designed by Frank J. Sprague. The need to use space efficiently led Boston to build the nation's first subway system. It opened in 1897.

Mass transit systems allowed cities to spread farther and farther outward. It was now possible for people to live miles away from where they worked. At the same time, new bridges were helping cities span rivers. The most impressive example was the steel-cabled Brooklyn Bridge, which connected Brooklyn with Manhattan Island. De-

This photograph from around 1900 shows the interior of a New York subway car. Note that this car has been designated for women only. **TECHNOLOGY** How did mass transit systems affect the way people in cities lived? 3A, 4E

signed by John A. Roebling, the bridge took 13 years to build and cost $15 million. When finished by Roebling's son in 1883, the Brooklyn Bridge was called "the eighth wonder of the world." With a span of nearly 1,600 feet, it was the longest suspension bridge in the world at the time.

PROVIDING CITY SERVICES 2A

Finding reliable transportation was only one of the problems facing the growing cities. Ways had to be found to combat disease, crime, and fire, all of which thrived in crowded urban conditions.

Poor sanitation made disease a constant worry. Many neighborhoods did not have regular garbage collection; rat-infested piles of garbage mounted in alleys and on street corners. Few cities had regulations banning the sale of spoiled food. Pollution control was almost unknown. Cities dumped sewage into rivers, lakes, or any other handy place.

Not surprisingly, outbreaks of disease were common. Cholera, tuberculosis, and influenza took a heavy toll on the young and the feeble. Yellow fever killed 5,000 in Memphis in 1878. Ten years later an outbreak of yellow fever in Jacksonville, Florida, caused desperate panic. When word of the epidemic spread, Jacksonville residents fled the city, overloading trains and boats in a desperate attempt to avoid the disease. No city in Florida or in Georgia would accept Jacksonville residents. Officials in one Georgia town threat-

Photo Caption Answer
People could live miles from their workplaces; transportation became less costly and time-consuming.

Background Eighty-five cities had telephone lines by 1880. By 1900 the entire country was linked by telephone lines, and there were 800,000 telephones in use, more than twice the number in all of Europe.

Environment
Ask students to discuss environmental issues created by urban life. Possible areas for discussion are air and water pollution, waste disposal, smog, and destruction of wildlife habitats. *How did solutions to past urban problems lead to environmental problems faced by cities today?* (Mass transit led to urban sprawl; improved roads led to more pollution caused by cars.)

Connecting with Literature
Ask students to reread the quotation from the play *The City,* on page 139, and discuss whether or not they agree with the speaker. Have students write a short speech answering the character quoted.

Science and Technology
Have students discuss ways in which the typewriter, telephone, and adding machine changed business practices. (Could work faster, communicate faster, be more productive.)
What office machines have changed the way people work today? (The computer, the fax machine, electronic voice mail.) Have students compare these innovations with those of the late 1800s.

Cooperative Learning

Divide the class into small groups. Have each group create a poster advertising a large American city at the turn of the century. Before designing the poster, the group should determine which aspects of urban life will be highlighted and what image would best symbolize the city. **LEP**

138

Addressing Individual Needs

Guided/ Independent Practice
Have students complete **Reinforcement Workbook** Worksheet 22, which asks them to graph the population of the largest cities in the United States in 1900.

Reteaching/Correctives
Have students form small groups and review the section, looking for examples of problems caused by the rise of cities, as well as the solutions to these problems. Have each group make a chart of these problems and solutions. Have groups try to find ways to categorize the problems.

Assign **Reteaching Resources** Worksheet 22, which will help students remember the main ideas of the section.

Enrichment and Extension
Have students complete **Enrichment and Extension Resources** Primary Source Worksheet 11, which helps them determine how Carl Sandburg's poem "Chicago" portrays a growing urban center of the new industrial age.

Assessment
You may wish to use the Section 1 Review, page 139, to see how well your students understand the main points in the lesson.

ened to wreck the railroad tracks if people from Jacksonville tried to come through their town, even in enclosed rail cars. The post office in a Florida town simply returned all mail with a Jacksonville postmark, even though Jacksonville officials had fumigated each piece.

Each day Jacksonville streets were cleaned, trash was burned, and infected houses were marked by yellow flags. Citizens were urged to stay in their homes from sunset to sunrise, since it was believed that the disease spread most easily during these hours. The city even fired cannons into the air, thinking that the force of the explosions would disperse the yellow fever germs. The only result was a couple of damaged buildings.

All these precautions proved unnecessary. Seven years earlier a Cuban doctor, Dr. Carlos Finlay, had argued that the disease was spread by mosquitoes, not humans. He was right, though no one believed him at the time. The epidemic finally came to an end in late November when a cold snap killed the mosquitoes. All told, the Jacksonville yellow fever epidemic took 427 lives.

To prevent such outbreaks, many cities in the 1880s improved their sanitation systems. Memphis built a modern sewer system in 1880, and other cities soon followed suit. New water treatment plants helped fight disease by providing city residents with cleaner drinking water.

City governments made other changes in the 1880s and 1890s to improve the quality of life for their residents. With the invention of the dynamo (page 95), it was now possible to light city streets with electric power. Improved street lighting, as well as larger, better-trained police forces, helped reduce crime. To fight fires more efficiently, many cities switched from volunteer to paid fire departments. They also installed hydrants and used steam-powered fire engines instead of hand pumps.

George Bellows, a leading American artist of the early 1900s, painted many scenes of poorer city neighborhoods and their inhabitants. He belonged to a group of painters that critics labeled the "Ash Can School" for their gritty, down-to-earth subject matter. **CULTURE** Why, do you think, did Bellows title this painting *Cliff Dwellers*? 4F, 9B

Photo Caption Answer
Students may suggest that the title echoes the primitive living conditions of the people in the painting, and that their apartment dwellings resemble caves in the face of a cliff.

PATTERNS OF URBAN GROWTH 2A, 8C

By the late 1800s the older American cities consisted of a series of rings of settlement. Nearest the central business section of the city were apartment buildings occupied by the poor. The next ring contained housing designed for residents with higher incomes. Neighborhoods farther away from the city were generally newer, less crowded, more attractive, and more expensive than those closer to the center of the city. The goal of ambitious residents living in the inner rings was to move to one of the outer rings.

Among those able to move farther away from city centers were members of the growing middle class. These people benefited from the widening job opportunities cities offered—such jobs as office workers, merchants, lawyers, and teachers. These jobs, which paid more than manual labor, gave people the chance to rise from the working class into more comfortable living conditions.

For many middle-class families, this meant a single-family home with a lawn. Searching for their own plot of land, people eventually moved beyond the last outer ring of the city to newly developed outlying areas called suburbs. Streetcars tied the suburbs to the city, allowing people to live in the suburb while working in downtown shops and offices. Real estate developers, hoping to lure people into the suburbs, described them as the best of all possible worlds. An 1873 booklet promoting North Chicago read:

> The charms of suburban life consist of qualities of which the city is in a large degree bereft [lacking], namely: its pure air, peacefulness, quietude, and natural scenery. . . . The controversy which is sometimes brought, as to which offers the greater advantage, the country or the city, finds a happy answer in the suburban idea which says, both—the combination of the two—the city brought to the country.

Where consumers moved, businesses followed. Banks, grocery stores, and shops of all kinds set up branches in the suburbs. Many suburbs became cities in their own right. This, in turn, created more outward pressure, as people moved yet farther from the city in search of living space.

PEOPLING THE CITIES 2D

Skyscrapers, elevators, mass transit, bridges—American cities were showcases of modern technology. But what made them work was people. Cities thrived, ultimately, because millions of people went there to labor and live.

Many of the new residents were farmers. Some had gone bankrupt, unable to compete with the expanding farms of the Plains. Others, especially young people, grew tired of rural life and longed for the excitement of the city. A character in a play called *The City* voiced the dreams of many:

> Who wants to smell new-mown hay, if he can breathe in gasoline on Fifth Avenue instead! Think of the theaters! The crowds! Think of being able to go out on the street and see some one you didn't know by sight!

> **"W**ho wants to smell new-mown hay, if he can breathe in gasoline on Fifth Avenue instead!"
> —*Character in "The City"*

An equally dramatic migration to the cities came from abroad. Millions of immigrants entered the United States in the late 1800s. Their story is the subject of the next section.

SECTION REVIEW

1. KEY TERM mass transit

2. PEOPLE William Le Baron Jenney, Elisha Otis, John A. Roebling

3. COMPREHENSION Why was disease such a problem for the cities? What efforts were made to fight disease?

4. COMPREHENSION In what ways did neighborhoods farther away from the city differ from those closer to the city?

5. CRITICAL THINKING Explain the connection between the expansion of industry and the growth of cities.

Section Review Answers

1. *mass transit*—Means to transport large numbers of people.

2. *William Le Baron Jenney*—Designed first metal frame skyscraper in 1885. *Elisha Otis*— Inventor of the elevator. *John A. Roebling*—Designer of the Brooklyn Bridge.

3. Lack of garbage collection, pollution control, and regulations against spoiled food led to outbreaks of disease which spread quickly because of crowded living conditions. To fight these outbreaks, cities introduced sewers and water treatment plants.

4. They were newer, less crowded, more expensive with single-family homes and yards, and inhabited by a growing middle class.

5. Industry needed the concentration of people as workers and as markets for products, so they located in cities; while people moved to cities to get jobs and then became urban consumers who needed to buy products.

Closure

Remind students of the pre-reading objectives in the section opener . Pose one or all of these questions again. Then have students read Section 2 for the next class period, noting the difference between the new immigrants and those who had arrived before the late 1800s.

Background Urban growth was unevenly distributed. In 1890 half the urban population was concentrated in the Northeast, while less than one tenth of the population of the South lived in cities.

Background The 1870s and 1890s were decades of severe agricultural depression. Between 1880 and 1910, 11 million Americans moved from farms to urban centers, more than the number of immigrants who came to America during the same period.

2 The New Americans

Section Focus

Key Terms old immigration ■ new immigration ■ steerage ■ parochial school ■ political machine ■ nativism

Main Idea Seeking opportunity and freedom, more than 10 million immigrants poured into the United States during the late 1800s.

Objectives As you read, look for answers to these questions:
1. Where did immigrants come from, and where did they settle?
2. Why did some native-born Americans resent the immigrants?

Section Objectives

■ identify the reasons for the upsurge in immigration in the late 1800s
■ describe the responses of city politicians and nativists to the new immigrants

Introducing the Section

Connecting with Past Learnings

Ask students to consider the fact that all Americans came from somewhere else, and have them note what "immigrant" groups came to the Americas before 1800. (American Indians came from Asia; colonists came from Spain, Portugal, France, the Netherlands, and Great Britain; black slaves were brought from Africa.)

Key Terms

Write the key terms for this section on the board. Help students find where the words are defined in the text. Then call on volunteers to define the terms in their own words. **LEP**

So at last I was going to America! The boundaries burst. The arch of heaven soared. A million suns shone out for every star. The winds rushed in from outer space, roaring in my ears, "America! America!"

How could America inspire such excitement—even awe—in the minds of those who came here? Part of the explanation lies in the poverty and oppression many immigrants had endured in their native lands. Mary Antin, who wrote the passage above, was a Russian Jew. Her family came to America looking for work and hoping to escape the hostility toward Jews that was common in Russia. For this young woman, America represented the future—a place where she and her family could prosper and be treated as equals.

Millions of newcomers to the United States shared Mary Antin's feelings. But the task that lay before them was by no means easy. Many immigrants arrived penniless, owning nothing more than the clothes on their back. Most spoke no English. What they had in abundance was the determination to carve out new lives in a young and growing nation. Their efforts helped shape modern America.

THE NEW IMMIGRATION 4B

Two distinct waves of immigration arrived in the United States during the 1800s. The first phase of immigration, lasting until about 1880, is called the old immigration. The bulk of these settlers were Protestants from northern and western Europe—from Germany, Great Britain, Ireland, and Swe-

den. Most were farmers leaving behind poverty, overcrowding, and (in the case of Ireland) famine. Attracted by the availability of land, they settled mainly in the Midwest and Great Plains.

GRAPH SKILLS 4B

This graph shows numbers of immigrants between 1821 and 1900. Which decade had the highest immigrant total? How many people arrived in that decade? **CRITICAL THINKING** Unemployment in 1890 was a relatively low 4 percent. What conclusion could you draw about the availability of jobs for immigrants at that time?

IMMIGRATION, 1821–1900

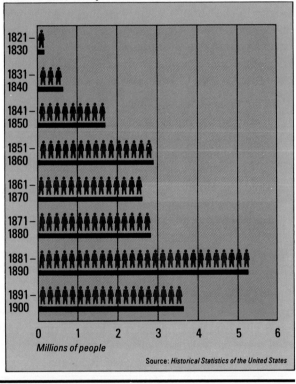

Source: *Historical Statistics of the United States*

SUPPORTING THE SECTION

Reinforcement Workbook: Worksheet 23
Reteaching Resources: Worksheet 23
Enrichment and Extension Resources: Primary Source Worksheet 12
Teaching Transparencies: Transparency 23

Graph Skills Answers
1881–1890. About 5.2 million. Many jobs were available due to the expanding economy.

Nevertheless, immigrant families often suffered from sharp generational differences. Immigrant children adjusted to life in America more easily than did their parents. They missed Europe less, did not feel so attached to European ways, and learned English more readily. Some children complained that their parents were tied to old ways of thinking. Some parents, in turn, complained that their children had lost respect for the family heritage. One parent sighed, "I can't talk to them about my problems and they can't talk to me about theirs."

Immigrants did have several organizations to turn to for support. Mutual-aid societies like the Sons of Italy helped people find jobs, paid for burials, and made loans. Churches and synagogues brought members of the community together on a regular basis. Parochial schools—schools run by religious groups—helped maintain the religious solidarity of new immigrant groups.

HELP FROM THE BOSSES 6B, 7C

Many immigrants also received much-needed help from city leaders known as "bosses." Bosses created political machines to dominate political life in many major American cities in the late 1800s. These leaders used bribes and favoritism to grab and hold on to power. They found ways to rig elections, often by buying votes. Then they appointed their friends to important jobs, creating small machines in the city's neighborhoods. At election time the boss would be assured that his candidates would win.

The bosses, while crooked, did perform important services. At a time when unemployment insurance and welfare were virtually unknown, the bosses helped city residents cope with their troubles—getting them jobs, paying for funerals, and so on. Even small favors like donating a turkey at Christmas or a basket of food during hard times made residents feel cared for. As an Irish boss in Boston explained, "There's got to be . . . somebody that any bloke can come to—no matter what he's done—and get help. Help, you understand, none of your law and justice, but help."

Recent immigrants in particular needed this help, for many of them had nowhere else to turn. One boss of Tammany Hall, the New York City machine, declared:

> People abuse Tammany for this and for that. But they forget what they owe to Tammany. . . . There is no such organization for taking hold of the untrained, friendless man and converting him into a citizen. Who else would do it if we did not?

For many, what mattered was not that bosses were crooked, but that they made things work.

Tenement houses and shops offering ready-made clothing line a street in an ethnic neighborhood in New York City known as "Little Italy." The photograph shows the crowded conditions in which many immigrants lived. Note also the gas lamps and peddlers with their pushcarts. ECONOMICS What businesses can you identify from the photograph?
9B

Patterns in History
Have students compare immigration at the turn of the century with immigration today. *Where do most immigrants to the United States come from today?* (Mexico, Central America, Asia.) *How is the situation of today's immigrants like that of the past? How is it different?* (Similarities—problems of language, difference in culture, often unskilled; differences—immigration today is much more regulated, so many immigrants enter and live here illegally.)

Impact of Geography
On a classroom map or the world map at the back of the book, have students identify the countries from which most early immigrants came: Germany, Great Britain, Ireland, and Sweden. Then have them find the countries immigrants came from in the late 1800s: Italy, Greece, Poland, and Russia. Discuss how these newer immigrants differed from immigrants from western Europe in language, religion, and culture. (Different foods, customs, clothes, etc.)

🄲 Cooperative Learning

Letters from friends and relatives already in America encouraged many immigrants to leave their native countries for a "better life" in the United States. Divide the class into small groups and have each group write a letter from a family already in America telling potential immigrants of what awaits them here. LEP

Photo Caption Answer
Bootmaker, brewery, bank, clothes store, and furniture store.

A nativist cartoon from the 1890s entitled "Where the Blame Lies" shows a judge persuading Uncle Sam that immigrant masses are responsible for a host of evils, including anarchy, socialism, and the Mafia. **ISSUES** To what extent does nativism still exist in the United States? **4B**

Chinese immigrants in Los Angeles display a dragon as part of a festival. An 1868 treaty allowed Chinese to immigrate in unlimited numbers, but when hard times struck in the 1870s, some Californians insisted "The Chinese must go!" and started anti-Chinese riots. **CULTURAL PLURALISM** Why might immigrants have lived together in communities like Los Angeles's Chinatown? **4B**

THE NATIVIST REACTION 4B

Hoping to make a good first impression, some bosses had representatives stand at the dock greeting immigrants as they landed. But immigrants did not always receive a warm welcome. Many of them encountered nativism—hostility from native-born Americans.

Nativism had been around a long time before the new immigrants arrived. As early as the 1840s groups of nativists had formed a secret society in New York. They pledged not to support any Catholics or immigrants running for public office. During the following decade, nativists across the country banded together in what was called the "Know-Nothing Party." (Its members were sworn to respond "I know nothing" when asked about the party. This gave the party its name.)

The Know-Nothings enjoyed a brief political life in the mid-1850s before fading away. Yet some Americans continued to hold nativist feelings. The increase in immigration after 1880 deepened their hostility toward newcomers. Nativists revived calls for restricting the flow of immigrants into the United States.

Much of the nativists' fear was economic. The sheer number of immigrants was too great, they claimed. The newcomers would steal jobs from other Americans. Willing to work for low wages and under poor conditions, the immigrants would encourage companies to exploit all American workers. There is no clear proof that the new immigration caused either unemployment or a decline in working conditions. Nevertheless, many Americans took these charges seriously at the time. People make exactly the same arguments today about newly arrived groups.

Nativists also claimed that many new immigrants came to the United States only to make a quick profit. Once they had saved enough, the immigrants would return to their home country.

Other nativist complaints dealt with immigration's effects on American society. Most of the new immigrants were Catholic or Jewish, and many did not speak English. Their customs also differed from those of earlier immigrants. For these reasons, nativists argued, the new immigrants could not—or would not—become "real" Americans. The ethnic neighborhoods in many American cities were proof, in nativists' eyes, that the new immigrants had failed to adapt to their new lives as Americans.

Religious prejudice often lay behind the nativists' complaints. Hostility toward Catholics and Jews became more visible as the size of these groups increased. The American Protective Association, an anti-Catholic group, was formed in 1887. By 1894 it had a million members. Jews likewise confronted a host of barriers. Clubs would not accept them as members. Private schools would not admit their children. People would not sell them homes.

Still another cause of nativism was racial prejudice directed at groups such as the Chinese. Immigrants from China had begun to arrive in the United States during the California gold rush of the 1850s. Thousands labored in mines or built railroads, while others remained in San Francisco, the main entry port for Asian immigrants. Spurred by racism as well as fears that Chinese immigrants were taking jobs from native-born Americans, nativists tried to restrict immigration. As you will read in Chapter 11, they succeeded: the Chinese Exclusion Act of 1882 cut off all immigration from China.

Nativist pressure also led to other restrictions on immigration. In 1882 Congress barred the immigration of convicts, the insane, and persons living on charity. In 1885, at the urging of labor unions, Congress forbade American companies to bring in skilled foreign workers under contract. In 1896 Congress passed a bill requiring that all immigrants pass a literacy test. President Cleveland vetoed the bill, arguing that what mattered was not literacy but a willingness to work.

BUILDING MODERN AMERICA 4B

Immigrants did indeed work. In countless ways, the newest Americans helped build a stronger nation. Poles and Italians labored in the flour mills and railroad yards of Buffalo. Jews worked in New York's garment industry. Slavs from Eastern Europe kept Pennsylvania's coal fields running. Chicago, a center of industry and transportation, became virtually an immigrant city. By 1890

BIOGRAPHY 4F

IRVING BERLIN (1888–1989), who emigrated with his family from Russia to New York City, was a self-taught musician. Berlin expressed his love for his new country in patriotic songs and musicals, including two musicals written about soldiers in World Wars I and II. Berlin wrote over 1,000 songs, many of which, such as "White Christmas" and "Easter Parade," have become classics.

nearly 80 percent of its residents were either immigrants or the children of immigrants.

Bringing with them the various cultures of Europe, the new immigrants broadened the cultural life of American cities. They set up thousands of foreign-language newspapers. They ran theater groups. (Several Broadway and Hollywood stars began their careers in the Yiddish-language theater in New York.) They opened restaurants serving foods from around the world. Immigrant artists, scientists, and intellectuals all thrived in the free atmosphere of the United States. One of these was a Russian-born composer named Israel Baline. Better known as Irving Berlin, he wrote a song of praise and thanks to his adopted country—"God Bless America."

SECTION REVIEW

1. KEY TERMS old immigration, new immigration, steerage, parochial school, political machine, nativism

2. PLACE Ellis Island

3. COMPREHENSION What factors helped encourage the new immigration?

4. COMPREHENSION According to nativists, what effects would the new immigration have on American workers?

5. CRITICAL THINKING In your opinion, does a country have the right to set different limits on immigration depending on the country of origin? Why or why not?

Biography
For further reading consider: Ewen, David. *The Story of Irving Berlin.* Holt, 1950.

Background To sell land and thus stimulate economic growth, individual states and territories and railroad companies conducted massive advertising campaigns to attract immigrants. The railroad campaigns were especially successful and played a large role in determining ethnic patterns in the Midwest.

An International Menu

Introducing the Feature

Ask students what they think the most "typical" American food is. (Likely answers are hamburgers, hot dogs, french fries, pizza, etc.) Explain to students that these foods have their origins in European cooking, as does most American food.

Have students examine the illustrations, identifying the various foods. (Squash, corn, potatoes; pretzels; French bread and cheese.)

Teaching the Expressions

Succotash: Ask students to describe this food. (Mixture of lima beans, kernels of corn, and tomatoes cooked together.) You may want to point out to students that in Great Britain, *corn* refers to all kinds of grains including wheat, rye, and oats. The British use the term *maize,* an American Indian word, to refer to the food we call *corn.* Ask students why this shift in meaning, using a word that used to describe all grains to describe only one, may have occurred in America.

Cookie: Ask students if they know what the British term for a *cookie* is. (Biscuit.) *What do Americans mean by the word biscuit?* (A small, round bread.)

Sauerkraut: Explain that the reason the Germans who settled in Pennsylvania were called "Pennsylvania Dutch" is because the German word for Germany is *Deutschland.*

An International Menu

From the time of Columbus's arrival, people in the Americas have encountered foods from several different cultures. As each new group arrived, its people brought different foods and words to describe them. By 1900, Americans were eating an "international" menu without realizing it.

North America had so many unfamiliar food plants that English and French settlers used—and mispronounced—the Indians' names for them. **Squash, succotash,** and **pecan** all come from Algonkian languages.

The English not only took over the Dutch colonies around New York, they also eagerly borrowed ideas from Dutch cooks and bakers. **Waffle** and **cookie** were originally words for Dutch treats.

In the Caribbean islands, the Carib Indians built frames of green wood and sticks for smoking fish and grilling meat. Spanish explorers called these *barbacoa,* which became, in English, **barbecue.**

The first settlers from Germany, usually called "Pennsylvania Dutch," introduced country dishes like **sauerkraut, pretzels,** and **noodles.** They also brought the custom of—and the word—**dunking** doughnuts.

In California and throughout the Southwest, early Spanish-speaking settlers brought with them a spicy cuisine from Mexico that included **tortillas, frijoles, tamales,** and **chili con carne.**

Some foods that were favorites of the Aztecs of Mexico were taken first to Spain, then brought back to America by European settlers. Along the way, their names changed only a little from the original Nahuatl language: *tomatl* to **tomato**, *chocolatl* to **chocolate**, *ahuacatl* to **avocado.**

Visitors to the 1893 World's Fair in Chicago could sample another Latin American custom—the **cafeteria,** or coffee-seller's shop. The word quickly came to mean a self-service eating place.

People from the German city of Hamburg are "Hamburgers." When immigrants from northern Germany first served a plate of raw or cooked chopped beef, it was called "Hamburger steak"—and then **hamburger.** During World War I, when German names were thought unpatriotic, restaurants renamed it "Salisbury steak."

No cook in China ever made **chop suey,** and no one can be sure what Chinese cook in the United States invented this dish to appeal to American tastes. In any case, he or she used the Mandarin Chinese term *tsa-sui* [zasui], which means "odds and ends."

The corner deli, or **delicatessen,** got its start in the United States among Jewish and German immigrants to large eastern cities. The word means "fine food."

What do you call a long sandwich of French bread filled with meat, cheese, and salad? It depends on where you live. In the South it's a **poor boy,** from the New Orleans French word *pourboire,* which means "a tip"—the price of a sandwich. In other cities you might ask for a **hero, submarine, grinder, Garibaldi,** or **hoagie.**

Italian immigrants brought many new American favorites—all kinds of **pasta** including **spaghetti, macaroni,** and **lasagna,** along with the sausages **salami** and **baloney** (named for the Italian city of Bologna). **Pizza**—which is really American—was based on a dish popular in Naples.

People who came from Germany called themselves *Deutsch* (DOYTCH), which was mispronounced by their English-speaking neighbors as *Dutch.* You might also note that during World War I many Americans referred to sauerkraut as "liberty cabbage." Ask students to suggest why that was true. (The United States was fighting Germany and Americans felt it was unpatriotic to use German words.)

Tortillas: Have students consider what European country influenced Mexican food. (Spain.) ***What other Mexican foods do you like to eat?*** (Some examples include guacamole, tostados, and fajitas.)

Tomatoes: Ask students to recall other fruits, vegetables, and crops that were once unique to the Western Hemisphere. You may wish to refer them to Chapter 1 for the answer. (Corn, pumpkins, peppers, beans, gourds, lima beans, potatoes, pineapples, bananas, peanuts, and tobacco.)

Hamburger: The Tartars, Asian people who invaded eastern Europe in the 1200s, originally brought the idea of eating raw, chopped meat into the Baltic region of Germany (thus, "steak tartar"). When the custom was brought to the United States in the 1880s, some health food advocates supported it. Most Americans, however, prefer their chopped meat cooked.

Poor boy: Ask students what this kind of sandwich is called in your community. Have them find out why it has that name.

3 City Life and Leisure

SECTION 3

City Life and Leisure
(pp. 148–155)

Section Objectives

- explain how an increase in the number of products, information, and entertainment changed American lifestyles
- describe how artistic styles reflected the urban age

Introducing the Section

Connecting with Past Learnings

Help students to see how American life changed in the 1800s. *What were some of the main features of daily life in the United States prior to the rapid expansion of industry in the late 1800s?* (Lived on farms or in small towns; food and clothes had to be made at home; work and chores took up almost all time; no electric lights, plumbing, etc.)

As students do this lesson, have them think about how rapidly life changed in the late 1800s.

Key Term

Write the key term for the section on the board. Ask students to define what journalism is. Then ask them to explain what characterizes yellow journalism and give examples of yellow journalism today. **LEP**

Section Focus

Key Term yellow journalism

Main Idea American cities offered their residents, rich and poor alike, a wide range of activities.

Objectives As you read, look for answers to these questions:
1. How did more products and information become available to the American people?
2. What forms of sports and entertainment gained wide popularity?
3. How did artistic styles reflect the urban age?

In 1893, to mark the 400th anniversary of Christopher Columbus's landing in the Americas, the city of Chicago held a World's Fair. Some 28 million visitors paid 50 cents apiece to view the 666 acres of exhibits. They came to see Europe's past and America's future. Plaster models of stately European buildings and statues stood alongside displays of the newest American inventions. The biggest attraction was the world's first Ferris wheel, a monstrous machine able to carry hundreds of people. The fair as a whole, one poster claimed, offered "the most Significant and Grandest Spectacle of Modern Times."

The grandeur of the fair contrasted sharply with the everyday lives of many who viewed it. But the fair did provide a glimpse of the variety and excitement an American city of the 1890s could offer.

CHAIN AND DEPARTMENT STORES 3C, 8D

Nowhere was the variety of city life more evident than in the field of consumer goods. A few companies set up huge networks of retail businesses to serve the growing consumer market. The first was The Great Atlantic & Pacific Tea Company, a grocery business founded in the 1860s. The company fully exploited the principle of economies of scale (page 97). Because it bought products in enormous volumes, A & P was able to lower its prices. The low prices attracted new customers. The company then used the profits to set up even more stores.

Other chains—businesses with more than one location—flourished as well. Some of the largest were department stores, providing customers with a wide range of goods. R. H. Macy and Company, which opened in New York City in 1858, became one of the largest. Frank Winfield Woolworth's five-and-ten-cent stores, the first of which opened in 1879, sold household goods to bargain-hunting shoppers.

Montgomery Ward, founded in 1872, carried the notion of chain stores one step further when it pioneered the mail-order catalog. The company could now reach customers from coast to coast without having to build stores in every town. The success of mail-order businesses such as Montgomery Ward and Sears, Roebuck helped spread urban styles all over the country.

City residents, of course, did not have to rely on catalogs. They could see the items offered by major retail companies first-hand. The largest companies built spacious, elegant stores in urban centers. There customers could spend an afternoon browsing and enjoying the atmosphere. For many people in cities, shopping became a form of recreation.

ADVERTISING: INVENTING DEMAND 8A

Advertising came of age in the American cities of the late 1800s. It was both easier and more necessary to advertise than in earlier times. Newspapers, magazines, posters, and billboards were readily available in urban areas. City residents could hardly avoid coming across some form of advertising during the course of the day.

Advertising became necessary because the supply of consumer goods now exceeded the demand. This had not been the case earlier in American history. A business of the late 1800s had to do more than tell the public about its product. It had

---

SUPPORTING THE SECTION

Reinforcement Workbook: Worksheet 24
Reteaching Resources: Worksheet 24
Teaching Transparencies: Transparency 24

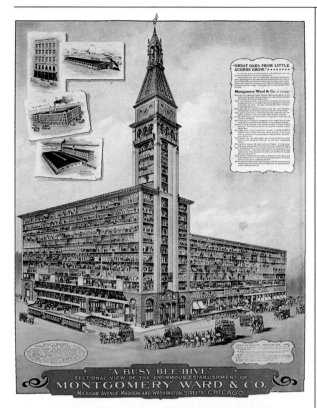

This poster advertises the Chicago headquarters of Montgomery Ward as "a busy bee hive." The store appears as if its outer walls had been removed. The store's many departments offered everything from baby carriages to violins. **TECHNOLOGY** Name the forms of transportation that appear on the poster. **3A, 4E**

to create a demand for that product. Advertising served to create demand.

Some ads, like those for Procter & Gamble or Singer Sewing Machine Company, were lavishly illustrated. As the technology of printing improved, large firms began to use color ads in mass-circulation magazines. Others concentrated on catchy songs or slogans. Whatever the method, the goals were the same: to catch the customers' attention and to fix the company or product name in their mind. Advertising could accomplish this through visual appeal, humor, or just plain repetition.

A good example of the last method was Sozodont, a tooth powder. By putting the name of the product everywhere, its makers hoped to have people think of the name Sozodont as a synonym for tooth powder. Foreign visitors to the United States saw the word Sozodont so much that they

thought it was another name for the nation. The makers of Sozodont used every excuse to get their product across to consumers, as illustrated by a newspaper ad on January 2, 1887:

> Hark! the New Year bells are ringing,
> How they laugh, as they are swaying in
>   the frosty air!
> Opening up a fortune golden
> To our hopes, though sight is holden
> In this world of care. . . .
> And this New Year fast advancing,
> Like a swift steed, gay and prancing,
> Must be sure to find
> Teeth well brushed each night and
>   morning
> With sweet SOZODONT, adorning
> Lips, whose words are kind.

The three advertisements above were some of the hundreds that bombarded city dwellers each day. By the mid-1800s, most magazines contained advertising. Some were started chiefly to earn advertising money. **CULTURE** What images did the Coca-Cola Company use to sell its product? **9B**

Focus

Have students name the new products, services, leisure-time activities, methods of selling, and jobs mentioned in the section. (Chain and department stores, mail order, advertising, cheap newspapers, greater opportunities for education, jobs for women, baseball, bicycling, popular entertainment, public parks, and realism in art.) *How did these change the way Americans lived?* (More free time; access to more ready-made products and information; more women in work force; more educated population.) *Where were these changes most prominent?* (In the cities.)

Discuss with students how the innovations of the late 1800s defined a national culture.

Developing the Lesson

After students have read the section, you may want to consider the following activities:

Economics

How does the growth of advertising reflect a society of abundance? (The supply of consumer goods exceeded demand, so advertisers had to create demand.) Ask students if they can think of products in today's market for which advertising has created a demand. (Many appliances, new perfumes and other personal goods, fashions.)

Have students compare the Sozodont campaign with today's advertisements. *Do you think that the Sozodont advertisements would be effective today? Why or why not?* Ask students to suggest advertising campaigns they find effective and to analyze what makes these ads work.

As advertising became more widespread and more sophisticated, businesses turned to advertising agencies for help. Agencies came up with a variety of sales pitches, a favorite being the use of testimonials from satisfied customers:

> I suffered fifteen years from a severe case of catarrh [head cold]; coughed incessantly day and night. I bought a Pillow-Inhaler, and since using it my cough is gone, my lungs are no longer weak and sore, and I am in better health than I have been for years.

This sounds impressive. But how would a customer know whether it was true? Some ads tried to mislead the public; the worst were downright lies. Among the frauds were liquid medicines, consisting largely of alcohol, which claimed to cure everything from sore feet to heart disease. As popular as they were ineffective, these products demonstrated the ability of shrewd advertising to manipulate the public.

In this cartoon critical of deceptive advertising, the Statue of Liberty has been plastered with advertisements for products like "Suredeath Cigarettes." **ETHICS** Describe the conflicting values represented in this cartoon.
7J

THE POPULAR PRESS 7B, 7J

Newspapers and magazines grew for many reasons in the late 1800s. Businesses needed a cheap, visible forum for their advertising. Better postal rates and service made it possible to send subscribers their copies quickly. The technology of printing—the linotype machine (invented in 1884),

cheaper paper, and the typewriter—made it possible to publish and sell papers and magazines more cheaply. Most of all, the press gave the public what it wanted: dramatic stories about the rich, the poor, the criminals, and the do-gooders. Little wonder that newspaper circulation increased from under 3 million in 1870 to 15 million by the century's end.

Urban life was full of dramatic events that could be presented in eye-catching headlines. Newspapers described crimes in gruesome detail. They wrote of poor people starving, of rich people holding lavish parties. They criticized government officials, charging that they did too little and were paid too much. Exposing the evils of society might or might not lead to reforms, but in any event it sold papers. Thus was born yellow journalism—journalism that exaggerates and exploits news in order to attract readers. (The term got its name from the yellow ink used by one New York City newspaper.)

The two masters of yellow journalism were Joseph Pulitzer and William Randolph Hearst. Pulitzer, a Hungarian immigrant, rose through the ranks to become a newspaper editor and owner. He devised the format, which is common today, of having separate sections for topics such as sports or national news. He also vowed that his papers, the *St. Louis Post Dispatch* and *The World*, would "expose all fraud and sham, fight all public evils and abuses."

> "
> **. . . expose all fraud and sham, fight all public evils and abuses."**
> —*Joseph Pulitzer*

Hearst, the son of a wealthy mining magnate, used the same techniques with his newspapers, the most famous of which was the *New York Journal*. Before long the two newspaper chains were in a fierce battle for readers. The competition drove both papers to even greater extremes of yellow journalism. Their reporting of events in Cuba in 1898, for example, helped bring about war between the United States and Spain, as you will read in Chapter 11.

EDUCATION FOR THE MASSES 4D, 8A

Newspapers, as well as giving information to city residents, also helped them learn to read. In the late 1800s, cities needed an educated population more than ever before. Industries were looking for skilled workers. Millions of immigrants could not read or write English; they also knew little about the American system of government.

Education, it was hoped, could equip people for life in American society. It could also help reduce differences among the many nationalities that had settled in the United States. With these goals in mind, the country began to devote more time and money to education for all classes of citizens. States passed laws requiring children to attend school. Massachusetts had passed the first such law in 1852; over the next four decades 27 states and territories followed suit.

Schooling grew more diverse. Kindergartens, a German invention, became widespread in urban areas. Public schools began offering new courses in addition to the traditional "three R's" ("reading, 'riting, and 'rithmetic"). Colleges also expanded their course offerings and worked to provide education of higher quality. The nation's first business school, the Wharton School of the University of Pennsylvania, opened in 1881. More women's colleges, such as Smith (1871) and Bryn Mawr (1880), were founded. The creation of co-educational institutions such as land-grant colleges (page 104) created still more openings for women.

Few African Americans shared in the growth of educational opportunities. Southern states gave little support to black education, for they had little money to begin with and spent most of it on white schools. Backed by private northern donors, institutions such as Howard University in Washington, D.C., were able to provide some black students with a quality education.

In spite of its failures, American public education made great strides during the late 1800s. School attendance more than doubled. The number of public high schools leaped by 60 times. The literacy rate for the country rose from 80 percent in 1870 to over 92 percent by 1910. In sum, millions of people received the education they needed to cope with a rapidly changing world.

This 1890 photograph by Jacob Riis shows immigrant children in a classroom of New York's P.S. 52, an industrial school. Riis, himself an immigrant from Denmark, publicized the lives of newly arrived Americans in photographs, books, and newspaper articles. He campaigned for improvements in urban life such as better housing, public parks, and playgrounds. **PARTICIPATION** Describe the students and their classroom. In what ways does it differ from your own? 4D

WOMEN IN THE WORK FORCE 4C, 8A

Among those who benefited from advances in education were women. More than five times as many women attended college in 1920 than in 1890; an even greater number of women received a high school education. Women were still expected to think of themselves primarily as wives and mothers. More women, however, were taking jobs outside the home. At the same time, helped by improved education, women were finding new professional opportunities.

There was nothing new, of course, about women entering the work force. Women workers had, for example, played a major role in the first New England textile mills. Poor women, especially immigrants, continued to take low-paying jobs in industry throughout the 1800s.

A more promising means of advancement for middle-class women came with the rise of huge business, finance, and government organizations. A great deal of clerical work was necessary to keep these organizations running efficiently. Firms realized that they could hire female office workers, train them at little cost, and pay them low wages. The number of women office workers leaped 2,700 percent between 1870 and 1900. By 1900 women held more than three-fourths of all stenographers' and typists' jobs.

Discrimination and lack of education usually kept poor and immigrant women out of office jobs. Instead these jobs went to middle-class women. These women still had household tasks to perform, but such tasks now took less time. Women could buy foods and clothes they once had to make themselves, and could also buy things like sewing machines and ice boxes to make housework more efficient. These developments freed many women to take jobs outside the home.

This photograph from the 1890s shows women clerical workers and their male supervisor at the offices of the Metropolitan Insurance Company. ECONOMICS What kind of work are the women performing? Why, do you think, were clerical workers traditionally women? 6B

This print by the lithographers Currier and Ives shows the first baseball game between two organized teams, the Knickerbockers and the New York Nine, in 1846. Union soldiers helped spread the game throughout the country during the Civil War. This game was held at Elysian Field in Hoboken, New Jersey. The Knickerbockers won, 23–1. **NATIONAL IDENTITY** Baseball became so popular after 1900 that French-born philosopher Jacques Barzun said, "Whoever wants to know the heart and mind of America had better learn baseball." Do you agree? Explain your answer. **6C, 8A**

LEISURE TIME 8A

Leisure had not been an important part of the average American's life before the 1890s. Farmers and workers had few opportunities for leisure, since making a living took so much of their time and energy. City life, on the other hand, started to give middle-class people more free time. A middle-class city worker like a clerk had fixed working hours and usually had some money left over after expenses to use for entertainment. Now he or she could begin to enjoy recreation, just as the wealthy had done for years. Sports, once geared to the rich, became popular among more average citizens as well.

Baseball is a good example. The game became an organized sport in 1845 when a group of rich New Yorkers formed the Knickerbocker Club. The club played baseball regularly, wearing uniforms of blue trousers, white shirts, and straw hats. The umpire was decked out in a stove-pipe hat and frock coat. A formal dinner followed each game. By 1856, however, middle-class clubs had formed, playing against such gentlemen's teams as the Knickerbockers. In 1869 the first professional team, the Cincinnati Red Stockings, was formed. The first World Series took place in 1903. By that time baseball had secured a place as one of America's favorite pastimes, its games attended by millions of spectators.

Bicycling likewise became a popular sport. The bicycles of the 1860s, with their enormous front wheels, were suited only for the daring. Bicyclists were an early version of today's race track drivers, even dressing for the part with knee pants, high-necked jackets, and round caps. After the 1880s, when a safer bicycle was invented, millions of Americans took to the streets on the new contraptions. People used bicycles to get to work, for exercise, and for weekend sightseeing tours.

A couple show off their "high-wheeler" bicycle in front of the White House. These models were hard to peddle and easy to fall off. **TECHNOLOGY** What were the bicycle's advantages over other nineteenth-century forms of private transportation? **3A, 4E**

Photo Caption Answers
(Top) Students may suggest that much of the game is individualistic, with a pitcher against a batter and that the lack of a time limit allows the underdog a chance to win. (Bottom) They were less expensive to own and maintain than a horse and carriage; they provided exercise.

The five Ringling brothers
started a circus in Wisconsin in 1884. They joined
with the Barnum and
Bailey show in 1907.
CULTURE Which circus
figures are on this poster?
8A

1886	First dinner jacket worn, at the Autumn Ball held at the Tuxedo Park Country Club, New York. A short black coat with satin lapels, it came to be known as a "tuxedo."
1890	First electrocution of a criminal, William Kemmler, a convicted murderer, in Auburn Prison, Auburn, N.Y.
	Journalist Nellie Bly completes first publicized tour of the world made by a woman traveling alone. (Jan. 25).
1895	First pizzeria opens at 53-1/2 Spring Street, New York City.
1896	First screen kiss—in the film *The Kiss*—brings on first screen censorship controversy.
1898	First professional basketball games are played by the National Basketball League, which has teams in New York, Philadelphia, Brooklyn, and New Jersey.

Like sports, other forms of entertainment came
within the reach of average Americans during the
late 1800s. The theater offered amazing variety.
For the cultured audience there were classic productions, such as Shakespearean tragedies. People
interested in simple entertainments could relax at
a musical comedy or a vaudeville show. This was
also the heyday of the circus. P. T. Barnum's
"Greatest Show on Earth," with its death-defying
acts and exotic animals, thrilled people of all ages.

City governments did their part to improve public entertainment. They established symphony orchestras and built public libraries and art
museums. They also reserved space—a city's most
valuable resource—for public parks. The leader in
this movement was a landscape architect named
Frederick Law Olmstead. He designed New York
City's Central Park as well as Washington Park in
Chicago, Back Bay Park in Boston, and others.
Parks gave city residents a bit of the feel of the
country. They also provided a place for sports, picnics, and long Sunday strolls.

NEW TRENDS IN THE ARTS 4F

Art, so often a mirror of society, reflected the
changes in the United States as the nation entered the urban age. Some artists, seeking to portray the United States as a modern, sophisticated
nation, sought to compete with the most up-to-
date European styles. Painters such as John
Singer Sargent and Mary Cassatt studied in Europe and then reflected European styles in their
own works. Writers such as Henry James described the lives of upper-class Americans; their
novels often took place in Europe. At the same
time, more and more American artists were heading in another direction. Their works stressed realism and practicality. The architect Louis
Sullivan, designer of one of the earliest skyscrapers, used the phrase "form follows function"
to describe his attitude toward architecture.

Painters such as Winslow Homer and Thomas
Eakins (AY–kinz) found beauty in America's common folk and surroundings. Homer became a master of detail in his paintings of people and places,
saying that "when I have selected [a subject], I
paint it exactly as it appears." Eakins became
known for the precision of his painting. He even

BIOGRAPHY 4C

MARY CASSATT (1844–1926)
was born in western Pennsylvania and moved to Paris to study
art. She became the first American artist to associate and
exhibit her work with French
impressionist painters, such as
Edgar Degas and Edouard Manet.
Cassatt's works, which featured
scenes of daily life, helped popularize the highly controversial
impressionist style in America.
Her self-portrait from around
1880 appears at right.

Photo Caption Answer
Horseback riders, clowns,
ringmasters.

Famous Firsts
Have students choose one of
the entries and create a
collage illustrating the ways
the product or idea introduced
has changed over time.

Biography
Have students find out more
information about the
impressionist school of
painting, and bring examples
of impressionist paintings to
class.

Mary Cassatt painted *Woman and Child Driving* in 1879. Cassatt often devoted her paintings to the theme of mothers and their children. CULTURE Describe the subjects of the painting. 4C, 9B

dissected animals in order to learn more about their structure.

Authors, most notably Mark Twain, wrote about everyday life. In *The Adventures of Tom Sawyer* (1876) and *The Adventures of Huckleberry Finn* (1884), Twain captured the flavor of rural America's life and manners. Other writers of the period included Stephen Crane, Frank Norris, and William Dean Howells. Crane painted a gloomy picture of tenement life, and Norris exposed economic wrongs. Howells dealt with social issues such as marriage, divorce, business success and failure, and the conflict between freedom and conformity for city residents. As you will read in Chapter 7, these were just a few of the problems confronting modern American society.

SECTION REVIEW

1. KEY TERM yellow journalism

2. PEOPLE Joseph Pulitzer, William Randolph Hearst, Frederick Law Olmstead

3. COMPREHENSION Why did advertising become important in the late 1800s?

4. COMPREHENSION Why did cities need an educated population?

5. CRITICAL THINKING Agree or disagree with the following statement, and explain your position: "The growth of the advertising and entertainment industries in the 1880s and 1890s was a sign of the growing wealth of the United States." 8A

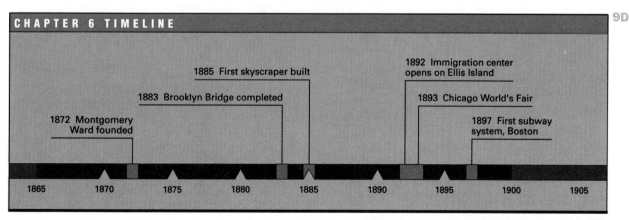

9D

CHAPTER 6 TIMELINE

1885 First skyscraper built

1892 Immigration center opens on Ellis Island

1883 Brooklyn Bridge completed

1893 Chicago World's Fair

1872 Montgomery Ward founded

1897 First subway system, Boston

1865   1870   1875   1880   1885   1890   1895   1900   1905

CHAPTER 6   URBAN AMERICAN SOCIETY, 1865–1900   **155**

Chapter 6 REVIEW

CHAPTER 6 SUMMARY

SECTION 1: American cities grew in size and population in the late 1800s.

■ Cities benefited from ties to industry and transportation.

■ The building of trolley lines, subway trains, and bridges helped cities expand.

■ Rapid growth caused problems such as disease, fire, and crime.

SECTION 2: A flood of immigrants in the years after the Civil War transformed American life.

■ In the late 1800s, most of the immigrants to the United States came from southern and eastern Europe.

■ Corruption became common in American cities as a result of rapid growth and the immigrants' need for help from those in power.

■ Some Americans tried to restrict immigration because they feared that the newcomers would not adapt well to American life or would take jobs from them.

SECTION 3: City life offered many opportunities.

■ Large department stores opened, offering consumers a wide array of goods.

■ Increasing competition among businesses led to the widespread use of advertising to attract customers.

■ Improved printing methods, lower postal rates, advertising, and the demand for entertainment and information greatly increased newspaper and magazine sales.

■ Educational opportunities increased for most people.

■ Middle-class women found office jobs open to them because of the need for clerical workers.

■ New trends in sports and entertainment reflected the greater leisure time of the American worker.

■ The realist movement in art and in literature tried to capture the details and flavor of everyday life.

KEY TERMS ●

Use the following terms to complete the sentences below.

mass transit
nativism
new immigration
old immigration
political machine
yellow journalism

1. Immigration before 1880 is often called the ____ .
2. ____ systems encouraged the growth of cities by allowing people to live far from their places of work.
3. Moves to restrict the flow of immigration were the result of ____ .

4. Newspaper owner Joseph Pulitzer used the technique of ____ to attract readers and to make his fortune.
5. New York's Tammany Hall was a famous example of a ____ .
6. During the period of immigration known as ____ , millions of people came to the United States from southern and eastern Europe.

PEOPLE TO IDENTIFY ●

Use the following names to complete the sentences below.

William Randolph Hearst
William Le Baron Jenney
Frederick Law Olmstead
Elisha Otis
John A. Roebling

1. ____ built the first passenger elevator in 1857.
2. ____ owned a vast newspaper chain that specialized in sensational stories.
3. The first metal frame skyscraper was a ten-story building designed by ____ .
4. The man who designed the Brooklyn Bridge was ____ .
5. ____ designed New York City's Central Park.

Match each of the letters on the map with the places that are listed below.

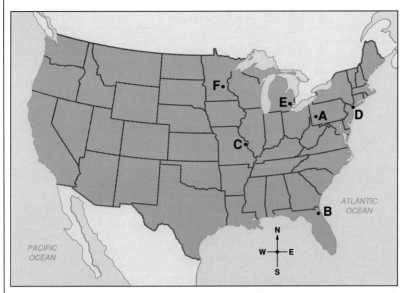

1. Ellis Island
2. St. Louis
3. Detroit
4. Pittsburgh
5. Jacksonville
6. Minneapolis

REVIEWING THE FACTS ▲

1. How did the right location enable small towns to develop into large cities?
2. What technological breakthroughs allowed rapid urban growth after 1850?
3. What were some of the problems that rapidly growing cities faced?
4. What factors encouraged the new immigration of the late 1800s?
5. How did the new immigrants to America differ from the old immigrants?
6. What problems did the new immigrants face in the United States?

7. What factors influenced the growth of nativism? What restrictions on immigration did nativists impose?
8. Why did advertising grow so rapidly during the late 1800s? What methods did advertisers use?
9. Why did education become a matter of wide public concern in the late 1800s?
10. Why did leisure time become more important to people in the late 1800s? What kinds of leisure-time pursuits did cities offer?

CRITICAL THINKING SKILLS ▲

1. **MAKING JUDGMENTS** Can advertising really create a demand for a product? Why or why not? Give examples from modern life.

2. **ANALYZING A QUOTATION** Architect Louis Sullivan described his attitude toward architecture with the phrase "form follows function." What do you think he meant?

3. **FORMING A HYPOTHESIS** How might the size and location of American cities be different today if industrialization had not occurred?

WRITING ABOUT TOPICS IN AMERICAN HISTORY ■

1. **CONNECTING WITH LITERATURE** A selection from "An Unfinished Story" by O. Henry appears on pages 781–782. Read it and answer the questions. Then answer the following question: What were some ways working men and women could spend leisure time in American cities in the early 1900s?

2. **APPLYING THEMES: PLURALISTIC SOCIETY** Find out about the steps an immigrant must go through to earn United States citizenship. If possible, attend a swearing-in ceremony for new citizens. Then write a report for the class summarizing the process.

3. **LOCAL HISTORY** If a political machine existed in your community or state in the late 1800s, do research and write a short essay about its time in power.

Critical Thinking Skills
1. Advertising introduces products that people may not be aware of and also suggests that a person's quality of life may be improved by purchasing such products.
2. Sullivan believed practical concerns dictated aesthetic decisions.
3. Students should mention that cities would most likely be smaller and less crowded, with most cities located close to ports in order to facilitate trade with other countries.

Writing About Topics in American History
1. They could attend sporting events, ride bicycles, go to the theater or musical comedies or vaudeville shows, hear symphony orchestras, or relax in public parks.
2. Students should discuss the process of naturalization; the establishment of residency; the need for knowledge of U.S. history and government; the ability to read, write, and speak English; and the pledging of the oath of loyalty.
3. Students might determine that rapid growth in city population, especially an influx of new immigrants, helped political machines come to power. They should find out about any reform movements or criminal investigations that contributed to the downfall of the local machines.

8. It became necessary as supply exceeded demand. Ads used visual appeal, wit, repetition.

9. Increased industrialization required skilled workers, and education helped assimilate immigrants.

10. Fixed working hours in factories and offices and higher salaries increased the possibility and affordability of leisure time. Opportunities for leisure included sports, theater, public parks, libraries, and museums.

Chapter Review exercises are keyed for student abilities:
● = Basic
▲ = Average
■ = Average/Advanced

Chapter 7 ■ Society and Politics in the Gilded Age

4 Sections, 4–6 Days

	SECTION OBJECTIVES	SECTION RESOURCES
Section 1 **The New Rich**	■ explain the impact of Social Darwinism on the United States in the late 1800s ■ describe the ways the very wealthy spent their money in the Gilded Age	● **Reteaching Resources:** Worksheet 25 ▲ **Reinforcement Workbook:** Worksheet 25 ■ **Enrichment and Extension Resources:** Primary Source Worksheet 13 ▲ **Teaching Transparencies:** Transparency 25
Section 2 **The Urban Poor**	■ describe the living and working conditions of the urban poor ■ evaluate the efforts made to improve the lives of the urban poor	● **Reteaching Resources:** Worksheet 26 ▲ **Reinforcement Workbook:** Worksheet 26 ▲ **Teaching Transparencies:** Transparency 26
Section 3 **Corruption in Party Politics**	■ identify examples of political corruption during the Gilded Age	● **Reteaching Resources:** Worksheet 27 ▲ **Reinforcement Workbook:** Worksheet 27 ■ **Enrichment and Extension Resources:** Primary Source Worksheet 14 ▲ **Teaching Transparencies:** Transparency 27
Section 4 **Hands-Off Government**	■ describe the weaknesses of national leadership in the late 1800s	● **Reteaching Resources:** Worksheet 28 ▲ **Reinforcement Workbook:** Worksheet 28 ▲ **Teaching Transparencies:** Transparency 28

The list below shows Essential Elements relevant to this chapter. (The complete list of Essential Elements appears in the introductory pages of this Teacher's Edition.)

Section 1: 3D, 4G, 8A, 8B, 8D, 8H, 9F
Section 2: 2A, 3A, 4D, 4G, 7J, 9A
Section 3: 2A, 3F, 4F, 5B, 7C, 7F, 7G, 9F
Section 4: 4C, 4D, 5B, 5C, 7C, 7J, 9B, 9D

> Section Resources are keyed for student abilities:
> ● = Basic
> ▲ = Average
> ■ = Average/Advanced

CHAPTER RESOURCES

Geography Resources: Worksheets 13, 14
Tests: Chapter 7 Test

Chapter Project: American Culture

Have students do a comparative study of cities in the late 1800s and today. These studies may take the form of photographs or art showing parallels and contrasts; skits illustrating several issues in common; or an in-depth discussion of problems and proposed solutions. Students may wish to focus on the city they live in, or a city nearby.

Homework Options

Each section contains activities labeled "Addressing Individual Needs." You may wish to choose from among these activities when assigning homework.

Provisions for Limited English Proficiency (LEP)
Several suggested activities may be particularly helpful for teachers of students with limited English proficiency. These activities have been marked throughout the Teacher's Annotated Edition with the symbol **LEP** .

BIBLIOGRAPHY AND AUDIOVISUAL AIDS

Teacher Bibliography

Josephson, Matthew. *The Robber Barons*. Harcourt Brace Jovanovich, 1962.

Morgan, H. Wayne. *From Hayes to McKinley: National Party Politics, 1877–1896*. Syracuse University Press, 1969.

Student Bibliography

Andrews, Wayne. *Architecture, Ambitions, and Americans: A Social History of American Architecture*. Free Press, 1979.

Katz, William Loren, and Jacqueline Hunt Katz. *Making Our Way: America at the Turn of the Century in the Words of the Poor and Powerless*. Dial, 1975.

Literature

Addams, Jane. *Twenty Years at Hull-House*. New American Library.

Carnegie, Andrew. *The Autobiography of Andrew Carnegie*. Northeastern University Press, 1986.

Howells, William Dean. *The Rise of Silas Latham*. Penguin, 1983. A businessman strives to break into society at the turn of the century.

Riis, Jacob. *How the Other Half Lives*. Darby Books, 1981.

Twain, Mark and Charles D. Warner. *The Gilded Age: A Tale of To-Day*. Dover, 1988.

Wharton, Edith. *The House of Mirth*. Penguin, 1985.

Films and Videotapes*

The 1880's. 32 min. KAW. Extensive survey of American life 100 years ago.

Filmstrips*

Industrial America (set of 3). GA. Titles include: The Gilded Age; Strike—The Growth of Organized Labor; and Shaping an Urban Society, 1870–1917.

Computer Software*

America's President Series: The Age of Growth–Presidents During the Late 19th and 20th Centuries (Apple with 48K; IBM with 64K). QUEUE. Each President is covered in a separate menu option and prominent Presidents have multiple sections on different phases of their lives and administrations. Presidents Hayes–Taft, 1877–1913.

*For a complete guide to audiovisual sources, see the introduction to this book (page Txx).

Chapter 7

Society and Politics in the Gilded Age

(pp. 158–175)

This chapter examines the life of the very rich and the urban poor during the late 1800s. It describes Social Darwinism and political corruption as responses to the social and economic forces at work during this period.

Themes in American History

- Economic development
- Pluralistic society
- American culture

Chapter Objectives

After students complete this chapter, they will be able to:

1. Explain the impact of Social Darwinism on the United States in the late 1800s.

2. Describe the ways the very wealthy spent their money in the Gilded Age.

3. Describe the living and working conditions of the urban poor.

4. Evaluate the efforts made to improve the lives of the urban poor.

5. Identify examples of political corruption during the Gilded Age.

6. Describe the weaknesses of national leadership in the late 1800s.

Chapter Opener Art
Theodore Robinson, *World's Columbian Exposition, Chicago*, 1894.

Industrialization and urbanization raised American society to new heights of wealth and sophistication. These elaborate buildings were constructed to house the World's Columbian Exposition in Chicago in 1893.

CHAPTER SUPPORT MATERIAL

Reinforcement Workbook: Worksheets 25–28

Reteaching Resources: Worksheets 25–28

Enrichment and Extension Resources: Primary Source Worksheets 13, 14

Geography Resources: Worksheets 13, 14

Teaching Transparencies: Transparencies 25–28

Tests: Chapter 7 Test

7 Society and Politics in the Gilded Age (1865–1893)

3D, 4G, 8A, 8B, 8D, 8H, 9F

1 The New Rich

★ Section Focus

Key Terms Gilded Age ■ natural selection ■ Social Darwinism ■ conspicuous consumption

Main Idea The country's prosperity brought forth a group of fabulously wealthy and confident individuals.

Objectives As you read, look for answers to these questions:
1. How were the ideas of Charles Darwin applied to society?
2. What were some signs of new wealth in the United States?
3. What dangers did the new wealth create?

September 17, 1887, was an absolutely perfect day in Philadelphia—delightfully cool and clear. Exactly 100 years earlier, the framers of the Constitution had put their final touches on that historic document. Now a crowd of thousands lined up to hear President Grover Cleveland. The President declared:

> Every American citizen should on this centennial day rejoice in his citizenship. . . . He should rejoice because the work of framing our Constitution and government has survived so long, and also because . . . [the American people] have demonstrated so fully the strength and value of popular rule.

In one sense, Cleveland's words were true. The United States had prospered for a full century, and its economic expansion had created vast amounts of wealth. Yet inequality and corruption lay beneath the shining surface of prosperity. For this reason, some people called the final decades of the 1800s the Gilded Age (*gilded* means "gold-

covered"). New ideas seemed to divide the nation into a land of the fit and unfit. While some Americans wallowed in luxury, many others lacked the basic necessities of life. Rich Americans bought politicians as they might buy a bar of soap. Politicians, in turn, used their power for shameless personal gain.

A PHILOSOPHY OF WEALTH 8A, 8B, 8H

The United States' economic growth during the late 1800s created a new class of extremely wealthy people. They had made their fortunes in a variety of industries—the Vanderbilts in railroads, the Rockefellers in oil, the Morgans in finance. In 1861 the United States had just 3 millionaires; by the end of the century that number had swelled to more than 3,800. Not surprisingly, new ideas surfaced to explain and justify this new wealth.

One such idea borrowed from a scientific theory that was very much in the news at that time. The English biologist Charles Darwin (1809–1882) published *The Origin of Species* in 1859. Darwin, who had extensively examined plant and animal life,

CHAPTER 7   SOCIETY AND POLITICS IN THE GILDED AGE, 1865–1893   **159**

SUPPORTING THE SECTION

Reinforcement Workbook: Worksheet 25

Reteaching Resources: Worksheet 25

Enrichment and Extension Resources: Primary Source Worksheet 13

Teaching Transparencies: Transparency 25

SECTION 1

The New Rich
(pp. 159–161)

Section Objectives

- explain the impact of Social Darwinism on the United States in the late 1800s
- describe the ways the very wealthy spent their money in the Gilded Age

Introducing the Section

Connecting with Past Learnings
What was happening to the American economy in the late 1800s? (Rapid growth of industry; creation of great wealth for some, growth of urban working class.)

Key Terms
Write the key terms on the board. Call on a student to define a term without naming it. Ask another student to identify the term. Continue until all terms have been covered. **LEP**

Focus
Ask students to suggest examples of Social Darwinism, the Gospel of Wealth, and conspicuous consumption. Invite them to add contemporary examples to those mentioned in the section.

Developing the Lesson
After students have read the section, you may want to consider the following activities:

Analyzing Controversial Issues
Many religious people are opposed to teaching the theory of evolution in public schools. Have students present both sides, explaining their feelings on the issue.

Religion
Ask students to explain Carnegie's Gospel of Wealth. The word *gospel* is often used to describe the teachings of Jesus. Discuss why Carnegie

159

Connecting with Literature
The success of Horatio Alger's hero did not truly reflect the life of the urban poor. *Given this contradiction, how do you explain the popularity of this character?* (Exemplified idea of America as land of opportunity for those willing to work hard.)

C Cooperative Learning

Divide the class into groups. Have each group discuss Social Darwinism from the point of view of: black or white southern leaders, business men, farmers, bankers, or factory workers. Conclude with a panel discussion composed of one representative from each group. **LEP**

Addressing Individual Needs

Guided/ Independent Practice
Have students complete **Reinforcement Workbook** Worksheet 25, which asks them to compare 18th and 19th century ideas.

Reteaching/Correctives
Direct students' attention to the objectives under the Section Focus on page 159. Have students work with partners to change each question into a statement and list the statements on a piece of paper. Beneath each statement, have students list important details that explain or add to it.

Instruct students to complete **Reteaching Resources** Worksheet 25.

Enrichment/Extension
Acquaint students with the writings of William Graham Sumner by having them read and complete **Enrichment and Extension Resources** Primary Source Worksheet 13.

160

---

called his philosophy natural selection. It stressed three main points. First, because of a lack of food, living things have always competed with each other for survival. Second, living things have evolved over millions of years as a result of genetic changes. Third, some plants and animals developed traits that helped them survive. Others, such as the dinosaur, perished.

An English philosopher, Herbert Spencer (1820–1903), applied Darwin's ideas to society. The result was the theory of Social Darwinism, which Spencer termed "survival of the fittest." He argued that in every human activity, individuals compete for success. The unfit or incompetent lose, and the strong or competent win. These winners make up a natural upper class.

Government, in Spencer's view, cannot do anything about this survival of the fittest. All that it can do is prevent the unfit from stealing from the fit. It cannot make the unfit rise into the natural aristocracy. It cannot eliminate slums any more than it can change the law of gravity. Social Darwinism, therefore, reinforced the idea of laissez faire by arguing that government should not interfere with the working of the economy.

ADVOCATES OF SOCIAL DARWINISM 4G, 8B, 8H
Spencer's Social Darwinism found a ready audience in the United States. In fact, his books sold more than 350,000 copies by 1900. Leading business tycoons accepted his views, with John D. Rockefeller arguing that "the growth of a large business is merely a survival of the fittest."

> "The growth of a large business is merely a survival of the fittest."
> —*John D. Rockefeller*

Some church leaders gave Social Darwinism a religious flavor. The Baptist minister Russell H. Conwell (1843–1925), who founded Temple University, was one such person. He gave a lecture entitled "Acres of Diamonds" over 6,000 times during a 55-year period, earning $8 million in fees. In his lecture, he said:

Money is power, and you ought to be reasonably ambitious to have it. You ought because you can do more good with it than you could without it. . . . It is an awful mistake of these pious people to think you must be awfully poor in order to be pious.

THE GOSPEL OF WEALTH 3D, 8B, 8H
Conwell's point—that people can use their money to perform good works—had plenty of supporters. Herbert Spencer had written that the fit had duties to the less fortunate. They should donate money to help the needy. Some of the giants of American industry, such as Andrew Carnegie (page 98), agreed. Carnegie, calling his theory the "Gospel of Wealth," argued that the wealthy had a duty to help others. As he put it, "Surplus wealth is a sacred trust which its possessor is bound to administer in his lifetime for the good of the community." Practicing what he preached, Carnegie gave away more than $350 million to libraries, universities, and other institutions.

Other wealthy businessmen followed Carnegie's example, donating money to a variety of worthy causes. The financier J. P. Morgan, as well as several other business leaders, contributed to art museums in the nation's cities. Ezra Cornell, who had made a fortune from the telegraph, founded Cornell University. Money rolled in to help build New York City's Metropolitan Opera House.

LIFESTYLES OF THE RICH AND FAMOUS 8D
Carnegie also called on the wealthy to "set an example of modest . . . living." Few listened. Proud of their wealth, they made a point of showing it off. This conspicuous consumption, as the social scientist Thorstein Veblen called it, led to a kind of competition among the wealthy to see who could live in the grandest style.

The wealthy built houses on fashionable city streets such as Fifth Avenue in New York. In places such as Newport, Rhode Island, they built "summer cottages"—actually mansions in the style of European country villas. The Breakers, the Vanderbilt mansion in Newport, had 70 rooms, two of which were built in France, torn apart, shipped to America, and rebuilt.

The photograph at the far left shows the marble-lined dining room in railroad tycoon Cornelius Vanderbilt's Newport mansion. At left, Mrs. Vanderbilt poses as "electricity" at a costume ball. **CULTURE** Why might the wealthy have imitated European architecture when building their mansions? **9F**

Lavish parties abounded. Mary Astor, a leader of New York society, wore so many diamonds when entertaining that someone suggested she carry them to her next ball in a wheelbarrow. At one dinner party the men were given cigars wrapped in hundred-dollar bills. Another man spent $10,000 on a dinner for his friends—72 of them. The enormous dinner table had a pond in it, in which four swans swam.

THE DANGERS OF WEALTH 8B

Rutherford B. Hayes, President from 1877 to 1881, warned after leaving office about the impact of great wealth on American society:

> It is time for the public to hear that there is a giant evil and danger in this country. The danger which is greater than all others is the vast wealth owned or controlled by a few persons. Money is power. In Congress, in state legislatures, in city councils, in the courts, in political conventions, in the press, in the pulpit, in the circles of the educated and talented, its influence is growing greater and greater. Great wealth in the hands of the few means extreme poverty, ignorance, vice, and wretchedness as the lot of the many.

Hayes did not argue that wealth in itself was a bad thing. Indeed, the American people as a whole, from the richest railroad tycoon to the poorest immigrant seamstress, believed that they had a right to profit from their labor. This right was widely seen as a fundamental part of individual liberty. The wildly popular dime novels of Horatio Alger reinforced the idea that gaining wealth was both possible and desirable. In Alger's stories, hard work and a bit of luck brought people from "rags to riches."

The danger lay instead in the inequality that extreme wealth helped maintain. Poor Americans still had reason to believe that they (or their children) might be able to rise into the expanding middle class. Yet in the 1890s, four of every five Americans remained trapped in poverty. Just 10 percent of the population owned 90 percent of the wealth. Such a concentration of wealth seemed to warp the process of government, encouraging corruption and stifling reform. Thoughtful people became concerned about the government's inability to respond to these problems.

SECTION REVIEW

1. KEY TERMS Gilded Age, natural selection, Social Darwinism, conspicuous consumption

2. PEOPLE Charles Darwin, Herbert Spencer, Russell H. Conwell, Andrew Carnegie, Thorstein Veblen

3. COMPREHENSION According to Social Darwinism, what is the proper role of government?

4. COMPREHENSION How did rich Americans of the late 1800s show off their wealth?

5. CRITICAL THINKING Do you think that the concentration of wealth in a few hands is dangerous to a country? Explain your answer. **9F**

Photo Caption Answer
Students may suggest that they wanted to appear cultured and were attracted to Europe because of its impressive cultural history.

Assessment
You may wish to use the Section 1 Review, on this page, to see how well your students understand the main points in this lesson.

Section Review Answers

1. *Gilded Age*—Final decades of the 1800s. *natural selection*—Darwin's theory that living things compete, and develop traits that help them survive. *Social Darwinism*—Survival of fittest. *conspicuous consumption*—Showing off one's wealth.

2. *Charles Darwin*—English biologist who proposed the theory of natural selection. *Herbert Spencer*—English philosopher who applied Darwin's ideas to human society. *Russell H. Conwell*—Minister, preached virtue of wealth. *Andrew Carnegie*—Tycoon, advocated the Gospel of Wealth. *Thorstein Veblen*—Social scientist.

3. Do nothing to impede free competition or redistribute wealth, and prevent the unfit from stealing from the rich.

4. Extravagant homes and lavish parties.

5. Some may argue that concentration of wealth leads to corruption, while others may say that acquiring wealth is a democratic right and allows for philanthropy.

Closure
Call students' attention to the boxed beige quotation (p. 160). How does this quotation relate to the main idea of the section? Then have students read Section 2 for the next class period, comparing the lives of the poor with those of the wealthy.

SECTION 2

The Urban Poor
(pp. 162–165)

Section Objectives

- describe the living and working conditions of the urban poor
- evaluate the efforts made to improve the lives of the urban poor

Introducing the Section

Connecting with Past Learnings

Review population shifts in the late 1800s. *How were cities changing during the Gilded Age and why?* (Growing rapidly because of industrialization and immigration.) *Where did the new urban population come from?* (Farms; immigrants from eastern and southern Europe.)

Key Terms

Write the key terms on the board. Have volunteers come up to the board and put a plus in front of those terms which describe things which helped the urban poor and a minus in front of terms describing things that made their lives difficult. Then ask students to suggest definitions. **LEP**

Focus

Ask students to describe a day in the life of a garment worker in New York City in the 1890s. Be sure they include a description of the worker's living and working conditions. (Living in a crowded room with limited sanitation facilities; working more than ten hours in a sweatshop; stopping by a settlement house on the way home from work; etc.)

---

2 The Urban Poor

★ Section Focus

Key Terms tenement ■ sweatshop ■ settlement house ■ Social Gospel

Main Idea Many poor people, crowded into city slums, lived in miserable conditions and had to struggle just to survive.

Objectives As you read, look for answers to these questions:
1. What was life like for the urban poor?
2. What efforts were made to ease the plight of the poor?

When the super-rich of 1880s Pittsburgh—the Carnegies, the Mellons, and others—wanted to get away from it all, they headed to the South Fork Fishing and Hunting Club in western Pennsylvania. The club sat on the shores of an artificial lake. Club members had dammed the Little Conemaugh River to create the lake for fishing.

A casualty of the Johnstown Flood of 1889, this house was pierced by a tree and swept onto a heap of ruined railway equipment. It took just ten minutes for the flood to destroy the town and kill 2,200 people. HISTORY Why did some people see the flood as a symbol of the nation's ills? 9A

On May 31, 1889, after a night of heavy rain, the dam broke. A wall of water rushed down on the nearby community of Johnstown, wrecking the town and killing over 2,200 persons.

The Johnstown Flood is remembered as a natural disaster. But as one commentator explained, it was also "a symbol for what was wrong with our country. Back when no one gets a vacation, these rich guys are spending a vacation up there. And their pleasure lake breaks and brings death down upon the city workers here in Johnstown."

THE TENEMENTS 2A

Ordinarily, of course, most city workers were not worried about floods. But they did have a number of critical concerns. Having enough to eat was one, and housing was another. Two forces combined to make housing a terrible problem for working-class families. On the one hand, the growing prosperity of the city as a whole caused property values to skyrocket. On the other hand, the steady stream of poor arrivals to the city ensured a strong market for low-cost housing. Entrepreneurs and established landlords alike took advantage of the situation to cram as many people as possible into each building.

At first, landlords divided single-family homes into apartments. Beginning in 1850 a new type of building appeared. This was the tenement—an apartment building designed to house large numbers of people as cheaply as possible. Tenements were a step up for people who had been homeless or living in rural shacks. Nevertheless, tenements lacked decent room, light, and fresh air. Plumbing systems were primitive and often in poor condition. Overcrowding and poor sanitation made tenements ideal breeding grounds for disease.

SUPPORTING THE SECTION

Reinforcement Workbook: Worksheet 26
Reteaching Resources: Worksheet 26
Teaching Transparencies: Transparency 26

Photo Caption Answer
It was thought that the self-indulgence of the rich caused death and hardship for common people.

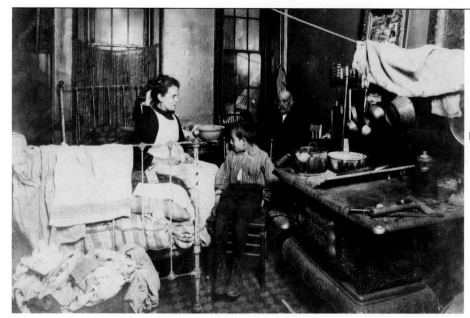

Tenements were designed to maximize the number of apartments they held. Photographer Lewis Hine recorded many scenes, such as this, of tenement life and gave his pictures to organizations fighting for improved living conditions. **HISTORY** Which problems of life in tenements does this photograph illustrate? **3A**

Tenement conditions were most appalling in New York City, one of the most densely populated places on earth in the late 1800s. Accordingly, New York took the lead in regulations designed to improve housing. In 1879 the city sponsored a contest to come up with a new design for tenements. The winning design, known as the "dumbbell tenement" because it was shaped like a dumbbell, offered modest improvements over earlier designs. Air shafts were built into the tenement to provide light and fresh air to interior rooms. Yet they also allowed noise and the smell of garbage to waft upward. The air shafts also gave fire a way of spreading quickly through the building.

Despite these shortcomings, New Yorkers built tens of thousands of dumbbell tenements. Nearly half the city's population lived in them by 1894. A Danish-born reporter named Jacob Riis toured New York's tenements, describing them in his classic work *How the Other Half Lives* (1890):

Be a little careful, please! The hall is dark and you might stumble. . . . Here where the hall turns and dives into utter darkness is . . . a flight of stairs. You can feel your way, if you cannot see it. Close? Yes! What would you have? All the fresh air that enters these stairs comes from the hall-door that is forever slamming. . . . The sinks are in the hallway, that all the tenants may have access—and all be poisoned alike by their summer stenches. . . . Here is a door. Listen! That short, hacking cough, that tiny, helpless wail—what do they mean? . . . The child is dying of measles. With half a chance it might have lived; but it had none. That dark bedroom killed it.

MAKING ENDS MEET 3A

For the poor, conditions at work were as grim as those at home. Employees labored for ten to twelve hours per day, six days a week. Pay averaged about $2 or $3 per day. The work itself consisted primarily of running machines. Those who let their minds wander could find their feet crushed or their fingers severed by the machines they operated. Speed, not safety, had top priority in these factories.

Some of the worst conditions existed in the garment industry. Workers toiled long hours in dimly lit, poorly ventilated factories called **sweatshops**. Others worked at home, hunched over sewing machines in their cramped tenement apartments. Similar conditions existed in other industries. Whole families might work dawn to dusk rolling cigars for less than $2 per day.

Photo Caption Answer
Crowding, unsanitary conditions, lack of light and fresh air.

How did middle class people help the urban poor? (Settlement houses taught English, job and living skills to immigrants; Social Gospel encouraged church members to help the poor.)

Developing the Lesson
After students have read the section, you may want to consider the following activities:

Geographic Themes: Place
Have students draw a floor plan or diagram, or create a model of a tenement. Ask them to present their drawings or models, and have the class discuss what life in one of these buildings would have been like.

Ethics
How did landlords justify the existence of squalid living conditions in tenements? (Principles of Social Darwinism.)

Economics
Have students look through this book or other material to find photographs of industrial workers. *What problems did industrial workers face in the late 1800s?* (Long hours, low pay, tedious and hazardous work.) Ask students to suggest reasons for these poor working conditions. (Large supply of workers kept wages down; lack of government regulations; workers not organized to demand better conditions.)

Cultural Pluralism
Why might new immigrants have been more likely to be members of the urban poor? (They often arrived with few job skills, were unable to speak English, and were unaware of their rights as citizens to approach government officials for help.) Discuss the ways that settlement houses attempted to correct those problems. (Taught English and citizenship skills.)

Child labor was a fact of life for the urban poor of the late 1800s. Employers found that children could perform many tasks—operating machines, running errands—for a fraction of the wages paid to adults. Some children began working as soon as they learned to walk. Several states had laws forbidding children under the age of fourteen from working. As a result, families concealed their children's ages to obtain jobs for them. Parents not only needed the money, but also had no other place to put their children during the long hours of the work day.

PRIVATE AID TO THE POOR 4D, 7J
Private citizens did what they could to ease the suffering of the needy. People set up various charitable societies to help the poor and other needy citizens. By 1892 there were 92 charities with branches in the major American cities.

At first, charities were usually run by volunteers, most of them women. In the 1890s, a professional group of college-educated social workers arose. Better trained than the volunteers, the social workers tried to look for long-term solutions to the problems of the poor. Part of this effort involved pressuring city and state governments to improve city housing. Social workers fought for

the establishment of safety and health standards in apartment buildings—running water, sanitation facilities, and so on.

Some social workers also became involved with **settlement houses**. These were centers providing various services to the poor. Educated middle-class women found in the settlement house movement an outlet for their talents. Many of them, especially single women, relished the opportunity to do useful work and improve society.

The most famous settlement house was Hull House in Chicago, founded by Jane Addams in 1889. Addams had grown up in a wealthy Illinois family and had attended medical school in Philadelphia. Choosing to care for Chicago's needy, Addams bought a run-down mansion in an immigrant neighborhood and called it Hull House.

Eventually Hull House owned thirteen buildings, including classrooms, a coffeehouse, theater, music school, nursery, and gymnasium. There was even a kindergarten for the children of working mothers. Determined to improve the quality of life for Chicago residents, Addams pushed the city to build parks and playgrounds. She also demanded better garbage collection, and even followed the garbage trucks herself to be sure that they were doing their job.

Lewis Hine traveled around the United States photographing the system of child labor. Children as young as ten labored in mines and factories for up to fourteen hours a day, six days a week. This photograph shows girls working in a textile mill. Hine often had to disguise himself from factory owners in order to take these photographs. **ECONOMICS** Why did many parents resist child labor laws? 2A

Photo Caption Answer
They needed the money and had no place to put their children during the workday.

Settlement houses performed invaluable services for city residents, especially immigrants. There they could learn English and learn how to vote. They could also spend time with other newcomers. If the need arose, the settlement house would provide them with food and clothing. At a time when government felt no obligation to lessen the misery of the poor, settlement houses were lifesavers.

THE SOCIAL GOSPEL 4D, 4G

Most American churches of the time did little to help the poor. They took the view that success in life was a sign of God's favor. Those who did not succeed in life had only themselves to blame. Social Darwinism, while not a religious doctrine, reinforced the belief that the poor were inferior to the rich.

A few members of the clergy in the late 1800s had other views. They developed what was called the Social Gospel, the idea that Jesus' teachings should be applied to society and not just preached in churches. Churches, they believed, should try to act as Jesus did in helping the poor.

An Englishman named William Booth started a chapter of the Salvation Army in the United States in 1880. (The organization was founded in England.) The Salvation Army set up shelters, nurseries, and children's homes in towns and cities. Maud Billington Booth, daughter-in-law of William Booth, described the operations of the army's "Slum Brigade":

Perhaps the duty which absorbs the greatest part of their time is . . . the systematic house-to-house and room-to-room visitation of all the worst homes in their neigh-

borhood. . . . These visits are often lengthened into prayer-meetings, which include singing and speaking, to a more interested audience, and certainly a more needy one, than can be found within the walls of many a church.

Some members of the clergy argued that political change was necessary to help the poor. One was Washington Gladden, a Congregational minister who wrote a book entitled *Applied Christianity* (1886). Gladden called on government to regulate corporations and urged churches to join together to solve industrial problems. In 1887 the Episcopal Church formed the Church Association for the Advancement of the Interests of Labor. The new group helped workers deal with employers and tried to improve workers' living conditions. Other religious denominations soon followed the example of the Episcopalians.

Even more radical in support of the Social Gospel was Walter Rauschenbusch, a Baptist minister whose church was located in one of the poorest sections of New York City. Claiming that capitalism was a system based on profit and greed, he argued that it was the opposite of Christianity or at best "semi-Christian." Ministers must never cease, said Rauschenbusch, to work for "a social foundation on which modern men individually can live and work in a fashion that will not outrage all the better elements in them."

SECTION REVIEW

1. KEY TERMS tenement, sweatshop, settlement house, Social Gospel

2. PEOPLE AND PLACES Jacob Riis, Jane Addams, Hull House, William Booth

3. COMPREHENSION Why were dumbbell tenements not much better than the tenements that they replaced?

4. COMPREHENSION How did the Salvation Army help the poor?

5. CRITICAL THINKING For what reason would government set limits on child labor? Who might oppose such limits? Why?

Biography
For further reading consider: Davis, Allen F. *American Heroine: The Life and Legend of Jane Addams.* Oxford University Press, 1973.

Background The Catholic Church had a long tradition of helping the poor. Under the leadership of James Cardinal Gibbons of Baltimore the Catholic Church helped millions of immigrants.

Background Walter Rauschenbush supported the movement for Christian Socialism, which proposed a collective society based on the teachings of Christ. This movement won few supporters.

---

essay on what they might have done to solve the problems described in those books.

Assessment
You may wish to use the Section 2 Review, on this page, to see how well your students understand the main points in this lesson.

Section Review Answers

1. *tenement*—Apartment building designed to house large numbers of people cheaply. *sweatshop*—Garment factory where employees worked long hours under bad conditions. *settlement house*—Center that provided services to the poor. *Social Gospel*—Idea that churches should help the poor, as Jesus did.

2. *Jacob Riis*—Journalist who wrote about slum conditions in New York. *Jane Addams*—Founder of settlement house in Chicago. *Hull House*—Famous settlement house in Chicago. *William Booth*—English founder of the Salvation Army.

3. In addition to light and air, they let in noise and the smell of garbage, and the air shafts allowed fires to spread quickly.

4. Provided shelters, nurseries, children's homes, and spiritual comfort.

5. Government might set limits on child labor for humanitarian reasons and to encourage widespread education. Factory owners would oppose such limits because children were a source of cheap labor.

Closure
Ask one student to transform the Main Idea of the section into a question, and have other students answer that question. Then have students read Section 3 for the next class period noting specific examples of government corruption.

165

3 Corruption in Party Politics

Section Focus

Key Terms Tweed Ring ■ Salary Grab Act
■ conflict of interest ■ money formula

Main Idea Government in the United States
suffered from corruption at both the local
and national levels.

Objectives As you read, look for answers to
these questions:
1. How did political machines take control
of major cities?
2. What forms of corruption plagued
Congress?
3. How did money influence national
politics?

Section Objective

■ identify examples of political corruption during the
Gilded Age

Introducing the Section

Connecting with Past Learnings
*What was the relationship be-
tween political machines and
the urban poor during the
Gilded Age?* (Political machines helped people get
jobs, housing, food, legal aid,
and education, in exchange
for their votes.)

Key Terms
Write each term on an index
card. Ask a volunteer to pick
a card, then answer ques-
tions from classmates with
either "yes" or "no" to determine which term it is. Follow
this procedure until all the
terms are defined. **LEP**

Focus
Have students imagine
themselves as reporters
breaking the news about
scandals in city or national
politics. Ask them to write a
lead paragraph (telling who,
what, where, when, and
why) about an episode de-
scribed in the text. Call on
students to read their paragraphs aloud, then discuss
similarities in these cases.
   *Why were there so many op-
portunities for government corruption at the local and
national level?* (Rapid growth
of cities made governments
powerful; federal govern-
ment's wealth attracted
corruption.)

Developing the Lesson
After students have read the
section, you may want to consider the following activities:

"I seen my opportunities and I took 'em." With
these words, George Washington Plunkitt spoke
for himself and many other politicians of the late
1800s. This was a time of unprecedented corruption in American politics. Taking advantage of
changing conditions in the country, such as the
plight of the urban poor and the expansion of industry, some politicians gained power and wealth
for themselves.

CORRUPTION IN THE CITIES 2A
One critic, disgusted by the extent of corruption
in American cities, labeled them "the worst in
Christendom." The cities' rapid growth was the
problem. Immigrants and farmers were pouring
into cities looking for jobs and housing. Businesses
of all sizes were looking for sites to make and sell
goods. Both residents and businesses were calling
for expanded services, such as transportation and
sanitation.

City governments stood at the center of all
these developments, for they alone could answer
the people's many needs. Whoever controlled the
city government also controlled the power and
wealth being generated by urban growth. Realizing this, political machines (often run by immigrants) sought and gained control of many city
governments.

The most famous machine in the nation was the
Tweed Ring in New York City, named after Boss
William Marcy Tweed. Tweed was a senator in the
New York legislature and a leader of Tammany
Hall, the local Democratic Party organization.
During the Tweed Ring's heyday, New York City
lost an estimated $200 million of tax money to

Tweed and his close friends. The city almost went
bankrupt before the ring was ousted in 1872. In
one year alone, for example, the city's debt skyrocketed from $36 million to $97 million.

It was hard to find an American city that did not
have corrupt politicians. Los Angeles's mayor in
1889 put his six sons on the police force. Indianapolis judges at the time worked on commission, receiving a cut from each fine they imposed on
lawbreakers. Politicians in many cities paid poor
residents for their votes. They rigged elections,
"voting the graveyards" by claiming the votes of
residents who had been dead for years. They demanded bribes from businesses seeking favors.
And they did all these things confident that they
could get away with them. As Boss Tweed himself
once told a reporter who accused him of corruption, "As long as I count the votes, what are you
going to do about it?"

> "**A**s long as I count the votes, what are
> you going to do about it?"
>   —*Boss Tweed, when accused
> of corruption*

TROUBLE IN WASHINGTON 3F
The main difference between corruption on the local and national levels was the amount of money
involved. In the national arena, there were simply
many more opportunities to make money illegally.
The federal government had plenty of sources of
money—tariffs, taxes, and land sales. And by mis-

SUPPORTING THE SECTION

Reinforcement Workbook: Worksheet 27
Reteaching Resources: Worksheet 27
Enrichment and Extension Resources: Primary
Source Worksheet 14
Teaching Transparencies: Transparency 27

This cartoon by Thomas Nast is entitled "Who Stole the People's Money?" The ring of accusations leads to Boss Tweed in the lower left-hand corner. Under Tweed's corrupt administration, contractors regularly overcharged the city for services and gave the money to the Tammany Hall boss. Nast's biting attacks eventually led to Tweed's overthrow and imprisonment. **ETHICS** Imagine you are trying to eliminate political corruption. What methods would you use? **9F**

using the spoils system, individuals were able to get their hands on these public funds. The party that won the White House and a majority of seats in Congress did what city bosses did. It made all the money it could from illegal schemes, rewarded its friends with money and jobs, and even stole from the public treasury.

Some of the worst examples of the spoils system occurred when Ulysses S. Grant was President (1869–1877). One was the Crédit Mobilier (moh-BEEL-yay) scandal, which surfaced in 1872. The Crédit Mobilier was a construction company hired to build the Union Pacific Railroad. It charged the railroad several times what the job actually cost. Lawmakers bought stock in the company and sold it at bargain rates to colleagues in Congress. Congress, in return, passed laws helping the company. Vice President Schuyler Colfax was involved, as were eight members of Congress. Even though the scandal came out into the open, no public official went to jail.

Then there was the example of William W. Belknap, Grant's Secretary of War. Belknap received a Cabinet position because he had once done a favor for one of Grant's relatives. He knew nothing about the duties of Secretary of War. While in office, he was accused of receiving bribes from traders at frontier Indian posts. The traders got goods from Indians at bargain prices in return. Money from the traders was funneled through Belknap's wife, who over six years took in $24,450—

equivalent to about a quarter of a million dollars today. Belknap was forced to resign. Although he was impeached by the House of Representatives, the Senate failed to convict him.

THE SALARY GRAB ACT 5B

No legislative body was less concerned about the public welfare than the 42nd Congress, which met from 1871 to 1873. In March 1873 it passed what came to be known as the Salary Grab Act. That legislation increased congressional salaries by 50 percent, effective two years earlier. Hoping to keep publicity at a minimum, Congress buried the pay raise in a bill dealing with other government spending projects. President Grant signed the bill, and on March 3, 1873—the last day of the Congress—members lined up to get their pay. The next day was Inauguration Day, and the festivities helped to camouflage the pay increase.

But not for long. Impoverished western farmers soon got wind of the raise and began to ask whether Congress had done more for itself than for the country. In state elections that fall, Congress's salary "steal" became a burning issue.

The new 43rd Congress felt the heat. Its members could not say enough bad things about the pay increase. One of its first actions was to scrap the Salary Grab Act and demand that the money be returned. Most members of Congress who had received the increased compensation either returned it to the U. S. Treasury or donated it to charity.

Have students work in small groups to create a booklet entitled "The Citizen's Guide to Corruption in Politics." Have groups base their guides on information from the section. Students may choose to use a factual, outraged, or satirical tone in their booklets. Have groups share their booklets with the class.

Have students complete **Reteaching Resources** Worksheet 27, in which they identify important terms introduced in the section.

Enrichment/Extension
Have students complete **Enrichment and Extension Resources** Primary Source Worksheet 14, to understand one politician's explanation of "honest graft."

Assessment
You may wish to use the Section 3 Review, page 169, to see how well your students understand the main points in this lesson.

Section Review Answers
1. *Tweed Ring*—New York City political machine. *Salary Grab Act*—Large congressional pay raise voted by 42nd Congress in 1873. *conflict of interest*—Mixing personal occupations with public responsibilities. *money formula*—The more money candidates spend, the more likely they are to win.
2. *William Marcy Tweed*—Boss of Tammany Hall in New York City. *Ulysses S. Grant*—President with scandal-ridden administration. *Schuyler Colfax*—Grant's Vice President, part of Crédit Mobilier railroad scandal. *William W. Belknap*—Grant's Secretary of War, forced to resign because of accusations of bribery. *Mark Twain*—Writer who satirized corruption in Washington. *Mark Hanna*—Chairman of the Republican National Committee and chief fund raiser.

168

MONEY TALKS 7C, 7G

Scandals involving individuals come and go. What made corruption in Washington so dangerous was that it extended far beyond a few crooked individuals. Politicians in both parties regularly did things that practically invited corruption.

Legislators engaged in conflict of interest—mixing personal occupations with public responsibilities. A member of Congress might, for example, have private investments in certain companies and vote on bills affecting those same companies. Lobbyists abounded in Washington. They provided willing legislators with every conceivable favor—including, on occasion, bags of cash—in return for votes on particular bills.

Mark Twain poked fun at the influence of money on politics in his novel *The Gilded Age* (1873). Twain stressed how costly it was to get Congress to pass bills that lobbyists wanted:

> Why the matter is simple enough. A congressional appropriation costs money. Just reflect, for instance.
>
> A majority of the House committee, say $10,000 apiece—$40,000; a majority of the Senate committee, the same each—say $40,000; a little extra to one or two chairmen of one or two such committees, say $10,000 each—$20,000; . . . seven male lobbyists, at $3,000 each—$21,000; one female lobbyist, $10,000; a high moral Congressman or Senator here and there—the high moral ones cost more, because they give tone to a measure—say ten of these at $3,000 each, is $30,000; then a lot of small-fry country members who won't vote for anything whatever without pay—say twenty at $500 apiece, is $10,000. . . .

By the 1880s the United States Senate was known as "The Millionaires' Club." Indeed, over half of its members were millionaires. Critics charged that the Senate represented only the views of special interests, such as steel, lumber, and railroads. Senators favoring big business controlled important committees. They made sure that bills hostile to business never made their way to the Senate floor for a vote. They also controlled their non-millionaire colleagues. These junior

MARK TWAIN (1835–1910) was the pen name of writer Samuel Clemens. Twain was a keen social critic. In his first novel, *The Gilded Age* (1873), he satirized American values. His best-known works, *Life on the Mississippi, Tom Sawyer,* and *Huckleberry Finn,* draw on Twain's childhood adventures in Hannibal, Missouri. His style of writing, full of homespun American humor and critical of pretense, made him one of America's most popular authors. **4F**

members knew that if they pushed for reform, the millionaires would block legislation they needed for their own states.

The power of money was most evident during election campaigns. The more money raised and spent, the more likely a candidate would win. In the late 1800s several candidates learned how well this so-called money formula could work. James Garfield was the first candidate for President to break the million-dollar mark. In 1880 he spent $1.1 million to Winfield Hancock's $335,000. From 1884 to 1900, spending in presidential elections ran from a low of $425,000 for William Jennings Bryan in 1900 (he lost) to a high of $3.3 million for William McKinley in 1896 (he won).

This cartoon, entitled "The American Bird of Freedom," shows Republican fund-raiser Mark Hanna as a bloated turkey making dollar-sign footprints. CIVIC VALUES Do you think the cartoonist viewed the money formula as supporting or corrupting American ideals? Explain. 7C

Biography
Mark Twain is considered a quintessential American writer. Discuss with the class the aspects of Twain's life and work that illustrate American qualities and values.

Photo Caption Answer
The cartoonist seems to be commenting ironically on the way the money formula undermines the ideal of political freedom and fair elections.

Candidates raised money in several ways. They used their own money, sought many small donations, or went to a few large donors such as business leaders. The best money-raiser was Mark Hanna, chairman of the Republican National Committee and a senator from Ohio. Hanna saw to it that all Republican friends and businesses had a quota of contributions to provide.

Some of the large donors to candidates expected to receive favors in return. Often they were not disappointed, but on occasion they were. As one businessman said of Theodore Roosevelt, who served as governor of New York and later as President, "He got down on his knees to us. We bought [him] and then he did not stay bought." Yet the practice of "buying" candidates went on. Not until 1907 did Congress begin to set up rules for campaign contributions.

4C, 4D, 5B, 5C, 7C, 7J, 9B, 9D

4 Hands-Off Government

Section Focus

Key Terms standpatter ∎ Civil Service Act of 1883 ∎ Mugwump ∎ logrolling

Main Idea The major political parties offered little leadership during the late 1800s.

Objectives As you read, look for answers to these questions:
1. Why were late nineteenth-century Presidents so lackluster?
2. What efforts were made at congressional reform?

Political campaigns in the late 1800s looked a lot like carnivals. Red, white, and blue banners waved in the breeze. Brass bands played patriotic songs. Strong-lunged orators delivered stirring speeches. And on Election Day, American voters trooped off to the polls in large numbers to select their leaders.

It was a perfect picture of a vibrant democracy, but there was one problem. Not much was being accomplished. Old habits die hard, and the federal government could not rouse itself to make reforms in the way it operated. Nor did it have the courage to deal with major issues facing the nation—the

growing influence of wealth, the plight of the needy, poor working conditions, the problems of the cities, and more. Those problems continued to fester, untackled and thus unsolved.

AN ERA OF STANDPATTERS 5B

The Presidents in the years after the Civil War were lackluster, in large part because neither the Democrats nor the Republicans offered American voters much of a choice. The two parties had roughly equal support among the voters. The Democratic Party was strongest in the South. The Republican Party, which called itself the "Grand

---

SUPPORTING THE SECTION

Reinforcement Workbook: Worksheet 28
Reteaching Resources: Worksheet 28
Teaching Transparencies: Transparency 28

---

3. Cities grew rapidly to become centers of wealth and power, often controlled by political machines. Corrupt politicians spent city funds for public works projects in which they had an interest.

4. Over half of all senators were millionaires who represented special interests and who blocked any reform.

5. Voters still had the power of the ballot, and western farmers who learned of the Salary Grab Act pressured their representatives to scrap it and return the money.

Closure

Use the Section 3 information in the Chapter 7 Summary (p. 174) to synthesize the important elements covered in Section 3. Then have students read Section 4 for the next class period. Ask them to compare the Presidents who served during the final decades of the 1800s.

SECTION 4

Hands-Off Government
(pp. 169–173)

Section Objective

∎ describe the weaknesses of national leadership in the late 1800s

Introducing the Section

Connecting with Past Learnings

Help students see the roots of political problems in the Gilded Age. *Who originated the spoils system? Why?* (Andrew Jackson, to reward supporters and bring "new blood" into government.)

Key Terms

Write the key terms on the board. Call on volunteers to use each term in a sentence. Ask other students to verify the correct usage of the term. **LEP**

Focus

In separate columns on the board, have students write the Presidents mentioned in the section. (Grant, Hayes, Garfield, Arthur, Cleveland, Harrison.) Have students brainstorm entries describing each presidency, including facts about elections, policies the President supported, scandals during office, and other information mentioned in the section as well as earlier sections of the book.

What were some causes of the weak presidential leadership of the late 1800s? (Corruption was rampant and voters seemed uninterested in reform; obstructionist Congress.)

Developing the Lesson

After students have read the section, you may want to consider the following activities:

Economics

Ask students where the following groups would stand on the issue of high tariffs: western farmers and ranchers (oppose tariffs because they raised prices), eastern factory workers (mixed response—opposed because raised prices, but in favor because helped U.S. industry), manufacturers (in favor because kept out foreign-made goods), Civil War veterans (in favor because tariff revenues supported pensions.)

170

Old Party" (GOP), was strongest in the North. Both feared angering the voters and upsetting the balance by taking controversial positions.

As a result, most candidates running for the nation's highest office were standpatters, not reformers. (A standpatter is someone who "stands pat"—who likes things as they are.) Standpatters did not want to tinker with the spoils system and preferred to let the economy run by itself. From their point of view, things seemed to be working fine. Why fix something that wasn't broken?

Some voters became frustrated with the lack of choice among the candidates. They turned to third parties, which were formed by those who felt strongly about a single, burning issue—such as the prohibition of liquor. But the two major parties continued to receive the bulk of the votes, and the margin of victory was often razor-thin.

In 1868, for instance, the Republicans nominated Ulysses S. Grant, while the Democrats chose Horatio Seymour, former governor of New York. Out of a popular vote of 5.7 million, Grant won by only 300,000 votes, because the political stands of the two men were so alike. In 1872, on the other hand, there was a meaningful difference among candidates. In that year the Democrats and a faction of the Republican Party called Liberal

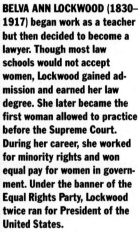

BIOGRAPHY 4C

BELVA ANN LOCKWOOD (1830–1917) began work as a teacher but then decided to become a lawyer. Though most law schools would not accept women, Lockwood gained admission and earned her law degree. She later became the first woman allowed to practice before the Supreme Court. During her career, she worked for minority rights and won equal pay for women in government. Under the banner of the Equal Rights Party, Lockwood twice ran for President of the United States.

Republicans nominated a candidate with a reform platform. The public, wanting no part of reform, re-elected Grant handily. Voters seemed to be saying this: being too different from mainstream politics was no way to win an election.

The major parties quickly learned that lesson, and the close elections resumed. It took a congressional committee to determine the winner of the 1876 election between Tilden and Hayes. In 1880, Republican James A. Garfield squeaked by his Democratic opponent, General Winfield Scott Hancock, by barely 7,000 popular votes out of more than 9 million cast. Four years later Democrat Grover Cleveland bested James G. Blaine by roughly 60,000 votes. Cleveland lost to Republican Benjamin Harrison in 1888, even though he got more popular votes. Next time around Cleveland won, again by a narrow margin.

The lesson was clear. The two major parties were not going to rock the boat, at least as long as the sea remained calm.

EFFORTS AT REFORM: CIVIL SERVICE 4D, 5C

It took the assassination of a President to bring about even a minimum of reform. This was in the area of government jobs.

Under the spoils system, elected leaders doled out jobs to their friends and supporters. Not surprisingly, corruption and incompetence thrived. President Hayes set out to change the system. Soon after his election, he announced new rules dealing with government appointments. Jobs were to be given to qualified people, not just to the friends of those in power.

In 1881 a man who was furious that he had not been given a government job assassinated Hayes's successor, James Garfield. The murder shocked the nation and shamed Congress into action. Congress passed the Civil Service Act of 1883 (also called the Pendleton Act), which set up a commission to come up with examinations for entry into government service.

The Civil Service Act was an important first step toward civil service reform. But it covered only about 10 percent of the jobs in the federal government. A group of Republicans known as Mugwumps (from an Indian word meaning "big shot") pushed for further reforms. In 1884 they

---

Biography
Ask students to suggest reasons why, in the 1800s, most law schools would not accept women. Then ask them to suggest how the increasing numbers of professional women has affected the role of women today.

THE PRESIDENTS

James A. Garfield

1881

20th President, Republican

- Born November 19, 1831, in Ohio
- Married Lucretia Rudolph in 1858; 7 children
- Representative and senator from Ohio
- Lived in Ohio when elected President
- Vice President: Chester A. Arthur
- Died September 19, 1881, in New Jersey after being shot by an assassin July 2, 1881
- Key event while in office: American Red Cross founded by Clara Barton

Grover Cleveland

1885–1889 and 1893–1897

22nd and 24th President, Democrat

- Born March 18, 1837, in New Jersey
- Married Frances Folsom in 1886; 5 children
- Lawyer; governor of New York
- Lived in New York when elected President
- Vice Presidents: Thomas Hendricks; Adlai Stevenson
- Died June 24, 1908, in New Jersey
- Only President to serve two nonconsecutive terms of office
- Key events while in office: Dawes Act; *(Second term) Plessy v. Ferguson*; Utah became a state

Chester A. Arthur

1881–1885

21st President, Republican

- Born October 5, 1829, in Vermont
- Married Ellen Herndon in 1859; 3 children
- Lawyer; Port of New York customs official; Vice President under Garfield
- Lived in New York when elected Vice President
- Vice President: none
- Died November 18, 1886, in New York
- Key events while in office: Standard time zones established; Civil Service Act

Benjamin Harrison

1889–1893

23rd President, Republican

- Born August 20, 1833, in Ohio
- Married Caroline Scott in 1853; 2 children
- Married Mary Dimmick in 1896; 1 child
- Lawyer; senator from Indiana
- Lived in Indiana when elected President
- Vice President: Levi Morton
- Died March 13, 1901, in Indiana
- Key events while in office: Sherman Antitrust Act; North Dakota, South Dakota, Montana, Washington, Idaho, and Wyoming became states; Battle of Wounded Knee

Why was the tariff a major concern of government during the Gilded Age? (Because it affected the economic welfare of all parts of American society, and provided money for federal projects which enriched congressional districts.)

Participating in Government

Discuss with students the frustration people felt over the perceived lack of choice between the two major political parties. *What types of third parties existed in the late 1800s?* (Usually formed around a single issue.) Ask students to describe their impressions of political parties today.

Civic Values

Make sure students understand the significance of the Civil Service Act of 1883 by asking them to describe the elements of an independent civil service. (People chosen to fill government jobs through blind testing; promotion by merit; inability for elected officials to fire civil servants.) Then have students present the pros and cons of an independent civil service.

Ask students to think of civil service jobs they know about, and list them. (Forest ranger, letter carrier, police officer, etc.) Students may wish to investigate how someone goes about getting such a job.

The Presidents
Have students examine the key events that occurred while these Presidents were in office, suggesting adjectives that describe the style of presidential leadership in the late 1800s.

This issue of *Puck*, a humor magazine, shows President Cleveland
uprooting a tree labeled "spoils system." The cartoonist Joseph
Keppler, an Austrian immigrant, was also *Puck*'s founder and
editor. Another example of his work appears on page 297. **ETHICS**
How did the spoils system hurt the nation's government? **7C**

broke with the GOP because its presidential candidate, James G. Blaine, was linked to corruption.
As one Mugwump put it, Blaine had "wallowed in
spoils like a rhinoceros in an African pool."
    Democrat Grover Cleveland defeated Blaine,
and while in office he extended the list of jobs covered by civil service. Yet Cleveland also caved in

to pressure from his party, firing many Republican officeholders and replacing them with Democrats. Despite this setback, the civil service
system was gradually strengthened.

NEW NEEDS, OLD POLITICS

Civil service reform meant a slightly more efficient, more honest government. But the nation
had other pressing needs, as well, that the federal
government failed to confront. What could be done
to restrain the influence of the wealthy? To ease
the suffering of the poor? Instead of answering
these questions, the federal government spent its
energy and taxpayers' money on other things.
    Debating the issue of tariffs took a lot of the
government's time. The positions were the same
as always. One side argued that tariffs helped
American manufacturers and filled the government treasury. The other side argued that tariffs
encouraged over-pricing and government waste.
In the years during and after the Civil War, supporters of tariffs won most of the the arguments.
    President Cleveland tried valiantly to lower the
tariff, which he called "unnecessary . . . vicious,
inequitable, and illogical." But in 1890 Congress
raised most rates. When Cleveland was re-elected
in 1892, he pushed a tariff cut through the House
of Representatives. The Senate rewrote the bill,
adding so many exceptions that tariffs remained

This cartoon appeared in *Puck*
in 1891. It shows a ragged
farmer intruding on a banquet
where industrialists are gorging
themselves on tariff-protected
luxuries. William McKinley
pours whiskey while other
congressmen provide music and
cigars. The farmer, whose
produce is not protected by
tariffs, asks, "Here, gents,
where do *I* come in?" **CULTURE**
Explain the cartoonist's point of
view. Is it expressed effectively? Why or why not?
7C, 9B

Photo Caption Answers
(Top) Politicians enriched
themselves at public expense,
and Americans lost faith in
their leaders in the process.
(Bottom) Students may
suggest that the cartoonist is
sympathetic to the farmer and
has effectively contrasted his
poverty with the rich lifestyle
of the politicians and
industrialists.

high. Though he disliked it, Cleveland let this bill—the Wilson-Gorman Tariff—become law.

Congress was also distracted by countless bills authorizing money for public projects. These generally wasteful, expensive projects had little value to the country as a whole. Yet logrolling kept them alive. This was a practice in which members of Congress backed each other's favorite projects. For example, a representative might want to build up his support among the voters by having a post office or harbor built in his district. Other representatives would support his bill, expecting that he would do them a similar favor later on. "You scratch my back, and I'll scratch yours" was a saying that described this system.

In 1882 alone, Congress passed a bill that supported nearly 500 such projects totaling nearly $19 million. When President Arthur vetoed the bill, Congress overrode his veto. One magazine commented: "Nobody denies that the bill was . . . a net of swindles and steals. . . . It is a huge logrolling bill, in which one job balances another, and one jobber is as deep in the mud as another to the mire."

The Republican-controlled Congress that met from 1889 to 1891 was the first peacetime Congress to authorize the spending of $1 billion. For that reason it became known as the "Billion Dollar Congress." Most of the money went to river and harbor projects and to pensions for Union army veterans of the Civil War.

The Dependent Pension Act of 1890 gave a pension to Union veterans with at least 90 days of military service who could lay claim to any disability. Their widows and children were also eligible for payment. That provision led to a bumper crop of marriages of young women to older vets. Within three years, the government was paying money to more than three times the number of actual surviving veterans. Not surprisingly, all the government's income from tariffs was spent—and then some. Red ink flowed.

Nevertheless, the Republicans still argued that what they had done in the "Billion Dollar Congress" was more significant than the work of any previous body. Never had any one party, they contended, done so much for so many with so little appreciation. No Republican was more spirited in his defense of the massive spending than House Speaker Thomas Reed. He contended that the Congress spent a billion dollars because the United States was a "billion dollar country."

SECTION REVIEW

1. KEY TERMS standpatter, Civil Service Act of 1883, Mugwump, logrolling

2. PEOPLE Rutherford B. Hayes, James A. Garfield, Grover Cleveland, Benjamin Harrison, James G. Blaine

3. COMPREHENSION Why did both major parties fail to deal with important issues?

4. COMPREHENSION What issues occupied the government's attention?

5. CRITICAL THINKING Do elected officials have a responsibility to tackle difficult issues even if the public is not demanding action? Explain your answer. 7J

9D

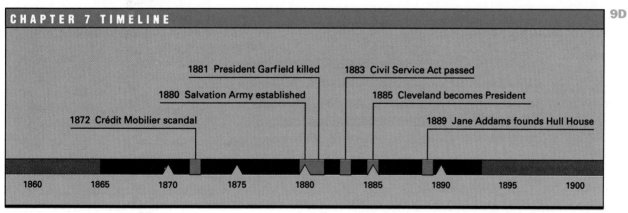

CHAPTER 7 TIMELINE

1881 President Garfield killed

1883 Civil Service Act passed

1880 Salvation Army established

1885 Cleveland becomes President

1872 Crédit Mobilier scandal

1889 Jane Addams founds Hull House

1860 1865 1870 1875 1880 1885 1890 1895 1900

Key Terms
1. settlement house
2. spoils system
3. standpatter
4. natural selection
5. conspicuous consumption

People to Identify
1. Ulysses S. Grant
2. William Marcy Tweed
3. Herbert Spencer
4. Jane Addams
5. Andrew Carnegie

Places to Locate
1. B   4. A
2. D   5. C
3. E

Reviewing the Facts
1. Social Darwinism is the theory that natural selection is the key to human progress.
2. The Gospel of Wealth was promoted by Andrew Carnegie who argued that the wealthy had a duty to help others.
3. The concentration of wealth was a threat to democracy as it encouraged corruption and stifled reform, thus making government unresponsive.
4. The urban poor faced the problems of unsafe, unhealthy tenements, and long workdays for little pay in dangerous factories and sweatshops. Government did not feel obligated to help the poor.
5. Private citizens set up charities, social workers and church groups fought for improved living and working conditions, settlement houses were created, and the Salvation Army was established to ease the suffering of the poor.
6. Rapid population growth, expansion of industry, and increasing wealth allowed the rise of political machines.

Chapter 7 REVIEW

CHAPTER 7 SUMMARY

SECTION 1: The economic growth of the United States produced a new class of wealthy people.

■ Herbert Spencer, an English philosopher, was the leading advocate of Social Darwinism, the theory that natural selection is the key to human progress.

■ Many wealthy Americans believed that they had a duty to use their money to help others and to improve the society in which they lived.

■ The wealthy also spent enormous sums of money competing to see who could live most lavishly.

■ Many Americans came to believe that the concentration of wealth in the hands of a tiny elite was dangerous to democracy and freedom.

SECTION 2: Millions of Americans were barely able to make ends meet.

■ A shortage of housing forced many poor people into unsafe, unhealthy tenements.

■ Workers labored long hours for little pay. Child labor was common.

■ Private charities tried to ease the suffering of poor Americans. Reformers pressed for the passage of laws to improve city life.

SECTION 3: Corruption was widespread in American government in the late 1800s.

■ High government officials benefited from the spoils system, using their authority to reward themselves and their friends.

■ Scandals plagued the federal government during the late 1800s.

■ People who donated money to fund political campaigns often expected to receive special treatment.

SECTION 4: The American political system proved incapable of dealing with the nation's major problems.

■ Neither party was willing to tackle controversial issues for fear of losing popular support.

■ The assassination of President Garfield led to modest civil service reforms.

■ Large sums of money were spent on questionable public works projects.

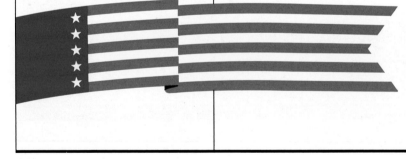

KEY TERMS ●

Use the following terms to complete the sentences below.

conspicuous consumption
natural selection
settlement house
spoils system
standpatter

1. A _____ was a private institution that aimed at improving life for poor city dwellers.
2. Under the _____, politicians used their power to help themselves and their friends.
3. A person in the late 1800s who opposed reforms was a

_____ .

4. The principle of _____ comes from the theory of evolution.
5. Spending money lavishly in order to show off one's wealth is known as _____ .

PEOPLE TO IDENTIFY ●

Match each of the following people with the correct description.

Jane Addams
Andrew Carnegie
Ulysses S. Grant
Herbert Spencer
William Marcy Tweed

1. President whose administration was ridden by scandal.
2. Boss of New York City's most famous political machine.
3. Leading proponent of Social Darwinism.
4. Founder of Hull House.
5. Industrialist who promoted the "Gospel of Wealth."

7. In national politics the election of candidates, job appointments, and the passage of laws were all influenced by bribery and corruption.

8. The civil service required entry examinations for government service and was designed to fight patronage.

9. The fear of angering voters and losing support kept political parties from tackling controversial issues.

PLACES TO LOCATE ●

Match each of the letters on the map with the places that are listed below.

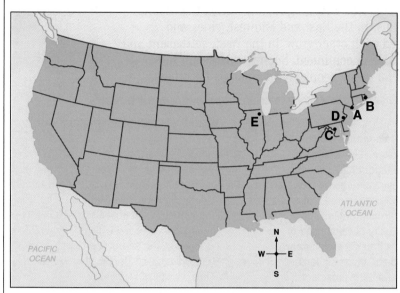

1. Newport, Rhode Island
2. Philadelphia
3. Chicago
4. New York City
5. Washington, D.C.

REVIEWING THE FACTS ▲

1. What was Social Darwinism?
2. What was the Gospel of Wealth?
3. Why did many people come to believe that the concentration of wealth in the hands of a few people was a threat to democracy?
4. What problems did the urban poor face? What was the government's attitude toward these problems?
5. What efforts did dedicated Americans make to relieve the suffering of the urban poor?

6. What conditions allowed powerful political machines to arise in many of the nation's major cities?
7. How did money influence national politics?
8. What is the civil service? What problem was it designed to remedy?
9. Why did the major political parties avoid addressing controversial issues?
10. What issues did Congress devote itself to in the late nineteenth century? What issues did Congress fail to address?

CRITICAL THINKING SKILLS ▲

1. **IDENTIFYING THE MAIN IDEA** How did Herbert Spencer apply Darwin's theories to human society?

2. **DRAWING CONCLUSIONS** Why might it be considered unethical for members of Congress to vote on bills affecting companies in which they own stock?

3. **MAKING A HYPOTHESIS** How might Andrew Carnegie or John D. Rockefeller have responded to the charge that the concentration of wealth in the hands of a few individuals was a threat to democracy?

WRITING ABOUT TOPICS IN AMERICAN HISTORY ■

1. **CONNECTING WITH LITERATURE** A selection from *The House of Mirth* by Edith Wharton appears on pages 783–785. Read it and answer the questions. Then answer the following question: How does Lily Bart's situation compare with that of her contemporary, Dulcie, in the O. Henry story (page 781)? How does each woman deal with her situation?

2. **APPLYING THEMES: CONSTITUTIONAL GOVERNMENT** Imagine that you are an adviser to President Grover Cleveland. He is under intense pressure from other members of his party to replace Republicans with Democrats in all government jobs under his control. Write a memo telling him how he should respond and why.

2. Members of Congress should not vote on bills which involve companies in which they own stock, as they may vote for personal interests rather than using their best judgment.

3. Rockefeller might point to Social Darwinism, stating that in a democracy everyone has a chance to be wealthy but only the fit survive. Carnegie might argue that the wealthy were not dangerous, but rather were there to help others and to contribute to the community.

Writing About Topics in American History
1. It is similar—both are poor and striving to take part in high society. Dulcie works to support herself, but Lily Bart seems to rely completely on the generosity of her wealthy friends.

2. Students should explain the background of these controversies, the different arguments used, and possible solutions.

10. Congress devoted much time to tariffs and wasteful public projects, rather than dealing with the problems of the poor and the influence of the wealthy.

Critical Thinking Skills
1. Spencer argued that individuals compete for success and only the strong or competent win, thus creating a natural upper class.

Chapter Review exercises are keyed for student abilities:
● = Basic
▲ = Average
■ = Average/Advanced

American Mosaic

Introducing the Feature

Have students explain how the settlement of the West both enriched and diminished American culture. (The culture was enriched by the experience of frontier explorers and adventurers and by cowboy traditions. However, government policies that subjugated and dislocated American Indians resulted in the near destruction of a valuable part of the nation's heritage.) ***How did the rise of industrialization and urbanization in the East and the Midwest affect the lives of immigrants?*** (Industry in the cities provided work for immigrants and created opportunities for enterprising and inventive newcomers to rise in society. But many urban dwellers labored in arduous jobs for low wages, without hope of improving their condition.)

Teaching Multiculturalism

History

Point out to students that by the second half of the 1800s it was not unusual to find women in such roles as nurse, teacher, or charitable worker. Many professions, however, remained the reserve of white males. ***In what non-traditional roles did Maggie Walker and Annie Oakley achieve prominence?*** (Maggie Walker: started an insurance fund and a newspaper, became the country's first female bank president; Annie Oakley: performing sharpshooter.)

Civic Values

Ask students to suggest alternative ways that Elfego Baca might have handled his confrontation with the cowboys. (He could have gone to the authorities; asked for help before attempting to arrest the cowboys; not gotten involved at all.)

176

UNIT 2: American Mosaic

★ *A Multicultural Perspective* ★

The United States was changing rapidly during the second half of the 1800s. In the East and Midwest, cities and industry helped each other grow. In the West, settlement and economic expansion continued. Such trends meant new opportunities for many people, but hardships for others.

Born a cook's daughter in Richmond, Virginia, in 1867, **Maggie Walker** (left) taught high school for a time and then volunteered to work for the Independent United Order of St. Luke, a self-help organization. Walker eventually became head of St. Luke's. She started an insurance fund and a newspaper and later formed a successful bank, thereby becoming the nation's first female bank president.

Immigrants whose success in business made their names famous as trademarks include E. I. **Du Pont** Nemours from France, Joseph **Bulova** from Czechoslovakia, and Maroun Hajjar from Lebanon whose name appears on the label of the clothing his company sells as **Haggar.** John Francis Queeny, the son of Irish immigrants, named his company after his Spanish American wife, Olga Mendez **Monsanto.**

Though **Annie Oakley** (left) never traveled west of the Mississippi River until she was in her mid-20s, she became a symbol of the independent woman of the frontier. She was born Phoebe Ann Moses in Ohio in 1860 and learned to handle a rifle at an early age. Her aim became so accurate that at the age of fifteen she outshot a traveling sharpshooter, Frank Butler. Butler and Oakley married a year later. The couple performed on their own before joining Buffalo Bill Cody's Wild West show. Touring in both the United States and Europe, Oakley became very famous indeed. One of her astounding tricks was to shoot away a cigarette from her husband's mouth. When she performed this feat for the German royal family in the 1890s, the Crown Prince volunteered to hold the cigarette in his own mouth. This was Wilhelm, the man who led his country into World War I. After that war broke out, Oakley regretted the accuracy of her shot. "If only my aim had been poorer," she said, "I might have averted the Great War."

Elfego Baca (right) became a county sheriff and a successful politician in New Mexico. His career in law enforcement began in 1884 when he was a teenager. Baca saw a group of rowdy cowboys harassing Mexican Americans in the town of Frisco. He tried to make a citizen's arrest of one of the cowboys, but was attacked by the man's friends. Baca killed one cowboy in the struggle that followed and took refuge in a friend's house. For more than a day a crowd fired shots into the building, but Baca refused to surrender until promised a fair trial. He got the promise and was acquitted.

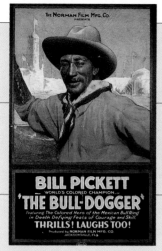

Bill Pickett (left), one of the many African American cowboys, popularized a sport called "bulldogging." A cowboy would jump from his horse onto the horns of a steer and then wrestle the huge animal to the ground. Pickett was regarded as the greatest rodeo performer of his day.

Polly Bemis (left) was born Lalu Nathoy in China in 1853. As a child she was sold to bandits for two bags of seed. Shipped to America as a slave, she wound up in an Idaho mining camp working for a Chinese saloon keeper. Then a man named Charlie Bemis won her in a poker game. The couple later married, settling down on a twenty-acre farm. Bemis twice saved her husband's life, and gained the respect and appreciation of her neighbors for her charitable works.

Hideyo Noguchi (right) had to borrow money from a friend to buy passage from Japan to the United States. As a man dedicated to what he called "the sweet realm of science," Noguchi was determined to pursue his career in a leading scientific nation. Though he had no job offer, he settled near the University of Pennsylvania and quickly impressed scientists there with his talent and dedication. In 1904 he took a research position in New York City and his work on antidotes to snake venom eventually won him international fame.

Factory owners in Lynn, Massachusetts, in 1877 were unimpressed when **Jan Matzeliger** (right) came looking for a job. Matzeliger, an immigrant from Surinam in South America, was turned down time after time. Undeterred, Matzeliger learned English and obtained a job as an apprentice in a shoe factory. There he got an idea for an invention—a machine that would shape and fasten the shoe upper to the sole. His invention, called the shoe laster, revolutionized the shoe industry.

In February 1866 **Mary Baker Eddy** (above) slipped on some ice near Boston and injured herself. She later reported that she had been healed while reading a passage from the New Testament. Out of that experience came a popular movement, led by Eddy, that proclaimed the healing powers of spirituality and prayer. "There is a law of God applicable to healing," Eddy declared. The Church of Christ, Scientist, which she founded, had 36,000 members by 1905.

In 1877 the federal government forcibly moved the Ponca Indians from their homes in Dakota and Nebraska to the Indian Territory. When the Ponca chief and some of his people tried to return to their homes two years later, they were arrested. An Omaha Indian named **Susette LaFlesche**

(right) went on a lecture tour through the East to rally public support for the Ponca. She later spoke before Congress and in Europe on behalf of Indian causes. A forceful and convincing public speaker, LaFlesche helped secure passage of the 1887 Dawes Act.

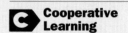

Historians' Corner

Vocabulary Preview

Be sure students understand the following terms:
bolster—Support. *ardent*—Enthusiastic. *enclave*—A distinctly bounded area enclosed within a larger unit.

Analyzing Historical Issues

In the first selection, Ray Allen Billington argues that the seemingly unlimited possibilities of the frontier produced the distinct and optimistic American character. Richard C. Wade, on the other hand, believes that cities provided the unifying element for national character amidst regional differences in the 1800s.

Is American identity the product of the frontier experience or the city? Explain your answer.

Critical Thinking Answers

1. Billington supports Turner's theory of the importance of the frontier.

2. The vast size of the frontier and its natural resources, combined with the pioneers' success in settling it, helped build a spirit of nationalism. The growth of cities contributed to nationalism by creating places of similar economic, political, and social organization.

3. Both explanations could be true because neither claims to be the only force in shaping American identity. The frontier may have had a greater effect on individuals, while the city may have had greater influence on institutions.

HISTORIANS' CORNER

The Frontier and the City

Historians have often tried to pinpoint the factors that have shaped the United States. One popular idea was Frederick Jackson Turner's theory that the existence of a vast frontier gave America a unique national character. This and other theories created a picture of America as a nation that was basically rural until the era of industrialization. Other historians, however, believe that the influence of cities has been underrated.

Ray Allen Billington

The quest for betterment, and the dream of a better life . . . helped bestow upon the pioneer the optimism that was another of his identifiable attitudes. As long as expansion was a fact of life, improvement was certain. . . . Expansion had given substance to such dreams in the past, and it would in the future. . . . Impatience to realize these dreams tended to speed up life along the frontiers; nowhere was the "go-ahead" spirit so extravagantly shown. . . .

Visions of the United States as the greatest nation on earth helped mold the nationalistic spirit. Everywhere in America during the nineteenth century, but most particularly in the West, travelers were buttonholed by natives who assured them that the United States had the best government, the rosiest future, the strongest army, and the handsomest people in the world. This faith was partly an outgrowth of frontier optimism, but it was bolstered by the pioneering experience. . . . The ardent nationalism that characterized the United States in the nineteenth century was the product of many forces, but one was the expansion of the frontier.

From Ray Allen Billington, *America's Frontier Heritage*. Copyright © 1963 by Holt Reinhart and Winston; copyright © 1974 by the University of New Mexico Press.

Richard C. Wade

Urbanization in the United States is not so recent a force as is often believed. In fact, cities have played an important role from the very beginning. . . . The port towns exerted a disproportionate influence in the seventeenth and eighteenth centuries. . . .

The rise of cities in the nineteenth century deepened the historic division between town and country; yet it also had, ironically, a profoundly nationalizing effect. In the first place, they appeared very rapidly in every part of the country, providing each section with important urban centers. When the "line of settlement" barely reached across the mountains in 1800, towns had already sprung up along the Ohio Valley and as far west as St. Louis. . . . In the West, Josiah Strong observed in 1884, "The city stamps the country, instead of the country stamping the city. It is the cities and towns which will frame constitutions, make laws, create public opinion." . . .

Second, this spread of urbanization fostered the growing nationalism by providing each region with enclaves of a similar environment. For nineteenth-century cities had much in common. They all stemmed from commercial necessity; they all developed similar political and social institutions.

From Richard C. Wade, "Urbanization" in *The Comparative Approach to American History*, ed. by C. Vann Woodward. Copyright © 1968 by C. Vann Woodward. Reprinted by permission of Basic Books, Inc., Publishers, New York.

Critical Thinking

1. Which of these historians supports Turner's theory of the importance of the frontier?

2. According to these historians, how was a spirit of nationalism encouraged by the frontier? By the cities?

3. Could both these explanations of American development be true? Explain.

Ray Allen Billington
(1903–1981) won the Bancroft Prize for American History. He was a supporter of Frederick Jackson Turner's frontier thesis and specialized in the history of the American West.

Richard C. Wade
(1922–   ) is a professor of history at the Graduate Center of the City University of New York, specializing in urban history.

UNIT THREE

Change and Reform

THEMES IN AMERICAN HISTORY

Economic Development During the late 1800s, both farmers and urban workers organized to deal with economic hardships.

Pluralistic Society African Americans formed national organizations to help improve their lives.

Geography The Progressive Presidents took important steps in the area of conservation.

Constitutional Government Constitutional amendments of the early 1900s furthered progressive causes in several areas.

Expanding Democracy In 1920, after a long struggle, women won the right to vote.

Unit Three

Change and Reform
(pp. 179–250)

Unit Three examines the growth of opposition to big business and laissez-faire government through the organization of labor unions and farmers' groups, and the rise of the Populist Party. It explains how conflicts over the money supply influenced presidential elections in the 1890s, and how the defeat of populism made way for the growth of progressivism. Several leading progressives are profiled, as well as their success in reforming city and state government and in passing constitutional amendments that created a more responsive and democratic federal government.

The unit also describes the personal motivations and political challenges of the three progressive Presidents who led the country in the first decades of the century, noting both their failure to address the problems of African Americans and their achievements in taking steps toward conserving the nation's natural resources.

Chapter 8 ▪ Rising Protests

	SECTION OBJECTIVES	SECTION RESOURCES
Section 1 **Organizing Labor**	▪ describe the development of early labor unions	● **Reteaching Resources:** Worksheet 29 ▲ **Reinforcement Workbook:** Worksheet 29 ■ **Enrichment and Extension Resources:** Primary Source Worksheet 15 ▲ **Teaching Transparencies:** Transparency 29
Section 2 **Striking Against Big Business**	▪ identify the causes and outcomes of the major strikes of the late 1800s	● **Reteaching Resources:** Worksheet 30 ▲ **Reinforcement Workbook:** Worksheet 30 ▲ **Teaching Transparencies:** Transparency 30
Section 3 **Organizing Farmers**	▪ describe the problems farmers faced in the last half of the nineteenth century and the ways in which they sought to improve their situation	● **Reteaching Resources:** Worksheet 31 ▲ **Reinforcement Workbook:** Worksheet 31 ■ **Enrichment and Extension Resources:** Primary Source Worksheet 16 ▲ **Teaching Transparencies:** Transparency 31
Section 4 **The Rise and Fall of Populism**	▪ define the issues of the 1896 presidential election and describe its outcome	● **Reteaching Resources:** Worksheet 32 ▲ **Reinforcement Workbook:** Worksheet 32 ▲ **Teaching Transparencies:** Transparency 32

The list below shows Essential Elements relevant to this chapter. (The complete list of Essential Elements appears in the introductory pages of this Teacher's Edition.)

Section 1:   2A, 2C, 3C, 3D, 3E, 4E, 9B
Section 2:   3C, 3D, 3E, 9F, 9G
Section 3:   3C, 3D, 3E, 3F, 5B, 5C, 8A, 8E, 9B
Section 4:   3E, 3F, 5B, 5D, 7E, 7H, 9A, 9D

Section Resources are keyed for student abilities:
● = Basic
▲ = Average
■ = Average/Advanced

CHAPTER RESOURCES

Geography Resources: Worksheets 15, 16
Tests: Chapter 8 Test

Chapter Project: Expanding Democracy
Have students choose one of the organizations mentioned in the chapter, such as a labor union, farmers' group, or political party, and create a pamphlet that could be used to solicit membership to the organization.

Homework Options
Each section contains activities labeled "Addressing Individual Needs." You may wish to choose from among these activities when assigning homework.

> **Provisions for Limited English Proficiency (LEP)**
> Several suggested activities may be particularly helpful for teachers of students with limited English proficiency. These activities have been marked throughout the Teacher's Annotated Edition with the symbol **LEP** .

BIBLIOGRAPHY AND AUDIOVISUAL AIDS

Teacher Bibliography
Bryan, William J., and Mary Bryan. *Memoirs of William Jennings Bryan.* Haskell, 1970.

Morgan, H. Wayne. *Eugene V. Debs: Socialist for President.* Greenwood, 1973.

Van Deusen, Glyndon G. *Horace Greeley: Nineteenth Century Crusader.* Hill and Wang, 1964.

Student Bibliography
Glad, Paul W. *The Trumpet Soundeth: William Jennings Bryan and His Democracy, 1896–1912.* Greenwood, 1986.

Meltzer, Milton. *Bread and Roses: The Struggle of American Labor, 1865–1911.* NAL Penguin, 1977.

Selvin, David. *Champions of Labor.* Abelard-Schuman, 1967.

Stiller, Richard. *Queen of Populists: The Story of Mary Elizabeth Lease.* Crowell, 1970.

Literature
Dreiser, Theodore. *Sister Carrie.* Bantam, 1982. The life of a nonconformist at the turn of the century.

London, Jack. *Martin Eden.* Airmont, 1969. A story of a seaman who rejects society's mores.

Twain, Mark. *The Man That Corrupted Hadleyburg: A Classic Story of Honesty.* Creative Education, 1986.

Films and Videotapes*
Masses and the Millionaires. 27 min. LCA. Dramatization of the strike at the Homestead steel mill in 1892.

Out of the Depths. 57 min. PBS. Recalls the struggles of miners and laborers in the American West.

Filmstrips*
The Growth of the Labor Movement (set of two). GA. Explores the historic development and current status of the labor movement in this country.

Computer Software*
Industrialism in America (Apple II). FOCUS. Titles include: *The Industrial Revolution Comes to the U.S.; The Age of Big Business;* and *Industrial America.* Introduces concepts and vocabulary.

*For a complete guide to audiovisual sources, see the introduction to this book (page Txx).

Rising Protests
(pp. 180–201)

Chapter 8 chronicles the struggles of labor unions, farmers, and Populists to protect their interests against the power of business in an age of laissez-faire national government.

Themes in American History

- Expanding democracy
- Economic development
- Geography

Chapter Objectives

After students complete this chapter, they will be able to:

1. Describe the development of early labor unions.

2. Identify the causes and outcomes of the major strikes of the late 1800s.

3. Describe the problems farmers faced in the last half of the nineteenth century and the ways in which they sought to improve their situation.

4. Define the issues of the 1896 presidential election and describe its outcome.

This 1885 poster by the Brotherhood of Locomotive Firemen of North America shows idealized scenes from the lives of union members. Farmers as well as industrial workers organized during the late 1800s to protect their interests and improve their lives.

CHAPTER SUPPORT MATERIAL	
	Reinforcement Workbook: Worksheets 29–32
	Reteaching Resources: Worksheets 29–32
	Enrichment and Extension Resources: Primary Source Worksheets 15, 16
	Geography Resources: Worksheets 15, 16
	Teaching Transparencies: Transparencies 29–32
	Tests: Chapter 8 Test

8 Rising Protests
(1865–1900)

2A, 2C, 3C, 3D, 3E, 4E, 9B

1 Organizing Labor

Section Focus

Key Terms business cycle ■ depression ■ recession ■ cooperative ■ anarchist ■ Haymarket Riot ■ closed shop ■ collective bargaining

Main Idea In the late nineteenth century, workers unhappy with working conditions began to organize unions.

Objectives As you read, look for answers to these questions:
1. How did American unions change after the Civil War?
2. What were some of the important unions of the late 1800s?

The growth of industry in the post–Civil War era produced revolutionary changes in the American economy and thus in American society. Government, at first, could not keep pace with these changes. As a result, workers and farmers formed organizations to defend their interests. At the same time, they pressured government to play a more active role in the economic life of the country. While their efforts never fully succeeded, they paved the way for new government policies in the early 1900s (Chapters 9 and 10).

GROWTH OF UNIONS 3C, 3E

Unions had been on the American scene since the late 1700s. The early unions were small, local organizations made up of skilled workers—tailors, carpenters, weavers, and so on. The building of factories brought into the work force many unskilled workers, who performed simple, monotonous chores that required little or no training. But few early unions recruited unskilled workers. In fact, the skilled workers regarded unskilled workers as rivals because they worked for lower wages. Partly because of this lack of worker unity, the

early unions were not strong enough to survive the Panic of 1837.

Not until after the Civil War did the labor movement again gather strength. A number of factors led to this revival. Most important was the need to bargain effectively with employers. The growth of industry produced a tremendous expansion in the labor force. Millions of new workers—immigrants, farmers, women—entered the factories. Skilled

This early photograph of a factory shows workers painting mowing-machine frames by hand. ECONOMICS Why did many workers in the late 1800s decide they needed to join unions? 3C

SUPPORTING THE SECTION

Reinforcement Workbook: Worksheet 29
Reteaching Resources: Worksheet 29
Enrichment and Extension Resources: Primary Source Worksheet 15
Teaching Transparencies: Transparency 29

Photo Caption Answer
The expanded labor force decreased job security, machines replaced skilled laborers, working conditions were often dangerous, wage-cutting and layoffs occurred during economic slumps.

SECTION 1

Organizing Labor
(pp. 181–185)

Section Objective
■ describe the development of early labor unions

Introducing the Section

Connecting with Past Learnings
Review with students the nature of the Industrial Revolution. *What changes in the conditions of work and the workplace resulted from the Industrial Revolution?* (Instead of a skilled artisan or a farmer doing a variety of tasks, working with the family or a few others, workers performed repetitive tasks away from home in large, crowded factories.)

Key Terms
Write the key terms for this section on the board. Call on volunteers to use each term in a sentence. Ask other students to verify the correct usage of each term. **LEP**

Focus
Ask students to explain the differences between the two philosophies of early labor unions. (Earlier labor unions united skilled and unskilled workers and demanded broad social reforms. The AFL, whose members were skilled workers only, bargained with employers for improved working conditions.)
If you had been a worker in the the mid-1800s, which philosophy would you have found more attractive? Why? Have students discuss which philosophy turned out to be more effective.

After students have read the section, you may want to consider the following activities:

Economics

Today, how does the U.S. government help failing banks and unemployed workers? (It insures depositors so that if a bank closes, depositors don't lose all their money; workers who lose their jobs get unemployment insurance payments and may get public assistance of some sort.) *How might these actions help the economy from falling into depressions?* (It keeps the amount of money in the economy from dropping dramatically.)

Have students discuss what it might be like to live in an economy where the government took no actions to help failing businesses or the unemployed.

History

Theodore Roosevelt said: "The old familiar relations between employer and employee were passing. A few generations before, the boss had known every man in his shop; he called his men Bill, Tom, Dick, and John; he inquired after their wives and babies; he swapped jokes and stories . . . with them." Ask students to compare this kind of relationship with that in large factories.

Science and Technology

The growth of industry meant that an increasing number of jobs were done by machines, which people tended. Ask students to discuss how this change might have affected the way people felt about their work. Have students role-play workers whose jobs have been taken over by machines.

workers forced out of business by machine-made goods also took factory jobs. Factory owners, meanwhile, knew that they could easily replace any workers who quit. Thus they had no incentive to raise wages or improve working conditions. As one cap maker explained:

> We were helpless; no one girl dared stand up for anything alone. Matters kept getting worse. The bosses kept making reductions in our pay. . . . One girl would say that she didn't think she could make caps for the new price, but another would say that she thought she could make up for the reduction by working a little harder, and then the first would tell herself: "If she can do it, why can't I?"

Even those who worked long and hard without complaint had no guarantees of long-term economic security. Laboring day after day at breakneck speed, factory workers suffered from fatigue and accidents. Between 1880 and 1900, accidents killed an average of five people each day.

CHART SKILLS 3E

This diagram outlines the phases of the business cycle. Economic changes, however, are not as regular as the diagram suggests. Which phase follows expansion? **CRITICAL THINKING** What effect might a recession have on purchases of consumer goods? Why?

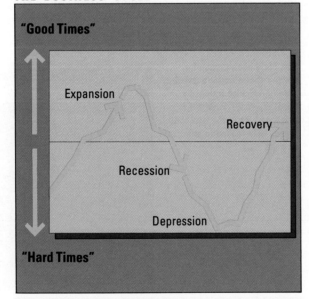

THE BUSINESS CYCLE

"Good Times"

Expansion

Recovery

Recession

Depression

"Hard Times"

Economic slumps also threatened the well-being of workers. In the 1800s, as today, the national economy operated according to the business cycle. A period of prosperity would be followed by hard times, a pattern sometimes called "boom and bust." In 1873 and 1893 the economy fell into a depression—a time of high unemployment, low consumer spending, and many business failures. There were also recessions, milder economic downturns. Today government is expected to take action to lessen the swings of the cycle—pumping up a sluggish economy or slowing an overheated one. But in the 1800s, the government's laissez-faire approach rejected these kinds of policies. Companies reacted to the economic slumps by cutting wages and firing workers, and government provided little help.

Unions offered workers a chance to join forces against the threats to their security. Some unions, eager to increase membership, began admitting the many new unskilled workers. They also tried to combine local unions into large national organizations. Only by gaining size and strength, union leaders realized, could they hope to compete with the growing size and strength of industry. For unions, as for industry, this was an era of "bigness."

THE NATIONAL LABOR UNION 3C

The first American union to unite skilled and unskilled workers was the National Labor Union (NLU). It was founded in 1866 by William Sylvis, a former head of the iron-molders union in Philadelphia. Sylvis was a dedicated leader. "I love this union cause," he once remarked. "I hold it more dear than I do my family or my life. I am willing to devote to it all that I am or have or hope for in this world." Within five years the NLU boasted a membership of 600,000. It included people who were not industrial laborers, such as farmers.

Sylvis saw the NLU as a broad-based popular movement. He believed that it should work to improve the lives of average Americans. Rather than confront employers with strikes, the NLU urged workers to become more self-sufficient by forming cooperatives—businesses owned and run by the workers themselves. Because these businesses would aim at breaking even, not making a profit,

Background Many Americans at this time harbored a deep suspicion toward labor unions. Although they thought that combinations and agreements among business were just good sense, they looked on the organization of labor with disapproval and tended to believe that unemployment was somehow "an act of God."

they would be able to charge workers lower prices.

The NLU also looked to government for help. Arguing that Chinese immigrants were taking jobs from native-born American workers, the NLU pushed Congress for a ban on Chinese immigration. (One was passed in 1882.) The union urged Congress to pass legislation setting an eight-hour limit to the work day. Finally, the NLU entered politics as an independent party. In 1872 it became the National Labor Reform Party and nominated a candidate for President. But the party received only two electoral votes in the election won easily by Ulysses S. Grant. Its membership and influence quickly faded.

THE KNIGHTS OF LABOR 3C

Already, however, there was a competing union. This was the Noble Order of the Knights of Labor, founded in 1869 by Uriah S. Stephens. The Knights of Labor began as a secret society. It had a special initiation ceremony and a secret password and handshake. The aims of the Knights were high-sounding:

> To secure to the toilers [workers] a proper share of the wealth that they create; more of the leisure that rightfully belongs to them; more societary advantages; more of the benefits, privileges, and emoluments [profits] of the world; in a word, all those rights and privileges necessary to make them capable of enjoying, appreciating, defending, and perpetuating the blessings of good government. . . .

Like the NLU, the Knights pinned their hopes on political action rather than strikes. Their political platform called for an end to child labor and for public ownership of railroads and telegraph lines. The Knights shared the NLU's goals of eight-hour work days and worker cooperatives. In fact, the union set up some 100 cooperatives, including a coal mine and a shoe-making plant. Most failed because of a lack of money or poor business decisions.

Membership in the Knights of Labor remained small until 1879, when Terence V. Powderly took over. Powderly reversed the union's emphasis on

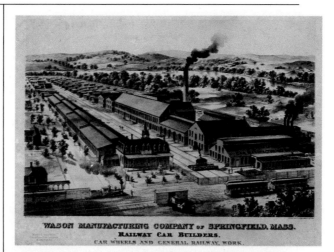

WASON MANUFACTURING COMPANY OF SPRINGFIELD, MASS.
RAILWAY CAR BUILDERS.
CAR WHEELS AND GENERAL RAILWAY WORK.

Throughout the 1800s, factories became increasingly frequent sights in the Northeast. Rivers provided their power. This print from 1872 shows a railroad car factory on the Connecticut River near Springfield, Massachusetts. ECONOMICS How might this factory have affected life in the town? 2A, 2C, 4E

secrecy and recruited thousands of new members. These included many blacks—one-tenth of the total members by 1886. Thousands of women also joined the union, some rising to leadership positions. For example, Elizabeth Flynn Rogers, a housewife and mother of twelve children, headed the Chicago branch of the union. The Knights attracted even more workers when some of its members struck against railroad baron Jay Gould in 1885 and won. Soon after the 1885 strike, the Knights were 700,000 strong.

BIOGRAPHY 3D

TERENCE POWDERLY (1849–1924), who worked as a machinist, joined the Knights of Labor in 1874. Five years later he became its Grand Master Workman. Powderly dreamed of a labor force in which "each man is his own employer." While many unions focused on such immediate demands as better wages and shorter hours, Powderly tried to promote more fundamental social changes. Powderly appears at right surrounded by other leaders of the Knights of Labor, including Uriah Stephens (top) and Samuel Gompers (left side, third from bottom).

Photo Caption Answer
Students may suggest that the economic life of the town revolved around the factory.

Biography
Have students compare Terence Powderly's goals with the goals of union leaders today.

Background The slogan of the Knights of Labor was "An injury to one is the concern of all." The union excluded from membership only lawyers, bankers, stockbrokers, liquor dealers, and professional gamblers.

This engraving of the 1886 Haymarket Riot appeared in *Harper's* magazine. A strike by the Knights of Labor at Chicago's McCormick-Harvester plant led indirectly to the riot. Most Americans blamed the violence on the labor movement. **HISTORY** To which group is this artist more sympathetic, the demonstrators or the police? How can you tell? 3C, 9B

THE HAYMARKET RIOT 3C

At first the Knights of Labor profited from strikes. But the union was losing control of its members. Union leaders did not dare criticize the strikers publicly for fear of splintering the union. They worried, however, that if their members became too radical, public opinion would swing against the union. That is exactly what happened.

On May 1, 1886, some Knights and other workers in Chicago went on strike in support of the eight-hour work day. Anarchists—people who oppose all forms of government—supported the strikers, hoping to take advantage of the rising tension. On May 3, police clashed with strikers at the McCormick-Harvester works. One striker was killed. The next day a demonstration was held in Haymarket Square to protest the violence.

The demonstration began as a typical rally: pamphlets were handed out and speeches were made. As a cold rain began to fall, 200 police officers arrived on the scene, sent there to break up the group. Suddenly a bomb exploded in the police ranks. The police fired into the crowd. Seven police officers and four workers died, and more than a hundred people were injured. Eight of the demonstrators were immediately arrested and charged with murder.

The public outcry was swift. *The Washington Post* argued that the defendants were a "horde of foreigners, representing almost the lowest stratum [level] found in humanity." *The Albany Law Journal* went even further, calling them "long-haired, wild-eyed, bad-smelling, atheistic, reckless foreign wretches who never did an honest hour's work in their lives."

Public opinion sealed the fate of the defendants. The prosecutor could not prove that any of them had actually thrown the bomb. Six of them, in fact, had not even been in Haymarket Square on May 4. No matter. All eight were convicted of conspiracy to kill a police officer. Four were hanged, another committed suicide, and the remaining three received long prison sentences. The governor of Illinois pardoned the surviving prisoners several years later, claiming they had not received a fair trial.

The Haymarket Riot dealt a fatal blow to the Knights of Labor. Powderly tried to distance the union from the violence. He declared that "Honest labor is not to be found in the ranks of those who march under the red flag of anarchy, which is the emblem of blood and destruction." Yet the public now linked the union with anarchists. Membership dropped sharply, and by the 1890s the union had all but disappeared.

THE AMERICAN FEDERATION OF LABOR 3C, 3D

The NLU and the Knights of Labor had followed the same basic strategy. This was to unite skilled and unskilled workers into one giant union, then to demand broad reforms from government. The failure of the NLU and the radicalism of the Knights led many in the union movement to abandon this strategy. Unskilled workers, many felt, weakened a union because an employer could easily replace them in the event of a strike. Unions should therefore include only skilled workers. Some union leaders also decided that unions should not try to push for sweeping social change. Instead, unions should bargain directly with employers and limit their demands to concrete issues such as wages. An organization that followed this new approach was the American Federation of Labor (AFL).

The AFL was founded in 1886. Samuel Gompers, a cigar-maker, was elected president; Peter J. McGuire, a carpenter, became secretary. Both men had colorful backgrounds. In 1863 Gompers had come to New York City from England at age 13. He got a job rolling cigars, and listened as other workers discussed ways to improve conditions. Some called on workers to take over industries from the owners. Others wanted government to take over industries. Gompers rejected these ideas as unrealistic. Unions, in his view, should work within the existing system, gaining improved conditions by bargaining with their employers.

McGuire had grown up in the East in the years after the Civil War. The son of Irish immigrants, he was forced to start working at age 11. He held almost every kind of job during his early years—except, he later joked, that of a sword swallower. "And sometimes," he said, "I was so hungry, a sword—with mustard, of course—would have tasted fine." McGuire finally found his trade as a carpenter and helped to set up the United Brotherhood of Carpenters in 1881.

Both Gompers and McGuire believed that only skilled unions joined together in a national federation could deal with employers. These unions would push for the establishment of a closed shop, meaning that the employer would agree to hire only union workers. The union's tactic would be collective bargaining—direct talks between organized workers and their employer. If the unions failed to gain their goals through collective bargaining, then they would use the strike. When Gompers was asked to summarize the philosophy of the AFL, he said, "More."

The AFL set up rules for its member unions. Each union was expected to admit only those workers who had gone through training to learn their skills. Unskilled workers, blacks, women, and recent immigrants were not allowed to join. Workers paid regular dues to their union so that the union would have money on hand to aid workers on strike. Unions were always reminded to devote their energy to reasonable, concrete goals.

The AFL grew steadily, becoming the nation's largest union. Its membership jumped from fewer than 200,000 in 1886 to 1,750,000 eighteen years later. However, that figure accounted for only a small fraction of the total number of industrial workers in the United States. The majority of industrial workers were unskilled and did not belong to any union. The American labor movement still had a long way to go.

SECTION REVIEW

1. KEY TERMS business cycle, depression, recession, cooperative, anarchist, Haymarket Riot, closed shop, collective bargaining

2. PEOPLE William Sylvis, Uriah S. Stephens, Terence V. Powderly, Samuel Gompers

3. COMPREHENSION In what ways did industrialization change American unions?

4. COMPREHENSION How did the AFL's strategy differ from that of the NLU and the Knights of Labor?

5. CRITICAL THINKING Why would a union want an employer to agree to a closed shop? Which workers might oppose the creation of a closed shop?

2. *William Sylvis*—Founder of the National Labor Union. *Uriah S. Stephens*—Founder of the Knights of Labor. *Terence V. Powderly*—Leader of the Knights of Labor. *Samuel Gompers*—First president of the American Federation of Labor.

3. Industrialization expanded the labor force, and factory jobs were often dangerous and difficult.

4. The AFL's strategy was to bargain with employers and limit demands to concrete issues instead of trying to accomplish broad social change.

5. A closed shop strengthened the union's bargaining position, since all workers would follow union-directed job action. Workers who did not agree with a union's position and unskilled workers who could not join the union might oppose closed shops.

Closure

Ask one student to transform the Main Idea of the section into a question, and have other students answer that question. Then have students read Section 2 for the next class period, noting the successes and failures of labor unions in achieving their goals.

2 Striking Against Big Business

Section Focus

Key Terms blacklist ▪ union contract ▪ Homestead Strike ▪ Pullman Strike

Main Idea Conflict between workers and owners over a number of issues led to many strikes. Most of the strikes were bitter, even violent.

Objectives As you read, look for answers to these questions:
1. What arguments were made against unions?
2. Why did major strikes in 1877, 1892, and 1894 fail?

The Presbyterian minister Henry Ward Beecher became well-known during the mid-1800s for his commentaries on American life. In one of his sermons he said that while the working class was oppressed, this condition was natural: "God has intended the great to be great and the little to be little."

> **"G**od has intended the great to be great and the little to be little."
> —*Henry Ward Beecher*

Beecher spoke for many Americans, and for their government as well. Most people did not believe that workers had the right to strike. Government leaders generally stayed out of labor disputes or sided with employers. For these reasons, workers had to rely on their own efforts. Lacking popular or government support, they usually suffered crushing defeats.

OPPOSITION TO UNIONS 3C

Business leaders repeatedly complained about unions. Unions violated the principle of free enterprise, they claimed. Workers were like any other product: their "price" (wages) should be determined by supply and demand. Unions, business leaders charged, were trying to monopolize the supply of workers in order to drive up wages.

For the most part, Americans sympathized with business leaders. Some felt that workers had a right to sell their labor for whatever price the market would bear, without having unions tell them what to do. Others resented the hardships caused by strikes. And many people were deeply frightened that labor unrest would lead to anarchy. When strikes shut down major industries, and especially when strikes turned violent, the public demanded that order be restored. This usually meant defeat for the strikers.

THE RAILROAD STRIKE OF 1877 3C

The railroad strike of 1877 is a case in point. The nation's economy had been struggling following a business panic in 1873. Since then, railroad owners had cut their workers' wages. They had also tried to discourage workers from joining unions by putting union members' names on blacklists—lists of people suspected of disloyalty. Blacklisted workers were often fired; other companies would not hire them because they were considered troublemakers.

On July 17, 1877, workers on the Baltimore and Ohio Railroad went on strike. This act let loose the pent-up anger of many other railroad workers. When word of the strike spread, railroad workers from New York to St. Louis joined the walkout. Soon two-thirds of the nation's railways had been shut down. Angry mobs lashed out at railroad owners, derailing trains and burning rail yards.

The worst violence took place in Pittsburgh. The local militia was ordered to break the strike. Instead it sided with the strikers, and troops were called in from Philadelphia to restore order. The Philadelphia militia waded into a crowd of demonstrators, killing about ten. Enraged, the crowd took up arms and trapped the soldiers inside a building. The next day the troops shot their way out of the building. They killed some twenty more strikers before fleeing the city.

Sidebar (left column)

SECTION 2

Striking Against Big Business
(pp. 186–188)

Section Objective
▪ identify the causes and outcomes of the major strikes of the late 1800s

Introducing the Section

Connecting with Past Learnings
Review with students the leading industries of the late 1800s. (Steel, mining, railroads.) *Which of these industries might unions find it most effective to strike against? Why?* (Railroads, because they affect most other industries.)

Key Terms
Have students define the key terms listed. Ask them to tell which of the first two terms is associated with each of the last two terms and explain the associations. **LEP**

Focus
On the board list: *Business, Laborer, Self-Employed Worker,* and *Government.* Discuss the attitude of people described by each one of the headings to the railroad strike of 1877, the Homestead Strike, and the Pullman Strike. (Big business opposed all strikes; laborers supported strikes as a way to improve conditions; self-employed workers were upset by the violence of strikes; government sided with business.)

Developing the Lesson
After students have read the section, you may want to consider the following activities:

Patterns in History
Discuss recent or ongoing major strikes and compare them with the strikes mentioned in the section.

186

SUPPORTING THE SECTION

Reinforcement Workbook: Worksheet 30
Reteaching Resources: Worksheet 30
Teaching Transparencies: Transparency 30

The railroad strike of 1877 may have inspired this painting of industrial workers confronting their boss. Factory owners often hired strikebreakers and armed guards to crush strikes. **PARTICIPATION** Imagine you are writing a play about the railroad strike. What might the people in the painting be saying? 9F

With the strike spreading and local militias proving unreliable, President Hayes called out federal troops. The strike was crushed, and the trains were running by August. But bitterness lingered on all sides, and more labor unrest seemed inevitable.

THE HOMESTEAD STRIKE 3C

Another confrontation came in 1892 at the Carnegie Steel Company in Homestead, Pennsylvania. The workers' union contract—an agreement in which the company recognizes the existence of the union—was coming to an end. Plant manager Henry Clay Frick saw a chance to save money and break the union at the same time. He announced cuts in the wages of certain skilled workers. He also declared that he would no longer deal with the union.

Late in June, all workers at the plant—union and nonunion—decided to strike. Frick hired 300 guards from the Pinkerton Detective Agency to protect the plant. When the guards arrived at the plant by barge on July 6, they were met by gunfire from angry workers. A pitched battle between the two groups followed. By day's end sixteen people had died—nine strikers and seven guards.

The strikers were soon in control of the plant. At Frick's request the governor of Pennsylvania called out 8,000 troops, who retook the plant. It reopened with nonunion workers. But for four months there were still outbreaks of violence as the troops remained at Homestead.

By mid-November the Homestead Strike had collapsed. The union strikers accepted the wage cut; their pay dropped from $2.25 per day to $1.89. Even then, the company agreed to rehire only about one-fifth of the strikers. The AFL-affiliated union would not receive another contract from the Carnegie firm for 45 years. Unionism in the steel industry had not died, but it was severely hurt.

Photo Caption Answer
Workers could be demanding higher wages or better working conditions, complaining about blacklisting or strikebreaking tactics. Owner might be asking for order, demanding a return to work, or providing assurances that workers' demands would be considered.

Background Andrew Carnegie once supported unions because they made wages uniform in the industry and took away any advantages in lower wages that his competitors might have enjoyed.

Have any of the following changed—types of demands made and actions taken by unions; attitude of employers; government actions? How?

Civic Values
Ask students to discuss their own attitudes toward labor unions. *Do you think unions were necessary in the late 1800s? Are they necessary today?*

Ethics
Discuss this description of life in Pullman, Illinois: "We are born in a Pullman house, fed from the Pullman shop, taught in the Pullman school, catechized in the Pullman church, and when we die we shall be buried in the Pullman cemetery and go to the Pullman hell."

C Cooperative Learning

Divide the class into groups and assign each group one of the three strikes described in the section. Have groups write editorials expressing their point of view on the strike, making sure that each member expresses his or her opinion before the group determines its position. **LEP**

Addressing Individual Needs

Guided/ Independent Practice
Have students complete **Reinforcement Workbook** Worksheet 30, which asks them to analyze a weekly family budget in the 1860s.

Reteaching/Correctives
Have the class create a cause-and-effect chart on the board, listing the reasons for and outcomes of the railroad strike of 1877, the Homestead Strike, and the Pullman Strike of 1894. Have students agree on a general statement of why all three of these strikes failed.

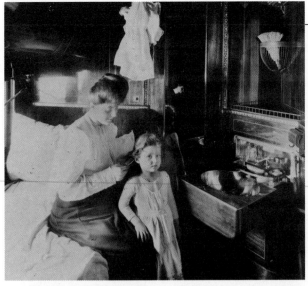

This photograph shows passengers inside a luxurious Pullman car. Wage cuts prompted Pullman workers to strike in 1894. President Cleveland used federal troops to break the strike. **CIVIC VALUES** What arguments might people have made both for and against the use of federal troops in the Pullman Strike? **9G**

THE PULLMAN STRIKE 3C, 3D, 3E

Hard times could bring labor unrest to any community. Still, few Americans would have expected a strike in 1893 at the Pullman Palace Car Company, which built railway passenger cars. In 1881 the firm's owner, George Pullman, had built a model town for his workers. Pullman, Illinois, was a beautiful town. It boasted modern housing, a new factory, a fine library, an enclosed shopping area, and recreational facilities.

In 1893 a depression struck, forcing George Pullman to lay off almost half his nearly 6,000 workers. The rest received wage cuts, although rents were not reduced. By mid-1894, an increase in business permitted Pullman to rehire 2,000 workers, but the wage cuts continued for all.

Workers noted that Pullman had continued to pay dividends to his stockholders. Therefore, they said, he should restore their wages. Pullman refused. More and more workers joined the American Railway Union (ARU), an independent union set up by Eugene V. Debs in 1893. Instead of organizing only skilled workers, as the AFL did, Debs let any railroad worker join the ARU.

Trouble started when three workers who had urged Pullman to listen to their grievances were fired. On May 11, 1894, the Pullman Strike be-

gan. Pullman then laid off all workers and shut down his plant. Workers tried to bargain with Pullman but failed. The union then urged all its members throughout the nation to boycott any train having Pullman cars on it. Railroad owners responded by firing any worker who refused to handle a Pullman car.

Before long, the strike and boycott had shut down most of the nation's trains. However, railroad owners had a plan for getting the government to support them. They hired new workers to run the trains and told them to attach a mail car to every Pullman car. Any striker who tried to disconnect a Pullman car would be stopping the movement of the mail, which was a federal crime.

The plan worked: federal troops were soon sent to keep the trains running. When strikers and their supporters tried to stop them, violence broke out. Some newspapers warned that the nation would split apart if order were not restored. Finally, the Attorney General of the United States obtained a court order under the Sherman Antitrust Act (page 107). The court order demanded that the strike be halted because it was hampering interstate commerce and the movement of the mail. Debs and other union leaders were jailed when they refused to obey.

With its leaders imprisoned, the strike collapsed. Many years would pass before railroad owners listened to the demands of their workers. Employers, backed by the power of the federal government, had triumphed again.

SECTION REVIEW

1. KEY TERMS blacklist, union contract, Homestead Strike, Pullman Strike

2. PEOPLE Henry Clay Frick, George Pullman, Eugene V. Debs

3. COMPREHENSION Why were federal troops used during the railroad strike of 1877?

4. COMPREHENSION What role did the courts play in the Pullman Strike?

5. CRITICAL THINKING In the strikes discussed in this section, which side, workers or employers, benefited from the outbreak of violence? Why?

3 Organizing Farmers

★ Section Focus

Key Terms mortgage ■ deflation ■ gold standard

Main Idea Farmers united to protect their interests, even creating a major political party.

Objectives As you read, look for answers to these questions:
1. What problems did farmers face?
2. How did farmers try to improve their conditions?

Wall Street owns the country. It is no longer a government of the people, by the people, and for the people, but a government of Wall Street, by Wall Street, and for Wall Street. . . . The great common people of this country are slaves, and monopoly is the master. . . . The parties lie to us, and the political leaders mislead us. . . . The people are at bay; let the bloodhounds of money who have dogged us thus far beware.

These fiery words came not from a Pittsburgh railroad worker or a Homestead steel worker, but from a farm leader named Mary Elizabeth Lease. Dubbed the "Kansas Pythoness," Lease became a well-known spokesperson for farmers' interests in the early 1890s. This colorful, outspoken woman is reported to have urged farmers to raise "less corn and more hell."

> **"W**all Street owns the country."
> —*Mary Elizabeth Lease*

Like industrial workers, farmers complained about the power of big business and the government's refusal to help the common person. The farmers' specific problems differed from those of industrial workers. But the mood—anger at their powerlessness—was the same. Their solution was the same as well: Unite!

PROBLEMS FACING THE FARMERS 3E

The farmers' basic problem can be summed up simply. Their incomes were falling, while their costs were rising. Several factors were at work:

(1) On the income side, bad weather often took its toll. The harsh winter of 1886–1887, which devastated many ranchers, ruined crops as well.

(2) Crop prices dropped sharply. The world's supply of farm products shot up as countries such as Argentina and Canada began large-scale farming. The United States' farm output also increased. As the world market became glutted with produce, prices sank. Wheat, for example, lost two-thirds of its value between 1886 and 1894. The price of cotton dropped by five-sixths between 1866 and 1894. Some farmers found it cheaper to burn their corn as fuel than to sell it.

(3) The cost of farm machinery, meanwhile, continued to climb. High tariffs on imported farm machinery enabled American manufacturers to charge high prices.

(4) Paying railroad companies to move crops to market took another sizable chunk of farmers'

BIOGRAPHY 3D

MARY ELIZABETH LEASE (1850–1933) was a Kansas lawyer who used her fiery personality and dramatic speaking voice on behalf of many reform movements. Lease helped found the Populist Party. She worked with the Farmers' Alliances to help farmers fight bank and railroad monopolies. Lease also lobbied for women's suffrage, labor unions, and a world peace movement.

SECTION 3

Organizing Farmers
(pp. 189–193)

Section Objective

■ describe the problems farmers faced in the last half of the nineteenth century and the ways in which they sought to improve their situation

Introducing the Section

Connecting with Past Learnings
Review the difficulties faced by the settlers of the Great Plains. *How did the expansion of the railroads help in the settlement of the western part of the United States?* (Brought settlers to the land and transported their produce to eastern markets. Railroads also encouraged settlement in order to sell land granted to them by the government.)

Key Terms
Have students find the definitions of the key terms in the text and then define the terms in their own words. Make sure they understand these important economic concepts by asking them to describe how a farmer might apply for a mortgage; explain why lenders prefer deflation; and explain the link between paper money and gold when the country was on the gold standard. **LEP**

Focus

What were the major problems facing farmers in the late 1800s? (Bad weather, low crop prices, expensive farm machinery and transportation, high debt.)

SUPPORTING THE SECTION

Reinforcement Workbook: Worksheet 31
Reteaching Resources: Worksheet 31
Enrichment and Extension Resources: Primary Source Worksheet 16
Teaching Transparencies: Transparency 31

Biography
Ask students to reread Mary Elizabeth Lease's speech, on this page, and discuss if her words have any validity today. You might point out that Wall Street is used to describe big business interests.

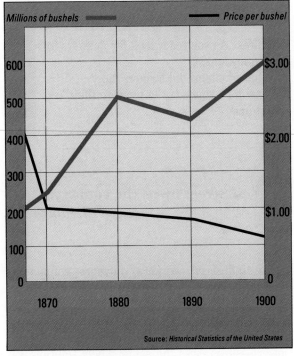

WHEAT OUTPUT AND PRICE, 1867–1900

Millions of bushels ▬▬▬   Price per bushel ▬▬▬

Source: *Historical Statistics of the United States*

GRAPH SKILLS 3E, 9B

This graph shows the relationship between wheat production and price. How many more bushels of wheat were produced in 1900 than in 1870? What happened to the price of wheat during this period? What caused this change? **CRITICAL THINKING** How does this graph illustrate the principle of supply and demand?

income. Farmers repeatedly pointed out that railroads charged higher rates in rural areas than in the more densely settled East. The railroads claimed that these higher rates were justified. In rural areas the railroads served fewer customers, and therefore had to charge each customer more in order to pay the cost of laying the rails. Yet railroads often raised their rates simply to increase profits. Because farmers had no other way to move their crops long distances, they were hostages to railroad demands.

All these factors combined to drive farmers deeply into debt. Even in the best of times, farmers must borrow in order to survive. They receive their income not steadily, as salaried workers do, but in one large lump when the crop is sold. They must borrow money to pay for seed, machinery, and farmland, hoping to earn enough money on that year's crop to repay the loans.

Many farmers could only meet these costs by getting a mortgage. In other words, they convinced a bank to lend them money by promising the bank that if they could not repay the loan, the bank could seize their land. When hard times came, thousands of farmers lost their farms. Some gave up farming altogether, while others became tenant farmers. By 1880 one-fourth of all American farms were operated by tenants.

THE GRANGE 3C, 8E

The first organization dedicated to solving farmers' problems was the Patrons of Husbandry, also known as the National Grange. It was founded in 1867 by Oliver H. Kelley, a former clerk in the Department of Agriculture. The Panic of 1873 drove thousands of farmers into the Grange. By 1875 the Grange boasted a membership of 800,000, mostly Great Plains farmers. This figure included many women, who had the same rights within the organization as men.

The Grange was founded in part as a social organization. Boredom and loneliness took their toll on farmers; Grange suppers and picnics gave them a chance to meet and discuss local issues and to hear speakers. The writer Hamlin Garland described how farmers came from miles around to attend Grange meetings:

> It was grand, it was inspiring to us, to see those long lines of carriages winding down the lanes, joining one another at the crossroads. . . . Nothing more picturesque, more delightful, has ever risen out of American rural life. Each of these assemblies was a most grateful relief from the loneliness of the farm.

In addition to this social function, the Grange worked to better the farmers' conditions. Like some industrial unions, the Grange set up cooperatives. By building and running their own grain elevators, for example, farmers believed that they could reduce their costs. These farmer cooperatives usually failed—just as the industrial cooperatives had—because of poor planning and lack of capital.

The Grange even entered politics. It backed candidates for state legislatures and Congress who sided with farmers. It also pushed for laws aiding farmers. During the 1870s several states passed laws, known as "Granger laws," that regulated railroad rates. These victories were short-lived, however. An 1886 Supreme Court decision in the case *Wabash, St. Louis and Pacific Railway Company v. Illinois* ruled that states could not regulate railroads passing through more than one state. The following year, the federal government created the Interstate Commerce Commission (ICC). In theory the ICC could satisfy the farmers' demand that the railroads be regulated. In practice, however, the railroads ran things pretty much their own way.

Even before the Supreme Court undercut the Granger laws, the Grange had begun to fade. The

This Granger poster from the 1870s includes idealized scenes of rural life. The Grange was strongest in Wisconsin, Minnesota, Iowa, and Illinois, where conflict flared between farmers and railroads over transport costs. ECONOMICS What words on the poster point out the country's dependence on farmers? 8E, 9B

failure of many of its cooperatives cost it support among farmers. However, the Grange had shown farmers what could be done if they worked together.

FARMERS' ALLIANCES 3C, 8E

As the Grange weakened, new farmers' groups arose. These were mostly local clubs called Farmers' Alliances. While the Alliances did try to set up cooperatives, they put more emphasis on government action than the Grange had. They pushed for lower taxes for farmers and higher taxes on railroad property. They also suggested a way to boost prices of farm products. In the Alliance plan, the federal government would build warehouses scattered across the country. Farmers would store crops in the warehouses until prices rose. Meanwhile, the government would lend farmers money to repay their debts. When the crops were finally sold, the farmers would repay the government.

Unlike the Grange, the Alliances were strong in the South. In fact, hundreds of small Alliances joined together in 1888 to form the Southern Alliance. It included some three million white farmers, as well as one million black farmers in the affiliated Colored Farmers' Alliance. About the same time, roughly one million Great Plains and Midwest farmers joined their local Alliances to form the Northern Alliance.

Several issues divided the two major Alliances. The Northern Alliance tended to back Republican candidates, and wanted blacks integrated into its organization. The Southern Alliance, on the other hand, backed Democrats and wanted black membership to be separate. Yet because their goals were similar, efforts were made to unify the two groups.

The growing Alliance movement flexed its muscles in the 1890 congressional elections. It won control of twelve state legislatures, elected six governors, and sent over fifty representatives to Congress. The effort succeeded so well, in fact, that Alliance members began to talk of forming their own political party. On July 4, 1892, representatives of the two Alliances came together in Omaha, Nebraska. Their aim was to create a party that would reshape American politics.

Patterns in History
In 1800 nearly 90 percent of Americans were farm workers. That figure dropped to 43 percent by 1886 and to less than 3 percent by 1980. Ask students to make a graph showing this information. Ask if they think this trend will continue and what it means for the United States.

Have interested students find out which, if any, of the problems facing farmers in the late 1800s still plague farmers today.

Economics
Help students understand how supply and demand affect the value of a product, including money, by drawing the graph of supply and demand, shown below, on the board.

What is the law of supply and demand? (As the price of a good goes up, more people are willing to sell it, but demand from buyers goes down. The market price of a good is determined when the number of suppliers willing to sell at a certain price is equal to the number of buyers interested in buying at that price.)

Geographic Themes: Place
Would you rather have lived in a rural or an urban setting in the last half of the nineteenth century? Have students explain their answers.

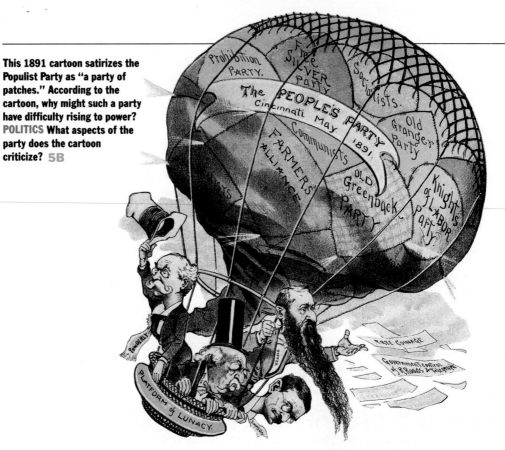

This 1891 cartoon satirizes the Populist Party as "a party of patches." According to the cartoon, why might such a party have difficulty rising to power? **POLITICS** What aspects of the party does the cartoon criticize? **5B**

THE POPULIST PLATFORM 5C

The new party was officially named the People's Party, but it became known as the Populist Party. The party's platform for the 1892 election called for sweeping changes in several areas.

One area was electoral reform: the Populists wanted to make government more responsive to the people. They demanded a constitutional amendment limiting the President and Vice President to one term. They called for the use of a secret ballot. (Up to that time each party had its own uniquely colored ballot, which made it easy to see how people voted.) Populists also called for senators to be elected directly by the people, not by the state legislatures. Other changes would make it easier for citizens to write their own laws, reject bills passed by the legislature, or remove public officials from office.

Another set of Populist demands concerned big business. Fed up with half-hearted government attempts to regulate banks, railroads, and telegraphs, the Populists called for government ownership of these industries. In addition, they wanted the government to reclaim all land given to railroad companies but not used for tracks; this land would go to farmers. Hoping to gain the backing of workers, the Populists supported labor's demands for an eight-hour work day. The Populist platform noted that "the interests of rural and civic labor are the same; their enemies are identical."

> "**T**he interests of rural and civic labor are the same; their enemies are identical."
>
> —*Populist Party platform, 1892*

THE MONEY ISSUE 3F, 8A, 8E

The most controversial Populist demand concerned the money supply. The value of money, like that of any other product, varies according to supply and demand. If the government keeps the money supply tight, or low, each dollar becomes worth more. The result is **deflation**—falling prices. If, on the other hand, the government de-

Photo Caption Answers
If one patch fails, the balloon (party) will fall. It is a "patchwork" composition of special-interest groups, some holding radical views.

cides to print more money, the supply of money increases. This causes each dollar to be worth less. The decline in money's value can be seen in inflation—rising prices.

Inflation helps some groups. People who sell goods benefit from inflation because they can charge higher prices. Debtors also benefit from inflation—the money they repay is worth less than the money they borrowed.

Farmers, being both sellers and debtors, saw inflation as a way to improve their standard of living. Thus they wanted to expand the money supply. Since the end of the Civil War, farmers had been asking the federal government to print more greenbacks, the paper money used during the war. The Panic of 1873 led to more calls for an expanded money supply. In 1876 the Greenback Party was formed to push for more greenbacks. The party ran candidates for President in 1876, 1880, and 1884 but never gained much support.

Congress had already decided against printing more greenbacks. In 1875 it voted to have the federal government buy back all the greenbacks in circulation, and not print any more. Congress disliked greenbacks because they were not backed by gold. Most people agreed that the money supply should operate according to the gold standard. That is, every paper dollar should be worth a specific amount of gold. The number of dollars in circulation, therefore, would be limited by the amount of gold held by the government. Because the American economy was then growing faster than the gold supply, the demand for money outstripped the supply of it. The gold standard thus produced deflation, exactly the opposite of what the farmers wanted.

Farmers knew that there was no way they could magically make more gold appear. They turned instead to something almost as "good as gold": silver, new sources of which were being found in the West. Farmers convinced the government to use silver as well as gold to back the money supply. In 1878 Congress passed the Bland-Allison Act, which called for the government to buy a set amount of silver each year and mint it into coins. The Sherman Silver Purchase Act of 1890 increased the amount of silver to be bought each year. It also permitted the government to print paper money backed by silver. Yet because the silver purchases remained small, the overall money supply did not expand much.

The Populist platform thus urged Congress to authorize "free and unlimited" minting of silver. The Populist goal was to have at least $50 in circulation for each person. That was a sizable increase. Critics of the proposal charged that it would lead to runaway inflation, the loss of public confidence in paper money, and financial ruin.

THE ELECTION OF 1892 5B

In spite of these warnings, voters found the Populists' platform appealing. In the farms and small towns of the nation's midsection, Populist speakers thundered against the many enemies of the farmer. People like "Sockless" Jerry Simpson, who got his nickname from criticizing his opponent's silk stockings, and Mary Elizabeth Lease brought farmers' anger to a boil. Eastern newspapers might laugh at these "calamity howlers," but farmers liked what they heard.

In the 1892 presidential election the Populist candidate was James B. Weaver, the Greenback Party's candidate in 1880. Weaver won over one million votes, carrying four states. This was the best showing by a third party since before the Civil War. Populist leaders believed that they had struck a chord with the American people—that millions more would join what they saw as a fight for economic and social justice. In 1896, they hoped, this message would sweep the Populist Party into the White House.

SECTION REVIEW

1. KEY TERMS mortgage, deflation, gold standard

2. PEOPLE Mary Elizabeth Lease, Oliver H. Kelley, James B. Weaver

3. COMPREHENSION List four of the problems facing farmers.

4. COMPREHENSION What did farmers stand to gain from inflation?

5. CRITICAL THINKING What is the common theme that links the different parts of the Populist platform?

Enrichment/Extension
Assign **Enrichment and Extension Resources** Primary Source Worksheet 16. Students will analyze a magazine article describing the situation of the American farmer in the 1800s.

Assessment
You may wish to use the Section 3 Review, on this page, to see how well your students understand the main points in this lesson.

Section Review Answers

1. *mortgage*—A promise to repay a bank loan, using land as security. *deflation*—Falling prices. *gold standard*—Guarantee that every paper dollar is worth a specific amount of gold.

2. *Mary Elizabeth Lease*—Spokesperson for farmers' interests. *Oliver H. Kelley*—Founder of the National Grange. *James B. Weaver*—Populist presidential candidate in 1892.

3. Bad weather; falling crop prices; rising cost of farm machinery; high prices charged by railroads.

4. They could charge higher prices and repay loans with money that would buy less than the amount of money they borrowed.

5. Making government more responsive to the average person.

Closure
Call students' attention to the boxed beige quotation (p. 192). Ask how this quotation relates to the main idea of the section. Then have students read Section 4 to see how populism fared in the elections of the 1890s.

4 The Rise and Fall of Populism

SECTION 4

The Rise and Fall of Populism
(pp. 194–199)

Section Focus

Key Term Coxey's Army

Main Idea Calls for new government policies reached a peak during the Depression of 1893, leading to a momentous presidential election in 1896.

Objectives As you read, look for answers to these questions:
1. How did the Cleveland administration try to deal with the economy?
2. Which Supreme Court cases angered Populists?
3. Why was the election of 1896 so important?

Section Objective

■ define the issues of the 1896 presidential election and describe its outcome

Introducing the Section

Connecting with Past Learnings
Review the growth of populism. *Why might the movement have become an influential third political party?* (It had a large base of support.) *What factors worked against the growth of populism?* (Supporters rarely had wealth or political power.)

Key Term
Have students define the key term in their own words. Ask them to suggest reasons why this group was called an "army." **LEP**

Focus
Have students determine which of the following would be "silverites" and "gold bugs": factory owner (gold bug), machine operator in factory (silverite), wealthy socialite (gold bug), unemployed person (silverite), farmer (silverite), and Northeast city dweller (gold bug).

Ask students to give reasons to support their choices. (People with money or those who needed to buy goods would want to stay on the gold standard and avoid inflation. Borrowers and those without money would want the value of money to go down and would favor silver.)

On Easter Sunday of 1894 an army of several hundred unemployed workers set forth from the small Ohio town of Massillon. Led by Jacob Coxey, a businessman and Populist, the army began a slow march to the nation's capital. People along the route emerged from their homes to view the ragtag marchers and to give them food. The group finally reached Washington, D.C., on April 30. They marched to the Capitol, and Coxey prepared to speak to the crowd. Suddenly police moved in, arresting Coxey and dispersing the crowd with clubs. Coxey's Army was smashed in a matter of minutes.

Coxey wanted to pressure the federal government to help the millions of Americans hurt by the

Jacob Coxey, a wealthy businessman who was also a Populist, appears in the center foreground of this photo of unemployed workers. **PARTICIPATION** Why, do you think, did Coxey and his followers decide to march to Washington? **7E, 7H**

Depression of 1893. The government, so effective in silencing Coxey, was having much less success dealing with the economy. Some 500 banks failed in the first year of the depression alone; over the next four years, 15,000 businesses went bankrupt. Three million workers—one of every five—lost their jobs. About 750,000 others went on strike, including those involved in the bloody disputes at Homestead and Pullman. The federal government floundered and popular anger rose.

CLEVELAND AND THE GOLD DRAIN 3E, 3F
Grover Cleveland may well have regretted running for President in 1892. His first term, from 1885 to 1889, had generally been a success. Defeated by Benjamin Harrison in the 1888 election, Cleveland spent the next few years practicing law in New York City. Upon returning to the White House in 1893 he confronted a rising Populist Party and a depression that was ravaging the nation's economy.

Many factors had contributed to the depression. Bad times in Europe had harmed American exports. Declining farm prices were wrecking the farm economy. Many industries and railroad companies had expanded too quickly, putting themselves dangerously in debt. Business closings had in turn ruined many banks.

Some people also blamed the depression on the government's silver policy. Under the Sherman Silver Purchase Act (page 193) the federal government had agreed to buy a fixed amount of silver each year. The government minted this silver at a ratio of sixteen to one. That is, there was sixteen times as much silver in a silver dollar as there was

---

Photo Caption Answer
To draw national attention to the plight of the unemployed during the Depression of 1893.

gold in a gold dollar. This reflected the relative value of silver and gold at the time.

As the supply of silver rose, however, its market value relative to gold declined. Yet the government continued to mint silver at the old ratio. Because the government operated on the gold standard, anyone who owned silver coins had the option of trading them in for gold. By minting silver at the old ratio, the government was in effect offering to buy silver coins for more than they were worth. Not surprisingly, people began trading in their silver dollars for gold ones.

This had two effects. One was to drain the government's gold supplies. The other was to weaken public confidence in the dollar and in the American economy as a whole. People saw that the government would soon run out of gold. It would then have to back its currency entirely with silver. Since silver was worth less than gold, the value of the dollar would drop, causing enormous inflation. While the thought of inflation appealed to farmers, it terrified bankers and business leaders. They rushed to unload their silver-backed dollars while they still had a chance. This, of course, only made the situation worse.

The thought of inflation also terrified Cleveland. A firm believer in the gold standard, he had criticized the minting of silver as a "dangerous and reckless experiment." Cleveland called a special session of Congress to repeal the Sherman Silver Purchase Act. Despite protests from farm interests, Congress went along. Yet the drain on the government's gold supplies continued. Even though the government had stopped buying silver from the mines, people could still return their silver to the government in exchange for gold.

In 1894, desperate to bolster the gold supply, the Cleveland administration sold bonds. By promising to pay high interest rates, the government hoped to convince people to use their gold to buy bonds. In 1895 a group of big banks, headed by banking tycoon J. P. Morgan, bought bonds at a bargain price. They then sold the bonds to the public for a much higher price, making huge profits. The government's gold reserves were replenished. The Populists, however, were outraged that the wealthy had been allowed to profit from the nation's troubles.

STRUGGLES IN THE COURTS 3F, 5D

It seemed to Populists that even the Supreme Court sided with the rich. An important court case in early 1895 dealt with the American Sugar Refining Company, which controlled about 90 percent of the nation's sugar refining. When the company tried to buy four other sugar refining firms, it was charged by the federal government with violating the Sherman Antitrust Act.

The Supreme Court, in *United States v. E. C. Knight*, ruled in favor of the company. The firm was a manufacturing business, said the Court, and not one engaged in interstate commerce. Congress, according to the Constitution, has power over interstate commerce but not over manufacturing. Therefore, the American Sugar Refining Company—or any manufacturing company, for that matter—was free to take over as much of the market as it could.

Also in 1895 the Supreme Court handed down a decision on an income tax passed by Congress the previous year. That tax, part of the Wilson-Gorman Tariff (page 173), was the first income tax

According to historian Richard Hofstadter, the Populists were "the first modern political movement . . . to insist that the Federal government has some responsibility for the common weal [good] . . ."

Do you agree with the Populists that it is the federal government's job to combat economic and social problems?

Impact of Geography
Ask students to look at the map on page 198 and tell why a candidate in the 1896 election might have paid more attention to the states in the Northeast than to those in the West. (Northeast states had a greater number of electoral votes.)

Have students compare the map of the 1896 election with the map of changes in electoral representation on page 646. *How might election strategies in the 1990s differ from those in the 1890s?* (The Northeast has lost many electoral votes while the South and West have gained, so southern and western concerns would play a larger role.)

---

imposed in peacetime. (Congress had passed an income tax in 1861 to pay for the Civil War.) Because the Populist Party held that the wealthy should pay a larger share of the cost of running the government, it supported the income tax.

To the dismay of the Populists, the Supreme Court in *Pollock v. Farmers' Loan and Trust Company* declared the 1894 income tax unconstitutional. Though the Court explained its decision on a fine point of constitutional law, politics may have played a role too. A lawyer arguing against the tax had called it "communistic, socialistic, . . . [and] populistic." In his ruling, Chief Justice Stephen J. Field seemed to agree:

> The present assault on capital is but the beginning. It will be but the stepping-stone to others, larger and more sweeping, till our political contests will become a war of the poor against the rich; a war constantly growing in intensity and bitterness.

Perhaps the most disturbing Supreme Court decision for Populists involved Eugene Debs, head of the American Railway Union. During the Pullman Strike, Debs had been sentenced to jail for violating a court order requiring workers to return to work (page 188). But Debs did not receive a jury trial; he was simply sentenced by a federal judge. He felt that his rights had been violated and sued. His case went all the way to the Supreme Court, which in 1894 unanimously voted against him. "The strong arm of the national government," said the Court, "may be put forth to brush away all obstructions to the freedom of interstate commerce or the transportation of the mails."

By now it was clear that the Supreme Court would not back Populist demands. Populists became convinced that the key to success lay not in the courts but in the ballot box. They looked to the presidential election of 1896 to give them the power they wanted.

THE CONVENTIONS OF 1896 5B

As the 1896 election approached, the issue of silver and gold loomed large. The Populists were united in favoring the minting of silver to expand the money supply. Most Democrats agreed with the Populist position; most Republicans, in contrast, favored the gold standard and a smaller money supply. The issue had become a symbol of cleavages within American society—rich against poor, urban against rural, Northeast against South and West. The "silverites" claimed that they stood for the working people against the wealthy. The "gold bugs" said that the silverites were radicals who would bring the country to ruin.

In June 1896 the Republican Party selected William McKinley of Ohio as its presidential nominee. McKinley had been a long-time member of the House of Representatives. There he had sided with business on important issues, favoring high tariffs and the gold standard. One tariff bill of 1890 was even named for him. McKinley's nomination was largely the work of Republican boss Mark Hanna (page 169), an Ohio banker who knew that McKinley would support big business against farm and labor protesters.

The Democrats, on the other hand, saw the Populists as potential allies. In the four years since the election of 1892, many Populist representatives had been elected in southern states. They were, for the most part, ex-Democrats who had defeated Democratic candidates. Democratic Party leaders realized that if they and the Populists could agree on a presidential candidate, that candidate might well win. Such an alliance would also lure Populists back into the Democratic Party, they hoped.

At their July convention, therefore, the Democrats adopted a platform that embraced many Populist ideas. It called for lower tariffs and for tighter government regulations on business. It supported an income tax. As for the silver issue, the Democratic platform was clear. It declared, "We demand the free and unlimited coinage of both silver and gold at the present legal ratio of sixteen to one."

One problem remained: Who would be the Democratic candidate for President? Definitely not Cleveland. He had sent troops to break the Pullman Strike. He had broken up Coxey's Army. He had stood by the gold standard. Cleveland was, in short, the Populists' sworn enemy. The convention rejected his renomination.

196 UNIT 3   CHANGE AND REFORM

Background   McKinley had the support of nearly all the nation's newspapers, as well a campaign chest of $3.5 million, compared to Bryan's $300,000.

The search for a Democrat acceptable to Populists ended when William Jennings Bryan stepped to the podium. A congressman from Nebraska, Bryan was a veteran of the unsuccessful fight to save the Sherman Silver Purchase Act. Only 36 years old, Bryan possessed a deep, booming voice and an unmatched gift for oratory. His statement in support of the Democratic platform, called the "Cross of Gold Speech," became one of the most famous in American history.

> You come to us and tell us that the great cities are in favor of the gold standard; we reply that the great cities rest upon our broad and fertile prairies. Burn down your cities and leave our farms, and your cities will spring up again as if by magic; but destroy our farms and the grass will grow in the streets of every city in the country.

Bryan concluded with a thundering warning against the pro-gold forces: "You shall not press down upon the brow of labor this crown of thorns, you shall not crucify mankind upon a cross of gold."

> "**Y**ou shall not press down upon the brow of labor this crown of thorns, you shall not crucify mankind upon a cross of gold."
>
> —*William Jennings Bryan*

Bryan's speech sparked wild celebration at the convention. Some delegates shouted themselves hoarse, while others cried in joy. They voted to nominate Bryan as the Democratic candidate for President.

When the Populist convention met two weeks later, the delegates were both pleased and frustrated. On the one hand, they liked Bryan and the Democratic platform. On the other hand, they detested the Democratic vice-presidential candidate, Maine banker Arthur Sewall. Nor did they like giving up their identity as a party. They compromised by endorsing Bryan, nominating their own

THE SACRILEGIOUS CANDIDATE.

Because William Jennings Bryan used biblical images in his speeches, *Judge* magazine accused him of sacrilege—disrespect toward anything sacred. In fact, Bryan believed strongly in fundamentalist Christianity. POLITICS Explain the main point of Bryan's "Cross of Gold Speech." 9A

candidate for Vice President (Thomas Watson of Georgia), and keeping their party organization intact.

THE CAMPAIGN OF 1896 5B

The last presidential campaign of the nineteenth century offered a stark contrast in styles. One hundred years earlier, in 1796, John Adams won the presidency without traveling a single mile. In 1896 William Jennings Bryan traveled 18,000 miles by train—a record up to that time. He made 600 speeches, also a record, before 5 million Americans. At stops from early morning to late at night, Bryan delivered slashing attacks on the rich and powerful. And his audiences responded. At one train stop, the crowd demanded to see Bryan although he was still shaving. Smiling broadly, he

---

Geographic Themes: Regions
Ask students if they agree with Bryan's statement that the cities rest on the farms, and have them justify their answers.

Religion
Discuss with students the imagery used by Bryan in his "Cross of Gold" speech. *To whom is he comparing working people?* (Jesus, who was crucified after being forced to wear a crown of thorns.) *How did this comparison strengthen Bryan's argument for free silver?* (By calling Jesus to mind, Bryan seemed to raise his cause to a religious crusade.)

C **Cooperative Learning**

Have students work together in small groups, with half the groups supporting Bryan and the other half McKinley. Explain that they are to act as campaign advisers and should prepare a campaign strategy for their candidate and come up with a campaign slogan. They can also produce campaign material, including buttons, signs, and posters. **LEP**

Photo Caption Answer
Farms and labor are essential to the country's well-being. The country as a whole would suffer by adherence to the gold standard.

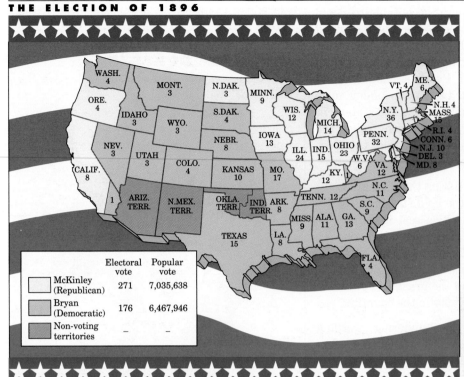

THE ELECTION OF 1896

	Electoral vote	Popular vote
McKinley (Republican)	271	7,035,638
Bryan (Democratic)	176	6,467,946
Non-voting territories	–	–

stepped into the group with his face covered with shaving lather and shook the hands of well-wishers.

McKinley's campaign looked more like John Adams's in 1796. He did not travel but stayed at his home in Canton, Ohio, and gave speeches on his front porch to Americans who came to hear him. Usually the audience had been sent by the Republican Party from various parts of the nation. His speeches, lacking the fire of his Democratic rival's, stressed patriotism and prosperity. Often McKinley would be joined on the front porch by his wife, who was an invalid, and his mother. Newspapers soon called McKinley's style of campaigning the "front porch campaign."

To ensure that McKinley's message reached the voters, the Republican Party sent out 250 million pieces of campaign literature to Americans. It also used 1,500 other speakers to comb the land. Never before had voters seen so much of one candidate and heard so much about another. The candidates' enthusiasm rubbed off on the voters, who went to the polls in record numbers that November.

McKINLEY TRIUMPHS 5B

Bryan received more votes—6.5 million—than any previous presidential candidate, but he still lost the election. McKinley won with 7.1 million votes. Bryan had swept the South and much of the West and had split the Midwest with McKinley. It was McKinley's control of the heavily populated Northeast that decided the election (map, above).

Bryan lost the Northeast because urban workers voted Republican. The Democratic platform had paid too little attention to the problems of workers and too much to the woes of farmers. Bryan's emphasis on the silver issue worked against him, for many urban workers feared that expansion of the money supply would cause prices to skyrocket. They, like voters in the Upper Midwest, were swayed by McKinley's calls for stability.

The Populists were in shock over their loss. "Our party, as a party," said Thomas Watson, "does not exist any more. . . . The sentiment is still there, . . . but the confidence is gone, and the party organization is almost gone. . . ."

THE PRESIDENTS

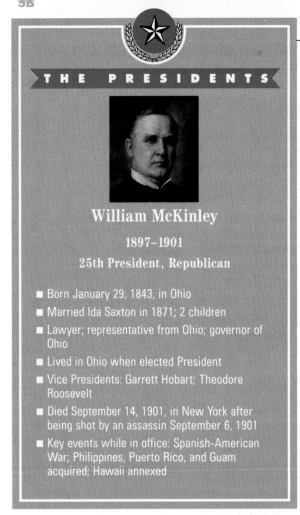

William McKinley

1897–1901

25th President, Republican

- Born January 29, 1843, in Ohio
- Married Ida Saxton in 1871; 2 children
- Lawyer; representative from Ohio; governor of Ohio
- Lived in Ohio when elected President
- Vice Presidents: Garrett Hobart; Theodore Roosevelt
- Died September 14, 1901, in New York after being shot by an assassin September 6, 1901
- Key events while in office: Spanish-American War; Philippines, Puerto Rico, and Guam acquired; Hawaii annexed

and farmers into a mass movement for economic reform had failed. In addition, the decades-long stalemate between the Republicans and Democrats was broken. The Republicans now controlled the White House. They also controlled both houses of Congress.

The greatest Populist victories came after the party had collapsed. Populist calls for a larger money supply were answered with the discovery of gold in Alaska's Klondike region in 1896 (page 127). The government bought more gold and put it into circulation, thereby pumping new life into the economy. Farmers benefited from better harvests and greater crop exports. And early in the new century, another wave of reform would sweep across the country, bringing about many of the changes Populists had demanded.

SECTION REVIEW

1. KEY TERM Coxey's Army

2. PEOPLE Jacob Coxey, Grover Cleveland, William McKinley, William Jennings Bryan

3. COMPREHENSION Why did many people trade in their silver dollars for gold ones?

4. COMPREHENSION Why was the Supreme Court's decision in *United States v. E. C. Knight* a defeat for Populists?

5. CRITICAL THINKING Which style of campaigning, Bryan's or McKinley's, more closely resembles that of today's presidential candidates? What are the advantages and drawbacks of this style?

The Populists had indeed lost their one great chance to realign American politics. Having joined with the Democrats in a losing cause, their party collapsed. The attempt to unite urban workers

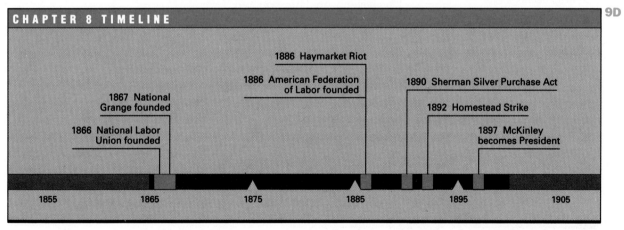

CHAPTER 8 TIMELINE

9D

1886 Haymarket Riot

1886 American Federation of Labor founded

1867 National Grange founded

1890 Sherman Silver Purchase Act

1892 Homestead Strike

1866 National Labor Union founded

1897 McKinley becomes President

| 1855 | 1865 | 1875 | 1885 | 1895 | 1905 |

Section Review Answers

1. *Coxey's Army*—Group of unemployed workers that marched on Washington, D.C., in 1894 to ask the federal government for help.

2. *Jacob Coxey*—Businessman and Populist who led Coxey's Army. *Grover Cleveland*—President during the depression of 1893. *William McKinley*—Republican candidate and victor in the election of 1896. *William Jennings Bryan*—Democratic and Populist candidate in 1896 election.

3. Because the federal government was buying silver for more than it was worth.

4. The decision favored big business interests by ruling that Congress did not have the power to regulate manufacturers, so the Sherman Antitrust Act did not apply to manufacturing monopolies.

5. Bryan's style was closer to today's candidates. Advantages: voters see and hear more about the candidate who has more opportunities to hear what the voters need and want. Disadvantages: modern-style campaigning requires huge expenditures of time and money. Other important national issues can be overshadowed by attention paid to a campaign.

Closure

The Section 4 information in the Chapter 8 Summary (p. 200) can be used to synthesize the important elements covered in Section 4. Then have students read Section 1 of Chapter 9 for the next class period and compare the rise of the Progressives with that of the Populists.

The Presidents

Of the eleven men elected President between the end of the Civil War and 1921, seven came from Ohio, including McKinley. Have students suggest explanations for that fact.

CHAPTER 8 SUMMARY

SECTION 1: In the late 1800s workers formed labor unions in an effort to improve working conditions and increase wages.

■ The National Labor Union, created in 1866, admitted both skilled and unskilled workers. It sought to better the lives of workers through political activity.

■ The Knights of Labor, founded in 1869, at first attracted many supporters with its calls for economic reforms.

■ The American Federation of Labor, created in 1886, restricted its membership to skilled workers and limited its demands to concrete issues such as wages and working conditions.

SECTION 2: Worker strikes led to bitter conflicts involving workers, employers, and the government.

■ Most Americans initially opposed labor unions. They supported government intervention to stop strikes.

■ Troops were used to halt the Homestead and Pullman strikes.

SECTION 3: Farmers united to deal with falling crop prices and other economic problems.

■ The Grange, formed in 1867, set up cooperatives and elected candidates to state legislatures and Congress.

■ In 1892 the Farmers' Alliance movement spawned the Populist Party, which pressed for far-reaching political and economic reforms.

SECTION 4: The Depression of 1893 led to increased calls for government action.

■ Farm and labor protesters called for the expansion of the nation's money supply.

■ The Populists bitterly denounced Supreme Court decisions that tended to benefit the wealthy.

■ Democrats and Populists joined forces behind William Jennings Bryan in the presidential election of 1896.

■ With its defeat in the presidential election of 1896, the Populist Party collapsed. Many of the reforms it had supported, however, were later adopted.

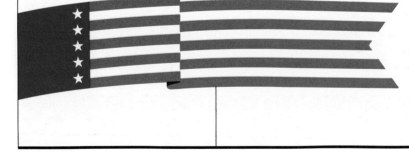

KEY TERMS ●

Use the following terms to complete the sentences below.

anarchist
blacklist
closed shop
cooperative
depression
recession

1. A _____ is one in which an employer agrees to hire only union members.
2. A period of high unemployment, low consumer spending, and business failures is a _____ .
3. A mild economic downturn is known as a _____ .
4. A business owned and operated by its workers is known as a _____ .
5. Dedicated labor unionists often found themselves on an employers' _____, which meant that no one would hire them.
6. An _____ is a person who is opposed to all forms of government.

PEOPLE TO IDENTIFY ●

Identify the following people and tell why each was important.

1. Jacob Coxey
2. Eugene V. Debs
3. Henry Clay Frick
4. Samuel Gompers
5. Oliver H. Kelley
6. Terence Powderly
7. William Sylvis

PLACES TO LOCATE ●

Match each of the letters on the map with the places that are listed below.

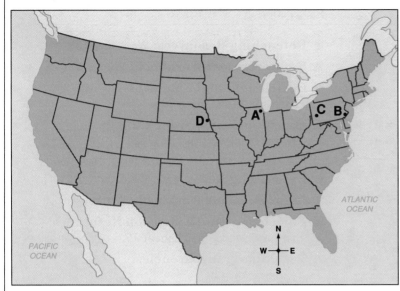

1. Pittsburgh
2. Omaha
3. Chicago
4. Philadelphia

REVIEWING THE FACTS ▲

1. What were some of the problems that led workers to unionize in the late 1800s, and how did unionization help workers?
2. What was the significance of the Haymarket Riot to the labor movement?
3. How did the American Federation of Labor differ from earlier labor unions? How did these differences help to make it successful?
4. Why did most Americans oppose labor unionism during the late 1800s? How did this hurt the labor union movement?
5. What was the impact of the Homestead Strike?

6. What problems did American farmers face during the late 1800s? What were the underlying causes of each of these problems?
7. What was the Grange? What legislation did the Grangers succeed in getting passed? On what grounds did the Supreme Court strike down this legislation?
8. What were the origin and goals of the Populist Party?
9. What problems did the Sherman Silver Purchase Act cause? Which groups favored the minting of silver coins? Which groups opposed it?
10. What voting blocs supported each candidate in the 1896 election?

CRITICAL THINKING SKILLS ▲

1. **DISTINGUISHING BETWEEN FACT AND OPINION** In 1892 the Populist platform included the following statement: "The interests of rural and civic [urban] labor are the same; their enemies are identical." Was this a statement of fact or a statement of opinion? Explain your answer.

2. **INFERRING** As you have read, farmers favored inflationary policies. Which groups probably opposed such policies? Explain your answer.

WRITING ABOUT TOPICS IN AMERICAN HISTORY ■

1. **CONNECTING WITH LITERATURE** Two selections from the poetry of Paul Laurence Dunbar appear on pages 785–786. Read them and answer the questions. Then answer the following question: Do you think it was harder for an African American writer to succeed in the 1890s than it is today? Why or why not?

2. **APPLYING THEMES: EXPANDING DEMOCRACY** Take notes from at least two sources on the life of Elizabeth Flynn Rogers, the leader of the Chicago branch of the Knights of Labor in the late 1800s. Then write a brief biographical sketch of her life.

3. **HISTORY** Obtain a copy of William Jennings Bryan's famous "Cross of Gold" speech. Then write a short essay analyzing its emotional appeal to American farmers.

8. Farmers' Alliance members formed the Populist Party and aimed for electoral reform, regulation of big business, land and labor reform, and an expanded money supply.

9. A drain in the government's gold supplies and loss of confidence in the dollar were caused by the Sherman Silver Purchase Act. Farmers favored the minting of silver coins, while urban workers opposed it.

10. The South and West supported Bryan, while McKinley controlled the Northeast.

Critical Thinking Skills
1. The statement is an opinion since the Populists were trying to unite two troubled groups, although farmers supported an expanded money supply and urban workers did not in fear of skyrocketing prices.
2. Urban workers favored a stable economy and low prices, as did bankers who made more money on loans during deflationary times.

Writing About Topics in American History
1. Most students will say yes. Writers in any era have a hard time succeeding. In the 1890s, when African Americans were barely accepted by society, the chance that their writings would gain a large audience was slim.
2. Students should use their school or local library to locate good sources for their assignment.
3. Students should recognize Bryan's support for farmers' concerns and his attempt to make Americans realize the great importance of farmers.

6. Farmers faced falling incomes caused by bad weather and dropping crop prices, and rising costs caused by machinery and transportation costs.

7. The Grange, organized to solve farmers' problems, got laws regulating railroad rates passed in several states. The Supreme Court ruled that states could not regulate railroads passing through more than one state.

Chapter Review exercises are keyed for student abilities:
● = Basic
▲ = Average
■ = Average/Advanced

Chapter 9 ▪ The Progressive Movement

	SECTION OBJECTIVES	SECTION RESOURCES
Section 1 **A Look at** **the Progressives**	▪ distinguish between populism and progressivism ▪ identify leading progressives and the actions they took to reform government activities	● **Reteaching Resources:** Worksheet 33 ▲ **Reinforcement Workbook:** Worksheet 33 ■ **Enrichment and Extension Resources:** Historian Worksheet 3 ▲ **Teaching Transparencies:** Transparency 33
Section 2 **Reforms in Cities** **and States**	▪ cite progressive reforms in cities and states and their enduring impact	● **Reteaching Resources:** Worksheet 34 ▲ **Reinforcement Workbook:** Worksheet 34 ■ **Enrichment and Extension Resources:** Primary Source Worksheet 17 ▲ **Teaching Transparencies:** Transparency 34
Section 3 **New Constitutional** **Amendments**	▪ identify the amendments passed between 1913 and 1920 and how they advanced progressive reforms	● **Reteaching Resources:** Worksheet 35 ▲ **Reinforcement Workbook:** Worksheet 35 ■ **Enrichment and Extension Resources:** Primary Source Worksheet 35 ▲ **Teaching Transparencies:** Transparency 18

The list below shows Essential Elements relevant to this chapter. (The complete list of Essential Elements appears in the introductory pages of this Teacher's Edition.)

Section 1:   3C, 3D, 4C, 4D, 4F, 5B, 5C, 7D, 7F, 7G, 7H, 8B, 8G, 9E
Section 2:   2E, 3F, 5C, 5D, 7E, 7F, 7H, 7I, 8G, 9A
Section 3:   4C, 4D, 5C, 5D, 6B, 7I, 9B, 9D

Section Resources are keyed for student abilities:
 ● = Basic
 ▲ = Average
 ■ = Average/Advanced

CHAPTER RESOURCES

Geography Resources: Worksheets 17, 18
Tests: Chapter 9 Test

Chapter Project: Constitutional Government

Have students put together an illustrated scrapbook of some aspect of the Progressive Movement. They may focus on muckrakers, methods used to achieve reform in government, or progressivism in various states. Encourage students to examine contemporary newspapers and magazine articles in composing their scrapbooks.

Homework Options

Each section contains activities labeled "Addressing Individual Needs." You may wish to choose from among these activities when assigning homework.

> **Provisions for Limited English Proficiency (LEP)**
> Several suggested activities may be particularly helpful for teachers of students with limited English proficiency. These activities have been marked throughout the Teacher's Annotated Edition with the symbol **LEP** .

BIBLIOGRAPHY AND AUDIOVISUAL AIDS

Teacher Bibliography

Hofstader, Richard. *The Age of Reform: From Bryan to F.D.R.* Knopf, 1960.

Goldman, Eric. *Rendezvous with Destiny: A History of Modern American Reform.* Random House, 1978.

May, Ernest R. *The Progressive Era.* Time-Life, 1974.

Student Bibliography

Boardman, Fon W., Jr. *America and the Progressive Era: 1900–1917.* Walck, 1970.

Cook, Fred J. *The Muckrakers: Crusading Journalists Who Changed America.* Doubleday, 1972.

Fleming, Alice. *Ida Tarbell: First of the Muckrackers.* (Women of America Series). Crowell, 1971.

La Follette, Robert M. *La Follette's Autobiography: A Personal Narrative of Political Experiences.* University of Wisconsin Press, 1960.

Literature

Gilman, Charlotte Perkins. *Herland: A Lost Feminist Utopian Novel.* Pantheon, 1979. A fantasy about a society of women.

Steffens, Lincoln. *The Shame of the Cities.* Hill and Wang, 1957. A classic muckraking work.

Van Vorst, John and Marie Van Vorst. *The Woman Who Toils.* University of California Industrial Relations, 1974.

Films and Videotapes*

Focus on 1900–1909. 58 min. COR/MTI. Events and key figures, including Teddy Roosevelt, the Wright Brothers, J.P. Morgan, Buffalo Bill, and Booker T. Washington.

Focus on 1909–1919. 58 min. COR/MTI. Events and key figures, including the presidency of Woodrow Wilson, the women's suffrage movement, and changes in the cities.

Progressive Era: Reform Works in America. 23 min. EBEC. Covers the election of 1912, the Pullman and Homestead strikes, the growth of populism, the formation of the Molly McGuires, and the building of self-defense armories by the rich.

Filmstrips*

Progressives, Populists and Reform in America (set of 2). GA. Examines specific objectives sought by reform groups between 1890 and 1917 and contrasts them with those of modern reformers. Also available in video.

Computer Software*

The Amendments of the Constitution (Apple with 128K; IBM with 128K). GEMSTAR. Simulations of actual case studies have students assume the role of a judge who examines the pros and cons and makes decisions based on evidence. A companion package, *U.S. Constitution,* is also recommended.

*For a complete guide to audiovisual sources, see the introduction to this book (page Txx).

This chapter discusses the nature and scope of the Progressive Movement, including profiles of key progressive leaders, changes in city and state governments, and the four progressive amendments added to the Constitution between 1913 and 1920.

Themes in American History

- Constitutional government
- Expanding democracy
- Pluralistic society

Chapter Objectives
After students complete this chapter, they will be able to:

1. Distinguish between populism and progressivism.

2. Identify leading progressives and the actions they took to reform government activities.

3. Cite progressive reforms in cities and states and their enduring impact.

4. Identify the amendments passed between 1913 and 1920 and how they advanced progressive reforms.

Chapter Opener Art
John Sloan, *Spring, Madison Square*, 1905–6.

The reform movement known as progressivism gathered strength in American cities around the turn of the century. A growing middle class provided the progressives with many of their supporters.

CHAPTER	**Reinforcement Workbook:** Worksheets 33–35
SUPPORT	**Reteaching Resources:** Worksheets 33–35
MATERIAL	**Enrichment and Extension Resources:** Primary Source Worksheets 17, 18; Historian Worksheet 3
	Geography Resources: Worksheets 17, 18
	Teaching Transparencies: Transparencies 33–35
	Tests: Chapter 9 Test

9 The Progressive Movement (1900–1920)

KEY EVENTS

1906	*The Jungle* published
1912	First minimum wage law
1913	Congress receives power to levy an income tax
1920	Prohibition takes effect
1920	Nineteenth Amendment gives women the vote

3C, 3D, 4C, 4D, 4F, 5B, 5C, 7D, 7F, 7G, 7H, 8B, 8G, 9E

1 A Look at the Progressives

Section Focus

Key Terms progressivism ■ consensus ■ muckraker ■ workmen's compensation ■ Wisconsin Idea

Main Idea A variety of people worked to reform American government in the early 1900s.

Objectives As you read, look for answers to these questions:
1. How did writers aid the cause of reform?
2. How did progressivism differ from populism?
3. Who were some progressive leaders?

A foreign visitor to the United States in late 1900 could easily have concluded that the country was entering a period of stability. William McKinley had just won re-election, trouncing the Populist firebrand William Jennings Bryan. The nation had recovered from depression, and Democratic calls for free silver and other reforms had fallen on deaf ears. It seemed a time of satisfaction, not protest. In fact, during the first two decades of the new century the United States would undergo the most thorough house-cleaning in its history.

THE ORIGINS OF PROGRESSIVISM 4D, 5C, 7D
The house-cleaning that began in the early 1900s was the work of a reform movement known as progressivism. It had roots in several earlier movements, such as the Liberal Republicans of the 1870s and the Mugwumps of the 1880s. Progressives also carried on the fight begun by the Populists in the last part of the 1800s.

Yet there were important differences between populism and progressivism:

(1) Populism drew its strength from rural areas, while progressivism centered in cities.

(2) Populists tended to be poor and uneducated, while most progressives were middle-class and well-educated.

(3) Populists flirted with radical ideas such as government ownership of major industries, while progressives stayed in the political mainstream. (Many people who became progressives had actually opposed the Populists in the 1890s because of their radical demands.)

(4) Perhaps the most important difference between the two movements is that while populism failed, progressivism succeeded.

Why? In part, populism helped pave the way for the success of progressivism. Populists made people aware of the debt-ridden farmer, the exhausted factory worker, the corrupt business leader or politician. The American people rejected the Populists' solutions, but could not ignore the problems they had raised.

The progressives' moderation also improved their chances for success. They aimed not to remake American society but merely to make the existing system work better—and to do this they were willing to make compromises. Populism had

---

SUPPORTING THE SECTION

Reinforcement Workbook: Worksheet 33
Reteaching Resources: Worksheet 33
Enrichment and Extension Resources: Historian Worksheet 3
Teaching Transparencies: Transparency 33

SECTION 1

A Look at the Progressives
(pp. 203–209)

Section Objectives
■ distinguish between populism and progressivism
■ identify leading progressives and the actions they took to reform government activities

Introducing the Section

Connecting with Past Learnings
Have students recall living and working conditions in the late 1800s. *What were some of the problems of industrial life?* (Sweatshops, slums, overcrowding, poverty, unsafe working conditions, child labor.) As students work through the lesson, have them note how these problems were addressed by progressive reforms.

Key Terms
Have students write definitions for the key terms. Call on volunteers to read a definition and have the class determine which term it defines. Continue until all terms have been defined more than once. Then have students agree on the best definition for each term. **LEP**

Run through the progressives profiled in the section, asking students to describe how these people tried to affect change. (Jones—used government money to help the poor; Low—improved public education system and civil service; Perkins—lobbied lawmakers to pass laws protecting worker safety; Johnson—reformed California politics and passed laws to help workers; La Follette—limited lobbying, improved civil service, and introduced laws to regulate businesses.)

Developing the Lesson
After students have read the section, you may want to consider the following activities:

Patterns in History
Tell students that the progressive notion that reform through legislation can and should improve social and political conditions is the basis of many public interest groups today. Ask students to identify public interest groups they have heard of and describe these groups' main area of concern and proposed solutions.

Do you think legislation is the best way to achieve social and political reforms?

scared off both the middle class, which feared inflation, and business leaders, who feared labor unrest. Progressivism offered these groups a safer kind of reform. By 1900 the American economy was strong. As a result, people of all classes felt more confident and more willing to compromise. A consensus—broad agreement—on how to improve American society now seemed possible.

THE PROGRESSIVES AND GOVERNMENT 8B, 8G
At the center of that consensus was the idea that the country had entered what one progressive called "a new social age, a new era of human relationships." The days in which government and business were small, personal institutions had passed forever. Now government had grown in size and complexity; it was often corrupt and ignored voters' concerns. Huge companies, meanwhile, had come to dominate many areas of industry. These companies often mistreated workers and misled customers. Both these developments threatened the rights of the individual, and thus the future of democracy.

Progressives offered two broad changes. First, government had to become more responsive to the voice of the people. This would be accomplished through reforms in the way government operated. Second, government had to play a greater role in protecting the well-being of all citizens. This required government action to regulate business, improve public health and safety, and ensure that every citizen had a reasonable chance to prosper.

THE MUCKRAKERS 4F
What inspired many people to join the Progressive Movement were the writings of muckrakers, journalists who exposed corruption in business and politics. These journalists, whose writings began to appear in the late 1800s, made it their job to anger readers. Jacob Riis (page 163) horrified those who read his descriptions of life in the New York City slums. Upton Sinclair shocked the nation with *The Jungle* (1906), which described in gory detail the unhealthy practices in meatpacking plants. Two sisters-in-law, Marie and Bessie Van Vorst, disguised themselves as workers to gain information for their startling book *The Woman Who Toils* (1903).

Helping the muckrakers reach a mass audience was the rise of inexpensive, popular magazines

This photograph shows workers stuffing sausages in a meatpacking plant in Chicago. These plants were notorious for their unsafe and unsanitary conditions. Upton Sinclair exposed these conditions in his muckraking novel *The Jungle*.
CULTURE How did writings by muckrakers affect reform movements in the United States? 4F, 5C

Photo Caption Answer
They gained popular support for reform movements.

Background The term *muckraking* was coined by Teddy Roosevelt in an allusion to the "man with a Muck-rake" in Bunyan's *Pilgrim's Progress*.

like *McClure's* and *Cosmopolitan*. In several articles for *McClure's*, Lincoln Steffens condemned the mismanagement of city governments. These articles were later collected into a book entitled *The Shame of the Cities* (1904). Ida Tarbell spent six years learning how John D. Rockefeller's Standard Oil Company had ruthlessly treated competitors, the government, and the public. Her articles helped *McClure's* sell thousands of copies to an eager public.

Other magazines, seeing how popular *McClure's* had become, also tried their hand at muckraking. An army of writers was sent out to report on crime, graft, and other abuses. Few of the muckrakers had specific ideas on how to solve the problems they pointed out. But they did spur the nation to deal with these problems.

WHO WERE THE PROGRESSIVES? 4D, 7F

Progressives came from a variety of backgrounds. Small business owners joined the progressive cause. So did teachers and social workers, as well as many politicians. The movement was strongest among the well-educated middle class that had emerged in the nation's cities.

Not all progressives had the same concerns. Some focused on improving working conditions, while others pushed for laws against unfair business practices. All, however, felt that government had to do something about the problems that plagued Americans. Here are a few of their stories.

SAMUEL M. "GOLDEN RULE" JONES 5C, 4D

Some progressives had only recently risen from poverty themselves. Samuel M. Jones was a typical American success story. Born in Wales in 1846, he came to the United States with his family three years later. By age ten he was a full-time worker. Jones saved his money and moved to Toledo, Ohio, where he started a successful business. Jones treated his workers fairly, giving them benefits far ahead of their day, such as paid vacations and an eight-hour work day.

Jones followed the "golden rule" when dealing with the people around him: Do unto others as you would have them do unto you. In 1897 Jones decided to run for mayor of Toledo on his "Golden Rule Platform." The workers at his plant set up the "Golden Rule Band" to lend stirring music to his campaign. Jones reached out to the average worker for support, and on Election Day won a stunning victory.

As mayor, Jones used government funds to build playgrounds, a golf course, free kindergartens, and even a night school for adults. A minimum wage for city workers was set at $1.50 per day, double the rate other cities paid. Jones built a shelter for the homeless and an open-air church for citizens of every faith.

Though business leaders disapproved of his pro-labor policies, Jones was re-elected mayor until his death in 1904. Another progressive succeeded him in office, keeping Jones's policies firmly in place.

SETH LOW 5C

Another well-known progressive mayor, Seth Low, came from a background totally different from that of Samuel Jones. His ancestors had arrived in Massachusetts in the 1600s; his father was the wealthy owner of an import business. Born in Brooklyn in 1850, Low attended private schools, traveled widely, and entered Columbia University in New York City.

After graduating with highest honors, Low entered his father's business and became active in civic affairs in Brooklyn. In 1878 he set up the city's Bureau of Charities. A short time later, he decided to run for mayor. He won and served two terms, from 1881 to 1885. Low improved the city's school system and expanded the list of city jobs to

This photograph by Jacob Riis shows a public playground built for the children of New York's Lower East Side, one of the city's poorest neighborhoods. Progressive reformers pushed for many such improvements in city life. **CULTURE** How did Riis's photographs contribute to the concern for children's welfare? **4D**

be filled on the basis of merit. Low was independent in his political views. "I am not a Republican mayor, as you say I am," he said in 1884. "I am mayor of the whole people of Brooklyn."

Low next served as president of Columbia University from 1890 to 1901. There he set up an adult education program and improved the gradu-

In this cartoon the Tammany Tiger, symbol of New York's political machine, mauls a woman representing the city. The cartoonist has given the tiger an Irish jacket and hat, since many Irish immigrants supported Tammany Hall. **CIVIC VALUES** How does the cartoon suggest voters should react to Tammany politicians? **7F**

ate school. He also continued his civic duties, aiding victims of a cholera epidemic that struck in 1893. In 1901 Low was able to beat the bosses of Tammany Hall and become mayor of New York City. During his term in office, Low improved the city's police department and civil service system. He also began planning the first subway to Brooklyn.

The political bosses were able to defeat Low in his re-election bid in 1903. Low, however, did not give up the fight to improve city government. In 1907 he became president of the National Civic Federation, a group devoted to improving urban government throughout the nation. He also became president of the New York Chamber of Commerce in 1914. Low remained an eloquent spokesman on urban issues until his death in 1916.

FRANCES PERKINS 4C, 4D, 7H

Women played a strong role in the Progressive Movement. One was Frances Perkins, born in 1882 in Boston. The daughter of a factory owner, Perkins was educated at Mount Holyoke College. After doing charity work for her local church, Perkins headed to Chicago to teach. There she became involved with Hull House (page 164), later taking graduate courses in the field of social work. Armed with a master's degree from Columbia University, in 1910 she became executive secretary of the New York Consumers' League.

206 UNIT 3 CHANGE AND REFORM

In 1911 Perkins witnessed one of the most notorious industrial accidents in American history: the Triangle Shirtwaist Company fire. Some 500 workers, mostly women, were trapped by fire on three floors of a New York City building. The company had locked the fire escapes to prevent employees from leaving work early. As a result, many workers either suffocated inside the building or jumped to their death. (The city's fire equipment did not reach high enough to save them.) In the end 146 died, yet the company was acquitted of any crime.

Appalled at the disaster, Perkins began looking into safety regulations in the workplace. She became executive secretary of the New York Commission on Safety and director of the New York State Factory Investigating Commission. Perkins took state lawmakers to visit the sweatshops and factories, showing them firsthand the conditions

Frances Perkins was a pioneer in the male-oriented world of politics. Her career led her into the highest circles of power in the United States government. This portrait of Perkins was painted in the 1930s, when she was Franklin Roosevelt's Secretary of Labor. **PARTICIPATION** How might Perkins's career have inspired other women? **4D, 9E**

workers faced. Her efforts paid off in the form of improved health and safety rules and a shorter work week for women (48 hours instead of 54).

Perkins spent the next half-century pursuing progressive ideals. She held high government positions at the state and federal level. In 1933 she became the nation's first female Cabinet member, serving as Secretary of Labor until 1945.

Progressives believed poor people needed help to overcome poverty and cope with its hardships. In this photograph a social worker visits a family in their slum dwelling. **CIVIC VALUES** What might motivate people to take up careers in social work? **7F, 7G, 7H**

Photo Caption Answers
(Top) Students may suggest that Perkins inspired other women to see government careers as an option. (Bottom) Possible answers include concern for others' welfare, and the rewards and challenges of helping other people.

Cooperative Learning

Divide students into groups. Tell each group they must choose a "Progressive of the Century" from among the muckrakers and reformers mentioned in the section. Each member of the group should state his or her choice before the group votes on its decision. Have the group write a speech about the reformer which explains why that reformer won. Then hold an "awards ceremony" where the speeches are presented. **LEP**

Addressing Individual Needs

Guided/ Independent Practice
Instruct students to complete **Reinforcement Workbook** Worksheet 33. This worksheet asks students to list examples of progressive reforms.

Reteaching/Correctives
Have students form groups of four or five and make a series of "Progressive biography cards," much like baseball cards, using the people discussed in the section as subjects. Each student may be responsible for a single card, or groups may choose to have each student do one step of the process.

Have students complete **Reteaching Resources** Worksheet 33, which asks students to note characteristics of progressivism.

Enrichment/Extension
Have students complete **Enrichment and Extension Resources** Historian Worksheet 3, which examines muckraking.

CAUSE AND EFFECT: THE PROGRESSIVE MOVEMENT

Causes
- Influence of populism
- Corrupt and unresponsive government
- Political machines
- Muckraker writings
- Growth of educated middle class

The Progressive Movement (1900–1920)

Effects
- More efficient city government
- More democratic state government
- Increased business regulation
- Improved working conditions
- New amendments to Constitution

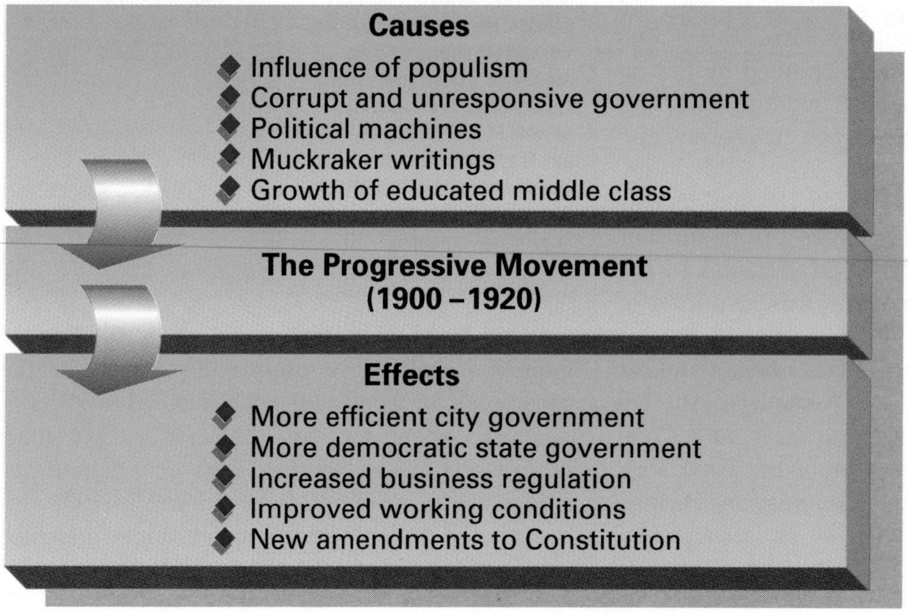

CHART SKILLS

This chart shows major causes and effects of the Progressive Movement. CRITICAL THINKING How, do you think, did the growth of an educated middle class further progressive goals? 7H, 9E

HIRAM W. JOHNSON 3D, 5C

Progressivism left its mark on the Pacific states as well as the East. Hiram W. Johnson, the son of a prominent railroad lawyer, was born in Sacramento, California, in 1866. He went to the University of California at Berkeley, but dropped out during his junior year. He then worked in his father's law office, and became a lawyer in 1888. But Johnson and his father soon clashed over politics. Hiram felt that government should regulate the railroads, while his father disagreed. Hiram decided to open his own law office.

Johnson later became an assistant district attorney in San Francisco. In 1908 he gained national fame in the trial of political boss Abe Ruef. In 1901 Ruef had convinced an orchestra leader named Eugene Schmitz to run for mayor. Schmitz knew little about politics and cared even less, but he ran anyway, and he won. Ruef's ties to Schmitz made Ruef the most popular lawyer in town. Businesses seeking contracts from the city hired Ruef to represent them. He used his influence with Schmitz to win the contracts, then split his fees with the mayor and other city officials. Eventually Ruef was brought to trial, but during the trial the prosecutor was shot in the courtroom. Johnson

took over the case and, despite Ruef's power and influence, had him convicted.

In 1910 Johnson ran for governor of California on a reform ticket and won. In his inaugural address, he noted the state's major problem:

> Nearly every governmental problem that involves the health, happiness, or the prosperity of the State has arisen because some private interest has intervened . . . to exploit either the resources or the politics of the State.

During Johnson's two terms as governor, California adopted a number of political reforms and passed wide-ranging labor laws. These included an eight-hour work day for women, limits on child labor, and workmen's compensation. This last reform was a state-run insurance system that supported workers injured on the job. Johnson created a railroad commission to set fair rates for trains operating within the state. Despite fierce opposition from business interests, he also worked for public control of utilities. "If you do not own them they will in time own you," he warned.

In 1912, when the Progressive Party was formed, Johnson served as its candidate for Vice

Cause and Effect Answer
Students may suggest that the more educated the middle class became, the more politically active it would be. Progressive reforms generally coincided with middle-class goals.

> "**I**f you do not own them [utilities] they will in time own you."
>
> —*Hiram Johnson*

President. He lost that election, but later left the governor's seat for the United States Senate. Johnson served there, working for progressive reforms, until his death in 1945.

3C, 5C

ROBERT M. "FIGHTING BOB" LA FOLLETTE

One of the most colorful of the progressives was Robert M. La Follette, nicknamed "Fighting Bob" for his energy and enthusiasm. Born on a Wisconsin farm in 1855, La Follette attended the University of Wisconsin and became a lawyer in 1880. He immediately went into politics, winning election as a local district attorney. At age 30 he ran for Congress and won, serving three terms in the House. At this point La Follette was anything but a reformer. He voted for high tariffs and generally

5B

This photograph from 1897 shows "Fighting Bob" La Follette speaking to a crowd in Cumberland, Wisconsin. He became the state's governor three years later. La Follette and his wife Belle, a noted journalist, fought vigorously for reform. POLITICS How did political campaigns in the late 1800s differ from those of today?

supported conservative principles. These stands cost La Follette his seat in Congress in the 1890 election.

While out of office, La Follette infuriated Republican leaders by claiming that a Republican senator had offered him a bribe. Shunned by the party organization, La Follette lost races for governor in 1896 and 1898. He ran again in 1900 as a reform candidate. Backed by small farmers and city workers, he won.

During his three terms as governor, La Follette led a successful progressive reform program that became known as the Wisconsin Idea. Wisconsin passed the first state income tax and a corporate tax. It set up a railroad rate commission. It also passed a conservation and waterpower act, regulated state banks, and put limits on lobbying.

Because many German immigrants lived in Wisconsin, La Follette looked to Germany for new ideas. (Germany at the time was a world leader in social legislation.) These included improving the civil service and strengthening the ties between universities and government. With the help of private experts, such as professors at the University of Wisconsin, state officials were able to deal with complex issues.

In 1906 La Follette moved on to the United States Senate, where he served until his death in 1925. He left behind in Wisconsin two sons and other followers who would keep the state a model of progressive reform for decades.

SECTION REVIEW

1. KEY TERMS progressivism, consensus, muckraker, workmen's compensation, Wisconsin Idea

2. PEOPLE Upton Sinclair, Lincoln Steffens, Ida Tarbell, Frances Perkins, Robert M. La Follette

3. COMPREHENSION List four differences between populism and progressivism.

4. COMPREHENSION What two broad changes did progressives demand?

5. CRITICAL THINKING Using some of the progressive leaders discussed in this section, explain the importance of education to the Progressive Movement.

Photo Caption Answer
Lack of radio and television meant that politicians relied on personal appearances to promote their campaigns.

2. *Upton Sinclair*—Muckraker whose novel, *The Jungle,* exposed the abuses of the meat-packing industry. *Lincoln Steffens*—Muckraker who attacked mismanagement of city governments. *Ida Tarbell*—Muckraker whose target was Standard Oil. *Frances Perkins*—Progressive who fought for health and safety rules in the workplace and became the first female Cabinet member. *Robert M. La Follette*—Three-term governor and later senator from Wisconsin, who led a series of progressive reforms.

3. Populism was mainly rural, while progressivism was urban; Populists tended to be poor and uneducated, while most progressives were middle-class and well-educated; populism was seen as more radical, while progressivism was seen as more mainstream; populism failed and progressivism succeeded.

4. Progressives wanted a more responsive government and for the government to take a more active role in protecting its citizenry.

5. Progressives saw education as a way for people to improve their own conditions, get better jobs, and so on. Samuel M. Jones backed free kindergartens; he and Seth Low supported adult education; and Robert La Follette demonstrated the value of education by enlisting universities' help in solving social problems.

Closure

Remind students of the pre-reading objectives in the section opener. Pose one or all of these questions again. Then have students read Section 2 for the next class period, noting progressive innovations.

2 Reforms in Cities and States

Section Focus

Key Terms city commission ■ city manager ■ initiative ■ referendum ■ recall ■ primary system ■ yellow dog contract

Main Idea Progressives made city and state governments more democratic. They also tightened regulations on business, which provoked several Supreme Court decisions.

Objectives As you read, look for answers to these questions:
1. What changes were made to improve city and state governments?
2. How did government seek to end abuses by business?
3. Which progressive laws were challenged in the courts?

Section Objective

■ cite progressive reforms in cities and states and their enduring impact

Introducing the Section

Connecting with Past Learnings
Review with students the two broad changes that progressives were trying to achieve. (To make the government more responsive to the people and to force the government to take a more active role in protecting citizens.)

Key Terms
Ask students which of the key terms were supported by progressives and which were opposed by them. Then have volunteers give examples of each term. Have students write definitions of the terms following the class discussion. **LEP**

Focus

Ask students to list the reforms mentioned in the section and put the list on the board. Then have students suggest the problem each reform was trying to solve. (Introduction of new forms of city government—rule by political bosses; initiative and referendum— state laws which ignored voter concerns; recall—inability to remove corrupt officials; primaries—choice of candidates by political bosses; business licenses and public utility commissions—lack of control over business; laws regulating working conditions—unsafe working conditions.)

Do you think progressive reforms were successful?

In the early 1900s, progressives pushed through changes in the way many American city and state governments operated. Official corruption was only one of their targets. The progressives also wanted government to become more efficient and more responsive to the needs of the people. And they wanted this stronger government to keep watch over business.

NEW FORMS OF CITY GOVERNMENT 7F, 7H, 7I
Corruption in city government was often easy to spot, but not so easy to fix. Some bosses were tried and convicted for their crimes. Reformers such as "Golden Rule" Jones and Seth Low worked hard to clean up their cities. But reformers could be voted out of office (as Low was) and replaced by bosses. Some progressives decided that the only way to make reforms last was to change the structure of city government.

Progressives came up with two new kinds of city government. One was the city commission—a board of perhaps five citizens elected by voters to run the city. The commission was not made up of professional politicians. Instead doctors, lawyers, business people, and others would serve in their spare time. The commission would meet a few evenings each month to make decisions.

The other kind of city government involved a city manager. This person was hired by the city council or city commission to run the city. City managers were experts in technical fields such as engineering. They had an understanding of the complex problems cities faced—sewer and bridge construction, public transportation, and so on. Highly paid and with few links to party leaders,

city managers would be insulated from bribes and other forms of corruption.

Two of the first cities to use these new forms of government did so to cope with natural disasters. In 1900 a hurricane devastated Galveston, Texas, killing more than 6,000 people. The city picked a commission to direct the rebuilding. Thirteen years later, a flood swept over Dayton, Ohio. Its residents hired a city manager to lead Dayton's recovery. Both experiments worked so well that hundreds of other cities followed suit.

The new city governments did face problems, though. In some cities, political machines hung on to power, blocking reform. Residents of other cities complained that their new leaders were less responsive to their needs than the bosses had been. While the bosses had often stolen public funds, they had also taken care of their supporters, even the poorest laborer. The commissions and managers, some people felt, only cared about efficiency.

CHANGES IN STATE GOVERNMENT 5C, 7E, 7I
City governments were not the progressives' only target. Many Americans felt that state governments had also lost touch with the people. Legislatures often sidetracked bills that voters wanted and passed bills that they did not want. Voters found themselves nearly helpless to remove lawmakers between elections. Even when election time did arrive, the list of candidates often left much to be desired. Using the slogan "Give the government back to the people!" progressives made far-reaching changes in how state governments worked.

SUPPORTING THE SECTION

Reinforcement Workbook: Worksheet 34
Reteaching Resources: Worksheet 34
Enrichment and Extension Resources: Primary Source Worksheet 17
Teaching Transparencies: Transparency 34

Background In 1906, San Francisco suffered a devastating earthquake. The corruption of the Ruef-Schmitz machine had allowed substandard construction in the city, and this contributed to the damage.

The Geographic Perspective: The San Francisco Earthquake and Fire

In 1900 San Francisco was the cultural and financial center of the Far West. Construction methods and styles in the fast-growing city resembled those in the Midwest or East. Commercial buildings were likely to be made of stone or brick, and other structures were of wood. Earthquakes caused by the nearby San Andreas Fault occasionally shook the region. However, most people agreed that "a good shake is not half so bad as a twister or a hurricane bearing down on you."

THE 1906 EARTHQUAKE

At 5:12 A.M. on April 18, 1906, northern California woke to a memorable shake. "Great gray clouds of dust shot up with flying timbers, and storms of masonry rained into the street," a reporter wrote. "Wild, high jangles of smashing glass cut a sharp note. Ahead of me a great cornice crushed a man as if he were a maggot."

This was the first major earthquake to strike a California city. In rural areas, dairy farmers commented on the amount of spilled milk. But in urban San Francisco the quake brought the city to a halt. Buildings collapsed. Streets were buckled and ripped. Broken gas lines and chimneys set the city on fire. The conflagration destroyed much of San Francisco.

Hundreds died. Thousands more were made homeless. A mountain of debris—including 6.5 billion fallen bricks—had to be removed in order to rebuild.

The challenges were immense, but San Franciscans seemed undaunted. Businesses quickly sprang up among the ruins. Citizen committees began to study all aspects of rebuilding. They addressed such problems as collecting taxes, condemning old buildings, widening streets, and rebuilding city services such as hospitals and sewers. Many saw the disaster as an opportunity to correct old problems and beautify the city. Such citizen involvement boosted the city-reform movement and contributed to the downfall of political boss Abe Ruef (page 208).

PLANNING AHEAD

Because fire had caused most of the destruction, new city codes emphasized measures to reduce the hazards of fire. In the downtown area, new buildings had to have exterior walls of stone or brick. Brick fire walls separated the buildings.

Ironically, though, these measures made the city even more vulnerable to earthquake damage. In an earthquake, brick walls can collapse as quickly as a house of cards. A quake-resistant building, on the other hand, has all its parts tied together into one unit. It can ride out an earthquake like a ship on rough seas.

After another disaster—the Long Beach earthquake of 1933—California required earthquake-resistant construction for schools. However, standards for other kinds of construction were not established until the 1960s. Such standards helped minimize the damage caused by a powerful earthquake in the San Francisco area in 1989.

2E, 7F

CRITICAL THINKING QUESTIONS

1. Why, do you think, did the people of San Francisco rebuild instead of leaving the area after the 1906 earthquake?
2. Why, after the earthquake, did San Francisco not require all buildings to be earthquake-proof?

The Geographic Perspective Answers
1. Because their friends and family lived in the area; because they enjoyed the area.
2. Because to do so would have been very costly.

Background Arnold Genthe, who shot this picture, has been called the "Father of Modern Photographers." The picture itself has been rated one of the ten best news photos of all time.

Geographic Themes
Geographic themes covered on this page:
✔ Location
___ Place
✔ Interactions
___ Movement
___ Regions

Developing the Lesson
After students have read the section, you may want to consider the following activities:

Civic Values
Ask students what form of government is used in your city or town. *Do you think it is responsive to the community?*
  Which form of city government do you think works best: city manager, city commission, or mayor/council?

Participating in Government
Ask students to suggest issues that might be the subject of a state initiative or referendum. Then have them find out if your state has provisions for these political actions and what they would have to do to be able to put their issues on the ballot.

Economics
Ask students to suggest public utilities. (Water, sewage, telephones, electricity.) *Why are utility companies likely to be monopolies?* (Business costs force out competitors; electric lines, sewage and water pipes, telephone lines, etc., can be built and operated more efficiently by one company.)
  Make sure that students understand that utilities are part of an economy's infrastructure. Then explain that utilities in many countries are run by the government. *Why might a government want total control of public utilities?* (To make sure that private businesses don't make large profits at public expense; to prevent any shutdown of service; to ensure all citizens access to service.)

Two reforms adopted in many states gave voters a larger role in the lawmaking process. One was the initiative, which gave voters the power to propose a bill and present it to the legislature for a vote. In this way, voters could force lawmakers to deal with difficult issues. The other reform was the referendum, in which the public voted on a bill offered by the legislature. Controversial bills—such as tax increases—could thus be put to a public vote before becoming law. Oregon made especially heavy use of the initiative and referendum. Between 1902 and 1910 that state's residents voted on 32 different measures.

Another set of reforms expanded voters' ability to choose their representatives. The recall allowed voters to remove a public official from office before the next scheduled election. The primary system gave party members a chance to choose their party's candidates for office. (Before the primary system came into use, party leaders had chosen the candidates.) Progressives also pushed states to adopt the secret ballot (page 192), long demanded by Populists. By 1910 every state used the secret ballot. A few states, nervous about the political influence of corporations, even limited the right of corporations to contribute money to political campaigns. In 1907 Congress passed a law banning corporate donations in all federal elections.

KEEPING AN EYE ON BUSINESS 3F, 8G

For progressives, honest and efficient government was an important goal, but not the ultimate one. They saw government as a tool to be used to promote the welfare of all citizens. Regulating business was, for both city and state governments, a major part of that task.

The simplest form of business regulation was the business license. Progressive city governments passed laws requiring every business person who wanted to work in the city to apply for a license. The applicant would provide the city with a name and address and a small license fee. Should the business try to cheat its customers, the city could refuse to renew its license. The practice of licensing would continue in cities throughout the twentieth century.

Vastly more complicated was the task of regulating public utilities (electricity, water and sewer fa-

This cover of *Puck* magazine from 1897 shows trusts and monopolies picking Uncle Sam's pockets. The picture is entitled "In the Hands of His Philanthropic Friends." ECONOMICS What harmful effect did unregulated trusts and monopolies have on consumers, according to their critics? 8G

cilities, and so on). Because it cost so much for a company to provide these services, in most cases a single company would drive its competitors out of business and establish a monopoly. The monopoly company was thus in a position to raise its rates. Customers, unable to buy from other suppliers or to do without needed services, would be forced to accept this exploitation.

There were two possible solutions. First, city governments could take over and run public utilities. Second, city governments could leave the utilities in private hands, but regulate them. Most cities chose the second solution, appointing public utility commissions to set fair utility rates. Ideally, these rates would balance the utility company's need to make a profit against the public's right to reasonable rates. This method of regulation would become the model for most American communities to the present day.

Some industries could not be regulated by cities because they did business beyond city limits. The telephone industry, for example, served people over a wide area. Railroads and insurance companies were two other examples. To regulate these businesses, state progressives used commissions similar to the public utility commissions in cities. The governor would appoint a state commission made up of lawyers or other professionals. It would listen to the arguments of the companies and consumers and then set rates it felt were fair.

PROGRESSIVISM TESTED IN THE COURTS 5C, 5D

Business leaders had mixed reactions to progressivism. Most preferred that the government maintain its laissez-faire attitude toward business. Yet many decided not to fight the progressives. They felt that it was wiser to accept some regulation now than risk even greater regulation later.

Business leaders realized, on the other hand, that certain progressive laws challenged ideas that had long been taken for granted. They had always assumed, for example, that companies would have complete control over working conditions—wages, hours, and so on. When progressive governments tried to regulate those areas, the battle for reform moved into the courts.

In 1896 the state of Utah passed a bill prohibiting workers in hazardous industries such as mines and steel mills from working more than eight hours a day. The bill's sponsors felt that worker fatigue caused many industrial accidents and hoped that a shorter work day would improve safety. In *Holden v. Hardy* (1898) the Supreme Court stated that the Utah law was constitutional. This was the first time the Court had approved a law limiting working hours.

Encouraged by the Court's decision, progressives in cities and states passed other similar laws. New York passed a bill forbidding bakers from working more than 10 hours a day or 60 hours a week. Yet in *Lochner v. New York* (1905), the Court stated that the bakery law was unconstitutional. Bakeries, the Court held, were not dangerous places to work, so there was no reason to limit working hours.

The debate over working conditions continued. In 1903 the Oregon legislature passed a bill limit-

Women workers labor in a textile factory in the early 1900s. In 1870, fewer than two million women were in the labor force. By 1910, there were more than eight million. **CONSTITUTIONAL HERITAGE** Why did Oregon forbid employment of women in certain industries? What might be the response to such a law today? 9A

ing the working hours of women in hazardous industries. Supporters of the law argued that if women were injured on the job they might not be able to have children. The birthrate would then decline, harming the nation as a whole.

The case quickly made its way to the Supreme Court. Two social workers who favored the law were able to convince the Oregon state government to hire Louis D. Brandeis, a famous Boston lawyer, to defend the law before the Court. Brandeis's written argument contained many statistics showing how long hours and poor working conditions harmed workers.

The Court decided, in *Muller v. Oregon* (1908), to uphold the law. It agreed with Brandeis that women needed special protection at work. As the Court put it, "The two sexes differ in . . . the self-

Photo Caption Answers
Work in hazardous industries might result in fewer children. Today the law might be challenged as unconstitutional because it discriminates on the basis of sex.

Enrichment/Extension
Assign **Enrichment and Extension Resources** Primary Source Worksheet 17. This worksheet asks students to analyze the attitude of employers toward employees.

Assessment
You may wish to use the Section 2 Review, page 214, to see how well your students understand the main points in this lesson.

Section Review Answers

1. *city commission*—Board of citizens elected by voters to run the city. *city manager*—Person hired by city council or commission to run the city. *initiative*—Gives voters power to propose a bill and present it to the legislature for a vote. *referendum*— Allows citizens to vote on a bill offered by the legislature. *recall*—Allows voters to remove a public official from office before the next scheduled election. *primary system*—Gives party members a chance to choose their party's candidates for office. *yellow dog contract*—Forces new employees to state that they did not belong to a union and would not join one.

2. *Louis D. Brandeis*— Boston lawyer who argued the *Muller v. Oregon* case successfully before the Supreme Court.

3. They saw it as the only way to make reforms last. Both the city commission and the city manager system had fewer links to party bosses and were better insulated from bribes and other forms of corruption.

4. They could take them over and run them, or they could leave them in private hands, but regulate them. Most cities did the latter.

5. Because it helped at least one group harmed by long hours and poor working conditions. Students' opinions about the decision will vary.

Closure

Use Section 2 information in the Chapter 9 Summary (p. 222) to synthesize the important elements covered in Section 2. Then have students read Section 3 for the next class period, noting what reforms were made at the federal level.

SECTION 3

New Constitutional Amendments
(pp. 214–219)

Section Objective

■ identify the amendments passed between 1913 and 1920 and how they advanced progressive reforms

Introducing the Section

Connecting with Past Learnings

Ask students to recall the constitutional amendments passed before 1900. *What three amendments were passed in the years just after the Civil War?* (Amendment 13 abolished slavery; Amendment 14 defined citizenship, representation, and voting rights for blacks; and Amendment 15 specifically established suffrage for black males.)

---

reliance which enables one to assert full rights." Progressives hailed the decision and passed more laws aimed at protecting various groups, especially children.

The Supreme Court also handled a host of other labor issues. It ruled that workmen's compensation laws, passed by four-fifths of the states by 1917, were constitutional. On other issues, it ruled against labor. In 1912 Massachusetts became the first state to pass a minimum wage law. Other states followed suit, but the Court struck down some of these laws. The Court further disappointed progressives by refusing to outlaw yellow dog contracts. Companies sometimes forced new workers to sign these contracts, which stated that the workers did not belong to a union and promised not to join one. In spite of these defeats, progressives continued to push for their goals.

SECTION REVIEW

1. KEY TERMS city commission, city manager, initiative, referendum, recall, primary system, yellow dog contract

2. PEOPLE Louis D. Brandeis

3. COMPREHENSION Why did progressives feel that the structure of city governments needed to be changed?

4. COMPREHENSION Which two choices did cities have in regulating public utilities? Which option did most of them choose?

5. CRITICAL THINKING Review the Supreme Court's decision in *Muller v. Oregon.* Why did progressives support this decision? What is your opinion about the decision?

4C, 4D, 5C, 5D, 6B, 7I, 9B, 9D

3 New Constitutional Amendments

Section Focus

Key Terms suffrage ■ progressive tax ■ prohibition ■ Equal Rights Amendment

Main Idea A series of progressive reforms came into law as constitutional amendments.

Objectives As you read, look for answers to these questions:
1. How did constitutional amendments change taxation and the election of senators?
2. What events led up to the passage of an amendment banning the sale of alcohol?
3. How did women win the vote?

This world taught woman nothing skillful and then said her work was valueless. It permitted her no opinions and said she did not know how to think. It forbade her to speak in public, and said there were no orators. It denied her the schools, and said women had no genius. It robbed her of every vestige of responsibility, and then called her weak.

These words came from a 1902 speech by Carrie Chapman Catt, then president of the National American Woman Suffrage Association. Catt was a leader in the drive for women's suffrage—voting rights. This was the best-known of several movements to amend the Constitution during the early 1900s. Only a total of five amendments (not counting the Bill of Rights) had been passed in all the years up to 1913. Between 1913 and 1920, four more amendments were passed. Each one represented a different area of concern to the Progressive Movement.

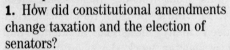
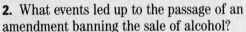

SUPPORTING THE SECTION

Reinforcement Workbook: Worksheet 35
Reteaching Resources: Worksheet 35
Enrichment and Extension Resources: Primary Source Worksheet 18
Teaching Transparencies: Transparency 35

Americans line up to pay the newly created federal income tax in 1913. Money gathered from this tax eventually became the main source of government income. ECONOMICS Why did progressives favor passage of the Sixteenth Amendment? 5C

AMENDMENT 16: INCOME TAX (1913) 5D

In its 1892 platform, the Populist Party had called for a federal income tax. It wanted that tax to be a progressive tax—one that assigns higher tax rates to people with higher incomes. Congress passed a federal income tax in 1894, but the following year the Supreme Court declared it unconstitutional.

Progressives liked the idea of a federal income tax. It would take money from the wealthy and give it to the government, which could then spend it on projects to benefit all the people. In 1913, with passage of the Sixteenth Amendment, Congress received the power to levy an income tax. Congress passed an income tax that same year. Those earning under $4,000 per year paid no taxes. (Most farmers and factory workers fell into this category.) Those earning over $4,000 paid taxes ranging from 1 percent to 6 percent of their income. While most government revenues still came from other sources, the income tax became a fact of life for the American people.

AMENDMENT 17: DIRECT ELECTION OF SENATORS (1913) 5D, 7I

The call for direct election of senators was another long-standing Populist demand picked up by the progressives. Under the Constitution (Article 1, Section 3), state legislatures were given the power to choose senators. Populists, and later progressives, complained that this system was undemocratic. They felt that senators should be chosen in the same way as members of the House of Representatives—by the voters themselves. Such a change would increase voters' power and also cut down on corruption in the Senate. A political boss or business tycoon might be able to bribe or bully a state legislature, but not the voters of an entire state.

The Seventeenth Amendment answered progressive demands by calling for the direct election of senators. Passed by Congress in 1912, it was ratified by the required number of states and became law the following year.

Photo Caption Answer
Progressives wanted the federal income tax because it took money from the wealthy and gave it to the government to benefit all the people.

Background   The first federal individual income tax was passed by Congress in 1861 as a method of raising money to fight the Civil War. The tax ended in 1872.

Key Terms
Have volunteers give one clue at a time about one of the key terms until other students guess which term is being described. Continue until students have guessed all the terms. **LEP**

Focus
Ask students to suggest reasons why progressives supported constitutional amendments instead of laws to bring about certain changes. (Laws progressives supported were declared unconstitutional; amendments brought about national change.)

How did the amendments passed between 1913 and 1920 further progressive goals? (Amendment 16—progressive income tax forced wealthier Americans to pay more for the government; Amendment 17—direct election of senators made government more responsive; Amendment 18—prohibition was seen as a way to make society better; and Amendment 19—women's suffrage broadened democracy.)

Developing the Lesson
After students have read the section, you may want to consider the following activities:

Constitutional Heritage
Ask students how amendments are added to the Constitution. (Passed by two thirds of both houses of Congress or a constitutional convention before being ratified by three quarters of the state legislatures.)

SOCIAL HISTORY
Famous Firsts

1869	Wyoming grants women suffrage.
1900	A New Haven, Connecticut lunch-counter owner invents the hamburger.
1902	*Al-Hoda,* first Arabic daily newspaper, New York City (Aug. 25).
1903	Maggie Lena Walker becomes first woman—and first black woman—president of a bank, the St. Luke Penny Savings Bank of Richmond, Virginia.
1908	Bibles in hotel rooms first distributed by the Gideons at Superior Hotel, Iron Mountain, Montana.
1909	Speaking on topic of women's suffrage, Harriet Stanton Black makes first speech broadcast on radio.
1910	Alice Wells is appointed to the Los Angeles Police Department as the nation's first policewoman (Sept. 12).
1914	First scheduled airline service begins, between St. Petersburg and Tampa, Florida.

AMENDMENT 18: PROHIBITION (1919) 4D, 5D

The progressives' campaign to reform the United States extended to moral issues. Personal habits such as smoking and drinking came under attack in many state legislatures. By 1913, thirteen states had banned the sale of cigarettes. When the problems of enforcing such a law became obvious, states began to tax cigarettes instead of outlawing them. Cigarette taxes became a major source of revenue for state governments.

The campaign against alcohol proved far more controversial. As early as the 1820s some groups had organized to discourage people from drinking. They argued that drinking harmed those who drank, their employers (who lost money because their workers became less productive), and their families (who had to put up with the misbehavior of drinkers). The movement drew strength from activists within Protestant churches. In 1874, for example, the Woman's Christian Temperance Union (WCTU) was founded. A WCTU leader named Carrie Nation became famous for her "raids" on Kansas saloons. Wielding a hatchet,

Nation smashed windows, bottles, and furniture to get her point across.

The idea of prohibition—banning the manufacture and sale of alcoholic beverages—picked up steam with the rise of progressivism. Reformers saw prohibition as a way to cut poverty, crime, and disease in one stroke. Even political corruption could be reduced, they argued, since many in the alcohol industry had ties to machine bosses.

In the mid-1800s several states, following the example set by Maine in 1846, passed laws banning alcohol. The Anti-Saloon League, formed in 1893, ran a well-organized lobbying operation to convince states to adopt prohibition. By 1915, more than a dozen states were totally "dry" (that is, they forbade alcohol). The rest gave their counties the option of banning alcohol. Looking for a nationwide ban, prohibition forces decided to push for a constitutional amendment against alcohol.

When the United States entered World War I (Chapter 13), popular support for prohibition grew. At a time when American soldiers were dying overseas, prohibitionists argued, going without alcohol was the least that Americans at home could do. Supporters of prohibition claimed that it would make American workers more efficient. They also pointed out that grain went into the making of many alcoholic beverages. Prohibition would therefore make more grain available for food. The Eighteenth Amendment was ratified in January 1919, and one year later prohibition was the law of the land.

4C, 4D, 5D
WOMEN'S STRUGGLE FOR VOTING RIGHTS

Of all the campaigns waged during the Progressive Era, none prompted more heated debate than the struggle for women's suffrage. The foundation for this struggle was laid during the abolitionist campaign of the pre-Civil War days. The drive to free the slaves drew into public life some of the most talented women of the time. These women learned how to organize and use their power to bring about change. Their involvement in the abolitionist movement also made women more aware of the discrimination they faced. For example, at the World Anti-Slavery Convention in 1840 the British and French delegates refused to admit female American delegates.

This engraving shows women in Cheyenne, Wyoming, casting their ballots in an 1888 election. Wyoming women were the first in the nation to have the right to vote. Women in Colorado and Idaho were next. **PARTICIPATION** What social factors fueled the women's movement of the late 1800s? **4D, 6B**

BIOGRAPHY 5D

SUSAN B. ANTHONY (1820–1906) was a hero of the movement for women's rights. In 1872 she was arrested for voting in a presidential election. At her trial, she made a stirring speech that ended with the words "Resistance to tyranny is obedience to God." Fourteen years after her death, the Nineteenth Amendment, also called the Susan B. Anthony Amendment, guaranteed a woman's right to vote.

With the outbreak of the Civil War, women's rights leaders concentrated their efforts on the struggle to end slavery. Thus they were disappointed when the Fourteenth and Fifteenth Amendments, drawn up after the war to ensure blacks' rights, made no specific mention of women. Stung by this exclusion, women intensified their struggle for voting rights.

In 1869 Elizabeth Cady Stanton and Susan B. Anthony formed the National Woman Suffrage Association (NWSA). It pushed the federal government for a broad range of reforms to help women, including the vote. Arguing that the Fourteenth Amendment applied to women, Anthony and others tried to vote in various elections. In 1872 Anthony and several other suffragists were arrested in Rochester, New York, for voting. After being denied the right to testify at her own trial, Anthony was convicted of "illegal voting." Two years later the Supreme Court agreed to hear a case challenging the law against voting by women. Yet the Court unanimously decided that women had no voting rights.

In 1869 another organization, the American Woman Suffrage Association (AWSA), was formed. Its head, a well-known women's rights leader named Lucy Stone, favored lobbying in the states rather than in Washington, D.C. The federal government's refusal to support women's demands convinced many women that Lucy Stone and the AWSA were correct. In 1890 the NWSA and AWSA joined forces.

Convincing states to give women the vote proved to be frustrating. The first success came in the Wyoming Territory, which let women vote beginning in 1869. When Wyoming applied for statehood in 1890, Congress seemed reluctant to admit a state that let women vote. Wyoming officials replied, "We will remain out of the union a hundred years rather than come in without woman suffrage." Congress backed down, and Wyoming became the first state with women's suffrage. Also in the 1890s Colorado, Idaho, and Utah gave women the vote.

In the rest of the country, the push for voting rights went nowhere. The women's suffrage movement faced formidable enemies. Some belonged to groups that feared how women would vote if given

218

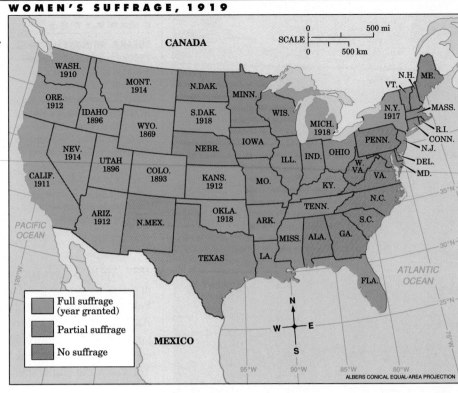

WOMEN'S SUFFRAGE, 1919

MAP SKILLS

By 1919, women in many southern and eastern states still had no voting rights. In much of the Midwest, women had partial voting rights—they could vote only in presidential elections or in primary elections. **CRITICAL THINKING** Which area of the country was the first to allow women's suffrage? Why, do you think, did this region give women the vote before other regions? 5D, 9B

the chance. Many women were active in the prohibition movement, for example. The liquor industry thus realized that the ballot could prove a more effective weapon against them than even Carrie Nation's axe. (It was.) Political leaders in the South, remembering the involvement of women in the antislavery movement, worried that they would use their votes to promote black rights. Business leaders did not want their female workers voting. Women were already gaining strength in the union movement. With the vote, they might push even harder for better wages and working conditions.

Simple prejudice also led people to oppose women's suffrage. Some assumed that the way things had been was the way they should be. Former President Grover Cleveland was one such person. In 1905 he wrote an article in *The Ladies' Home Journal*, arguing that "sensible and responsible women do not want to vote. The relative positions to be assumed by man and woman in the working out of our civilization were assigned long ago by a higher intelligence than ours."

218 UNIT 3 CHANGE AND REFORM

4D, 5D

AMENDMENT 19: WOMEN'S SUFFRAGE (1920)

Still, several factors were working in women's favor by the early 1900s. More women than ever before had taken jobs in industry, gaining a small measure of power and independence in the outside world. The Progressive Movement, by challenging many existing ideas and institutions, created the kind of atmosphere in which women's demands could more easily be heard.

The women's movement itself also benefited from a new generation of leaders. People such as Alice Paul and Carrie Chapman Catt brought fresh energy to the movement. They brought fresh ideas with them as well, including dramatic public demonstrations. From 1910 on, suffragists held parades in New York City. They also picketed in front of the White House, holding signs that read "How Long Must Women Wait For Liberty?" Angry crowds shoved and yelled at the demonstrators; police arrested them for blocking the sidewalk. While in prison, some of them went on hunger strikes. The whole nation heard of the dignity and resolve of the protesters.

"How Long Must Women Wait For Liberty?"

—Suffragist sign

Using the publicity of these events, women's leaders redoubled their efforts in the states. In 1916 Carrie Chapman Catt drew up a "Winning Plan" that targeted states where victory was most likely. She then laid out a strategy to "capture" those states one by one.

United States entry into World War I made Catt's task easier. As men left offices and factories to join the war, women took their places. Women built weapons, directed traffic, and performed countless other tasks normally done by men. Their contributions to the war effort gave added strength to the demand for the vote. By 1919, fifteen states had granted women full suffrage, and many others had granted partial suffrage (map, page 218).

This groundswell of support gave new life to a constitutional amendment granting women the vote. The Susan B. Anthony Amendment, which in every year since 1878 had been presented to Congress and then ignored, was passed in 1919. With the backing of Congress and Woodrow Wilson (President at that time), women's leaders went back to the states seeking ratification of the amendment. By August 1920 the needed number of states had approved it, and the Nineteenth Amendment became law.

Amidst their joy, women's leaders recalled the frustrations of the long struggle. Carrie Chapman Catt noted:

> It was a continuous, seemingly endless, chain of activity. Young suffragists who helped forge the last links were not born when it began. Old suffragists who forged the first links were dead when it ended.

Some women's leaders, such as Alice Paul, vowed to press forward for greater protection against discrimination. In 1923 she submitted the **Equal Rights Amendment** to Congress. It stated that "equality of rights under the law shall not be denied or abridged [reduced] by the United States nor by any State on account of sex." Efforts to ratify this amendment have continued to this day.

SECTION REVIEW

1. KEY TERMS suffrage, progressive tax, prohibition, Equal Rights Amendment

2. PEOPLE Carrie Chapman Catt, Carrie Nation, Elizabeth Cady Stanton, Susan B. Anthony, Lucy Stone, Alice Paul

3. COMPREHENSION Why did the Populists and progressives favor direct election of senators?

4. COMPREHENSION How did the entry of the United States into World War I aid the Prohibition Movement?

5. CRITICAL THINKING Compare and contrast the processes by which women and black men received the vote.

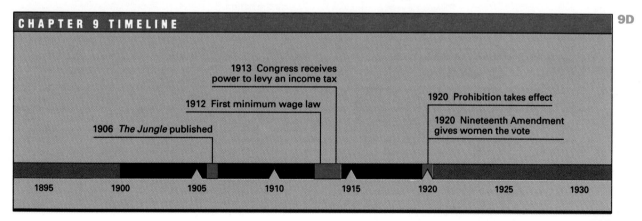

CHAPTER 9 TIMELINE

9D

1906 *The Jungle* published

1912 First minimum wage law

1913 Congress receives power to levy an income tax

1920 Prohibition takes effect

1920 Nineteenth Amendment gives women the vote

1895 1900 1905 1910 1915 1920 1925 1930

2. *Carrie Chapman Catt*—Leader in the drive for women's suffrage. *Carrie Nation*—Hatchet-wielding leader of the Woman's Christian Temperance Union. *Elizabeth Cady Stanton*—One of the founders of the National Woman Suffrage Association (NWSA). *Susan B. Anthony*—Founder of the NWSA who submitted a women's suffrage amendment in 1878. *Lucy Stone*—Head of the American Woman Suffrage Association. *Alice Paul*—Submitted the Equal Rights Amendment in 1923.

3. They felt direct election of senators was more democratic and that it would cut down on corruption.

4. Prohibitionists argued that at a time when American soldiers were dying overseas, going without alcohol was the least Americans at home could do.

5. Students' answers should acknowledge that both came about by constitutional amendment, but that women faced fewer secondary obstacles, such as poll taxes and literacy tests, in order to exercise their vote. Students might also note that women originally claimed inclusion under the Fourteenth Amendment, but their rights were denied by the courts.

Closure

Ask one student to transform the Main Idea of the section into a question, and have other students answer that question. Then have students read Section 1 of Chapter 10 for the next class period, noting how presidential leadership helped shape the Progressive Era.

Continental United States in 1900

Background

This map offers a visual summary of the information presented in the chapters on the United States up to 1900. The activities and cultures shown are far from exhaustive; they have been chosen to give a flavor of the variety that existed. Because of issues of scale, it has not always been possible to place symbols in precise locations. Though Arizona, New Mexico, and Oklahoma were still territories in 1900, their state boundaries are shown for geographic reference. The projection, developed for this map by cartographer Howard S. Friedman, is based on an oblique view of a polyconic projection.

Examining the Map for Content

Review the labeled symbols on the map and help students identify symbols that have not been labeled. Have them note the Mississippi River steamboat and the bridge over the river. Explain to students that many rail bridges were built over the Mississippi in the late 1800s. *How might the rise of railroads have affected the importance of riverboats?* (Railroads decreased the significance of river travel.)

Review the development of the cattle industry. *What does the map's railroad tracks to the ranch represent?* (Railheads, where cattle was driven to be shipped to urban markets.)

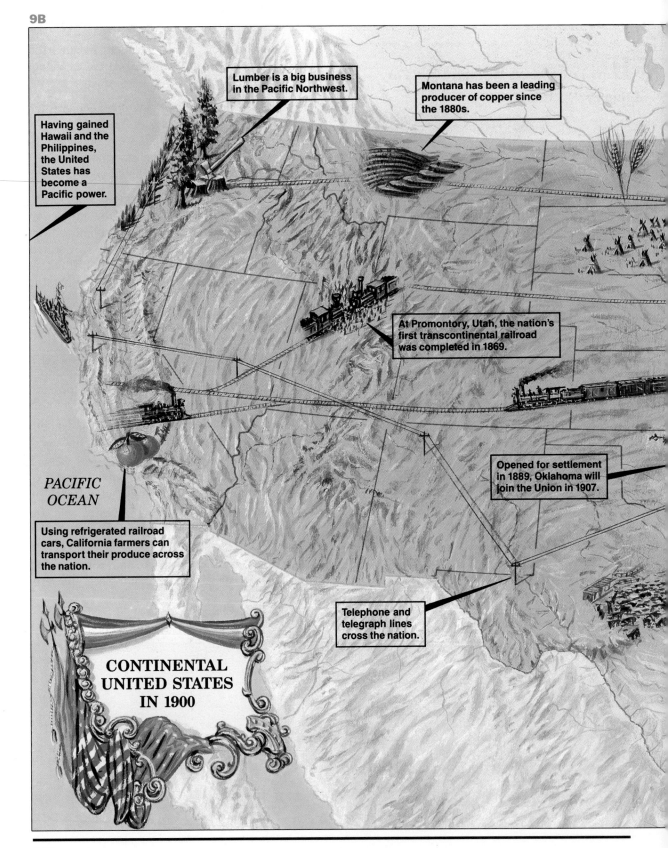

Lumber is a big business in the Pacific Northwest.

Montana has been a leading producer of copper since the 1880s.

Having gained Hawaii and the Philippines, the United States has become a Pacific power.

At Promontory, Utah, the nation's first transcontinental railroad was completed in 1869.

Opened for settlement in 1889, Oklahoma will join the Union in 1907.

PACIFIC OCEAN

Using refrigerated railroad cars, California farmers can transport their produce across the nation.

Telephone and telegraph lines cross the nation.

CONTINENTAL UNITED STATES IN 1900

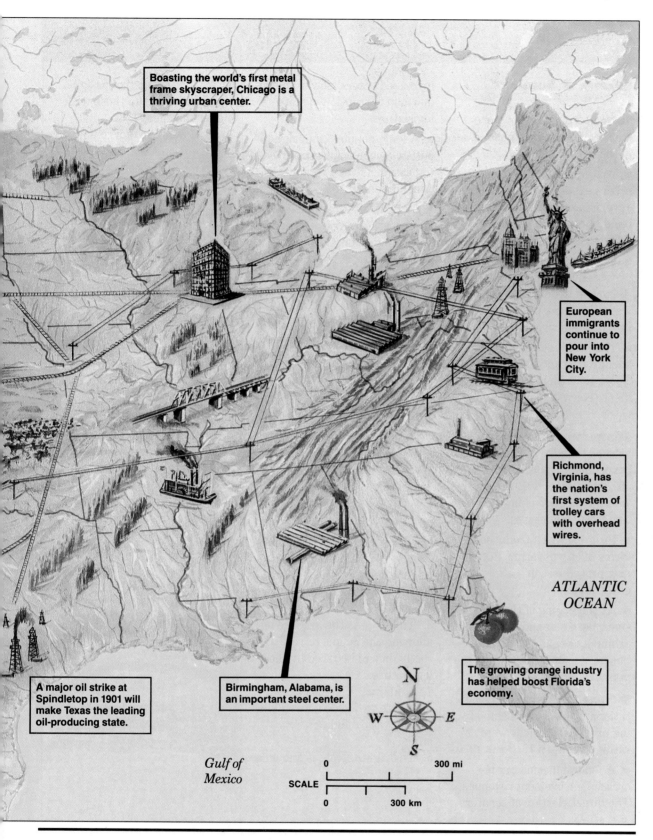

Boasting the world's first metal frame skyscraper, Chicago is a thriving urban center.

European immigrants continue to pour into New York City.

Richmond, Virginia, has the nation's first system of trolley cars with overhead wires.

ATLANTIC OCEAN

A major oil strike at Spindletop in 1901 will make Texas the leading oil-producing state.

Birmingham, Alabama, is an important steel center.

The growing orange industry has helped boost Florida's economy.

N
W · E
S

Gulf of Mexico

SCALE

0   300 mi

0   300 km

CHAPTER 9   THE PROGRESSIVE MOVEMENT, 1900–1920   **221**

Have students find the Great Lakes and identify the symbol representing boat traffic. Ask them to note the economic activities shown on the map. (Manufacturing, lumbering, farming, ranching, mining.) Have them identify the symbols used to show agriculture. (Oranges in Florida, cattle in Texas, produce in California, wheat in North Dakota.)

Connecting Geography and History

Have students find the symbol representing American Indians. (In South Dakota.) *What was the situation of Plains Indians at the turn of the century?* (Indian resistance had died out, surviving Indians had been forced onto reservations, the Dawes Act encouraged assimilation.) Challenge students to identify the other symbol shown on the map which implies a loss of Indian land. (Settlement of Oklahoma, which had been part of Indian Territory.)

Point out that several railroad lines intersect at Chicago. *How might Chicago's location on one of the Great Lakes have led to its becoming the second largest city in the United States in 1900?* (It was an important transportation center. Shipping connected it with other Great Lakes industrial centers and with the East through the Erie Canal. Railroads linked it to agricultural centers in the West and to urban centers around the country.)

Discuss with students what the map shows about the role of transportation and communications in the development of the United States.

Chapter 9 Review Answers

Key Terms
1. initiative
2. recall
3. referendum
4. primary system
5. suffrage
6. progressive tax
7. Prohibition

People to Identify
1. Frances Perkins
2. Carrie Nation
3. Susan B. Anthony
4. Upton Sinclair
5. Robert La Follette

Places to Locate
1. E 4. C
2. A 5. D
3. B

Reviewing the Facts

1. Progressivism was centered in the cities, involved the well-educated middle-class, remained in the political mainstream, and succeeded.

2. Progressives believed government should play a greater role in regulating business and helping the needy.

3. The city manager was a person experienced in technical fields hired to run the city. The city commission was a board of citizens elected to make decisions concerning the city.

4. Progressives urged such reforms as the initiative, the referendum, and the recall, which forced lawmakers to be more responsive.

5. Governments used business licenses, public utility commissions, and other such commissions to regulate business.

6. Businesses challenged the attempt of government regulation of working conditions, such as wages, hours, the employment of women, and workers' compensation.

CHAPTER 9 SUMMARY

SECTION 1: A reform movement called progressivism rose in the early 1900s.

■ Writers known as muckrakers exposed business and government corruption, helping build public support for the Progressive Movement.

■ Unlike the earlier Populists, progressives came mainly from the urban middle class. They wanted reform, but most did not propose radical change.

■ The progressives varied in background and priorities. Their goals included government reform and protection of workers and consumers.

SECTION 2: Progressives worked to make city and state governments more democratic, efficient, and active. They also won the passage of laws regulating many businesses.

■ Progressives introduced new forms of city government and new procedures in state government.

■ At the urging of the progressives, both city and state governments began to regulate business in order to protect the public interest.

SECTION 3: A series of constitutional amendments embodying progressive ideas were ratified between 1910 and 1920.

■ A federal income tax increased government revenues. The direct election of senators increased voters' power and cut down on corruption in state legislatures.

■ A long, popular campaign to outlaw alcoholic beverages led to passage of the Prohibition Amendment in 1919.

■ In 1920, after many decades of protest, feminists succeeded in winning a constitutional amendment that gave voting rights to American women.

KEY TERMS ●

Use the following terms to complete the sentences below.

> **initiative**
> **primary system**
> **progressive tax**
> **prohibition**
> **recall**
> **referendum**
> **suffrage**

1. The _____ is the procedure by which the people of a state can introduce legislation.
2. The _____ allow voters to remove a public official from office before the next scheduled election.
3. The _____ is the practice of allowing the people to vote directly on a bill offered by the legislature.
4. Under a _____, party members vote to decide who will be the party's candidates for office.
5. The right to vote is known as _____ .
6. A _____ is one that assigns higher tax rates to those with higher incomes.
7. _____ was the movement to ban the production and consumption of alcohol.

PEOPLE TO IDENTIFY ●

Match each of the following people with the correct description.

> **Susan B. Anthony**
> **Robert La Follette**
> **Carrie Nation**
> **Frances Perkins**
> **Upton Sinclair**

1. New York social worker who campaigned for safe working conditions.
2. Member of the Kansas WCTU whose axe-wielding saloon raids made her famous.
3. Co-founder of the National Woman Suffrage Association whose name was eventually given to the Nineteenth Amendment.
4. Muckraking author who exposed unhealthy practices in the meatpacking industry.
5. Reform governor of Wisconsin who later served as senator.

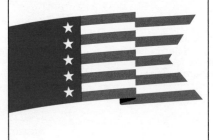

7. The Populists called for an income tax in 1892, Congress passed a federal income tax in 1894, the Supreme Court declared the income tax unconstitutional in 1895, and in 1913 Congress received the power to levy an income tax with the passage of the Sixteenth Amendment.

PLACES TO LOCATE ●

Match each of the letters on the map with the places that are listed below.

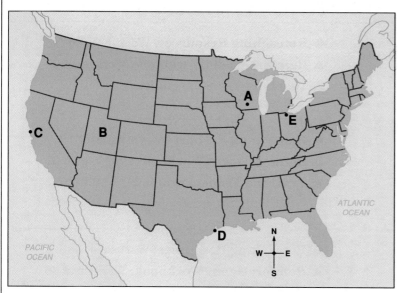

1. Toledo, Ohio
2. Madison, Wisconsin
3. Utah
4. San Francisco, California
5. Galveston, Texas

REVIEWING THE FACTS ▲

1. How did the Progressive Movement differ from the earlier Populist Movement?
2. What was new about the progressives' attitude toward the role of government?
3. Describe the city manager and city commission forms of government.
4. What procedural reforms did progressives urge on state governments? What was the purpose of each of these reforms?
5. What methods did city and state governments invent to regulate business?

6. In what areas did businesses challenge attempts at government regulation?
7. What were the steps by which the federal income tax became law?
8. How were senators selected before and after passage of the Seventeenth Amendment?
9. What were some of the arguments made by those who favored the banning of alcohol?
10. How did the passage of the Fifteenth Amendment foster the growth of the women's suffrage movement? How did World War I help the women's suffrage movement?

CRITICAL THINKING SKILLS ▲

1. MAKING A VALUE JUDGMENT
Some Americans oppose the progressive income tax. They argue that people with larger incomes already pay higher taxes when taxed on a flat rate, and it is unfair to ask them to pay a higher percentage of their income. What do you think of this argument?

2. FORMING A HYPOTHESIS Why might the Progressive Movement have been more attractive to the middle class than to the working class?

3. ANALYZING A QUOTATION Reread the quotation from Carrie Chapman Catt on page 219. How would you describe the tone of Catt's statement? Is it a statement of fact or a statement of opinion?

WRITING ABOUT TOPICS IN AMERICAN HISTORY ■

1. CONNECTING WITH LITERATURE
A selection from "Boy on Horseback" by Lincoln Steffens appears on pages 786–788. Read it and answer the questions. Then answer the following question: How did conditions like those Steffens saw in the California legislature help bring about the Progressive movement?

2. APPLYING THEMES: EXPANDING DEMOCRACY Return to the quotation by Carrie Chapman Catt on page 219. Write a paragraph that explains what you think the main point of the quotation was.

More women entered the workforce during World War I, performing tasks normally done by men. Their new independence strengthened the demand for the vote.

Critical Thinking Skills
1. Students who support the argument could point to the fact that the tax is reverse discrimination. Those opposed could argue that the wealthy would still have more money remaining than the poor.
2. Progressivism offered reforms which did not challenge the essential rules of the capitalist system, a system that was tougher on the working class than the middle class.
3. Students should recognize the tone of frustration and realize that Catt's statements emphasize the fact that women had few opportunities to change their position in society.

Writing About Topics in American History
1. Because of the rampant corruption in government, the people's needs were not being met. Voters were eager to reform the system, so they supported progressive candidates.
2. Students should explain that the suffragists, through their dedication to a just cause, fought a long battle to win women the right to vote.

---

8. The Constitution gave state legislatures the power to choose senators but the Seventeenth Amendment called for the direct election of senators.

9. Prohibitionists argued that prohibition would ease poverty, crime, political corruption, and disease.

10. The Fifteenth Amendment, which ensured blacks' rights, made no mention of women thus intensifying their struggle for voting rights.

Chapter Review exercises are keyed for student abilities:
● = Basic
▲ = Average
■ = Average/Advanced

Chapter 10 ▪ The Progressive Presidents

4 Sections, 4–6 Days

	SECTION OBJECTIVES	SECTION RESOURCES
Section 1 **The Square Deal**	▪ describe Theodore Roosevelt's rise to the presidency and his accomplishments as President	● **Reteaching Resources:** Worksheet 36 ▲ **Reinforcement Workbook:** Worksheet 36 ▲ **Teaching Transparencies:** Transparency 36
Section 2 **Filling TR's Shoes**	▪ contrast Taft's successes and failures as President with Theodore Roosevelt's presidency ▪ describe how the Taft-Roosevelt split affected the 1912 election	● **Reteaching Resources:** Worksheet 37 ▲ **Reinforcement Workbook:** Worksheet 37 ▲ **Teaching Transparencies:** Transparency 37
Section 3 **The Presidency of Woodrow Wilson**	▪ list reforms achieved by Wilson ▪ describe the situation of African Americans under progressive Presidents	● **Reteaching Resources:** Worksheet 38 ▲ **Reinforcement Workbook:** Worksheet 38 ■ **Enrichment and Extension Resources:** Primary Source Worksheet 19 ▲ **Teaching Transparencies:** Transparency 38
Section 4 **The Progressives and Conservation**	▪ describe the influence of progressive Presidents on the growth of the conservation movement	● **Reteaching Resources:** Worksheet 39 ▲ **Reinforcement Workbook:** Worksheet 39 ■ **Enrichment and Extension Resources:** Primary Source Worksheet 20 ▲ **Teaching Transparencies:** Transparency 39

The list below shows Essential Elements relevant to this chapter. (The complete list of Essential Elements appears in the introductory pages of this Teacher's Edition.)

Section 1: 3C, 3F, 4D, 4F, 5B, 8F, 8G, 9A
Section 2: 3F, 5B, 5C, 5D, 8B, 8F, 8G, 9B
Section 3: 3F, 3G, 4C, 4D, 4F, 5B, 5D, 7E, 7J, 8G
Section 4: 2B, 2C, 5E, 7G, 9D

Section Resources are keyed for student abilities:
● = Basic
▲ = Average
■ = Average/Advanced

CHAPTER RESOURCES

Geography Resources: Worksheets 19, 20
Tests: Chapter 10 Test

Chapter Project: Constitutional Government

Have students choose one of the Presidents discussed in this chapter and prepare a campaign strategy for the election of 1912. Students should write policy statements on the key issues facing the country, as well as identify groups that support their candidate.

Homework Options

Each section contains activities labeled "Addressing Individual Needs." You may wish to choose from among these activities when assigning homework.

> ### Provisions for Limited English Proficiency (LEP)
> Several suggested activities may be particularly helpful for teachers of students with limited English proficiency. These activities have been marked throughout the Teacher's Annotated Edition with the symbol **LEP** .

BIBLIOGRAPHY AND AUDIOVISUAL AIDS

Teacher Bibliography

Cooper, John Milton, Jr. *The Warrior and the Priest: Woodrow Wilson and Theodore Roosevelt.* Harvard University Press, 1983.

Link, Arthur S. *Woodrow Wilson and the Progressive Era, 1910–1917.* Harper and Row, 1963.

Morris, Edmond. *The Rise of Theodore Roosevelt.* Ballantine, 1980.

Student Bibliography

McCullough, David. *Mornings on Horseback.* Simon and Schuster, 1982.

Peare, Catherine O. *The Woodrow Wilson Story: An Idealist in Politics.* Crowell, 1963.

Steinberg, Alfred. *Woodrow Wilson.* G.P. Putnam's Sons, 1961.

Literature

Spargo, John. *The Bitter Cry of the Children.* Johnson Reprint, 1969.

Sinclair, Upton. *The Jungle.* Penguin, 1985. An eastern European immigrant's experiences working in the stockyards of Chicago.

Films and Videotapes*

America Spreads Its Wings, 1901–1910 (Indomitable Teddy Roosevelt Series). 30 min. CF. Roosevelt's presidency from 1901 to 1909.

A Different World, 1910–1916 (Indomitable Teddy Roosevelt Series). 30 min. CF. Although Roosevelt left the presidency in 1909, he retained an important place in American politics and national life.

Rise to Power, 1858–1901 (Indomitable Teddy Roosevelt Series). 30 min. CF. Presents Roosevelt's early years from his birth in 1858 to his swearing in as President in 1901.

United States in the 20th Century: 1900–1912. 12 min. COR/MTI. Highlights of U.S. history under the Roosevelt and Taft administrations.

Filmstrips*

Woodrow Wilson: Idealism and American Democracy (set of 2). GA. Artwork, photography, speeches, and written works document the life and influence of Woodrow Wilson.

Computer Software*

America's Presidents Series: World Wars, Prosperity and Depression—Presidents During and Between Two World Wars (Apple with 48K; IBM with 64K). QUEUE. Each President is covered in a separate menu option, and prominent Presidents have multiple sections on different phases on their lives and administrations. Presidents Wilson–Truman, 1913–1953.

*For a complete guide to audiovisual sources, see the introduction to this book (page Txx).

Chapter 10

The Progressive Presidents
(pp. 224–247)

This chapter describes the concerns and accomplishments of domestic policy during the Theodore Roosevelt, Taft, and Wilson administrations.

Themes in American History

- Constitutional government
- Pluralistic society
- Geography

Chapter Objectives

After students complete this chapter, they will be able to:

1. Describe Theodore Roosevelt's rise to the presidency and his accomplishments as President.

2. Contrast Taft's successes and failures as President with Theodore Roosevelt's presidency.

3. Describe how the Taft-Roosevelt split affected the 1912 election.

4. List reforms achieved by Wilson.

5. Describe the situation of black Americans under progressive Presidents.

6. Describe the influence of the progressive Presidents on the growth of the conservation movement.

Chapter Opener Art
Photograph taken 1912; oil over photograph, c. 1912.

President from 1901 to 1909, Theodore Roosevelt was a forceful and colorful spokesman for Progressive causes. Here he campaigns before a crowd of supporters.

CHAPTER SUPPORT MATERIAL

Reinforcement Workbook: Worksheets 36–39
Reteaching Resources: Worksheets 36–39
Enrichment and Extension Resources: Primary Source Worksheets 19, 20
Geography Resources: Worksheets 19, 20
Teaching Transparencies: Transparency 36–39
Tests: Chapter 10 Test

3C, 3F, 4D, 4F, 5B, 8F, 8G, 9A

1 The Square Deal

★ Section Focus

Key Terms Square Deal ■ "trustbusting"
■ Pure Food and Drug Act

Main Idea Theodore Roosevelt initiated national progressive reforms. The desire to be fair to all Americans underlined his policies as President.

Objectives As you read, look for answers to these questions:
1. How did Theodore Roosevelt rise to the presidency?
2. How did Roosevelt view the office of President?
3. What progressive reforms did Roosevelt make?

Leaders of the Republican Party in New York state had a problem on their hands in the summer of 1900. His name was Theodore Roosevelt, Jr., New York's Republican governor. Ambitious, strong-willed, and intelligent, Roosevelt had all the makings of a leader. That was the problem. Party chiefs worried that Roosevelt was too independent, too difficult to control. Many disliked his progressive policies. Then they came up with an idea. Why not find Roosevelt a job with no real power—one in which they could keep an eye on him? Why not offer him the vice presidency? As President McKinley's loyal Vice President, Roosevelt would have no choice but to behave.

This seemingly clever idea did not appeal to Mark Hanna, the prominent Ohio Republican. "Don't any of you realize that there's only one life between that madman and the presidency?" he warned. But Roosevelt was offered the nomination, took it, and he and McKinley won the election that fall. Less than one year later, Hanna's warning became reality. President McKinley was

shot by an anarchist in Buffalo, New York, in September 1901. McKinley died eight days after the shooting, and Roosevelt became the nation's twenty-sixth President. Party regulars, trying to wreck Roosevelt's career, had instead made him the most powerful man in the country. And as they feared, he would indeed turn out to be a powerful voice for the Progressive Movement.

ROOSEVELT'S ROAD TO THE WHITE HOUSE 5B

Theodore Roosevelt, Sr., a big, athletic man, was overjoyed on October 27, 1858. His wife had given birth to a son who would bear his proud name. Yet the happiness of the Roosevelt family would soon fade. As a child Theodore was short, skinny, and prone to illness. He was also nearsighted and spoke in a high, squeaky voice. "Teedie," as he was called at home, was determined to strengthen his body as well as his mind. "I'll make my body," twelve-year-old Teedie told his father.

Roosevelt wasted no time in proving his ability to overcome obstacles. As a student at Harvard

---

SECTION 1

The Square Deal
(pp. 225–230)

Section Objective

■ describe Theodore Roosevelt's rise to the presidency and his accomplishments as President

Introducing the Section

Connecting with Past Learnings
What is meant by progressivism? (Movement that held that social problems could be solved through legislation.) Review with students progressive reforms, first at the local level, then at the state level. *To what level was progressive reform carried next?* (National.)

Key Terms
List key terms on the board. Have students suggest definitions for them. As you come across terms in the lesson, compare definitions given by students to those in the text. Modify student definitions if necessary. **LEP**

Focus

Ask students to list adjectives which describe Theodore Roosevelt's presidency. (Active, reformist, dynamic.) Compare that image with other major Presidents such as Washington, Jefferson, and Lincoln. *Do you think Theodore Roosevelt helped change the nature of the presidency?*

225

University he made the boxing team and reached the finals in competition in his junior year. After graduation he studied law and then, at the age of 23, won a seat in the New York state legislature. But in 1884, when both his wife and mother died (on the same day), Roosevelt gave up politics. He headed west to the raw frontier of Dakota Territory and became a cowboy. One day a rowdy cowboy in a hotel bar bellowed to his friends that Roosevelt—"four eyes"—was going to buy drinks for everyone. Roosevelt responded with several quick punches that felled the cowboy and silenced the room.

His cattle ranch ruined by the harsh winter of 1885–1886, Roosevelt moved back east, remarried, and re-entered politics. From 1889 to 1895 he was a member of the United States Civil Service Commission. He then became president of the New York City Board of Police Commissioners. Never one to be chained to his desk, Roosevelt roamed city streets to make certain that the men in blue were doing their jobs. Thanks to his efforts the city police force became more efficient and honest.

Roosevelt next entered national politics. Campaigning hard for McKinley in the 1896 presidential election, Roosevelt was rewarded with the position of Assistant Secretary of the Navy. When the Spanish-American War broke out in 1898, he organized a voluntary cavalry unit. The press called the unit the Rough Riders because its members were rough-and-tumble cowboys, sheriffs, and football players. Colonel Roosevelt and his men won fame with their dramatic charge up Cuba's San Juan Hill. His image as a hard-charging leader carried Roosevelt to victory in the 1898 race for governor of New York.

As governor, Roosevelt followed progressive policies, including a tax on corporations and new civil service laws. He also took the first steps to preserve the state's natural resources. These moves made Roosevelt popular and led to his offer of a spot on the Republican national ticket in 1900. In the campaign, Roosevelt traveled some 21,000 miles to greet voters. People loved his toothy grin and squeaky voice, and began referring to him as "Teddy" or "TR." The Republican ticket won handily, and Roosevelt became Vice President.

This portrait shows President Theodore Roosevelt with his family in 1903. Roosevelt knew both tragedy and happy times. His first wife died after giving birth to their daughter Alice (center). Roosevelt had five children with his second wife, Edith (second from right). As President, Roosevelt allowed his children to bring their pets, including a pony and snakes, into the White House. **POLITICS** What aspects of Roosevelt's personality and political career contributed to his popularity? 5B

Photo Caption Answer
Students may suggest his ability to overcome physical obstacles, his experience of personal tragedy, his image as a forceful leader and war hero, and his progressive policies.

ROOSEVELT AND THE PRESIDENCY 8G

President McKinley died from an assassin's bullet on September 14, 1901. After taking the oath of office as President, Roosevelt said solemnly: "I wish to say that it shall be my aim to continue, absolutely unbroken, the policy of President McKinley for the peace, prosperity, and the honor of our beloved country."

Roosevelt's remarks proved to be only partially true. William McKinley had been an "Old Guard" Republican—that is, a member of the conservative branch of his party. He had believed that the federal government should follow laissez-faire policies. Roosevelt, on the other hand, felt that government needed to take a more active role in society. In his view, the presidency had a special role to play. He called it a "bully pulpit," meaning that as President he could speak for the country as a whole, defining national goals, problems, and solutions.

Roosevelt also believed that the President could do much more than speak to the nation. The President had a great deal of power to act—to take the initiative in setting new policies, rather than waiting for Congress. Presidents of the Gilded Age had for the most part been passive, but Roosevelt intended to change that. He would *lead*.

ROOSEVELT AND THE TRUSTS 8F, 8G

Roosevelt once called the President the "steward of the people." A steward manages other people's business affairs with their best interests in mind. Roosevelt wanted to work for the people's needs—to do what was right and fair. He called this goal a Square Deal.

One example of the Square Deal concerned trusts (large business combinations). Roosevelt did not oppose all trusts. He saw that in some cases, trusts worked to the advantage of the consumer: compared to smaller companies, they provided better products at lower prices. These "good" trusts Roosevelt preferred to leave alone. But there were other, "bad" trusts—those that used unfair methods to gain a monopoly and then exploited helpless customers. These trusts, Roosevelt decided, must be broken up. As he later explained, "We drew the line against misconduct, not against wealth."

The new President's first attempt at "trustbusting"—breaking up trusts—was directed at the Northern Securities Company. This was a large, powerful firm, run by some of the biggest names in the railroad and finance industries. Its control of three major northwestern railroads gave Northern Securities a stranglehold over rail traffic in the area. In 1902 the federal government filed an antitrust suit against the company. J. P. Morgan, one of Northern Securities' heads, said to Roosevelt: "If we have done anything wrong, send your man [the Attorney General] to my man [Morgan's lawyer] and they can fix it up." But Roosevelt wanted no secret deals. He took Northern Securities to court and won. "The most powerful men in this country were held to accountability before the law," Roosevelt exclaimed.

A cartoon from 1904 shows Theodore Roosevelt wielding his "trustbusting" stick at the railroad and oil industries and "everything in general." During his presidency Roosevelt brought suits against 44 corporations. ECONOMICS Does the cartoonist approve of Roosevelt's trustbusting policies? How can you tell? 8G

Civic Values
Discuss TR's attitude toward the presidency. Have students compare it to their own attitudes toward their civic responsibilities. *How are we all "stewards of democracy"?*

Economics
Have students explain how Roosevelt distinguished between "good" trusts and "bad" trusts. (Good trusts provided better products at lower prices; bad trusts used unfair methods to gain monopolies and exploit consumers.) *Do you agree that there is such a thing as a good trust and a bad trust?*

Have students consider mergers taking place in the economy today. *Do you think that corporate mergers are good or bad for the economy?*

Photo Caption Answer
The cartoon seems to criticize Roosevelt's approach as indiscriminate and overly enthusiastic.

Background In 1901 James J. Hill and J. P. Morgan battled against E. H. Harriman for control of western railroads. Neither side could prevail, so they merged interests, forming the Northern Securities Company.

Background The adjective *bully* means "excellent, dashing," and was a popular expression at the turn of the century.

Roosevelt's victory over Northern Securities signaled the start of a new kind of relationship between government and business. Ever since the Supreme Court's decision against the government In *United States v. E. C. Knight* (page 195), many people had assumed that the Sherman Antitrust Act was an ineffective tool against monopoly. Roosevelt proved them wrong. Spurred on by his victory, he went on to file more than 40 suits against various companies.

Roosevelt also made it clear to the "good" trusts that the federal government would keep watch over their actions. At Roosevelt's urging, Congress created the Bureau of Corporations in 1903. The Bureau collected information on firms so that the Department of Justice could decide whether or not to take them to court. Congress also passed laws that strengthened the Interstate Commerce Act of 1887. One such law—the Elkins Act (1903)—barred railroads from giving refunds to favored customers. Another—the Hepburn Act (1906)—gave the government the power to cut railroad rates it felt were too high. The Hepburn Act also permitted the government to regulate such means of transportation as pipelines.

GIVING WORKERS A SQUARE DEAL 3C

Roosevelt's policy toward trusts was based on the principle of fairness. As he saw it, only firms that were behaving unfairly should be broken up. This same principle was applied to disputes between companies and their workers. Here too Roosevelt looked for a fair solution—a Square Deal.

During a long coal strike in 1902, Roosevelt put his Square Deal into practice. Over 150,000 Pennsylvania miners walked off the job demanding higher pay, shorter hours, and recognition of their union. Instead of taking sides with either the mine owners or workers, the President called both parties to the White House to work out an agreement. No President had ever tried to help settle a strike, but both sides obeyed his call. When the owners appeared unwilling to compromise, Roosevelt insisted that they tone down their demands. Otherwise, he said, the government would take over their mines.

Roosevelt's threat frightened the mine owners into making a compromise. In the end, each side

This picture from 1900 shows young workers in a Pennsylvania coal mine. Long working hours and hazardous conditions led to the coal strike of 1902. Roosevelt's handling of the strike won many miners' approval. ECONOMICS Do you think the government should take a role in solving labor disputes? Why or why not? 3F

received some of what it wanted. Roosevelt thus had proven that the government could act as an umpire to solve disputes. Unlike several earlier Presidents, he had also shown a concern for the

228 UNIT 3   CHANGE AND REFORM

demands of working people. "While I am President," Roosevelt stated, "I wish the laboring man to feel that he has the same right of access to me that the capitalist has; the doors swing open as easily to the wage-worker as to the head of a big corporation—and no easier."

> "**I** wish the laboring man to feel that he has the same right of access to me that the capitalist has."
>
> —*Theodore Roosevelt*

A SQUARE DEAL FOR CONSUMERS 8F, 8G

Consumers, like workers, deserved fair treatment, Roosevelt felt. They had a right to pure, healthy foods and medicines. Yet as Upton Sinclair pointed out in *The Jungle*, the meat Americans ate was anything but pure. Sinclair had written the novel to make people understand the harsh conditions faced by workers in meat-packing plants. But what struck Roosevelt—and the American people as a whole—was Sinclair's descriptions of the meat products themselves. Sinclair, for example, pointed out that the packing plants were overrun with rats:

> There would be meat stored in great piles in rooms; and the water from the leaky roofs would drip over it, and thousands of rats would race about on it. . . . These rats were nuisances, and the packers would put poisoned bread out for them, they would die, and then rats, bread, and meat would go into the hoppers together.

The President appointed a commission to investigate the plants and recommend federal regulation. The result was the Meat Inspection Act (1906). It gave inspectors from the Department of Agriculture the power to see that meat shipped across state lines came from healthy animals and had been packed under sanitary conditions.

Meat was not the only food product often tainted by poor processing. Studies by Dr. Harvey W. Wiley, chief of the Bureau of Chemistry in the De-partment of Agriculture, showed that many food preservatives contained harmful chemicals. Even worse was the widespread use of harmful drugs in over-the-counter medicines. Many of these so-called cures had a high alcohol content. Many others contained cocaine.

Cocaine had been widely praised in the United States in the decades before 1900. Physicians regarded cocaine as a cure for alcoholism and morphine addiction; they also claimed that it could treat sore throats, fatigue, depression, seasickness, and nervousness. The Hay Fever Association regarded cocaine as a miracle drug. Surgeons noted that cocaine was especially useful as an anesthetic in eye operations. In 1885 one American drug company contended that cocaine would be the most important drug of its time, benefiting humanity in ways too numerous to count.

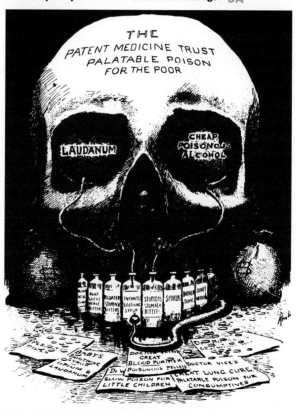

This grim cartoon from 1905 warns of the dangers of drugs such as laudanum (a form of opium), poisonous alcohol, and fraudulent medicines. Many popular "cure-alls," peddled by quack doctors, contained harmful drugs. ETHICS Who, according to the cartoon, were the principal victims of these harmful drugs? 9A

2. *Theodore Roosevelt—* Progressive President. *J. P. Morgan—*Financier, one of the heads of Northern Securities Company. *Upton Sinclair—* Author of *The Jungle,* which exposed unhealthy meat-packing practices. *Harvey W. Wiley—* Chief of the Bureau of Chemistry in the Department of Agriculture.

3. William McKinley was a conservative Republican who believed that the federal government should follow laissez-faire policies. Roosevelt believed that government needed to take a more active role in society and that Presidents should define national goals, problems, and solutions.

4. Actions that aided workers: helped workers and owners of coal mines settle strike, promised workers same access as business leaders. Actions that aided consumers: Meat Inspection Act; Pure Food and Drug Act; "trustbusting"; Bureau of Corporations to collect information on firms.

5. Yes; easier; because television and other communications systems allow the President to appeal directly to the public and the voters expect the President to do that.

Closure

Call students' attention to the beige boxed quotation (p. 229). Ask them to relate this quotation to the main idea of the section. Then have students read Section 2 for the next class period, comparing Taft's presidency with Roosevelt's.

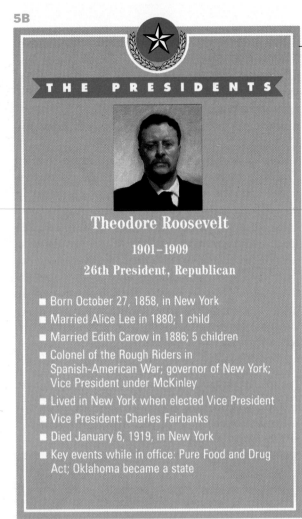

THE PRESIDENTS

Theodore Roosevelt

1901–1909

26th President, Republican

- Born October 27, 1858, in New York
- Married Alice Lee in 1880; 1 child
- Married Edith Carow in 1886; 5 children
- Colonel of the Rough Riders in Spanish-American War; governor of New York; Vice President under McKinley
- Lived in New York when elected Vice President
- Vice President: Charles Fairbanks
- Died January 6, 1919, in New York
- Key events while in office: Pure Food and Drug Act; Oklahoma became a state

Cocaine found its way into numerous products. These included cola drinks bearing such names as Doctor Don's Kola, Delicious Dopeless Koca Nola, Inca Cola, and Kumforts Coke Extract. An early ad for Coca-Cola stressed the drink's value as a "valuable Brain Tonic, and a cure for all nervous affections—Sick Headache, Neuralgia, Hysteria, Melancholy, &c."

By the turn of the century, however, praise for cocaine had turned to horror. People began to realize that cocaine was not a cure for disease. Rather, the drug was so addictive that it ruined the health of those who fell under its power. As one medical journal pointed out, "There is no such thing as an occasional or moderate cocaine user." What had been hailed as a wonder drug became one of the greatest enemies of humanity.

UPTON SINCLAIR (1878–1968) wrote muckraking novels about corruption in big business. Sinclair criticized both capitalism and communism in his description of tensions between the social classes. His novel *The Jungle* tells of a Lithuanian immigrant who works in the Chicago stockyards. The barbaric environment there turns him toward socialism. The book pushed Congress to pass the Pure Food and Drug Act of 1906. Sinclair also helped found the American Civil Liberties Union. **4D, 4F**

Roosevelt recognized the need to protect the American people from harmful drugs. Under the Pure Food and Drug Act (1906), the federal government took the first steps toward banning badly prepared foods and dangerous drugs. The new law required manufacturers to put the contents of foods and drugs on labels. Meanwhile, states were taking their own steps to outlaw cocaine and other addictive drugs. By 1914 nearly every state had passed anti-cocaine laws. With the passage of the Harrison Narcotic Act in 1914, the federal government joined the battle against harmful drugs.

SECTION REVIEW

1. KEY TERMS Square Deal, "trustbusting," Pure Food and Drug Act

2. PEOPLE Theodore Roosevelt, J. P. Morgan, Upton Sinclair, Harvey W. Wiley

3. COMPREHENSION How did Roosevelt's idea of the presidency differ from that of McKinley?

4. COMPREHENSION Which of Roosevelt's actions aided workers? Which actions aided consumers?

5. CRITICAL THINKING Do Presidents today use the presidency as a "bully pulpit"? Is that easier or harder now than it was in Roosevelt's day? Why?

The Presidents
As a child, Teddy Roosevelt was sickly and asthmatic. For students interested in finding out more about TR's early life, recommend *Mornings on Horseback* by David McCullough. Simon and Schuster, 1982.

Biography
Ask students to consider what issues Upton Sinclair might investigate if he were alive today.

2 Filling TR's Shoes

Section Focus

Key Terms New Nationalism ■ Bull Moose Party ■ New Freedom

Main Idea William Howard Taft succeeded Roosevelt as the second progressive President, but found himself opposed both by Roosevelt and the Democrats.

Objectives As you read, look for answers to these questions:
1. How did Taft come to succeed Roosevelt as President?
2. What success did Taft have as President?
3. How did the Roosevelt-Taft split affect the 1912 presidential election?

Roosevelt proved himself a popular as well as active President. In the 1904 election he defeated his rival, Democrat Alton B. Parker, by more than two million votes. Three years later, when a business panic caused the collapse of hundreds of businesses, most people stuck by their President. Roosevelt could well have won re-election in 1908, but he had promised not to seek another term.

With the approach of the 1908 election, therefore, Roosevelt picked William Howard Taft, then Secretary of War and a close friend, to succeed him. Roosevelt wanted Taft to carry on the progressive policies he had begun during his years in the White House. With Roosevelt's backing, Taft easily defeated the old Democratic war horse, William Jennings Bryan.

TAFT'S ROAD TO THE WHITE HOUSE 5B

William Howard Taft contrasted strikingly with his predecessor. Roosevelt had a small frame but the muscular build of a former boxer, Taft was large and stout. While Roosevelt was energetic and aggressive, Taft was slow-moving and cautious. Roosevelt relished the world of politics; Taft came to loathe it.

Born in Cincinnati in 1857, Taft graduated from Cincinnati Law School. His greatest wish, both as a young man and later on in life, was for a career in law. His first job was as assistant prosecuting attorney. At age 30, Taft was appointed to fill a vacancy on the Superior Court of Ohio. Three years later President Harrison appointed him Solicitor General of the United States and then made him a federal judge.

Other opportunities, however, drew Taft away from the field of law. After the Spanish-American War (Chapter 11), President McKinley chose Taft to run the Philippines, which the United States had just acquired from Spain. Taft served as governor of the territory from 1901 to 1904, leaving behind a record of fair and effective leadership. Then in 1904 President Roosevelt elevated Taft to the position of Secretary of War. The two became good friends, and Roosevelt decided that Taft would make a good successor in 1908.

This cartoon by Joseph Keppler appeared in a 1906 issue of *Puck* magazine. It shows Teddy Roosevelt designating William Howard Taft, his Secretary of War, as his successor. POLITICS What impression does the cartoon give of Taft? 9B

SECTION 2

Filling TR's Shoes
(pp. 231–235)

Section Objectives

■ contrast Taft's successes and failures as President with Theodore Roosevelt's presidency
■ describe how the Taft-Roosevelt split affected the 1912 election

Introducing the Section

Connecting with Past Learnings
Review tariff issues by asking students to describe the reasons for tariffs. (Protect U.S. manufacturers and raise money for the government.) *Which groups opposed tariffs? Why?* (Farmers, consumers, and progressives because tariffs created high prices for goods.)

Key Terms
Have students look up the key terms in their texts and write definitions for each term. Ask them to identify the person most associated with each term. Then have them use the terms in a paragraph about the 1912 election. **LEP**

Focus
What does the title of this section imply? (TR left a giant hole when he left the presidency.) Have students create a chart of Taft's achievements and failures as President. Referring to the list if necessary, have students write editorials for or against Taft's re-election in 1912.

Photo Caption Answer
Students may suggest that Taft seems smaller and less impressive than Roosevelt, upon whose shoulder he rests.

Taft's inauguration on March 4, 1909, was a memorable occasion. It was snowy and cold, forcing Taft to take his oath of office inside. "I knew it would be a cold day when I was made President of the United States," he said with a jovial laugh. Then he went on to give one of the longest inaugural addresses in history—much too long for any audience to sit through. Onlookers already had one clue to Taft's presidential abilities: the new President lacked Roosevelt's speaking talent. He also lacked Roosevelt's political instincts, a failing that would cost him dearly.

TAFT AND THE TARIFF 3F, 8F
Taft was a lawyer, not a politician. He had been appointed to his earlier jobs, not elected. Thus it was not until he arrived in the White House that Taft began to learn how to be a politician.

Taft's political education began on the rocky issue of tariffs. Taft believed that tariffs should be reduced. By 1900, American products could compete well against imports and no longer needed special protection. Lowering tariffs thus would not wreck American industry, and it would bring lower prices to consumers. Since the revenue from tariffs went to the government, a drop in tariffs would cost the government money. However, income taxes on corporations could make up the difference.

Many in Congress rejected this reasoning. Earlier Presidents, such as Grover Cleveland, had tried without success to lower tariffs. Backers of the high tariff lay ready to ambush President Taft if he should try to do the same. They did not have long to wait.

Shortly after his inauguration, Taft called Congress into special session to deal with tariffs. The House of Representatives passed a lower tariff bill sponsored by Henry Payne of New York. When the bill got to the Senate, Nelson Aldrich of Rhode Island, a supporter of high tariffs, rewrote it. Instead of a tariff reduction bill, it became a tariff increase bill. When the bill—now called the Payne-Aldrich Tariff—finally came to Taft's desk, it showed much more of Aldrich's influence than Payne's.

Taft was trapped. If he vetoed the bill, he would upset conservative Republicans. If he signed it, he

In this cartoon, President Taft pleads with Senator Nelson Aldrich for a tariff decrease. Theodore Roosevelt's big stick gathers dust in the background. **POLITICS** The cartoonist has hung Roosevelt's portrait on the wall. Why? What message is the cartoonist trying to communicate? 9B

would infuriate progressives. Had he been an experienced politician, Taft might have chosen a third option: to call Senator Aldrich to the White House for some "arm twisting." That is, he could have pointed out to Aldrich that both men were Republicans, and that a senator who rebelled against the head of his own party usually paid a stiff price. He could have hinted that if Aldrich opposed him, the President might ignore Aldrich's recommendations in making federal job appointments in Rhode Island.

Even if Taft had decided not to veto the bill, he could have let the bill become law without his signature. Instead, Taft signed the bill. To add insult to injury, he called it "the best tariff bill that the Republican Party has ever passed." Progressives were in a rage, convinced that Taft simply could not fill Roosevelt's shoes.

MORE TROUBLE FOR TAFT 5B
Another controversy arose in 1909 to drive a wedge between Taft and the progressives. This had to do with Joseph G. "Uncle Joe" Cannon,

Speaker of the House of Representatives. In those days, the Speaker had near-total control over what went on in the House. He appointed all committees and headed the committee that decided when issues would be brought up for a vote. He could muzzle opponents simply by not letting them speak before the House. An "Old Guard" Republican, Cannon used his power to block progressive legislation.

First in 1909, then again in 1910, progressives in the House tried to strip Cannon of his power. As in the tariff dispute, Taft found himself caught in the middle—progressives on one side, conservatives on the other. He never took a clear stand on the issue. In the end the progressives defeated Cannon, but the damage had been done. Taft's standing with progressives sank still further, and the tension between conservative and progressive Republicans was as high as ever.

SOME TAFT VICTORIES 5D, 5C, 8G

While progressives never forgave Taft for his political blunders, he did oversee some important progressive victories. One was the passage of an income tax amendment to the Constitution. With Taft's backing, Congress approved an income tax amendment in 1909. The amendment faced tough opposition in the states, but final ratification came in 1913.

In a host of other ways the Taft administration tried to prove that the Square Deal was alive and well. The Department of Justice launched even more antitrust suits against corporations than Roosevelt had. Under the Mann-Elkins Act of 1910, the Interstate Commerce Commission gained the power to regulate telephone, telegraph, cable, and wireless companies. The Federal Children's Bureau was created to look after the welfare of the nation's youngest citizens. Government employees received an eight-hour work day. A Department of Labor was created to look after the needs of workers.

Taft also pushed for reforms in the election process. Congress passed two critical bills to clean up congressional campaigns. The first, in 1910, forced House members to state publicly how much money their campaigns spent. The second, passed in 1911, made senators do the same.

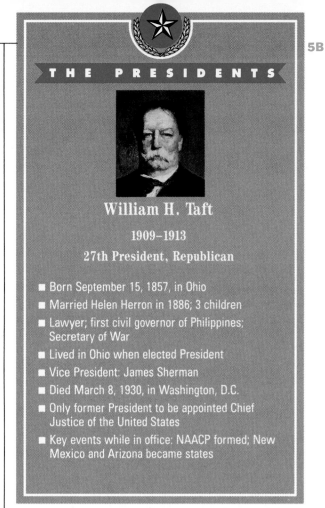

THE ROUGH RIDER'S RETURN 8G, 5C

After leaving the White House, Theodore Roosevelt took a world tour that included an African safari. In mid-1910 he returned to the United States and went on a speaking trip that put him back into the news. The former President's speeches showed that a rift was brewing with Taft. Roosevelt may have been angry that Taft had replaced some of Roosevelt's appointees. Roosevelt had also heard many progressives complain that Taft had abandoned their cause.

Perhaps most importantly, Roosevelt's own views had changed. Instead of sticking to his Square Deal, Roosevelt had moved on to what he called the New Nationalism. This philosophy stressed more liberal reform than the Square Deal: more safety and welfare laws, more taxation of business, and more government regulation of

Civic Values
Ask students to recall important third parties which participated in presidential elections before 1912. (Examples: Know-Nothing; Populist.) Have them examine the map of the election of 1912. *Which political party lost the most through the creation of a third party in 1912?* (Republican.)

Have students discuss their feelings about the two-party system in the United States. Ask them what interests might be represented by a third political party. *Do you think the country would be better or worse off if there were a strong third party?*

Connecting with Literature and Music
Have students reread the words the delegates to the Progressive Party convention sang and consider what sort of message the song communicated. Ask students to suggest political songs or slogans which they feel have been particularly effective in getting a message across. If possible, have students bring in tapes or records of these songs.

Students may wish to write their own songs or slogans on an issue about which they feel strongly.

The Presidents
Taft had the misfortune of serving between two of America's greatest Presidents. For students interested in reading more about Taft's life, suggest "Big Bill Taft" by Stephen Hess, in *American Heritage* magazine, Vol. VII, No. 6 (Oct. 1966).

Background The Taft administration filed 90 antitrust suits in 4 years, as compared with TR's 44 suits in 7.5 years.

APOSTLE OF PROSPERITY.

HE WHO SOWS WIND WILL REAP STORM — BUT FROM GOOD SEED SPRINGS PROSPERITY !

TAKE SPADE AND HOE THYSELF; DIG ON — GREAT SHALT THOU BE THROUGH PEASANT TOIL.

This poster pictures Theodore Roosevelt as the "Apostle of Prosperity." POLITICS What images does the poster use to appeal to voters? What specific political issues, if any, does it address? 8B

large corporations. At a famous speech in Kansas he stated, "property shall be the servant and not the master" of the people.

Roosevelt's new position went well beyond what Taft and his followers could stomach. But many progressives—those frustrated with Taft—loved Roosevelt's New Nationalism. In the 1910 congressional elections, the split between Taft and Roosevelt cost the Republican Party dearly. Many "Old Guard" Republicans lost, and the Democrats gained control of the House of Representatives. Progressive Republicans, feeling that public opinion was moving away from Taft, decided to oppose him in 1912. They formed the National Progressive Republican League and began pushing Senator La Follette for President.

Roosevelt had his eye on the White House too. Ambitious, vigorous, and still young, Roosevelt longed for a return to power. When La Follette collapsed from exhaustion while giving a speech in early 1912, Roosevelt jumped into the race saying, "My hat is in the ring."

> **"M**y hat is in the ring."
>
> —*Theodore Roosevelt, 1912*

The clash between Roosevelt and Taft took place at the Republican convention. As a sitting President, Taft controlled a majority of the convention

delegates. He therefore defeated Roosevelt on the first ballot. By now the two men were personal as well as political enemies. Roosevelt could not bear to let Taft return to the White House, and he was willing to split the Republican Party to bring Taft down. Roosevelt and his followers stormed out of the convention and formed a new party, the Progressive Party. (It was also called the Bull Moose Party because Roosevelt had announced that he was "fit as a bull moose.")

The Progressive Party convention met in August. It chose Roosevelt for President and Hiram Johnson of California (page 208) for Vice President, and approved a platform that reflected the ideas of the New Nationalism. Roosevelt was the star of the show. Resembling an army readying to march to war, the delegates sang:

> Thou wilt not cower in the dust,
> Roosevelt, O Roosevelt!
> Thy gleaming sword shall never rust,
> Roosevelt, O Roosevelt!

Meanwhile the Democrats, after an exhausting 46 ballots, finally chose a candidate. He was a former college professor and governor of New Jersey named Woodrow Wilson. Wilson's program of reform, which he called the New Freedom, stressed the need to protect small businesses from being wiped out by larger companies.

THE ELECTION OF 1912 5B

American voters now faced an odd spectacle. A former President was challenging a sitting President—a man of his own party, a man he had personally chosen to succeed him. A little-known governor was opposing them both. Yet each of the three men called himself a progressive.

Differences did exist among the candidates. Roosevelt felt that only the federal government could achieve progressive reforms, while Wilson placed more faith in actions by the individual states. Taft, despite a solid record of progressive achievements, had the most conservative outlook of the three.

The candidates also differed in style. Roosevelt and Taft spent much of their time attacking each other—Roosevelt showing his usual energy, Taft showing his usual lack of it. Wilson, in contrast,

THE ELECTION OF 1912

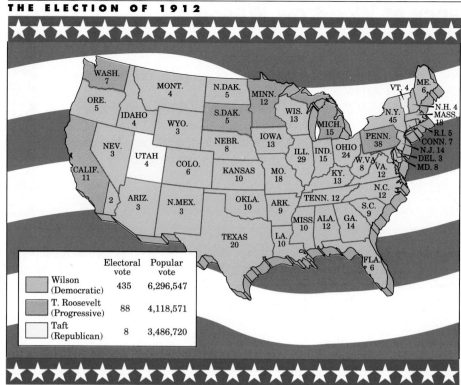

	Electoral vote	Popular vote
Wilson (Democratic)	435	6,296,547
T. Roosevelt (Progressive)	88	4,118,571
Taft (Republican)	8	3,486,720

MAP SKILLS

Woodrow Wilson won the election of 1912 by a landslide. Taft, the incumbent President, won only two states, worth just eight electoral votes. **CRITICAL THINKING** If Theodore Roosevelt had not split the Republican ranks by forming the Progressive Party, how might the results have differed? Why?

5B

spoke directly to the people. Using lofty and stirring words, he said:

> If Jefferson were living in our day he would see what we see: that the individual is caught in a great confused nexus [web] of all sorts of complicated circumstances, and that to let him alone is to leave him helpless as against the obstacles with which he has to contend; . . . therefore, law in our day must come to the assistance of the individual.

Wilson's speaking skills gained him support, as did his message. His program of reform, less radical than Roosevelt's, appealed to voters. Wilson also seemed to be a fresher, more desirable candidate than his veteran opponents. Most importantly, the expected split among Republican voters almost guaranteed him victory.

The November results thus were no surprise. Wilson won 435 electoral votes, compared with 88 for Roosevelt and 8 for Taft. A fourth candidate, Socialist Eugene V. Debs, received no electoral votes but nearly a million popular votes.

The real victor in 1912 was the Progressive Movement. Wilson could count on the support of congressional Democrats (who now controlled both houses of Congress) as well as of liberal Republicans. This gave the new President plenty of muscle to achieve his goals. No wonder many Americans looked forward to Inauguration Day, March 4, 1913.

SECTION REVIEW

1. KEY TERMS New Nationalism, Bull Moose Party, New Freedom

2. PEOPLE William Howard Taft, Joseph G. Cannon, Robert M. La Follette, Woodrow Wilson

3. COMPREHENSION Why did Roosevelt select Taft to succeed him? What weakness of Taft's hampered his ability to govern?

4. COMPREHENSION Why was the Payne-Aldrich Tariff a defeat for Taft?

5. CRITICAL THINKING What steps might Taft have taken to improve his chances for re-election?

Map Skills Answer
Had all of those who voted for Roosevelt voted for Taft, Taft would have had a popular majority. He might have defeated Wilson.

Background   In 1921 Taft became the Chief Justice of the United States, a position he held until 1930. He is the only person to have served as both President and Chief Justice.

Assessment
You may wish to use the Section 2 Review on this page to see how well your students understand the main points in this lesson.

Section Review Answers

1. *New Nationalism*—TR's political policy by 1912. *Bull Moose Party*—Progressive Party, headed by TR. *New Freedom*—Wilson's policy of reform, which stressed the need to protect small businesses.

2. *William Howard Taft*—President after TR. *Joseph G. Cannon*—Powerful speaker of the House of Representatives. *Robert M. La Follette*—Senator who campaigned for presidential nomination of Progressive Party. *Woodrow Wilson*—Defeated Taft and Roosevelt in 1912 to become President.

3. Taft was a friend of Roosevelt's and TR thought Taft would carry on progressive policies. Taft was not a good politician.

4. It was rewritten in the Senate to become a tariff increase bill. Taft would alienate some of his supporters whether he vetoed it or signed it. He signed it and thereby lost support of progressives.

5. Taft could have tried to reconcile opposing factions in the Republican Party; he also could have tried to heal the rift with TR.

Closure
Remind students of the pre-reading objectives in the section opener. Pose one or all of these questions again. Then have students read Section 3 for the next class period, noting the groups helped and ignored during Woodrow Wilson's presidency.

235

Introducing the Section

Connecting with Past Learnings

Review Woodrow Wilson's election in 1912 by asking students to distinguish between Wilson's New Freedom and Roosevelt's New Nationalism. (Wilson wanted less centralization of government.) *Was Wilson considered a progressive?* (Yes.)

Key Terms

Write the key terms on the board and have students create a timeline of the terms, writing the date each act or organization was created, the term, and a short definition. **LEP**

Focus

Have students debate the relative merits of TR, Taft, and Wilson, comparing the three Presidents' actions on such progressive issues as tariffs, regulating business, protecting consumers, and improving working conditions. (TR—activist President who did not take on tariffs, busted "bad" trusts, got Pure Food and Drug Act passed, and acknowledged unions; Taft—unsuccessful at lowering tariffs, continued antitrust fight, got income tax amendment passed, and gave government workers eight-hour day; Wilson—lowered tariffs, cleaned up banking system, strengthened antitrust laws, worked to end child labor.)

236

3F, 3G, 4C, 4D, 4F, 5B, 5D, 7E, 7J, 8G

3 The Presidency of Woodrow Wilson

Section Focus

Key Terms Underwood Tariff ■ Federal Reserve Act ■ Clayton Antitrust Act ■ Federal Trade Commission ■ NAACP

Main Idea Woodrow Wilson followed in the progressive path of Roosevelt and Taft. He had several important victories in Congress, but like his predecessors ignored the needs of African Americans.

Objectives As you read, look for answers to these questions:
1. What reforms did Woodrow Wilson achieve as President?
2. How did African Americans fare under Wilson and the other progressives?

Woodrow Wilson's gifts as a public speaker had helped bring him to the White House. In his Inaugural Address in 1913, those gifts were on full display:

> This is not a day of triumph. It is a day of dedication. Here muster, not the forces of party, but the forces of humanity. Men's hearts wait upon us; men's lives hang in the balance; men's hopes call upon us to say what we will do. Who shall live up to the great trust? Who dares fail to try? I summon all honest men, all patriotic, all forward-looking men, to my side. God helping me, I will not fail them, if they will but counsel and sustain me!

Historians of that time felt that with the possible exception of Jefferson and Lincoln, no President had ever given so moving an address. But who was this spectacled, studious man who had gone from college professor to President in only a few years?

THE CAREER OF WOODROW WILSON 5B

Thomas Woodrow Wilson was born in Virginia in 1856. His father was a Presbyterian minister; his mother's father had been a minister as well. Wilson's parents instilled in their son a deep sense of duty and morality, qualities he would retain throughout his life.

Wilson attended Davidson College in North Carolina for a year, then moved on to Princeton University, where he graduated in 1879. After receiving a law degree, Wilson practiced law for a

short time. Finding little challenge in legal work, he entered Baltimore's Johns Hopkins University. He emerged with a Ph.D. in political science and a desire to teach. After teaching at Bryn Mawr College in Pennsylvania and Wesleyan University in Connecticut, Wilson returned to Princeton.

Wilson loved Princeton. Students called him the best teacher in the university as well as the biggest supporter of the football team. Wilson also did much research and published books and articles that were widely praised. When Princeton needed a new president, Wilson became the obvious choice.

As head of Princeton, Wilson made a number of reforms. He raised academic standards and tightened student discipline. He copied the English practice of having professors tutor students. But when Wilson proposed changes in the basic structure of the university, Princeton's alumni and trustees joined forces against him.

Just when Wilson was running into opposition in Princeton, a new opportunity arose. Democratic party bosses in New Jersey, looking for a candidate they could control, invited him to run for governor. But after his election in 1910, Wilson drove out corrupt officials as he carried out a program of reform. He instituted a direct primary system, a public utility commission, antitrust laws, and workmen's compensation. Wilson also made it possible for the state's cities and towns to adopt the commission form of government (page 210).

Even before his first term as governor had expired, Wilson was recognized as a potential candidate for President. An unknown compared with

---

SUPPORTING THE SECTION

Reinforcement Workbook: Worksheet 38
Reteaching Resources: Worksheet 38
Enrichment and Extension Resources: Primary Source Worksheet 19
Teaching Transparencies: Transparency 38

other Democratic contenders, such as Champ Clark (speaker of the House of Representatives), Wilson had the advantage of having fewer enemies. He won the nomination after a long struggle. In the general election, Taft and Roosevelt split the Republican vote, bringing victory to Wilson.

WILSON AS PRESIDENT 3F, 3G

Wilson resembled Roosevelt in some respects. Like TR, he was strong-willed, intelligent, and well-educated. He also shared Roosevelt's opinion that the President should be a powerful, active leader. On the other hand, Wilson lacked Roosevelt's personal charm. His perfectionism too often came across as snobbery, and he had trouble putting people at ease. One person complained that Wilson's handshake "felt like a ten-cent pickled mackerel in brown paper—irresponsive and lifeless."

One of Wilson's first acts in office was to break a long-standing custom. Presidents traditionally sent messages to Congress in written form and had them read aloud before Congress. Wilson went up to Capitol Hill himself, speaking directly to Congress to demand lower tariffs, his first priority.

Despite Wilson's dramatic show of commitment, he still faced a hard fight. The House passed a bill cutting tariff rates on most goods and eliminating them altogether on a few. To prevent the Senate from rewriting the bill (as it had done before), Wilson went over the heads of the senators and appealed directly to the American people. The public pressure forced the Senate to go along with the House bill. Thus the first bill since the Civil War to dramatically lower tariff rates, the Underwood Tariff, became law in 1913. To make up for the loss in revenues caused by the lower tariffs, the Underwood Tariff included an income tax.

Wilson next turned to bank reform. There were several problems with the nation's banking system. The National Banking Act of 1863 required banks to keep a certain amount of money on hand for their customers. Yet there was no central money supply from which banks could borrow. In times of trouble (such as the Panic of 1907), people rushed to withdraw their deposits, causing banks

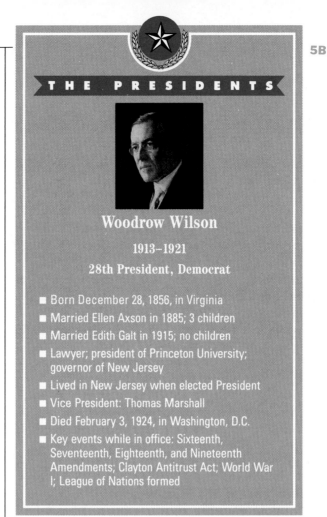

THE PRESIDENTS

Woodrow Wilson

1913–1921
28th President, Democrat

- Born December 28, 1856, in Virginia
- Married Ellen Axson in 1885; 3 children
- Married Edith Galt in 1915; no children
- Lawyer; president of Princeton University; governor of New Jersey
- Lived in New Jersey when elected President
- Vice President: Thomas Marshall
- Died February 3, 1924, in Washington, D.C.
- Key events while in office: Sixteenth, Seventeenth, Eighteenth, and Nineteenth Amendments; Clayton Antitrust Act; World War I; League of Nations formed

to fail. An added problem was that a few huge banks, dominated by finance tycoons such as J. P. Morgan, controlled a large share of the nation's money supply. Critics demanded that this "money trust" be broken up.

People in both parties recognized the need for bank reform, but disagreed over the form it should take. Progressives wanted the federal government to regulate the banking system, while conservatives preferred private control. Politicians also disagreed over whether control over the banking system should be concentrated in one place or divided among several agencies.

Wilson worked with Congress for months carving out a compromise plan—the Federal Reserve Act—that finally became law on December 23, 1913. It set up a three-layered system of regulation. At the top was a Federal Reserve Board,

---

Finally, discuss black Americans' exclusion from progressivism. *What groups were created to help blacks at this time?* (NAACP, National Urban League.)

Developing the Lesson
After students have read the section, you may want to consider the following activities:

Participating in Government
The Democratic sweep in the election of 1912 gave them control of Congress as well as the presidency. In addition, Wilson had made no binding campaign promises to any economic or political group. In light of these facts, have the class discuss the implications of the following statement by historian Arthur Link: "Few Presidents have entered office so completely free to serve the general interest."

Economics
Have students consider the front side of U.S. currency. *What does Federal Reserve Note at the top of the bill mean?* (Issued by Federal Reserve Bank.) Have students find the large letter shown on the left side of the front of the bill to find out which Federal Reserve Bank issued the note.

The Presidents
Have students discuss how Wilson's experience as a university administrator prepared him to run the country.

Background   The panic of 1907 made the country aware of the need to reform its banking system. The National Monetary Commission, headed by Senator Nelson W. Aldrich, was formed and gave testimony to Congress in 1911 and 1912. The Aldrich plan was very favorable to bankers, and therefore was opposed by progressives.

whose members were appointed by the President. On the second level were twelve Federal Reserve Banks located in various cities throughout the nation. These were "bankers' banks," serving private banks rather than individual customers.

On the third and bottom level were local banks in communities across the nation that agreed to belong to the system. These banks could buy stock in the twelve Federal Reserve Banks. They could also borrow money from them. To control the money supply, the Federal Reserve Board set the rate of interest the Federal Reserve Banks would use in lending money to member banks. For example, if the Federal Reserve wished to pump more money into the economy, it would lower its interest rate. That would encourage member banks to borrow money, which they in turn would lend to private customers.

The nation's new banking system did little to reduce the power of the financial tycoons. Yet it did give American banks more flexibility, allowing them to deal with changing conditions in the nation's economy. With a few modifications, this banking system has continued to serve the country to the present day.

REGULATING BIG BUSINESS 8G
Another important economic issue addressed by Wilson was monopoly. Seeing monopolies as a mortal threat to small businesses of every kind, Wilson had demanded in the 1912 campaign that they be broken up. After his election, Wilson moved to strengthen the Sherman Antitrust Act of 1890.

The result was the Clayton Antitrust Act of 1914. The law spelled out in clear terms what corporations could *not* do. They could not, for example, purchase the stock of a competitor. A person who served on the board of directors of one firm could not serve on the board of a competing company. These and other provisions helped both government and business understand the rules governing corporate actions.

To put more teeth into government antitrust efforts, Wilson persuaded Congress in 1914 to create the Federal Trade Commission (FTC). This was an improved version of Roosevelt's Bureau of Corporations, which it replaced. Commission members, appointed to lengthy terms, were in a strong position to do their jobs honestly regardless of political pressure. This made it less likely that any corporation could use its influence to gain special treatment from the government.

Moreover, the FTC filled a gap in government regulation. The Sherman Antitrust Act and the Clayton Act could break up monopolies, but something else was needed to halt unfair practices in everyday business. The FTC had the power to examine corporate practices (such as advertising) and issue "cease and desist orders" when such practices were unfair to competitors. For example, if a firm advertised that its product would last for twenty years and the FTC determined that the claim was false, the FTC could force the firm to stop the ads.

HELPING WORKERS 4D
A key goal of Wilson's New Freedom program was to help American workers. No abuse of working people was more shocking than the institution of child labor. John Spargo's 1906 book, *The Bitter Cry of the Children*, told thousands of readers of the terrible conditions faced by child workers, such as the young boys who labored in coal mines. Spargo wrote:

> The coal is hard, and accidents to the hands, such as cut, broken, or crushed fingers, are common among the boys. Sometimes there is a worse accident: a terrible shriek is heard, and a boy is mangled and torn in the machinery, or disappears in the chute to be picked out later smothered and dead. Clouds of dust . . . are inhaled by the boys, laying the foundation for asthma and miners' consumption.

Wilson supported the Keating-Owen Child Labor Act of 1916, which prevented goods produced by child labor from moving across state lines. When the act was declared unconstitutional by the Supreme Court, Congress passed another bill in 1919. The Court then struck down this law. Opponents of child labor then sponsored a constitutional amendment prohibiting it, but this too failed. Federal protection of child workers would not come until the 1930s.

President Wilson supported federal laws regulating child labor. The Supreme Court, however, ruled that the laws' provisions, including a fourteen-year minimum age for most work and an eight-hour day, violated states' rights and personal freedom. **CONSTITUTIONAL HERITAGE** What arguments could be made against the Court's position? **5D**

Wilson had more success in helping adult workers. His choice for the nation's first Secretary of Labor was sympathetic to labor's concerns. Labor leaders especially liked a part of the Clayton Antitrust Act that exempted labor unions from antitrust laws. Ever since the Pullman Strike of 1894

(page 188), the courts had held that unions were like any other business. They ruled that strikes and boycotts violated the Sherman Antitrust Act, and ordered an end to these worker actions. Now the Clayton Antitrust Act stated that the courts could halt strikes only in cases where property might be damaged. (Later court rulings, however, continued to favor employers in labor disputes.)

For farmers the Wilson administration set up twelve Federal Farm Loan Banks that lent money on more favorable terms than private banks did. These banks provided another example of progressive compromise. Populists too had seen the need for farmers to gain access to money, but their solution had been for the federal government to take over all the banks. Progressives chose a more careful solution, bringing in the federal government only where it was needed.

4C, 4D, 7E

AFRICAN AMERICANS AND PROGRESSIVISM

One area where the federal government did not take action concerned the status of blacks. At the turn of the century, nine-tenths of American blacks lived in the South. They faced discrimination in every area of life—housing, employment, voting. Some blacks moved to the North beginning in the 1880s. This migration increased after

4F, 4C

African American artist Jacob Lawrence created a series of 60 paintings on the theme of black migration. In this scene, black families move from the South to the major northern cities. **CULTURAL PLURALISM** What factors motivated black migration after 1900?

THE PHILLIPS COLLECTION, WASHINGTON, D.C.

Photo Caption Answers
(Top) Students may suggest that the harmful effects of child labor on society necessitated federal regulation where states would not act, and that personal freedom was less an issue than freedom from exploitation. (Bottom) Search for better jobs and a life free from racial discrimination.

Background The first Secretary of Labor, William B. Wilson, worked in coal mines when he was nine years old. He was elected to Congress after serving as secretary-treasurer of the United Mine Workers.

Interested students might find out if there is an office of the National Urban League or the NAACP in your community and call the office to find out what its priorities are today.

C **Cooperative Learning**

Divide the class into small groups. To each group assign a piece of legislation discussed in this section—for example, the Federal Reserve Board Act or the Clayton Antitrust Act. Have each group find more information on the law and paraphrase its main points. Groups can make a bulletin board display of their rewritten acts or present them orally. **LEP**

Addressing Individual Needs

Guided/ Independent Practice
Assign **Reinforcement Workbook** Worksheet 38, which helps students analyze a diagram of the Federal Reserve system.

Reteaching/Correctives
Divide the class into groups of four, and have students in each group assume these roles: an African American, a banker, a business person, and a laborer. Have students evaluate the Wilson presidency from their assumed point of view, and try to persuade other group members to agree with them.

Instruct students to complete **Reteaching Resources** Worksheet 38, which asks them to make a chart listing progressive reforms.

Enrichment/Extension
Instruct students to complete **Enrichment and Extension Resources** Primary Source Worksheet 19. This worksheet guides students in analyzing excerpts from the Niagara Movement's Declaration of Principles.

Assessment

You may wish to use the
Section 3 Review, page 241,
to see how well your students
understand the main points
in this lesson.

Section Review Answers

1. *Underwood Tariff*—Law
that lowered tariff rates in
1913. *Federal Reserve Act*—
Law regulating national
banking system. *Clayton Antitrust Act*—Law specifying
actions forbidden to corporations. *Federal Trade Commission*—Agency
created to strengthen government's antitrust efforts.
NAACP—Group devoted to
securing blacks' legal rights.

2. *Woodrow Wilson*—
President, 1913–1921. *John Spargo*—Author of *The Bitter Cry of the Children*,
which described poor conditions of child laborers.
Booker T. Washington—
Black leader who encouraged
blacks to learn trades.
W.E.B. Du Bois—Black leader who urged blacks to work
against discrimination.
Niagara Falls—Site of meeting in 1905 of Du Bois and
other black leaders.

3. He went directly to
Congress to demand lower
tariffs; and prevented Senate
opposition by appealing
directly to the American
people.

4. Lengthy terms of commission members made them
less susceptible to political
pressure; could issue "cease
and desist orders" when corporate practices were unfair
to competitors.

1900, with black southerners moving in large numbers to northern cities in search of work. Yet conditions there were not much better, for blacks still had to deal with a variety of official and unofficial rules against them.

In fact, violence against African Americans became more common in the North as well as the South. In 1908 a white mob in Springfield, Illinois, rampaged through black neighborhoods, burning homes, looting stores, and beating any black residents they could find. As they marched down the streets, the crowd shouted "Lincoln freed you, we'll show you where you belong." The Illinois militia had to be called out to restore order.

Angry and frustrated, blacks looked to new leaders. Booker T. Washington (page 78), the best-known African American leader of the late 1800s, remained a powerful figure after 1900. Yet many believed his views were outdated. Washington wanted blacks to concentrate first on learning a trade. He thought social and political equality could only come later. But of what use was a job without decent pay, without a decent place to live, without protection against mob violence?

One person asking these questions was the historian W.E.B. Du Bois, a Harvard-educated professor. Du Bois charged that Washington was teaching blacks how to go along with the existing system of racial discrimination. Discrimination would not disappear by itself, said Du Bois; blacks had to fight to get rid of it. In his words, "The way for a people to gain their reasonable rights is not by voluntarily throwing them away." He wanted immediate political action to overturn Jim Crow laws and other forms of discrimination.

> "**T**he way for a people to gain their reasonable rights is not by voluntarily throwing them away."
>
> —*W.E.B. Du Bois*

In 1905 Du Bois and other black leaders met at Niagara Falls. The group published a statement demanding equal opportunities for all blacks, and formed an organization called the Niagara Move-

W.E.B. DU BOIS (1868–1963)
was the first African American
student to receive a doctorate
from Harvard University. By urging blacks to become politically
involved in the fight against
segregation, he departed from
the ideas of Booker T.
Washington. Later in life, disillusioned with the slow pace
of racial progress at home, he
joined the Communist Party and
became a citizen of the West
African nation of Ghana.

4C, 7J

ment. While this group did not attract much national attention, a later group did. In 1909 the National Association for the Advancement of Colored People (NAACP) was formed in New York City. Du Bois and other members of the Niagara Movement joined the NAACP, Du Bois becoming editor of the organization's journal, *The Crisis*. The NAACP devoted its energy to securing blacks' legal rights. It provided blacks with lawyers, pushed for laws against discrimination, and tried to have some existing laws overturned.

While the NAACP concentrated on legal issues, another organization dedicated itself to improving economic conditions for urban blacks. This was the National Urban League, founded in 1910. It helped blacks work for good jobs and fair housing, and tried to make life easier for newcomers to the city.

Blacks needed such organizations in part because the federal government was doing little to help them. The progressive Presidents, for all their talk about fairness and equality, turned a blind eye to racial problems. Roosevelt briefly raised hopes in 1901, when he invited Booker T. Washington to the White House for a meeting. But later, Roosevelt seemed to be more interested in winning the support of white southerners than

---

Biography
Du Bois also advocated that
blacks pursue academic
achievement. Booker T.
Washington wanted blacks to
concentrate on a trade. Ask
students to explain which
proposal they favor.

Background Members of the
Niagara Movement tried to
meet in Buffalo, New York, but
were denied hotel rooms. They
therefore went across the
Niagara River to Niagara,
Canada, for their first
conference.

Background At the time of
its formation, almost all the
officers of the NAACP were
white. Within five years of its
formation, the NAACP had
over 6,000 members and
offices in 50 American cities.

in correcting racial discrimination. In 1906 some black soldiers, whose unit had fought alongside the Rough Riders, were involved in a riot in Brownsville, Texas. Without waiting for a full investigation, Roosevelt had the entire unit kicked out of the army.

If anything, Taft and Wilson were even worse. Taft not only failed to protect blacks' rights, but told a black audience that whites and blacks could never live together on friendly terms. The only solution, he argued, was for blacks to leave the country. In the 1912 election many blacks supported Wilson, attracted by his promise of fair treatment. But once in office, Wilson took a giant step backward. He ordered that black and white workers in the federal government be segregated from one another. Those who objected to this policy lost their jobs. For many African Americans, the political slogans of the day—"Square Deal," "New Nationalism," "New Freedom"—seemed a cruel joke.

SECTION REVIEW

1. KEY TERMS Underwood Tariff, Federal Reserve Act, Clayton Antitrust Act, Federal Trade Commission, NAACP

2. PEOPLE AND PLACES Woodrow Wilson, John Spargo, Booker T. Washington, W.E.B. Du Bois, Niagara Falls

3. COMPREHENSION How did Wilson's handling of the tariff issue prove his leadership qualities?

4. COMPREHENSION In what ways did the Federal Trade Commission strengthen the government's ability to regulate business?

5. CRITICAL THINKING Booker T. Washington and W.E.B. Du Bois had nearly opposite backgrounds: Washington was born a slave, while Du Bois had a college education. How, do you think, did each man's experiences shape his views on the issue of equal rights?

2B, 2C, 5E, 7G, 9D

4 The Progressives and Conservation

Section Focus

Key Terms National Reclamation Act
■ National Park Service Act

Main Idea All three progressive Presidents advanced the cause of conservation. The federal government assumed a central role in both protecting and managing natural resources.

Objectives As you read, look for answers to these questions:
1. Why was conservation necessary?
2. Why is Roosevelt seen as the foremost conservationist among progressives?
3. How did Roosevelt's successors continue his policies?

In December 1901, during his first Christmas as President, Roosevelt broke White House tradition by refusing to put up an official tree at 1600 Pennsylvania Avenue. A strong believer in conservation, Roosevelt shared some Americans' fear that the practice of installing Christmas trees would wipe out the nation's supply of evergreens. Much to his embarrassment, word leaked out the following year that two of his sons had secretly put a

Christmas tree in one of their rooms. In good progressive fashion, Roosevelt compromised for the remainder of his term in office. No official White House tree was allowed, but a small tree was put up in one of the children's rooms.

More than any other person, Theodore Roosevelt made conservation a duty of the federal government. An outdoorsman himself, Roosevelt saw first-hand how easily humans could harm nature.

SUPPORTING THE SECTION

Reinforcement Workbook: Worksheet 39
Reteaching Resources: Worksheet 39
Enrichment and Extension Resources: Primary Source Worksheet 20
Teaching Transparencies: Transparency 39

---

5. Washington's experiences as a slave could have influenced his sense that blacks could only make gains slowly, while Du Bois's achievements taught him that a black man could make progress and that social and legal battles could be won.

Closure

Call students' attention to the beige boxed quotation (p. 240). Ask them to relate this quotation to the main idea of the section. Then have students read Section 4 for the next class period, noting the growth of the conservation movement.

SECTION 4

The Progressives and Conservation
(pp. 241–245)

Section Objective
■ describe the influence of the progressive Presidents on the growth of the conservation movement

Introducing the Section

Connecting with Past Learnings
Discuss with students early American attitudes toward resources. *Why did few Americans in the 1700s and 1800s worry about conservation?* (They felt there were unlimited natural resources, such as land.)

Key Terms
Write the key terms on the board. Have students use their texts to define the terms. Then have them compare and contrast the two acts. **LEP**

Ask students how TR raised the issue of conservation in the national consciousness. (He spoke to Congress on the issue; reserved federal land; got conservation acts passed; created commissions for inland waterways and conservation; called for a National Conservation Congress.) Have them list actions of Taft and Wilson that aimed to preserve and conserve resources. (Taft—protected more land; Wilson—got National Park Service Act passed.) *How did conservation policies of these Presidents exemplify the changing role of government?* (Government became more active regarding the control of resources.)

Discuss with students their feelings about conservation today. *Do you think that environmental issues are treated as important national priorities?*

Developing the Lesson
After students have read the section, you may want to consider the following activities:

Patterns in History
The issue of conservation in the United States has grown, not diminished, in importance. Ask students to describe recent news events which involve environmental issues.

He believed that a national conservation policy would protect the nation's resources better than individual state laws could. Roosevelt knew, however, that such a policy—like his White House Christmas tree policy—had to be reasonable. It had to balance nature's need for protection with the nation's need for resources.

THE IMPORTANCE OF CONSERVATION 2B

Some people recognized the importance of conservation long before Roosevelt took office. As early as the 1870s Secretary of the Interior Carl Schurz opposed the cutting of trees on federal land. During that same decade the American Association for the Advancement of Science warned that Americans were wasting their natural resources.

The damage took many forms. Lumber companies cut forests without replanting. Oil companies let oil and natural gas gush out of the ground unused. Ranchers overgrazed valuable grasslands. Mining companies gouged huge holes in the earth in their search for ores. The federal and state governments, interested more in development than conservation, gave and sold millions of acres of land to individuals and corporations.

Conservationists were divided on how to respond to these problems. Some, such as Sierra Club founder John Muir (page 131), wanted lands protected from development altogether. Others felt that it was more important to develop resources carefully so that they would last longer.

In the late 1800s the federal government took the first steps to meet both groups' demands. Yellowstone became the world's first national park in 1872, and in 1891 the Forest Reserve Act allowed the President to set aside forest lands that would be protected from private development. Using the new law, Presidents Harrison and Cleveland set aside millions of acres of land. Meanwhile, the effort to manage resources received a boost with the creation of the Division of Forestry within the Department of Agriculture. Gifford Pinchot, a leading conservationist named to the position of Chief Forester, tried to teach lumber companies how to harvest trees without destroying forests. These steps marked a promising beginning, but most Americans still did not believe conservation was an important national issue.

ROOSEVELT AND CONSERVATION 2B, 2C

Theodore Roosevelt changed all that. Using the "bully pulpit" of the presidency, he *made* conservation a national issue. In a speech to Congress he demanded that the nation "look ahead" and understand that unless efforts were made to conserve natural resources, those resources would soon be exhausted.
5E

⭐ **Historical Documents**

For an excerpt from a presidential message to Congress on conservation, see page 722 of this book.

Roosevelt backed up his words. With the strong backing of Pinchot, he used his authority under the 1891 act to reserve 150 million acres of federal lands. (That area was larger than the entire nation of France.) Private developers complained to Congress that both Roosevelt and Pinchot were acting without legal authority. Congress responded by limiting Roosevelt's power to reserve land, but before the new law went into effect Roosevelt signed orders protecting even more land.

Roosevelt took other steps to protect resources. The Antiquities Act (1906) allowed him to set aside landmarks of great historical importance as national monuments. Arizona's Petrified Forest, as well as other sites, received protection under the act. To protect wildlife, he created several big-game refuges and over 50 bird refuges.

At the same time, Roosevelt supported attempts to manage resources more efficiently. He got Congress to pass the National Reclamation Act in 1902. Under this law, the President could use money from the sale of federal lands in the West to build dams and other irrigation projects. In this way more land would be made available for farming. Millions of acres of farmland were eventually created. Roosevelt also established the Inland Waterway Commission to come up with a plan for the nation's water resources.

Most of Roosevelt's conservation efforts called for action by the federal government. But he saw an important role for the states as well. Roosevelt brought the message of conservation to the states in 1908 by calling a National Conserva-

Background Many fortunes had been built on the exploitation of the West's natural resources. Lumbermen, mine operators, ranchers, and power companies were among the opponents of conservation.

Background Teddy bears came into being in 1903. They were named after President Theodore Roosevelt. On one of TR's hunting trips, he refused to shoot a bear cub, and the toy was created in his honor.

tion Congress, attended by most governors. "I have asked you to come together now," said Roosevelt at the meeting, "because the enormous consumption of these resources, and the threat of imminent exhaustion of some of them, due to reckless and wasteful use, once more calls for common effort, common action." The governors responded to Roosevelt's call by setting up conservation commissions in their states. Roosevelt in turn created a National Conservation Commission, headed by Pinchot, to assist these state efforts.

2B, 2C

CONSERVATION UNDER TAFT AND WILSON

Taft shared Roosevelt's commitment to conservation, but he received little credit for it at the time because of a controversy that had emerged under Roosevelt. In his desire to protect unspoiled land,

Roosevelt had walked on the edge of (if not over) the law at times. Specifically, he had withdrawn lands other than forest lands from development.

Taft's new Secretary of the Interior, a lawyer named Richard A. Ballinger, felt that Roosevelt had overstepped his authority. He decided to return some non-forest lands Roosevelt had withdrawn. Pinchot was livid. He appealed to Taft to retake the lands in question, and Taft agreed. But Pinchot now regarded Ballinger as an enemy of conservation. When some coal fields in Alaska were sold to private developers, Pinchot demanded that Taft fire Ballinger. Taft, convinced that Ballinger had acted properly, fired Pinchot instead.

The Ballinger-Pinchot controversy soured relations between Taft and conservationists. (It also

This photograph from a 1916 issue of *National Geographic* shows conservationists linking hands around a giant sequoia tree threatened by the lumber industry. ENVIRONMENT Why did Theodore Roosevelt believe conservation deserved national attention? 2C

Photo Caption Answer
He worried that rapid consumption and wasteful use of the nation's resources threatened to exhaust them.

Background   Richard Ballinger had been a popular mayor of Seattle until 1907, when he came to Washington to be Commissioner of the Land Office. In 1909 President Taft asked him to be the Secretary of the Interior. His most avid supporters were Old-Guard, conservative

Republicans who wanted to lessen the centralized conservation movement.

Analyzing Controversial Issues
On the board, write the names *John Muir, Gifford Pinchot,* and *Richard A. Ballinger.* Have students describe each man's point of view on conservation. (Muir—wanted a total ban on use of resources; Pinchot—called for management of resources; Ballinger—strict legal interpretation of conservation laws.) **Which point of view is closest to your own? Which, do you think, is most prevalent today?**

Impact of Geography
Have students examine the map on page 244. **Why does Alaska have so many large national parks?** (The conservation movement had gained strength by the time it became a state, and much of the land is inhospitable to settlement so there is less conflict over its preservation.)

Environment
Have students create a visual image using pictures, photographs, three-dimensional illustrations, or any similar means to express their feelings about the environment. **LEP**

C   Cooperative Learning

Divide the class into small groups. Have each group choose a park or other piece of land in your community which they believe should be conserved. Ask the group to compose a list of reasons why conservation of this land is important and present their arguments. Students may wish to find out from local officials about the legal status of the land. **LEP**

Guided/Independent Reading

Instruct students to complete **Reinforcement Workbook** Worksheet 39. This worksheet guides students in comparing contemporary points of view regarding the Ballinger-Pinchot Affair.

Reteaching/Correctives

Have students work in pairs to develop timelines of important events in the conservation movement during this time period. Have them use the text to develop a list of dates and events to include. Have them explain why conservation was an important issue in the late 1800s and early 1900s.

Instruct students to complete **Reteaching Resources** Worksheet 39, which helps them observe details about the conservation movement.

Enrichment/Extension

Instruct students to complete **Enrichment and Extension Resources** Primary Source Worksheet 20. This worksheet guides students in analyzing TR's ideas on the importance of conservation.

Assessment

You may wish to use the Section 4 Review, page 245, to see how well your students understand the main points in this lesson.

Section Review Answers

1. *National Reclamation Act*— Allowed President to use money from sale of federal lands in the West to build irrigation projects. *National Park Service Act*—Created federal agency to oversee national parks.

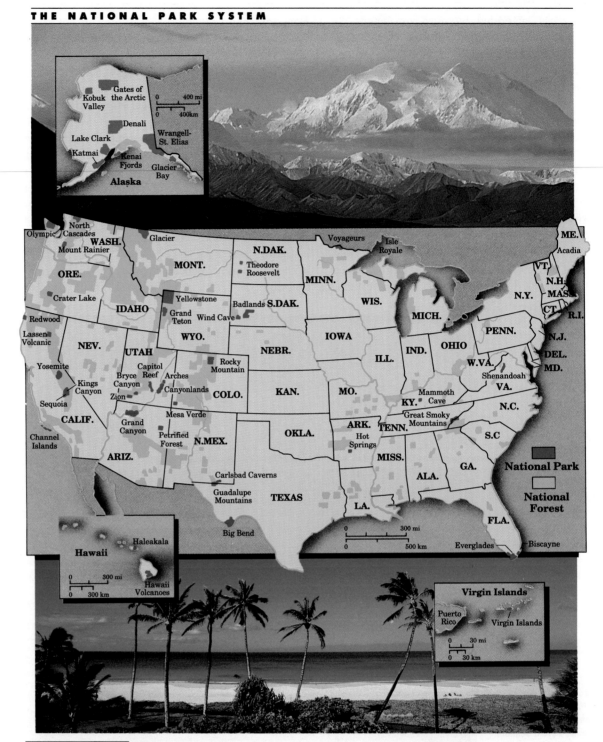

THE NATIONAL PARK SYSTEM

MAP SKILLS 2C

The United States pioneered the preservation of areas of natural beauty and scientific importance. This map shows the location of America's national parks and forests. **CRITICAL THINKING** In which regions do most of the nation's national parks and forests lie? Why, do you think, is this the case?

244 UNIT 3 CHANGE AND REFORM

Map Skills Answers
The West and Alaska. Students may suggest that by the time the government passed conservation legislation, most of the East and South were already developed.

helped wreck Taft's friendship with Roosevelt. After being fired, Pinchot visited Roosevelt, then out of the country, and gave him the full details of this unpleasant episode.) Most of all, the controversy overshadowed Taft's achievements in conservation. Having received permission from Congress to withdraw even more federal land from sale, Taft protected tens of millions of additional acres of land.

Woodrow Wilson's greatest contribution to con-

servation was the National Park Service Act (1916). Yellowstone, the nation's first national park, had been established in 1872. Several more national parks were created in the 1880s and 1890s. The National Park Service Act created a federal agency—the National Park Service—to oversee these areas and other parks to be created later. By the middle of the century the National Park Service would manage more than 23 million acres of parks. The National Park Service dedicated itself to a vital task for the nation's future:

> To conserve the scenery and the natural and historic objects and the wild life therein, and to provide for the enjoyment of the same in such manner and by such means as will leave them unimpaired for the enjoyment of future generations.

SECTION REVIEW

1. KEY TERMS National Reclamation Act, National Park Service Act

2. PEOPLE Gifford Pinchot, Richard A. Ballinger

3. COMPREHENSION List three ways in which natural resources were being wasted in the late 1800s.

4. COMPREHENSION How did Roosevelt use the power of the presidency to advance the cause of conservation?

5. CRITICAL THINKING To what degree is conservation an issue of national importance today? Give two examples of how citizens can conserve natural resources. 2C, 7G

2. *Gifford Pinchot*—Conservationist and Chief Forester. *Richard A. Ballinger*—President Taft's Secretary of the Interior, whose actions alienated conservationists.

3. Lumber companies did not replant; oil companies let oil and natural gas gush, unused; ranchers overgrazed grasslands; mining companies gouged holes in the earth; the government gave and sold land to private individuals and corporations.

4. Delivered message to Congress demanding attention for conservation; reserved over 150 million acres of federal lands; supported Antiquities Act; influenced Congress to pass National Reclamation Act; established Inland Waterway Commission; created National Conservation Congress to help states with conservation.

5. Conservation is of critical national importance. Examples of how citizens can conserve natural resources include: recycling of waste; only using electricity when needed; conserve oil by carpooling, using mass transit, or riding bikes or walking; fix appliances instead of buying new ones.

Closure

Remind students of the pre-reading objectives in the section opener. Pose one or all of these questions again. Then have students read Section 1 of Chapter 11 for the next class period, noting changes in Americans' attitude toward foreign affairs.

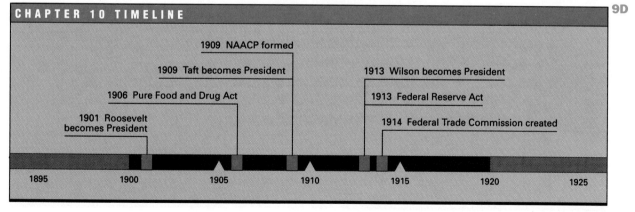

CHAPTER 10 TIMELINE

9D

1909 NAACP formed

1909 Taft becomes President

1913 Wilson becomes President

1906 Pure Food and Drug Act

1913 Federal Reserve Act

1901 Roosevelt becomes President

1914 Federal Trade Commission created

| 1895 | 1900 | 1905 | 1910 | 1915 | 1920 | 1925 |

CHAPTER 10 THE PROGRESSIVE PRESIDENTS, 1900–1920 **245**

Famous Firsts
Ask students to consider which of these events was most significant when it occurred and which of these events is most significant today.

Background In 1901 there were 45 million acres in government preserves; by 1908, there were almost 195 million.

Chapter 10 Review Answers

Key Terms
1. Pure Food and Drug Act
2. Federal Reserve Act
3. NAACP
4. National Reclamation Act
5. Underwood Tariff
6. Clayton Antitrust Act
7. Federal Trade Commission

People to Identify
1. Taft's Secretary of Interior who supported development.
2. Speaker of the House who blocked progressive legislation.
3. NAACP member who called for political action to overturn discrimination.
4. Chief Forester, appointed head of the National Conservation Commission by Roosevelt.
5. Writer who exposed the terrible conditions of child labor.
6. Black leader who said that blacks should work within the system to gain equality.
7. Chief of the Bureau of Chemistry whose studies exposed harmful chemicals.

Places to Locate
1. B   4. A
2. E   5. C
3. D

Reviewing the Facts
1. Roosevelt believed that the government needed to take an active role in society and that the President should take initiative in setting new policies.
2. A "good" trust provided products at lower prices, while a "bad" trust used unfair methods to gain a monopoly. He took companies to court, established the Bureau of Corporations, and called for regulatory laws.
3. He appointed a commission, resulting in the Meat Inspection Act and the Pure Food and Drug Act.

CHAPTER 10 SUMMARY

SECTION 1: Theodore Roosevelt brought progressivism to the White House.

- Roosevelt was an activist President. His "Square Deal" included vigorous business regulation and government intervention to resolve disputes between companies and their workers.

- Investigations of meatpacking plants and the contents of foods and medicines led to consumer protection laws.

SECTION 2: William Howard Taft succeeded Roosevelt in 1909.

- Although he supported and won many progressive reforms, Taft's political inexperience led to several controversies that undermined his leadership.

- In the 1912 presidential election, progressive Republicans supported Roosevelt's third-party candidacy. As a result, the Republican vote was split, and Woodrow Wilson, the Democratic candidate, won the election.

SECTION 3: Woodrow Wilson continued the progressivism of his two predecessors.

- Wilson pursued tariff reduction, banking and business regulation, and aid to farmers and laborers.

- African Americans, most of whom lived in the South, faced segregation and severe racial discrimination in every area of their lives.

- Progressivism fueled increased demands for full civil rights for African Americans. These demands went unheeded by the progressive Presidents.

SECTION 4: Conservation of the nation's natural resources was pursued by all three progressive Presidents.

- Rapidly growing industries had used resources carelessly and wastefully, doing severe damage to the environment in many areas.

- Roosevelt made conservation a high priority, establishing national parks and refuges to protect wildlife and natural resources. Taft and Wilson followed Roosevelt's lead.

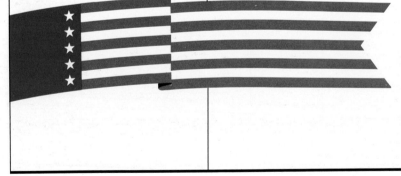

KEY TERMS ●

Use the following terms to complete the sentences below.

Clayton Antitrust Act
Federal Reserve Act
Federal Trade Commission
NAACP
National Reclamation Act
Pure Food and Drug Act
Underwood Tariff

1. Upton Sinclair's *The Jungle* sparked passage of the _____ .
2. The nation's banking system was brought under federal regulation by the _____ .
3. The _____ was formed in 1909 to promote legal rights for blacks.
4. The _____ made more land available for farming.
5. The first bill to dramatically lower tariff rates after the Civil War was the _____ .
6. The _____ clearly spelled out illegal corporate practices.
7. The _____ was formed to stop businesses from using unfair practices.

PEOPLE TO IDENTIFY ●

Identify the following people and tell why each was important.

1. Richard A. Ballinger
2. Joseph G. Cannon
3. W.E.B. DuBois
4. Gifford Pinchot
5. John Spargo
6. Booker T. Washington
7. Harvey W. Wiley

---

4. Tariffs and the Speaker of the House caused problems. He got the income tax amendment passed, continued antitrust suits, and adopted reforms in the election process.
5. It caused a split in the Republican party, resulting in the election of Woodrow Wilson.
6. Wilson won passage of the Federal Reserve Act, which included the Federal Reserve Board, twelve Federal Reserve Banks, and local banks.

PLACES TO LOCATE ●

Match each of the letters on the map with the places that are listed below.

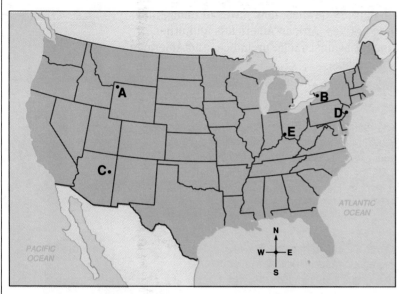

1. Buffalo, New York
2. Cincinnati, Ohio
3. Princeton, New Jersey
4. Yellowstone National Park
5. Petrified Forest National Park, Arizona

REVIEWING THE FACTS ▲

1. How did Roosevelt's policies as President differ from those of McKinley?
2. According to Roosevelt, what was a "good" trust? A "bad" trust? What steps did he take to regulate corporations?
3. What steps did the Roosevelt administration take to protect consumers?
4. What issues caused problems between President Taft and progressive Republicans? What successes did Taft have as President?
5. How did the rift between Taft and Roosevelt affect the 1912 presidential election?

6. What reforms did Woodrow Wilson make in the nation's banking system?
7. What steps did Wilson take to regulate large corporations? To help organized labor?
8. How did W.E.B. DuBois differ from Booker T. Washington in his assessment of how African Americans could best improve their status?
9. What factors encouraged the rise of the conservation movement?
10. How did Theodore Roosevelt affect the conservation movement in the United States?

CRITICAL THINKING SKILLS ▲

1. **ANALYZING A QUOTATION** Reread the Wilson quotation on page 235. Against what criticism is he defending himself? Why does he mention Jefferson?

2. **FORMING A HYPOTHESIS** On what grounds might the Supreme Court have struck down laws designed to ban child labor?

3. **WEIGHING BOTH SIDES OF AN ISSUE** What are the pros and cons of electing officials who have extensive experience in government as opposed to candidates who have no experience in government?

WRITING ABOUT TOPICS IN AMERICAN HISTORY ■

1. **CONNECTING WITH LITERATURE** A selection from *Ragtime* by E. L. Doctorow appears on pages 788–790. Read it and answer the questions. Then answer the following question: What groups of people in American society gave the strongest support to laws protecting workers?

2. **APPLYING THEMES: PLURALISTIC SOCIETY** Find out more about the views of African American leaders W.E.B. Du Bois and Booker T. Washington. Then write an imaginary exchange of letters between the two men. On what points might the two leaders agree? On what might they disagree?

9. The settlement of the frontier made Americans aware of the space limitations and the need to conserve.
10. He got Congress to pass the National Reclamation Act and the Antiquities Act, and he called a National Conservation Congress.

Critical Thinking Skills
1. Critics charged progressive government with being radical and meddling in the economy. Jefferson had radical ideas for his time, such as democracy.
2. Congress did not have the power to regulate labor under the Tenth Amendment.
3. Continuity and knowledge of the system are pros for the experienced candidate, while distance from voters' concerns and likelihood for corruption are cons. A new candidate has a fresh viewpoint, but is inexperienced and has fewer political connections.

Writing About Topics in American History
1. Working people and people with progressive ideas were likely to support laws protecting workers.
2. Students might note that Washington and Du Bois would agree that economic and social advancement was a worthy goal. However, Washington felt blacks should achieve such advancement first; Du Bois felt it could only be achieved after equality with whites was achieved.

7. The Clayton Antitrust Act and the Federal Trade Commission were created to regulate business. The Clayton Antitrust Act helped organized labor, as it exempted labor unions from antitrust laws.

8. Du Bois felt that Washington was teaching blacks to go along with the existing system of racial discrimination. Du Bois called for immediate political action and believed blacks must fight discrimination.

Chapter Review exercises are keyed for student abilities:
● = Basic
▲ = Average
■ = Average/Advanced

Introducing the Feature

Have students compare the reasons why European settlers came to America in the early colonial period with the reasons why immigrants came to the United States at the beginning of the twentieth century. (In both eras, the promise of economic opportunity and of religious and political freedom drew immigrants to America.) *In what ways did women and ethnic and racial minority groups participate in the reforms of the Progressive Era?* (Students should consider the issues of equality of citizenship rights, broadened participation in urban politics, and labor reforms.)

Teaching Multiculturalism

Citizenship

How did Mary Tape secure her daughter's right to enroll in public school in San Francisco? (By bringing a lawsuit against the city and winning.) *How did the city continue to deny equality to Chinese children?* (It built a separate school for them.)

Constitutional Heritage

Remind students that during the 1890s "Jim Crow" laws authorized segregation in the South, and that the Supreme Court sanctioned such laws in its 1896 *Plessy v. Ferguson* decision by declaring "separate but equal" facilities constitutional. *What form of segregation did Dr. Daniel Hale Williams challenge in 1891?* (Segregation in hospitals, by opening an integrated hospital in Chicago.) *What contributions did Mary Church Terrell make to the cause of equal rights for African Americans?* (She helped found the National Association of Colored Women; she lectured on civil rights and worked for equal rights for women.)

UNIT 3: American Mosaic

★ *A Multicultural Perspective* ★

As the twentieth century dawned, new waves of immigrants came to the United States, African Americans and other ethnic groups fought against racial prejudice, and American women won voting rights.

In 1884 **Mary Tape** (right) tried to enroll her daughter in a public school in San Francisco. The Board of Education, reflecting the widespread practice of discriminating against Chinese Americans, rejected her application. Tape refused to give in. "Will you please tell me!" she asked in a letter to the Board. "Is it a disgrace to be born a Chinese?" Tape took the city to court and won. However, the city maintained segregation by building a separate school for Chinese children.

Even after the abolition of slavery, racial segregation touched every aspect of American life, including medicine. Not until 1891 were there any hospitals that would treat both black and white patients. The first such hospital was founded in Chicago by **Daniel Hale Williams** (left), an African American doctor. Williams also started a school to train African American nurses, since no white nursing school would accept them. Williams is best known, however, for performing the first successful open-heart operation in history in 1893.

Madame C. J. Walker (above), the first self-made millionaire among American women, was an unlikely success story. Born a sharecropper's daughter in Louisiana in 1867, married at fourteen and widowed at twenty, she joined thousands of other African Americans seeking jobs in the North. Walker settled in New York and started a thriving cosmetics firm that propelled her into the ranks of the city's wealthiest, best-known citizens.

In the United States, where ability mattered more than formal training, scientific research flourished. **Josef Murgas** came to the United States from Hungary in 1896 and settled in Pennsylvania. A Catholic priest, Murgas performed numerous community services. Yet he also found time to satisfy his lifelong interest in experimentation. In 1905, using a wireless telegraph system that he had devised, Murgas transmitted the first wireless signals. (Guglielmo Marconi's advances in wireless technology were based on Murgas's work.) Later, when his native Czechoslovakia became independent, Murgas offered to work for the new government. Citing his lack of formal training, the Czech government turned him down.

Passed in 1913, California's Webb Act specifically denied Japanese Americans the right to own land in that state.

Science and Technology

Point out to students that Rev. Joseph Murgas obtained a patent for his "wireless telegraphy apparatus" in 1904, and that Guglielmo Marconi and Dr. R. A. Fessenden used many of Murgas's ideas in a radio they marketed in 1912. *What explanation did the Czech government give for refusing Murgas's offer of his scientific talents?* (Murgas's lack of formal training.)

"OVER THE FALLS AND STILL ALIVE!"

shouted newspaper headlines in October 1901. **Annie Edson Taylor** (left), a 43-year-old Michigan schoolteacher, had just become the first person to go over Niagara Falls in a barrel and live. Taylor thought the stunt would make her rich. Instead she wound up nearly penniless, living near Niagara Falls and autographing postcards for tourists.

Fittingly, the life of **Mary Church Terrell** (above) spanned the years from the Emancipation Proclamation (1863) to the Supreme Court's ruling against school segregation (1954). A tireless fighter for the rights of African Americans, Terrell helped found the National Association of Colored Women in 1896 and made numerous lecture tours. She also worked for equal rights for all women. In 1953, at the age of 89, Terrell led a successful fight to desegregate lunch counters in Washington, D.C.

In April 1912 the luxury liner *Titanic* struck an iceberg and sank in the Atlantic. **Isidor** and **Ida Straus** (shown right, on the cover of Yiddish sheet music) were among the 1,500 victims. Isidor Straus, once a Jewish immigrant from Germany, was now an immensely rich owner of Macy's department store in New York City. On the *Titanic,* when the order was given to board the lifeboats, Isidor and Ida chose to stay behind. They declared that they had lived happily together for 40 years and that younger people should take their places.

In their often bitter struggles against management, workers of the late 1800s and early 1900s had a powerful ally in Mary Harris Jones. **Mother Jones** (right), as she was called, was an Irish immigrant whose experiences as a poor dressmaker brought her into the labor movement. "Labor," she later wrote, "must bear the cross for others' sins." For decades she traveled the country, organizing workers and fighting the use of child labor.

Geographic Themes: Movement

Have students prepare a memoir that Madame C. J. Walker might have written about her rise from poverty to wealth. Memoirs should consider Walker's reasons for moving from the rural South to the North, her response to life in urban New York, and the obstacles she overcame as an African American woman to achieve success in business.

Ethics

Discuss with students the decision of Isidor and Ida Straus to give up their places in the *Titanic*'s lifeboats to younger passengers. Have students consider what they might have done if they were in the couple's place. Ask students to think of comparable examples of Americans acting selflessly in times of disaster.

Students might be interested to know that the ship *California* was close enough to the *Titanic* (about 19 miles away) to have saved all of its passengers, but the *California*'s wireless operator had retired for the night just minutes before the *Titanic* sent out its first distress call.

Economics

Discuss with students what Mother Jones meant when she wrote "Labor must bear the cross for others' sins." ***Who are the "others" to whom she was referring?*** (Students might suggest factory owners, management, and politicians.) ***What contributions did Mother Jones make to the labor movement in the United States?*** (She organized workers and fought against the use of child labor.)

Historians' Corner

Vocabulary Preview

Be sure students understand the following terms: *utilitarian*—Stressing the value of practical qualities. *ministration*—The act of aiding. *philanthropic*—Charitable. *manifestation*—Demonstration of existence. *encroachment*—Gradual intrusion.

Analyzing Historical Issues

These passages present the personal interests of three reformers during the Progressive Era. W.E.B. Du Bois reflects the desire to apply scientific method to improving society. Jane Addams discusses the mutual interests of politicians and philanthropic women. Robert M. La Follette focuses on making government the instrument of the people, not of the "powerful few."

How do the concerns of these reformers reflect the attitudes of their times? Are any of these concerns relevant today?

Critical Thinking Answers

1. Du Bois was interested in applying a scientific attitude to solving the problems of black Americans. Addams's interest in "big human needs" found expression in settlement work. La Follette's interest in restoring political power to voters took shape in reforms he sponsored as governor and senator.

2. Women did not yet have the right to vote or the tradition of participating in politics.

3. On the need for citizen participation in government to solve society's problems.

HISTORIANS' CORNER

Voices of Progressivism

The histories of reform movements such as progressivism are shaped by the goals and ideals of dedicated people. Locally and nationally, the Progressive Movement addressed many different issues. These reflected the individual concerns of the men and women who took part in it. Here, three well-known progressives describe some issues that concerned them.

W.E.B. Du Bois

The main result of my schooling had been to emphasize science and the scientific attitude. . . . The triumphs of the scientific world thrilled me: the X-ray and radium came during my teaching term. . . .

On the other hand the difficulties of applying scientific law and discovering cause and effect in the social world were still great. . . . But . . . facing the facts of my own social situation and racial world, I determined to put science into sociology through a study of the problems of my own group. . . .

I entered this primarily with the utilitarian object of reform and uplift; but nevertheless, I wanted to do the work with scientific accuracy.

From W.E.B. Du Bois, *Dusk of Dawn* (New York: Harcourt, Brace, 1940); reprinted in *The Progressives,* ed. by Carl Resek (Indianapolis: Bobbs-Merrill, 1967), pp. 44-45.

Jane Addams

When a great political party asks women to participate in its first convention, and when a number of women deliberately accept the responsibility, it may indicate that public-spirited women are ready to . . . go back to the long historic role of ministration to big human needs. After all, our philanthropies have cared for the orphans whose fathers have been needlessly injured in industry; . . . solaced men and women [who] could find no work to do. . . . Remedial legislation for all these human situations is part of the Progressive Party platform; and as the old-line politician will be surprised to find . . . that politics have to do with such things, so philanthropic women . . . will be surprised to find that their long concern for the human wreckage of industry has come to be considered politics.

From Jane Addams, "My Experiences as a Progressive Delegate," *McClure's,* 1913, reprinted in *The Progressives,* ed. by Carl Resek (Indianapolis: Bobbs-Merrill, 1967), pp. 327-328.

Robert M. La Follette

With the changing phases of a twenty-five-year [political] contest I have been more and more impressed with the deep underlying singleness of the issue. It is not railroad regulation. It is not the tariff, or conservation, or the currency. It is not the trusts. These and other questions are but manifestations of one great struggle. The supreme issue, involving all the others, is *the encroachment of the powerful few upon the rights of the many.* This mighty power has come between the people and their government. Can we free ourselves from this control?

From Robert M. La Follette, *La Follette's Autobiography,* p.321. Copyright © 1960. Reprinted by permission of the University of Wisconsin Press.

Critical Thinking

1. What specific aspects of social reform interested each of these writers? How can you relate these to their careers?

2. What do Addams's comments reveal about women's political status in 1913 when the progressives had their party convention?

3. On what general ideas would these three progressives agree?

W.E.B. Du Bois

(1868–1963) taught history and economics at Atlanta University after getting his doctorate at Harvard University. His research as a historian and sociologist is still used by historians today.

Jane Addams

(1860–1935) was a leading progressive reformer who believed in the need for research into the causes of poverty and crime. She wrote and lectured on a wide variety of social problems.

Robert M. La Follette

(1855–1925) served as a congressman from Wisconsin, and then governor and senator. He ran as the Progressive Party's candidate in the presidential elections of 1924.

UNIT FOUR

Becoming a World Power

CHAPTERS IN THIS UNIT

THEMES IN AMERICAN HISTORY

 Geography   By the end of the 1800s, with the West settled and industrial output rising, the United States looked abroad for new resources and markets.

 Economic Development   The nation's commercial interests in Latin America produced active American involvement in the region.

Global Interactions   A war with Spain and American entry into World War I were signs of a growing American willingness to use force abroad.

 Pluralistic Society   Government efforts to enforce loyalty during World War I proved controversial; still, Americans from all backgrounds joined together to support the war effort.

Constitutional Government   The task of mobilizing for World War I gave the federal government an expanded role in the life of the nation.

This unit examines the nation's growing involvement in international affairs, beginning in the late 1800s when interest in exporting American culture and finding new markets led to expansion in the Pacific, United States support of free trade in Asia, and restricted Asian immigration. The causes and effects of the Spanish-American War are detailed as well as the debate it raised over America's role as an imperial power.

Students will learn about the increasing involvement of the United States in Latin American affairs, the significance of the construction of the Panama Canal, and United States economic and military intervention in the region in the first decades of the 1900s.

The unit also describes the movements and events in Europe leading to the outbreak of World War I, the early course of the war, the reasons for United States entry, the American experience in battle and on the home front, the global effects of the war, and the postwar movement in the United States away from international involvement.

Chapter 11 ■ A Force in the World

	SECTION OBJECTIVES	SECTION RESOURCES
Section 1 **Interest** **in Expansion**	■ explain the arguments for and against American expansion in the late 1800s	● **Reteaching Resources:** Worksheet 40 ▲ **Reinforcement Workbook:** Worksheet 40 ▲ **Teaching Transparencies:** Transparency 40
Section 2 **The "Splendid** **Little War"**	■ explain the significance of the Spanish-American War	● **Reteaching Resources:** Worksheet 41 ▲ **Reinforcement Workbook:** Worksheet 41 ■ **Enrichment and Extension Resources:** Primary Source Worksheet 21 ▲ **Teaching Transparencies:** Transparency 41
Section 3 **The Debate** **over Imperialism**	■ explain the debate over the acquisition of overseas territory and its outcome	● **Reteaching Resources:** Worksheet 42 ▲ **Reinforcement Workbook:** Worksheet 42 ■ **Enrichment and Extension Resources:** Primary Source Worksheet 22 ▲ **Teaching Transparencies:** Transparency 42
Section 4 **Involvement** **in Asia**	■ analyze the role of the United States in Asian affairs	● **Reteaching Resources:** Worksheet 43 ▲ **Reinforcement Workbook:** Worksheet 43 ▲ **Teaching Transparencies:** Transparency 43

The list below shows Essential Elements relevant to this chapter. (The complete list of Essential Elements appears in the introductory pages of this Teacher's Edition.)

Section 1:   1A, 1B, 1C, 4C, 4F, 9A
Section 2:   1A, 1B, 1C, 9A, 9G
Section 3:   1A, 1B
Section 4:   1A, 1B, 1C, 4B, 9A, 9D

Section Resources are keyed for
student abilities:
● = Basic
▲ = Average
■ = Average/Advanced

CHAPTER RESOURCES

Geography Resources: Worksheets 21, 22
Tests: Chapter 11 Test

Chapter Project : Global Interactions

Have students work in groups to write skits on American expansion between 1895 and 1910. They may choose to write about economic causes of expansion, causes of the Spanish-American War, expansion in Asia, or the conflict between imperialism and American democratic ideals. Characters in the skits should include historic figures, such as Henry Cabot Lodge, Queen Liliuokalani, President Cleveland, Carl Schurz, and John Hay. Students may present their skits as a videotape.

Homework Options

Each section contains activities labeled "Addressing Individual Needs." You may wish to choose from among these activities when assigning homework.

Provisions for Limited English Proficiency (LEP)

Several suggested activities may be particularly helpful for teachers of students with limited English proficiency. These activities have been marked throughout the Teacher's Annotated Edition with the symbol **LEP** .

BIBLIOGRAPHY AND AUDIOVISUAL AIDS

Teacher Bibliography

Dulles, Foster R. *Prelude to World Power: American Diplomatic History, 1860–1900.* Macmillan, 1971.

Karnow, Stanley. *In Our Image: America's Empire in the Philippines.* Random House, 1989.

Mahan, Alfred Thayer. *The Influence of Sea Power upon History, 1660–1783.* Little, Brown, 1890.

Pearce, Jenny. *Under the Eagle: U.S. Intervention in Central America and the Caribbean.* South End Press, 1983.

Rosenberg, Emily S. *Spreading the American Dream: American Economic and Cultural Expansion 1890–1945.* Hill and Wang, 1982.

Student Bibliography

Crane, Stephen. *The War Dispatches of Stephen Crane.* R. W. Stallman and E. R. Hagemann, eds. Greenwood, 1977.

Swanberg, W. A. *Citizen Hearst.* Scribners, 1961.

Werstein, Irving. *Eighteen Ninety-Eight: The War and the Philippine Insurrection Told with Pictures.* Cooper Square, 1966.

Literature

Michener, James. *Hawaii.* Random House, 1959.

Films and Videotapes*

United States Expansion: Overseas (revised). 13 min. COR/MTI. The United States becomes a world power with its expansion to the Hawaiian Islands, Cuba, Puerto Rico, the Philippines, the Panama Canal, and the Virgin Islands.

Filmstrips*

Emergence of the United States as a World Power (set of 3). GA. Reviews early American neutrality, the growth of imperialism, the impact of World War I, and subsequent policy developments. Also available in video.

Nationalism (set of 2). GA. American nationalism during the nineteenth and twentieth centuries. Also available in video.

United States as a World Power: 1890s–1970s (set of 3). NATGEO. Introduces diplomatic efforts, and military conflicts and foreign policies that helped define the role of the U.S. in international affairs. Titles include: Before 1921; 1921–1945; After WW II.

Computer Software*

American History: Becoming a World Power, 1865–1912 (Apple with 48K; Commodore with 64K; IBM with 128K). WORD. Options focus on different topics: Reconstruction, industrial growth, the frontier, the farm, the cities, and foreign policy. No graphics. Questions can be taken in either test or tutorial mode.

*For a complete guide to audiovisual sources, see the introduction to this book (page Txx).

Chapter 11

A Force in the World

(pp. 252–269)

This chapter examines American involvement in world affairs in the late 1800s. It discusses how United States expansion, war with Spain, and involvement in Asia led to internal debate over imperialism.

Themes in American History

- Global interactions
- Economic development
- Geography

Chapter Objectives

After students complete this chapter, they will be able to:

1. Explain the arguments for and against American expansion in the late 1800s.
2. Explain the significance of the Spanish-American War.
3. Explain the debate over the acquisition of overseas territory and its outcome.
4. Analyze the role of the United States in Asian affairs.

Chapter Opener Art

In Memory of My Cruise, China, Japan, and Philippine Islands, silk, gold, and silver thread on a silk ground with watercolor and photograph.

An expanded navy was one sign of growing American interest in overseas expansion. In 1904 an American sailor created this remarkable textile painting to commemorate his voyage to Asia.

CHAPTER SUPPORT MATERIAL	**Reinforcement Workbook:** Worksheets 40–43
	Reteaching Resources: Worksheets 40–43
	Enrichment and Extension Resources: Primary Source Worksheets 21, 22
	Geography Resources: Worksheets 21, 22
	Teaching Transparencies: Transparencies 40–43
	Tests: Chapter 11 Test

11 A Force in the World
(1880–1910)

SECTION 1

Interest in Expansion
(pp. 253–256)

1A, 1B, 1C, 4C, 4F, 9A

1 Interest in Expansion

Section Focus

Key Terms imperialism ■ protectorate

Main Idea By the late 1800s Americans were showing new interest in world affairs.

Objectives As you read, look for answers to these questions:
1. What factors led to a growing interest in expansion in the late 1800s?
2. How did the United States take possession of Samoa? Hawaii?

In the decades following the Civil War, few Americans had much interest in foreign affairs. Rapid economic growth and the settlement of the West absorbed the energy and attention of Americans. When it came to foreign affairs, the American people and their government preferred having as few ties as possible with other nations.

Then, in the 1890s, Americans began to "look outward." An article from the *Washington Post* in 1898 expressed this new international outlook:

> A new consciousness seems to have come upon us—the consciousness of strength—and with it a new appetite, the yearning to show our strength. . . . Ambition, interest, land hunger, pride, the mere joy of fighting, whatever it may be, we are animated by a new sensation.

THE EUROPEAN EXAMPLE 1B
What accounted for this change in outlook? One factor was the desire to compete with Europe. Since the 1870s countries in Europe—especially Great Britain and France—had been setting up colonies around the world. By 1900 they controlled

much of Africa and Asia. Europeans held most of the Pacific islands as well. Great Britain was "reaching out for every island in the Pacific," warned Senator Henry Cabot Lodge in 1895. "As one of the great nations of the world, the United States must not fall out of the line of march." Theodore Roosevelt agreed that America must meet the challenge. "If we shrink from the hard contests," said TR, "then the bolder and stronger peoples will pass us by, and will win for themselves the domination of the world."

> " **A**s one of the great nations of the world, the United States must not fall out of the line of march."
> —*Senator Henry Cabot Lodge*

THE POWER OF NEW IDEAS 1B, 4F
As Roosevelt's words suggest, the ideas of Social Darwinism (page 160) encouraged expansionism. "The rule of the survival of the fittest applies to nations as well as to the animal kingdom,"

CHAPTER 11   A FORCE IN THE WORLD, 1880–1910   **253**

SUPPORTING THE SECTION

Reinforcement Workbook: Worksheet 40
Reteaching Resources: Worksheet 40
Teaching Transparencies: Transparency 40

Section Objective
■ explain the arguments for and against American expansion in the late 1800s

Introducing The Section

Connecting with Past Learnings
Review Social Darwinism by having students explain its major tenets. (People are always competing to get ahead, the ones who succeed are the best while those that fail are unfit.) Ask students to consider how Social Darwinism might apply to international affairs.

Key Terms
List the key terms on the board. Have students find where those words are defined in context and then ask volunteers to define the terms in their own words. **LEP**

Focus
Have students state the opinions of the following people on the U.S. role in world affairs: Henry Cabot Lodge (need to expand role to prevent Great Britain from complete domination), Theodore Roosevelt (involvement in world affairs shows U.S. strength), Josiah Strong (God chose America to rule others), Alfred Thayer Mahan (must expand role by developing a powerful navy), and Grover Cleveland (did not feel the country should control territories, such as Hawaii).

Who do you agree with, the expansionists or those who opposed overseas expansion? Why?

U.S. naval power declined after the Civil War. Then, in the late 1800s, the nation began building steam-driven, steel-hulled battleships. Alfred Thayer Mahan's idea that America needed an ocean-going navy like Britain's influenced many Americans, including Assistant Secretary of the Navy Theodore Roosevelt. **GLOBAL AWARENESS** What connection was there between the desire for a large navy and overseas colonies? **1C**

Developing the Lesson

After students have read the section, you may want to consider the following activities:

Religion
Have students consider how Josiah Strong interpreted Christianity to support his view of racial superiority and ask students to explain their response to that interpretation.

Connecting with Literature
Write the opening lines of Kipling's poem "The White Man's Burden" on the board:
   "Take up the White Man's burden,
   Send forth the best ye breed—
   Go, bind your sons to exile
   To serve your captives' need."
Ask students why Kipling characterizes imperialism as a "burden." (Imperial country must send its people abroad, to administer foreign territories.) *What emotional response is Kipling trying to evoke in his poem?* (Patriotism, a sense of honor.) *What values are implied in his view?* (Superiority of white race; right of "superior" people to dominate others.)

Global Awareness
The end of the 1800s is often called the "Age of Imperialism." Assign students to find out which areas of the world were controlled by Britain, France, Belgium, the Netherlands, and Germany in 1900. Have them report their findings so that the class can create a map of world imperialism in 1900.

Patterns in History
Have students compare the build-up of naval power in the late 1800s with the build-up of nuclear weapons in the late 1900s. *How are these situations similar? How are they different?* (Both were

explained one American diplomat. A number of writers assured white Americans that they were indeed the "fittest."

One such writer was a Congregational minister named Josiah Strong. In his influential book *Our Country*, Strong argued that God had chosen the "Anglo-Saxon race" (people of English ancestry) to "prepare the way for the full coming of His kingdom on the earth." British poet Rudyard Kipling advanced much the same message when he used the famous phrase "take up the white man's burden." According to this view, white people had a duty to civilize and Christianize the "backward" peoples of the world.

Yet another voice calling for more involvement overseas was Captain Alfred Thayer Mahan. In 1890 Mahan wrote a book that led to a massive program of shipbuilding. In *The Influence of Sea Power Upon History, 1660–1783*, he argued that great nations were always seafaring nations with powerful navies. Mahan insisted that the United States build a large merchant fleet and strong navy. These ships would require bases and fueling stations. Thus, he reasoned, the United States needed to establish colonies around the world.

Mahan's ideas aroused enormous interest in Congress. What had been a sluggish program of shipbuilding became a dynamo throughout the 1890s. By the end of the century the United States had the world's third largest navy.

THE SEARCH FOR NEW MARKETS 1C
Mahan felt that expansion would bring the United States power and prestige. But he also saw a practical need for expansion. "The growing production of the country demands it," he wrote. Increasingly efficient machines and workers created a surplus of goods. Americans, for example, mined more coal than could be sold at home. Farmers grew more tobacco, wheat, and cotton than people could buy. Factories made more goods than the country needed. Producers, as a result, began to look abroad for new markets. The value of American exports jumped from $450 million in 1870 to nearly $1.4 billion by 1900.

The outside world also offered places to invest. Many foreign countries needed capital to build factories, roads, and railroads. American businesses and banks thus began investing overseas, hoping to make large profits.

A RELUCTANT EXPANSIONIST 1B
Prestige, racial theories, economic growth—these and other factors whetted Americans' appetite for expansion. Some people talked about a "new manifest destiny." Henry Cabot Lodge, for instance, thought that "from the Rio Grande to the Arctic Ocean there should be but one flag and one country." The poet Walt Whitman predicted, "There will be some 40 to 50 great states, among them Canada and Cuba."

Photo Caption Answer
Overseas colonies could supply and harbor the fleet which, in turn, could defend the colonies.

Background In 1880 the United States ranked twelfth among the world's naval powers. Reforms initiated by Secretary of the Navy William C. Whitney advanced the rapid construction of modern steel ships in the 1880s.

U.S. FOREIGN TRADE, 1865–1915

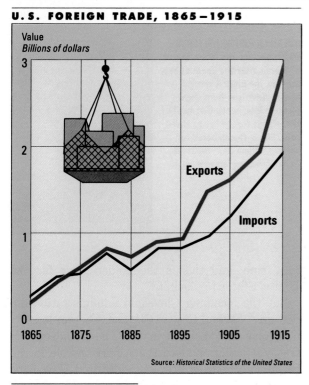

Value
Billions of dollars

Exports

Imports

1865 1875 1885 1895 1905 1915

Source: *Historical Statistics of the United States*

GRAPH SKILLS 1B, 1C

This graph shows the growth of trade between the United States and other nations during the late 1800s and early 1900s. When did export levels first top $1 billion? By how much did exports exceed imports in 1915? CRITICAL THINKING Is it preferable for a country to have greater imports than exports? Why or why not?

These things never came to pass. Never, in fact, did the nation enter the race for colonies with enthusiasm. Two major arguments worked against colonization. First, the United States was a vast country, with plenty of outlets for American energies. There was, in short, plenty to do at home. Second, Americans had once been the subjects of a foreign power—Britain. Most Americans felt that as heirs to the first great anti-colonial rebellion, they should not rule other peoples. They opposed imperialism, the exerting of control over another nation.

On the other hand, Americans did support greater economic contacts, such as trade and investment, with other nations. Occasionally these economic ties grew into political ties. The United States found itself drawn deeper and deeper into world affairs.

RIVALRY OVER SAMOA 1A

Samoa was one example. Strategically located in the South Pacific on the way to Australia, the Samoan Islands had long been popular resting places for whaling and fishing ships. The islanders were pleased to have American ships refuel in Samoa. As early as 1872, their chieftains discussed making Samoa a protectorate of the United States. Under the arrangement, Samoa would be protected and partly controlled by the United States. It would not be an American territory, but neither would it be wholly independent.

Congress refused to approve the agreement, feeling that it smacked of imperialism. Still, the United States did have an important interest in Samoa. Steamships now carried American goods across the Pacific. Those steamships needed coaling stations where they could refuel. In 1878 the United States and Samoa signed a new agreement. In exchange for fueling rights in the port of Pago Pago, the United States promised to help Samoa in any dispute with other countries.

German interference in Samoan affairs almost led to war with the United States in 1889. Instead of fighting, however, the two countries joined Great Britain in setting up a protectorate over Samoa. Britain later withdrew, and the United States and Germany divided the islands. For the first time the United States had committed itself to helping rule another people.

AMERICAN INVOLVEMENT IN HAWAII 1A, 1C

Other Pacific islands drew American attention. As early as the 1780s, American trading ships had stopped at the Hawaiian Islands for food and supplies. These islands, located more than 2,000 miles southwest of San Francisco, were a useful refueling station for vessels on their way to China.

In the 1820s American missionaries began to settle in Hawaii to spread Christianity. Their descendants bought large amounts of land, which they turned into cattle ranches and sugar plantations. Closer economic ties between Hawaii and the United States were established by an 1875 treaty in which the United States eliminated import duties on Hawaiian sugar. The United States renewed the treaty in 1887. In return, Hawaii gave it the use of Pearl Harbor as a naval base.

implemented to defend allies and American interests abroad. Today the United States is a significant world power. The potential for destruction has led to attempts to limit nuclear weapons.)

Economics
Why did Americans favor foreign investments in the late 1800s? (Had more money than they could invest at home; foreign investments had the potential for large profits.)

C **Cooperative Learning**

Divide the class into small groups. Assign each group responsibility for either Samoa or Hawaii. Have the groups draw up treaties between the U.S. government of the late 1800s and the territory for which they are responsible. **LEP**

Addressing Individual Needs

Guided/ Independent Practice
Ask students to complete **Reinforcement Workbook** Worksheet 40, which relates causes and effects of events from this section.

Reteaching/Correctives
With the class, read and discuss the stated main idea of the section, under the Section Focus on page 253. Then have students find ten details in the section that support this idea. On a piece of paper, have students write the section's main idea, and beneath it, list the ten details that they found.

Have students complete **Reteaching Resources** Worksheet 40, which helps them understand American interest in expansion.

Enrichment/Extension
Have students research the history of Hawaii. Students might prepare a timeline of Hawaiian history.

Graph Skills Answers
After 1895. About $1 billion. No, since exports bring money into a country and imports take it out.

Background The threatened naval battle over Samoa in 1889 was averted by a hurricane that wrecked American and German warships.

Background Americans established cattle ranches as well as plantations in Hawaii and imported Mexican cowboys to work on the ranches.

The Hawaiian monarchy used this coat of arms. The design later formed the basis for the state seal. The stripes on the central shield represent Hawaii's eight inhabited islands. HISTORY Who established Hawaii's first plantations? 9A

BIOGRAPHY 4C

QUEEN LILIUOKALANI (1838–1917) became the last monarch of Hawaii after the death of her brother, the king. A revolt among American-born sugar planters who controlled most of the islands forced her to abdicate. She is remembered for writing "Aloha Oe," the traditional Hawaiian farewell song.

Relations between the United States and Hawaii soon soured. In 1890 Congress passed new tariff legislation that wiped out the advantages enjoyed by Hawaiian sugar planters. The following year, a new ruler, Queen Liliuokalani (lee–LEE–oo–oh–kah–LAH–nee), took the Hawaiian throne. She tried to curb American influence and put Hawaiians back in control of their own economy.

In 1893 the American sugar planters struck back. Aided by marines from an American warship, they deposed "Queen Lil." They then asked that Hawaii be annexed, or added, to the United States. (Among other things, this would exempt Hawaiian sugar from American import tariffs.) The American diplomatic minister in Hawaii, John Stevens, supported them. "The Hawaiian pear," wrote Stevens to the State Department, "is now

Cultivation of sugar cane and pineapples in Hawaii began in the 1870s and 1880s. Hawaii continues to lead the United States in their production. The island chain's rich volcanic soil, mild climate, and abundant rainfall aid agriculture. ECONOMICS Why did sugar planters want to depose Queen Liliuokalani? 9A

fully ripe, and this is the golden hour for the United States to pluck it."

But the incoming Cleveland administration did not agree. When Grover Cleveland began his second term as President in 1893, he withdrew the treaty. Having opposed the American role in the revolt, he removed Stevens and urged Hawaiians to restore their queen to the throne. The American planters, however, would not yield. They declared Hawaii a republic and elected Sanford Dole as president. Cleveland formally recognized the new government in 1894, but still opposed annexation. In 1898, however, when the United States went to war with Spain, Hawaii's strategic value became clear. Congress then agreed to annex Hawaii.

SECTION REVIEW

1. **KEY TERMS** imperialism, protectorate

2. **PEOPLE AND PLACES** Josiah Strong, Alfred Thayer Mahan, Samoa, Hawaii, Liliuokalani

3. **COMPREHENSION** What three factors increased Americans' interest in overseas expansion?

4. **COMPREHENSION** Why did President Cleveland refuse to annex Hawaii? When and why was Hawaii annexed?

5. **CRITICAL THINKING** "Once the United States committed itself to economic expansion, it could not avoid engaging in imperialism." Do you agree or disagree with this hypothesis? Explain. 1B

2 The "Splendid Little War"

Section Focus

Key Terms Spanish-American War ■ Teller Amendment

Main Idea Events in Cuba led to war between the United States and Spain in 1898.

Objectives As you read, look for answers to these questions:
1. Why did the United States go to war with Spain?
2. What was the outcome of the war?

In the 1890s reports about Spain's harsh rule in Cuba filled American newspapers. Joseph Pulitzer's *The World* asked these questions about Cuba in 1897:

> How long are the Spaniards to drench Cuba with the blood and tears of her people? . . . How long shall old men and women be murdered by the score, the innocent victims of Spanish rage against the patriot armies they cannot conquer?

Such articles angered the American public. In this heated atmosphere, one spark was enough to ignite war: the Spanish-American War of 1898.

BACKGROUND TO WAR 1B

American interest in Cuba went back to the early 1800s, when John Quincy Adams proposed annexation of the island. Nothing came of that idea. In 1853 the United States even offered Spain $130 million for Cuba. The Spanish responded that they "would prefer seeing it [Cuba] sunk in the ocean."

One of Spain's oldest colonies, Cuba had stayed loyal during the period of Latin American revolutions in the early 1800s. Hard economic times led to revolts in 1868 and in 1895. In 1895, Cuban patriots took to the hills to carry on savage guerrilla warfare against the Spanish. The rebels struck the Spanish soldiers in surprise attacks and burned many sugar plantations and mills, most of them American-owned. The rebels hoped that these attacks would provoke the United States into entering the conflict. But the United States did not intervene.

WAR FEVER RISES 1B

American opinion shifted as Spanish policies in Cuba became increasingly brutal. Convinced that Cuban civilians were helping the guerrilla fighters, Spanish military commander Valeriano Weyler put thousands of people in squalid detention centers. As many as 200,000 Cubans died of starvation and disease in these camps. Following a visit to Cuba in 1898, a United States senator described life in the camps:

> Torn from their homes, with foul earth, foul air, foul water, and foul food or none, what wonder that one-half have died and one-quarter of the living are so diseased that they cannot be saved?

Words like these were tame compared to reports in the daily newspapers that practiced yellow journalism. The newspapers put out by Joseph Pulitzer and William Randolph Hearst reported every gruesome detail of events in Cuba. But in their frantic efforts to win readers and whip up public anger, Pulitzer's and Hearst's papers ran stories that were exaggerated and often untrue. Some reporters wrote articles without seeing the places they described. Hearst once told artist Frederick Remington, who could not find the site of a battle he was supposed to sketch: "You furnish the pictures, and I'll supply the war."

American expansionists also called for action. Theodore Roosevelt declared that failure to help the Cuban rebels would be an "unpardonable sin." The Republican Party announced in 1896, "We believe that the government of the United States should [try] to restore peace and give independence to the island." But both Presidents Cleveland and McKinley followed a cautious policy. Hopes for peace rose when a new Spanish government came to power in 1897 and removed Weyler. In early 1898, however, two events heightened war fever.

SUPPORTING THE SECTION

Reinforcement Workbook: Worksheet 41
Reteaching Resources: Worksheet 41
Enrichment and Extension Resources: Primary Source Worksheet 21
Teaching Transparencies: Transparency 41

SECTION 2

The "Splendid Little War"
(pp. 257–260)

Section Objective

■ explain the significance of the Spanish-American War

Introducing the Section

Connecting with Past Learnings

Review students' understanding of American foreign policy in the early 1800s. *How had the United States reacted to Latin American revolutions in the early 1800s?* (Supported independence of former Spanish colonies; Monroe Doctrine stated that the Western Hemisphere was closed to European colonization.)

Key Terms

List the key terms from this section on the board. Ask students to find each term in their text and state its meaning. Then ask students to describe the connection between the two terms. **LEP**

Focus

Have students create a chart of the causes and effects of the Spanish-American War using the book's charts as models. (Causes—American desire to be a world power, concern over Spanish actions in Cuba, press coverage, Spanish insults to U.S. President, sinking of the *Maine*; effects—Cuba became independent, U.S. prestige increased, and the United States gained control of the Philippines, Puerto Rico, and Guam.)

When the battleship *Maine* exploded in Havana harbor, American newspapers failed to report Spanish efforts to rescue the crew. By blaming Spain for the blast, newspapers helped start the war with Spain. Modern researchers, however, blame the explosion on an accidental fire that spread to ammunition supplies. ETHICS What influence do newspapers have in society? Should the government set standards for newspaper reporting? Why or why not? 9G

Developing the Lesson

After students have read the section, you may want to consider the following activities:

Civic Values

Discuss the role of the press in the Spanish-American War. *What are the responsibilities of a free press?* (To report the news accurately.) *What values influenced journalism in the late 1800s?* (Competition among leading newspapers.) *Do you think the press is more responsible today than it was at the turn of the century? Why or why not?*

Analyzing Controversial Issues

Have students suggest reasons why the Spanish-American War marked the emergence of the United States as a world power. (It defeated a European power and gained territory abroad.) *Do you think the United States made the right decision in going to war? Explain.* (Yes— involvement in world affairs was inevitable, given economic interests; no—if the U.S. had chosen to remain isolated it might have been able to avoid involvement in later wars.)

Global Awareness

Discuss President McKinley's statement about the location of the Philippines. *Are Americans today generally better informed about world geography than they were in McKinley's time? Explain.* (International news stories cause Americans to be more aware of their world, but many lack knowledge of geography.)

What was the significance of the Spanish-American War? (United States defeated a European power in an overseas war and became an international power.)

On February 9, 1898, Hearst's *New York Journal* published a letter by Dupuy de Lôme, Spanish minister to the United States. This private letter had been stolen by a Cuban rebel in Havana and released to the American press. It described President McKinley as "weak and a bidder for the admiration of the crowd." The embarrassed Spanish government apologized and the minister resigned. Still, Americans were outraged over the insults to their country and their President.

"REMEMBER THE *MAINE*!" 1A

Six days later, Americans learned of a more shocking incident. On February 15, 1898, the United States battleship *Maine*, which had been sent to Cuba to protect American citizens, suddenly blew up in Havana harbor. A total of 260 sailors were killed. Though an American inquiry could not find who sank the vessel, Americans blamed the Spanish. "Remember the *Maine*!" became the slogan of a public bent on war.

Spain saw that something needed to be done. To pacify the Americans, the Spanish government agreed to an armistice in Cuba. But it was too late, for the American public now demanded war. McKinley gave in to public pressure, and on April 11, 1898 he delivered a War Message to Congress. The President asked for authority to stop the hostilities in Cuba and to end a conflict which was "a constant menace to our peace."

After nine days of debate, Congress granted McKinley's request for war against Spain. At the same time, it adopted a resolution that included the Teller Amendment. This amendment stated that once the war was over and Cuba independent, the United States would "leave control of the island to its people."

VICTORY IN MANILA 1A

The first battle of the Spanish-American War did not take place in Cuba. Rather, fighting broke out half a world away, in the Spanish-controlled Philippine Islands.

When war had seemed likely, Assistant Secretary of the Navy Theodore Roosevelt sent orders to George Dewey, commander of the Pacific squadron. He told Dewey to keep the fleet "full of coal." Upon news of war, Dewey was to sail from Hong Kong to the Philippines and fight the Spanish.

On May 1, 1898, Dewey attacked the Spanish fleet in Manila Bay. The superior American naval forces quickly destroyed Spain's antiquated warships without losing a single man. Dewey became an American hero.

Having sunk the Spanish fleet, the Americans could now seize the Philippines. Aiding them was Emilio Aguinaldo (ah–gee–NAHL–doh), a popular Filipino patriot. Aguinaldo organized a Filipino army that helped the Americans capture Manila in August 1898. This was a great military victory, but it would have serious consequences in the long run.

Photo Caption Answers
Students may suggest that newspapers help shape many people's awareness of political events. Some may suggest that while irresponsible reporting is harmful, preservation of free speech is also important.

THE UNITED STATES BECOMES A WORLD POWER

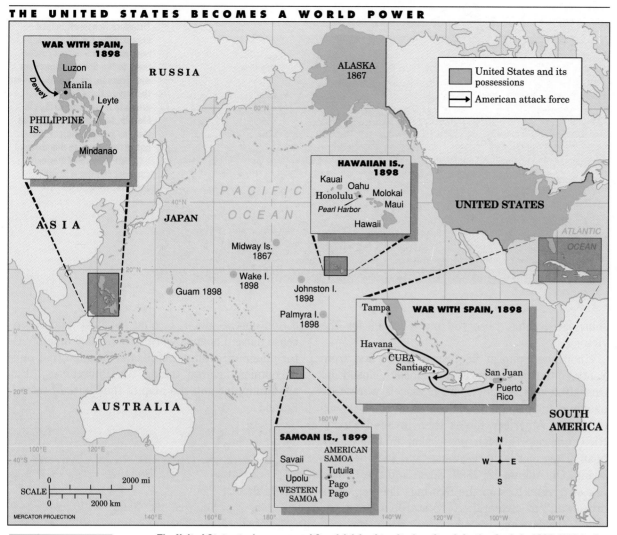

WAR WITH SPAIN, 1898
Luzon
Dewey
Manila
Leyte
PHILIPPINE IS.
Mindanao

RUSSIA

ALASKA 1867

United States and its possessions

American attack force

ASIA

JAPAN

PACIFIC OCEAN

HAWAIIAN IS., 1898
Kauai
Oahu
Honolulu • Molokai
Pearl Harbor • Maui
Hawaii

UNITED STATES

ATLANTIC OCEAN

Midway Is. 1867
Wake I. 1898
Guam 1898
Johnston I. 1898
Palmyra I. 1898

Tampa
WAR WITH SPAIN, 1898
Havana
CUBA
Santiago
San Juan
Puerto Rico

SOUTH AMERICA

AUSTRALIA

SAMOAN IS., 1899
Savaii
AMERICAN SAMOA
Upolu
Tutuila
WESTERN SAMOA
Pago Pago

SCALE
0   2000 mi
0   2000 km
MERCATOR PROJECTION

MAP SKILLS

1A

The United States took over several Spanish island territories after defeating Spain in 1898. Which of these islands lie between the Asian mainland and Australia? **CRITICAL THINKING** How did its new possessions in the Pacific help make America a world power?

THE CUBAN CAMPAIGN 1A

After Dewey's victory, the scene shifted to Cuba. There the Americans had a rougher time. The American army was ill-trained and ill-prepared for war. Worse, the War Department issued heavy woolen uniforms to soldiers who would fight in a tropical climate. One American veteran later described the summer of 1898:

It's remarkable what our bodies can stand, when I think back on our . . . days in Tampa, Florida [the departure point for American forces]—raw men in a heavy

rain, . . . our clothing soaked to the skin. Then came the issue of corned beef at sea that stunk so that we had to throw it into the sea, . . . heavy rains pouring down, no tents for cover, . . . standing in trenches in a foot of water and mud, day and night. . . .

The hardest fighting in Cuba took place near the port city of Santiago. The American army, including Theodore Roosevelt's Rough Riders, captured San Juan Hill and other fortified positions around the city. The victory made Roosevelt a hero—though in truth the Tenth Negro Cavalry, led by

CHAPTER 11   A FORCE IN THE WORLD, 1880–1910   **259**

CHICAGO HISTORICAL SOCIETY

Theodore Roosevelt helped organize the Rough Riders, a regiment of U.S. cavalry volunteers in the Spanish-American war. Transportation problems on the way to Cuba forced the group to leave their horses in Florida, so they had to fight on foot, as this painting of the battle for San Juan Hill shows. **HISTORY** Why did Americans consider the war a great success? 9A

John J. Pershing, deserved much credit for the victory.

When the Spanish fleet tried to escape from Santiago harbor, American gunboats closed in. One after another the Spanish vessels were crippled and sunk by gunfire. Soon after, the city surrendered. American forces then invaded Puerto Rico, another Spanish possession in the Caribbean. They met little resistance and soon held the island. On August 12, 1898, Spain and the United States agreed to stop the fighting. The "splendid little war," as Secretary of State John Hay had called it, was over.

AFTER THE WAR 1A

Americans saw the war as a great success. Fewer than 400 American soldiers had died in combat. (More than 5,000 soldiers, however, had died from disease caused by bad food and poor sanitation.) By the terms of the Treaty of Paris, signed on December 10, 1898, Cuba gained its independence. Spain also gave Puerto Rico to the United States, along with Guam (a small island in the Pacific). Spain reluctantly agreed to sell the Philippines for $20 million.

President McKinley, like most Americans, knew little about the Philippines and was unsure what to do with them. He later confessed, "When we received the cable from Admiral Dewey telling of the taking of the Philippines, I looked up their lo-

cation on the globe. I could not have told where those darned islands were within 2,000 miles." After much uncertainty, McKinley decided that public opinion favored taking the Philippines. "Put the Philippines on the map of the United States," he said.

> "**P**ut the Philippines on the map of the United States."
>
> —*William McKinley, 1898*

SECTION REVIEW

1. **KEY TERMS** Spanish-American War, Teller Amendment

2. **PEOPLE AND PLACES** Cuba, Valeriano Weyler, Philippine Islands, George Dewey, Santiago, Puerto Rico

3. **COMPREHENSION** How did the sinking of the *Maine* affect public opinion in 1898?

4. **COMPREHENSION** What were the terms of the Treaty of Paris?

5. **CRITICAL THINKING** To what extent can the "splendid little war" be called a turning point in United States history? Explain your answer.

3 The Debate over Imperialism

★ Section Focus ★

Key Terms Anti-Imperialist League ■ Platt Amendment

Main Idea Opinion was split over the question of United States imperialism. Some Americans favored it, while others opposed it.

Objectives As you read, look for answers to these questions:
1. What arguments did Americans use in favor of imperialism? In opposition?
2. What problems did the United States face in the territories acquired in the Spanish-American War?

The Treaty of Paris, with McKinley's backing, now went to the Senate for ratification. The acquisition of the Philippines raised the most debate. The real issue was imperialism.

THE DEBATE OVER IMPERIALISM 1A

In the Senate debate over the Treaty of Paris, familiar arguments were raised in favor of annexation. Some senators called for new markets, new places for investment, and new sites for naval bases—all of which the Philippines could provide. Others agreed with President McKinley when he said that the United States should take over the islands in order to "uplift and civilize and Christianize them." (In fact, most Filipinos already were Roman Catholics.) Senator Beveridge expressed similar ideas in discussing Cuba:

> Think of the hundreds of thousands of Americans who will build a soap-and-water, common-school civilization in Cuba, when a government of law replaces the double reign of anarchy and tyranny!

Besides, people argued, leaving the Philippines would only encourage other foreign powers to fight over the islands.

Many Americans, however, opposed the acquisition of overseas territory. Carl Schurz, a German immigrant with a distinguished career in the United States government, was one such opponent. He thought that ruling people against their will was immoral. He also argued that acquiring new territory would cost too much money. Each colony would need defense forces to protect it from rival nations. Schurz also opposed the idea of spreading American civilization to other nations.

He said that other peoples were "utterly alien to us, not only in origin and language, but in habits, traditions, ways of thinking, principles, ambitions."

Mark Twain agreed. One of Twain's essays was a tongue-in-cheek commentary about some Americans' desire to bring the "light of civilization" to people living in "darkness." He wrote:

> Shall we go on conferring our Civilization upon the People that Sit in Darkness, or shall we give those poor things a rest?

Twain and Schurz joined with other opponents of annexation—including Andrew Carnegie, Jane Ad-

President McKinley tailors a new suit of clothes for an expanding Uncle Sam in this cartoon from *Puck* magazine in 1900. Which territories contributed to Uncle Sam's growth? POLITICS Does the cartoonist seem to favor adding more territory to the United States? How can you tell? 1B

SUPPORTING THE SECTION

Reinforcement Workbook: Worksheet 42
Reteaching Resources: Worksheet 42
Enrichment and Extension Resources: Primary Source Worksheet 22
Teaching Transparencies: Transparency 42

Photo Caption Answers
Hawaii, Alaska, Puerto Rico, Texas, California, Florida, Louisiana. Pro-expansion because of Uncle Sam's confident appearance. Some students may suggest that weight is unhealthy.

SECTION 3

The Debate over Imperialism
(pp. 261–262)

Section Objective
■ explain the debate over the acquisition of overseas territory and its outcome

Introducing the Section

Connecting with Past Learnings
Ask students to list the ways by which the U.S. had acquired overseas possessions. (Treaty, war, purchase, annexation.)

Key Terms
Have volunteers define terms until the class feels that the definitions are correct. **LEP**

Focus

Divide the class into two teams, representing imperialists and anti-imperialists. Have each team take turns presenting arguments in a debate.

Developing the Lesson
After students have read the section, you may want to consider the following activities:

Patterns in History
The question of whether Puerto Rico should become a state or be given independence has frequently been raised. Have students suggest arguments for and against all possibilities.

Ⓒ Cooperative Learning

Instruct class groups to create a banner, poster, or slogan representing anti-imperialist or imperialist viewpoints. **LEP**

dams, and Samuel Gompers—to form the Anti-Imperialist League. "We regret," the League declared, "that it has become necessary in the land of Washington and Lincoln to reaffirm that all men, of whatever race or color, are entitled to life, liberty, and the pursuit of happiness."

THE FILIPINO UPRISING 1A

Despite the efforts of the Anti-Imperialist League, the Senate narrowly ratified the Treaty of Paris on February 6, 1899. The Filipinos, however, were not about to trade Spanish rule for American rule. When Emilio Aguinaldo and his followers learned the terms of the peace treaty, they felt betrayed. They vowed to continue the fight for their independence.

The United States was soon fighting a bitter guerrilla war. Both sides resorted to burning villages and torturing prisoners. Americans who opposed annexation were quick to point out that these were the same tactics that Spain had used against the Cubans.

It took the Americans nearly three years to put down the rebellion. American soldiers suffered more than 7,000 casualties, while Aguinaldo's forces lost as many as 20,000 men. More than 200,000 Filipino civilians also died. American tactics against the rebels caused long-lasting bitterness among the Filipino people.

In the years that followed, the Philippines repeatedly asked for independence. In 1934 a ten-year period was agreed upon, after which independence would be granted. The outbreak of World War II delayed fulfilling the promise. Finally, on July 4, 1946, the Republic of the Philippines was born.

RULING CUBA AND PUERTO RICO 1B

The United States faced a different situation in the Caribbean. Though officially independent, Cuba was occupied by American troops when the war with Spain ended. Cuba faced many problems. It had no strong government, and thousands of people faced death from starvation, disease, and crime. According to the Teller Amendment of 1898, the United States had agreed not to take over Cuba. Still, not wanting to abandon the impoverished island entirely, American leaders de-

cided to hang on to Cuba for the moment, both to improve conditions there and to strengthen American influence.

In 1900 Cubans wrote a constitution for an independent state. The United States, however, expected to have some control over the new nation. Before it withdrew its troops in 1902, it made Cuba accept the Platt Amendment. This agreement gave the United States the right to intervene in Cuban affairs, if necessary, "for the protection of life, property, and individual liberty." It also forced Cuba to lease harbors to the United States for naval stations. (Accordingly, in 1903 the United States leased the land around Guantánamo Bay for the construction of a naval base.) Cubans opposed this interference, but could do nothing about it.

Unlike Cuba, Puerto Rico became a United States possession after the Spanish-American War. There was no thought of bringing independence to its people. American government and trade helped improve living conditions. Still, Puerto Ricans resented American control. In 1900 Congress adopted the Foraker Act, which gave Puerto Rico a form of self-government. Unhappiness with this plan led to passage of the Jones Act in 1917. Under this act, the people of the island became United States citizens with the right to elect their leaders. Later, in 1952, Puerto Rico became a self-governing commonwealth under United States protection.

SECTION REVIEW

1. KEY TERMS Anti-Imperialist League, Platt Amendment

2. PEOPLE Carl Schurz, Emilio Aguinaldo

3. COMPREHENSION Why did Senator Beveridge, among others, favor imperialism?

4. COMPREHENSION What arguments did anti-imperialists use to oppose annexation of territory?

5. CRITICAL THINKING Did the results of American imperialism in the late 1800s justify the arguments of the imperialists or of the anti-imperialists? Explain your answer.

Background Research by doctors Carlos Finlay and Walter Reed determined that yellow fever was carried by mosquitos. Under the direction of Major William C. Gorgas (page 277), the United States Army drained swamps to destroy mosquito breeding areas in Cuba.

4 Involvement in Asia

Section Focus

Key Terms Chinese Exclusion Act ■ sphere of influence ■ Open Door Policy ■ Boxer Rebellion ■ reparations ■ Gentlemen's Agreement ■ Russo-Japanese War

Main Idea Long interested in Asia, the United States took a more active role in Asian affairs by 1900.

Objectives As you read, look for answers to these questions:
1. What were the main issues in the United States' relationship with China?
2. What issues raised tensions between the United States and Japan?

By 1900, the United States had established a strong presence in the Pacific, controlling Samoa, Guam, Hawaii, and the Philippines. These islands, lying between North America and the Far East, had great strategic value for the United States, especially as American contacts with the Far East grew. From the earliest days of the American nation, the United States had been interested in trade and other contacts with countries such as China and Japan. As the United States expanded and prospered, its involvement with China and other Asian nations deepened.

THE CHINA TRADE 1C

In August 1784 the American ship *Empress of China* sailed to China. On the trip back to New York, it carried tea, silk, and other Chinese goods, which were sold for a hefty profit. The success of this enterprise led to greater Chinese-American trade in the late 1700s and early 1800s. Trading ships leaving from New York and Boston sailed around South America. They stopped to pick up furs in the Northwest before sailing on to China, where the furs were sold and the ships reloaded with Chinese exports. The trip became much

The fan shown above commemorates the *Empress of China*'s visit to the port of Canton in 1784. The dark-hulled vessel appears at the far left of the fan. The painting at left depicts the process of tea production in China: hillside cultivation (top), transport down-river for drying and sifting in sheds (center), packing for sale to buyers (such as the American in top hat at lower left), and transfer to ocean-going ships for export (right center). GEOGRAPHY What route did American ships take to China? 1C

CHAPTER 11   A FORCE IN THE WORLD, 1880–1910   **263**

SUPPORTING THE SECTION

Reinforcement Workbook: Worksheet 43
Reteaching Resources: Worksheet 43
Teaching Transparencies: Transparency 43

Photo Caption Answer
They sailed from the eastern United States around the southern tip of South America to the West Coast, and from there across the Pacific to China.

Who benefited more from
American involvement in
Asia—the United States or the
Asian countries? Explain your
answer.

Developing the Lesson

After students have read the
section, you may want to consider the following activities:

Economics

Have students suggest Chinese goods Americans would
have been interested in buying. (Tea, silk, porcelain,
ivory, jade.) *Why might these
goods have been highly prized
in the United States?* (They
were not produced at home
and were obviously imported
from China.) *Why do you think
interest in luxury goods from
China increased in the late
1800s?* (Americans had more
money to spend; fast clipper
ships made the journey easier than before.)

Analyzing Controversial
Issues

Discuss the Chinese Exclusion Act and the Gentlemen's
Agreement with Japan. *What
point of view do they reflect?*
(Prejudice against Asians; a
sense of racial superiority.)
Have students suggest what
the goals of immigration
laws should be.

shorter after the 1840s, when fast clipper ships
began crossing the Pacific.

In the years that followed, the most significant
exchange between the United States and China
was in people. American missionaries flocked to
China to spread Christianity. Chinese workers,
seeking a better life, came to the United States to
work on such projects as the transcontinental
railroad.

THREATS TO CHINA AND THE CHINESE 4B

European nations shared the United States' interest in trade with China. The Chinese government,
on the other hand, feared that Western influence
would disrupt the traditional Chinese way of life.
China therefore tried to restrict trade with the
outside world. But it lacked the power—especially
the modern technology—to force Western nations
out. By the mid-1800s, both the British and
French had gained tight control over China's
trade.

America's first foreign minister to China, Anson
Burlingame, worried about the power of the European nations. In 1867 he resigned from his post,
hoping to help China by serving in its diplomatic
corps.

As a representative of China, Burlingame negotiated a treaty with the United States. The
Burlingame Treaty of 1868 was a model agreement providing for fair play between the two nations. The United States, needing workers to help
build the Central Pacific Railroad, agreed to unlimited immigration from China. It also promised
not to meddle in Chinese domestic affairs.
Burlingame tried to get the European powers to
approve similar agreements. None of them would
do so.

The Burlingame Treaty led to more Chinese immigration to the United States. Business leaders
in California and other western states favored immigration because it provided a large labor pool.
Unions, on the other hand, opposed immigration,
claiming that it lowered wages. Chinese laborers,
they said, were willing to work for less money
than American laborers.

Anti-Chinese feeling finally resulted in passage
of the Chinese Exclusion Act (1882), which suspended Chinese immigration for ten years. This
was the first time the United States had ever
barred immigrants on an ethnic basis. The law
was later revised to permit certain Chinese—such
as students, teachers, and travelers—to enter the
United States.

Those people who favored exclusion of the Chinese from the United States used racial arguments as well as economic ones. In testimony
offered in 1902, the American Federation of Labor
added racial reasons to its usual economic arguments for Chinese exclusion:

> The free immigration of Chinese would be
> for all purposes an invasion by Asiatic bar-
> barians, against whom civilization . . . has
> been frequently defended, fortunately for
> us. It is our inheritance to keep it pure
> and uncontaminated.

Congress agreed, and in 1902 it ended the matter
once and for all by barring all Chinese immigration. What had begun as a free flow of peoples
between the United States and China ended in total restriction.

THE OPEN DOOR NOTES 1B, 1C

Throughout the late 1800s Britain, Germany, Russia, France, and Japan carved out spheres of
influence in a weakened China. These were areas
in which each country had sole rights to trade and
invest. Americans, wanting to protect their own
trading rights, tried to stop these other countries
from gaining unfair advantages in China.

Secretary of State John Hay stated America's
opposition to further foreign meddling in China in
the Open Door Notes of 1899–1900. These letters,
sent to the major trading powers, proposed an
Open Door Policy. Under this policy, all nations
would have equal trading rights in China. The European powers did not agree to this idea, but they
did not flatly reject it either. Hay announced that
the major powers had accepted the Open Door
Policy.

THE BOXER REBELLION 1A

Meanwhile, a tide of resentment against foreigners was rising in China. Chinese patriots
known as Boxers demanded that all foreigners be
expelled from the country. In 1900 they started a

264 UNIT 4 BECOMING A WORLD POWER

Background Early American
ships sailing to China carried
ginseng, a root that the Chinese used for medicine. Later
exports consisted of furs such
as fox, raccoon, and otter.

rebellion, attacking and murdering missionaries and other foreigners. Scores of people trapped in the capital city of Beijing (bay–JING) took refuge in the residences of foreign diplomats. Westerners called this uprising the Boxer Rebellion.

The United States and several other nations sent military forces to Beijing. They arrived just in time to put down the Boxers and save the besieged diplomats and missionaries. Now a new problem arose: Would the European powers use their victory to take even greater control of China? Secretary of State Hay hoped not. He committed the United States "to seek a solution which may bring about permanent safety and peace to China."

Hay's efforts paid off. China suffered no further loss of territory but was forced to pay more than $332 million in reparations—money for war damages—to the various nations. The United States later returned almost half its share of the money. This sum was used to set up a fund to send Chinese students to American schools.

This photograph shows a captured Boxer, so named because he belonged to a secret society whose members practiced martial arts. The Boxer Rebellion climaxed a late-1800s movement to rid China of foreigners. **CULTURAL PLURALISM** What factors might account for anti-foreign feelings in a society? **9A**

FOREIGN INFLUENCE IN CHINA

RUSSIA

Russia 1896–1898

MANCHURIA

KOREA

Japan 1876–1910

Port Arthur

Beijing

Tokyo
JAPAN

SCALE
0 — 500 mi
0 — 500 km

CHINA

Britain 1898

Germany 1898

Japan 1895

INDIA (Br.)

FORMOSA
Hong Kong
Macao (Port.)

Britain 1842

BURMA (Br.)

1898

PACIFIC OCEAN

SIAM

Manila

PHILIPPINE IS. (U.S.)

1858–1895 France

INDOCHINA

OBLIQUE PARABOLIC EQUAL-AREA PROJECTION

MAP SKILLS 9A

Foreign nations took advantage of China's weakness to grab land and impose unequal treaties. This map shows colonial territories in East Asia and foreign possessions in China. Which Southeast Asian territory belonged to France? **CRITICAL THINKING** Why did foreign powers want to control China's coastal cities?

OPENING JAPAN 1A, 1C

Another Asian country of great interest to outside powers was Japan. Since the 1600s the Japanese government had allowed very little trade with the outside world. This policy did not sit well with the American government. American whalers wanted to land in Japan to get fresh food and water, and other supplies. Americans also wanted to buy Japanese goods, such as silk.

In 1852 the United States government sent Commodore Matthew C. Perry to Japan to open trade. Perry's warships, painted black and belching smoke from their funnels, terrified the Japanese. In 1854 they agreed to a treaty letting American ships enter Japanese ports. Soon other countries reached similar agreements with Japan.

As with China, the issue of immigration strained

Geographic Themes: Regions
Direct students' attention to the map on this page. **Which nations had the greatest geographic advantage for gaining power in China?** (Russia and Japan because of their proximity.) **What territory gave the United States a presence in the region?** (The Philippines.)

Have students compare the map with a map of Asia today, noting the modern names of Siam and Indochina. (Thailand and Vietnam, Cambodia, and Laos.) **Who controls Manchuria and Formosa today?** (China controls Manchuria and Formosa is the country of Taiwan.)

Science and Technology
Discuss with students the role of technology in opening up U.S. trade with Asia. (Clipper ships made trade faster and easier; superior technology gave Europeans power in China, which encouraged the United States to become more involved in affairs there; U.S. warships terrified the Japanese, convincing them to open their country to foreigners.)

Global Awareness
In the 1600s Japanese leaders ordered Christian missionaries to leave the country, banned Christianity, cut its ties with other countries, and forbade Japanese people to live abroad. Explain this to students and have them imagine how a Japanese person might have reacted when he or she saw Perry's warships. Ask them to create a story, poem, picture, or collage that expresses those thoughts and feelings. **LEP**

Photo Caption Answer
Students may suggest that the Chinese feared foreigners might take control of their country. Other factors may include fear, ignorance, and racism.

Map Skills Answers
Indochina. Control of the port cities enabled foreign powers to control China's trade.

Background Japan had been so tightly closed to outsiders before Perry, that its leaders ruled that any foreigners shipwrecked on its shores were to be killed. Contact was limited to one Dutch ship each year.

relations with the United States. After 1885 the Japanese emperor allowed citizens to leave the nation for Hawaii. Then, when the United States annexed Hawaii in 1898, many Japanese moved to the West Coast. Native-born Americans soon protested this influx of workers, and western states passed laws discriminating against the Japanese.

The situation came to a head in 1906. In that year San Francisco's mayor, Eugene Schmitz, ordered that Japanese (as well as Chinese and Korean) students be placed in a separate "Oriental Public School." Newspapers in Japan called this an insult, and anti-American riots broke out. Diplomats from both nations agreed to try to solve the problem. In 1907–1908 they came to an understanding. Under what was called the Gentlemen's Agreement, Japanese immigration was greatly restricted. At the same time, San Francisco canceled its plan for a separate Asian school. Yet relations between the United States and Japan remained chilly.

SOCIAL HISTORY
Famous Firsts

1883	Steel vessels authorized by U.S. Navy.
1884	Naval War College opens (Sept. 3).
1889	First Pan American Conference, Washington, D.C. (Oct. 2).
1890	Pan American Union established (April 14). First battleship of importance—the *Maine*—launched, Brooklyn Navy Yard (Nov. 18).
1901	First naval coaling station completed on foreign soil, in Baja California, Mexico.
1902	S.B.M. Young begins service as first president of Army War College (July 10).
1908	U.S. government contracts for a dirigible balloon.
1912	First parachute jump from an airplane, at Jefferson Barracks, Missouri (March 1).

This Japanese painting shows curious residents of Yokohama rowing out to inspect Commodore Matthew C. Perry's black warships. What was Perry's mission and how did he accomplish it? TECHNOLOGY Explain what Perry's arrival might have meant to the Japanese. 1A

266 UNIT 4 BECOMING A WORLD POWER

JAPAN'S WAR WITH RUSSIA 1B

Another source of Japanese-American friction was Japan's growing strength. Unlike China, which had become weaker as a result of Western influence, Japan had adopted Western ideas and was becoming a powerful industrial nation. With this new strength came an eagerness to expand its influence in Asia and the Pacific. The United States, likewise interested in those areas, looked with concern on Japanese moves.

Once again China was the scene of foreign intrigue. Both Japan and Russia had exploited China's weakness to extend their influence in Korea and in Manchuria (a large, mineral-rich territory in northeastern China). Soon the imperialists were fighting each other. Aiming to drive the Russians out of Manchuria, Japan launched a surprise attack against Russia in 1904.

On land and at sea, the modern Japanese forces won victory after victory in the Russo-Japanese War. Yet Japan, now running out of money, could not force Russia to its knees. When President Roosevelt offered to help settle the conflict, both countries gladly accepted. Roosevelt was interested in settling the war for two reasons. (1) He wanted both Russia and Japan to uphold the Open Door Policy. (2) He feared that if Japan won the war, it might become too strong. Such a situation, he believed, might "possibly mean a struggle between them [Japan] and us in the future."

Delegates from Russia and Japan met at Portsmouth, New Hampshire, in 1905. They signed a peace treaty requiring both countries to withdraw from Manchuria. Roosevelt later won the Nobel Peace Prize for his part in ending the war. But many Japanese, expecting a better settlement, thought Roosevelt had let them down.

Roosevelt took several steps to maintain a stable relationship with Japan. The two countries signed agreements in 1905 and 1908 in which they promised to respect each other's interests in Asia and the Pacific. To show that the United States could fight for its interests if need be, Roosevelt sent the United States Navy on a global cruise in 1907. The sixteen battleships of the Great White Fleet—so called because the vessels were painted white—provided an impressive display of strength. They demonstrated beyond doubt that the United States was indeed a Pacific power.

SECTION REVIEW

1. KEY TERMS Chinese Exclusion Act, sphere of influence, Open Door Policy, Boxer Rebellion, reparations, Gentlemen's Agreement, Russo-Japanese War

2. PEOPLE AND PLACES Anson Burlingame, John Hay, Beijing, Matthew C. Perry, Manchuria

3. COMPREHENSION Why was the United States concerned about China remaining independent? What did it do about it?

4. COMPREHENSION Why did Roosevelt fear a Japanese victory over Russia?

5. CRITICAL THINKING Should a nation ever restrict immigration? If so, under what circumstances? 4B

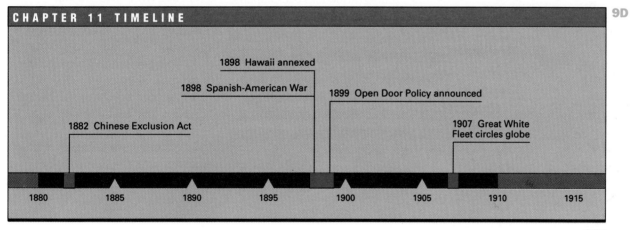

CHAPTER 11 TIMELINE

- 1882 Chinese Exclusion Act
- 1898 Hawaii annexed
- 1898 Spanish-American War
- 1899 Open Door Policy announced
- 1907 Great White Fleet circles globe

1880 · 1885 · 1890 · 1895 · 1900 · 1905 · 1910 · 1915

9D

Chapter 11 Review Answers

Key Terms

1. The Open Door Policy was a proposal that all nations had equal trading rights in China. The Boxer Rebellion was an uprising of Chinese patriots.

2. The Gentlemen's Agreement restricted Japanese immigration to the U.S. The Chinese Exclusion Act was a law suspending Chinese immigration to the U.S. for ten years.

3. The Platt Amendment gave the U.S. the right to intervene in Cuban affairs. The Teller Amendment was part of a declaration of war against Spain which stated that the U.S. would not attempt to control Cuba after the war.

4. Imperialism is the controlling of another nation. Sphere of influence is an area in which a foreign country has exclusive rights to trade and invest.

People to Identify

1. Emilio Aguinaldo
2. John Hay
3. Matthew C. Perry
4. Anson Burlingame
5. Valeriano Weyler
6. Carl Schurz
7. George Dewey

Places to Locate

1. E   **4.** D
2. A   **5.** B
3. C

Reviewing the Facts

1. The desire to compete with Europe, the ideas of Social Darwinism, and a search for new markets.

2. Samoa provided a strategic refueling stop for merchant ships. Hawaii offered a strategic port in the Pacific and was a major source of sugar and beef.

CHAPTER 11 SUMMARY

SECTION 1: During the late 1800s Americans became increasingly interested in foreign affairs.

■ New ideas about America's destiny as a world power and the need for new markets overseas caused an interest in empire-building. This was countered by a tendency toward avoiding involvement in world affairs and a belief that imperialism was wrong.

■ The United States acquired Samoa and Hawaii because of their strategic locations and usefulness as bases and refueling stations.

SECTION 2: The United States went to war against Spain in 1898.

■ American support for Cuba's fight to throw off colonial rule led to war between Spain and the United States.

■ The Spanish-American War ended in victory for the United States. The spoils of war included the Philippines, Puerto Rico, and Guam.

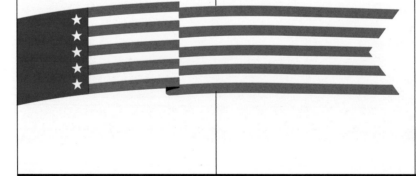

SECTION 3: The proposal to annex the Philippines sparked a debate over imperialism.

■ Imperialists argued that American rule would benefit the U.S. as well as the people of Spain's former colonies.

■ Anti-imperialists argued that ruling people against their will was immoral and un-American. They did not think Americans should impose their institutions and beliefs on people from different backgrounds.

■ Congress voted to annex the Philippines. American troops then had to put down a Filipino revolt against American rule.

SECTION 4: American relations with China and Japan broadened during the late 1800s.

■ The United States expanded trade with China while trying to preserve China's independence from foreign control.

■ Labor's resentment of Chinese workers led to a ban on immigration from China.

■ Tensions between Japan and the U.S. rose over Japanese immigration and over Japan's growing influence in Asia.

KEY TERMS ●

Define the terms in each of the following pairs.

1. Open Door Policy; Boxer Rebellion
2. Gentlemen's Agreement; Chinese Exclusion Act
3. Platt Amendment; Teller Amendment
4. imperialism; sphere of influence

PEOPLE TO IDENTIFY ●

Match each of the following people with the correct description.

Emilio Aguinaldo
George Dewey
Anson Burlingame
John Hay
Matthew C. Perry
Carl Schurz
Valeriano Weyler

1. Leader of Filipino independence movement.
2. Author of the Open Door Policy.
3. American naval officer who opened trade with Japan.
4. American diplomat who resigned his post in order to serve China.
5. Spanish military commander in Cuba.
6. German-born American government official who opposed American imperialism.
7. American commander whose forces sank the Spanish fleet in Manila Bay.

---

3. The brutal treatment of Cubans, enhanced by yellow journalism reporting that the Spanish sunk the *Maine*.

4. The Spanish-American War began in the Philippines, where Dewey's forces wiped out the Spanish fleet. Fighting resumed in Cuba where the Spanish fleet was again smashed. After the invasion and swift takeover of Puerto Rico, the war ended.

Match each of the letters on the map with the places that are listed below.

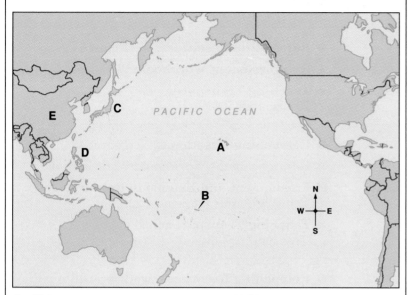

1. China
2. Hawaii
3. Japan
4. Philippines
5. Samoa

REVIEWING THE FACTS ▲

1. What were the causes of American interest in empire-building?
2. How did economic forces and strategic considerations lead the United States to take possession of Samoa? Hawaii?
3. What factors turned American public sentiment against Spanish policy in Cuba during the 1800s?
4. Describe the course of the Spanish-American War. How did the war begin? Where were the main battles fought? How did United States forces fare in these battles?

5. What territory did the United States gain as a result of its victory in the Spanish-American War?
6. What arguments were presented opposing the acquisition of overseas territory?
7. What problems arose in the Philippines after the Spanish-American War?
8. Why did business leaders favor Chinese immigration? Why did labor leaders oppose it?
9. How and why did the United States open trade with Japan?
10. What were Roosevelt's reasons for helping settle the Russo-Japanese War?

CRITICAL THINKING SKILLS ▲

1. **FORMING A HYPOTHESIS** What connection might there have been between the closing of the frontier and growing American interest in overseas expansion? Write one or two sentences clearly stating this possible connection.
2. **INFERRING** Why did Congress pass the Teller Amendment?
3. **WEIGHING BOTH SIDES OF AN ISSUE** Which do you find more convincing, the arguments of the imperialists or the anti-imperialists? Write a brief essay making the best possible case for the *other* side.

WRITING ABOUT TOPICS IN AMERICAN HISTORY ■

1. **CONNECTING WITH LITERATURE** A selection from "Versos Sencillos" ("Simple Poetry") by José Martí appears on page 791. Read it and answer the questions. Then answer the following question: How could simple verses such as these help inspire people to fight for their freedom?

2. **APPLYING THEMES: GLOBAL INTERACTIONS** Read Rudyard Kipling's famous poem "The White Man's Burden." Then write a brief essay paraphrasing the ideas he expressed in the poem.

3. **HISTORY** Choose an incident from the late 1800s or early 1900s in American history and write an account of it in the style of yellow journalism.

8. Business leaders favored it because it provided a plentiful and inexpensive labor pool. Labor leaders opposed it because the Chinese drove down wages.
9. The U.S., wanting to establish a supply port and hoping to benefit from Japanese markets, had Commodore Perry negotiate a treaty with the Japanese.
10. Roosevelt wanted to protect the Open Door Policy and he feared Japan might get too strong.

Critical Thinking Skills
1. The tradition of moving on to find new opportunities encouraged overseas expansion after the frontier closed.
2. It wanted to make it clear that the United States was not in the war to gain territory.
3. Answers should reflect an understanding of the financial, philosophical, and moral issues involved in imperialism.

Writing About Topics in American History
1. The simplicity of the poems suggests simple, basic values. Such poems gave people a sense of pride and an identity worth fighting to protect.
2. Students should note Kipling's sense of service as well as his patronizing attitude.
3. Students' accounts should choose an incident and describe it in exaggerated and untruthful terms.

5. Puerto Rico, Guam, and the Philippines.

6. Two arguments against empire-building were that it was immoral to rule people against their will and that maintaining distant territories was too costly.

7. The Philippine people demanded their independence. When the U.S. refused to grant it a guerrilla war broke out.

Chapter Review exercises are keyed for student abilities:
● = Basic
▲ = Average
■ = Average/Advanced

Chapter 12 ▪ Expanding in Latin America

3 Sections, 2–3 Days

	SECTION OBJECTIVES	SECTION RESOURCES
Section 1 **Background** **to American** **Involvement**	▪ explain the roots of Latin America's economic problems in the late 1800s ▪ analyze the impact of U.S. involvement in Central America	● **Reteaching Resources:** Worksheet 44 ▲ **Reinforcement Workbook:** Worksheet 44 ▲ **Teaching Transparencies:** Transparency 44
Section 2 **"Big Stick** **Diplomacy"**	▪ describe the events leading to the construction of the Panama Canal ▪ describe United States policy toward Latin America during Theodore Roosevelt's presidency	● **Reteaching Resources:** Worksheet 45 ▲ **Reinforcement Workbook:** Worksheet 45 ■ **Enrichment and Extension Resources:** Primary Source Worksheet 23 ▲ **Teaching Transparencies:** Transparency 45
Section 3 **Dollars and Morals** **in Foreign Affairs**	▪ compare the foreign policies of Presidents Taft and Wilson	● **Reteaching Resources:** Worksheet 46 ▲ **Reinforcement Workbook:** Worksheet 46 ■ **Enrichment and Extension Resources:** Primary Source Worksheet 24 ▲ **Teaching Transparencies:** Transparency 46

The list below shows Essential Elements relevant to this chapter. (The complete list of Essential Elements appears in the introductory pages of this Teacher's Edition.)

Section 1:   1A, 1B, 3A, 6A
Section 2:   1A, 1B, 2E, 3A, 4E
Section 3:   1A, 1B, 3F, 9A, 9B, 9D

Section Resources are keyed for
student abilities:
  ● = Basic
  ▲ = Average
  ■ = Average/Advanced

CHAPTER RESOURCES

Geography Resources: Worksheets 23, 24
Tests: Chapter 12 Test

Chapter Project : Global Interactions

Have students choose one of the nations of Latin America and develop a policy paper on United States relations with that country between 1900 and 1920. The paper should have some information on the government and economy of the country, as well as recommendations for future U.S. policy toward that country.

Homework Options

Each section contains activities labeled "Addressing Individual Needs." You may wish to choose from among these activities when assigning homework.

> **Provisions for Limited English Proficiency (LEP)**
> Several suggested activities may be particularly helpful for teachers of students with limited English proficiency. These activities have been marked throughout the Teacher's Annotated Edition with the symbol **LEP** .

BIBLIOGRAPHY AND AUDIOVISUAL AIDS

Teacher Bibliography

Bell, Sidney. *Righteous Conquest: Woodrow Wilson and the Evolution of the New Diplomacy.* Kennikat, 1972.

Collin, Richard H. *Theodore Roosevelt, Culture, Diplomacy and Expansion: A New View of American Imperialism.* Louisiana State University Press, 1985.

Kennan, George. *American Diplomacy, 1900–1950.* University of Chicago Press, 1985.

Minger, Ralph E. *William Howard Taft and United States Foreign Policy: The Apprenticeship Years, 1900–1908.* University of Illinois Press, 1975.

Hogan, J. Michael. *The Panama Canal in American Politics: Domestic Advocacy and the Evolution of Policy.* Southern Illinois University Press, 1986.

Student Bibliography

Beale, Howard K. *Theodore Roosevelt and the Rise of America to World Power.* Johns Hopkins University Press, 1984.

Keller, Ulrich, ed. *The Building of the Panama Canal in Historic Photographs.* Dover, 1983.

McCullough, David. *The Path Between the Seas: The Creation of the Panama Canal, 1870–1914.* Touchstone Books, 1978.

Films and Videotapes*

A Man, A Plan, A Canal: Panama (Nova Series) 57 min. COR/MTI. Examines the evolution and significance of the Panama Canal.

Filmstrips*

The Monroe Doctrine Applied: U.S. Policy Toward Latin America (set of 2). GA. Explores Roosevelt's 1904 corollary which declared the intent of the United States to intervene in Latin American affairs when necessary.

The Panama Canal: Past, Present and Future (1 filmstrip). GA. Traces the growth of the United States as an economic and political world power by the turn of the century. Describes events leading up to the decision to build a canal, including debates over whether to build it through Panama or Nicaragua.

Computer Software*

TIME TRAVELER: Spanish War, Etc. 1886–1912 (IBM). MVP. Multiple choice, true/false, and short-answer questions within the context of a time travel adventure. Includes questions about contributions made by women and minorities. Up to 300 additional questions can be added.

*For a complete guide to audiovisual sources, see the introduction to this book (page Txx).

Chapter 12

Expanding in Latin America
(pp. 270–285)

This chapter explores the origins of United States interest in Latin America and the instances of U.S. intervention there from 1900 to 1917.

 Themes in American History

- Global interactions
- Economic development
- Geography

Chapter Objectives

After students complete this chapter, they will be able to:

1. Explain the roots of Latin America's economic problems in the late 1800s.

2. Analyze the impact of U.S. involvement in Central America.

3. Describe the events leading to the construction of the Panama Canal.

4. Describe United States policy toward Latin America during Theodore Roosevelt's presidency.

5. Compare the foreign policies of Presidents Taft and Wilson.

Chapter Opener Art
Charles Sheeler, *Panama Canal*, 1946.

270

To protect its economic interests, the United States has long played an active role in Latin American affairs. The Panama Canal is the most concrete symbol of United States involvement in Latin America. A vital commercial and military waterway, the canal cuts across the Isthmus of Panama and links the Atlantic Ocean and the Pacific Ocean.

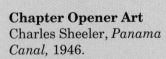

CHAPTER SUPPORT MATERIAL	
	Reinforcement Workbook: Worksheets 44–46
	Reteaching Resources: Worksheets 44–46
	Enrichment and Extension Resources: Primary Source Worksheets 23, 24
	Geography Resources: Worksheets 23, 24
	Teaching Transparencies: Transparencies 44–46
	Tests: Chapter 12 Test

12 Expanding in Latin America (1900–1920)

SECTION 1

Background to American Involvement
(pp. 271–273)

Section Objectives
- explain the roots of Latin America's economic problems in the late 1800s
- analyze the impact of U.S. involvement in Central America

1A, 1B, 3A, 6A

1 Background to American Involvement

★ Section Focus

Key Terms *caudillo* ■ Clayton-Bulwer Treaty

Main Idea Americans, long interested in Latin America, were increasingly drawn to the region by the early 1900s.

Objectives As you read, look for answers to these questions:
1. What was the political and economic situation in Latin America in the nineteenth century?
2. What interests did the United States have in Latin America?
3. How did interest grow in building a canal across Central America?

In 1870 a Yankee sea captain named Lorenzo Dow Baker loaded 160 bunches of bananas on board his ship in Jamaica. Eleven days later he sold the bananas in Jersey City for a profit of $2 a bunch. Baker had discovered the profits that could be made in Latin America. He was not alone. In the middle and late 1800s, many Americans looked south to do business. Later on, these economic interests would spur the United States to take a dominant role in Latin America.

LATIN AMERICA IN THE 1800s 6A

By 1830 almost all of Latin America had gained independence. However, independence did little to change the great inequalities in the region. In Spain's former colonies, for example, the population was divided into distinct social classes. People born in Spain, and Creoles (the children of Spaniards born in the colonies), controlled most of the wealth. These groups also held the most impor-

tant positions in the government and in the Roman Catholic Church. Those at the bottom of society—Indians, blacks, and people of mixed ancestry—remained trapped in grinding poverty.

Spain had given its colonies little or no experience in self-government. As a result, the new Latin American republics were ill-prepared to manage their own affairs. In country after country, harsh leaders called *caudillos* (kow–DEE–yoz) seized power. The worst dictators became cruel tyrants who used terror to keep power.

The history of Central America in the 1800s illustrates the instability of Spain's former colonies. In 1838 the United Provinces of Central America—a political union made up of Costa Rica, Guatemala, Nicaragua, Honduras, and El Salvador—fell apart. Confusion followed. Honduras, for example, had twenty presidents between 1862 and 1872. Five Salvadoran presidents were deposed by force; two others were executed.

Introducing the Section

Connecting with Past Learnings
Ask students to list territorial gains made as a result of the Mexican War, 1846–1848. (California, Utah, and Nevada, and parts of Colorado, Wyoming, New Mexico, and Arizona.)

Key Terms
Write the first key term on the board and circle the double *l*. Explain that in Spanish this has the sound of *y*. Have students pronounce the term and then define it and the other term in their own words. **LEP**

Focus
Ask students to list the reasons Americans became involved in Latin America. (Wanted to buy the region's raw materials; to invest capital; to run a transportation network across the isthmus of Panama, shortening travel time between the East and West Coast; slave owners wanted to set up slave states.)

Why didn't U.S. investments help the poor of the region? (Most of the money ended up in the hands of foreign investors and the upper classes.)

Developing the Lesson
After students have read the section, you may want to consider the following activities:

SUPPORTING THE SECTION

Reinforcement Workbook: Worksheet 44
Reteaching Resources: Worksheet 44
Teaching Transparencies: Transparency 44

271

THE ECONOMIES OF LATIN AMERICA 6A

Many of the social problems of the Latin American republics were rooted in the economic life of the region. A few wealthy families owned almost all the usable farmland. To make matters worse, the produce of the land, rather than the land itself, was taxed. Once a tenant farmer fell into debt to the landowner, the debtor was required by law to remain on the estate and work until the debt was repaid. Sinking even deeper into debt, most tenants became virtual slaves to the landowners.

For the most part, the Latin American republics concentrated on producing food and raw materials. When the United States and Europe began to industrialize, they provided a ready overseas market for these products. The money of foreign investors also flowed into Latin America. It was used to improve transportation, provide public utilities, and modernize mines. American and European technicians and business managers moved to the region to run mines and factories.

Foreign capital and skilled workers increased the output of the Latin American economies. But the profits did little to improve standards of living. Foreign investors received a lion's share of the profits. The upper classes took most of what remained. The rich grew richer; the vast majority of the people grew poorer.

EARLY AMERICAN INVOLVEMENT 1A

American interest in the lands to its south went back many years. In pre–Civil War days, slave-owners wanted to set up slave states in the Caribbean. American adventurers were drawn to the region too. One was William Walker, a southern journalist. With the United States on the brink of the Civil War, Walker's plan to bring slavery to Nicaragua added fuel to the abolitionists' fire. Central American and British troops drove Walker out of Nicaragua.

Walker tried twice more to gain power in Central America—once in Nicaragua and another time in Honduras. He was finally captured by the British and turned over to the Hondurans. He was executed by a firing squad in 1860.

Another American active in Central America was Minor Cooper Keith. At about the same time that Lorenzo Dow Baker discovered the American market for bananas, Keith built a railroad in Costa Rica. Finding fewer passengers than he expected, Keith searched for another use for his railroad. He began to grow bananas, transporting them north by rail. By 1899 Keith was the biggest banana grower in Central America.

Together with Baker and another partner, Keith helped build the Boston Fruit Company. United Fruit, as the company was later called, became a

This engraving shows William Walker drilling troops in Nicaragua in 1856. Walker was able to take over the country's presidency later that year. A conflict with the American investors who supported him soon led to Walker's removal from office. **ECONOMICS** How did foreign investment affect the economies of Latin American nations? 1A

huge corporation. The largest employer in Central America, it wielded substantial power over Central American governments. Soon the Latin American press began to target the company as a symbol of American greed and power. Newspapers called the company *el pulpo*—the octopus.

CROSSING THE ISTHMUS 1B

Enterprising Americans sometimes stumbled into very profitable businesses in Central America. George Law, a New York builder, and William H. Aspinwall, a steamship operator, set up a transportation link across the Isthmus of Panama in 1848. Law's ships carried mail and passengers from New York to New Orleans and then to Panama's Caribbean coast. Aspinwall operated a shipping line from Oregon and California to Panama. The two lines were connected by canoe and mule and then, in 1855, by railroad.

When gold was discovered in California, Law and Aspinwall had a "gold mine" of their own. The "forty-niners" who traveled to California from the East were willing to pay handsomely for passage across Central America. Still, this was not a pleasant trip. Passengers were packed into foul-smelling steamships for the trip to Panama. They went ashore in frail canoes, often losing all their possessions in the process. Then they battled insects, sunstroke, and disease as they rode up the Chagres River to the Pacific side of the isthmus.

When business tycoon Cornelius Vanderbilt learned of the profits Law and Aspinwall were making, he decided to grab a piece of the action. Vanderbilt planned to take away Law's and Aspinwall's business by digging a canal across Nicaragua. But the canal project fell through. Vanderbilt clashed with William Walker over control of the Nicaraguan enterprises. Although Vanderbilt helped to force Walker out of Nicaragua, the canal scheme collapsed in a tangled mess of claims and counterclaims.

The United States and Great Britain had also seen the need for a waterway linking the Atlantic and Pacific oceans. Neither country, however, wanted to confront the other. In 1850 the two sides signed the Clayton-Bulwer Treaty. In the treaty, both countries promised that any canal in Central America would be politically neutral.

CONNECTING THE AMERICAS 3A

Though Vanderbilt's plan failed, other Americans dreamed of building a canal across Central America. They argued that a canal would boost the nation's economy by bringing the resources of the West to the industrial centers of the East. It would also shorten the journey from eastern factories to Asian markets by thousands of miles.

France too found the idea of a canal tempting. In 1880 a French company began work on a sea-level canal across Panama. The head of this company had already conquered the Egyptian desert to build the Suez Canal in the 1860s. But the disease-ridden swamps of Panama and the challenge of the terrain were too much. After a decade of work and thousands of deaths, the project was canceled. The disastrous venture ruined its French investors.

In spite of the French failure, the United States showed new interest in a canal after the Spanish-American War. The war reminded Americans of the strategic importance of such a waterway. When war was declared on Spain, the navy had ordered its battleship *Oregon*, then harbored in San Francisco, to sail to Cuba. The perilous journey around Cape Horn, the southernmost tip of South America, took 68 days. For weeks no one knew where the vessel was. The *Oregon's* dangerous race around South America strengthened the case of those pushing for an American-controlled canal. One such person, President Theodore Roosevelt, would take the decisive action to make the canal a reality.

SECTION REVIEW

1. KEY TERMS *caudillo*, Clayton-Bulwer Treaty

2. PEOPLE AND PLACES William Walker, Minor Cooper Keith, Cornelius Vanderbilt, Panama

3. COMPREHENSION What problems did Latin American nations face after independence?

4. COMPREHENSION Why did the United States want to build a canal across Central America?

5. CRITICAL THINKING Why, do you think, did Latin American countries concentrate on producing food and raw materials rather than manufactured goods?

Enrichment/Extension
Ask students to do biographical research on an entrepreneur in this section and report on an incident that reveals the person's character.

Assessment
You may wish to use the Section 1 Review, on this page, to see how well your students understand the main points in this lesson.

Section Review Answers

1. *caudillo*—Latin American dictator. *Clayton-Bulwer Treaty*—Agreement that any canal across Central America would be neutral.

2. *William Walker*—Adventurer who tried to gain power in Central America. *Minor Cooper Keith*—Built a railroad in Costa Rica and started a banana business. *Cornelius Vanderbilt*—Business tycoon who planned a canal across Nicaragua. *Panama*—Site where the French tried to build a canal.

3. Their economies were sharply divided between rich and poor; they lacked experience in self-government and often *caudillos* took power.

4. After the discovery of gold in California, a canal seemed the best way to shorten the trip West. The *Oregon* incident convinced the U.S. of the strategic importance of a canal.

5. Industrialization requires capital, and much of the money produced in the region was taken out by foreign investors.

Closure
Remind students of the pre-reading objectives in the section opener. Pose one or all of these questions again. Then have students read Section 2 for the next class period, noting the events leading to the building of the Panama Canal.

2 "Big Stick Diplomacy"

SECTION 2

"Big Stick
Diplomacy"
(pp. 274–279)

Section Focus

Key Terms Hay-Pauncefote Treaty ■ Roosevelt Corollary

Main Idea During Theodore Roosevelt's presidency, the United States began to intervene more actively in Latin American affairs.

Objectives As you read, look for answers to these questions:
1. How did the United States build the Panama Canal?
2. Why did the United States intervene in Latin American countries?

Section Objectives

■ describe the events leading to the construction of the Panama Canal
■ describe United States policy toward Latin America during Theodore Roosevelt's presidency

Introducing the Section

Connecting with Past Learnings
Have students recall Theodore Roosevelt's domestic policies and personal style. *What kind of a person was Theodore Roosevelt?* (He was energetic and aggressive, had implemented progressive policies, was a "take-charge" kind of person.)

As students work through the lesson, ask them to consider how the force of Roosevelt's personality both shaped and exemplified U.S. policy in Central America in the early 1900s.

Key Terms
Have students define the key terms in their own words. Explain to students that a *corollary* is a proposition that follows from one that already exists. Ask them what proposition the Roosevelt Corollary followed, and have them explain the relationship. **LEP**

When Theodore Roosevelt became President in 1901, he quickly made known his goals for Latin America. First, he wanted to build a canal across Central America. Second, he was determined to keep the European powers from interfering in the affairs of Latin American countries. In pursuing his goals, Roosevelt sometimes quoted a West African proverb: "Speak softly and carry a big stick, you will go far." He did not always speak softly in Latin America, but he did use a "big stick" to get what he wanted.

> "**S**peak softly and carry a big stick, you will go far."
>
> —*Theodore Roosevelt*

PLANS FOR A CANAL   1A

Before the United States could proceed with plans for a Central American canal, it had to remove a political obstacle—the Clayton-Bulwer Treaty. Britain, tied down with other problems and eager to improve relations with the United States, was ready to let the United States have its way. In 1901 Secretary of State John Hay reached a new agreement with the British ambassador, Sir Julian Pauncefote. The Hay-Pauncefote Treaty granted the United States sole right to construct, control, and defend a Central American canal. It further said that the canal was to remain free and open to ships from all nations on equal terms.

The question that remained was where to build the canal. Studying the matter, a presidential commission recommended a canal across Nicaragua.

The proposed route had fewer of the technical problems the French had faced in Panama. Much of the route could follow the San Juan River and Lake Nicaragua. That would leave about 50 miles of actual canal to be dug. Nicaragua was also relatively free of disease, something not to be ignored in light of the French experience.

In early 1902 the House of Representatives voted 308 to 2 to build a Nicaragua canal. In the same week, however, the French company that had failed in Panama offered to sell its canal assets to the United States for $40 million. Theodore Roosevelt wanted to accept the deal. He had been impressed by an engineer's conclusion that by building a dam and using locks, the Panama route would be the cheaper and better choice.

With Roosevelt's involvement, the canal route suddenly became an issue. The strongest supporters of the Nicaragua route were southerners. John Tyler Morgan, senator from Alabama, had lobbied for a Nicaragua canal since the 1870s. He sincerely believed Nicaragua to be the best route from both a technical and health standpoint. Morgan also pointed out that a Nicaragua canal would be 700 to 800 miles closer to Gulf ports than a Panama canal. He predicted that Gulf ports such as New Orleans and Galveston would flourish and that southern exports would increase.

Congress probably would have stuck by the Nicaragua route had not the unexpected happened. In May 1902 a volcano exploded on the Caribbean island of Martinique, killing 40,000 people. That inspired the French company's chief agent, Philippe Bunau-Varilla. Bunau-Varilla had been head engineer in Panama and was passionately devoted to seeing the Panama Canal finished. Preying

The Geographic Perspective: Selecting a Canal Site

The dream of a canal across Central America dates back to the Spanish conquistadors. Not until the age of the steamships, however, did the dream begin to approach reality.

During the 1860s and 1870s, both American and French expeditions searched out every possible route. These included paths across Tehuantepec (the narrowest part of Mexico), Nicaragua, and Panama—the three shortcuts to California's gold fields. Other possible routes led through Darién, the region south of Panama. In 1876 a canal commission established by President Grant reviewed all the facts and decided in favor of the Nicaragua route.

AN INTERNATIONAL CONGRESS

In France, meanwhile, Ferdinand De Lesseps, builder of the sea-level Suez Canal, proposed a congress to share information on a Central American canal route. Experts from 22 nations came to the congress, which was held in May 1879. American delegates presented the case for a Nicaragua canal. The highest point along the route was 153 feet. In contrast, the Culebra Gap in Panama was 275 feet above sea level. The proposed Nicaragua canal would use locks at each end but for most of its course would follow Lake Nicaragua and the San Juan River.

Another reason for choosing Nicaragua was that a canal in Panama would face a critical

CENTRAL AMERICA: PROPOSED CANAL ROUTES

SCALE
0 — 300 mi
0 — 300 km

ATLANTIC OCEAN
Gulf of Mexico
20°N
Yucatán Peninsula
CUBA
JAMAICA
MEXICO
Isthmus of Tehuantepec
BELIZE
Caribbean Sea
GUATEMALA
HONDURAS
EL SALVADOR
NICARAGUA
Managua
Brito
Greytown (San Juan del Norte)
Isthmus of Panama
Cartagena
Colón
COLOMBIA
COSTA RICA
PANAMA
Panama City
Panama Canal
PACIFIC OCEAN

☐ Proposed canal routes

LAMBERT CONFORMAL CONIC PROJECTION
90°W
10°N
80°W

problem: what to do with the Chagres River. The river could become a raging flood in the rainy season. At such time the Chagres could rise 10 feet an hour and measure 1,500 feet across. A sea-level canal at Panama was physically impossible, said the engineers.

THE FRENCH IN PANAMA

De Lesseps did not want to hear such judgments. He wanted the congress to endorse a sea-level canal across Panama. By the sheer force of his personality, De Lesseps persuaded the delegates to vote for the Panama route. He then organized a company to build the canal.

Even when his best engineers later concluded that a sea-level canal was impossible, De Lesseps remained blind to the geographic reality of Panama. He still thought in terms of the desert of Suez and insisted on a sea-level route. In the end, De Lesseps had to accept the idea of locks, but it was too late. Disease and delays had bankrupted the company. It was the Americans who would carry on the dream of a canal.

CRITICAL THINKING QUESTIONS 2E

1. Why did interest in a Central American canal increase with the coming of steamships?

2. What causes geographic blindness?

The Geographic Perspective Answers

1. Unlike sailing ships, steamships were not dependent on winds and ocean currents; steamships burned fuel for energy and therefore, the less distance they traveled, the less fuel they used.

2. An assumption that one place is like another; not understanding the geographic forces that make a place unique.

Geographic Themes
Geographic themes covered on this page:

✔ Location
___ Place
✔ Interactions
✔ Movement
___ Regions

Focus
In the center of the board, write the words *Panama Canal* and circle them. Have the class suggest policies and actions which relate to the United States' desire to build a canal. On top of the original circle put the suggestions that led to the creation of the canal. (Hay-Pauncefote Treaty; French company's failure; volcanoes in Martinique; Panamanian revolution). Below the circle put the results of the canal's completion. (Shortened travel time between the East and West coasts; stimulated trade; American military bases built in the Canal Zone; Roosevelt Corollary.)

Developing the Lesson
After students have read the section, you may want to consider the following activities:

Geographic Themes: Interaction
What was the connection between the Suez Canal and the Panama Canal? (The French company that built the Suez Canal was led by the same man who directed the French attempt at building a Panama Canal.)

Using a classroom map or the world map at the back of the book, have students find the Suez Canal and the Panama Canal. *How does the Suez Canal function in the Middle East in much the same way that the Panama Canal functions in the Western Hemisphere?* (Both cut short the distance between major bodies of water, making travel easier.) Discuss with students the value of canals in times of war. (They allow the countries controlling the canals to move their warships quickly to where they are needed.)

on American fears about the destructive power of volcanoes, he came up with a clever plan:

> I was lucky enough to find . . . 90 Nicaraguan stamps, that is, one for every [U.S.] senator, showing a beautiful volcano belching forth in magnificent eruption. . . .

These ominous stamps helped convince Congress to choose the route across Panama, which was then part of Colombia. The House reversed its earlier vote and agreed to buy the French rights if a suitable arrangement could be made with Colombia.

REVOLUTION IN PANAMA 1A
Colombia asked for more money than the United States was willing to pay. Philippe Bunau-Varilla, however, knew that some Panamanians were unhappy with Colombian rule. He reasoned that an independent Panama might agree to a canal treaty with the United States. Bunau-Varilla thus took it upon himself to help a small group of Panamanians to rebel against Colombia.

Roosevelt supported Bunau-Varilla by sending a warship to Panama. The *Nashville* arrived on November 2, 1903. On the next day, the revolt broke out. With marines from the *Nashville* blocking Colombian troops from crushing the rebels, the revolution succeeded. The United States quickly recognized the new nation. It also negotiated a canal treaty with Panama's new foreign minister—none other than Philippe Bunau-Varilla.

Opponents at home and abroad blasted Roosevelt for his role in the affair. Although the Senate ratified the treaty, many Americans felt that the government had violated Colombia's rights. The New York *American* said it would "rather forego forever the advantage of [a canal] than gain one by such means as this." Roosevelt denied any wrongdoing, but he later boasted:

> If I had followed traditional conservative methods, I would have submitted a dignified state paper of probably 200 pages to Congress and the debates on it would have been going on yet; but I took the Canal Zone and let Congress debate; and while the debate goes on the Canal does also.

Criticism of Roosevelt's methods continued, however. In 1921, after TR's death, the United States paid Colombia $25 million. This was a diplomatic way of apologizing to that country.

BUILDING THE PANAMA CANAL 1A
No area of the Western Hemisphere was more hostile to human life than the Panama Canal Zone. Its swamps teemed with disease-carrying mosquitoes. Humidity so filled the air that even light work was difficult, and at night the chorus of frogs made more noise than passing cars on city streets. Yet a New York reporter who was among the first to arrive remained optimistic:

> There is nothing in the nature of the work to daunt an American. . . . I should say that the building of the canal will be a comparatively easy task for knowing, enterprising, and energetic Americans.

This somber cartoon shows death awaiting builders of the Panama Canal in the disease-infested swamps of Panama. People who worked on the canal risked catching malaria or yellow fever from mosquitoes and bubonic plague from rats. TECHNOLOGY How was the Canal Zone made livable? 3A

> **"I** am going to make the dirt fly!"
> —*Theodore Roosevelt*

At the height of construction, more than 43,000 laborers from nations around the world were employed on the canal project. Many of them were black workers from the West Indies and from the United States. They did the bulk of the pick-and-shovel work of the canal. The food was as tough as the work. One worker recalled the "cooked rice which was hard enough to shoot deer; sauce spread all over the rice; and a slab of meat which many men either spent an hour trying to chew or eventually threw away."

More than 61 million pounds of dynamite were used in the construction of the Panama Canal. Dynamite blasted through rock and removed huge trees. One West Indian worker described the danger of clearing trees in this way:

> Each man, torches in both hands, dashed from tree to tree, lighting fuses as fast as possible, then ran for cover. . . . It was something to watch and see the pieces of trees flying in the air.

President Roosevelt was just as hopeful. "I am going to make the dirt fly!" he shouted. First, however, Americans had to cope with the problem of disease. William C. Gorgas, who had wiped out yellow fever in Cuba, was sent to Panama. He drained swamps and ponds in the ten-mile-wide strip leased to the United States. After eighteen months the Canal Zone was free of mosquitoes, and deaths from malaria and yellow fever declined. Work could now begin.

This cartoon's title is "The News Reaches Bogota." (Bogota is the capital of Colombia.) According to the cartoonist, how did news of Panamanian independence and the Panama Canal's construction reach Colombia? **GLOBAL AWARENESS** What does the cartoon imply about President Roosevelt's treatment of Colombia? **1A**

Photo Caption Answers
They found out when dirt started flying. Roosevelt's tossing of dirt in Bogota's direction suggests that Columbia suffered from ill-treatment.

Biography
Discuss the role of the Surgeon General, asking students to suggest public health challenges facing today's Surgeon General.

Background A famous palindrome describes Roosevelt's strategy for building the Panama Canal: "A man, a plan, a canal—Panama."

Science and Technology
Have students suggest reasons why the canal was considered the greatest engineering feat of its time. (Had to drain swamps and ponds over large area; used large amounts of dynamite and concrete; moved enormous amounts of dirt, etc.) Interested students may draw diagrams or create dioramas illustrating the construction or operation of the canal.

Global Awareness
Ask students to study the Roosevelt Corollary on page 278 of their text. *What does it say about Roosevelt's opinion of Latin American countries?* (He implied that they are somehow less civilized than the United States.) Discuss why many Latin American countries might have objected to the United States taking on the role of regional police officer. (They had no say in that decision; it implies the United States has "ownership" of the entire hemisphere.) Ask students how they feel about the United States taking on that role.

C Cooperative Learning

Divide students into groups and have each group consider one of the following situations in a Central American country: a revolution is impending; the government is initiating land reform; a European nation is threatening intervention to collect on a debt. Have the groups discuss possible United States responses and the rationale they would use for each response. **LEP**

As many as 60 steam shovels were used daily, with trains taking the dirt to dumping grounds. If all the dirt had been placed in a shaft the width of a city block, it would have been 19 miles tall. About 5 million cubic yards of concrete were used in construction. Little wonder that the canal was called the greatest engineering feat of all time!

Work ended in 1914. No project had ever cost more: $365 million. The human cost too was great. Accidents and disease killed more than 5,600 workers. Yet in the end, the canal was a success.

IMPORTANCE OF THE CANAL 2E
The 50-mile canal changed the economic history of the world. The water route from New York to San Francisco was now 8,000 miles shorter. Travel through the canal took only about 12 hours, while the journey around Cape Horn took weeks to complete. Ships from around the globe could get goods to consumers faster than before. The canal also allowed navies to move their ships quickly between the Atlantic and the Pacific. The motto of the Canal Zone says it best: "The Land Divided, the World United."

The building of the Panama Canal profoundly affected relations between the United States and Latin America as well. Some Latin Americans saw the canal as proof that the United States felt free to meddle in their affairs. The American government, wanting to protect its new investment, took actions that only heightened Latin American

Judge magazine honored Theodore Roosevelt's guiding role in the construction of the Panama Canal. **ISSUES** What might Roosevelt's supporters and critics have said about his handling of the canal project? **1A**

concerns. The United States built American military bases in the Canal Zone, and leased Great Corn and Little Corn islands from Nicaragua. The Virgin Islands were purchased from Denmark in 1917 for $25 million. Also, to maintain stability in Central America and the Caribbean, the United States insisted that nations have orderly governments. Instability in the region, Americans feared, might result in European intervention.

POLICING LATIN AMERICA 1B
The threat of European intervention had long been on the minds of American Presidents. In 1895 President Cleveland was drawn into a border dispute between Venezuela and its neighbor, the British colony of British Guiana. After gold was discovered near the border, Britain seemed to be extending its claim. The Monroe Doctrine forbade the establishment of new colonies in the Americas. Was Britain violating the Monroe Doctrine?

The United States demanded that Great Britain agree to arbitration—settling the dispute by a board of neutral persons. Eventually the British agreed. Acceptance of the United States' role in the dispute showed increasing American power in the hemisphere.

A second Venezuelan crisis indicated continued American determination to uphold the Monroe Doctrine. In 1902, warships from Germany, Britain, and Italy blockaded Venezuela for its failure to pay debts. Venezuela requested United States arbitration. The European powers accepted this proposal, and the crisis was resolved diplomatically.

Roosevelt feared that there would be more threats to the Monroe Doctrine. Other Latin American nations suffered from problems, such as foreign debt, that might provoke European intervention. In 1904 Roosevelt delivered a policy statement that became known as the **Roosevelt Corollary**. It said that the United States would intervene in any Latin American nation whose stability was in question. The Corollary stated:

> Chronic wrongdoing . . . may in America, as elsewhere, ultimately require intervention by some civilized nation, and in the Western Hemisphere the adherence of the

This 1901 cartoon depicts Uncle Sam as a rooster protecting chickens, which represent Latin American nations. **GLOBAL AWARENESS** How did Roosevelt try to "coop up" European roosters with his corollary to the Monroe Doctrine? 1B

United States to the Monroe Doctrine may force the United States, however reluctantly, . . . to the exercise of an international police power.

The United States first exercised this "police power" in the Dominican Republic in 1905. This poorly run country was in debt to European creditors. American officials took over the collection of customs duties, a responsibility they held until 1941. They also arranged for payment of the country's debts.

To critics of the Roosevelt Corollary, the President replied that he was actually protecting the independence of Latin American countries. Unlike European nations, he said, the United States had no desire to set up more colonies. Describing the Dominican crisis, he declared:

I want to do nothing but what a policeman has to do in Saint Domingo. As for annexing the island, I have about the same desire to annex it as a gorged boa constrictor might have to swallow a porcupine wrong end to.

Under the Roosevelt Corollary the United States also intervened in Cuba, Nicaragua, and Haiti. Not surprisingly, few Latin Americans welcomed United States intervention. They complained that the United States was not letting them conduct their own affairs.

SECTION REVIEW

1. KEY TERMS Hay-Pauncefote Treaty, Roosevelt Corollary

2. PEOPLE AND PLACES Colombia, Philippe Bunau-Varilla, Venezuela, Dominican Republic

3. COMPREHENSION How did the United States succeed in negotiating a treaty for a canal across Panama?

4. COMPREHENSION How did the Roosevelt Corollary change United States policy toward Latin America?

5. CRITICAL THINKING "I took the Canal Zone and let Congress debate," recalled Theodore Roosevelt. Do you think Roosevelt was right or wrong to bypass Congress in this affair? Explain. 9G

2. *Colombia*—Panama was part of this South American country prior to a revolution in 1903. *Philippe Bunau-Varilla*—French canal company's main agent, who convinced the U.S. Senate to build in Panama and not Nicaragua. *Venezuela*—South American nation threatened twice by European intervention. *Dominican Republic*—Caribbean nation where the United States took over collection of customs duties from 1905 to 1941.

3. By sending a gunboat to ensure the success of a revolution in which Panama separated from Colombia.

4. It stated that the United States intended to act as a police power in this hemisphere to maintain stability, whereas the policy before had been only to act to keep out new foreign influence in the region.

5. Right—Roosevelt's pragmatic, "get things done" approach meant the canal was completed sooner rather than later; wrong—by ignoring Congress, he ignored the constitutional principle of a balance of powers.

Closure

Ask one student to transform the Main Idea of the section into a question, and have other students answer that question. Then have students read Section 3 for the next class period, noting the foreign policy of Presidents Taft and Wilson.

Photo Caption Answer
The U.S. tried to prevent European nations from intervening in Latin America by taking complete responsibility for policing the region.

3 Dollars and Morals in Foreign Affairs

SECTION 3

Dollars and Morals in Foreign Affairs
(pp. 280–283)

Section Objective

■ compare the foreign policies of Presidents Taft and Wilson

Introducing the Section

Connecting with Past Learnings

Have students characterize the foreign policy of President Theodore Roosevelt. (Students may mention big stick diplomacy and the use of force to promote U.S. interests.)

Key Term

Write the key term on the board and invite students to free associate words or phrases related to the term. For example, "money," "intervention," "foreign policy," and so on. Write them on the board. Then have them develop a definition of the key term incorporating the appropriate ideas. **LEP**

Focus

Privately, assign three volunteers to play one of the following Presidents: Roosevelt, Taft, Wilson. Have them use slogans, stories, and descriptions of their actions in Latin America to provide clues to their identity. Have the class guess which President each student represents.

Why and where did Presidents Taft and Wilson intervene in Latin America? (To restore and maintain order and protect U.S. investments—Taft in Nicaragua and Wilson in Haiti, the Dominican Republic, and Mexico.)

280

★ Section Focus

Key Term dollar diplomacy

Main Idea Presidents Taft and Wilson continued the policy of intervening in Latin America to defend American interests.

Objectives As you read, look for answers to these questions:
1. What changes did Presidents Taft and Wilson make in American foreign policy?
2. Why did Wilson intervene in Mexico?

Each of the two Progressive Presidents following Roosevelt brought his own style to foreign policy. Taft, a less forceful man than Roosevelt, shied away from "big stick diplomacy." Peaceful activities like trade and investment, Taft hoped, would produce stability and prosperity—not just for the United States, but for all nations. President Wilson too rejected imperialist policies. To Wilson, morality—not power—must lie at the heart of American foreign policy.

Yet while the style of the three Progressive Presidents differed, their policies generally did not. This is because the three men agreed on two basic points. First, the United States had important interests in Latin America. Second, the United States should intervene in Latin America when it felt those interests were threatened. A variety of troubles in Latin America thus prompted American intervention in the early 1900s.

DOLLAR DIPLOMACY 1B, 3F

Taft went even further than Roosevelt in intervening in Latin America. Under a policy called **dollar diplomacy**, he urged American banks and businesses to invest in Latin America. Such investments would both help build the local economies and bring in a hefty profit for the American investors. The United States would step in, Taft promised, if unrest in Latin America threatened these investments.

Taft applied dollar diplomacy to several countries. In 1912, for example, when Nicaragua was torn by financial problems and the threat of a revolution, Taft sent in the United States marines. Their mission was to restore order and protect American lives and property. "We were not welcome," one marine recalled. "We could feel it dis-

tinctly." Yet the marines remained in Nicaragua until 1933.

Taft tried, without great success, to extend dollar diplomacy to Asia. By encouraging American investment in China, he hoped to limit European and Japanese expansion there. He proposed, for example, that American bankers invest in a railroad scheme in central China. American investors had little enthusiasm for this and other projects. Only a small amount of American money was invested in China by the time Taft left office.

A MORAL FOREIGN POLICY 1B

President Wilson held a different view of dollar diplomacy. He feared that heavy American investment might actually harm weak nations. That is, the foreign investors could take all the profits out of the country, leaving the host country as poor as before. And these investors could gain influence over the government of the host country. Wilson also declared himself to be firmly against imperialism. "The United States," he declared in 1913, "will never again seek one additional foot of territory by conquest."

Wilson did not rule out the use of force in certain situations. In 1915, for example, France, Great Britain, and Germany threatened to intervene in Haiti to insure payment of debts owed to them. At the same time, during a popular uprising, a mob killed Haiti's president. Wilson sent American troops to restore order. In 1916 the United States took over the running of Haiti's customs office.

A similar situation took place in the Dominican Republic in 1916. Marines were sent to that country to put down political unrest. For the next eight years an American military government ruled the Dominican Republic.

SUPPORTING THE SECTION

Reinforcement Workbook: Worksheet 46

Reteaching Resources: Worksheet 46

Enrichment and Extension Resources: Primary Source Worksheet 24

Teaching Transparencies: Transparency 46

This satiric view of Porfirio Díaz portrays the Mexican dictator's self-coronation. Foreign investment during Díaz's rule contributed to Mexico's industrial development but benefited only the wealthy. POLITICS What does the cartoon say about popular support for Díaz?

9B

THE MEXICAN REVOLUTION 1B

Relations with Mexico proved to be one of President Wilson's greatest challenges. Mexico had been ruled for nearly 35 years by a dictator, Porfirio Díaz (DEE–ahs). Díaz, a friend of the United States, had long encouraged foreign investment in his country. He sold some 75 percent of Mexico's mineral resources to foreigners, most of them American. Americans owned a large share of Mexico's mines, oil resources, rubber plantations, and railroads. While foreign businesses and some Mexican politicians grew rich, the common people remained desperately poor.

Revolutionaries led by Francisco Madero overthrew the aged Díaz in 1911. Before he could carry out his promised reforms, Madero was challenged by other rebel leaders. They arrested Madero in 1913 and had him executed. Victoriano Huerta (WAYR–tah), who proclaimed himself ruler of Mexico, was assumed to be responsible for Madero's death.

President Wilson faced a dilemma. Should he recognize Huerta's undemocratic government? Or should he refuse to do so and thereby risk American investments? The President's response was clear. "I will not recognize a government of butchers," he insisted. This refusal marked a change in American policy. Wilson wanted to establish diplomatic relations only with governments chosen in free elections. Until then the United States had recognized governments no matter how they had taken power.

> "**I** will not recognize a government of butchers."
>
> —*Woodrow Wilson, 1913*

INTERVENTION IN MEXICO 1A

Wilson was determined to bring about Huerta's downfall. He allowed American weapons to reach Venustiano Carranza and Pancho Villa (VEE–yah), rebel leaders who opposed Huerta. Then, an incident in 1914 gave Wilson the chance he wanted to oust Huerta. Some American sailors were arrested in the Mexican port of Tampico. The sailors were quickly let go, but the American admiral in charge demanded an apology and a 21-gun salute to the American flag. When Huerta refused, Wilson directed an American fleet to set sail for Mexico.

Wilson now learned that a German ship carrying arms to Huerta was heading for the port of Vera Cruz. Wilson quickly ordered United States marines to occupy the city. To his surprise, Mexican citizens joined the fight against the American in-

Photo Caption Answer
That he lacked popular support.

Developing the Lesson
After students have read the section, you may want to consider the following activities:

Economics
Why did several European nations threaten to intervene in Latin America? (They wanted to collect on debts owed them by Latin American nations.)
How do you think dollar diplomacy affected the Latin American debt problem? (If U.S. investment improved local economies, countries would be better able to repay their debts, but might get deeper in debt to the U.S.)

Patterns in History
Have the class discuss recent United States involvement in Central America and compare activity in the region today with actions earlier in the century. *Do you think the policy of the United States is better today than it was 80 years ago?*

Impact of Geography
Discuss with students how Mexico's history has been influenced by its neighbor to the north. (Mexico lost half its territory to the U.S. in the 1840s, U.S. investment may have contributed to the revolution, and U.S. policy from 1914 to 1917 may have made an unstable situation worse.) Have students suggest ways that proximity to the United States influences Mexico today.

Global Awareness
How and why did Villa set out to draw the United States into Mexico? (Villa murdered U.S. citizens, knowing that would provoke a military response.) *What reaction did Mexicans have to the U.S. invasion?* (They rallied behind Villa, seeing him as a hero.) Discuss the Mexican reaction to that invasion and U.S. interventions in Tampico and Vera Cruz, asking students to consider why smaller nations might resent U.S. interventions.

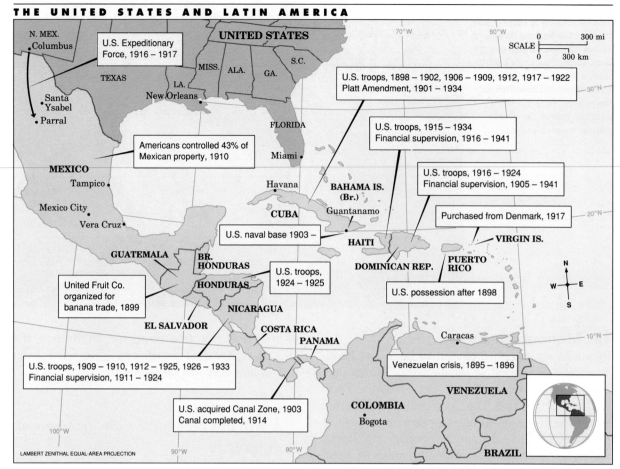

THE UNITED STATES AND LATIN AMERICA

U.S. Expeditionary Force, 1916 – 1917

U.S. troops, 1898 – 1902, 1906 – 1909, 1912, 1917 – 1922
Platt Amendment, 1901 – 1934

Americans controlled 43% of Mexican property, 1910

U.S. troops, 1915 – 1934
Financial supervision, 1916 – 1941

U.S. troops, 1916 – 1924
Financial supervision, 1905 – 1941

Purchased from Denmark, 1917

U.S. naval base 1903 –

U.S. troops, 1924 – 1925

U.S. possession after 1898

United Fruit Co. organized for banana trade, 1899

U.S. troops, 1909 – 1910, 1912 – 1925, 1926 – 1933
Financial supervision, 1911 – 1924

Venezuelan crisis, 1895 – 1896

U.S. acquired Canal Zone, 1903
Canal completed, 1914

SCALE 0 – 300 mi / 0 – 300 km

LAMBERT ZENITHAL EQUAL-AREA PROJECTION

MAP SKILLS
9B

The United States has a history of extensive interests and intervention in Latin America. Which countries were occupied by U.S. troops? In which country did the United Fruit Company play a leading role? **CRITICAL THINKING** Why might the Caribbean Sea have been called "an American lake"?

Pancho Villa, shown here with his wife, became famous through his legendary guerrilla exploits. He is also remembered for supporting demands for reform by Mexico's poor. **HISTORY** Why did Villa try to provoke American intervention in Mexico? **9A**

vasion. Carranza also condemned the American action. The Mexican people clearly preferred to handle their own problems.

Huerta was soon overthrown and fled to Spain. Carranza took control of the government, but he soon had a new opponent. This was Pancho Villa, his former ally. Born Doroteo Arango, the barrel-chested Villa dominated northern Mexico. Before one battle this passionate revolutionary wrote, "We put in motion the plans to reach a great victory or die in the trying."

Villa and Carranza split shortly after Huerta's overthrow. Villa, determined to oust Carranza, decided to provoke American intervention in Mexico. In 1916 Villa's troops took over a dozen Americans off a train in northern Mexico and executed them.

282 UNIT 4 BECOMING A WORLD POWER

Two months later, his forces raided Columbus, New Mexico, and killed seventeen more Americans. With the American public demanding revenge, Wilson ordered General John J. Pershing and 6,000 American troops into Mexico to "get Villa dead or alive."

Unimpressed by Wilson's threat, Villa launched another daring raid across the Rio Grande, killing three soldiers and a boy. Members of Congress cried out for an invasion of Mexico. Mexicans, on the other hand, rallied behind Villa. They regarded him as a hero who fought for the people against overwhelming odds. The wily Villa even gained the respect of his American opponents. In his memoirs, General Hugh L. Scott wrote:

> He always impressed me as a man of great force and energy and willing to do right. . . . After all, he was a poor peon without any advantages in his youth, persecuted and pursued through the mountains, his life always in danger; but he had the cause of the [Mexican peasants] at heart. He was fully aware of his own deficiencies and even at the height of his power had no desire for the presidency.

War between Mexico and the United States seemed imminent for a time. But in the end, both sides backed off. Pershing withdrew his troops, never having found Villa, and the two nations agreed to try to work out their differences peacefully. The United States needed calm on its southern border, for the nation was preparing to jump headlong into a world war.

OROZCO, JOSE. "ZAPATISTAS." 1931. COLLECTION, THE MUSEUM OF MODERN ART, NEW YORK. GIVEN ANONYMOUSLY.

This painting by the Mexican artist José Clemente Orozco shows peasant supporters of Emiliano Zapata. Zapata favored giving land to Mexico's peasants. He fought with Pancho Villa against Carranza and became a Mexican hero. NATIONAL IDENTITY Name some modern-day heroes. What makes them heroic? 9A

SECTION REVIEW

1. KEY TERM dollar diplomacy

2. PEOPLE AND PLACES Haiti, Dominican Republic, Mexico, Porfirio Díaz, Victoriano Huerta, Pancho Villa, John J. Pershing

3. COMPREHENSION On what two basic points did Taft and Wilson agree with Roosevelt?

4. COMPREHENSION Why did Wilson refuse to recognize the Huerta government in Mexico?

5. CRITICAL THINKING Do you think foreign policy can ever be based on moral principles? Why or why not?

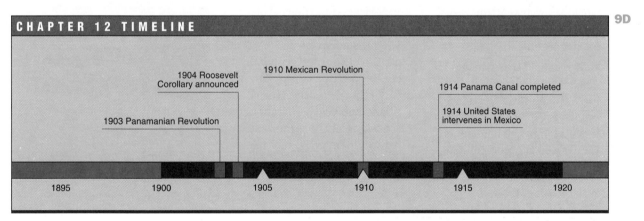

CHAPTER 12 TIMELINE   9D

1903 Panamanian Revolution

1904 Roosevelt Corollary announced

1910 Mexican Revolution

1914 Panama Canal completed

1914 United States intervenes in Mexico

1895   1900   1905   1910   1915   1920

Photo Caption Answer
Students may suggest prominent figures in medicine, sports, civil and human rights, politics, etc.

Background The Americans that Villa pulled off the train and murdered were engineers and technicians who worked in a Mexican mine owned by Americans. The fact that they were returning to Mexico to reopen a mine was taken by Villa as a provocation—foreign ownership of mines and

foreign control of mineral profits having been a major issue in the 1910 revolution.

Section Review Answers

1. *dollar diplomacy*—Taft's policy urging American banks and businesses to invest in Latin America.

2. *Haiti*—Caribbean nation, occupied by U.S. troops in 1915. *Dominican Republic*—Caribbean nation occupied by the U.S. for eight years. *Mexico*—Nation in which the U.S. intervened in 1914 and again in 1916. *Porfirio Díaz*—Leader of Mexico for 35 years and a friend of the United States, overthrown in 1911. *Victoriano Huerta*—Rebel leader responsible for the death of Mexico's reform president in 1913. *Pancho Villa*—Mexican revolutionary whose murder of U.S. citizens provoked military retaliation. *John J. Pershing*—U.S. general assigned to capture Villa.

3. The United States had important interests in Latin America and should intervene when they were threatened.

4. Huerta was held responsible for the death of Francisco Madero, the reform president who had led the revolution against Díaz's dictatorship.

5. Students' answers may mention that it is difficult to apply moral standards to situations which may be unclear or rapidly changing, or where the application of moral standards goes against U.S. economic interests. Equally, it is difficult to support regimes Americans consider immoral.

Closure
Call students' attention to the beige boxed quotation (p. 281). Ask them to relate this quotation to the main idea of the section. Then have students read Section 1 of Chapter 13 for the next class period, noting why the United States maintained neutrality as Europe went to war.

Chapter 12 Review Answers

Key Terms
1. Hay-Pauncefote Treaty
2. Roosevelt Corollary
3. *caudillo*
4. dollar diplomacy
5. Clayton-Bulwer Treaty

People to Identify
1. William Walker
2. Cornelius Vanderbilt
3. Minor Cooper Keith
4. Porfirio Díaz
5. Pancho Villa
6. Philippe Bunau-Varilla

Places to Locate
1. C   4. A
2. E   5. B
3. F   6. D

Reviewing the Facts
1. Severe poverty in the lower classes and no experience in self-government made the Latin American nations politically unstable.

2. Food and raw materials were the main Latin American exports to the U.S.

3. The discovery of gold in California, the recognized potential of Asian markets, and the military importance of such a waterway peaked interest in building a canal across Central America.

4. After some questionable negotiations, a staged revolution, and the hasty recognition of Panama as a sovereign nation the U.S. signed a treaty with Panama's foreign minister Bunau-Varilla.

5. The builders of the canal had to contend with the massive physical undertaking of digging through swamps, jungles, and mountains. Builders also had to contend with tropical diseases and critical public opinion.

284

Chapter 12 REVIEW

Chapter 12 Summary

Section 1: American interest in Latin America grew during the early 1900s.

■ After winning independence in the 1800s, Latin America was plagued by a rigid class structure, wide divisions between rich and poor, and political instability.

■ Latin America's economies were based on agriculture and raw materials.

■ Political and economic opportunities attracted American adventurers and entrepreneurs to Latin America. Foreigners benefited most from these projects.

Section 2: During the early 1900s, the United States became the dominant force in the Western Hemisphere.

■ Theodore Roosevelt supported a revolt against Colombia to gain rights to build a canal across the Isthmus of Panama.

■ The Panama Canal, completed in 1914, revolutionized world trade by cutting travel time between the Atlantic and Pacific oceans.

■ The canal strengthened American determination to enforce the Monroe Doctrine. In order to prevent European intervention in the hemisphere, the United States assumed police power in Latin America.

Section 3: Under Presidents Taft and Wilson, the United States continued to intervene in the internal affairs of Latin American nations.

■ Taft encouraged private investment in Latin America and intervened to protect those investments.

■ President Wilson sent troops into Mexico to overthrow a dictator and protect American investments.

Key Terms ●

Use the following terms to complete the sentences below.

> *caudillo*
> **Clayton-Bulwer Treaty**
> **dollar diplomacy**
> **Hay-Pauncefote Treaty**
> **Roosevelt Corollary**

1. Through the _____, the United States gained the right to build a Central American canal.
2. The _____ stated that the United States would exercise police power in Latin America.
3. Political instability in Latin America led to the rise of _____ rule.
4. Taft's policy of _____ was a plan to encourage economic development in Latin America.
5. In the _____, the United States and Great Britain agreed that any Central American canal would be politically neutral.

People to Identify ●

Use the following names to complete the sentences below.

> **Philippe Bunau-Varilla**
> **Porfirio Díaz**
> **Minor Cooper Keith**
> **Cornelius Vanderbilt**
> **Pancho Villa**
> **William Walker**

1. The American adventurer who tried to take power in Nicaragua and Honduras was _____ .
2. The American tycoon who attempted to build a canal across Nicaragua was _____ .
3. _____ helped to found the United Fruit Company.
4. The Mexican dictator overthrown by Francisco Madero in 1911 was _____ .
5. The Mexican revolutionary who made raids across the American border was _____ .
6. The French businessman who persuaded Congress to build the canal across Panama was _____ .

6. The Panama Canal allowed consumer goods and raw materials to be moved faster between the Atlantic and Pacific. It caused the U.S. to be more concerned with the stability of Latin American governments.

7. The policies of all three Presidents were similar because they all believed the U.S. had important interests in Latin America and if those interests were threatened the U.S. should intervene.

8. Taft believed that American investment in Latin America would build up local economies, reap profits, and build stronger ties with the United States.

Match each of the letters on the map with the places that are listed below.

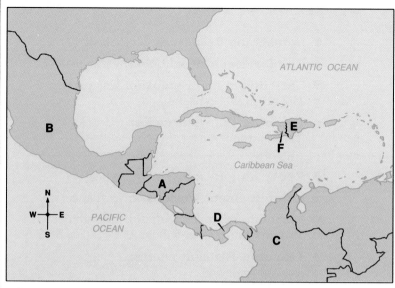

1. Colombia
2. Dominican Republic
3. Haiti
4. Honduras
5. Mexico
6. Panama

REVIEWING THE FACTS ▲

1. What were some of the problems that Latin American nations faced after they gained their independence?
2. What were Latin America's main exports to the United States?
3. Why was there interest in building a canal across Central America?
4. How did the United States gain the right to build a canal through Panama?
5. Why was the building of the Panama Canal such a difficult project?

6. How did the Panama Canal change world trade? Why? How did the canal affect relations between the United States and Latin America?
7. Why were the Latin American policies of Roosevelt, Taft, and Wilson similar?
8. What were the aims of dollar diplomacy?
9. Describe the course of the Mexican Revolution. What role did the United States play?
10. How was the crisis between Mexico and the United States resolved?

CRITICAL THINKING SKILLS ▲

1. IDENTIFYING SIGNIFICANCE
Why might it be difficult for a people who had no experience in self-government to establish an orderly democratic system?

2. ANALYZING A QUOTATION
Reread Roosevelt's defense of American policy in the Dominican Republic (page 279). Do you think the analogy of a policeman was misleading? Explain your answer.

3. IDENTIFYING ADVANTAGES AND DISADVANTAGES What might be the advantages and disadvantages of President Wilson's policy of refusing to recognize undemocratic governments?

WRITING ABOUT TOPICS IN AMERICAN HISTORY ■

1. CONNECTING WITH LITERATURE
A selection from *Complete Book of Marvels* by Richard Halliburton appears on pages 791–793. Read it and answer the questions. Then answer the following question: Why does Halliburton call the opening of the Panama Canal "one of the greatest days in the history of geography"?

2. APPLYING THEMES: GLOBAL INTERACTIONS Do research on a current controversial issue in U.S.–Latin American relations. Then write a concise letter to your representative in Congress expressing your views.

3. GEOGRAPHY Find out more about the building of the Panama Canal. Then write an essay describing the impact it had on the world economy.

Critical Thinking Skills
1. A democratic system requires the participation of a knowledgable citizenry.
2. The United States did more than maintain peace; it enforced its will by taking over the collection of customs duties.
3. Students should point out that by only recognizing democratic governments, the U.S. may promote democracy throughout the world. Such a policy, however, may severely restrict its diplomatic relations with many nations.

Writing About Topics in American History
1. The canal was a geographic marvel—it had connected the two greatest oceans. The canal had also turned everyone's attention to how important geography is. Before the canal, ships had had to sail way around South America.
2. Letters should reflect an understanding of the issues involved and an explanation of the student's opinion.
3. Students should consider the major ports, trade routes, and the type and amount of international trade before the building of the canal, and how these changed after the canal was opened.

9. Years of injustice came to a head when Madero overthrew Díaz in 1911. Madero was later overthrown and executed by Huerta, who was in turn overthrown by Carranza. The U.S. did not recognize the government of Huerta and supplied opposing rebel forces with arms.

10. It was resolved when both sides backed off and agreed to work out their differences peacefully.

Chapter Review exercises are keyed for student abilities:
● = Basic
▲ = Average
■ = Average/Advanced

Chapter 13 ■ World War I

	SECTION OBJECTIVES	SECTION RESOURCES
Section 1 **Roots of the** **Conflict**	■ explain the causes of World War I ■ define United States policy during the early years of the war	● **Reteaching Resources:** Worksheet 47 ▲ **Reinforcement Workbook:** Worksheet 47 ■ **Enrichment and Extension Resources:** Historian Worksheet 4 ▲ **Teaching Transparencies:** Transparency 47
Section 2 **The United States** **Goes to War**	■ explain why the United States entered World War I ■ describe the role of American troops in ending the war	● **Reteaching Resources:** Worksheet 48 ▲ **Reinforcement Workbook:** Worksheet 48 ■ **Enrichment and Extension Resources:** Primary Source Worksheet 25 ▲ **Teaching Transparencies:** Transparency 48
Section 3 **On the Home Front**	■ explain how American efforts on the home front helped make an Allied victory possible	● **Reteaching Resources:** Worksheet 49 ▲ **Reinforcement Workbook:** Worksheet 49 ■ **Enrichment and Extension Resources:** Primary Source Worksheet 26 ▲ **Teaching Transparencies:** Transparency 49
Section 4 **Peacemaking,** **Mapmaking,** **Policymaking**	■ describe the impact of World War I on the world and the United States	● **Reteaching Resources:** Worksheet 50 ▲ **Reinforcement Workbook:** Worksheet 50 ▲ **Teaching Transparencies:** Transparency 50

The list below shows Essential Elements relevant to this chapter. (The complete list of Essential Elements appears in the introductory pages of this Teacher's Edition.)

Section 1: 1A, 1B, 3A, 9A, 9B
Section 2: 1A, 1B, 2D, 4F, 5B, 9A, 9B
Section 3: 2C, 3B, 3D, 3F, 5D, 7B, 7F, 7G, 7J, 9A
Section 4: 1A, 1B, 3B, 5B, 5E, 9A, 9B,9D, 9E

> Section Resources are keyed for student abilities:
> ● = Basic
> ▲ = Average
> ■ = Average/Advanced

CHAPTER RESOURCES

Geography Resources: Worksheets 25, 26
Tests: Chapter 13 Test

Chapter Project : Global Interactions

Have students write a journal of a teenager between the years 1914 and 1918. Students should include accounts of World War I the teenager may have read in the newspaper as well as the war's effects on America. Encourage students to focus on how the war changed the world in terms of national identity, economics, and technology.

Homework Options

Each section contains activities labeled "Addressing Individual Needs." You may wish to choose from among these activities when assigning homework.

> **Provisions for Limited English Proficiency (LEP)**
> Several suggested activities may be particularly helpful for teachers of students with limited English proficiency. These activities have been marked throughout the Teacher's Annotated Edition with the symbol **LEP** .

BIBLIOGRAPHY AND AUDIOVISUAL AIDS

Teacher Bibliography

Darracott, Joseph, ed. *The First World War in Posters: From the Imperial War Museum, London.* Dover, 1974.

Marshall, S.L.A. *World War I.* Houghton Mifflin, 1985.

Tuchman, Barbara. *The Guns of August.* Macmillan, 1962. A history of the period leading up to World War I, focusing on military alliances and the people who formed them.

Student Bibliography

Everett, Suzanne. *World War I: An Illustrated History.* Rand McNally, 1980.

Nordhoff, C. B. and J. N. Hall. *Falcons of France: A Tale of Youth and the Air.* Ayer, 1979.

Literature

Dos Passos, John. *Three Soldiers.* Houghton Mifflin, 1964. Three American soldiers' lives are broken by their experiences in the Army during World War I.

Faulkner, William. *Soldier's Pay.* Liveright, 1954. In Faulkner's first novel, a wounded pilot returns to his hometown to die.

Hemingway, Ernest. *A Farewell to Arms.* Scribner, 1987. A moving story of the effects of World War I on an American in Europe.

Remarque, E. M. *All Quiet on the Western Front.* Fawcett, 1987.

Films and Videotapes *

Clouds of War, 1916–1917. 25 min. AIMS. An account of the events leading to United States entry into World War I.

1914–1918. 56 min. FFH. Documents World War I from its beginning to its end, using film clips from the archives of all of the combatants.

Versailles: The Lost Peace. 26 min. FI. Woodrow Wilson's idealistic hopes for world peace through collective security clashed with the harsher European stance that sought to punish Germany after World War I.

Filmstrips *

Witness to History: The U.S. in World War I (1 filmstrip). GA. Chronicles America's involvement in World War I from the homefront to the trenches.

Computer Software *

The Tragedy of War: A Simulation (Apple with 48K). FOCUS. Simulated game program introduces the realities of fighting a war. The background is World War I from the perspective of frontline soldiers. Encourages students not only to examine the everyday reality of war but to try to understand some of the reasons wars are fought in the first place.

*For a complete guide to audiovisual sources, see the introduction to this book (page Txx).

Chapter 13

World War I
(pp. 286–311)

This chapter provides a detailed study of World War I from the roots of the conflict to the results of the Treaty of Versailles. It examines United States involvement on the battlefront, on the home front, and on the diplomatic front.

Themes in American History

- Global interactions
- Constitutional government
- Pluralistic society
- Geography

Chapter Objectives

After students complete this chapter, they will be able to:

1. Explain the causes of World War I.

2. Define United States policy during the early years of the war.

3. Explain why the United States entered World War I.

4. Describe the role of American troops in ending the war.

5. Explain how American efforts on the home front helped make an Allied victory possible.

6. Describe the impact of World War I on the world and the United States.

*B*reaking its long-held policy of neutrality in European conflicts, the United States entered World War I in 1917. Recruiting posters such as the one above sought to attract volunteers for military service in Europe.

Chapter Opener Art
James Montgomery Flagg, *I Want You,* 1918.

CHAPTER SUPPORT MATERIAL	
Reinforcement Workbook: Worksheets 47–50
Reteaching Resources: Worksheets 47–50
Enrichment and Extension Resources: Primary Source Worksheets 25,26; Historian Worksheet 4
Geography Resources: Worksheets 25, 26
Teaching Transparencies: Transparencies 47–50
Tests: Chapter 13 Test

1A, 1B, 3A, 9A, 9B

1 Roots of the Conflict

Section Focus

Key Terms World War I ■ Triple Alliance ■ Triple Entente ■ Central Powers ■ Allies ■ U-boat

Main Idea A complex system of alliances helped draw the nations of Europe into war in 1914, but the United States declared its neutrality. While fighting deadlocked on the Western Front, submarine warfare threatened American trade and neutrality.

Objectives As you read, look for answers to these questions:
1. What trends in Europe contributed to the outbreak of war?
2. What was trench warfare?
3. How did the United States deal with the nations at war?

June 28, 1914. Sarajevo, Bosnia. Flags waved in the bright morning sun, and people gathered to celebrate the feast of St. Vitus. Happy crowds lined the streets as Archduke Franz Ferdinand, heir to the Austrian throne and future leader of Bosnia, drove by. Suddenly, shots rang out. "It's nothing," murmured Franz Ferdinand, but within an hour he and his wife were dead.

At first, the terrorist killings seemed little more than a minor tragedy. World leaders, including President Wilson, sent their condolences to Emperor Franz Josef in Vienna but did not expect anything more to come of the incident. A month later, however, what had begun as "nothing" triggered the worst war the world had ever known.

In the end, World War I (1914–1918) would redraw national boundaries on three continents and shift the world balance of power. The United States, a reluctant combatant, would emerge as an economic and political giant. But the war would last four years, destroy much of Europe, and take more than 10 million lives in combat, disease, and famine.

This photograph of Austrian Archduke Franz Ferdinand (far right) was taken minutes before his assassination by a Slavic nationalist. The killing provided the spark that ignited World War I in a Europe already primed to explode. GLOBAL AWARENESS Why, do you think, did this one event trigger a world war? 9A

Section Objectives
■ explain the causes of World War I
■ define United States policy during the early years of the war

Introducing the Section

Connecting with Past Learnings
Have students discuss the roots of United States policy towards Europe by asking them to recall the advice Washington gave in his Farewell Address on dealing with Europe. (Avoid foreign entanglements.) How did the Spanish-American War mark a change from traditional foreign policy? (It marked the start of greater American involvement in foreign affairs.)

Key Terms
Write the key terms for this section on the board. Referring to the map on page 296, have students identify the location and countries connected to each one of the terms. Then ask students to use each term in a sentence related to the causes of World War I. **LEP**

SUPPORTING THE SECTION

Reinforcement Workbook: Worksheet 47
Reteaching Resources: Worksheet 47
Enrichment and Extension Resources: Historian Worksheet 4
Teaching Transparencies: Transparency 47

Photo Caption Answer
Students may suggest that the assassination caused a political chain reaction because of international treaties and alliances.

Write the following headings on the chalkboard: *Nationalism, Imperialism, Militarism.* Instruct students to list as many examples as possible to indicate how each heading contributed to conflict in Europe. (Nationalism—tension between Germanic and Slavic peoples; Serbian nationalist assassinated Franz Ferdinand; imperialism—rivalry for land between Ottomans, Austria-Hungary, Russia, France, and Germany; militarism—nations were heavily armed, with large, conscript armies.)

What were people's expectations about the war? (That they would win a quick and easy victory.) *How was the nature of the war different from what people expected?* (It stretched on past the first summer, was very bloody, and was mostly a stalemate.)

Developing the Lesson

After students have read the section, you may want to consider the following activities:

Impact of Geography

Have students study the map of World War I in Europe on page 296, noting the influence of geography on the war. *Why were German U-boats so threatening to Great Britain?* (It is an island nation, and therefore very dependent on shipping.) *Why was the war fought on so many fronts?* (Members of the alliances were separated by geographic boundaries, which became battle fronts.)

CAUSES OF THE WAR 1A

The opening round of this cataclysmic carnage came from a small pistol. The assassin's motive, however, was a large and powerful idea—nationalism. By 1900 great waves of nationalist feeling were sweeping across Europe. The pan-German movement, led by Germany and including Austria, hoped to bring together all German-speaking peoples. The pan-Slavic movement, led by Russia, tried to unite Slavic peoples. Such passionately held beliefs were bound to lead to conflicts over territory. Bosnia, a small state in the Balkans, was one of these contested lands. Although many of its people were Slavs, it had been annexed by German-speaking Austria.

Bosnia's annexation was part of another form of international rivalry—imperialism. For years, European nations had competed for territory throughout the world in search of raw materials and markets. They also competed for lands closer to home, creating flash points throughout Europe. Both Russia and Austria wanted power in the Balkans. Italy disputed Austria's claim to certain territories. France wanted to reclaim the provinces of Alsace and Lorraine from Germany, while Germany wanted to expand eastward. To everyone, bigger meant better.

To protect their growing empires and display their national pride, the European powers engaged in an enormous military buildup. Each nation (except Britain) had a conscription system requiring young men to serve in the military. The drafts produced huge standing armies. By 1914, Russia had more than 8 million men in uniform. Germany had the best-trained army, however, and raced to expand its navy to compete with Great Britain. All nations stockpiled new weapons and ammunition. Militarists—people who glorify the military—called on their governments to use force to settle international problems.

Under the pressures of nationalism, imperialism, and militarism, the nations of Europe formed alliances to maintain a balance of power. Germany joined Austria-Hungary and Italy in the Triple Alliance, while France, Russia, and Great Britain formed the Triple Entente. In each case, the countries agreed to aid their allies in a crisis.

These international arrangements worked for a while; war seemed unthinkable. Yet the system of mutual defense agreements, designed to keep the peace in Europe, ultimately destroyed it. The web of entangling alliances turned a small shooting incident into global violence on an unprecedented scale.

CHAIN REACTION 1A

Franz Ferdinand had been murdered by a Slavic nationalist who thought that Bosnia should belong to its neighbor Serbia. Austria blamed the government of Serbia for the killing and, with a pledge of support from Germany, declared war. Serbia's powerful ally, Russia, mobilized its armies to protect its fellow Slavs. To Germany, this mobilization meant only one thing—war. Germany declared war on Russia on August 1, 1914, and two days later on Russia's ally, France.

The Germans hoped to knock out the French quickly, then concentrate their forces on the Eastern Front against the massive Russian army. To

The British government used posters like this to recruit replacements for the thousands of soldiers who died in the first months of World War I. NATIONAL IDENTITY Compare this poster with the one on page 286. In what ways are they similar? 9B

BRITONS

"WANTS" YOU

JOIN YOUR COUNTRY'S ARMY!
GOD SAVE THE KING

Reproduced by permission of LONDON OPINION

Photo Caption Answer
Each poster uses a stern masculine symbol of the nation to appeal directly to the viewer's patriotism.

Background Gavrilo Princip, Archduke Ferdinand's assassin, was a member of a terrorist group whose goal was to free Slavic peoples living under Austrian rule. He died in prison the year the war ended.

In August 1914, thousands of citizens of Paris thronged the city's boulevards in celebration of France's entry into the war against Germany. **NATIONAL IDENTITY** Why, do you think, were the people in the painting happy about going to war? **9B**

Science and Technology
Discuss with students the effects of the "new instruments of death." *Why were traditional strategies of war ineffective in the face of new technology?* (Armies had to devise different strategies of offense and defense because new weapons were more powerful than before.) *Which weapon do you think had the greatest impact on the development of modern warfare?* (Students may point out that the use of airplanes and submarines revolutionized methods of war.)

Patterns in History
Discuss the ethics of using chemical weapons. Tell students that chemical weapons have been called "the poor man's nuclear weapon." In the late 1980s both George Bush and Mikhail Gorbachev proposed banning at least some types of chemical weapons. *Why might chemical weapons be difficult to regulate?* (They are cheap and relatively easy to make and use and are very effective.) *Do you think they should be banned completely? Why or why not?*

this end, German troops invaded neutral Belgium on August 4 on their way to France. This invasion brought Great Britain into the war, for that country had pledged to defend Belgium.

Now the unthinkable had happened—war had come. Opposing the Central Powers of Germany and Austria-Hungary were the Allies—France, Russia, and Great Britain. About twenty other countries would join the Allies, while the Ottoman Empire (present-day Turkey) and Bulgaria would side with the Central Powers as the world tumbled into madness.

STALEMATE IN THE TRENCHES 1A

Everyone thought the war would be brief—"all over before Christmas," a British slogan said. But everyone misjudged the intensity of the fighting. The Germans swiftly pushed south to the Marne River 40 miles from Paris. By October Allied troops had forced them back to the Belgian town of Ypres (EE–pruh).

Casualties were enormous, and winter was setting in. To consolidate the Allied position, French general Ferdinand Foch told his officers, "You must dig in; it's the only way of staying out of sight and cutting losses." From the North Sea south for 400 miles to Switzerland, Allied soldiers dug trenches in which to live and fight. German troops did the same.

Sometimes the trenches were so close that soldiers could hear the enemy talking. Yet such nearness did not bring the two sides any closer to peace. With the move to the trenches, fighting on the Western Front became a bloody stalemate that was to last nearly four years.

"Nothing to see but bare mud walls, nowhere to sit but on a wet muddy ledge; no shelter of any kind against the weather except the clothes you are wearing; no exercise you can take in order to warm yourself." This was a soldier's life in the trenches. And as one soldier put it, "There doesn't seem the slightest chance of leaving except in an ambulance."

Daytime in the trenches was bleak, uncomfortable, and often boring. Action came at night. Under cover of darkness, troops and supplies were moved into the trenches. Soldiers repaired their dugouts and the barbed wire in front of them.

Photo Caption Answer
Students may suggest that they were glad for a chance to prove their patriotism and that they believed the war would be easily won.

This picture shows one of the trenches that zigzagged along the Western Front. Trenches were wide enough for two men to pass. Dugouts in the walls sheltered men from enemy fire. Supplies and troops reached the front through communications trenches. **HISTORY** What hardships did soldiers in the trenches face? **9A**

Spies set out on patrol, wary of snipers and grenades.

Attacks usually came before dawn. One side would blast the other with heavy artillery, then send its soldiers "over the top," bayonets fixed on rifles, to attack the enemy's trenches. Few ever reached the trenches, for most were cut down by a hail of machine gun fire. During one two-week battle in 1915, for example, the Allies gained about 1,200 yards at the cost of 17,000 men.

NEW INSTRUMENTS OF DEATH 3A

Such slaughter continued year after year because the generals clung to obsolete battlefield tactics. The combination of old ideas and new technology produced a bloodbath.

The old tactic of charging enemy lines proved futile against machine guns and heavy artillery. Some machine guns had greater fire power than an entire company of riflemen. Field guns and howitzers rained destruction on their enemies. At the Battle of the Somme, 2,000 pieces of artillery fired 2 million shells from June to November 1916. So intense was their power that the shelling could be heard nearly 300 miles away in London!

In an attempt to break the stalemate in the trenches, the Germans began using poison gas in 1915. Soldiers feared its deadly greenish-yellow

cloud. "It burned in my throat," wrote a French survivor, "caused pains in my chest, and made breathing all but impossible. I spat blood and suffered dizziness. We all thought that we were lost."

Against the horrors of artillery and gas, the British devised an ingenious weapon. From the Somme came this German report:

> When the German pickets crept out of their dug-outs . . . their blood chilled. Mysterious monsters were crawling towards them over the craters. . . . The monsters approached slowly, hobbling, rolling and rocking, but they approached. Nothing impeded them. . . . Tongues of flame leapt from the sides of the iron caterpillars.

The "monsters" were tanks, which could smash through barbed wire and clear the way for waves of infantry. Yet the early tanks were unreliable, and commanders did not know how best to use them. Tanks did not decisively affect the war's outcome.

Airplanes, too, played a part in the war. At first used only for observation, they were later equipped with machine guns. Brave pilots engaged in aerial dogfights with enemy planes. The most famous of these was the German ace, Manfred von Richthofen. Called the "Red Baron," he scored 80 victories before being shot down.

BIOGRAPHY

EDDIE RICKENBACKER (1890–1973) raced automobiles before volunteering as a pilot in World War I. He became the leading American flying ace of the war, shooting down 22 enemy planes and 4 balloons. After the war, Rickenbacker became the owner of the Indianapolis Speedway and president of Eastern Airlines. He wrote three books about his experiences as a pilot.

290 UNIT 4 BECOMING A WORLD POWER

Gassed is the title of this painting by American artist John Singer Sargent. It shows British soldiers blinded by a poison gas attack clinging together as they retreat from a battlefield. Germany first used gas against Russia on the Eastern Front in 1915. Russia did not report the attack to the other Allies, who were later surprised by the use of gas on the Western Front. **CULTURE** What attitudes toward war does Sargent's painting convey? **9B**

THE WAR AT SEA **3A**

Perhaps the most dreaded of the new weapons was the German submarine, or U-boat, for it changed the nature of war at sea. In defiance of international law, the U-boats attacked without warning, sinking both military and commercial ships.

Germany used submarines to retaliate against the British naval blockade of the Central Powers. The British wanted to cut off supplies bound for Germany. They even searched and seized neutral vessels bound for neutral ports to prevent any food or weapons from reaching the enemy. In return, German submarines began sinking merchant ships in an attempt to starve the British, who depended on imported food.

In February 1915, Germany declared a war zone around the British Isles. Enemy merchant ships were sunk without warning in this zone; neutral ships entered at their own risk. The effects were devastating. At one point, the English had only enough food to last three weeks. German submarines destroyed one-fourth of the British fleet. In one month alone they sank about one million tons of shipping.

SUBMARINES THREATEN AMERICAN TRADE **1B**

At the beginning of the war, President Wilson had declared American neutrality. He expected Americans to be "neutral in fact as well as in name." He also expected the countries at war to honor the rights of neutrals, under the principles of international law. One of these rights stated that warships were to warn neutral ships before attack, then take on surviving passengers. Submarines, small craft whose success depended upon surprise, could do neither.

This watercolor shows F-2A "flying boats" bombing a German U-boat. Scientists applied new technologies to weaponry, and the machines they designed changed the nature of warfare. **TECHNOLOGY** What were each side's goals in naval warfare during World War I? **9A**

As a neutral nation, the United States sold arms, ammunition, and food to both sides. Because of the British blockade, however, the United States conducted much more trade with the Allies than with the Central Powers. The United States did hundreds of millions of dollars of business with the Allies, which greatly boosted the American economy. Submarines, however, threatened this trade and violated the rights of neutral nations.

When the Germans declared their naval war zone, President Wilson warned that they would be held to "strict accountability" for any loss of American life or property. He further stated that the United States would take action to protect the rights of American citizens to travel on the high seas. All too soon his warning would be tested.

1A, 1B, 2D, 4F, 5B, 9A, 9B

2 The United States Goes to War

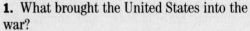

Section Focus

Key Terms Sussex Pledge ■ Zimmermann Note ■ American Expeditionary Forces ■ convoy ■ Treaty of Brest-Litovsk

Main Idea No longer willing to remain neutral in the face of German provocations, the United States entered the war and helped bring victory to the Allies.

Objectives As you read, look for answers to these questions:
1. What brought the United States into the war?
2. What did President Wilson hope to accomplish by joining the fight?
3. How did American troops help end the war?

May 1, 1915. A dance band played as the luxury liner *Lusitania* sailed out of New York harbor, bound for England. Six days later, passengers filled the deck after lunch to look at the approaching coast of Ireland. Lurking beneath the surface, a German submarine spotted the ship. The Germans knew that the *Lusitania*, though a civilian ship, was secretly carrying munitions. The German captain took aim at the oncoming ship and fired a torpedo into its hull. Within 18 minutes the *Lusitania* went to the bottom, taking with it 1,198 passengers. Of these, 128 were Americans, most of them women and children.

WILSON RESPONDS 1A, 5B

Americans were outraged. To many, the war had seemed a European problem, one in which the United States was wise to remain neutral. Yet the sinking of the *Lusitania* made the war a problem for Americans as well. Some, like Theodore Roosevelt, called for war, but President Wilson refused to abandon neutrality. Instead, he demanded from Germany an apology, money damages, and a commitment not to use submarines again.

When Germany agreed to all but the last condition, most Americans were satisfied. For the next year Wilson tried to end the war through diplo-

This American cartoon appeared after the *Lusitania* was sunk. It shows Germany's leader, Kaiser Wilhelm, paying reparations to President Wilson while a humiliated eagle stands in the background. POLITICS What point does the cartoon make about the kaiser's handling of the incident and Wilson's reaction? 1B

macy. At the same time, the *Lusitania* incident convinced him of the need to prepare for national defense. In November 1915 Wilson made public a plan to build up the army and the navy. Congress, however, did not support it.

Events of the following March would change the legislators' minds. A German submarine sank the French passenger ship *Sussex*, killing several passengers. Although he did not want war, President Wilson was furious and threatened to break off relations with Germany. To keep the United States from entering the war, the Germans agreed to the Sussex Pledge. In it they promised not to sink merchant ships "without warning and without saving human lives."

The Sussex Pledge, in effect, bought more time for the Germans. But the sinking of the *Sussex* showed Congress how little time there was to prepare for war. Congress soon passed laws to build up the army and navy, and set up the Council of National Defense to organize industries and resources in case of war.

Wilson's goal was to work for peace but be pre-

pared for war. In the election of 1916, he appealed to most Americans' desire for neutrality with the campaign slogan "He kept us out of war." His opponent, Charles Evans Hughes of New York, did not want war either. But Hughes was hurt by splits within the Republican Party, and by support from prowar Theodore Roosevelt. Democrats ran this ad to win working class votes:

> You are Working;
> —Not Fighting!
> Alive and Happy;
> —Not Cannon Fodder!
> Wilson and Peace with Honor?
> or
> Hughes with Roosevelt and War?

THE UNITED STATES ENTERS THE WAR 1A

Wilson narrowly won the election in November and continued to work for an end to the war. In January 1917 he suggested that the European powers negotiate a "peace without victory," in which neither side gained territory or lost power. Wilson believed that "Only a peace between equals can last." But the Europeans rejected his idea—nothing less than victory would do after so much bloodshed.

> "**O**nly a peace between equals can last."
>
> —*Woodrow Wilson, 1917*

Events beyond America's borders would soon pull the United States into the war. The Germans won stunning victories over the Russians on the Eastern Front and then turned their attention to the west, where trench warfare was deadlocked. On February 1, 1917, they resumed unrestricted submarine warfare, gambling that they could crush the British at sea before the United States had time to enter the war.

Thus the Germans violated the Sussex Pledge. In response, President Wilson broke off diplomatic relations with Germany and decided to arm American merchant ships with naval guns. The United States was now practicing "armed neutrality."

Neutrality was strained to the limit when British intelligence intercepted a coded message from the German foreign secretary, Arthur Zimmermann, to the German ambassador in Mexico. It instructed him to offer Mexico a deal. If Mexico would join Germany in an alliance against the United States, Germany would restore territory in New Mexico, Texas, and Arizona to Mexico. Wilson made public the Zimmermann Note on March 1, 1917, causing a storm of anti-German feeling in the United States.

Public opinion turned even more decisively against Germany when submarines sank several American merchant ships. Wilson faced a hard choice: keeping up his efforts for peace through diplomacy and armed neutrality or going to war against Germany. On the one hand, he hated war, believing that it would promote intolerance and weaken American democracy. On the other hand, he feared that a German military victory would destroy democracy altogether.

A revolution in Russia in mid-March helped Wilson decide. Czar Nicholas II was overthrown, and a democratic government was set up. No longer a dictatorship, Russia became an acceptable ally for the United States.

On April 2, 1917, Wilson asked a joint session of Congress for a declaration of war. He presented the state of affairs not as an American problem but a world problem, the issue not one of politics but of morality. "The present German submarine warfare against commerce is a warfare against mankind," Wilson said. "Our object . . . is to vindicate the principles of peace and justice in the life of the world. . . . Neutrality is no longer feasible or desirable where the peace of the world is involved and the freedom of its peoples. . . . The world must be made safe for democracy."

> "**T**he world must be made safe for democracy."
>
> —*Woodrow Wilson, 1917*

On April 6, 1917, Congress voted to go to war. The President hoped that it would be the war to end all wars.

General John J. Pershing organized the 2 million American soldiers, most of them inexperienced, who fought in World War I. Pershing had earlier fought in Cuba, in the Philippines, and against Pancho Villa in Mexico. CULTURE To what historical figures does this poster compare Pershing and his army? 9A

THE YANKS ARE COMING 1A

June 14, 1917. With flag-bedecked streets and brass bands playing "The Star-Spangled Banner," Paris greeted General John J. Pershing, commander of the American Expeditionary Forces. After a huge welcoming ceremony, Pershing wanted to make a small visit before he began his military mission. A few days later he drove to a cemetery on the outskirts of Paris. As Pershing placed a wreath on a marble tomb, his aide said quietly, "Lafayette, we are here."

Repaying the French for their support of liberty in the American Revolution, American troops began arriving in France in the summer of 1917. British and American warships guarded troop carriers across the Atlantic. Through this convoy system soldiers and supplies reached Europe safely.

Although their numbers were limited at first,

the "Yanks," as they were called, bolstered the morale of the Allies. It was not until 1918 that the United States could send more than a million soldiers to Europe, and by then they were desperately needed.

THE LAST YEAR OF THE WAR 1A

Despite heavy fighting in 1917, the Germans remained in control of northern France and Belgium. Germany and Austria crushed Italy, a member of the Allies since 1915, at the Battle of Caporetto in October 1917. In November 1917, Russia shook with another revolution—the Bolshevik Revolution. Promising the war-weary Russians "Peace, Land, Bread," the Bolshevik wing of the Communist Party took control, under the leadership of V. I. Lenin. In March 1918, Russia signed the Treaty of Brest-Litovsk with Germany and dropped out of the fight.

With no opposition in the east, the Germans then began an all-out assault on the Western Front. In one week in March 1918 they marched 30 miles to the west, more than either side had achieved since 1914.

To help the British and French forces stop the German advances, the United States rushed troops across the Atlantic. By the end of March, 85,000 "doughboys," as they were also dubbed, reached Europe; 120,000 more came a month later. American forces would number 1 million by July 1, 1918, and 2 million by early November.

On June 1, 1918, American soldiers helped block the Germans at Château-Thierry, about 50 miles from Paris. Intense Allied fighting throughout June and July stopped the German advance and began to push the enemy eastward. By August the tide of war had turned.

GEOGRAPHY AS ENEMY 2D

The critical battle to end the war began in September. The goal was to cut off the German rail lines near Sedan, which supplied enemy troops. To do so required attacking through the Argonne Forest, a "vast network of uncut barbed wire, . . . deep ravines, dense woods, myriads of shell craters, . . . [obscured by] heavy fog," in General Pershing's words.

For 47 days, 1.2 million American soldiers pushed toward the German lines, under heavy enemy fire. In one month, more ammunition was used than in the entire Civil War. Troops often moved at night in order to surprise the Germans.

A million American troops took part in the offensive in the Argonne Forest in September 1918. Here, machine gunners advance through a war-blasted section of forest. TECHNOLOGY How did the machine gun make previous military strategy obsolete? 9A

Photo Caption Answer
Its firepower could wipe out enemy forces when they charged in close-grouped formations.

Background   To weaken Russia, Germany helped Lenin return from Switzerland. Lenin gained control and called for peace with Germany. The Brest-Litovsk Treaty forced Russia to give up large amounts of territory.

pipe clay dough. A third possible origin is from *adobe*, used in the Southwest because soldiers were sometimes housed in adobe buildings. Ask students if they know nicknames used to describe soldiers in other wars. (*Yanks* for Union troops during the Civil War and *Johnny Reb* or just *Reb* for a southern soldier. *G.I.* during World War II and *grunt* during the Vietnam War.)

Geographic Themes: Place
Instruct students to locate each of the following places on the map on page 296 and explain its significance:
(1) Caporetto, Italy;
(2) Château-Thierry, France;
(3) Argonne Forest. (1— battle in which Germany and Austria defeated Italy; 2— battle at which Americans helped block Germans; 3— scene of last critical battle of World War I.)

Connecting with Literature
Explain to students that the two heads in this section, "THE YANKS ARE COMING" and "ALL QUIET ON THE WESTERN FRONT" refer, respectively, to a popular World War I song and a famous book about the war. "The Yanks Are Coming" is from the chorus of "Over There," a song by George M. Cohan. Have interested students find a recording or the lyrics of that song or other World War I songs.

A former German soldier, Erich Maria Remarque, wrote *All Quiet on the Western Front*, about the horror of the war in the trenches. Students may be interested in reading that book, or the poetry of Englishmen Siegfried Sassoon or Wilfred Owen, for a sense of the common soldier's experiences in World War I.

Divide the class into small groups. Have each group generate two lists: reasons for the United States to enter World War I, and reasons for the country to remain neutral. Make sure each member of the group contributes at least one suggestion to each list. Then have the group decide whether the United States should have entered the war or not. **LEP**

Addressing Individual Needs

Guided/Independent Practice

Have students complete **Reinforcement Workbook** Worksheet 48, which requires students to make judgments about issues related to World War I.

Reteaching/Correctives

Have students work in small groups to create illustrated timelines of important events discussed in the section. First have students scan the section to decide which events to list and how best to illustrate them. Be sure that each group member contributes in some way to the project.

Ask students to complete **Reteaching Resources** Worksheet 48. This worksheet helps students sequence and understand events leading to American involvement in World War I.

Enrichment/Extension

Assign **Enrichment and Extension Resources** Primary Source Worksheet 25, which examines President Wilson's war message.

Assessment

You may wish to use the Section 2 Review, page 297, to see how well your students understand the main points in this lesson.

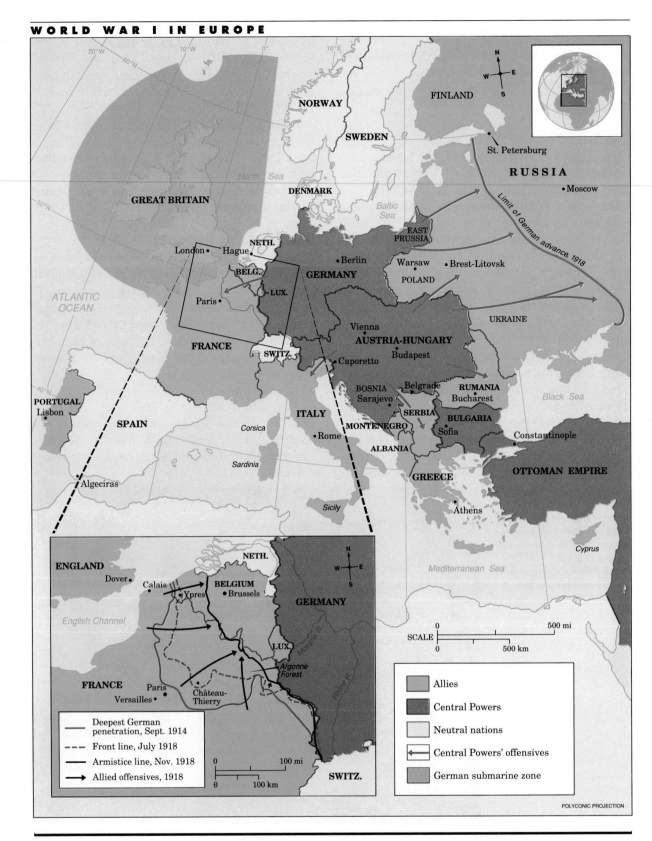

WORLD WAR I IN EUROPE

Map Skills Answers

The distance ranges from 250 miles (402 km) to 700 miles (1126 km). Less than 40 miles (64 km). The distance was short because trench warfare allowed neither side to gain significant territory.

Harry S. Truman, a future President, fought in the Argonne Forest. He wrote home:

> There were some three or four weeks, from September 10 to October 6, that I did nothing but march at night and shoot or sleep in daylight. . . . The infantry—our infantry—are the heroes of the war. There's nothing—machine guns, artillery, rifles, bayonets, mines, or anything else—that can stop them when they start.

Among the unstoppable infantrymen at the Argonne were several units of black troops. Black soldiers fought bravely in all the major battles; two were the first Americans to be honored with the Croix de Guerre (a French medal). Three black regiments also received this award. Yet of the 200,000 African Americans sent to France, only 20,000 saw action. Army policy kept black troops separated from whites and assigned most of them to menial noncombat duties.

ALL QUIET ON THE WESTERN FRONT 1A

By mid-October 1918, the German lines were crumbling. Not wanting to give them time to regroup their forces, General Pershing told his troops, "We must strike harder than ever." American soldiers fought their way forward and on November 7 captured the high ground above Sedan. The next day the Germans asked for the Allied terms of armistice.

In the chill mists of dawn on November 11, 1918, the armistice was signed, and at the eleventh hour of the eleventh day of the eleventh month the fighting stopped. At first the soldiers were dazed. Wrote a sergeant, "It really was beyond comprehension, this glorious news—too much to grasp all at once. No more whizz-bangs [light artillery shells], no more bombs, no more mangled, bleeding bodies, no more exposure to terrifying shell fire in the rain and cold and mud!"

MAP SKILLS 9B

About how far from the German border did the Central Powers push into Russia? CRITICAL THINKING Use the inset map to determine the greatest distance between the German front line in September 1914 and in July 1918. Why, do you think, had the line moved so little in four years?

Americans celebrated in the streets on Armistice Day in 1918. This impressionistic painting by Gifford Reynolds Beal captures the joy and excitement of the moment. CULTURE How does the painting suggest a new international outlook among Americans?
1A, 4F

With more than 8 million soldiers dead, at long last the killing was over. Soldiers climbed out of foxholes to celebrate, and telegraph cables flashed the good news around the world. As one historian described it, "Never in history perhaps have such great multitudes experienced such restoration of joyousness in the twinkling of an eye."

SECTION REVIEW

1. KEY TERMS Sussex Pledge, Zimmermann Note, American Expeditionary Forces, convoy, Treaty of Brest-Litovsk

2. PEOPLE AND PLACES Charles Evans Hughes, John J. Pershing, V. I. Lenin, Château-Thierry, Sedan, Argonne Forest

3. COMPREHENSION What were the events that brought the United States into the war?

4. COMPREHENSION Why was the Allied need for American troops especially great after March 1918?

5. CRITICAL THINKING Compare Wilson's call in January 1917 for a "peace without victory" with his statement in April 1917 that "The world must be made safe for democracy." Are the two statements consistent? Explain your answer.

Photo Caption Answer
Flags of many nations appear in the streets.

Closure

Call students' attention to the beige boxed quotation (p. 294). Ask them to relate this quotation to the main idea of the section. Then have students read Section 3 for the next class period, noting how the war affected life in the United States.

3 On the Home Front

Section Objective

■ explain how American efforts on the home front helped make an Allied victory possible

Introducing the Section

Connecting with Past Learnings

Discuss reasons why the United States stayed neutral for the first few years of World War I. (Traditional policy of staying out of European affairs; divided loyalties among Americans of different European backgrounds; lack of preparedness.)

Key Terms

Write the key terms for this section on the board. Have students underline the names of agencies and circle the names of laws. Ask volunteers to locate each term in the text and write a brief definition on the board. **LEP**

Focus

Have students create a hypothetical American family in 1918: a husband, wife, son and daughter in their late teens or early twenties, another child in high school. Write the names and ages of family members on the board. Then have students list the ways in which the war affected each family member. Ask volunteers to role play family members at dinner time, discussing activities on the home front.

Section Focus

Key Terms Selective Service Act ■ War Industries Board ■ Liberty Loan ■ Trading with the Enemy Act ■ Sedition Act ■ Espionage Act ■ American's Creed

Main Idea Efforts on the home front helped make Allied victory possible. Wilson won public support with a crusading appeal, but the need for wartime conformity led to some restrictions on civil rights.

Objectives As you read, look for answers to these questions:
1. How did the federal government regulate production during the war?
2. What volunteer efforts did Americans make to help win the war?
3. How and why were civil rights affected by the war?

Wilson the idealist wanted to make the world safe for democracy, but Wilson the realist knew that winning the war would take an enormous effort from everyone in the United States. Soon after Congress declared war, he told the American people:

> In the sense in which we have been [used] to think of armies there are no armies in this struggle, there are entire nations armed. Thus, the men who remain to till the soil and man the factories are no less a part of the army that is in France than the men beneath the battle flags. It must be so with us. It is not an army that we must shape and train for war—it is a Nation.

Mobilizing troops and the nation's resources, industries, workers, and will to fight was a tremendous task. Its successful completion brought victory in Europe and profound changes at home.

YOU'RE IN THE ARMY NOW 7B

The Germans were counting on knocking out the British before the Americans were ready to fight. To defeat their plan, the United States had to raise an army fast. With no time to wait for enough volunteers, Congress voted to pass the Selective Service Act in May 1917. It required all men between ages 21 and 30 to sign up for military service.

Historically, Americans had not liked the idea of conscription. There had been draft riots during the Civil War, and only volunteers had fought the

This picture was on a World War I recruitment poster for the U.S. Navy. Though the need for volunteers was enormous, only 73,000 men had signed up six weeks after war was declared. HISTORY How did the government respond to the lack of volunteers? 7G

Spanish-American War. Now there was opposition to the Selective Service Act. In Congress, Speaker of the House Champ Clark argued that "there is precious little difference between a conscript and a convict." Yet the law was passed, and registration for the draft went smoothly. Later the law would be broadened to include men between 18 and 45.

Eventually the Selective Service listed more than 24 million men and drafted about 3 million of them by lottery. Another 2 million men volun-

SUPPORTING THE SECTION

Reinforcement Workbook: Worksheet 49
Reteaching Resources: Worksheet 49
Enrichment and Extension Resources: Primary Source Worksheet 26
Teaching Transparencies: Transparency 49

Photo Caption Answer
It passed the Selective Service Act in 1917.

teered. Among the nearly 5 million men in uniform were 370,000 blacks. Women volunteered for the military by the thousands and served as clerks, stenographers, and radio operators.

To prepare this overnight army, the War Department hastily built sixteen training camps throughout the nation—most were unfinished when the first trainees arrived in September 1917. Officers, mostly college students, were trained for duty in a short 90 days. Never was so much done so quickly to build up a fighting force.

ORGANIZING INDUSTRY 3B, 3D, 3F

Arming and transporting this fighting force was an immense challenge. It required centralized organization and a planned economy, which the federal government had never undertaken before. Congress gave President Wilson the power to create new agencies to coordinate the war effort.

The most important was the War Industries Board, headed by financier Bernard Baruch. The board regulated the supply of raw materials to manufacturers and the delivery of finished products. Iron and steel went into tanks and guns instead of cars and corsets. Textiles were turned into uniforms instead of civilian clothes.

Leaders of big business, who had opposed government regulation before the war, rolled up their sleeves and went to work in Washington to help run the War Industries Board. They became known as "dollar-a-year men" for the token salaries they received.

Their efforts paid off. It has been estimated that through the organization of the War Industries Board, the industrial capacity of the country grew 20 percent. Factories worked around the clock to pour forth mountains of supplies, including 89 million pairs of socks and 19 million blankets. American shipyards launched the amazing total of 95 vessels in a single day—appropriately enough, the Fourth of July in 1918. Without American industry, there would not have been an Allied victory.

"LABOR WILL WIN THE WAR" 3B, 3F

This wartime slogan, meant to encourage hard work, proved correct. America's astonishing level of production would not have been possible without the cooperation of working people.

Samuel Gompers and other leaders of organized labor cooperated with the federal government to keep up production. The War Labor Board settled labor disputes and determined wages, hours, and working conditions. In the booming wartime economy, there was work for everyone, and membership in labor unions soared.

One union, however, opposed the war. The Industrial Workers of the World, or IWW, claimed the war was being fought to enrich big business and Wall Street, not to make the world safe for democracy. The Wobblies, as members of the IWW were called, advocated sabotage and engaged in some strikes, but they were an exception among American workers.

With millions of men in the armed forces, American employers looked for new employees. Women began filling jobs once thought fit only for men. Answering the call "A woman's place is in the war," they became factory workers, auto mechanics, streetcar conductors, telegraph messengers, traffic cops, and farmers (called "farmerettes" at the time).

> "**A** woman's place is in the war."
> —*Wartime slogan*

Pleased to have new jobs open up to them, women still did not forget the patriotic reason for their work. Wrote one woman of her job in a gas mask factory:

> It has been one of the richest experiences of my life—meeting all the wonderful women who are there . . . who have given up their old work to do their bit—and all the time feeling that I was being really useful to the boys on the other side.

The shortage of workers also lured southern blacks to northern and western cities. There they found jobs in war-related industries. Many of these jobs had previously been closed to blacks. But while employment opportunities opened up and blacks could earn more money, discrimination still faced them in every other aspect of life.

What efforts on the home front contributed to Allied victory overseas? (Raising and training an army, coordinating and increasing production, conserving materials needed for war, and financing the war through bond purchases.)
How did the war effort affect American attitudes and values at home? (Inspired patriotism and loyalty; suppressed freedom of speech.)

Developing the Lesson

After students have read the section, you may want to consider the following activities:

Economics

Discuss the ways that the federal government took control of the economy during the war. (The War Industries Board regulated manufacturing; the War Labor Board settled disputes and determined wages, hours, and working conditions.) *What were the results of the planned economy coordinated by the government?* (Industrial capacity increased about 20 percent.)

Ask students to list positive and negative consequences of government regulation of the war effort. (Positive—Allied victory, increased employment opportunities, higher wages; negative—increased role of federal government in private industry and people's lives, possible problems of return to peacetime economy.)

Ethics

Discuss sacrifices Americans made for the war effort. (Voluntary food conservation, less use of coal and gasoline, bought liberty bonds, young men joined the army.) *Do you think Americans are willing to make such sacrifices today?* Discuss with students the causes for which they would be willing to make personal sacrifices.

CONSERVATION 2C

Heatless, wheatless, and meatless—these were watchwords to encourage conservation during the war. Resources were limited, and frugality became the norm.

To win the war, Americans would have to feed their European allies as well as themselves. President Wilson named Herbert Hoover to head the Food Administration. Hoover, a mining engineer, was an excellent organizer. His Food Administration set crop prices and regulated food exports to Europe.

To make sure there was enough to send abroad, Hoover asked Americans to give up wheat on Mondays and Wednesdays, meat on Tuesdays, and pork on Thursdays and Saturdays. This voluntary food conservation came to be known as "Hooverizing." Also part of Hoover's program to save food for export was the victory garden. He encouraged Americans, especially Boy Scouts, to plant a home vegetable garden. "Every scout to feed a soldier," was a popular saying.

Another saying was "Fuel Will Win the War,"

Herbert Hoover's Food Administration issued this poster encouraging Americans to avoid wasting food. NATIONAL IDENTITY To which aspects of American identity and experience does the poster appeal? 2C

FOOD WILL WIN THE WAR
You came here seeking Freedom
You must now help to preserve it
WHEAT is needed for the allies
Waste nothing
UNITED STATES FOOD ADMINISTRATION

for fuel was absolutely essential to run factories and to transport goods and troops. The Fuel Administration encouraged greater coal production and at the same time urged citizens to use less coal. To save an hour's use of lighting each day, the Fuel Administration established daylight saving time. To be patriotic, Americans participated voluntarily in "heatless Mondays" and "lightless nights." They willingly gave up family drives on "gasless Sundays."

FINANCING THE WAR 3B

Voluntarism also played a large part in paying for the war. By November 1918 the war cost $44 million a day. Increased taxes paid for only about one-third of war expenditures. The rest came from bonds bought by citizens rich and poor.

The government sold these bonds in four large Liberty Loan drives. Bonds went on sale everywhere, from big city theaters to small-town banks. Famous entertainers urged people at crowded rallies to buy bonds. Posters rallied popular support. In each of the Liberty Loans, bond sales exceeded their goal, and the number of subscribers grew. More than 21 million people eventually bought bonds.

RALLYING PUBLIC OPINION 7B

Liberty Loans and Hooverizing succeeded because they made the war a personal effort. Recruiting posters like the famous Uncle Sam saying "I Want You" attempted to do the same thing. But such massive popular support was not at all a sure thing at the time Congress declared war.

When war broke out in Europe in 1914, Wilson had called on Americans to be neutral and impartial. That was not easy for everyone. As Wilson himself said, "We have to be neutral. Otherwise, our mixed populations would wage war on each other." German Americans were the largest foreign-born ethnic group in the country, and many felt loyalty to their relatives abroad. Many Irish Americans supported the Central Powers against their old enemy, England.

On the other hand, a great many Americans sympathized with the Allies. A common language with England and a belief in democracy led them to favor the Allies. So did anti-German propaganda spread by the British, who controlled the telegraph cables linking Europe with the United States.

As the war in Europe dragged on and German submarines threatened American interests, more people favored the Allies. But favoring the Allies was one thing; actually going to war for them was another. Since Washington's time, Americans had been told to avoid "entangling alliances" with Europe. Many had trouble understanding a war against Germany, which had not attacked the United States. Transforming Americans from neutrals to belligerents would require changing hearts and minds. With Wilson it would take on the tone of a moral crusade.

A propaganda poster by James Montgomery Flagg (who also designed the poster on page 286) shows a woman representing America asleep in a chair while smoke rises in the background. NATIONAL IDENTITY Why, do you think, was it necessary to persuade Americans to support the nation's role in World War I? 9A

ENFORCING LOYALTY 5D

Wilson explained the war as more than a matter of shipping interests. To him it was a struggle between good and evil, between righteous democracy and the forces of "selfish and autocratic power," who were the "natural foe to liberty." With the goals of war stated so idealistically, disagreement with the government was seen as disloyalty, intolerable in time of war.

To suppress criticism, Congress passed three laws. Under the Trading with the Enemy Act, the Postmaster General gained the power to censor any publications exchanged with other countries. The controversial Sedition Act prohibited any speech that was "disloyal, profane, scurrilous, or abusive" about the government, flag, Constitution, or armed forces. The Espionage Act punished anyone found guilty of helping the enemy, hindering recruitment, or inciting revolt.

In a landmark case—*Schenck v. U.S.* (1919)—the Supreme Court upheld the Espionage Act. Justice Oliver Wendell Holmes declared that there were circumstances in which the First Amendment right of free speech could be limited. These included the existence of a "clear and present danger" to public safety, as in wartime.

Americans who criticized the government went to prison. The Supreme Court upheld the conviction of Eugene V. Debs for an antiwar speech. Anarchist Emma Goldman spent two years in jail for opposing the draft. Radical labor leader William D. Haywood and 94 other members of the IWW were also convicted of sedition.

Here indeed was a paradox. Fighting in Europe to make the world safe for democracy, the United States was stifling differences of opinion at home. As historian David Kennedy explained it, "fear corrupted usually sober minds." First Amendment rights were sacrificed to the crusade for public support of the war.

PROMOTING PATRIOTISM 7F, 7J

Entry into the war prompted a national writing contest to bring forth a stirring statement of America's values. About 3,000 contestants vied for the prize of $1,000 offered by the mayor of Baltimore, the city where Francis Scott Key had written "The Star-Spangled Banner."

Addressing Individual Needs

Guided/Independent Practice
Ask students to complete **Reinforcement Workbook** Worksheet 49, which helps them recognize the use of propaganda to support the war effort.

Reteaching/Correctives
Have students work in pairs to create posters illustrating American efforts on the home front that helped make an Allied victory possible. Have students use at least four subjects covered in the section. Have them title their posters and display them in the classroom.

Instruct students to complete **Reteaching Resources** Worksheet 49. This worksheet helps students identify the problems of mobilizing for war and the solutions implemented by the federal government.

Enrichment/Extension
Assign **Enrichment and Extension Resources** Primary Source Worksheet 26. This worksheet examines the food conservation effort on the home front.

Assessment
You may wish to use the Section 3 Review, page 302, to see how well your students understand the main points in this lesson.

Section Review Answers
1. *Selective Service Act*—Required men between 21 and 30 to sign up for military service. *War Industries Board*—Regulated supply of raw materials and delivery of finished products. *Liberty Loan*—Drive to sell government bonds, raising money to pay for the war. *Trading with the Enemy Act*—Law censoring publications exchanged with other

William Tyler Page, a clerk of the House of Representatives, wrote the winning entry. In it he
wove together words from the Declaration of Independence, the Constitution, the Gettysburg Address, and one of Daniel Webster's most famous
speeches to create the American's Creed:

> I believe in the United States of America
> as a government of the people, by the peo-
> ple, for the people; whose just powers are
> derived from the consent of the governed;
> a democracy in a Republic; a sovereign
> Nation of many sovereign States; a perfect
> Union, one and inseparable; established
> upon those principles of freedom, equality,
> justice, and humanity for which Ameri-
> can patriots sacrificed their lives and
> fortunes.
>
> I therefore believe it is my duty to my
> country to love it; to support its Constitu-
> tion; to obey its laws, to respect its flag;
> and to defend it against all enemies.

After the contest received national publicity, the
Creed became quite popular. Millions of schoolchildren memorized it and recited it daily. With his
prize money, Page bought war bonds, which he
gave to charities.

BUILDING SUPPORT FOR THE WAR 7J

Wilson knew that promoting patriotism was not
enough. To promote the war itself, the President
authorized formation of the Committee on Public
Information, headed by the muckraking journalist
George Creel. Plunging into his task, Creel used
millions of posters and leaflets to rally support for
the war. He also trained a group of spirited citizens to give brief speeches about war. These
"Four-Minute Men" totaled 75,000 and had millions of listeners.

Songs too were used to stir public enthusiasm.
Before the war, Americans rarely sang "The Star-
Spangled Banner." By war's end, thanks to the
Creel Committee, the song would be sung at
almost every public occasion, from baseball games
to school assemblies.

Despite its patriotic intentions, the Committee
on Public Information became a propaganda mill
that played on people's fears. It had writers make

up stories of the crimes German soldiers would
commit if they ever invaded the United States. It
also encouraged people to spy on their fellow citizens. One leaflet said, "Report the man who
spreads pessimistic stories, divulges—or seeks—
confidential military information, cries for peace,
or belittles our efforts to win the war."

> "**R**eport the man who . . . cries for
> peace, or belittles our efforts to win the
> war."
>
> —*Government leaflet*

The Committee also used "100 percent Americanism" to build support for the war and to denounce anything or anyone connected with
Germany. Many school districts stopped teaching
the German language. Doctors referred to German measles as "liberty measles," and grocers
sold "liberty cabbage" instead of sauerkraut.

Passions ran high against the enemy. To wage
war, Wilson had succeeded in mobilizing public
support in thought as well as in action. Once the
fighting stopped, however, he would not meet with
the same success in his plans for peace.

SECTION REVIEW

1. KEY TERMS Selective Service Act, War Industries Board, Liberty Loan, Trading with the Enemy Act, Sedition Act, Espionage Act, American's
Creed

2. PEOPLE Bernard Baruch, Herbert Hoover,
Emma Goldman, William Haywood, William Tyler
Page, George Creel

3. COMPREHENSION What steps did the federal government take to guarantee high levels of production during the war?

4. COMPREHENSION In what ways did civilians contribute to the war effort?

5. CRITICAL THINKING Do you think that wartime
circumstances ever justify limiting civil rights?
Explain your answer.

---

4 Peacemaking, Mapmaking, Policymaking

Section Focus

Key Terms Fourteen Points ■ League of Nations ■ Treaty of Versailles ■ mandate ■ Balfour Declaration ■ genocide ■ Weimar Republic

Main Idea Although Wilson wanted a peace among equals, the peace treaty punished Germany. The Senate rejected the treaty.

Objectives As you read, look for answers to these questions:
1. What were Wilson's goals for the peace treaty?
2. What were the final terms of the peace treaty?
3. Why did the United States Senate refuse to ratify the treaty?

November 11, 1918. The magnificent Cloth Hall of Ypres lay in ruins. Once it stood at the heart of Belgium's thriving textile industry. Now it bore witness to the ravages of war and the destruction of European economies.

Across the Atlantic, the Woolworth Building looked out over New York City. The gleaming 792-foot skyscraper, the tallest building in the world, stood as a fitting symbol of the new colossus, America. The war had made the United States rich and powerful. Now it remained to be seen how the new giant would use that power.

WILSON'S PLAN FOR PEACE 1B

In January 1918, while the fighting raged, President Wilson announced a fourteen-point plan for peace. In the Fourteen Points he sought to eliminate the causes of the war. He would ban secret treaties, guarantee freedom of the seas, remove international tariff barriers, reduce armaments, and adjust colonial claims while respecting the rights of colonial peoples. He also suggested specific territorial changes based on the principle of national self-determination. Polish people, for example, should live under a Polish government.

To preserve world peace, Wilson proposed the creation of an international organization to be called the League of Nations. This was to be a "general association of nations . . . under specific covenants for the purpose of affording mutual guarantees of political independence and territorial integrity to great and small states alike."

The Fourteen Points were an eloquent expression of Wilson's idealism. With several changes, they became the basis for the terms of the German surrender. Late in 1918 Wilson headed for the peace talks in Paris. He was confident that he could shape a lasting peace for the world.

5E

> ★ **Historical Documents**
>
> For an excerpt from Woodrow Wilson's Fourteen Points speech, see page 723 of this book.

THE PARIS PEACE TALKS 1A

But Wilson made several miscalculations that would undermine all his efforts. During the war, Democrats and Republicans had agreed to work together for the good of the nation. Wilson violated this arrangement in the 1918 congressional campaign by asking voters to elect Democrats to show their support for his policies. Republicans were furious at this breach of the political truce. After recapturing control of Congress, they were further outraged when Wilson refused to take any major Republican leader with him to Paris.

Wilson also misjudged the international climate in Paris. He went with the loftiest intentions of creating world peace. The other Allied leaders, however, were far more interested in punishing the enemy and dividing the spoils of war. As a result, the peace talks dragged on for months.

Furthermore, Wilson's personality did not endear him to the other leaders, who saw him as a stubborn, self-righteous man. At one point, Georges Clemenceau of France refused even to talk to Wilson. "Talk to Wilson?" he fumed. "How can I talk to a fellow who thinks himself the first man for 2,000 years who has known anything about peace on earth?"

SUPPORTING THE SECTION

Reinforcement Workbook: Worksheet 50
Reteaching Resources: Worksheet 50
Teaching Transparencies: Transparency 50

SECTION 4

Peacemaking, Mapmaking, Policymaking
(pp. 303–309)

Section Objective
■ describe the impact of World War I on the world and the United States

Introducing the Section

Connecting with Past Learnings
Discuss steps President Wilson took to avoid war. Then help students recall how Wilson's attitudes toward the war affected his decision to enter the conflict. *What were Wilson's goals for United States participation in World War I?* (To make the world safe for democracy; to end all wars.) As students work through the lesson, have them note how these goals affected the plan for peace after the war.

Key Terms
Write the key terms for this section on slips of paper and put them in a bag, making sure to include several copies of each term. Ask volunteers to pick one term from the bag. Have the class play "Twenty Questions" with each volunteer, asking yes or no questions about the term until it is identified. Follow this procedure until all the terms have been identified at least once. **LEP**

On the board, write two
headings: *The Fourteen
Points* and *The Treaty of Versailles*. Referring to the text,
and the document on page
723, have students list the
major elements of the treaty
and Wilson's Fourteen
Points. (Fourteen
Points—ban secret treaties,
guarantee freedom of the
seas, remove tariffs, grant
self-determination, reduce
armaments, adjust colonial
claims, organize a League of
Nations; Treaty of Versailles
—created new countries and
mandates, stripped Germa-
ny of its colonies, demanded
German reparations, created
League of Nations.)

   ***How did the Treaty of Ver-
sailles differ from Wilson's plan
for peace?*** (Wilson wanted a
peace among equals; the
treaty made Germany bear
responsibility for the war.)

NEW NATIONS FROM OLD EMPIRES 1A

As the Allied leaders prepared the Treaty of Versailles, the formal agreement to end the war, territorial issues took up much of their time. Four empires had collapsed during the war—Russia, Austria-Hungary, the Ottoman Empire, and Germany. For months, Wilson, Clemenceau, Vittorio Orlando of Italy, and David Lloyd George of Great Britain argued over how to divide the territory of these fallen empires.

While Russia had not been one of the Central Powers, military defeats and the Bolshevik Revolution had knocked it out of the war early in 1918. Germany had seized much of western Russia. The nations of Finland, Latvia, Lithuania, Estonia, and Poland were created out of these lands.

From the Austro-Hungarian Empire, Austria and Hungary emerged as separate nations. The new nations of Czechoslovakia and Yugoslavia were also created out of the old empire. Some Austrian lands went to Italy and to Poland, while some Hungarian territory went to Rumania.

Part of the Ottoman Empire was cut up into mandates, lands to be supervised by the Allies under the direction of the League of Nations. France received Syria, and Britain received Palestine and Iraq.

On the whole, the settlement was a victory for self-determination. As Wilson had wanted, many ethnic groups were freed from foreign rule. Still, there remained the question of how to treat the German Empire.

Allied leaders signed the Treaty of Versailles in the elegant mirrored hall of a palace near Paris. Wilson, Georges Clemenceau, and David Lloyd George (seated center, left to right) look on as German representatives sign in the foreground. HISTORY How did the treaty affect the old empires of Europe and Asia? 9E

304 UNIT 4 BECOMING A WORLD POWER

Photo Caption Answer
Austria-Hungary and the
Ottoman Empire were
dissolved; Germany and
Russia lost territory; Great
Britain and France gained new
territory, but were greatly
weakened by the war.

A TREATY OF PEACE OR VENGEANCE? 3B

In April 1919 the Allies called representatives of Germany to France. For weeks the Germans were kept waiting in a small house surrounded by barbed wire. They expected to get a treaty based on the Fourteen Points; the barbed wire should have tipped them off to what lay ahead.

When they first heard the terms of the Treaty of Versailles, the Germans refused to accept it. The Allies, however, would not change a word. Finally, on June 28, 1919, the Germans signed the treaty. It forced Germany to accept full responsibility for the war. The treaty stripped Germany of its colonies, coal fields, and the provinces of Alsace and Lorraine. Moreover, it reduced Germany's army, crippled its navy, and forced Germany to pay reparations to the Allies. The reparations would eventually total $33 billion but Germany only managed to pay about $4.5 billion.

Wilson had not wanted so harsh a peace settlement, but he had to compromise in order to achieve his most important goal, the establishment of the League of Nations. Wilson did succeed in making the League part of the Versailles Treaty. It remained for him to sell the treaty to the Senate—and the American people.

THE TREATY IN THE SENATE 5B

On July 10, 1919, the President appeared before the Senate. With fiery passion he presented the Treaty of Versailles:

> Dare we reject it and break the heart of the world? The stage is set, the destiny disclosed. It has come about by no plan of our conceiving but by the hand of God who led us into this way.

Most senators could accept the peace treaty's creation of new nations based on ethnic groups. They could accept the harsh terms dictated to the Central Powers. But many could not accept the League of Nations. They opposed one article of its covenant, or charter, which called for members of the League to defend one another's territory against aggression. To the opposing senators, led by Republican Henry Cabot Lodge, this provision would restrict America's independent authority to make foreign policy decisions.

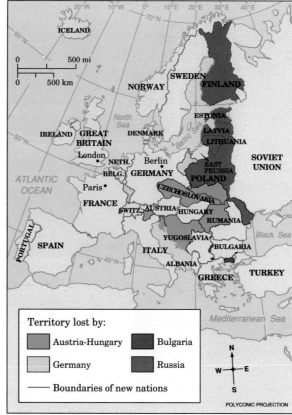

EUROPE AFTER WORLD WAR I

Territory lost by:
- Austria-Hungary
- Germany
- Bulgaria
- Russia
- Boundaries of new nations

POLYCONIC PROJECTION

MAP SKILLS 9B

Many new European nations were formed in the war's aftermath, including Czechoslovakia, Yugoslavia, Lithuania, Latvia, and Estonia. **Which two powers lost the most territory? What other nations lost territory? CRITICAL THINKING What future problems for Europe does the redrawn map suggest?**

Lodge and others were wary of Wilson as well as the League. Said Senator Lawrence Sherman, "He is no longer Wilson the American President of the United States. Now he is Wilson the internationalist, aspirant for the first President of the World's League of Nations." These senators wanted to revise the treaty, but Wilson would not hear of it. To drum up support, the President went on a speaking tour throughout the nation.

The tour nearly killed him; it could not save the treaty. In Colorado, Wilson collapsed from exhaustion, then suffered a stroke a few days later. He remained ill and partially paralyzed for the rest of his presidency. Twice the treaty came up for a vote before the Senate but never received the two-thirds support necessary for ratification.

Map Skills Answers
Russia and Austria-Hungary. Germany and Bulgaria. Problems may include resentment over lost territories and unrest in newly formed states.

Background   Senator Lodge favored participation in the League with reservations. A group of senators, including Hiram W. Johnson and Robert La Follette, advocated complete rejection.

Background   In the final months of Wilson's presidency, Mrs. Edith Wilson controlled access to the President and even guided his hand in signing legislation.

Developing the Lesson

After students have read the section, you may want to consider the following activities:

Geographic Themes: Regions

Have students examine the map of Europe on this page, noting the new countries that were created by the Treaty of Versailles. *What was the basis for redrawing national boundaries?* (Ethnic self-determination; the desire to punish Germany by reducing its territory.) Have students speculate why Russia lost so much territory after World War I. (It left the war early, while it was losing; other nations were hostile towards its Communist government after the war.)

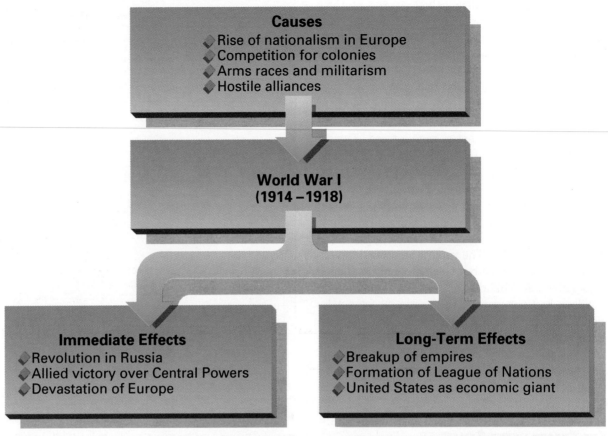

Causes
◆ Rise of nationalism in Europe
◆ Competition for colonies
◆ Arms races and militarism
◆ Hostile alliances

**World War I
(1914 – 1918)**

Immediate Effects
◆ Revolution in Russia
◆ Allied victory over Central Powers
◆ Devastation of Europe

Long-Term Effects
◆ Breakup of empires
◆ Formation of League of Nations
◆ United States as economic giant

CHART SKILLS

9E

Many factors contributed to the outbreak of fighting in Europe in 1914. Name two of them. Which factors, if any, directly involved the United States? **CRITICAL THINKING** Why, given the war's European origins, did the United States decide to enter World War I?

Ethics

Present the following statement for students' consideration: "Idealism and morality have no place in international relations." Invite students to defend or reject the statement. (Students may defend the principle of striving for perfection in an imperfect world; or they may reject idealism because it has failed in the past.)

Constitutional Heritage

President Wilson's illness and partial paralysis raised serious questions concerning his ability to carry out the duties of his office. The Constitution had no provision for determining presidential disability and succession. Refer students to the 25th Amendment to find out when and how this issue was resolved. (In 1967 the Constitution was amended to provide for a majority of the Cabinet to determine whether a President is capable of carrying out the duties of office.)

Cause and Effect

Have students choose which of the effects of World War I, shown on the chart on this page, they feel was most important and write a short essay justifying their choice.

THE GLOBAL IMPACT OF THE WAR 9E

Thus the League of Nations was formed without the United States, which made it a much weaker organization than it might have been. The League faced a staggering number of problems. Throughout war-torn Europe, people were starving. Piles of rubble stood where factories and railroads had once hummed. Scarred battlefields replaced once-fertile farmland. Beneath the soil lay millions of young men, whose talents and energies were now desperately needed.

Added to economic chaos were many political problems, in Europe and elsewhere:

(1) The Middle East. During the war, the British had promised support for Arabs who wanted in-dependence from the Ottomans. In the Balfour Declaration, they also promised support for the establishment of a national homeland for Jews in Palestine. After the war, the British set up Iraq and Trans-Jordan for the Arabs and Palestine for the Jews. Disputes over this territory, however, led to numerous outbursts of ethnic fighting.

(2) Armenia. Armenia was another part of the old Ottoman Empire where bloodshed continued after the war. Since 1894, Muslim Turks had been massacring thousands of Christian Armenians. When the Ottoman Empire joined the Central Powers in 1914, it feared that Armenians would support their enemies. The Ottomans therefore murdered 1.5 million Armenians in a campaign of

Cause and Effect Answers
Students may mention two of the following: a rise in nationalism, competition for colonies, an arms race, and hostile alliances. None of these factors directly involved the United States. Students may suggest that U.S. entry into the war was based on financial ties to Allied countries and the desire to make the United States a global power.

genocide—the systematic destruction of an entire people. The historian David Marshall Lang described the horror: "Infants were forcibly removed from their families to 'orphanages,' which turned out to be pits dug in the ground, into which the children were hurled alive, to be covered with piles of stones." The slaughter of Armenians continued until 1922, when the Turkish and Russian governments split up Armenia.

(3) Russia. Russia itself became a battlefield again after World War I. Communists fought anti-Communists in a bloody civil war from 1918 to 1920. Fearing Communist dictatorship in Russia, the United States, France, Great Britain, and Japan sent troops to support the anti-Communists, but to no avail. Russian peasants supported the Communists against the foreigners and the members of the old regime who had kept them in poverty. Gradually the Communists solidified their control of Russia. In 1922 the Communists organized the diverse peoples within the old Russian Empire into the Union of Soviet Socialist Republics (also called the USSR or Soviet Union).

(4) Germany. At war's end, the Kaiser fled Germany and a democratic government was set up in the city of Weimar (VY–mahr). But this new government, called the Weimar Republic, was swamped with problems. Still reeling from the wartime blockade, the German people had no food and no fuel. They also had no lack of humiliation

SOCIAL HISTORY
Famous Firsts

1915 Edward Stone of Chicago, member of the French Foreign Legion, is first American to die in World War I.

First American ship—the *Nantucket Chief*—is torpedoed by German submarines (May 1).

1917 Navy appoints David Goldberg of Corsicana, Texas, as first Jewish chaplain.

Jeannette Rankin of Montana seated as first woman member of U.S. House of Representatives.

1918 First shots to land on American soil fired by a German submarine off Orleans, Mass. (July 21).

First German spy—Lothar Witzke, alias Pablo Waberski—given death sentence by American forces during World War I.

1919 First Medal of Honor in World War I awarded to Ernest Janson of Brooklyn, N.Y.

and rage at the Treaty of Versailles. The Allies had wanted the impossible: to destroy Germany and at the same time make it pay war damages. This, noted military historian S.L.A. Marshall, was "like mining for gold in a slag heap."

These Armenian orphans await an uncertain fate after their parents were killed by Turkish forces. Thousands of Armenians fled Turkey during and after World War I. **HISTORY** What factors led to the Armenian genocide? 9E

Assessment

You may wish to use the Section 4 Review, page 309, to see how well your students understand the main points in this lesson.

Section Review Answers

1. *Fourteen Points*—President Wilson's proposal for ways to eliminate future wars. *League of Nations*—Organization proposed by Wilson to preserve world peace. *Treaty of Versailles*—Peace treaty that forced Germany to accept full responsibility for World War I. *mandate*—Nation supervised by an Allied country under the direction of the League of Nations. *Balfour Declaration*— Agreement by which the British promised support for the establishment of a national homeland for Jews in Palestine. *genocide*—Systematic destruction of an entire people. *Weimar Republic*—German government after World War I.

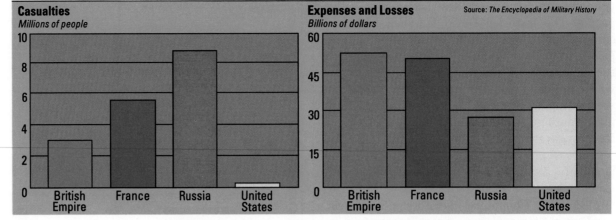

COSTS OF WORLD WAR I FOR THE ALLIES

Casualties
Millions of people

Expenses and Losses
Billions of dollars

Source: *The Encyclopedia of Military History*

GRAPH SKILLS

3B, 9B

This graph shows Allied losses in lives and wealth. Casualties among the Central Powers totaled about 15 million. Which Allied nation had the highest casualties? How many people did it lose? **CRITICAL THINKING** Why did the United States have relatively low casualties yet relatively high expenses?

Radical groups like the Communists and their enemies, the National Socialists, took to the streets to protest, and the Weimar government lacked the strength to suppress them. Nor could it gain the loyalty of the German people. Commenting on the Versailles Treaty, France's General Foch had said, "This is not peace. It is an armistice for twenty years." In due time, Adolf Hitler would turn Foch's words into prophecy.

> "This is not peace. It is an armistice for twenty years."
>
> —*General Foch, on the Versailles Treaty*

THE WAR'S IMPACT ON THE UNITED STATES 3B

In contrast to Europe, the United States had not suffered enormously from the war. It had lost 116,000 fighting men, while the war had cost France more than a million men and Russia almost two million. American civilians were not starving, for wheatless and meatless days had required only small personal sacrifices. And the American economy was anything but devastated, for wartime production had made the United States the richest country in the world.

With this new wealth and power came the poten-

tial for world leadership, as Woodrow Wilson clearly saw. But with the defeat of the Treaty of Versailles, the United States shifted instead toward a policy of isolation. The wartime crusade for "100 percent Americanism" turned into postwar distrust of foreigners and especially of foreign ideas such as communism. Americans had whipped themselves into a frenzy to support the war effort. Now they were tired of the crusade and just wanted their lives to return to normal, untroubled by world affairs.

But life would never be the same as before the war. Progressivism was dead, some of its goals forgotten and some accomplished. Big businessmen, once the target of muckraking reformers, were now heroes, for industry had helped to win the war. On the other hand, government regulation of the economy, once feared as a threat to free enterprise, had worked remarkably well during the crisis. The federal government had even instituted many practices demanded by labor and progressives for years.

The war had also brought higher wages to working people. Despite inflation, Americans had achieved a higher standard of living. Wrote journalist William Allen White, "We have raised the laboring man into middle-class standards of living and he is not going back."

Both whites and blacks had made money in war industries, but blacks were not to share the fruits

Graph Skills Answers
Russia. About 9 million people. Since the war was not fought on American territory, there were virtually no civilian casualties. America also entered the war late. At the same time, the country's industries produced huge quantities of war materials.

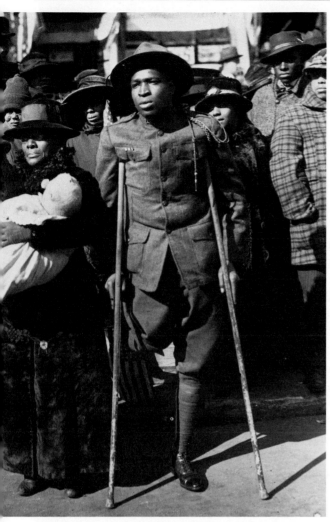

A black veteran of World War I watches a parade of the 309th Colored Infantry from the sidelines. **CULTURAL PLURALISM** How might black soldiers who had fought abroad in the name of liberty have felt on returning to a segregated society? **9A**

of prosperity. Vicious race riots broke out in 1919 when blacks tried to integrate white neighborhoods. Blacks who had fought for democracy abroad would not find it when they returned home. Racism and competition from returning soldiers edged them out of postwar jobs.

Unlike blacks, women made solid progress toward equality as a result of the war. Women had gained experience and recognition in the workplace. Their outstanding contributions to the war effort had helped them to win the right to vote.

The war had been a sobering time for all Americans. American idealism had not been able to change the world—indeed, participation in the war had changed America. As in the years following the Civil War, the mood of the country was about to undergo a shift from idealism to materialism.

SECTION REVIEW

1. KEY TERMS Fourteen Points, League of Nations, Treaty of Versailles, mandate, Balfour Declaration, genocide, Weimar Republic

2. PEOPLE AND PLACES Vittorio Orlando, Georges Clemenceau, David Lloyd George, Armenia, Henry Cabot Lodge

3. COMPREHENSION What were the terms of the Treaty of Versailles?

4. COMPREHENSION Why did the Senate turn down the treaty?

5. CRITICAL THINKING What might the peacemakers have done to create a more stable Europe?

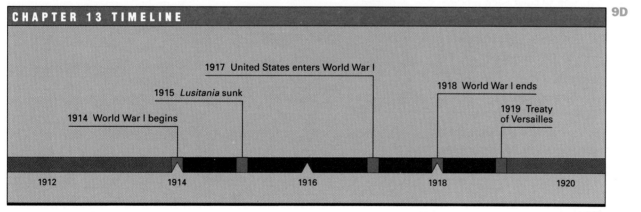

CHAPTER 13 TIMELINE   9D

1917 United States enters World War I

1915 *Lusitania* sunk

1918 World War I ends

1914 World War I begins

1919 Treaty of Versailles

| 1912 | 1914 | 1916 | 1918 | 1920 |

Photo Caption Answer
Students may suggest that black soldiers might have felt the bitterness of racism at home more keenly after fighting for liberty abroad.

Chapter 13 Review Answers

Key Terms
1. Triple Entente
2. Central Powers
3. Zimmermann Note
4. Treaty of Versailles
5. Treaty of Brest-Litovsk
6. League of Nations
7. Balfour Declaration

People to Identify
1. Head of the War Industries Board.
2. Representative from France at the Paris Peace Conference.
3. Labor leader convicted of sedition.
4. Head of the Food Administration.
5. Senator who led opposition to the League of Nations.
6. Commander of American Expeditionary Forces

Places to Locate
1. D   4. C
2. F   5. E
3. B   6. A

Reviewing the Facts
1. The growing international tensions created by conflicting nationalistic, imperialistic, and militaristic policies sparked by the assassination of Archduke Ferdinand triggered World War I.

2. Trench warfare is the digging of trenches by opposing armies. Combatants plan attacks from the trenches and charge enemy lines. This old tactic of fighting was ineffective against modern weapons such as machine guns and heavy artillery.

3. The sinking of passenger ships and attacks on United States shipping by German submarines threatened American neutrality.

Chapter 13 REVIEW

CHAPTER 13 SUMMARY

SECTION 1: At the outbreak of World War I, the United States tried to remain neutral.

- Nationalism, imperialism, militarism, and a complex set of alliances had combined to cause World War I. The war pitted the Allies—France, Britain, and Russia—against Germany and Austria-Hungary.

- On the Western Front, the fighting quickly reached a bloody stalemate, with both sides dug into trenches.

- Submarine warfare in the Atlantic threatened American neutrality.

SECTION 2: In 1917 the United States entered the war on the side of the Allies.

- German provocations early in 1917 and a democratic revolution in Russia led to United States entry into the war.

- A second revolution in Russia prompted Russian withdrawal from the war in March 1918.

- Tens of thousands of American soldiers were rushed to Europe to turn back a huge assault launched by Germany.

- The war ended in an Allied victory on November 11, 1918.

SECTION 3: The war called for an all-out effort on the home front to support the Allies.

- The federal government undertook strict economic planning, massive conscription, and propaganda campaigns.

- The labor shortage created new opportunities for women and brought many blacks from the South to northern cities.

- Voluntary efforts by citizens did much to help the war effort.

- Determined to enlist public support for the war, the federal government sometimes violated citizens' individual liberties.

SECTION 4: Wilson's hopes for a fair and lasting peace were frustrated.

- The Treaty of Versailles, while it brought self-rule to some European states, harshly punished Germany.

- The Senate rejected the treaty because senators opposed American entry into the League of Nations.

- As Europe faced new problems, the United States turned away from international commitments.

KEY TERMS ●

Use the following terms to complete the sentences below.

Balfour Declaration
Central Powers
League of Nations
Treaty of Brest-Litovsk
Treaty of Versailles
Triple Entente
Zimmermann Note

1. The _____ included France, Russia, and Great Britain.
2. The _____ included Germany and Austria-Hungary.
3. The _____ offered to return American territory to Mexico in return for an alliance.
4. The _____ was the formal agreement ending the war.
5. The _____ set the terms for Russian withdrawal from the war.
6. The _____ was an international organization created after the war.
7. The _____ stated British support for a Jewish state.

PEOPLE TO IDENTIFY ●

Identify the following people and tell why each was important.

1. Bernard Baruch
2. Georges Clemenceau
3. William Haywood
4. Herbert Hoover
5. Henry Cabot Lodge
6. John J. Pershing

4. After the Zimmermann Note established that Germany was preparing to fight the U.S., Wilson presented the war as a fight for democracy.

5. The Allies cut off the German supply lines near Sedan and the Germans were forced to surrender.

6. The War Industries Board, operating under the authority of the President, regulated the economy from raw materials to finished products.

7. Seeing the war as a struggle between good and evil, the government guarded against any acts that appeared disloyal.

8. The Allies wanted to punish Germany and divide the spoils of war.

PLACES TO LOCATE ●

Match each of the letters on the map with the places that are listed below. Then explain the importance of each place.

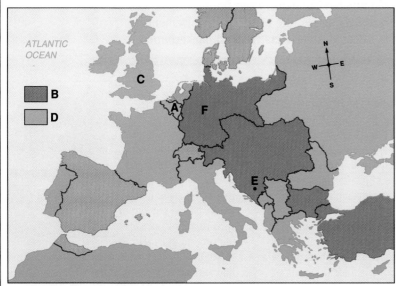

1. Allies
2. Germany
3. Central Powers
4. Britain
5. Sarajevo
6. Belgium

REVIEWING THE FACTS ▲

1. What was the immediate cause of World War I? What were the other important causes of the war?
2. Describe trench warfare. How were the military tactics used in World War I out of step with new technology?
3. What actions by the Germans threatened to bring an end to American neutrality?
4. Why did the United States finally enter the war? How did President Wilson present the war to the American people?
5. How did the war end?

6. What did the federal government have to do in order to mobilize the United States' economy for war?
7. Why did the government restrict civil rights during the war?
8. Why did the leaders of the other Allied nations reject Wilson's call for a lenient peace settlement?
9. Why did the Senate of the United States reject the Treaty of Versailles?
10. What was the impact of World War I on Europe? What was the impact of the war on the United States?

CRITICAL THINKING SKILLS ▲

1. **PARAPHRASING** Reread the section of this chapter headed "Causes of the War" (page 288). Then write a paragraph paraphrasing its contents.

2. **MAKING CONTRASTS** From the perspective of the United States government, how did the challenges posed by World War I differ from those posed by the Civil War?

3. **MAKING A GENERALIZATION** What might cause a nation to shift its focus from idealism to materialism in the years following a war?

WRITING ABOUT TOPICS IN AMERICAN HISTORY ■

1. **CONNECTING WITH LITERATURE** A selection from *Three Soldiers* by John Dos Passos appears on pages 793–795. Read it and answer the questions. Then answer the following question: Why, do you think, was this book criticized for presenting too realistic a picture of army life?

2. **APPLYING THEMES: AMERICAN CULTURE** Read two of the many poems or short stories that came out of the experience of World War I. One should be a favorable view toward the United States' participation in the war; the other should be unfavorable. Then write a few paragraphs contrasting the two points of view.

3. **CIVIC VALUES** Submit an entry to the essay-writing contest described on page 301 by writing your own American's Creed.

Introducing the Feature

Discuss whether American involvement in Latin America was an extension of the nineteenth century idea of manifest destiny that had inspired Americans to expand the nation west to the Pacific and south to Texas. *Why did some Americans strongly object to U.S. participation in World War I?* (Many Americans of European heritage did not want the U.S. to become involved in the European political turmoil that they had come here to escape. Some Americans of German descent were opposed to U.S. intervention on Britain's behalf.)

Teaching Multiculturalism

Politics

Remind students that the United States was not only a land of opportunity but also a refuge for political dissidents. *Why did José Martí come to the United States?* (Spanish authorities had deported him from Cuba because of his revolutionary activities.) *How did Martí take advantage of the freedom of expression he found in America?* (He achieved international acclaim as a political writer, poet, and essayist.) *How did Martí fulfill his commitment to Cuban independence?* (He returned to Cuba as a leader of the revolution of 1895.)

Analyzing Controversial Issues

Have students write a critical review of Kelly Miller's ideas about the progress of race relations in the United States. Reviews should agree or disagree with Miller's belief in the unprecedented advancement of African Americans in the fifty years following the Civil War. Have students support their opinions by citing the impact of such historical events as

UNIT 4: American Mosaic

★ *A Multicultural Perspective* ★

By the end of the nineteenth century the United States was playing an increasingly active role overseas. Involvement in foreign conflicts affected Americans from all backgrounds.

Born in Cuba in 1853, **José Martí** (left) devoted his life to freeing Cuba from Spanish rule. Spanish authorities deported Martí from Cuba because of his revolutionary activities. Settling in New York City in 1881, Martí achieved international fame as a writer. Besides his political writings, which emphasized the importance for Cuba of education and economic development, Martí composed numerous poems and essays. In 1895 Martí returned to Cuba to lead a revolution, but was killed by Spanish troops. In death he became a powerful symbol of the Cuban people's struggle for independence.

Kelly Miller (right) worked his way through school, graduating from Howard University in 1886 and becoming a professor there. He wrote many books on the subject of race relations, stressing that no people in world history had made as rapid advances as had African Americans in the 50 years following the Civil War. Miller believed that African Americans would eventually gain full equality in American society. Miller's writings also included protests against American imperialism overseas. He called on African Americans to oppose moves to control overseas territory.

The West Coast had its own Ellis Island—Angel Island in San Francisco Bay, where an immigration center was built in 1910 (above). Here government officials examined and questioned immigrants from Asia before allowing them to settle in the United States. Some immigrants, frustrated by the long delays in processing their cases, carved messages on the wooden walls of the buildings. Questioned one, "How was anyone to know that my dwelling place would be a prison?"

During the Spanish-American War six African Americans were awarded the Medal of Honor, the nation's highest military honor. Four of them—**Dennis Bell, Fitz Lee, William H. Thompkins,** and **George H. Wanton** (below)—earned this medal in a single battle. Fighting Spanish troops in Cuba, the four men went ashore in the face of enemy fire and rescued wounded comrades.

When explorer Robert Peary prepared for his final attempt to reach the North Pole, he asked along the man he called "my most valuable companion." This was **Matthew Henson** (left), who had the skills necessary for Arctic exploration. He could hunt, and he knew how to build and drive a dogsled. Henson also knew the language of the Inuit guides who took part in the expedition. On April 6, 1909, the members of the expedition became the first people to stand at the top of the earth.

The coming of World War I posed special problems for the nation's Mennonites. (A Mennonite family in Kansas is shown above.) A plain-living, deeply religious group living mostly in Pennsylvania and several Plains states, the Mennonites were committed pacifists. The Selective Service Act of 1917 exempted Mennonites from combat assignments, but most Mennonites refused to enter the armed forces at all. A law passed the following year allowed Mennonites to remain on their farms. Still, their pacifism and German heritage made Mennonites frequent targets of harassment.

The seeds of **Emma Goldman's** rebellion against authority were sown early in life. As a Lithuanian Jew she faced both foreign (Russian) rule and religious discrimination. After coming to the United States, Goldman (above) struggled for justice and better conditions for working people. During the Homestead Steel strike, Goldman became convinced that violent revolution was necessary to produce lasting change. She plotted unsuccessfully to kill Carnegie Steel manager Henry Frick. Goldman later renounced violence, but was often jailed for her political activities, including her opposition to United States entry into World War I. In 1919, during the Red Scare, she was deported to Russia.

When the United States entered World War I a young congressman from New York City joined the army. **Fiorello La Guardia** (left) rose to the rank of major. Returning to politics at war's end, La Guardia served another decade in Congress and later became mayor of New York City. A part-Jewish, part-Italian Protestant whose heritage reflected the diversity of his city, La Guardia is widely regarded as New York's greatest mayor.

Some American soldiers returned from the Spanish-American War with Filipino wives. These brides were the first Asian women to come to the United States after a war married to American servicemen who had fought in their country.

Reconstruction, the Fifteenth Amendment, the Compromise of 1877, the Ku Klux Klan, "Jim Crow" laws, *Plessy v. Ferguson,* and the founding of the NAACP.

Cultural Conflict
Have students write a letter that an Asian immigrant might have written from Angel Island to a relative back home. Letters should include the newcomer's accounts of the attitude of American officials toward Asians, the experience of being processed for admission, and his or her hopes and fears about life in the new country.

History
Have students imagine that they are reporters assigned to interview Matthew Henson on his return from Robert Peary's expedition to the North Pole. Interviews should focus on the skills Henson brought to Peary's effort, and explain how these skills helped make the expedition a success.

Politics
What event in the United States influenced Emma Goldman to advocate violent revolution? (The Homestead Steel Strike.) *Why was Goldman deported to the Soviet Union?* (For political activities associated with her opposition to U.S. entry into World War I.)

Point out to students that Goldman found little comfort in the Soviet Union in the 1920s. At first a great admirer of the Soviet regime, she later voiced strong criticism of its policies and was expelled from that country.

Participating in Government
Have students draw political cartoons depicting some aspect of life in New York during the era of Fiorello La Guardia. Cartoons should demonstrate the increasing influence and participation of new immigrant groups in American politics, particularly in the big cities.

Historians' Corner

Vocabulary Review

Be sure students understand the following terms: *tactical*—Of the technique of securing objectives designated by strategy. *militate*—Have influence. *inextricably*—Being impossible to escape. *chateau*—French country mansion.

Analyzing Historical Issues

In this selection, John Keegan and Richard Holmes describe problems facing military leadership that arose during World War I. These included rejecting heroic actions in favor of less glorious but more practical maneuvers, managing enormous armies, supplying these armies, and maintaining communications.

How does this military history of World War I differ from the diplomatic or political history of the war? How do military historians help us to understand the course and outcome of World War I?

Critical Thinking Answers

1. "Heroic" ideal of leadership leads generals to pursue short-term glory rather than long-term strategic success.

2. They needed toughness of character, insensitivity to losses, mental flexibility, and adaptiveness.

3. Radios, walkie talkies, spy satellites, and other wireless communications devices.

HISTORIANS' CORNER

Changing Styles of War

Some writers concentrate on military history. They may study the tactics and strategy of a war or a single battle. Or they may look at the soldiers who fought the war and the commanders who led them. In this excerpt, two military historians examine how a new style of leadership developed in World War I.

John Keegan and Richard Holmes

By 1914 the peacetime armies of the industrial world exceeded in size those which states had with difficulty raised for war a hundred years before. France maintained an army of half a million, Germany of 800,000, Russia of 1,400,000. . . .

Officering armed forces of this size at all levels had become a major call upon the . . . resources of every state possessing them. . . . Only since the beginning of the nineteenth [century] had academies for infantry and cavalry officers become established. And . . . the quality of education and training offered within their walls continued to be inspired by the essentially "heroic" ethos. . . . But mere heroism is a recipe for tactical disaster, since the urge to display bravery militates against the cultivation of skill and ingenuity in the face of the enemy. . . .

At the end of 1914, though Europe was inextricably locked in war with itself, its generals found themselves without either means or ideas to wage it.

Many [generals] had already been broken by the strain of grappling with forces as large and unfamiliar as the war had released. . . .

Those who were to take their places, men like Foch and Pétain, were notable for their toughness of character and insensitivity to losses. But they also revealed mental flexibility and adaptiveness to the new warfare. . . . Foch had used the railways in an ingenious way to provide himself with reinforcements at the Marne. . . . Pétain would use convoys of motor trucks to keep Verdun supplied when he had to fight that battle in 1916. Both accepted, as did counterparts in other armies . . . that it would be numbers that counted in trench warfare, numbers of men, of guns, of shells and that the side which could assemble the largest quantity and maintain discipline longest would win.

European and American industry rose to the challenge . . . so that by mid-1915 [equipment was] again becoming available to the armies. . . . The war grumbled back into life. But it was a strange war, in no way more unfamiliar than in the style of generalship it encouraged—what has been called "chateau generalship.". . . Their function had become essentially organizational, and a station miles to the rear of the front, from which material and reinforcements could be sent forward, seemed more logical than one placed close to a narrow section of the trenches. . . .

"Chateau generalship" might have worked . . . had the premise on which it rested—smooth telephonic and telegraphic communication with the front—held good. . . . In practice, it worked very well as far as the front line, but there its wires were so frequently cut by shellfire that communication ceased, precisely at the place and time most needed. . . . Every battle of the war . . . was thus fought beyond rather than under the control of the responsible general's hand.

From *Soldiers: A History of Men in Battle* by John Keegan and Richard Holmes. Copyright © 1985 by John Keegan, Richard Holmes and John Gau Productions. Reprinted by permission of Viking Penguin.

Critical Thinking

1. What is the authors' attitude toward the "heroic" ideal of leadership in warfare?

2. What characteristics were important for successful generals in World War I?

3. What modern forms of technology could have given "chateau generals" better control of their armies?

John Keegan (1934–) is a senior lecturer in war studies at the Royal Military Academy, Sandhurst, England.

Richard Holmes (1946–) is the deputy head of war studies at the Royal Military Academy, Sandhurst.

UNIT FIVE

From Boom to Bust

CHAPTERS IN THIS UNIT

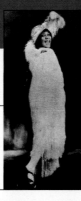

THEMES IN AMERICAN HISTORY

 Pluralistic Society   Conflicts between urban and rural values, as well as racial divisions, plagued American society during the 1920s.

 Economic Development   Though the American economy expanded during the 1920s, underlying problems plus a stock market crash in 1929 produced a severe depression.

Global Interactions   The Great Depression, caused in part by worldwide economic problems, brought hardship to nations around the world.

American Culture   The 1920s and 1930s were decades of tremendous artistic innovation.

 Constitutional Government   President Franklin Roosevelt expanded the size and role of the federal government in an attempt to lift the economy out of depression.

Unit Five

From Boom to Bust
(pp. 315–388)

Unit Five describes the 1920s, a decade of economic prosperity, political conservatism, and social experimentation. It details the scandals, fads, artistic trends, religious revivals, and strengthening of prejudices which arose, as well as the agricultural crisis and failure of prohibition.

The unit explains the economic events leading to the stock market crash in 1929, attempts by President Hoover to control the growing economic Depression, and the impact on American life of widespread unemployment. Franklin Roosevelt's election and the various programs of his New Deal are discussed, as well as criticisms of his policies. Students will also learn about the immediate impact and long-term effects of the New Deal on American society and government.

Chapter 14 ■ The Roaring Twenties   4 Sections, 4–6 Days

	SECTION OBJECTIVES	SECTION RESOURCES
Section 1 **The Search for** **Peace at Home**	■ describe the social tensions that arose in the United States after World War I	● **Reteaching Resources:** Worksheet 51 ▲ **Reinforcement Workbook:** Worksheet 51 ■ **Enrichment and Extension Resources:** Primary Source Worksheet 27 ▲ **Teaching Transparencies:** Transparency 51
Section 2 **The Politics** **of Normalcy**	■ explain how the policies of Presidents Harding and Coolidge encouraged business expansion and prosperity	● **Reteaching Resources:** Worksheet 52 ▲ **Reinforcement Workbook:** Worksheet 52 ▲ **Teaching Transparencies:** Transparency 52
Section 3 **A Revolution in** **Styles and** **Manners**	■ describe new sources of popular entertainment during the 1920s ■ describe the messages and forms of artistic expression in the 1920s	● **Reteaching Resources:** Worksheet 53 ▲ **Reinforcement Workbook:** Worksheet 53 ▲ **Teaching Transparencies:** Transparency 53
Section 4 **Divisions in** **American Society**	■ identify and explain the reasons for divisions in American society	● **Reteaching Resources:** Worksheet 54 ▲ **Reinforcement Workbook:** Worksheet 54 ■ **Enrichment and Extension Resources:** Primary Source Worksheet 28 ▲ **Teaching Transparencies:** Transparency 54

The list below shows Essential Elements relevant to this chapter. (The complete list of Essential Elements appears in the introductory pages of this Teacher's Edition.)

Section 1:   3B, 5C, 7J, 9A
Section 2:   3C, 3D, 3E, 3F, 5B, 8A, 8C, 8D, 8F, 8H, 9B
Section 3:   3A, 4B, 4F, 8A, 9B
Section 4:   2A, 3E, 4B, 4C, 4D, 4G, 9D, 9E

Section Resources are keyed for
student abilities:
● = Basic
▲ = Average
■ = Average/Advanced

CHAPTER RESOURCES

Geography Resources: Worksheets 27, 28
Tests: Chapter 14 Test

Chapter Project: American Culture

Have students create a short visual or oral report on some aspect of American society during the 1920s. For example, students may create a tape of popular songs or music, a poster of famous sports figures, examples of fashions in clothing, or a model of a speakeasy. Allow time for students to present their reports to the class.

Homework Options

Each section contains activities labeled "Addressing Individual Needs." You may wish to choose from among these activities when assigning homework.

> **Provisions for Limited English Proficiency (LEP)**
> Several suggested activities may be particularly helpful for teachers of students with limited English proficiency. These activities have been marked throughout the Teacher's Annotated Edition with the symbol **LEP** .

BIBLIOGRAPHY AND AUDIOVISUAL AIDS

Teacher Bibliography

Baritz, Loren. *The Culture of the Twenties: 1920–1929.* Macmillan, 1970.

May, Ernest R. *Boom and Bust, 1917–1932.* Silver, Burdett and Ginn, 1974.

Student Bibliography

Allen, Frederick L. *Only Yesterday: An Informal History of the 1920s.* Harper and Row, 1986.

American Heritage History of the Twenties and Thirties. American Heritage, 1970.

Literature

Fitzgerald, F. Scott. *The Great Gatsby.* Arion Press, 1984. A coming-of-age story illustrating the moral emptiness of society during the 1920s.

Hemingway, Ernest. *The Sun Also Rises.* Scribner, 1984.

Hughes, Langston. *I Wonder as I Wander: An Autobiographical Journey.* Hill and Wang, 1964.

Lewis, Sinclair. *Babbitt.* Harcourt Brace Jovanovich, 1949. The classic novel of an American businessman.

Parker, Dorothy. *The Portable Dorothy Parker.* Penguin, 1976. Short stories, poems, and critical essays by a member of the Algonquin Round Table.

Films and Videotapes*

The Best of Times, 1920-1924 (American Diary Series). 24 min. AIMS. During this period of rapid growth, Americans flocked to see the "stars" of motion pictures, radio became popular, and Harding was elected President.

Coming of Age, 1924-1928 (American Diary Series). 25 min. AIMS. The flapper era of peace, prosperity, and prohibition. Includes scenes on Charles Lindbergh's transatlantic flight.

The Flapper Story. 30 min. CG. Historical developments that gave rise to the "new woman" of the 1920s—the flapper. Examines ways in which she rebelled against prevailing social mores.

The Twenties (A Walk Through the 20th Century with Bill Moyers Series). 57 min. PBS. Nineteen Americans who lived through this era recall the events of the time.

Filmstrips*

The Reckless Years, 1919–1929 (set of 2). GA. Demonstrates how corruption and government inaction contributed to the worst depression in the nation's history. Also available in video.

Computer Software*

America's Presidents Series: World Wars, Prosperity and Depression—Presidents During and Between Two World Wars (Apple with 48K; IBM with 64K). QUEUE. Each President is covered in a separate menu option, and prominent Presidents have multiple sections on different phases on their lives and administrations. Presidents Wilson–Truman, 1913–1953.

TIME TRAVELER: Wilson—New Freedom 1913–1945 (IBM). MVP. Multiple choice, true/false, and short-answer questions within the context of a time travel adventure. Includes questions about contributions made by women and minorities. Up to 300 additional questions can be added.

*For a complete guide to audiovisual sources, see the introduction to this book (page Txx).

The Roaring Twenties

(pp. 316–339)

This chapter describes the changes that occurred in American society and politics after World War I. It includes an explanation of the business expansion and political conservatism of the 1920s, as well as a discussion of the labor unrest, troubles for farmers, revolution in manners and morals, failure of prohibition, threats to civil liberties, and political scandals which marred the era of peace and prosperity.

Themes in American History

- Economic development
- Pluralistic society
- American culture

Chapter Objectives

After students complete this chapter, they will be able to:

1. Describe the social tensions that arose in the United States after World War I.

2. Explain how the policies of Presidents Harding and Coolidge encouraged business expansion and prosperity.

3. Describe new sources of popular entertainment during the 1920s.

4. Describe the messages and forms of artistic expression in the 1920s.

5. Identify and explain the reasons for divisions in American society.

Chapter Opener Art
The Cathedrals of Broadway, Florine Stettheimer.

When the aftershocks of World War I had subsided, the nation entered a decade remembered for prosperity and style. Broadway in New York City, the topic of this painting, was a symbol of the dazzle of the 1920s.

CHAPTER SUPPORT MATERIAL	
Reinforcement Workbook: Worksheets 51–54	
Reteaching Resources: Worksheets 51–54	
Enrichment and Extension Resources: Primary Source Worksheets 27, 28	
Geography Resources: Worksheets 27, 28	
Teaching Transparencies: Transparencies 51–54	
Tests: Chapter 14 Test	

14 The Roaring Twenties (1919–1929)

3B, 5C, 7J, 9A

1 The Search for Peace at Home

 Section Focus

Key Terms Red Scare ■ Palmer raids

Main Idea Social tensions rose as the United States tried to adjust to life after World War I.

Objectives As you read, look for answers to these questions:
1. What led to a wave of strikes in industry?
2. Why was there so much fear of political radicalism?

In 1917, several weeks before asking Congress to declare war against Germany, Woodrow Wilson reportedly told a friend about one of the dangers of war:

> Once lead this people into war and they'll forget there ever was such a thing as tolerance. To fight you must be brutal and ruthless, and the spirit of ruthless brutality will enter into every fiber of our national life, infecting Congress, the courts, the policeman on the beat, the man in the street. . . . A nation cannot put its strength into a war and keep its head level; it has never been done.

While Wilson's fears were exaggerated, there was some truth to his prediction. The United States did have trouble adjusting to postwar life; discontent and intolerance threatened social order. While the majority of Americans hoped for nothing more than peace and quiet, troubling economic and political issues demanded action.

THE SHAKY POSTWAR ECONOMY 3B

When World War I ended, most Americans had money to spend. Wartime shortages had forced civilians to save much of what they had earned during the war. Many soldiers were returning home with back pay in their pockets. People wanted houses, cars, and appliances.

However, production could not meet this new demand. It took time for the nation's factories to switch from "guns to butter"—from war materiel to consumer goods. There were too many dollars and too few goods, and the result was inflation. In 1919 prices ballooned by 77 percent. The following year they went up another 28 percent. This meant that by 1920 most goods cost more than twice what they had cost just two years earlier.

Workers believed that wages had to rise to keep pace with prices. They also wanted to be allowed to form unions. For the good of the war effort, workers had agreed not to strike during the war. Now that the war was over, it was time to make their demands known. In 1919 alone some 3,600 strikes took place, many of them violent.

In September 1919 Boston's police commissioner fired a group of police who had joined the American Federation of Labor. Most of the city's police force then walked off the job. Massachusetts Governor Calvin Coolidge called out the National Guard to keep the peace, and all striking police officers were fired. Coolidge declared,

SECTION 1

The Search for Peace at Home
(pp. 317–319)

Section Objective
■ describe the social tensions that arose in the United States after World War I

Introducing the Section

Connecting with Past Learnings
Why were Americans disillusioned with the outcome of World War I? (They had fought for democracy and lasting peace and were disappointed by the Treaty of Versailles, which did not seem to create a democratic world.)

Key Terms
Write the key terms on the board and have volunteers define them. **LEP**

Focus
Have students create a newspaper called *The Tense Times* by suggesting headlines for events mentioned in the text. Then have students write stories to match the headlines. Students may want to assemble the stories into newspaper form and put it on display.

Developing the Lesson
After students have read the section, you may wish to consider the following activities:

Economics
With the class, create a diagram describing the cause of inflation after World War I. (Production could not rise fast enough to meet demand. Inflation resulted from too many dollars chasing too few goods.)

317

"There is no right to strike against the public safety by anyone, anywhere, anytime." Coolidge's stand made national headlines, and he was widely praised as a strong defender of public order.

Hard on the heels of the Boston strike came a strike in the steel industry. Steel workers were fed up with their 69-hour, 7-day work week, and wanted to form an AFL-affiliated union. When the steel owners refused to deal with the union, more than 300,000 workers across the country struck. As in the 1892 Homestead Strike, violence erupted between workers and private security guards. Local police and state militia sided with the owners, and the strike was crushed. Eighteen workers died.

Coal miners joined the wave of strikes in November 1919. Led by John L. Lewis, the United Mine Workers called for higher wages and a shorter work week. Through arbitration the union did gain a wage increase, but the demand for shorter hours went unanswered.

> "**T**here is no right to strike against the public safety by anyone, anywhere, anytime."
>
> —*Calvin Coolidge, on the Boston police strike*

THE RED SCARE 5C

Strikes, even violent strikes, had occurred in the United States before. Yet the strikes of 1919 seemed especially threatening to many Americans because they took place at a time of widespread anxiety and fear, the Red Scare of 1919–1920.

The Bolshevik takeover in Russia in 1917 and revolutionary uprisings in Germany and Hungary terrified many Americans. The Bolsheviks, predicting the violent destruction of the capitalist system, called on the world's workers to revolt. Some Americans regarded strikes in their own country as the opening blows of a revolution.

Terrorist incidents inflamed the high emotions sweeping the nation. In April 1919 some 36 bombs were mailed to business and political leaders. This

This photograph from 1920 records the scene after a bomb exploded in front of the New York Stock Exchange. CIVIC VALUES Describe the reaction of government officials to terrorist incidents in the United States. How did this reaction affect constitutional liberties? 9A

act was probably the work of a handful of anarchists and not related to any of the labor unrest. The public, however, saw striking workers, Communists, and anarchists as part of a giant conspiracy against the United States government.

Beginning in 1919, the federal government staged a crackdown on suspected radicals. On January 2, 1920, Attorney General A. Mitchell Palmer ordered the arrest of several thousand suspected Communists in 33 cities across the country. The Palmer raids, as they were called, involved many violations of civil rights. Suspects were arrested without warrants and were often denied lawyers. There was little or no evidence against most of them. Most were simply working-class immigrants. In response to the raids, a group of Progressives, including Jane Addams (founder of Hull House), formed the American Civil Liberties Union to provide legal defenses for those jailed.

Palmer signed up 200,000 worried Americans to watch for Communist threats in their neighborhoods and to report the names of people who looked suspicious. People began to see the Red menace at every turn. "Bride Thinks Red Kidnapped Missing Groom," shouted a headline in the *Boston Herald*. Yet no evidence was found of a Communist plot to overthrow the American government. The Justice Department seized only 3 pistols from the 5,000 radicals that it arrested.

This painting by artist Ben Shahn is one of a series he created on the trial and execution of Sacco and Vanzetti. It shows the two accused men awaiting their trial with patience and dignity. **HISTORY** Explain the constitutional significance of the judge's statement that Sacco was guilty even though he may not actually have committed the crime. **9A**

SACCO AND VANZETTI 7J

The Communist revolution that Palmer predicted never took place, but the effects of the Red Scare lingered. In 1920 two Italian immigrants, Nicola Sacco and Bartolomeo Vanzetti, were accused of murdering a paymaster and a guard during a payroll holdup near Boston. The evidence against them was flimsy. Still, the two men were anarchists, and as far as the judge was concerned, that meant they were guilty. To the jury the judge explained, "This man [Sacco], although he may not actually have committed the crime, is nevertheless morally culpable [guilty], because he is the enemy of our existing institutions." The two men were found guilty and sentenced to death.

Sacco and Vanzetti appealed to higher courts, and the case raised an international furor. Leftists organized huge rallies to protest their death sentence. The struggle went on until 1927, when their conviction was upheld. Vanzetti once again declared his innocence. He added:

My conviction is that I have suffered for things that I am guilty of. I am suffering because I am a radical, and indeed I am a radical; I have suffered because I was an Italian, and indeed I am an Italian.

The two men were put to death in the electric chair.

Critics compared the Red Scare and the prosecution of Sacco and Vanzetti to the Salem witch trials of 1692. They argued that the government, overcome by fear, had trampled the rights of its citizens. Critics would make this same argument about another wave of anti-Communist fear that took place after World War II. Others would defend government actions, pointing out that events during these times made Communist subversion a legitimate danger. What is certain is that, as Wilson warned, war and the emotions it arouses pose delicate problems for any democratic society.

SECTION REVIEW

1. KEY TERMS Red Scare, Palmer raids

2. PEOPLE AND PLACES Boston, Calvin Coolidge, John L. Lewis, A. Mitchell Palmer, Nicola Sacco, Bartolomeo Vanzetti

3. COMPREHENSION Why was there so much labor unrest in 1919?

4. COMPREHENSION What foreign events caused alarm in the United States? Why?

5. CRITICAL THINKING Do you agree or disagree with Coolidge's statement that "There is no right to strike against the public safety by anyone, anywhere, anytime?" Explain your answer.

Photo Caption Answer
The assertion that Sacco could be found guilty on the basis of his beliefs rather than his actions contradicts the First Amendment guarantee of freedom of speech.

Background The term "leftist" meaning someone who is politically liberal and reformist derives from the French National Assembly of 1789–1791. Moderate members were seated in the center of the Assembly. Conservatives were seated on the right and radicals on the left.

Assessment
You may wish to use the Section 1 Review, on page 319, to see how well your students understand the main points in this section.

Section Review Answers

1. *Red Scare*—Widespread anxiety and fear resulting from revolutionary uprisings abroad, radical political activity at home, and labor violence. *Palmer raids*—Crackdown on suspected radicals.

2. *Boston*—City where police went on strike in 1919. *Calvin Coolidge*—Governor of Massachusetts who called out the National Guard to break up the Boston police strike. *John L. Lewis*—Head of the United Mine Workers. *A. Mitchell Palmer*—Attorney General who led the effort to rid the country of radicals. *Nicola Sacco and Bartolomeo Vanzetti*—Italian immigrants accused of and executed for participation in a robbery.

3. Much of it was the result of inflation and the inability of wages to keep pace with prices. Also, workers wanted the right to form unions.

4. The Bolshevik Revolution in Russia in 1917 and revolutionary uprisings in Germany and Hungary caused Americans to fear the spread of communism.

5. Agree—individual gain should not come at the cost of public safety. Disagree—public officials should not have to give up the right to decent pay and working conditions.

Closure
Call students' attention to the beige boxed quotation (p. 318). Ask them to relate this quotation to the main idea of the section. Then have students read Section 2 for the next class, noting the economic policies of Harding and Coolidge.

319

SECTION 2

The Politics of Normalcy
(pp. 320–325)

Section Objective

■ explain how the policies of Presidents Harding and Coolidge encouraged business expansion and prosperity

Introducing the Section

Connecting with Past Learnings

Ask students to suggest words describing Woodrow Wilson's presidency. (Idealistic, strong leadership, progressive, Democrat, world leadership, wartime leader, rigid, internationalist, intellectual.) Have them compare Wilson with Presidents Harding and Coolidge as you work through this section.

Key Terms

Write the key terms on the board. Ask students to find the terms in the book and define them in their own words. Then have students write one or two sentences showing how the last two terms relate to President Harding. **LEP**

Focus

Have students construct a cause and effect chart. In the first column have them list the main points of the Republican formula for prosperity. After each point, have students write in the second column the effect each element had on the economy. (Lower government spending meant less need for revenue; lower taxes on business

2 The Politics of Normalcy

Section Focus

★ **Key Terms** American Plan ■ Ohio Gang ■ Teapot Dome scandal

Main Idea Under Presidents Harding and Coolidge, the government encouraged business expansion, and the United States entered an era of prosperity.

Objectives As you read, look for answers to these questions:
1. What were Warren G. Harding's goals as President?
2. What political scandals troubled the Harding administration?
3. Why was Calvin Coolidge such a popular President?

As the turbulent events of 1919–1920 show, the United States continued to live in the shadow of World War I even after the war had ended. Throughout the 1920s, the American people tried in a number of ways to put the war behind them. In politics, Americans reacted against the war by looking for peace, prosperity, and limited government.

ELECTING A PRESIDENT: 1920 5B

In 1920 the Democrats nominated the governor of Ohio, James M. Cox, for President. Franklin D. Roosevelt, Assistant Secretary of the Navy, was the vice presidential candidate. Both were capable leaders, but their political views were not in line with the times. They supported the League of Nations, which most Americans wanted nothing to do with. They were also progressives who wanted to increase the role of the government in the economy. Tired of wartime wage and price controls, most Americans were looking in just the opposite direction.

The Republicans were much more in tune with the public mood. They nominated Warren G. Harding, a senator from Ohio, as their candidate for President. For Vice President, they chose Massachusetts Governor Calvin Coolidge, who had won instant fame by breaking the Boston police strike of 1919.

Harding was a handsome man who looked like a President. He had simple, small-town tastes, and he made most of his campaign speeches from his front porch in Marion, Ohio. He promised to let the United States run itself without too much government interference. There would be no

great sacrifices ahead, only quiet prosperity—in his word, "normalcy." By mid-October 1920, the journalist H. L. Mencken was sure Harding would win:

> The overwhelming majority of Americans are going to vote for him. They tire, after twenty years, of a steady diet . . . of protestations. . . . They are weary of hearing highfalutin . . . words; they sicken of idealism.

Mencken's forecast was right on target. Harding won the election—the first in which women were able to vote—by a landslide. In March 1921 he was sworn in as President of the United States.

THE REPUBLICAN FORMULA 3D, 3F

Although government management of business had worked remarkably well during the war, most Americans opposed it on principle. They also remained suspicious of heavy federal spending. They wanted a policy of laissez faire, and Harding was the man to give it to them. He believed that the government could help the United States best by keeping its hands off the economy. He also wanted to make the government run more efficiently.

Harding appointed the banker Andrew Mellon—one of the six richest men in America—as Secretary of the Treasury. Mellon was determined to spur economic growth by cutting taxes on industry. Harding chose another banker, Charles G. Dawes, to direct the newly created Bureau of the Budget. Dawes's job was to bring federal spending under tighter control. During his first year in

320 UNIT 5 FROM BOOM TO BUST

SUPPORTING THE SECTION

Reinforcement Workbook: Worksheet 52
Reteaching Resources: Worksheet 52
Teaching Transparencies: Transparency 52

Background In 1923 Mellon presented Congress with a plan to lower income taxes. Taxes on the rich would drop from 50 percent to 25 percent.

Artist Georgia O'Keeffe painted this view of New York City's East River in 1928. The skyscrapers and smokestacks in the picture show how industrial expansion changed the face of American cities. **ECONOMICS** What methods did President Harding use to help American businesses? **3F**

office, Dawes cut government expenses by one-third and recorded a surplus equal to almost one-fourth of the total budget. He then used the surplus to chip away at the national debt, which had leaped by nearly 25 times as a result of World War I.

Congress followed Harding's lead, passing laws to encourage and protect American business. The Revenue Act of 1921 eliminated taxes placed on businesses during World War I. The Fordney-McCumber Tariff set tariffs far above the existing level, and gave the President the power to raise protective tariffs on his own in some situations.

The Republican formula of lower spending, lower taxes, and higher tariffs seemed to work. After a brief postwar depression the economy began rising steadily.

THE PLIGHT OF LABOR 3C

With the approval of the federal government, the owners of industry stepped up their opposition to labor unions. Employers advocated an anti-labor policy they called the American Plan. They said that it was un-American for a worker to have to join a union in order to get a job in a particular plant. They claimed that by refusing to deal with unions, they were protecting employees' right to work. Owners tried to break troublesome unions by firing workers who went on strike.

To convince workers that unions were unnecessary, companies that followed the American Plan offered benefits such as higher wages or stock ownership. They also formed company unions that had little independence and no association with labor groups in other parts of the same industry. Between 1920 and 1925, the number of workers in unions dropped from 5 million to 3.5 million.

Yet Harding himself was not rigidly opposed to labor. He pardoned most of the union and labor leaders who had been jailed during World War I. These included 27 members of the radical Industrial Workers of the World. It also included Eugene Debs, the leader of the Socialist Party, who had spent two years in jail for speaking out against American involvement in World War I. Debs was released from prison on December 24, 1921, because Harding wanted him to be able to eat Christmas dinner with his wife.

POLITICAL SCANDALS 7K

Harding was a hard-working President who hoped that his good intentions would make up for his limited abilities. "I can't hope to be the best President this country's ever had," he told reporters one evening before taking office. "But if I can, I'd like to be the best-loved." For a time, he succeeded. Yet Harding is now remembered largely for the scandals that battered his administration.

Photo Caption Answer
He cut taxes on business and passed high tariffs to protect industry from foreign competition.

freed more money for investment; higher tariffs provided government revenue and protected American businesses from foreign competition; the Bureau of the Budget brought federal spending under tighter control and used the surplus to pay off the national debt accumulated during the war.)

How successful was the Republican formula for economic prosperity? (Business flourished and so did the economy during the Harding and Coolidge years.)

Developing the Lesson
After students have read the section, you may wish to consider the following activities:

Participating in Government
Have students make a chart to organize information about Harding and Coolidge. They should use information in Section 2 and the biographical information in The Presidents features in the section. Include political party, political experience, personal appeal, presidential goals, successes and failures.

Do you think Harding and Coolidge were successful Presidents? (Students may point out that both men succeeded in making the economy prosper with little government interference by encouraging business expansion. Political scandals battered Harding's administration. Coolidge was popular, but he ignored serious problems in American society.)

Do you think Harding and Coolidge could have been elected President today? Why or why not?

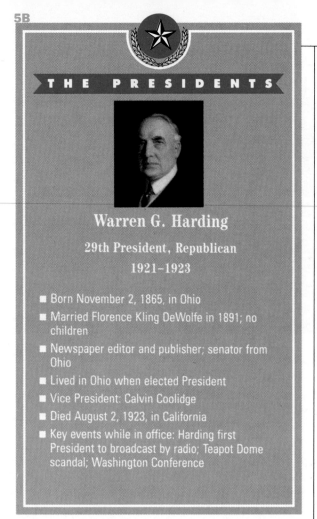

THE PRESIDENTS

Warren G. Harding

29th President, Republican

1921–1923

- Born November 2, 1865, in Ohio
- Married Florence Kling DeWolfe in 1891; no children
- Newspaper editor and publisher; senator from Ohio
- Lived in Ohio when elected President
- Vice President: Calvin Coolidge
- Died August 2, 1923, in California
- Key events while in office: Harding first President to broadcast by radio; Teapot Dome scandal; Washington Conference

When Harding came to Washington, he brought with him a group of friends and political advisers known as the Ohio Gang. Harding saw them as men of proven loyalty who shared his background and who would stand behind him. He failed to see that most of them were not qualified for the important government jobs they held. Worse, many of them were just plain corrupt, and within two years tales of their misconduct began to seep out. Harding was distraught. He told the editor William Allen White, "I have no trouble with my enemies. I can take care of them all right. But my friends, White, they're the ones that keep me walking the floors nights."

In 1923 a federal investigation revealed that Charles R. Forbes, head of the Veterans' Bureau, had swindled the country out of $200 million. (This was at a time when thousands of veterans still lay in hospitals that were desperately short of supplies.) Forbes resigned his post and fled to Europe. He later returned and was sentenced to two years in prison.

The public also learned that the Ohio Gang had been selling all manner of favors, including pardons and appointments to office. When this news came out, one of Harding's advisers, Jess Smith, committed suicide. Drained by these scandals and exhausted by overwork, Harding decided to take a trip to Alaska. On the journey home he became ill, and he died (possibly from a heart attack) in San Francisco on August 2, 1923.

The most embarrassing scandals did not come to light until after Harding's death. His right-hand man, Attorney General Harry Daugherty, was forced to resign in 1924 after being charged with bribery and fraud. Worst of all was the Teapot Dome scandal. The Secretary of the Interior, Albert B. Fall, was found to have leased government oil reserves—including one in Teapot Dome, Wyoming—to oilmen who paid him kickbacks worth hundreds of thousands of dollars. Other members of the administration were also linked to the scandal, and investigations and trials went on until 1930. By then, the Harding administration had earned a reputation as one of the most corrupt in American history.

COOLIDGE TAKES OFFICE 5B

When Harding died, Vice President Coolidge was on vacation at his birthplace in Plymouth, Vermont. The news that he was now President reached him in the middle of the night. His father, a justice of the peace, administered the oath of office to him by the light of a kerosene lamp.

Coolidge was a dry, quiet man with a sour expression. He had always held on to the values of his New England boyhood. To some he seemed an unlikely hero, yet he became one of the most popular Presidents in American history. He remained untouched by the scandals of the Harding administration, and his integrity won him many followers. In a decade remembered for the giddy enjoyment of wealth and the abandonment of the moral values of the past, Coolidge was a reassuring reminder of old ways. The journalist Walter Lippmann wrote, "At the time when Puritanism as a way of life was at its lowest ebb among the people, the people were delighted with a Puritan as their national symbol."

THE ELECTION OF 1924 5B

Less than a year after Coolidge succeeded Harding, it was time to prepare for the 1924 election. Coolidge was already so much admired that he easily captured the Republican nomination on the first ballot.

The Democrats were badly split. On one side were the eastern, big-city Democrats who wanted Governor Al Smith of New York. Facing them were the rural forces from the South and West who backed former Treasury Secretary William G. McAdoo. After 102 grueling ballots Smith and McAdoo gave up, and on the next ballot the nomination went to a compromise candidate, John W. Davis of West Virginia. Davis was a corporation lawyer and a conservative; his nomination signaled a Democratic shift away from the progressivism of Woodrow Wilson.

The voters who wanted to continue the fight for progressive ideals turned to Senator Robert M. La Follette of Wisconsin, the nominee of the Progressive Party. The party platform called on the federal government to spend more time regulating business and less time fighting labor unions. La Follette had many followers in rural America, where a farm crisis was prompting many farmers to demand government subsidies.

Coolidge won the 1924 presidential election easily, with a two-to-one margin over Davis in the popular vote. La Follette made a decent showing with 17 percent of the popular vote. Yet it was clear that the majority of American voters were happy with Coolidge and with government policies as they stood.

THE COOLIDGE YEARS 8F, 8H

Coolidge did little active campaigning in 1924, and during the next four years he showed himself to be a man of few words. He often refused to comment on controversial issues. He also used his wry sense of humor to deflect questions he did not want to answer. Known as "Silent Cal," he did not cultivate political friendships and had little contact with Congress.

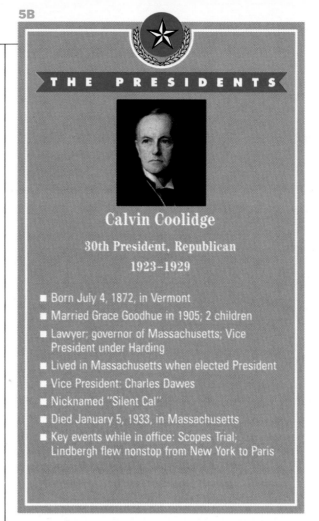

THE PRESIDENTS

Calvin Coolidge
30th President, Republican
1923–1929

- Born July 4, 1872, in Vermont
- Married Grace Goodhue in 1905; 2 children
- Lawyer; governor of Massachusetts; Vice President under Harding
- Lived in Massachusetts when elected President
- Vice President: Charles Dawes
- Nicknamed "Silent Cal"
- Died January 5, 1933, in Massachusetts
- Key events while in office: Scopes Trial; Lindbergh flew nonstop from New York to Paris

Coolidge's reputation is that of a "hands-off" President. He usually worked only four hours a day, with a nap in the afternoon and about ten hours of sleep at night. When informed of his death in 1933, the New York writer and wit Dorothy Parker asked, "How could they tell?" Coolidge's relaxed style reflected his belief that the government did not have to do much to make America prosper. He spent most of his energy in opposing legislation that he believed to be harmful or unnecessary.

Like Harding, Coolidge wanted to create a climate in which business could flourish. "The business of America is business," he once declared. Coolidge agreed with Harding that business performed best when the government stayed out of its affairs. Along with Secretary of the Treasury Andrew Mellon, Coolidge followed in Harding's footsteps by reducing the national debt. It dropped by a billion dollars a year during most of the 1920s.

> "**T**he business of America is business."
> —*Calvin Coolidge*

PROSPEROUS TIMES 3E, 8A

Most Americans accepted Coolidge's ideas because the country was in the midst of an economic boom. Wages were rising and, thanks to new technology, so was productivity. Americans had more money to spend and more things to buy than ever before. Now that the war was over, Americans could choose from a parade of consumer goods—radios, washing machines, vacuum cleaners, telephones, and especially cars.

The automobile industry was a key part of the nation's prosperity. In 1913, Henry Ford had made mass production possible through the use of the assembly line. Now, by making the assembly line faster, Ford was able to lower the price of his cars. His Model T cost $950 in 1909. Its price fell to

These salespeople in Louisville, Kentucky, pose in front of their store with some of the household appliances that Americans bought in great quantities after World War I. The large item at right center is an early washing machine. **ECONOMICS** Explain the term *consumer goods*. 8A, 8C, 8D

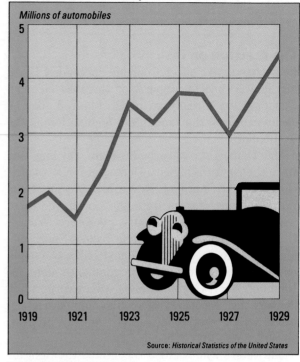

AUTOMOBILE SALES, 1919–1929

Millions of automobiles

Source: *Historical Statistics of the United States*

GRAPH SKILLS 8H

Automobile sales increased during the 1920s because of lower prices and increased purchasing power among many consumers. About how many more autos were sold in 1929 than in 1919? **CRITICAL THINKING** Why, do you think, are automobile sales often used as an indicator of how the economy is doing?

$360 in 1916 and to $290 by 1925. Cars, once considered luxuries that only the wealthy could afford, came to be seen as necessities. By 1930 there were 23 million registered cars on the road, more than double the number in 1920.

The phenomenal success of the automobile industry had a ripple effect on the economy. The steel, rubber, and glass industries flourished because their products were needed to make cars. The construction industry also enjoyed a boom. Federal and state governments built new roads and highways to keep up with growing auto traffic. Developers built more houses in the suburbs, which cars made convenient to the city. People opened motels and gas stations to serve the auto traveler.

The economic growth of the 1920s led to a greater demand for white-collar workers. More

324 UNIT 5 FROM BOOM TO BUST

Oh, memories that bless and burn . . .

LISTERINE
ends halitosis

Are you sure about yourself?

It hasn't a single belt, fan or drain pipe . . . .

Refrigerator
GENERAL ELECTRIC

and more people were needed for sales and management. As a result, education became more important to the work force. Enrollment in high schools doubled between 1920 and 1930. College enrollment showed similar gains for the same period, rising from 582,000 to 1,054,000. New business schools were opened to train managers for the nation's growing industries.

ADVERTISING AND CREDIT 8A, 8C

The 1920s also witnessed growth in the advertising industry. None of the new products of the decade was an actual necessity of life. As a result, Americans had to be convinced that they would be happier and more admired by their neighbors if they bought them. This was the job of the advertising industry, into which more and more money flowed with each passing year. At the turn of the century, advertising was an $800 million a year business. By 1920 it was up to $3 billion a year.

One result of this barrage of advertising was that Americans became more willing to buy on credit. Before the 1920s, most Americans felt that it was wrong to go into debt except in an emergency. But with the rise of the automobile and other expensive, long-lasting consumer goods, businesses began to urge customers to buy on the installment plan. By 1928 more than two-thirds of all furniture, phonographs, and washing machines were bought on credit. So were more than half of all sewing machines, pianos, and vacuum cleaners.

Personal debts were rising two and a half times faster than income. All this credit-buying stimulated production, but it also meant that some consumers were getting in over their heads.

Because the nation was enjoying such prosperity, people were surprised and disappointed when the popular Coolidge announced that he would not run for another term. "I do not choose to run for President in 1928," he said, with his usual brevity. Some historians suspect that he had a feeling that economic troubles lay ahead. Indeed, Grace Coolidge, the First Lady, is said to have remarked, "Papa thinks a depression is coming."

SECTION REVIEW

1. KEY TERMS American Plan, Ohio Gang, Teapot Dome scandal

2. PEOPLE Warren G. Harding, Calvin Coolidge, Robert M. La Follette, Henry Ford

3. COMPREHENSION What were the three parts of Warren G. Harding's "Republican formula"? Were they successful?

4. COMPREHENSION How did the automobile industry affect the economy?

5. CRITICAL THINKING Explain what Calvin Coolidge meant by the statement "The business of America is business."

---

2. *Warren G. Harding*— President of the United States, elected in 1920. *Calvin Coolidge*—Vice President who became President upon Harding's death in 1923. *Robert M. La Follette*— Senator from Wisconsin, Progressive Party candidate in the 1924 presidential election. *Henry Ford*—Made mass production of cars possible through the use of the assembly line.

3. Lower government spending, lower taxes, and higher tariffs led to a steady rise in the economy.

4. The automobile caused a boom in the industries that provided raw materials such as rubber and steel, as well as the construction industry which built roads, highways, and houses in the suburbs.

5. Coolidge believed that it was government's job to create a climate where business could flourish. The benefits would trickle down to society as a whole.

Closure

Remind students of the pre-reading objectives in the section opener. Pose one or all of these questions again. Then have students read Section 3 for the next class period. Ask them to note the changes in society during the decade of the 1920s.

---

3 A Revolution in Styles and Manners

Section Focus

Key Terms flapper ■ Lost Generation ■ Harlem Renaissance

Main Idea In the 1920s Americans looked for new sources of popular entertainment and new forms of artistic expression.

Objectives As you read, look for answers to these questions:
1. What kinds of entertainment became popular?
2. How did Charles A. Lindbergh win his fame?
3. What developments characterized the literature of the 1920s?

Section Objectives
■ describe new sources of popular entertainment during the 1920s
■ describe the messages and forms of artistic expression in the 1920s

Introducing the Section

Connecting with Past Learnings
Discuss the prosperity of the 1920s with the class. *How were the lives of workers affected by economic growth in the 1920s?* (Wages rose, factories produced large numbers of consumer goods such as family cars and telephones, more managerial positions opened up.)

Key Terms
Write each key term on an index card. Assign each card to a student. Have the student write a definition of the term on the board, and let the class decide which term is being defined. Students may wish to suggest modifications to the original definition. When the class has agreed on a definition's accuracy, have the student write that definition on the back of the index card. Cards may be saved and added to other "term cards" to make flash cards for review. **LEP**

In the 1920s Americans had an abundance of leisure and a thirst for entertainment. In his essay *Commentary on New York, 1926*, the writer F. Scott Fitzgerald described the mood of the times:

> The restlessness approached hysteria. The parties were bigger. The pace faster, the shows broader, the buildings were higher, . . . but all these benefits did not really bring about much delight. Young people wore out early—they were harder and languid at twenty-one. . . . The city was bloated, glutted, stupid with cake and circuses, and a new expression "Oh yeah?" summed up all the enthusiasm evoked by the announcement of the last super-skyscrapers.

The pace of life did indeed quicken during the 1920s—literally, because of the automobile, and figuratively, because of new forms of entertainment. For millions of Americans this was a time of great excitement. But as Fitzgerald pointed out, for some Americans it was also a time of dissatisfaction.

POPULAR ENTERTAINMENT 4F, 8A
In the 1920s shorter working hours and higher wages gave Americans more spare time and spending money than ever before. Plenty of promoters were ready to take advantage of this wealth. Radio, movies, and sports became the focus of American popular culture.

The first radio station, KDKA in Pittsburgh, went on the air in November 1920 to report the presidential election returns. When President Coolidge put a radio set in the White House, even skeptics were convinced that the product was worth buying. By 1929, almost 40 percent of American families had radios in their homes.

At first, radio stations did not carry advertising. Within a few years, however, the airwaves were filled with catchy advertising jingles. Many companies sponsored radio programs, such as the "A & P Gypsies" and "The Eveready Hour." Stations broadcast popular music every day, and they helped to make jazz respectable and to give it a wide audience.

A rival that radio could never outshine was the moving pictures. Before World War I, silent movies were shown in small "nickelodeons," where admission cost only a nickel. Now entrepreneurs began to build deluxe movie houses, known as "picture palaces," lavishly decorated with velvet curtains and gilt trim. More and more Americans made a weekly habit of going to the pictures. They thrilled over the exploits of such stars as Rudolph Valentino, Mary Pickford, Douglas Fairbanks, Charlie Chaplin, and Clara Bow. The silent film era came to an end in 1927 with the release of the first talking picture, *The Jazz Singer.*

The only idols who matched movie stars in popularity were the heroes of American sports. The increase in leisure time meant that more Americans could go to boxing matches and football and baseball games. Play-by-play accounts of these sports were also broadcast on the radio.

Sports promoters built huge football stadiums and baseball parks. To arouse interest in upcoming sporting events, they billed every big event as the most thrilling in history. When the heavy-

SUPPORTING THE SECTION

Reinforcement Workbook: Worksheet 53
Reteaching Resources: Worksheet 53
Teaching Transparencies: Transparency 53

Background The greatest football hero of the decade was Harold "Red" Grange, nicknamed "The Galloping Ghost." Playing for the University of Illinois in 1924, he once made four touchdowns in twelve minutes.

This painting of Broadway in New York City portrays the brightly lit theater marquees and signs that led people to call this avenue the "Great White Way." **CULTURE** What impression does the painting give of life in the city? **4F**

weight champion Jack Dempsey fought the challenger Gene Tunney in 1926 and 1927, the spectacle brought in $4 million in revenues. In 1920 the baseball hero Babe Ruth of the New York Yankees set a new record for home runs. People began pouring into the new Yankee Stadium—"The House that Ruth Built"—to watch him break his own records. In 1927 he hit 60 home runs and made almost as much money as the President.

BIOGRAPHY

GEORGE HERMAN RUTH (1895–1948), known as "Babe," was the best-known baseball player of the 1920s. Ruth began his career as a pitcher, but then switched to outfield. His home run blasts and colorful personality attracted huge crowds. He and Lou Gehrig, his teammate on the New York Yankees, formed the greatest one-two hitting combination in baseball.

MUSIC AND DANCING 4F

The radio and the phonograph gave a big boost to the music business. Americans hummed popular songs like "Yes, We Have No Bananas," "It Ain't Gonna Rain No More," and "My Blue Heaven." Some of the best songs played on the radio came from the musical stage. Outstanding composers such as Irving Berlin, George Gershwin, Jerome Kern, and Cole Porter wrote musical comedies that became American classics.

Perhaps the most important musical development of the 1920s was jazz. In fact, the decade came to be known as the "Jazz Age." Rooted in black spirituals and African folk rhythms, jazz had begun with black musicians in New Orleans in the late 1800s. Jazz had an energy and style all its own, allowing musicians to improvise on certain themes each time they played a tune. According to the legendary trumpet player Louis Armstrong, "If you have to ask what jazz is, you'll never know."

Louis Armstrong and Duke Ellington were two of the founders of modern jazz. After Ellington and his band opened at the Cotton Club in Harlem, the nightclub became one of the most famous in the country. Bessie Smith, the "Empress

Photo Caption Answer
Students may suggest excitement and wealth.

Biography
By 1930 Babe Ruth was making more money than the President. Today star athletes routinely make more than our political leaders. Ask students to discuss the fairness of these salaries.

Focus
Ask volunteers in the class to play the role of "social secretaries" for members of an average American family in the 1920s: a husband and wife; their 21-year-old unmarried daughter; a seventeen-year-old son; and a ten-year-old son. *How might the different members of this family spend a Saturday afternoon? A Saturday night?* (Possible answers for Saturday afternoon—parents reading a popular book or magazine, doing crossword puzzles; kids listening to the radio, going to a sports game. Saturday night— Parents going to Mah Jong party, the movies; daughter and older son going out on dates to dance, listen to music.)

Why is this period described as a "revolution"? (It brought dramatic changes in behavior, literature, films, music, and dance. Young people in particular broke out of the pre-World War I mold. Americans enjoyed unprecedented leisure and new forms of entertainment.)

Developing the Lesson
After students have read the lesson, you may wish to consider the following activities:

Connecting with Literature
Read the F. Scott Fitzgerald quotation on page 326. Have students compare the quotation with the poem by Langston Hughes on page 332. *How do these two authors show dissatisfaction with life in the 1920s?* (Fitzgerald shows the restlessness of a generation looking for the benefits of prosperity but finding little of real value. Disillusioned black writers like Hughes felt closed out of the American dream altogether.)

Bessie Smith began singing in honky-tonks and tent shows, but after coming to New York in 1923 she became one of the world's most famous jazz and blues stars. She died after an automobile accident in Mississippi when a hospital refused her admission because she was black. **CULTURE** How did the feeling of jazz match America's mood in the 1920s? **4F**

of the Blues," made recordings with Armstrong and other jazz greats.

By the mid-1920s white band leaders such as Paul Whiteman were playing jazz in concert. Whiteman called jazz "the folk music of the machine age." George Gershwin wrote classical compositions that borrowed heavily from jazz, including "Rhapsody in Blue" and "An American

This *Life* magazine cover shows a woman in flapper dress doing an unrestrained Charleston with a high-society partner. Such short skirts, short haircuts, and use of makeup upset traditionalists. **CULTURE** What image of the 1920s does this picture convey? **9B**

in Paris." Big-band leaders like Guy Lombardo and Rudy Vallee began to play a quieter style of jazz geared to white audiences.

Big-band music was perfect for dancing, and Americans danced as they never had before. Young women nicknamed flappers wore short skirts and danced the fox-trot, the camel-walk, and the tango. In 1924 they learned the Charleston, a fast dance that came from a black show on Broadway called *Runnin' Wild*. Preachers called jazz and dancing sinful, but few young people cared. The band was playing, and they were having the time of their lives.

FADS AND FANCIES 4F

Americans in the 1920s also amused themselves with an assortment of games and fads. In 1923 the country was swept by the craze for Mah Jong, a Chinese game played with colored tiles. The tiles could be bought one for a dime at many stores, but manufacturers sold fancy sets priced as high as $200. Upper-class Mah Jong fanatics even wore imported Chinese clothing while playing.

Another fad of the day was crossword puzzles. The idea started in Sunday newspapers, which usually printed a word puzzle that people used to kill time. It became a craze in 1924 after Richard L. Simon and Max Schuster published a book of crossword puzzles, which sold 750,000 copies within the year. (The profits from this book helped build Simon & Schuster into one of the nation's leading publishing companies.) Crosswords became so popular that some railroads even equipped their cars with dictionaries to help passengers when they were stumped. Dictionary and thesaurus sales skyrocketed. Like Mah Jong, however, the fad peaked within a few years.

The magazines founded in the 1920s had a more lasting effect on American popular culture. The weekly news magazine *Time* was launched in 1923 to bring news from home and around the world to the general public. *Reader's Digest* also aimed at the general reader. It offered articles from other magazines, often condensing them to aid the busy city resident whose time was valuable. A different audience turned to the *New Yorker*, founded in 1925. The *New Yorker* printed articles on the cultural and political life of the nation, as well as

The Geographic Perspective: The California Dream

The California dream began with gold in 1849 and flourished with images of orange groves in the 1880s. In the minds of many, California was a golden dreamland, a land of abundance and endless summers.

In the 1920s California continued to symbolize the good life. Its history, its climate, even its location at the western edge of the continent, made California seem a place of opportunity.

The rise of Hollywood as the center of movie-making added to the California legend. The movie industry made a business of fantasy. Films about romance, wealth, and adventure helped gild the California dream. Even the state's architecture began to reflect Hollywood fantasy. Images of Dutch windmills, medieval castles, Chinese pavilions, and Hansel-and-Gretel cottages became part of the southern California cityscape.

An effective advertising campaign by southern California boosters—clubs, Chambers of Commerce, realtors—also nurtured the dream. One of the things they sold was the weather: "Sleep under a blanket every night all summer in southern California."

PEOPLE ON THE MOVE

California was not the only state to attract newcomers during the 1920s. While two-thirds of the states lost population from migration, sixteen grew. Of these Michigan, New York, and California were the leaders.

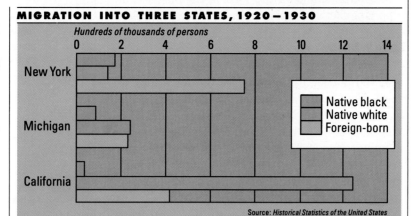

MIGRATION INTO THREE STATES, 1920–1930

Hundreds of thousands of persons

Legend: Native black, Native white, Foreign-born

Source: *Historical Statistics of the United States*

Michigan's growth reflected the boom in auto manufacturing, which provided thousands of new jobs. New York's growth was caused primarily by immigrants who landed in New York and chose to settle there. California's population surged because native-born Americans were pursuing a dream—a dream that took them away from the toil of farm work, the boredom of small towns, the blizzards of winter, and the sultry heat of summer. The California dream was responsible for the largest internal migration yet seen in American history.

BOOM TIMES

About 1,300,000 native-born Americans headed for California in the 1920s. Three-fourths of them settled in southern California. "Like a swarm of invading locusts, migrants crept in over all the roads," an observer wrote. "For wings, they had rattletrap automobiles, their fenders tied with string, and curtains flapping in the breeze." The new migrants "came with no funds and no prospects, apparently trusting that heaven would provide for them."

In fact, a booming economy did provide jobs. By 1926, Hollywood movies had become the nation's fifth-largest industry. Not far away, oil derricks dotted the landscape. Major oil fields had been discovered in the Los Angeles basin during the previous decade. The movie and oil businesses in turn encouraged finance, manufacturing, and shipping.

The California dream is still powerful. Each year more people move into the state than leave it.

CRITICAL THINKING QUESTIONS 4B

1. Is geography always a factor in the image of a dreamplace? Explain.
2. How does the California migration compare to earlier migrations such as the Puritan migration or westward movement?

National Identity
Why was Lindbergh given a hero's welcome when he returned to the United States? (His solo trans-atlantic flight was a feat of courage. His clean-cut character captured the imagination of the public.) Have the class suggest people who might be considered heroes today. Ask students to reflect on what makes them heroes. *How do heroes today compare with Lindbergh?*

Connecting with Literature
Writers of the "Lost Generation" gathered in Paris as literary exiles from America. Black writers worked in Harlem. *What were the literary themes of their work?* (Disillusionment with materialism, dissatisfaction with prosperity, attacks on the narrowness of small-town America, criticism of political and religious leadership, spiritual poverty, physical and emotional scars of war, the black experience in America.) Have students work in groups of three to create a poem that captures one of the literary themes of the 1920s. Have a student from each group read the group's poem. Post finished works on a bulletin board.

The Geographic Perspective Answers
1. Every place, even a dreamplace, has a climate. Certain features are idealized, negative features are overlooked.
2. Puritans migrated to establish an ideal society and often moved as a congregation. Pioneer families, searching for land, brought the means to make it productive. The 1920s migrants wanted urban opportunities, but were unsure of how they would make a living.

Geographic Themes
Geographic themes covered on this page:
___ Location
✔ Place
___ Interactions
✔ Movement
___ Regions

short stories from the country's finest writers. All three magazines joined *The Saturday Evening Post, Collier's,* and *Vanity Fair* in the business of supplying fact and fiction to the American people.

LUCKY LINDY 3A

The greatest public enthusiasm of the decade was reserved not for passing fancies but for a man of merit. That man was Charles A. Lindbergh, a 25-year-old pilot from Minnesota. In the mid-1920s no pilot had yet flown the Atlantic alone. There was a standing offer of $25,000 for a nonstop flight between New York and Paris. Lindbergh, a quiet young man with a streak of daring, decided to take up the challenge.

On May 20, 1927, Lindbergh took off from Roosevelt Field, Long Island, in his single-engine plane, *The Spirit of St. Louis.* Just getting off the ground was a victory for the tiny plane, which was loaded down with fuel for the long journey. (Lindbergh had to leave his radio and parachute behind in order to carry more gasoline.) Thirty-three hours later, having fought off numbing fatigue,

This 1927 magazine cover illustrates America's admiration for airplane pilots, such as Charles Lindbergh. Lindbergh was a mail plane pilot before his historic trans-Atlantic flight. **NATIONAL IDENTITY** How does this cover portray pilots as part of a great American tradition? **9B**

Lindbergh landed in Paris to the roar of a crowd of spectators.

Lindbergh returned to the United States by navy ship, and he was met by an uproar unknown in American history. Four destroyers, two army blimps, and forty airplanes escorted the ship into the Navy Yard at Washington, D.C. "Every rooftop, window, old ship, wharf, and factory floor was filled with those who simply had to see Lindbergh come home," a reporter wrote. "Factory whistles, automobiles, church bells, and fire sirens all joined the pandemonium."

Lindbergh then rode down Pennsylvania Avenue in a ticker tape parade. People wept openly as the shy, handsome pilot passed by. At the White House Lindbergh was honored by President Coolidge, who presented him with the Distinguished Flying Cross.

The public adulation that greeted Lindbergh verged on hysteria, and it is hard to understand even in view of his remarkable achievement. The best explanation is that people found different symbols in Lindbergh's feat. His flight showed

330

Americans that individual effort still mattered even in the machine age. It proved that there were still adventures to be had and frontiers to be tamed. Lindbergh himself also became a symbol—a hero in an age that worshiped heroes.

The Literary Life 4F

To many American writers of the 1920s, however, the heroic qualities credited to Lindbergh were rare indeed. Discontented with American society, writers were eager to experiment with new styles and explore new themes.

One group of writers aimed their attacks at small-town, middle-class America. Sinclair Lewis wrote about the narrowness of small-town life in *Main Street* (1920) and made fun of Midwestern businessmen in *Babbitt* (1922). The first American novelist to win the Nobel prize, Lewis even faulted Protestant clergymen in *Elmer Gantry* (1927), the story of a revivalist who had more sins than virtues. The greatest journalist of the time, H. L. Mencken, also had a taste for satirizing American life. Mencken was the self-appointed critic of the whole American scene. He used his column in the *Baltimore Sun* and his magazine, *American Mercury*, to air his ideas on the political and cultural life of the nation.

Another group of writers, accusing American society of hypocrisy and greed, settled in Paris or in New York City's Greenwich Village. The two

most important writers of the time, Ernest Hemingway and F. Scott Fitzgerald, were drifters whose lives were anchored only by their art. Gertrude Stein, an American writer in Paris, once remarked to Hemingway, "Ernest, you are all a lost generation."

> ## "You are all a lost generation."
> —*Gertrude Stein to Ernest Hemingway*

Stein's label stuck. The term Lost Generation came to be applied to the group of American writers who came of age between the wars. Their prose was realistic, and they often used profanity and sexual themes that shocked their readers. But what really set them apart from other writers was their sense of disillusionment. They, like the characters in their stories, found little in life worth believing in.

Hemingway, an ambulance driver during World War I, often wrote about men crippled physically or emotionally by the war. Hemingway's writing style—urgent and simple, like a news story—had a great influence on the other writers of his generation.

Fitzgerald, in contrast, wrote in a more elaborate manner better suited to the flamboyant lifestyle of his characters. Yet like Hemingway, Fitzgerald focused on people's inability to find happiness in postwar society. Fitzgerald's best-known novel, *The Great Gatsby* (1925), described a world that was materially wealthy but spiritually poor.

Black writers, many of whom had their own grievances against American society, also made valuable contributions to the literature of the 1920s. Their gathering place in New York City was not Greenwich Village but Harlem, and the literary movement that took root there was known as the Harlem Renaissance. For the first time, black poets and novelists could celebrate black life and still find a market for their work. Claude McKay, a Jamaican-born writer who had traveled around America working jobs on the railroads, wrote a best-selling novel called *Home to Harlem* (1928). Poets such as Countee Cullen and

BIOGRAPHY 4C

GERTRUDE STEIN (1874–1946) studied philosophy at Radcliffe College before moving to Paris in 1903. Her apartment there became a gathering place for writers such as Sherwood Anderson and Ernest Hemingway and painters such as Henri Matisse and Pablo Picasso (whose famous portrait of her appears here). Stein encouraged these artists to experiment and go beyond conventional styles. In this way, and through her own writing, Stein helped lay the foundation of modern art.

Biography
Ask students to consider why many American artists and writers lived abroad at this time.

You may wish to use the Section 3 Review, page 332, to see how well your students understand the main points in this section.

Section Review Answers

1. *flapper*—Young woman who dressed in short skirts and danced the new dances of the 1920s. *Lost Generation*—Group of American writers who came of age between the wars and wrote of American society's hypocrisy and greed. *Harlem Renaissance*—Group of black writers in New York's Harlem who celebrated and examined black life in America.

2. *Rudolph Valentino*—Early silent film idol. *Babe Ruth*—New York Yankee baseball star who set a record for home runs. *Louis Armstrong and Duke Ellington*—Famous musicians and founders of modern jazz. *Charles A. Lindbergh*—Pilot who made the first nonstop flight between New York and Paris. *Ernest Hemingway*—Writer whose simple and urgent style influenced many other writers. *F. Scott Fitzgerald*—Writer who focused on people's inability to find happiness in postwar society. *Harlem*—New York City neighborhood that was home to many black artists.

3. In the 1920s shorter working hours and higher wages gave Americans a combination of prosperity and leisure to devote more time to entertainment.

4. Hemingway's style was simple and urgent, and his characters were often men crippled physically or emotionally by war. In contrast, Fitzgerald's style was more elaborate to match the flamboyant and disillusioned characters he described. Both focused on people's inability to find happiness in postwar society.

5. Students may mention that every age finds its own heroes, and people celebrate great accomplishments and personal courage or success. Television and mass media may make heroic accomplishments more widely known. On the other hand, some students may point out that Americans have become more cynical and less able to agree on a hero.

Closure

Call students' attention to the beige boxed quotation (p. 331). Ask them to relate this quotation to the main idea of the section. Then have students read ahead to Section 4 for the next class period, noting the conflicts in American society in the 1920s.

SECTION 4

Divisions in American Society
(pp. 332–337)

Section Objective

■ identify and explain the reasons for divisions in American society

Introducing the Section

Connecting with Past Learnings

Help students see the changing conditions of the farmers. *How well did farmers do during World War I? Why?* (Farmers prospered because of the high demand generated by the war.)

Key Term

Have students define the Volstead Act and relate it to prohibition. Discuss with the class why it was necessary for Congress to pass a law to enforce a constitutional amendment. **LEP**

Langston Hughes examined the place of blacks in a white world. In his poem "Harlem," Hughes wondered how black Americans would respond if their demands for social justice were not met:

What happens to a dream deferred?

Does it dry up
like a raisin in the sun?
Or fester like a sore—
And then run?
Does it stink like rotten meat?
Or crust and sugar over—
like a syrupy sweet?

Maybe it just sags
like a heavy load.

Or does it explode?

2A, 3E, 4B, 4C, 4D, 4G, 9D, 9E

4 Divisions in American Society

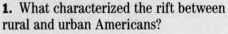

Section Focus

Key Term Volstead Act

Main Idea The 1920s witnessed a clash between rural and urban values.

Objectives As you read, look for answers to these questions:
1. What characterized the rift between rural and urban Americans?
2. What threats to civil liberties took place in the 1920s?
3. Why did prohibition fail?

The prominent writers of the 1920s who harshly criticized American society believed that the United States was neither as prosperous nor as free as was commonly thought. Indeed, the prosperity of the decade did bypass groups such as farmers and blacks. Issues concerning race, religion, immigration, and even alcohol also divided the American people during the 1920s.

THE FARM CRISIS 3E

In 1900, roughly 42 percent of all Americans were farmers. By 1929 only 25 percent of Americans were farmers, and that number was dropping all

the time. Young people, lured by industrial wages and by the excitement of urban life, were moving from the countryside to the cities.

Many people left the farms because farmers were not sharing in the prosperity of the decade. Life had changed since World War I, when farmers made big profits selling food to the European allies. When the war ended, the demand for agricultural exports went down. Europeans began to grow more of the food they needed.

Also, urbanization changed Americans' eating habits. People ate less when they did not have to do hard physical labor. By 1920 the average Amer-

---

SECTION REVIEW

1. KEY TERMS flapper, Lost Generation, Harlem Renaissance

2. PEOPLE AND PLACES Rudolph Valentino, Babe Ruth, Louis Armstrong, Duke Ellington, Charles A. Lindbergh, Ernest Hemingway, F. Scott Fitzgerald, Harlem

3. COMPREHENSION What economic changes allowed many Americans to devote more time to entertainment?

4. COMPREHENSION How did the writings of Hemingway and Fitzgerald differ? How were they similar?

5. CRITICAL THINKING Can there ever be a hero as famous today as Lindbergh was? Explain.

SUPPORTING THE SECTION

Reinforcement Workbook: Worksheet 54

Reteaching Resources: Worksheet 54

Enrichment and Extension Resources: Primary Source Worksheet 28

Teaching Transparency: Transparency 54

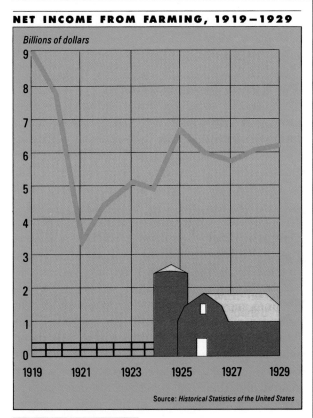

NET INCOME FROM FARMING, 1919–1929

Billions of dollars

Source: *Historical Statistics of the United States*

GRAPH SKILLS 3E

This graph shows the changes in U.S. farm income during the 1920s. In which year did farm income fall lowest? By how much did farm income decline between 1919 and 1921? **CRITICAL THINKING** Imagine yourself as a farmer in 1929. Would you feel optimistic about your economic future? Why or why not?

ican ate 75 pounds of food *less* a year than a decade before. Less grain was needed for livestock because the automobile had replaced horses for transportation. Even prohibition laws hurt the farm economy—farmers could no longer sell their grapes for wine or their barley for beer.

The result was overproduction of farm goods and a plunge in prices. In 1920, wheat brought $2.46 per bushel. A year later it brought $1.33 per bushel. Corn and cotton prices were cut in half during the same period. Advancements in technology—including fertilizers, pesticides, new types of seeds, and scientific breeding of livestock—only added to overproduction.

Farmers also had to worry about paying off mortgages on land they had bought during the

war. Falling food prices made it hard for many farmers to meet mortgage payments. Even if farmers chose to sell their extra land, they were still not in the clear. Land prices had been unnaturally high during the inflationary war years. They fell in the 1920s, making it impossible to pay off mortgages by land sales.

These hardships forced many farmers into bankruptcy. During a depression in 1920–1921, nearly half a million farmers lost their farms. Every year more and more farm families left the land and moved to towns and cities. During the 1920s, for the first time in the history of the United States, the total number of farms decreased.

Congress struggled with the farm crisis throughout the decade. The Federal Farm Loan Banks created under President Wilson (page 239) were increased in number. Farmers were given the legal right to work together to market their crops without fear of prosecution under antitrust laws. Congress also drafted the McNary-Haugen Bill. The bill proposed that the government buy farm surpluses and sell them abroad. Twice President Coolidge vetoed the proposal, objecting to government price-fixing. By the time Coolidge left office in 1929, farmers were in the midst of a depression of which few others were aware.

FARMERS AND CITY SLICKERS 2A

It was not just the economy that set farmers apart from city people. Social values were changing too—more so in the cities than in small towns or the countryside. Women found that more choices were open to them in the cities. On farms they had done back-breaking work that wore them out and sometimes killed them. But now city jobs offered them a new kind of independence. A city woman could work a fixed number of hours and earn enough money to rent an apartment of her own. By 1930 there were eleven million working women in America, more than double the number in 1900. Many women, as a result, no longer accepted the idea that they should defer to men.

This did not mean that marriage was going out of style. On the contrary, more Americans were getting married than ever before. In frontier times, half the male adult population never married. Now the figure was down to one-third and

Focus
If the muckrakers had continued to write in the 1920s, they would have found many problems deserving their journalistic attention. *What significant issues might an investigative reporter have written about in the 1920s?* (The plight of the farmers, black migration to northern cities, religion, KKK threats to liberty, growing sentiment to limit immigration, crime linked to prohibition, and the failure of the Volstead Act.)

Why were there so few muckraking journalists examining the problems in American society? (People were tired of the moral exertions of the progressives and the muckrakers. They preferred to enjoy prosperity of the times and not to look for trouble.)

Developing the Lesson
After students have read the section, you may wish to consider the following activities:

Economics
Have students look at the graph on this page, noting the trends in farm income in the 1920s. *What caused a decline in farm income?* (Overproduction, declining demand, inflated land prices.) *What measures did the government use to help the farmers?* (Farm banks; Congress introduced the McNary-Haugen farm bill, but President Coolidge vetoed it.) *Do you think the government did enough to help the farmers?*

Discuss the situation of farmers today, and ask interested students to find out about existing government agriculture programs.

Religion
Why were religious revival meetings popular in the 1920s? (Many people who had moved from farms to the cities felt a loss of religion in their lives.)

Analyzing Controversial Issues
Have the class re-enact the Scopes trial, with students playing John Scopes, William Jennings Bryan, Clarence Darrow, and witnesses for and against Scopes. Then have students discuss the case and decide whether they would have found Scopes guilty or declared the Tennessee law unacceptable.

Discuss with students the relationship between religion and what is taught in public schools. *Should schools be able to teach subjects that conflict with students' religions? Should religious leaders be able to determine what is taught in public schools? Explain your answers.*

Geographic Themes: Movement
What major migrations occurred in the United States in the 1920s? (Farmers moved to the cities, black people moved to the North, native-born Americans moved to California.) *How did these migrations affect American society?* (The United States became more urban, with a culture more at odds with traditional values; black people brought their culture to neighborhoods in northern cities; California became a leading state.)

Civic Values
Discuss with the class the actions and growth of the Ku Klux Klan in the 1920s. *Why, do you think, did the Klan gain power in the 1920s?* (Some people, worried about the erosion of traditional values,

dropping steadily. At the same time, however, the divorce rate was shooting upward. In 1890 there had been one divorce for every seventeen marriages; by the late 1920s there was one for every six. Most Americans, especially outside the cities, looked with dismay at this change in morals.

Religion, for the most part, played a more important role in farming communities than in cities. City people did not always know their neighbors. They could sleep late on Sunday without feeling that they would be missed at church. Moreover, the amusements of city dwellers included things that many country people considered sinful. City slickers drank liquor and danced the Charleston. Women wore short skirts and used cosmetics, which had not been accepted in "respectable society" only a few years before.

To combat what they saw as a decline in public morality, the American Protestant churches rallied to win sinners back. Charismatic preachers such as Billy Sunday and Aimee Semple McPherson held huge revival meetings. At these meetings they made highly dramatic pleas for sinners to pledge themselves to clean Christian living. Many of their followers were people who had moved to cities from the countryside and felt lost in their new surroundings. One year, during the annual Iowa Day that she held at her temple in

Artist John Steuart Curry painted this scene of a baptism in a Kansas farmyard in 1928. Curry was well-known for his dramatic paintings of midwestern rural life. **RELIGION** What are some of the values Curry portrays these rural folk as having? **4G**

Los Angeles, Aimee Semple McPherson asked how many people had once lived on a farm. The entire audience stood up.

THE SCOPES MONKEY TRIAL 4G

Perhaps the most celebrated conflict between country and city values involved the theory of evolution. In 1925 the state legislature of Tennessee passed a law making it illegal "to teach any theory that denies the story of the Divine creation of man as taught in the Bible, and to teach instead that man is descended from a lower order of animals." A number of other states passed similar laws. Darwin's theory of evolution, which was basic to the study of modern biology, was not to be taught in those states' public schools or universities.

John Scopes, a young biology teacher in Dayton, Tennessee, was one of the many educators who ignored the law and continued to teach evolution. The American Civil Liberties Union was determined to overturn the anti-evolution law. With Scopes's consent, they arranged for him to be arrested and then put together his defense. The foremost criminal lawyer in the nation, Clarence Darrow, volunteered his services as counsel for the defense. William Jennings Bryan, a wholehearted fundamentalist and a three-time candidate for President, joined the prosecution.

The trial, held during a heat wave in July 1925, drew national attention. The judge in the case made his own sympathies clear. He had a ten-foot banner hung behind his head facing the jury. It said, "READ YOUR BIBLE!" He refused to let Darrow call scientists as witnesses for the defense. They were not around during the Creation, the judge said, and their opinions would only be hearsay.

To nobody's surprise, the jury found John Scopes guilty of teaching evolution and fined him $100. The Tennessee law remained in force. Bryan's side had won, yet he did not feel like a victor. Darrow had gotten the better of him a dozen times during the trial. The national press was not kind. "Once he had one leg in the White House and the nation trembled under his roars," H. L. Mencken wrote in the *Baltimore Sun.* "Now he is a tinpot pope in the Coca-Cola belt. . . ." Bryan died only five days after the trial ended.

Photo Caption Answer
Students may suggest faith and simplicity.

Background Clarence Darrow called Bryan as a witness during the Scopes trial, as an expert on the Bible. Because the number of people who wanted to hear Bryan's

testimony was so large, the judge moved the trial to the lawn. It was during this questioning that many observers thought Darrow made Bryan look foolish.

AFRICAN AMERICAN MIGRATION 4C

Blacks as well as whites moved from the countryside to the cities throughout the 1920s. During and after World War I, southern rural blacks began to move—first by the thousands and later by the millions—to northern industrial cities. Blacks looked to the North as a place where there might be less racial prejudice. They, like their rural white counterparts, were also eager to trade the drudgery of sharecropping for the steady wages of industry. They settled in cities such as Philadelphia, Chicago, and New York. By 1930, 49 percent of Manhattan's black population had been born in the South. Many migrants were homesick, but they were comforted by the distinctive black culture that grew up in these northern cities.

Black migrants, however, found that racial prejudice followed them wherever they went. Most lived in poverty. Frozen out of jobs in shipping, construction, and in many factories, blacks confronted high levels of unemployment. Some black leaders concluded that blacks could never have justice in a land where they were in the minority. These leaders, known as black nationalists, argued that blacks needed a nation of their own, preferably in Africa.

The most popular black nationalist was Marcus Garvey, who founded the Universal Negro Improvement Association in his native Jamaica in 1914. Garvey saw himself as a black Moses leading his people out of bondage to an African promised land. At its peak his organization had 4 million members. It also had a widely circulated newspaper, *Negro World*.

Garvey caused a great deal of excitement among black Americans when he announced the formation of a steamship company, the Black Star Line, to carry blacks to a new homeland in Africa. Black Americans sent in money for tickets before the ships had even been bought. The money was soon wasted in mismanagement and stolen by some of Garvey's advisers. Garvey, himself penniless, was convicted of mail fraud and jailed for two years. He was later deported to Jamaica, and his organization collapsed. A few black nationalists continued his work, scornful of the efforts of moderate black leaders to win racial justice in the United States.

THE RETURN OF THE KU KLUX KLAN 9E

At the same time that some blacks sought solace in dreams of returning to Africa, they faced a new threat at home. This was the rebirth of the Ku Klux Klan, a group devoted to persecuting minorities in American society.

The Klan, which had flourished in the South

The influence of the Ku Klux Klan, a terrorist organization dedicated to white supremacy, revived in the 1920s and spread to northern states. Here Klan members in their traditional uniforms march in Washington, D.C., in 1925. **PATTERNS IN HISTORY** What factors may have boosted the Klan's popularity in the years after World War I? Why, do you think, are white supremacist organizations still a part of American society? 9E

looked for scapegoats and were willing to believe the racist teachings of the Klan.) Tell students that the KKK helped elect senators in such states as Oregon, Ohio, Tennessee, and Texas. *Do you think that a party which advocates racism should be allowed to participate in elections?*

Cultural Pluralism
On a classroom map or the map at the back of the book, have students identify the countries of northern and western Europe. (Great Britain, Ireland, Germany, Scandinavian countries such as Sweden, Denmark, and Norway.) Then have them identify southern and eastern European countries. (Italy, Poland, Czechoslovakia, Russia, etc.) Have students consider the cultural distinctions between these two areas and suggest reasons why immigration laws made it easier for northern and western Europeans to immigrate to the U.S. (More likely to be Protestant, speak English or a language like it, be lighter skinned, etc.)

Patterns in History
Ask students to suggest the positive and negative effects of prohibition. (Positive— tried to stamp out alcoholism and problems caused by drinking; negative—undermined respect for authority, increased organized crime, caused many people to suffer from drinking poisonous alcohol.) Have students compare prohibition with drug laws today. *What can prohibition teach us about how to control illegal substances effectively?* (Need public support and sufficient resources for enforcement.)

Photo Caption Answers
Racism and anti-immigrant feeling. Students may suggest that racial and ethnic prejudices have not yet been eliminated.

during Reconstruction, was revived in Georgia in 1915. Membership grew from 100,000 in 1919 to more than 2 million by 1924. Though its greatest influence was in rural areas, the Klan tried to appeal to bigots all over the country. In the South it vowed to "Keep the Negro in his place"; in the Midwest and West it attacked Catholics; in the East it stressed hatred of Jews. And everywhere the Klan blamed immigrants for many of the nation's troubles.

Terror was the Klan's favorite tactic. Dressed in white robes that hid their identity, Klan members used threats and violence to frighten people they considered undesirable. In a single year the Oklahoma Klan was held responsible for 2,500 floggings. Klansmen also branded, tarred and feathered, and lynched many victims. (Victims included a number of black soldiers—veterans of World War I—who were still in uniform.)

The Klan had some startling successes in politics, electing many state officials and several members of Congress. Its influence declined after 1925, however. In that year the leader of the Indiana Klan was convicted of murder, and a number of other scandals discredited Klan politicians.

IMMIGRATION RESTRICTIONS 4B

Some of the Klan's prejudice against immigrants was shared by mainstream American society. For decades, immigrants had been pouring into the United States by the millions. By 1920 more than 10 percent of all Americans were foreign-born. Many others were the children of immigrants, still steeped in the culture of their parents.

Americans had always prided themselves on their "melting pot" society. But the 1920s witnessed an upsurge in anti-immigrant feeling. It came from a variety of motives: racism, fear of competition for jobs, worries about political radicals. Newspapers printed editorials arguing that the "racial stock" of America was being watered down. The Red Scare added to the mistrust of foreigners. Some people claimed that the newcomers were bringing subversive ideas with them, like some sort of plague from abroad.

Responding to popular protests, Congress passed a law in 1921 to limit immigration. In 1924 the Johnson-Reed Act set even tighter immigra-

tion levels. Under this new law, quotas were highest for those countries that had already sent the greatest number of immigrants to the United States—namely, northern and western Europe. "America must be kept American," President Coolidge declared when he signed the law. Yet the Johnson-Reed Act by no means shut the door to all immigration. It did not, for instance, restrict immigration from Canada or Latin America. As a result, more than 4 million immigrants came to the United States during the 1920s.

PROHIBITION 4D

Controversies came and went in the 1920s, but the one that lasted longest was the debate over prohibition. After the Eighteenth Amendment was ratified in January 1919, it became illegal to manufacture, sell, or transport alcoholic beverages in the United States. Congress backed up the amendment by passing the Volstead Act in October 1919. The Volstead Act provided for enforcement of prohibition. The Anti-Saloon League of New York announced, "Now for an era of clean living and clear thinking!"

> "**N**ow for an era of clean living and clear thinking!"
> —*Anti-Saloon League of New York, 1919*

Few people in 1920 had any idea how difficult it would be to enforce prohibition. Illegal bars known as "speakeasies" sprang up everywhere. By 1929 there were 32,000 speakeasies in New York City alone. "Bootlegging"—the sale of illegal liquor—had become big business. Liquor was smuggled over the border from Mexico and Canada. Respectable middle-class Americans brewed homemade liquor in their cellars. Others paid their doctors to write prescriptions for liquor, which was still legal for medicinal purposes. Doctors wrote 11 million such prescriptions each year during the Prohibition Era, which lasted from 1920 to 1933.

The failings of prohibition were soon painfully obvious. Some of the home-brewed liquor was little better than poison, and a number of people

Texas agents pose with alcohol confiscated during Prohibition. ISSUES What similarities and differences exist between Prohibition and the recent war on drugs? 4D

died or went blind after drinking it. Also, because so many Americans preferred to break the law rather than give up drinking, prohibition undermined respect for authority. It even encouraged the spread of organized crime. Criminal gangs made fortunes distributing illegal liquor. The profits were so high that gangs fought over territory with pistols and submachine guns. The most famous gangster of the day was "Scarface" Al Capone. His Chicago gang took in several million dollars a month during its heyday.

Prohibition was never properly enforced because it was not well-funded. There were simply not enough courts and jails to process and keep the 40,000 to 50,000 people who violated the Volstead Act every year. As a result, violators were often let off with little or no punishment.

Prohibition dragged on for fourteen years, in spite of its lack of success. It still had many supporters, especially in rural America. Prohibition was not repealed until 1933, when the country was in the midst of a depression. By then the country simply did not have enough money to enforce an unworkable law.

SECTION REVIEW

1. KEY TERM Volstead Act

2. PEOPLE John Scopes, Clarence Darrow, William Jennings Bryan, Marcus Garvey, Al Capone

3. COMPREHENSION What four groups did the Ku Klux Klan attack?

4. COMPREHENSION Why was prohibition so difficult to enforce?

5. CRITICAL THINKING Do you think that rural areas tend to be more conservative than urban areas? Why or why not?

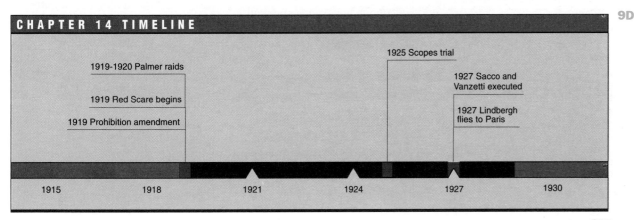

CHAPTER 14 TIMELINE

1919-1920 Palmer raids

1919 Red Scare begins

1919 Prohibition amendment

1925 Scopes trial

1927 Sacco and Vanzetti executed

1927 Lindbergh flies to Paris

| 1915 | 1918 | 1921 | 1924 | 1927 | 1930 |

CHAPTER 14   THE ROARING TWENTIES, 1919–1929   **337**

Chapter 14 REVIEW

CHAPTER 14 SUMMARY

SECTION 1: The nation had difficulty making the adjustment to peacetime after World War I.

■ Thousands of labor strikes erupted in the years after the war. Many of these strikes were violent.

■ Fears grew that there might be a Communist or anarchist conspiracy to overthrow the United States government. Efforts to crack down on radical groups led to violations of civil liberties.

SECTION 2: Under Presidents Warren G. Harding and Calvin Coolidge, the United States enjoyed unprecedented prosperity.

■ Harding took a laissez-faire attitude towards the nation's economy, cutting federal spending, encouraging business growth, and reducing the national debt.

■ Corruption plagued Harding's administration. When he died in office, he was succeeded by Vice President Coolidge.

■ The growth of the automobile industry both reflected and enhanced the nation's prosperity.

SECTION 3: Forms of entertainment and styles of life in the United States changed radically during the 1920s.

■ Americans had more money to spend and more leisure time than ever before. Radio, movies, and sports became national pastimes.

■ Some writers, however, attacked life in America.

SECTION 4: Changes that affected urban America were slow to come to rural areas.

■ Farmers did not share in the nation's prosperity during the 1920s. Their way of life contrasted sharply with that of city dwellers.

■ Many blacks migrated to northern cities in search of opportunities denied them in the South.

■ Prejudice against blacks and immigrants increased during the 1920s.

■ A law banning the sale of alcoholic beverages sparked crime and controversy throughout the 1920s.

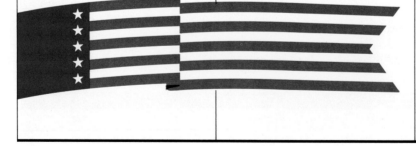

KEY TERMS ●

Define the terms in each of the following pairs.

1. Lost Generation; Harlem Renaissance
2. Palmer raids; Red Scare
3. Ohio Gang; Teapot Dome scandal

PEOPLE TO IDENTIFY ●

Use the following names to complete the sentences below.

Al Capone
F. Scott Fitzgerald
Henry Ford
Marcus Garvey
Charles A. Lindbergh
John Scopes
Bartolomeo Vanzetti

1. _____ was the teacher who was arrested and brought to trial in 1925 for teaching the theory of evolution.

2. _____ was the first person to fly alone across the Atlantic Ocean.

3. _____ was an anarchist found guilty of murder in 1920 and executed in 1927.

4. _____ was a black nationalist leader.

5. _____ was an automobile manufacturer who pioneered mass production.

6. _____ was the author of *The Great Gatsby*.

7. _____ was a Chicago gangster whose illegal activities brought in millions of dollars a month during Prohibition.

338

PLACES TO LOCATE ●

Match each of the letters on the map with the places that are listed below. Then explain the importance of each place.

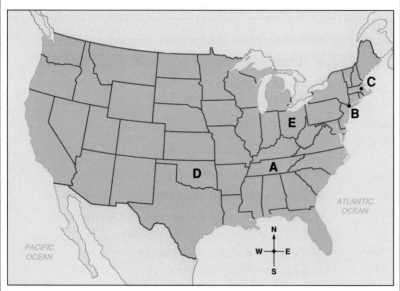

1. Boston
2. New York City
3. Ohio
4. Oklahoma
5. Tennessee

REVIEWING THE FACTS ▲

1. Why were there many labor strikes in the period after World War I?

2. What were the causes of the Red Scare?

3. What political scandals embarrassed the Harding administration?

4. What was Coolidge's style of leadership?

5. Describe the American economy during the 1920s.

6. What new forms of entertainment became popular during the 1920s?

7. What new trends developed in literature during the 1920s? Who were some of the most prominent authors of the decade?

8. What were the main factors that caused the farm crisis of the 1920s?

9. How did life change for black Americans during and after World War I? What minority groups, targeted by the Ku Klux Klan, became the objects of racial and cultural intolerance?

10. How did people get around the restrictions of the Eighteenth Amendment?

CRITICAL THINKING SKILLS ▲

1. **ANALYZING A QUOTATION** Reread the statement by the judge in the Sacco and Vanzetti case on page 319. Was this statement justified? Explain.

2. **FORMING A HYPOTHESIS** Harding claimed that while he could never be the nation's best President, he wanted to be the best-loved President. How would the qualities needed to be a popular President differ from those necessary to be an effective one?

3. **MAKING COMPARISONS** Compare and contrast the issue of restricting immigration in the 1920s with the issue as it exists today.

WRITING ABOUT TOPICS IN AMERICAN HISTORY ■

1. **CONNECTING WITH LITERATURE** A selection from *The Great Gatsby* by F. Scott Fitzgerald appears on pages 796–797. Read it and answer the questions. Then answer the following question: What influence do you think this portrayal of Gatsby's lifestyle might have had on readers in the 1920s?

2. **APPLYING THEMES: ECONOMIC DEVELOPMENT** Choose one of the technological advancements of the early 1900s that helped bring prosperity in the 1920s, such as the assembly line. Explain how it came about, how it was used, and why it helped increase economic efficiency.

9. While many blacks moved to northern cities hoping to earn industrial wages, their social status did not change. Intolerance was also directed at Catholics, Jews, and immigrants.

10. Some people brewed homemade liquor while others bought from bootleggers.

Critical Thinking Skills

1. Justified—opposing the government incites social unrest that may lead to violence; unjustified—Americans enjoy the right to freedom of conscience.

2. Presidents need to be unafraid to make unpopular decisions and to have strong personal convictions which might clash with popular opinion.

3. Concern over immigrants taking jobs from American workers remains, but today racial quotas are no longer followed in determining who is allowed to immigrate.

Writing About Topics in American History

1. Some students might say that readers would have tried to copy Gatsby's lifestyle, thinking that it was very modern. Others might suggest that readers would react unfavorably to such an extravagant lifestyle.

2. Students should do research to find out more about which technological advances helped the 1920s to prosper and why.

6. Radio, silent movies, publicized sporting events, jazz, new dances, and a variety of board games.

7. The Lost Generation, represented by Ernest Hemingway and F. Scott Fitzgerald; and the Harlem Renaissance, represented by Claude McKay and Langston Hughes.

8. The exodus from the farms of the young who preferred the excitement of urban life and industrial wages, the fall in the price of farm products, and the need to pay high debts incurred during the war.

Chapter Review exercises are keyed for student abilities:
● = Basic
▲ = Average
■ = Average/Advanced

Chapter 15 ■ Hoover and the Great Depression

3 Sections, 3–5 Days

	SECTION OBJECTIVES	SECTION RESOURCES
Section 1 **The Bubble Bursts**	■ describe the 1929 stock market crash ■ identify the causes of the Depression	● **Reteaching Resources:** Worksheet 55 ▲ **Reinforcement Workbook:** Worksheet 55 ■ **Enrichment and Extension Resources:** Historian Worksheet 5 ▲ **Teaching Transparencies:** Transparency 55
Section 2 **Daily Life in Hard Times**	■ describe how Americans coped with unemployment ■ identify problems faced by farmers in the 1930s	● **Reteaching Resources:** Worksheet 56 ▲ **Reinforcement Workbook:** Worksheet 56 ■ **Enrichment and Extension Resources:** Primary Source Worksheet 29 ▲ **Teaching Transparencies:** Transparency 56
Section 3 **The Hoover Response**	■ analyze Hoover's failure to stem the Depression ■ explain how the Depression influenced the 1932 election	● **Reteaching Resources:** Worksheet 57 ▲ **Reinforcement Workbook:** Worksheet 57 ■ **Enrichment and Extension Resources:** Primary Source Worksheet 30 ▲ **Teaching Transparencies:** Transparency 57

The list below shows Essential Elements relevant to this chapter. (The complete list of Essential Elements appears in the introductory pages of this Teacher's Edition.)

Section 1: 3E, 3F, 3G, 5B, 9E
Section 2: 2C, 3E, 4C
Section 3: 3E, 5B, 8H, 9D, 9E

Section Resources are keyed for student abilities:
● = Basic
▲ = Average
■ = Average/Advanced

CHAPTER RESOURCES

Geography Resources: Worksheets 29, 30
Tests: Chapter 15 Test

Chapter Project: American Culture

Have students devise a multi-media project focusing on the early years of the Great Depression. Students may include illustrated scrapbooks, tapes of interviews with people who lived through the Depression, and reports analyzing causes. Encourage students to use photographs, art, literature, and music of the Depression to enhance their project.

Homework Options

Each section contains activities labeled "Addressing Individual Needs." You may wish to choose from among these activities when assigning homework.

Provisions for Limited English Proficiency (LEP)

Several suggested activities may be particularly helpful for teachers of students with limited English proficiency. These activities have been marked throughout the Teacher's Annotated Edition with the symbol **LEP** .

BIBLIOGRAPHY AND AUDIOVISUAL AIDS

Teacher Bibliography

Bernstein, Irving. *The Lean Years: A History of the American Worker, 1920–1933.* Da Capo, 1983.

Burner, David. *Herbert Hoover: The Public Life.* Knopf, 1978.

Galbraith, John Kenneth. *The Great Crash of Nineteen Twenty-Nine.* Avon, 1980.

McElvaine, Robert. *The Great Depression: America 1929–1941.* Times Books, 1985.

Terkel, Studs. *Hard Times: An Oral History of the Great Depression in America.* Pantheon, 1986.

Student Bibliography

Hunt, Irene. *No Promises in the Wind.* Berkley-Pacer, 1987. A story of the Depression.

McElvaine, Robert S., ed. *Down and Out in the Great Depression: Letters from the "Forgotten Man."* University of North Carolina Press, 1983.

Meltzer, Milton. *Brother, Can You Spare a Dime? The Great Depression, 1929–1933.* Mentor Books, 1977.

Literature

Baker, Russell. *Growing Up.* Signet, 1984. A boy's life during the Depression.

Saroyan, William. *My Name Is Aram.* Harcourt Brace Jovanovich, 1950. Stories about an Armenian boy growing up in California.

Steinbeck, John. *The Grapes of Wrath.* Penguin, 1986.

Wolfe, Thomas. *You Can't Go Home Again.* Buccaneer Books, 1981.

Films and Videotapes*

America Lost and Found. 59 min. DCL. Rare footage conveys the psychological impact of the Great Depression.

Growing Up in the Great Depression. 28 min. COR/MTI. Shared memories of five Americans who survived the Great Depression.

Filmstrips*

The Great Depression, 1929–1939 (set of 3). GA. Begins with "Black Tuesday" and the panic on Wall Street; describes the effects of unemployment and traces Roosevelt's New Deal; concludes with the coming of World War II and the return to prosperity.

Computer Software*

America's Presidents Series: World Wars, Prosperity and Depression—Presidents During and Between Two World Wars (Apple with 48K; IBM with 64K). QUEUE. Each President is covered in a separate menu option, and prominent Presidents have multiple sections on different phases on their lives and administrations. Presidents Wilson–Truman, 1913–1953.

*For a complete guide to audiovisual sources, see the introduction to this book (page Txx).

Chapter 15

Hoover and the Great Depression
(pp. 340–359)

This chapter describes the events that led to the Great Depression and discusses the impact of the Depression on American life. It explains the loss of confidence in President Hoover's leadership and the election of Franklin Delano Roosevelt.

Themes in American History

- Global interactions
- Economic development
- Pluralistic society
- American culture

Chapter Objectives

After students complete this chapter, they will be able to:

1. Describe the 1929 stock market crash.

2. Identify the causes of the Depression.

3. Describe how Americans coped with unemployment.

4. Identify problems faced by farmers in the 1930s.

5. Analyze Hoover's failure to stem the Depression.

6. Explain how the Depression influenced the 1932 election.

Chapter Opener Art
J. Porter, *Transients Cooking Their Dinner in the Snow near a Coal Chute, DeKalb, Illinois* (detail), from a photograph taken of the scene in 1938 by Ivan E. Prall.

In the years after the nation's terrifying plunge into the Great Depression, countless Americans suffered from cold, hunger, and lack of work. Many people ended up homeless, as shown in this painting of transients in a barren field outside DeKalb, Illinois. To an increasingly frustrated public, President Hoover appeared cold and indifferent to such scenes of suffering.

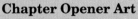

CHAPTER SUPPORT MATERIAL	
	Reinforcement Workbook: Worksheets 55–57
	Reteaching Resources: Worksheets 55–57
	Enrichment and Extension Resources: Primary Source Worksheets 29, 30; Historian Worksheet 5
	Geography Resources: Worksheets 29–30
	Teaching Transparencies: Transparencies 55–57
	Tests: Chapter 15 Test

15 Hoover and the Great Depression (1929–1933)

KEY EVENTS	
1929	Hoover takes office
1929	Stock market crashes
1929	Great Depression begins
1930	Congress passes Smoot-Hawley Tariff
1932	Bonus Army marches on Washington

3E, 3F, 3G, 5B, 9E

1 The Bubble Bursts

Section Focus

Key Terms Dow Jones Industrial Average
■ Black Thursday ■ institutional investor
■ margin buying ■ stock pool ■ Great
Depression ■ Smoot-Hawley Tariff

Main Idea After the crash of the stock market in October 1929, the United States sank into the most serious depression of its history.

Objectives As you read, look for answers to these questions:
1. What were the issues in the 1928 presidential campaign?
2. Why did the stock market crash?
3. What caused the American economy to sink into a depression?

In 1928 and 1929 the rising stock market tempted more and more Americans into speculation. Once the stock market had been of interest only to rich investors. Now ordinary people used their savings to buy stocks. Many people turned to the financial section of the newspaper even before they looked at the front page. The head of a New York bank remarked, "You ride in an elevated train or a streetcar and the conductor asks you: 'How is General Motors?'"

The economic policies of the Republicans were behind the rise in the market, but even Democrats approved. In the summer of 1929, the chairman of the Democratic National Committee made the following claim:

> If a man saves $15 a week, and invests in good common stocks, and allows the dividends and rights to accumulate, at the end of twenty years he will have at least $80,000 and an income from investments of around $400 a month. He will be rich. And

because income can do that, I am firm in my belief that anyone can not only be rich, but ought to be rich.

Americans expected decades of lasting prosperity, but they were sadly mistaken. A time of hardship was coming that would be harsher than anything the nation had yet known.

THE ELECTION OF 1928 5B

In 1928 Franklin Delano Roosevelt was getting ready to run for governor of New York. He did not envy his friend Al Smith, who was a candidate for President. "I am doubtful whether any Democrat can win in 1928," Roosevelt remarked. He knew that most Americans were satisfied with the previous eight years of Republican leadership. Employment was steady, wages were high, and the stock market was rising. Apart from the farm crisis, there was little a Democratic challenger could point to that required reform. The newspaper columnist Will Rogers wrote, "You can't lick this

---

SECTION 1

The Bubble Bursts
(pp. 341–346)

Section Objectives
■ describe the 1929 stock market crash
■ identify the causes of the Depression

Introducing the Section

Connecting with Past Learnings
Review with the class the definition of *corporation* (business organization owned by stockholders), and *dividend* (portion of corporate profits paid to stockholders).
How did the increase in the supply of capital in the late 1800s help the American economy? (Businesses used the capital to expand production, hiring more workers and producing more goods.) *How do businesses raise capital?* (Through borrowing or by selling stock.)

Key Terms
Write terms on the board and divide the class into teams. Tell them that when you say, "Go!" they are to determine the best definition for each term. The first team to finish will stand and recite the words and the definitions. Tell the other teams that they can challenge the definitions and suggest their own. **LEP**

Challenge students to create flow charts illustrating the stock market crash. (Margin buying, unethical practices, and higher interest rates led to a sharp drop on October 23, 1929; stockholders reacted with panic the next day and prices plunged; bankers bought up stocks after noon on October 24, calming fears; bankers sold those stocks and the market continued to drop; institutional investors sold and stocks dropped even lower.) Have volunteers share their charts with the class, then combine the best features into one diagram on the board.

What were the causes of the Depression? (Uneven distribution of wealth; high tariffs; farm crisis; over-production in industry; shaky banking system.)

Developing the Lesson

After students have read the section, you may wish to consider the following activities:

Participating in Government

What disadvantages did Al Smith have as the Democratic nominee for President in 1928? (Smith was Irish Catholic, from an immigrant family, and not well-known outside his own state.) **Which of these, do you think, would still be obstacles today?** (Lack of voter recognition.)

Prosperity thing. Even the fellow that hasn't got any is all excited over the idea."

As the Democratic nominee for 1928, Alfred E. Smith was not exactly the man to snatch victory from the jaws of defeat. Smith was an Irish Catholic from an immigrant family in New York City. He had served four terms as governor of New York, where he instituted reforms in the Progressive tradition. He fought for workmen's compensation and shorter working hours for women, and he reformed the state's financial system. Outside his state he failed to win much popularity. "Never heard of him," a Maine farmer said when one of Smith's supporters asked him about the candidate. "What happens in New York doesn't make any difference here."

Smith's religion proved to be another drawback. The rise in immigration from southern and eastern Europe had brought many Catholics to the United States. But the majority of Americans belonged to Protestant churches, and anti-Catholic prejudice was common. The Ku Klux Klan came out against Smith, lining railroad tracks near Oklahoma City with flaming crosses when the candidate was scheduled to speak there. "I am unable to understand how anything I was taught to believe as a Catholic could possibly be in conflict with what is good citizenship," Smith responded.

The Republicans nominated Herbert Hoover as their candidate for President. Hoover was a shy, modest man, who had been raised a Quaker. He had devoted himself to public service after making millions as a mining engineer, and he had gained fame for his skillful administration of relief operations in Europe after World War I.

Republican Herbert Hoover and his running mate, Charles Curtis, appear on this button from the 1928 presidential campaign. Hoover, a Quaker who became an orphan at age nine, had a reputation as a humanitarian and an able administrator for his role in European relief efforts following World War I. **POLITICS** What political advantages did Hoover possess in his campaign against Smith? **5B**

Hoover had served as Secretary of Commerce under Presidents Harding and Coolidge, but he had never run for elective office. He found it hard to make small talk and had little taste for the theatrical side of campaigning. His good reputation spoke for him, however, and his ideas on American politics were in line with the times. He stressed "Republican prosperity" and promised "a chicken in every pot and a car in every garage." He was in favor of maintaining prohibition, while Smith argued for its repeal. He wanted to limit the role of government in the economy, while Smith wanted more government programs.

> "**A** chicken in every pot and a car in every garage."
> —*Hoover campaign slogan, 1928*

Near the end of his campaign, Hoover told an audience of 20,000 at Madison Square Garden in New York City:

> Even if governmental conduct of business could give us more efficiency instead of less efficiency, the fundamental objection to it would remain unaltered and unabated. . . . It would undermine the development of leadership. It would cramp and cripple the mental and spiritual energies of our people. It would extinguish equality and opportunity. It would dry up the spirit of liberty and progress.

The majority of Americans seemed to agree, because Hoover won the election by a landslide. He captured 444 electoral votes to Smith's 87. Smith did not even carry his home state of New York. Americans were happy with things as they stood, and they hoped to preserve the status quo by electing another Republican President.

THE CRASH 3E

On a cold and rainy day in March 1929, Herbert Hoover was sworn in as President of the United States. "I have no fears for the future of our country," he told the listening crowd. "It is bright with hope." In the early months of his administration,

Photo Caption Answer
Most Americans were satisfied with the state of the economy; anti-Catholic prejudice hurt his less well-known opponent.

the confidence of the new President seemed justified. The economy was in fine shape, and the stock market continued to rise. By September 1929, the Dow Jones Industrial Average—the average value of stocks from 30 of the nation's largest firms—had reached 381, nearly 300 points higher than it had been five years before.

> "**I** have no fears for the future of our country. It is bright with hope."
> —*Herbert Hoover, 1929*

Most people thought the good times would go on forever. The Yale economist Irving Fisher declared, "Stock prices have reached what looks like a permanently high plateau." Only one economist warned of danger. "There is a crash coming, and it may be a terrific one," Roger W. Babson predicted in early September, but the financial journals laughed at him.

On Wednesday, October 23, 1929, in the space of five hours, stock prices dropped so sharply that investors lost about $5 billion. On the next day, October 24, known as Black Thursday, panic gripped Wall Street and prices plunged even lower. Everyone tried to sell their stocks and get out of the market, afraid that within days their holdings would be worthless.

At noon Thursday, word spread that New York's biggest bankers were meeting to stop the panic. They stepped in to buy stocks at prices higher than the going rate, and relieved brokers cheered them on the floor of the Stock Exchange. By day's end, trading had stabilized and the fall in stock prices had been slowed to a drop of only 12 points. The press hailed the bankers as "Saviors of the Market." Yet what the bankers had really done was to force prices up temporarily. They then sold their own securities and got out of the market. The fall continued.

During Monday and Tuesday of the following week, the market dropped another 92 points. On Tuesday more shares were traded than ever before in the history of the Exchange. This was because institutional investors—pension companies and insurance firms that bought stocks in large volume—were rushing to unload blocks of 10,000 shares. Losses for the day were estimated at between $6 billion and $9 billion.

The next day the market rallied, gaining 31 points. Hoping to calm fears, *The New York Times* reported, "Many bankers, brokers, and industrial leaders expressed the belief . . . that [the downturn] had now run its course." Yet the country was badly shaken. Millionaires had seen enormous fortunes melt away. Ordinary people had gambled their savings and lost their security for the future. The worst, however, was yet to come.

Investors crowd Wall Street on Black Thursday—the day of the worst stock market crash in United States history. Traders anxiously watched ticker tape machines (above) as stock prices fell. **ECONOMICS** Explain Hoover's statement that the future was "bright with hope." What factors made him confident of the nation's economic health? **3E**

Economics
Help students understand the stock market crash by giving each student five pieces of paper with the words "Stock in X Corporation" on each. Explain that you have issued them stock. Then tell them that the economy is strong and X Corporation is doing well. Tell students who want to sell their stock to go to one side of the room, and students who want to buy more stock to go to the other side. *According to the law of supply and demand, will the cost of the stock go up or down?* (Probably up.)

Now explain that interest rates are rising, Corporation X cannot afford to borrow money to start a new advertising campaign, its products are not selling well, and the economy in general is weak. Have students rearrange themselves according to who wants to buy and who wants to sell. *Will the cost of the stock go up or down?* (Probably down.)

You may want to have students actually barter with each other to buy and sell the stock, noting how the price of the stock changes.

Patterns in History
Have students find out what the Dow Jones Industrial Average is today. Then have them create a graph showing its ups and downs over the past week. Based on their graphs and news reports, ask them if the stock market has been going up or down. Have them find out reasons for this trend.

Photo Caption Answer
Relatively steady employment, high wages, and rising stock prices.

Background   Wall Street is actually a short, narrow street in downtown New York City, which borders the area where the New York Stock Exchange and a number of banks and brokerage houses are located. It is the heart of U.S. banking and business and has become an international symbol of finance.

Ethics

Have students consider brokerage practices before the stock market crash. *Do you think margin buying or forming a stock pool was unethical? Why or why not?* Ask students if they feel that most stock market traders today behave ethically.

Global Awareness

Have students write a diplomatic dispatch from London reporting on the worldwide effects of the American economic crisis. The dispatch should explain the impact of the American Depression on the European economy. (American banks had fewer dollars to lend, higher tariffs stifled trade, war debts had to be paid.)

What were the results of the worldwide economic crisis? (Banks abroad failed; European nations entered a cycle of poverty and political instability.)

C Cooperative Learning

Prepare eight large index cards, each with an underlying cause of the Depression written on one side: unequal distribution of wealth, high tariffs, war debts, farm crisis, over-production, credit buying, weakness in the banking system, the domino effect. Divide the class into groups, assigning each group an index card. On the back of the card, each group should create a cause and effect chart for the problem. Display the cards. **LEP**

5B

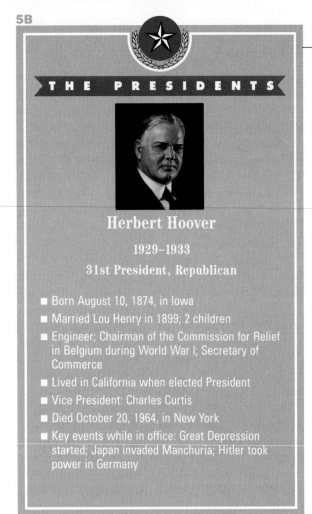

THE PRESIDENTS

Herbert Hoover

1929–1933

31st President, Republican

- Born August 10, 1874, in Iowa
- Married Lou Henry in 1899; 2 children
- Engineer; Chairman of the Commission for Relief in Belgium during World War I; Secretary of Commerce
- Lived in California when elected President
- Vice President: Charles Curtis
- Died October 20, 1964, in New York
- Key events while in office: Great Depression started; Japan invaded Manchuria; Hitler took power in Germany

WHAT CAUSED THE CRASH? 9E

The most important reason behind the Crash was overspeculation. Prices had risen far above the stocks' actual value. Brokers used financial practices that were unsound and even unethical, and the government did not try to stop them.

Margin buying was one of the most dangerous of these practices. Investors who bought on margin gave their brokers a fraction of the real value of the stocks they wanted to purchase. The broker then borrowed the rest of the money to buy the stocks. In this way, people were able to invest money that they did not really have. As demand for stocks rose, so too did stock prices.

The schemes of greedy investors also boosted stock prices during the 1920s. Some investors used illegal or barely legal methods to make quick profits for themselves. One of these methods was

the stock pool, in which a group of wealthy investors got together and bought a large block of a certain stock. They then traded shares back and forth, driving up the price and pulling in outsiders who thought they had spotted a good thing. At an agreed-upon point, the members of the stock pool would pull out, dumping their shares on the market and pocketing the profits. The price of the stock would then drop, and the outsiders would lose money.

A crash was bound to come sooner or later. But what triggered it in the fall of 1929 will never be known for sure. The Federal Reserve Board (page 237) may accidentally have helped cause the crisis. During the 1920s, the Federal Reserve had tried to promote economic growth by lowering the interest rates it charged member banks. These banks in turn lowered the interest rates they charged individual customers, thereby putting more money into circulation.

Unfortunately, much of this money was not used for things like housing construction and new industrial machinery—investments that would have fueled solid, long-term growth. Rather, it went into get-rich-quick schemes, especially in the stock market. In August 1929 the Federal Reserve, worried that speculation was getting out of control, decided to raise interest rates. Investors feared that the higher rates would stifle economic growth, and so they sold their stocks.

Once prices began to fall in New York, mob psychology took over. Brokers and investors panicked, selling all their stocks before prices fell even further. This, of course, only worsened the situation. The lower stocks fell, the more people wanted to unload the stocks they still had.

THE DEPRESSION TAKES HOLD 3E

Soon the nation found itself in the midst of the Great Depression, a time of economic hardship that would last from 1929 to 1941. Economists have long debated the relationship between the Crash and the Great Depression. Some claim that the Crash caused the Depression. Others, however, argue that the Depression was a result of underlying problems in the American economy. The Crash, they argue, was merely a symptom of these deeper problems.

The Presidents
Have students create a cause and effect chart on how the stock market crash affected Hoover's presidency.

Background Buying on margin allowed purchasers of securities to use those securities as collateral when borrowing money to buy the securities themselves. If the securities went up in price, they could sell, pay off the loan, and still have a profit. If the securities went down, purchasers had to scramble to

pay the borrowed money. In 1929, there were $6 billion outstanding in brokers' loans because of people buying on margin.

As rumors of bank failures spread, panicked Americans, such as this crowd at Cleveland's Union Trust Company, rushed to withdraw their savings. Five thousand banks and thousands of businesses failed during the early 1930s, and millions of people lost their savings. **ECONOMICS** Why might bank failures also have forced many businesses to close?

3E, 3G

Whatever the role of the Crash in causing the Depression, there is no doubt that the American economy faced serious problems in the years leading up to 1929. The unequal distribution of wealth was one. Too many people in the United States had only a little money, and too few had a lot. The richest 1 percent of Americans had 14.5 percent of the nation's annual income. These wealthy few invested their money in stocks or placed it in savings accounts. Not enough of the national income went to farmers and workers, who would have bought consumer goods and thereby kept the money in circulation.

High tariffs and war debts were another problem. In 1922 Congress had passed the Fordney-McCumber Tariff, setting high tariff rates that discouraged European companies from selling to the American market. This made it hard for Europeans to repay war debts, and nearly all of Europe was in debt to the United States. The high tariffs also prompted European nations to raise their own tariffs in retaliation, slowing international trade.

The farm crisis too helped to undermine the economy. Farmers had bought more land and new equipment to meet the demand for farm products during World War I. In the 1920s there was widespread overproduction, and farmers found themselves in financial trouble during an otherwise prosperous decade.

Overproduction was a problem in industry as well as in agriculture. The nation's productive capacity increased rapidly after World War I. But because workers' wages did not keep pace with the price of goods, many people could not afford these new products. This problem was masked but not cured by the expansion of credit during the 1920s. Thousands of people bought goods on the installment plan, helping boost the economy in the short run. Yet installment buying put consumers in debt, thereby reducing their buying power for the future.

The banking system too was vulnerable. Many banks were poorly managed, and there was little government regulation. Bank failures became common during the 1930s. Five thousand banks failed and nine million people lost their savings accounts during the first three years of the Depression. Some of these bank failures were the result of the Crash, since banks had made loans to investors who could not repay them after stocks fell. Some were the result of panics, as people who feared a failure rushed to withdraw their savings while they still had the chance. Even healthy banks were forced to shut down when all their depositors demanded their money at the same time.

SOME ECONOMIC INDICATORS OF THE GREAT DEPRESSION

Indicator	1928	1929	1930	1931	1932	1933
Unemployment (in millions)	2.0	1.6	4.3	8.0	12.1	12.8
Average weekly earnings for production workers in manufacturing (constant dollars)	$27.80	$28.55	$25.84	$22.62	$17.05	$17.71
Bank suspensions because of financial difficulties	499	659	1,352	2,294	1,456	4,004
Federal government spending (in billions of dollars)	$2.9	$3.1	$3.3	$3.6	$4.7	$4.6
Value of United States exports (in billions of dollars)	$5.8	$5.4	$4.0	$2.9	$2.3	$2.1

Source: *Historical Statistics of the United States*

CHART SKILLS

3F, 9E

This chart shows some of the effects of the Depression on the American economy. What trend can you identify in average earnings? In value of exports? How many in the work force were unemployed in 1932? **CRITICAL THINKING** How do you account for the trend in government spending?

Finally, the Depression was the product of the domino effect. Because of the countless ties among various sectors of the American economy, problems in one sector eventually affected others. Workers who lost jobs no longer had the money to buy consumer products. Sales fell and more businesses shut down, causing a fresh wave of workers to lose their jobs. The cycle went on. By 1930 four million people were out of work, and by 1932 it was twelve million.

WORLDWIDE CRISIS 3E

The onset of the Great Depression sent shock waves throughout the world. European nations had especially close economic links to the United States. When American banks no longer had money to lend them, European nations suffered. Many of them were already on the verge of economic collapse.

Congress did not help matters by raising tariffs soon after the Crash. In June 1930 Congress passed the Smoot-Hawley Tariff, setting the highest tariff rates in history. Confused by the plunge in stock prices and eager to protect American trade, members of Congress did not realize that high tariffs would only make the situation worse.

The tariffs reduced European imports by making imported goods more expensive. European na-

tions retaliated by raising their own tariffs. This hurt United States exports and brought international trade to a virtual standstill. The problem was compounded when Europe suffered an economic crisis of its own in the spring of 1931. Hoover sponsored a moratorium on the payment of war debts in June 1931, giving the European nations a year's grace. Yet this was not enough to save the European economy. Many banks failed, and much of Europe entered a cycle of poverty and political instability.

SECTION REVIEW

1. **KEY TERMS** Dow Jones Industrial Average, Black Thursday, institutional investor, margin buying, stock pool, Great Depression, Smoot-Hawley Tariff

2. **PEOPLE AND PLACES** Alfred E. Smith, Herbert Hoover, Wall Street

3. **COMPREHENSION** What part did religion play in the 1928 election?

4. **COMPREHENSION** How did overspeculation affect the stock market?

5. **CRITICAL THINKING** What changes in policy do you think would have helped the United States avoid the Depression?

2 Daily Life in Hard Times

Section Focus

Key Terms Hooverville ■ Dust Bowl ■ Okie

Main Idea The Depression was a time of great hardship for both urban and rural Americans.

Objectives As you read, look for answers to these questions:
1. How did urban Americans cope with poverty?
2. What problems faced farmers in the 1930s?
3. What crisis gripped the Great Plains?

The Depression, arriving at a time of widespread confidence in the United States' future, came as a great shock to the American people. In the hard times that followed the Crash, some people became disillusioned about American democracy. In April 1932 Senator Huey Long of Louisiana announced that America had lost the light that once guided it:

> This great and grand dream of America, that all men are created free and equal, endowed with the inalienable right of life and liberty and the pursuit of happiness, this great dream of America, this great light, and this great hope, have almost gone out of sight in this day and time, and everybody knows it. There is a mere candle flicker here and yonder to take the place of what the great dream of America was supposed to be.

Senator Long was not the only person voicing such concerns. Many people at that time believed that the Depression represented the permanent breakdown of the American economy. In 1932 nearly a quarter of the nation's labor force was out of work. Four-fifths of the steel mills were shut down, and farm income had fallen to less than half of what it had been in 1929. The mood of the country was grim. The goal of most Americans was simply to survive. So they held on, impatient with Hoover, nostalgic for the past, eager for a change.

COPING IN THE CITY 3E

Most city people had to retrench during the Depression, cutting out luxuries and making old things last longer. The telephone was often the first thing to go. People also stopped buying household appliances, furniture, jewelry, and candy. Yet some other items seemed indispensable. Sales of gasoline, radios, electric refrigerators, and cigarettes were brisk throughout the Depression. Movies too were popular, as people looked to Hollywood as an escape from their troubles. The novelist Anita Loos remarked, "Motion picture houses throughout the nation were jammed. Folks were skimping on the bare necessities of life to buy distraction."

Families had to use their ingenuity to save money. They cut down on their food budgets by planting gardens in vacant lots. In Gary, Indiana, for example, 20,000 families raised gardens on land lent by the city. Women often sewed clothes instead of buying them. Younger children wore the hand-me-downs of their older siblings. In an effort to make clothing more affordable, clothing manufacturers began to simplify styles, selling men's suits without vests and socks without garters. Styles also became more sober. Women's hemlines went down—a sign that the wild and carefree mood of the 1920s was at an end.

The Depression made people turn back to their families. Children could not afford to leave home, and many people had to move in with relatives when they lost their own homes or apartments. The divorce rate went down during the Depression, perhaps because couples could not afford to split up. Yet the constant shortage of money and worry about the future created new tensions within families.

Some Americans suffered more than others. People who were out of work often could not afford medical care or proper food. In 1933 the

---

SUPPORTING THE SECTION

Reinforcement Workbook: Worksheet 56
Reteaching Resources: Worksheet 56
Enrichment and Extension Resources: Primary Source Worksheet 29
Teaching Transparencies: Transparency 56

SECTION 2

Daily Life in Hard Times
(pp. 347–351)

Section Objectives
■ describe how Americans coped with unemployment
■ identify problems faced by farmers in the 1930s

Introducing the Section

Connecting with Past Learnings
Remind students of daily life in the 1920s by asking them to describe important social trends of the decade. (Greater prosperity, more leisure than before, greater freedom for women.) *What problems did farmers face in the 1920s?* (Overproduction from World War I had led to lower farm prices. Many farmers lost their land and moved to the city.)

Key Terms
List key terms on the board. Ask students to define the terms. Then have students relate each term to one of the hardships brought about by the Great Depression. LEP

Focus
Make two columns on the board labeled *Hardships* and *Coping*. Have students fill in the columns with lists of hardships during the Great Depression and people's attempts to cope with them. (Hardships—unemployment, inability to buy food and pay rent, suffering of urban blacks, overproduction and drought on the farm. Coping—traveling to find work, selling apples and shining shoes, raising gardens in cities, using old clothes, living in Hoovervilles, "block aid," "rent parties," killing off livestock, letting crops rot in the fields, moving to California.)

What did the Depression do to Americans' image of their country? (Americans lost confidence in the political system.)

Developing the Lesson

After students have read the section, you may want to consider the following activities:

National Identity

Have students contact grandparents, relatives, or others who remember the Great Depression and interview them. Tell students to find out where their subjects lived during the Depression, what hardships their families faced, how they coped, and their most vivid memories of the Depression. Ask students to write up their interviews and read them to the class.

Cultural Pluralism

What efforts did the NAACP focus on during the Depression? (The effort to end discrimination and promote black education.) *What was W.E.B. Du Bois's criticism of that focus?* (He felt that the poverty of blacks, caused by the Depression, was more important.) *With whom do you agree? Why?*

Environment

How were farmers' problems affected by forces of nature? (Drought and the Dust Bowl contributed to the ruin of farmers as well as overproduction and falling prices.) *How was the delicately balanced ecology of the Great Plains disrupted by farming?* (When grasslands of the Great Plains were plowed under, topsoil was no longer held by the deep tangled roots of the grass. In dry years the topsoil blew away.) *What might farmers have done to avert disaster?* (Better use of dry farming and crop rotation might have kept more of the topsoil in place.)

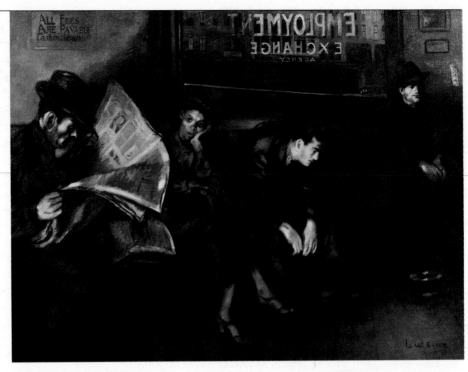

During the Depression, millions of jobless Americans searched desperately for work. Isaac Soyer's realistic painting shows job seekers waiting at an employment agency. **CULTURE** What emotions does the painting communicate on the part of its subjects? **3E**

Children's Bureau reported that one out of every five children was not getting enough of the right things to eat. Families substituted cheap starches like bread and potatoes for milk, meat, and fresh fruit. In 1933, starvation claimed the lives of 29 people in New York City alone.

THE HOMELESS 3E

People who had no relatives to turn to could not even find decent shelter when they were out of work. Some slept in flophouses—large buildings run by cities or by private charities that provided a bed at night for homeless people. In his novel *You Can't Go Home Again*, Thomas Wolfe described the population of drifters who came to these shelters:

> Some were those shambling hulks that one sees everywhere, in Paris as in New York. . . . But most of them were just the flotsam of the general ruin of the time—honest, decent middle-aged men with faces seamed by toil and want, and young men, many of them mere boys in their teens, with thick, unkempt hair. These were the wanderers from town to town, the riders of freight trains, the thumbers of rides on highways, the uprooted, unwanted male population of America. They drifted across the land and gathered in big cities when winter came, hungry, defeated, hopeless, restless. . . .

Other people who lost their homes moved into shacks without heat or running water. Every large city had a dozen or more Hoovervilles—shantytowns patched together out of old crates and cartons, where homeless people lived. They were named after Hoover because people did not believe that he was doing enough to help the poor and fight the Depression. About one million Americans lived in Hoovervilles by 1933.

The federal government did little to provide direct relief to unemployed and homeless people during Hoover's administration. The burden fell instead on state and local governments and on charitable groups such as the Red Cross. There was never enough help for the many who needed it. Bread lines were a common sight in large cities; in 1931 there were 82 breadlines in New York City alone, serving 85,000 meals every day. People were shocked to see children standing in soup

Photo Caption Answer
Anxiety, discouragement.

lines with their parents. They could no longer tell themselves that those who went hungry did so because they were too lazy to work.

Most Americans believed in the work ethic and would do anything to show they were trying. On big-city streets, unemployed men stood by crates of apples, selling them for a nickel apiece. Shoeshining was another popular last resort.

The restless desire to get somewhere and to find some kind of employment was also behind the custom of "riding the rails." Single men and even families would ride in empty freight cars across the country, looking for seasonal work or just hoping that conditions would be better elsewhere. Langston Hughes wrote:

> Everybody in America was looking for work . . . everybody moving from one place to another in search of a job. People who lived in the West were hoboing on trains to the East. . . . Sometimes they wouldn't go any further than Reno, whichever way they were going, and none of them had any money, they'd build those big fires near the railroad tracks . . . and they'd just live collected around those fires until they could make enough money at odd jobs to move further on their way.

AFRICAN AMERICANS IN THE CITIES 3E

At the time of the Crash, about half of all African Americans lived in cities. They got an extra helping of the troubles that the Depression dished out to everyone. In 1931 a survey by the Urban League reported that "with a few notable exceptions . . . the proportion of Negroes unemployed was from 30 to 60 percent greater than whites." One reason was that many blacks were unskilled workers who held jobs as household servants. When hard times hit, the wealthy saved money by firing their servants. Another reason was discrimination. Some white employers believed that in bad times, white workers should be employed before blacks, regardless of the job involved. Many blacks found themselves fired from jobs once considered too menial for white workers.

The Depression slowed the struggle for black rights and sometimes divided black groups. The

BIOGRAPHY 4C

MAHALIA JACKSON (1911–1972) was born in New Orleans and sang gospel music in the church choir directed by her father, a Baptist minister. In 1928 she moved to Chicago and began to record and perform as a soloist. Jackson's powerful voice and dignified presence made her the world's best-known gospel singer.

National Association for the Advancement of Colored People (NAACP) continued to focus on the effort to end discrimination and to promote black education. Some of its members, including W.E.B. Du Bois, argued that the NAACP was not concerned enough with the poverty of blacks in America. Du Bois charged that the NAACP was missing "the essential need," which was "to enable the colored people of America to earn a living."

The Depression was hard on blacks all over the country, but it was urban blacks who suffered the most. The singer Mahalia Jackson later recalled how the Depression affected blacks in Chicago and in other northern cities:

> The Depression was much harder on city Negroes up North than it was on the Negroes down South because it cost them all the gains they had struggled for. Many of the Negroes in the South didn't feel the Depression too much. Some of them could hardly tell the difference from prosperity. They never had much for themselves and still had their little vegetable gardens and their chickens and maybe a pig or two, so they could still get enough to eat.
>
> But in Chicago the Depression made the South Side a place of broken dreams. It was so sad that it would break your heart to think about it.

Yet African Americans made an effort to stand by each other in these difficult times. Neighbors organized "block aid," encouraging people to

Connecting with Literature
Have students consider why Steinbeck chose to write about the problems of Okies in a novel, although he had researched their situation for a magazine article. *What other novels have played an important role in American history?* (*Uncle Tom's Cabin, The Jungle, Babbitt,* etc.) Ask students to suggest novels they have read that describe social, political, or economic issues.

C **Cooperative Learning**

Have students work in groups to create a script for an audio tape entitled "Voices of the Depression." Each group will represent one segment of American society during the Great Depression: an Okie, a resident of Hooverville, a hobo teenager who rides the rails, a farmer, a black city-dweller, a white city-dweller. Explain to the groups that they should create a first-person account of the effects of the Depression on their lives. If possible, make a recording of the scripts. **LEP**

Biography
If possible, play a recording of Jackson and have students discuss why gospel music developed in the American black community.

contribute whatever amount of money they could spare each week to help the poorest people on the block. In Harlem, "rent parties" became common affairs, as people organized parties with a nickel or dime admission at the door to help them get their rent together for the next day. Crowds of people in black neighborhoods also protested evictions. In some cases, landlords allowed tenants to stay simply because they feared a riot.

CRISIS IN RURAL AMERICA 3E
The irony of the Great Depression is that while thousands were going hungry in the nation's towns and cities, farmers had more food than they could sell. Many consumers simply did not have the money to buy much food. As consumer demand shrank, prices for farm products fell—in some cases, farmers could not even afford to pay the freight to send them to market. They had no choice but to shoot and bury their livestock and to let their crops rot in the fields. One farmer described the situation to a congressional committee in February 1932:

> I saw men picking for meat scraps in the garbage cans in the cities of New York and Chicago. I talked to one man in a restaurant in Chicago. He told me of his experience in raising sheep. He said that he had killed 3,000 sheep this fall and thrown them down the canyon, because it cost $1.10 to ship a sheep, and then he would get less than a dollar for it. He said he could not afford to feed the sheep, and he would not just let them starve, so he just cut their throats and threw them down the canyon.

Unable to sell their crops, farmers could not pay their mortgages, and many had their farms repossessed by the bank. In 1930 parts of the South suffered a severe drought, and farmers there could not even feed their families. The nation was alarmed when a group of 500 farmers in drought-ravaged Arkansas entered the town of England armed with shotguns and demanded food from local shopkeepers. "Paul Revere just woke up Concord. Those birds woke up America," Will Rogers

Hoeing, an oil painting by Virginia artist Robert Gwathmey, depicts impoverished white and black sharecroppers in a bleak landscape featuring withered plants and a weather-beaten church.
ECONOMICS What factors created hardships for southern farmers during the early 1930s? 3E

wrote in his column. Such incidents were a sign of the desperation that farmers felt during the Depression.

Farmers in some states tried to organize in order to stop foreclosures. When the bank auctioned off a farm, a group of local farmers would sometimes show up and bid only a few cents for each piece of land and property. In this way, the entire farm would be bought for a couple of dollars, and it would then be turned over to the bankrupt farmer who owned it originally. Yet the foreclosures went on, as the cycle of overproduction and falling prices continued unchecked.

DROUGHT ON THE GREAT PLAINS 2C
On the Great Plains, farmers were ruined not only by low prices but by the forces of nature. Year after year in the 1930s, this region—the high, semiarid grasslands that stretch from the Rocky Mountains to the Mississippi Valley—was struck by drought. An area covering part of Texas, Oklahoma, Kansas, Colorado, and New Mexico became so dry that it was known as the **Dust Bowl**

Human activities were partly to blame for the Dust Bowl. The soil of the Great Plains region is held in place by the deep, tangled roots of the prairie grass. Starting in the late 1800s, farmers

Drought and dust storms, some so severe they buried houses, forced thousands of farm families such as this one to leave the Dust Bowl. Eventually, the federal government was able to reclaim the land by planting grass and trees and by using scientific agricultural methods. **ENVIRONMENT** What harmful farming practices helped cause the Dust Bowl? 2C

plowed up the soil and planted crops, such as wheat, whose roots were not strong enough to hold the soil. Other grasslands were destroyed by overgrazing. In dry years, the strong winds that blew over the Plains stirred up the loose soil, causing fierce dust storms. These storms filled the air with choking dust, forcing schools and businesses to close and making noon look more like midnight.

Because the dust storms also ruined crops, many farmers decided to move elsewhere. They packed their belongings and drove west to California in search of better living conditions and jobs picking fruit. These migrants, called Okies because there were so many Oklahomans among them, were retracing the paths of earlier pioneers. But unlike the westward migrants of the 1800s, the Okies were driven much more by desperation than by any promises of future success.

A young writer named John Steinbeck observed the Okies firsthand for a magazine assignment. Later he wrote a novel about them, called *The Grapes of Wrath* (1939). He was impressed by the way the migrants stuck together and helped one another:

The cars of the migrant people crawled out of the side roads on the great cross-country highway, and they took the migrant way to the West. In the daylight they scuttled like bugs to the westward; and as the dark caught them, they clustered like bugs near to shelter and water.

And because they were lonely and perplexed, because they had all come from a place of sadness and worry and defeat, and because they were all going to a new mysterious place, they huddled together; they talked together; they shared their lives, their food, and the things they hoped for in the new country.

Unfortunately, the Okies did not find the things they hoped for. California too was locked into the cycle of overproduction and falling prices, and farmers were letting their crops rot in the fields. The Okies settled in refugee camps, living in poverty nearly as great as that which they had left behind. Like the rest of the country, the Okies could only wait for times to change.

SECTION REVIEW

1. KEY TERMS Hooverville, Dust Bowl, Okie

2. PEOPLE AND PLACES Huey Long, Great Plains, John Steinbeck

3. COMPREHENSION Why did many people continue to go to movies even when money was short?

4. COMPREHENSION How did human activities help cause the Dust Bowl?

5. CRITICAL THINKING What are two ways in which the government can help farmers escape the cycle of overproduction and falling prices? 3E

Photo Caption Answer
Ploughing and planting crops with weak roots; overgrazing.

SECTION 3

The Hoover Response
(pp. 352–357)

Section Objectives

■ analyze Hoover's failure to stem the Depression
■ explain how the Depression influenced the 1932 election

Introducing the Section

Connecting with Past Learnings

Help students understand the historical precedents for Hoover's policies. *When had there been other economic crises?* (Panics of 1873, 1893, farming crisis of the 1920s.) *Did the federal government help the needy then?* (No.)

Key Terms

Have students write down the terms and their definitions on a piece of paper. Discuss the fact that these terms are made up of two words, asking students to define the words used in each term. Then have students explain how these words relate to the terms. **LEP**

Focus

Ask volunteers to come to the board and list measures Hoover took to deal with the Depression. Then have another group of volunteers list reasons why those measures failed to stem the tide of the Depression. (Hoover set up the Presidential Commission for Unemployment to coordinate private charities, but community chests could not keep up with the problem; he provided indirect relief through public works, but there were too few projects to lower unemployment; he used federal funds to help stop bank failures through the Reconstruction Finance Corporation, but that did not help the poor and homeless.)

352

---

3 The Hoover Response

Section Focus

Key Terms community chest ■ Bonus Army

Main Idea President Hoover failed in his efforts to defeat the Great Depression.

Objectives As you read, look for answers to these questions:
1. What was President Hoover's political philosophy?
2. Why did veterans march on Washington?
3. What were the main issues in the 1932 presidential campaign?

By 1932 Herbert Hoover was the most unpopular man in the country. He had done little to ease the suffering of the poor, and he was widely disliked for his failure to end the Depression. On vaudeville stages, comedians cried out, "What? You say business is better? You mean Hoover died?" Cartoonists drew caricatures of him with starched collars up to his chin and his hands over his ears to shut out the pleas of the hungry and unemployed.

Once known as a humane and efficient leader, Hoover was now thought to be a hard-hearted and distant man who sympathized only with business. "What Mr. Hoover wants," one Democratic critic declared, "is bigger and better opportunities for rich men to inherit the earth. It is the plight of the banks and the railroads and the great corporations that stirs his heart most deeply."

RUGGED INDIVIDUALISM 8H

Hoover's response to the Great Depression was rooted in his political philosophy. He had traveled widely in Europe and Asia before and after World War I. He noticed that nearly all of the countries he visited had undergone some economic and political crisis and had turned to the government for its solution. These countries, therefore, routinely gave economic aid to citizens in need. Hoover believed that this practice, which he called the "European philosophy of . . . state socialism," would not work in the United States. He argued that accepting these foreign ideas would undermine "the individual initiative and enterprise through which our people have grown to unparalleled greatness."

Hoover never surrendered his belief in what he called "the American system of rugged individualism," even during the depths of the Depression. He did not think that the unemployed should be "on the dole"—receiving government relief—or that controls should be placed on the economy to keep farm prices from falling. He believed that these measures would only slow the recovery. If the economy was in a slump, then the people of the United States would just have to wait it out.

Hoover's Cabinet members agreed with him. "It will purge the rottenness out of the system," Secretary of the Treasury Andrew Mellon said of the economic collapse. "High costs of living and high living will come down. People will work harder, live a more moral life. Values will be adjusted and enterprising people will pick up the wrecks from less competent people." This philosophy did not sit well with most of the country. For them the "adjustment of values" meant that poor people would have nothing to eat for dinner.

Hoover called for private initiatives to cushion the blow of the Depression. In October 1930 he created the President's Committee for Unemployment Relief. The Committee was to help raise funds for the needy in towns and cities across the nation. People would contribute to privately organized welfare funds called community chests to help their needy neighbors. While the community chests did provide some help for the poor, they simply could not keep pace with the growing need.

Hoover kept hoping that the economy would bounce back on its own. He usually referred to the Depression as a "recession" in his speeches, and in 1930 he announced, "I am convinced we have

---

SUPPORTING THE SECTION

Reinforcement Workbook: Worksheet 57
Reteaching Resources: Worksheet 57
Enrichment and Extension Resources: Primary Source Worksheet 30
Teaching Transparencies: Transparency 57

Background Throughout the 1920s the federal budget had a surplus. Starting in 1931, the government began to run a deficit. Hoover felt that for confidence to be restored, the nation had to balance the budget.

passed the worst and with continued effort we shall rapidly recover." But the financial crisis in Europe in 1931 sent the United States further into its downward spiral.

Hoover still believed that "direct relief to individuals from the federal government would bring an inevitable train of corruption and waste such as our nation had never witnessed." Yet he was willing to accept indirect relief through public works programs to build federal roads, buildings, and dams. These programs would provide jobs and stimulate the economy, while establishing long-term sources of income for the government. Annual public works appropriations rose from $250 million in 1930 to $750 million by 1933.

THE DEPRESSION DEEPENS 3E

During his final year in office, President Hoover decided to use federal funds to try to stem the flood of bank and business failures. He found considerable support for this measure in Congress. Democrats had controlled the House since the 1930 elections and were continually calling for stronger measures against the Depression.

In 1932 Congress set up the Reconstruction Finance Corporation (RFC), an organization with the power to lend money from the national treasury. It was authorized to lend $2 billion to banks, insurance companies, loan associations, railroads, and other businesses.

Like increased public works spending, the RFC was a form of indirect relief. It did not help poor people find food or shelter. Rather, it aimed to stabilize the entire economy by saving the major institutions from bankruptcy. In time, RFC backers hoped, the benefits would work their way down to the nation's needy. But critics, led by New York Congressman Fiorello La Guardia, promptly attacked the bill, calling it the "millionaire's dole." They argued that people who were out of work could not afford to wait for such indirect benefits. They needed help now.

Although the RFC aided 5,000 firms in 1932, the number of business failures continued to rise. Farmers were assisted by loans from the Federal Farm Banks, but the foreclosure rate still climbed. By this time, most community chests were empty, and state and local governments did not have enough money to provide food for all the citizens who came to them for aid.

Lines of unemployed people waiting for free soup and bread became a common sight in most American cities during the Depression. Most early relief efforts, such as this one at St. Peter's Mission in New York City, were sponsored by churches or community chests. **ECONOMICS** Why, if food was available, did many Americans go hungry during the Depression? 3E

Photo Caption Answer
Many Americans were unable to afford to buy food for as much as it cost farmers to grow and transport it, and relief efforts were inadequate to feed all those in need.

Why did Hoover fail to enlist the resources of government to give direct aid to people in need? (He felt it would undermine American individualism and the spirit of free enterprise.) **How did Roosevelt's philosophy differ from Hoover's?** (He felt that it was government's job to help citizens in need.)

Developing the Lesson
After students have read the section, you may want to consider the following activities:

Patterns in History
Discuss Hoover's attitude toward government involvement in giving economic aid. **How did Andrew Mellon explain why government should do little to end economic hard times?** (He felt it would help the economy by lowering inflation, force people to work harder and live more morally, and hurt only those who deserved to be hurt.) **Do you agree with Hoover and Mellon that government aid to the unemployed, homeless, and farmers undermines people's desire to work?**

Ask students to list programs that exist today to help the homeless, unemployed, poor, and farmers. **Do you think the government does enough or too much to help those groups?**

Economics
With the class, create a flow chart showing how the RFC was supposed to help the needy. (Lent money to large institutions to keep them from going bankrupt and closing; these, in turn, were able to employ people and to lend money to other businesses to prevent them from closing; employed people would be able to buy groceries and pay their rent; the money that employed people spent would help maintain other jobs.) **What were the criticisms of the RFC?** (It helped the rich first, and poor people could not wait for relief.)

Constitutional Heritage
What authority did Hoover have to break up the Bonus Army?
(He was commander-in-chief of the military and had the right to call out the Army to disperse the crowd.)

Have students write a newspaper editorial for July 17, 1932, on the Bonus Army. Editorials should include the desperation of the marchers, their attempt to pressure Congress into appropriating a bonus for veterans and Hiram Johnson's sense that Congress was under siege.

History
What were the results of the 1932 election? (Roosevelt won by a landslide with 472 electoral votes and all but six states.) *How did Hoover explain why he lost the election?* (He told his secretary that he was opposed by six million unemployed, ten thousand bonus marchers, and ten-cent corn.) *What did Hoover mean by his statement?* (He had been defeated by economic conditions.)

Civic Values
How might Franklin Roosevelt's physical handicap have influenced his decision to run for President? (On the one hand, he might have questioned his stamina and ability to be elected because of it; on the other, it would convince him that he could overcome great despair and terrible odds to help the country in that difficult time.) Have students consider personal setbacks they have faced, and how those setbacks have affected their attitude toward other challenges.

Philadelphia was just one of the many cities that had run out of relief funds by the spring of 1932. A city official there described the poverty he had witnessed:

> One woman said she borrowed 50 cents from a friend and bought stale bread for 3½ cents per loaf, and that is all they had for eleven days except for one or two meals. . . . One woman went along the docks and picked up vegetables that fell from the wagons. Sometimes the fish vendors gave her fish at the end of the day. On two different occasions this family was without food for a day and a half.

It was ironic that President Hoover could do nothing for these people, since he had built his reputation as head of a relief project in postwar Europe. Aware that his efforts were falling short, Hoover became increasingly desperate, working eighteen hours per day in search of solutions. However, he refused to visit soup kitchens or private relief stations. "This is not a showman's job," he said. "I will not step out of character."

THE BONUS ARMY 3E

A clear sign of the nation's impatience with Hoover's policies was the controversy in 1932 over the veterans' bonus. At issue was the law that Congress had passed in 1924 to give each World War I veteran an insurance policy as a bonus. It was a reward to veterans for their loyal service and an attempt to make up for the relatively low wages that soldiers had been paid during the war. They would get the money from their policies in 1945.

When the Depression hit, however, many veterans lost their jobs. They were middle-aged men, most of them with families to support, and they said it was now the government's turn to help them out. They asked that the bonus be paid immediately.

In May 1932, thousands of jobless veterans marched on Washington, D.C., to urge Congress to pass a bill to pay the bonus. Many brought their wives and children with them, and soon the group numbered 15,000. Nicknamed the Bonus Army, the veterans set up tents, built shacks, and occupied vacant buildings on the outskirts of the city.

Police in Washington, D.C., attack members of the Bonus Army in their camp near the White House. Shortly afterward, army troops under Douglas MacArthur broke up the veterans' camp with cavalry, tanks, and tear gas. ECONOMICS What was the goal of the Bonus Army? 3E

Photo Caption Answer
Economic relief through early payment of money due to them in 1945.

"We'll stay here until 1945 if necessary to get our bonus," their leader, Walter Waters, declared. The writer John Dos Passos visited one of their camps and listened to the men making speeches and debating with one another. "Give us the money and we'll buy their bread and their corn and their radios," he overheard one man say. "We ain't holding out because we don't want those things; can't get a job to make money to buy 'em is all."

Every day the members of the Bonus Army held demonstrations and military drills. There was much concern in Washington over what they would do if their demands were not met. Rumors spread that Communists were trying to infiltrate their ranks. On July 17, when the bill to pay the bonus was defeated in the Senate, the veterans were waiting on the steps of the Capitol. Inside, the members of Congress were uneasy. "This marks a new era in the life of our nation," Senator Hiram Johnson told one of his colleagues. "The time may come . . . when fat old men like you and me will be lined up against a stone wall." The senator's fears proved to be unfounded. When the veterans heard that the bill had been defeated, Waters told them to sing "America" and they obeyed. They then returned to their camps.

Yet no one knew how to get the Bonus Army to leave the city. They vowed to stay until the legislators changed their minds. Congress voted funds to lend each veteran money for the journey home, but only a few hundred veterans accepted the offer. The administration decided to step up the pressure against the veterans, ordering the evacuation of abandoned buildings that they had occupied. During the evacuation, a fight broke out and police fired in self-defense, killing two veterans. Hoover then called out the army.

On July 28, 1932, General Douglas MacArthur (who would later gain fame in World War II) led 1,000 soldiers and 6 tanks in clearing out all the veterans' camps around the city. The soldiers rushed into crowds of men, women, and children, waving sabers and throwing cans of tear gas. Sixty-three people were injured. "A challenge to the authority of the United States had been met, swiftly and firmly," Hoover declared.

Most Americans did not agree with Hoover. The press had shown pictures of soldiers clearing out

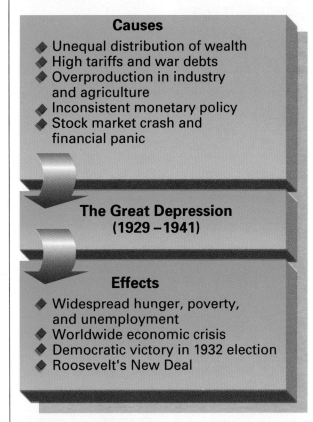

CAUSE AND EFFECT: THE GREAT DEPRESSION

Causes
◆ Unequal distribution of wealth
◆ High tariffs and war debts
◆ Overproduction in industry and agriculture
◆ Inconsistent monetary policy
◆ Stock market crash and financial panic

The Great Depression (1929–1941)

Effects
◆ Widespread hunger, poverty, and unemployment
◆ Worldwide economic crisis
◆ Democratic victory in 1932 election
◆ Roosevelt's New Deal

CHART SKILLS 9E

The Great Depression was one of the most critical periods in the nation's history. **CRITICAL THINKING** Which of the causes of the Great Depression were outgrowths of government policies?

the camps, dubbing the sad scene the "Battle of Washington." It was clear that the situation had been mishandled. Hoover became more unpopular than ever. The whole nation looked to the coming election for new leadership.

THE CANDIDATES FOR PRESIDENT IN 1932 5B
In June 1932 the Republican National Convention met in Chicago and nominated Herbert Hoover for President. He had no real rival in the Republican Party, and it would have been an extreme step to deny the nomination to a President already in office. Yet the mood of the convention was glum. The delegates knew that with the country as it

Cause and Effect
Explain to students that "inconsistent monetary policy" on the chart on this page refers to the Federal Reserve Bank's raising of interest rates to tighten the amount of money in the economy.

Have students create a flow chart showing how the causes listed on the chart led to the Great Depression. (Stock market speculation led to strict monetary policy because the Fed worried speculation was getting out of control; uneven distribution of prosperity led to overproduction because people could not afford to buy goods; all these factors led to the stock market crash.)

C Cooperative Learning

Divide the class into three groups to set up a presidential debate in 1932. Group one will select members to play Hoover and two of his advisers. Group two will select members to play Franklin D. Roosevelt and two advisers. The third group will chose three members to play reporters. Have each group prepare its representatives with appropriate questions and answers. Set up the room with space for the journalists, candidates, and advisers. Allow other members of the groups to help out while the debate is in progress. **LEP**

Cause and Effect Answer
High tariffs, war debts, and inconsistent monetary policies were direct outgrowths; some students may suggest that unequal distribution of wealth and overproduction were indirect outgrowths.

Background Two other officers who later gained fame in World War II were also involved in pushing the Bonus Army out of Washington, D.C.: Dwight Eisenhower and George Patton.

This photograph shows Franklin Delano Roosevelt relaxing in New York City's Biltmore Hotel as he reads of his re-election as governor of New York in 1930. It was rare for photographers to show the leg braces Roosevelt wore as a result of polio. POLITICS What factors made Roosevelt such an appealing candidate in the 1932 presidential election? 5B

356 UNIT 5 FROM BOOM TO BUST

was, Hoover had little chance of being re-elected. The announcement of Hoover's selection was met with only scattered applause.

Two weeks after the lackluster Republican convention, the Democrats came to town. They were full of hope, knowing that the right candidate—in fact, almost *any* candidate—could defeat Hoover. Three politicians vied for the nomination. One was Al Smith, who had lost to Hoover in 1928. Another was Speaker of the House John Nance Garner of Texas. The third candidate was Franklin Delano Roosevelt.

Franklin Roosevelt was a distant cousin of Theodore Roosevelt, the former President. Like his famous cousin, Franklin Roosevelt came from a wealthy family and had gone to Harvard College and Columbia Law School. He served as Assistant Secretary of the Navy and later became governor of New York.

Also like his cousin, who had been a sickly child, Franklin Roosevelt drew strength of character from his battle to overcome illness. He had been struck with polio in 1921, one year after losing the race for Vice President. At first completely paralyzed, he slowly regained the use of his arms and upper body. Therapy at Warm Springs, Georgia, where he founded a polio rehabilitation clinic, gave him the ability to walk with crutches and heavy leg braces. Given a friend's arm to lean on, he could walk to a podium without other visible support, though each step caused him great pain.

Roosevelt did not allow his disability to disrupt his political career. When polio first struck, he felt, as he said later, "utter despair." He had great courage and ambition, however, and his naturally buoyant temperament helped him recover his health and spirits. He won the governor's seat in New York in 1928. He had always been energetic and outgoing, and those qualities came across to voters as much as ever. The Roosevelt charm was famous, and mixed with it was a sympathy for ordinary people. That quality led him to become a champion of the poor in spite of his privileged background. He once explained:

The duty of the State toward the citizen is the duty of the servant to its master. The people have created it; the people, by common consent, permit its continual existence. One of these duties of the State is that of caring for those of its citizens who find themselves the victims of such adverse circumstances as make them unable to obtain even the necessities for mere existence. . . . To these unfortunate citizens aid must be extended by government—not as a matter of charity but as a matter of *social duty.*

Roosevelt's ideas and personality impressed the delegates of the 1932 Democratic convention, and he won the nomination on the fourth ballot. By tradition, candidates did not attend the convention but waited to be notified formally of the nomination several weeks later. Roosevelt broke this tradition, flying to Chicago to accept the nomination. This was an especially dramatic gesture, because air travel was still a novelty. The band played "Happy Days Are Here Again," which was to be Roosevelt's theme song. "I pledge you, I pledge myself, to a new deal for the American people," he declared.

THE ELECTION OF 1932 5B

Hoover was so unpopular that the election results were almost a foregone conclusion. Hoover tried to portray Roosevelt as a dangerous radical, saying that his was "the same philosophy of government which had poisoned all Europe . . . the fumes of the witch's cauldron which boiled in Russia." Yet no one seemed to listen. On the eve of the election, Hoover remarked to his secretary, "I'll tell you what our trouble is. We are opposed by

> "**I** pledge you, I pledge myself, to a new deal for the American people."
> —*Roosevelt campaign pledge, 1932*

six million unemployed, ten thousand bonus marchers, and ten-cent corn." He was right about that, except that he underestimated the number of unemployed.

Roosevelt won the election by a landslide, taking 472 electoral votes to Hoover's 59. Hoover carried only six states. "A Vote for Roosevelt Is a Vote Against Hoover," had been one Democratic slogan. But for many Americans, a vote for Roosevelt was also a vote for his "new deal," which they eagerly awaited during the cold and dreary Depression winter of 1932.

SECTION REVIEW

1. KEY TERMS community chest, Bonus Army

2. PEOPLE Andrew Mellon, Walter Waters, Douglas MacArthur, Franklin Roosevelt

3. COMPREHENSION What did the Bonus Army want from Congress?

4. COMPREHENSION What made Franklin Roosevelt such an attractive candidate in the 1932 presidential campaign? What factors hurt Hoover?

5. CRITICAL THINKING Do you agree or disagree with Hoover's philosophy? Explain your answer.

---

2. *Andrew Mellon*— Treasury Secretary who said the Depression would lead to an "an adjustment of economic values." *Walter Waters*—Leader of the Bonus Army. *Douglas MacArthur*— General dispatched to clear the Bonus Army out of Washington. *Franklin Roosevelt*—Democratic candidate for President in 1932.

3. The Bonus Army wanted Congress to advance them the bonus payment, promised in 1924 to veterans of World War I. The payment was supposed to be made in 1945.

4. Roosevelt was charming and energetic. His sympathy for people was expressed in his belief that it was the government's job to help the needy. Hoover was much less charming, and unwilling to commit vast government resources to solve the Depression. Also, Hoover had been President when the Depression hit, and was therefore held responsible for it.

5. Students who agree may point to the problems caused when everyone looks to government to solve social problems. The budget deficit is one result of such government involvement. Those who disagree with Hoover may point to the need for government to be humane and help those who cannot help themselves.

Closure

Use the Chapter Review Summary for Section 3 (p. 358) to synthesize the important elements in the section. Then have students read Section 1 of Chapter 16 for the next class period. Ask them to note how Roosevelt's approach to the Depression differed from Hoover's.

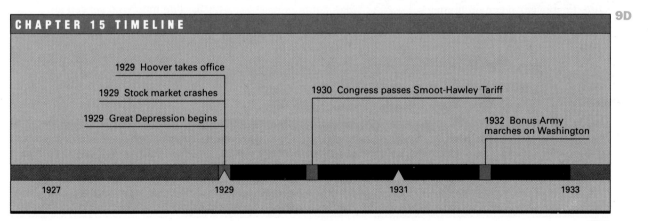

CHAPTER 15 TIMELINE   9D

1929 Hoover takes office

1929 Stock market crashes

1929 Great Depression begins

1930 Congress passes Smoot-Hawley Tariff

1932 Bonus Army marches on Washington

1927   1929   1931   1933

CHAPTER 15   HOOVER AND THE GREAT DEPRESSION, 1929–1933   **357**

CHAPTER 15 SUMMARY

SECTION 1: A stock market crash in October 1929 helped drive the United States into a severe economic depression.

■ Herbert Hoover was elected President in 1928 on a promise to continue the Republican policies of the 1920s.

■ The underlying causes of the stock market crash were over-speculation, margin buying, and shady business practices. When stock prices began to fall, panic took over and made the situation much worse.

■ Underlying economic problems, such as uneven distribution of wealth, high tariffs, war debts, overproduction, overuse of credit, and a weak banking system, contributed to the Great Depression.

■ Economic crisis in the United States helped plunge Europe into depression as well.

SECTION 2: The Depression caused great hardship.

■ Economic hard times had important effects on ways of life. People cut down on luxuries and turned to their families for support. Many people ended up homeless.

■ The burden of helping the poor fell on state and local governments and private charities.

■ Black Americans suffered even greater unemployment than whites.

■ Drought in the Plains states worsened the crisis for farmers, forcing many to leave their farms.

SECTION 3: President Hoover's efforts to halt the Depression were unsuccessful.

■ Hoover's philosophy of limited government and "rugged individualism" made him reluctant to undertake emergency measures.

■ Hoover's popularity plunged as people blamed him for not doing enough to combat the Depression. A march to Washington by angry veterans also hurt Hoover.

■ In 1932 Hoover's opponent was the Democrat Franklin D. Roosevelt, who promised a more active government role in ending the Depression. Roosevelt won by a landslide.

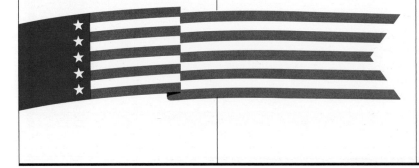

KEY TERMS ●

Define the terms in each of the following pairs.

1. Bonus Army; Hooverville
2. Dust Bowl; Okie
3. margin buying; stock pool
4. Black Thursday; Great Depression

PEOPLE TO IDENTIFY ●

Use the following names to complete the sentences below.

Douglas MacArthur
Andrew Mellon
Franklin D. Roosevelt
Alfred E. Smith
John Steinbeck
Walter Waters

1. The Democratic candidate for the presidency in 1928 was _____ .
2. _____ wrote *The Grapes of Wrath*.
3. The officer who led the attack on the Bonus Army was _____ .
4. _____ was the victorious Democratic candidate for President in 1932.
5. The man who served as Hoover's Secretary of the Treasury was _____ .
6. The leader of the Bonus Army of World War I veterans was _____ .

PLACES TO LOCATE ●

Match each of the letters on the map with the places that are listed below.

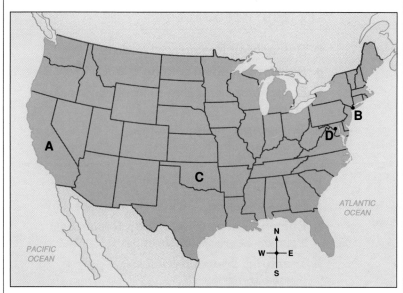

1. California
2. New York City
3. Oklahoma
4. Washington, D.C.

REVIEWING THE FACTS ▲

1. What factors affected the outcome of the 1928 presidential election?
2. What were the causes of the stock market crash?
3. What underlying weaknesses in the American economy contributed to the Great Depression?
4. What effects did the Great Depression have on ways of life in America?
5. How did the Depression divide some black groups? Why were black Americans in the cities harder hit than whites were?
6. How did the Depression affect American farmers?
7. What natural disaster worsened the effects of the Depression on the farmers of the Great Plains? How did this disaster come about?
8. Why was Hoover reluctant to use the power of the federal government to relieve the suffering of the poor or to direct economic recovery? What steps did Hoover take?
9. What did the members of the Bonus Army want? What was the outcome of the crisis?
10. Describe the issues and the candidates of the election of 1932.

CRITICAL THINKING SKILLS ▲

1. **INFERRING** Why might advisers have urged President Hoover to visit soup kitchens? Why did he refuse?
2. **ANALYZING A QUOTATION** Reread the excerpt from Herbert Hoover's 1928 campaign speech on page 342. Would this argument have been less convincing after the Crash and the beginning of the Great Depression? Explain.
3. **MAKING JUDGMENTS** How might the President have handled the situation with the Bonus Army differently? Why, do you think, did he act as he did?

WRITING ABOUT TOPICS IN AMERICAN HISTORY ■

1. **CONNECTING WITH LITERATURE** A selection from *Their Eyes Were Watching God* by Zora Neale Hurston appears on pages 797–799. Read it and answer the questions. Then answer the following question: How do Janie's attitudes and behavior reflect the changes in women's status during the 1930s?
2. **APPLYING THEMES: CONSTITUTIONAL GOVERNMENT** Pretend that you are a speechwriter for one of the presidential candidates in the 1932 election. Write the best speech you can for him. The speech should both represent the candidate's views and appeal to the voters.
3. **RELIGION** Write a brief essay about the role churches played in relieving the suffering of the poor during the Depression.

8. Hoover believed that government action would diminish individualism, slow recovery, and lead to corruption. He called for private intervention and indirect relief through increased public works spending.

9. They wanted immediate payment of bonuses promised for 1945. The U.S. Army drove the protesting veterans out of their camps.

10. Republican President Hoover believed private initiative would bring the country out of the Depression. Democrat Franklin D. Roosevelt believed government needed to direct the economic recovery.

Critical Thinking Skills

1. Advisers wanted positive publicity to rally support, but Hoover thought such actions were hypocritical.

2. The hands-off philosophy of Hoover's speech would not have been as appealing during a time of crisis.

3. He might have negotiated with the Bonus Army, instead of trying to show he was in control with the use of force.

Writing About Topics in American History

1. Janie's attitudes and behavior reflect a breaking with tradition and an independent spirit. That same spirit was alive in such women as Eleanor Roosevelt and Frances Perkins.

2. Students may define the problems faced in 1932 and present a strategy that would remedy the situation.

3. Students may research the aid a church in their area offered during the Depression.

5. Some blacks wanted to focus on discrimination while others wanted to focus on ending poverty. Discrimination and a lack of skills caused blacks to suffer more than whites during the Depression.

6. Overproduction and falling prices caused widespread despair for the American farmer.

7. A series of droughts coupled with poor farming practices created the Dust Bowl, which further devastated farmers.

Chapter Review exercises are keyed for student abilities:
● = Basic
▲ = Average
■ = Average/Advanced

	SECTION OBJECTIVES	SECTION RESOURCES
Section 1 **Roosevelt Takes Office**	■ describe the major relief, recovery, and reform programs initiated by Roosevelt in the early days of his administration	● **Reteaching Resources:** Worksheet 58 ▲ **Reinforcement Workbook:** Worksheet 58 ■ **Enrichment and Extension Resources:** Historian Worksheet 6 ▲ **Teaching Transparencies:** Transparency 58
Section 2 **Critics from the Right and Left**	■ identify critics of the New Deal and their proposals for coping with the Depression	● **Reteaching Resources:** Worksheet 59 ▲ **Reinforcement Workbook:** Worksheet 59 ■ **Enrichment and Extension Resources:** Primary Source Worksheet 31 ▲ **Teaching Transparencies:** Transparency 59
Section 3 **The Second New Deal**	■ identify and describe the major programs of the Second New Deal ■ describe the controversy involving Roosevelt and the Supreme Court	● **Reteaching Resources:** Worksheet 60 ▲ **Reinforcement Workbook:** Worksheet 60 ▲ **Teaching Transparencies:** Transparency 60
Section 4 **Life During the Roosevelt Years**	■ identify the effects of the New Deal on American society and culture in the 1930s	● **Reteaching Resources:** Worksheet 61 ▲ **Reinforcement Workbook:** Worksheet 61 ■ **Enrichment and Extension Resources:** Primary Source Worksheet 32 ▲ **Teaching Transparencies:** Transparency 61
Section 5 **The Legacy of the New Deal**	■ identify the long-term effects of the New Deal	● **Reteaching Resources:** Worksheet 62 ▲ **Reinforcement Workbook:** Worksheet 62 ▲ **Teaching Transparencies:** Transparency 62

The list below shows Essential Elements relevant to this chapter. (The complete list of Essential Elements appears in the introductory pages of this Teacher's Edition.)

Section 1: 3E, 3F, 3G, 4D, 5B, 8I, 9A, 9B
Section 2: 3F, 4D, 5B, 8F
Section 3: 3C, 4D, 4F, 5B, 5E, 5F, 9A, 9B, 9E
Section 4: 4C, 4F, 6A, 6C, 7J
Section 5: 3B, 3E, 5F, 9D, 9E

Section Resources are keyed for
student abilities:
● = Basic
▲ = Average
■ = Average/Advanced

CHAPTER RESOURCES

Geography Resources: Worksheets 31, 32
Tests: Chapter 16 Test

Chapter Project: Economic Development

Have students create an illustrated report focusing on the local impact of the New Deal. Students may include information on local WPA projects such as public works, art, and writing; statistics on employment at a local level during the 1930s; and information on the changing government structure as a result of the New Deal.

Homework Options

Each section contains activities labeled "Addressing Individual Needs." You may wish to choose from among these activities when assigning homework.

> ### Provisions for Limited English Proficiency (LEP)
> Several suggested activities may be particularly helpful for teachers of students with limited English proficiency. These activities have been marked throughout the Teacher's Annotated Edition with the symbol **LEP** .

BIBLIOGRAPHY AND AUDIOVISUAL AIDS

Teacher Bibliography

Lash, Joseph P. *Eleanor and Franklin: The Story of Their Relationship Based on Eleanor Roosevelt's Private Papers.* Norton, 1971.

Leuchtenburg, William E. *Franklin D. Roosevelt and the New Deal, 1932–1940.* Harper and Row, 1963.

Rauch, Basil. *History of the New Deal: 1933–1938.* Octagon, 1975.

Wilson, Edmund. *The Thirties: From Notebooks and Diaries of the Period.* Leon Edel, ed. Farrar, Straus, Giroux, 1980.

Student Bibliography

Israel, Fred L. *Franklin D. Roosevelt.* Chelsea House, 1985.

Lawson, Don. *FDR's New Deal.* Crowell, 1979.

Rosen, Elliot. *Hoover, Roosevelt and the Brain Trust: From Depression to New Deal.* Columbia University Press, 1977.

Literature

Faulkner, William. *Light in August.* Random House, 1965.

Lee, Harper. *To Kill a Mockingbird.* Warner Books, 1982. A six-year-old girl narrates events in a small Depression-era Alabama town when her father, a lawyer, defends a black man accused of raping a white woman.

Warren, Robert Penn. *All the King's Men.* Barron, 1985. A Pulitzer Prize-winning story of the rise and fall of Willie Stark, a southern demagogue based on Louisiana politician Huey Long.

Wright, Richard. *Lawd Today.* Northeastern University Press, 1986. Wright describes one day in the life of an embittered black postal clerk in Depression-era Chicago.

Films and Videotapes*

The Helping Hand (A Walk Through the 20th Century with Bill Moyers). 56 min. PBS. Shows how the concept of "big government" grew during the Depression of the 1930s.

Roosevelt: The Fireside Chats and the New Deal. 27 min. COR/MTI. Chronicles the period from 1932 to 1938, introducing the main points of Roosevelt's New Deal and its significance on the American economy.

Roosevelt: Hail to the Chief. 24 min. LCA. Franklin D. Roosevelt faced the nation's economic collapse as well as the military threat of Germany and Japan. Shows how he used his popularity with the people to achieve his New Deal.

Computer Software*

America's Presidents Series: World Wars, Prosperity and Depression—Presidents During and Between Two World Wars (Apple with 48K; IBM with 64K). QUEUE. Each President is covered in a separate menu option, and prominent Presidents have multiple sections on different phases on their lives and administrations. Presidents Wilson–Truman, 1913–1953.

TIME TRAVELER: Wilson—New Freedom 1913–1945 (IBM). MVP. Multiple choice, true/false, and short-answer questions within the context of a time travel adventure. Includes questions about contributions made by women and minorities. Up to 300 additional questions can be added.

*For a complete guide to audiovisual sources, see the introduction to this book (page Txx).

The New Deal
(pp. 360–385)

This chapter describes the New Deal legislation and programs of President Roosevelt and their effects on American labor, industry, agriculture, and the arts. It also examines criticism of the New Deal from both the right and left, and the lasting influence of the New Deal in the United States.

Themes in American History

- Constitutional government
- Economic development
- Pluralistic society
- American culture

Chapter Objectives

After students complete this chapter, they will be able to:

1. Describe the major relief, recovery, and reform programs initiated by Roosevelt in the early days of his administration.

2. Identify critics of the New Deal and their proposals for coping with the Depression.

3. Identify and describe the major programs of the Second New Deal.

4. Describe the controversy involving Roosevelt and the Supreme Court.

5. Identify the effects of the New Deal on American society and culture in the 1930s.

6. Describe the long-term effects of the New Deal.

Chapter Opener Art
William Gropper,
Construction of a Dam.

President Franklin Roosevelt's New Deal programs used federal government spending in an effort to lift the nation out of the Great Depression. This mural, financed by the government, celebrates the spirit of American workers.

CHAPTER	
SUPPORT	**Reinforcement Workbook:** Worksheets 58–62
	Reteaching Resources: Worksheets 58–62
MATERIAL	**Enrichment and Extension Resources:** Primary Source Worksheets 31, 32; Historian Worksheet 6
	Geography Resources: Worksheets 31, 32
	Teaching Transparencies: Transparencies 58–62
	Tests: Chapter 16 Test

SECTION 1
Roosevelt Takes Office
(pp. 361–367)

3E, 3F, 3G, 4D, 5B, 8I, 9A, 9B

1 Roosevelt Takes Office

★ Section Focus

Key Terms fireside chat ■ New Deal

Main Idea Upon taking office in 1933, President Roosevelt proposed a program of legislation to help the poor and prevent economic collapse.

Objectives As you read, look for answers to these questions:
1. How did Roosevelt address the banking crisis?
2. What public programs did Roosevelt set up during his first hundred days in office?
3. How did Roosevelt try to bring about agricultural and industrial recovery?

Section Objective

■ describe the major relief, recovery, and reform programs initiated by Roosevelt in the early days of his administration

Introducing the Section

Connecting with Past Learnings
Have students describe the effects of the stock market crash of 1929 and the resulting Depression. (Students may recall that many businesses collapsed and millions of people were without work, homes, and economic resources.) *What solutions had President Hoover proposed to alleviate the Depression?* (Had created the President's Committee on Unemployment Relief, supported the creation of the Reconstruction Finance Corporation, encouraged the activities of community chests, and maintained that the economy would fix itself.)

Key Terms
Write the key terms on the board and ask students to list images that come to mind for each one of the terms. Then have them find the terms in the section and define them in their own words. **LEP**

The winter of 1932 was a bleak time for the United States. Roosevelt would not take office until March, and Herbert Hoover, the outgoing President, had lost the faith of the American people. A fourth of the labor force was out of work. Heavy snows and record cold added to the hardships of the homeless. Many cities ran out of money to pay public employees or fund local relief programs. Hungry people demonstrated in New York and Chicago, and in Detroit unemployed auto workers smashed windows and overturned cars.

Roosevelt adviser Rexford Tugwell later wrote, "There is no doubt in my mind that during the spring of 1933 the army felt that the time was approaching when it might have to 'take over.'" Even Hoover could not deny that the situation was critical. "We are at the end of our string," he remarked grimly.

ROOSEVELT'S INAUGURATION 5B
Roosevelt too had risks to face that winter. On February 15, 1933, just two weeks before Inauguration Day, he decided to give a speech at Bay Front Park in Miami. Seated in an open car, he had only just begun his remarks when a series of pistol shots rang out. An assassin, Giuseppe Zangara, fired at close range, wounding several people. Among them was Anton Cermak, the mayor of Chicago, who later died. None of the bullets struck Roosevelt, but it had been a close call.

Roosevelt took the oath of office on the cold and rainy afternoon of March 4, 1933. He did not try to downplay the nation's crisis. The new President said:

> This is pre-eminently the time to speak the truth, the whole truth, frankly and boldly. Nor need we shrink from honestly facing conditions in our country today. This great nation will endure as it has endured, will revive and will prosper. So first of all let me assert my firm belief that the only thing we have to fear is fear itself.

"**T**he only thing we have to fear is fear itself."

—*Franklin Roosevelt, 1933*

SUPPORTING THE SECTION

Reinforcement Workbook: Worksheet 58
Reteaching Resources: Worksheet 58
Enrichment and Extension Resources: Historian Worksheet 6
Teaching Transparencies: Transparency 58

Background Rexford Tugwell and Harry Hopkins were two of the many well-educated advisers nicknamed Roosevelt's "brain trust."

361

Focus

Focus

Create an annotated time-line of the New Deal for the year 1933 by having students note important dates, including dates when major legislation passed, and describe what each program was set up to accomplish and what its effects were. (3/4—FDR inaugurated; 3/6—bank holiday; 3/9—FDR calls Congress into special session, Congress passes Emergency Banking Bill supporting FDR's measures; 3/12—first fireside chat; 5/12—Farm Mortgage Act provided funds to keep farmers from losing their land, AAA regulated farming to prevent overproduction; 5/18—TVA created to help region by bringing flood control and electricity; 5/27—Securities Act, step toward regulating the stock market; 6/13—HOLC established, helped homeowners make payments and keep their homes; June—CCC gave work to young men and helped to conserve natural resources; Fall—CWA established to give people jobs while they were on relief.)

Why were these measures seen as a radical shift in the role of government? (The government was directly involved in employing people and in the economy.)

Developing the Lesson

After students have read the section, you may want to consider the following activities:

Analyzing Controversial Issues

Ask students what aspects of programs passed in the Hundred Days might be criticized as "creeping socialism"? (Possible answers include government ownership of a utility, the TVA; government regulation of farming production; the NRA's system of setting prices and minimum wages.)
Do you agree with this criticism?

362

Roosevelt rode to his inauguration with outgoing President Hoover. This magazine cover, drawn before the event, was never published. Officials worried it could reveal information that might make the two Presidents vulnerable to assassins. **POLITICS** What contrast does the artist make between the personalities of the two men? **9B**

The new President pledged to "act and act quickly," and he carried out his promise, taking a dramatic step in the week that followed.

5E

⭐ **Historical Documents**

For the text of Roosevelt's First Inaugural Address, see page 723 of this book.

A BANK HOLIDAY 3E, 3G

Roosevelt's most immediate challenge was the banking crisis. The nation's entire banking system was near collapse. To stop panicky depositors from demanding their deposits in gold, banks in the nation's major cities had been forced to close.

Roosevelt's first official act was to declare a holiday for every bank in the nation beginning Mon-

day, March 6. Only those banks that had been examined and found solvent—able to meet their financial obligations—would be allowed to reopen. This would reassure people that open banks could be trusted and keep them from withdrawing their money out of panic. On March 9, Roosevelt called Congress into special session. Within hours it passed the Emergency Banking Bill, backing up his emergency measures.

The banks remained closed for a week. Many Americans had to make do without cash, borrowing money from friends or using IOUs. But the American public supported the President.

On Sunday, March 12, Roosevelt delivered the first of his fireside chats. These were radio talks in which he explained his policies in a simple, friendly way, as a father would to his family. Roosevelt used his first fireside chat to discuss the banking crisis. He pointed out that banks do not put customer deposits in safety deposit boxes. Instead they invest them, leaving only a relatively small sum in the banks to tend to customers' daily needs. No bank, the President went on, could withstand the massive withdrawal of funds that occurred before he took office. "I can assure you that it is safer to keep your money in a re-opened bank than under the mattress," Roosevelt said.

Franklin Delano Roosevelt became the first President to make use of the radio to communicate directly with the public. He broadcast informal reports known as fireside chats to explain and gain public support for his policies. **POLITICS** Explain why fireside chats were effective. **9A**

Roosevelt's speech worked. When the banks re-opened, millions of Americans lined up to redeposit the money they had been hoarding. The banking system still required reform, and the economy was still at rock bottom, but the mood of the country was changing. The journalist Walter Lippmann wrote, "In one week, the nation, which had lost confidence in everything and everybody, has regained confidence in the government and in itself."

THE BIRTH OF THE NEW DEAL 4D
In accepting the Democratic nomination in 1932, Roosevelt, known to many as "FDR," had pledged that he would provide a "new deal for the American people." Roosevelt had not yet worked out the specifics of his plan. But during the first hundred days of his term, the New Deal—Roosevelt's program to end the Great Depression—took shape. The bills passed during the "Hundred Days" reflected FDR's practical approach to politics. As he remarked during the campaign, "It is common sense to take a method and try it. If it fails, admit it frankly and try another. But above all, try something."

What finally emerged was a three-pronged strategy, sometimes called the "three R's." Roosevelt proposed *relief* programs to ease the suffering of the needy, *recovery* programs to lay the foundation for economic growth, and *reform* programs to help prevent future economic crises. Some of these programs succeeded. Others failed. Together they profoundly altered the government's role in American society.

RELIEF FOR THE NEEDY 4D
Most of Roosevelt's relief programs were not simple handouts. Rather, they used government money to fund projects that performed useful work. Roosevelt had long been interested in conservation, and the first work relief program he organized was the Civilian Conservation Corps (CCC). By August 1933 more than 300,000 young men between the ages of 18 and 25 were at work planting trees, setting up firebreaks, and building dams to stop soil erosion.

The CCC aided its workers as well as the environment. Many of the men who joined the CCC

were ill-nourished, and the average weight gain for Corps members was from eight to fourteen pounds. A number of camps also offered courses that allowed members to develop job skills and earn high school diplomas. By 1941 about 2.5 million men had passed through the camps, finding work and fellowship at a time when they might otherwise have drifted into political extremism.

Another relief organization was the Federal Emergency Relief Administration (FERA). Congress set aside $500 million for FERA to hand out in direct relief to states, cities, and towns. Harry Hopkins, the head of FERA, believed that work programs should replace direct relief. He persuaded Roosevelt to set up the Civil Works Administration (CWA) in the fall of 1933. Hopkins was put in charge of CWA, which took over many

Have students imagine they are members of Congress considering the NRA, and ask them to debate the measure.

Science and Technology
Tell students that radio served as a unifying activity for large numbers of Americans in the 1930s, as television does today. *How did Roosevelt use radio to fight the Depression?* (He spoke directly to the people in a simple, friendly way, convincing them to have more confidence in the banking system and the country.) *How was FDR's use of the radio different from traditional methods of gaining support for presidential programs?* (It allowed him to appeal directly to the people, not through Congress, and he did not have to travel around the country.) Ask students to compare Roosevelt's use of radio with the way the President uses television today.

Environment
What environmental problems did the U.S. face in the 1930s? (Poor farming practices had led to soil erosion and the creation of a Dust Bowl over many of the Great Plains states.) *What did the CCC do to help the U.S. environment?* (Planted trees, set up firebreaks, and built dams to stop soil erosion.) *Do you think the United States could use a CCC today? What would its tasks be?*

The Presidents
Franklin D. Roosevelt was the only President elected to four terms. In 1951 the 22nd Amendment was established declaring a President can be elected to no more than two terms. Ask students to consider why this amendment was enacted and whether they agree with it.

Background Harry Hopkins became FDR's chief adviser and directed the massive Works Progress Administration, created in 1935. He lived in the White House for a time and died only nine months after Roosevelt.

Impact of Geography
Have students consider how much influence a geographical landform or body of water can have on the people in a region. This was the case for the people in the Tennessee River Valley and explains why the TVA had such a widespread effect on the region. *What geographical realities affect your lives in your community? How?* (Students may name a mountain range, river, ocean, Great Lake, coastal area, plain, desert, etc. Effects should include crops, transportation, how people make a living, etc.)

Patterns in History
Remind students that the New Deal was a response to a period of crisis. *Do you think there are any problems in today's world that are critical enough to merit a New Deal approach? What are they?*

Economics
What earlier group argued in favor of the United States going off the gold standard? (Populists.) *What were the Populists' arguments?* (Tying the money supply to the gold standard kept the money tight, which hurt farmers and other debtors.) *Why did the United States finally go off the gold standard in 1933?* (The U.S. was losing large amounts of gold to foreign investors; FDR wanted to put more money into circulation and encourage inflation.)

Ask students to explain why, though high inflation is considered an economic threat, deflation is also damaging to the economy. (It discourages businesses from borrowing and expanding. If prices are falling, businesses will get less money for their products in the future.)

of the functions of FERA. By January 1934, Hopkins had placed four million people in CWA jobs. CWA workers built roads, parks, schools, and airports. They cleared and cleaned wasteland and helped fix up run-down neighborhoods. Some critics complained that CWA jobs, such as raking leaves, were often "make-work" projects. Yet the chance to work and earn wages boosted the morale of many unemployed people.

SPURRING ECONOMIC RECOVERY 3E, 4D

Relief programs like the CWA were designed to pump more money into the economy as well as aid individuals. Encouraging economic recovery was also an aim of the Public Works Administration (PWA), headed by Harold L. Ickes. PWA jobs were usually on large-scale engineering projects, such as highways, bridges, power plants, and dams. The accomplishments of PWA included the Hoover Dam on the Colorado River, completed in 1936, and the Grand Coulee Dam on the Columbia River, finished in 1942. The Grand Coulee Dam is the largest concrete structure in the world.

An even larger—and more controversial—recovery program was an effort to revive the economy of the Tennessee Valley. The Tennessee River ran through seven southern states, and the valley that surrounded it suffered from widespread poverty. Deforestation and frequent flooding had caused severe erosion, leaving much of the land infertile. Nearly half of the families were on relief.

In 1933, Senator George W. Norris of Nebraska proposed a development project that would help the whole valley. FDR backed Norris's plan, and on May 18, 1933, Congress passed the Tennessee Valley Act, creating the Tennessee Valley Authority (TVA). The TVA would produce and sell cheap electrical power, control floods, replant forests, practice soil conservation, and encourage small private industries to come to the valley.

The TVA was a resounding success. It lifted the people of the Tennessee Valley out of poverty and provided them with long-term resources for a better life. Even today the TVA generates more electricity than any other competitor in the power industry. Yet critics vehemently opposed the TVA, calling it "creeping socialism." Charging that gov-

This photograph shows the Fort Loudoun Dam, one of several built on the Tennessee River by the TVA. Today, water power supplies only about one-sixth of the electricity generated by the TVA. The rest comes from nuclear and coal-burning plants. ECONOMICS On what grounds did its critics oppose the TVA? 8I

ernment ownership of industry violated the spirit of free enterprise, they blocked Roosevelt's efforts to build more TVAs elsewhere in the country.

3E 4C

HOUSING AND AGRICULTURAL RECOVERY

When FDR took office, the housing industry was in a tailspin. Even worse, more than 1,000 families in the United States were losing their homes to foreclosures each day. On June 13, 1933, Congress established the Home Owners Loan Corporation (HOLC). The HOLC bought up mortgages from banks and refinanced them in a way that allowed homeowners to meet their payments. By the time the Depression was over, the HOLC had saved one out of every five mortgaged homes.

Foreclosure was only one of the many threats facing American farmers. Roosevelt believed that agricultural recovery could not occur without fundamental changes in economic policy. The problem of overproduction and falling prices had plagued farmers throughout the 1920s. It had grown worse after the Crash, and farm income had fallen by 60

364 UNIT 5 FROM BOOM TO BUST

Photo Caption Answer
Private power companies opposed government production of electric power.

Background One reason for opposition to the TVA was that once the government got into the electricity business, it would find out how much it cost to generate electricity. Those figures could then be used as a yardstick to judge whether private utilities were charging fair rates.

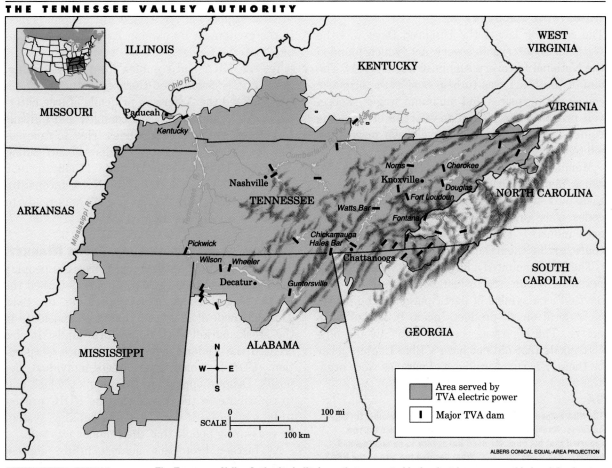

ALBERS CONICAL EQUAL-AREA PROJECTION

MAP SKILLS

8I, 9B

The Tennessee Valley Authority built dams that generated hydroelectric power, provided an inland water-way system, and created lakes. What states were served by TVA programs? CRITICAL THINKING In which general direction do the major rivers dammed by the TVA flow? How can you tell?

Cooperative Learning

Divide students into small groups. Have the members of each group choose a problem they consider to be important today. Then have the groups design programs to address the problems. Programs should include the people or problem to be helped, what levels of government are to be involved, how the program is to be financed, etc. Each group may elect a spokesperson who will present its program to the larger class, or "Congress." The "Congress" may then vote on the program. **LEP**

Addressing Individual Needs

Guided/Independent Practice
Instruct students to complete **Reinforcement Workbook** Worksheet 58. This worksheet asks students to write a newspaper editorial on the NRA.

Reteaching/Correctives
Have students work in small groups to develop problem-solution charts based on the section. Each New Deal program should be viewed as a solution. In the column "Problems," students should list the problems that the programs aimed at remedying. In a third column, have students evaluate the success of the solution.

Have students complete **Reteaching Resources** Worksheet 58, in which they complete a chart on major New Deal programs.

Enrichment/Extension
Assign **Enrichment and Extension Resources** Historian Worksheet 6.

percent since 1929. In an effort to raise farm income, Congress passed the Agricultural Adjustment Act on May 12, 1933.

This act included the emergency Farm Mortgage Act, which provided funds to keep farmers from losing their lands to foreclosure. It also included a system of farm subsidies designed to lower production and raise prices. Each spring the Agricultural Adjustment Administration (AAA) would estimate how many acres of crops and how much livestock the nation needed that year. The AAA would then work with farmers to set quotas for the coming year. It would pay farmers to let part of their land lie fallow—remain unplanted.

The biggest problem of the AAA was what to do with existing crops and livestock. To prevent a glut on the market in the fall of 1933, farmers had to plow under millions of acres of corn and slaughter millions of pigs. There was a great public outcry over this wastefulness. But Henry H. Wallace, the Secretary of Agriculture, refused to be swayed. He mocked his critics for thinking that "every little pig has the right to attain before slaughter the full pigginess of his pigness." Wallace argued that farmers, like industrialists, had to pay attention to the laws of supply and demand.

The system of farm subsidies helped save farmers from economic disaster. Within two years farm income jumped by more than 50 percent, even though 40 million acres of land had been taken out of cultivation.

CHAPTER 16   THE NEW DEAL, 1933–1941   **365**

Map Skills Answers
Tennessee, North Carolina, Georgia, Alabama, Mississippi, Kentucky, and Virginia. The rivers flow east to west as indicated by the eastern mountains where they originate and by their outlet into the Ohio and Mississippi Rivers to the west; also, all the lakes created by the dams are to the east, behind the dams.

You may wish to use the Section 1 Review, page 367, to see how well your students understand the main points in this lesson.

Section Review Answers

1. *fireside chat*—One of a series of radio talks delivered by President Roosevelt in which he explained his policies to listeners in a friendly manner. *New Deal*—Program of legislation put into effect by the Roosevelt administration in an effort to end the Depression.

2. *Harry Hopkins*—Director of FERA and then CWA. *Harold L. Ickes*—Director of the PWA. *George W. Norris* —Senator from Nebraska who helped develop the Tennessee Valley Authority project.

3. To prevent continued withdrawals and to assure depositors that only solvent institutions would be allowed to reopen. Both results were necessary to save the banking industry.

4. Relief—the immediate and direct help of those in need; recovery—the stimulation of economic growth; and reform— the prevention of further economic crises.

5. Possible answers include large employment programs by the government, government ownership of the TVA, government regulation of farming production, and the NRA's system of setting prices and minimum wages. All of these are examples of government attempts to control important parts of the economy.

INDUSTRIAL RECOVERY 3E

The crowning law of the Hundred Days was the National Industrial Recovery Act, which founded the National Recovery Administration (NRA). The aim of the NRA was to help businesses organize codes setting prices and minimum wages. Roosevelt proposed the plan in an effort to prevent the ruinous competition that drove down prices and led to business failures.

Membership in NRA was made voluntary, because Roosevelt feared that forcing industries to take part would be unconstitutional. The NRA codes were drawn up by the businesses within each industry. The President then approved the codes, giving them the force of law.

The NRA mounted a huge publicity campaign to persuade businesses to join. The Blue Eagle was devised as a symbol of participation, to be placed as a decal on all products made by coded businesses. The hope was that the public would boycott goods that did not have a Blue Eagle sticker on it. Enormous rallies and parades were organized in support of NRA, and Philadelphia joined in the excitement by naming its professional football team the Eagles.

Yet the NRA had troubles from its beginning. Some critics complained that restricting competition violated the American principle of free enterprise. Also, the codes were complex and difficult to enforce, and some industries tried to take advantage of workers. Labor leaders began calling NRA the "National Run-Around." Finally, in 1935 the Supreme Court declared the NRA unconstitutional. By then, however, Roosevelt was ready to try other ways of regulating business.

9A

The NRA helped produce jobs but was beneficial mainly to big business. A review board headed by lawyer Clarence Darrow reported that big business used the agency to dominate small business and labor. **POLITICS** What decided the fate of the NRA?

REFORMING BANKS AND THE STOCK MARKET 3G

To prevent future crashes and to restore people's faith in the banking system, Congress passed the Glass-Steagall Banking Act on June 16, 1933. This act made it illegal for banks to speculate in the stock market with depositors' funds. It also created the Federal Deposit Insurance Corporation (FDIC), which guaranteed individual deposits. Despite opposition from banks, which had to contribute to the insurance, the FDIC proved to be a success. It stabilized the banking system by reassuring people that their money was safe.

As further protection against future depressions, the New Deal also reformed the stock market. The Securities Act, passed on May 27, 1933, required all firms that issued stock to provide investors with accurate information about their finances. A year later Congress created the Securities and Exchange Commission (SEC). Its five members, appointed by the President, monitored corporations to make sure they provided proper information to investors.

GOING OFF THE GOLD STANDARD 3F

The most dramatic change in economic policy during the New Deal was Roosevelt's decision to take the United States off the gold standard. This meant that the government would no longer pay gold in exchange for dollars. Most of Europe had already gone off the gold standard, and the United States was losing large amounts of gold through shipments to foreign investors.

Roosevelt was determined to stop this outflow of gold. He also wanted to raise prices, which had

Photo Caption Answer
The Supreme Court declared it unconstitutional.

Background Clarence Darrow, mentioned on page 334 in connection with the Scopes trial, had a reputation as an advocate of liberal causes by the time he served as the head of the NRA review board.

sunk so low that many manufacturers could not break even, let alone make a profit, on the goods they sold. If the government abandoned the gold standard, it could print and circulate more dollars, thereby creating inflation.

Some Americans criticized Roosevelt's action, claiming that no one would have faith in the dollar if it were not redeemable in gold. "This is the end of Western civilization," one of Roosevelt's advisers, Lewis Douglas, cried when he heard of the decision. Yet world leaders praised the move, and prices began to climb. People knew that the United States still had substantial gold reserves, and they did not lose faith in paper currency.

SECTION REVIEW

1. KEY TERMS fireside chat, New Deal

2. PEOPLE Harry Hopkins, Harold L. Ickes, George W. Norris

3. COMPREHENSION Why did Roosevelt declare a bank holiday?

4. COMPREHENSION What were the three main parts of the New Deal strategy?

5. CRITICAL THINKING Which parts of the New Deal would you regard as examples of socialism? Explain your answer.

3F, 4D, 5B, 8F

2 Critics from the Right and Left

Section Focus

Key Terms American Liberty League
■ Share-Our-Wealth program ■ Townsend Plan ■ EPIC

Main Idea By 1934 the New Deal had aroused criticism both from conservatives, who wanted to overturn its laws, and from radicals, who wanted to extend them.

Objectives As you read, look for answers to these questions:
1. Why did some conservatives oppose the New Deal?
2. What measures did Huey Long and Father Coughlin propose to defeat the Depression?
3. How did Dr. Townsend and Upton Sinclair plan to end the Depression?

During the first year of his administration, President Roosevelt was hailed as a hero. By 1934 his political opponents were beginning to complain. Conservatives argued that FDR had gone too far in his reforms, while radicals claimed that he had not gone far enough. Nearly all his critics were ready to step in with solutions of their own. In March 1934 Justice Stone of the Supreme Court wrote of Roosevelt, "It seems clear that the honeymoon is over."

THE AMERICAN LIBERTY LEAGUE 8F

Business leaders objected to the New Deal both on practical grounds and on principle. They pointed out that the government did not have the

money to pay for New Deal programs and that the budget deficit was mounting. They opposed the expansion of the New Deal because they believed it would be paid for by new taxes on business and on the rich. They also argued that the New Deal undermined the American traditions of individual responsibility and local initiative. They said that Roosevelt was claiming too much power for the presidency. Some even accused him of wanting to become a dictator.

In 1934 a group of Republicans and conservative Democrats, including FDR's old friend and rival Al Smith, formed the American Liberty League. Their goal was to defend the principles of laissez-faire, which called for government to leave busi-

Developing the Lesson

After students have read the section, you may want to consider the following activities:

Religion
Have students compare Father Coughlin with today's television evangelists. *Do you think religious leaders should preach political points of view?*

Cooperative Learning

Divide the class into five groups, each one representing the programs and constituents of one of the following: the American Liberty League, Huey Long, Father Coughlin, Dr. Townsend, and Upton Sinclair. Have each group prepare a political poster for their leader, using a slogan and suggestions for a graphic. **LEP**

Addressing Individual Needs

Guided/ Independent Practice
Have students complete **Reinforcement Workbook** Worksheet 59, in which they make judgments about the political scene.

Reteaching/Correctives
Have students develop a chart comparing the points of view of Roosevelt's critics. In the first column have students list the critic's name; in the second column, the critic's program; in a third, the program's criticism of FDR; and in a fourth, its suggestions for change.

Have students complete **Reteaching Resources** Worksheet 59, in which they compare the critics of the New Deal.

Enrichment and Extension
Assign students **Enrichment and Extension Resources** Primary Source Worksheet 31, which helps them understand Huey Long's proposals.

368

ness alone, so they opposed Roosevelt and the New Deal. The League insisted that it welcomed all classes of people, but the organization was dominated by northern industrialists, especially executives of Du Pont and General Motors. Many League members disliked Roosevelt so much that they never referred to him by name, calling him only "that man in the White House."

The members of the American Liberty League believed that limiting free enterprise would undermine the basic freedoms of all Americans. Business regulation, they claimed, threatened the liberty of manufacturers; high taxes threatened the property rights of the rich. "If one thing . . . has been proved by historical experience," said the League's president, "it is that the denial of property rights has always been the prelude to a denial of human rights."

RADICAL CRITICS: HUEY LONG AND CHARLES COUGHLIN 5B

Other political threats to FDR came from the left. Senator Huey Long of Louisiana was one of the few politicians in the nation to rival FDR in popularity. Noisy and ungrammatical, Long was described by one critic as being "like an overgrown

Louisiana Senator Huey Long, known as the "Kingfish," is shown here criticizing the NRA in a 1935 speech. Initially one of Roosevelt's supporters, Long turned against the New Deal because it was not radical enough. His candidacy in 1935 threatened to split the Democratic vote. POLITICS Why was Long popular? 5B

368 UNIT 5 FROM BOOM TO BUST

small boy with very bad habits indeed." But though Long lacked polish, he possessed enormous power. As governor of Louisiana, he had used bribery, violence, and blackmail to bring the entire state under his control. He won the gratitude of the poor by building schools and paving roads. He also abolished the poll tax so that poor whites and blacks could vote. One observer said of the common people of Louisiana, "They do not merely vote for him, they worship the ground he walks on. He is part of their religion."

Long was elected to the United States Senate in 1930. He supported Roosevelt in 1932, but by the following year he was already complaining that the New Deal had not gone far enough and that FDR had sold out to Wall Street. In 1934 Huey Long announced his Share-Our-Wealth program. He proposed that the federal government confiscate all incomes over one million dollars and use this money to guarantee a $5,000 home and a $2,000 annual income to every American.

Long's scheme attracted several million followers, and it had the following jingle to popularize it:

Ev'ry man a king, ev'ry man a king,
For you can be a millionaire
But there's something belonging
 to others.
There's enough for all people to share.
When it's sunny June and December too,
Or in the winter or spring.
There'll be peace without end
Ev'ry neighbor a friend
With ev'ry man a king.

> "**E**v'ry man a king."
> —*Huey Long slogan*

In 1935 Long announced his candidacy for President, but he did not live to see the election. He was assassinated in September 1935 in Baton Rouge by the son-in-law of an obscure political opponent. "I wonder what they shot me for?" he said after the bullet hit him.

Another powerful critic of FDR was the "Radio

Photo Caption Answer
His Share-Our-Wealth program and other efforts that benefited the poor won him great popularity.

Priest," Father Charles Coughlin (CAWG–lin). Coughlin was a Roman Catholic priest who began to broadcast sermons from a Detroit radio station in 1926. With his Irish humor and his charming radio voice, Coughlin was a great success. In the fall of 1930, CBS began to carry his talks over a national network. His subject matter was more often politics than religion, and by 1934 he was receiving more mail than any person in the United States—including Roosevelt.

Like Huey Long, Coughlin was an early supporter of the New Deal. He turned against it after a year, claiming that Roosevelt had gone over to the side of the bankers. Coughlin's persuasive manner gained him many followers, even though his political views had no coherent direction. He was openly prejudiced against Jews and often claimed that Roosevelt and other New Dealers had Jewish backgrounds. In 1934, arguing that capitalism was dead, he called for the nationalization of banks and utilities. CBS dropped his program when it became too controversial, but Coughlin started his own radio network, which reached about 40 million people.

THE TOWNSEND PLAN 3F

Long and Coughlin were not the only New Deal critics to call for radical economic changes. Another highly popular radical of this era was Dr. Francis E. Townsend, a 66-year-old physician from California. Concerned about the plight of the elderly, Townsend came up with a plan he claimed would help the aged and cure the nation's economic ills at the same time. Under the Townsend Plan, the federal government would pay every person over age 60 a pension of $200 a month. The money had to be spent before another monthly check would be issued. In theory, this would not only make it possible for the elderly to live a decent life, but would also stimulate the economy and thereby end the Depression.

Townsend's scheme attracted millions of followers among the elderly, who founded Townsend Clubs across the country. But when a California Democrat put the Townsend Plan before Congress, economists called it impractical. Townsend did not help matters. "I'm not in the least interested in the cost of the plan," he told a congressional committee. Finally, someone pointed out that the plan would channel about half of the national income into the pockets of one-eleventh of the population. The bill was dropped, and Townsend's influence faded.

UPTON SINCLAIR AND EPIC 4D

Another movement for radical political change emerged in California. This one was led by the novelist and reformer Upton Sinclair. Sinclair, best known for his 1906 novel *The Jungle*, was a Socialist who ran for governor of California on the Democratic ticket in 1934. His plan to defeat the Depression was called EPIC, which stood for End Poverty in California. Sinclair's plan called for the state of California to buy up closed factories and unused land and put unemployed citizens to work manufacturing goods and raising food. The workers would be paid in special currency that could be spent only on food and goods produced within this "production-for-use" system.

Sinclair won the Democratic primary in August 1934, piling up so many votes that the Republicans were seriously worried. His opponents mounted a huge publicity campaign against him, and the leading newspapers in California refused to print any news about EPIC. Many Democratic politicians decided to endorse Sinclair's Republican rival for governor, as did Dr. Townsend. Within six months of Sinclair's defeat, EPIC was dead, and some observers joked that what it had really stood for was Empty Promises in California.

SECTION REVIEW

1. KEY TERMS American Liberty League, Share-Our-Wealth program, Townsend Plan, EPIC

2. PEOPLE Huey Long, Charles Coughlin, Dr. Francis E. Townsend, Upton Sinclair

3. COMPREHENSION What group dominated the American Liberty League?

4. COMPREHENSION Why did Huey Long oppose Roosevelt?

5. CRITICAL THINKING Which threat to the New Deal do you think was more serious, that from the right or from the left?

Background Father Coughlin blamed Jewish bankers for U.S. entry in World War II, prompting the Catholic Church to order him to cease all nonreligious activities in 1942.

Assessment
You may wish to use the Section 2 Review, page 369, to see how well your students understand the main points in this lesson.

Section Review Answers

1. *American Liberty League*— Group that criticized the New Deal because it threatened laissez-faire economics. *Share-Our-Wealth program*—Proposal by Huey Long guaranteeing each American a home and basic income. *Townsend Plan*—Proposal that the government pay every citizen over 60 years of age a monthly income. *EPIC*—End Poverty in California, proposal that California buy closed factories and unused land and re-employ people.

2. *Huey Long*—Senator from Louisiana, he proposed the Share-Our-Wealth program. *Charles Coughlin*—"Radio Priest," he called for nationalization of banks and utilities. *Dr. Francis E. Townsend*—California physician who proposed a plan to help the elderly. *Upton Sinclair*—Socialist and novelist, he ran for governor of California in 1934.

3. Northern industrialists, particularly executives of Du Pont and General Motors.

4. Long claimed that Roosevelt's New Deal programs did not go far enough.

5. The right—the country's traditional free enterprise system favored Liberty League arguments; the left—the Depression encouraged many people to look to radical answers.

Closure

Ask one student to transform the Main Idea of the section into a question, and have other students answer that question. Then have students read Section 3, noting the ways the New Deal changed.

Section Objectives

- identify and describe the major programs of the Second New Deal
- describe the controversy involving Roosevelt and the Supreme Court

Introducing the Section

Connecting with Past Learnings

Have students recall the basic criticisms from the left regarding the New Deal programs of the Hundred Days. (New Deal programs did not go far enough, reach enough people, or offer a radical enough alternative to the problems of the Depression.)

Key Terms

Help students identify the key terms by finding their definitions in context. Ask them to explain the connection between the first terms and the other two terms. **LEP**

Focus

Have students create a chart listing the legislation of the Second New Deal, what programs it created, the responsibilities of these programs, and whether they strengthened or replaced earlier New Deal programs. (FHA: encouraged banks to make housing loans; strengthened HOLC. WPA: created jobs in construction and jobs for writers, artists, and young people; replaced the CWA.

370

3C, 4D, 4F, 5B, 5E, 5F, 9A, 9B, 9F

3 The Second New Deal

★ **Section Focus**

★ **Key Term** Second New Deal ■ Social Security Act ■ National Labor Relations Act

★ **Main Idea** In 1934 President Roosevelt sought to extend and improve the New Deal with a second major legislative program.

Objectives As you read, look for answers to these questions:
1. What further programs and reforms did Roosevelt propose in 1935?
2. What controversy arose over the Supreme Court?

In spite of the complaints of critics such as Huey Long and Father Coughlin, the majority of Americans were still solidly behind President Roosevelt. The overwhelming victory of the Democratic Party in the 1934 congressional elections was a clear sign of approval for the New Deal and for FDR. "The President," historian William Allen White wrote, "has all but been crowned by the people."

With an even greater Democratic majority in Congress than before, Roosevelt had strong backing for his plans to extend the New Deal. He now believed that the permanent machinery of government—not just temporary legislation—should protect Americans from economic hardship. His new programs answered some of his critics' demands for a fairer distribution of wealth.

HOUSING REFORM 4D

One tool that Roosevelt used to change economic conditions was the Federal Housing Administration (FHA), created in 1934. The FHA aimed to improve the housing market by encouraging banks to make housing loans and by encouraging customers to apply for them. The FHA offered banks insurance on loans they made to families buying new homes. This meant that if a homeowner failed to pay his mortgage and the bank foreclosed, the bank would be guaranteed repayment.

To boost sales of new homes, the FHA required banks to offer customers low down payments on housing loans. The FHA also had banks change the loan repayment schedule, spreading out the payments more evenly.

The FHA was an ingenious answer to New Deal critics who wanted every American family to be able to own a home. More families could afford to buy homes when only a small down payment was necessary. Fewer families would lose their homes to foreclosure now that mortgages were easier to pay. Roosevelt hoped that the FHA would revive the housing market by encouraging Americans to start buying and selling again.

MORE PUBLIC WORKS 4D

Roosevelt's effort to improve the housing market was especially important because one-third of all jobless workers were in the building industry. The programs established during the Hundred Days had not done much to bring down the unemployment rate. The CWA had been terminated in 1934, when Roosevelt had become concerned about its cost and possible corruption. As a result, the government had once more returned to direct relief for the unemployed.

In his State of the Union Address on January 4, 1935, Roosevelt announced his plan to end direct relief by the federal government and to replace it with public works. "We have a human problem as well as an economic problem," he said. "To dole out relief is to administer a narcotic, a subtle destroyer of the human spirit. . . . We must preserve not only the bodies of the unemployed from destruction but also their self-respect and courage and determination."

> "To dole out relief is to administer a narcotic, a subtle destroyer of the human spirit."
>
> —*Franklin Roosevelt, 1935*

SUPPORTING THE SECTION

Reinforcement Workbook: Worksheet 60
Reteaching Resources: Worksheet 60
Teaching Transparencies: Transparency 60

Many artists and writers received commissions from the WPA, as well as state agencies, that helped them through the Depression and enriched the nation culturally. This scene from a 1931 mural by Thomas Hart Benton uses strongly sculptured shapes and bright colors to depict workers building a city. Benton's work was influenced by Mexican mural painters such as José Orozco (painting, page 283). **ECONOMICS** How did the WPA differ from direct relief?

4F, 9A

COPYRIGHT © THE EQUITABLE LIFE ASSURANCE SOCIETY OF THE UNITED STATES.

The result was the Works Progress Administration (WPA), created on May 6, 1935. The WPA put people to work in their home towns, building roads, bridges, playgrounds, swimming pools, sidewalks, and sewers. It also gave jobs to artists, scholars, writers, and students, who had been largely overlooked in the concern for farmers and blue-collar workers. Under the sponsorship of the WPA, writers researched local histories, artists painted murals in post offices and other public buildings, and photographers tried to capture the human face of the Depression.

The WPA also set up the National Youth Administration to give work to students aged 16 to 25. Students performed such chores in their high school or college as mowing lawns, painting walls, fixing furniture, or serving as clerks. The chores were done after school or on weekends to ensure that students' education was not interrupted.

Between 1935 and 1943, when the WPA came to an end, about one out of ten adult Americans had held a WPA job. More than 2.5 million young people had also worked for the WPA. WPA workers built 122,000 public buildings, 77,000 bridges,

664,000 miles of roads, and 285 airports. The WPA was supported by $11 billion of federal government funds—the largest expenditure of any New Deal program.

Some members of Congress opposed the enormous expense of the WPA. Others thought that it was not right to pay workers who might spend more time loafing on the job than working. These "shovel-leaners" even became the object of critical cartoons and jokes. But most Americans felt good about being able to work for wages once again. One North Carolina farmer declared, "I'm proud of our United States, and every time I hear 'The Star-Spangled Banner' I feel a lump in my throat. There ain't no other nation in the world that would have sense enough to think of WPA."

> "There ain't no other nation in the world that would have sense enough to think of WPA."
>
> —*North Carolina farmer*

Social Security Act: provided compensation for the unemployed, disabled, widows and children, and pension for the elderly. Resettlement Administration: helped farmers move to better land; extended farm assistance. REA: brought electricity to the countryside; extended farm assistance. Wagner Act: reaffirmed the right of labor to organize; replaced NIRA provision.)

What was the relationship between Roosevelt's proposal to pack the Supreme Court and the New Deal? (The Supreme Court, made up of older, more conservative justices, struck down many New Deal programs. Roosevelt wanted to prevent that trend from continuing by getting younger, more liberal justices on the Court.)

Developing the Lesson
After students have read the section, you may want to consider the following activities.

Economics
Have students create charts showing how the FHA helped more Americans buy homes. (It insured home loans so that banks were more willing to make them; and required banks to accept lower down payments and to schedule payments more evenly.)

Photo Caption Answer
Under the WPA, the government paid people for constructive projects.

Background   Artists Ben Shahn and Jackson Pollock were employed by the WPA's Federal Art Project. John Steinbeck, John Cheever, Richard Wright, and Conrad Aiken are just a few of the writers who worked for the Federal Writer's Project. The WPA also sponsored the Federal Theatre, which performed all over the country, and the Federal Music Project which employed 15,000 musicians.

SOCIAL SECURITY 4D

The flood of reform legislation that Congress passed in the summer of 1935 was a major addition to the New Deal. For this reason it is often called the Second New Deal. As Roosevelt put together these laws, he looked back to the goals of the progressives at the turn of the century: unemployment insurance, old-age pensions, and the protection of the rights of labor.

One of the most important laws of the Second New Deal was the Social Security Act, passed in August 1935. The Social Security Act was intended to protect Americans who were unable to support themselves. It used a tax levied on employers to provide unemployment compensation to workers who were laid off from their jobs. It also gave compensation to disabled workers and offered assistance to widows and children in case of a worker's death.

The Social Security Act is now best known for its old-age insurance plan. During their working years, employees were to pay a certain percentage of their wages, known as payroll contributions, into the old-age fund. The employer paid the same percentage. Upon retirement, workers would receive monthly payments for the rest of their lives. This plan worked because it was funded, not by the federal government, but by workers and their employers. As Roosevelt explained, "We put those payroll contributions there so as to give the contributors a legal, moral, and political right to collect their pensions. . . . With those taxes in there, no politician can ever scrap my social security program."

OTHER PROGRAMS 4D

The Second New Deal offered more support to American farmers, especially the poorest ones—laborers, tenant farmers, and sharecroppers. In 1935 the Resettlement Administration was created to help poor farmers move from worn-out land to more fertile regions. This agency, later called the Farm Security Administration, offered grants and loans for the purchase of new farmland. It also provided short-term loans to help farmers purchase farm equipment, seed, and fertilizer.

At the time of the Second New Deal, nine out of ten American farms did not have electricity. Private utilities had always argued that running power lines to isolated farms was too expensive to be worthwhile. In May 1935, Roosevelt created the Rural Electrification Administration (REA), which made loans to farm communities that wanted to build public utilities. By 1943 the REA had loaned more than $300 million to farm communities. Worried that public utilities would take over the market, private electrical companies had also begun to provide more power to rural areas. By 1941, four out of ten American farms had electricity.

The United States was one of the last industrialized nations to create a social security system. Most Americans believed the government should not take responsibility for caring for the aged, disabled, or needy. The Depression changed many people's attitudes. ISSUES How much responsibility do you think the government should take for citizens' welfare? 9G

MAJOR NEW DEAL PROGRAMS

	PROGRAM	PURPOSE
Finance		
FDIC	Federal Deposit Insurance Corporation 1933–	To protect money of depositors in insured banks
SEC	Securities and Exchange Commission 1934–	To regulate the stock exchanges
FHA	Federal Housing Administration 1934–	To insure loans to homeowners for mortgages or home repairs
Agriculture		
AAA	Agricultural Adjustment Administration 1933–1936	To regulate farm production and promote soil conservation
FSA	Farm Security Administration 1937–1946	To help tenant farmers and migrant workers to own farms
Business and Labor		
NRA	National Recovery Administration 1933–1935	To regulate industry and raise wages and prices
NLRB	National Labor Relations Board 1935–	To regulate and protect unions
Employment and Public Works		
CCC	Civilian Conservation Corps 1933–1942	To employ young men to plant trees, set up firebreaks, and build dams
TVA	Tennessee Valley Authority 1933–	To develop the Tennessee Valley region
PWA	Public Works Administration 1933–1939	To create jobs building highways, bridges, power plants, and dams
WPA	Works Progress Administration 1935–1943	To create jobs for and sponsor artists
Social Insurance		
SSA	Social Security Administration 1935–	To provide workers with unemployment insurance and retirement benefits

CHART SKILLS 4D

This chart summarizes the major programs introduced under President Roosevelt's New Deal. What was the purpose of the SEC? Which Americans participated in the CCC? CRITICAL THINKING Why might the government have decided to terminate its agricultural programs?

To help pay for the Second New Deal, Congress had to raise taxes. Many New Deal critics had called for a fairer distribution of income, and in 1935 and 1936 Congress passed legislation to increase income taxes on corporations and on the rich. Estate taxes and gift taxes were also raised.

GROWTH OF LABOR UNIONS 3C

Roosevelt was a strong and lasting supporter of labor. For decades, labor unions had sought government backing of their right to organize and to strike. The National Industrial Recovery Act had contained a provision, called Section 7a, that

Constitutional Heritage
Why did the Supreme Court declare many New Deal programs unconstitutional? (It tended to believe that neither the federal nor the state government had the right to regulate industry and agriculture.) ***What was FDR's justification for changing the composition of the Supreme Court?*** (He claimed that younger justices would bring new ideas, work faster, and be more familiar with the problems facing the country.) ***How would FDR's plan have affected the constitutional balance of power?*** (It would have given the President more power at the expense of the Court.)

Analyzing Controversial Issues
Remind students that public opinion was seen as a reason for the Court's increasing responsiveness to FDR's New Deal legislation. ***To what degree should the Supreme Court remain independent of public opinion in making its decisions?*** Have students suggest current controversial issues before the Supreme Court, and ask them if they feel the Court is affected by public opinion in these cases.

Civic Values
Why did FDR criticize the justices serving on the Supreme Court during his first administration? (He said they were too old.) Ask students if they think people should be removed from office on the basis of age. They may wish to find out the ages of the present Supreme Court justices. ***Do you think the present Court is too old?***

Chart Skills Answers
To regulate the stock exchanges. Young men. Students may suggest that agricultural programs were intended to provide temporary help to farmers rather than effecting permanent changes.

Critics in the 1930s frequently satirized the New Deal's alphabet soup of federal agencies. This image by William Gropper is based on a famous scene from the book *Gulliver's Travels*. **POLITICS** What, according to Gropper, was the effect of New Deal programs on the United States? **9B**

guaranteed workers' right to organize unions and to bargain collectively with employers. As a result of this provision, union membership jumped from 2.8 million in 1933 to 3.7 million a year later. But many employers ignored the law and refused to bargain with unions.

In July 1935 Congress passed the most important law in American labor history, the National Labor Relations Act. This law is often called the Wagner Act because it was sponsored by Senator Robert F. Wagner of New York. The Wagner Act reaffirmed the right of labor to organize. It also gave enforcement powers to the National Labor Relations Board (NLRB), which Roosevelt had set up the year before. The NLRB would continue to hear testimony about unfair labor practices by employers, and it could now issue "cease and desist" orders requiring employers to stop those practices. With the NLRB to protect them, labor unions flourished, and union membership rose to 11 million by 1941.

As the union movement grew, workers began to look for an alternative to the American Federation of Labor. The AFL was still sticking to its policy of admitting only skilled workers. Ambitious labor leaders were eager to bring unskilled workers into labor unions. John L. Lewis of the United Mine Workers pulled his union and others out of the AFL to form the Congress of Industrial Organiza-

tions (CIO). The CIO organized workers by industry rather than by craft. Lewis was determined to unionize the steel and automobile industries, no matter what resistance he encountered.

The CIO used a new tactic known as the "sit-down strike," in which workers simply sat down in their factories. The strategy was successful. Large corporations like U.S. Steel and General Motors were forced to bargain with the CIO. By 1937, CIO membership was even larger than that of the AFL.

ROOSEVELT WINS RE-ELECTION 5B

As Roosevelt prepared for his re-election bid in 1936, he knew that he had alienated many of the business interests. He could still look for support, however, from the middle-class and working-class people who had benefited from New Deal programs. He was especially popular among urban voters and union members. In a campaign speech at Madison Square Garden, Roosevelt denounced the forces of "organized money." He told the crowd, "I should like to have it said of my first administration that in it the forces of selfishness and of lust for power met their match. . . . I should like to have it said of my second administration that in it these forces met their master."

When Roosevelt ran for re-election in 1936, his opponents accused him of taking over congressional powers, undermining free enterprise, and violating the Constitution. **POLITICS** What factors, do you think, accounted for Roosevelt's decisive victory? **5B**

The Republicans chose Governor Alfred Landon of Kansas, a moderate, as their presidential candidate. Landon had gained national attention for balancing his state's budget at a time when government deficits were commonplace. The Republican platform ignored the views of the American

Liberty League. Instead it endorsed many New Deal measures, including unemployment insurance, old-age pensions, and benefits for farmers.

The followers of Huey Long and Father Coughlin formed a third party, the Union Party, and ran William "Liberty Bill" Lemke for the presidency. But the party's call for a socialist America fell on deaf ears. Lemke won only 880,000 popular votes and not one electoral vote.

Roosevelt won the election easily, swamping Alf Landon and capturing 61 percent of the popular vote. He won every state except for Maine and Vermont. "As Maine goes, so goes the nation," was an old political saying. One observer now joked that it should read, "As Maine goes, so goes Vermont."

FDR's BATTLE WITH THE SUPREME COURT 5F

With his enormous victory behind him, Roosevelt proposed to take on an issue that had troubled him throughout the previous year: the decisions of the Supreme Court. In 1935 the Court declared five New Deal laws, including the NRA and the program of farm debt relief, to be unconstitutional. In 1936 four more Court decisions went against the New Deal, the last of which concerned a law establishing a minimum wage in New York. The Court seemed to believe that neither the federal nor the state governments had the right to impose regulations on industry and agriculture.

Roosevelt saw the Supreme Court as an enemy of the New Deal. He was impatient with the "Nine Old Men," as the justices were sometimes called. None had retired or died during his entire first term, so he was dealing with a conservative Court appointed during the previous decade of Republican leadership.

In 1937 Roosevelt proposed that whenever a justice failed to retire at the age of 70, the President should have the right to add a new justice. This would raise the number of justices in the Supreme Court, though Roosevelt added that the total should not exceed fifteen.

Roosevelt did not tell the public that he wanted to establish a pro–New Deal majority on the Supreme Court. Instead he used more careful language to describe the plan. He explained that it had two chief purposes:

By bringing into the judicial system a steady and continuing stream of new and younger blood, I hope, first, to make the administration of all federal justice speedier and, therefore, less costly; secondly to bring to the decision of social and economic problems younger men who have had personal experiences and contact with modern facts and circumstances under which average men have to live and work. This plan will save our national Constitution from hardening of the judicial arteries.

Most people saw through this strained explanation. It was clear that Roosevelt simply wanted to warn the six justices over the age of 70 that if they did not retire, he would appoint new justices to outvote them on important issues. To many people, this "court-packing plan" smacked of dictatorship. The President had gone too far.

Even Democrats refused to support the bill. "Boys, here's where I cash in my chips," said one Democratic congressman. FDR submitted a compromise version that would allow two, rather than six, new appointments. But the Senate killed the bill by a vote of 70 to 20 in July 1937. It was FDR's first major legislative defeat.

5E

★ **Historical Documents**

For an excerpt from the Senate Judiciary Committee's rejection of President Roosevelt's plan to reform the federal judiciary, see page 724 of this book.

AFTERMATH OF THE COURT FIGHT 9E

The Supreme Court controversy did Roosevelt lasting political damage. It weakened his popular support, and it alienated some members of Congress. Roosevelt began to find it harder to get Congress to pass laws that he wanted.

However, Roosevelt did win some battles in his war with the judiciary. After the spring of 1937 the Court began to make decisions in favor of the New Deal. It upheld the National Labor Relations Act as well as the Social Security Act. In Roosevelt's words, "The Court yielded. The Court

and read or display it to the class, making a short statement about what the material shows about life during the New Deal years.

Assessment

You may wish to use the Section 3 Review, page 376, to see how well your students understand the main points in this lesson.

Section Review Answers

1. *Second New Deal*—Reform legislation passed by Congress in 1935 to extend and strengthen the New Deal. *Social Security Act*—Law passed in 1935 to provide for Americans unable to support themselves; its chief provisions were for those laid off, disabled, and retired, and their dependents. *National Labor Relations Act*—Protected labor unions and their right to organize and strike, and created the National Labor Relations Board.

2. *Robert F. Wagner*—New York Senator who sponsored National Labor Relations Act. *John L. Lewis*—President of United Mine Workers who formed the Congress of Industrial Organizations. *Alfred Landon*—Governor of Kansas, Republican presidential candidate in 1936. *William Lemke*—The Union Party candidate for President in 1936, he represented the followers of Huey Long and Father Coughlin.

3. The Social Security Act provided funding through payroll deductions from workers and matching contributions by employers.

4. The FHA required banks to offer low down payments and more equitable repayment schedules in order to attract buyers, and guaranteed loans. The FHA made mortgages easier to acquire, encouraging people to buy and sell homes.

5. Students may suggest that the acceptance of FDR's plan may have set a bad precedent for executive interference in the judiciary and might have made the Court more responsive to popular opinion.

Closure

Call students' attention to the beige boxed quotation (p. 370). Ask them to relate this quotation to the main idea of the section. Then have students read Section 4 for the next class, noting how the Depression affected books, newspapers, and radio programs in the 1930s.

SECTION 4

Life During the Roosevelt Years
(pages 376–380)

Section Objective

■ identify the effects of the New Deal on American society and culture in the 1930s

Introducing the Section

Connecting With Past Learnings

Ask students to recall how the Depression affected African Americans. (They were hard hit because racial prejudice often meant that they were the first workers laid off and the last hired back.) *What political party did African Americans traditionally support? Why?* (Republican, because that party was in power when the slaves were freed and because the Radical Republicans had pushed for Reconstruction. White Democrats in the South had instituted racist policies there.)

changed. The Court began to interpret the Constitution instead of torturing it."

Many observers believed that the sudden switch in the direction of Court decisions was indeed a response to FDR's attack. Chief Justice Hughes had decided that the Court would have to be more responsive to the political climate of the time if it were to survive.

In May 1937 one 70-year-old justice decided to retire, and the President appointed a liberal justice, Hugo Black of Alabama, to replace him. In January 1938 a second justice retired, and the next year another died. By 1942 Roosevelt had appointed seven new justices, all strongly pro–New Deal. The Court had been packed all right, but according to tradition and the law.

4C, 4F, 6A, 6C, 7J

4 Life During the Roosevelt Years

Section Focus

Key Term black Cabinet

Main Idea Hard times dominated daily life during the 1930s, slowing progress by minorities and women and providing themes for art, literature, and popular culture.

Objectives As you read, look for answers to these questions:
1. What gains did minorities make during the New Deal?
2. How did the role of women change during the 1930s?
3. What effect did the Depression have on art, literature, and popular culture?

The pace of social change was slower during the Depression than it had been in the hectic 1920s. Economic hardship made people pull back and retrench. Minorities and women found it difficult to make new gains because their goals were considered secondary to the objectives of the New Deal. Yet most people looked to the future with hope and were willing to take small steps forward as proof that the country was changing for the better. "Man is a long time coming," the poet Carl Sandburg wrote during this period. "Man will yet win."

AFRICAN AMERICANS 4C

African Americans were slow to support FDR's run for President in 1932. The Republicans had held the allegiance of blacks ever since the Civil War. Most blacks regarded the Democratic Party with suspicion, associating it with the racism of southern Democrats. By the 1936 election, however, Roosevelt had won the support of large numbers of blacks. Robert L. Vann, the publisher of the Pittsburgh Courier, told black voters, "My friends, go turn Lincoln's picture to the wall. That debt has been paid in full."

SUPPORTING THE SECTION

Reinforcement Workbook: Worksheet 61
Reteaching Resources: Worksheet 61
Enrichment and Extension Resources: Primary Source Worksheet 32
Teaching Transparencies: Transparency 61

BIOGRAPHY 4C

MARY McLEOD BETHUNE
(1875–1955) was born in South Carolina, the youngest of seventeen children of former slaves. She graduated from Chicago's Moody Bible Institute and devoted the rest of her life to improving educational opportunities for black Americans. In 1935 Bethune founded the National Council of Negro Women and later served as vice-president of the NAACP. Under Franklin Roosevelt, she became the first black woman to head a federal agency.

Roosevelt placed more blacks in federal positions than any President before him. By 1936 these advisers were being called the President's black Cabinet. Among those appointed were Mary McLeod Bethune, Robert Vann, and Robert C. Weaver. William Hastie, the dean of Howard University's law school, was the first black judge to serve in a federal court.

Another reason why blacks swung to Roosevelt was the government's role in providing help. Blacks were hit harder by the Depression than almost any other group. Thousands found jobs in work programs such as the CCC and the WPA. Blacks were also influenced by symbolic acts of solidarity. When the black opera star Marian Anderson was refused permission to sing in Constitution Hall, owned by the Daughters of the American Revolution, Secretary of the Interior Ickes invited her to sing at the Lincoln Memorial. On Easter Sunday, 1939, Anderson performed before a crowd of 75,000 in an impressive ceremony.

The New Deal, however, was not always favorable to blacks. Government work programs usually paid blacks lower wages than whites. The policies of the Agricultural Adjustment Agency often drove black tenant farmers and sharecroppers from the land, while white landowners pocketed government checks. Nor did the New Deal offer legal protection for the rights of blacks. Not a single piece of civil rights legislation was enacted during the Roosevelt years.

Roosevelt even refused to speak out for an anti-lynching bill that was put before Congress in 1934. He was afraid of antagonizing the white southerners who held key positions on the Senate and House committees. "If I come out for the anti-lynching bill now, they will block every bill I ask Congress to pass to keep America from collapsing. I just can't take that risk," he said. Southern Democrats defeated the bill.

MEXICAN AMERICANS   6A, 4C

Mexican Americans were another group that suffered greatly during the Depression. Two decades of political upheaval had forced many Mexicans to leave their country in search of a better life. By the 1930s there were a million Mexican Americans in the United States. Some held jobs in mining, railroad construction, and the steel industry. Most, however, toiled as migrant farm workers.

Because Mexican Americans took low-paying jobs that few other Americans wanted, there was little prejudice against them at first. As the economy fell, however, the competition for jobs rose. To make matters worse, established labor groups often resented migrant workers for accepting low wages, not recognizing that the newcomers did so out of necessity. The outcry against Mexican Americans was so great that the United States and Mexico agreed on a program to encourage them to return to their native land.

AMERICAN INDIANS   6A, 4C, 6C

One minority group that made clear gains under the New Deal were the American Indians. The Dawes Act, passed in 1887, had broken up their tribes and deepened their poverty. Although they gained citizenship in 1924, the 1920s brought no prosperity to the Indians. In fact, between 1920 and 1930 the amount of tribal land shrank. The Depression brought further hardship, and the Bureau of Indian Affairs did not devise a relief program for Indians until 1931, two years after the Crash.

In 1933 Roosevelt appointed John Collier to be Commissioner of Indian Affairs. Under Collier's guidance, Congress passed the Indian Reorganization Act in 1934. The act halted the allotment of land to individuals and re-established tribal

Biography
Bethune also served as President of Bethune-Cookman College. Ask students to consider the many positions she held and to explain which one they believe was most significant.

Background   Mary McLeod Bethune was the director of the Division of Negro Affairs of the National Youth Administration. Robert Vann served as Special Assistant to the United States Attorney General. Robert C. Weaver was an economist in the Interior Department.

Key Terms
Remind students that *cabinet* has multiple meanings and that in this context it refers to a group of presidential advisers. Have them define the term, and contrast it with FDR's official Cabinet. **LEP**

Focus
Have students work as a class to prepare a "score sheet" report on the New Deal from the point of view of four segments of the population: women, blacks, American Indians, and Mexican Americans. The score sheets should list any positive and negative effects of the New Deal on the lives of the members of each group, and suggestions for improvement.

Why do you think members of these groups were not more vocal in their demands for their rights and recognition during the Depression? (Students may suggest that times were so hard that these groups felt that their goals would not be addressed; people made to feel second class often have difficulty speaking up; etc.)

Developing the Lesson
After students have read the section, you may want to consider the following activities:

Ethics
Why did Roosevelt refuse to speak out in favor of the anti-lynching bill? (He was afraid that powerful white southerners in Congress would block other New Deal legislation in revenge.) *Do you agree with his decision? Why or why not?* Discuss with students the ethical questions involved in making political compromises.

ownership. It also provided for local tribal government, made loans available for Indian-owned businesses, and set up programs to teach new methods of farming and land development. The goal was to improve economic conditions among Indians and to permit a return to the rich heritage of communal work and life. Indians were encouraged to hold tribal festivals and even speak native languages. Collier also saw to it that more than a quarter of all employees for the Bureau of Indian Affairs were American Indians.

WOMEN AND THE NEW DEAL 4C

Women too made gains during the Roosevelt years. Roosevelt's Secretary of Labor, Frances Perkins, was the first woman Cabinet member, and she remained one of his closest advisers during his years in office. First Lady Eleanor Roosevelt also became active in politics and served as a symbol of the changing role of women in American society.

Mrs. Roosevelt was born into a wealthy New York family. As a young woman she shunned the world of high society, working instead with the poor on New York City's East Side. After her marriage to Franklin Roosevelt, Eleanor became

Eleanor Roosevelt, the President's wife, became a widely admired public figure. Here she meets with Reverend B.C. Robeson, brother of singer Paul Robeson, at a meeting of ministers. CIVIC VALUES How did Eleanor Roosevelt symbolize the changing role of women in American society? 7J

an invaluable aide to him. When Franklin lost the ability to walk, he sent her on fact-finding missions all over the country. A *New Yorker* cartoon of this period showed a coal miner peering down a mine tunnel and exclaiming, "For Gosh sakes! It's Mrs. Roosevelt." She also became an expert political organizer, using press conferences and newspaper columns to push for the rights of women and minorities. In 1937 she wrote that "no one can make you feel inferior without your consent."

> **"N**o one can make you feel inferior without your consent."
> —*Eleanor Roosevelt*

Eleanor Roosevelt knew from experience how difficult it could be for women to break out of traditional roles. The homely daughter of a famous beauty, she had to overcome intense shyness to become a successful public figure. "You gain strength, courage, and confidence," she wrote, "by every experience in which you really stop to look fear in the face. You are able to say to yourself, 'I lived through this horror. I can take the next thing that comes along. . . .' You must do the thing you think you cannot do."

Mrs. Roosevelt and Frances Perkins had some success in advancing the interests of women in the New Deal. Most of the NRA codes setting minimum wages in various industries did not discriminate against women. The WPA organized a special division to focus on work projects for women. Women also suffered setbacks, however, most notably in 1933 when female employees of the federal government were fired if their husbands held federal jobs.

ART OF THE 1930s 4F

Painters and writers had their own responses to the economic upheaval of the 1930s. Some noted American painters, such as William Gropper, rejected capitalism, charging that America's economic system had failed. Gropper's paintings depicted sinister businessmen and corrupt politicians. Perhaps the most respected of the "protest" artists was Ben Shahn, who won fame in 1932 for

378 UNIT 5 FROM BOOM TO BUST

Like Grant Wood and John Steuart Curry, his fellow artists of the regionalist school, Missouri-born Thomas Hart Benton chose rural life as the subject of many paintings. In *Cradling Wheat,* Benton portrayed lean and vigorous Midwestern farmers. **NATIONAL IDENTITY** What images do people have of farmers today? **4F**

a series of paintings on the Sacco and Vanzetti case of the 1920s (painting, page 319).

Another group of painters, known as regionalists, had a greater faith in the ability of the United States to endure. Thomas Hart Benton said that his aim was to paint "American life as known and felt by ordinary Americans." In works such as *Cradling Wheat* and *Country Dance* he showed the beauty of country life, though he was capable of criticizing it as well. In a mural on the history of Indiana, he painted scenes of the Ku Klux Klan along with other episodes in the state's history. Grant Wood's painting *American Gothic* was immediately recognized as an American classic. John Steuart Curry painted scenes from his native Kansas (painting, page 334).

Writers also struggled to come to terms with the times. Some wrote novels clearly influenced by politics. John Steinbeck's *The Grapes of Wrath* (1939) protested the hard lot of Dust Bowl farmers. Erskine Caldwell showed the plight of the southern poor in *God's Little Acre* (1933). John Dos Passos offered a sweeping and critical portrait of American life in his trilogy *U.S.A.* (1937).

Other writers of the period were less political. William Faulkner explored the southern past in a stunning group of novels set in Mississippi, including *Light in August* (1932) and *Absalom, Absalom!* (1936). The poet Robert Frost wrote spare, lyrical celebrations of rural New England. Hart Crane, in his long poem *The Bridge* (1930), described the beauty and grace of the Brooklyn Bridge and summoned up figures from the American past such as Columbus and Pocahontas.

This poster advertises the film version of John Steinbeck's famous novel. Henry Fonda starred as a member of an "Okie" family in California who struggle for decent working conditions and social justice. Another Steinbeck novel, *In Dubious Battle* (1936), deals with the violent labor strikes that took place in California during the 1930s. **LITERATURE** Why, do you think, did many writers during the 1930s include political themes in their work? **4F**

Photo Caption Answers
(Top) Students may suggest that farmers are seen as representative of traditional American values. (Bottom) Students may suggest that they wrote in response to the dire social problems facing the nation during the Depression.

C Cooperative Learning

Divide students into small groups. Tell the groups they can create any one of the following: a scenario for a light-hearted escape film; a comic book sequence using heroes and villains and an "everything works out in the end" plot line; a newspaper ad or poster for a movie theater seeking to attract customers; a radio news broadcast of a major event which took place during the Depression. Then have the groups present their creations by acting them out or putting them on display. **LEP**

Addressing Individual Needs

Guided/ Independent Practice
Instruct students to complete **Reinforcement Workbook** Worksheet 61. This worksheet helps students learn about society and culture during the Depression.

Reteaching/Correctives
Have students form small groups to create "New Deal population cards," much like baseball cards, in which they evaluate the well-being of the segments of the population discussed in the section. Have them include artists in addition to the minority groups that are mentioned.

Have students complete **Reteaching Resources** Worksheet 61, in which they review information about life during the Roosevelt years.

Enrichment and Extension
Have students complete **Enrichment and Extension Resources** Primary Source Worksheet 32, in which they interpret an excerpt about black Americans written by Richard Wright.

POPULAR CULTURE 4F

One of the greatest sources of escape from the troubles of the Depression was the radio. The radio offered a cheap source of entertainment at a time when most people were on a tight budget. It also linked the nation together more closely than any medium of communication had yet done. People could now enjoy a greater diversity of radio programs than had been available in the 1920s. They listened not only to big band music and concert music, but also to news reports and political speeches. They followed comedy and drama such as *Fibber McGee and Molly*, the *March of Time*, and the *Lux Radio Theater*. Children followed the adventures of heroes such as the Lone Ranger, who served (according to the show's sponsors) "as an example of good living and clean speech."

Movies too became more elaborate, and the silent film stars of the 1920s survived only if their voices sounded good in the talking pictures. The subject matter was wide-ranging, from mystery to comedy to romantic drama. Whether the star was

Californian Shirley Temple made her movie debut at age three and became the most popular star of the 1930s. In this photograph she holds a doll replica of herself. **CULTURE** Why were movies, and musicals in particular, so popular during the 1930s? 4F

Shirley Temple, Greta Garbo, Cary Grant, James Cagney, or Gary Cooper, two themes nearly always emerged: Good triumphs over Evil, and everything works out in the end. This optimism was important to a nation that needed to overcome the Depression blues. Hollywood musicals offered an even bigger vacation from reality, as actors such as Fred Astaire and Ginger Rogers sang and danced their way through luxurious settings.

Movies were such a popular pastime that small towns of 10,000 often had a movie theater big enough to hold a quarter of their population. Many people went to the movies at least once a week and sometimes two or three times. To draw in even more customers, theaters held "bank nights" when patrons could win prizes at the door. Many theaters offered "double features"—two movies for the price of one.

Many Americans turned to comic strips to forget their troubles. *Dick Tracy*, *Lil' Abner*, and *Krazy Kat* were some of the most popular. People also followed professional sports, admiring Joe Louis in boxing and Lou Gehrig in baseball, as well as taking part in amateur sports of their own. Elmer Davis, a writer for *The New York Times*, complained that while the rest of the world was in turmoil and Europe was falling into the hands of dictators, the people of the United States were busy playing miniature golf. "Here," he wrote, "where the disaster might have been expected to have the worst repercussions, the citizens find solace . . . by knocking a little ball across a surface of crushed cottonseed hulls and through a tin pipe."

SECTION REVIEW

1. **KEY TERM** black Cabinet
2. **PEOPLE** William Hastie, John Collier, Eleanor Roosevelt, Frances Perkins
3. **COMPREHENSION** Why did blacks support the Democratic Party after 1936?
4. **COMPREHENSION** What part did Eleanor Roosevelt play in the Roosevelt administration?
5. **CRITICAL THINKING** Many Depression-era movies were set in high society. Why, do you think, was this so?

3B, 3E, 5F, 9D, 9E

5 The Legacy of the New Deal

Section Focus

Key Terms deficit spending ∎ welfare state

Main Idea The New Deal ended in 1941, but its effects can still be felt today.

Objectives As you read, look for answers to these questions:
1. Why did President Roosevelt propose few reform laws after 1937?
2. What were the long-term effects of the New Deal?

Roosevelt had a hard year in 1937. The Supreme Court battle had cost him much support in Congress, and critics were complaining that the New Deal had not ended the Depression. They pointed to the bulging federal budget deficit and to the millions of people who were still unemployed or on relief. When, they asked, would the situation return to normal? Even Roosevelt and his advisers began to rethink the New Deal. In 1937 Harry Hopkins, head of the WPA, declared that it was "reasonable to expect a probable minimum of 4 million to 5 million unemployed even in future 'prosperity' periods."

THE NEW DEAL ENDS 3B

In June 1937 Roosevelt, concerned about the budget deficit, decided to cut spending sharply. He persuaded Congress to slash funding for public works and to eliminate thousands of workers from the public payroll. The budget was balanced for the first time since the Crash, but the result was a severe recession. The stock market fell sharply, and 10 million Americans were out of work by early 1938. To defeat the recession, FDR was forced to renew his "lend and spend" policies. He quickly put more money into government programs like the WPA and the CCC.

In earlier years Roosevelt had pushed law after law through Congress, thanks to his own popularity and political momentum. Now the times had changed. Alienated by the Supreme Court battle and concerned about big deficits, Republicans and southern Democrats firmly opposed any expansion of the New Deal. Roosevelt managed to get only one major reform bill through Congress after 1937. This was the Fair Labor Standards Act, which passed in June 1938. It set the first federal guidelines for minimum wages and maximum hours.

In the late 1930s, domestic affairs were increasingly overshadowed by foreign policy issues, as events in Europe made headlines. Though the rise of nazism in Germany alarmed Americans, most

---

GRAPH SKILLS 3E

This graph illustrates the partial success of New Deal programs in dealing with high levels of unemployment during the Great Depression. About how many fewer Americans were unemployed in 1940 than in 1933? **CRITICAL THINKING** What caused the increase in unemployment in 1938?

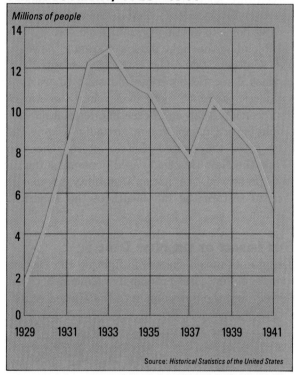

UNEMPLOYMENT, 1929–1941

Millions of people

Source: *Historical Statistics of the United States*

SUPPORTING THE SECTION

Reinforcement Workbook: Worksheet 62
Reteaching Resources: Worksheet 62
Teaching Transparencies: Transparency 62

Graph Skills Answers
About five million. The administration's decision to balance the budget forced cuts in funding for public works projects that caused thousands of workers on the public payroll to lose their jobs.

SECTION 5

The Legacy of the New Deal
(pages 381–383)

Section Objective
∎ describe the long-term effects of the New Deal

Introducing the Section

Connecting with Past Learnings
How was the Second New Deal different from programs initiated during FDR's first years in office? (Earlier legislation was aimed at solving critical problems of high unemployment and financial collapse. The Second New Deal was an attempt to reform society by establishing more permanent solutions to unemployment, labor issues, and care of the elderly.)

Key Terms
Have students define the key terms in their own words and note the connection between them. **LEP**

Focus
In the middle of the board, list the seven changes to American society and government caused by the New Deal. Then, on one side of the list, have volunteers come to the board and write examples of New Deal programs or 1930s trends which illustrate these changes. On the other side of your list, have volunteers enter examples of programs and trends that exist today which illustrate the legacy of the New Deal.
Do you think that the legacy of the New Deal is a positive or negative one?

After students have read the section you may wish to consider the following activities:

Economics
Discuss FDR's decision to slash spending in 1937, creating a chart on how cuts led to a rise in unemployment and a fall in the stock market. (Government workers lost their jobs; as confidence in the economy fell, people sold their stocks.)

Although FDR cut spending, the 1938 deficit was $1 billion. Have students suggest why. (FDR based his budget on taxes collected from the number of people working in 1937. The higher unemployment rate meant lower tax revenue.)

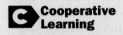

Cooperative Learning

Have students work in groups, and assign each group to be responsible for one of the major effects of the New Deal discussed in the section. Have the members of the group decide whether the effect has been good or bad for the country. Then have them create a list of reasons. **LEP**

Addressing Individual Needs

Guided/ Independent Practice
Instruct students to complete **Reinforcement Workbook** Worksheet 62, which helps them interpret a political cartoon about the New Deal.

Reteaching/Correctives
With the class, read and discuss the stated main idea of the section, under the Section Focus on page 381. Then have students find ten details in the section that support this main idea. On a piece of paper, have students write the section's main idea, and beneath it, list the ten details that they found.

One effect of New Deal programs was increased government paperwork. Here, under the watchful eye of New York City's postmaster, postal workers send out the first social security forms in 1936. POLITICS How did the New Deal increase government involvement in the lives of American citizens? 5F

people opposed American involvement in European affairs. But by the end of 1941, as you will read in the next chapter, the United States was forced into another world war. At that moment, the nation's top priority shifted from fighting poverty at home to fighting tyranny overseas.

In joining the fight against tyranny, however, the United States also struck a major blow against domestic poverty. The shift to wartime production pumped more money into the American economy than any peacetime legislation ever would have. Unemployment virtually disappeared soon after the United States entered the war. While the New Deal had eased personal suffering and preserved the nation's stability, it took a war to restore the full health of the American economy.

THE IMPACT OF THE NEW DEAL 9E
Despite its mixed success in fighting the Depression, the New Deal profoundly changed both the society and the government of the United States. These changes include:

(1) *Extension of the power of the federal government.* New Deal agencies came to the rescue of banking, industry, and agriculture in the early

years of the Depression. While government involvement in private business existed long before Roosevelt, the extent of that involvement increased greatly during the New Deal.

Such involvement was not merely extensive; it was permanent. Five decades after the Depression ended, the government continues to play an important role in the lives of Americans. The Federal Housing Administration still insures mortgage loans. The Agricultural Adjustment Agency still pays farm subsidies. The TVA still provides electricity. Bank deposits are still federally insured, and the Securities and Exchange Commission still watches over the stock exchange. The lasting effects of financial and banking reforms have been especially important, assuring citizens of the long-term stability of the American economy.

(2) *Extension of the power of the President.* FDR was probably the best-loved and most-hated President since Lincoln. Not only his policies but also his forceful style of leadership aroused strong emotions on both sides. Critics, pointing to the Court-packing scheme and other Roosevelt policies, sometimes accused FDR of wanting to be a dictator. Even today he remains a controversial figure.

Without question, Roosevelt believed in an active presidency and did much to broaden the President's power. Later Presidents continued the trend, helping to create what is often called an "imperial presidency." Defenders of presidential power have replied that as a large and complex nation, the United States cannot afford to be without strong executive leadership.

(3) *Deficit spending.* One of Roosevelt's most controversial tactics was deficit spending, that is, spending more money than the government raises in taxes. Roosevelt was not the first President to fail to balance the budget. He was, however, the first to consistently use deficit spending as a method of stimulating the economy. This tactic, advocated by the British economist John Maynard Keynes, is sometimes called Keynesian economics. By the time Roosevelt left office the national debt was nearly $260 billion. (However, much of this debt reflected wartime spending rather than New Deal programs.) Presidents after Roosevelt have

Photo Caption Answer
Many citizens were employed by the government in public works; government regulation was introduced into finance, farming, and business and labor relations; the government assumed responsibility for some aspects of social security.

sometimes tried to balance the budget, but deficit spending has been more typical.

(4) Federal social programs. The New Deal established the welfare state—government based on the view that the state is responsible for the economic security of its people. The Social Security Act has continued to provide aid to the elderly, the disabled, and the unemployed. Later administrations have used it as a precedent for extending aid to other groups, such as students, the handicapped, and mothers with dependent children. Like Roosevelt, however, later Presidents have favored "modified" social welfare programs that do not guarantee complete economic security. Few Social Security recipients can live entirely on their pensions. Recipients of unemployment compensation eventually have to find work. FDR's modified welfare approach was intended to help people in their time of need, not make them permanent dependents of the government.

(5) Greater concern for workers. The National Labor Relations Act of 1935 gave workers the right to join unions and to bargain with their employers. The Fair Labor Standards Act was another milestone in labor history. Later administrations built upon these two laws to provide workers with safer workplaces, rights to company pensions, and freedom from racial and sexual discrimination.

(6) Conservation gains. The New Deal made conservation a permanent part of the political agenda. New Deal programs changed the face of the country, as government workers practiced soil conservation, built dams to prevent flooding, and reclaimed the grasslands of the Great Plains. After the 1930s Americans would never wholly forget that farmlands and forests could not be used without thinking of the future.

(7) Renewal of faith in democracy. Perhaps most importantly, the New Deal carried the United States through a time when the success of democracy itself seemed to be in question. "The only bulwark of continuing liberty," Roosevelt once declared, "is a government strong enough to protect the interests of the people, and a people strong enough and well enough informed to maintain its sovereign control over its government." By reviving the faith and strength of the American people, Roosevelt ensured that the United States would be strong enough to defend democracy if the need arose. With a world war at hand and the survival of freedom itself at stake, the United States was ready to play a fateful role in the course of world history.

SECTION REVIEW

1. KEY TERMS deficit spending, welfare state

2. PEOPLE John Maynard Keynes

3. COMPREHENSION What groups opposed Roosevelt in Congress after 1937? Why?

4. COMPREHENSION List seven ways in which the New Deal affected American life.

5. CRITICAL THINKING How did the New Deal change the way in which Americans think about government?

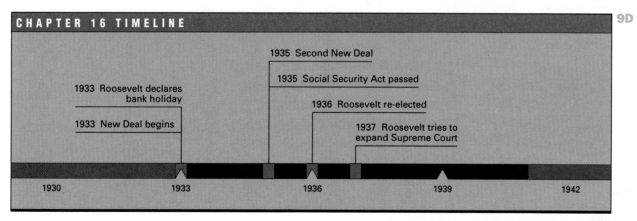

CHAPTER 16 TIMELINE

1935 Second New Deal

1935 Social Security Act passed

1933 Roosevelt declares bank holiday

1936 Roosevelt re-elected

1933 New Deal begins

1937 Roosevelt tries to expand Supreme Court

1930   1933   1936   1939   1942

9D

Have students complete **Reteaching Resources** Worksheet 62.

Enrichment/Extension
Have students research the 1939 World's Fair in either New York or San Francisco and write an essay on how the fair represented a new confidence in the future.

Assessment
You may wish to use the Section 5 Review, on this page, to see how well your students understand the main points in this lesson.

Section Review Answers

1. *deficit spending*— Government spending more money than it raises. *welfare state*—Government which takes responsibility for the economic welfare of its citizens.

2. *John Maynard Keynes*— British economist who advocated deficit spending to stimulate the economy.

3. Republicans and southern Democrats who were critical of his court-packing plan and of the huge deficits caused by New Deal spending.

4. It extended the power of the federal government and the President; introduced deficit spending as an economic tactic; established the welfare state; gave legal support to the rights of workers; made conservation a political issue; renewed people's faith in democracy.

5. Students may suggest that Americans began to accept much more government involvement and regulation, and that they looked to the government to solve social and economic problems.

Closure
Use the Chapter Review Summary for Section 5 (p. 384) to synthesize the important elements in the section. Then have students read Section 1 of Chapter 17.

Chapter 16 Review Answers

Key Terms

1. Share-Our-Wealth program
2. National Labor Relations Act
3. Second New Deal
4. Social Security Act
5. Townsend Plan
6. American Liberty League
7. welfare state

People to Identify

1. "Radio priest" who criticized FDR and called for the nationalization of banks and utilities.
2. Director of the PWA.
3. Republican presidential candidate in 1936.
4. Senator from Louisiana who proposed the Share-Our-Wealth program.
5. Roosevelt's Secretary of Labor and the first woman named to the Cabinet.

Places to Locate

1. C   3. B
2. D   4. A

Reviewing the Facts

1. It reassured people that banks were trustworthy and kept depositors from withdrawing money out of panic.

2. Relief, recovery, and reform were the three main parts of the New Deal.

3. Critics on the right felt that the New Deal undermined the American tradition of individual responsibility. Critics from the left believed that the New Deal did not go far enough.

4. The Second New Deal went further in protecting people from economic hardship and redistributing wealth. Programs such as the FHA, the WPA, and Social Security instituted

Chapter 16 REVIEW

CHAPTER 16 SUMMARY

SECTION 1: President Roosevelt came to office committed to reviving the nation's economy.

■ Roosevelt restored people's faith in the banking system—and the government—by temporarily closing all banks and allowing only those that were solvent to reopen.

■ Roosevelt's New Deal was a three-part strategy based on relief programs to ease suffering, recovery programs to rebuild the economy, and reform programs to ensure that such a crisis could never occur again.

SECTION 2: By 1934 the New Deal was being criticized from both right and left.

■ Conservatives thought the New Deal was too costly and would undermine the American traditions of individual responsibility and local control.

■ Radicals wanted FDR to go further, redistributing wealth and taking over industries.

SECTION 3: Democratic victories in the 1934 elections led Roosevelt to propose a Second New Deal in 1935.

■ New programs helped more Americans to buy houses, provided work for the unemployed, and gave aid to the elderly and disabled.

■ In 1937, after being reelected by a large margin, Roosevelt tried but failed to "pack" the Supreme Court.

SECTION 4: The Depression dominated American culture during the 1930s.

■ Hard times slowed the progress of women and minority groups toward equality.

■ Some writers and artists rejected capitalism and used their work to convey political messages.

■ Radio, movies, comic strips, and sports provided escape and encouragement to Americans.

SECTION 5: The New Deal has had lasting effects on American life.

■ The powers of the federal government and of the President were increased.

■ Greater government efforts to help needy citizens, workers, and the environment continue.

■ The New Deal helped to preserve American democracy.

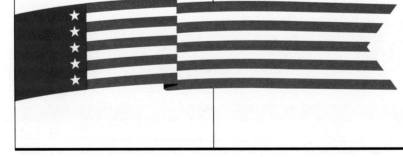

KEY TERMS ●

Use the following terms to complete the sentences below.

> **American Liberty League**
> **National Labor Relations Act**
> **Second New Deal**
> **Share-Our-Wealth program**
> **Social Security Act**
> **Townsend Plan**
> **welfare state**

1. The _____ was a radical proposal to redistribute incomes over a million dollars.
2. Another term for the Wagner Act was the _____ .
3. The _____ was a set of programs put forward by Roosevelt in 1935.
4. The _____ provided old-age insurance for working people.
5. The _____ called for the federal government to pay all older Americans $200 per month.
6. The _____ criticized Roosevelt's programs as a threat to Americans' basic freedoms.
7. A nation in which the government is responsible for the economic security of citizens is known as a _____ .

PEOPLE TO IDENTIFY ●

Identify the following people and tell why each was important.

1. Charles Coughlin
2. Harold L. Ickes
3. Alfred Landon
4. Huey Long
5. Frances Perkins

permanent changes in the U.S. economy.

5. The Supreme Court had declared some New Deal laws unconstitutional. Roosevelt tried to "pack" more supportive justices onto the Court. His proposal was rejected and he lost popularity and support.

6. The goals of women and minorities were considered secondary to the objectives of the New Deal.

7. Artists and writers developed a more political focus, while others celebrated American life. Radio shows and movies became popular pastimes offering temporary escape.

PLACES TO LOCATE ●

Match each of the letters on the map with the places that are listed below.

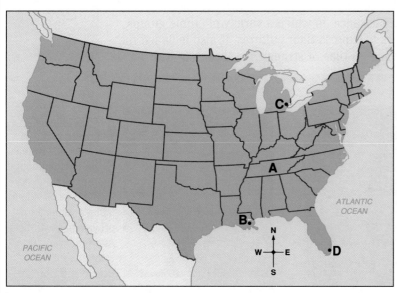

1. Detroit
2. Miami
3. New Orleans
4. Tennessee

REVIEWING THE FACTS ▲

1. What were the results of the "bank holiday" declared by Roosevelt in 1933?
2. What were the three basic parts of the New Deal?
3. What criticisms did the New Deal draw from the right? From the left?
4. In what way did the Second New Deal differ from the First? What were some of its programs?
5. Why did Roosevelt try to "pack" the Supreme Court? What were the results of this proposal?

6. How did the Great Depression affect women and minority groups?
7. Describe the effects of the Great Depression on art, on literature, and on popular culture.
8. How did the Roosevelt administration's policies change after 1937? Why did these policies change?
9. How did the New Deal permanently affect the role of the federal government?
10. How did the New Deal help to restore Americans' faith in democracy?

CRITICAL THINKING SKILLS ▲

1. **FORMING A HYPOTHESIS** How might Liberty Leaguers have defended their claim that New Deal programs were a threat to the liberties of all Americans?
2. **ANALYZING A QUOTATION** What did Roosevelt mean when he said "To dole out relief is to administer a narcotic, a subtle destroyer of the human spirit"? Do you agree or disagree? Why?
3. **IDENTIFYING SIGNIFICANCE** Why did black Americans shift their allegiance from the Republican to the Democratic Party during the 1930s? What was the significance of this shift?

WRITING ABOUT TOPICS IN AMERICAN HISTORY ■

1. **CONNECTING WITH LITERATURE** A selection from *Point of No Return* by John P. Marquand appears on pages 799–801. Read it and answer the questions. Then answer the following question: If you had received one of the letters from Charles's company advising you to sell all your stocks, what might have been your reaction?
2. **APPLYING THEMES: GEOGRAPHY** Imagine you are a staff assistant to Senator George Norris of Tennessee. He has asked you to write a memo convincing the Congress that the TVA would provide great benefits to the people of the Tennessee Valley. Write the memo, supporting your argument with factual information.

Critical Thinking Skills

1. The Liberty Leaguers would have said that the New Deal, through its social welfare and regulatory agencies, squelched individual initiative and limited free enterprise.
2. Roosevelt believed that simply handing out aid would diminish self-esteem. Students should consider the challenge of administering aid without creating a cycle of dependence.
3. Roosevelt's placement of blacks in federal positions and his programs for the poor swung the black vote to the Democratic Party, where they formed a powerful block.

Writing About Topics in American History

1. Such a letter might well lead to a sense of panic in the stockholders. If enough people were so advised, a general panic might follow.
2. Students should do research on the formation of the TVA and arguments used in support of it. Criticisms could be responded to as well.

---

8. The loss of political support that followed the Supreme Court battle and the rise of fascism in Europe caused the Roosevelt Administration to shift its focus from domestic policy issues.

9. It created social welfare and regulatory agencies that are still in existence today, permanently increasing the government's power and scope.

10. The New Deal restored America's faith in democracy by coping with an enormous crisis without curtailing democracy or civil liberties.

Chapter Review exercises are keyed for student abilities:
● = Basic
▲ = Average
■ = Average/Advanced

Introducing the Feature

Discuss with students the reasons why disillusioned Americans turned to the diversions of "Roaring Twenties" after World War I. **What were some of the consumer goods and types of mass entertainment that captured the imagination of the American people?** (Radios, phonographs, automobiles, magazines, talking movies, jazz.)

Have students suggest reasons why Americans of diverse backgrounds looked to Franklin D. Roosevelt to deliver their nation from the ravages of the Depression. (Students should consider Roosevelt's personal charm and energy, his courage in confronting physical disability, and the confidence with which he presented his New Deal programs.) Discuss Eleanor Roosevelt's role in reaching out to women, minorities, and the poor.

Teaching Multiculturalism

History

Students may be interested to know that Jim Thorpe was forced to give up his Olympic medals in 1913 because officials ruled that he had lost his amateur status by having earlier played semiprofessional baseball. Thorpe subsequently played professional baseball with the New York Giants and the Boston Braves.

Have students work in groups to prepare a series of posters of Thorpe competing in each of the many sports in which he excelled.

Civic Values

Have students make a list of the positive forces in Helen Keller's life that helped her become an example to other physically challenged people, and a leader in the effort to give the disabled educational opportunities. (Students

---

UNIT 5: American Mosaic

★ *A Multicultural Perspective* ★

The period between the world wars included the Jazz Age and the Harlem Renaissance, in which a variety of ethnic groups found new ways to express their cultures. It also included the Great Depression—a time of struggle for sheer survival.

It seems unbelievable that one person could be a major league baseball player, an Olympic track and field champion, and in the pro football Hall of Fame. Such a person would have a good claim to the title of "World's Greatest Athlete." In fact, many sports fans consider **Jim Thorpe** (right) to have been just that. Thorpe was born in Oklahoma. His great-grandfather, Black Hawk, was a famous Sauk Indian chief. At his small technical high school for Indians, Thorpe led the football team to national fame. In the 1912 Olympic games, he became the first athlete to win the pentathlon and decathlon events. Thorpe went on to help establish pro football as a popular sport and became president of the American Professional Football Association (now the NFL) in 1920.

A serious illness when she was two years old left **Helen Keller** (left) without sight or hearing. Fortunately, her Alabama family was able to provide her with help. Anne Sullivan, her tutor, taught Keller Braille and sign language. The two struggled long and hard so that Keller could communicate with other people. Keller eventually learned to speak and attended Radcliffe College, where she graduated with honors in 1904. She devoted the rest of her life to improving conditions for blind people around the world. Her many books helped the public learn what disabled people can achieve with determination and understanding. Her life was the subject of the play *The Miracle Worker,* which later became a successful film.

Eleanora Fagan grew up in Baltimore, her early years scarred by poverty and child abuse. As **Billie Holiday** (right), she became one of the greatest vocalists in American music. Holiday moved to New York City and began singing at Harlem jazz clubs. Her voice lacked the range of other great singers, but the sweet and sad feeling "Lady Day" put into the music more than made up for it. Throughout her career, Holiday faced racism and struggled with drug addiction. Among her most haunting recordings is "Strange Fruit" (1939)—a protest song against the lynching of black southerners. Her autobiography, *Lady Sings the Blues,* appeared in 1956.

Filipinos make up one of the largest groups of Asian Americans. Because the Philippines was a colony of the United States, Filipinos were allowed to immigrate freely to the United States from 1898 until 1934. Then, prejudice toward Asians and economic hardships of the Great Depression prompted Congress to severely restrict immigration.

---

should consider such forces as her family's support; the skill and devotion of her tutor, Anne Sullivan; the development of the communication methods of Braille and sign language; the opportunity for higher education offered by Radcliffe College; and especially Keller's own intelligence and determination.)

Connecting with Music

Have students imagine that they are music reviewers for a New York City newspaper assigned to cover a Billie Holiday concert. Reviewers should describe her performance and discuss how Holiday's music was affected by the experience of rural and urban blacks in the early decades of the twentieth century, as well as by her own personal history.

Harry Houdini (right) was the stage name of Erich Weiss, son of a Hungarian rabbi, and the greatest escape artist of all time. Audiences around the world jammed theatres to see him get out of handcuffs and straitjackets while submerged in a tank of water. Houdini became the most popular and highest paid performer of the 1920s, as well as a symbol of individual power and determination to be free. Although magicians know how several of his feats were accomplished, some of his famous tricks remain mysteries to this day.

"Which is the best airplane engine?" **Igor Sikorsky** (right) asked a pilot in 1909. "They are all bad," the aviator replied. Sikorsky, a Russian, put his engineering skills and imagination to work and by 1911 had created the world's fastest plane. Sikorsky grew rich selling his planes to the czar in World War I. He fled Russia during the 1917 Revolution and came to the United States. Here he became a pioneer of the aircraft industry, designing the world's largest planes and inventing the helicopter.

The first black woman to graduate from Yale Law School, Jane M. Bolin, was also the first black woman admitted to the Bar Association of New York City. In 1939 Bolin became the first black woman judge in the United States.

A "Renaissance Man" is someone who is accomplished in many different fields. It is fitting, therefore, that **James Weldon Johnson** (right) is known as a leader of the Harlem Renaissance. After graduating from Atlanta University, Johnson headed a school for African Americans in his hometown of Jacksonville, Florida. He later became the first black lawyer to practice in Florida. After serving as a diplomat in Latin America, Johnson worked as an editor, author, and literature professor. He is best known for his book of poetry, *God's Trombones,* which combined Biblical sermons with black folklore. Johnson also helped found the NAACP.

> James Weldon Johnson
> 22
> Lift ev-'ry voice and sing
> **Black Heritage USA**

When New Mexico became a state in 1912, about half its citizens were Spanish-speaking. Among them was **Octaviano Larrazolo** (left), a long-time community leader. Larrazolo helped draft the state's new constitution, seeing to it that the rights of Spanish-speaking New Mexicans were protected. (For example, the constitution recognized both Spanish and English as the official languages of the state.) Larrazolo was elected governor of New Mexico in 1918 and United States senator in 1928.

History
Tell students that although he was a master of illusion, Harry Houdini took pains to inform the public that there were rational explanations for his feats of magic. Houdini was eager to discredit the "spiritualists" who claimed that their magic feats were attributable to supernatural powers.

Have students draw an advertising poster for a performance by Houdini.

Science and Technology
Remind students that many immigrants came to America in the early decades of the twentieth century brimming with ideas and skills to contribute to the dynamic young nation. *Why did Igor Sikorsky immigrate to the United States?* (He was fleeing the Russian Revolution of 1917.) *What contributions did Sikorsky make to the American aviation industry?* (He developed the world's fastest and largest planes, and invented the helicopter.)

History
Remind students of the period described by the term *Renaissance.* (The revival of classical art, literature, and learning that originated in Italy in the 1300s and later spread throughout Europe.) Explain that the term *Renaissance man* derives from the talented individuals of that period who were knowledgable in many different areas.

Why can James Weldon Johnson be considered a true "Renaissance Man"? (He was a leader of the Harlem Renaissance; he headed a school for African Americans in Florida; he became the first black to practice law in Florida; he was a diplomat to Latin America; he was an editor, author, poet, and professor of literature; and he was a founder of the NAACP.)

Historians' Corner

Vocabulary Preview

Be sure students understand the following terms:
repudiate—Reject.
watershed—Critical dividing line. *palliate*—Make less severe.

Analyzing Historical Issues

Carl N. Degler believes that the New Deal made fundamental changes in the role of government in the United States. Since FDR, Degler says, the government has become the protector of human welfare. Gabriel Kolko argues that the New Deal did not, in fact, change the basic system or even do much to alleviate suffering. Kolko, a historian of the New Left, believes that the New Deal was not revolutionary but conservative.

How would each of these historians view the impact of the Works Progress Administration?

Critical Thinking Answers

1. Gabriel Kolko.

2. To Degler, the best proof of the lasting importance of the New Deal is that no party has claimed that the government does not have a role in providing for social well-being.

3. Students who agree with Degler might point to the near-sacred status of Social Security. Those supporting Kolko might cite the many cuts in social service programs in recent years.

HISTORIANS' CORNER

How Effective Was the New Deal?

The Great Depression of the 1930s was the most serious economic crisis the United States has ever faced. President Franklin D. Roosevelt took unprecedented steps to counteract the crisis. The federal government's New Deal programs drastically changed American life—or did they? As these two excerpts show, historians disagree about the long-term effects of New Deal programs.

Carl N. Degler

Few areas of American life were beyond the touch of . . . the New Deal. . . . To achieve that minimum standard of well-being which the Depression had taught the American people to expect of their government, nothing was out of bounds.

But it is not the variety of change which stamps the New Deal as the creator of a new America; its significance lies in the permanence of its program. . . . The New Deal Revolution has become so much a part of the American Way that no political party which aspires to high office dares . . . repudiate it. . . .

The conclusion seems inescapable that . . . the New Deal . . . was a revolutionary response to a revolutionary situation. In its long history America has passed through two revolutions since . . . 1776, but only the last two, the Civil War and the Depression, were of such force as to change the direction of the relatively smooth flow of its progress. . . .

The searing ordeal of the Great Depression purged the American people of their belief in the limited powers of the federal government and convinced them of the necessity of the guarantor state. . . . And as the Civil War constituted a watershed in American thought, so the Depression and its New Deal marked the crossing of a divide from which, it would seem, there could be no turning back.

From Carl N. Degler, *Out of Our Past*, pp. 415-416. Copyright © 1959, 1970 by Carl N. Degler. Reprinted by permission of Harper & Row, Publishers, Inc.

Gabriel Kolko

The magnitude of the Depression defies description of the human suffering and consequences, just as it defied the New Deal's efforts to find means to terminate it. . . . In the simplest terms . . . the government and the men it listened to had answers only to their immediate concerns of profitability and competition . . . and scarcely tried to do more than palliate the human consequences of the collapse. . . .

Not for a moment did the New Deal endanger the existing distribution of income and wealth, and hence it could not cope successfully with the collapse of American Capitalism.

The enlarged system of welfare and social security institutions established during the 1930s also reflected a persistent conservatism prevalent in the Executive and Congress. The Social Security Act . . . played no economic role at all during this decade. . . . Its unemployment insurance measures were no less conservative, and its provisions reflected the ideas of a coalition of politicians, moderate social reformers, and businessmen.

From Gabriel Kolko, *Main Currents in Modern American History*. Copyright © 1976 by Gabriel Kolko. Reprinted by permission of Gabriel Kolko.

Critical Thinking

1. Which historian's point of view do you believe is best expressed by the following statement? "The New Deal failed to make fundamental changes in the American economy."

2. What does Degler consider to be the best proof of the New Deal's lasting importance?

3. Which historian's argument do you believe is more valid? Explain your answer.

Carl N. Degler (1921–) taught at Stanford University and won the Bancroft and Pulitzer prizes in 1972 for his work in social history.

Gabriel Kolko (1932–) is a professor of history at York University, Ontario, Canada, who specializes in political history and foreign policy studies.

UNIT SIX

World Leadership

CHAPTERS IN THIS UNIT

17 Between the Wars (1920–1941)
18 The World at War (1941–1945)

THEMES IN AMERICAN HISTORY

 Global Interactions Despite the United States' wariness of foreign commitments, the rise of extremism in Europe and Japan ultimately brought the United States into World War II.

 Geography American forces in World War II fought on different continents and under a variety of conditions.

 Pluralistic Society Though the coming of war brought discrimination against Japanese Americans, other minority groups and women enjoyed new job opportunities during wartime.

Economic Development Mobilization for World War II brought the American economy out of depression and into a new period of high growth.

UNIT 6   WORLD LEADERSHIP   **389**

Unit Six

World Leadership
(pp. 389–442)

This unit tracks United States foreign policy from isolationism to the nation's emergence as a superpower after World War II. It begins with a discussion of American disarmament initiatives in the 1920s, notes the movement away from direct intervention in Latin American affairs in the 1930s, and explains how the growth of fascism and militarism overseas brought the world closer to war. Japanese and German expansionism and the outbreak of World War II are described, as well as American attempts to remain at peace and yet prepare for war.

The unit discusses the Japanese attack on Pearl Harbor and United States entry into the war and then details the initial defeats and later military victories in Europe and Japan, as well as the war's impact on the economy, ethnic minorities, and women. It describes the development of atomic weapons and the decision to drop them on Japan, noting the enormous costs of the war and the tense and fragile peace that emerged after the Axis was defeated.

389

Chapter 17 ■ Between the Wars

	SECTION OBJECTIVES	SECTION RESOURCES
Section 1 **Searching for** **Peace**	■ evaluate the influence of isolationism on American foreign policy	● **Reteaching Resources:** Worksheet 63 ▲ **Reinforcement Workbook:** Worksheet 63 ▲ **Teaching Transparencies:** Transparency 63
Section 2 **Changing** **Relations with** **Latin America**	■ describe changes in U.S. policy toward Latin America in the 1930s	● **Reteaching Resources:** Worksheet 64 ▲ **Reinforcement Workbook:** Worksheet 64 ▲ **Teaching Transparencies:** Transparency 64
Section 3 **The Rise** **of Dictators**	■ explain how fascism took hold in Italy, Germany, and Japan	● **Reteaching Resources:** Worksheet 65 ▲ **Reinforcement Workbook:** Worksheet 65 ■ **Enrichment and Extension Resources:** Primary Source Worksheet 33 ▲ **Teaching Transparencies:** Transparency 65
Section 4 **From Neutrality** **to War**	■ describe how World War II began and how the United States entered the war	● **Reteaching Resources:** Worksheet 66 ▲ **Reinforcement Workbook:** Worksheet 66 ■ **Enrichment and Extension Resources:** Primary Source Worksheet 34 ▲ **Teaching Transparencies:** Transparency 66

The list below shows Essential Elements relevant to this chapter. (The complete list of Essential Elements appears in the introductory pages of this Teacher's Edition.)

Section 1: 1B, 3B
Section 2: 1A, 1B
Section 3: 1B, 3D, 4D, 7D, 7I, 7J, 9A, 9E
Section 4: 1A, 1B, 5E, 9A,9B, 9D, 9F

Section Resources are keyed for
student abilities:
  ● = Basic
  ▲ = Average
  ■ = Average/Advanced

CHAPTER RESOURCES

Geography Resources: Worksheets 33, 34
Tests: Chapter 17 Test

Chapter Project: Global Interations

Have students do research and write a biography on one of the world leaders discussed in the chapter: Adolf Hitler, Joseph Stalin, Anastasio Somoza, Benito Mussolini, Hideki Tojo, or Winston Churchill. Encourage students to describe personal qualities that helped each man rise to power and to discuss how each leader met the needs of his country.

Homework Options

Each section contains activities labeled "Addressing Individual Needs." You may wish to choose from among these activities when assigning homework.

Provisions for Limited English Proficiency (LEP)
Several suggested activities may be particularly helpful for teachers of students with limited English proficiency. These activities have been marked throughout the Teacher's Annotated Edition with the symbol **LEP** .

BIBLIOGRAPHY AND AUDIOVISUAL AIDS

Teacher Bibliography

Abel, Theodore. *Why Hitler Came to Power.* Harvard University Press, 1986.

Ferrell, Robert H. *American Diplomacy in the Great Depression: Hoover-Stimson Foreign Policy, 1929–1933.* Shoe String, 1969.

Johnson, Walter. *The Battle Against Isolation.* Da Capo, 1973.

Shirer, William. *The Rise and Fall of the Third Reich.* Touchstone Books, 1981.

Student Bibliography

Elson, Robert T. *Prelude to War.* Time-Life Books, 1977.

Rauch, Basil. *Roosevelt: From Munich to Pearl Harbor.* Da Capo, 1975.

Smith, Bradley F. *Adolf Hitler: His Family, Childhood and Youth.* Hoover Institution Press, 1967.

Literature

Hemingway, Ernest. *For Whom the Bell Tolls.* Scribner, 1940. An idealistic American goes to Spain to fight the fascists.

Wouk, Herman. *The Winds of War.* Little, Brown, 1971. An American naval family's experiences in the years before U.S. entry into World War II.

Films and Videotapes*

The Darkest Hour, 1939–1941. 25 min. AIMS. Chronicles events leading to World War II through the bombing of Pearl Harbor.

The Inevitable War, 1939–1940. 13 min. COR/MTI. Chronicles the early years of World War II.

Roosevelt: Manipulator-in-Chief. 24 min. LCA. Focuses on Roosevelt as he assumed his third term in office, with Europe at war.

Computer Software*

America's Presidents Series: World Wars, Prosperity and Depression—Presidents During and Between Two World Wars. (Apple with 48K; IBM with 64K) QUEUE. Each President is covered in a separate menu option, and prominent Presidents have multiple sections on different phases on their lives and administrations. Presidents Wilson–Truman, 1913–1953

---

*For a complete guide to audiovisual sources, see the introduction to this book (page Txx).

Chapter 17 traces the development of Fascist governments in Italy, Germany, and Japan and describes the events leading to the start of World War II and America's entry into the war.

Themes in American History

- Global interactions
- Economic development
- Geography

Chapter Objectives

After students complete this chapter, they will be able to:

1. Evaluate the influence of isolationism on American foreign policy.

2. Describe changes in U.S. policy toward Latin America in the 1930s.

3. Explain how fascism took hold in Italy, Germany, and Japan.

4. Describe how World War II began and how the United States entered the war.

Chapter Opener Art
Oil over photograph of Secretary of the Navy Claude Swanson, FDR, former Secretary of the Navy Josephus Daniels, 1934.

In the years after World War I, Americans watched anxiously as events abroad pushed the world toward another global conflict. Here President Franklin Roosevelt (center) inspects a navy cruiser.

CHAPTER SUPPORT MATERIAL	
Reinforcement Workbook: Worksheets 63–66	
Reteaching Resources: Worksheets 63–66	
Enrichment and Extension Resources: Primary Source Worksheets 33, 34	
Geography Resources: Worksheets 33, 34	
Teaching Transparencies: Transparencies 63–66	
Tests: Chapter 17 Test	

SECTION 1

Searching for Peace
(pp. 391–393)

Section Objective
- evaluate the influence of isolationism on American foreign policy

Introducing the Section

Connecting with Past Learnings
At the end of World War I, how did the United States show its desire to distance itself from European affairs? (Refused to ratify Treaty of Versailles or join the League of Nations.)

Key Terms
List the key terms on the board. Have students find the terms in their texts and come to an agreement on a definition for each term. **LEP**

Focus
Ask students to list actions taken by the United States in the 1920s to prevent future overseas involvement. Have them explain their answers. (Ended the draft; called the Washington Conference to prevent an arms race; signed the Five-Power and Four-Power treaties to prevent hostile actions; signed the Nine-Power Treaty to keep China independent and open to foreign trade; signed the Kellogg-Briand Pact renouncing war; implemented the Dawes Plan to help the European economy.)

Why were Americans worried about getting involved in future European conflicts? (Americans felt that Europe was unstable, and were disillusioned by the results of the war.)

1B, 3B

1 Searching for Peace

★ Section Focus

Key Terms isolationism ■ Washington Conference ■ Kellogg-Briand Pact ■ debtor nation ■ creditor nation ■ Dawes Plan

Main Idea During the 1920s and 1930s, Americans were determined not to be drawn into another foreign war. To this end, they worked for international agreements on war prevention and arms control.

Objectives As you read, look for answers to these questions:
1. What were American foreign policy goals in the years after World War I?
2. What steps did the United States take to reduce the risks of another war?

On Armistice Day, November 11, 1921, the Tomb of the Unknown Soldier was dedicated at Arlington National Cemetery near Washington, D.C. A crowd of 100,000 persons gathered to hear President Harding deliver the main address. In honoring the unknown soldier, Harding reflected Americans' yearning for a peaceful world:

> We know not whence he came, but only that his death marks him with the everlasting glory of an American dying for his country. The loftiest tribute we can bestow today . . . is commitment of this Republic to an advancement never made before . . . to put mankind on a little higher plane . . . with war's distressing and depressing tragedies barred from the stage of righteous civilizations.

Harding, who had promised "normalcy" at home, was making a plea for "normalcy" abroad as well. The United States had no intention of repeating the experience of World War I.

A FREE HAND IN FOREIGN AFFAIRS 1B

The desire to remain free from European conflicts had long been a central part of American foreign policy. In his Farewell Address in 1796, George Washington warned against "foreign entanglements." He declared that "the great rule of conduct for us in regard to foreign nations is, in extending our commercial relations, to have with them [European nations] as little political connection as possible." In his 1921 Inaugural Address, Harding echoed Washington's words. "We do not mean to be entangled," Harding stated.

> "**W**e do not mean to be entangled."
> —*Warren Harding*

The policy of avoiding entanglements came to be known as isolationism. Despite its name, isolationism did not attempt to isolate the United States from other nations. Rather, the goal was for States from other nations. Rather, the goal was for

SUPPORTING THE SECTION

Reinforcement Workbook: Worksheet 63
Reteaching Resources: Worksheet 63
Teaching Transparencies: Transparency 63

Developing the Lesson

After students have read the section, you may want to consider the following activities:

Economics

Ask students to describe the balance of trade between the United States and Europe after World War I. (The U.S. economy grew stronger as European nations borrowed dollars to rebuild.) Have students explain how the Dawes Plan helped in the economic recovery of Europe. (It encouraged American banks to lend money to Germany so that the Germans could rebuild their economy and pay reparations.)

Cooperative Learning

Divide the class into small groups. Have each group create a cartoon interpretation of United States foreign policy during the 1920s. Have them refer to details from the text to use in their cartoons. **LEP**

Addressing Individual Needs

Guided/ Independent Practice

Have students complete **Reinforcement Workbook** Worksheet 63, which asks them to analyze a response to the Kellogg-Briand Pact.

Reteaching/Correctives

Have students form small discussion groups and explain what the United States' main objective was following World War I. Then have them state the various ways in which the United States tried to meet this objective. Have a group member take notes, and make these notes available to the group.

Instruct students to complete **Reteaching Resources** Worksheet 63, which guides them in finding the main ideas of the section.

392

the United States to keep a free hand in foreign affairs. In 1919, fear of becoming trapped in future European conflicts had helped kill the Versailles Treaty in the Senate. That fear continued in the 1920s. Troubled by Europe's continuing problems—communism in Russia, unrest in Germany—Americans wondered whether their great sacrifices in World War I had been worthwhile. They had little enthusiasm to become more deeply involved in Europe.

Support for isolationism killed proposals to continue the military draft after World War I. Nor was there much support for building up the armed forces in peacetime. The American army remained smaller than that of most European nations. Isolationists argued that America should devote its energies instead to economic growth.

AMERICAN PEACE INITIATIVES 1B

American leaders believed that the United States' economic growth in the postwar era depended on worldwide stability. To achieve stability, the United States took part in several international peace conferences in the 1920s.

In 1921, President Harding invited delegates from Europe and Japan to meet in Washington, D.C. At the time of the Washington Conference, the United States was on the verge of a naval arms race with Japan and Great Britain. No one wanted an arms race. Everyone recalled that similar competition had helped trigger World War I.

At the start of the conference, Secretary of State Charles Evans Hughes proposed that no

BIOGRAPHY

CHARLES EVANS HUGHES (1862–1948) achieved an illustrious career of government service. Defeated in the 1916 presidential race by Woodrow Wilson, Hughes later served as Secretary of State under Harding and organized the Washington Conference in 1921. As Chief Justice of the United States during the 1930s, Hughes fought FDR's plan to pack the court but approved other New Deal measures.

new battleships be built for ten years. Hughes also called for limits on total naval tonnage. This plan required that many existing ships be scrapped. One observer said that Hughes wanted to sink "in 35 minutes more ships than all the admirals of the world have sunk in a cycle of centuries."

Negotiations led to the Five-Power Treaty, named for the five great sea powers. Signed in 1922, it provided for a ten-year ban on the building of large warships. The delegates also agreed to a fixed ratio of naval strength. Under the treaty, Japan could only have three-fifths as many large warships as the United States and Britain; France and Italy could only have one-third as many.

In the Four-Power Treaty, signed that same year, Japan, Great Britain, France, and the United States agreed not to attack each other's possessions in the Pacific. Another agreement, the Nine-Power Treaty, was also reached. In it, all the conference delegates agreed to respect China's independence. The doctrine of the Open Door (Chapter 11) was thus recognized.

The Washington Conference was the first successful disarmament conference in American history. The treaties it produced limited American naval power to the Atlantic Ocean, but preserved stability in East Asia and the Pacific—at least for a time.

The United States signed an even bolder peace plan when Calvin Coolidge was President. In 1927, French diplomat Aristide Briand (bree–AHN) proposed that France and the United States agree never go to war with each other. The American Secretary of State, Frank B. Kellogg, feared that such an agreement might be viewed as an alliance. He suggested instead that *all* nations be invited to sign a peace treaty.

In 1928, fifteen nations signed the Kellogg-Briand Pact. (In time, more than 60 nations signed.) In signing, they pledged to "renounce [war] as an instrument of national policy." Most Americans, imagining a world without war, cheered the Kellogg-Briand Pact. However, critics pointed out that the treaty said nothing about enforcement. Nor did it rule out wars for self-defense. One country could attack another and simply claim to be acting in self-defense. These

Biography
Ask students to research Charles Evans Hughes further and then write a resume for him.

Background At the time of the Washington Conference, Japan was spending almost one third of its budget on naval construction. A disarmament agreement was to its advantage, since that money could then be spent elsewhere.

This cartoon shows the reaction of some members of Congress to Secretary of State Frank B. Kellogg's peace treaty, known as the Kellogg-Briand Pact. **POLITICS** Judging from the cartoon, describe the reaction from Capitol Hill. What were some of the treaty's flaws? **1B**

loopholes caused one senator to claim that the pact was not even "worth a postage stamp."

WAR DEBTS AND REPARATIONS 3B

Peace conferences were one legacy of World War I. American economic power was another. Before the war, the United States was a debtor nation—one that owes money to other nations. By war's end it had become a creditor nation—one to which money is owed. By 1919, as a result of wartime borrowing, European nations owed the United States more than $10 billion. The United States became known as the "banker to the world."

Britain and France owed the most. These nations hoped to pay off their loans by collecting reparations from Germany. But Germany was bankrupt and could not pay the reparations. Without money from Germany, Britain and France could not pay the United States.

Many Europeans called on the United States to cancel some or all of the debt. After all, they argued, the United States had entered the war late. Its losses had been light, and no battles had been fought on its soil. It could afford to be charitable.

American leaders, however, refused to forgive the debt. Why should the United States cancel the debt, they asked, when Britain and France still demanded payments from Germany? Instead, American bankers devised several plans in the 1920s to improve the German economy and enable it to pay reparations. In 1924 Coolidge adopted a plan suggested by Chicago banker Charles B. Dawes. The Dawes Plan eased the debt burden on Germany by allowing Germany to stretch out its payments over a longer period of time. It also called on American banks to lend Germany money to rebuild its economy. The Dawes Plan gave a temporary boost to European economic recovery. However, the plan was derailed after 1929, when an economic crisis struck the United States and Europe.

SECTION REVIEW

1. KEY TERMS isolationism, Washington Conference, Kellogg-Briand Pact, debtor nation, creditor nation, Dawes Plan

2. COMPREHENSION What factors encouraged the growth of isolationism in the postwar era?

3. COMPREHENSION What were the results of the Washington Conference?

4. COMPREHENSION What criticism was raised against the Kellogg-Briand Pact?

5. CRITICAL THINKING Why might isolationists support government involvement in international peace and disarmament efforts?

CHAPTER 17 BETWEEN THE WARS, 1920–1941 **393**

Photo Caption Answers
Hostile. It was unenforceable and contained a large loophole allowing wars for self-defense.

2 Changing Relations with Latin America

★ Section Focus

Key Term Good Neighbor Policy

Main Idea During the 1930s the United States sought to use political influence rather than military force to protect its interests in Latin America.

Objectives As you read, look for answers to these questions:
1. Why did the United States look for alternatives to direct intervention in Latin America?
2. How did the United States retain influence in the region?

Section Objective

■ describe changes in U.S. policy toward Latin America in the 1930s

Introducing the Section

Connecting with Past Learnings
Have the class recall U.S. relations with Latin America following the Spanish-American War. (The "big stick" policy justified U.S. occupation of some countries; the U.S. had economic interests in Latin America.)

Key Term
Have the students find the key term in the text and discuss the meaning of the term and agree upon a definition. **LEP**

Focus

Have the class create a "Before and After" chart of the Good Neighbor Policy, listing actions of the United States toward Latin America in the 1910s and 1920s on one side of the board, and U.S. action in the 1930s on the other.
How did the Good Neighbor Policy affect United States relations with Latin America?
(Latin American nations had more control over their own affairs.)

Developing the Lesson

After students have read the section, you may want to consider the following activities:

Economics
What forms of economic aid did the Good Neighbor Policy make available? (Reduced tariff rates; billions of dollars lent to governments.) *How can economic aid lead to political stability?* (People with a higher standard of living are less likely to change governments.)

394

In 1915 United States marines landed on the Caribbean island of Haiti. Their mission was to protect American property, reorganize the Haitian government, and force it to pay its bills. One of the Americans involved was the jaunty young Assistant Secretary of the Navy. He is said to have boasted later, "I wrote the constitution of Haiti, and if I say so myself, it's a darned good one." His name was Franklin D. Roosevelt. Nineteen years later, as President, he ordered the marines withdrawn from Haiti. United States policy toward Latin America had entered a new phase.

PROBLEMS WITH INTERVENTION 1A
Actually, the new American policy toward Latin America did not begin with Roosevelt. The shift away from intervention had been going on since the end of World War I, for two reasons. First, no European nation dared challenge American authority in the Western Hemisphere. The United States thus had little need to intervene in Latin American countries to keep out meddling Europeans.

Second, intervention in Latin America had created several problems for the United States. It was expensive—too expensive, said many in Congress. Later, as the nation's economy slid downhill during the Great Depression, more and more people felt that the United States could no longer afford to keep troops stationed overseas. Furthermore, many people in the United States and elsewhere opposed intervention on moral grounds. What right had the United States to rule other peoples? they asked. Latin Americans in particular took a very dim view of "Yankee imperialism."

Still, the United States had no intention of sur-

rendering its influence in Latin America. After all, Secretary of State Henry Stimson declared in 1931, the region was "the one spot external to our shores which nature has decreed to be most vital to our national safety, not to mention our prosperity." The American goal was to retain influence in the region without the use of troops. The case of American involvement in Nicaragua shows how the United States tried to solve that problem.

NICARAGUA: A CASE STUDY 1A
Direct American involvement in Nicaragua began in 1909. In that year President Taft supported a rebellion against Nicaragua's ruler, who was unfriendly to United States business interests. With American backing he was driven from office, and Adolfo Díaz became Nicaragua's new president in 1911. Díaz was a strong supporter of American investment.

When a revolt threatened his government in 1912, Díaz asked the United States for help. Taft sent in 2,600 troops. After defeating the rebels, marines remained in Nicaragua for the next 21 years.

Many Nicaraguans hated the marine presence. Beginning in 1927, a Nicaraguan named Augusto Sandino led a guerrilla war against American forces. For five years, he and his followers evaded the marines and Nicaraguan forces. Peasants in the countryside fed and protected Sandino's troops.

By the early 1930s, President Hoover had grown disillusioned with the occupation. Shortly before leaving office in 1933, he withdrew the American troops. However, they left behind an American-trained Nicaraguan National Guard to take their

394 UNIT 6 WORLD LEADERSHIP

SUPPORTING THE SECTION

Reinforcement Workbook: Worksheet 64
Reteaching Resources: Worksheet 64
Teaching Transparencies: Transparency 64

place. Anastasio Somoza was the National Guard's first commander. American officials liked Somoza, in part because he had attended school in the United States and spoke fluent English.

The Nicaraguan National Guard was supposed to stay out of the country's politics. However, after the marines left, Somoza seized power and ordered Sandino killed. Somoza and his sons became corrupt and brutal—but pro-American—dictators. The Somoza family ruled Nicaragua until 1979. In that year leftist revolutionaries overthrew the dictatorship. They called themselves Sandinistas, after Sandino, the revolutionary leader of the 1920s and 1930s.

Training local military forces like the Nicaraguan National Guard seemed a more efficient way to protect American interests than using U.S. troops. The United States adopted a similar policy in the Dominican Republic and Haiti, two other nations under American occupation. As in Nicaragua, the legacy of American involvement was harsh, dictatorial governments.

This Marine recruiting poster by James Montgomery Flagg portrays armed service as an exotic and exciting career. Flagg also designed the posters shown on pages 286 and 301. **GLOBAL AWARENESS** Describe the Marines' role in countries such as Nicaragua, Haiti, and the Dominican Republic. **1A**

Roosevelt's Good Neighbor Policy won praise in Latin America. When FDR visited Argentina in 1936, he was hailed as *el grand democrata* ("the great democrat"). The sheet music at the right is for a song praising Roosevelt, set to a Latin beat. **GLOBAL AWARENESS** How, in place of direct intervention, did the United States retain its influence in Latin America? **1B**

BECOMING A GOOD NEIGHBOR 1B

Americans saw the trend away from intervention as a positive development that would improve relations with Latin America. In his 1933 Inaugural Address, President Roosevelt gave the new policy a name. He said that he would follow "the policy of the good neighbor who . . . respects the rights of others." Under the Good Neighbor Policy, the United States avoided direct intervention in Latin American affairs. Congress also revoked the Platt Amendment, which had given the United States the right to intervene in Cuba.

The new policy was tested in 1938 when the Mexican government seized the property of American oil companies. Once, that might have meant an American invasion. This time, FDR's diplomats worked out a deal by which Mexico paid the companies for their lost property.

The Good Neighbor Policy also aimed to improve economic relations between the United States and Latin America. The Trade Agreements Act of 1934 allowed the President to reduce tariff rates in the hemisphere. As a result, during the 1930s this trade increased by more than 50 percent.

Increasing trade, Roosevelt hoped, would raise standards of living in Latin America, thus helping to promote stability in the region. Toward the same end, the United States lent billions of dollars to Latin American governments to build roads, bridges, hospitals, schools, and water and sewer systems. Finally, to increase public understanding

Cooperative Learning

Divide the class into groups. Have each group discuss the Good Neighbor Policy as applied to either Cuba, Mexico, Nicaragua, or Haiti. Ask groups to develop a list of criteria for a good neighbor, in terms of countries. **LEP**

Addressing Individual Needs

Guided/ Independent Practice
Have students complete **Reinforcement Workbook** Worksheet 64, which guides them in analyzing data.

Reteaching/Correctives
Have students form groups of four or five. Have them role-play a situation, based on information from the text, in which the U.S. influences the politics of a Latin American country. Possible roles include a United States and Latin American diplomat or general; a common person of each country; a leftist political opponent.

Instruct students to complete **Reteaching Resources** Worksheet 64, which helps students understand the changing relations with Latin America.

Enrichment/Extension
Ask students to research and write a timeline of relations between the United States and a Central American or Caribbean country from the 1930s to the present day.

You may wish to use the Section 2 Review, page 396, to see how well your students understand the main points in this lesson.

Section Review Answers

1. *Good Neighbor Policy*—Plan by which the U.S. refrained from direct intervention in Latin American affairs.

2. *Nicaragua*—Central American nation occupied by the United States from 1912 to 1933. *Adolfo Díaz*—Nicaraguan president. *Augusto Sandino*—Guerrilla leader in Nicaragua. *Anastasio Somoza*—Nicaraguan commander who seized power.

3. It was too expensive and considered immoral.

4. United States would no longer intervene directly in Latin American affairs.

5. The oppressive actions of dictators prevented change, and these dictators were often pro-American. The United States supported these dictators for those reasons.

Closure

Remind students of the pre-reading objectives in the section opener. Pose one or all of these questions again. Then have students read Section 3 for the next class period, noting the rise of fascism in Europe.

SECTION 3

The Rise of Dictators
(pp. 396–401)

Section Objective

■ explain how fascism took hold in Italy, Germany, and Japan

---

of Latin America, Roosevelt promoted cultural exchanges. Artists, writers, actors, and dancers came to this country, making many Americans more aware of Latin American viewpoints and cultures.

Despite the move away from direct intervention, the United States retained huge influence in Latin America. The U.S. Army patrolled the American-owned Panama Canal Zone. American banks and businesses still controlled Latin American plantations and politicians. But the Good Neighbor Policy did win some new friends in Latin America. These were friendships the United States would sorely need at a time of rising international tension.

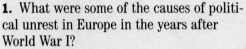

SECTION REVIEW

1. **KEY TERM** Good Neighbor Policy

2. **PEOPLE AND PLACES** Nicaragua, Adolfo Díaz, Augusto Sandino, Anastasio Somoza

3. **COMPREHENSION** What were the arguments against direct American military involvement in Latin America?

4. **COMPREHENSION** How did the Good Neighbor Policy differ from the Latin American policies of previous administrations?

5. **CRITICAL THINKING** How did the United States' desire to bring political stability to Latin America sometimes lead to dictatorship?

1B, 3D, 4D, 7D, 7I, 7J, 9A, 9E

3 The Rise of Dictators

★ **Section Focus**

★ **Key Terms** Nazi Party ■ anti-Semitism ■ puppet state

★ **Main Idea** In the years after World War I, the United States watched with concern as extremists took hold in Italy, Germany, and Japan.

Objectives As you read, look for answers to these questions:
1. What were some of the causes of political unrest in Europe in the years after World War I?
2. Why did Fascist leaders come to power in Europe?
3. What action did Japan take that concerned the United States?

Many people had hoped that the end of World War I would bring peace and democracy. But the Versailles Treaty created more problems than it solved. For instance, the treaty tried to satisfy the hunger of various peoples for self-rule. Under the new boundaries, however, many Slavs, Greeks, Turks, and Germans still lived in nations dominated by others. The breakdown of the old social order also led to violence. Loyalty to the old ruling dynasties, now toppled, no longer united different social classes.

Another source of unrest was fear of communism. In 1917 V. I. Lenin had led a Communist revolution in Russia. Lenin claimed that this was the start of a worldwide revolt of the working classes against capitalism. Many people, fearing Lenin was right, struck at Communists in their own countries. Communist-led movements in Germany and Hungary in 1919 were stamped out by force. As violence mounted, writer Arthur Koestler declared that the political language of the twentieth century was spoken by machine guns.

SUPPORTING THE SECTION

Reinforcement Workbook: Worksheet 65
Reteaching Resources: Worksheet 65
Enrichment and Extension Resources: Primary Source Worksheet 33
Teaching Transparencies: Transparency 65

This photograph shows Italian dictator Benito Mussolini gesturing theatrically during a speech in 1935. Known to Italians as *Il Duce* ("the leader"), Mussolini was a former Socialist who founded Italy's Fascist Party. HISTORY What policies made Mussolini popular among the Italian people? 9A

MUSSOLINI AND ITALIAN FASCISM 7D

Postwar Italy was a country in crisis. Italians felt betrayed by the Versailles Treaty. Italy had fought on the winning side but had gained little of the Austrian territory it had hoped for. Italy also struggled with internal problems. Its economy was failing, and political and class tensions divided its people.

In 1919, unemployment and inflation produced bitter strikes, some Communist-led. Communist ideas spread among the country's poor. The following year, peasants inspired by communism's triumph in Russia began seizing land. Workers took over factories. Alarmed by these threats, the middle and upper classes demanded stronger leadership.

Benito Mussolini, a blacksmith's son and a combat veteran, took advantage of this situation. Mussolini was a powerful speaker and demagogue—a leader who plays to popular fears and hatreds. He knew how to appeal to Italy's wounded national pride. He also played on fears of economic collapse and of communism. Mussolini blamed Italy's problems on Communists, corrupt business and labor leaders, and weak politicians. He promised to restore to Italy the honor, glory, and prosperity of the ancient Roman Empire.

Mussolini founded the Fascist Party in 1919. (Its name came from the word *fasces*—a bundle of rods tied around an ax handle. The fasces had been a symbol of unity and authority in ancient Rome.)

The Fascists openly scorned democracy. Power, they said, should rest with a single leader. They promised to rebuild Italy into a great empire. "We will turn the Mediterranean into an Italian lake," Mussolini boasted. This vision attracted many army officers and veterans.

Mussolini also organized a private army of angry young men. The "Black Shirts," as they were known, broke up left-wing rallies and beat up political opponents. Their violent actions increased the sense of crisis in Italy.

In 1922 Mussolini led thousands of Black Shirts in a march on Rome. "Either they will give us the government," he proclaimed, "or we will take it." As Mussolini had hoped, Italy's King Victor Emmanuel III refused to use the army to stop the march. A few days later, the king made Mussolini prime minister.

Once in power, Mussolini outlawed all political parties but his own. Officials, business leaders, and union chiefs all had to be members of the ruling Fascist Party. Mussolini's secret police crushed political dissent. The Fascists imposed censorship and flooded Italy with pro-Fascist propaganda. Fascist slogans told Italians to "Believe! Obey! Fight!"

> "**B**elieve! Obey! Fight!"
> —*Italian Fascist slogan*

Participating in Government

Ask students to compare the Fascist governments in Italy, Germany, and Japan and the Communist government in the Soviet Union with the representative democracy that exists in the United States. Have them note how the non-democratic governments took power. *What influence did the average citizen have in the governing of Fascist and Communist governments?* (Very little, if at all.) *What personal liberties did people lose under these governments?* (The right to protest government actions; freedom of religion, expression, and the press.)

Ethics

Read aloud this statement, attributed to the eighteenth century British politician Edmund Burke: "The only thing necessary for the triumph of evil is for good men to do nothing." *Why might "good people" have not opposed the cruel governments of Italy, Germany, and Japan?* (Fear of government reprisals; the belief in the need for a strong government, even if that government was unjust.) Have students consider what actions they might have taken if they had been living in one of those countries at that time.

THE RISE OF NAZISM IN GERMANY 7I

Popular discontent and economic problems also brought radical change to Germany. The burdens of reparations and rebuilding after the war caused hard times in Germany. Inflation skyrocketed. Middle-class Germans panicked as they saw their life savings become worthless.

These problems overwhelmed the democratic Weimar government ruling Germany. Like modern Italy, Germany had no democratic tradition. Many Germans despised the Weimar Republic as weak and ineffective, and shifted their support to extremist groups promising strong leadership. Some workers turned to the Communists. Many in the military and upper class longed to return to monarchy. During the 1920s and early 1930s a third choice emerged—the National Socialist German Workers' Party, or Nazi Party, led by Adolf Hitler.

Hitler, who had fought as a corporal in World War I, blamed Germany's defeat in that war on traitors, cowards, Jews, and Communists. Hitler never forgave the Weimar government for signing the Versailles Treaty. He was furious over the humiliating terms of the surrender. Many Germans agreed when he said that it had been internal political weakness and treachery, and not the Allied armies, that had defeated Germany. Germany, they said, had not really lost the war.

Like Mussolini, Hitler gained much of his success from his charismatic personality. A spellbinding, magnetic speaker, he gave his followers a sense that they were part of a vast movement to bring new glory to the German people. He also organized Nazi gangs, following the example of Mussolini's blackshirts. They beat up Jews and other "enemies."

Nazi party leader Adolf Hitler gives the Nazi salute at a parade of brown-shirted members of his "security police," later known as the SS, in 1927. HISTORY Describe the relationship between the Treaty of Versailles and the Nazi rise to power. 9E

Photo Caption Answer
Hitler used German dissatisfaction with the treaty's terms to gain political support for the Nazi's ultra-nationalist policies.

In 1923 the Nazis tried to overthrow the Weimar government. The plot fizzled, and Hitler was thrown in jail. There Hitler wrote down his political views in a book called *Mein Kampf* ("My Struggle"). Playing on anti-communism and anti-Semitism—prejudice against Jews—he blamed Communists and Jews for all of Germany's problems. Even more ominously, Hitler claimed that Germans were a superior race who had the right to conquer and rule over other peoples.

Mein Kampf became a best-seller in Germany. The Nazi Party, however, received few votes during the 1920s, for the Dawes Plan had briefly revived the German economy. But the worldwide depression beginning in 1929 doomed the Weimar government. By 1932, millions of hungry, jobless people roamed the streets. Under these circumstances, Germans were quick to listen to extremists with easy answers. Both the Communists and the Nazis gained seats in the German parliament.

In January 1933 a group of bankers, business leaders, and generals persuaded Germany's president to name Hitler chancellor (prime minister). During a faked emergency, Hitler soon got "temporary" unlimited power. This gave him a chance to eliminate political opponents and pack the government with Nazis loyal to *Der Führer* (FYOO-rur)—"the Leader."

HITLER IN POWER 7J

Once in power, Hitler promised to create a new German empire and give Germans a sense of national unity. He also began a massive rearmament program, which not only swelled national pride but also pumped up the German economy. Unemployment plummeted. The Nazi Party also offered many new opportunities to people from modest backgrounds. For these reasons, most of the German people were devoted to Hitler.

At the same time, Hitler proceeded with the program outlined in *Mein Kampf*. Members of the Weimar government who had signed the Versailles Treaty were hunted down and murdered. Gangs of Nazis burned books by Jewish authors as well as those that praised democracy. The government also brought schools under its control. Students learned only those things that would make them good Nazis.

Anti-Semitism became the official government policy of Germany. New laws deprived Jews of their citizenship and their jobs. Jews also became targets for brutal attacks. On November 10, 1938, Nazi thugs went on a rampage, destroying synagogues and looting Jewish homes and stores. Many Jews were killed or wounded during this *Kristallnacht* (kris–TAHL–nahkt), "the night of broken glass."

Jewish shopkeepers in Berlin clean up their damaged storefronts following attacks by Nazi thugs on *Kristallnacht*. The attacks were only one part of the systematic persecution of German Jews. POLITICS What accusations did Hitler make against the Jews? How did this help him politically? 9E

Photo Caption Answers
Hitler claimed Jews were responsible for all of Germany's problems. Jews became convenient scapegoats and that anti-Semitic prejudice helped unite Germans behind Hitler.

Background Hitler's racism extended to blacks as well as Jews. In the 1936 Olympics, held in Berlin, the Olympic Committee asked Hitler if gold-medal winning black American Jesse Owens could sit in Hitler's box. Not only did Hitler say no, but he even refused to shake hands with Owens.

Religion
Discuss anti-Semitism in Nazi Germany. Make sure students understand that Hitler defined Jews as a race, not just a religion, just as he defined Germans as a race, not just a nationality. *What, do you think, is at the root of prejudice against those of a different race or religion?* (Possible responses may include fear, economic competition, dislike of differences.)

Patterns in History
Discuss how Japan's lack of resources influenced its move toward militarism and territorial expansion. (To keep its economy growing and serve its expanding population, Japan needed an increasing amount of natural resources.)

Explain to students that today Japan has more than 125 million people and one of the strongest economies in the world, yet it has no more natural resources than it had in the 1930s—and it spends very little of its gross national product on defense. Have students suggest how Japan has managed to expand economically today and compare that method with the militarism of the 1930s. (Japan depends on trade today, which has made it a far more prosperous and free society.)

Global Awareness
Have students review the text and other sources to find out information about Joseph Stalin and his rule of the Soviet Union in the 1930s. Have them report back to the class, and list the information on the board. Conclude by having the class agree upon a general statement about the Soviet Union in the 1930s based on the list of details.

JAPANESE MILITARISM 7D

As Hitler's power grew in Germany, militarism was on the rise in Japan. During the prosperous 1920s, Japan had maintained close ties with the West. In 1922, for example, Japanese leaders had moved to reduce tensions in Asia by accepting the agreements made at the Washington Conference. At home, Japan was developing a democratic system.

There were, however, many Japanese who opposed these trends. Extreme nationalists in the military glorified their country's past. They called for a return to absolute rule by the emperor. Like the Italian Fascists, they preached the virtues of territorial expansion. Military leaders claimed that Japan's destiny was to drive out the Western colonial powers and rule all of Asia. Many Japanese business leaders, who were linked to the military by defense contracts, supported expansion for economic reasons.

In fact, Japan had much to gain from expansion. Japan's population was booming. Over 70 million Japanese lived in an area the size of Montana. Japan also lacked natural resources like oil, coal, and iron for its industries.

Like the Nazis, Japan's extremists remained in the background until the Great Depression. When economic problems beset the democratic government, the extremists gained popular support. Right-wing military officers bullied and murdered democratic leaders in the 1930s. Unlike their European counterparts, Japanese extremists were not led by a lone demagogue. Instead, a small group of leaders made policy. They allowed no opposition to government views. They censored the media and demanded total obedience to the state.

This 1931 photograph shows Japanese troops and artillery in Manchuria—a region in northern China. Japanese army officers in Manchuria ordered the occupation, and the Japanese civilian government in Tokyo proved too weak to stop them. **GLOBAL AWARENESS** Name some of the factors that motivated Japan's expansionist policies during the 1930s. **9E**

JAPAN INVADES MANCHURIA 1B

In 1931 military officers took matters into their own hands. Acting without orders from the civilian government, they invaded the resource-rich Chinese province of Manchuria. Then they turned Manchuria into a puppet state—one formally independent but dominated by another nation.

This land grab was a direct slap at the United States, which had invented and defended the principle of the Open Door. Secretary of State Stimson wanted a strong response. The Depression-stricken United States, however, preferred not to tangle with Japan. Stimson could only announce that America would not recognize Japanese rule in Manchuria or any transfer of territory by conquest. This announcement, called the Stimson Doctrine, had moral power but could not be enforced.

The League of Nations, to which Japan belonged, also condemned the conquest of Manchuria. Japan responded by withdrawing from the League. Japanese leaders had gambled that no Western power would come to China's aid. Their gamble paid off.

RECOGNIZING THE SOVIET UNION 1B

Rising right-wing extremism in Europe and Asia helped produce a thaw in relations between the United States and the Soviet Union (formerly Russia). At the start of the 1920s, fear and hatred of the Soviet Union had run high. Yet shared interests—economic as well as strategic—began to draw the United States and the Soviet Union together.

The new Soviet leader, Joseph Stalin, focused less on world revolution and more on modernizing his nation's backward economy. Communist or not, Stalin admired American productivity and was eager to learn from U.S. experts. In turn, American business leaders saw that a developed Soviet Union could make a profitable client. Companies like Ford, General Electric, and DuPont began to sell equipment to Soviet farm managers. American engineers helped the Soviets build factories and dams. For both sides, profits began to push aside politics.

Presidents Harding, Coolidge, and Hoover had refused to recognize the Moscow dictatorship. In

BIOGRAPHY

ARMAND HAMMER (1898–1990) traveled to Russia in 1921 to help fight famine. There he impressed Soviet leader Lenin, who offered him a mining concession. Hammer paved the way for other Americans to obtain Soviet sales concessions and for cultural exchanges with the United States. **3D, 4D**

1933, however, Franklin Roosevelt decided to scrap the non-recognition policy. For one thing, few other countries treated the Soviet Union as an outcast. It had even joined the League of Nations. Also, FDR believed increased trade with the Soviet Union could assist the Depression-hit economy. Finally, he thought it wise to make allies of the Soviets. They might be used to counter Japanese ambitions in Asia.

In December 1933 an American ambassador flew to Moscow. The air was chilly but Stalin's reception was warm. Meanwhile, a Soviet ambassador arrived to smile for Washington cameras. The ideological gulf between the two nations—one a capitalist democracy, the other a Communist dictatorship—remained huge. But both were united by economic need and by a common fear of Germany, Italy, and Japan. Their stormy marriage would last through World War II.

SECTION REVIEW

1. KEY TERMS Nazi Party, anti-Semitism, puppet state

2. PEOPLE AND PLACES V. I. Lenin, Benito Mussolini, Adolf Hitler, Manchuria, Henry Stimson, Joseph Stalin

3. COMPREHENSION How did Fascist dictators rise to power in Europe?

4. COMPREHENSION How did Japan threaten world peace in 1931? What was the response of the League of Nations?

5. CRITICAL THINKING What connection is there between hard economic times and the rise of dictators?

Biography
For further reading consider:
Bryson, John. *The World of Armand Hammer.* Harry N. Abrams, 1985.

Background Japan's invasion of Manchuria in 1931 was a violation of the Nine-Power Treaty, the Kellogg-Briand Pact, and the League of Nations Charter.

Section Review Answers

1. *Nazi Party*—Hitler's political party, which gained control of Germany in 1933. *anti-Semitism*—Prejudice against Jews. *puppet state*—State that is supposedly independent but in reality is dominated by another country.

2. *V. I. Lenin*—Leader of Communist Revolution in Russia. *Benito Mussolini*—Leader of Fascists in Italy. *Adolf Hitler*—Leader of Nazi Party, seized control of Germany in 1933. *Manchuria*—Chinese province, overrun by Japanese in 1931. *Henry Stimson*—Secretary of State, who announced the United States would not recognize Japanese rule of Manchuria. *Joseph Stalin*—Soviet leader in the 1920s and 1930s.

3. By blaming their countries' problems on groups such as Jews or Communists, by promising to restore their countries to a glorious state, and by taking advantage of economic crises.

4. By overrunning Manchuria, where they created a puppet state. The League condemned the action, but did nothing more.

5. When times are hard economically, people are more willing to sacrifice political freedom if it will bring them economic prosperity.

Closure

Call students' attention to the beige boxed quotation (p. 397). Ask them to relate this quotation to the main idea of the section. Then have students read Section 4 for the next class period. As they read, ask them to note how the United States moved away from neutrality and finally entered World War II.

4 From Neutrality to War

Section Focus

Key Terms Spanish Civil War ■ appeasement ■ Munich Conference ■ nonaggression pact ■ World War II ■ blitzkrieg ■ Lend-Lease Act

Main Idea Fascist aggression mounted throughout the 1930s, until Germany's invasion of Poland in 1939 plunged the world into another global war. The United States stayed out of the war until Japan attacked it in December 1941.

Objectives As you read, look for answers to these questions:
1. What were the major events leading to war in Europe?
2. What was America's attitude toward the war, and how did it change over time?
3. How did the United States enter the war?

Section Objective
■ describe how World War II began and how the United States entered the war

Introducing the Section

Connecting with Past Learnings
Review reasons for American isolationism in the 1930s. *Why was America unwilling to get involved in a European war?* (Did not believe it affected the United States; disillusionment and pacifism after World War I.) Have students note American interests in Asia and the Pacific. (American possessions, such as Guam and the Philippines; trade with China and other nations.)

Key Terms
List the key terms on the board and have students write sentences using the terms. Ask volunteers to read their sentences aloud, leaving out the key term, and have the rest of the class suggest the omitted term. Follow this procedure until all terms have been used at least once. **LEP**

During the second half of the 1930s, dictators in Europe began a program of territorial conquest. As bystanders, Americans debated their country's role. Should the United States once again become involved in Europe's struggles?

FASCISM GAINS IN EUROPE 1B
By 1935 fascism had not solved Italy's problems of poverty and unemployment. Mussolini, however, had a solution for his failures at home. He began rebuilding Italy's armed forces with plans of conquering new territory in Africa.

In 1935 the Italian army invaded Ethiopia, one of Africa's few independent nations. The League of Nations condemned the invasion and voted limited economic sanctions against Italy. However, neither Great Britain nor France was eager to pick a fight with Mussolini. In addition, neither country wanted to sacrifice its trade with Italy. In any case, the economic sanctions had little effect. They did not prohibit the sale of oil—the lifeblood of modern war machines.

The conquest was a disaster for Ethiopia. It also crushed the League of Nations. Italy had defied the League and gotten away with it. Faith in the League's ability to guard world peace faded.

Roosevelt and other Western leaders had feared that a tough stand against Mussolini might push him into the arms of Hitler. Despite their caution, Mussolini soon quit the League. In 1936 he joined Hitler in an alliance known as the Rome-Berlin Axis.

CIVIL WAR IN SPAIN 1B
Meanwhile, new trouble erupted, this time in Spain. In 1931, Spain had changed from a monarchy to a republic. Though the republicans had fairly won control of the government, they still faced much political unrest in the country. In 1936 a group of Spanish army officers, led by General Francisco Franco, rebelled against the government. This began the Spanish Civil War (1936–1939), which aroused passions not only in Spain but throughout the world. Many American leftists supported the Loyalists—those who stayed loyal to the Spanish republic. More than 3,000 Americans fought for the Loyalists.

The Spanish Civil War became an international struggle. Germany and Italy helped arm Franco's forces. Meanwhile, the Soviet Union aided the Loyalists with officers and technicians. After two years of fighting, however, Stalin withdrew Soviet support. Stalin's withdrawal and non-intervention by Britain, France, and the United States allowed Franco to sweep to victory in 1939. In a sense, Spain was the first battleground of the coming world war. Democracy had lost.

GERMANY EXPANDS, 1935–1938 1B
The Western democracies' failure to stand up to fascism had even more serious consequences in Germany. In 1935 Hitler announced that he would no longer obey the Versailles Treaty's requirement that Germany stay disarmed. Germany would again become a great military power. This

---

SUPPORTING THE SECTION

Reinforcement Workbook: Worksheet 66
Reteaching Resources: Worksheet 66
Enrichment and Extension Resources: Primary Source Worksheet 34
Teaching Transparencies: Transparency 66

amounted to canceling part of the Allied victory. Still, no reaction came from London or Paris.

Next, Hitler took a more dangerous step. In March 1936, he sent his army into the Rhineland, a demilitarized area on the border with France. Even Hitler feared France would react to this breach of the Versailles Treaty. Knowing the German forces were no match for the French army, Hitler later admitted, "If the French had then marched into the Rhineland, we would have had to withdraw with our tails between our legs." But his gamble worked; nothing happened. An early chance to stop Hitler was lost.

There were many reasons for British and French inaction:

(1) *The memory of World War I.* Exhausted by the last war, neither Britain nor France wanted a new one. World War I had demonstrated the dangers of arms races, hair-trigger defenses, and harsh rhetoric. No one wanted to stumble yet again into a bloody conflict.

(2) *Fear of Soviet communism.* Some British and French conservatives thought a strong Germany would be a good balance against the Soviets. Communism appeared to be at least as great a threat to democracy as fascism was.

(3) *Unease with the Versailles Treaty.* Many people felt that Germany had valid objections to the Versailles Treaty. Hitler played on this fact to make German demands sound reasonable.

(4) *Hope for compromise with Germany.* Partly because some of his demands did sound reasonable, Hitler convinced many Europeans that he had only limited ambitions. He could be bought off, they believed, by giving him part of what he wanted. This strategy was called appeasement.

Hitler's ambitions, however, knew no bounds. He claimed he wanted to unite all of Europe's German-speaking people in one empire. He began in March 1938 by sending his army to annex Austria, once again without opposition.

Next, Hitler turned on another neighbor, Czechoslovakia. Its boundaries, created by the Treaty of Versailles, contained three million Germans. Hitler used the claim that these Germans were oppressed as an excuse for war threats.

Unlike the Austrians, the Czechs wanted to resist Hitler. Czechoslovakia had a defense treaty with France, which gave it a fighting chance. France, however, would not risk war with Germany without support from Britain.

In September 1938 Britain's prime minister, Neville Chamberlain, flew to Munich, Germany, to talk with Hitler. If Chamberlain stood firm on Czechoslovakia, war would likely come. But he thought the whole matter was a "quarrel in a faraway land between people of whom we know nothing." At the Munich Conference, Chamberlain and French Premier Edouard Daladier agreed to permit Germany to absorb the Sudetenland, a German-speaking part of Czechoslovakia. In return, Hitler promised to make no more territorial demands in Europe. On his return to England, Chamberlain insisted that the agreement guaranteed "peace in our time." But Hitler's word was worthless, and Munich soon became a code word for surrender and betrayal.

This poster commemorates the "steel pact" between Hitler (left) and Mussolini. A swastika, the Nazi symbol, appears on the German flag at left. POLITICS What were some of the elements shared by nazism and Italian fascism? 9A

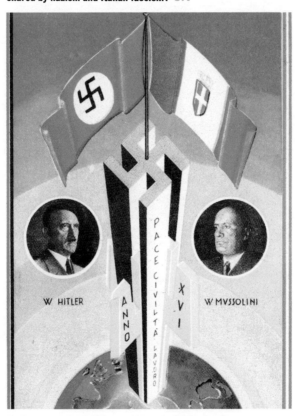

Focus
With the class, create a flow chart of Axis actions and Allied and American responses from 1935 to December 1941. (Example shown below.)

ACTION	RESPONSE
Italian invasion of Ethiopia, 1935	League of Nations condemnation
Spanish Civil War, 1936–1939	volunteers fought against fascism
Hitler militarizes the Rhineland, 1936	no response
Japanese invasion of China, 1937	American embargo of iron and steel, 1940
Hitler annexes Austria and claims Sudetenland, 1938	Munich Conference
German invasion of Poland, 1939	start of World War II
German victory over western Europe, 1940	passage of Selective Service Act in the United States and start of military build-up
Battle of Britain and German submarine warfare in the Atlantic, 1940–1941	Lend-Lease Act and Atlantic Charter
German invasion of the Soviet Union, 1941	American and British aid offered to Soviets
Japanese invasion of French Indochina	American seizure of Japanese money and property and embargo of oil exports
Japanese attack on Pearl Harbor	U.S. enters World War II

Photo Caption Answer
They were both anti-democratic ideologies that invested power in a single demagogic leader. Each made popular appeals to prejudice and fear of communism. Each tried to establish one-party states in which the government exercised tight control over all aspects of life.

WAR BEGINS, 1939 1B

Hitler began to speed up his timetable. Seizing the rest of Czechoslovakia, he then began his familiar refrain. He must "liberate" suffering Germans in Poland, he claimed. Meanwhile, Mussolini's army invaded the tiny Balkan nation of Albania.

Appeasement had failed, as even Chamberlain now recognized. Against Hitler, the only real choices were to fight or be crushed. Britain and France promised to defend Poland. They began talks with Stalin to convince the Soviet Union to join the effort. Instead, Hitler and Stalin sprang one of the century's greatest diplomatic surprises. In August 1939 they signed a **nonaggression pact**, with each side promising not to attack the other. The Communist and Nazi dictators, once sworn enemies, had become allies.

The nonaggression pact sealed Poland's fate. On September 1, 1939, German tanks thundered across the Polish frontier. True to their promises, Britain and France declared war on Germany, and **World War II** began. Yet British and French help came too slowly, for Germany had developed a revolutionary method of attack. This was the **blitzkrieg**, or "lightning war," which used highly mobile ground forces supported by dive-bombers to punch holes in enemy defenses. Polish resistance was crushed in less than four weeks.

After the German attack, the Soviet Union occupied eastern Poland. (During the occupation, the Soviets massacred some 4,000 Polish officers, whose bodies were later found in the Katyn Forest.) Hitler and Stalin had secretly agreed in their 1939 pact to divide Poland between them. Stalin also received a free hand to take over the Baltic states—Estonia, Latvia, and Lithuania. In November 1939 the Soviets invaded Finland. The Finns fought fiercely, but were defeated by spring.

German troops roll through a destroyed area of Poland during the *blitzkrieg* in September 1939. Poles fought bravely against the invaders, but their resistance was ultimately crushed. **GLOBAL AWARENESS** What agreement did Hitler and Stalin make regarding Poland? **9A**

HITLER TRIUMPHANT 1B

At first, Germany made no attacks on France or Britain. Some observers called the situation a "phony war" that would end in another deal with Hitler. Isolationist feeling in the United States was strengthened by the "phony war."

In April 1940 the "phony war" exploded, and Americans saw the true extent of Germany's power and ambition. Once again using blitzkreig tactics, Hitler's armies made the conquest of Western Europe look easy. First they poured into neutral Denmark and Norway. Then Belgium and the Netherlands—also neutral—went under. Within two weeks, France's armies were sent reeling. By May 1940 a British army that had been rushed to France was trapped at the French port of Dunkirk. Hundreds of boats ferried the battle-weary soldiers back to England.

The Germans slashed their way to Paris through a French army once thought to be the world's best. On June 17, 1940, France surrendered. German forces took control of the northern half of the country. In southern France a puppet government was run from the town of Vichy (VEE–shee).

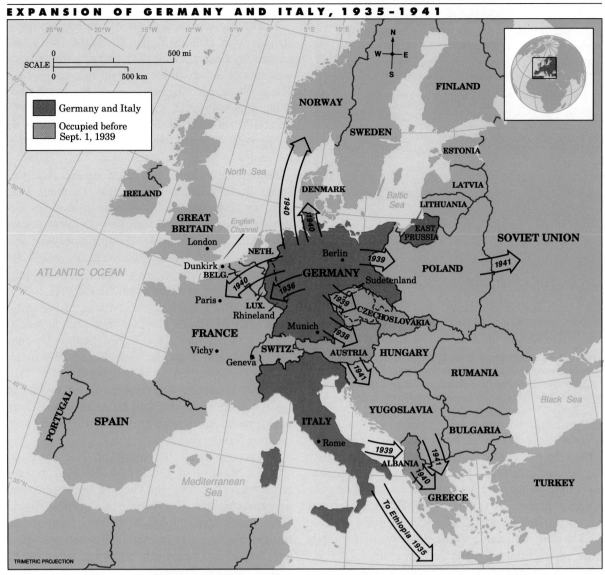

This map shows European military conquests by the Axis powers beginning in the 1930s. Which two countries did Germany occupy before September 1939? What countries did German armies invade in 1940? **CRITICAL THINKING** Why might Hitler have waited until 1941 to attack the Soviet Union?

Great Britain suddenly stood alone against Germany. An invasion was expected almost hourly. Few believed the island could hold out. But Britain's new prime minister, Winston Churchill, loathed the Nazis and growled defiance. "We shall fight on the beaches," Churchill vowed, "we shall fight in the fields and in the streets, we shall never surrender."

> "**W**e shall fight on the beaches, we shall fight in the fields and in the streets, we shall never surrender."
> —*Winston Churchill, 1940*

CHAPTER 17   BETWEEN THE WARS, 1920–1941   **405**

Global Awareness
Discuss how the nonaggression pact between Germany and the Soviet Union affected the world's balance of power in 1939. *How might the balance of power have changed if the Soviets had become allies of Britain and France at that time?* (Germany would no longer have had an advantage.) *How would United States entry affect balance of power?* (Give much greater strength to the Allies.)

Participating in Government
The election of 1940 marked the first time in United States history that a President ran for a third term—and won. Discuss why Roosevelt remained in office. (It was a time of crisis, requiring strong leadership; he was extremely popular.) *Would you have voted for him in that election? Why or why not?*

Analyzing Controversial Issues
Explain to the class that there were many Americans who opposed any steps to prepare for war. Ask students to suggest reasons why Americans would oppose aid to Britain. (Too expensive; would draw the United States into war; some Americans supported the Axis.) Explain to students that other Americans, just as opposed to U.S. entry into the war, felt that aid to Britain, and the build-up of arms, were the only means by which the United States could stay out of the war. Have the class debate this issue. *Do you think that having a strong military is the best way to prevent war?*

Map Skills Answers
Czechoslovakia and Austria. Norway, Denmark, Netherlands, Belgium, and France. Students may suggest that he wanted to solidify his conquests of less powerful states before attacking a stronger adversary. They might also mention that it was not until the end of 1940 that Hitler gave up on his plan to invade Britain.

Britain's King George VI and Queen Elizabeth inspect damage done by German bombs during the Battle of Britain in 1940.
HISTORY Why did England and Germany bomb each other's civilian population? Did this strategy succeed? Why or why not? **9F**

Hitler sent waves of bombers over Britain to soften up its defenses. The Battle of Britain was under way. Outnumbered British pilots, warned by radar of air attacks, shot down hundreds of German planes. By October 1940, Hitler had given up on the invasion. Still, German bombers continued to pound Britain's cities. They wanted to disrupt production and break civilian morale. British pilots also bombed German cities. Amidst heavy casualties and blazing wreckage, civilians in both countries stubbornly carried on.

DEBATING THE AMERICAN ROLE 1B
The world had turned upside down for the United States. The Nazis now dominated Europe. If Britain fell, they would control the Atlantic too.

Roosevelt, though gravely concerned, had been forced to bow to isolationist sentiment in the United States. When war broke out, he declared, "This nation will remain a neutral nation, but I cannot ask that every American remain neutral in thought as well. . . . Even a neutral cannot be asked to close his mind or his conscience."

At the very least, Roosevelt wanted to supply Britain with arms to fight the Nazis. But a law passed by Congress in 1935 forbade the sale of weapons to any country engaged in war. In 1939 Roosevelt asked Congress to repeal the embargo. What he got, instead, was a compromise: the Neutrality Act of 1939. It allowed the sale of arms to belligerents—warring nations—but forbade American ships to enter the war zone.

Though isolationism remained strong, Nazi victories in 1940 changed American thinking. One sign of change was the passage in 1940 of the Selective Training and Service Act—the first peacetime draft in U.S. history. In just one year, the size of the army tripled. Roosevelt also called for and received a huge increase in defense spending, from $1.8 billion in 1940 to $6 billion in 1941.

This military buildup worried many Americans. Most wanted Hitler stopped, but still hoped to stay out of the war. Possible American entry into the war became a central issue in the 1940 presidential election (just as it had been in the 1916 election). Roosevelt was re-elected, but he had to make a promise he doubted he could keep. "Your boys," he told America's parents, "will not be sent into any foreign war."

Yet even during the campaign, Roosevelt did what he could to aid the British. He kept in close touch with Churchill, and the two leaders became personal friends. He transferred surplus World War I arms and supplies to Britain. Britain also needed destroyers to fight off German submarines and defend its lifeline—the shipping lanes to the United States. In September 1940, FDR gave Britain 50 aging destroyers. In return, the United States received free lease of British naval bases in Canada and the Caribbean.

MOVING TOWARD WAR 1B
Roosevelt saw his re-election in 1940 as an endorsement of his policy of aid to Britain. In the winter of 1940–1941, Britain needed all the help it could get. Neutrality acts, however, prevented the United States from lending Britain money. President Roosevelt then hit upon the idea of lending Britain goods instead of money. In a radio "fireside chat," Roosevelt compared his plan to lending a garden hose to a neighbor whose house was on

fire. It was, he suggested, the only sensible thing to do. Isolationists warned against the plan, but most Americans favored it.

In March 1941 Congress passed the Lend-Lease Act. The act allowed the President to sell, lend, or lease war materials to any nation whose defense he thought vital to American security. Lend-Lease aid stripped away the last pretense of neutrality. The United States would be what Roosevelt called "the arsenal of democracy."

Another sign of growing British-American ties was the Atlantic Charter, signed by Roosevelt and Churchill in August 1941. The Atlantic Charter spelled out the two leaders' hopes for a better world after the defeat of fascism. All peoples, Roosevelt and Churchill declared, should be free to live in peace and choose their own government.

UNDECLARED WAR IN THE ATLANTIC 1A

The principles of the Atlantic Charter were a far cry from reality in 1941. German submarines—the feared U-boats—had sunk millions of tons of shipping. Britain's navy was stretched to the limit. American ships were badly needed.

Roosevelt met the threat in gradual stages. First he launched "neutrality patrols" to watch for U-boats in American waters. Then he allowed American destroyers to accompany British convoys halfway across the Atlantic. Inevitably, U-boats fired on the American destroyers. Finally, Roosevelt announced that the navy would shoot any U-boat in the western Atlantic.

In October, U-boats torpedoed two more American destroyers. The first uniformed Americans to die in 1941 were sailors who drowned in the Atlantic waves during "peacetime." But real war was not far off.

GERMANY INVADES THE SOVIET UNION 1A

While the United States was trying to bolster Britain's defenses, Hitler's attention was elsewhere. Having stamped out most resistance in Western Europe, he decided that the moment had come to strike eastward. "We have the chance to smash Russia while our own back is free," he told his generals. In June 1941, German forces blitzed through Soviet defenses in a surprise attack. Hitler hoped unhappy Soviet citizens might welcome

his troops as liberators. At least, he did not expect fierce resistance from the Soviet army.

The German invasion was a stunning success at first. But the Soviet Union was a huge country, not easily conquered. And the Soviets soon had outside help. Acting on the principle that "the enemy of my enemy is my friend," Roosevelt and Churchill offered Stalin supplies. Hitler's attack on the Soviet Union changed the nature of the war. Germany would have to fight on two fronts.

RELATIONS WITH JAPAN 1B

Germany's European victories created new openings for Japanese expansionists. Holland, France, and Britain could no longer guard their colonies in the Pacific or on the Asian mainland. Those colonies and their resources—oil, rubber, and tin—offered tempting targets. Japan already controlled Manchuria, and in 1937 had launched an invasion of China. Japanese leaders now saw an opportunity to unite all of East Asia under Japanese control. Only the United States stood in the way.

Roosevelt, who regarded the United States as a Pacific power and China's protector, was determined to halt Japanese expansion. By 1940, American public opinion was beginning to agree. In September 1940, Roosevelt embargoed iron and steel exports to Japan. He demanded that the Japanese abandon their aims in China and in the colonies of Southeast Asia.

The embargo infuriated the Japanese, who felt the United States was trying to strangle their economy. Despite growing tension, however, each side wished to avoid a showdown. Roosevelt feared a war in the Pacific might disrupt his program to help defeat Hitler. Japan likewise hoped to avoid a potentially disastrous conflict with the much-larger United States. Diplomats on both sides agreed to talk.

Meanwhile, each nation took steps that pushed the other toward war. The Japanese remained in China, and in July 1941 moved troops into French Indochina (the present-day nations of Laos, Cambodia, and Vietnam). That same month, Roosevelt seized all Japanese money and property in the United States. The United States also cut off oil exports to Japan. Without oil, Japan's war machine would grind to a halt. Japan would either

Background The America First Committee was America's most powerful isolationist group. The Committee tried to influence public opinion through speeches and publications. At its peak, the Committee boasted more than 800,000 members. It was dissolved on December 11, 1941, four days after the bombing of Pearl Harbor.

C Cooperative Learning

Divide the class into small groups, assigning each the role of one of the following countries: the United States, Britain, France, the Soviet Union, Germany, Japan. Have each group put together a short "status" report for its country dated December 1941. The groups should include a history of the previous decade, the present leader or occupier of their countries, the immediate problems their countries face, and possible future courses of action. Then have one member of each group present the report. LEP

Addressing Individual Needs

Guided/ Independent Practice

Instruct students to complete **Reinforcement Workbook** Worksheet 66. This worksheet guides students in analyzing a political cartoon.

Reteaching/Correctives

Provide students with an outline of a world map, or have them trace the map on pages 848–849. Have students review the section. Then, on their maps, have them pinpoint sites of conflict resulting from United States entry into World War II. Have students explain their choices.

Instruct students to complete **Reteaching Resources** Worksheet 66, which requires students to sequence historical information.

Enrichment/Extension

Have students complete **Enrichment and Extension Resources** Primary Source Worksheet 34, in which students read and critique a speech by Charles Lindbergh reflecting the isolationist point of view.

JAPAN EXPANDS IN ASIA, 1930–1941

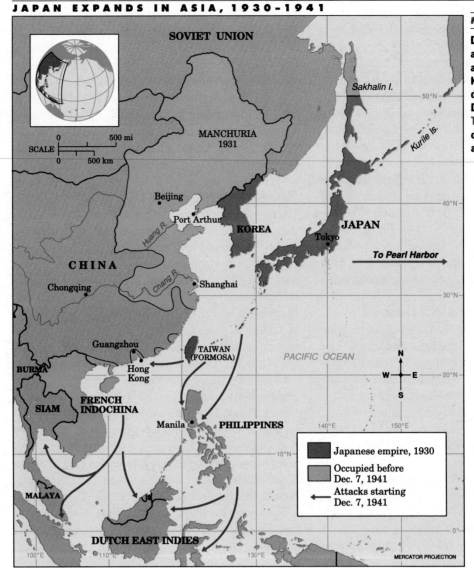

MAP SKILLS 9B

During the 1930s, Japan added areas on the Asian mainland to an empire that already included Korea and Taiwan. What areas did Japan attack beginning on December 7, 1941? CRITICAL THINKING Describe the extent of Japanese influence in China as shown on the map.

have to meet American demands or grab the oil of the Dutch East Indies. This would mean war.

Japan's War Minister, Hideki Tojo, thought war with the United States was inevitable. He argued that Japan should strike first before U.S. forces could mobilize. In the fall of 1941, Japan prepared for war while continuing talks in Washington. What the Japanese did not know was that American experts had broken the Japanese code. Eavesdropping on Japanese radio messages, the United States learned of Japan's war preparations. But the precise time and place of the coming attack remained a mystery.

THE ATTACK ON PEARL HARBOR 1A

American intelligence picked up messages to the Japanese embassy indicating that something was going to happen on December 7, 1941. They assumed, however, that if there were an attack, it would come in the Philippines.

Pearl Harbor, Hawaii, was America's largest naval base. On Sunday morning, December 7, 1941, thousands of American sailors at the base were beginning a quiet day. In the middle of the previous night, 353 Japanese bombers, fighters, and torpedo planes had taken off from aircraft carriers several hundred miles from Hawaii. At 7:55 A.M.

408 UNIT 6 WORLD LEADERSHIP

Sailors from the battleship *West Virginia* are rescued by motorboat after their vessel was bombed during the Japanese surprise attack on Pearl Harbor. **HISTORY** How did the attack change American attitudes toward World War II? **9E**

they attacked the American ships, which lay anchored in the harbor like sitting ducks. Years later Admiral Gene Larocque recalled the morning:

> At first I thought the U.S. Army Air Corps was accidentally bombing us. We were so proud, so vain, and so ignorant of Japanese capability. . . . It took a long time to realize how good these fellows were.

The Japanese killed more than 2,300 American servicemen and destroyed 18 ships. More than 150 aircraft were caught on the ground and destroyed. The Japanese suffered few losses. Their forces also attacked other American bases in the Pacific as well as British and Dutch possessions.

The day after the attack on Pearl Harbor, Roosevelt asked Congress for a declaration of war against Japan. He gravely observed that December 7, 1941, was "a date which will live in infamy." Both houses of Congress complied within hours, by votes of 82-0 and 388-1. Pearl Harbor had swayed isolationist feelings where the threat of fascism had not. Three days later, Japan's allies—Germany and Italy—declared war on the United States. There was now no turning back. For the second time in a half-century, the United States was part of a world war. **5E**

★ **Historical Documents**

For an excerpt from President Roosevelt's War Message to Congress, see page 725 of this book.

SECTION REVIEW

1. KEY TERMS Spanish Civil War, appeasement, Munich Conference, nonaggression pact, World War II, blitzkrieg, Lend-Lease Act

2. PEOPLE AND PLACES Rhineland, Dunkirk, Vichy, Winston Churchill, French Indochina, Hideki Tojo, Pearl Harbor

3. COMPREHENSION Why did appeasement fail to prevent war in Europe?

4. COMPREHENSION What steps did Roosevelt take to help Britain in 1941? Why did he have to act cautiously?

5. CRITICAL THINKING Was United States entry into World War II inevitable? Explain your answer.

2. *Rhineland*—Area near France that Hitler militarized in 1936. *Dunkirk*—Port in France, from which British army retreated in 1940. *Vichy*—City in southern France where a puppet government was established. *Winston Churchill*—Prime minister of Britain during World War II. *French Indochina*—Territory invaded by Japan in 1941. *Hideki Tojo*—Japan's war minister. *Pearl Harbor*—American naval base, attacked by Japan, 1941.

3. Through appeasement, Britain and France had hoped to stop continued German expansion, but Hitler continued to make more territorial demands after each compromise.

4. He proposed the Lend-Lease Act, signed the Atlantic Charter, and sent American warships to protect British convoys. He had to proceed cautiously because many Americans opposed any U.S. involvement in the war.

5. Yes, because both Germany and Japan were interested in domination of areas of the world where the United States had a vital interest.

Closure

Remind students of the pre-reading objectives in the section opener. Pose one or all of these questions again. Then have students read Section 1 of Chapter 18 for the next class period, noting the changes that World War II brought to American society.

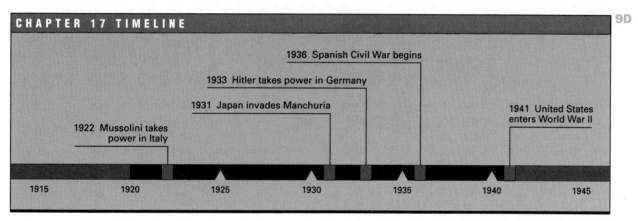

CHAPTER 17 TIMELINE

1936 Spanish Civil War begins

1933 Hitler takes power in Germany

1931 Japan invades Manchuria

1941 United States enters World War II

1922 Mussolini takes power in Italy

1915   1920   1925   1930   1935   1940   1945

Photo Caption Answer
The attack convinced Americans to enter World War II on the side of the Allies.

Background Jeannette Rankin, who in 1917 had been the first woman elected to the House of Representatives, cast the only vote against declaring war on Japan. She had also voted against entering World War I.

Chapter 17 REVIEW

CHAPTER 17 SUMMARY

SECTION 1: After World War I, Americans were determined not to become involved in another European war.

■ Avoiding war was the main theme of American foreign policy during the postwar period.

■ To prevent war, the United States joined international disarmament efforts.

■ The issues of war debts and reparations created tensions among the world powers.

SECTION 2: During the 1930s the United States used diplomacy rather than force to achieve its goals in Latin America.

■ The earlier American policy of armed intervention was rejected as unnecessary, expensive, and to some, immoral.

■ Franklin Roosevelt tried to promote stability in Latin America through aid and economic development.

SECTION 3: By the 1930s extremist governments had come to power in Italy, Germany, and Japan.

■ Postwar bitterness over the peace settlements, economic woes, political instability, and fear of communism created fertile ground for extremists.

■ Mussolini gained power in Italy by promising to restore the glory of ancient Rome and by playing on fears of communism and economic collapse.

■ Adolf Hitler capitalized on German feelings of humiliation and resentment to become ruler of Germany. He promised to build a new German empire.

■ In Japan, the Depression ended a trend toward democracy and brought extreme nationalists to power. The new leaders urged expansionism.

SECTION 4: The outbreak of fighting in Europe and Asia pulled the United States into World War II.

■ Fascist dictators, encouraged by the weakness of the democracies, captured territory in Europe, Africa, and Asia during the late 1930s.

■ Britain and France declared war on Germany when it invaded Poland in 1939.

■ Americans' isolationism weakened as they came to appreciate the Fascist threat.

■ The Japanese attack on Pearl Harbor in December 1941 brought the United States into World War II.

KEY TERMS ●

Use the following terms to complete the sentences below.

appeasement
Dawes Plan
Good Neighbor Policy
Lend-Lease Act
Munich Conference
nonaggression pact
Weimar Republic

1. Roosevelt's attempt to improve relations with Latin America was called the _____ .
2. The _____ allowed the United States to supply Britain with war materials.
3. The _____ gave Hitler control of part of Czechoslovakia.
4. Hitler's rise to power in Germany signaled the fall of the
_____ .
5. In 1939 Hitler successfully concluded a _____ with the Soviet Union.
6. The _____ slowed the schedule for Germany's payment of war reparations.
7. The strategy of giving in to Hitler in order to preserve the peace was known as _____ .

PEOPLE TO IDENTIFY ●

Identify the following people and tell why each was important.

1. Winston Churchill
2. Francisco Franco
3. Hideki Tojo
4. Anastasio Somoza
5. Joseph Stalin

PLACES TO LOCATE ●

Match each of the letters on the map with the places that are listed below.

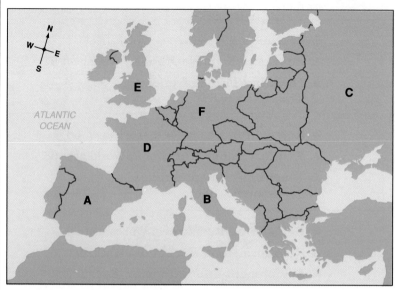

1. France
2. Germany
3. Great Britain
4. Italy
5. Soviet Union
6. Spain

REVIEWING THE FACTS ▲

1. Why did the United States turn to isolationism after World War I?
2. In what international peace efforts did the United States take part during the 1920s?
3. How did United States policy in Latin America change after World War I?
4. What conditions in Europe led to the rise of fascism during the 1920s and 1930s?
5. Explain how Mussolini and Hitler came to power.
6. How did militarists come to power in Japan? What reasons did Japan have for wanting to expand?

7. How did United States policy toward the Soviet Union change under President Roosevelt?
8. What was the policy of appeasement? Why did both France and Britain follow the policy?
9. Describe the course of Hitler's aggression in Europe. What finally caused the outbreak of World War II?
10. How did American attitudes toward the war change between 1939 and 1941? What finally brought the United States into the war?

CRITICAL THINKING SKILLS ▲

1. **DRAWING CONCLUSIONS** Why did the measures taken during the 1920s to prevent war fail? What other measures might have been more successful?

2. **MAKING A GENERALIZATION** Which nations—powerful ones or weak ones—would be more likely to follow isolationist policies? Explain your answer.

3. **IDENTIFYING CAUSE AND EFFECT** How did the policy of appeasement encourage Fascist aggression?

4. **FORMING A HYPOTHESIS** If Germany and Italy had not declared war on the United States, do you believe that the United States would have joined the war in Europe? Why or why not?

WRITING ABOUT TOPICS IN AMERICAN HISTORY ■

1. **CONNECTING WITH LITERATURE** A selection from *Babbitt* by Sinclair Lewis appears on pages 801–802. Read it and answer the questions. Then answer the following question: What is the "ideal type" of American that Babbitt thinks the rest of the world should imitate?

2. **APPLYING THEMES: PLURALISTIC SOCIETY** Write a report on the response of Italian Americans to the rise of Mussolini, or on the response of German Americans to the rise of Hitler. Your research might include interviews with Italian Americans or German Americans who were alive at that time.

Critical Thinking Skills
1. Peace treaties and arms limitation pacts have little meaning to aggressive militarists. Policies promoting economic stability might have kept militarists from taking power.
2. Strong, self-sufficient nations can avoid foreign entanglements. Weaker nations cannot afford the cost of foreign entanglements.
3. Fascists perceived appeasement as a weak response.
4. Students should point out that the U.S. had all but declared war against Germany and Italy, and that continued offensives against the Allies would have forced the U.S. to take greater action.

Writing About Topics in American History
1. The "ideal type" is a male businessman with a family, a house on the edge of town, and a car. He is generous, efficient, optimistic, hardworking and determined to be a success.
2. Students may contact family, relatives, neighbors, or local organizations for firsthand accounts.

9. He militarized the Rhineland, annexed Austria, seized Czechoslovakia, and started World War II by invading Poland.

10. Initially, Americans favored an isolationist policy, but that faded with attacks against American shipping and requests for support from Britain. The Japanese attack on Pearl Harbor brought the United States into the war.

Chapter Review exercises are keyed for student abilities:
● = Basic
▲ = Average
■ = Average/Advanced

Chapter 18 ■ The World at War

	SECTION OBJECTIVES	SECTION RESOURCES
Section 1 **Times of Crisis**	■ describe how the Allies halted the expansion of the Axis during 1942	● **Reteaching Resources:** Worksheet 67 ▲ **Reinforcement Workbook:** Worksheet 67 ▲ **Teaching Transparencies:** Transparency 67
Section 2 **War and the Home Front**	■ describe the impact of World War II on the U.S. economy and on women, Japanese Americans, and other minority groups	● **Reteaching Resources:** Worksheet 68 ▲ **Reinforcement Workbook:** Worksheet 68 ▲ **Teaching Transparencies:** Transparency 68
Section 3 **Toward Victory in Europe**	■ explain how the Allies defeated Germany and Italy	● **Reteaching Resources:** Worksheet 69 ▲ **Reinforcement Workbook:** Worksheet 69 ■ **Enrichment and Extension Resources:** Primary Source Worksheet 35 ▲ **Teaching Transparencies:** Transparency 69
Section 4 **Advancing on Japan**	■ describe Allied advances on Japan in the Pacific ■ discuss the decision to develop and use the atomic bomb	● **Reteaching Resources:** Worksheet 70 ▲ **Reinforcement Workbook:** Worksheet 70 ■ **Enrichment and Extension Resources:** Historian Worksheet 7 ▲ **Teaching Transparencies:** Transparency 70
Section 5 **The Wreckage of War**	■ describe the political and social effects of World War II	● **Reteaching Resources:** Worksheet 71 ▲ **Reinforcement Workbook:** Worksheet 71 ■ **Enrichment and Extension Resources:** Primary Source Worksheet 36 ▲ **Teaching Transparencies:** Transparency 71

The list below shows Essential Elements relevant to this chapter. (The complete list of Essential Elements appears in the introductory pages of this Teacher's Edition.)

Section 1: 1A, 9A, 9B, 9E, 9F
Section 2: 1A, 3B, 3F, 4C, 6B, 7G, 9B, 9F
Section 3: 1A, 1B, 2E, 9A, 9B, 9D
Section 4: 1A, 3A, 4E, 7A, 7J, 9B
Section 5: 1B, 3B, 4C, 6A, 7A, 7B, 9A, 9D, 9E

Section Resources are keyed for student abilities:
● = Basic
▲ = Average
■ = Average/Advanced

CHAPTER RESOURCES

Geography Resources: Worksheets 35, 36
Tests: Chapter 18 Test

Chapter Project: Global Interactions

Have students create an illustrated scrapbook of World War II. Students may focus on such topics as war and technology, changes in the United States as a result of the war, or its effect on American foreign policy. Have students use photographs, art, literature, movies, and music of the war period.

Homework Options

Each section contains activities labeled "Addressing Individual Needs." You may wish to choose from among these activities when assigning homework.

> ### Provisions for Limited English Proficiency (LEP)
> Several suggested activities may be particularly helpful for teachers of students with limited English proficiency. These activities have been marked throughout the Teacher's Annotated Edition with the symbol **LEP** .

BIBLIOGRAPHY AND AUDIOVISUAL AIDS

Teacher Bibliography

Blum, John M. *V Was for Victory: Politics and American Culture During World War II.* Harcourt Brace Jovanovich, 1977.

Gilbert, Martin. *The Holocaust: A History of the Jews of Europe During the Second World War.* Henry Holt and Co., 1987.

Keegan, John, ed. *The Times Atlas of the Second World War.* Harper and Row, 1989.

Student Bibliography

American Heritage and E. L. Sulzberger, eds. *The American Heritage Picture History of World War II.* American Heritage, 1966.

Bernbaum, Israel. *My Brother's Keeper: The Holocaust Through the Eyes of an Artist.* G. P. Putnam's Sons, 1985.

Terasaki, Gwen. *Bridge to the Sun.* Wakestone, 1986. The American wife of a Japanese diplomat tells the story of internment in the United States and her later war years in Japan.

Literature

Frank, Anne. *Diary of a Young Girl.* Doubleday, 1967.

Heller, Joseph. *Catch Twenty-Two.* Dell, 1985. A dark comedy on the absurdities of the World War II military bureaucracy.

Piercy, Marge. *Gone to Soldiers.* Summit Books, 1987. A novel that follows several characters in the United States and Europe through the war.

Shaw, Irwin. *The Young Lions.* Dell, 1984. Three soldiers in World War II: a German and two Americans.

Wiesel, Elie. *Night.* Bantam, 1982. A searing account of the Holocaust as witnessed by a fifteen-year-old boy.

Films and Videotapes*

D-Day. 27 min. LUCERNE. Film classic tells of the Allies' military build-up, strategies leading to D-Day, and the Allied invasion of Europe.

The Homefront. 90 min. CF. Social changes that occurred in the United States during the war, including the effect on family life, the beginning of the civil rights movement, and the growth of the American economy.

The Lost Generation. 20 min. FI. Visual diary of the U.S. atomic bombing of Hiroshima and Nagasaki in 1945. Interviews, drawings, and historical footage document its tragic effects.

1942–1943: America the Way We Were (War Years Series). 58 min. PBS. Captures the determination of the nation as it geared up to fight World War II.

Topaz. 58 min. ONEWEST. Documentary about American citizens of Japanese descent who were forced from their homes during World War II.

The Turning Point, 1941–1944 (American Chronicles Series). 23 min. AIMS. General MacArthur leads U.S. forces in the Pacific against Japan as Hitler declares war on America.

Computer Software*

The European Theater (Apple). HS. Nazi Germany is rapidly taking over Europe, and Allied forces must find a way to stop them. Students make decisions regarding troop movement, weaponry, joining forces with other nations, etc.

Patton vs. Rommel (Apple Macintosh). ELEC. Allied troops have landed at Omaha Beach. Features realistic battle conditions and sound effects. Historically accurate game map.

*For a complete guide to audiovisual sources, see the introduction to this book (page Txx).

Chapter 18

The World at War
(pp. 412–439)

This chapter focuses on the role of the United States in World War II between 1941 and 1945. It describes the events leading to Allied victory on the European and Pacific fronts. The chapter also discusses the effects of the war on American society.

 Themes in American History

- Global interactions
- Economic development
- Pluralistic society
- Geography

Chapter Objectives

After students complete this chapter, they will be able to:

1. Describe how the Allies halted the expansion of the Axis during 1942.

2. Describe the impact of World War II on the U.S. economy and on women, Japanese Americans, and other minority groups.

3. Explain how the Allies defeated Germany and Italy.

4. Describe Allied advances on Japan in the Pacific.

5. Discuss the decision to develop and use the atomic bomb.

6. Describe the political and social effects of World War II.

Chapter Opener Art
Ogden Placner, *Sweating in the Mission.*

*A*ir *power proved to be a decisive factor in World War II. It also became a symbol of the United States' growing reach around the world.*

CHAPTER	**Reinforcement Workbook:** Worksheets 67–71
SUPPORT	**Reteaching Resources:** Worksheets 67–71
MATERIAL	**Enrichment and Extension Resources:** Primary Source Worksheets 35, 36; Historian Worksheet 7
	Geography Resources: Worksheets 35, 36
	Teaching Transparencies: Transparencies 67–71
	Tests: Chapter 18 Test

18 The World at War (1941–1945)

SECTION 1

Times of Crisis
(pp. 413–417)

Section Objective
- describe how the Allies halted the expansion of the Axis during 1942

Introducing the Section

Connecting with Past Learnings
Review the events of World War II up to the entry of the United States. *By the end of 1941, what had happened on the European front?* (Germany dominated Europe, with only Britain and the Soviet Union still fighting the Axis powers.) *In December 1941, what areas in Asia and the Pacific had Japan attacked?* (Manchuria, China, French Indochina, American bases in the Pacific, British and Dutch possessions.)

Key Terms
List the key terms on the board. Have students locate the terms in their texts and define them in their own words. Then ask them to write a short paragraph on the year 1942 using all the terms. **LEP**

Focus
Create a timeline on the board, asking volunteers to fill in major battles and military actions discussed in the section. Have students differentiate between Allied and Axis victories. *What battle was the turning point of the war against Germany, on the Western Front?* (Battle of El Alamein.) *The Eastern Front?* (Battle of Stalingrad.) *Against Japan?* (Battle of Midway.) *Why were these victories so important?* (They were massive defeats for forces which, up until that point, had experienced only victory.)

1A, 9A, 9B, 9E, 9F

1 Times of Crisis

Section Focus

Key Terms Axis Powers ■ Allies ■ Battle of El Alamein ■ Battle of Stalingrad ■ Bataan Death March ■ Battle of Midway

Main Idea The Allies formed an alliance that, by the end of 1942, halted the expansion of Axis power.

Objectives As you read, look for answers to these questions:
1. Why did the Allies adopt a "Europe first" policy?
2. What were some of the low points suffered by the Allies in 1941 and 1942?
3. When and why did the tide of the war turn in the Pacific and in Europe?

In the first months after Pearl Harbor, the Axis Powers—Germany, Italy, and Japan—seemed unstoppable. Japan quickly occupied most of Southeast Asia and seized strategic islands throughout the Pacific. In the Atlantic, German submarines sank three or four ships every day. And in Eastern Europe, Hitler's forces stormed into the Soviet Union, pushing all the way to the city of Stalingrad on the Volga River.

To fight back, the United States, Britain, and the Soviet Union forged a strong alliance. They (and a host of smaller nations) called themselves the Allies, with a capital "A." Believing that Germany and Italy posed a greater threat than Japan, the Allies agreed on a "Europe first" policy. They would devote the bulk of their resources to the European war. In the Pacific, they would buy time with an "aggressive defense." Once the Allies had gained the upper hand in Europe, the planners agreed, they could pour more resources into the Pacific war.

DARK DAYS IN EUROPE 1A

Hitler's invasion of the Soviet Union in June 1941 (page 407) met with great success at first. German forces swept rapidly eastward, capturing more than a million Soviet soldiers and driving the Red Army back to the edge of Moscow.

As diplomats and panicky citizens fled the capital, the Soviets launched an impressive counter-offensive. Aided by heavy December snows and frigid temperatures, for which the Germans were not prepared, the Red Army saved Moscow and stopped the Germans from advancing farther.

To the north, however, the Germans had surrounded Leningrad and held it under siege from September 1941 to January 1944. Residents, having run out of food, starved to death at a horrendous rate of 4,000 a day. By the time the Red Army finally broke the siege of Leningrad, more than 600,000 civilians had died.

Meanwhile, German troops had occupied the Balkan nations in southeastern Europe, driving

SUPPORTING THE SECTION

Reinforcement Workbook: Worksheet 67
Reteaching Resources: Worksheet 67
Teaching Transparencies: Transparency 67

In this picture a German firing squad appears to be killing a resistance fighter. In reality the "execution" was faked to try to scare
the resistance fighter into talking. HISTORY How did the resistance
hinder German conquests in Europe? **9A**

A Soviet poster from 1942 declares, "The Big Three Will Tie the
Enemy in Knots." The Big Three were the United States, the
Soviet Union, and Great Britain. HISTORY Why, do you think, is the
poster concerned with Germany rather than Japan? **9B**

British forces off the Greek mainland and the
Mediterranean island of Crete. In the southern
part of the Soviet Union, the Nazis broke through
the Soviet defenses and swept toward the oil-rich
region near the Caspian Sea.

The conquered nations felt the full force of Hitler's ruthless policies. To free Germans for military service, the Nazis rounded up hundreds of
thousands of men and women to work as slave laborers in German war industries. Such brutality
drove thousands of European civilians into resistance movements in Poland, France, and other occupied countries. Resistance agents used
sabotage, assassination, and other weapons to harass the German occupiers.

THE MEDITERRANEAN AND AFRICA 1A
The Russians, desperately trying to stem the tide
of the Nazi advance, pleaded with the United
States and Britain to attack Hitler from the west.
By establishing a second front, the Allies might
divert German forces from their assault on the Soviet Union. But in 1942 the Western Allies felt
they did not yet have the resources to risk a full-
scale invasion of the European mainland. Instead,
they would attack Axis forces in North Africa.

German and Italian forces had seized a great
stretch of North Africa, from Tunisia to eastern
Libya. By so doing, they threatened British-
controlled Egypt and the Suez Canal—Britain's

lifeline to its Asian and African empire. Leading
the Axis forces was the Nazis' most skillful general, Erwin Rommel, nicknamed "the Desert
Fox." Rommel sent his famed Afrika Korps
smashing eastward toward Egypt in May 1942.
British forces retreated deep into Egypt. Mussolini was so sure of an Axis victory that he had his
white horse shipped in to be ready for a victory
parade through Cairo, the Egyptian capital.

At the Battle of El Alamein in October 1942,
however, British forces under General Bernard
Law Montgomery halted the German advance.
Rommel, outnumbered and desperately short of
supplies, retreated hundreds of miles across the
North African desert. The tide of war was begin-
ning to turn—and not just in North Africa. In
Churchill's words, "Up to Alamein we survived.
After Alamein we conquered."

ALLIED VICTORIES ON TWO FRONTS 1A
As Rommel's retreat churned up the Egyptian
dust, the Allies stopped Axis offensives in two key
places, the Soviet Union and North Africa. In
the Soviet Union, the German invasion came to a
bloody halt at the city of Stalingrad. The Battle
of Stalingrad saw some of the fiercest fighting of
the war. Beginning in September 1942, small units
of German and Soviet troops fought hand to hand
in almost every building and alley. All the while,
constant bombing and artillery fire were reducing

the city to rubble. A Nazi lieutenant wrote, "The street is no longer measured by meters but by corpses. Stalingrad is no longer a town. It is an enormous cloud of burning, blinding smoke; it is a vast furnace."

Then in November 1942, a Soviet armored attack surrounded the German forces in Stalingrad. After three months of fighting, the tattered and freezing German survivors surrendered in February 1943. Having lost some 300,000 front-line troops in the Stalingrad campaign, Germany would never again be able to mount a major successful offensive on the Eastern Front. But the Soviets had paid a steep price for victory. In the fight for Stalingrad they had lost more than 500,000 soldiers and civilians—more people than the United States would lose in the entire war.

Meanwhile, in North Africa, General Dwight D. Eisenhower of the United States led a British-American invasion of Axis-controlled Morocco and Algeria. Eisenhower pushed eastward and Montgomery advanced westward from Egypt, trapping Rommel's Africa Korps between them. The Axis forces surrendered in May 1943. Rommel escaped, but some 349,000 German and Italian soldiers had been killed or captured.

The North African victory meant that the southern coast of Europe now lay open to Allied attack. By mid-1943 the Allies were everywhere on the offensive.

Soviet survivors of a Nazi attack in the Crimea search for relatives among the dead. Germans deliberately killed Russian noncombatants. This policy resulted in millions of Soviet civilian deaths. **GLOBAL AWARENESS** How might the loss of so many of its civilians have affected the Soviet Union? **9E**

Photo Caption Answer
Students may suggest damage to the economy and lowering of productivity, reduced future population, and intense mistrust of Germany.

Background   Throughout the war, despite Germany's vicious attacks on Soviet civilians, the Soviet Union never lost its capacity for production. In 1941 Stalin ordered hundreds of factories to be dismantled and moved piecemeal to areas east of the Ural Mountains, where they were safe from attack. During the war, women in the USSR made up over half of the industrial work force.

Enrichment/Extension
Have students find out more about the role of cryptographers during World War II. Notable code-breaking operations include Operation Magic in the Pacific and Operation Ultra on the European front, whose secrets have just been revealed in the past few years. Students may also research the use of the Navajo language for coded messages in the Pacific. Have students write reports describing their findings.

Assessment
You may wish to use the Section 1 Review, page 417, to see how well your students understand the main points in this lesson.

Section Review Answers
1. *Axis Powers*—Alliance of Germany, Italy, and Japan. *Allies*—U.S., Britain, Soviet Union, and other nations allied against the Axis. *Battle of El Alamein*—Battle that marked the turning point of the war in North Africa. *Battle of Stalingrad*—Bloody battle, marked turning point of war on Russian front. *Bataan Death March*—Forced march of American and Filipino prisoners of war. *Battle of Midway*— American victory that marked the turning point in the Pacific.

JAPAN'S PACIFIC OFFENSIVE 1A

Like Germany, Japan enjoyed tremendous success in the early part of the war. Japan's attack on Pearl Harbor was part of an offensive against British and American positions throughout Asia and the Pacific. Key targets included American bases in the Philippines and the important British naval base at Singapore.

When Japanese troops seized Manila, capital of the Philippines, in January 1942, American and Filipino troops had to withdraw to the Bataan Peninsula and Corregidor Island (map, page 431). They fought on, taking many losses. At last, greatly outnumbered and cut off from outside support by air or sea, roughly 12,000 American and 65,000 Filipino forces surrendered to the Japanese in April and May.

The Japanese led the prisoners on a brutal forced march of 65 miles over tortuous terrain to a prisoner-of-war camp. Between 7,000 and 10,000 Allied prisoners were clubbed, shot, or starved to death. News of the Bataan Death March, as it was called in the United States, further enraged an American public already infuriated by Pearl Harbor.

This picture of Allied prisoners was taken at the start of the Bataan Death March. Thousands died, in part because the Japanese were not prepared to deal with so many exhausted prisoners, and in part from brutal treatment. HISTORY What effect did Japanese atrocities have on American public opinion? 9F

BIOGRAPHY

CHESTER NIMITZ (1885–1966) of Fredericksburg, Texas, graduated from the U.S. Naval Academy in 1905. He served with the U.S. submarine force during World War I. After Japan crushed the U.S. naval force at Pearl Harbor, Nimitz rebuilt the fleet. As the Pacific chief of operations for the Navy and Marines, Nimitz developed the island-hopping strategy that helped win the war in the Pacific.

HALTING THE JAPANESE 1A

The surrender of the Philippines was the bleakest hour of the Pacific war for Americans. Japan seemed unbeatable. It had seized 300,000 square miles of ocean in six months. It was poised to attack Australia, and might even invade the United States. Americans on the West Coast kept a nervous lookout for Japanese invaders. At this early point, with the American war machine just getting into gear, the Japanese navy had three times as many ships as the United States.

Two crucial battles in mid-1942 halted Japan's expansion in the Pacific. In May, at the Battle of the Coral Sea, Allied forces blocked a Japanese push toward Australia. This battle, fought entirely by aircraft, was the first in naval history in which opposing ships never came within sight of each other. The next month, in June 1942, a Japanese armada of more than 100 ships attacked an American naval base on Midway Island, a stepping-stone on the way to the Hawaiian Islands. Included in the fleet, which was led by Admiral Isoroku Yamamoto, were five aircraft carriers loaded with hundreds of warplanes.

The United States Navy gained control of the Battle of Midway because Admiral Chester Nimitz knew exactly where the Japanese fleet was going. American code-breakers had intercepted key messages. Unlike the decoded messages prior to the attack on Pearl Harbor, this information was used successfully.

As at Coral Sea, the fighting at Midway was done by warplanes. Both sides suffered heavy

---

Photo Caption Answer
It produced an outpouring of hostile feeling against Japan.

Biography
For further reading consider: Driskill, Frank A., and Dede Cassad. *Admiral of the Hills: Chester W. Nimitz.* Eakin Press, 1983.

This painting of the Battle of Midway by an American naval commander shows the scene of Japan's first major setback of World War II. American dive-bombers sank the aircraft carrier *Kaga* (at right) in an inferno that killed 800 sailors. **HISTORY** What made this United States victory possible? **1A**

losses. But the decisive moment came when American dive-bombers attacked and sank four Japanese carriers in a matter of minutes. The crippled Japanese fleet was forced to retreat, and Midway Island remained in American hands.

TAKING THE OFFENSIVE 1A

The American triumph at Midway marked a turning point in the Pacific war. Henceforth, American forces began to drive the Japanese back to their home islands.

As the Allies advanced on key Japanese possessions, these remote, jungle-choked islands became scenes of death and destruction. William Manchester, a marine who fought in the Pacific, recalled:

Some islands were literally uninhabitable . . . and the battles were fought under fantastic conditions. Guadalcanal was rocked by an earthquake. Volcanic steam hissed through the rocks at Iwo. On Bougainville, bulldozers vanished in the spongy, bottomless swamps, and at the height of the fighting on Peleliu the temperature was 115 degrees in the shade.

The first Allied offensive took place at Guadalcanal, one of the Solomon Islands. Guadalcanal's importance lay in its location—close to both Australia and New Guinea. In August 1942 a force of 20,000 American marines stormed ashore. Their goal was to root out the Japanese and seize control of the island.

The marines suffered agonizing setbacks. When the Japanese sank four out of five Allied cruisers, support ships withdrew, stranding American troops on Guadalcanal without naval gunfire and supplies. For four months they remained isolated, under Japanese bombardment from sea, air, and ground. After some of the toughest fighting of the war, much of it hand-to-hand, the marines began to gain the advantage. The surviving Japanese fled the island in February 1943. Victory over Japan, however, was far in the future.

SECTION REVIEW

1. KEY TERMS Axis Powers, Allies, Battle of El Alamein, Battle of Stalingrad, Bataan Death March, Battle of Midway

2. PEOPLE AND PLACES Leningrad, Erwin Rommel, Bernard Law Montgomery, Dwight D. Eisenhower, Philippines, Chester Nimitz, Isoroku Yamamoto, Guadalcanal

3. COMPREHENSION Which Allied nation bore the brunt of the fighting against Hitler in 1942?

4. COMPREHENSION What two battles turned the tide of war against the Japanese in the Pacific? Describe how they were fought.

5. CRITICAL THINKING Why, do you think, would the Soviet Union have pushed for a "Europe first" policy? Why might some Americans have preferred an "Asia first" policy?

Photo Caption Answer
Cracking the Japanese secret code.

2. *Leningrad*—Soviet city under siege 1941–1944. *Erwin Rommel*—Nazi general who scored early victories in North Africa. *Bernard Law Montgomery*—British general who won at El Alamein. *Dwight D. Eisenhower*—American general who led invasion of Morocco and Algeria. *Philippines*—American-controlled islands in the Pacific, captured by the Japanese in 1942. *Chester Nimitz*—American admiral during the Battle of Midway. *Isoroku Yamamoto*—Japanese admiral during the Battle of Midway. *Guadalcanal*—One of the Solomon Islands, where the first Allied offensive in the Pacific took place.

3. The Soviet Union.

4. The Battles of Midway and Guadalcanal. Midway was a naval battle fought with aircraft carriers, in which American dive-bombers sank Japanese carriers. At Guadalcanal, stranded U.S. troops fought for months.

5. The greatest threat to the Soviet Union was Germany, which already controlled a great deal of Soviet territory by 1942. The United States, on the other hand, had been attacked by Japan at Pearl Harbor, and Japan had captured the American territory of the Philippines.

Closure

Ask one student to transform the Main Idea of the section into a question, and have other students answer that question. Then have students read Section 2 for the next class period, noting the ways the war affected Americans' way of life.

Section Objective

■ describe the impact of World War II on the U.S. economy and on women, Japanese Americans, and other minority groups

Introducing the Section

Connecting with Past Learnings

Have students recall the war's effect on the home front. *How did World War I change American society?* (Farm production soared; labor profited; women gained status; repression of dissent; agencies created to deal with war; propaganda against Germans.)

Key Terms

List the key terms on the board. Have students find the terms in their texts and explain how each is related to World War II. You may ask the class to create a special list of World War II terms, using the key terms and other terms introduced in the section, such as *GI, Nisei,* and *WAAC.* **LEP**

Focus

To review the changes in American society caused by World War II, play a matching game. On the board list these groups: Japanese Americans, women in the armed forces, women civilians, businesses, blacks in the armed forces, black civilians, national economy, Hispanics. Have individual students describe the situation of each of these groups without naming the group, and have the class identify who is being described.

418

1A, 3B, 3F, 4C, 6B, 7G, 9B, 9F

2 War and the Home Front

Section Focus

Key Terms internment ■ War Production Board

Main Idea World War II brought sweeping changes to American society.

Objectives As you read, look for answers to these questions:
1. What special hardships did Japanese Americans suffer during the war?
2. How did the American economy respond to the overwhelming demands of the war?
3. What were the war's effects on women and minorities?

In many ways, World War II's effects on American society mirrored those of World War I. The economy boomed as industry began churning out war supplies. The federal government took a more active role in economic planning. Groups such as blacks and women found new opportunities for advancement. And wartime tensions threatened the civil liberties of some Americans.

7G

THE INTERNMENT OF JAPANESE AMERICANS

American involvement in the war changed many lives. Among those affected almost immediately were Japanese Americans. The war inflamed a long tradition of racism against people of Asian ancestry. The governor of Idaho said, for example, "A good solution to the Jap problem would be to send them all back to Japan, then sink the island."

Many believed that Japanese Americans would act as spies or saboteurs, although there was little evidence to back such beliefs. Most people of Japanese descent living in the United States at the time of Pearl Harbor had been born as American citizens.

In February 1942, President Roosevelt ordered the army to round up some 110,000 citizens and aliens of Japanese ancestry. These people, most of whom lived along the West Coast, were put in "relocation centers"—in effect, concentration camps. Families being relocated were not allowed to take any of their major possessions with them. Many lost homes and businesses during their period of internment (imprisonment). There was little privacy in the camps, and whole families were made to live in single rooms.

Peter Ota, age 15, was one such Japanese American who was forced to leave his Los Angeles home. Together with his 12-year-old sister and his father, Peter was sent to a camp in Colorado. His mother was too ill to go. After a while, Peter was released occasionally to work on a farm or in a factory. When Peter's mother died, he went to California, under military guard, to get her body. "When they marched me through the train stations," Peter recalled, "the people recognized me as being Oriental. . . . I heard 'dirty Jap' very distinctly."

This photograph shows the anxiety Japanese American families felt as they left their homes for remote internment camps. **ETHICS** Why, do you think, were Japanese Americans treated differently from German Americans or Italian Americans? **9F**

SUPPORTING THE SECTION

Reinforcement Workbook: Worksheet 68
Reteaching Resources: Worksheet 68
Teaching Transparencies: Transparency 68

Photo Caption Answer

Students may suggest that racism played a role. Also, there were not as many Japanese Americans as there were members of the other groups, therefore they possessed less political power.

Like some 33,000 other Japanese Americans, Peter Ota eventually joined the armed forces. Beginning in 1943 the American government began recruiting Japanese Americans for military service. Nisei (nee–SAY) battalions—units made up of second-generation Japanese Americans—served with distinction on European battlefields.

The Supreme Court upheld internment throughout the war. Four decades later a federal commission determined that the internment "was not justified by military necessity." In 1988 Congress apologized for the wartime mistreatment and voted to pay $20,000 in compensation to each person still living who had been interned. Spark Matsunaga of Hawaii, a Japanese American who was among 69 senators supporting the apology, rejoiced. The action, he said, removed "one great blot" on the Constitution.

BUILDING UP THE ARMED FORCES 1A

At the time of Pearl Harbor about 1.5 million Americans served in the armed forces. By the end of the war the armed forces were 12 million strong. Fifteen million men and women of every color and creed served at some point in the war. Almost every family had at least one member in the military. Not since the Civil War had so many Americans been so personally touched by war.

After Pearl Harbor, thousands volunteered for service. Despite overwhelming support for the war, however, most "GIs" entered the military through the selective service system—the draft. (GI, an abbreviation for "government issue," was a common wartime nickname for American servicemen.) The average age of American soldiers in World War II was 26. In the Vietnam War, by contrast, the typical soldier would be 19.

In earlier wars, women had served with the military as clerks or as nurses. In World War II they received full status. Creation of forces like the WAAC (Women's Auxiliary Army Corps) came over loud objections from people such as a congressman who wondered who would be left at home to do "the humble homey tasks to which every woman has devoted herself." One writer reported, "At most bases the WAACs lived in guarded, barbed-wire compounds which they could leave only in groups escorted by armed

Women pilots flew support missions for the Air Corps in World War II. These WAAC pilots are returning from a training mission in their B-17 flying fortress nicknamed "Pistol Packin' Mama." PARTICIPATION Present arguments for and against participation of women in the military. 4C

guards." Such precautions were thought necessary to keep soldiers from constantly trying to socialize with them.

Despite such obstacles, women made a significant contribution to the American war effort. They worked as nurses, ambulance drivers, radio operators, mechanics, and pilots—nearly every duty not involving direct combat.

MOBILIZING THE ECONOMY 3B

World War II put an end to the Great Depression, and once again the economy boomed. The gross national product jumped from $91 billion in 1939 to $212 billion in 1945. In 1940, more than 8 million workers had no jobs. By 1944 unemployment had dropped to 670,000. Employers were desperate for help. Signs urged restaurant patrons, "Please be polite to our waitresses. They are harder to get than customers."

Of course, the armed forces provided many of the jobs. Equally important were the industries that made weapons and war supplies. As these industries grew, so did their need for workers. Many employers found people with handicaps to

Developing the Lesson
After students have read the section, you may want to consider the following activities:

Constitutional Heritage
Roosevelt's order to round up all people of Japanese descent is an example of the extraordinary powers of the President in times of war. **Why did Senator Matsunaga call the internment a blot on the Constitution?** (Because it used the President's constitutional power to wage war to limit constitutionally protected rights of Americans.) Ask students if they think the Constitution should be amended to limit the President's ability to restrict civil rights during wartime.

Economics
Create a balance sheet on the board, illustrating the good and bad effects of the war on the U.S. economy. (Good—unemployment went down; GNP went up; increase in productivity. Bad—shortages; taxes increased; most growth experienced by only a few companies.) **How did the war change the relationship between the government and the economy?** (The government took more active control of the economy.)

Photo Caption Answer
Some students may suggest that women can make important military contributions. Others may suggest that women should not have to face the dangers of combat.

Background The Pentagon, completed in 1943, was the largest building in the world. Yet it was already too small to house the military bureaucracy by the time it was finished.

Background The "government issue" on which the nickname GI is based refers to the uniforms and supplies issued to draftees.

Ask students to suggest resources which were necessary materials. (Rubber, gasoline, metal products.) Have students find out what parts of the world are sources of these products. (Rubber—Southeast Asia, Latin America, Africa; oil—the Middle East, the United States, Southeast Asia; metal ores—the United States and other places around the globe.) *Why were many of these resources scarce during the war?* (Supplies from Japanese-controlled areas were shut off; submarine warfare made all overseas trade difficult.)

Why might butter and meat have been in short supply? (Much of it went to soldiers overseas; there were fewer people to work on farms.)

Civic Values
Have students consider how the war brought the issue of civic responsibility to daily life. Ask them to suggest how their lives might be different if the year were 1943.

Cultural Pluralism
Discuss the impact of World War II on black Americans. *How did racial discrimination follow blacks into the army?* (They were given low-level jobs and rarely saw combat; refused service at segregated businesses.) *What advances were blacks able to make during the war?* (FDR signed an executive order ending discrimination in war industries and created the FEPC; some black soldiers did fight and distinguish themselves in battle.) Have students suggest how the war led to the civil rights movement.

History
Have students discuss the role fashion played in the riots between Mexican Americans and white servicemen. Ask students if there are styles of clothing today which distinguish groups of people and lead to social tensions.

420

KEEP THESE HANDS OFF!

BUY the New VICTORY BONDS

This 1942 propaganda poster encourages citizens to purchase government bonds. **CULTURE** What images does the poster use? How effective are they? Why? **9B**

be excellent war workers. For example, some factories hired the deaf to work around loud machines. Airplane-makers hired midgets to inspect the interior of airplane wings.

To a greater extent than ever before in American history, the federal government managed the economy. It decided what to make, who would make it, and how certain scarce products should be distributed. Presiding over this enormous enterprise was the War Production Board (WPB), which President Roosevelt created in 1942. The War Production Board organized the shift of the economy to wartime production. Factories that had made nylon hose began to make nylon parachutes. Manufacturers of cars turned out tanks and airplanes. A gigantic Ford plant at Willow Run, Michigan, began work on its first B-24 bomber a week before the Japanese attack on Pearl Harbor. Soon it was sending forth a new airplane every 63 minutes.

Government contracts most often went to large corporations like Ford and General Motors. WPB

officials said those firms were best suited to produce war goods quickly and in great volume. Critics replied that smaller companies could have produced just as efficiently. In any event, the result was to sharply increase the power of big corporations. In 1940 the 100 largest companies made 30 percent of all manufactured goods. By 1945 that figure had jumped to 70 percent.

"WE WILL FIGHT ON TO VICTORY!" 3B, 3F
Where did the government get all the money it spent on the war? About 40 percent came from taxes. Congress raised the income tax and extended it to millions more people. In 1939 only 4 million Americans—people like bankers and professionals—paid income tax. By 1945, factory workers and others of modest means also had to pay taxes. Some 42 million Americans were on the tax rolls.

The government had to borrow the rest of the money it needed. Patriotic citizens bought billions of dollars worth of war bonds to finance the war effort. As in World War I, national debt rose dramatically during the war years.

The government set up a system of rationing to help hold down prices and manage shortages of scarce products. Each family got a supply of ration tickets to hand over whenever it bought goods like meat, butter, and gasoline. People grumbled about the inconvenience, but it was better to have some of those goods than none at all.

To get more food, people spaded up lawns and planted "Victory gardens." A woman in Long Beach, California, recalled, "There was a large vacant lot and everybody got together and had a gigantic communal Victory garden. . . . They'd give things away to everybody. Nobody said, 'This is mine.'"

But not everyone was high-minded. Some advertisers saw patriotism as a sales gimmick and tried to persuade consumers that even everyday products aided the war effort. A maker of women's hair pins took this effort to extraordinary lengths: "She wears it proudly—this badge of courage. It helps her face a shattered world with calm valor and deep faith. . . . It's a silent eloquent way of saying, 'There must be no letting down. We will fight on to Victory!'"

Photo Caption Answers
The poster uses the image of clawed hands representing Germany and Japan, reaching out to threaten an innocent mother and child. Students may suggest the poster successfully makes use of the urge to protect a nation's women and children from harm at the hands of foreigners.

A TURNING POINT FOR WOMEN

Most women had more to think about than hair pins. Vast numbers took jobs vacated by men who had gone to war. During the Depression, with jobs scarce, Americans had discouraged women from seeking jobs. "Don't take a man's place," was the attitude. But with the boom in wartime manufacturing and the loss of millions of male workers to the military, employers eagerly recruited women.

Peggy Terry was a Kentucky woman who went to work in a plant that loaded anti-aircraft shells with gunpowder. "My mother, my sister, and myself worked there," she later recalled. "Each of us worked a different shift because we had little ones at home. We made the fabulous sum of $32 a week. . . . To us it was just an absolute miracle. Before that, we made nothing."

About 18 million American women worked in war plants during World War II. Some industries created child-care programs so that mothers would be free to work. CULTURAL PLURALISM How, do you think, did women's wartime experiences affect their attitudes regarding work outside the home? **6B**

SOLDIERS *without guns*

The female labor force swelled by about 5 million during the war, a jump of about one-third. Like Peggy Terry, about half of the new workers went into industrial jobs. Women worked as welders, taxicab drivers, crane operators, police officers, chemists—wherever there was a need.

Women seized these new opportunities with enthusiasm, but their experience was not entirely positive. They usually earned much less than men, even in jobs that were exactly the same. Another grievance was the lack of day care for children. And finally, women were told in a variety of ways to think of their work merely as a temporary necessity, a wartime duty. Psychologists and magazine writers said women should be happy to return to the home at war's end. But many women resisted. If they were fired from a wartime job to make room for a returning soldier, they kept looking until they found a new job.

AFRICAN AMERICANS ON THE HOME FRONT 4C

"V for Victory" was everybody's slogan. It appeared on countless posters, and people greeted one another with a two-fingered V salute. African Americans called for a Double V—a victory against fascism overseas and against racial discrimination at home.

In 1941, as military spending began to climb, the jobs that opened up were mainly for whites. One aircraft plant told job applicants that blacks "will be considered only as janitors and in other similar capacities." The military, meanwhile, segregated black soldiers and generally assigned them to low-level, rear-area jobs. As one black recruit put it, "We can take no pride in our armed forces. We can become no more than flunkies in the army and kitchen boys in the navy."

A. Philip Randolph, president of the Brotherhood of Sleeping Car Porters, vowed to fight job discrimination. He planned a giant march on Washington for July 1941 to demand equal access to defense jobs and the "right to fight" in the military. A few weeks before the march was to take place, President Roosevelt met with Randolph and made a deal. Roosevelt issued Executive Order 8802. The order prohibited discrimination in war industries—although not in the armed forces. In return, Randolph agreed to cancel the march.

Photo Caption Answer
Some women were eager to return to their homes or to their former jobs, while others realized that they were fully capable of holding what had formerly been considered a man's job.

Background The city of Washington became crowded with women during the war. The armed services recruited young women from across the country to take military service jobs at salaries that seemed like fortunes to most. From the high school graduating class of Alma, Arkansas, for example, fully one-fourth of the young women boarded a train and left for Washington.

C **Cooperative Learning**
Divide the class into small groups. Have each group create a propaganda poster designed to win the support for the war effort of one of the following: women, blacks, Hispanics, the business community, labor. Have each group explain its poster to the class. **LEP**

Addressing Individual Needs

Guided/ Independent Practice
Instruct students to complete **Reinforcement Workbook** Worksheet 68, which requires students to analyze a table of data about federal government finances during World War II.

Reteaching/Correctives
Have students form small groups. Have each member of the group assume one of these roles: Japanese American, black civilian or soldier. Ask students to imagine that they are attending a reunion, held this year, of people who lived through World War II. Have them use the text as a basis for talking about their war experiences.

Have students complete **Reteaching Resources** Worksheet 68. This worksheet guides students in organizing information presented in the section.

Enrichment/Extension
Have students ask family members who were alive during World War II about how the war affected their lives, creating tapes or transcripts to present to the class. If that is not possible, have them read excerpts from Studs Terkel's *The Good War: An Oral History of World War Two.* Pantheon, 1984. Have them choose a selection they find particularly moving and write a paragraph describing that person's recollections of the war.

Members of an all-black Fighter Group are briefed at their base in Italy. The group received a citation for their role in a 1,600-mile air raid on a Berlin tank factory. **CULTURAL PLURALISM** What special hardships did blacks face in the armed forces? 4C

By creating a Fair Employment Practices Committee (FEPC) to enforce his order, Roosevelt helped to open up new jobs for blacks. But the FEPC had few enforcement powers, and many white employers and union leaders continued to discriminate. Randolph and other black leaders kept up the pressure throughout the war.

Blacks in the armed forces were never allowed to forget their "second-class" status. A soldier named Lloyd Brown recalled the time he and other blacks were refused service at a lunch counter in Salina, Kansas. "We just stood there inside the door, staring at the German prisoners of war who were having lunch at the counter. . . . The people of Salina would serve these enemy soldiers and turn away black American GIs."

About one million black men and women served in the armed forces during World War II. The military remained segregated, and most black units had non-combat duties. As the war went on, however, blacks made slow gains. Some black units distinguished themselves in battle, and during the Battle of the Bulge (page 427) blacks and whites fought side by side in integrated units.

MOBILITY AND SOCIAL TENSION 3B

Americans have always been restless, but World War II caused major population shifts. Many men and women went off to war. Wives moved in with relatives or headed to cities to find work. Many southerners, white and black, moved north or west to the nation's booming industrial centers.

California and Michigan, with their abundant defense jobs, attracted the largest numbers of migrants. The mobility and competition for jobs frequently heightened already tense relations among America's diverse ethnic groups. In the summer of 1943 almost 250 racial conflicts broke out across the country. The worst was in Detroit on a hot June night:

> Early in the evening, when sporadic fights broke out between white and black teenagers, rumors of violence spread like prairie fire. Within a few hours race war had engulfed the ghetto. Negroes smashed windows, stoned cars and attacked white workers returning from a night shift. Whites dragged Negroes off trolley cars and beat them.

Authorities brought in 6,000 federal troops to restore order. Before peace returned, the fighting had killed 26 blacks and 9 whites.

Trouble also flared between whites and other minorities, such as Hispanics. With war industries desperately seeking workers, many Mexicans crossed the border (by government invitation) to take jobs at farms and factories in the Southwest. Many long-time residents resented the newcomers. In the summer of 1943, violence flared. White servicemen home on leave roamed Los Angeles streets beating up young Mexican Americans who wore flamboyant "zoot suits" and "duck tail" haircuts. Rioting went on for a week.

SECTION REVIEW

1. KEY TERMS internment, War Production Board

2. PEOPLE A. Philip Randolph

3. COMPREHENSION How did Congress later express its regret for the treatment of Japanese Americans during World War II?

4. COMPREHENSION How did the war cause population shifts within the United States?

5. CRITICAL THINKING Do you think the war made American society more democratic or less democratic? Explain your answer.

Photo Caption Answer
They faced discrimination and segregation.

3 Toward Victory in Europe

Section Focus

Key Terms Battle of the Atlantic ▪ unconditional surrender ▪ D-Day ▪ Battle of the Bulge ▪ Yalta Conference

Main Idea Even as they fought to victory against Germany and Italy, the Allied nations maneuvered for political advantage in a postwar Europe.

Objectives As you read, look for answers to these questions:
1. What Allied moves brought victory over Germany?
2. How did wartime decisions by Allied leaders cause postwar tensions?

By 1943 the Allies had brought the Axis advances to a halt. Now they were ready to take the offensive against Germany and Italy.

A Sea and Air War 1A

The North Atlantic was a death-trap during World War II. A sudden torpedo could send any ship to the ocean floor in a matter of moments. Scrambling into a life raft, a sailor might be machine-gunned by an enemy aircraft or submarine. Or he might be blown into the ocean, to flounder alone in an icy swell and die quickly of the cold.

The German aim in the Battle of the Atlantic was to prevent food and war materiel from reaching Great Britain and the Soviet Union. At the start of the war, groups of German submarines—called "wolf-packs"—almost drove Allied shipping from the Atlantic Ocean. In 1942 alone they sank more than 900 Allied ships, some within view of the American coast. At stake was nothing less than the Allied lifeline to Europe. If German subs had continued to sink ships at the rate they achieved in 1942, Britain and the Soviet Union would not have received enough food and arms to continue fighting.

With grim determination, the United States and Britain fought back. Destroyers stepped up escorts of merchant-ship convoys. Air patrols helped to spot and attack enemy subs. New inventions also helped. For example, radar and sonar used radio and sound waves to locate enemy subs. By the spring of 1943 the Allies had gained control of the Atlantic, and the supply ships ran with only occasional losses.

Meanwhile, Allied air forces based in Britain were striking deep into the German heartland. The Allies hoped to cripple the German war economy with attacks on military targets. They also pulverized such major cities as Cologne, Hamburg, and Berlin in an attempt to sap the German people's will to fight. Despite massive destruction and heavy loss of life, German morale held firm.

Taking Italy 1A

At a January 1943 conference in Casablanca, Morocco, Churchill and Roosevelt agreed to continue fighting until they won an unconditional surrender from the Axis Powers. That is, enemy nations would have to accept whatever terms of peace the Allies dictated. (This was in contrast to World War I, which had ended with a negotiated armistice.) The two leaders also agreed to postpone for another year the full-scale invasion of France that Stalin was demanding. First, they would strike from the south against what Churchill called "the soft under-belly" of Hitler's Europe.

BIOGRAPHY

GEORGE PATTON (1885–1945), of San Gabriel, California, came from a prominent military family. Patton participated in tank warfare during World War I. In World War II he promoted the use of armored vehicles and mobile tactics. Patton was often at odds with the Army and the public. However, his combat daring helped win important Allied victories.

SUPPORTING THE SECTION

Reinforcement Workbook: Worksheet 69
Reteaching Resources: Worksheet 69
Enrichment and Extension Resources: Primary Source Worksheet 35
Teaching Transparencies: Transparency 69

Biography
For further reading consider: Blumenson, Martin. *Patton: The Man Behind the Legend, 1885–1945.* William Morrow, 1985.

SECTION 3

Toward Victory in Europe
(pp. 423–428)

Section Objective
▪ explain how the Allies defeated Germany and Italy

Introducing the Section

Connecting with Past Learnings
Review the military situation in Europe at the start of 1943. *How much of Europe did German forces control?* (Almost all of western Europe from Norway to France and Greece; in the east, they controlled the western part of the Soviet Union.) *What European powers were still fighting the Axis?* (Britain and the Soviet Union.)

Key Terms
Write the key terms on the board. Beside each word have a volunteer write a definition with which the class agrees. **LEP**

Focus
Help students compare different countries' attitudes about events in Europe between 1942 and 1945 by having volunteers express the viewpoints of the Soviet Union, Britain, the United States, and Germany. Starting with 1942, have different students express each country's assessment of the military and political situation for each year. Other class members could contribute by asking questions of these representatives.

What Allied strategies contributed to victory in Europe? (Use of radar and sonar to gain control of the Atlantic; air raids on German cities; attacking Italy; invasion on D-Day; continued Soviet fighting on the east.)

423

After students have read the section, you may want to consider the following activities:

Impact of Geography

Discuss the Battle of the Atlantic. *Why were shipping lanes across the Atlantic important to the war effort?* (Provided Britain and the Soviet Union food and arms to continue fighting; later, U.S. armed forces crossed the ocean to fight.) *How did the United States and Britain fight the Battle of the Atlantic?* (Destroyers escorted convoys, air patrols spotted and attacked enemy subs, and radar and sonar located enemy submarines and ships.) Working in pairs or small groups, have students create models or diagrams illustrating how one of these methods worked.

Science and Technology

Be sure students understand the difference between radar and sonar. (Radar detects objects above ground; sonar detects objects under water.) *What are peacetime uses of radar and sonar?* (Radar is used by vessels to avoid other ships; sonar is used for medical sonograms and by ships to detect underwater obstructions.)

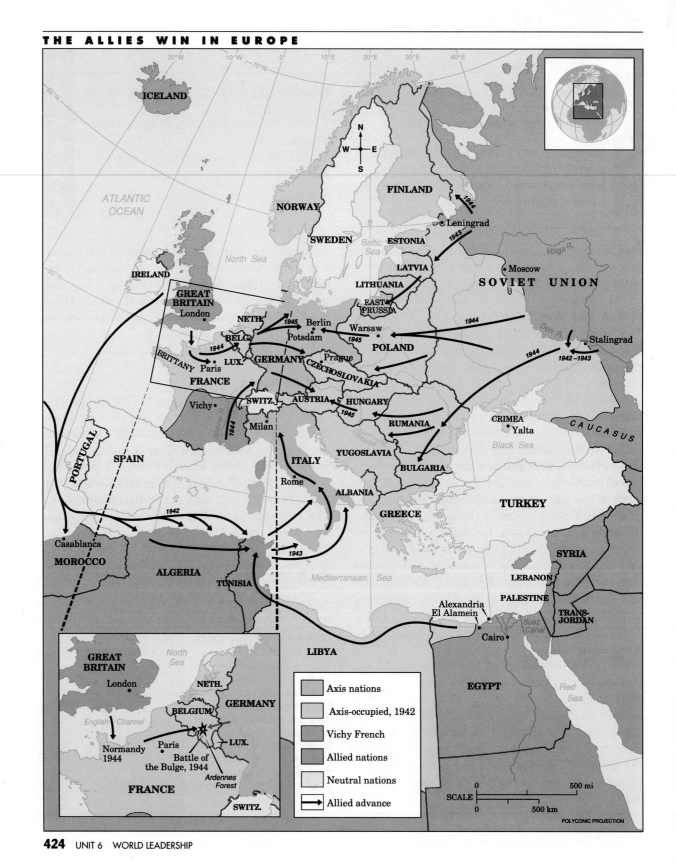

THE ALLIES WIN IN EUROPE

	Legend
	Axis nations
	Axis-occupied, 1942
	Vichy French
	Allied nations
	Neutral nations
	Allied advance

SCALE
0   500 mi
0   500 km

POLYCONIC PROJECTION

424   UNIT 6   WORLD LEADERSHIP

Map Skills Answers
Belgium. Its central location helped it expand rapidly into neighboring territories; however, Germany was also exposed to attacks on several fronts.

American tanks roll past the Roman Colosseum in June 1944, nine months after landing in southern Italy. In the picture at right, an Italian woman warmly welcomes a GI. **HISTORY** What happened in Italy after the fall of Mussolini's Fascist government? **9D**

In July 1943 a huge force of 160,000 American and British troops left North Africa, heading for the Italian island of Sicily. Meeting little resistance, the Allies moved on to attack the Italian mainland. Mussolini's government crumbled, and a new Italian government surrendered to the Allies and offered to help fight the Germans.

Hitler was determined not to lose Italy. He ordered a large German force to block the Allied march up the Italian peninsula. Aided by skilled generals and mountainous terrain, the Germans slowed the Allied advance to a crawl. The Allies did not take Rome until June 1944, and German forces continued to fight in northern Italy until the final surrender.

The invasion of Italy eased the pressure on Soviet forces by engaging Germans who might otherwise have fought on the Eastern Front. But Stalin would not be satisfied until the Western Allies had mounted a full-scale invasion of France.

INVADING EUROPE 1A

At Tehran, Iran, late in 1943, the "Big Three" Allied leaders met together for the first time. Roosevelt tried his best to win Stalin's favor, playfully

MAP SKILLS 9B

Allied forces from Britain and the United States attacked the Axis in North Africa and then pushed north into Italy and France. Russian armies advanced toward Germany through Eastern Europe. In which country were the battles of the Bulge and the Ardennes Forest fought? **CRITICAL THINKING** What military advantages and disadvantages did Germany's central location in Europe present?

calling him "Uncle Joe" and backing his plea for an early invasion of France across the English Channel. Roosevelt and his generals were eager to finish off Germany. Churchill, on the other hand, wanted British and American troops to attack southeastern Europe first. Churchill feared that if Soviet troops reached southeastern Europe before the Western Allies did, British influence in that region would be ended. Nevertheless, Churchill finally agreed to an invasion of France.

As the date for the invasion (code-named "Operation Overlord") approached, nearly 3 million Allied soldiers, sailors, and airmen crowded into southern England. Makeshift camps dotted the countryside, and men and women in uniform swarmed through the streets. While preparations for such a massive operation could not be kept secret, General Eisenhower, supreme commander of the Allied forces, managed to keep the Germans guessing about where the Allies would strike. Thus German commanders were unprepared on D-Day—June 6, 1944—when the largest seaborne invasion force in history landed in the Normandy region in northwestern France.

Under cover of dark, paratroopers dropped behind German lines to sabotage lines of communication and transportation. At dawn, with 11,000 planes providing air cover, the first wave of Allied

On D-Day, 176,000 Allied troops landed on the northern coast of France. Many soldiers drowned accidentally during the enormous operation. However, "Operation Overlord" succeeded in giving the Allies a foothold in western Europe. **GEOGRAPHY** Why did the Allies choose to mount the invasion from England? **9A**

Divide the class into small groups. Have each group choose to focus on the invasion of Normandy or the Battle of the Bulge. Relying on information in the book or additional research, have them illustrate some aspect of the battle by creating a battle map, a poster, a diary of a soldier or civilian, or a skit. Allow time for the groups to share their projects with the rest of the class. **LEP**

Addressing Individual Needs

Guided/ Independent Practice

Instruct students to complete **Reinforcement Workbook** Worksheet 69. This worksheet will help students understand contrasting points of view regarding the Yalta Conference.

Reteaching/Correctives

Direct students' attention to the objectives under the Section Focus on page 423. Have students work with partners to change each question into a statement and list the statements on a piece of paper. Beneath each statement, have students list important details that explain or add to it.

Have students complete **Reteaching Resources** Worksheet 69, which deals with the Allied wartime conference.

Enrichment/Extension

Instruct students to complete **Enrichment and Extension Resources** Primary Source Worksheet 35. This worksheet guides students in analyzing an eyewitness account, by journalist Ernie Pyle, of the day following D-Day.

The Geographic Perspective: The Invasion of Normandy

Wide beaches of sand and pebbles line the coast of the French region of Normandy. In some places, rugged cliffs rise from the sea. In others, tall beach grasses grow on sand dunes behind the high tide mark. Beyond the beaches are quiet fishing villages and well-kept farms. In June 1944 this tranquil area was the site of the largest military operation in history.

THE CHOICE OF NORMANDY

The aim of the Allied invasion was to liberate France and the rest of Western Europe from German occupation. The Germans expected an invasion in France, but they did not know exactly where. Allied planners kept the location secret while leading the Germans to believe that the landing would take place near Calais. Calais was on the narrowest part of the English Channel and would be the easiest place for seaborne troops to reach. Thus German defenses were strongest at Calais.

The Allies chose Normandy, however, because it was *not* ideal for an invasion. It had cliffs, strong currents, inadequate harbors, and frequent storms. By choosing the site, Allied leaders hoped to catch the Germans off guard.

The beach terrain of Normandy demanded special military planning. British and American commandos were trained in cliff climbing. To provide protection and docking for

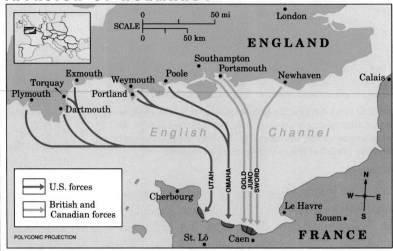

INVASION OF NORMANDY

Allied ships, engineers devised two massive artificial harbors that would be towed across the English Channel and put in position off shore. The harbors, code-named "Mulberry," had docks where ships could unload. Jeeps and other equipment moved to shore across floating roadways.

THE D-DAY LANDINGS

D-Day began hours before dawn on June 6, 1944. The seas were heavy, the skies overcast, and the weather so stormy that the Germans relaxed their watch. When the first British and American paratroopers landed behind the German coastal defenses about 1 A.M., the Germans thought the attack was only a diversion. By about 6:30 A.M., they knew differently as the first of several thousand ships began to unload soldiers on the Normandy beaches.

At Utah Beach, American units

met light opposition and quickly joined the airborne troops inland. The British and Canadians also were able to establish early beachheads at Juno, Sword, and Gold beaches. At Omaha Beach, though, the invading forces met unexpected resistance. Deadly gunfire from Germans bunkers raked troops as they sought to scramble up the cliffs. A thousand Americans died that day at Omaha Beach.

By day's end the Allies had a secure beachhead on the Normandy coast. The great success of the invasion had depended on courage, on secrecy, on cooperation, and on adequate preparation for the difficult landing site.

CRITICAL THINKING QUESTIONS 2E

1. How did the Allies turn geographical handicaps into assets in the D-Day invasion?
2. To what extent were the Germans victims of their own assumptions?

The Geographic Perspective Answers
1. The Germans were surprised because they did not expect an attack on such tough terrain; the Allies trained commandos in cliff climbing and built artificial harbors.

2. The Germans were not as well prepared in Normandy because they assumed the Allies would attack near Calais. They also doubted that the attack would take place on a day with such poor weather.

Geographic Themes
Geographic themes covered on this page:
✔ Location
✔ Place
___ Interactions
✔ Movement
___ Regions

troops stormed ashore. The Germans put up heavy resistance, but the Allies still landed more than 300,000 men in the first week alone. Within a month the number rose to 1 million.

Having gained a foothold on the continent, the Allies punched across northern France. Another Allied force landed in southern France and pushed northward. On August 25, 1944, the Allies marched into Paris, ending four long years of Nazi occupation of the French capital. A few days later, British and Canadians took the cities of Brussels and Antwerp in Belgium. Within a few months of D-Day the Allies had liberated all of France and massed 3 million soldiers along Germany's western border.

By the winter of 1944, Allied forces were closing in on Hitler from both sides—the British and Americans from the west, the Soviets from the east. It seemed that victory was just a month or two away. But in mid-December 1944, Germany made one last-ditch counteroffensive, attacking along a weakly defended stretch of the Ardennes Forest in Belgium.

The German drive caught the Allies off guard. Allied troops beat a hasty retreat, creating a huge bulge in their lines, and so the fighting became known as the Battle of the Bulge. Despite heavy losses, the Allies finally managed to regroup and drive the Germans back.

A MEETING AT YALTA 1B

As the Allies pushed toward victory in Europe, they worked out plans for the future. In February 1945 an ailing Roosevelt met Churchill and Stalin at Yalta, a Soviet resort on the Black Sea. The Big Three made decisions at the Yalta Conference that helped to shape the postwar world. Some of those decisions contained the seeds of future troubles.

Roosevelt's top priority at Yalta was to work out the details of a new international body to help maintain the peace. The League of Nations had failed, Roosevelt believed, because the world's major powers had not supported it. He got Stalin and Churchill to agree with him on the basic structure of a new peacekeeping body.

Roosevelt also won Stalin's secret pledge that the Soviet Union would declare war on Japan within three months after Germany surrendered. American military advisers believed this to be crucial. For if the Japanese mainland had to be attacked by American forces alone, as many as a million American soldiers might die. In exchange for Stalin's promise to help defeat Japan, Roosevelt and Churchill gave Stalin territorial concessions. They agreed that the Soviet Union could occupy Outer Mongolia and several important Japanese islands.

The leaders also discussed new postwar borders for Poland and Germany. They agreed to divide Germany into four military zones, with the Big Three and France each controlling a zone.

Finally, the Yalta Conference produced some vague agreements on the fate of Eastern Europe. The Big Three promised to set up governments there that were "broadly representative of all democratic elements." When Stalin later imposed pro-Soviet governments in Eastern Europe, some Americans would accuse Roosevelt of "selling out" to communism at Yalta. Others would claim that because Stalin would never have accepted anything less than total control over Eastern Europe, the Yalta agreements represented the best deal possible at the time.

Winston Churchill (left) and Joseph Stalin (right) flank Franklin Roosevelt at the 1945 Yalta Conference. The leaders discussed strategy for the final phase of the war and made plans for the postwar era. HISTORY What, do you think, were each leader's primary political concerns at the time of the Yalta Conference? 1B

2. *Casablanca*—Moroccan city, site of conference between FDR and Churchill in 1943. *Sicily*— Italian island, first place Allies invaded in Europe in 1943. *Tehran*—Iranian city where first "Big Three" meeting was held. *English Channel*—Water separating France and England, crossed by Allied forces on D-Day. *Normandy*—Site of Allied invasion of France. *Harry S. Truman*—Vice President who became President when Roosevelt died in 1945. *Ardennes Forest*—Site of Battle of the Bulge. *Yalta*—Soviet resort where Churchill, FDR, and Stalin met in 1945. *Elbe River*—German river where American and Soviet forces met in 1945.

3. Sicily and then Italy.

4. Tehran—to invade France across the English Channel; Yalta—made plans for UN, USSR would declare war on Japan and would get territory, new borders for Poland and Germany, vague agreements about Eastern Europe's governments.

5. Victory over Germany seemed assured, while the United States was worried about fighting Japan and wanted Soviet help. Also, the Soviet Union was already occupying nations of Eastern Europe; plans had to be made quickly so that new governments could be established.

Closure

Use the Section 3 information in the Chapter 18 Summary (p. 438) to synthesize the important elements covered in the section. Then have students read Section 4 for the next class period. As they read, have them note how the United States won the war in the Pacific.

This navy musician's face expressed what many Americans felt as FDR's body was carried to the train at Warm Springs, Georgia, the day after the President's death. **NATIONAL IDENTITY Describe Roosevelt's importance to the American people.** 9A

VICTORY IN EUROPE 1A

As the Allied leaders left for home, Churchill noticed that Roosevelt seemed "placid and frail." Yet no one realized just how frail. Two months later, on April 12, 1945, Roosevelt died of a stroke while at Warm Springs, Georgia.

Harry Truman took over as President. This former Missouri senator had been picked as Roosevelt's running mate in 1944. Truman, who had served as Vice President for just a few months before Roosevelt's death, had not even been involved in top policy decisions. Suddenly, he was in charge. All too aware of the terrible burden he was assuming, Truman remarked, "I felt like the moon, the stars, and all the planets had fallen on me."

"**I** felt like the moon, the stars, and all the planets had fallen on me."
—*Harry Truman, 1945*

Hitler's propaganda minister jubilantly announced, "My Führer, I congratulate you! Roosevelt is dead! It is written in the stars that the second half of April will be a turning point for us." But the stars did not favor Hitler. As infantry units squeezed Germany on the ground, Allied bombers rained down destruction from the sky.

Already in February of that year, Allied fire-bombings had turned the city of Dresden into an inferno, killing 135,000 people.

Collapsing German resistance in the west presented the Western Allies with a dilemma: How far eastward should they push? Though the Soviets were wartime allies, some Western leaders foresaw a postwar rivalry with the Soviet Union. Churchill argued that the farther east the Western Allies got before shaking hands with the Soviets, the less power Stalin would wield in Eastern Europe after the war. Supreme Allied Commander Dwight D. Eisenhower had a different view. He wanted to end the war as quickly as possible and with the fewest casualties. This meant mopping up German forces left in the west rather than launching new offensives. Eisenhower's position carried the day.

On April 25, 1945, American troops met Soviet forces along the Elbe River, 60 miles south of Berlin. A few days later, Adolf Hitler committed suicide in a Berlin bunker as Soviet troops were battling to capture the Nazi capital. On May 7, at Eisenhower's headquarters in France, a German commander signed an unconditional surrender, ending the war in Europe. On May 8, 1945, people around the world celebrated V-E (for Victory in Europe) Day.

SECTION REVIEW

1. KEY TERMS Battle of the Atlantic, unconditional surrender, D-Day, Battle of the Bulge, Yalta Conference

2. PEOPLE AND PLACES Casablanca, Sicily, Tehran, English Channel, Normandy, Harry S. Truman, Ardennes Forest, Yalta, Elbe River

3. COMPREHENSION After their conquest of North Africa, where did the Americans and British strike next against Hitler's forces?

4. COMPREHENSION What decisions did the Big Three leaders make at the Tehran and Yalta conferences?

5. CRITICAL THINKING How might the military situation of February 1945 have affected the decisions made at Yalta?

Photo Caption Answer
Students may suggest that FDR had helped end the Depression and led the country through the war.

Background Harry S. Truman was a moderate Democrat who was acceptable to southern conservatives and who had served successfully as chairman of a Senate committee that had investigated military spending.

4 Advancing on Japan

Section Focus

Key Terms island-hopping ■ Battle of Leyte Gulf ■ kamikaze ■ Battle of Iwo Jima ■ Battle of Okinawa ■ Manhattan Project

Main Idea The Allies pushed on to victory in the Pacific, but the United States faced a grave moral decision over the use of the atomic bomb on Japan.

Objectives As you read, look for answers to these questions:
1. What strategy did the Allies follow in the Pacific after their victory at Guadalcanal?
2. How did the Allies finally force Japan to surrender?

By 1943 the Allies were beginning to push the Japanese back to their home islands. The Allied drive followed two main paths. One, led by Admiral Chester Nimitz, approached Japan from the east directly across the islands of the central Pacific. The other, led by General Douglas MacArthur, advanced toward Japan from the south—through New Guinea and the Philippines.

ISLAND-HOPPING IN THE PACIFIC 1A

Nimitz used a strategy called island-hopping. Rather than invade every Japanese-held island, the Allies planned to capture only a few strategic ones. The rest, cut off from resupply, would no longer pose a threat. Starting with Guadalcanal, the Allies attacked important island groups one after another, using each new group as a base from which to attack the next.

Nimitz's forces began their campaign in the Gilbert Islands late in 1943, advancing to the Marshall Islands early in 1944. In the summer of 1944 the Allies moved on to the Mariana Islands, capturing Guam and Saipan. Now, Allied forces were within striking distance of Japan. Soldiers began building airfields in the Marianas from which B-29 bombers could attack Japan.

RETURN TO THE PHILIPPINES 1A

General MacArthur had been commander of Allied forces in the Philippines at the time of the Japanese invasion in December 1941. When American and Filipino forces had their backs to the wall on Bataan, President Roosevelt ordered MacArthur to go to Australia. MacArthur went, but he pledged, "I shall return."

> **"I shall return."**
> —*General Douglas MacArthur*

In October 1944, after two years of bloody fighting in the malaria-ridden swamps of New Guinea, MacArthur fulfilled his promise. Wading ashore on Leyte (LAY-tee) Island in the Philippines, he made one of the most famous statements of World War II: "People of the Philippines! I have returned. . . . Rally to me."

But the Philippines were not easily regained. Japan scraped together most of its remaining ships and planes in a desperate attempt to block the American invasion. What followed—the Battle of Leyte Gulf—proved to be the largest naval engagement in history. The United States won a smashing victory, wiping out Japan's fleet once and for all.

As the Battle of Leyte Gulf raged, a bomb-laden Japanese plane zoomed straight at the U.S. ship *St. Lo*, crashing through the flight deck and touching off explosions that sank the ship. For the first time the Japanese were resorting to attacks by kamikazes—suicide pilots who intentionally crashed their planes into American ships. (*Kamikaze*, meaning "divine wind," refers to a typhoon that destroyed a Mongol fleet trying to invade Japan in the 1200s.) During the final year of the war, kamikaze attacks sank or severely damaged more than 300 U.S. ships and killed 15,000 American servicemen.

With the Japanese fleet destroyed, U.S. troops

SUPPORTING THE SECTION

Reinforcement Workbook: Worksheet 70
Reteaching Resources: Worksheet 70
Enrichment and Extension Resources: Historian Worksheet 7
Teaching Transparencies: Transparency 70

SECTION 4

Advancing on Japan
(pp. 429–432)

Section Objectives

■ describe Allied advances on Japan in the Pacific
■ discuss the decision to develop and use the atomic bomb

Introducing the Section

Connecting with Past Learnings
Why was the Battle of Midway the turning point of the war in the Pacific? (Because the Japanese advance was halted.)
What was the significance of the fighting in Guadalcanal? (It took place near New Guinea and Australia; it foreshadowed the difficult fighting in the Pacific.)

Key Terms

Write the key terms on the board. Have students circle the terms that identify military strategies and underline terms that identify battles. Then have the class agree on a definition for each term. **LEP**

Focus

Have students create an annotated timeline of the Allies' progress in the Pacific. Be sure they include explanations of the strategic importance of the Marianas, Leyte Gulf, Burma Road, Iwo Jima, and Okinawa. On a parallel timeline, have students note dates in the development of the atomic bomb.
What choices did Truman face in using the atomic bomb? (Could drop it on Japan or explode it in a remote area in front of official Japanese witnesses.) *Why did he choose to drop it on Japan?* (Afraid the bomb might have been a dud; wanted to avoid the costs of a full-scale invasion.)

Developing the Lesson

After students have read the section, you may want to consider the following activities:

Impact of Geography

Discuss the role geography played in the Pacific. *How did geography affect the nature of battle?* (Naval forces were important in the Pacific; airplanes also played an important role because distances were great.) *How might the climate have affected soldiers?* (Heat and humidity made life uncomfortable and increased the likelihood of disease.)

Analyzing Controversial Issues

How might United States have believed that use of the atomic bomb would affect its relations with the Soviet Union in the postwar world? (It believed that possession of such a powerful weapon could force concessions from the Soviets.) Have students list this and other arguments in favor of dropping the bomb on Japan. Then have them list reasons not to drop the bomb. (In favor—would end the war faster; would save American and Japanese lives lost in an invasion of Japan. Against—would cost thousands of innocent lives; could just demonstrate the bomb.)

Do you think that the United States should have dropped the bomb on Japan? Why or why not?

Science and Technology

Since the end of World War II, scientists have worked to find ways of using nuclear power for peaceful means. *What are some peaceful uses of nuclear energy?* (Nuclear medicine; nuclear generated electricity.) *What are some problems of uses of nuclear power?* (Waste disposal; possibility of explosion.) Discuss with students varying points of view regarding the use of nuclear power.

---

cleared the Japanese from Leyte and in January 1945 invaded the main Philippine island of Luzon. After weeks of bitter combat, much of it in the streets of Manila, American forces gained control of the Philippines.

MAINLAND ASIA 1A

The Allies battled Japan on the Asian mainland as well as in the Pacific, but progress in Asia came more slowly. Driven all the way back to India by the Japanese attacks of 1941 and 1942, the Allies struggled doggedly to recapture northern Burma. Their aim was to reopen the Burma Road and bring supplies to Chiang Kai-shek's Nationalist Chinese government, which was resisting the Japanese invaders in China. With the Japanese in control of the Burma Road, the Chinese depended on courageous American pilots who flew supplies "over the hump" of the Himalaya Mountains.

By early 1944, U.S. General Claire Chennault had set up airbases in China from which to fly bombing raids against the Japanese. Later in the year, Allied troops advanced into northern Burma from the west and north. With island-hopping forces closing in on Japan from the Pacific, Japanese commanders had to shift troops to meet the Pacific threat, and the tide of war on the mainland began to turn.

In Asia, as in Europe, the war had brought Communist and non-Communist forces into alliance. Two Communist leaders—Mao Zedong in China and Ho Chi Minh in Indochina—had thrown their efforts into the struggle against Japan. But as victory approached, Allied leaders feared that wartime alliances might break down. Chinese Communists and Nationalists had only papered over their differences, and a full-scale Chinese civil war might break out at any moment. Indochina's future too seemed clouded. Ho Chi Minh was a popular figure opposed to any return of his homeland to French colonial control, and he was determined to win independence. You will read more about Mao and Ho in later chapters.

ON TOWARD TOKYO 1A

While MacArthur's troops approached Japan from the southwest and Nimitz's forces battled their way across the Pacific, American submarines and

bombers were wrecking the Japanese war economy. Because Japan had few natural resources of its own, it depended on shipping for food and raw materials. Submarine attacks took a deadly toll on Japanese merchant ships. Meanwhile, beginning in November 1944, lumbering B-29 bombers began flying regular bombing raids from Saipan, Tinian, and Guam against Japanese cities. By the start of 1945 Japan was hard put to supply itself with food, let alone war materiel.

In February 1945 U.S. marines landed on the tiny island of Iwo Jima (EE–woh JEE–mah), just 750 miles from Japan. The marines advanced without air cover against a honeycomb of underground Japanese positions. In the Battle of Iwo Jima they suffered 25,000 casualties, including 6,800 killed. In some units as many as three men out of four were killed or badly wounded. But the Americans finally triumphed, with heroic marines planting the Stars and Stripes atop Mt. Suribachi, the island's highest point.

The next steppingstone to Japan, the island of Okinawa (oh–kih–NAH–wah), was a mere 350 miles from Japan. The Battle of Okinawa began in April 1945 and turned into the bloodiest island fight of the Pacific war. Eventually some 300,000 Americans poured ashore, supported by 1,300 ships. By the time the marines gained control of the island in June, 110,000 Japanese and some 12,000 Americans had been killed.

The capture of Okinawa provided the United States with more airbases for raids against Japan. American pilots began systematic fire-bombing of the cities of Tokyo, Yokohama, and Osaka.

This memorial to soldiers who fought in the Battle of Iwo Jima is located in Washington, D.C. It shows marines planting the American flag after one of the costliest battles of the war. CULTURE What does the sculptor appear to be celebrating in this work? 7J

Photo Caption Answer Determination, courage, endurance, teamwork, patriotism.

Background The bombing of Japan was even more intense than that against Germany. Japan's navy and industrial plants and the bulk of its cities were destroyed. In just one week, for example, nearly 200,000 residents of Tokyo were killed.

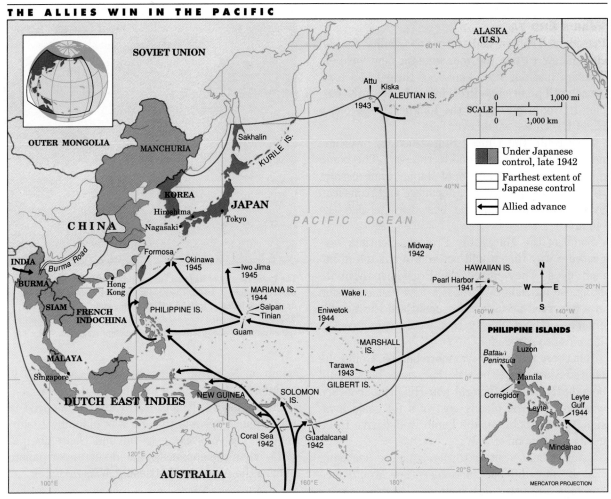

Cooperative Learning

Have students form small groups to role play the situation of Truman and his advisers in making the decision to use the atomic bomb. Have them follow this paradigm: identify the problem; consider alternatives; consider consequences and merits of each alternative; make a decision. Each student can advocate a particular point of view. **LEP**

MAP SKILLS American naval victories beginning in 1942 marked the turning point in the war against Japan. The island of Midway lies next to which island group? What large islands border the Coral Sea? CRITICAL THINKING Explain the strategic importance of the Philippine Islands in the war against Japan. 9B

THE MANHATTAN PROJECT 3A, 7A

To understand the next step in the Pacific war, we must look back to the year 1938. In that year, an Austrian physicist, Lise Meitner, and her colleagues discovered a way to split uranium atoms. By breaking the microscopic atoms into even smaller particles, the physicists could release a sudden burst of energy. Scientists around the world were quick to see the military potential of this discovery. If the energy of the atom were harnessed in a bomb, it could be the most destructive weapon ever invented.

Many of the scientists who fled Hitler's Nazi regime feared that Germany might make such a bomb. Albert Einstein, one such refugee, was the most famous scientist of the age. In 1939 he signed a letter to President Roosevelt, warning him of the atom's potential and suggesting that the United States begin to develop an atomic bomb.

Roosevelt put teams of scientists to work on a crash project to build such a bomb before Hitler's scientists could do so. To mask the nature of the top-secret undertaking, authorities gave it an innocent name—the Manhattan Project. Four years of frantic efforts produced an awesome weapon. In a blinding flash of light on July 16, 1945, the first atomic bomb exploded in a successful test over the New Mexico desert. The Atomic Age had dawned.

CHAPTER 18   THE WORLD AT WAR, 1941–1945   **431**

Addressing Individual Needs

Guided/ Independent Practice
Instruct students to complete **Reinforcement Workbook** Worksheet 70. This worksheet guides students in analyzing a political cartoon focusing on the atomic bomb.

Reteaching/Correctives
Divide the class into groups and have each group choose a battle mentioned in the text. Have the groups create battle maps illustrating the strategies and course of the battle.

Have students complete **Reteaching Resources** Worksheet 70, in which students make an outline about the war in the Pacific.

Enrichment/Extension
Have students complete **Enrichment and Extension Resources** Historian Worksheet 7.

Assessment
You may wish to use the Section 4 Review, page 432, to see how well your students understand the main points in this lesson.

Map Skills Answers
Hawaiian Islands. Australia and New Guinea. Their location, near both Japan and mainland Asia, made them excellent bases for attacks against Japanese-held territory in Southeast Asia and against Japan's home islands.

Background Two colors are used on this map to show the Japanese empire in 1942 so that students can see the area under Japanese control before and after 1931, the start of its expansionist policies.

1. *island-hopping*—Island-by-island advance on Japan. *Battle of Leyte Gulf*—Largest naval battle in history, a U.S. victory. *kamikaze*—Japanese suicide pilot who intentionally crashed into an American ship. *Battle of Iwo Jima*—Battle for an island near Japan. *Battle of Okinawa*—Bloodiest fight of the Pacific War. *Manhattan Project*—Top-secret undertaking to develop an atomic bomb.

2. *Chester Nimitz*—Admiral who led island-hopping naval forces. *Douglas MacArthur*— Army general who led attack to regain the Philippines. *Chiang Kai-shek*—Head of Nationalist Chinese government. *Lise Meitner*—Austrian physicist who discovered a way to split uranium atoms. *Albert Einstein*—Scientist, suggested that U.S. develop an atomic bomb. *Hiroshima*—City in Japan where first atomic bomb was dropped. *Nagasaki*—City in Japan where second atomic bomb was dropped.

3. From the Marianas, B-29 bombers could attack Japan.

4. Many scientists feared that the Nazis would develop the bomb first, and then use it to gain worldwide domination. They convinced Roosevelt that the U.S. needed to develop the powerful weapon first.

5. Yes—it would prevent a costly invasion of Japan. No—it unleashed a weapon that killed many innocent civilians.

Closure

Ask one student to transform the Main Idea of the section into a question, and have other students answer that question. Then have students read Section 5 for the next class period, noting the effects of the war on the United States and the world.

432

WAR'S END 7A

President Truman had the responsibility for deciding how to use the monumental new weapon. Truman had not even known of the bomb's existence until he became President a few months earlier. It would be one of the toughest decisions a Chief Executive would ever face.

How could the United States use its awesome new weapon to put an end to the war? The bomb might make an invasion of Japan unnecessary, thereby saving millions of Japanese and American lives. But what was the best way to use the bomb?

Some of the Manhattan Project scientists suggested a way that would not add to the toll in human lives. They urged the President to invite Japanese officials to witness a new test explosion in a deserted area, so they could see the bomb's immense power. Surely that would convince the Japanese to surrender.

But there were only two more bombs. Could the United States take the risk that one or both would be a dud? Truman thought not. His prime concern was avoiding the bloody cost of a full-scale invasion, and he believed the bomb would have to be used as a weapon of war.

Truman sent a letter to the Japanese declaring that if they did not surrender they would face "prompt and utter destruction." Japan's premier wanted to accept the ultimatum, but he was unable to persuade military leaders to surrender.

Therefore, Truman ordered that the bomb be dropped on a Japanese city. On August 6, 1945, a B-29—the *Enola Gay*—took off from Tinian Island in the Marianas carrying one atomic bomb. It headed for Hiroshima, an industrial city of 245,000. The plane dropped its bomb without warning at 8:15 A.M. The fierce blast devastated the city and sent a mushroom cloud 50,000 feet into the air. Americans estimated the blast killed 80,000 civilians; the Japanese put the figure at 200,000. Tens of thousands more suffered the painful and lingering effects of radiation poisoning.

Still, Japanese military leaders refused to surrender. Two days after the destruction of Hiroshima, the Soviet Union declared war on Japan and invaded Japanese-occupied Manchuria. A day later, on August 9, a U.S. plane dropped an atomic

The Japanese city of Nagasaki lies in ruins following the nuclear blast of August 9, 1945. The second and last atomic bomb ever used in war killed or injured a third of Nagasaki's population of 250,000. Japan sued for peace the following day. ISSUES Discuss the advantages and disadvantages of nuclear weapons. 4E, 7A

bomb on Nagasaki. That city too disappeared in an inferno of pulverized buildings and bodies.

On August 14, Emperor Hirohito announced to the Japanese people that he was planning to surrender. The war came to an end September 2, 1945, when the Japanese signed surrender papers aboard the American battleship *Missouri*.

SECTION REVIEW

1. KEY TERMS island-hopping, Battle of Leyte Gulf, kamikaze, Battle of Iwo Jima, Battle of Okinawa, Manhattan Project

2. PEOPLE AND PLACES Chester Nimitz, Douglas MacArthur, Chiang Kai-shek, Lise Meitner, Albert Einstein, Hiroshima, Nagasaki

3. COMPREHENSION What was the importance of the Mariana Islands in the Allied victory over Japan?

4. COMPREHENSION How did fear of Nazi Germany contribute to the decision to build an atomic bomb?

5. CRITICAL THINKING If you had been in President Truman's place, would you have ordered the atomic bombing of Japan? Why or why not?

Photo Caption Answers
Advantages include a threat so great that the weapons discourage war. Disadvantages include great destructiveness so that the world now lives with the risk of nuclear catastrophe.

Background Truman believed that possession of the atomic bomb could help win concessions from the Soviet Union on the fate of Eastern Europe. Truman's decision to use the weapon on Japan may have been influenced by a desire to demonstrate American might to the Soviet Union.

5 The Wreckage of War

Section Focus

Key Terms Holocaust ∎ Nuremberg Trials ∎ GI Bill of Rights ∎ superpower ∎ United Nations

Main Idea The devastation and changes wrought by the war had vast effects. Peace was restored, but world tensions remained.

Objectives As you read, look for answers to these questions:
1. What were the costs of World War II?
2. What war crimes did the Nazis commit?
3. How did the war alter the world balance of power?

In 1945 the world emerged from the ruins of war to confront a new age. Tens of millions had died, either from battle or from deliberate murder. The balance of power in Europe and Asia had been overturned. There existed new opportunities for peace, but also new dangers of conflict.

THE COSTS OF WAR 3B, 7A

No one knows how many people died as a direct result of World War II. Estimates of the total war dead range from 40 to 60 million people. One thing is certain: at least as many civilians died as combatants. The Soviet Union, for example, lost 18 to 20 million people, at least 10 million of whom were civilians. At least 6 million Germans died, as did 2 million Japanese. China lost more than 2 million and Britain about 400,000.

On the fighting fronts, the United States suffered 291,000 killed and 670,000 wounded. But the home front also sustained heavy casualties. The rush to churn out planes and tanks and other goods contributed to job accidents that killed nearly 100,000 American workers and permanently disabled 1 million more. An astounding 3 million workers suffered lesser injuries. On-the-job injuries are not just a wartime problem, of course. However, World War II temporarily reversed a trend toward greater job safety that had gathered speed in the 1930s.

The cost in material resources was incalculable. In Europe and Asia, the war reduced cities to rubble and demolished railroads, highways, and factories. It destroyed priceless works of art and turned majestic cathedrals into piles of stone. But the United States escaped such damage. Of the major powers, it alone emerged unscathed. In

fact, the massive government spending of the wartime years had stimulated the American economy and spread a glow of prosperity.

THE HOLOCAUST 6A

People had known all along that the war was taking a terrible toll. Still, the full agony only became apparent when Allied forces entered Nazi territory and liberated dozens of concentration camps. Soldiers could not believe their eyes. They found prisoners so emaciated that they resembled living corpses. They found gas chambers, crematoriums (ovens in which bodies were burned), and thousands of corpses stacked like cordwood in boxcars and open pits. One soldier recalled:

> The odors, well there is no way to describe the odors. . . . Many of the boys I am talking about now—these were tough soldiers, there were combat men who had been all the way through the invasion—were ill and vomiting, throwing up, just at the sight of this.

News of the mass murders had filtered out of Germany early in the war. Most people, however, had found the reports unbelievable—too terrible to be true.

After *Kristallnacht* in 1938 (page 399), Hitler's ruthless anti-Semitism should have been clear to the world. Nevertheless, Jews fleeing Germany had trouble finding nations that would accept them. The United States, having adopted tough immigration restrictions in the 1920s, showed little desire to make exceptions for European Jews. Other nations were just as hard-hearted.

By 1939 only about a quarter of a million Jews

SUPPORTING THE SECTION

Reinforcement Workbook: Worksheet 71
Reteaching Resources: Worksheet 71
Enrichment and Extension Resources: Primary Source Worksheet 36
Teaching Transparencies: Transparency 71

SECTION 5

The Wreckage of War
(pp. 433–437)

Section Objective
∎ describe the political and social effects of World War II

Introducing the Section

Connecting with Past Learnings
Have the class recall the United States after World War I. *What were the results of World War I in the U.S.?* (Isolationist attitude, unemployment, Red Scare.)

As students work through the lesson, have them compare the United States in 1919 with the United States after World War II.

Key Terms
Have students find the terms in their texts and agree upon a definition for each term. The word *holocaust* refers to total destruction by fire. Have students discuss why this term is appropriate for what happened to the Jews of Europe. **LEP**

These photographs of Holocaust victims and their clothing are on display at a memorial in Auschwitz, Poland. ETHICS What motivated Germany's genocidal campaign against Europe's Jews? 9A

remained in Germany. But other nations that Hitler occupied, especially Poland and Russia, had millions more. Obsessed with a desire to rid Europe of the Jews, Hitler backed a policy of genocide against the Jewish people.

When Germany invaded Russia in 1941, Hitler sent *Einsatzgruppen*—mobile killing units—to kill as many civilians as possible, especially Jews. The *Einsatzgruppen* alone murdered about 1.5 million Jews. But this solution to "the Jewish problem" was too slow for Hitler. He ordered the construction of death camps to kill masses of people more efficiently. The Nazis rounded up Jews, put them on trains, and sent them to concentration camps at Dachau, Buchenwald, Treblinka, Auschwitz, and other places. Age and gender did not matter. The Nazis killed women, men, children, infants, and the elderly.

Some of the camps used prisoners as slave laborers. Prisoners built or worked in factories to profit the Nazi regime. But as soon as they weakened or grew sick, they were murdered.

At Auschwitz, the Nazis killed hundreds of thousands who had been shipped in by train. Whip-wielding guards herded the Jews into buildings, had them strip naked, and forced them into the gas chambers. The Nazis were able to gas more than 12,000 people *per day* at Auschwitz.

Of the 12 million civilians the Nazis killed, about 6 million were Jews—a third of the world's Jewish population. This program of mass murder has become known as the Holocaust.

DEFINING INTERNATIONAL LAW 7A
The Allied nations expressed outrage at the horrors of the Holocaust and vowed to punish those responsible. They pointed to other international crimes too—the aggressions that began the war, the atrocities of the Japanese in Bataan and China, and more. But what court could conduct the trials?

Soon after peace came, the Allies formed two International Military Tribunals—one at Nuremberg, Germany, and one at Tokyo—to put enemy leaders on trial. They charged the defendants with violating international law by committing "crimes against peace," "war crimes," and "crimes against humanity." Because of the hideous revelations about the Nazi death camps, attention focused mainly on the Nuremberg Trials. Of 24 leading Nazis placed on trial at Nuremberg, 12 received the death sentence. In less-publicized trials throughout the occupation zone, U.S. judges convicted more than 500,000 lesser Nazis. Their penalties ranged from small fines to imprisonment in labor camps.

The Tokyo court sentenced Japan's wartime premier, Hideki Tojo, and six Japanese generals to be hanged. Several hundred other Japanese convicted of war crimes were also hanged.

Some people have argued that the war crimes trials did not go far enough in seeking out and punishing war criminals. Many Nazis who took part in the Holocaust did indeed go free. Some re-entered German civilian life and others found refuge in foreign countries, including the United States.

However imperfect the trials may have been, they did establish an important principle—the idea that individuals are ultimately responsible for their own actions, even in time of war. Nazi executioners could not escape punishment by showing that they were "merely following orders." The principle of individual responsibility is now firmly entrenched in international law.

RETURNING FROM WAR 7B

By the time of the war crimes trials, Americans were drifting back to the everyday life that the war had disrupted. Some would look back on the war years as a time of adventure and daring excitement. Others who had lost limbs or loved ones would feel the heartbreak and anguish for years to come. But few would be unmarked by their wartime experience.

For some, the war had revealed a dark side of human nature. Japanese Americans like Peter Ota could not shake the bitter memories from their minds:

> I think of my father. . . . After all those years, having worked his whole life to build a dream—an American dream mind you—having it all taken away. . . . His [fruit and vegetable] business was worth more than a hundred thousand. He sold it for five. . . . He died a very broken man.

Yet the war also evoked human kindness and hope. Alex Shulman, a U.S. Army surgeon, recalled the time during the Battle of the Bulge when he treated a teenage German soldier whose skull had been punctured:

> He . . . started to cry. I said, "What are you crying about?" He said, "They told me I'd be killed. And here you are, an American officer, washing my hands and face and my hair." I reminded him that I was a Jewish doctor, so he would get the full impact of it.

For many, the war meant a chance to break out of old molds. "The war changed our whole idea of how we wanted to live when we came back," said a soldier from the New York area. "All my relatives worked in factories. They didn't own any business. They worked with their hands. High school was about as far as they went." Taking advantage of a 1944 law called the GI Bill of Rights, that soldier and thousands of others went to college and built

> "The war changed our whole idea of how we wanted to live when we came back."
>
> —Army veteran, 1945

successful careers. They became accountants, engineers, pharmacists. Said the soldier, "We just didn't want to go back and work in a factory in the hometown. The GI Bill was a blessing."

The GI Bill bought books, paid tuition, and provided living expenses for veterans who attended high school or college. It was one of several laws that offered a broad range of benefits to veterans—loans for buying a home or setting up a business, preference in seeking a government job, and so on.

Mexican Americans had won more medals for valor than any other ethnic minority. From their war experiences they had gained skills and confidence. No longer willing to accept second-class citizenship, they began to organize politically. A leader in this struggle was Dr. Hector García, a Texas veteran who created the GI Forum. Its aim was to fight discrimination against Mexican American veterans.

Analyzing Controversial Issues

Explain to students that some people criticized the International Military Tribunals, stating that there are no such things as laws regulating the conduct of war. Ask students to suggest arguments supporting and opposing that point of view. (Support—war is inherently immoral; laws are always determined by the victor. Oppose—there are some actions that are unacceptable, even in wartime; international organizations can make fair international laws.) *With which arguments do you agree? Why?*

Patterns in History

Why didn't the United States and the Soviet Union remain allies after the war? (They had strong ideological differences, which had only been suspended while they fought a common enemy.) *How did World War II create two superpowers?* (The intense fighting had destroyed traditional powers, leaving just the United States and the Soviet Union as great powers.) *Do you think the world is still divided between superpowers today? Explain your answer.*

Global Awareness

Provide encyclopedias and books on the United Nations. Have students draw a diagram explaining the functions of the different branches of the UN and the relationships between the branches.

Cause and Effect

Have students examine the chart on page 436 and suggest a specific example of each of the long-term causes of World War II. (Economic instability—inflation in the Weimar Republic; rise of extremists—Hitler, Mussolini, Tojo; failure of appeasement—invasion of Poland after Munich.)

Do the effects of World War II still play a role in the world today?

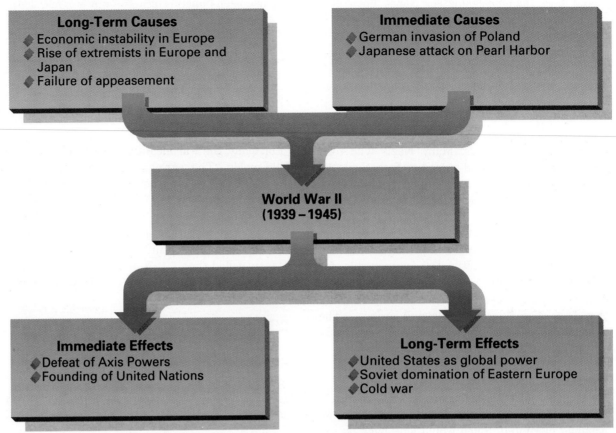

Long-Term Causes
◆ Economic instability in Europe
◆ Rise of extremists in Europe and Japan
◆ Failure of appeasement

Immediate Causes
◆ German invasion of Poland
◆ Japanese attack on Pearl Harbor

World War II (1939 – 1945)

Immediate Effects
◆ Defeat of Axis Powers
◆ Founding of United Nations

Long-Term Effects
◆ United States as global power
◆ Soviet domination of Eastern Europe
◆ Cold war

CHART SKILLS World War II made the United States a superpower but put it on a collision course with the Soviet Union.
CRITICAL THINKING Which of the causes listed above stemmed from World War I? 9E

A CLOUDED FUTURE 1B

The end of the war also brought new evaluation of America's place in the world. By 1945 two nations—the United States and the Soviet Union—stood head and shoulders above the rest. Despite its great losses in the war, the Soviet Union wielded colossal military strength. The United States possessed even greater power, as the atomic bomb confirmed. Truly, these were two superpowers—as they in fact came to be called.

Although the superpowers had fought as allies against a common enemy, they still eyed each other with deep-seated suspicion. Ideological differences—communism versus democracy—were only part of the problem. The economic and political goals of the superpowers clashed in Europe, Asia, and other parts of the world. One man returning to the United States in the spring of 1945

observed, "War with Russia is unthinkable, yet it is being thought about constantly. It is, in fact, America's great fear."

It was to avoid a "postwar war" that President Roosevelt had championed a world body to replace the League of Nations. He saw the new United Nations (UN) organization as a sort of police force for the world. He thought the UN would only succeed, however, if the victorious Allies worked together.

The UN's structure reflected Roosevelt's belief that great-power cooperation would be essential. Five major powers from the anti-Axis coalition—the United States, the Soviet Union, Britain, France, and China—had a veto in the decision-making Security Council. The veto allowed any of the five to block a UN action it opposed.

Two weeks after Roosevelt's death, the founding

1941 First air hero is Second Lieutenant George S. Welch of Wilmington, Delaware, who shoots down four Japanese airplanes during Pearl Harbor attack (Dec. 7).

Jeannette Rankin, Republican of Montana, is only representative to vote twice against American entry into war (Dec. 8).

Glenn Miller's "Chattanooga Choo-Choo" is first gold record (having sold more than a million copies).

1942 First cross-country helicopter flight (May 13).

1943 First warship named for a black hero is the U.S.S. *Harmon,* in honor of Leonard Roy Harmon (killed in action during the Battle of Guadalcanal).

1944 First ship-launching telecast, of U.S.S. *Missouri,* New York City (Jan. 29).

1945 First conference of the United Nations, at San Francisco (April 25).

BIOGRAPHY 4C

ELEANOR ROOSEVELT (1884–1962) became a delegate to the United Nations and helped write its Universal Declaration of Rights. She began her lifelong crusade for humanitarian causes working with the poor in New York City. As First Lady, she made fact-finding trips to provide FDR's administration with information on world problems.

conference of the UN opened in San Francisco. Delegates from almost 50 nations quickly drafted a charter, and in July 1945 the Senate approved American membership by a vote of 89 to 2. This time there was none of the quarreling that had kept the United States out of the League of Nations after World War I. The American people believed that their nation, which played such a crucial role in the war, had an equally crucial role to play in the peace.

SECTION REVIEW

1. KEY TERMS Holocaust, Nuremberg Trials, GI Bill of Rights, superpower, United Nations

2. PEOPLE AND PLACES Auschwitz, Hideki Tojo

3. COMPREHENSION How many deaths and injuries did the American home front suffer? What caused them?

4. COMPREHENSION What important principle did the Nuremberg Trials establish?

5. CRITICAL THINKING Compare the United States' world position at the end of World War II with its position at the end of World War I. What factors would have made it more difficult for Americans in 1945 to argue against United States participation in an international organization?

Section Review Answers

1. *Holocaust*—Program of mass murder of Jews by Nazis. *Nuremberg Trials*—Trials of Nazi leaders for crimes against humanity. *GI Bill of Rights*— Law that helped veterans to continue their education. *superpower*—Nation with enormous military might. *United Nations*—World peacekeeping organization.

2. *Auschwitz*—Nazi concentration camp. *Hideki Tojo*—Japan's wartime premier.

3. On-the-job accidents killed about 300,000 Americans, permanently disabled 1 million, and injured 3 million more.

4. The idea that individuals are responsible for their own actions, even in time of war.

5. Possible answers include: afraid that isolationism would lead to another war; the United States was a superpower after World War II, which had not happened after World War I; the Soviet Union was more powerful, and U.S. isolationism could encourage the spread of communism.

Closure

Call students' attention to the beige boxed quotation (p. 435). Ask how this quotation relates to the main idea of the section. Then have students read Section 1 of Chapter 19 for the next class period. Ask students to look for ways to characterize postwar America.

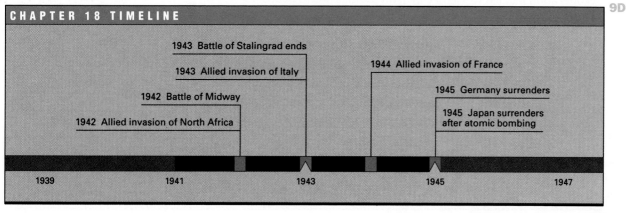

CHAPTER 18 TIMELINE   9D

1943 Battle of Stalingrad ends

1943 Allied invasion of Italy

1944 Allied invasion of France

1942 Battle of Midway

1945 Germany surrenders

1942 Allied invasion of North Africa

1945 Japan surrenders after atomic bombing

1939   1941   1943   1945   1947

CHAPTER 18 THE WORLD AT WAR, 1941–1945 **437**

Famous Firsts
Ask students to research one of the events and present their findings to the class.

Biography
As First Lady, Eleanor Roosevelt proved to be an important member of the Roosevelt administration. Discuss with students other First Ladies they may know about and ask them to write a job description for the First Lady's position.

Chapter 18 REVIEW

CHAPTER 18 SUMMARY

SECTION 1: At first the Axis Powers made great gains. By 1942 the Allies had begun to halt Axis advances.

■ The Axis Powers made rapid gains during the first months after Pearl Harbor.

■ The Nazi invasion of the Soviet Union was blocked at Stalingrad in 1943.

■ American naval victories over Japan turned the tide in the Pacific.

SECTION 2: World War II transformed American society.

■ Racism and fears of disloyalty led the United States government to intern thousands of Japanese Americans.

■ War production created an economic boom.

■ Blacks and women gained economic opportunities.

■ Major population shifts resulted from the migration of job-seekers to industrial centers.

SECTION 3: By 1945, Allied cooperation had led to victory in Europe.

■ In 1943 Allied forces invaded Italy from North Africa. On June 6, 1944, Allied forces invaded France.

■ Soviet forces fought their way into Germany and captured Berlin.

■ In May 1945 Germany surrendered, ending the war in Europe.

SECTION 4: Fierce Japanese resistance could not withstand Allied advances.

■ Allied forces "island-hopped" across the Pacific toward Japan.

■ In September 1945, after the atomic bombing of Hiroshima and Nagasaki, Japan surrendered.

SECTION 5: The effects of World War II lasted long into peacetime.

■ The war resulted in unprecedented loss of life.

■ The Allies punished some Axis officials for committing war crimes.

■ Tensions between the Soviet Union and Western democracies threatened world peace.

KEY TERMS ●

Use the following terms to complete the sentences below.

Battle of the Atlantic
Battle of the Bulge
Battle of Leyte Gulf
Battle of Midway
Battle of Stalingrad
D-Day
El Alamein

1. Japan failed to stop an American invasion of the Philippines at the _____ .
2. The Allied invasion of France in June 1944 is known as _____ .
3. The final German offensive of World War II was the _____ .
4. More than half a million Russian people were killed in the _____ .
5. The turning point of the war in North Africa came at _____ .
6. The fight for control of shipping lanes connecting the United States and Great Britain was called the _____ .
7. The Japanese advance in the Pacific was turned back after the _____ in 1942.

PEOPLE TO IDENTIFY ●

Identify the following people and tell why each was important.

1. Albert Einstein
2. Dwight D. Eisenhower
3. Douglas MacArthur
4. A. Philip Randolph
5. Erwin Rommel

PLACES TO LOCATE ●

Match each of the letters on the map with the places that are listed below. Then explain the importance of each place.

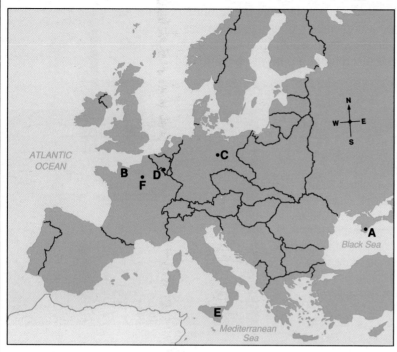

1. Paris
2. Ardennes Forest
3. Yalta
4. Berlin
5. Sicily
6. Normandy

REVIEWING THE FACTS ▲

1. Which nations made up the Axis Powers? The Allies?
2. How and when was the Axis offensive halted in North Africa? In the Pacific?
3. What effects did American entry into the war have on the U.S. economy?
4. In what ways did the U.S. government become more involved in the everyday lives of citizens during the war?
5. Why did Stalin ask Churchill and Roosevelt to attack Germany from the west? Why did they delay in doing so?
6. What important agreements were reached by the Big Three at the Yalta Conference?
7. Why did Churchill want the troops of the Western Allies to proceed as far to the east as possible before meeting the Soviet troops? What did Eisenhower do instead?
8. What strategy did the Allies follow in the Pacific after Guadalcanal?
9. When and under what conditions did Italy, Germany, and Japan surrender?
10. Why did the United States use the atomic bomb against Japan?

CRITICAL THINKING SKILLS ▲

1. **FORMING A HYPOTHESIS** Why, in your opinion, did the Allied leaders believe that Germany and Italy were more dangerous enemies than Japan?

2. **DRAWING CONCLUSIONS** Why, do you think, did union leader A. Philip Randolph agree to the deal Roosevelt offered him (page 421)?

3. **MAKING COMPARISONS** Compare Allied military strategy in Europe in World Wars I and II. (See Chapter 13 for the history of World War I.)

WRITING ABOUT TOPICS IN AMERICAN HISTORY ■

1. **CONNECTING WITH LITERATURE** A selection from *The Wall* by John Hersey appears on pages 803–804. Read it and answer the questions. Then answer the following question: How does this selection help you *feel* what it must have been like inside the Warsaw ghetto?

2. **APPLYING THEMES: EXPANDING DEMOCRACY** Imagine you are a woman who, after working to raise a family for 20 years, has found a job as a welder in a shipyard. Write a letter to your parents describing the new opportunity and the changes it has brought to your life.

3. **GEOGRAPHY** Write a report on an important battle or campaign in World War II. Focus on the effects of geography on the fighting and its outcome.

9. Italy surrendered in September 1943 when the Allies invaded. The Germans surrendered May 7, 1945, after the taking of Berlin. Japan surrendered on September 2, 1945, after two atomic bombs were dropped on it.

10. The atomic bomb was used to end the war quickly, avoiding the bloody cost of a full-scale invasion.

Critical Thinking Skills
1. Germany and Italy appeared more dangerous because they invaded or tried to invade Allied countries—the Soviet Union and Britain.

2. Possible answers are Randolph agreed to the deal because it was the best offer he could get and he did not want to appear unpatriotic.

3. The Allied strategy during World War I was one of trench warfare and little movement on the Western Front. During World War II, planes allowed greater mobility along the fronts, civilian targets were hit, and commanders waited to invade until they were confident their forces could make a strong move.

Writing About Topics in American History
1. Students should note how the use of a first-person journal and the detailed description of the sights and sounds of the ghetto allow the reader to experience what life was like in the ghetto.

2. Students may want to search for primary sources of women who began working for wages during the war.

3. Students should consider the effects of environment and weather on the battles and how commanders adapted strategies and weapons to geography.

7. Churchill believed the further east the Western Allies got, the less power Stalin would have in postwar Europe. Eisenhower mopped up pockets of resistance rather than launch a new offensive.

8. Island-hopping.

Chapter Review exercises are keyed for student abilities:
● = Basic
▲ = Average
■ = Average/Advanced

UNIT 6: American Mosaic

★ *A Multicultural Perspective* ★

World War II created a labor shortage in the United States. As a result, women and members of ethnic minorities were able to move into job areas from which they had traditionally been excluded. Racial discrimination, however, continued.

The automobile industry made big profits in America during the 1930s. Its management was fiercely opposed to unions. The family of **George Addes** (left) was among the many Arab American families that had come from Syria to work in Michigan's auto factories. Addes joined the labor movement and helped form the United Auto Workers (UAW). After a hard struggle with manufacturers, the entire industry was unionized by 1941. Addes became the first secretary-treasurer of the UAW. During World War II, Addes helped auto workers increase the output of weapons in line with government policies.

After Japan's attack on Pearl Harbor, many doubted the patriotism of Japanese Americans. However, most second generation Japanese Americans (or *Nisei*) felt fully as patriotic as other Americans. To prove it they joined the U.S. armed forces in large numbers. One Nisei army regiment, the 442nd, fought in Italy during World War II and earned over 18,000 medals for bravery. (Members of the brigade are shown above.) The 442nd became the most decorated unit in United States military history.

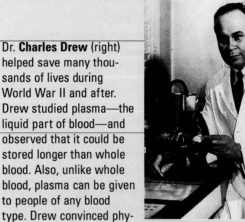

Dr. **Charles Drew** (right) helped save many thousands of lives during World War II and after. Drew studied plasma—the liquid part of blood—and observed that it could be stored longer than whole blood. Also, unlike whole blood, plasma can be given to people of any blood type. Drew convinced physicians to use plasma for battlefield and other emergency blood transfusions. During the war he also organized many blood bank programs, despite the fact that because blood from African Americans was not accepted by blood banks, he could not have donated his own blood.

In 1942 **Maggie Gee** left school to take a job as a welder and later as a draftswoman in a California shipyard. Long interested in aviation, Gee took flying lessons and then joined the air force as a pilot. During the remainder of the war she flew military aircraft wherever they were needed in the United States. She later returned to school and became a physicist.

After fleeing his native Italy in 1938 to escape its Fascist government, physicist **Enrico Fermi** (left) continued his work in the United States. He produced the world's first nuclear chain reaction in his laboratory at the University of Chicago. He also contributed to the Manhattan Project, which built the first atomic bomb in 1945.

Born in Los Angeles, Iva Toguri (right) was visiting relatives in Japan when Japan attacked Pearl Harbor. Unable to return home, she worked as a disc jockey for Radio Tokyo in order to survive. Meanwhile, in the United States, her parents were moved to a detention camp for Japanese Americans where her mother died. After the war Toguri was accused of being **Tokyo Rose,** who the army claimed had spread anti-American propaganda. Toguri had actually done little more than spin records. In spite of the lack of evidence against her, Toguri was convicted of treason in 1949. President Ford pardoned Toguri in 1977 citing "the unfortunate web of circumstance" in which she was caught.

More than 400 Navajo Indians served as radio operators in World War II, transmitting top secret messages in their language —a "code" the Japanese were unable to break.

Arturo Toscanini (left) gained fame as a conductor of classical music while working with an Italian opera company on tour in Brazil in 1886. The company's regular conductor quit and the nineteen-year-old Toscanini stepped in to lead Verdi's *Aïda* without a musical score. Toscanini came to the United States in 1908 and worked with its best orchestras, including the NBC Symphony, created especially for him. The U.S. government sponsored Toscanini on a 13,000-mile goodwill tour of South America in 1940. A strong opponent of fascism, Toscanini refused to return to Italy while Mussolini was dictator and boycotted concerts in Austria while it was under Nazi rule.

A native of Brownsville, Texas, **Américo Paredes** (left) worked as a reporter for the army newspaper *Stars and Stripes* and covered the war crimes trials of Japanese leaders in 1946. After returning to Texas, he received degrees from the University of Texas and stayed to become a professor of English. In his writing, Parades examines Mexican American culture through its folk tales, songs, and popular beliefs. His work has earned him the title of "dean of Mexican American scholars."

Ruth Benedict (right) studied the religious beliefs and practices of different societies around the world, including those of the Plains Indians. She concluded that cultures show the same characteristics as the individuals who belong to them—only on a larger scale. During World War II the U.S. government asked Benedict to study the culture of Japan. Her ideas influenced America's policy toward Japan during the postwar period of occupation.

Historians' Corner

Vocabulary Preview

Be sure students understand the following terms: *craven*—Cowardly. *augment*—Increase. *coup d'etat*—Sudden overthrow of a government. *concoct*—Invent. *fait accompli*—An accomplished and irreversible deed or fact.

Analyzing Historical Issues

These contemporary accounts reveal different journalists' responses to the news from Munich. Alice Marquis recounts how American radio networks in Europe tried to give impartial coverage of events, while Dorothy Thompson's newspaper column denounces the agreement.

What should the role of the news media be in covering foreign affairs—simply to report events or to analyze them and present a point of view? Which form would be more useful to future historians? Why?

Critical Thinking Answers

1. Thompson makes her opinion of the Munich agreement very clear, while Murrow was trying to be impartial.

2. American news coverage was not controlled by government pressure. While Britain and France were limiting the news, American radio networks were expanding and upgrading their coverage.

3. Modern news reporting has the advantage of live television coverage, so people can see events as well as just read and hear about the news.

HISTORIANS' CORNER

Reporting the News from Munich, 1938

Some of the headlines from five or ten or fifty years ago eventually become history. In the 1930s, although the United States wanted to stay out of Europe's troubles, Hitler's actions in Czechoslovakia were clearly a threat. These two excerpts show how Americans got the news of the Munich "appeasement" agreement. The first tells how radio covered the news. The other quotes a respected newspaper columnist of the 1930s.

Alice G. Marquis

When the [Munich] crisis broke on September 12, both networks [NBC, CBS] were ready for live coverage at a level never before attempted. . . .

Not only correspondents, but the participants themselves became familiar voices to American listeners: Mussolini from Trieste, Premier Milan Hodza from Prague, Pope Pius XI from Rome, Hitler personally attacking President Benes, and Chamberlain's craven "How horrible . . . that we should be digging trenches and trying on gas masks here, because of a quarrel in a faraway country. . . ."

Reporters and commentators were careful to avoid editorializing: "We are trying to provide material on which an opinion may be formed," [Edward R.] Murrow explained, "but we are not trying to suggest what that opinion may be.". . .

For both networks, the Munich crisis coverage . . . caused them to augment and professionalize their news staffs, preparing for the war that now seemed inevitable.

From Alice G. Marquis, *Hope and Ashes*. Reprinted by permission of The Free Press. Copyright © 1986 by The Free Press.

Dorothy Thompson

[Oct. 1, 1938] What happened on Friday [the Munich agreement] is called "Peace." Actually it is an international Fascist *coup d'etat*.

The "Four-Power Accord" is not even a diplomatic document. . . . It is difficult to describe except as a hurriedly concocted armistice made in advance of a war to permit the occupation by German troops of a territory which by sheer threat . . . they have conquered by "agreement.". . .

On Friday Czechoslovakia was disposed of by four men who in four hours made a judgment of the case in which the defendant was not even allowed to . . . be heard. . . .

What ruled that conference was Nazi law. Not one of the four men who thus arbitrarily disposed of a nation had ever set foot in Czechoslovakia. . . .

In this whole affair, described as an attempt to keep peace, the democratic process has been completely suspended. In both Britain and France the facts have been suppressed by . . . government pressure on the controlled radio and on the newspapers. The people of

England and France are confronted with a *fait accompli* without . . . possession of the facts on which it is based. . . .

Let us not call this peace. Peace is not the absence of war. Peace is a positive condition—the rule of law.

This peace has been established by dictatorship, and can only maintain itself by further dictatorship. . . .

This is not peace without victory, for the victory goes to Mr. Hitler.

From Dorothy Thompson, *Let the Record Speak* (Boston: Houghton Mifflin, 1939), pp. 223, 225-227.

Critical Thinking

1. How does Thompson's report differ from the approach described by Edward R. Murrow?

2. According to these two reports, how was American news coverage of the crisis different from that in Britain and France?

3. Compare the reporting of foreign news in 1938 with news reporting today.

Alice G. Marquis

(1930–), born in Munich and a naturalized U.S. citizen, is a journalist and former history instructor at the University of California at San Diego.

Dorothy Thompson

(1893–1961) was known as the "first lady of American journalism." She served as a European correspondent during the 1930s and 1940s, and helped shape American attitudes toward events of the time.

UNIT SEVEN

A Cold Peace

CHAPTERS IN THIS UNIT

19 The Truman Years (1945–1952)
20 The Eisenhower Years (1953–1960)

THEMES IN AMERICAN HISTORY

 Global Interactions Following World War II, the United States assumed leadership in the West's battle against communism.

 Economic Development The American economy was immensely powerful after World War II, and American economic aid helped rebuild the shattered nations of Western Europe.

 Constitutional Government Fear of Communist subversion threatened to limit Americans' civil liberties in the late 1940s and early 1950s.

American Culture American culture of the 1950s reflected not only the stability and prosperity of the decade but also some signs of rebellion.

This unit examines the economic advancements and international insecurities of the United States in the years following World War II. It traces the course of Harry S. Truman's presidency: his relationship with Congress, American attempts to limit the threat of growing Communist influence in Europe and Asia, the impact of fears of Communist subversion at home, and the outbreak of the Korean War.

The unit discusses President Dwight Eisenhower's role in ending the Korean War and his administration's response to the major international crises of the 1950s. The influence of economic prosperity, suburban growth, and increased consumer goods on American society is described. They are contrasted with such underlying tensions as the threat of nuclear war, the rise and fall of Joseph McCarthy, a growing rift between young Americans and their parents, the success of the Soviet launch of *Sputnik*, television and radio scandals, and corruption in labor unions.

Chapter 19 ■ The Truman Years

	SECTION OBJECTIVES	SECTION RESOURCES
Section 1 **Postwar America**	■ describe the United States' adjustment to a peacetime economy and society	● **Reteaching Resources:** Worksheet 72 ▲ **Reinforcement Workbook:** Worksheet 72 ▲ **Teaching Transparencies:** Transparency 72
Section 2 **The Cold War**	■ determine the postwar events that led to the development of the cold war	● **Reteaching Resources:** Worksheet 73 ▲ **Reinforcement Workbook:** Worksheet 73 ■ **Enrichment and Extension Resources:** Primary Source Worksheet 37 ▲ **Teaching Transparencies:** Transparency 73
Section 3 **The Age of Suspicion**	■ explain how fear of communism created a climate of suspicion that affected American society in the postwar period	● **Reteaching Resources:** Worksheet 74 ▲ **Reinforcement Workbook:** Worksheet 74 ▲ **Teaching Transparencies:** Transparency 74
Section 4 **The Korean War**	■ identify the causes of the Korean War ■ explain how American involvement in Korea affected political and social conditions at home	● **Reteaching Resources:** Worksheet 75 ▲ **Reinforcement Workbook:** Worksheet 75 ■ **Enrichment and Extension Resources:** Primary Source Worksheet 38 ▲ **Teaching Transparencies:** Transparency 75

The list below shows Essential Elements relevant to this chapter. (The complete list of Essential Elements appears in the introductory pages of this Teacher's Edition.)

Section 1: 1A, 3B, 3D, 3E, 4D, 5B, 6A, 7B, 8E
Section 2: 1A, 1B, 3F, 5E, 9A, 9B
Section 3: 6B, 7E, 7J, 9A
Section 4: 1A, 1B, 7A, 9A, 9B, 9D, 9E

Section Resources are keyed for student abilities:
● = Basic
▲ = Average
■ = Average/Advanced

CHAPTER RESOURCES

Geography Resources: Worksheets 37, 38
Tests: Chapter 19 Test

Chapter Project: Global Interactions

Have students write the script for a news documentary focusing on an important issue during the Truman years, such as demobilization, the elections of 1948, the cold war, the Truman Doctrine, the Marshall Plan, the Berlin blockade, the formation of NATO, the Chinese Revolution, the spy trials, or the Korean War. Students may choose to act out or film their documentaries.

Homework Options

Each section contains activities labeled "Addressing Individual Needs." You may wish to choose from among these activities when assigning homework.

> ### Provisions for Limited English Proficiency (LEP)
> Several suggested activities may be particularly helpful for teachers of students with limited English proficiency. These activities have been marked throughout the Teacher's Annotated Edition with the symbol **LEP** .

BIBLIOGRAPHY AND AUDIOVISUAL AIDS

Teacher Bibliography

Ferrell, Robert H., ed. *Off the Record: The Private Papers of Harry S. Truman.* Penguin, 1982.

Kalb, Marvin, and Elie Abel. *Roots of Involvement: The U.S. in Asia 1784–1971.* Norton, 1971.

Ridgway, Matthew. *The Korean War.* Da Capo, 1986.

Schlesinger, Arthur M. *Dynamics of World Power: A Documentary History of U.S. Foreign Policy, 1945–73.* Chelsea House, 1983.

Student Bibliography

Donovan, Robert J. *Conflict and Crisis: The Presidency of Harry S. Truman, 1945–1948.* Norton, 1977.

Leuchtenburg, William E. *Age of Change, from 1945.* Silver, Burdett and Ginn, 1974.

Miller, Merle. *Plain Speaking: An Oral Biography of Harry S. Truman.* Berkley, 1986.

Literature

Lowell, Robert. *The Collected Prose.* Farrar, Straus and Giroux, 1987.

Miller, Arthur. *Death of a Salesman.* Penguin, 1976. Pulitzer Prize-winning play.

O'Connor, Flannery. *Wise Blood.* NAL Penguin, 1987. A fanatic tries to establish the Church Without Christ but is driven to using violence to prove God's existence.

Salinger, J. D. *Catcher in the Rye.* Bantam, 1977.

Films and Videotapes*

Are We Winning the War Mommy? 85 min. FRF. Historical review of the cold war from its origins in World War I.

Cold War Confrontation. 21 min. FI. Examines two events that created a confrontation between East and West—the Berlin airlift and the Korean War.

The Korean War: Aggression. 15 min. COR/MTI. *The Korean War: Escalation.* 15 min. COR/MTI. *The Korean War: Negotiation.* 15 min. COR/MTI. Series chronicles key events during the Korean War.

Korean War: The Untold Story. 34 min. PYR. Powerful story of America's first "undeclared" war, told by survivors who fought in Korea.

Truman: A Self Portrait. 23 min. NAVC. Rare archival footage documents the life of Harry Truman.

Truman: Years of Decision. 24 min. LCA. Present-day consequences of Truman's European policies of military alliance and economic assistance.

Filmstrips*

Harry S. Truman: Man of Decision (set of 3). GA. Documents the life and influence of Harry S. Truman, drawing upon speeches, written works, and other primary sources. Also available in video.

Modern U.S. History: Unit 1, 1945–1960 (set of 4). GA. Covers the Truman-Eisenhower years. Also available in video.

Computer Software*

DECISIONS, DECISIONS: Foreign Policy—The Burdens of World Power (Apple II and IBM). TS. Students confront realistic international relations dilemmas. Though the story lines are fictional, the program provides advice based on factual information. Materials are for use by groups and are designed to encourage class discussion and problem solving. Excellent support materials; good software.

TIME TRAVELLER: After World War II (IBM). MVP. Multiple-choice, true/false, and short-answer questions within the context of a time-travel adventure. Includes questions about contributions by women and minorities. Up to 300 additional questions can be added.

*For a complete guide to audiovisual sources, see the introduction to this book (page Txx).

This chapter deals with the social, economic, and political situation of postwar America. It focuses on the return to a peacetime economy, the roots of the cold war, the fear of communism, and the Korean War.

Themes in American History

- Global interactions
- Constitutional government
- Economic development

Chapter Objectives

After students complete this chapter, they will be able to:

1. Describe the United States' adjustment to a peacetime economy and society.

2. Determine the postwar events that led to the development of the cold war.

3. Explain how fear of communism created a climate of suspicion in the postwar period.

4. Identify the causes of the Korean War.

5. Explain how American involvement in Korea affected political and social conditions at home.

The end of World War II allowed Americans—including thousands who had fought overseas—to resume normal lives. In this cover for The Saturday Evening Post, *Norman Rockwell shows a returning soldier describing his wartime experiences.*

Chapter Opener Art
Norman Rockwell, *The War Hero,* 1945.

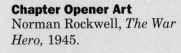

CHAPTER SUPPORT MATERIAL	
	Reinforcement Workbook: Worksheets 72–75
	Reteaching Resources: Worksheets 72–75
	Enrichment and Extension Resources: Primary Source Worksheets 37, 38
	Geography Resources: Worksheets 37, 38
	Teaching Transparencies: Transparencies 72–75
	Tests: Chapter 19 Test

SECTION 1

Postwar America
(pp. 445–448)

1A, 3B, 3D, 3E, 4D, 5B, 6A, 7B, 8E

1 Postwar America

★ **Section Focus**

Key Terms demobilization ■ Fair Deal ■ Taft-Hartley Act ■ Dixiecrat

Main Idea After World War II, Americans sought to maintain prosperity as they adjusted to peacetime.

Objectives As you read, look for answers to the following questions:
1. What were the effects of World War II on the American economy?
2. Why was the 1948 presidential election remembered as a great upset?
3. What were the results of Harry Truman's struggles with Congress?

August 14, 1945. "JAPAN SURRENDERS," "THE WAR IS OVER"—the newspapers blared the news. President Harry Truman declared a two-day national holiday of jubilation. People danced in the streets. The war had ended and the Allied victory promised a bright future.

There was good reason to be optimistic. "No country in history ever emerged from a major war in better shape," one historian has written. America was by far the richest and most powerful nation on earth. But the joy of victory was mixed with uncertainty. People remembered the hard times of the Great Depression before World War II. Would a return to peace also bring back the high unemployment and low wages of the 1930s?

COMING HOME 1A

At the end of World War II, millions of American soldiers were stationed around the world waiting eagerly to come home. Many of them thought the wait was lasting too long. Thousands wrote to Congress to protest. Scores of others took part in "Send Us Home" demonstrations. After all, they thought, wasn't the war over? Many stateside relatives joined the call to "bring the boys home."

President Truman, however, wanted to keep some forces based around the globe. He believed they were needed to preserve American power in the postwar world. Truman was also concerned about a possible war with the Soviet Union. But the cry for demobilization—reduction in the size of the armed forces—was too great to ignore. By late 1946, American forces had dropped from 12 million to 3 million.

This reduction left behind the largest peacetime military in American history. (Before the war only 300,000 Americans were in uniform.) Still, the return of so many soldiers in search of civilian jobs proved a challenge to a peacetime economy.

THE PEACETIME ECONOMY 3B, 3E

As the government spent less on war production, it began to spend billions on postwar programs to help veterans adjust to civilian life. The GI Bill of Rights (page 435) was passed in 1944. It gave veterans preference for federal and state jobs and provided money for almost 2.5 million veterans to go to college.

The economy was further stimulated by a rush of spending by American consumers. During the

Section Objective
■ describe the United States' adjustment to a peacetime economy and society

Introducing the Section

Connecting with Past Learnings
Review the changes in the economy at the start of World War II. (Factories stopped producing consumer goods and began producing war materials. Women took over jobs traditionally held by men. Goods needed for the military were rationed or salvaged.)

Key Terms
Write the key terms for this section on the board. Call on volunteers to come to the board and write a sentence using one of the terms in context. Ask the rest of the class to verify the meaning of the terms by looking them up in the text. **LEP**

Focus
Ask students to discuss what they might be looking forward to and what they might worry about if the date were August 15, 1945. (Positives— return of friends and relatives from the armed forces, peace, more consumer goods, end of rationing; negatives— fear of unemployment, inflation, labor unrest.)

Looking back at that time, do you think that Americans adjusted well or poorly to peacetime conditions?

SUPPORTING THE SECTION

Reinforcement Workbook: Worksheet 72
Reteaching Resources: Worksheet 72
Teaching Transparencies: Transparency 72

Background The Federal Employment Act of 1946 pledged the federal government to promote full employment by creating and maintaining employment opportunities.

war, the economy produced bullets and tanks, not houses and cars. Rationing made even basic products like butter and sugar scarce. Many people responded to shortages by saving money for the future. After the war, America was ready for a shopping spree. Money poured into the economy, starting a postwar economic boom.

The negative side to all the spending was a spurt of inflation. Because people wanted to buy more than they could find in the stores, prices rose. Also fueling inflation was the removal of wartime price controls. Between 1945 and 1948, prices rose 48 percent.

BIOGRAPHY 3D

JOHN L. LEWIS (1880–1969) promoted unionization of the industries—including steel, rubber, and automobile—that used mass-production methods. He served as president of the United Mine Workers of America from 1920 to 1960. During World War II, Lewis led the mine workers in controversial strikes that won them medical and retirement benefits.

As in the years following World War I, inflation touched off labor unrest. Poor and working people were hit hardest by inflation because wages did not meet rising prices. Workers in many industries walked off their jobs to demand wage increases. About 4.5 million people went on strike in 1946; no other year has seen so many strikes.

Truman viewed the strikes as a threat to postwar economic growth. He used his wartime powers to seize several industries. Taking control of the coal fields, oil refineries, and meat-packing houses, he forced labor and management to accept settlements designed by the government.

When negotiations broke down in the railway industry, Truman even threatened to draft railroad workers into the military. Then, as commander-in-chief, he could order them back to work. When the Attorney General warned Truman that such action would be unconstitutional, the President re-

sponded, "We'll draft 'em first and think about the law later." A settlement was reached before Truman had a chance to carry out his threat. Still, Truman's tough stand against strikers showed a hostility toward labor unknown since the 1920s.

> "**W**e'll draft 'em first and think about the law later."
>
> —*Harry Truman, on striking railroad workers, 1946*

Truman's action in the railway strike also showed his take-charge, no-nonsense style of leadership. When Truman took office in 1945, many people doubted that he could handle the job. But the fast pace of events—wartime decisions such as dropping the atomic bomb, as well as peacetime crises such as the railroad strike—demanded firm presidential leadership. Truman's motto, "The buck stops here," showed that he was prepared to make the tough decisions. He was also prepared to fight for his policies if need be.

> "**T**he buck stops here."
>
> —*Harry Truman*

TRUMAN VERSUS CONGRESS 4D, 8E

In 1946 the Republican Party won votes by claiming that Democratic policies had caused the postwar strikes and inflation. The Republicans' campaign slogan was "Had Enough?" They used it to gain control of both houses of Congress for the first time since 1928.

The election put the President and Congress on a collision course. Truman, a New Deal Democrat in the tradition of FDR, called his domestic program the **Fair Deal**. Truman wanted the government to create jobs, build public housing, and end job discrimination against African Americans.

The 80th Congress, in contrast, was one of the most conservative of the twentieth century. Many of its members opposed Fair Deal efforts to distribute wealth more equally. These efforts, they believed, had discouraged Americans from gaining wealth. So they passed a tax cut that favored the wealthy. They also rejected civil rights reforms. And they viewed almost every bill for federal aid to housing, health care, and education as too much government intervention.

In 1947 Congress passed the Taft-Hartley Act. This bill overturned many rights won by unions under the New Deal. It outlawed closed shops but allowed the union shop (in which new workers had to join a union) if most workers voted for it. The bill also banned sympathy strikes (walkouts by workers in support of strikers in other industries). Finally, it allowed states to pass right-to-work laws. Such laws let workers obtain and keep jobs without joining a labor union at all.

Supporters of Taft-Hartley said it kept a balance of power between labor and management that had been upset (in favor of labor) by the Wagner Act (1935). Critics called it the "Slave Labor Act." Truman vetoed the bill, but Congress overrode the veto. The bill became law.

THE UPSET OF 1948 5B

The Republicans were in an excellent position to win the presidency in 1948. They had scored a great victory in the 1946 congressional races. The 80th Congress had been able to block many of Truman's liberal proposals. It had also passed a number of conservative laws (such as Taft-Hartley) over Truman's vetoes. Thus, the Republicans thought their candidate—New York Governor Thomas E. Dewey—would easily defeat Truman.

The Democrats had trouble rallying party support for Truman. In 1948 two factions broke away from the Democratic Party. Southern conservatives formed the States' Rights Democratic Party. Supporters of racial segregation, they were angered by a civil rights plank in the Democratic Party platform. The States' Rights Democrats, nicknamed the Dixiecrats, nominated Strom Thurmond, governor of South Carolina, as their presidential candidate.

On the left wing of the Democratic Party, a new Progressive Party was formed. It called for improved relations with the Soviet Union and an extension of New Deal legislation. Its candidate for

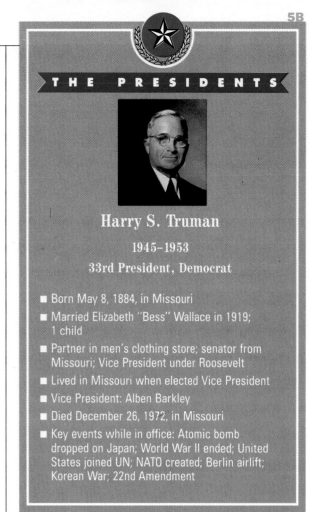

President, Henry Wallace, had been Vice President during Franklin Roosevelt's third term.

The splits in the party did not seem to bother Truman. An energetic campaigner, he traveled all over the country by train, giving "whistle-stop" speeches in dozens of small towns and villages. He stirred the crowds by lashing out at the Republican-dominated 80th Congress. He claimed it was a "do-nothing" Congress that had no compassion for ordinary Americans. "The Republicans," he warned, are "gluttons of privilege . . . all set to do a hatchet job on the New Deal." Delighted crowds egged him on with shouts of "Give 'em hell, Harry!"

Though Dewey waged a lackluster campaign, most people were sure he would win. Six weeks before the election, *Newsweek* polled 50 experts asking who they thought would win. All 50

The Presidents
Truman was the only President elected in the twentieth century who did not attend college. Have students discuss the importance of a college education to a President.

Background   The demands of labor unions caused growing resentment on the part of business leaders. New Deal labor laws had strengthened the power of unions. Conservative Republicans wanted to limit that power by means of the Taft-Hartley Act.

Truman's domestic program based on extending social welfare policies. *Taft-Hartley Act*—Outlawed closed shops and sympathy strikes and gave management the power to seek federal injunctions to end strikes. *Dixiecrat*—Supporter of racial segregation and states' rights who broke away from the Democratic Party in 1948.

2. *Thomas E. Dewey*—Republican presidential candidate in 1948. *Strom Thurmond*—Dixiecrat presidential nominee. *Henry Wallace*—Vice President during FDR's third term, nominated by the Progressive Party in 1948.

3. Americans feared a return to the high unemployment and low wages of the 1930s. After the war, Americans fueled an economic boom by spending money saved during the war. However, a high rate of inflation led to an unprecedented number of strikes.

4. Republicans already controlled Congress; Truman had very little success getting many of his social programs passed; the Democratic Party split into factions; people seemed tired of Democratic control.

5. Helped—keeps any one point of view from gaining too much power, forces more compromises; harmed—prevents many important decisions from being made because of fights between the legislative and executive branches.

Closure

Remind students of the prereading objectives in the section opener. Pose one or all of these questions again. Then have students read Section 2 for the next class period. Ask them to consider the definition of *cold war* based on the information in the section.

A jubilant Harry Truman holds aloft a newspaper mistakenly proclaiming his opponent's victory in the 1948 election. Newspaper editors, like many others, were certain Dewey would win. This newspaper went to press before all the returns were counted. Blacks, union members, and farmers all helped Truman retain office. **POLITICS** What advantages did Truman have over Dewey that helped him win the election? **5B**

picked Dewey. On Election Day it became clear that Truman had pulled off the political upset of the century. He took 49.5 percent of the vote to Dewey's 45 percent. The splits within the Democratic Party had not done the expected damage. The States' Rights and Progressive parties won only about a million votes each.

MORE CONFLICTS WITH CONGRESS 6A, 7B

His surprise victory in 1948 gave Truman new hope for passing liberal social legislation—his Fair Deal. However, most of his proposed bills were blocked in Congress by Republicans and southern Democrats.

Truman supported, for example, the first comprehensive plan for national health insurance for all citizens. That initiative, bitterly opposed by the medical profession, was killed by Congress. But Congress did increase the number of people who could benefit from Social Security. It also raised the minimum hourly wage from 40 to 75 cents.

Truman's Fair Deal went well beyond the New Deal in calling for racial justice. Congress failed to pass much civil rights legislation. Truman did, however, publicly criticize violence against blacks, job discrimination, and racial bigotry.

Truman's most significant step against discrimination came in 1948. In that year he issued an executive order banning racial segregation in the armed forces. This move was a tribute to the long struggle by blacks for equal participation in the military. It was also an acknowledgment, long overdue, of black Americans' contributions to the defense of their nation.

SECTION REVIEW

1. KEY TERMS demobilization, Fair Deal, Taft-Hartley Act, Dixiecrat

2. PEOPLE Thomas E. Dewey, Strom Thurmond, Henry Wallace

3. COMPREHENSION Why did many Americans worry that the economy would falter after World War II? What actually happened?

4. COMPREHENSION Why did so few people expect Truman to win the 1948 election?

5. CRITICAL THINKING Do you think the United States is helped or harmed by strong disagreements between the President and Congress? Explain your answer.

Photo Caption Answer
He campaigned more energetically and had more personal dynamism than Dewey; he presented himself as FDR's heir and guardian of the New Deal.

Background In 1947 Jackie Robinson became the first black player in the major leagues. Robinson's courage in the face of prejudice and his skill on the baseball field helped pave the way for other black athletes.

Background By executive order, Truman banned racial discrimination in the hiring of federal employees.

2 The Cold War

★ Section Focus

Key Terms cold war ■ satellite ■ iron curtain ■ containment ■ Truman Doctrine ■ Marshall Plan ■ Berlin blockade ■ NATO

Main Idea After World War II, relations between the United States and the Soviet Union turned icy cold. The two superpowers often seemed on the verge of open warfare.

Objectives As you read, look for answers to these questions:
1. What events soured relations between the superpowers?
2. How did the United States respond to fears of Soviet expansion?
3. How did events in China heighten American fears?

Since World War II the fate of the world has hinged on relations between the Soviet Union and the United States. These superpowers have engaged in a costly arms race for almost 50 years. They have viewed each other with suspicion and open hostility. War has never broken out directly between them. However, they have competed around the world for resources, markets, prestige, and political strength.

Hostility between the two nations really began with the Bolshevik Revolution in 1917. During World War II there was hope that the two nations might build the foundation for a peaceful world. After all, they fought together against fascism, and in wartime meetings the two powers tried to settle their differences. But strains in the alliance were developing even during the war. Soon after the war's end, Soviet-American cooperation all but collapsed.

A CRISIS IN IRAN 1A

Iran was the scene of the first postwar crisis between the United States and the Soviet Union. Both nations had occupied parts of Iran during World War II to protect Allied supply routes running through that country. The superpowers had agreed to leave Iran when peace came. But in 1945 the Soviets, lured by Iran's vast oil supplies, refused to withdraw.

Encouraged by the United States, Iran complained about the Soviet occupation before the UN Security Council. When the Security Council began looking into the complaint, Soviet delegates walked out of the UN. This was the first of several times that the Soviet Union boycotted the United Nations.

The crisis ended in 1946 when the USSR agreed to pull its troops out of Iran in return for the right to drill Iranian oil. A year later, however, the United States persuaded Iran to take back the oil rights. The Soviets felt cheated, and suspicion grew between the two nations.

EASTERN EUROPE 1A

Europe was the center stage for superpower conflict. Tensions would reach a point where observers started talking about a cold war. A cold war is not a direct confrontation. It is, rather, a battle of diplomacy, of propaganda, and of nerves.

In the final years of World War II, the Soviet Red Army drove German forces out of Eastern Europe. Thus, at war's end the Soviet Union controlled a vast stretch of land on its western border. At the Yalta Conference (page 427), Soviet leader Joseph Stalin had promised to allow free elections in Eastern Europe. As it turned out, free elections were the last thing Stalin had in mind.

First, the Soviet Union annexed the Baltic nations of Estonia, Latvia, and Lithuania, which it had seized during the war. In Poland, Stalin installed a regime loyal to him. Elsewhere, there seemed some hope for democracy. In some nations the Soviets set up coalition governments that included non-Communist representatives. However, as time went on, Stalin consolidated power. In nation after nation, Communists eliminated all dissent. There was no freedom of speech, assembly,

---

SUPPORTING THE SECTION

Reinforcement Workbook: Worksheet 73
Reteaching Resources: Worksheet 73
Enrichment and Extension Resources: Primary Source Worksheet 37
Teaching Transparencies: Transparency 73

Background A 1941 agreement provided for the stationing of British troops in the south of Iran and Soviet troops in the north. U.S. troops arrived after U.S. entry into the war. British and American troops withdrew in 1945.

SECTION 2

The Cold War
(pp. 449–454)

Section Objective
■ determine the postwar events that led to the development of the cold war

Introducing the Section

Connecting with Past Learnings
Ask students to list reasons why the Soviet Union and the United States emerged as superpowers after World War II. (Both were large and populous countries; the United States escaped the devastation of the war and built up its industrial strength; after the war the Soviet Union occupied or controlled many countries in Asia and Eastern Europe.)

Key Terms
Write the key terms for this section on the board and have students write down definitions. Call on volunteers to share one of the definitions, and have the class guess which term is being defined. Follow this procedure until all the terms have been defined a few times. Have the class determine the best definition for each term and write that on the board. **LEP**

Direct students to work in pairs to create two posters illustrating differences between the United States and the Soviet Union after World War II. Encourage students to design symbols or other visual interpretations to illustrate differences in political, economic, and social values between the two countries. Display and discuss the completed posters.

Were tensions between the superpowers inevitable? Why or why not?

Developing the Lesson

After students have read the section, you may want to consider the following activities:

Global Awareness

Have students list the countries mentioned in the section controlled by Communists or which were threatened by Communist takeover. (Soviet Union, Iran, Estonia, Latvia, Lithuania, Poland, Yugoslavia, Rumania, Bulgaria, Greece, Turkey, France, Italy, East Germany, West Germany, China.) Have students discuss why communism spread so quickly in those years. (The war had destroyed many legitimate governments, leaving countries vulnerable.)

What did the United States do to prevent the spread of communism? (Initiated policy of containment, the Truman Doctrine, and the Marshall Plan, aided West Berlin during the blockade, helped form NATO.) ***Do you think the policy of containment worked the way Kennan predicted it would?***

or petition. Government critics were jailed or shot. The borders were sealed so that no one could flee to the West.

By the end of 1948, seven Eastern European nations had become Soviet satellites. (A satellite nation is officially independent but controlled by a foreign power.) Only Yugoslavia, under its strong-willed leader, Marshal Tito, gained a measure of independence from Moscow.

Stalin insisted that his actions were merely defensive. He argued that the Soviet Union needed friendly states on its borders as protection from possible future attack from the West.

CONTAINING SOVIET POWER 1B

In March 1946, Winston Churchill came to the United States to warn about Soviet aggression. The former British prime minister stated, "From Stettin in the Baltic to Trieste in the Adriatic an iron curtain has descended across [Europe]." Behind that iron curtain, Churchill warned, the Soviets were tightening their grip. Even more frighteningly, he claimed the Russians meant to expand their power around the world.

5E

★ **Historical Documents**

For an excerpt from Churchill's iron curtain speech, see page 725 of this book.

President Truman shared Churchill's views. But how should the United States respond? Truman decided on a policy first expressed by George Kennan. A State Department expert on the Soviet Union, Kennan said the United States could block Soviet expansion with a "policy of firm containment." The idea was to halt further Communist expansion, with force if necessary. Kennan believed that if this effort were successful, in time the Soviet system would mellow and the Soviet Union would become less dangerous. The containment policy became the cornerstone of postwar American foreign policy. As Truman put it, "Unless Russia is faced with an iron fist, another war is in the making."

Most Americans supported containment because it seemed to correct the error of appeasement made before World World II. Everyone recalled

how diplomacy had failed to stop Hitler's aggression. In the early postwar years, American leaders believed the Soviet Union represented the same kind of threat. What remained unclear, however, was just how and where the United States should draw the line.

> "Unless Russia is faced with an iron fist, another war is in the making."
> —*Harry Truman, 1946*

THE TRUMAN DOCTRINE 1B

The policy of containment was first brought to bear in the Mediterranean. Since the end of World War II, Greek Communists had fought to overthrow the Greek monarchy. The revolutionaries received arms from Communist Yugoslavia. Britain backed the Greek government with military aid. But Britain, its finances exhausted by the war against Hitler, was in no position to maintain its commitments around the world. In 1947 the British announced that they were suspending all aid to the Greek royalist government.

President Truman believed the United States should step in to help crush the rebellion. To do so would require a massive aid program. At the same time Truman called for assistance to Turkey. Its government was seeking to block Soviet demands for a naval base in Turkish territory. Congressional leaders at first held back. "If we assume a special position in Greece and Turkey," Senator Robert Taft warned, "we can hardly . . . object to the Russians continuing their domination in Poland, Yugoslavia, Rumania, and Bulgaria."

However, Truman persuaded a majority in Congress (Taft included) that if communism triumphed in Greece, the Soviet Union would spread revolution elsewhere. He described the crisis in Greece as part of a global struggle between freedom and communism. "I believe it must be the policy of the United States to support free peoples who are resisting attempted subjugation by armed minorities or by outside pressures," he said. This statement became known as the Truman Doctrine.

Congress approved $400 million in aid to Greece and Turkey. And, in those cases, the policy worked. The Greek revolution was crushed, and Turkey stood up to the Communist threats. The Truman Doctrine would guide American policy for years to come.

5E

 Historical Documents

For an excerpt from the Truman Doctrine, see page 726 of this book.

THE MARSHALL PLAN 1A, 3F

The Truman Doctrine was a military approach to the policy of containment. But containment also had an economic side. In June 1947, during a speech at Harvard University, Secretary of State George Marshall made a dramatic offer. The Marshall Plan proposed that the United States begin a program of massive economic aid to Europe.

Marshall had several aims. One was to help Europe. Ravaged by the war, the economies of most nations were shattered. Poverty and hunger were widespread, and many cities lay in ruins. Another of Marshall's goals was to contain communism. American policymakers believed that economic despair boosted the popular appeal of communism (just as it had boosted the Nazis' appeal in 1930s Germany). Communists could point to the hardship as a sign of capitalism's failure. People might begin to think that a radical change would bring relief. And there were already strong Communist parties in Western Europe, especially in France and Italy.

A third goal of the Marshall Plan was to ensure the continued health of the American economy. The United States needed Europe as a trading partner. As European countries recovered, they would be able to buy more American products, thereby helping the American economy.

Marshall's offer of economic aid applied to the Soviet Union and Eastern Europe as well as to Western Europe. However, the Soviet government and its satellites rejected the plan, charging that it was an effort to create economic dependence on the United States.

Over a three-year period the Marshall Plan sent

This promotional poster for the Marshall Plan advertises "Inter-European Cooperation for a Higher Living Standard." Under the plan, the United States sent billions of dollars worth of food, machinery, and other goods to Europe. **GLOBAL AWARENESS** What do the images in the poster represent? 9B

$12 billion of aid to 16 nations in Western Europe. The program was a great success. The Western economies surged, and the influence of communism in the participating nations lessened.

STANDOFF IN BERLIN 1A

In the German city of Berlin, the cold war threatened to turn hot. Germany had been divided into four occupation zones at the end of World War II. The Soviets occupied eastern Germany. The United States, France, and Britain controlled zones in the western part of Germany. The Western Allies, seeking to rebuild Germany as an ally, promoted the creation of an independent West Germany. Established in 1949, it was called the Federal Republic of Germany.

CHAPTER 19 THE TRUMAN YEARS, 1945–1952 **451**

Refer students to the map on page 453. Based on Churchill's speech on page 725, have students indicate the approximate location of the "iron curtain." **Why did Eastern Europe fall under Communist control?** (Soviet forces occupied Eastern Europe by the end of World War II; Stalin eliminated dissent by jailing or shooting opponents and closing the borders.)

C Cooperative Learning

Divide the class into small groups and assign one of the following crises to each group: occupation of Iran by the Soviet Union, Greek civil war, Berlin blockade, struggle between Nationalist and Communist forces in China. Instruct the members of each group to brainstorm alternative solutions to their assigned problem. Each member should suggest one solution. Then the group should discuss the advantages and disadvantages of each course of action and choose the best solution. Have each group report its decision to the class. **LEP**

By that time, Stalin had tightened his grip on eastern Germany. He had set up a Communist government there and removed as much wealth as he could from the German economy to strengthen the Soviet Union. But the city of Berlin posed a problem for him. Berlin had also been divided among the Allies into separate zones. However, the city lay deep inside the Soviet zone, far from the centers of Western power.

In June 1948, Stalin made a move to grab all of Berlin. He blocked the highways, rivers, and railroads into West Berlin to try to seal off the city within the Soviet zone. This effort to force the West from the former German capital became known as the Berlin blockade.

Since West Berliners depended on trade with Western nations, a blockade would leave them without food and fuel. They would be at the mercy of the Soviet Union. But the United States and its allies were not about to give up West Berlin. They considered sending an armed convoy to break the blockade, but feared that this would provoke war. Instead, America and Britain decided to use a massive airlift of food and supplies.

Every day for almost a year, British and U.S. cargo planes flew tons of goods to West

A U.S. Air Force artist painted this view of the Berlin airlift. It shows an American plane flying over a cemetery as it approaches Berlin's Tempelhof airport. Such flights kept West Berlin supplied with food and fuel during the Soviet blockade of land routes. **GLOBAL AWARENESS** Why did the United States and its allies choose to use an airlift rather than some other method to get supplies to Berlin? **9A**

Photo Caption Answer
It provided a means of circumventing the blockade without using force. The Soviet Union could not stop the planes without starting a war.

Background The Berlin blockade lasted 321 days. British and American pilots made 272,264 flights, bringing 2.3 million tons of food and other supplies to Berlin.

Member of NATO, 1955

Member of Warsaw Pact, 1955

MAP SKILLS

9B

The cold war divided Europe into East and West. To which alliance did Hungary belong, NATO or the Warsaw Pact? To which alliance did West Germany belong? **CRITICAL THINKING** What role did most of the European nations that joined *neither* alliance play in World War II?

Berlin. It was an extraordinary effort, and it worked. At the peak of the airlift, planes were landing in Berlin at the rate of one every 3 minutes. The Soviets could not stop the planes without starting a war. The blockade failed, and in May 1949 Stalin re-opened Western access to the city.

MILITARY COOPERATION IN EUROPE 1A

Stalin's gamble in Berlin backfired. It stiffened Western resolve in Berlin and also led to greater cooperation among the Western powers. While the Berlin blockade was under way, the United States, Canada, Iceland, and nine Western European nations formed the North Atlantic Treaty Organization (NATO). Each nation pledged to defend the others in the event of outside attack. The treaty also created a permanent NATO military force in Europe. (In 1955 the Soviet Union and other Com-

munist nations in Eastern Europe formed an opposing alliance, the Warsaw Pact.)

Along with the Truman Doctrine and the Marshall Plan, the United States' entry into NATO marked a new era of American involvement in world affairs. NATO was the first peacetime military pact with Europe that the United States had made since its alliance with France in 1778. Congressional opponents of the treaty argued that it would provoke an arms race with Russia. They also claimed it would raise defense costs and allow the President to send troops into battle without Congress declaring war. However, Truman stressed that NATO would take some of the burden of the cold war off the United States. Europeans would take on more responsibility in the stand against communism. The Senate ratified the treaty by a vote of 82 to 13.

CHAPTER 19   THE TRUMAN YEARS, 1945–1952   **453**

Map Skills Answers
Warsaw Pact. NATO. They were neutral.

Background The original NATO members were Belgium, Britain, Canada, Denmark, France, Iceland, Italy, Luxembourg, the Netherlands, Norway, Portugal, and the United States. Greece and Turkey joined the alliance in 1951, and West Germany joined in 1954. Differences

among members caused France to withdraw in 1966. Spain joined NATO in 1982.

Addressing Individual Needs

Guided/Independent Practice
Have students complete **Reinforcement Workbook** Worksheet 73. This worksheet helps them locate and describe "hot spots" that contributed to cold war tensions.

Reteaching/Correctives
On the board, help students develop a cause-and-effect chart of issues discussed in the section. For causes, have them list actions of the Soviet Union, economic despair in Western Europe, and the revolution in China. Have students agree on a general statement about United States foreign policy following World War II.

Instruct students to complete **Reteaching Resources** Worksheet 73, which helps students organize the main ideas of this section.

Enrichment/Extension
Assign **Enrichment and Extension Resources** Primary Source Worksheet 37, in which students read excerpts from the Marshall Plan.

Assessment

You may wish to use the Section 2 Review, page 454, to see how well your students understand the main points in this lesson.

Section Review Answers

1. *cold war*—Battle of diplomacy, of propaganda, and of nerves, not a direct confrontation. *satellite*—Officially independent country controlled by another. *iron curtain*—Invisible barrier between eastern and western Europe created by differing governing ideologies. *containment*—American foreign policy aimed at stopping the spread of communism.

Portraits of Lenin and Marx hang on the wall behind Mao Zedong as he addresses members of the Red Army. This romanticized painting shows Mao as a young Communist leader during the fight against Chiang Kai-shek. **GLOBAL AWARENESS** Was American support for Chiang's Nationalist government a good decision or a mistake? Explain your answer. **1A**

Truman Doctrine—Policy of the United States to support free peoples in resisting communism. *Marshall Plan*—Program of massive economic aid to European countries. *Berlin blockade*—Soviet effort to isolate Berlin from Western support. *NATO*—Peacetime military alliance between the United States, Canada, and ten western European nations.

2. *George Kennan*—State Department official who first expressed the policy of containment. *George Marshall*—Secretary of State who proposed program of economic aid to Europe. *Chiang Kai-shek*— Leader of Nationalist Chinese. *Mao Zedong*—Leader of Chinese Communists.

3. The Soviets wanted to control Iran's oil and refused to withdraw from that country. The United States supported Iran when Iran took its grievance to the UN.

4. To help war-ravaged Europe, contain communism, and ensure European trading partners to help the American economy.

5. Students may point out that maintaining diplomatic relations with Latin American dictators was not the same as controlling their governments. Other students may argue that the United States did train, install, and maintain rulers in some Latin American countries.

Closure

Call students' attention to the beige boxed quotation (p. 450). Ask how this quotation relates to the main idea of the section. Then have students read Section 3 for the next class period, noting the domestic response to the spread of communism abroad.

REVOLUTION IN CHINA 1A

In the summer of 1949, United States leaders were generally happy with the world situation. The cold war was tense as ever, but they believed America was gaining an edge. The Truman Doctrine had stopped communism in Greece. The Marshall Plan was reviving Western Europe, and the Berlin blockade had been broken. A strong NATO alliance had been forged. Within months, however, the United States would suffer a jolt.

For two decades Chinese Communists had struggled against the Nationalist government of Chiang Kai-shek. The United States supported Chiang. Between 1945 and 1949, he received $3 billion in American military and economic aid. However, Chiang's regime had grown corrupt, incompetent, and unpopular. Communist forces led by Mao Zedong gained strength throughout the vast country.

Chiang ignored American advice to begin land reform, end corruption, and increase democracy. Nor would he seek a ceasefire with the Communists, as Secretary of State Marshall counseled. Finally, in the fall of 1949 Mao forced Chiang to flee China for the island of Formosa (Taiwan).

The Communist victory caused a storm of debate in the United States. Republican critics blamed Truman for "losing China." But the President said that nothing short of all-out war could have stopped the revolution.

To many Americans, the Chinese revolution was viewed as proof of a Communist conspiracy to control the world. The world's largest country in area—Russia—had been Communist since 1917. Now the largest country in population, containing one-fourth of the world's people, had gone Communist. On top of that came the news in September 1949 that the Soviet Union had exploded its first atomic bomb.

America's confidence was shaken. Many wondered if the blame for communism's gains might be found in the United States. As you will read in the next section, some Americans began fighting the cold war at home as well as abroad.

SECTION REVIEW

1. KEY TERMS cold war, satellite, iron curtain, containment, Truman Doctrine, Marshall Plan, Berlin blockade, NATO

2. PEOPLE George Kennan, George Marshall, Chiang Kai-shek, Mao Zedong

3. COMPREHENSION Why did the United States and the Soviet Union clash over Iran in 1945?

4. COMPREHENSION What were the three goals of the Marshall Plan?

5. CRITICAL THINKING Stalin once said that Communist control of Eastern Europe was no different from U.S. support for Latin American dictators. How would you respond to this argument?

---

454 UNIT 7 A COLD PEACE

454

Photo Caption Answer
Some students may say that support was a mistake since Chiang's corrupt government was unpopular. Others may suggest that even a corrupt government was better than communism.

Background For many decades, the United States recognized the Nationalist government of Taiwan as China's legal government and supported Nationalist representation in the UN. Britain, France, the Soviet Union, and several other nations recognized the People's Republic of China (Chinese Communist government). Formal U.S. recognition of mainland China came in 1979.

3 The Age of Suspicion

Section Focus

Key Terms HUAC ■ perjury ■ McCarthyism

Main Idea Concern about communism abroad touched off a fervent anti-Communist crusade at home.

Objectives As you read, look for answers to these questions:
1. Why is the period after World War II called an "age of suspicion?"
2. How did Senator Joseph McCarthy gain widespread attention?

As concern about communism overseas gathered steam, many Americans became afraid that Communists were a threat to life at home. Citizens were encouraged to expose and denounce anyone thought to have Communist leanings. A climate of fear developed that resembled the Red Scare of 1919–1920. These words of alarm came from Truman's Attorney General, J. Howard McGrath:

> There are today many Communists in America. They are everywhere—in factories, offices, butcher shops, on street corners, in private business—and each carries in himself the germs of death for society.

American Communists 7J

Despite McGrath's warning, the number of actual Communists in the United States was never very large. Although more than 100,000 people voted for the Communist candidate for President in 1932, communism soon lost its appeal. This was in large part because of the American Communist Party's close ties to the Soviet government. In the mid-1930s Stalin began massive purges among his own people, executing thousands of imagined enemies. Over the years, millions of Soviet citizens lost their lives. As news of these horrors reached the West, support for the American Communist Party dropped.

The American Communist Party regained some support when the United States allied itself with the Soviet Union in the fight against Germany. However, after the war it dwindled to a small underground movement that still clung to the views of the Soviet Communist Party.

Nevertheless, the fear of Communist subversion affected the entire society. People were so suspicious that almost any unusual opinion might be labeled "un-American." The climate of suspicion was most severe in the years 1947–1954, but it lasted throughout the 1950s.

Testing Loyalty 7J

In 1947 Truman responded to fears about radicals in government by creating a Loyalty Review Board. Federal employees could be fired for having once belonged to a group, or signed a petition, that the Board deemed "subversive." While Truman was in office, some 1,200 federal workers were fired for being "disloyal" or "bad security risks." About 5,000 more resigned under pressure.

Rarely were the accused allowed to challenge the claims made against them. The head of the Loyalty Board said, "The government is entitled to dismiss any employee . . . without extending to such employee any hearing whatsoever." Those who kept their jobs had to sign loyalty oaths.

Communist influence anywhere raised public concerns. The House Committee on Un-American Activities (HUAC) began to investigate Hollywood in 1947. The committee believed Communists were sneaking propaganda into films. Witnesses called to testify were asked, "Are you now, or have you ever been, a member of the Communist Party or a fellow traveler?" (A fellow traveler is sympathetic to communism but not a party member.)

> "**A**re you now, or have you ever been, a member of the Communist Party?"
>
> —*Question posed by HUAC investigators*

SUPPORTING THE SECTION

Reinforcement Workbook: Worksheet 74
Reteaching Resources: Worksheet 74
Teaching Transparencies: Transparency 74

Background A National Security Act, passed in 1947, created the Central Intelligence Agency (CIA). The original purpose of this agency was to collect and evaluate intelligence information relating to national security.

SECTION 3

The Age of Suspicion
(pp. 455–457)

Section Objective
■ explain how fear of communism created a climate of suspicion in the postwar period

Introducing the Section

Connecting with Past Learnings
Review Communist gains in the world in the 1940s. (Takeover of Eastern Europe and China; threats to Greece and Turkey; large Communist parties in Italy and France; Soviet explosion of atomic bomb.)

Key Terms
Have students write sentences using each of the key terms. Instruct them to leave a blank for the term in each sentence. Then have students exchange papers and use context clues to fill in the key terms. **LEP**

Focus

Divide the board into two halves. On one half, have students suggest events which caused the fear of communism. (Communist takeovers in Eastern Europe and China; detonation of atomic bomb; Alger Hiss case; Rosenberg case.) On the other half, list responses to those fears. (Loyalty Review Board; HUAC investigations; McCarthyism.)

Do you think that the response to the fear of communism helped or harmed the nation? Why?

Developing the Lesson

After students have read the section, you may want to consider the following activities:

455

As head of an actor's union, Ronald Reagan worked to keep suspected Communists out of the film industry. Here, Reagan testifies before HUAC in 1947. HUAC probes targeted liberals, artists, and intellectuals. **CONSTITUTIONAL HERITAGE** Did Loyalty Boards and blacklisting violate constitutional rights? Why or why not? **9A**

Some witnesses refused to answer, because they believed such questions were illegal. Hollywood studios took silence as an admission of guilt and blacklisted those witnesses. That is, the studios refused to hire them, and circulated their names to other employers so they could not get jobs anywhere. The careers of many writers, actors, and directors were ruined.

SPY TRIALS

In 1948 HUAC began investigating Alger Hiss, a former State Department official. Whittaker Chambers, a former Communist Party member, accused him of having been a Communist agent in the 1930s. He testified that Alger Hiss had given him secret documents in 1937 and 1938 to pass along to the Soviet Union.

By the time the case went to trial, Hiss could not be convicted for spying since the statute of limitations had run out. He was, however, convicted of **perjury**—lying under oath—in 1950 for claiming that he had not known Chambers in the 1930s. The Hiss case left many Americans thinking there were Communist spies in government. (It also boosted the career of a future President—the young California congressman named Richard Nixon, a HUAC member who spearheaded the investigation of Hiss.)

Fear of spies grew with another shocking charge. Had Americans given Soviet scientists help in building an atomic bomb?

The Soviet Union tested its first atomic bomb in 1949, just four years after the United States began the Atomic Age. In 1950 Klaus Fuchs confessed to taking part in a spy ring that sent atomic secrets to the Soviets. Fuchs had worked on the American atomic bomb project at Los Alamos, New Mexico. His confession led to the arrest of two Americans: Ethel and Julius Rosenberg.

The espionage trial of Julius and Ethel Rosenberg split public opinion. While many Americans protested the guilty verdict and death sentences as unjust, others agreed with the words of the demonstrator in the foreground. **ETHICS** Do you support the use of the death penalty in certain cases? Why or why not? **7E**

In 1951, after a long and controversial trial, a jury found the couple guilty of spying. Two years later the Rosenbergs were executed at Sing Sing prison. They were the first civilians in American history put to death for espionage.

McCARTHYISM 6B

In 1950 Joseph R. McCarthy was an unknown Republican senator from Wisconsin, serving his first term. When he asked friends for a good re-election issue, they suggested anticommunism. Within a few weeks McCarthy began making shocking claims about the Communist menace.

At a Lincoln Day speech in Wheeling, West Virginia, McCarthy said there were 205 Communists in the State Department. A Senate subcommittee looked into McCarthy's charges. The Democratic chairman of the committee, Millard Tydings, had little patience with McCarthy's accusations. He called them "a hoax and a fraud . . . an effort to inflame the American people with a wave of hysteria and fear on an unbelievable scale."

Nevertheless, Republicans generally backed McCarthy's investigations. (Most of his targets were Democrats.) McCarthy also gained public support with his simplistic explanations of foreign policy failures. For example, he blamed the victory of Communist forces in China on "Communists" in the State Department. He ruined the careers of several China experts who had accurately reported the corruption in Chiang Kai-chek's government.

Some historians believe McCarthy tried to win support by stirring up resentment of the rich. His accusations often focused on wealth and privilege. He charged:

> It has not been the less fortunate or members of minority groups who have been selling this nation out, but rather those who have had all the benefits—the finest homes, the finest college education, and the finest jobs in government.

Though McCarthy failed to find facts to support his charges, his accusations continued to make headlines. For over four years he held the national spotlight. Eventually the term McCarthyism emerged to describe McCarthy's practice of ad-

Senator McCarthy charged that Communists had infiltrated many areas of American life. As in the Salem witch trials, McCarthy's investigations relied on rumor. He succeeded in ruining many careers and reputations but never uncovered a single Communist spy. POLITICS Why did many people believe in McCarthy? 6B

vancing one's political career by making unproven accusations of disloyalty. And just as overseas events had helped launch the campaign against Communist influence, Communist aggression in Korea would help to sustain it.

SECTION REVIEW

1. KEY TERMS HUAC, perjury, McCarthyism

2. PEOPLE Alger Hiss, Ethel and Julius Rosenberg, Joseph R. McCarthy

3. COMPREHENSION What touched off the crusade against Communist subversion at home?

4. COMPREHENSION What shocking claims did Senator McCarthy make in 1950 that gained him national headlines?

5. CRITICAL THINKING Agree or disagree with the following statement, and give reasons for your position: "In the long run, false accusations cause no damage because innocent people will eventually be cleared of suspicion."

CHAPTER 19   THE TRUMAN YEARS, 1945–1952   **457**

457

4 The Korean War

Section Objectives

■ identify the causes of the Korean War

■ explain how American involvement in Korea affected political and social conditions at home

Introducing the Section

Connecting with Past Learnings

Have students consider American fears of Communist expansion overseas during Truman's presidency. *What policy had pledged the United States to aid free peoples in resisting outside pressures?* (Truman Doctrine.)

Key Term

Write the key term from this section on the board and have a volunteer define it. Ask students to suggest examples of limited wars, starting with Korea, and explain their examples. **LEP**

Section Focus

Key Term limited war

Main Idea The United States entered the Korean War to contain communism. Yet the war turned into a frustrating stalemate that left the American people confused and disillusioned.

Objectives As you read, look for answers to these questions:
1. What was the situation in Korea at the end of World War II?
2. What happened to South Korea in June 1950?
3. Why did President Truman fire General MacArthur?

In 1950, American troops were once again in the thick of battle. This time they were fighting in Korea. Colonel Gilbert Cleck, a tank commander, recalled one desperate clash in the early days of the war:

> Antitank guns caught us on a curve several miles short of our objective. The tanks caught partially afire and the crews were wounded. But three of the tanks were still operable. . . . I was not going to let several hundred thousand dollars' worth of American equipment sit back there on the road. I yelled, "Who around here thinks he can drive a tank?" A couple of ex-bulldozer operators and an ex-mason volunteered. They got about three minutes' checking out and off they went.

Cleck's column was led through ambush after ambush back to safety. The drive back taught them valuable lessons about Korea. The fighting would be tough and gritty—and there would be no easy victories.

BUILDING A NEW JAPAN 1A

The story of American involvement in Korea goes back to World War II. During the war, Japan ruled much of Asia and the Pacific. With its defeat in 1945, however, it lost not only its empire but also its independence. Who would govern the land once dominated by Japan? Who would govern Japan itself?

Since the United States had played the biggest part in winning the Pacific war, it claimed the right to occupy Japan and shape its future.

Backed by an American occupation force, General Douglas MacArthur ruled Japan for seven years. He took power away from the emperor and abolished the armed forces. MacArthur also wrote a new Japanese constitution that called for representative government. Though the United States and Japan had been bitter enemies, they became strong allies. American aid helped to ease the humiliation of Japanese defeat.

KOREA DIVIDED 1A

Korea was a more complex problem. Japan had ruled Korea from 1910 to 1945. United States and Soviet troops moved in, in August 1945, to accept Japanese surrender. Afterwards, neither nation wanted to remove its troops.

At wartime conferences, the Allies agreed to divide Korea into two zones at the 38th parallel. The Soviet Union would occupy the North and the United States the South. Plans were made to reunify Korea with national elections. But these plans—like the plans to reunify Germany—fell victim to the tensions of the cold war.

By the time Soviet and American forces left Korea in 1949, there was little hope for peaceful reunion. Korea was deeply divided. North Korea was now a well-armed Communist satellite, ruled by Kim Il-Sung. In the South, the United States had built up the dictatorial government of an American-educated Korean, Syngman Rhee.

NORTH KOREA INVADES THE SOUTH 1B

Both of these aggressive rulers sought to reunify Korea by force. Each side had started a number of border skirmishes. Rhee frequently threatened a

Background The Japanese Constitution, drafted by the occupation authorities, went into effect in 1947. It supported the formation of political parties, farm reform, and the emancipation of women.

full-scale invasion of the North. His forces were no match for the Communists, however, and he never followed through on his threats.

In 1950, American intelligence services reported a massive build-up of North Korean forces along the 38th parallel. On June 25, the North Koreans struck, crossing the 38th parallel in force. The South Korean Army was soon in full retreat.

Kim Il-Sung may have believed he could defeat the South without drawing the United States into the war. Earlier that year, Secretary of State Dean Acheson had outlined American policy in the region. He said the United States would keep communism behind a "defensive perimeter" that stretched from the Aleutian Islands to the Philippines. Korea was not included within the perimeter. Critics later charged that Acheson's speech had encouraged the Communists to attack. Yet, Acheson was not alone in his view that Korea was of secondary importance to American policy. General MacArthur and other military leaders had also indicated that Korea was not vital to American interests.

When fighting broke out, however, American leaders quickly agreed that the United States should intervene. The occupation of Japan was scheduled to end soon, and American officials feared that a Communist victory in Korea might threaten Japan. Perhaps more important, Truman had been accused of "losing" China in 1949. Another Communist victory, even in a small country such as Korea, would be political suicide.

TRUMAN RESPONDS 1A

Truman received news of the North Korean invasion while resting at his home in Missouri. For a few days it was unclear how he would respond. Then, on June 27, 1950, Truman ordered air strikes against North Korean forces. He also sent arms to South Korea. Truman, however, did not want American forces acting alone in Korea. He asked the UN Security Council to seek a resolution calling on other nations to help the South.

The Soviet Union probably would have vetoed the action, had the Soviet delegate been present for the vote. However, at this time the Soviets were boycotting the Security Council to protest the Council's refusal to recognize the new Communist government of China. The failure to veto the Korean resolution proved a serious blunder for the Soviets. Now, the effort to defend South Korea had gained support from other nations.

On June 30, 1950, Truman ordered American troops to South Korea, calling the move a "police action." He appointed General MacArthur commander of UN forces. The confident MacArthur announced, "If Washington will not hobble me, I can handle it with one arm tied behind my back."

UN pilots in Korea flew fighter planes like this F4U Corsair, which had originally been built for use in World War II. Newer jet aircraft such as the F-86 Sabre dueled with Soviet-built MIG-15s, often flown by Chinese pilots. GLOBAL AWARENESS What factors prompted American intervention in Korea? 9E

Have students write a series of newspaper headlines reflecting major events of the Korean War. (Examples: "North Korean Troops Cross the 38th Parallel"; "Victory at Inchon.") Have volunteers write one of their headlines on the board and ask the class to discuss the story that would go with it.

After most of the major events of the war have been discussed, ask: *Why did the United States intervene in Korea?* (Officials feared that a Communist victory in Korea would threaten Japan, and Truman did not want to "lose" another country to the Communists.) *What was America's original goal in Korea?* (To push North Korean forces back to the 38th parallel.) *How did the American objective change after the victory at Inchon?* (Truman called for an invasion of North Korea to liberate the territory under Communist rule.)

Have students sum up by explaining how Truman's decisions during the Korean War affected his popularity. (Many Americans viewed him as inept; congressional support for Fair Deal legislation dropped even lower than before.)

Photo Caption Answer
The "loss" of China and a perceived threat to Japan.

Background   Truman justified sending troops to Korea without consulting Congress by arguing that the atomic age required quick decisions that could not wait for lengthy congressional debates.

Patterns in History
What was the United States relationship with Japan in the years immediately after World War II? (Occupied Japan; wrote a new constitution; helped ease postwar bitterness, became strong allies.)

Have students characterize the relationship with Japan today. *Do you think the United States and Japan are still strong allies? What issues have strained their alliance?*

Geographic Themes: Location
Refer students to the maps on page 462. Ask them to speculate about reasons why Korea was a target for conflict. (Korea borders on China and the Soviet Union; lies close to Japan; was a divided country.)

FROM PUSAN TO INCHON 1A

The first weeks of the war were grim for the Americans. It looked as if the North Koreans might push them and their South Korean allies right into the ocean. By the end of July 1950 the enemy was within a few miles of the city of Pusan, on the southern tip of the Korean peninsula.

Heavy reinforcements began arriving in the South in August. Along with several large American divisions, small contingents of British, French, and Canadian troops set up positions in the South. All told, sixteen nations sent soldiers to South Korea. Americans, however, comprised 90 percent of the UN forces.

The arrival of more troops shored up the defensive line in the South. At that point, General MacArthur made a daring move. Leaving part of his forces in Pusan, he decided to strike at the North Korean rear. He landed a large naval force at Inchon, on the western border near the 38th parallel.

Many military experts thought MacArthur's assault was a crazy gamble. It would weaken the still-vulnerable forces in Pusan. And the ocean tides around Inchon were dangerous. Unless the landing were perfectly timed, the landing forces might drown or be exposed on open beaches, making them easy prey for North Korean units on shore.

The gamble worked. On the morning of September 15, MacArthur's forces stormed the beaches of Inchon. They quickly regained the South Korean capital of Seoul, and drove south. At the same time UN forces advanced north from Pusan. The

United Nations soldiers herd North Korean prisoners from a blazing section of the city of Inchon. Although sixteen allied countries were involved in Korea, the United States provided most of the troops and supplies for the UN force. **HISTORY** What were the results of MacArthur's landing at Inchon? **9E**

Photo Caption Answer
The landing temporarily changed the course of the war by enabling UN forces to repulse the North Korean army and regain Seoul.

Background At their greatest strength, there were 1.1 million South Korean and UN troops: 590,000 South Korean, 480,000 American; and another 39,000 UN soldiers from Australia, Belgium, Britain, Canada, Colombia, Ethiopia, New Zealand, France, Greece, the Netherlands, the Philippines, Luxembourg, South Africa, Thailand, and Turkey. They were fighting 260,000 North Korean soldiers and 780,000 Chinese troops.

North Koreans were caught in between. Within two weeks half of their troops were either killed or imprisoned. The others fled back to North Korean territory.

NORTH TO THE YALU RIVER 1B

The American goal at the start of the war was to push back North Korean forces to the 38th parallel. That was in keeping with the policy of containment. After Inchon, Truman changed his mind. It was not enough, he believed, to hold communism at the 38th parallel. He called for the liberation of territory that was already under Communist rule. Thus, with Communist forces in retreat, Truman gave MacArthur the green light to invade North Korea.

For a short time it looked as if UN forces might win a complete victory. MacArthur's forces moved rapidly north. He confidently promised to "have the boys home by Christmas." American soldiers, not expecting to meet heavy resistance, began to lighten their load by discarding extra supplies and ammunition.

In November 1950, American planes bombed bridges on the Yalu River, the border between North Korea and China. The Chinese threatened to enter the war if the bombing continued. MacArthur assured Truman that the threat was meaningless. Or, he said, if the Chinese did enter the war, they could be handily defeated.

MacArthur was wrong on both counts. The Chinese did join the war, and their entry wrecked the American plan for victory. Several hundred thousand Chinese soldiers crossed the Yalu, driving UN forces south. When MacArthur called for the bombing of mainland China, Truman rejected the proposal. The Chinese invasion raised the possibility of a further widening of the war. Wanting to avoid another global war, Truman once again began to call for the limited goal of containing communism.

MACARTHUR FIRED 1B, 7A

In the winter of 1950–1951, Chinese troops drove UN forces back below the 38th parallel. By March 1951, MacArthur regained some ground. Military lines hardened around the border between North and South. Truman began to think about ending the war without a further effort to invade the North.

The long stalemate angered MacArthur. He believed strongly that he could achieve victory if Truman would allow him to use the full weight of American firepower in Korea. He called for attacks on China. He even suggested the use of atomic bombs. A proud, strong-willed man, MacArthur felt that he knew best how to handle the war. Truman, he said, was fighting a **limited war**—a war in which nations limit their objectives or the resources they use. MacArthur called it "an entirely new war," a war fought with "one hand tied behind our back." "In war," he said, "there is no substitute for victory."

> "**I**n war there is no substitute for victory."
>
> *—General Douglas MacArthur*

Global Awareness
Have students suggest why Truman went to the UN to gain support for aid to South Korea. *Why did Truman prefer to have American troops fight under UN sponsorship?* (Made fighting communism a global issue, not simply one of American interest.) *How did the Soviet Union's absence from the UN Security Council affect the course of the Korean War?* (Soviet representatives were not there to veto the UN resolution supporting South Korea, so troops were from many nations.)

Interested students may investigate UN peacekeeping activities in the world today.

Constitutional Heritage
Refer students to Article II, Section 2, Clause 1 of the Constitution, found on page 748. *What powers did President Truman exercise as commander-in-chief during the Korean conflict?* (He ordered air strikes against North Korea, ordered American troops to South Korea, approved invasion of North Korea, rejected proposal to attack China, and fired General MacArthur.)

Then refer students to Article I, Section 8, Clause 11, found on page 744. *Why was the Korean conflict called a "police action" rather than a war?* (Only Congress can declare war; fighting in Korea was ordered by the President and supported by a vote of the United Nations.)

Famous Firsts
Have students create a collage illustrating these items.

THE KOREAN WAR

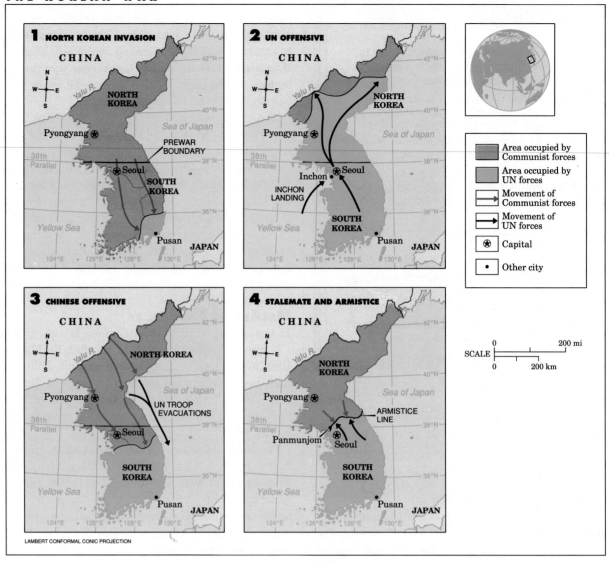

MAP SKILLS

7A, 9B, 9E

Map 1 shows the extent of the successful North Korean invasion of 1950. UN forces counterattacked, landing at Inchon and advancing to the Yalu River (Map 2). UN forces retreated as a result of China's entry into the war (Map 3). The last map shows where the two sides stood when they signed the armistice in 1953. How did the armistice line (Map 4) differ from the prewar boundary (Map 1)? **CRITICAL THINKING** Why did UN forces advance to the Yalu River? How did this decision affect the war's course?

His superiors informed MacArthur that he had no authority to make policy. Despite repeated warnings to follow orders, MacArthur continued to criticize the President. Worse, he made his criticisms public. Truman, just as stubborn as MacArthur, refused to stand for this sort of behavior. He was trying to put together a settlement of the war and could no longer tolerate a military commander who was trying to sabotage his policy. On April 11, 1951, Truman made the shocking announcement that he had fired MacArthur.

   The firing of MacArthur sparked a furious debate in the United States about the war. Just what *were* American objectives in Korea, people wondered. Few protested involvement in the war, but the changes in policy confused people.

462 UNIT 7   A COLD PEACE

This cartoon shows Harry S. Truman (H.S.T.) and members of the Pentagon and State Department feeling the heat of public opinion after Truman fired MacArthur. **POLITICS** What accounted for MacArthur's popularity with the American public? **9A**

Truman came across as indecisive and inept. By contrast, MacArthur appealed to many Americans as a strong champion of national pride and power. When he returned to the United States, he received a hero's welcome.

Yet there was also widespread support of the principle that the President was commander-in-

chief. MacArthur had clearly disobeyed his superior. Furthermore, few Americans really wanted to risk nuclear war by invading China. To do that, warned General Omar Bradley (a World War II hero), would be to fight "the wrong war, in the wrong place, at the wrong time, with the wrong enemy."

Truman survived his clash with MacArthur, but he remained trapped in an unpopular war. His Fair Deal legislation had never received much congressional support. Now, as the fighting dragged on and his popularity sank, his domestic programs were hardly even debated.

In 1951, with a presidential election approaching, both political parties began to look for a leader who could restore national confidence. The Republicans did not have to look far. They chose one of the biggest heroes of World War II— General Dwight Eisenhower.

SECTION REVIEW

1. KEY TERM limited war

2. PEOPLE AND PLACES Douglas MacArthur, Kim Il-Sung, Syngman Rhee, Pusan, Inchon, Yalu River

3. COMPREHENSION How did war break out in Korea? What was the response of the United Nations?

4. COMPREHENSION What did MacArthur find frustrating about American strategy in Korea?

5. CRITICAL THINKING What are the advantages and disadvantages of fighting a limited war rather than an all-out war?

9D

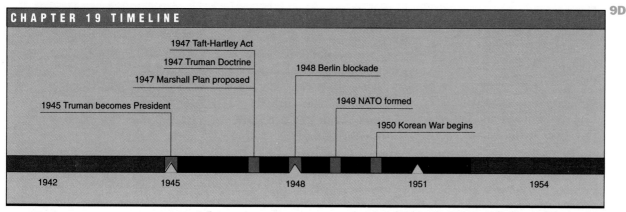

CHAPTER 19 TIMELINE

1947 Taft-Hartley Act
1947 Truman Doctrine
1947 Marshall Plan proposed
1948 Berlin blockade
1945 Truman becomes President
1949 NATO formed
1950 Korean War begins

1942   1945   1948   1951   1954

463

Chapter 19 REVIEW

CHAPTER 19 SUMMARY

SECTION 1: The end of World War II brought changes to American society.

■ Postwar inflation contributed to labor unrest.

■ In 1946 a conservative Republican Congress was elected. It reversed New Deal reforms, cut taxes, and limited the power of labor unions.

■ Truman won a surprising victory in the 1948 presidential election.

■ Conservatives in Congress blocked many of Truman's efforts to pass liberal social legislation during his second term.

SECTION 2: In the aftermath of World War II, the United States and the Soviet Union became bitter enemies.

■ Tension arose over Soviet expansion in Eastern Europe and other areas. The United States responded with a policy of containment.

■ Under the Marshall Plan, the United States sent billions of dollars in aid to rebuild Western Europe.

■ Stalin's failed attempt to seize West Berlin led to the formation of a Western mutual-defense organization.

■ Communist victory in the Chinese civil war and Soviet testing of atomic weapons fueled Western fears.

SECTION 3: Fear of Communist spies led to violations of civil liberties during the late 1940s and early 1950s.

■ Widely publicized cases of espionage led to concern about Communist infiltration of the American government.

■ Senator Joseph McCarthy's accusations ruined the careers and reputations of many people.

SECTION 4: American influence in East Asia remained strong after World War II.

■ In 1950 the United States sent troops to South Korea to defend against a North Korean invasion.

■ Entry of Communist China into the war on North Korea's side brought the conflict to a stalemate.

KEY TERMS ●

Use the following terms to complete the sentences.

Berlin blockade
Marshall Plan
NATO
Taft-Hartley Act
Truman Doctrine

1. The _____ allowed management to hire non-union workers.
2. The _____ said that the United States would aid any nation threatened by Communists.
3. The _____ was an economic aid program that rebuilt Western Europe.
4. Stalin tried to force Westerners out of West Berlin in the _____.
5. _____ was a mutual-defense pact among Western nations.

PEOPLE TO IDENTIFY ●

Match each of the following people with the correct description.

Thomas E. Dewey
Alger Hiss
Douglas MacArthur
Strom Thurmond
Mao Zedong

1. State Department official convicted of perjury in 1950.
2. Republican whom Truman defeated in 1948 presidential election.
3. Leader of Communist revolution in China.
4. Leader of American forces in Korea.
5. States' Rights Party presidential candidate in 1948.

6. The Alger Hiss and Ethel and Julius Rosenberg cases convinced many Americans that the country's internal security was threatened.

7. The Loyalty Review Board checked government employees for connections to groups considered subversive. HUAC investigated cases of suspected Communists. McCarthy grabbed attention by making unproven accusations of disloyalty.

PLACES TO LOCATE ●

Match each of the letters on the map with the places that are listed below.

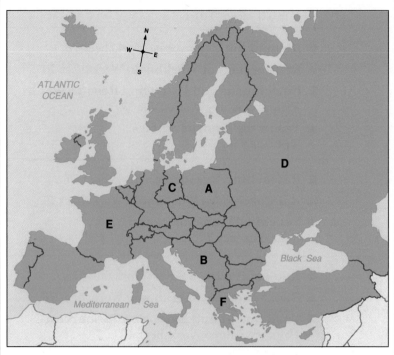

1. Soviet Union
2. Poland
3. East Germany
4. Yugoslavia
5. Greece
6. France

REVIEWING THE FACTS ▲

1. What concerns did Americans have about the postwar economy? What different problems actually developed?
2. What were President Truman's successes and failures in domestic policy? Why were many of his legislative proposals defeated?
3. What was the cold war? How did it start?
4. What was the policy of containment? Why did the United States adopt it? How did the Marshall Plan bolster it?

5. What two armies fought in the Chinese civil war? What led to the downfall of Chiang's government?
6. What events during the late 1940s caused Americans to worry about internal security?
7. What were the Loyalty Review Board and the House Committee on Un-American Activities? What tactics did Joseph McCarthy use to gain publicity?
8. What reforms did Douglas MacArthur institute in Japan during the occupation?

9. What two sides fought in the Korean War? What were the roles of the United States, the United Nations, and Communist China?
10. Why was Truman's policy in Korea controversial?

CRITICAL THINKING SKILLS ▲

1. **PARAPHRASING** In your own words, describe the situation in Korea in 1950 and explain why the United States decided to enter the war.

2. **RECOGNIZING A FRAME OF REFERENCE** Describe the disagreement between Truman and MacArthur in terms of their differing responsibilities and views of the Korean War.

3. **FORMING A HYPOTHESIS** Why, do you think, did Stalin agree at Yalta to hold free elections in Eastern Europe and then refuse to honor his commitment?

WRITING ABOUT TOPICS IN AMERICAN HISTORY ■

1. **CONNECTING WITH LITERATURE** A selection from *Maud Martha* by Gwendolyn Brooks appears on pages 804–806. Read it and answer the questions. Then answer the following question: How, in a quiet way, was Maud Martha leading a small civil rights movement?

2. **APPLYING THEMES: CONSTITUTIONAL GOVERNMENT** HUAC's investigation of communism in Hollywood trampled on certain constitutional principles. What were some of these principles and how were they affected?

Critical Thinking Skills

1. Postwar Korea had been cut in half, with North Korea under Communist control. North Korean hostilities brought the U.S. into the conflict in order to protect its interests in Asia and its image at home.

2. Truman was responsible for the larger implications of events in Korea and did not wish to escalate war into nuclear conflict, while MacArthur, who was responsible for fighting the war, favored any actions which might help the United States win the war.

3. Students may argue that Stalin simply lied to Western leaders in order to tighten the Soviet grip on Eastern Europe, or suggest that Stalin under-estimated Western support for democracy in Eastern Europe.

Writing About Topics in American History

1. Maud Martha and her husband were integrating an all-white movie theater and refusing to be limited to one particular area of the city or one type of entertainment.

2. Students may note that principles such as freedom of speech, right to a fair trial, and due process of the law were often disregarded by HUAC.

---

8. MacArthur limited the emperor's power, abolished the armed forces, and wrote a new constitution that called for representative government.

9. South Korea fought Communist North Korea. The U.S. military fought as part of the UN forces helping South Korea. Communist China supported the North Koreans.

10. Truman's objectives seemed unclear and his policy kept changing.

Chapter Review exercises are keyed for student abilities:
● = Basic
▲ = Average
■ = Average/Advanced

Chapter 20 ■ The Eisenhower Years

5 Sections, 5–7 Days

	SECTION OBJECTIVES	SECTION RESOURCES
Section 1 **Eisenhower** **Takes Office**	■ identify reasons for Eisenhower's popular appeal ■ describe the resolution of the Korean War	● **Reteaching Resources:** Worksheet 76 ▲ **Reinforcement Workbook:** Worksheet 76 ■ **Enrichment and Extension Resources:** Primary Source Worksheet 39 ▲ **Teaching Transparencies:** Transparency 76
Section 2 **The Cold War** **at Home**	■ explain how fear of communism affected American society during the 1950s	● **Reteaching Resources:** Worksheet 77 ▲ **Reinforcement Workbook:** Worksheet 77 ▲ **Teaching Transparencies:** Transparency 77
Section 3 **The Cold War** **Around the World**	■ discuss the effectiveness of American foreign policy during the 1950s	● **Reteaching Resources:** Worksheet 78 ▲ **Reinforcement Workbook:** Worksheet 78 ■ **Enrichment and Extension Resources:** Primary Source Worksheet 40 ▲ **Teaching Transparencies:** Transparency 78
Section 4 **The Boom Years**	■ explain the causes and effects of the economic boom of the 1950s	● **Reteaching Resources:** Worksheet 79 ▲ **Reinforcement Workbook:** Worksheet 79 ▲ **Teaching Transparencies:** Transparency 79
Section 5 **Signs of Change** **and Doubt**	■ identify events and movements in the 1950s that challenged American society	● **Reteaching Resources:** Worksheet 80 ▲ **Reinforcement Workbook:** Worksheet 80 ■ **Enrichment and Extension Resources:** Historian Worksheet 8 ▲ **Teaching Transparencies:** Transparency 80

The list below shows Essential Elements relevant to this chapter. (The complete list of Essential Elements appears in the introductory pages of this Teacher's Edition.)

Section 1: 1A, 5B, 9E
Section 2: 3A, 4C, 4E, 5E, 6B, 7A, 7D, 7J, 7K, 9A
Section 3: 1A, 1B, 6C, 9A, 9E
Section 4: 2D, 3A, 3C, 3E, 3F, 4E, 4F, 4G, 8A, 8B, 8C, 8E, 8I, 9B
Section 5: 3A, 4E, 4F, 8G, 9D

Section Resources are keyed for student abilities:
● = Basic
▲ = Average
■ = Average/Advanced

CHAPTER RESOURCES

Geography Resources: Worksheets 39, 40
Tests: Chapter 20 Test

Chapter Project: Civic Values

Have students create a journal of a student attending high school during a period of four years between 1953 and 1959. Ask them to make entries on personal issues that reflect the society of that time as well as entries that describe their reactions to important events that occurred during those years.

Homework Options

Each section contains activities labeled "Addressing Individual Needs." You may wish to choose from among these activities when assigning homework.

Provisions for Limited English Proficiency (LEP)

Several suggested activities may be particularly helpful for teachers of students with limited English proficiency. These activities have been marked throughout the Teacher's Annotated Edition with the symbol **LEP** .

BIBLIOGRAPHY AND AUDIOVISUAL AIDS

Teacher Bibliography

Alexander, Charles C. *Holding the Line: The Eisenhower Era, 1952–1961.* Indiana University Press, 1975. Recalls how the cold war intensified as the President tried to contain Russia.

Ambrose, Stephen E. *Ike: Abilene to Berlin.* Harper and Row, 1973.

Student Bibliography

Archer, Jules. *Battlefield President: Dwight D. Eisenhower.* Messner, 1967.

Goldman, Eric F. *The Crucial Decade and After: America 1945–1960.* Random House, 1961.

Lederer, W. and E. Burbick. *The Ugly American.* Norton, 1965.

Literature

Bellow, Saul. *Seize the Day.* Penguin, 1984. A powerful novella that chronicles one day in the life of an alienated man torn between love and hate for his impossible father.

Kerouac, Jack. *On the Road.* Buccaneer Books, 1976. A classic of the "beat generation," detailing a trip across the United States by rebels in search of the American experience.

McMurtry, Larry. *The Last Picture Show.* Penguin, 1979.

Malamud, Bernard. *The Natural.* Avon, 1980. An allegory about the rise and fall of a baseball hero.

Plath, Sylvia. *Collected Poems.* Harper and Row, 1981.

Updike, John. *Rabbit, Run.* Fawcett, 1980. An immature young man, a former star athlete, abandons his wife and child to search for the meaning of life.

Films and Videotapes*

The Age of Anxiety, 1952–1958 (American Chronicles Series). 24 min. AIMS. Key events of the Eisenhower administration, including the end of the Korean War, the beginning of the U.S.-Soviet arms race, Castro in Cuba, and the expansion of China.

Postwar Hopes, Cold War Fears (A Walk Through the 20th Century with Bill Moyers Series). 57 min. PBS. The economy was strong and America was optimistic during the 1950s. However, the growth of communism cooled the nation's hopes for a peaceful world.

Filmstrips*

Dwight D. Eisenhower: Soldier and Statesman (set of 2). GA. Colorful portrait of a popular President.

Computer Software*

War or Peace? You Decide (Apple with 48K; IBM with 256K). BRI. Thought and discussion on nuclear weapons and the threat of conflict between the superpowers are stimulated through this simulation of processes through which war might begin or be avoided. Especially good for small groups.

*For a complete guide to audiovisual sources, see the introduction to this book (page Txx).

The Eisenhower Years

(pp. 466–489)

This chapter examines the forces that influenced American attitudes and values during the 1950s. It deals with Eisenhower's style of leadership regarding domestic issues and international crises. It explores the social and economic impact of the baby boom, automation, and television.

Themes in American History

- Global interactions
- Economic development
- American culture

Chapter Objectives

After students complete this chapter, they will be able to:

1. Identify reasons for Eisenhower's popular appeal.

2. Describe the resolution of the Korean War.

3. Explain how fear of communism affected American society during the 1950s.

4. Discuss the effectiveness of American foreign policy during the 1950s.

5. Explain the causes and effects of the economic boom of the 1950s.

6. Identify events and movements in the 1950s that challenged American society.

Chapter Opener Art
Robert Bechtle, *'58 Rambler*, 1967.

Middle-class Americans reaped the fruits of a thriving economy during the years of Dwight D. Eisenhower's presidency. Owning a home and an automobile, once only a dream, became a reality for millions of people in the United States.

CHAPTER SUPPORT MATERIAL	
Reinforcement Workbook: Worksheets 76–80	
Reteaching Resources: Worksheets 76–80	
Enrichment and Extension Resources: Primary Source Worksheets 39, 40; Historian Worksheet 8	
Geography Resources: Worksheets 39, 40	
Teaching Transparencies: Transparencies 76–80	
Tests: Chapter 20 Test	

20 The Eisenhower Years

(1953–1960)

1A, 5B, 9E

1 Eisenhower Takes Office

★ Section Focus

Main Idea Dwight Eisenhower returned the Republicans to the White House for the first time in twenty years. His first priority as President was to end the Korean War.

Objectives As you read, look for answers to these questions:
1. Why did the Republicans win the presidential election of 1952?
2. How was a settlement to the Korean War reached?

The reputations of American Presidents change with the times. Harry Truman's popularity has gone up and down like a yo-yo. Many people now look back fondly on the former President. They remember that he talked straight to the American people, that he took responsibility for his actions. They admire him for guiding this nation through a dangerous, turbulent period.

What people forget, however, is that by 1952 Truman was one of the least popular Presidents in American history. Critics called him weak and uncertain. They blamed Truman for the victory of communism in China and for the stalemate in Korea. They also accused him of being blind to the Communist menace within the United States.

THE ELECTION OF 1952 5B

The anti-Truman sentiments reflected a deep desire for new leadership. The Democrats had controlled the White House for twenty years. These were years of great stress and crisis—the Depression, World War II, and the early cold war. The Republicans hoped to regain the White House by promising a new age of peace and stability. Their candidate for President was General Dwight D. Eisenhower.

Eisenhower entered the race with enormous ad-

vantages, most of which resulted from his achievements during World War II. As the historian Stephen Ambrose explained:

> By [1945] Eisenhower had become the most famous and successful general of the war. . . . He had become the symbol of the forces that had combined to defeat the Nazis, and of the hopes for a better world. His worldwide popularity was immense. He inspired a confidence that can only be marveled at, rather than accurately measured.

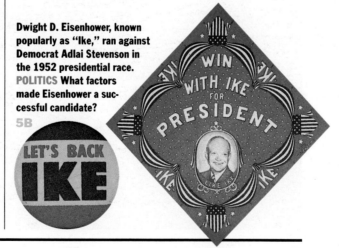

Dwight D. Eisenhower, known popularly as "Ike," ran against Democrat Adlai Stevenson in the 1952 presidential race. POLITICS **What factors made Eisenhower a successful candidate?**
5B

SUPPORTING THE SECTION

Reinforcement Workbook: Worksheet 76
Reteaching Resources: Worksheet 76
Enrichment and Extension Resources: Primary Source Worksheet 39
Teaching Transparencies: Transparency 76

Photo Caption Answer
Ike's popularity was immense due to his success as a general in World War II, his values fit the times, and his manner charmed voters.

Section Objectives
- identify reasons for Eisenhower's popular appeal
- describe the resolution of the Korean War

Introducing the Section

Connecting with Past Learnings
Review the start and course of the Korean War. *In what ways did the war affect Truman's popularity?* (The war was unpopular and his firing of MacArthur as commander also made Truman less popular.)

Focus
Have students list the important issues in the election of 1952. (Fear of the spread of communism; desire for new leadership; stalemate of the Korean War.) *If you were a voter between the ages of 30 and 35 in 1952, why would you be likely to vote for Eisenhower?* (May have served in World War II and felt that Eisenhower could end the Korean War and could halt the spread of communism; tired of "old," Democratic leadership.)

Why was Eisenhower successful at ending the Korean War? (Threatened the Chinese and North Koreans with great destruction; was a more adept military leader than Truman.)

Developing the Lesson
After students have read the section, you may want to consider the following activities:

Refer students to the 22nd
Amendment, which limits
the presidential term. *Could
Harry Truman have run again in
1952?* (Yes. The amendment
did not apply to him because
he was in office.)

Civic Values
Have students suggest why
Eisenhower was popular.
(He symbolized the victory of
World War II; was strongly
anti-Communist and
pro-business; patriotic;
friendly and relaxed.) *Do you
think Eisenhower would be popular today? Why or why not?*

Impact of Geography
Have students look at the
maps of Korea on page 462
and consider Syngman
Rhee's desire to invade
North Korea. *Why, do you
think, did Eisenhower oppose
an invasion of North Korea?*
(UN forces had tried before
and failed; China would retaliate; Americans might not
support it.) *Do you agree with
Eisenhower or Rhee? Why?*

**Ⓒ Cooperative
Learning**

Candidates in 1952 took
advantage of television to
reach voters. Have students
work in small groups to
prepare a 30-second television commercial for either
Eisenhower or Stevenson.
Allow groups to present their
commercials. **LEP**

**Addressing Individual
Needs**

**Guided/
Independent Practice**
Have students complete
Reinforcement Workbook
Worksheet 76 to analyze
statistics and attitudes to-
ward the Korean War.

Reteaching/Correctives
Have students review the
section, then work in small
groups to create cause-and-
effect charts of the section.
Have them include at least
four actions that clearly led

So great was Eisenhower's appeal that both parties urged him to run for President in 1948. Instead, he served as president of Columbia
University and later as commander of NATO
forces in Europe.

Voters were charmed by "Ike's" easy-going
manner and friendly appearance. Eisenhower also
had values that fit the times. His deep patriotism,
passionate anticommunism, and faith in American
business expressed the mood of America in the
1950s.

The Republican choice for Vice President was
Richard M. Nixon. Known mainly as an anti-
Communist, Nixon had gained national attention
in 1948 as a congressman investigating the Alger
Hiss case. He had won election to the Senate in
1950 after a bitterly fought campaign against a
New Deal Democrat, Helen Gahagan Douglas.

Recognizing his poor odds for winning again,
Truman retired from politics in 1952. The Democrats then chose Adlai Stevenson, governor of Illinois, to run for President. Noted for his intelligence and dry sense of humor, Stevenson appealed
to voters looking for a leader with much the same
political outlook as Truman but a more sophisticated style.

The Republicans won the 1952 election in a landslide. Frustrated by the stalemate in the Korean
War, Americans found Eisenhower's military record reassuring. As one Korean war veteran recalled, "We thought if anyone could win in Korea,
Ike could. And if he couldn't, he'd know how to
get us out in one piece." Just before the election,
Eisenhower promised, "I shall go to Korea." He
did not say what he would do when he got there,
but most Americans believed he would end the
war. They were right.

> **"I shall go to Korea."**
> —*Dwight Eisenhower, 1952*

A white Cadillac carried Dwight
and Mamie Eisenhower to the
1953 inauguration, where Ike
was sworn in as the first Republican President since Herbert
Hoover. Republicans also won
control of both houses of Congress. POLITICS How did United
States involvement in the Korean War affect the 1952
election? 1A, 5B, 9E

Photo Caption Answer
Many Americans, frustrated by
the bloody stalemate in Korea,
believed Eisenhower could
guide U.S. forces to victory
there.

Background Eisenhower
won 55 percent of the popular
vote in 1952. The electoral
vote was 442 to 89 in
Eisenhower's favor.

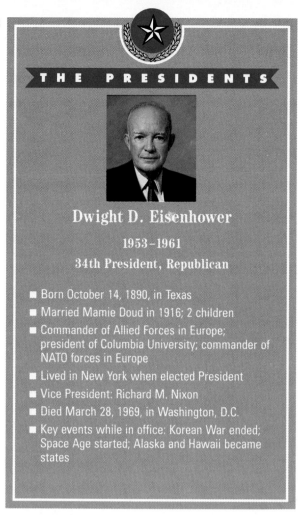

THE PRESIDENTS

Dwight D. Eisenhower

1953–1961

34th President, Republican

- Born October 14, 1890, in Texas
- Married Mamie Doud in 1916; 2 children
- Commander of Allied Forces in Europe; president of Columbia University; commander of NATO forces in Europe
- Lived in New York when elected President
- Vice President: Richard M. Nixon
- Died March 28, 1969, in Washington, D.C.
- Key events while in office: Korean War ended; Space Age started; Alaska and Hawaii became states

THE KOREAN SETTLEMENT 1A

After the election, Eisenhower fulfilled his promise to go to Korea. The trip confirmed what he had already suspected—a stalemate was about the best the United States could expect. South Korean President Syngman Rhee believed that another invasion of North Korea by UN forces would succeed. Eisenhower was not convinced. He thought it more practical to negotiate.

Truce talks had begun in the summer of 1951 but had made little progress. Neither side could agree on where the ceasefire line should be and how the truce would be enforced. There was also deadlock over the issue of prisoners of war. Thousands of North Korean and Chinese prisoners did not want to return home after the war. Their governments insisted that they be repatriated (sent home). The United States refused.

Hoping to break the deadlock with a show of force, Eisenhower increased bombing raids on North Korea. He also sent a secret message to the Chinese, warning that the United States might use nuclear weapons if an agreement were not reached.

Some people have argued that Eisenhower's threat made China and North Korea back down. In truth, both sides were willing to compromise. The United States had lost 54,000 soldiers. More than a million Koreans, many of them civilians, had died. The Chinese too had suffered huge losses—perhaps a million dead. There seemed little point in continuing the bloodshed.

On July 27, 1953, an armistice was signed in the Korean village of Panmunjom. A ceasefire line was set just above the thirty-eighth parallel (the pre-1950 boundary). A prisoner exchange program allowed captives to accept or refuse repatriation.

In the United States, the end of the war brought relief, but little joy. The American public had found the war troubling, confusing, and wasteful. Unlike World War II, in which the threat to American security had been clear, the conflict in Korea seemed only a distant concern of the United States. Americans were pleased that the United States had stood up to Communist aggression. But for the most part, Korea had seemed like someone else's war.

SECTION REVIEW

1. PEOPLE AND PLACES Richard M. Nixon, Adlai Stevenson, Panmunjom

2. COMPREHENSION What concerns had brought Harry Truman's popularity to a low point by 1952?

3. COMPREHENSION What promise did Dwight Eisenhower make regarding the war in Korea? How did Americans interpret that promise?

4. COMPREHENSION What was the outcome of the Korean War?

5. CRITICAL THINKING How do you account for the fact that an unpopular President like Truman can now be regarded as a great leader?

CHAPTER 20   THE EISENHOWER YEARS, 1953–1960   **469**

to reactions by a second party. Have students share their charts with the class.

Have students complete **Reteaching Resources** Worksheet 76, which reviews the steps Eisenhower took to end the Korean War.

Enrichment/Extension
Assign students **Enrichment and Extension Resources** Primary Source Worksheet 39, which examines Eisenhower's Inaugural Address.

Assessment
You may wish to use the Section 1 Review, on this page, to see how well your students understand the main points in the lesson.

Section Review Answers
1. *Richard M. Nixon*— Eisenhower's Vice President. *Adlai Stevenson*— Democratic candidate for President, 1952. *Panmunjom*—Village where armistice ending the Korean War was signed.
2. Stalemate in Korea; fear of the spread of communism.
3. That he would visit Korea; they believed that Ike would end the war.
4. The 38th parallel boundary was re-established; a prisoner exchange program was implemented.
5. Students should recognize the importance of historical perspective. After a period of time, people are able to judge Truman's accomplishments as well as his failures.

Closure
Remind students of the pre-reading objectives in the section opener. Pose one or all of these questions again. Then have students read Section 2 for the next class period, and ask them to identify domestic issues during Eisenhower's presidency.

The Presidents
In 1948, in a letter to a New Hampshire newspaper publisher, Eisenhower wrote that it was "necessary and wise" that professional soldiers "abstain from seeking high political office." Ask students if they agree with this statement. Have them suggest why Eisenhower may have changed his mind and run for President.

Background Hostilities formally ceased at 10 PM on July 26, 1953. South Korea gained about 1,500 square miles of territory.

2 The Cold War at Home

SECTION 2

The Cold War at Home
(pp. 470–472)

Section Objective

■ explain how fear of communism affected American society during the 1950s

Introducing the Section

Connecting with Past Learnings
Review the rise of Joseph McCarthy. (McCarthy made unsubstantiated claims that there were Communists in the government.)

Key Terms
Have students find the key terms in context and define them in their own words. Then ask students to write sentences that show how each term relates to the cold war. **LEP**

Focus

To help students understand the impact of the civil defense campaign, conduct a mock air-raid drill. *What assumption is implied by such drills?* (That people could survive a nuclear attack.) *What effect do you think the civil defense campaign had on Americans?* (It increased their fear of nuclear war.)

Developing the Lesson

After students have read the section, you may want to consider the following activities:

Connecting with Literature
Make sure students understand the importance of the writers Thoreau and Emerson. Have them suggest circumstances under which literature might be labeled subversive.

★ **Section Focus**

Key Terms Army-McCarthy hearings ■ censure ■ hydrogen bomb

Main Idea Despite the end of the Korean War, the cold war went on. Americans remained concerned about communism and fearful of nuclear war.

Objectives As you read, look for answers to these questions:
1. What led to Joseph McCarthy's downfall?
2. What steps were taken to tighten internal security?
3. What precautions were taken against nuclear attack?

The Korean settlement did not put an end to American anxiety about communism. Stories of Communists undermining American society continued to fill newspapers and magazines. In time, however, Americans grew more skeptical about wild charges of political radicalism and disloyalty.

McCarthy's Downfall 7D, 7J, 7K

Senator Joseph McCarthy had become famous in 1950 by charging that the U.S. State Department employed scores of Communists (page 457). Throughout the Korean War years, McCarthy continued to insist that American foreign policy was controlled by the Soviet Union.

BIOGRAPHY 4C

MARGARET CHASE SMITH (1897–   ) of Maine worked as a teacher before entering politics. Smith became the first woman to be elected to both houses of Congress. Her 1950 "Declaration of Conscience" was the first formal rejection of McCarthyism by a Republican senator. A member of the Senate until 1973, Smith campaigned actively for her party's presidential nomination in 1964—the first woman to do so.

5E

★ **Historical Documents**

For an excerpt from Senator Margaret Chase Smith's "Declaration of Conscience," see page 727 of this book.

When Dwight Eisenhower took office, some people thought McCarthy would stop making claims about Communists in government. After all, they believed, no one would attack the executive branch if it were run by his own party. But McCarthy had no such loyalty. His charges simply got wilder.

One of his more infamous campaigns was to "clean up" the libraries run by the State Department in foreign countries. McCarthy sent two of his assistants to Europe to search these libraries for "subversive" books. Works by Ralph Waldo Emerson and Henry Thoreau, among others, disappeared from the shelves.

Eisenhower privately expressed disapproval of McCarthy. Yet he never denounced McCarthy in public. He justified his silence by claiming that it would be out of place for a President to "get down in the gutter with that guy."

In the end, McCarthy self-destructed. When he claimed that even the army was riddled with Communists, his public backing plunged.

McCarthy's assault on the military began when the army refused to promote one of his former assistants. An angry McCarthy launched a broad investigation. The Army-McCarthy hearings were shown live on television, and millions of Americans got their first close look at McCarthy in action.

What they saw was not a heroic defender of the American way of life, as McCarthy presented himself, but a schoolyard bully. His power, like that of all bullies, evaporated when someone stood up to him. In McCarthy's case that person was the army's attorney, Joseph Welch. Fed up with

SUPPORTING THE SECTION

Reinforcement Workbook: Worksheet 77
Reteaching Resources: Worksheet 77
Teaching Transparencies: Transparency 77

Biography
Ask students to list Margaret Chase Smith's "firsts" and then discuss which was the most significant at the time and which is the most significant today.

Reporters jam the hearing room as Senator Joseph McCarthy (at far left) asks a witness to testify during the Senate investigation of the Army-McCarthy hearings in 1954. **POLITICS** What was the Senate's decision regarding McCarthy? How did this decision affect McCarthy's influence? **7A, 9A**

McCarthy's insults and abuse, Welch at one point blurted out, "Until this moment, senator, I think I never really gauged your cruelty or your recklessness. . . . Have you no sense of decency, sir, at long last?" The spectators, and no doubt many television viewers, burst into applause. McCarthy's spell had been broken.

> **"H**ave you no sense of decency, sir, at long last?"
> —*Joseph Welch to Senator McCarthy, 1954*

In 1954 the Senate condemned, but did not censure McCarthy for "conduct unbecoming a member." (A censure is Congress's most severe way of condemning the behavior of a fellow member.) McCarthy's influence faded, and he died in 1957.

INTERNAL SECURITY 6B

It would be a mistake to link fear of communism with McCarthy alone. Almost all institutions in the United States took steps to purge their ranks of members judged radical, un-American, or disloyal. Universities, trade unions, newspapers, television networks—all took part.

Under Eisenhower, the government expanded Truman's internal security program. Truman had fired employees considered disloyal. Eisenhower added another group of workers to be fired—those thought to be security risks. Not only persons suspected of radical political ties, but heavy drinkers, homosexuals, and other people judged by employers to have "character defects" were included. In the Eisenhower years 1,500 federal employees were fired for such reasons. Another 6,000 were forced to resign.

Later in the 1950s, a series of Supreme Court decisions helped curb the excesses of this latest Red Scare. One such decision was *Yates v. United States* (1957). In it the Court held that believing and teaching an idea—even the idea of revolution—was not a crime, but that urging others to break the law could be. Membership in subversive organizations thus was protected by the First Amendment. Organizing a revolution or planting a bomb was not.

THE NUCLEAR AGE 3A

While the thought of Communist subversion made people anxious and distrustful, the fear of nuclear war terrified them. In the early 1950s, American scientists developed a nuclear bomb 150 times more powerful than the one dropped on Hiroshima. This superweapon was called the H-bomb, or hydrogen bomb.

The first nuclear weapons were atomic bombs, often called "A-bombs." The power of A-bombs came from fission, the splitting of uranium atoms.

Hydrogen bombs work by fusion, the uniting of hydrogen atoms. The process requires extremely high temperatures. For that reason, hydrogen bombs are also known as thermonuclear weapons.

Scientists who had worked on the first atomic bombs asked the government to stop research on the hydrogen bomb. They feared that the explosion of great numbers of H-bombs might destroy the planet. Famed atomic scientist Albert Einstein warned the nation, "Radioactive poisoning of the atmosphere and hence annihilation of any life on earth has been brought within the range of technical possibilities. . . . General annihilation beckons."

In spite of these warnings, President Truman gave full support to the development of thermonuclear weapons. The Soviet Union's development of atomic weapons in 1949 had shocked American officials, who had expected to enjoy an atomic monopoly for years. The H-bombs promised the United States a temporary edge in the nuclear arms race.

American scientists conducted the first H-bomb test on a small Pacific island on November 1, 1952. The island simply disappeared. Nothing was left but a huge hole in the ocean floor. Within a year the Soviet Union had its own hydrogen bomb. The nuclear arms race had reached a new, higher level of terror.

SURVIVING NUCLEAR WAR 4E
The threat of nuclear attack was unlike any the American people had ever faced. Even if only a few bombs reached their targets, millions of civilians could die. Civil defense workers held air-raid drills, stocked shelters, and kept the public informed of where to go and what to do. A best-selling novel called *Tomorrow* described an American town hit by nuclear bombs. The heroes of the book were civil defense workers who rushed people into shelters and later led survivors in rebuilding their town.

Schoolchildren heard similar messages. During air-raid drills, they had to crawl under their desks and cover their heads. Metal name tags were given out in many schools to help identify bodies in case of nuclear war.

The Federal Civil Defense Administration gave

During the post–World War II arms race, America built weapons a thousand times more destructive than the atomic bombs dropped on Japan. This picture records the first American hydrogen bomb test in 1952. **POLITICS** What is meant by an "arms race"? **7A, 9A**

schools comic books about nuclear war, featuring "Burt the Turtle." The books read, in part:

> The atomic bomb is a new danger. . . . Things will be knocked down all over town. . . . You must be ready to protect yourself. So, like Burt, you DUCK to avoid things flying through the air and COVER to keep from getting cut or even badly burned.

The warnings of the 1950s seem naive today—schoolchildren cannot "duck" a nuclear bomb—but the fears they reflected were very real. The psychological impact of the 1950s civil defense drills is a subject of some debate. Did they provide a sense of security, or did they make people more anxious?

SECTION REVIEW

1. **KEY TERMS** Army-McCarthy hearings, censure, hydrogen bomb
2. **PEOPLE** Joseph McCarthy
3. **COMPREHENSION** Why did the Senate censure Joseph McCarthy?
4. **COMPREHENSION** Describe some of the civil defense measures of the 1950s.
5. **CRITICAL THINKING** Do you think the Constitution protects people's right to join political parties that call for the overthrow of the government? Explain.

3 The Cold War Around the World

Section Focus

Key Terms rollback ■ massive retaliation ■ Third World ■ nationalize ■ U-2 incident

Main Idea Throughout the 1950s, tensions between the Soviet Union and the United States remained high. As many nations in Asia and Africa gained independence, the scene of the cold war shifted to these unstable areas.

Objectives As you read, look for answers to these questions:
1. What changes in foreign policy did John Foster Dulles propose?
2. What challenges did the emergence of new nations offer the United States?
3. What event shattered hopes for better relations with the Soviet Union?

During the 1952 campaign, some of the Republicans' most stinging criticisms of Truman dealt with foreign policy. Republicans blasted Truman for failing to produce a clear-cut victory in Korea. They also rejected the policy of containment. It was not enough, they argued, to hold the line against Communist advances. Such a policy left the people in Communist nations enslaved. Instead, the Republicans wanted to liberate the nations under Communist rule. This policy, called rollback, was the rallying cry of the Republican Party as Eisenhower took office.

DULLES AND THE BATTLE AGAINST WORLD COMMUNISM 1A

Advocates of the rollback policy were heartened when Eisenhower named John Foster Dulles as his Secretary of State. Dulles came from a distinguished family with a long history of experience in politics, diplomacy, law, and finance. His critics found him pompous, stuffy, and boring—"dull, duller, Dulles," was a popular joke of the day. But Eisenhower admired Dulles's knowledge. Ike once told an adviser, "There's only one man I know who has seen more of the world and . . . knows more than [Dulles] does—and that's me."

There was one topic on which Dulles was passionate: communism. For him, the cold war was a moral crusade. He never tired of preaching against dictatorship and atheism. He also called for the rollback of communism to its pre-World War II boundaries. However, with the Soviet Union in firm control of Eastern Europe, calls for

a rollback of communism were more talk than action. Containing communism, not rolling it back, continued to be the centerpiece of American foreign policy under Eisenhower.

Dulles did announce changes in the American strategy for containing communism. One change was to build up a network of alliances among non-Communist nations around the world. In 1954, Dulles helped create the Southeast Asia Treaty Organization (SEATO). Another alliance—called CENTO—was formed in the Middle East, and the United States also made defense agreements with such nations as Taiwan and South Vietnam.

A second change dealt with American military strategy. Dulles and Eisenhower feared that the Korean War would be the first of many limited wars around the globe. Through such wars, they believed, the Soviets intended to sap American resources and morale. In the end, the Soviets would win the cold war by forcing the United States to spend so much money on defense that its economy would collapse.

Dulles announced to the world that in the future, the American response to Soviet aggression would be massive retaliation. That is, the United States would no longer be dragged into costly, frustrating limited wars like the Korean War. Instead, the United States would punish the Soviet Union with an all-out nuclear attack. Dulles believed this threat would deter Soviet aggression.

Dulles also argued that massive retaliation would save money. The administration did not plan to fight another limited war like that in Korea.

SUPPORTING THE SECTION

Reinforcement Workbook: Worksheet 78
Reteaching Resources: Worksheet 78
Enrichment and Extension Resources: Primary Source Worksheet 40
Teaching Transparencies: Transparency 78

SECTION 3

The Cold War Around the World
(pp. 473–478)

Section Objective
■ discuss the effectiveness of American foreign policy during the 1950s

Introducing the Section

Connecting with Past Learnings
What was Truman's policy toward communism? (Containment.) *Was the policy successful? If so, how?* (The United States helped Greece and Turkey fight the spread of communism, and the Marshall Plan reduced Communist influence in Western Europe. However, China became a Communist country.)

Key Terms
Play "Jeopardy" with the class by announcing each key term as if it were an answer. Have students ask a question answered by the term. Follow this procedure for all terms. **LEP**

Focus
On the board, write *Middle East, Eastern Europe,* and *Central America.* Have students create a chart summarizing the issues, actions, and results of United States foreign policy in those areas in the 1950s. (Middle East—war between Jews and Arabs in 1948; nationalization of Iranian oil fields, 1951, causes a boycott of Iranian oil and an American role in putting the Shah in power; Suez War ends with United States condemnation of the actions of Britain, France, and Israel. Eastern Europe—Hungarian uprising, United States unable to help revolution. Central America—Guatemala seizes American-owned property, CIA-led invasion puts different government in power.)

474

What was the goal of Dulles's policy regarding communism? (To roll back communism to its pre-World War II boundaries.) **Was it more successful than containment?** (No.)

Developing the Lesson

After students have read the section, you may want to consider the following activities:

Analyzing Controversial Issues

Discuss the policy of massive retaliation with the class. Have students explain how the policy was designed to save money for the United States. (The country would not have to support a large, standing army and keep it armed with conventional weapons. Instead, less money would be spent on nuclear weapons that would threaten any possible attacker.) **Why did some people criticize that policy?** (They felt that it would only work if the United States showed itself willing to fight a nuclear war, which they did not want to happen.) **Do you think massive retaliation is a good policy? Do you think it is one the United States follows today?**

"DON'T BE AFRAID—I CAN ALWAYS PULL YOU BACK"—FROM *HERBLOCK'S SPECIAL FOR TODAY* (SIMON & SCHUSTER)

Secretary of State John Foster Dulles pushes Uncle Sam to "the brink" of war in this 1956 cartoon by Herbert Block, known as Herblock. The caption reads "Don't be afraid—I can always pull you back!" POLITICS How, judging from the cartoon, does Herblock regard Dulles's brinkmanship policy? **1B**

Therefore, it could afford to cut back on the forces designed to fight such a war—army divisions, navy warships, and so on. Nuclear weapons, administration officials explained, provided "more bang for the buck."

The threat of massive retaliation may have frightened Soviet leaders into more moderate behavior. It certainly did frighten some Americans, who charged that "brinkmanship"—Dulles's willingness to go to the brink of all-out war—was irresponsible in the nuclear age. In any case, events outside Europe continued to pose problems for American leaders throughout the 1950s. The cause was not Soviet expansion but the rise of nationalism.

THE RISE OF THIRD WORLD NATIONALISM **6C**

During the cold war, American leaders began to think of the globe as being divided into three parts, or "worlds." The First World included the Western democracies, such as the United States, Britain, and France. The Second World was made up of the Soviet Union, China, and the Communist nations of Eastern Europe.

All the other nations were considered part of the Third World. The Third World included dozens of countries, large and small, on several continents. They had much in common: an agricultural way of life, widespread poverty and illiteracy, and a history of Western colonial rule.

Throughout Africa and Asia, new nations began to emerge in the 1940s and 1950s. Great Britain, France, the Netherlands, and other Western nations had once ruled them as colonies. After World War II, facing large war debts at home and strong independence movements in the colonies, the Europeans could not afford to keep their empires. One by one the colonies gained independence.

For many Third World nations the coming of independence posed a new set of problems. These problems—poverty, social inequality, domination by foreign investors—were similar to those the Latin American countries faced after their independence in the 1800s. And like Latin America, the newly independent Third World nations wanted to control their own destiny—to become independent in fact as well as name.

The Third World's desire for independence often clashed with the aims of the First and Second worlds. The Western democracies sought to maintain influence in the Third World, both for economic reasons and to guard against Soviet expansion. The Soviet Union, in turn, regarded the Third World as fertile ground for the world-wide spread of communism. Thus, beginning in the 1950s the Third World became the prime battleground of the cold war.

TROUBLES IN THE MIDDLE EAST **1A**

The Middle East was especially explosive. Both the Western democracies and the Soviet Union were tempted by this region's strategic location—it links the continents of Africa, Europe, and Asia—and by its vast oil reserves.

Hostility among Middle Eastern nations heightened tensions. Jewish settlers living in the former British mandate of Palestine founded the state of Israel on May 14, 1948. They intended Israel to be

474 UNIT 7   A COLD PEACE

Photo Caption Answer
He views it as dangerous and irresponsible.

Jewish refugees from Europe arrive at the Israeli port of Haifa in this 1949 picture by famed photographer Robert Capa. The horrors experienced by European Jews during the Holocaust helped persuade international leaders to create the state of Israel in 1948. **GLOBAL AWARENESS** Why, do you think, did Arabs living in Palestine object to Israel's creation? **9A**

a homeland for Jews. The next day, armies from neighboring Arab countries invaded Israel. Though heavily outnumbered, the Israelis held on. A UN mission led by an American, Ralph Bunche, arranged an armistice in 1950. However, the Arab states still refused to accept Israel's existence. The conflict over Israel continues to this day.

A year after the end of the Arab-Israeli war, American attention shifted to Iran. Mohammed Mossadegh, the 71-year-old prime minister of Iran, aimed to gain control of Iran's oil. A British firm owned most of Iran's oil fields, earning some $350 million in oil sales each year while paying Iran a fee of just $50 million. In 1951 Mossadegh seized the oil fields and nationalized them. That is, he placed these formerly private industries under government control. This action outraged Western leaders. Britain, with United States backing, called for a boycott of Iranian oil.

In 1953, Eisenhower, believing Mossadegh to be a tool of Iranian Communists, approved a secret plan to overthrow him. The plan—called Operation Ajax after an American cleaning product—had been devised by Allen Dulles, head of the Central Intelligence Agency (CIA) and the brother of John Foster Dulles. The CIA gave several million dollars to anti-Mossadegh military leaders. It also hired mobs to stage protests against Mossadegh. The goal was to replace the nationalist leader with

the pro-American Shah of Iran, Reza Pahlavi, who had recently been forced to flee the country.

Operation Ajax worked. Mossadegh was arrested and the Shah was returned to power. He quickly turned over control of the Iranian oil fields to Western companies, mostly American ones.

The Shah held power for the next 25 years. The long-term costs, however, were great. As the Shah's regime became increasingly corrupt, more and more Iranians turned against him. They blamed the U.S. for installing and supporting him. When the Shah was overthrown in 1979, a wave of bitter anti-Americanism swept Iran.

THE SUEZ WAR 1A

In Egypt, the United States had a different response to Third World nationalism. Egypt had gained partial independence from Britain in 1922 and full independence in 1936. For years afterward, however, British troops remained in Egypt to protect the Suez Canal. The waterway, owned by a British and French investment company, was the key route for shipping oil from the Middle East to Europe. When Egypt demanded that Britain withdraw its troops, Eisenhower supported Egypt. In 1954, British troops left the country.

Secretary of State Dulles hoped this gesture would draw Egypt into the Western camp. He also offered the Egyptian leader, Gamal Abdel Nasser,

This photograph shows the reopening of the Suez Canal at Port Said, Egypt, after attacks by Israel, Britain, and France in 1956 had shut it down. Eisenhower's handling of the Suez Crisis helped him win re-election the same year. The President's decisiveness re-stored public confidence in his ability after a heart attack had raised questions about his health. POLITICS Why did Eisenhower respond to the Suez Crisis as he did? 1A

a $56 million loan to help build a large dam on the Nile River. However, Nasser tried to play the Soviets and the Americans off against each other, improving relations with both sides in order to gain more aid. In 1956, after learning that Nasser was making deals with the Soviet bloc, Dulles withdrew his offer of a loan.

Nasser responded by nationalizing the Suez Canal. He also denied Israeli ships the right to use the waterway. In response, Israel invaded Egypt in October 1956 and the Suez War began. France and Britain joined in and bombed Egyptian air bases. They also dropped paratroopers who retook the canal.

Eisenhower shared many of the concerns that led the three allies to invade Egypt. He agreed that Nasser posed a threat to Western interests. Yet he was convinced that the invasion would only inflame anti-Western sentiment in the Third World. He was also furious that the allies had invaded Egypt without consulting him.

Eisenhower backed a resolution in the United Nations condemning the invasion. The resolution passed, and Britain, France, and Israel reluctantly agreed to a ceasefire. The crisis ended.

THE HUNGARIAN UPRISING 1B
Even as fighting was raging in the Middle East, a revolt was breaking out in Hungary. Dominated by the Soviet Union since the end of World War II, the Hungarian people rose in fury in October 1956. They called for the withdrawal of Soviet troops and for a democratic government.

The Soviet response was swift and brutal. Soviet tanks rolled in to crush Hungary. The rebels fought heroically, but they had few weapons and no outside support. The Soviets soon regained control.

Eisenhower gave some thought to helping the rebels, but Hungary lay deep inside Soviet-held territory. As Ike put it, "Hungary is as inaccessible to us as Tibet." The American non-response to the Hungarian uprising made it clear that rollback was a slogan, not a policy.

GUATEMALA 1A
In contrast, the United States was both willing and able to influence events in the Americas. In 1954 Jacobo Arbenz, the popular Guatemalan leader, seized property of the United Fruit Company, Guatemala's largest landowner. Arbenz of-

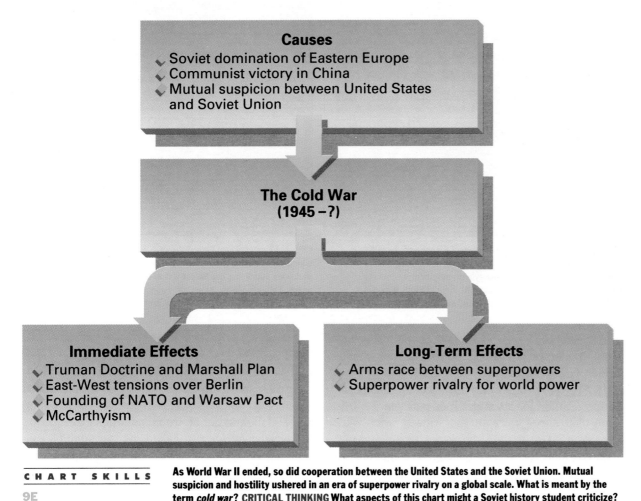

Causes
- Soviet domination of Eastern Europe
- Communist victory in China
- Mutual suspicion between United States and Soviet Union

The Cold War
(1945 – ?)

Immediate Effects
- Truman Doctrine and Marshall Plan
- East-West tensions over Berlin
- Founding of NATO and Warsaw Pact
- McCarthyism

Long-Term Effects
- Arms race between superpowers
- Superpower rivalry for world power

CHART SKILLS
9E

As World War II ended, so did cooperation between the United States and the Soviet Union. Mutual suspicion and hostility ushered in an era of superpower rivalry on a global scale. What is meant by the term *cold war*? CRITICAL THINKING What aspects of this chart might a Soviet history student criticize?

fered to pay United Fruit for the land. But he would pay only the value claimed by the company on its tax forms, which was far below the land's real value. United Fruit, charging that Communists controlled the Arbenz government, called on Washington for help.

Eisenhower ordered the CIA to lead a group of anti-Arbenz Guatemalans. They invaded from neighboring Honduras and ousted Arbenz. The new regime returned the land to the United Fruit Company.

As in Iran, the secret mission succeeded. Yet it too inflamed anti-American feelings. Later, when Vice President Nixon toured Latin America, he was met by angry crowds in one city after an-

other. They hurled stones at his car and chanted slogans calling for an end to U.S. intervention in Latin America.

HOPES FOR SUPERPOWER NEGOTIATIONS 1A

Throughout the 1950s, relations between the Soviet Union and the United States remained chilly. With the development of hydrogen bombs on both sides, the two superpowers became locked in a thermonuclear arms race. Yet there were some signs that relations might improve.

In 1953 Joseph Stalin died. His iron-fisted dictatorship had been a disaster not only for the Soviet Union and its people, but for the prospects of peace throughout the world. With his death, there

CHAPTER 20   THE EISENHOWER YEARS, 1953–1960   **477**

Cause and Effect Answers
Cold war is competition between hostile nations that falls short of direct military conflict. Students may suggest that the chart implies that the Soviet Union caused the cold war, whereas a Soviet student might assert that the superpowers were equally responsible, or that the United States was more so. For example, the Truman Doctrine could be viewed as a cause rather than an effect.

Addressing Individual Needs

Guided/ Independent Practice
Direct students to work through **Reinforcement Workbook** Worksheet 78. This worksheet analyzes a political cartoon dealing with the Eisenhower Doctrine.

Reteaching/Correctives
Provide students with a world map, or have them trace the map on pages 848–849. Have students review the section, then on their maps identify the sites of conflict described in the text. Have students include the name of the country involved, and the date(s) of the conflict.

Have students complete **Reteaching Resources** Worksheet 78. This worksheet will help students identify and locate crisis spots discussed in this section.

Enrichment/Extension
Have students complete **Enrichment and Extension Resources** Primary Source Worksheet 40, which helps students interpret the U-2 incident.

Assessment
You may wish to use the Section 3 Review, page 478, to see how well your students understand the main points in the lesson.

Section Review Answers
1. *rollback*—Policy of liberating nations under Communist rule. *massive retaliation*—Response to aggression with an all-out nuclear attack. *Third World*—Countries with an agricultural way of life, widespread poverty and illiteracy, and a history of colonial Western rule.

nationalize—Put formerly private industries under government control. *U-2 incident*—The shooting down over the USSR of an American spy plane in 1960.

2. *John Foster Dulles*—Eisenhower's Secretary of State. *Israel*—Country in Middle East, created to be a homeland for Jews. *Ralph Bunche*—American who led a UN mission to end war between Israel and its neighbors in 1950. *Iran*—Oil-rich country in the Middle East. *Suez Canal*—Key route for shipping oil from the Middle East to Europe. *Gamal Abdel Nasser*—Egyptian leader who nationalized Suez Canal in 1956. *Nikita Khrushchev*—Soviet premier who came to power in the mid-1950s.

3. He wanted to rollback communism by liberating Communist nations instead of just containing communism by keeping it from spreading to non-Communist countries.

4. The Soviet Union canceled a summit conference when Eisenhower refused to apologize for U-2 flights over Soviet territory.

5. Students should consider how powerful a threat a foreign leader may pose to the nation.

Closure

Ask one student to transform the Main Idea of the section into a question, and have other students answer that question. Then have students read Section 4 for the next class period, noting how the economic boom of the 1950s affected family life.

Nikita Khrushchev poses with President Eisenhower in 1959 during the Soviet leader's historic visit to the United States. Khrushchev wanted to visit Disneyland, but security concerns prevented him from doing so. **GLOBAL AWARENESS** Why did Stalin's death raise hopes for reduced superpower tensions? **1A**

CIA pilot Francis Gary Powers holds a model of the U-2 plane in which he was shot down over the Soviet Union in 1960. The U.S. had been overflying the Soviet Union on spy missions for four years. Today, such missions are entrusted to spy satellites. **POLITICS** How did the U-2 affair affect U.S.-Soviet relations? **1A**

was hope that the Soviet leadership might become more moderate. In the mid-1950s a new Soviet leader, Nikita Khrushchev (nih–KEE–tah kroosh–CHOFF) came to power. Khrushchev publicly denounced Stalin for his murderous policies.

In 1959 hopes were further raised when Vice President Nixon visited the Soviet Union and met with Khrushchev. The two engaged in spirited debates about the relative strengths of the two societies. No agreements were made, but at least the two sides were speaking.

A few months later Khrushchev visited the United States. This was the first time a Soviet head of state had come to this country. He and Eisenhower met and announced plans for a summit conference to settle international differences.

THE SUMMIT CANCELED 1A

Hopes for a summit were soon dashed by the U-2 incident. In May 1960 Khrushchev announced that an American spy plane had been shot down over Soviet territory. The United States, it turned out, had routinely flown U-2 flights high over the Soviet Union. The planes photographed troop movements and missile sites. This time, however, a Soviet missile struck the American plane. The pilot, Francis Gary Powers, safely parachuted to the ground and was captured by the Soviets.

Eisenhower denied at first that the U-2 had been spying. The Soviets had evidence, however, and Eisenhower finally had to admit it. Khrushchev demanded an apology for the flights and a promise to halt them. Eisenhower agreed to stop the U-2 flights, but he would not apologize.

Khrushchev angrily called off the summit conference. He also withdrew his invitation to Eisenhower to visit the Soviet Union. Thus, after fifteen years of cold war, the conflicts between the superpowers seemed as dangerous as ever.

SECTION REVIEW

1. KEY TERMS rollback, massive retaliation, Third World, nationalize, U-2 incident

2. PEOPLE AND PLACES John Foster Dulles, Israel, Ralph Bunche, Iran, Suez Canal, Gamal Abdel Nasser, Nikita Khrushchev

3. COMPREHENSION How did Dulles's strategy for containing communism differ from Truman's?

4. COMPREHENSION Why did the U-2 incident dash hopes for world peace?

5. CRITICAL THINKING Should a nation have the right to remove a foreign leader by force? If so, under what circumstances?

Photo Caption Answers
(Left) Khrushchev, the new leader, denounced Stalin's policies and allowed Nixon to visit the Soviet Union. Later, Khrushchev visited the United States. (Right) It ended a thaw in the cold war by causing Khrushchev to cancel his invitation to Eisenhower to visit the Soviet Union and by breaking off their proposed summit conference.

Background In 1958 Khrushchev gave Western powers six months to withdraw from Berlin or, he warned, the East Germans would take control of the city. Eisenhower refused to give in to Khrushchev's demands.

4 The Boom Years

Section Focus

Key Terms modern Republicanism ■ gross national product ■ conglomerate ■ automation ■ baby boom ■ Highway Act of 1956

Main Idea During the Eisenhower years the economy enjoyed one of the greatest economic booms in its history.

Objectives As you read, look for answers to these questions:
1. What was Eisenhower's approach to government and the economy? How did the economy perform during his years in office?
2. What contributed to the growth of suburbs?
3. What were some other aspects of American society during the 1950s?

The cold war, unrest in the Third World, fears of nuclear war—all these were part of the 1950s. But they were not the only parts, nor even the best-remembered. Today, Americans recall the 1950s as a time of prosperity, stability, and confidence. Most (though certainly not all) Americans enjoyed unprecedented wealth during the 1950s. Government was stable, with Eisenhower winning a second term by another landslide in 1956. And the nation as a whole remained confident in itself and its future throughout most of the decade. For these reasons, one historian has labeled the 1950s "The American High."

A BUSINESS GOVERNMENT 8A

During Eisenhower's years in office, he chose successful business leaders for most of his Cabinet posts. Eisenhower preferred business leaders to politicians and scholars because he felt success in business and success in government went hand-in-hand. His first Secretary of Defense, Charles E. Wilson, summed up that creed. A former president of General Motors, Wilson said, "What is good for our country is good for General Motors, and vice versa."

> **"W**hat is good for our country is good for General Motors, and vice versa."
> —*Charles E. Wilson*

MODERN REPUBLICANISM 3F, 8E, 8I

Like most Republicans since the 1920s, Eisenhower criticized government efforts to solve social problems. When the Republicans regained the White House in 1953, many people thought Eisenhower would scrap the liberal programs of the New Deal and Fair Deal.

At first there were signs that Eisenhower would do just that. He complained that the federal government had grown too large, and he criticized the New Deal for what he termed its "creeping socialism." In his first year in office Eisenhower did away with thousands of federal jobs.

Eisenhower also wanted to limit the federal government's role in the economy. For example, the government owned great reserves of offshore oil. Past Presidents had kept these deposits in public hands, but Eisenhower wanted to turn them over to the states closest to the oil—California, Texas, and Louisiana. Congress agreed. The reserves were then leased to private oil companies. Eisenhower planned to sell the Tennessee Valley Authority to get the government out of the utility business. That plan met resistance, and Eisenhower kept the TVA in public hands.

For the most part, Eisenhower did not tamper with social programs already in place. He was a practical leader who avoided rocking the boat. Though he proposed almost no new social welfare laws, Eisenhower did agree to extend social security benefits. This willingness to accept some federal responsibility for the well-being of the people became known as modern Republicanism.

SUPPORTING THE SECTION

Reinforcement Workbook: Worksheet 79
Reteaching Resources: Worksheet 79
Teaching Transparencies: Transparency 79

The Boom Years
(pp. 479–484)

Section Objective

■ explain the causes and effects of the economic boom of the 1950s

Introducing the Section

Connecting with Past Learnings
Review economic conditions during the postwar years. *What caused the postwar economic boom in the United States?* (Americans spent wartime savings on consumer goods.) *What was the major economic problem during the Truman years?* (High inflation.)

Key Terms
Write the key terms for this section on the board. Have students define each term as it relates to the 1950s. Then ask students to discuss how each term affects American life today. **LEP**

Focus
Have students work individually or in pairs to create a cause and effect chart dealing with one of the major topics in this section: prosperity, automation, suburban growth, poverty in the inner cities, the move toward security, the growth of television, or the religious revival. Have them share these charts with the class and then ask students to consider how economic prosperity affected American values. (Students should mention the materialistic values of a consumer economy as well as the social values of family and community.)

PROSPEROUS TIMES 3C, 3E

During Eisenhower's presidency, the economic trend was upward. Indeed, the economy continued the boom it had begun during World War II. The gross national product—the total output of all goods and services produced by a nation in a year—rose 250 percent from 1945 to 1960. The United States, with 6 percent of the world's population, produced fully *half* of the world's goods and consumed about one-third. Unlike the Truman years, the Eisenhower period enjoyed prosperity without high inflation. From 1953 to 1961, inflation averaged just 3 percent per year.

As the American economy expanded, so did major American companies. A wave of mergers swept the business world beginning in the early 1950s. Some of these mergers resulted in the creation of conglomerates—corporations made up of companies in widely different fields. Because their assets were spread over separate industries, conglomerates could ride out a downturn in any one field. These businesses were huge. The largest had bigger budgets than many countries.

TRANSFORMATION OF THE WORKPLACE 3A, 3C

In the years after World War II the American economy moved away from manufacturing. Steelworkers, coal miners, dressmakers—these were typical workers of the early twentieth century. Such jobs remained, of course, but by the 1950s the biggest growth was in sales and service.

One reason for this trend was automation—the use of machines instead of human labor. The development of advanced machinery greatly reduced the number of people needed to harvest crops, mine natural resources, and assemble products. In the 1940s and 1950s, machines replaced the labor of millions of workers. In 1955, for example, a radio manufacturer installed automatic machinery that enabled 2 workers to assemble 1,000 radios a day. Before automation, the same task had required 200 people.

This replacement of human labor by machines created problems for workers. Many workers lost their jobs. They had to move to other parts of the country in search of work, or seek training in different fields. Those workers who kept their jobs had to speed up their work in order to keep pace with the new machines. Yet few union leaders resisted automation. Instead, they accepted it in return for higher wages for the workers who were not fired.

One bright spot for labor came in 1955. In that year the American Federation of Labor (AFL) and the Congress of Industrial Organizations (CIO) merged, ending a long rivalry. Workers in strong AFL-CIO unions made big gains in the postwar years. However, only one-fourth of American workers were represented by unions.

SUBURBAN GROWTH 4E, 8A, 8B, 8C

From 1945 to 1960 new housing construction mushroomed outside the cities. Suburbs seemed to pop up overnight. Almost all new housing built during the period took place in the areas around American cities.

The move to the suburbs had several causes. One was the pent-up demand for housing. Little housing had been built during the Depression and World War II. Another cause was the enormous growth in the American population. During the hard times of the 1930s, the birth rate had dropped to about two children per family. But the postwar years brought new hope about the future. As a result, families had more children. In the 1950s, as families with three and four children became the norm, people started talking about a baby boom. In the fifteen years after the war, the nation grew from 140 million people to 180 million. That kind of growth rivaled India's.

Federal government support also spurred the growth of suburbs. A federally insured loan often made the difference for a family seeking to build or buy a house in the suburbs. The federal government provided more help by financing a huge surge in highway construction. The Highway Act of 1956 committed $32 billion to the construction of 41,000 miles of highways. These high-speed highways allowed people to commute long distances to their jobs. For the first time, people could live in suburbs that were as far as 50 or 60 miles from their place of work.

With the rise of suburbs came another boom—an explosion in car ownership. Automobiles were essential to suburbanites. City dwellers could walk to neighborhood grocery stores and take a bus to

The Geographic Perspective: Growth of the Sunbelt

THE POPULATION SHIFT TO THE SOUTH AND WEST, 1950-1970

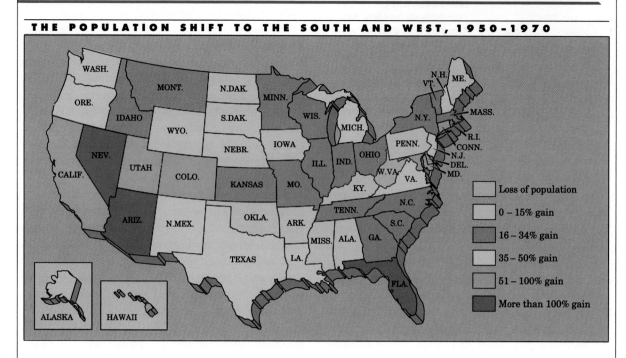

Legend:
- Loss of population
- 0 – 15% gain
- 16 – 34% gain
- 35 – 50% gain
- 51 – 100% gain
- More than 100% gain

In 1952 a new word entered our language: *sunbelt*. The word was coined to describe the generally sunny states of the south and southwest. The region extends from the southern Atlantic coast to California.

SHIFT TOWARD THE SUNBELT
Today over half the American population lives in the sunbelt. The population shift toward the sunbelt began in the 1950s and continued into the 1980s.

Between 1950 and 1970 the United States population leaped 35 percent, from about 150 million to over 200 million. A state that did not show close to a 35 percent gain in this period was probably losing population to migration. States with a greater than 35 percent gain were gaining population from migration.

SOME REASONS FOR GROWTH
The growth of the sunbelt states mirrors the growth of new air and highway transportation networks. These networks spurred the development of areas far from established rail and water routes. Between 1950 and 1970 trucking volume grew 138 percent. In the same years the number of miles flown by commercial aircraft expanded by five times.

Associated with the airplane industry was the new aerospace industry. Like *sunbelt*, the word *aerospace* was invented in the 1950s. The development and testing of military aircraft, of rockets and missiles, and of space vehicles would take place primarily in the sunbelt states.

Although most people do not move when they retire, those who do are likely to head for a sunbelt state. Beginning in the 1950s special retirement communities were developed in the sunbelt states to attract retirees. Florida's retirement-age population tripled between 1950 and 1970.

New technology also made it easier to work and live in the high summer temperatures of the sunbelt. Air conditioning for homes and cars was introduced in the 1950s and had become common by the 1960s.

CRITICAL THINKING 2D
1. How did new technology contribute to the growth of such desert states as Arizona and Nevada?
2. What would it take to reverse the population growth of the sunbelt?

The Geographic Perspective Answers
1. The aerospace industry needed to have sunny skies and open spaces. Air cargo allowed manufacturers to get supplies and distribute lightweight products. Air conditioning made living there more feasible.

2. Decline of economic opportunities there, new technology making northern states more attractive, a perception that life is better elsewhere.

Geographic Themes
Geographic themes covered on this page:
- ✔ Location
- ___ Place
- ___ Interactions
- ✔ Movement
- ✔ Regions

Cultural Pluralism
Discuss with students the link between American prosperity and the rise in immigration from Puerto Rico and Mexico. Tell students that during the 1950s the number of immigrants from the Americas came close to matching the number of immigrants from Europe. Ask them to suggest the reasons for this pattern. (Western Europe was recovering from the war and growing more prosperous. Communism had effectively closed emigration from Eastern Europe. Poor people in the Americas were attracted by the proximity of the United States and its prosperity.)

Patterns in History
Have students identify the chief goals of young people in the 1950s. (Job security, family life.) Then ask them to discuss the goals of young people today. Have them suggest the factors that explain the differences and similarities between individual goals today and in the 1950s.

Science and Technology
Refer students to the graph, on page 483, showing television ownership. **What impact do you think television had on family life?** (Changed recreation and communication; influenced values.)

History
Provide the following list of 1950s teenage slang: *cool* (worthy of approval); *hang loose* (don't worry); *hairy* (formidable); *square* (a dull person); *drag* (dreary person or event); *wheels* (a car). Ask students to identify the present-day equivalents of these slang terms.

work. In the suburbs, however, houses were usually a long distance from stores, offices, and factories. Americans bought cars like never before. Car sales jumped from 2 million in 1946 to nearly 8 million in 1955.

Young families moved from cities to suburbs in search of more space, cleaner and quieter neighborhoods, and modern schools for their children. There were, however, many types of suburban communities. Some suburbs were located far from the central cities. They had large homes of varying design on lots of at least one-quarter acre. These were the most expensive suburbs. Yet there were also far more modest developments, usually closer to the big cities.

Developers like Levitt and Sons even mass-produced suburbs. The first "Levittowns" consisted of thousands of small four-room houses with few variations in design. Critics called them "little boxes made of ticky-tacky." But they brought the "American dream" of owning one's own home to many middle-class Americans.

THOSE PROSPERITY MISSED 3A, 4E

Not all Americans were able to fulfill their dreams during the 1950s. Almost all suburbs, North and South, wealthy and modest alike, were exclusively white. Discrimination kept out blacks, Hispanics, and other minority groups. Real estate agents routinely refused to show blacks houses in white neighborhoods, and banks routinely denied them loans.

Nor did rural America and the inner cities share in the nation's prosperity. Driven from the land by the mechanization of farming and mining, millions of rural Americans entered the central cities. Several million, black and white, came from the rural South and Appalachia. They were joined by a new wave of immigrants from Puerto Rico, Mexico, and other Spanish-speaking areas. But the cities did not have jobs for all the newcomers. A study made in 1958 found that more than 40 million Americans—nearly one in four—lived in families making less than $3,000 per year.

A writer of the period who pointed out the great gap between rich and poor was the economist John Kenneth Galbraith. In *The Affluent Society* (1958), Galbraith criticized society's inattention to the problems of the poor and the lack of government aid for education and public housing.

In 1947, developer William Levitt revolutionized the concept of suburban housing, which until then was too expensive for most Americans. Using mass-produced, nearly identical units, Levitt turned potato fields on Long Island, New York, into the tract-housing development pictured here. Levitt's three-bedroom houses sold for between $11,000 and $15,000—prices that middle-class families could afford. **TECHNOLOGY** How was suburban growth related to increased use of the automobile? 4E

THE SEARCH FOR SECURITY 4E

With the Depression still a vivid memory, middle-class Americans placed a high priority on economic security. In 1949, *Fortune* magazine found that "security was the one big goal of college graduates." Only one in fifty male graduates wanted to start a business, a rewarding but potentially risky undertaking. The rest preferred to work for large, established corporations. As one graduate put it, "I know AT & T might not be very exciting, but there will always be an AT & T."

Young people wanted secure family lives as well. In the 1950s, most Americans married early. The average age of marriage was 23 for men and 21 for women. Popular books, magazines, and television shows painted a picture of the ideal family. It consisted of a father who served as "breadwinner," a nurturing wife, and several children.

By the late 1950s many television programs featured such families. Comedies such as *Father Knows Best* and *Leave It to Beaver* revolved around the lighthearted complications of suburban family life. Each morning, Father left in a business suit for the office. The viewer rarely saw what he did there, but it did not seem to matter, for life was centered in the home. Mother was almost always in the kitchen. The kids busied themselves with school and friends. And despite his job, Father always seemed to have plenty of time to share with his family.

For the most part, these shows reflected how Americans wished to live rather than how they did live. A great many women had roles besides that of mother. At the start of the 1950s, women made up one-fourth of the work force; this figure had risen to one-third by the end of the decade. Still, women were counseled not to take work too seriously. Magazines of the time emphasized that women's jobs should not interfere with family life or the economic prospects of men.

THE AGE OF TELEVISION 4E, 4F, 8A

The appearance of television shows praising suburban life points to another development of the 1950s: the rise of television. The first television sets began to appear on the market in the late 1940s. They were very expensive, costing $500 or $600 (the equivalent of $2,500 today). As the indus-

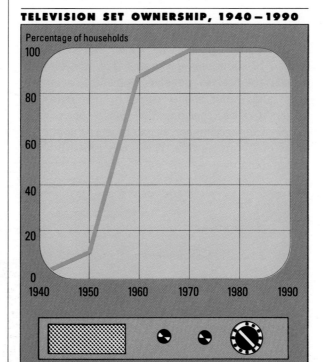

TELEVISION SET OWNERSHIP, 1940–1990

Percentage of households

Source: *Historical Statistics of the United States*

GRAPH SKILLS 8A, 9B

As television sets grew more affordable, their popularity increased. About what percentage of American households owned television sets in 1950? During which decade did television ownership increase the most? **CRITICAL THINKING** Why does the graph show a leveling-off around 1970?

try grew and technology improved, prices dropped. From 1949 to 1959, the number of households with TV sets increased from 1 million to 44 million.

Historians of popular culture believe that the early 1950s were the best years of television. Most programs were filmed live and had a fresh, unrehearsed look. Along with variety shows and situation comedies, early television presented some of the best serious drama of the age.

Of course, television was a business, and it made money by selling advertising time. In 1949 American companies paid $58 million to run commercials on TV. Only one decade later they bought $1.5 billion of television advertising.

As television became a booming business, the

Graph Skills Answers
10 percent. 1950s. As ownership approached 100 percent of households, it could no longer increase much.

Enrichment/Extension
Ask students to make a comparison of television programming/viewing in the 1950s and today. Students should compare the programs mentioned in the text with their favorite shows and other popular television shows of this decade. Provide time for students to share and discuss their findings.

Assessment
You may wish to use the Section 4 Review, page 484, to see how well your students understand the main points in the lesson.

Section Review Answers
1. *modern Republicanism*—Willingness of the Republican Party to support some federal responsibility for the well-being of the people. *gross national product*—A nation's total annual output of goods and services. *conglomerate*—Corporation made up of companies in widely different fields. *automation*—Replacement of workers with machines. *baby boom*—Increase in birth rate after World War II. *Highway Act of 1956*—Law that provided $32 billion for 41,000 miles of highway construction.

commercial networks took fewer risks. They needed large audiences to please advertisers. With so much money at stake, the networks tended to show only programs that had already proven themselves popular. Comedies, soap operas, and game shows came to dominate the screen. Critics, charging that most shows were mindless entertainment, began to worry about the effect of TV on viewers. It is a concern still being voiced today.

Americans began their fascination with television during the 1950s. Popular stars included comedians Milton Berle, Lucille Ball, and Jackie Gleason. The average American now watches television for seven hours each day. **CULTURE** What are your favorite TV shows? Why do you think people watch so much TV? **4F**

THE REVIVAL OF RELIGION 4G

Television also revolutionized communication, playing a part in the revival of religious faith in the United States. During the first half of the twentieth century, fewer than half of the American people belonged to a church or temple. By the end of the 1950s, two-thirds of the population belonged to a religious group. Even more—96 percent—claimed a religious faith.

Historians have many explanations for this surge of religious feeling. Some stress the fears of the cold war and the nuclear age. Others believe the search for spiritual meaning was a response to the consumerism and status-seeking of the time. Still others argue that the growth of religion showed not only a faith in God, but faith in the American way of life. To some people, such as Sec-

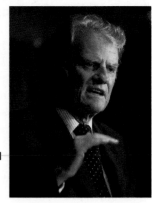
retary of State John Foster Dulles, the cold war was a religious struggle—one between "Judeo-Christian civilization" and "godless communism."

Beginning in the late 1940s, charismatic preachers such as Billy Graham began drawing huge audiences for their religious meetings. Like other preachers, Graham used radio and then television to get his message across to the American people. Not everyone shared Graham's highly emotional approach to religion, but the idea of religion itself took hold. In 1954 President Eisenhower said, "Our government makes no sense unless it is founded on a deeply felt religious faith—and I don't care what it is." That same year Congress added the words "under God" to the Pledge of Allegiance.

SECTION REVIEW

1. KEY TERMS modern Republicanism, gross national product, conglomerate, automation, baby boom, Highway Act of 1956

2. COMPREHENSION What evidence is there of prosperity in the United States during the Eisenhower years?

3. COMPREHENSION Name three causes of the rise of suburbs. Why was the automobile important to suburban growth?

4. COMPREHENSION Why was there a surge in religious activity during the 1950s?

5. CRITICAL THINKING Describe the ideal family as presented in the 1950s. How, if at all, does it differ from today's ideal family?

5 Signs of Change and Doubt

Section Focus

Key Terms rock 'n' roll ■ *Sputnik* ■ military-industrial complex

Main Idea A number of events and movements in the late 1950s raised doubts about American society.

Objectives As you read, look for answers to these questions:
1. How did young Americans rebel against society in the 1950s?
2. What blows were there to American confidence in the late 1950s?

Most Americans regarded the 1950s as something like a golden age. Many still do. Yet a closer look suggests a more troubled and rebellious decade. The most important rebellion came from African Americans struggling for civil rights and racial equality. Because the civil rights struggle was the most important social movement of the period, it will be discussed in a full chapter (Chapter 22). There were other signs of conflict and change throughout American culture.

THE SILENT GENERATION?

Some observers in the 1950s noted the complacency of young people. The writer Thornton Wilder labeled them "the silent generation." Indeed, in 1957, commencement speakers all over the country warned graduates about the dangers of conformity.

It was certainly true that most teenagers did not challenge the political views of their time. However, in other ways they showed a deep desire to find forms of expression of their own.

One such form of expression was rock 'n' roll. A hybrid music, rock evolved out of a mix of black blues, white country music, and black gospel. The new music was rough, rhythmic, and, above all, loud. It gave young people throughout the nation a sense of common identity.

The style of dancing that accompanied rock 'n' roll was offensive to much of the adult world. That made it all the more exciting to the young. Rock also broke with convention by crossing racial boundaries.

The most famous rock star of the age was Elvis Presley, a white Mississippian who learned rhythm and blues from black musicians in Memphis. He proved to be the answer to record producer Sam Phillips's dream. "If I could find a white man who had the Negro sound and the Negro feel," Phillips once said, "I could make a million dollars." Presley would go on to sell more than a billion records.

For a few years in the mid-1950s, black rock 'n' rollers like Chuck Berry and Little Richard held the spotlight with white artists such as Buddy Holly and Jerry Lee Lewis. White "teen idols" like Pat Boone began to dominate the pop music market in the late 1950s. A number of their hits were softer versions of songs first recorded by black groups. Yet even their watered-down rock reflected a profound change from the popular music of the 1940s, sung by performers such as the Andrews Sisters and Frank Sinatra.

Elvis Presley adapted blues music, formerly sung only by black musicians, to a rock beat. Black artists even wrote many of his hits, such as "That's Alright Mama" and "All Shook Up." Elvis's records spun on jukeboxes everywhere, but television host Ed Sullivan called him "unfit for a family audience." **CULTURE** Name some of the other rock stars of the 1950s. 4F

SUPPORTING THE SECTION

Reinforcement Workbook: Worksheet 80
Reteaching Resources: Worksheet 80
Enrichment and Extension Resources: Historian Worksheet 8
Teaching Transparencies: Transparency 80

Photo Caption Answer
Chuck Berry, Little Richard, Buddy Holly, Jerry Lee Lewis, etc.

SECTION 5

Signs of Change and Doubt
(pp. 485–487)

Section Objective
■ identify events and movements in the 1950s that challenged American society

Introducing the Section

Connecting with Past Learnings
Ask students to identify issues and events that were sources of anxiety during the 1950s. (Cold war, threat of nuclear war, fear of communism, automation, poverty in rural areas and inner cities.)

Key Terms
List the key terms for this section on the board. Ask students to define each term. Then have them identify one positive effect and one negative effect of each term. **LEP**

Focus
On the board, create three columns and label them *Positive Effects, Movement/Event,* and *Negative Effects.* Have students fill in the columns by suggesting important trends and events discussed in the section and their good and bad effects. (Students may suggest such trends and events as rock 'n' roll, criticism of American values, *Sputnik,* public scandals, and the growth of the military-industrial complex.)

Developing the Lesson
After students have read the section, you may want to consider the following activities:

Science and Technology
Ask the class to suggest reasons why the launching of *Sputnik* was such a blow to Americans. (They feared nuclear weapons launched from space; they believed that American technology was superior.)

485

SOCIAL HISTORY
Famous Firsts

1954 *The Tonight Show*, with Steve Allen as host, premieres on NBC (Sept. 27).

C. A. Swanson and Sons sell their first "TV Brand Dinners."

Bill Haley and the Comets record "Rock Around the Clock," first rock 'n' roll smash hit (April 12).

1955 Esther Pauline Friedman Lederer of Chicago publishes her first confidential column, "Ann Landers Says," in the *Chicago Sun-Times*.

1957 Ford Motor Company introduces the Edsel—Detroit's first major flop.

1958 First bank card, BankAmericard, introduced.

Hula-Hoops go on sale, quickly becoming the biggest toy fad in history.

THE FEAR OF DELINQUENCY 4F

While rock 'n' roll worried some parents, concern about teen-age crime became something of a national obsession. There is little evidence that young people engaged in more criminal behavior in the 1950s than in other times in American history. But many adults believed young hoodlums were on the rampage and that "good" kids could easily be seduced into a life of crime. One best-selling book of the time argued that comic books were a major cause of juvenile delinquency.

What particularly frightened parents was that their children idolized movie stars who portrayed rebels and delinquents. Some of this parental concern can be understood by watching the *The Wild One*. In that 1954 movie Marlon Brando played the leader of a motorcycle gang. At one point the Brando character is asked, "What are you rebelling against?" He responds, "Whaddya got?"

The "wild one" rejected the values of the age—security, status, respectability, patriotism, and organized religion. James Dean presented a similar message in *Rebel Without a Cause* (1955). Yet as that movie title suggests, the rebel lacked a clear vision of an alternative way of life.

Doubts about the idealized vision of the American way of life can also be found in the pages of the most popular youth magazine of the time: *Mad*. In one poll, 58 percent of college students identified it as their favorite magazine.

Mad offered no vision of how students might change their society for the better. It attracted readers simply by making fun of American culture. One issue included the lines, "Hey, the Lone Ranger, Wonder Bread, and TV commercials . . . are *ridiculous*! Clark Kent is a creep! Superduperman can't get off the ground."

Some of the most severe critics of the American way of life in the 1950s were the poets and writers known as the "beats" (the media called them "beatniks"). Writers like Allen Ginsberg and Jack Kerouac professed nonconformity and freedom from social constraints. They urged people to search for spiritual meaning rather than material success.

A SOVIET BREAKTHROUGH IN SPACE 4E, 3A

A series of events in the late 1950s gave new force to the criticisms of American society. First there was the success of the Soviet space program. In 1957 the Soviet Union launched the world's first space satellite, called *Sputnik*. The American people, who regarded their nation as the world leader in technology, were stunned to learn of the Soviet success. Clare Booth Luce, former Republican congresswoman from Connecticut, called *Sputnik* a blow "to a decade of American pretensions that the American way of life is a gilt-edged guarantee of our national superiority."

Some critics charged that the nation had fallen behind the Soviet Union because of failures in education. Improving education now became a matter of national security. In 1958, Congress passed the National Defense Education Act. It gave over half a billion dollars in aid to improve education in science, mathematics, and foreign languages.

SCANDALS AND CORRUPTION 4F

Examples of scandal and corruption also surfaced. In 1958, Americans learned that several of their favorite television game shows were rigged. Winners were picked in advance and given the correct answers. It was especially shocking that Charles Van Doren had taken part in the fixed shows. A Columbia University instructor, Van Doren had become a national celebrity while a contestant.

That same year another scandal broke, this one in the radio world. Investigations revealed that several well-known disc jockeys had accepted bribes in return for playing certain records frequently.

Union corruption also troubled the nation. In the late 1950s, Dave Beck, president of the International Brotherhood of Teamsters, was charged with misusing union funds. A jury convicted him and sent him to jail. The Teamsters then elected Jimmy Hoffa as Beck's successor, despite evidence that Hoffa had ties with organized crime. In response, the AFL-CIO expelled the Teamsters in 1957.

None of these events by itself threatened the United States. Together, however, they pointed to lingering problems in American society. As the nation entered a new decade—the 1960s—the chorus of demands for change would only grow.

EISENHOWER'S FAREWELL ADDRESS 8G

President Eisenhower also struck a warning note in his Farewell Address in January 1961. Eisenhower pointed out that since World War II, for the first time in its history, the United States had developed a "permanent armaments industry" and an "immense military establishment." Eisenhower was especially concerned about the friendly relationship between the military and the giant corporations that built its weapons. He told Americans to keep a close eye on this military-industrial complex. "We must never let the weight of this combination endanger our liberties or democratic processes," he stated.

In addition, Eisenhower called for progress toward world disarmament:

> Disarmament, with mutual honor and confidence, is a continuing imperative. Together we must learn how to compose differences, not with arms, but with intellect and decent purpose. As one who has witnessed the horror and lingering sadness of war . . . I wish I could say tonight that a lasting peace is in sight.

SECTION REVIEW

1. KEY TERMS rock 'n' roll, *Sputnik*, military-industrial complex

2. PEOPLE Elvis Presley, Marlon Brando, Allen Ginsberg, Dave Beck

3. COMPREHENSION Describe the 1950s rebel as portrayed in such films as *The Wild One* and *Rebel Without a Cause*.

4. COMPREHENSION How did Congress respond to the news that the Soviet Union had launched a space satellite?

5. CRITICAL THINKING How might Eisenhower's concern about the military be linked to his call for progress toward world disarmament?

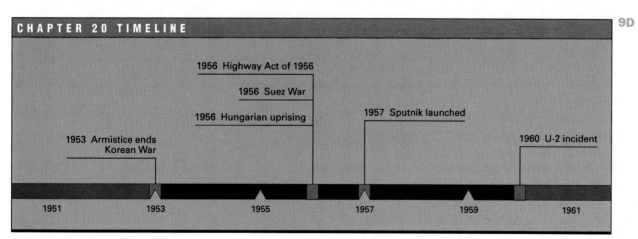

CHAPTER 20 TIMELINE   9D

- 1953 Armistice ends Korean War
- 1956 Highway Act of 1956
- 1956 Suez War
- 1956 Hungarian uprising
- 1957 Sputnik launched
- 1960 U-2 incident

1951   1953   1955   1957   1959   1961

Chapter 20 Review Answers

Key Terms

1. The Army-McCarthy hearings were televised Senate hearings on McCarthy's allegations that Communists were in the Army. Censure is Congress's most severe way of condemning a member's behavior.

2. A hydrogen bomb is a nuclear weapon. *Sputnik* was the world's first space satellite, launched by the USSR in 1957.

3. Rollback was Eisenhower's policy for the liberation of nations under Communist rule. Massive retaliation is a response to aggression with an all-out nuclear attack.

4. The Third World includes developing countries. To nationalize is to place formerly private industries under government control.

5. Gross national product is the annual output of goods and services. Military-industrial complex is the relationship between the military and corporations that build weapons.

People to Identify

1. Adlai Stevenson
2. Joseph McCarthy
3. Gamal Abdel Nasser
4. John Foster Dulles
5. Richard M. Nixon
6. Marlon Brando

Places to Locate

1. D   3. B
2. C   4. A

Reviewing the Facts

1. Democrat Adlai Stevenson shared many of the same views as Truman. Republican Dwight Eisenhower, a war hero, won by promising an end to the Korean War.

2. Eisenhower increased bombings and threatened the use of nuclear weapons. The truce established a cease-fire line and freed prisoners of war.

CHAPTER 20 SUMMARY

SECTION 1: Dwight Eisenhower was elected President in 1952. His first major accomplishment was to end the war in Korea.

■ The public was tired of years of crisis. Voters responded to Eisenhower's promise of peace and prosperity.

■ The Korean War ended in a stalemate. The boundary of North and South Korea remained almost exactly where it had been before the fighting broke out.

SECTION 2: Cold war tensions continued to affect life in the United States.

■ McCarthy's wild charges of Communist influence in government finally led to his downfall in 1954.

■ Concern with internal security was widespread during the 1950s. Many federal workers deemed "risks" were forced out of their jobs.

■ The development of the hydrogen bomb heightened fears of nuclear attack.

SECTION 3: The arena of cold war conflict shifted away from Europe to the Third World during the 1950s.

■ Secretary of State Dulles tried to contain Soviet growth through the establishment of regional alliances and through threats of nuclear retaliation.

■ The West and Communist nations fought for power and influence in newly independent Third World nations.

SECTION 4: Despite the cold war, the 1950s is remembered as a time of prosperity, stability, and confidence.

■ Eisenhower moderated but did not undo the trends toward social spending and big government that had characterized the 1930s and 1940s.

■ The economy performed well during the 1950s, with high growth and low inflation.

■ Lifestyles changed as the result of increased prosperity, the shift to service occupations, automation, the growth of suburbs, and the spread of television and automobile ownership.

SECTION 5: A number of events and trends in the late 1950s undermined Americans' confidence in the future.

■ Some people worried that youths were too conformist, others that they were rebels.

■ Soviet successes in space seemed to threaten American security.

KEY TERMS ●

Define the terms in each of the following pairs.

1. Army-McCarthy hearings; censure
2. hydrogen bomb; *Sputnik*
3. rollback; massive retaliation
4. Third World; nationalize
5. gross national product; military-industrial complex

PEOPLE TO IDENTIFY ●

Match each of the following people with the correct description.

Marlon Brando
John Foster Dulles
Joseph McCarthy
Gamal Abdel Nasser
Richard M. Nixon
Adlai Stevenson

1. Democratic candidate for President in 1952, who lost to Eisenhower.
2. Wisconsin senator censured by the Senate in 1954 for "conduct unbecoming a member."
3. Egyptian leader who nationalized the Suez Canal in 1956 and denied Israeli ships the right to use the waterway.
4. Secretary of State under Eisenhower.
5. Vice President under Eisenhower.
6. Movie actor who portrayed rebellious youth.

---

3. They gave Americans a close look at McCarthy's bullying tactics.

4. Internal security called for firing employees thought to be risks. *Yates v. United States* protected the right to belong to opposition groups.

5. Dulles was not content with Truman's policy to contain communism. He advocated a policy of massive retaliation and rollback of communism.

PLACES TO LOCATE ●

Match each of the letters on the map with the places that are listed below. Then explain the importance of each place.

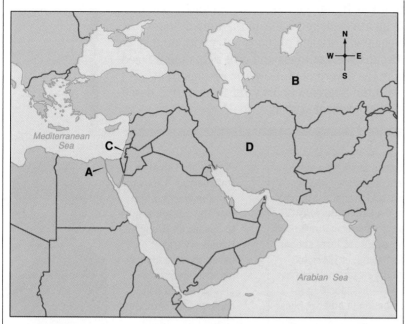

1. Iran
2. Israel
3. Soviet Union
4. Suez Canal

REVIEWING THE FACTS ▲

1. Describe the candidates, issues, and outcome of the 1952 presidential election.
2. What steps did President Eisenhower take to end the Korean War? What settlement was reached among the warring parties?
3. How did televised hearings help to bring an end to Joseph McCarthy's power?
4. What steps were taken to protect internal security? What was the Supreme Court's ruling in the case of *Yates v. United States*?

5. Describe the foreign policy of John Foster Dulles. How did it differ from that of the Truman administration?
6. Why did the Third World become a battleground in the cold war? Give two examples of Third World unrest during the 1950s.
7. Describe Eisenhower's approach toward government social programs.
8. Describe the trends in the economy during the 1950s.
9. How did unions react to automation? What danger did it pose to American workers?
10. What events and trends shook Americans' confidence in the future during the 1950s?

CRITICAL THINKING SKILLS ▲

1. IDENTIFYING THE MAIN IDEA
What was the main purpose of the strategy of massive retaliation?

2. IDENTIFYING CAUSE AND EFFECT
Why did the foreign policy of the United States lead to anti-American feelings in places such as Latin America and the Middle East?

3. ANALYZING A QUOTATION
What did Secretary of Defense Wilson mean when he said, "What is good for the country is good for General Motors"? Do you agree or disagree with the statement? Why?

WRITING ABOUT TOPICS IN AMERICAN HISTORY ■

1. CONNECTING WITH LITERATURE
A selection from *Chicano* by Richard Vasquez appears on pages 806–808. Read it and answer the questions. Then answer the following question: How might the "1950s ideal" of the Eisenhower era have affected the children in Mrs. Weimer's class?

2. APPLYING THEMES: AMERICAN CULTURE Write a report on the writings of one of the "beat" poets. Or watch a video recording of either *The Wild One* or *Rebel Without a Cause*, and then write an essay telling why you think it appealed to the young people of the 1950s.

3. POLITICS Compare and contrast the policy of massive retaliation with that of fighting limited wars. Which do you find easier to support? Why?

9. Unions accepted automation in return for higher wages though, by replacing human labor with machines, automation cost many workers their jobs.

10. The idolization by teenagers of rock 'n' roll stars and movie rebels, the challenge to American technological superiority of *Sputnik,* and a series of popular culture scandals.

Critical Thinking Skills
1. Dulles established massive retaliation in the hopes that such an extreme threat would deter any Soviet aggression.
2. America's installation and support of pro-American leaders threatened the sovereignty of newly independent nations and caused anti-American feelings.
3. Wilson believed that the goals of big business and the government were the same. Students may say that helping business means more jobs, or they may point to examples such as tariffs that benefit business but hurt consumers.

Writing About Topics in American History
1. Students might note that the 1950s were a time of conformity and conservatism, and that the children were trying to conform by all claiming to speak English.
2. Students may consider how the poets or actors depict a rebellion against hypocrisy and a search for new values.
3. Students should define what each of the policies is, and discuss their pros and cons.

6. Democracies and the Soviet Union tried to extend their influence in such countries as Guatemala and Iran.

7. Eisenhower did not support new social programs, but did not tamper with those programs already in place.

8. The U.S. was prosperous, with large-scale corporate mergers crossing markets and industries.

Chapter Review exercises are keyed for student abilities:
● = Basic
▲ = Average
■ = Average/Advanced

American Mosaic

Introducing the Feature

Discuss with the class why Americans began to doubt United States power during the postwar period. *What events of the cold war led Americans to support the tactics of Senator Joseph McCarthy?* (The Soviet achievement of the atomic bomb, the Communist Revolution in China, the Korean War, and the disclosure of Westerners spying for the Soviet Union.)

Have students explain the differences between the Supreme Court's 1896 *Plessy v. Ferguson* decision allowing "separate but equal" facilities for blacks, and its 1954 *Brown v. Board of Education* ruling. (In *Brown*, separate educational facilities were declared to be inherently unequal, which meant that public schools would have to be integrated.)

Teaching Multiculturalism

Civic Values

Discuss with students how one individual, Gonzolo Mendez, set in motion a process that ended the practice of segregating Mexican American children in his town. *What organizations backed Mendez in his desegregation suit?* (The NAACP and the American Jewish Congress.) *What other forms of segregation besides separate schools did Mendez's victory call into question?* (Segregation in public facilities such as swimming pools and parks.)

Participating in Government

Remind students that the first woman to be appointed to a Cabinet position was Frances Perkins, who was President Franklin D. Roosevelt's Secretary of Labor. *To what newly created Cabinet position did President Dwight D. Eisenhower appoint Oveta Culp Hobby?* (Secretary of Health,

---

★ *A Multicultural Perspective* ★

Following World War II, the cold war with the Soviet Union helped create an atmosphere of fear in the United States. Many people equated criticism of the country with attacks on its security. Groups seeking to expand civil rights often faced opposition from the government. However, an important advance came with the Supreme Court's 1954 ruling that desegregated the nation's school system.

During the mid-1940s, the town of Westminster, California, had two schools. One was a modern, well-funded school for Anglo-American children. Mexican American children attended the other school with its older, shabbier building and equipment. **Gonzolo Mendez,** a Westminster resident, wondered why his three children had to attend an inferior school just because they had Hispanic backgrounds. Mendez, with the help of the NAACP and the American Jewish Congress, sued local school officials and, in 1947, they won. His victory helped pave the way for opposition to segregation in other public facilities such as swimming pools and parks.

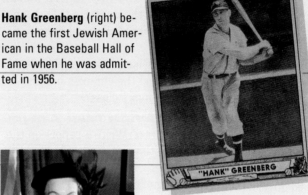

Hank Greenberg (right) became the first Jewish American in the Baseball Hall of Fame when he was admitted in 1956.

"HANK" GREENBERG

Playwright **Lorraine Hansberry's** *A Raisin in the Sun* was the first work by a black woman to appear on Broadway. Hansberry (right) believed that the complex personalities she created would help counter the "cardboard characters and hip-swinging musicals with exotic scores" in which blacks typically appeared. Her play was produced, directed, and acted by African Americans, and became a successful film. Through it, Hansberry helped gain wider acceptance for the work of other black playwrights.

Many of the best-known American cartoonists come from a variety of cultural backgrounds. **Stan Lee,** the son of Romanian immigrants, dreamed up Spiderman and others for Marvel Comics. "Peanuts" is created by **Charles Schulz,** a German American. **Garry Trudeau,** the creater of "Doonesbury," has French Canadian ancestors.

Oveta Culp Hobby (left) was born in Killeen, Texas, where her father was a lawyer. Interested in politics and the law, Hobby worked for the Texas House of Representatives and ran unsuccessfully for the state legislature. In 1931 she married William Pettus Hobby, publisher of the *Houston Post* and a former governor of Texas. During World War II, Hobby headed the Women's Army Auxiliary Corps (WAAC). Though a Democrat, she campaigned for Dwight Eisenhower's election in 1952. President Eisenhower named her to his Cabinet as the first Secretary of Health, Education, and Welfare.

An Wang (left), a native of Shanghai, China, worked as a radio engineer for the Chinese government during World War II. Wang came to the United States in 1945 and earned a Ph.D. from Harvard. At a time when few engineers were even thinking about computers, Wang became an expert on them and set up a tiny corporation. Wang Laboratories introduced calculators, computers, and word processors, and grew into an industry giant. Wang used his wealth to benefit hospitals, the performing arts, and the homeless.

The city of San Antonio, Texas, was sharply divided between Anglo-Americans and Mexican Americans in the 1950s. The divisions are fewer today, and some of the credit belongs to **Henry González** (right). After serving on the city council and the Texas Senate during the 1950s, González won election to Congress in 1961. He became known for his support for civil rights. He also insisted that minorities seek opportunity within American society as a whole, not by forming separatist groups.

John H. Johnson (above) was born in rural Arkansas. His mother took him to Chicago in 1933 to visit the World's Fair, and they decided to stay. Johnson took a job with a black-owned life insurance company during the Depression. There, Johnson gathered African American news for a company newsletter. Thinking the public would also be interested in such news, Johnson began to publish his own *Negro Digest*. He went on to publish *Ebony* and *Jet,* magazines read by hundreds of thousands of Americans. These magazines, focusing on what Johnson calls "the brighter side of Negro life and success," have been a source of pride to many African Americans.

Evangelist **Oral Roberts** (left) is descended from Cherokee Indians on his mother's side. His father was a Pentecostal preacher who held revival meetings along Oklahoma's pioneer trails. Believing that prayer had cured his childhood tuberculosis, Roberts dedicated himself to religion in 1935 at age 17. Reports of his healing powers spread. By 1955 he was holding crusades across the country. Roberts pioneered the use of radio and television programs to become the first of the new wave of "televangelists."

One day, a New York City recreation official saw **Althea Gibson** playing paddle ball in the Harlem streets and encouraged her to apply her talent to tennis. Members of a local tennis club raised money for lessons, and Gibson won her first tournament in 1941 at age fourteen. Professional tennis, like many sports in the 1940s, was off-limits to African Americans. Gibson and her sponsors determined to break the color barrier. In 1957 she became the first African American to win the English and American championships.

AMERICAN MOSAIC **491**

Historians' Corner

Vocabulary Preview

Be sure students understand the following terms: *conformity*—Behavior in keeping with customs and styles. *residual*—Remaining. *withal*—In addition. *deride* —Speak of contemptuously.

Analyzing Historical Issues

These selections present opposing viewpoints of the 1950s. William L. O'Neill defends the decade by saying that it accomplished postwar reconstruction and paved the way for later assaults on social problems. John Patrick Diggins cites four social commentators who view the 1950s as an era of mind-numbing materialism.

Can both of these assessments of the 1950s be accurate? How?

Critical Thinking Answers

1. O'Neill views the 1950s as a time of hope, growth, and glory in which the nation developed postwar prosperity and the seeds of tolerance which would enable it to tackle social problems in later decades.

2. The events of the times in which a historian lives might influence his or her interpretation of the past. Also, economic, cultural, and political historians might evaluate the decade in different terms.

3. Students who agree might point to the obsession with making money in order to purchase status items during both decades. Those who disagree might cite the change in the status of women in the 1980s from that of the 1950s.

HISTORIANS' CORNER

The Fifties—Decade of Conformity?

The passing of time often alters historians' views of an era and its mood. While many people see the 1950s as a time when conformity was the rule, others point to the many accomplishments of the period. As you compare these excerpts, remember that differing points of view are not necessarily "right" or "wrong."

William L. O'Neill

Criticisms of American society in the postwar era were largely misplaced. . . . The degree of conformity was overstressed, as were the horrors of mass culture and mass society. The educational system was much more effective than critics thought, and perhaps more effective than it is today judging by achievement test scores and other objective indexes. . . . Social evils certainly did exist, racism, sexism, and residual poverty in particular. These received surprisingly little attention. Sexism was ignored, racism underplayed, and poverty obscured by the general preoccupation with abundance.

This can be excused to some extent by the fact that no society, however rich, can attend to everything at once. Reconstruction was the first priority after World War II and was triumphantly accomplished. Perhaps that was enough to expect from a single generation. Further, some reforms must necessarily precede others. There could be no war on poverty, which affected perhaps one in four or five Americans, until the needs of the many were met. . . . There could be no assault on racism until ethnic and religious prejudices had been overcome. Before World War II it was rare to find Catholics and Jews in the higher reaches of American life. . . . In 1960 the first Roman Catholic became president of the United States. Not by coincidence that was also the year of the first sit-ins against racial segregation. . . .

Failures and blindspots notwithstanding, the years of the American High were in many ways among the nation's best. There had been McCarthyism yet also Joseph Welch, racism yet also Martin Luther King, the frustration of Korea, yet also the heroism. . . . Withal, it had been a time of hope, a time of growth, and in its best moments, even a time of glory.

From William L. O'Neill, *American High: The Years of Confidence 1945-1960*, pp. 289-291. Reprinted by permission of The Free Press, a Division of Macmillan, Inc. Copyright © 1986 by Catherine L. O'Neill and Cassandra O'Neill.

John Patrick Diggins

[Some writers] looked back wistfully on the fifties as a period of peace and prosperity. Many [others] . . . passed a different verdict. "Good-bye to the fifties—and good riddance," wrote the historian Eric Goldman, "the dullest and dreariest in all our history." "The Eisenhower years," judged columnist William Shannon, "have been years of flabbiness and self-satisfaction and gross materialism. . . . The loudest sound in the land has been the oink-and-grunt of private hoggishness. . . . It has been the age of the slob." The socialist Michael Harrington called the decade "a moral disaster, an amusing waste of time," and the novelist Norman Mailer derided it as "one of the worst decades in the history of man."

From John Patrick Diggins, *The Proud Decades: America in War and in Peace, 1941-1960* (New York: W.W. Norton, 1988), pp. 177-178.

Critical Thinking

1. In your own words, summarize O'Neill's view of the 1950s.

2. What, do you think, might account for the radically different ways in which historians see the 1950s?

3. It has been suggested that the 1980s were similar to the 1950s in their emphasis on material things. Do you agree with this judgment? Why, or why not?

William L. O'Neill (1935–) is a professor of history at Rutgers University specializing in American social and intellectual history.

John Patrick Diggins (1935–) is a professor of history at the University of California at Irvine.

UNIT EIGHT

Times of Turmoil

CHAPTERS IN THIS UNIT

THEMES IN AMERICAN HISTORY

 Global Interactions   The cold war—including the war in Vietnam—dominated American foreign policy through the 1960s. The early 1970s, however, brought improved superpower relations.

Expanding Democracy   African Americans' long struggle for civil rights produced many successes during the 1960s.

Constitutional Government   Abuses of power under President Richard Nixon produced a crisis for the American system of government.

 Pluralistic Society   Social tensions over race, the war in Vietnam, and other issues boiled over during the late 1960s.

 American Culture   Young Americans, critical of American society, supported a "counterculture" that emphasized love and freedom.

UNIT 8   TIMES OF TURMOIL   **493**

Unit Eight

Times of Turmoil
(pp. 493–592)

Unit Eight examines the political and social upheaval of the 1960s and early 1970s, beginning with the election of John F. Kennedy, his handling of major cold war confrontations, attempts to effect important social reforms, and his assassination. It notes President Lyndon Johnson's success in implementing liberal social programs.

The unit also examines two important struggles which started before the 1960s and continued after that decade's close: the civil rights movement and the Vietnam War. The cultural issues of these times are discussed as well, including the rise of ethnic pride, the development of the counterculture, and increased interest in environmental issues. Unit Eight describes President Richard Nixon's foreign policy breathroughs, as well as the role of Watergate in shattering his presidency.

493

	SECTION OBJECTIVES	SECTION RESOURCES
Section 1 **Kennedy and** **the Cold War**	▪ describe how anti-communism influenced Kennedy's foreign policy	● **Reteaching Resources:** Worksheet 81 ▲ **Reinforcement Workbook:** Worksheet 81 ■ **Enrichment and Extension Resources:** Primary Source Worksheet 41 ▲ **Teaching Transparencies:** Transparency 81
Section 2 **A Thousand Days**	▪ determine the obstacles to the adoption of President Kennedy's domestic policies	● **Reteaching Resources:** Worksheet 82 ▲ **Reinforcement Workbook:** Worksheet 82 ■ **Enrichment and Extension Resources:** Primary Source Worksheet 42 ▲ **Teaching Transparencies:** Transparency 82
Section 4 **"All the Way** **with LBJ"**	▪ explain President Johnson's success in gaining congressional approval of social legislation ▪ describe the major cases decided by the Supreme Court under Chief Justice Earl Warren	● **Reteaching Resources:** Worksheet 83 ▲ **Reinforcement Workbook:** Worksheet 83 ▲ **Teaching Transparencies:** Transparency 83

The list below shows Essential Elements relevant to this chapter. (The complete list of Essential Elements appears in the introductory pages of this Teacher's Edition.)

Section 1: 1A, 1B, 2B, 2C, 5B, 5E, 6A, 6C, 9A, 9E
Section 2: 3E, 3F, 4D, 4E, 5B, 6B, 9A
Section 3: 1A, 1B, 4C, 4D, 5B, 5D, 6A, 7B, 7F, 7G, 7H, 7J, 9A, 9D

Section Resources are keyed for
student abilities:
● = Basic
▲ = Average
■ = Average/Advanced

CHAPTER RESOURCES

Geography Resources: Worksheets 41, 42
Tests: Chapter 21 Test

Chapter Project: American Culture

Have students do an in-depth study of either Kennedy or Johnson, comparing how they were perceived during their tenure in office and how historians view them now. Students may use political cartoons, books, and journal articles for their study.

Homework Options

Each section contains activities labeled "Addressing Individual Needs." You may wish to choose from among these activities when assigning homework.

> **Provisions for Limited English Proficiency (LEP)**
> Several suggested activities may be particularly helpful for teachers of students with limited English proficiency. These activities have been marked throughout the Teacher's Annotated Edition with the symbol **LEP** .

BIBLIOGRAPHY AND AUDIOVISUAL AIDS

Teacher Bibliography

Caro, Robert A. *The Years of Lyndon Johnson: The Path to Power.* Random House, 1984.

Donald, Aida Di Pace. *John F. Kennedy and the New Frontier.* Hill and Wang, 1966.

Kennedy, John F. *"Let the Word Go Forth."* Delacorte, 1988.

Manchester, William. *One Brief Shining Moment: Remembering Kennedy.* Little, Brown, 1983.

Student Bibliography

Cook, Fred J. *The Cuban Missile Crisis, October 1962: The U.S. and Russia Face a Nuclear Showdown.* Watts, 1972.

Johnson, Lady Bird. *A White House Diary.* Dell, 1971.

Kurland, Gerald. *Lyndon Baines Johnson: President Caught in an Ordeal of Power.* SamHar Press, 1982.

Wofford, Harris. *Of Kennedys and Kings: Making Sense of the Sixties.* Farrar, Straus and Giroux, 1980.

Literature

Capote, Truman. *In Cold Blood.* Random House, 1966. A realistic novel about a gruesome multiple murder by two men that addresses the larger social issues of the crime.

Didion, Joan. *Slouching Towards Bethlehem.* Washington Square Press, 1983. Essays about contemporary culture that center on California as the author's metaphor for the lost American dream.

Kesey, Ken. *One Flew Over the Cuckoo's Nest.* Penguin, 1977. A funny, poignant story of one man's rebellion against a sadistic nurse in a mental hospital.

Roth, Philip. *Goodbye Columbus.* Houghton Mifflin, 1959. A witty novella that deals with various aspects of contemporary Jewish identity.

Wolfe, Tom. *The Right Stuff.* Bantam, 1984. Wolfe describes the early years of the U.S. space program and America's first seven astronauts, the men who had "the right stuff."

Films and Videotapes*

America Remembers John F. Kennedy. 100 min. WOMBAT. Documents the journey of JFK from the West Virginia primary to his assassination in Dallas. Recalls the confluence of history and personality that created the Camelot legend around his administration.

The Cuban Missile Crisis: 1962. 20 min. FFH. Explores the events that led up to the Cuban missile crisis; documenting Castro's rise to power, his economic policies, and his relationship with the Soviet Union.

The Sixties. 15 min. PYR. A visual portrait of a decade of change, which includes famous footage of key events, movements, and statements.

Computer Software*

DECISIONS, DECISIONS: Foreign Policy—The Burdens of World Power (Apple II and IBM). TS. Students confront realistic international relations dilemmas. Though the story lines are fictional, the program provides advice based on factual information. Materials are for use by groups and are designed to encourage class discussion and problem solving. Excellent support materials; good software.

*For a complete guide to audiovisual sources, see the introduction to this book (page Txx).

This chapter examines John F. Kennedy's election and foreign and domestic policies, as well as the domestic accomplishments of Lyndon B. Johnson.

 Themes in American History

- Global interactions
- Constitutional government

Chapter Objectives

After students complete this chapter, they will be able to:

1. Describe how anti-communism influenced President Kennedy's foreign policy.

2. Determine the obstacles to the adoption of President Kennedy's domestic policies.

3. Explain President Johnson's success in gaining congressional approval of social legislation.

4. Describe the major cases decided by the Supreme Court under Chief Justice Earl Warren.

Chapter Opener Art
Elaine de Kooning, *John F. Kennedy.*

The first President born in the twentieth century, John F. Kennedy brought grace and wit to the White House. To many Americans—especially young Americans—his election in 1960 seemed to signal a new era in American politics.

CHAPTER SUPPORT MATERIAL	
Reinforcement Workbook: Worksheets 81–83	
Reteaching Resources: Worksheets 81–83	
Enrichment and Extension Resources: Primary Source Worksheets 41, 42	
Geography Resources: Worksheets 41, 42	
Teaching Transparencies: Transparencies 81–83	
Tests: Chapter 21 Test	

CHAPTER

21 The Politics of Conflict and Hope
(1960–1969)

KEY EVENTS

1961	Bay of Pigs invasion
1962	Cuban missile crisis
1963	Kennedy assassinated
1964	Great Society launched
1965	U.S. intervenes in Dominican Republic
1969	Astronauts land on the moon

1A, 1B, 2B, 2C, 5B, 5E, 6A, 6C, 9A, 9E

1 Kennedy and the Cold War

Section Focus

Key Terms flexible response ■ Peace Corps ■ Alliance for Progress ■ Berlin Wall ■ Nuclear Test-Ban Treaty

Main Idea John F. Kennedy, elected President in 1960, devoted much of his time in office to foreign policy. His administration witnessed some of the most dangerous Soviet-American confrontations of the nuclear age.

Objectives As you read, look for answers to these questions:
1. What foreign policy changes did President Kennedy propose?
2. Why did the United States back plans for an invasion of Cuba?
3. What international crises raised fears of nuclear war?

"We like Ike!" Americans had proclaimed during the 1950s, but by 1960 many people felt the need for a change. The politics of the Eisenhower years had come to seem stand-pat and boring. The economy was lagging. The Soviet Union had launched a space satellite and shot down the U-2 spy plane, causing U.S. prestige abroad to slip.

People hungered for an active President, one who would make the United States a better and more exciting nation. The candidates in 1960 gave voters the vision of such a presidency. The promises of Democrat John F. Kennedy and Republican Richard M. Nixon were quite similar, and the contest between them led to one of the closest elections in American history.

A NARROW VICTORY 5B
Kennedy and Nixon had entered Congress in the same year—1946. Both were young veterans of World War II. Both rose to prominence in their respective parties. In 1952, Kennedy advanced to

the Senate and Nixon to the vice presidency. Eventually both men would be President.

John F. Kennedy of Massachusetts was the son of a very wealthy businessman and ambassador. His father instilled in him self-confidence and a passion for competition. Young Kennedy was charming and talented; he also had been decorated for heroism during World War II. His family's wealth and influence helped ease his path to political power.

In contrast, Richard Nixon was always an outsider in the world of wealth and power. His California family was not poor, but it was never prosperous. His father had merely a sixth-grade education and moved constantly from one job to another. At an early age, Nixon set out to advance himself through sheer hard work. His discipline and ambition amazed his classmates.

Both candidates pledged to build up the nation's military might and ensure continued prosperity. Kennedy's personal charm and his promise to "get

CHAPTER 21   THE POLITICS OF CONFLICT AND HOPE, 1960–1969   **495**

SECTION 1

Kennedy and the Cold War
(pp. 495–500)

Section Objective
■ describe how anti-communism influenced Kennedy's foreign policy

Introducing the Section

Connecting with Past Learnings
Help students remember American foreign policy before Kennedy. *What policies did Truman and Eisenhower support to deal militarily with the threat of Communist expansion?* (Truman supported containment, while Eisenhower and his Secretary of State, John Foster Dulles, wanted to roll back communism.) *How did the Marshall Plan help prevent the spread of communism to Western Europe?* (It offered economic aid to rebuild war-torn Europe, which lessened the appeal of communism.)

Key Terms
Ask students to define the key terms in their own words. Then have them create a timeline using the last four terms, noting the dates and definitions on the timeline. **LEP**

SUPPORTING THE SECTION

Reinforcement Workbook: Worksheet 81
Reteaching Resources: Worksheet 81
Enrichment and Extension Resources: Primary Source Worksheet 41
Teaching Transparencies: Transparency 81

495

Senator John F. Kennedy greets enthusiastic supporters during his 1960 presidential campaign. Kennedy's opponent, Richard Nixon, won California and 25 other states but ultimately lost one of the nation's closest elections. POLITICS What advantages did Kennedy possess in the campaign? 5B

the country moving again" hit the right note with voters. Wherever JFK toured, crowds swarmed to glimpse his dashing good looks and listen to his inspiring speeches. And in his televised debates with Nixon—the first televised debates in an American election—Kennedy came across as poised and confident, while Nixon appeared tired and ill-at-ease.

Kennedy's Catholicism posed one of the great questions about the campaign. Religious prejudice was still strong, and many people felt a Catholic should not be President. They argued that a Catholic President would respond to the wishes of the Pope, not the American people. However, Kennedy managed to calm most such fears.

On Election Day 69 million votes were cast. Kennedy won by only 120,000 ballots. At age 43, he was the youngest man ever elected President. Kennedy's choice of Texas Senator Lyndon B. Johnson as his running mate proved to be a great help, as the Democrats won Texas by a slim margin. Had a few thousand more people voted Republican in Texas and Illinois, Nixon would have been the victor.

496 UNIT 8 TIMES OF TURMOIL

FIGHTING THE COLD WAR 1B

The cold war and its many dangers—arms races, competition in the Third World—were on everyone's mind as Kennedy took office. "We will bury you," Soviet leader Nikita Khrushchev had promised the United States in 1956. There was every reason to believe that he meant what he said.

> "We will bury you."
> —*Soviet leader Khrushchev, 1956*

In his Inaugural Address Kennedy declared, "In the long history of the world, only a few generations have been granted the role of defending freedom in its hour of maximum danger." The greatest threat to freedom, in Kennedy's view, was posed by the "iron tyranny" of communism. To fight communism, Kennedy declared, the

★ **Historical Documents**   5E

For an excerpt from John F. Kennedy's Inaugural Address, see page 728 of this book.

American people must be willing to "pay any price" and "bear any burden."

Part of the price was a large increase in defense spending. Kennedy had claimed during the 1960 campaign that the American military was becoming dangerously weak. Eisenhower had cut spending on non-nuclear forces, arguing that massive retaliation—the threat to use nuclear weapons—would deter Soviet aggression around the world. But now the Soviets had more nuclear weapons of their own, as well as new intercontinental missiles to deliver them. Would a President really use nuclear weapons if he knew that the United States would suffer nuclear devastation in return?

Kennedy did not want to face such a terrible decision; he wanted more choices. The policy he advocated, called flexible response, aimed to give the President a range of options for dealing with international crises. Kennedy increased the American nuclear stockpile, expanded non-nuclear forces, and bolstered an elite branch of the army called the Special Forces (or Green Berets). These changes, Kennedy felt, would give the United States the capacity to fight limited wars around the world. Thanks to its nuclear superiority, the United States would also be able to fight an all-out nuclear war with the Soviet Union.

A PEACEFUL REVOLUTION 1A, 6A, 6C

Kennedy understood that winning the cold war required far more than a strong military. He knew that communism fed on poverty and social injustice. Kennedy urged America to offer poor nations a "peaceful revolution" against the "common enemies of man: tyranny, poverty, disease, and war itself."

The Peace Corps proved the most successful example of the "peaceful revolution." Created in 1961, the Peace Corps sent young men and women to do volunteer work in developing countries. By 1966, 10,000 Americans had served in the Peace Corps, moved to do so by the idea, as one volunteer said, "of giving, not getting." The Peace Corps remains active today, its volunteers spreading goodwill as well as knowledge among people in dozens of countries.

Another Kennedy proposal to fight poverty was the Alliance for Progress. The Alliance aimed to

A Peace Corps volunteer checks the weight of a young girl in the West African nation of Senegal. Peace Corps volunteers work in the fields of health, agriculture, and education in 60 countries around the world. CIVIC VALUES Why did Kennedy promote the Peace Corps? What are some of its benefits? 1A

stop communism in Latin America by offering economic and technical aid to nations in the region. While the aid program brought some progress to Latin America, the Alliance was mostly a failure. Too much of the money ended up in the hands of the wealthy and strengthened the rule of dictators.

THE INVASION OF CUBA 1A

Kennedy faced one of his toughest foreign policy problems in Cuba. In 1959, Cubans overthrew the dictatorship of Fulgencio Batista. Though the United States had supported Batista, many Americans sympathized with the revolution. As one journalist put it, "Batista's Cuba was a police state run by terrorists and corrupt bureaucrats."

A bearded young lawyer named Fidel Castro led the uprising. American public opinion supported Castro at first, hoping he would bring greater democracy to Cuba. Before long, however, Castro was jailing and murdering his opponents. He also seized property owned by American companies. Over harsh American objections, Cuba signed a

Global Awareness
Have students look at a map of the world and note the areas of the world where there were Communist countries in the 1960s. (Cuba, Eastern Europe and the Soviet Union, China, North Korea, North Vietnam.) Mention that in 1960 Khrushchev claimed that one-third of the world's people lived under Communist rule.

Explain to students that many Third World nations were gaining their independence in the 1960s. *How did the emergence of so many new nations affect Kennedy's concern with stopping the spread of communism?* (Kennedy feared that these new, often poor, nations would come under Communist domination and upset the balance of power between the free and Communist worlds.)

Civic Values
Have students read Kennedy's Inaugural Address on page 728. Discuss with them the idea of a "new generation," asking students to contrast Kennedy's vision with that of Eisenhower. (The new generation was young, had fought in World War II, were activist not reactive.) Tell students that many young people who heard this speech were inspired to join the Peace Corps and become involved in government. Ask students to describe their feelings about the speech. *Is Kennedy's message similar to the message presented by today's leaders?*

Photo Caption Answers
He wanted to provide alternatives to communism through a "peaceful revolution." Americans can experience life in developing countries first hand; their work may improve the lives of people in these countries and spread goodwill toward the United States.

Background The idea for the Peace Corps was first proposed in 1904 by William James. He developed the notion of a peaceful "army" of young people who would tackle important civilian projects.

trade agreement with the Soviet Union. Eisenhower retaliated by canceling imports of Cuban sugar and soon broke diplomatic ties.

Eisenhower also put the Central Intelligence Agency to work on a secret plan to overthrow Castro. The idea was to train and equip a group of anti-Castro Cuban exiles living in the United States. This force would be landed on Cuba to establish a foothold on the island and inspire the Cuban people to rise up against Castro.

From a military standpoint, the plan was risky at best. Moreover, the invasion would be an overt act of war that would break several treaties the United States had signed with Latin American nations. On the other hand, the prospect of a Communist regime located so close to the American mainland was unthinkable. Eisenhower approved the plan. When Kennedy took office, he and his advisers continued to support it.

Thus, on the morning of April 17, 1961, the Cuban exile force went ashore at Bahia de Cochinos (the Bay of Pigs). The invasion proved a complete disaster. The expected popular uprising never materialized, and Castro's troops made short work of the rebels. Kennedy considered an air strike to support the rebels, but decided against it. Within two days most of the 1,400 invaders were killed or captured.

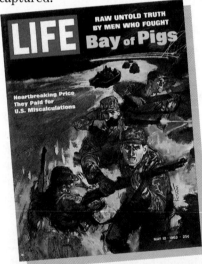

A magazine takes a hard look back at the 1961 Bay of Pigs invasion. The United States trained and transported Cuban exiles who hoped to topple Castro's government. The invasion damaged the prestige of the Kennedy administration. **POLITICS** How did the plan originate? Why did Kennedy support the invasion? **9E**

The Bay of Pigs disaster left the administration looking weak and foolish. Still, Kennedy and his advisers remained determined to rid themselves of Castro. The CIA hatched plans to disrupt the Cuban economy, undermine Castro's support, and even to assassinate Castro. Nothing worked. Looking back on this period, former Secretary of Defense Robert McNamara said, "We were hysterical about Castro."

CRISIS IN BERLIN 1A
Kennedy worried that the Soviet Union, emboldened by the American failure in Cuba, would undertake new adventures abroad. When he was invited to meet Soviet leader Khrushchev in Vienna, Austria, in June 1961, Kennedy meant to prove himself a tough opponent.

The chief subject of debate between the two leaders was Berlin. Berlin had been a focus of cold war tension since the 1940s. West Berlin, a non-Communist outpost in the heart of Communist East Germany, was a symbol of freedom to Western nations. It also served as a gateway for thousands of East Germans to escape to the West. At Vienna, Khrushchev tried to push the West out of Berlin, but Kennedy would not budge. "It is going to be a cold winter," Kennedy told Khrushchev as the meeting ended.

President Kennedy speaks to a crowd in West Berlin in 1963. Kennedy's anticommunism and expressions of support for the residents of the divided city made him very popular there. After Kennedy's death, the square where he spoke was renamed for him. **GEOGRAPHY** What circumstances made Berlin a unique city? **9A**

Upon his return to the United States, Kennedy told the American people that the crisis over Berlin could lead to war. He called for more defense spending and mobilized the National Guard. He also urged Americans to build fall-out shelters to protect themselves in case of nuclear war. Seized by a fear bordering on panic, many Americans did construct crude shelters for themselves and their families. War seemed imminent.

Rather than attack West Berlin, the Communists decided to wall it off. In August 1961 the East Germans began work on a barrier between East and West Berlin. The Berlin Wall became a frightening symbol of the cold war's division of Europe. But by stopping the flight of East Germans to the West, the Wall enabled the Soviet Union to avoid a showdown over West Berlin. The crisis eased. Then, a year later, the most dangerous confrontation of the cold war brought the world to the brink of nuclear war.

THE CUBAN MISSILE CRISIS 1A

The crisis began on October 16, 1962. That was the day President Kennedy received spy-plane photographs showing Soviet missiles being installed in Cuba. Kennedy had vowed not to allow offensive weapons in Cuba. Faced with the prospect of nuclear warheads a mere 90 miles from Florida, Kennedy felt he had to do something to eliminate them.

What could be done? For six days Kennedy huddled with close advisers in secret meetings while news of the missiles was kept from the public. Most advisers favored an air strike on the missile sites. Kennedy thought this too risky. What if some Soviet workers were killed? Would Khrushchev feel that he had to retaliate?

On October 22, 1962, the President went on television to tell the public about the Soviet missiles in Cuba. He announced that the United States was blockading Cuba. Navy ships would stop all approaching vessels and search them for weapons. Kennedy warned the Soviets to remove the missiles already in place or further steps would be taken.

Two days later, as the world held its breath, Soviet ships approached the blockade. A message finally arrived at the White House, announcing that

Aerial photographs taken from a U-2 spy plane in 1962 revealed a Soviet-built missile launch site in Cuba. In the ensuing crisis the superpowers came as close as they have ever come to a nuclear war. **POLITICS** What connection existed between the Soviet missiles in Cuba and American missiles in Turkey? 9A

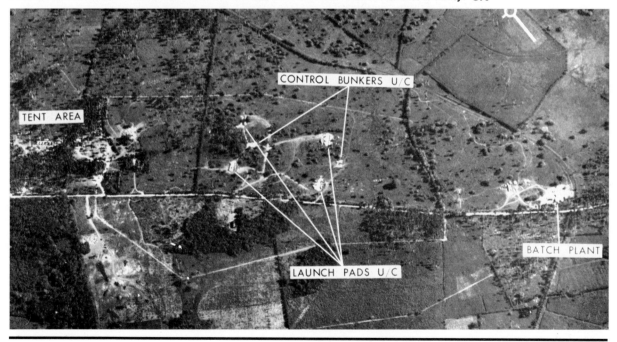

Photo Caption Answer
Each country considered the stationing of enemy missiles in a neighboring country unacceptable. The United States agreed to remove its missiles in Turkey as part of the resolution of the Cuban missile crisis.

Background   In 1963 JFK visited West Berlin and said, "All free men, wherever they may live, are citizens of Berlin. And therefore, as a free man, I take pride in the words 'Ich bin ein Berliner.'"

Addressing Individual Needs

Guided/ Independent Practice
Instruct students to complete **Reinforcement Workbook** Worksheet 81, in which students complete a chart showing causes and outcomes of Kennedy's major foreign policy confrontations.

Reteaching/Correctives
Have students work in pairs to develop illustrated timelines of the events described in this section. Have students make sure that their drawings illustrate Kennedy's foreign policy and the cold war. Display student timelines on a wall of the classroom.

Have students complete **Reteaching Resources** Worksheet 81, which helps them remember the main ideas and supporting details in the section.

Enrichment/Extension
Assign **Enrichment and Extension Resources** Primary Source Worksheet 41, in which students analyze a campaign speech by Kennedy about American foreign policy towards the newly emerging nations of Africa.

Assessment
You may wish to use the Section 1 Review, page 500, to see how well your students understand the main points in this lesson.

Section Review Answers

1. *flexible response*—Policy of building up both nuclear and non-nuclear forces to meet foreign crises. *Peace Corps*—Government group which sent American volunteers to help developing nations. *Alliance for Progress*—U.S. foreign aid to Latin American nations to develop their economies and counteract the appeal of communism. *Berlin Wall*—Erected by Communists to prevent

500

escape from East Berlin.
Nuclear Test-Ban Treaty—Agreement with Soviet Union to stop nuclear testing in the air and under water.

2. *John F. Kennedy*—Elected President in 1960. *Richard M. Nixon*—Republican candidate for President in 1960. *Lyndon B. Johnson*—JFK's Vice President, had been a Texas senator. *Fidel Castro*—Communist leader of Cuba. *Bay of Pigs*—Failed invasion of Cuba by anti-Castro emigres, sponsored by CIA. *Nikita Khrushchev*—Soviet leader during Kennedy's presidency. *Robert Kennedy*—JFK's brother and the U.S. Attorney General.

3. Massive retaliation required the willingness to use nuclear weapons to stop Communist threats while flexible response gave the United States the option of using non-nuclear forces.

4. An expected popular uprising did not occur and Castro's troops easily defeated the invaders.

5. Students might note that both events triggered military mobilization, but there was no actual military confrontation. Students should understand that the existence of nuclear weapons causes nations to try very hard to prevent all-out war.

Closure

Use the Chapter Review Summary for Section 1 (p. 512) to synthesize the important elements in the section. Then have students read Section 2 for the next class period, noting Kennedy's domestic policies.

---

the Soviet ships had stopped, and some were turning back.

But the crisis was not over. Four more days passed before a cable arrived from Khrushchev offering a deal. If the United States pledged not to invade Cuba, the missiles would be removed. Then a second cable arrived, bearing a new demand. The United States had nuclear missiles in Turkey, and now the Soviets wanted those missiles dismantled.

In fact, the United States already planned to remove the outdated missiles in Turkey. However, most of Kennedy's advisers were dead set against making a deal. Kennedy should not even *appear* to be making concessions to Khrushchev, they argued. That would only encourage more Soviet recklessness. Instead, these advisers repeated the call for a bombing strike on Cuba. National Security Adviser McGeorge Bundy said, "If we appear to be trading the defense of Turkey for the threat in Cuba, then we will face a radical decline."

The President's brother, Robert Kennedy, then offered another idea. Robert Kennedy was the Attorney General and JFK's most trusted adviser. Like his brother, Robert believed that an attack on Cuba should be the last option. He suggested that the President privately assure the Soviets that the United States would remove its missiles from Turkey. In return, the Soviet Union would withdraw its missiles from Cuba but would agree not to say that a deal had been made. The Soviets accepted the proposal, and the crisis passed.

THE MISSILE CRISIS ANALYZED 2B, 2C

During that week and a half in October 1962, the world came closer to nuclear destruction than ever before—or since. What lessons can we draw from the crisis? Some historians say that Kennedy was too soft. They believe that the United States should have invaded Cuba and ousted Castro, and should never have given up its missiles in Turkey. Others say that Kennedy was too tough. They argue that since the United States had nuclear missiles based just outside the Soviet Union, it should have accepted Soviet missiles based near the United States.

Defenders of Kennedy, on the other hand, argue that he achieved the best result possible. An air

strike or invasion of Cuba would almost certainly have prompted a Soviet attack somewhere else, such as Berlin. Doing nothing about the missiles in Cuba would have demoralized American allies and destroyed public confidence in Kennedy. What Kennedy did, his backers claim, was combine firmness and flexibility to lead the world out of the crisis.

While the debate over the Cuban missile crisis continues, few can doubt that it marked the peak of the cold war. In the years that followed, while the United States and the Soviet Union remained far apart on many issues, there were hopeful signs of progress. In June 1963 Kennedy delivered a speech at American University in which he called for improved superpower relations. That same year the United States, the Soviet Union, and Great Britain agreed to stop testing nuclear weapons in the air and under water. The agreement was called the Nuclear Test-Ban Treaty. Underground testing continued, but it did not threaten the environment as much as these other tests.

In his speech at American University, Kennedy made one of his most eloquent statements on global peace. "In the final analysis," he said, "our most basic link is that we all inhabit this small planet. We all breathe the same air. We all cherish our children's future. And we are all mortal."

SECTION REVIEW

1. KEY TERMS flexible response, Peace Corps, Alliance for Progress, Berlin Wall, Nuclear Test-Ban Treaty

2. PEOPLE AND PLACES John F. Kennedy, Richard M. Nixon, Lyndon B. Johnson, Fidel Castro, Bay of Pigs, Nikita Khrushchev, Robert Kennedy

3. COMPREHENSION How did flexible response differ from the Eisenhower administration's idea of massive retaliation?

4. COMPREHENSION Why did the Bay of Pigs invasion fail?

5. CRITICAL THINKING Compare the ways in which the crises over Berlin and the Cuban missiles were solved. What lessons can you draw regarding crisis diplomacy in the nuclear age?

Background In August 1963, Kennedy and Khrushchev set up a hot line (direct telephone communication) between Washington and Moscow as a further effort to reduce the chances of accidental nuclear war.

2 A Thousand Days

Section Focus

Key Terms New Frontier ■ urban renewal ■ Warren Commission

Main Idea Kennedy called for a new direction in government, but he could not move many reform measures through Congress.

Objectives As you read, look for answers to these questions:
1. Why did Kennedy face trouble in getting his domestic programs through Congress?
2. What were Kennedy's goals for the economy and the space program?
3. What event cut short the Kennedy administration?

Kennedy brought a charm, eloquence, and wit to the presidency that fascinated the American people. Nobel Prize winners, poets, movie stars, and musicians flocked to the White House to attend a series of glittering banquets hosted by the young President and his dazzling wife Jacqueline.

6B

President Kennedy's daughter, Caroline, holds her father's hand as she skips along the White House veranda. Not only was Kennedy the youngest elected President, but his children were the youngest to live in the White House for over 60 years. **CULTURE** What did the Kennedy White House represent for the American public?

Under the Kennedys, the White House became the center of American art and culture as well as power.

Critics of Kennedy's presidency argued that below "the Kennedy style" there was not enough substance. He lacked, they said, the courage and skill to make the reforms he called for so eloquently. There may be some truth to this criticism. Yet Kennedy's greatness lay in his ability to inspire political commitment in others. In the words of his Inaugural Address, "Ask not what your country can do for you—ask what you can do for your country." Kennedy convinced people—especially the young—that they could accomplish great things. He made them see that they could make the world more decent, more just, and more beautiful.

> "**A**sk not what your country can do for you—ask what you can do for your country."
>
> —*John F. Kennedy, 1961*

THE NEW FRONTIER 4D

"We stand today on the edge of a new frontier," Kennedy announced in accepting the nomination for President. He called upon Americans to be "new pioneers" and explore "uncharted areas of science and space, . . . unconquered pockets of ignorance and prejudice, unanswered questions of poverty and surplus."

SUPPORTING THE SECTION

Reinforcement Workbook: Worksheet 82
Reteaching Resources: Worksheet 82
Enrichment and Extension Resources: Primary Source Worksheet 42
Teaching Transparencies: Transparency 82

Photo Caption Answer
Students may suggest youth, charm, elegance, and culture.

SECTION 2

A Thousand Days
(pp. 501–505)

Section Objective
■ determine the obstacles to the adoption of President Kennedy's domestic policies

Introducing the Section

Connecting with Past Learnings
Review domestic policy in the 1950s by asking students to describe President Eisenhower's modern Republicanism. (Eisenhower did not scrap the liberal programs of the New Deal, but he tried to keep the role of government limited, especially in connection with the economy.)

Key Terms
Call on students to define the key terms in their own words. Be sure students know the literal meaning of *frontier,* the edge of settlement. **LEP**

Focus
On the board draw a scorecard with win and loss columns for President Kennedy. Call on students to identify the problems he attempted to solve through legislation and indicate in which column it should be listed. *On which issues was Kennedy successful in getting legislation passed?* (Increased minimum wage, funds for urban renewal.) *Why was he not more successful?* (Much of his legislation was blocked by Republicans and conservative southern Democrats.) Have students copy the chart into their notebooks, to be used in the next lesson.

Remind students that Kennedy had called for leadership to solve the problems of the New Frontier. Ask students to rate his leadership.

501

Developing the Lesson

After students have read the section, you may want to consider the following activities:

National Identity

Help students understand how JFK inspired Americans by describing his vision as a "New Frontier." **What qualities were American pioneers on the western frontier supposed to have?** (Courage, strength, inventiveness, honesty, etc.) Discuss why *frontier,* with all its connotations of fearless problem-solving, was a good choice of words to label Kennedy's goals.

Economics

Help students understand why Kennedy's proposed tax cut was supposed to raise revenues to be used for social programs by having the class draw a flow chart showing the impact of the tax cut on the economy and on federal revenues. (Tax cut would mean more money to spend, which would increase demand and expand the economy; increased economic activity would generate more taxes to pay for social programs.)

Analyzing Controversial Issues

Discuss with students the questions raised by Kennedy's assassination. Have them consider why many private citizens doubted the findings of the Warren Commission. Interested students may research and report on other theories on the assassination.

Kennedy's New Frontier program suggested grand reforms, but provided few plans for achieving them. Kennedy had little patience with the details of government. He distrusted bureaucracy and believed he could get things done with an executive branch filled with smart, aggressive achievers.

Kennedy chose people, as one adviser put it, who were "young and vigorous and *tough.*" Members of his Cabinet—one of the youngest in history—had an average age of 47. Robert McNamara, president of the Ford Motor Company, became Secretary of Defense. Dean Rusk, president of the Rockefeller Foundation, was named Secretary of State. The President also worked closely with a circle of advisers outside the Cabinet—a group of long-term associates and Ivy League academics.

No matter how talented the executive branch, only Congress can pass laws. And while Kennedy's advisers may have been "tough," they were mostly tough in foreign policy, not in pursuit of domestic legislation. Kennedy had plans to improve housing, education, and health care, but he could not get the votes he needed in Congress. A combination of Republicans and conservative southern Democrats, the same combination that defeated much of Truman's Fair Deal, blocked most of his social programs.

Kennedy did win an increase in the minimum wage from $1 to $1.25 an hour. He also got Congress to approve $5 billion in urban renewal—programs to rebuild run-down areas of the nation's cities. Proposals of aid for education and health insurance for the elderly met defeat, however.

In the area of civil rights, Kennedy failed to press hard for new laws. With an eye toward winning re-election in 1964, he feared losing support from white southerners who opposed federal enforcement of civil rights for blacks. Yet Kennedy could not ignore the energy and commitment of the civil rights movement. As we will see in Chapter 22, the early 1960s was a key period in the growth of a mass movement calling for an end to discrimination.

In 1963 Kennedy finally made a strong plea for civil rights legislation. Addressing the nation, he asked, "Are we to say to the world and . . . to each

---

THE PRESIDENTS

John F. Kennedy

1961–1963

35th President, Democrat

- Born May 29, 1917, in Massachusetts
- Married Jacqueline Bouvier in 1953; 2 children
- Representative and senator from Massachusetts
- Lived in Massachusetts when elected President
- Vice President: Lyndon B. Johnson
- Assassinated November 22, 1963, in Dallas, Texas
- Key events while in office: 23rd Amendment; Bay of Pigs invasion; Berlin Wall built; Cuban missile crisis; Peace Corps and Alliance for Progress created

---

other that this is a land of the free except for Negroes; that we have no second-class citizens except Negroes?"

KENNEDY'S ECONOMIC PROGRAM 3E, 3F

Kennedy took office during a recession. The economy, which had performed splendidly through most of the 1950s, had slowed at the end of the decade. Unemployment hovered at one of the highest levels since World War II—around 7 percent. Now, under Kennedy, the economy moved upward, fueled by heavy federal spending on military and space projects.

In his economic views, Kennedy was a moderate. He shared with liberals a desire to see government do more to relieve hardship and sickness.

502 UNIT 8   TIMES OF TURMOIL

The Presidents
JFK was the youngest man ever elected President. His Cabinet was also one of the youngest in history. Ask students to discuss the pros and cons of such a young administration.

Background In addition to Rusk and McNamara, JFK's Cabinet included C. Douglas Dillon (Treasury), Robert F. Kennedy (Attorney General), J. Edward Day (Postmaster General), Stewart L. Udall (Interior), Orville L. Freeman (Agriculture), Luther H. Hodges (Commerce), Arthur J.

Goldberg (Labor), Abraham A. Ribicoff (Health, Education, and Welfare).

Yet his chief aim was to spur economic growth by encouraging cooperation between business and labor.

The focus of this cooperation was on wages and prices. During the 1950s, workers had demanded higher and higher wages from their employers. Business leaders had granted these demands, passing off their higher labor costs in the form of higher prices. As a result, American goods were more expensive and thus more difficult to sell abroad.

Kennedy wanted both sides to agree to guidelines in wages and prices. That is, workers would limit their salary demands, and businesses would limit their price increases. In 1962, steelworkers honored the guidelines by accepting a small wage increase. However, the U.S. Steel Company promptly raised the price of steel by $6 per ton. This increase outraged Kennedy. Believing the price hike would cause inflation, he called it "an irresponsible defiance of the public interest." JFK had the Department of Defense cancel its millions of dollars worth of contracts with U.S. Steel. That, and other forms of pressure, led the company to withdraw its price hike.

For the most part, however, Kennedy was not anti-business. Later in 1962 he offered corporations a large tax break. He also pushed for a trade bill that would increase American exports. When steel companies began raising prices in 1963, Kennedy took no action against them.

FIGHTING POVERTY 3F

While JFK spent the rest of his presidency improving his relations with the business community, he also became more concerned about poverty. In 1962, Michael Harrington wrote a book called *The Other America*. It told of the terrible pockets of poverty that existed throughout the country. Using government statistics, Harrington found more than 42 million "other" Americans—families making do on less than $1,000 per person for a whole year.

Many Americans, like Kennedy, knew little about poverty in the United States. Most middle-class and wealthy people lived in the suburbs. Poor people were clustered in urban slums and remote rural areas. Prosperous Americans, who traveled on superhighways and by plane, simply had not seen what was going on around them. Like Jacob Riis's *How the Other Half Lives* of 1890, *The Other America* described the squalor amidst prosperity. As one writer put it, "We seem to have suddenly awakened, rubbing our eyes like Rip van Winkle, to the fact that mass poverty persists."

In 1963, JFK called for a "national assault on the causes of poverty." Yet he did not offer a strong program to fight poverty. His major economic goal at the time was to cut personal income taxes. He believed that would stimulate the economy and produce more jobs. However, the federal government was already spending more than it was taking in. Congress rejected the tax cut.

NEW FRONTIERS IN SPACE 4E

Launching the United States into space exploration was one of Kennedy's top priorities. In 1961 the Soviet Union made history by sending a man into space—the cosmonaut Yuri Gagarin. Kennedy was determined to overtake the Soviets in space. Shortly after taking office, JFK made a daring proposal. "I believe that this nation should commit itself to achieving the goal, before this decade is out," he said, "of landing a man on the moon and returning him safely to earth."

Space flight was largely the outgrowth of the cold war. The missiles developed to carry capsules into space were based on the technology used to carry nuclear warheads to their targets. However, the goal of sending *people* into space had little military significance. Nor did it promise great scientific discoveries. Machines existed that could collect data more efficiently, and far more cheaply, than humans. But in the highly charged atmosphere of the cold war, manned space flight became a matter of pride—a sign of national courage and achievement. Both the United States and the Soviet Union believed their world reputation depended on supremacy in space.

The space program fascinated the American people. In the early 1960s, whenever space flights were launched during school hours, students would gather in gyms and auditoriums to watch the lift-offs on television. The early astronauts, such as John Glenn (who in 1962 became the first

Background Almost twenty years after Kennedy proposed a tax cut to raise revenues, President Ronald Reagan offered a tax cut of his own. Reagan's supply-side economics were aimed at stimulating the private sector, however, not at raising money to fund social programs.

Background Kennedy also succeeded in getting Congress to approve aid to economically depressed areas in April 1961.

Impact of Geography
Have students locate the major space centers—Cape Canaveral, Florida; Huntsville, Alabama; Houston, Texas—on a map. Discuss reasons for locating space centers there. (Good weather, access to water transportation for moving rockets on barges, good launch site.) *Why might conservative southern members of Congress have supported President Kennedy's space program?* (The space program meant a huge boost to the economies of their states.)

C **Cooperative Learning**

Divide students into small groups and ask each group to brainstorm ways in which President Kennedy might have been more effective in getting his legislation through Congress. Have each group report its suggestions to the whole class. Students should begin to see the complexities of "horse trading" that would be necessary to pass so much new social legislation. **LEP**

Addressing Individual Needs

Guided/ Independent Practice
Have students complete **Reinforcement Workbook** Worksheet 82. In this worksheet students analyze federal expenditures during the Kennedy years for an understanding of national priorities.

Reteaching/Correctives
Direct students' attention to the objectives under the Section Focus on page 501. Have students change each question into a statement and list the statements on a piece of paper. Beneath each statement, have students list important details that explain or add to it.

American to orbit the earth), were national heroes. Their courage and optimism recalled the exploits of earlier American pioneers.

The race to the moon continued through the
1960s. Besides the Vietnam War (Chapter 23), it
was the nation's single most expensive project of
the decade, costing $25 billion.

> # "That's one small step for a man, one giant leap for mankind."
> —*Astronaut Neil Armstrong*

Then, on July 16, 1969, three astronauts took off
in a spacecraft named Apollo 11. A Saturn 5
rocket the height of a 36-story building thrust
their capsule into space. The voyage to the moon
took three days. More than 500 million people
around the world gathered around television sets
showing live pictures of the moon landing. They
watched as Neil Armstrong descended a small ladder to step onto the moon's surface. Placing his
foot into the lunar dust, Armstrong proclaimed,
"That's one small step for a man, one giant leap
for mankind."

TRAGEDY IN DALLAS 5B

John Kennedy never lived to see the space voyage
he had set in motion. On November 22, 1963, he
was assassinated in Dallas, Texas.

Kennedy had gone to Texas to build support for
his 1964 re-election campaign. He rode through
the streets of Dallas in the back of an open limou-
sine, waving and smiling at the crowds, when
shots rang out. The President slumped over in his
seat. The driver raced to a hospital, but there was
no hope. A bullet had shattered his brain.

It is difficult to describe the effect that John
Kennedy's death had on the American people. For
a President so young and full of vitality to die so
suddenly seemed unbelievable. The nation went
into shock, as did people around the globe. Long
after his death, in remote villages of the world,
visitors would find pictures of John Kennedy in
the homes of even the poorest peasants. And practically all Americans who were alive on November

22, 1963, remember exactly what they were doing
when they first heard the news of the President's
death.

The suspected assassin was Lee Harvey Oswald. Two days after Kennedy's death, while being transferred to another jail, Oswald too was
murdered, by a Dallas nightclub owner named
Jack Ruby. With Oswald dead, many questions
went unanswered. Was Oswald the assassin? Had
he acted alone? Had there been a conspiracy to
murder the President?

On the plane carrying the slain President's body
back to Washington, Vice President Lyndon Johnson was sworn in as the new President. One of his
first acts was to appoint a commission, headed by
Chief Justice Earl Warren, to investigate Kennedy's assassination.

The Warren Commission concluded that Oswald had been the assassin and that he had acted
on his own. However, many questions remained
unanswered. Private citizens have launched their

This photograph shows John F. Kennedy's coffin inside the rotunda
of the Capitol in Washington, D.C. People around the world
mourned the loss of a leader who seemed to embody intelligence,
courage, and hope for the future. POLITICS Evaluate the success
of Kennedy's domestic programs. 9A

own investigations. Many still claim that Oswald was part of a conspiracy. Still, no convincing proof of a conspiracy exists.

President for just "a thousand days," Kennedy met with many failures in office. He mishandled the Bay of Pigs invasion, had a poor legislative record, and responded slowly to the challenges of civil rights and poverty. Yet Kennedy also left a positive legacy, one that has overshadowed his failures. He understood the power of words and ideas. He knew that the President has the unique ability—perhaps even the duty—to pull Americans together. Would his abilities have helped the United States cope with the challenges it would face during the late 1960s? The answer can be guessed at, but never known.

1A, 1B, 4C, 4D, 5B, 5D, 6A, 7B, 7F, 7G, 7H, 7J, 9A, 9D

3 "All the Way with LBJ"

★ Section Focus

Key Terms Civil Rights Act of 1964 ■ Office of Economic Opportunity ■ judicial activism ■ Great Society ■ Medicare

Main Idea After Kennedy's assassination, Lyndon Johnson took the reins of power and maneuvered both JFK's proposals and his own programs through Congress. In time, however, a conflict in Southeast Asia crippled Johnson's domestic program.

Objectives As you read, look for answers to these questions:
1. How successful was President Johnson in getting domestic legislation passed?
2. Why did the decisions of the Warren Court stir controversy?
3. How did Johnson's foreign policy affect his domestic programs?

Five days after Kennedy's assassination, the nation was still in mourning. Both houses of Congress gathered to hear the new President—the tall, somber-looking Lyndon Baines Johnson. LBJ had been a major figure in American politics for years. Yet there was great uncertainty about how he would act as President.

Johnson began his speech on a humble note: "All I have, I would have given gladly not to be stand-

ing here today." But Johnson was not a humble man. He had enormous ambition and a passion for political power. Fate had thrust him into the highest office, and he was not about to be a passive caretaker. He wanted to put his own stamp on American life, and the sooner the better.

Johnson's speech before Congress, his first major address as President, reflected his great political skill. He promised to continue the programs

---

SECTION REVIEW

1. KEY TERMS New Frontier, urban renewal, Warren Commission

2. PEOPLE Robert McNamara, Dean Rusk, Michael Harrington, Yuri Gagarin, John Glenn, Neil Armstrong, Lee Harvey Oswald, Jack Ruby

3. COMPREHENSION Why did Kennedy have trouble getting Congress to pass his domestic legislation?

4. COMPREHENSION How did the cold war affect the nation's space program?

5. CRITICAL THINKING How, in your opinion, might Kennedy's assassination have influenced the public's view of him and his presidency?

---

5. Kennedy died before he had a chance to get many of his programs passed by Congress, so people remember his upbeat style more than the substance of his accomplishments. Also, because he was killed in office, he is remembered as a slain hero, not a politician.

Closure

Call students' attention to the beige boxed quotation (p. 501). Ask them to relate this quotation to the main idea of the section. Then have students read Section 3 for the next class period. Tell them to look for specific differences between Kennedy and Johnson.

SECTION 3

"All the Way with LBJ"
(pp. 505–511)

Section Objectives
■ explain President Johnson's success in gaining congressional approval of social legislation
■ describe the major cases decided by the Supreme Court under Chief Justice Earl Warren

Introducing the Section

Connecting with Past Learnings
Remind students that Lyndon Johnson entered politics as a New Deal congressman. *What were the goals of New Deal legislation?* (To end high unemployment and insure a decent standard of living for Americans.)

Kennedy had proposed. Although Congress had already rejected most of Kennedy's proposals, LBJ called for immediate action. "The ideas and ideals [Kennedy] so nobly represented," he said, "must and will be translated into effective action."

Johnson used national grief to build support for legislation. Nothing, said Johnson, "could more eloquently honor President Kennedy's memory than the earliest possible passage of the civil rights bill for which he fought." Johnson used the same words to demand quick passage of a tax cut. How could Congress refuse? To do so, Johnson suggested, would be to reject the ideals of a national hero. "Let us here highly resolve that John Fitzgerald Kennedy did not live—or die—in vain."

It was a moving and effective speech. Some members of Congress wept openly. In one stroke, Johnson had both honored Kennedy and established himself as a forceful leader. LBJ later told some senators, "They say Jack Kennedy had style, but I'm the one who got the bills passed."

> "**T**hey say Jack Kennedy had style, but I'm the one who got the bills passed."
> —*Lyndon Johnson*

JOHNSON'S PATH TO POWER 7H

Who was this man "who got the bills passed"? LBJ liked to describe himself as a poor boy from the Texas hill country. Johnson, in fact, had not been poor. Still, he had grown up among poor people and had a keen sense of the pain and insecurity poverty brings. His father was a state legislator who fought on behalf of struggling farmers and small ranchers. His mother grew up in a once-prosperous family that lost much of its money. She devoted herself to Lyndon, pushing him to gain the education and respect she so much wanted for herself.

After graduating from college, Johnson taught high school. But his true interest lay in politics. When a congressional seat opened in 1937, he jumped into the race with great energy. He visited almost every voter in his district, building an

This 1937 photograph shows LBJ (center) conversing with President Franklin Roosevelt (left) and Texas governor James V. Allred. LBJ supported Roosevelt's New Deal and received the President's support in his 1937 campaign for representative from Texas. POLITICS Describe LBJ's political style. 9A

image as a Roosevelt New Dealer. At 29, he became one of the youngest members of Congress.

In Congress, Johnson gained the help of wealthy Texas businessmen. They helped him win election to the Senate in 1948. With his talent for behind-the-scenes maneuvering, Johnson was able to bring together people with very different political views. He mastered the art of political compromise, and in 1955 became Senate Majority Leader.

Johnson's ability to influence people in private became a legend. Whatever it took to win his way, LBJ tried it—praise, ridicule, humor, gifts, threats, appeals to patriotism, appeals to power. This "Johnson treatment" was always a physical ordeal. Johnson surrounded his targets with his huge body, pawing, poking, and getting so close you could feel his breath. Sometimes people gave in from sheer exhaustion.

DOMESTIC LEGISLATION 6A, 7B, 7J

Johnson himself never seemed to tire. He worked at least fourteen hours a day, and demanded the same of his staff. In keeping with his pledge to continue where Kennedy had left off, Johnson decided to keep Kennedy's Cabinet and advisers. He knew that he needed the loyalty of Kennedy Democrats to succeed with his legislative plans.

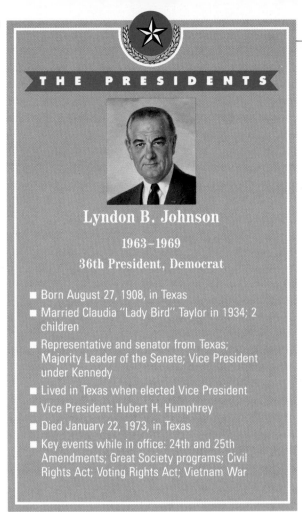

THE PRESIDENTS

Lyndon B. Johnson

1963–1969

36th President, Democrat

- Born August 27, 1908, in Texas
- Married Claudia "Lady Bird" Taylor in 1934; 2 children
- Representative and senator from Texas; Majority Leader of the Senate; Vice President under Kennedy
- Lived in Texas when elected Vice President
- Vice President: Hubert H. Humphrey
- Died January 22, 1973, in Texas
- Key events while in office: 24th and 25th Amendments; Great Society programs; Civil Rights Act; Voting Rights Act; Vietnam War

Since less than a year remained before the next presidential election, Johnson had to move quickly. He needed immediate results, and he sought them at home, in domestic reform. Kennedy had always been a bit bored by domestic legislation, reserving his passion for world affairs. Johnson was the opposite. He thrived on national politics and viewed the international scene as a source of trouble.

The Civil Rights Act of 1964 was Johnson's first important piece of legislation. The act made it illegal for employers to deny someone a job because of race, sex, or religion. It also gave the government the power to use the courts to desegregate schools and other public places.

He also quickly won the tax cut Kennedy had proposed. Conservative Republicans opposed the tax cut, fearful that it would deprive the government of money needed to balance the budget.

Democrats argued that the tax cut would stimulate the economy. If the economy boomed, they said, people would make more money. Thus, even if tax rates were lower, the government would receive more money in total.

The economy did boom. There was a surge of faith in the capacity of government to improve society. As LBJ put it to one of his advisers, "I'm sick of all the people who talk about the things we can't do. We're the richest country in the world, the most powerful. We can do it all, if we're not too greedy."

What Johnson most wanted to do was to end human suffering. At the beginning of 1964, he declared a war on poverty and created an Office of Economic Opportunity (OEO). Headed by Sargent Shriver, a Kennedy in-law, the OEO launched an ambitious variety of programs. Many were designed for disadvantaged children and teenagers. Head Start, for example, offered preschool education to children in poor neighborhoods. The most innovative idea was a Community Action Program. This program tried to involve poor people in creating their own projects to improve local neighborhoods.

7F, 7G, 7H

The Johnson administration oversaw the creation of public service programs including VISTA (Volunteers in Service to America). Here, VISTA volunteers work with young schoolchildren. Other VISTA jobs included food distribution and health care. **CIVIC VALUES** What are some of the rewards of volunteer work?

Developing the Lesson
After students have read the section, you may want to consider the following activities:

Economics
Write these budget statistics on the board:

	Income	Expenditures
1963	$106,560 million	$111,311 million
1968	153,671 million	178,833 million

What is happening to the level of total federal spending? (Increasing.) *Where is the money coming from and where is it going?* (Greater tax revenue from booming economy; spent on space, social programs, Vietnam War.) *Is there enough money to pay for these expenditures?* (No.) *What happened to the federal budget deficit between 1963 and 1968?* (More than quintupled.) *Why did Johnson support this high level of spending?* (He was willing to create an enormous deficit, as the New Deal had done.)

Patterns in History
One of the most serious problems facing the United States in the 1990s is its huge budget deficit. *How did Johnson's economic policies help create today's large deficits?* (He created expensive programs which still exist today and must be paid for.) Have students compare the U.S. economy of this decade with that of the 1960s, noting the similarities and difference leading to deficit spending by the government.

Civic Values
In accepting the Republican nomination in 1964, Goldwater said, "I would remind you that extremism in the defense of liberty is no vice. And let me remind you also that moderation in the pursuit of justice is no virtue." Have students discuss what Goldwater meant and whether they agree with him.

Constitutional Heritage
How did the Warren Court extend the rights of people accused of crimes? (It required states to provide lawyers for poor defendants, allow lawyers present when people were questioned, and read people their rights as they were being arrested.) In recent years, some people have argued that the Supreme Court went too far in extending the rights of the accused at the expense of the safety and security of the general public. Have students give examples of this, and ask them if they agree with the Warren Court or its critics.

THE ELECTION OF 1964 5B

As Johnson was pushing ahead with social welfare programs, the Republican Party was moving in the opposite direction. Its nomination of Arizona Senator Barry Goldwater to represent the party in the 1964 presidential election marked a sharp move to the right. A crusty, straightforward man, Goldwater supported "rugged individualism" and believed the federal government had no business trying to end poverty or advance civil rights. He even attacked such long-standing federal programs as Social Security as being the first steps toward socialism.

There was one area in which Goldwater did call for more spending—defense. He accused the Democrats of backing down in the face of Communist uprisings, especially in Vietnam. LBJ had carried on Kennedy's efforts to build up a non-Communist government in South Vietnam (Chapter 23), but he had pledged not to use combat soldiers. Goldwater wanted all-out United States intervention to defeat the Communists in Vietnam. His talk was so blunt and tough that many feared he would lead the nation into nuclear war.

Republicans nominated Barry Goldwater for President in 1964, but the Arizona senator's candidacy came at the wrong time. Goldwater won only his home state and part of the Deep South. POLITICS What were some of Goldwater's positions on political issues? 5B

Goldwater hoped that his strong views would bring him public support. His campaign offered "a choice, not an echo," according to one ad. The choice was indeed clear, but so was the preference of the American people. Goldwater's extreme conservatism did not match the political mood of the 1960s. Liberalism was at its high point in modern American history. Most people believed that the American government, backed by a strong economy, could and should work for greater fairness and equality. On Election Day, Johnson demolished Goldwater, winning by a whopping sixteen million votes. Just as important, Democrats increased their majorities in both houses of Congress.

AN ACTIVIST COURT 5D

The Supreme Court mirrored the nation's liberal leanings during these years. President Eisenhower had named Earl Warren as Chief Justice in 1953. Eisenhower thought that Warren, a fellow Republican, would be pro-business, tough on crime, and moderate on civil rights. Instead Warren, who remained on the bench for sixteen years, led the most liberal (and perhaps the most powerful) Court in history.

In one key case, the Court showed that it intended to play a role in determining the makeup of legislatures. By 1960 about 80 percent of Americans lived in cities and suburbs. Nevertheless, many states continued to overrepresent rural areas. For example, a rural district with 100,000 people might have the same number of representatives as an urban district that had 300,000 people. *Baker v. Carr* (1962) was the first of several Supreme Court decisions that made such arrangements illegal. These decisions upheld the principle of "one person, one vote."

Other cases strengthened the rights of people accused of crimes. In *Gideon v. Wainwright* (1963) the Court required state courts to provide a lawyer in criminal cases to anyone who could not afford to hire one. In *Escobedo v. Illinois* (1964) the Court declared that an accused person has a right to have a lawyer present when being questioned by police. And in *Miranda v. Arizona* (1966) the Court ruled that police must inform suspects of their legal rights at the time of arrest.

508 UNIT 8 TIMES OF TURMOIL

Photo Caption Answer
He opposed social welfare programs and government involvement in civil rights. He supported an all-out military commitment to South Vietnam.

Background Johnson appointed the first black justice to the Supreme Court, Thurgood Marshall (page 517). Marshall had led the attack on school segregation in *Brown v. Board of Education* in 1954.

Outraged conservatives attacked Chief Justice Earl Warren's views on racial integration and suspects' rights. Warren kept his seat on the bench until 1969. **CONSTITUTIONAL HERITAGE** Would you have supported the Court's decision in *Gideon v. Wainright*? Why or why not? **5D**

Liberals praised the Court, arguing that it was simply placing necessary limits on police power and protecting citizens' right to a fair trial. Conservatives were livid. They claimed that the rulings handicapped the police and put hard-core criminals back on the streets. Billboards appeared urging, "Impeach Earl Warren." Republican office-seekers hammered away at the crime issue, presenting the Supreme Court (and the Democratic Party) as being soft on crime.

There was a certain irony to conservatives' attacks on the Warren Court. Thirty years earlier, Franklin Roosevelt had blasted the Supreme Court for declaring some of his New Deal programs unconstitutional. He had argued then that the Court should not overturn laws passed by a democratically elected legislature. Now, in the 1960s, conservative Republicans were making much the same argument. They accused the Court of *judicial activism*—making laws instead of interpreting them.

The debate over the wisdom of judicial activism continues today. People tend to support judicial activism when they agree with the Court's rulings and oppose it when they disagree with those rulings.

BUILDING THE GREAT SOCIETY 4D

As Johnson's legislative proposals took shape, he began to describe his overall vision of change. In 1964 he urged Americans to seek a **Great Society**. "The Great Society," he said, "demands an end to poverty and racial injustice." But it should also be a place that serves "the desire for beauty and the hunger for community," a place where people "are more concerned with the quality of their goals than the quantity of their goods."

> "The Great Society demands an end to poverty and racial injustice."
>
> —*Lyndon Johnson*

Johnson's vision of the Great Society included neighborhood beautification programs. Here, the President's wife, known as "Lady Bird," drops a shovelful of dirt around a newly planted tree on a rainy day in 1966. **POLITICS** With what issue did the majority of Great Society programs deal? **2C, 4D**

Cooperative Learning

Divide the class into teams. Each team must make up ten questions (with answers) on this section; each team member must contribute at least one question. Pair off teams and have them quiz each other. When they have finished all questions, switch pairs and repeat. **LEP**

Addressing Individual Needs

Guided/Independent Practice
Have students complete **Reinforcement Workbook** Worksheet 83, which helps them make judgments about the section.

Reteaching/Correctives
Divide the class into small groups. Have students imagine that they are political analysts and are evaluating Johnson's domestic policies. Have students begin by taking notes on the important actions in Johnson's administration; then reshape these notes into an opinion paper.

Assign **Reteaching Resources** Worksheet 83, in which students will make a chart about LBJ.

Enrichment/Extension
Have students do research on one of the Supreme Court cases mentioned in the section and report back their findings to the class.

In the years 1964–1966, with huge Democratic majorities in Congress, Johnson had a chance to advance his Great Society programs. In those years Congress passed more reform legislation than at any time since the New Deal of the 1930s. Many of these laws dealt with civil rights issues and will be discussed in Chapter 22.

Great Society programs did not end poverty, but they began to reduce it. The Food Stamp Act of 1964 helped poor people buy food. Medicaid, a program established in 1965, provided medical care to those who could not otherwise afford it.

The elderly poor received the most help from the Great Society. In 1960, about 40 percent of the nation's senior citizens were poor. Beginning in 1965, a program called **Medicare** provided medical insurance for those over 65. That, along with greater Social Security benefits, brought the number of elderly poor below 20 percent.

Less successful were efforts to rebuild American cities. The explosive economic and population growth of the 1950s created a host of new problems for the cities. One was a severe shortage of safe, affordable housing. The growing popularity of automobiles created two other problems—pollution and traffic. To handle the problems of the cities, Johnson created a new Cabinet department, the Department of Housing and Urban Development (HUD). It was guided by Robert Weaver, the first black Cabinet head. HUD did make improvements in public housing and mass transit systems. But urban problems were huge, and most of the programs were short on funds.

BIOGRAPHY 4C

ROBERT WEAVER (1907–   ), a great-grandson of slaves, received a Ph.D in economics from Harvard and worked in public housing during the New Deal. He was administrator of the federal Housing and Home Finance Agency when President Johnson expanded the agency into the Department of Housing and Urban Development. Appointed secretary of the new department, Weaver in 1965 became the first African American Cabinet officer.

SOCIAL HISTORY
Famous Firsts

1961   Squibb makes first electric toothbrush.

Alan Shepard, whose flight reaches an altitude of 114 miles and a speed of 5,181 mph, is first American in space.

1963   First privately built and operated nuclear reactor is opened by New Jersey Power and Light at Oyster Creek, New Jersey.

1964   U.S. Surgeon General reports that cigarette smoking is dangerous to one's health.

California surpasses New York as most populous state.

1967   In first football Super Bowl, Green Bay Packers defeat Kansas City Chiefs, 35-10.

1969   The Boeing 747 flies for first time, ushering in the age of jumbo jets.

Richard Nixon places first phone call to moon, when he speaks to astronauts Neil Armstrong and Buzz Aldrin, 240,000 miles away (July 21).

The Great Society had many other goals as well. One was improving American education. The Elementary and Secondary Education Act of 1965 directed more than a billion dollars to needy schools. It was the first large-scale program of federal aid to grade-school education. The administration also made the first significant federal effort to clean up the environment. In response to the pressure of consumer groups, new laws required companies to make safer products.

In recent years the Great Society has received a great deal of criticism but little serious study. To critics, it was a costly and wasteful attempt to solve social and economic problems the federal government has no business handling. On the other hand, some have said that the Great Society fell short of its goals because it did not receive adequate funding. They point out that the money spent on ending poverty was never very great, especially when compared with the tens of billions spent on the space program or the war in Vietnam. However incomplete its success, the Great Society did represent a sincere effort to lift millions of Americans out of poverty.

Biography
Ask students to consider why an advanced degree in economics would be an asset to any contemporary politician. Discuss what other fields of study would be beneficial to a political career.

Famous Firsts
Ask students to write newspaper headlines for each of the items.

Background   Johnson also established the Department of Transportation in 1966.

CONTINUING THE COLD WAR 1B

Although Johnson would gamble on creative domestic legislation, in foreign policy he was more cautious. While in Congress, Johnson had never challenged America's cold war policies. He saw how Republicans had often won votes by claiming that Democrats were not tough enough in foreign policy. Johnson also realized that Kennedy's strong anticommunism had helped him in the 1960 campaign.

Johnson's cold war thinking can be seen in his response to a rebellion in the Dominican Republic. In April 1965, a popular leader named Juan Bosch led a revolt against a Dominican dictator. LBJ, convinced that Bosch was a Communist and would become another Castro, ordered American troops to crush the uprising. The troops remained while support was rallied for a conservative candidate. One year later, when a pro-American government was elected, U.S. troops were called home.

The Dominican intervention further damaged United States relations with Latin America. Yet Johnson could at least claim to have achieved a quick victory. He would not be so lucky in Vietnam. As you will read in Chapter 23, Johnson launched the United States into a major war in Vietnam. As the cost of that war mounted, money had to be drawn away from the ambitious programs of the Great Society. The American people became more and more divided among themselves, and the nation lost faith in its leadership. By 1967, the civil rights leader Martin Luther King, Jr., began to denounce the war in Vietnam. "The Great Society," he claimed, "has been shot down on the battlefields of Vietnam."

U.S. Marines fire at supporters of Juan Bosch during their 1965 intervention in the Dominican Republic. **POLITICS** How might the Bay of Pigs invasion have influenced Johnson's decision to intervene in the Dominican Republic? 1A

SECTION REVIEW

1. KEY TERMS Civil Rights Act of 1964, Office of Economic Opportunity, judicial activism, Great Society, Medicare

2. PEOPLE AND PLACES Sargent Shriver, Barry Goldwater, Earl Warren, Robert Weaver, Dominican Republic

3. COMPREHENSION What arguments were made defending and attacking the decisions of the Warren Court?

4. COMPREHENSION Explain the statement by Martin Luther King, Jr., that "The Great Society has been shot down on the battlefields of Vietnam."

5. CRITICAL THINKING Explain why Johnson had greater success in advancing Kennedy's domestic programs than Kennedy himself enjoyed.

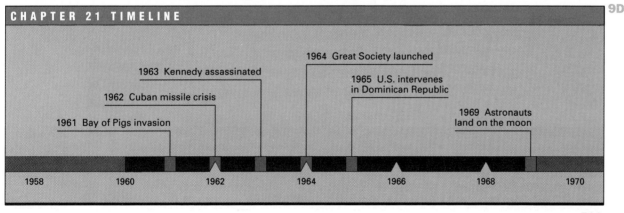

CHAPTER 21 TIMELINE 9D

1961 Bay of Pigs invasion

1962 Cuban missile crisis

1963 Kennedy assassinated

1964 Great Society launched

1965 U.S. intervenes in Dominican Republic

1969 Astronauts land on the moon

1958   1960   1962   1964   1966   1968   1970

Section Review Answers

1. *Civil Rights Act of 1964*—Outlawed discrimination on basis of race, religion, or sex. *Office of Economic Opportunity*—Administered programs of LBJ's war on poverty. *judicial activism*—Courts making laws, not just interpreting them. *Great Society*—LBJ's vision for improving America. *Medicare*—Health insurance for the elderly.

2. *Sargent Shriver*—Administrator of Office of Economic Opportunity. *Barry Goldwater*—Republican candidate for President in 1964. *Earl Warren*—Chief Justice of the United States, appointed by Eisenhower. *Robert Weaver*—First Secretary of HUD and the first black Cabinet member. *Dominican Republic*—Caribbean nation, U.S. troops sent there to put down a revolt.

3. Liberals praised the Court for limiting the power of the police, while conservatives accused it of handicapping the ability of the police to enforce the law.

4. The war took money away from social programs and divided the nation, causing people to question Johnson's leadership.

5. Johnson had more experience and ability at handling Congress. He also used the nation's desire to honor JFK as a means to get his legislation passed.

Closure

Call students' attention to the beige boxed quotation (p. 509). Ask them to relate this quotation to the main idea of the section. Then have students read Section 1 of Chapter 22 for the next class, noting the major events of the early civil rights movement.

511

Chapter 21 REVIEW

CHAPTER 21 SUMMARY

SECTION 1: The cold war between the United States and the Soviet Union reached its height under the presidency of John F. Kennedy.

■ Kennedy's personal charm and his promise to "get the country moving again" after eight years of Republican rule led to his election as President in 1960.

■ To prevent Communist expansion, Kennedy built up American defenses and supported efforts for peaceful reform in the Third World.

■ Crises involving Cuba and Berlin during the years 1961 and 1962 brought the world dangerously close to war.

SECTION 2: Kennedy called for new social spending programs but did not succeed in getting much legislation through Congress.

■ Heavy federal spending on military and space projects lifted the economy out of an early recession.

■ The space program was a top priority during the Kennedy years, and Kennedy pledged that the nation would put a man on the moon before the decade's end.

■ Kennedy's assassination in 1963 shocked the nation. Questions about the tragedy persist to this day.

SECTION 3: Lyndon Johnson, the new President, had many successes with Congress but became bogged down in a war in Vietnam.

■ Johnson was a skilled legislator and politician with a strong interest in domestic reform. He supported civil rights measures and antipoverty programs known as the Great Society.

■ During the 1960s an activist Supreme Court promoted liberal causes through its legal decisions.

■ Johnson's intervention in the Dominican Republic and escalation of the war in Vietnam showed the nation's continuing cold war concerns.

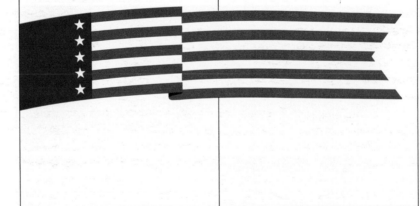

KEY TERMS ●

Match each of the following terms with its correct definition.

> Alliance for Progress
> Berlin Wall
> Civil Rights Act of 1964
> Great Society
> New Frontier
> Peace Corps

1. The result of a Communist attempt to block the flow of refugees escaping to Western Europe.
2. Kennedy's term for his domestic programs.
3. Kennedy's aid program for Latin America.
4. Law that banned racial discrimination in employment.
5. Organization that sent volunteers to work in developing nations.
6. Johnson's term for his domestic programs.

PEOPLE TO IDENTIFY ●

Identify the following people and tell why each was important.

1. Neil Armstrong
2. Fidel Castro
3. Nikita Khrushchev
4. Robert McNamara
5. Lee Harvey Oswald
6. Dean Rusk
7. Earl Warren

PLACES TO LOCATE ●

Match each of the letters on the map with the places that are listed below.

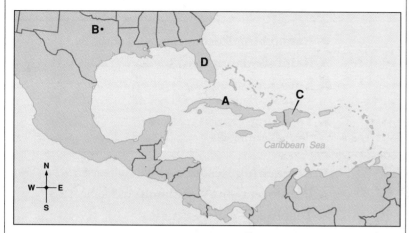

1. Florida
2. Cuba
3. Dallas
4. Dominican Republic

REVIEWING THE FACTS ▲

1. Who was the Republican candidate for President in 1960? How did Kennedy's choice of a running mate help bring him victory?
2. Why did President Kennedy maintain that he needed more military options for dealing with international crises?
3. How did the Peace Corps and the Alliance for Progress fit into Kennedy's plan for fighting the cold war?
4. Describe the events of the Cuban missile crisis.
5. Why did Kennedy have trouble getting his domestic programs through Congress? What legislation was passed?

6. Why was the space program a top priority for the Kennedy administration?
7. What questions were raised about the assassination of President Kennedy? What were the findings of the official investigation?
8. How did Lyndon Johnson reach the office of President? Describe Johnson's background and skills.
9. What were some of the controversial decisions of the Warren Court? What charges did conservatives make about these rulings?
10. What were the major components of Johnson's domestic policy? What were his main foreign policy initiatives?

CRITICAL THINKING SKILLS ▲

1. ANALYZING A QUOTATION What did John Kennedy mean when he urged Americans to "Ask not what your country can do for you—ask what you can do for your country"?

2. STATING BOTH SIDES OF AN ISSUE Make the best case you can for and against the following statement: President Kennedy was justified in taking steps to overthrow Fidel Castro.

3. MAKING COMPARISONS Compare the foreign policies of the four postwar Presidents you have now read about—Truman, Eisenhower, Kennedy, and Johnson.

WRITING ABOUT TOPICS IN AMERICAN HISTORY ■

1. CONNECTING WITH LITERATURE A selection from *The Mambo Kings Play Songs of Love* by Oscar Hijuelos appears on pages 808–811. Read it and answer the questions. Then answer the following question: Why does Cesar Castillo think of the Cuban revolution as "the rose that sprouted a thorn"?

2. APPLYING THEMES: AMERICAN CULTURE Imagine you are a newspaper reporter covering the 1960 presidential race. Your editor has assigned you to write an article describing the controversy over Kennedy's Roman Catholicism. Write the article, being sure to include what the public's fears were and how Kennedy addressed them.

10. The Food Stamp Act, Medicare, and HUD were Great Society programs. Stopping a revolt in the Dominican Republic and escalating the conflict in Vietnam were Johnson's major foreign policy initiatives.

Critical Thinking Skills
1. Kennedy called on the American people to selflessly serve the needs of the country rather than expecting the government to answer their individual concerns.
2. Support—the existence of a Communist regime so close to the American mainland could pose a security threat. Opposing—such an overthrow broke several treaties and was an overt act of war.
3. Truman sought to contain communism by supplying massive aid to countries where it was a threat. Eisenhower was more forceful, attempting to drive communism back with the threat of nuclear weapons. Kennedy incorporated flexible and creative responses. Johnson followed more established cold war policies.

Writing About Topics in American History
1. Students should note that the revolution was successful because Fidel Castro promised to help the poor and needy. The thorn, however, was the Communist government that he set up.
2. Students may want to learn more about religious prejudice in this country, especially during Kennedy's campaign. They should note how Kennedy allayed those fears.

8. Johnson became President when JFK was killed. An effective speaker, a forceful leader, and a skilled negotiator, Johnson rose through the political ranks to become Senate Majority Leader and Vice President.

9. Conservatives complained that *Miranda v. Arizona, Escobedo v. Illinois,* and *Gideon v. Wainwright* were overly concerned with a suspected criminal's rights and hindered law enforcement.

Chapter Review exercises are keyed for student abilities:
● = Basic
▲ = Average
■ = Average/Advanced

	SECTION OBJECTIVES	SECTION RESOURCES
Section 1 **Origins of the Civil Rights Movement**	■ explain the significance of *Brown v. Board of Education* in the history of the civil rights movement ■ identify key events of the 1950s which led to changes in the status of southern blacks	● **Reteaching Resources:** Worksheet 84 ▲ **Reinforcement Workbook:** Worksheet 84 ■ **Enrichment and Extension Resources:** Primary Source Worksheet 43 ▲ **Teaching Transparencies:** Transparency 84
Section 2 **Freedom Now**	■ identify examples of nonviolent tactics used by civil rights workers to end discrimination	● **Reteaching Resources:** Worksheet 85 ▲ **Reinforcement Workbook:** Worksheet 85 ▲ **Teaching Transparencies:** Transparency 85
Section 3 **High Hopes and Tragic Setbacks**	■ describe how the methods and goals of the civil rights movement shifted during the 1960s	● **Reteaching Resources:** Worksheet 86 ▲ **Reinforcement Workbook:** Worksheet 86 ■ **Enrichment and Extension Resources:** Primary Source Worksheet 44 ▲ **Teaching Transparencies:** Transparency 86

The list below shows Essential Elements relevant to this chapter. (The complete list of Essential Elements appears in the introductory pages of this Teacher's Edition.)

Section 1: 4A, 4C, 5A, 5D, 5E, 6A, 7B, 7E, 7F, 7G, 7I, 7K, 9A, 9E
Section 2: 4D, 4G, 5A, 5E, 6A, 6B, 7E, 7F, 7G, 7H, 7J
Section 3: 2A, 4C, 5A, 6A, 6B, 7B, 7E, 7F, 7G, 7H, 7I, 7J, 9A, 9D, 9E

> Section Resources are keyed for student abilities:
> ● = Basic
> ▲ = Average
> ■ = Average/Advanced

CHAPTER RESOURCES

Geography Resources: Worksheets 43, 44
Tests: Chapter 22 Test

Chapter Project: Expanding Democracy

Have students research and report on how the civil rights movement affected your community. Encourage them to interview family members, friends, and community leaders and to read local newspapers from the 1950s and 1960s.

Homework Options

Each section contains activities labeled "Addressing Individual Needs." You may wish to choose from among these activities when assigning homework.

> **Provisions for Limited English Proficiency (LEP)**
> Several suggested activities may be particularly helpful for teachers of students with limited English proficiency. These activities have been marked throughout the Teacher's Annotated Edition with the symbol **LEP** .

BIBLIOGRAPHY AND AUDIOVISUAL AIDS

Teacher Bibliography

Farmer, James. *Lay Bare the Heart: An Autobiography of the Civil Rights Movement.* Arbor House, 1985.

Garrow, David J. *Bearing the Cross: Martin Luther King, Jr., and the Southern Christian Leadership Conference, 1955–1968.* Morrow, 1986.

Katz, William L. *Minorities in American History, Vol. 6: Modern America: 1957–Present.* Watts, 1974.

Student Bibliography

Archer, Jules. *1968: Year of Crisis.* Messner, 1971.

King, Coretta Scott. *My Life with Martin Luther King.* Avon, 1980.

Williams, Juan. *Eyes on the Prize: America's Civil Rights Years, 1954–1965.* Penguin, 1986.

Literature

Douglas, Ellen. *The Rock Cried Out.* Harcourt Brace Jovanovich, 1979. A young man returns to his native Mississippi and becomes involved in a traumatic event that happened years before.

Haley, Alex. *Roots.* Dell, 1977.

Hansberry, Lorraine. *A Raisin in the Sun.* Random House, 1969. Drama of a black family's struggle to escape the poverty of the Chicago ghetto.

Malcolm X. *The Autobiography of Malcolm X.* Ballantine, 1977.

Moody, Ann. *Coming of Age in Mississippi.* Dell, 1970.

Wright, Richard. *Native Son.* Harper and Row, 1969. A black youth from a Chicago slum is victimized by prejudice and his own errors.

Films and Videotapes*

Ain't Scared of Your Jails, 1960–1961 (Eyes on the Prize Series). 60 min. PBS. Depicts the changing focus of black protest during the early 1960s, including personal and group challenges to a broad range of inequities.

Awakenings, 1954–1956 (Eyes on the Prize Series). 60 min. PBS. Two events helped focus the nation's attention on the civil rights of black Americans: the 1955 lynching of Emmett Till and the bus boycott in Montgomery, Alabama.

Daughters of the Black Revolution. 28 min. FFH. Daughters of slain civil rights leaders Martin Luther King, Jr., Medgar Evers, and Malcolm X discuss what their fathers' dreams and struggles appear to have achieved a generation later.

Great Americans: Martin Luther King, Jr. (2nd ed). 23 min. EBEC. Traces King's actions as he commits his life to the civil rights crusade. Includes commentary by his widow and close friends.

The Torch Is Passed. 30 min. FL. Examines the origins of the 1960s student political movement in the United States.

Computer Software*

Civil Rights, 1964 (1 disk, IBM). NCSC. Simulation and tutorial on major civil rights events, including passage of the Civil Rights Act of 1964.

*For a complete guide to audiovisual sources, see the introduction to this book (page Txx).

Chapter 22

The Civil Rights Movement
(pp. 514–535)

Chapter 22 traces the struggle for equality in the United States from the battles to end segregation and disfranchisement in the South in the 1950s, through the challenges from black power advocates in the late 1960s, to issues faced by minorities in the country today.

Themes in American History

- Constitutional government
- Expanding democracy
- Pluralistic society
- American culture

Chapter Objectives

After students complete this chapter, they will be able to:

1. Explain the significance of *Brown v. Board of Education* in the history of the civil rights movement.

2. Identify key events of the 1950s which led to changes in the status of southern blacks.

3. Identify examples of non-violent tactics used by civil rights workers to end discrimination.

4. Describe how the methods and goals of the civil rights movement shifted during the 1960s.

Chapter Opener Art
Civil rights marcher, Selma, Alabama, 1965.

The road to political equality for African Americans was long and lonely. However, the civil rights movement achieved historic gains during the 1950s and 1960s.

CHAPTER SUPPORT MATERIAL

Reinforcement Workbook: Worksheets 84–86
Reteaching Resources: Worksheets 84–86
Enrichment and Extension Resources: Primary Source Worksheets 43, 44
Geography Resources: Worksheets 43, 44
Teaching Transparencies: Transparencies 84–86
Tests: Chapter 22 Test

SECTION 1

Origins of the Civil Rights Movement
(pp. 515–521)

Section Objectives
- explain the significance of *Brown v. Board of Education* in the history of the civil rights movement
- identify key events of the 1950s which led to changes in the status of southern blacks

Introducing the Section

Connecting with Past Learnings
Review the origins of legislation supporting segregation in the South. *What were Jim Crow laws? When and why were they passed?* (Jim Crow laws were passed after Reconstruction to segregate blacks from whites in the South and to restore white political, economic, and social supremacy.)

Key Terms
Write the key terms for this section on the board. Have students play "Jeopardy" by asking one student to supply the definition of a term, and then call on another student to supply the question. The question must contain the key term. Continue until all key terms have been used. **LEP**

4A, 4C, 5A, 5D, 5E, 6A, 7B, 7E, 7F, 7G, 7I, 7K, 9A, 9E

1 Origins of the Civil Rights Movement

Section Focus

Key Terms *Brown v. Board of Education of Topeka* ■ Southern Manifesto ■ Montgomery bus boycott ■ White Citizens Council

Main Idea The struggle against racial injustice gathered force in the years after World War II. The Supreme Court declared segregation in schools unconstitutional, and African Americans continued to search for new ways to overcome discrimination.

Objectives As you read, look for answers to these questions:
1. What was it like to be a black southerner in the 1950s?
2. How did a historic decision by the Supreme Court affect the struggle for civil rights?
3. What lessons did African Americans learn from events in Montgomery and Little Rock?

We've been 'buked and we've been scorned,
We've been talked about, as sure as you're born.
But we'll never turn back, no,
We'll never turn back,
Until we've all been freed and
We have equality.

　　　—Civil rights freedom song, adapted
　　　　from a nineteenth-century spiritual

Their ancestors were born into slavery. The generations that followed suffered the wrongs of racism and exclusion. African Americans had been "rebuked and scorned" throughout United States history. Then, in the mid-1900s, the long struggle for racial equality developed into a remarkable mass movement.

What did black Americans want? They wanted to be able to use public places as freely as white people. They wanted enforcement of their consti-

tutional right to vote. They wanted a fair chance when applying for jobs and housing.

SECOND-CLASS CITIZENS 4A, 5A, 6A
Imagine that you are a black person living in the American South of the 1950s. You are now "colored" or "Negro." Many white people call you "girl" or "boy," even if you are an adult. Some call you names much worse than that. You are expected to "know your place." That means never disobeying the laws and customs of a segregated society. You are on the bottom of a divided world. You are a second-class citizen.

At every turn, southern blacks were reminded of their second-class status. They had to attend schools that were separate and of inferior quality. They had to drink from "colored" water fountains, eat at "colored" restaurants, ride in "colored" railroad cars. At concerts and movies, black and white teenagers had to sit in separate sections, divided by ropes.

SUPPORTING THE SECTION

Reinforcement Workbook: Worksheet 84
Reteaching Resources: Worksheet 84
Enrichment and Extension Resources: Primary Source Worksheet 43
Teaching Transparencies: Transparency 84

Draw a "Mason-Dixon Line" dividing the class. Have one half list arguments in favor of the Topeka Board of Education; the other half list arguments in favor of Linda Brown. Students should support their positions with past precedents, present conditions, and predictions for the future. Discuss each side, listing the main points on the board.

What are the advantages of working for social change through the courts? (It puts the power of the federal government behind the decision.)

Developing the Lesson

After students have read the section, you may want to consider the following activities:

Ethics

Ask students to list the effects of segregation on blacks in the South. (Had to attend separate schools, restaurants, public facilities; worked at low-status, low-paying jobs; had no representation in government.)

How do you think white southerners justified the system of racial segregation? (Possible answers include the background of slavery in the South; a belief in the inferiority of blacks; and the half-century tradition of Jim Crow laws.)

Segregation, or separation on the basis of race, appeared in all aspects of daily life in the South. **CULTURAL PLURALISM** What might have happened to the man in the photograph if he had used the facility marked "white"? How might he have felt about using a separate water fountain?
4A, 5A, 6A

As adults, most blacks entered low-status, low-paying jobs. They had no representation in government, because only a few blacks were allowed to vote. If they were charged with a crime, they had to face an all-white jury. If they were sick or injured, they had to find a "colored" emergency room. When they died, they were buried in a "colored" cemetery.

The southern system of racial segregation was backed by state and local laws, known as Jim Crow laws. Passed in the late 1800s, these laws were firmly in place a half-century later.

In the North and West, blacks did not face segregation laws. However, while there was racial equality in the law books, there was not equality in practice. Throughout the North and West, blacks were prevented from living in white neighborhoods. They were discriminated against on the job, and treated like second-class citizens. The racist belief that blacks were inferior to whites was common in every state.

In fact, some people believe blacks and whites had closer personal relations in the South than in other regions. They were unequal relationships, but in some ways they were warm and caring. Virginia editor James J. Kilpatrick, in a book published in 1962, presented the point of view of white southerners:

What is so often misunderstood, outside the South, is this delicate intimacy of human beings whose lives are so intricately bound together. I have met Northerners who believe, in all apparent seriousness, that segregation in the South means literally that: *segregation*, the races stiffly apart, never touching. . . .

In plain fact, the relationship between white and Negro in the segregated South, in the country and in the city, has been far closer, more honest, less constrained, than such relations generally have been in the integrated North.

Kilpatrick and others argued that outside the South few whites had day-to-day contact with people of other races. Thus, they argued, segregation and racial stereotyping were really national problems. Nevertheless, in the South racial injustice had the force of state and local law. That is, people were breaking the law if they did *not* discriminate racially. As a result, civil rights leaders devoted most of their early efforts to the southern states.

Photo Caption Answers
He might have been arrested. Students may suggest that separate facilities were insulting and degrading.

CRUSADING LAWYERS 4C

Since the early 1900s, lawyers of the National Association for the Advancement of Colored People (NAACP) had fought racial injustice in the courtroom. These efforts were advanced in the 1930s by a remarkable group of lawyers trained at the all-black Howard University in Washington, D.C.

Howard University became a top-notch law school under the leadership of Charles Houston. Houston knew that white judges and lawyers were not likely to abolish Jim Crow laws on their own. They needed a tireless, highly trained corps of black lawyers to push them. Houston worked toward that dream by making Howard one of the toughest law schools in the nation.

"He was so tough we used to call him 'Iron Shoes,'" recalled Thurgood Marshall, one of Houston's students. "There must have been 30 of us in that class when we started, and no more than 8 or 10 of us finished." From the 1930s to the 1950s Marshall and many of his classmates brought dozens of important civil rights cases to court. In 1967 Thurgood Marshall became the first African American to serve on the Supreme Court.

The major legal obstacle facing blacks was the precedent established in 1896 by the *Plessy v. Ferguson* case (page 78). The *Plessy* decision said the states could segregate public facilities as long as the separate facilities were equal for both

BIOGRAPHY 4C

CHARLES H. HOUSTON (1895–1950) served in France and Germany during World War I. In 1923 he became the first African American to receive a Doctor of Laws degree from Harvard. As vice-dean, Houston worked to strengthen Howard University's Law School, from which his father had graduated. Together with Thurgood Marshall, his former student, Houston fought legal battles for fair representation of minority workers by unions. His work during the 1930s and 1940s as a lawyer and teacher helped pave the way for civil rights victories after his death.

BIOGRAPHY 4C

THURGOOD MARSHALL (1908–   ) graduated first in his class at Howard University Law School in 1933. He served as chief counsel for the NAACP from 1938 to 1961. During that time, Marshall argued 32 civil rights cases before the Supreme Court and won 29 of them, including the historic *Brown v. Board of Education.* In 1967 Marshall became the first African American justice on the Supreme Court. In 1991 he retired from the Court.

races. This became known as the "separate-but-equal" doctrine. In practice, blacks rarely enjoyed public facilities equal to those of whites.

Charles Houston traveled all over the South to gather evidence. He found that for every dollar southern states spent on educating a black child, they spent five dollars on a white child. Civil rights lawyers used this evidence to show that segregation made the races separate-and-unequal. They won some cases, and a few states had to improve their "colored" schools. But by the 1940s the NAACP believed the best way to fight legal segregation was to attack *Plessy* head-on. Their efforts paid off in one of the most important Supreme Court decisions of the twentieth century.

A HISTORIC DECISION 5D, 7B

It was May 17, 1954, and civil rights backers rejoiced. The Supreme Court had outlawed racial segregation in public schools. The landmark case was called *Brown v. Board of Education of Topeka.* Though the case involved several black school children, it got its name from just one: nine-year-old Linda Brown of Topeka, Kansas. Linda went to an all-black elementary school across town. Her parents believed she should have the right to go to a white school closer to home.

The Court agreed that most black schools were worse than those provided for whites. To overturn *Plessy* and outlaw segregation, however, the NAACP lawyers had to persuade the justices of

Constitutional Heritage
Refer students to the Thirteenth, Fourteenth, and Fifteenth Amendments on pages 757–759. *What rights did these amendments guarantee to blacks?* (Freedom from slavery, rights of citizenship and equal protection under the law, right to vote.) *How did Plessy v. Ferguson allow segregation to exist in the South despite these guarantees?* (It declared that separating the races was constitutional as long as the separate facilities were equal.) Discuss with the class how prevailing attitudes may have influenced the Supreme Court's decision in that case.

Have students read the excerpt from *Brown v. Board of Education* on page 727, noting how the Supreme Court's attitude toward segregation had changed since *Plessy v. Ferguson.*

Geographic Themes: Regions
Help students understand the difference between *de jure* segregation (according to the law) and *de facto* segregation (actually existing, whether lawfully or not). Ask the class to compare living conditions of black people in the North, West, and South. (North and West did not have laws segregating the races, but blacks still did not enjoy the rights of other Americans. Laws and customs made life difficult for blacks in the South, but there was more day-to-day contact between the races.)

Biography
Ask students which aspect of Houston's career they think was more significant: his role as a lawyer or as a teacher. Have them explain their answers.

Biography
For further reading consider: Bland, Randall W. *Private Pressure on Public Law: The Legal Career of Justice Thurgood Marshall.* Associated Faculty Press, 1973.

This photograph from 1953 shows Linda Brown (foreground) as a fourth grader in her class at the segregated Monroe School in Topeka, Kansas. Brown's parents sued the Topeka school system in *Brown v. Board of Education of Topeka.* **CONSTITUTIONAL HERITAGE** Explain the significance of the *Brown* case's outcome. **5D, 7K**

another point. They had to show that separate schools were unequal—*by definition.*

Racially separate schools could never be equal, the lawyers argued, because segregation degraded black children. It taught young blacks that white society considered them inferior, not worthy of mixing with white children. After studying years of testimony in dozens of related cases, the Supreme Court agreed.

Chief Justice Earl Warren wrote the Court's decision. He stated, "To separate [black children] from others of similar age . . . solely because of their race generates a feeling of inferiority . . . that may affect their hearts and minds in a way unlikely ever to be undone."

The decision was a triumph for legal equality. But it is one thing to make new law, and another thing to enforce it. The *Brown* decision struck down legal segregation without clearly saying when or how schools had to desegregate. **5E**

★ Historical Documents

For an excerpt from the *Brown v. Board of Education* decision, see page 727 of this book.

Some whites denounced the *Brown* decision. Others, including President Eisenhower, disapproved of it privately, hoping to avoid a confrontation over desegregation. In Congress, meanwhile, southern representatives signed the so-called Southern Manifesto. That document called *Brown* a "clear abuse of judicial powers." It also argued that the decision increased the power of the federal government at the expense of the rights and powers of the states.

The *Brown* decision raised the hopes of African Americans. Yet most of them knew it would take a long struggle to win their rights. Soon after *Brown,* a brutal murder in Mississippi led to a sense that a showdown was coming.

THE LYNCHING OF EMMETT TILL 7I

In the summer of 1955, a fourteen-year-old Chicago student named Emmett Till boarded a "colored" car of the Illinois Central Railroad. He was headed for Money, Mississippi, to spend his vacation with relatives.

One night in the small southern town, Emmett and some other black teenagers were talking outside a country store. Emmett bragged about a white girlfriend back in Chicago. In 1955 dating across racial lines was extremely rare; in Mississippi it was unheard of. The others doubted Emmett's story. Then one of them pointed to a white woman inside the store and dared him to talk to her. Within earshot of his friends, Emmett called out to her.

The angry woman told her husband, Roy Bryant, about the incident. Bryant and his brother-in-law tracked down Emmett at the home of 64-year-old Mose Wright. They forced Emmett into the back seat of their car and threatened to murder Wright if he complained. Three days later Emmett Till's lifeless body was dragged from the Tallahatchie River. He had been so badly beaten that his family barely recognized him.

Pictures of Till's body, published in national magazines, shocked the nation. Charles Diggs of Chicago, the first African American congressman since Reconstruction, recalled their impact.

> I think the picture in *Jet* magazine showing Emmett Till's mutilation was probably

Photo Caption Answer
It overturned the doctrine of "separate-but-equal" in education.

the greatest media product in the last forty or fifty years, because that picture stimulated a lot of interest and anger on the part of blacks all over the country.

When the case came to trial, an all-white jury found Bryant and his brother-in-law innocent. The accused men later admitted they had killed Till.

During the trial, several black people had stood up in court and accused the white defendants of murder. To do so was to risk death. Mose Wright was one of those people. On the witness stand he pointed at the two men who had dragged Emmett Till away that day. Afterward Wright said, "It was the first time in my life I had the courage to accuse a white man of a crime." Congressman Diggs added, "For someone like Mose Wright and others to testify against white defendants in a situation like this was historic."

Around the country, commentators denounced the state of justice in Mississippi. The *Delta Democrat Times* of Greenville spoke for many Mississippians. It claimed that the prosecutor's case had been weak. It also pointed out that "to blame two million Mississippians for the irresponsible acts of two is about as illogical as one can become."

MONTGOMERY BUS BOYCOTT 7E, 7F, 7G

Not long after the Emmett Till case, a new controversy arose in the South. On December 1, 1955, a black woman named Rosa Parks chose to defy a law that required black passengers to give up their seats to whites and move to the back of the bus. Mrs. Parks later recalled the bus driver's anger: "He said, 'If you don't stand up, I'm going to have to call the police and have you arrested.' I said, 'You may do that.'" Rosa Parks was taken in a police car to the city jail. Her act sparked one of the great rebellions of the civil rights movement—the Montgomery bus boycott of 1955–1956.

A seamstress, Rosa Parks had long been active in the local branch of the Alabama NAACP. In fact twelve years earlier, in 1943, Parks had been thrown off another bus for refusing to enter through the rear door. She and many others worked for years to build a movement against segregation. By 1955, Montgomery's 50,000 blacks were ready to unite in protest.

As news of Rosa Parks's arrest spread, people flew into action. A group of black women organized a boycott of the city buses. They circulated thousands of leaflets urging blacks to stay off the buses. Since most of the bus company's passengers were black, a boycott would hurt their business. With the loss of profits, they might pressure the city to change its segregation laws. That was the hope.

On the first day of the boycott, a young Baptist minister got up before dawn to see what would happen. He and his wife stood at the window to watch as the day's first bus rumbled down the street. It was empty—and so was the next, and the next. The minister, Martin Luther King, Jr., was thrilled. King had been born in Atlanta, Georgia, and had received a divinity degree and a doctorate in theology from Boston University. He had moved to Montgomery in 1954 to become pastor of the Dexter Avenue Baptist Church. He had not expected to get involved in the civil rights struggle. But local black leaders quickly recognized his eloquence and political skill. They named King, age 27, leader of the boycott movement.

The first night of the boycott, King spoke at a black church before an overflow crowd of more than 4,000. "One of the great glories of democracy is the right to protest for right," he preached. "If you will protest courageously and yet with dignity and Christian love, . . . future generations . . . will pause and say, 'There lived a great people—a black people—who injected new meaning and dignity into the veins of civilization.'"

> "**O**ne of the great glories of democracy is the right to protest for right."
> —*Martin Luther King, Jr., 1955*

It took great sacrifice to carry on the boycott. Many people walked miles each day to avoid the buses. Thousands participated in a complex system of car-pooling. Leaders were arrested and charged with conspiracy. And one month into the boycott, someone bombed Reverend King's house. Meanwhile, more than 10,000 of Montgomery's whites joined the White Citizens Council. These

Background At the time of the bus boycott, Montgomery had more than 50,000 black citizens. This large black community had no political, economic, religious, or cultural unity or leadership. One long-range effect of the boycott was the development of leaders and strategies that would become the basis of the Southern Christian Leadership Conference.

Addressing Individual Needs

Guided/ Independent Practice
Have students complete **Reinforcement Workbook** Worksheet 84, in which they will compare methods and results of early activities of the civil rights movement.

Reteaching/Correctives
Have students work in small groups to create posters illustrating some of the origins of the civil rights movement as discussed in the section. Have them include at least four important events. Each event should be accompanied by an explanatory sentence. Display student posters in the classroom.

Assign **Reteaching Resources** Worksheet 84, which has students review individual connections to the struggle for civil rights.

Enrichment/Extension
Assign **Enrichment and Extension Resources** Primary Source Worksheet 43. This worksheet will help students understand the principles of nonviolent resistance as described by Martin Luther King, Jr.

Assessment
You may wish to use the Section 1 Review, page 521, to see how well your students understand the main points in this lesson.

Section Review Answers

1. *Brown v. Board of Education of Topeka*—Supreme Court decision declaring school segregation unconstitutional. *Southern Manifesto*—Statement by southern members of Congress that the Supreme Court had abused its powers in the *Brown* decision. *Montgomery bus boycott*—Blacks' refusal to ride city buses until public transportation was desegregated. *White Citizens Council*—Group of southern whites who opposed integration.

2. *Charles Houston*—Leader of Howard University Law School. *Linda Brown*—Plaintiff in *Brown v. Board of Education*. *Emmett Till*—Black teenager whose murder in Mississippi aroused national attention. *Rosa Parks*—Woman whose refusal to give up her seat on a Montgomery bus sparked a boycott. *Martin Luther King, Jr.*—Baptist minister and leader of Montgomery bus boycott. *Orval Faubus*—Governor of Arkansas who refused to let Little Rock schools be integrated.

3. They went to separate schools and states spent less money on those schools; they were insulted and treated without respect; they had to use separate facilities; they had low-status, low-paying jobs; they were unable to vote.

4. It led to a Supreme Court case which outlawed segregation on buses. It also succeeded in organizing the black community of Montgomery, in developing black leadership, and in accelerating the push for civil rights.

This picture shows seamstress and civil rights worker Rosa Parks on a bus in Montgomery, Alabama, after the city's buses were desegregated. Her arrest for refusing to move to the back of a bus had sparked a 382-day bus boycott led by Martin Luther King, Jr. PARTICIPATION What factors helped the bus boycott succeed? **7E, 7F, 9E**

councils were formed throughout the South in the 1950s to oppose integration.

Montgomery's blacks maintained the boycott for more than a year. Meanwhile, Rosa Parks's arrest became a test case in the courts. Late in 1956, the Supreme Court ruled that segregation on buses was illegal. It was another great victory for the civil rights movement.

CONFRONTATION AT LITTLE ROCK

Despite *Brown v. Board of Education* (1954), most southern states kept black children out of white schools. One exception came in Arkansas. The city of Little Rock had quietly approved a plan in 1957 to begin integrating its schools. During the first year, 9 black students were assigned to Central High School (along with 2,000 white students).

Orval Faubus, the governor of Arkansas, opposed the plan. On the first day of classes, he surrounded the high school with members of the Arkansas National Guard. Guard members kept the black students from entering the high school.

A mob of angry whites screamed at the black students. Elizabeth Eckford was one of the nine black students who tried to enter the school that day. She recalls approaching a guard. "When I tried to squeeze past him, he raised his bayonet.

[Then] somebody started yelling, 'Lynch her! Lynch her!'" The black students managed to escape the mob and return home. Integration in the face of such opposition seemed impossible.

For several weeks President Eisenhower hesitated to act. He did not believe in using the federal government to defeat segregation. "You cannot change people's hearts merely by laws," he once said. But in the face of Faubus's challenge, Eisenhower felt he had no choice. He sent federal troops to Little Rock to maintain order while the law was carried out. "Mob rule cannot be allowed to override the decisions of our courts," he said. "[Most southerners] do not sympathize with mob rule. They, like the rest of the nation, have proved in two great wars their readiness to sacrifice for America. And the foundation of the American way of life is our national respect for law."

Day after day the troops escorted the black students through angry mobs. By the end of the school year, the situation was still tense. Continuing to fight integration, Governor Faubus ordered Little Rock's public schools closed in 1958. The

Arkansas governor Orval Faubus ordered these National Guardsmen to forcibly prevent black children from entering Little Rock's all-white high schools. CONSTITUTIONAL HERITAGE Was Eisenhower's use of troops in Little Rock constitutional? Explain. **9A**

Photo Caption Answers
(Top) The bus company's dependence on black riders, unity within the black community, good organization, and courage in the face of arrests and violence. (Bottom) The Constitution declares the supremacy of national law over state law and gives the President responsibility for enforcing the law.

Supreme Court soon ruled, however, that "evasive schemes" to avoid integration were illegal. In 1959 the Little Rock public schools were peacefully reopened and integrated.

Opposition to school integration remained fierce. In a poll taken late in 1958, Americans named Orval Faubus as one of the ten most-admired men in the nation. The federal government, moreover, seemed eager to avoid another confrontation at all costs. True, Congress did pass a civil rights bill in 1957 to ensure that blacks could vote. But the act included such weak enforcement measures that it had very little impact. By 1960 more and more blacks believed that the federal government would not take the lead in advancing civil rights. The movement would have to go back to the grass roots.

4D, 4G, 5A, 5E, 6A, 6B, 7E, 7F, 7G, 7H, 7J

2 Freedom Now

Section Focus

Key Terms sit-in ■ freedom rider ■ March on Washington

Main Idea In the early 1960s, the civil rights movement became a mass movement. Throughout the South, thousands of people participated in nonviolent protests against segregation.

Objectives As you read, look for answers to these questions:
1. What nonviolent tactics did demonstrators use to protest discrimination?
2. What factors gave people courage and hope to pursue the struggle for civil rights?
3. What was the impact of events in Mississippi and Birmingham, Alabama?

In Nagpur, India, a young African American named James Lawson was reading a newspaper. Suddenly he jumped to his feet, shouting with joy. Ordinarily a quiet man, Lawson rarely let his emotions show. Yet the news he had read was thrilling. Black people in Montgomery were boycotting the segregated buses.

Lawson had dreamed of such a day. He had gone to India as a Methodist missionary, filled with a devout faith in the Christian values of love and peace. But he had also gone to learn about Mohandas Gandhi. Gandhi's policies of nonviolent resistance—including boycotts and peaceful demonstrations—had set the pattern for India's successful struggle for independence from Britain. Those tactics, Lawson felt, could be a tool for African Americans.

Reverend Lawson would return to the United States and become one of the many heroes of the civil rights movement. Like King, he taught the principles of nonviolent protest. Lawson's students learned to remain calm even when they were spat on, screamed at, beaten, and jailed.

Peaceful challenges to segregation were crucial

Have the class list methods used by the civil rights movement in the 1960s to end segregation in the South, and write the list on the board. (Sit-ins, wade-ins, etc.; freedom rides; boycotts; protest marches; court orders; March on Washington.) Then have students grade each method, determining how effective it was.

How was the civil rights movement in the 1960s different from that in the 1950s? (Gained wide support; became a mass movement.) *In what ways did the movement succeed in the early 1960s?* (Supreme Court ended segregation in public travel; Civil Rights Act of 1964 outlawed racial discrimination and gave the federal government power of enforcement.)

Developing the Lesson
After students have read the section, you may want to consider the following activities:

Civic Values
Review forms of protest Americans have used in the past. (Written statement, speech, boycott, strike, public gathering, demonstration, riot.) Discuss the reasons why civil rights leaders chose to use nonviolent methods in their struggle. *Was nonviolent resistance successful in the civil rights movement? Why or why not?* (Nonviolent methods, such as sit-ins and freedom rides, helped eliminate legal segregation.) Have students consider whether they would have been able to remain nonviolent in the face of a violent response.

---

to the civil rights movement. All over the South, demonstrators faced violence. And they did so, almost always, without striking back. In the end, they led the way to the final elimination of legal segregation.

LUNCH-COUNTER SIT-INS 5A, 7E, 7F

On February 1, 1960, four black students from North Carolina Agricultural and Technical College headed into downtown Greensboro. David Richmond, Franklin McCain, Ezell Blair, and Joseph McNeil had a simple goal. They would go to Woolworth's, sit down at the whites-only lunch counter, and order coffee. They knew that this simple demand could land them in jail.

"I'm sorry," said the waitress, "but we don't serve coloreds here." The students stayed seated in silent protest until the store closed. They came back the next day, and 23 more students joined them. Sixty-six came the following day. At week's end, 1,000 students were participating. The movement spread like wildfire. By the end of 1960 there were sit-ins in more than 100 southern cities. As many as 50,000 people took part.

Hostile crowds often surrounded the demonstrators. Sometimes hecklers poured ketchup over the heads of the seated protesters, or spat on them. Some demonstrators had cigarettes ground out on their backs. In many cases the police moved in—to arrest the nonviolent protesters.

The sit-in movement won its most dramatic victory in Nashville, Tennessee. Led by James Lawson, the Nashville movement was large and disciplined. At first, the protesters were met with severe abuse and frequent arrests. However, the movement reached a turning point in April 1960 when it organized a large protest march on City Hall. Diane Nash, only 21 years old, was a march leader. When the mayor came out to speak with the demonstrators, Nash asked, "Mayor West, do *you* feel it is wrong to discriminate against a person solely on the basis of their race or color?" The mayor agreed that it was wrong. Taking his statement as the new policy, several stores began to serve blacks at their lunch counters.

In the midst of the sit-in movement, several hundred participants gathered at a meeting called by the Southern Christian Leadership Conference

(SCLC). The SCLC had been formed in 1957, with Martin Luther King, Jr., as its president. Working through the churches, the SCLC became one of the major civil rights organizations in the South. However, many of the young students of the sit-in movement believed the SCLC was too cautious. Sit-in leaders like Diane Nash wanted an organization that would take the nonviolent movement into the streets. Later that year they formed their own group: the Student Nonviolent Coordinating Committee (SNCC, pronounced "Snick").

As the sit-in movement grew, other nonviolent challenges to Jim Crow developed. There were "sleep-ins" at all-white motels, "kneel-ins" at all-white churches, "wade-ins" at all-white beaches. Public facilities were integrated in some cities. In most of the South, however, Jim Crow laws remained firmly in place.

FREEDOM RIDING 5A, 7E, 7F

We took a trip on a Greyhound bus,
Freedom's comin' and it won't be long
To fight segregation, this we must
Freedom's comin' and it won't be long.
Judge say local custom shall prevail
Freedom's comin' and it won't be long
We say "no" and we land in jail
Freedom's comin' and it won't be long.

—Civil rights freedom song

In 1961, groups of protesters called freedom riders boarded buses that would take them across the South. The freedom riders, some of whom were white, sought to call attention to Jim Crow laws requiring segregation on buses and trains engaged in interstate travel. The freedom riders sang songs to keep their spirits high. But they knew their trips would be dangerous. And so they were. At several stops white mobs dragged them from their buses and beat them.

As news of the violence spread around the world, demands mounted for an end to segregation in transportation. In September 1961 the Interstate Commerce Commission outlawed segregation in interstate buses and terminals. The next year, the Supreme Court ordered an end to segregation in all public travel accommodations.

Freedom riders watch in sorrow after their bus was burned by an angry white mob in Anniston, Alabama, in 1961. The mob stoned the bus, slashed its tires, and then followed it out of town and threw gas bombs inside it when it stopped for repairs. **CULTURAL PLURALISM** Why, do you think, did many white people resist desegregation so violently? **6B**

The freedom riders had brought more people into the civil rights movement. They had clung to the faith that "freedom's comin' and it won't be long."

THE SOURCES OF A MASS MOVEMENT 7E

What gave people the courage to risk their lives in nonviolent protest? Part of the explanation is that blacks were unwilling to accept second-class citizenship any longer. Outrage fueled their protest. But anger alone does not give life to a mass movement for social change. People must also feel hope, and must believe that change is possible. In the years after World War II, several factors gave hope to the civil rights movement:

(1) Black urbanization. Until World War II most black people lived in the rural South. Isolated on country farms, individual blacks had little power to challenge white authority. In the 1940s many thousands of rural blacks moved to the cities of the South and North. There they saw what they had in common. They also saw that together they had the power to challenge discrimination. The civil rights movement, as a result, was strongest in southern cities.

(2) Religious faith. Religion was crucial to the civil rights movement. The faith that all people are equal before God gave many people greater determination in their struggle for equality on earth. Black churches, along with black colleges, were at the center of the movement. They provided places to meet, plan, and pray. They also produced inspirational leaders such as Martin Luther King, Jr.

(3) Constitutional rights. Blacks drew hope from the belief that the Constitution guaranteed their basic civil rights. That faith was strengthened by Supreme Court decisions such as *Brown v. Board of Education.* Although these rights were denied in many places, blacks were confident that the Constitution justified their protests.

(4) Media coverage. By the late 1950s most American homes had a television. For the first time, camera crews could bring live news stories into people's living rooms. Shocked by what they saw, many viewers became supporters of the civil rights movement. Growing numbers of whites, in fact, took part in civil rights demonstrations.

In addition, televised news stories were broadcast around the world. Many white Americans grew uncomfortable about the denial of rights to citizens of color at home. They said it would harm

Photo Caption Answer
Students may suggest that desegregation threatened a way of life and a system of values which they considered essential.

the United States in its cold war competition with the Soviet Union.

(5) African independence. By 1960, scores of African countries had gained their independence from European nations. This inspired American blacks and challenged them to work harder for their own freedom. After all, if black African nations could vote in the United Nations, why couldn't black Americans vote in the South?

VIOLENCE IN MISSISSIPPI 4D, 7F

Medgar Evers, a civil rights leader in Mississippi, was especially moved by the African example. Evers pointed out in 1963 that a black man in the Congo "can be a locomotive engineer, but in Jackson he cannot even drive a garbage truck."

As a soldier in World War II, Medgar Evers fought in Normandy on D-Day (page 425). He risked his life in the name of democracy. Like many black veterans, he returned home determined to win his full rights as an American citizen. Born and raised in Mississippi, Evers became the NAACP's first field director in that state. Throughout the 1950s Evers devoted himself to the civil rights movement. He investigated lynchings (like Emmett Till's), helped blacks register to vote, and challenged segregation.

One of Evers' many projects was to help a black student gain admission to the University of Mississippi. "Ole Miss" was an all-white school that was proud of its southern traditions—including segregation. But in the fall of 1962, a federal court ordered the university to admit James Meredith, an air force veteran.

When Governor Ross Barnett refused to obey the court order, President Kennedy sent in federal marshals to protect the black student. During Meredith's first night on campus, an angry mob gathered outside his dorm. The school became a war zone as the crowd attacked the marshals. By dawn 2 people had been killed and 375 injured. Federal marshals had to remain on campus until Meredith graduated in 1963.

The violent response to the admission of one black man to "Ole Miss" revealed the depth of racial hostility among segregationists. Another example came a year later. Late one night, as Medgar Evers pulled into his driveway, shots rang

out from a speeding car. Evers was killed. A suspect in the Evers murder was arrested, but the charges against him were dropped after two trials ended in hung juries. Meanwhile, the struggle between segregationists and the growing civil rights movement was reaching a head. The most dramatic clash came in Birmingham, Alabama.

THE STRUGGLE IN BIRMINGHAM 7E

Some people were starting to call it "Bombingham." Between 1957 and 1963, blacks were the victims of at least twenty bombing attacks. Birmingham was one of the most segregated cities in America. Fear of racial mixing was so strong that the city even banned a children's book showing black and white rabbits playing together.

The governor of the state, George Wallace, was a fierce segregationist. Like Ross Barnett, Wallace tried to keep black students out of his state's largest university. At the start of 1963, Wallace declared, "I say segregation now, segregation tomorrow, and segregation forever."

> "**I** say segregation now, segregation tomorrow, and segregation forever."
> —*George Wallace, 1963*

Martin Luther King, Jr., and the SCLC decided to launch an all-out nonviolent challenge to segregation in Birmingham. In April 1963 they began sit-ins, boycotts, and protest marches. Police Chief Eugene "Bull" Connor responded by arresting the demonstrators. The jails began to fill. Soon, thousands of blacks were protesting. Journalists from around the world began to cover the Birmingham story.

Bull Connor's officers became more aggressive as the demonstrations mounted. They used high-pressure fire hoses, police dogs, and electric cattle prods to break up the demonstrations. Around the world millions of people saw film footage of black children being blasted with water and snapped at by police dogs.

Reverend King was one of those arrested. In jail he wrote a long letter to a group of clergymen who said he should halt the demonstrations and be more patient. King explained:

> For years now I have heard the word "Wait!" It rings in the ear of every Negro. . . . This "Wait" has almost always meant "Never." . . .
>
> Perhaps it is easy for those who have never felt the stinging darts of segregation to say, "Wait." But when you have seen hate-filled policemen curse, kick, and even kill your black brothers and sisters; when you see the vast majority of your 20 million Negro brothers smothering in an airtight cage of poverty in the midst of an affluent society; . . . when you are humiliated day in and day out by nagging signs reading "white" and "colored"; . . . when you are forever fighting a degenerating sense of "nobodiness"—then you will understand why we find it difficult to wait.

The protests worked. In May 1963 a group of Birmingham business leaders agreed to desegregate their stores and begin hiring more black employees. Events in Birmingham also raised President Kennedy's commitment to civil rights. He went on television to give a dramatic speech:

> If an American, because his skin is dark, cannot eat lunch in a restaurant open to the public; if he cannot send his children to the best public school available; if he cannot vote for the public officials who represent him; if, in short, he cannot enjoy the full and free life which all of us want, then who among us would be content to have the color of his skin changed and stand in his place?

Kennedy then proposed a strong civil rights bill. To support the bill, civil rights leaders planned a massive rally in the nation's capital.

Civil rights demonstrators faced police beatings and attack dogs as well as imprisonment. Here, firemen under orders from police chief Bull Connor turn high-powered hoses on protesters in Birmingham, Alabama, in 1963. Television news coverage of police violence helped raise a national outcry against segregation. RELIGION How did the black church help inspire and sustain the civil rights movement? 4G, 7B

Photo Caption Answer
Religious concepts of equality and justice provided a moral foundation for the movement. The church organization helped coordinate the movement's activities, and people's faith gave them courage to act in the face of adversity.

C Cooperative Learning

Divide the class into groups. Ask each group to design a poster characterizing the civil rights movement of the early 1960s. Posters might feature a photograph, song, quotation, or slogan from the period. **LEP**

Addressing Individual Needs

Guided/ Independent Practice
Assign **Reinforcement Workbook** Worksheet 85, which helps students identify and explain factors that influenced the civil rights movement.

Reteaching/Correctives
Have students imagine that they were participants in a sit-in, freedom ride, or the movement between 1960 and 1963.

Have students complete **Reteaching Resources** Worksheet 85, which helps them sequence major events in the history of civil rights.

Enrichment/Extension
Have students imagine that they were participants in a sit-in, freedom ride, or the integration of a southern university. Ask them to write a diary entry for the night before their actions to promote integration.

Assessment
You may wish to use the Section 2 Review, page 526, to see how well your students understand the main points in this lesson.

Section Review Answers

1. *sit-in*—Method by which demonstrators sat at all-white lunch counters to protest segregation. *freedom rider*—Protester who rode buses across the South to call attention to segregation in transportation. *March on Washington*—Peaceful rally in which 250,000 Americans gathered to support civil rights legislation in 1963.

2. *James Lawson*—Black minister who led sit-in movement. *Nashville*—Tennessee city where sit-ins led to desegregation of lunch counters. *Medgar Evers*—Civil rights leader in Mississippi who was murdered in 1963. *Ross Barnett*—Governor who refused to obey a court order to integrate the University of Mississippi. *Birmingham*—Alabama city targeted by civil rights leaders, massive demonstrations there succeeded in desegregating stores and attracting national attention. *George Wallace*—Segregationist governor of Alabama. *Bull Connor*—Police chief who used violence against demonstrators in Birmingham.

3. Interstate Commerce Commission declared segregation on interstate buses and in terminals illegal. Supreme Court ordered all public travel accommodations to be integrated.

4. Martin Luther King and SCLC launched sit-ins, boycotts, and protest marches. These were met by vicious actions by the police department to put down demonstrations. Many demonstrators, including King, were arrested. Birmingham business leaders agreed to desegregate their stores and hire blacks.

5. Students may choose black urbanization, religious faith, constitutional rights, media coverage, or the inspiration of African independence.

Closure

Remind students of the pre-reading objectives in the section opener. Pose one or all of these questions again. Then have students read Section 3 for the next class period, noting how the civil rights movement changed in the mid-1960s.

Martin Luther King, Jr., won a Nobel Peace Prize for his use of Gandhi's techniques of nonviolent protest. King's political activism made him a target of the FBI, which sought to discredit him and other black leaders. **CIVIC VALUES** Explain King's belief that "injustice anywhere is a threat to justice everywhere." **6A, 7J**

THE MARCH ON WASHINGTON **7E, 7F, 7G, 7H**

In August 1963 "freedom buses" and "freedom trains" brought marchers from across the country to Washington, D.C. In all, some 250,000 Americans—60,000 of them white—gathered in Washington, D.C. Chanting "Pass that bill! Pass that bill!" they were taking part in what was, at the time, the largest political rally in American history.

Though journalists had predicted violence, the March on Washington was peaceful. Perhaps on no other day had Americans felt so hopeful about relations between the races. The day of songs and speeches ended with a speech by Martin Luther King, Jr. King put aside his prepared text and spoke from the heart. "I have a dream today!" he called out. King foresaw a day when people would "not be judged by the color of their skin, but the content of their character." The Baptist minister called on Americans to "stand up for freedom together." When that happened, he promised, "all

God's children, black men and white men, Jews and Gentiles, Protestants and Catholics, will be able to join hands and sing in the words of the old Negro spiritual: 'Free at last. Free at last. Thank God Almighty, we are free at last.' "

5E

★ **Historical Documents**

For an excerpt from Martin Luther King, Jr.'s, "I Have a Dream" speech, see page 729 of this book.

There was reason to hope that King's dream would come true. Congress passed Kennedy's civil rights bill after the President's assassination. The Civil Rights Act of 1964 marked the legal death of Jim Crow. It outlawed racial, religious, and sex discrimination in public places and by employers. Perhaps most importantly, it gave the federal government more power to enforce all the laws governing civil rights.

Yet there was also reason to fear that harmony between the races was still far off. Just two weeks after the exultation of the March on Washington, violence erupted again in Birmingham. Four black girls were killed when someone hurled dynamite into their church.

SECTION REVIEW

1. KEY TERMS sit-in, freedom rider, March on Washington

2. PEOPLE AND PLACES James Lawson, Nashville, Medgar Evers, Ross Barnett, Birmingham, George Wallace, Bull Connor

3. COMPREHENSION What success did the freedom riders have in protesting segregation in interstate transportation?

4. COMPREHENSION What events related to the civil rights movement took place in Birmingham in 1963?

5. CRITICAL THINKING Which of the factors listed on pages 523–524 do you think was *most* important in explaining why people risked their lives by taking part in the civil rights movement?

Photo Caption Answer
Students may suggest that the values of society as a whole are threatened by discrimination and prejudice, and that a truly just society does not permit its members to experience injustice.

Background Ten leaders of the March on Washington addressed the crowds at the Lincoln Memorial. Among them were A. Philip Randolph, Martin Luther King, Jr., Roy Wilkins, Whitney M. Young, Jr., and Walter Reuther. The ten leaders later met with President Kennedy at the White House.

2 A Divided Vietnam

Section Focus

Key Terms domino theory ■ Vietcong ■ coup

Main Idea From 1954 to 1963 the United States tried to make South Vietnam independent and non-Communist under Ngo Dinh Diem.

Objectives As you read, look for answers to these questions:
1. What decisions did the Geneva Conference make about Vietnam?
2. What was South Vietnam like under the Diem regime?
3. What was the situation in South Vietnam when Lyndon Johnson became President?

During the siege of Dienbienphu, diplomats in Geneva, Switzerland, were working on a settlement to end the Korean War. With the French defeat, the Geneva Conference turned its attention to Vietnam.

A DIVIDED NATION 1B

The Vietminh had, for all practical purposes, won the war. Ho Chi Minh had good reason to hope for a peace treaty that would give the Vietminh authority over all of Vietnam. Yet Chinese and Soviet delegates persuaded the Vietminh to compromise. Both Communist powers were concerned that the United States might go to war to prevent the Vietminh from taking all of Vietnam. With cold war tensions high, they wanted to avoid open conflict with the United States.

Thus the Vietminh accepted a temporary division of Vietnam at the seventeenth parallel. According to the agreements reached in Geneva, Hanoi would be the capital of the North, with Ho Chi Minh as its leader. Saigon would be the capital of the South, under the leadership of the anti-Communist Ngo Dinh Diem (NOH DIN dee–EM). But the division was only supposed to last for two years. In 1956 a nationwide election was to be held to reunify Vietnam under one government.

No elections were held. American leaders opposed a nationwide election because they believed Ho Chi Minh would win and all of Vietnam would become Communist. As President Eisenhower wrote later, "I have never talked or corresponded with a person knowledgeable in Indochinese affairs who did not agree that had elections been held . . . possibly 80 percent of the population

would have voted for the Communist Ho Chi Minh." In place of elections, the United States worked to establish a permanent non-Communist South Vietnam under Ngo Dinh Diem.

When Vietnam was divided in 1954, hundreds of thousands of northerners fled south to avoid Communist rule. These refugees formed a political base for the Diem government. **GLOBAL AWARENESS** For what reasons do refugees leave their homes? **9A**

REASONS FOR AMERICAN POLICY 1B

Opponents of United States policy have long criticized American leaders for opposing an all-Vietnam election. It was hypocritical, they say, to attack Communists as undemocratic, and then refuse to allow elections for fear of the results.

Supporters of American policy argued that Communists could not be trusted to preserve democracy. If Ho had won nationwide control, they claimed, he would have crushed all opposition.

CHAPTER 23   THE VIETNAM WAR, 1945–1975   **541**

SUPPORTING THE SECTION

Reinforcement Workbook: Worksheet 88
Reteaching Resources: Worksheet 88
Teaching Transparencies: Transparency 88

Photo Caption Answer
Students may suggest persecution, search for a better life, war, famine, and natural disaster.

SECTION 2

A Divided Vietnam
(pp. 541–544)

Section Objective

■ identify American objectives in Vietnam between 1954 and 1963

Introducing the Section

Connecting with Past Learnings
Review U.S. involvement in Vietnam up to 1954. (It was paying for 80 percent of France's war costs with Vietnam, but had not sent any troops.)

Key Terms
Write each key term on a file card and give the file cards to volunteers. The volunteers should lead a class discussion on the definitions of the terms, until students agree on a definition. Student leaders should write that definition on the back of the file card, adding to the set of flash cards. **LEP**

Focus

On one side of the board, have students list adjectives describing Ho Chi Minh's leadership of the Vietminh. (Dedicated, Communist, ruthless, revolutionary, etc.) Then, on the other side of the board, have them list Diem's leadership qualities. (Corrupt, unpopular, Catholic, anti-Communist, etc.) Ask them to consider who they might have chosen to follow if they had lived in Vietnam during the 1950s and 1960s.
What was the United States trying to achieve in Vietnam between 1954 and 1963? (To keep South Vietnam non-Communist and independent.) *How did Diem's leadership undercut American goals?* (His actions lost support for his anti-Communist government.)

After students have read the section, you may want to consider the following activities:

Global Awareness
During the period 1954–1963, what were other cold war "hot spots"? (Iran, Hungary, the Middle East, Guatemala, Berlin, Cuba, emerging African nations.) Have students create a timeline of U.S. foreign affairs during that period.

Impact of Geography
Have students examine a classroom map of Asia or the world map at the back of the book and identify Communist-controlled Asian countries in 1960. (China, North Korea, North Vietnam.) *According to the domino theory, what might be the next countries to become Communist?* (Students may suggest South Korea, South Vietnam, Laos, Cambodia, Burma, etc.) Have students write their suggestions on the board, creating a flow chart of the perceived spread of communism.

Analyzing Controversial Issues
Ask students to list examples of the undemocratic nature of Diem's government. (He threw opponents in jail, refused to hold elections, imprisoned or killed former Vietminh.) *Do you think the United States should have supported his regime?* (Possible answers include yes, because it was against communism; or no, because it was undemocratic.) *Are there any circumstances under which the United States should support a foreign government that is undemocratic?*

Religion
Discuss with the class the impact of the public suicides of Buddhist monks protesting Diem's regime. Ask students to consider the monks' motivations. *Do you think the monks were courageous or foolish? Why?*

They cited Ho's ruthless land reform campaign waged in North Vietnam from 1955 to 1956, in which thousands of landholders were executed. Ho finally stopped the executions and admitted that "errors" had been made. Nevertheless, North Vietnam remained a tightly controlled and undemocratic society.

Criticism of North Vietnam was deserved. Yet the American position would have been stronger if the United States had made a genuine effort to promote democracy in South Vietnam. Washington's main concern, however, was not that the Saigon government be democratic; it simply had to be anti-Communist. If South Vietnam fell to communism, Eisenhower claimed, other nations in Southeast Asia would also fall, toppling one after another like dominoes. This domino theory reflected American leaders' desire to learn the lessons of the 1930s. As Lyndon Johnson later explained, "We learned from Hitler at Munich that success only feeds the appetite for aggression."

> "**W**e learned from Hitler at Munich that success only feeds the appetite for aggression."
>
> —*Lyndon Johnson*

SUPPORTING DIEM 1A

After the Geneva Conference, the United States threw its weight behind Ngo Dinh Diem. Diem was a wealthy, Western-educated Catholic. American leaders saw him as the best hope for building a lasting non-Communist South Vietnam. While living in the United States during the early 1950s, Diem had won the admiration of many powerful people, including Senator John F. Kennedy.

Diem's American supporters admired the fact that he was a devout Catholic and a critic of both French colonialism and communism. They hoped he would ignite a non-Communist nationalism in the hearts of the South Vietnamese. Instead, he built a government that proved to be unpopular, corrupt, and dictatorial. He used massive American military and economic aid to enlarge his own

Members of South Vietnam's air force pledge their support for President Ngo Dinh Diem (left) following a failed military rebellion and an attempt on Diem's life in 1962. Diem had little popular support and staged fraudulent elections to stay in power. GLOBAL AWARENESS Why did his American supporters admire Diem? 1A

power and that of a small circle of loyal supporters—family members, generals, and wealthy landlords.

To American officials, Diem promised to end corruption, introduce democratic reforms, and help the peasants. The changes never came about. Meanwhile, Diem continued to rule with an iron fist, jailing those who criticized his regime. He also imprisoned or killed thousands of former Vietminh. Anyone who had fought against the French was accused of being a Communist. In May 1957 *Life* magazine, usually supportive of Diem, sharply criticized his government:

> Behind a facade of photographs, flags and slogans there is a grim structure of decrees, political prisons, concentration camps, milder "re-education centers," secret police. . . . The whole machinery of security has been used to discourage active opposition of any kind from any source.

542 UNIT 8 TIMES OF TURMOIL

plan" to end the war. He would not say what the plan was, but however the war ended, he vowed to "win the peace" abroad and restore it at home.

With the Democrats badly divided, Nixon won the election. He received just 43 percent of the popular vote, but his victory in the Electoral College was decisive. Now Nixon had to find a way to fulfill his promise of bringing "peace with honor."

> **"P**eace with honor."
>
> —*Richard Nixon, 1968*
> *campaign slogan*

SECTION REVIEW

1. KEY TERMS Tet Offensive, hawk, dove

2. PEOPLE AND PLACES Hué, Eugene McCarthy, Robert F. Kennedy, Hubert H. Humphrey, Richard M. Nixon, George Wallace, Richard Daley

3. COMPREHENSION What was the military impact of the Tet Offensive? What was its political impact?

4. COMPREHENSION What pressures confronted President Johnson early in 1968?

5. CRITICAL THINKING What reasons help to explain the victory of Richard Nixon and the defeat of the Democrats in 1968?

1A, 1B, 3B, 4B, 7B, 7C, 9A, 9D, 9E, 9G

5 Nixon and the End of the War

Section Focus

Key Terms Vietnamization ■ My Lai massacre ■ Khmer Rouge ■ War Powers Act

Main Idea Under President Nixon, American troops were gradually withdrawn from Vietnam, but the bombing increased and fighting spread to Cambodia. Though a peace treaty was signed in 1973, final victory went to the Communists two years later.

Objectives As you read, look for answers to these questions:
1. How did Nixon bring about American withdrawal from Vietnam?
2. How and why did the Communists win the war?
3. What was the legacy of the war for Southeast Asia? For the United States?

Despite Nixon's pledge to end the war, 1969 brought some of the war's bloodiest fighting and some of the largest antiwar demonstrations. Millions of Americans took part in peaceful protests. The nation's capital twice filled with more than 250,000 demonstrators.

The protesters called for an end to the bloodshed, an end to a war that seemed to them more pointless every day. In houses of worship across the land, people held candlelight services to read

off the names of Americans killed in Vietnam. It took hours and days to read them all.

VIETNAMIZATION 1B, 7C

Nixon claimed to be unmoved by the protests, but they did affect American policy. Nixon and his key foreign policy adviser, Henry Kissinger, knew that they needed to show some progress toward ending the war. If not, the nation might come apart at the seams.

---

5. The polarization and increasingly violent confrontations within the country made it seem like the Democrats had lost control and people wanted new leadership; the war seemed stalemated and Nixon promised he had a way for the United States to end it.

Closure

Use the Chapter Review Summary for Section 4 (p. 564) to synthesize the important elements in the section. Then have students read Section 5 for the next class period, noting how United States involvement in Vietnam ended.

SECTION 5

Nixon and the End of the War
(pp. 557–563)

Section Objective

■ describe how the United States ended its involvement in Vietnam

Introducing the Section

Connecting with Past Learnings
Discuss with students the mood of the country at the end of 1968. *How did the Vietnam War help Richard Nixon win the presidency?* (Johnson had lost a great deal of support because he escalated American involvement in Vietnam. Vice President Humphrey ran for President, but lost support because of his closeness to Johnson. Nixon claimed he had a secret plan to end the war.)

Nixon and Kissinger's response was a policy of **Vietnamization**—building up South Vietnamese forces and making them do more of the fighting while gradually withdrawing American troops. Nixon announced that American forces would be reduced to 480,000 by the end of 1969. In 1970 the troop level dropped to about 235,000. At the end of 1971, it was under 160,000.

By withdrawing troops, Nixon hoped to reduce the number of Americans killed and thereby quiet protests against the war. In time casualties did drop, and many Americans were persuaded that the war was winding down. Yet, because the withdrawal was so slow, almost as many Americans died *after* Nixon took office as before.

As American manpower went down, American firepower went up. Nixon ordered large-scale bombing raids on North Vietnam to reassure the South Vietnamese of continued American backing.

Nixon believed his plan was the best way to preserve a non-Communist South Vietnam. Troop withdrawals would quiet the peace movement, buying time to bolster the South Vietnamese military. At the same time, by stepping up the bombing he hoped to convince the Communists of his commitment to victory. Nixon did not want to use nuclear weapons, but he wanted North Vietnam to think he would. In effect, he wanted to scare the enemy into compromise.

To this end, Nixon ordered the bombing of neighboring Cambodia early in 1969. Cambodia had not taken sides in the war, but North Vietnamese troops had been using Cambodia to stage attacks against South Vietnam. Nixon wanted to wipe out these bases. He also wanted to pressure North Vietnam to agree to American terms at the bargaining table. The bombing of Cambodia continued off and on until August 1973.

THE MY LAI MASSACRE REVEALED 1B

Nixon did not tell the American people of the bombing of Cambodia. The success of his overall strategy depended in large part upon keeping the war out of the news. News of the bombing, he feared, would set off protests. This part of his plan suffered a setback in November 1969. Journalists learned that more than a year earlier, American

soldiers had killed hundreds of unarmed civilians in the village of My Lai (MEE LY). Officers had covered up the **My Lai massacre** by reporting that there had been a battle in My Lai in which 128 Vietcong died.

In truth, there had been no battle. American soldiers had entered the village, looking for a Vietcong unit. The soldiers, having recently suffered many casualties to mines and booby traps, attacked My Lai in a spirit of revenge. Even though they found only women, children, and old men, they opened fire. The killing went on for several hours. American military investigators later concluded that at least 350 civilians were killed.

The shocking news of the My Lai massacre further divided Americans. It made many even more opposed to the war. Others were angry because they thought reporting My Lai hurt the war effort.

THE INVASION OF CAMBODIA 1B

Nixon believed he could rally Americans behind a tougher policy. Once again he saw Cambodia as crucial, because the secret bombing had not destroyed the Communist bases there. Without consulting Congress or the Cambodian government, Nixon ordered an invasion of Cambodia in April 1970. Nixon claimed that the attack would wipe out Communist bases, shorten the war, and save American lives. Unless this tough measure were taken, Nixon warned, America would be seen as a "pitiful helpless giant."

The 20,000-man invasion did not produce the expected results. Most Communist troops simply pulled back deeper into Cambodian territory. While the Americans seized large amounts of enemy supplies, this was not enough to cripple the North Vietnamese war effort.

However, the invasion did spark a new round of protests at home. Congress voted to repeal the Gulf of Tonkin Resolution, and more than 200 employees of the State Department signed a letter protesting the invasion. Outraged students held strikes and demonstrations at more than 400 colleges and universities.

Kent State University in Ohio saw the most tragic confrontation. The governor had called in the National Guard to keep the peace. When demonstrators were ordered to disperse, they responded by throwing rocks. Suddenly a few guardsmen opened fired, killing four students and wounding ten.

The killings at Kent State split the nation even more deeply. Nixon heightened the tension by calling the war protesters "bums." His view was supported by 100,000 demonstrators who marched in New York City carrying signs that said "America, Love It Or Leave It."

THE VIETNAM GENERATION 1A

Some people *were* leaving, for the prospect of being drafted and sent to Vietnam concerned an entire generation. As many as 30,000 young men went to Canada and other countries to avoid the draft. Joining them were about 20,000 men who deserted the military. Meanwhile, millions more evaded the draft by going to college. (College students were exempt from the draft.) Fewer than one in ten American soldiers in Vietnam were college graduates.

Three million young Americans eventually fought in Vietnam. Of these, most came from poor and working-class backgrounds. Many hoped that the military would give them training for better jobs. But whatever their background, many who fought believed that military service was their duty as citizens—something to be performed, not questioned.

AMERICAN SOLDIERS IN VIETNAM 1A

All wars are traumatic, but Vietnam was an especially brutal shock. The average soldier was only 19 years old, barely out of high school. He fought an enemy he could rarely see, lived among "allies" he could not trust, and moved through jungles and rice paddies that were as exhausting and dangerous as combat.

As the frustrating war dragged on, troop morale declined. After Tet, American soldiers found the war more and more pointless. By 1970 drug use was commonplace, and some units even began refusing to go on combat missions. Dozens of officers were killed or wounded by their own men. In June 1971 journalist Robert Heinl wrote in *Armed Forces Journal*, "Our army that now remains in Vietnam is in a state of approaching collapse."

This photograph shows American nurses and soldiers at Cam Ranh Bay—the major entry point for U.S. supplies and troops in South Vietnam. The majority of the approximately 10,000 American women who served in Vietnam were medical personnel. ISSUES There were no women combat soldiers in Vietnam. Do you believe women should fight in war? Why, or why not? 9G

Photo Caption Answers
Some students may say that women are capable of fighting a modern-day technological war and they should have the right to choose how to serve their country. Others may say that combat still requires great physical strength and that the world is accustomed to male soldiers being killed, but the idea of someone's daughter or mother dying in battle is too offensive.

History
Why didn't President Nixon tell the American people about the bombing of Cambodia? (He wanted to quiet the peace movement by winding down U.S. involvement, at the same time keeping up pressure on the Communists.) *Did his strategy work?* (No, when Americans heard about the My Lai massacre and the invasion of Cambodia, many protested.) Have students discuss reasons why the President might keep secrets from the American public, citing other examples if they can.

Have students consider the idea that generals are often accused of fighting the previous war. *How do you think the American experience in Vietnam might influence today's generals?*

National Identity
Discuss the My Lai massacre. *Why was news of the massacre so upsetting to the American public?* (It undercut Americans' image of themselves as liberators who were helping the Vietnamese.) *How do you think it affected the morale of soldiers fighting in Vietnam?* (Caused great harm, because many antiwar critics viewed them as the "bad guys.") *How might stories such as My Lai and reports of drug use among soldiers have affected American attitudes toward returning Vietnam veterans?*

Civic Values
Have students debate whether the First Amendment provision for freedom of the press should extend to possibly damaging stories in times of war, such as the My Lai massacre. Then have them consider whether the students who protested against the invasion of Cambodia were acting as responsible citizens. Ask students to express their opinions of the deaths at Kent State.

THE END OF THE WAR 1A

In 1972, after so many years of bloodshed, an end
to the war appeared to be in sight. On October 26,
1972, National Security Adviser Henry Kissinger
announced that "peace is at hand." After three
years of talks, Kissinger and Le Duc Tho of North
Vietnam had agreed to a ceasefire under which all
remaining American troops would be withdrawn.
Communist forces would be allowed to remain in
place with the promise of forming a coalition government in South Vietnam.

However, South Vietnamese president Nguyen
Van Thieu (nuh–WIN VAN TYOO) wanted Nixon
to promise that the United States would step in if
the Communists broke the terms of the agreement. Nixon offered his word, but Thieu still insisted on other changes. Le Duc Tho responded
by suspending the peace talks. Nixon, eager to
show Thieu that American force was still behind
him, decided to unleash American firepower one
more time.

On December 18, 1972, Nixon ordered a massive
two-week bombing attack on the cities of Hanoi
and Haiphong. Nixon believed that these "Christmas bombings" were necessary to force the North
Vietnamese to sign the agreement. The raids were
also meant to demonstrate American backing for
South Vietnam. Meanwhile, China and the Soviet
Union were pressuring North Vietnam to settle
the war. Both Communist giants had been working to improve ties with the United States. They
believed that an end to the war would go a long
way toward smoothing relations.

The final settlement was signed on January 27,

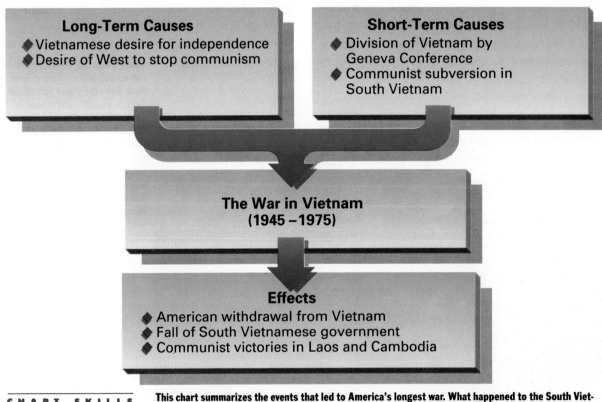

CAUSE AND EFFECT: THE WAR IN VIETNAM

Long-Term Causes
◆ Vietnamese desire for independence
◆ Desire of West to stop communism

Short-Term Causes
◆ Division of Vietnam by Geneva Conference
◆ Communist subversion in South Vietnam

The War in Vietnam (1945 – 1975)

Effects
◆ American withdrawal from Vietnam
◆ Fall of South Vietnamese government
◆ Communist victories in Laos and Cambodia

CHART SKILLS
9E

This chart summarizes the events that led to America's longest war. What happened to the South Vietnamese government as a result of the war? CRITICAL THINKING Was American participation in the war
inevitable? What might have happened had the United States not intervened?

South Vietnamese civilians race to board a U.S. evacuation helicopter during the fall of Saigon.
POLITICS Explain former Vice President Humphrey's comment that big powers often "miscalculate, . . . overestimating our power to control events. . . . Power tends to be a substitute for judgment and wisdom." 9A

1973. As part of the agreement, more than 500 American prisoners of war were released from the prison they had dubbed the "Hanoi Hilton." The sight of the POWs stepping off planes in California marked for many Americans the end of the Vietnam War. Still, the fragile ceasefire agreement left little hope for peace. With armed Communist and

A former prisoner of war returns home to an emotional welcome. In 1973, North Vietnam agreed to release several hundred POWs, but over 2,000 Americans remain unaccounted for. **NATIONAL IDENTITY** What problems did Vietnam veterans face after returning to the United States? 9A

non-Communist troops still in place, fighting was sure to resume.

Early in 1975, North Vietnamese forces made some cautious military probes in South Vietnam. Emboldened by success, they began a steady advance toward Saigon. Gerald Ford, Nixon's successor as President, asked for more military aid to save South Vietnam from collapse. But Congress refused. In the words of historian George C. Herring, that vote "seems to have reflected the wishes of the American people." As one American said of the war, "My God, we're all tired of it, we're sick to death of it."

Its American backers gone, the South Vietnamese army dissolved in the face of Communist attacks. Saigon fell on April 30, 1975. While the Communists were celebrating their victory, helicopters hastily evacuated the American ambassador and his staff.

SOUTHEAST ASIA AFTER THE WAR 1A
As the departing helicopters rose above the embassy compound, crowds of South Vietnamese

---

Analyzing Controversial Issues
Have the class debate the lessons of the Vietnam War by asking them if they agree with the point of view of William Westmoreland, Paul Warnke, or James Stockdale.

Cultural Pluralism
Why have many Southeast Asians come to the United States since the war? (To escape repressive regimes.) *What kind of background or beliefs were these refugees likely to have had? What were they looking for when they left?*

C Cooperative Learning

Divide the class into four groups representing Nixon, Le Duc Tho, an American antiwar protester, and a South Vietnamese soldier. Have the groups write down their person's version of how the Vietnam War ended and what effect it had on his or her country. Convene the class and have each group report its version. Challenge students to identify areas of agreement and disagreement. **LEP**

Addressing Individual Needs

Guided/Independent Practice
Instruct students to complete **Reinforcement Workbook** Worksheet 91. This worksheet asks students to use information from a table to understand the cost of the Vietnam War.

In the aftermath of war, more than one million desperate Vietnamese fled their country by boat. Their voyages were very dangerous, and tens of thousands died at sea. More than half the refugees from Vietnam eventually settled in the United States. ISSUES What role do immigrant groups play in today's society? 4B

Reteaching/Correctives

Have students imagine they are historians evaluating the Vietnam War and its effects on United States history. Have them write several paragraphs on this topic. Have students use facts from the text as well as the chart on page 560 to support their opinion.

Have students complete **Reteaching Resources** Worksheet 91, which asks them to identify people and places discussed in the section.

Enrichment/Extension

Have students complete **Enrichment and Extension Resources** Primary Source Worksheet 46. This worksheet asks students to analyze congressional testimony given by a representative of Vietnam Veterans Against the War.

Assessment

You may wish to use the Section 5 Review, page 563, to see how well your students understand the main points in this lesson.

Section Review Answers

1. *Vietnamization*—Policy of building up South Vietnamese forces and making them do more of the fighting while gradually withdrawing American troops. *My Lai massacre*—The slaughter of unarmed Vietnamese civilians by American soldiers in the village of My Lai. *Khmer Rouge*—Cambodian Communists. *War Powers Act*—Passed by Congress in 1973 to prevent future wars from starting without congressional approval.

struggled to join them. These Vietnamese were terrified at the thought of life under the Communists—justly, it turned out. Over the next few years many tens of thousands of people suffered brutal treatment in "re-education camps." Soon, scores of "boat people" began fleeing Vietnam, risking their lives on dangerous waters as they sought refuge in such distant places as Thailand or Hong Kong. Many made their way to the United States.

The Vietnamese had suffered enormous casualties during the war. Well over a million people had died, and countless others had lost their homes and belongings. For Cambodia, the horror was only just beginning. The United States had stopped bombing Cambodia in August 1973. Without American support, the Cambodian government fell to a Communist group called the Khmer Rouge. Under the leadership of Pol Pot, the Khmer Rouge undertook a campaign of mass terror against the Cambodian people. They murdered at least one million Cambodians in an effort to wipe out all traces of Western influence.

Pol Pot's fanatical rule ended in 1979 when Vietnam invaded Cambodia. A Vietnamese-backed government was installed in Cambodia, but the Khmer Rouge and other armed groups remained active. The withdrawal of Vietnamese troops in 1989 promised continued unrest in Cambodia, as the Khmer Rouge renewed its effort to regain power.

562 UNIT 8 TIMES OF TURMOIL

THE UNITED STATES AFTER THE WAR 3B, 7B

The American defeat in Vietnam was a profound shock, shattering Americans' belief that their nation was invincible. The defeat also shook many Americans' confidence in their system of government. People especially lost faith in the elected leaders who had misled them about the war.

In this spirit, Congress tried to reclaim some control over American foreign policy. Overriding Nixon's veto, it passed the War Powers Act on November 7, 1973. The aim of this act was to prevent future wars from starting without congressional support. It requires the President to inform Congress within two days of any use of American troops in a foreign country. Those troops must be withdrawn within 60 days if Congress does not support their deployment.

Meanwhile, another casualty of the Vietnam War was the American economy. Fighting the war had cost vast sums of money. President Johnson, refusing to increase taxes to pay for the war, had let the budget deficit rise instead. This policy produced a huge national debt and mounting inflation.

In a more literal sense, returning soldiers were also casualties, with wounds both visible and invisible. Unwelcome in South Vietnam, they did not receive a hero's welcome when they came back to the United States. Many had a hard time finding jobs and readjusting to life at home. According to the Department of Veterans Affairs, as many as

Photo Caption Answer
Students may suggest that immigrants are highly motivated members of society who generally work hard to succeed economically and academically.

500,000 veterans have suffered psychological problems related to the war.

It took years for the nation to recognize the contributions of its soldiers in Vietnam. The Vietnam Veterans Memorial in Washington, D.C., was dedicated in 1982 to honor the nation's 58,000 war dead. During the 1980s support groups were formed around the country to help veterans.

Long after the fighting stopped, Americans still disagree over why the United States lost the war. Some accept the view of General Westmoreland, who said, "The war was lost by congressional actions withdrawing support to the South Vietnamese government despite commitments by President Nixon." Others agree with Paul Warnke, former General Counsel to the Defense Department. Warnke stated, "We became involved because we viewed the Indochinese conflict as part of our global struggle with the Soviet Union and the People's Republic of China. It was, instead, a . . . revolution in which we had no legitimate role."

Americans also disagree over the meaning of events in Indochina since the end of the war. Some point to the Communist takeover of Cambodia and neighboring Laos in 1975 as proof that the domino theory was correct. And, in their opinion, the flood of refugees from the region since 1975 confirms what American leaders had always been saying—that communism would be a disaster for the people of Indochina. Others disagree. They argue that because the Communists in Cambodia and Vietnam became enemies, the domino theory does not apply. They also contend that wartime destruction, much of it caused by the United States, was largely responsible for the miserable conditions in Indochina.

Both sides seem to agree that the American people should have had a larger voice in the war. Admiral James Stockdale, who took part in the Gulf of Tonkin incident and later spent eight years as a prisoner of war in Hanoi, summed up this lesson of the war:

> The Founding Fathers were correct in writing into the Constitution the provision that only the Congress, only the people, can declare war. If people don't understand a war, if they don't support it, our armed conflicts will degenerate into half-hearted, deceptive measures. These usually spell defeat.

SECTION REVIEW

1. KEY TERMS Vietnamization, My Lai massacre, Khmer Rouge, War Powers Act

2. PEOPLE AND PLACES Kent State, Nguyen Van Thieu, Gerald Ford, Pol Pot

3. COMPREHENSION Why did Nixon order the bombing of Cambodia? What effects did it have?

4. COMPREHENSION What were the effects of the war on Southeast Asia and on the United States?

5. CRITICAL THINKING Should leaders conducting a war ever be allowed to keep secrets from their people? Why or why not?

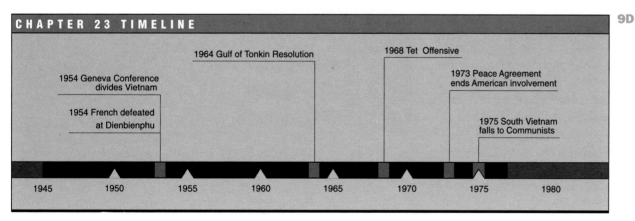

CHAPTER 23 TIMELINE

1954 Geneva Conference divides Vietnam

1954 French defeated at Dienbienphu

1964 Gulf of Tonkin Resolution

1968 Tet Offensive

1973 Peace Agreement ends American involvement

1975 South Vietnam falls to Communists

1945   1950   1955   1960   1965   1970   1975   1980

---

2. *Kent State*—Ohio university where the National Guard killed four student antiwar demonstrators. *Nguyen Van Thieu*—South Vietnamese president at the time of South Vietnam's fall. *Gerald Ford*— President in 1975, when Communists gained control of South Vietnam. *Pol Pot*—Leader of the Khmer Rouge.

3. He wanted to wipe out bases which North Vietnamese troops had been using to stage attacks against South Vietnam; it did not wipe out the bases.

4. Answers should indicate that there was enormous loss of life and disruption of families in Southeast Asia, livelihoods were threatened by the damage done to the land, and the economies of the countries were in shambles. In the United States, the war created a loss of faith in U.S. invincibility and in the truthfulness of our leaders. It also left a huge debt, and thousands of veterans with physical, emotional, and psychological scars.

5. Some students may say that in a democracy the people must have all the information to make proper decisions. Others may note that in times of war, national security could be compromised if every decision were publicized.

Closure

Remind students of the pre-reading objectives in the section opener. Pose one or all of these questions again. Then have students read Section 1 of Chapter 24 for the next class period, noting the domestic issues faced by the United States in the late 1960s and early 1970s.

Chapter 23 Review Answers

Key Terms
1. Vietnamization
2. Khmer Rouge
3. War Powers Act
4. Gulf of Tonkin Resolution
5. domino theory

People to Identify
1. U.S.-supported leader of South Vietnam until his assassination in 1963.
2. Communist leader of the Vietnamese independence movement.
3. Democratic presidential candidate in 1968.
4. Democratic peace candidate who challenged Johnson in 1968.
5. Leader of the Khmer Rouge.
6. South Vietnamese president at the time of its fall.
7. Commander of U.S. forces in South Vietnam.

Places to Locate
1. F   4. D
2. A   5. B
3. C   6. E

Reviewing the Facts
1. During the war, Ho Chi Minh's forces fought the Japanese. Later, they fought the French.
2. To avoid a Communist takeover of Vietnam.
3. The Geneva agreement divided Vietnam at the seventeenth parallel into a Communist and a non-Communist country. U.S. officials opposed elections because they believed Ho Chi Minh, a Communist, would win.
4. Diem's repression and corruption made him unpopular, but the U.S. supported him because of his anti-Communist stance. The escalation of Diem's oppressive tactics, especially attacks against Buddhists, caused the U.S. to withdraw its support.

Chapter 23 REVIEW

CHAPTER 23 SUMMARY

SECTION 1: Vietnam, which had long been dominated by colonial powers, fought for independence from France after World War II.

■ Ho Chi Minh, a Communist, led the Vietnamese independence movement.

■ The United States supported the French because of concern over the spread of communism.

■ The French withdrew from Vietnam after their defeat at Dienbienphu in 1954.

SECTION 2: The United States backed an independent non-Communist government in South Vietnam.

■ Vietnam was temporarily divided in 1954. The North was controlled by Communists. In the South, Ngo Dinh Diem established an anti-Communist regime.

■ A Communist-led guerrilla movement gathered strength in the south. In the early 1960s, the United States increased aid and sent military advisers to help the government.

SECTION 3: Under the Johnson administration, the United States made a major military commitment to Vietnam.

■ American troops and planes supported South Vietnam.

■ The war was fought under difficult conditions and with little support from the South Vietnamese population.

SECTION 4: By 1968 Americans were sharply divided over the Vietnam War.

■ Though it was a military failure for the North, the Tet Offensive led many Americans to decide the war could not be won.

■ Antiwar protests increased during the late 1960s. President Johnson, battered by criticism, announced in 1968 that he would not seek re-election.

■ Richard Nixon won the 1968 presidential election with the pledge that he would reunite Americans and end the war honorably.

SECTION 5: Under Nixon, American troops were gradually withdrawn from Vietnam.

■ The last American troops left Vietnam in 1973. The war ended in a Communist victory in 1975.

■ The Vietnam War claimed almost 60,000 American lives. It also damaged the United States' self-image, its image abroad, and its economy.

KEY TERMS ●

Use the following terms to complete the sentences below.

domino theory
Gulf of Tonkin Resolution
Khmer Rouge
Vietnamization
War Powers Act

1. Nixon's plan to train ARVN forces to take over the fighting was known as _____.
2. The vicious Communist group that came to power in Cambodia in 1975 was known as the _____.
3. The _____ aimed to prevent the United States from involvement in future wars without congressional support.
4. The _____ gave President Johnson authority to commit American combat troops to fight in Vietnam.
5. The _____ stated that if Vietnam fell to the Communists, all of Southeast Asia would follow.

PEOPLE TO IDENTIFY ●

Identify the following people and tell why each was important.

1. Ngo Dinh Diem
2. Ho Chi Minh
3. Hubert H. Humphrey
4. Eugene McCarthy
5. Pol Pot
6. Nguyen Van Thieu
7. William Westmoreland

5. Because the government of South Vietnam was too weak to stop the Vietcong.

6. American troops fought a war of attrition using search-and-destroy missions and massive bombing raids. The Communists fought with hit-and-run and ambush tactics.

PLACES TO LOCATE ●

Match each of the letters on the map with the places that are listed below.

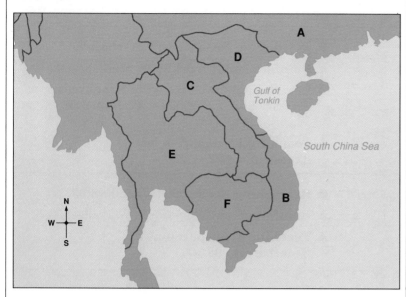

1. Cambodia (Kampuchea)
2. China
3. Laos
4. North Vietnam
5. South Vietnam
6. Thailand

REVIEWING THE FACTS ▲

1. Whom did Ho Chi Minh's forces fight during World War II? After the war?
2. Why did the United States support the French effort to maintain control of Vietnam?
3. What agreement was reached at the Geneva Conference? Why did the United States not push for elections in South Vietnam in 1956?
4. Why was Ngo Dinh Diem unpopular with his people? Why did the United States support him? Why did it withdraw that support in 1963?
5. Why did President Johnson increase American involvement in Vietnam?

6. What tactics were used by the American troops? The Communists?
7. What events at home and abroad significantly affected the outcome of the 1968 presidential election?
8. Describe the positions taken on the Vietnam War by hawks and by doves.
9. What strategy did President Nixon use in conducting the war? What was the effect of the peace agreement signed in 1973?
10. Which side finally won the war in Vietnam? What lasting effects did the war have on the United States?

CRITICAL THINKING SKILLS ▲

1. **MAKING JUDGMENTS** Some analysts believe that television coverage of the fighting in Vietnam turned Americans against the war. How might television coverage have affected public opinion? Would television coverage of earlier wars have produced a different effect?

2. **IDENTIFYING THE MAIN IDEA** Reread the quote from *Life* on page 542. What is the main idea the author is expressing?

WRITING ABOUT TOPICS IN AMERICAN HISTORY ■

1. **CONNECTING WITH LITERATURE** A selection from *Going After Cacciato* by Tim O'Brien appears on pages 813–814. Read it and answer the questions. Then answer the following question: In what ways, do you think, is literature about the Vietnam War different from other types of war literature?

2. **APPLYING THEMES: GLOBAL INTERACTIONS** Pretend that it is Inauguration Day 1969 and you are an adviser to President Nixon. Write a memo telling him how you think he should handle the war over the next four years. Consider both public opinion at home and foreign policy objectives abroad.

3. **ISSUES** Do research about Vietnam antiwar protests in the United States. Who were the protesters? What tactics did they use? To what degree did their actions affect public opinion?

9. Nixon adopted a policy of Vietnamization, building up South Vietnamese forces while withdrawing U.S. troops. The peace agreement established a temporary ceasefire and freed American POWs.

10. The Communists eventually won. The war shattered the American belief that the U.S. was invincible and left a huge national debt and thousands of veterans who remain physically and emotionally scarred.

Critical Thinking Skills

1. Television brought the horrors of war home, heightening awareness and polarizing public opinion. This horror might have resulted from watching other wars; on the other hand, U.S. victories would have made such scenes more palatable.

2. The reporter describes South Vietnam as a ruthless dictatorship and not the democratic state that Americans hoped to establish.

Writing About Topics in American History

1. Students might mention that heroism, honor, and the importance of the cause for which soldiers were fighting would play a much more important role in the literature of earlier wars.

2. Students, while acknowledging the growing resentment towards the war at home, should consider how to get out of Vietnam without giving the Communists a free hand.

3. Students may research the nonviolent protests of such people as the Berrigans and consider how they attracted national attention.

7. The demoralizing attacks of the Tet Offensive and the social unrest caused by antiwar protesters and the Kennedy and King assassinations influenced the 1968 presidential elections.

8. Hawks saw the war as part of the worldwide struggle against communism. The doves saw the war as a civil war among the Vietnamese people and believed the United States had no right to intervene.

Chapter Review exercises are keyed for student abilities:
● = Basic
▲ = Average
■ = Average/Advanced

Chapter 24 ■ From Vietnam to Watergate

	SECTION OBJECTIVES	SECTION RESOURCES
Section 1 **A Divided Nation**	■ identify issues that caused tensions in American society during the Nixon years	● **Reteaching Resources:** Worksheet 92 ▲ **Reinforcement Workbook:** Worksheet 92 ■ **Enrichment and Extension Resources:** Primary Source Worksheet 47; Historian Worksheet 10 ▲ **Teaching Transparencies:** Transparency 92
Section 2 **Toward a Cleaner and Safer World**	■ analyze the effects of movements toward protection of the environment, health and safety in the workplace, and consumer rights	● **Reteaching Resources:** Worksheet 93 ▲ **Reinforcement Workbook:** Worksheet 93 ▲ **Teaching Transparencies:** Transparency 93
Section 3 **World Affairs in the Nixon Years**	■ identify major events in foreign affairs during the early 1970s	● **Reteaching Resources:** Worksheet 94 ▲ **Reinforcement Workbook:** Worksheet 94 ▲ **Teaching Transparencies:** Transparency 94
Section 4 **The Watergate Scandal**	■ identify the major scandals of the Nixon administration ■ analyze the constitutional basis for the impeachment of President Richard Nixon	● **Reteaching Resources:** Worksheet 95 ▲ **Reinforcement Workbook:** Worksheet 95 ■ **Enrichment and Extension Resources:** Primary Source Worksheet 48 ▲ **Teaching Transparencies:** Transparency 95

The list below shows Essential Elements relevant to this chapter. (The complete list of Essential Elements appears in the introductory pages of this Teacher's Edition.)

Section 1: 1A, 3E, 3F, 4C, 4F, 5B, 5C, 5D, 5F, 7J, 8I, 9A
Section 2: 2B, 2C, 4C, 8D, 8G
Section 3: 1A, 1B, 8F, 9B, 9E, 9F
Section 4: 5B, 5D, 7A, 7B, 7I, 9A, 9D, 9E

Section Resources are keyed for student abilities:
● = Basic
▲ = Average
■ = Average/Advanced

CHAPTER RESOURCES

Geography Resources: Worksheets 47, 48
Tests: Chapter 24 Test

Chapter Project: Constitutional Government

Have students construct an illustrated report dealing with some aspect of American political life between 1969 and 1974. Topics for students to focus on include the environmental reawakening of the 1970s, the Watergate scandal, or changes in foreign affairs.

Homework Options

Each section contains activities labeled "Addressing Individual Needs." You may wish to choose from among these activities when assigning homework.

> **Provisions for Limited English Proficiency (LEP)**
> Several suggested activities may be particularly helpful for teachers of students with limited English proficiency. These activities have been marked throughout the Teacher's Annotated Edition with the symbol **LEP** .

BIBLIOGRAPHY AND AUDIOVISUAL AIDS

Teacher Bibliography

Ambrose, Stephen. *Nixon: The Triumph of a Politician, 1962–1972.* Simon and Schuster, 1989.

Harward, Donald W., ed. *Crisis in Confidence: The Impact of Watergate.* Little, Brown, 1974.

Jaworski, Leon. *The Right and the Power: The Prosecution of Watergate.* Gulf Publishing, 1976.

Kissinger, Henry. *Years of Upheaval.* Little, Brown, 1982. Kissinger's view of Watergate, the Middle East, and the Vietnam War.

White, Theodore H. *Breach of Faith: The Fall of Richard Nixon.* Dell, 1986.

Student Bibliography

Archer, Jules. *Watergate: America in Crisis.* Crowell, 1975.

Dean, John. *Blind Ambition.* Pocket Books, 1979.

Wheeler, John. *Touched with Fire: The Future of the Vietnam Generation.* Avon, 1985.

Woodward, Bob, and Carl Bernstein. *All the President's Men.* Warner Books, 1976.

Woodward, Bob, and Carl Bernstein. *The Final Days.* Avon, 1976.

Literature

Mailer, Norman. *Of a Fire on the Moon.* Grove, 1979. An account of the Apollo 11 moon shot including the technology, engineering, and people at NASA which made it possible.

Pirsig, Robert. *Zen and the Art of Motorcycle Maintenance: An Inquiry into Values.* Morrow, 1979.

Silko, Leslie M. *Ceremony.* Penguin, 1986. A World War II veteran is haunted by the war until he discovers his identity through Navajo rituals.

Films and Videotapes*

Focus on the Seventies: The Nixon Years. 23 min. COR/MTI. Documents the turbulent climate in the United States when Richard Nixon took office; evaluates Nixon's policies and the events leading to Watergate.

Nixon: Checkers to Watergate. 20 min. PYR. Archival stills, speeches, interviews, and press conferences highlight the triumphs and tragedies of Richard Nixon's career.

Filmstrips*

Watergate (set of 2). GA. Examines the events that led to the downfall of Richard Nixon and the realignment of the balance of power among the three branches of American government. Also available in video.

Computer Software*

Watergate Simulation (Apple). NCSC. An elaborate decision-making game/tutorial in which the student plays the roles of journalists Woodward and Bernstein during the Watergate investigation. Illustrates political dynamics and journalistic strategies.

*For a complete guide to audiovisual sources, see the introduction to this book (page Txx).

Chapter 24

From Vietnam to Watergate
(pp. 566–589)

This chapter traces the events and issues of the Nixon years, including social and political conflicts, the rise of the environmental movement, President Nixon's foreign policy, and the Watergate scandal.

Themes in American History

- Global interactions
- Constitutional government
- Pluralistic society
- American culture

Chapter Objectives

After students complete this chapter, they will be able to:

1. Identify issues that caused tensions in American society during the Nixon years.

2. Analyze the effects of movements toward protection of the environment, health and safety in the workplace, and consumer rights.

3. Identify major events in foreign affairs during the early 1970s.

4. Identify the major scandals of the Nixon administration.

5. Analyze the constitutional basis for the impeachment of President Richard Nixon.

Richard Nixon's presidency was highlighted by his historic trip to China in 1972. Nixon's foreign policy advances were soon overshadowed by the Watergate affair, however, which led to his resignation two years later.

CHAPTER SUPPORT MATERIAL

Reinforcement Workbook: Worksheets 92–95
Reteaching Resources: Worksheets 92–95
Enrichment and Extension Resources: Primary Source Worksheets 47, 48; Historian Worksheet 10
Geography Resources: Worksheets 47, 48
Teaching Transparencies: Transparencies 92–95
Tests: Chapter 24 Test

SECTION 1

A Divided Nation
(pp. 567–572)

Section Objective

■ identify issues that caused
tensions in American society during the Nixon years

**Introducing the
Section**

**Connecting with
Past Learnings**
Help students identify
controversial issues of the
late 1960s. *During the Johnson
years, what were the main issues dividing the nation?*
(Blacks' struggle for civil
rights, Vietnam War.) As
students work through the
lesson, have them analyze
how some of the issues that
divided the nation during
the Nixon era related to
those earlier issues.

Key Terms
Write the key terms on the
board. Explain that *stagflation* is a combination of the
words *stagnation* and *inflation*. Ask volunteers to define
each of the root words and
then the key term. Using the
example of *counterclockwise*,
ask students to suggest what
the prefix *counter* in *counterculture* means. (Opposite.)
Then have them define that
term, and the other key
term, in their own words. **LEP**

1A, 3E, 3F, 4C, 4F, 5B, 5C, 5D, 5F, 7J, 8I, 9A

1 A Divided Nation

★ Section Focus

Key Terms stagflation ■ American Indian
Movement ■ counterculture

Main Idea During the Nixon era, divisions
over political and social policies brought
conflict and change to America.

Objectives As you read, look for answers to
these questions:
1. What were Richard Nixon's goals as
President?
2. How did American Indians and Hispanic
Americans seek to gain justice?
3. How did young people in America break
with traditional social values?

November 6, 1968. A beaming Richard M. Nixon
steps before the microphones to celebrate his narrow victory over Hubert Humphrey. He calls for a
new spirit of national unity: "We want to bridge
the generation gap. We want to bridge the gap
between the races. We want to bring America
together."

The newly elected President had his work cut
out for him. The Vietnam War had opened up political divisions that threatened to tear apart
American society. The idealism of the Kennedy-
Johnson years had faded. Racial tensions remained high. The enormous cost of war was
threatening the economy.

THE PRESIDENT'S MEN 1A, 5F

"I don't want a Cabinet of yes-men," Nixon said
shortly after his election. He promised to appoint
a Cabinet that was strong and diverse, but like
others before him, he ended up doing just the opposite. Nixon's Cabinet members were white,

male, and Republican. Seven out of the twelve
were millionaires. Nixon's Cabinet, though, had
little influence on the President, and it rarely even
saw him. The only Cabinet member with real
clout was Nixon's former law partner, Attorney
General John Mitchell.

President Nixon relied on his personal staff instead of the Cabinet. Henry Kissinger was
Nixon's primary adviser on foreign policy. Domestic issues were overseen by Chief of Staff Bob
Haldeman and domestic adviser John Ehrlichman.
These advisers felt an intense loyalty to the President, and Nixon in turn trusted almost no one
else.

The President's chief interest was foreign policy.
He saw himself as a statesman and a man of
peace. On the domestic front, Nixon's ability to
lead was limited by the Democrats' control of both
houses of Congress. The Democrats pursued their
own legislative aims, and Nixon could do little to
initiate new bills.

SUPPORTING THE SECTION

Reinforcement Workbook: Worksheet 92

Reteaching Resources: Worksheet 92

Enrichment and Extension Resources: Primary
Source Worksheet 47; Historian Worksheet 10

Teaching Transparencies: Transparency 92

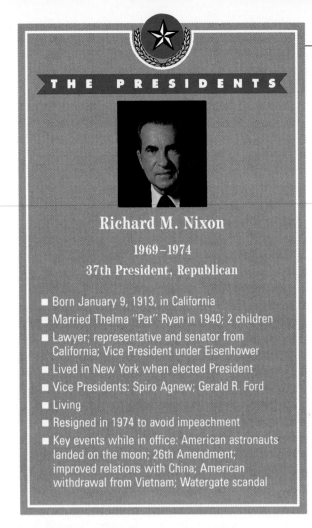

THE PRESIDENTS

Richard M. Nixon

1969–1974
37th President, Republican

- Born January 9, 1913, in California
- Married Thelma "Pat" Ryan in 1940; 2 children
- Lawyer; representative and senator from California; Vice President under Eisenhower
- Lived in New York when elected President
- Vice Presidents: Spiro Agnew; Gerald R. Ford
- Living
- Resigned in 1974 to avoid impeachment
- Key events while in office: American astronauts landed on the moon; 26th Amendment; improved relations with China; American withdrawal from Vietnam; Watergate scandal

ECONOMIC PROBLEMS 3E, 3F

The 1960s were boom years for the American economy. But the social programs of the Great Society, together with the Vietnam War, weighed heavily on the federal budget. By the time Nixon took office in 1969, the economy was in trouble.

Nixon pledged to cut government spending. However, the war in Vietnam continued to eat up billions. By 1971 slow economic growth had caused unemployment to rise. In addition, inflation was increasing rapidly.

In August 1971, Nixon responded by imposing wage and price controls—a temporary freeze on wages, rents, and prices—on the American economy. In 1951 the Truman administration had imposed similar controls to combat inflation during the Korean War. President Nixon's decision, however, came as a surprise. Just one month earlier,

Nixon had rejected such controls, saying that they would "snuff out" economic growth.

Wage and price controls kept inflation under control, but the underlying problem—high government spending—remained. When Nixon removed the controls shortly after his re-election in 1972, prices shot back up. Then, in 1973 and 1974, high oil prices helped push the annual inflation rate over 10 percent.

What made inflation such a frustrating problem during the 1970s was that unemployment levels were high as well. According to traditional economic models, this should not happen. An active economy should produce high inflation but low unemployment; a sluggish economy would show low inflation and high unemployment. But by the mid-1970s, the United States faced high inflation and high unemployment. Economists produced a name for the situation—stagflation—but no sure way to cure it. Trying to solve one of the problems only made the other one worse.

THE BURGER COURT 5D

President Nixon's economic policies may have been cloudy, but his agenda for the Supreme Court was clear. In his 1968 campaign, Nixon had accused the Court of being too liberal and lenient. He claimed that the Court was too quick to defend the rights of criminals and protesters. He promised that as President he would appoint more conservative justices. Nixon kept that promise.

Congress rejected two of Nixon's nominees for the Court. Nixon's first successful appointment came in 1969, when Earl Warren retired after sixteen years as Chief Justice. Nixon replaced him with Warren Burger, a conservative judge from Minnesota.

During the next three years, President Nixon appointed three new Justices. All of them tended to have conservative views, and the character of the Supreme Court changed substantially.

On at least one key issue, however, the Burger Court ruled against the President's views. It supported school busing laws. These laws required school systems to integrate by busing children out of racially segregated neighborhoods. School busing became one of the most controversial issues of Nixon's presidency.

Busing proved to be an effective and peaceful policy in some places. It worked especially well in rural areas, where busing had always been the norm. Elsewhere, particularly in the North, it met with stiff opposition. Thousands of white parents placed their children in private schools to avoid busing. In Boston, white opponents of busing staged bitter and violent protests.

President Nixon was a vocal critic of school busing. He ordered the Department of Health, Education, and Welfare (HEW) to continue granting federal aid to school districts that resisted desegregation. HEW Secretary Robert Finch resigned in protest against this policy.

Demonstrators in Boston protest court-ordered school busing. The sign calls for keeping children out of school rather than sending them out of their neighborhoods by bus.
CONSTITUTIONAL HERITAGE What was the goal of busing? Describe President Nixon's view of the Court's busing decision. **5D**

THE AMERICAN INDIAN MOVEMENT 4C, 8I

School desegregation grew out of the movement for civil rights for black Americans. Other American minorities became more involved with politics in the 1960s as well. Perhaps more than any other minority group, American Indians had reason to demand change. Indians were, by many measures, the nation's most deprived and troubled minority. Their unemployment rate was an astounding ten times above the national average. Indians died, on average, twenty years sooner than other Americans. And most disturbingly, they committed suicide at a rate 100 times that of white Americans.

Many of the Indians' difficulties stemmed from the federal government's policies after World War II. In 1953, for example, the government slashed federal aid to Indian reservations and confiscated valuable Indian lands. Officials claimed the cuts in aid would make Indians more self-sufficient. In reality, the policy forced many Indians off the reservations and into urban ghettos. By 1961 about one-third of the approximately one million American Indians lived in cities. Many simply could not cope with city life, which was so unlike the life they had known.

A group of young urban Indians formed a political organization to fight for better treatment from the government. They called their group the American Indian Movement (AIM). Inspired by the black power movement, AIM called for "red power" and demanded a role in forming federal Indian policy. According to AIM, the government's Bureau of Indian Affairs treated Indians as though they were incapable of governing themselves.

In 1973 a group of AIM members took over the town of Wounded Knee, South Dakota. The site of an 1890 massacre of Sioux Indians by government soldiers, Wounded Knee formed part of a Sioux reservation. Most of the Indians there lived in desperate poverty. For 70 days the Indian activists occupied the town until they agreed to surrender their weapons to United States marshals. Other Indians occupied Alcatraz Island in San Francisco Bay to protest government seizure of Indian lands, restriction of Indian hunting and fishing rights, and pollution of their environment.

These demonstrations gained Indians national

Economics
Help students understand the puzzle of stagflation by drawing a Phillips curve, shown below, on the board.

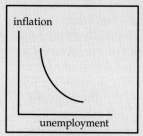

Phillips Curve

Explain to students that before the 1970s, economists felt this curve illustrated the connection between unemployment and inflation. *According to the graph, what happens to inflation when unemployment goes up?* (Inflation goes down.) Ask students to suggest why that might be true. (People who are out of work have less money to spend and can buy less. Suppliers must lower their prices to be able to sell their goods.) *What actually happened in the 1970s when unemployment went up?* (Inflation stayed high.)

Constitutional Heritage
How many justices are there are on the United States Supreme Court? (Nine.) *How many justices did President Nixon appoint during his two terms?* (Four.) Discuss how Nixon's appointment of almost half the Supreme Court compensated in many ways for having a Congress controlled by an opposition party.

Photo Caption Answers
Busing was used to integrate school systems. Nixon opposed busing and ordered the continuation of federal aid to school districts that resisted desegregation.

A member of the American Indian Movement (AIM) waits behind a makeshift barricade during the 1973 takeover of the South Dakota town of Wounded Knee. **HISTORY** Why did AIM members occupy Wounded Knee? What was the outcome of this incident? **9A**

attention but little public support. However, in the 1970s Indian groups won some important legal battles. Over the years the United States government had broken most of the treaties it had signed with Indians. Judges required the government to return some of the land it had taken from the Indians years before.

THE HISPANIC MOVEMENT 5C

Hispanics—people of Spanish and Latin American background—formed the fastest-growing minority group in the United States during the 1970s. The largest number of Hispanic Americans are of Mexican descent.

During the 1960s, Hispanic groups focused on grassroots campaigns for elective office and for better jobs, pay, and housing. The Hispanic movement was strongest in the barrios (Hispanic neighborhoods) of cities such as Denver and San Antonio. In the countryside, however, the movement achieved its most stunning success: a union of farm workers.

In 1962 in the vineyards of California, Cesar Chavez began organizing farm workers, most of whom were Mexican American. To gain recognition for his union, Chavez used strikes and called for consumer boycotts of produce harvested by non-union workers. Under such pressure, major growers finally negotiated with the union. In 1973 it became

known as the United Farm Workers (UFW).

Like civil rights leader Martin Luther King, Jr., Chavez promoted change through nonviolence. In 1968 he explained:

> When we are really honest with ourselves, we must admit that our lives are all that really belong to us. So it is how we use our lives that determines what kind of men we are. I am convinced that the truest act of courage . . . is to sacrifice ourselves for others in a totally nonviolent struggle for justice.

From the Hispanic struggles of the 1960s emerged a new political and cultural awareness. *Chicano*, which once meant a Mexican farm worker, became a term of ethnic pride adopted by many Mexican Americans. A new political party, *La Raza Unida*, "the united people," was organized in 1970 by José Angel Gutiérrez of Crystal City, Texas. Party candidates began to win elected positions.

Hispanic arts also showed new vigor. Inspired by Mexican muralists, artists began to paint bold murals on the drab walls of the barrios. Chicano theater flourished when Luis Valdez organized the Teatro Campesino for farm workers. Valdez now has a national reputation for such productions as *Zoot Suit*.

BIOGRAPHY 4C

CESAR CHAVEZ (1927–   ), a renowned spokesman for migrant farm workers, founded a union in 1962 to help the workers negotiate with the growers. Chavez organized nationwide boycotts of grapes and lettuce to force growers to bargain with the union, which in 1973 became the United Farm Workers.

YOUTH IN THE 1960s 4F

"Come on people now/Smile on your brother/Everybody get together/Try to love one another right now." This song, by a rock group called The Youngbloods, carried a message shared by much of the exciting new music of the 1960s. The message was that young people could make the world more loving, more joyous, and more cooperative.

The youth of the 1960s formed the largest generation in American history. Members of the baby boom that followed World War II, they had grown up in the prosperous 1950s. Few worried about finding jobs. That very security gave them the freedom to search for alternative ways of life.

Many young people were disillusioned with the bland conformity of life in the 1950s. They rejected what they saw as the dominant values in American society—money, status, and power. Those values, they said, had done little to stop war, poverty, or racism.

It was Vietnam that angered them the most. To critics of American society, the Vietnam War was the most vivid symbol of what had gone wrong

with the United States. In their view, the United States was defending not freedom but its own power and profits. Some "New Left" historians reflected this cynicism, arguing that the United States had been an aggressive, selfish power for decades. They rejected the traditional view that Soviet expansion had produced the cold war. Rather, they claimed, the cause was American threats to Soviet security. The atomic bombings of Japan in August 1945 were meant to frighten Soviet leaders as well as the Japanese, they argued.

Since young people were the ones called upon to fight in Vietnam, resistance to the war was an especially potent rallying cry. Musician Country Joe McDonald made fun of blindly patriotic, militaristic values when he sang, "There ain't no time to wonder why/Whoopie! We're all gonna die."

THE COUNTERCULTURE 4F

The result of young people's rebellion against their parents' values was a counterculture—a culture with values opposed to those of the established culture. The counterculture of the late

Many young Americans of the 1960s were attracted to counterculture ideals of peace and personal liberation. Rock music helped spread the message. Here, audience members watch the 1969 Woodstock festival from atop a brightly painted bus. CULTURE What aspects of society did youth in the 1960s rebel against? 4F

Photo Caption Answer
The bland conformity of life in the 1950s and its values of money, status, and power; also the Vietnam War.

1960s and early 1970s stressed love and individual freedom. Millions of young people responded enthusiastically to the music and styles of the counterculture. Young people wore their hair long and dressed in bell-bottom jeans, miniskirts, long peasant dresses, and even Civil War uniforms. Counterculture fashions featured headbands, love beads, peace symbols, and Day-Glo body paint.

The most memorable flowering of counterculture ideals occurred in August 1969, on a farm in upstate New York. About 500,000 young people gathered for a three-day rock concert called "The Woodstock Festival of Life." Many adults feared Woodstock would turn into a gigantic riot, but *Time* magazine assured its readers that the event produced "no rapes, no assaults, no robberies." A local sheriff went so far as to say, "This was the nicest bunch of kids I've ever dealt with."

Yet the euphoria of Woodstock masked a darker side of the counterculture. Its celebration of "mind-expanding" drugs led many young people (and some of the greatest rock musicians) to addiction and even death. Also, while "dropping out" was an effective way to reject society, it could do nothing to improve it.

NIXON'S APPEAL TO MIDDLE AMERICA 7J

President Nixon was deeply disturbed by the attitudes of young people. He believed that their antiwar protests and the ideals of the counterculture posed a threat to society. Nixon had pledged to bridge the generation gap between adults and rebellious youths. However, the President labeled every critic of his administration an enemy of the traditional American values of hard work, family, and patriotism. In the summer of 1969 he said:

> Our fundamental values are under bitter and even violent attack. We live in a deeply troubled and profoundly unsettled time. Drugs, crime, campus revolts, racial discord, draft resistance—on every hand we find old standards violated.

Nixon called for support from what he termed the "silent majority" of Americans. Many people, sharing Nixon's views, responded to his call. Suspicious of change, they believed that young people and demonstrators were simply trying to tear down the United States. Since many of Nixon's supporters came from the middle class and from the South and Midwest, the media began to call them "Middle Americans."

Vice President Spiro Agnew was given the task of rallying support for Nixon among Middle Americans. Agnew not only defended Nixon's policies but also attacked the President's critics. He tried to win the support of working Americans by insisting that Nixon's critics were "intellectual snobs." Agnew's speeches were so colorful that he soon became a figure of great controversy, harshly attacked by some, defended by others.

Vice President Agnew called critics of the Vietnam War "nattering nabobs of negativism." Agnew's zeal helped inflame an already heated national debate. **CIVIC VALUES** Why did the Nixon administration believe America's fundamental values were under attack? **9A**

SECTION REVIEW

1. KEY TERMS stagflation, American Indian Movement, counterculture

2. PEOPLE AND PLACES Warren Burger, Cesar Chavez, Woodstock, Spiro Agnew

3. COMPREHENSION In what ways did Nixon change the Supreme Court?

4. COMPREHENSION How did Hispanic Americans try to achieve their goals?

5. CRITICAL THINKING Do you think the values of the counterculture, and the expression of those values, still exist today? Explain your answer.

2 Toward a Cleaner and Safer World

★ Section Focus

Key Terms Environmental Protection Agency ■ OSHA

Main Idea In the early 1970s Americans worked to conserve resources and to improve the safety and quality of the goods and services available to consumers.

Objectives As you read, look for answers to these questions:
1. Why did the public become concerned about pollution?
2. In what ways were safety threats to workers and consumers reduced?

During the Nixon years, more and more Americans began to hear the ticking of the environmental clock. Time, they feared, was running out. People were steadily consuming the earth's irreplaceable natural resources—burning its fossil fuels, polluting its water and air, and killing off the plants that produce oxygen.

Concerned citizens began to call for private efforts to reduce waste and conserve resources. They also believed that government regulation of business was needed to protect the health and safety of workers and consumers. Industries, they argued, could not be relied on to protect the environment without laws and penalties to guide them. So, like the Progressives of the early 1900s, environmentalists called on the federal government to step in.

ENVIRONMENTAL PROBLEMS 2C

If you visit American city,
You will find it very pretty.
Just two things of which you must beware:
Don't drink the water and don't breathe
the air.

These song lyrics from social critic Tom Lehrer were, of course, an overstatement. But they pointed to a problem whose time had come by the late 1960s. Pollution from growing cities and factories had caused concern as early as the 1800s. Not until well after World War II, however, did people see environmental destruction as a global problem demanding immediate attention.

In the boom years following the war, the United States produced and consumed goods faster than it ever had before. The rapid production caused

pollution levels to skyrocket. By the 1960s the United States was releasing some 139 million tons of pollution into the air every year. (This weight is equivalent to 1,500 of the navy's largest aircraft carriers.) Even greater amounts of waste were being buried in the soil or dumped into rivers and oceans.

Some people argued that increased pollution was an unavoidable result of population growth. A fuller explanation was advanced in a groundbreaking book called *The Closing Circle* (1971). The author, Barry Commoner, found that levels of pollution were rising ten times faster than either the population or the economy. Thus, Commoner reasoned, the crisis was not a simple matter of more people consuming more products. The major sources of pollution were new kinds of products and new ways of making them. Plastics, synthetic fibers, fertilizers, pesticides, detergents, nuclear power, bigger automobiles—all involved new and

BIOGRAPHY 4C

RACHEL CARSON (1907–1964), who worked for the U.S. Fish and Wildlife Service most of her life, wrote several influential books and articles on ecology and the environment. *The Sea Around Us* (1951) won the National Book Award. *Silent Spring* (1962) called public attention to the harmful effects of pesticides, such as DDT, that poison the food supplies of animals and humans. Her arguments led to restrictions against pesticide use in many parts of the world.

SUPPORTING THE SECTION

Reinforcement Workbook: Worksheet 93
Reteaching Resources: Worksheet 93
Teaching Transparencies: Transparency 93

Biography
Have students consider how Rachel Carson's life illustrates the democratic ideal that an individual can make a difference. Ask them to suggest other examples.

Toward a Cleaner and Safer World
(pp. 573–575)

Section Objective
■ analyze the effects of movements toward protection of the environment, health and safety in the workplace, and consumer rights

Introducing the Section

Connecting with Past Learnings
What conditions were the targets of Progressive Era outrage? (Corrupt government and business; living conditions of the poor; unsafe working conditions; impure food and drugs.) *How did progressives propose to solve these problems?* (By making government more responsive.)

Key Terms
Write the two key terms on the board. Ask students to explain when and why each agency was created. **LEP**

Focus
Working individually or in small groups, have students create cause and effect charts on environmental problems and occupational safety.

Developing the Lesson
After students have read the section, you may want to consider the following activities:

Patterns in History
Ask students to compare their community's values today with the "throwaway society" of the 1960s. *What do you think has changed? How did that change come about? What remains the same?*

Economics
Why might businesses be opposed to legislation which regulates their activities? (Restricts their freedom to make

573

decisions; often requires added expenses.) *Why might businesses, workers, and consumers welcome environmental protection?* (Business leaders are affected by impure water and air, consumers are more willing to buy safe products, and workers will be attracted to safe jobs.)

Tell students that critics of Ralph Nader claim that many of his demands are very costly to industry, but provide only a small increase in safety.

Divide the class into groups and assign each one of the following topics: air quality, water quality, waste, safety in the workplace, consumer rights. Ask each group to synthesize the information on their topic in the text, identifying the main problem and the solutions that were implemented. Have each group turn its information into a diagram with pictures and text. **LEP**

Addressing Individual Needs

Guided/ Independent Practice
Instruct students to complete **Reinforcement Workbook** Worksheet 93. This worksheet has students analyze a cartoon on an environmental issue.

Reteaching/Correctives
Allow students to choose from a variety of media to translate the material in the section into another form. Some possibilities are poetry, a ballad, or a found-art collage. Students should begin by reviewing the section and extracting the most important information.

Have students complete **Reteaching Resources** Worksheet 93, which asks them to examine trends discussed in their text.

574

dangerous sources of pollution. New packaging materials, especially plastic and aluminum, did not disintegrate naturally over time. They contributed to the ever-growing waste sites around the nation.

People's wasteful habits worsened the problem. Few people tried to limit the amount of garbage they produced. Recycling was still a new idea that many considered impractical. Social critics called America a "throwaway society." For a short time, the fashion industry even produced throwaway paper dresses.

Industry too treated the environment carelessly. Manufacturers marketed new chemicals without clearly understanding their effects. Powerful pesticides such as DDT seemed to be the perfect solution to insect control. But DDT and similar chemicals did not vanish after they had served their purpose. Instead they entered the food chain, contaminating the bodies of fish and animals and eventually reaching human beings. In 1962, marine biologist Rachel Carson directed public attention to the waste and destruction caused by pesticides with her book *Silent Spring.*

Responding to pressure from environmental activists like Carson, the government banned almost all use of DDT by 1972. However, American corporations increased exports of the chemical to Third World nations. DDT was not the only dangerous chemical to be exported. Few government regulations existed in the Third World, and unscrupulous companies could "dump" chemicals there that could not be sold in the United States.

THE ENVIRONMENTAL MOVEMENT 2B, 2C
Regulations on harmful chemicals such as DDT were signs of the rising influence of the environmental movement during the late 1960s and early 1970s. The movement gained strength in part because the pollution problem kept getting worse—and more noticeable. Oil spills from tankers and wells polluted the shores of Louisiana, Florida, Maryland, New Jersey, and Massachusetts. A 1970 oil spill in southern Alaska killed tens of thousands of wild animals. Automobile smog fouled the air in major cities like Baltimore and Los Angeles, forcing authorities to warn the sick and elderly to remain indoors. Pollution was wiping out the plants and fish in Lake Erie and Lake Ontario. A river in Cleveland contained so many flammable chemicals that it actually caught fire.

Environmentalists found many allies among young people whose ideals included respect for nature and distrust of big business. By staging demonstrations and "teach-ins," environmentalists rallied support for conservation. In April 1970, Americans celebrated the first Earth Day with a nationwide trash cleanup. Environmental-

A haze caused by air pollution obscures the skyline of Denver, Colorado. Smoke from automobiles, power plants, and factories is responsible for most air pollution. ISSUES How much involvement do you think government should have in the regulation of pollution from businesses and automobiles? **2B**

Photo Caption Answer
Some students may suggest that government regulation should be minimal so as not to interfere with business. Others may note that since the welfare of its citizenry is affected, the government should make regulation a priority.

Background Although it was organized largely on college and university campuses, the concept for Earth Day actually originated with Senator Gaylord Nelson of Wisconsin.

Demonstrators in New York City's Central Park rally support for the environmental movement on Earth Day in 1970. **ENVIRONMENT** What caused Congress to pass environmental legislation in the early 1970s?

2B, 2C

ists also lobbied Congress to establish limits on industrial pollution.

Responding to pressure from the environmental movement, Congress passed the Clean Air Act and the Water Quality Improvement Act in 1970. These laws limited the amounts of poisonous chemicals and gases that companies were allowed to release into the environment. Also in 1970, President Nixon established the Environmental Protection Agency (EPA). The EPA is responsible for enforcing laws on water and air pollution, toxic waste, pesticides, and radiation.

8D, 8G

PROTECTION FOR WORKERS AND CONSUMERS

Government regulation of industry aimed at more than environmental protection. In the late 1960s, Americans demanded higher safety standards in the workplace. They called for the elimination of health hazards such as cotton dust, asbestos, toxic chemicals, and noise. They also urged that machinery and working methods be made safer in order to reduce the number of job-related accidents.

The need for safety improvements was not limited to a few industries. In 1970 a House committee added up the cost to the nation of industrial accidents. It found the following for a single year:

[There were] 15,500 workers killed, 2,700,000 workers injured, 390,000 cases of occupational disease (lung cancer, asbestosis, etc.); 250,000 man-days of work lost (ten times as many as by strikes). More

than $1.5 billion in lost wages. More than $8 billion loss to GNP.

Responding to this evidence, Congress established the Occupational Safety and Health Administration (OSHA) in 1970. Its tasks were to carry out inspections and maintain safe conditions in the workplace.

Other political activists stressed the rights of consumers. They worked to improve the quality and safety of American goods. They also pressed Congress to pass safety regulations. Ralph Nader emerged as the leading figure in the consumer movement. After graduating from law school, Nader chose to represent the public instead of taking a high-paying job with private industry. His example led hundreds of young people to take up what was called "public interest law."

Nader first targeted the automobile industry. Fifty thousand Americans were dying in car accidents every year. Nader believed that unsafe cars were part of the problem. He found, for example, that most car bumpers were not strong enough to offer protection against an impact of more than three miles per hour.

Nader and his supporters (who became known as "Nader's Raiders") took on dozens of other causes. They opposed contamination of the water supply, unsafe children's toys, and nuclear power. In all their efforts they gained support through tireless lobbying, grassroots organizing, and skillful use of the media.

SECTION REVIEW

1. KEY TERMS Environmental Protection Agency, OSHA

2. PEOPLE Barry Commoner, Rachel Carson, Ralph Nader

3. COMPREHENSION For what reasons did pollution levels rise rapidly after World War II?

4. COMPREHENSION Why was DDT banned in the United States?

5. CRITICAL THINKING Why is cooperation from private individuals, as well as government action, necessary to reduce waste and pollution?

Enrichment/Extension
Ask students to identify a key environmental issue today and report on the problem and possible solutions.

Assessment
You may wish to use the Section 2 Review, on this page, to see how well your students understand the main points in this lesson.

Section Review Answers
1. *Environmental Protection Agency*—Agency created in 1970 to enforce environmental laws. *OSHA*—Occupational Safety and Health Administration, created in 1970 to maintain safe working conditions.
2. *Barry Commoner*—Environmentalist who publicized the problem of pollution. *Rachel Carson*—Marine biologist who directed attention to the waste and destruction caused by pesticides. *Ralph Nader*—Consumer activist who spurred a consumer movement.
3. The United States was producing and consuming goods faster than ever before. In addition, new materials and products were more dangerous sources of pollution.
4. Because Rachel Carson and others showed that DDT was harmful to human beings as well as other animals.
5. Individuals are responsible for a great deal of pollution. Individual actions to conserve resources can make a difference.

Closure
Remind students of the pre-reading objectives in the section opener. Pose one or all of these questions again. Then have students read Section 3 for the next class period, noting the direction of U.S. foreign policy during the Nixon years.

Photo Caption Answer
Political pressure from the environmental movement.

Background The environmental movement was not universally popular, especially among blue collar workers who felt the warnings against consumption threatened their ability to get what others in America already had. In addition, the environmentalists were often very critical of the automobile industry—an industry upon which thousands of jobs depended.

SECTION 3

World Affairs in the Nixon Years
(pp. 576–581)

Section Objective

■ identify major events in foreign affairs during the early 1970s

Introducing the Section

Connecting with Past Learnings

Help students see how Nixon tried to avoid his predecessors' mistakes. *What major foreign policy entanglement occupied Presidents Kennedy, Johnson, and Nixon?* (The war in Vietnam.) *Which President was "defeated" by the war?* (Johnson.) As you teach the lesson, have students note how President Nixon used foreign policy initiatives to take people's attention away from the war and build a positive image for himself.

Key Terms

Pronounce each key term, noting the German origins of the term *realpolitik* and the French origins of *détente*. Explain that *SALT* and *OPEC* are acronyms, or words formed from initials. Call on volunteers to use each term in a sentence, and have other volunteers give definitions of the terms. **LEP**

3 World Affairs in the Nixon Years

Section Focus

Key Terms realpolitik ■ SALT ■ détente ■ OPEC ■ embargo

Main Idea President Nixon hoped to boost American prestige and international stability by improving relations with the major Communist powers.

Objectives As you read, look for answers to these questions:
1. Why did President Nixon try to improve relations with China?
2. Why was the summit meeting between Nixon and Brezhnev of historic importance?
3. How did events in the Middle East affect Americans?

"It will be a safer world and a better world," President Nixon said in 1971, "if we have a strong, healthy United States, Europe, Soviet Union, China, Japan—each balancing the others." This vision of a world with many power centers marked a change in American diplomacy. Since World War II, most Presidents had seen foreign policy as a two-way competition between the United States and the Soviet Union. By the 1960s, however, China had become a third major power armed with nuclear weapons. With American help, Europe and Japan had risen from the ashes of wartime destruction to become powerful economic forces in the Western alliance. President Nixon hoped that these five centers of power could maintain a more stable global order.

President Nixon converses with Henry Kissinger, his key adviser on foreign policy. Kissinger's family fled Nazi Germany in 1938. He later gained fame for a book he wrote in 1957 on the role of nuclear weapons in defense strategy. Kissinger served as a consultant to the Kennedy and Johnson administrations before joining Nixon's staff. Nixon made him Secretary of State in 1973. **GLOBAL AWARENESS** Explain Kissinger's policy of realpolitik. 1B

KISSINGER AND REALPOLITIK 1B

Nixon's most trusted foreign policy adviser was Henry Kissinger, the National Security Adviser. Kissinger had studied and admired the nineteenth-century European diplomats who engaged in realpolitik, a German word meaning "practical politics." According to realpolitik, foreign policy should be based solely on considerations of power, not ideals or moral principles. Whether you liked them or not, the enemies of your enemies were your friends. Such ideas appealed to Nixon. With the President's backing, Kissinger launched a breathtaking series of diplomatic missions.

THE CHINA BREAKTHROUGH 1A

February 21, 1972. Beijing, the capital of the People's Republic of China. Richard Nixon, the President of the United States, raises his glass to toast Mao Zedong, leader of Communist China. After 23 years of hostility, the two nations begin to speak to each other as friends.

Few people would have predicted such an event. The United States was still fighting China's ally, the Vietnamese Communists. Moreover, the man toasting the Chinese—Richard Nixon—had long been a harsh critic of Mao's China. However, for this very reason, Nixon was in an ideal position to transform Chinese-American relations. Because he was such an outspoken anti-Communist, Nixon was immune to charges of being "soft on communism."

The China breakthrough followed a change in cold war politics. For years, policymakers in the

---

SUPPORTING THE SECTION

Reinforcement Workbook: Worksheet 94
Reteaching Resources: Worksheet 94
Teaching Transparencies: Transparency 94

Photo Caption Answer
Foreign policy should be based solely on considerations of power, not ideals or moral principles.

President Nixon reviews Chinese troops at Beijing airport during his historic 1972 visit. To Nixon's right is China's premier, Zhou Enlai, and behind them is First Lady Pat Nixon. **GLOBAL AWARENESS** Why did Nixon want better relations with China? **1A**

Focus
Divide the board in half, writing *Improvements* on one side and *Problems* on the other. Then ask the class: ***What improvements in foreign relations occurred as a result of realpolitik? What problems occurred?*** (Improvements: more open relations with China; SALT, which ushered in détente. Problems: a CIA-sponsored coup against the elected leader of Chile, followed by support for his repressive successor.)

Developing the Lesson
After students have read the section, you may want to consider the following activities:

Global Awareness
Tell students that Henry Kissinger said, "In traditional diplomacy, the aim was, through an accumulation of small advantages, to gain a qualitative edge over your major rivals. In the nuclear age, the most dangerous thing to aim for is a qualitative edge. . . ." Ask students to explain this statement. (The act of trying to achieve an edge could drive an enemy to strike.) ***How did this philosophy lead to the signing of the SALT agreement?*** (U.S. and Soviet forces were fairly equal, neither side had a significant "edge," and the agreement would maintain that balance.)

United States had assumed that China was merely a pawn of the Soviet Union. By the late 1960s, however, that view seemed out of date. Although China had allied itself with the Soviet Union during the early 1950s, the two leading Communist powers had since become bitter rivals. The Soviet Union refused to trust China with its advanced technology, especially nuclear weapons. For its part, China accused the Soviet Union of betraying Socialist ideals. China's leaders said the Soviet government had become corrupt. The two nations competed fiercely for influence among Third World leaders.

By the 1970s more than a million troops faced each other along the Chinese-Soviet border, and war seemed possible. Chinese leaders now pushed for better relations with the United States. They hoped the United States might provide them with modern technology as well as protection against the Soviet Union.

Nixon and Kissinger tried to take advantage of the tension between China and the Soviet Union. By negotiating with each side, they hoped to play the two Communist giants off against one another. Nixon had one additional motive. The most serious obstacle to his re-election in 1972 was the continuing nightmare of Vietnam. He desperately needed a foreign policy success. It would draw attention away from Vietnam and cast him as a man of diplomacy and peace.

The major obstacle to normal relations between China and the United States was the issue of Taiwan. This island nation was ruled by Chinese who had fled the mainland when the Communists came to power. Since 1949 the United States had supported Taiwan with economic and military aid. It claimed that Taiwan, rather than the People's Republic, was the only legitimate Chinese government. The Chinese demanded that the United States withdraw the troops it had stationed in Taiwan. In secret negotiations before Nixon's Beijing visit, Kissinger agreed to gradually withdraw American forces from Taiwan. In exchange, the Chinese promised to push the North Vietnamese to accept a peace settlement in Vietnam.

Few people were aware of the arrangement. Media coverage focused instead on the pageantry of Nixon's historic visit. Cameras clicked as the American party visited the Great Wall and attended a revolutionary opera written by Chairman Mao's wife. This was just as Nixon and Kissinger had planned. If details of the bargain became public, Nixon feared he might be accused of abandoning Taiwan to a possible Chinese invasion.

The opening to China was indeed a political risk for Nixon. But the potential payoffs were mind-boggling. They included economic, scientific, and cultural relations with the world's most populous nation. In addition, by exploiting the rivalry between the Soviets and Chinese, the United States could increase its leverage over both of them.

Photo Caption Answer
Nixon wanted to play China off against its rival, the Soviet Union. He also wanted a foreign policy success to draw national attention away from Vietnam.

Background Richard Nixon's visit to China was truly dramatic, not only because he had for so long been a critic of that country, but also because it marked the first time an American President had ever visited China. The scheduling of this event, followed so closely by Nixon's trip to the Soviet Union, ensured that these foreign policy successes would dominate the 1972 presidential campaign.

THE MOSCOW SUMMIT 1B
The visit to Beijing was one-half of Nixon's diplomatic plan. An improvement in Soviet-American ties was the other. Just two months after the China visit, Nixon was scheduled to meet with Soviet leader Leonid Brezhnev in Moscow. The two heads of state hoped to sign an agreement limiting their arsenals of nuclear weapons.

Until the last minute, it remained uncertain whether the summit would actually take place. In early May 1972, Nixon angrily denounced the Soviet shipment of arms to North Vietnam. He ordered air strikes against Vietnam to halt the flow of arms. However, both superpowers decided to set aside the issue of Vietnam for the moment. Nixon's trip went forward as scheduled.

Like the United States, the Soviet Union was eager for an arms agreement. After their humiliation in the Cuban missile crisis of 1962, the Soviets had spent ten years expanding and modernizing their nuclear forces. Those forces were now roughly equal to the United States'. An arms control agreement, the Soviets hoped, would stabilize the arms race and perhaps lower their defense costs.

The threat posed by the United States' new relationship with China also motivated the Soviets to sign an arms agreement. The Soviets could ill afford to drive those two nations into an outright alliance.

The treaty that Nixon and Brezhnev signed in Moscow grew out of the Strategic Arms Limitation Talks (SALT), which had begun in 1969. For the first time in history, the two superpowers agreed to limit the production of nuclear weapons. The agreement, however, contained many loopholes. It placed limits on the total numbers of intercontinental missiles but not on the number of nuclear warheads each missile could carry. Nor did it limit the development of nuclear weapons systems other than missiles, such as bombers. Still, the SALT agreement was a crucial first step toward ending the arms race.

Food was another area of growing Soviet-American agreement. The Soviet Union was suffering food shortages caused by crop failures. At the same time, American storehouses were overflowing with grain. Surplus corn was actually piling up in the streets of several midwestern towns. The United States agreed to sell the Soviet Union about a billion dollars' worth of grain.

CALMING SUPERPOWER TENSIONS 1B
Agreements on arms control and grain sales marked a new relationship between the United States and the Soviet Union. The period of cooperation that emerged under Nixon became known as détente (day-TAHNT), a French term meaning "relaxation of tensions." Détente led to cultural and scientific exchanges between the superpowers. Citizens in both countries worried less about the possibility of nuclear war.

Yet while in Washington and Moscow the cold war seemed to have eased, it raged more strongly than ever in the Third World. Around the globe—in Southeast Asia, in southern Africa, and in Latin America—the Communist and anti-Communist tug-of-war continued. Both superpowers backed the sides they favored with large doses of economic and military aid.

A COUP IN CHILE 1A
Smaller nations were often caught up in the superpower struggle. One such case was the South American nation of Chile. In 1970 Chile's citizens elected a Socialist government. The new President, Salvador Allende (ah-YEN-day), proposed a radical economic program. Allende wanted the government to nationalize key industries in Chile, such as copper mining. American corporations controlled several of these industries. Corporations such as International Telephone and Telegraph (ITT) lobbied the White House to protect their interests by opposing Allende's government. At the same time, conservatives argued that the United States should not allow socialism to advance in Latin America.

President Nixon decided to cut off all aid to Allende's government. He then approved sending $10 million to anti-Allende forces within Chile's military. The President also ordered the CIA to secretly "destabilize" Chile by encouraging strikes, sabotage, and disorder.

Chile's economy went into a tailspin. In September 1973, right-wing military officers overthrew the Socialist government and murdered Allende.

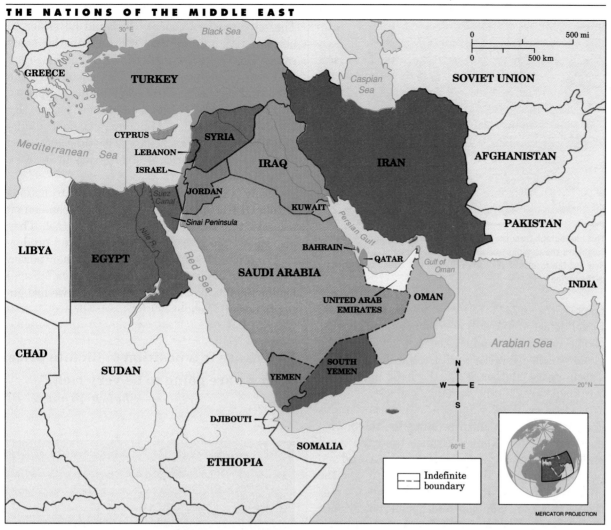

MAP SKILLS
9B

The Middle East is sometimes called a global crossroads because of its location between Europe, Asia, and Africa. The region contains most of the world's oil reserves. CRITICAL THINKING What factors might encourage continued unrest in the Middle East?

When Kissinger was asked why the United States had supported the overthrow of a democratically elected government, he replied, "I don't see why we have to let a country go Marxist just because its people are irresponsible."

The new government of Chile was led by General Augusto Pinochet (peen–oh–CHET). Because he was a fierce anti-Communist, Pinochet received generous American support. Yet Pinochet was soon known as one of the most repressive dictators in Latin America. Americans are still unsure whether the overthrow of Allende represented a success or failure for American foreign policy.

WAR IN THE MIDDLE EAST 1A

The danger of world war erupting over events in Chile was small. The same could not be said of the Middle East, a region prized by both superpowers. In 1973, long-standing hostilities between Israel and its Arab neighbors once again led to war. In this fresh outbreak of fighting, the United States supported Israel while the Soviets sided with the Arab states.

The 1973 war was a renewal of the brief but intense conflict of 1967. That summer, Israel had been alarmed by the mobilization of Egyptian troops. Launching a surprise attack, the Israelis

CHAPTER 24   FROM VIETNAM TO WATERGATE, 1969–1974   **579**

Map Skills Answers
Hostilities between Israel and its Arab neighbors; the region's strategic location and its oil wealth.

C Cooperative Learning

Divide class into groups representing: China or the United States during Nixon's visit to China; the Soviet Union or the United States during Nixon's visit to the Soviet Union; Israel, the Arab side, or the United States during the October War. Ask students to set an agenda for a meeting based on what their group's priorities are and to determine the demands or issues their group would put forth. Call the class back together and review agendas. **LEP**

Addressing Individual Needs

Guided/ Independent Practice
Instruct students to complete **Reinforcement Workbook** Worksheet 94, which asks them to create a map of the nations of the Middle East.

Reteaching/Correctives
Provide students with an outline of a world map, or have them trace the map on pages 848–849. On their maps, have students pinpoint sites of United States foreign policy action in the early 1970's. Have students label each area and explain the reasons for United States concern in a brief accompanying statement.

Have students complete **Reteaching Resources** Worksheet 94, which asks them to relate causes and effects of various foreign policy events and initiatives during the Nixon years.

Enrichment/Extension
Have students compare the boundaries on the map on this page with those on a present-day political map of the Middle East. Have them note which boundaries have changed and then do research to find out why these boundaries have changed.

579

This photograph from the 1973 war between Israel and its Arab neighbors shows tanks massing near Israel's border. **HISTORY** How had the results of the earlier Six-Day War added to tensions in the region? **9E**

bombed the airfields of Egypt, Syria, and Jordan. Israel defeated its Arab neighbors so quickly that people called the conflict the Six-Day War. The victory tripled Israel's territory, but did not bring lasting peace. Rather, it left the Arab nations determined to regain the land they had lost.

In October 1973, Egyptian and Syrian troops launched their own surprise attack on the Jewish holy day of Yom Kippur. Armies from the Arab nations made early gains, but Israel recovered and pushed them back. When Israel began to take the offensive, the Soviet Union threatened to enter the war on the Arab side. Both superpowers put their forces on military alert. Eager to defuse this dangerous situation, President Nixon sent Henry Kissinger to persuade the Arabs and Israelis to accept a ceasefire. Kissinger's negotiations succeeded, and the superpowers breathed more easily.

THE OIL EMBARGO 8F

The 1973 ceasefire was only a temporary halt in the fighting. The underlying conflict between Arabs and Jews remained. Moreover, the October War had brought a new element into the situation: oil.

For decades, Western companies had dominated the world market in oil. In 1960, at the urging of these companies, the oil-producing nations formed a collective bargaining group called the Organization of Petroleum Exporting Countries (OPEC).

The oil companies thought it would be easier to bargain with a group than with each nation separately. But the plan backfired. OPEC nations realized that by acting together they could force the industrialized nations to accept higher oil prices. In time OPEC's profits and power soared. By 1973, Libyan leader Muammar Qaddafi (kuh-DAHF-ee) was announcing, "The time has come for us to deal America a strong slap in its cool, arrogant face."

During the October War, the Arab nations within OPEC imposed an embargo—a ban—on oil sales to the Western supporters of Israel. They also raised the price of oil and decreased production to remind the rest of the world of their power. "We are in a position to dictate prices," Saudi leader Sheikh Yamani remarked, "and we are going to be very rich."

> **"We** are in a position to dictate prices, and we are going to be very rich."
> —*Sheikh Yamani, 1973*

The OPEC embargo and the resulting price increases prompted construction of the Trans-Alaska Pipeline (pictured above). The pipeline extends 800 miles from Prudhoe Bay in the Arctic to the port of Valdez, site of a major oil spill in 1989. **GLOBAL AWARENESS** How did OPEC benefit oil-producing nations? **9F**

Photo Caption Answers
(Top) The Arab nations wanted to regain territory that Israel had captured from them in 1967. (Bottom) By acting together, the producing nations could force the industrialized nations to accept higher oil prices.

Yamani was right. Accustomed to an endless river of cheap gasoline, Americans were shocked to find themselves short of fuel. Suddenly drivers had to sit for hours in long lines at gas stations. In the short run, there was not much the government could do to end the crisis. President Nixon called on the nation to conserve energy. Over the objections of environmentalists, he also signed the Alaskan Pipeline Act. This act authorized the building of a huge pipeline to move oil south from northern Alaska.

OPEC ended the embargo the following year, and the energy crisis soon eased. However, fuel prices continued to climb. The industrialized nations simply could not curb their appetite for vast quantities of oil.

---

1. KEY TERMS realpolitik, SALT, détente, OPEC, embargo

2. PEOPLE Henry Kissinger, Mao Zedong, Leonid Brezhnev, Salvador Allende, Augusto Pinochet

3. COMPREHENSION What was the major obstacle to the improvement of relations between China and the United States? Why?

4. COMPREHENSION What were the effects of the Arab oil embargo on the United States?

5. CRITICAL THINKING Explain why both Nixon and Brezhnev were acting on the basis of realpolitik in the meeting at Moscow.

5B, 5D, 7A, 7B, 7I, 9A, 9D, 9E

4 The Watergate Scandal

Section Focus

Key Terms Watergate scandal ■ Pentagon Papers ■ Saturday Night Massacre

Main Idea During Nixon's second term, investigations revealed that his administration had been involved in criminal activities. Nixon resigned to avoid facing an impeachment trial.

Objectives As you read, look for answers to these questions:
1. What was the link between Vietnam and Watergate?
2. Why was Nixon re-elected in 1972?
3. What events led to Nixon's resignation?

Readers of *The Washington Post* on June 17, 1972, might easily have missed a small story on the back pages. It reported that five men had been arrested while breaking into the headquarters of the Democratic National Committee. The headquarters was located in a Washington, D.C., building complex called Watergate. The burglars had been carrying equipment used to wiretap phones and photograph papers.

Two young reporters from *The Washington Post*, Bob Woodward and Carl Bernstein, dug deeper into the story. They learned that one of the suspects had carried an address book with the name and phone number of a White House official in it. They began to suspect that the break-in had been ordered by White House officials.

In an August 1972 press conference, President Nixon declared that "no one on the White House staff . . . was involved in this very bizarre incident." Most of the media accepted Nixon's word and dropped the story. That fall he was re-elected in a landslide (page 583). However, when the Watergate burglars went to trial four months later, what had been a small story ballooned into a national scandal. It ended only when Richard Nixon was forced from office.

SUPPORTING THE SECTION

Reinforcement Workbook: Worksheet 95

Reteaching Resources: Worksheet 95

Enrichment and Extension Resources: Primary Source Worksheet 48

Teaching Transparencies: Transparency 95

---

5. Neither nation liked or trusted the other, but practical politics motivated them. The United States wanted to prevent the Soviets from continuing to build up their arms. The Soviets wanted to prevent the U.S. from getting too close to China, and they wanted to lower their own defense costs.

Closure

Use the Chapter Review Summary for Section 3 (p. 588) to synthesize the important elements in the section. Then have students read Section 4 for the next class period, noting the development of the Watergate scandal.

SECTION 4

The Watergate Scandal
(pp. 581–587)

Section Objectives

■ identify the major scandals of the Nixon administration

■ analyze the constitutional basis for the impeachment of President Richard Nixon

Introducing the Section

Connecting with Past Learnings
Ask students to recall the main themes of the Nixon campaign in 1968. (Law and order, bringing the nation together.) As students work through the lesson, have them note how far from his campaign ideals Nixon went in trying to win re-election and, later, in protecting his administration.

Focus

Beginning with June 1971, and ending with August 1974, create a timeline of the Watergate scandal.

June 1971	Pentagon Papers published
1972	Plumbers play "dirty tricks" on Muskie
June 17, 1972	Watergate break-in
June 23, 1972	In private meeting, Nixon tells advisers to prevent the FBI from involvement in Watergate investigation
August 1972	Nixon denies White House connection with break-in
November 1972	Nixon re-elected
January 1973	Burglars go on trial
April 1973	Top aides resign
May 1973	Senate Watergate hearings begin
October 1973	Vice President Agnew resigns
October 20, 1973	Saturday Night Massacre
October 1973	House Judiciary Committee begins impeachment proceedings
April 1974	Nixon releases transcripts of office tapes
July 1974	Committee votes for impeachment
August 9, 1974	Nixon resigns

THE VIETNAM CONNECTION 7B

The Watergate trial eventually exposed a long series of illegal activities in the Nixon administration. The President and his staff were found to have spied on and harassed political opponents, accepted illegal campaign contributions, and covered up their own misdeeds. This series of crimes became known as the Watergate scandal.

Actually, the Nixon administration had carried on these activities for years before they were discovered. Watergate really began in 1969, when the White House staff compiled an "enemies list." President Nixon's "enemies" included some 200 liberal politicians, black political activists, actors, and journalists. Most of the people on the list had taken a public stand against the war in Vietnam. The President's aides ordered the Internal Revenue Service to conduct tax audits on people on the list. Undercover agents were hired to dig up damaging information about them.

President Nixon was especially concerned about government employees "leaking," or revealing, secret information to the press. The President's aides illegally wiretapped reporters' telephones to discover the sources of leaks. When news of the secret bombing of Cambodia leaked out, Nixon even ordered wiretaps placed on the telephones of his own staff members.

In June 1971, *The New York Times* began to publish a history of the Vietnam War known as the Pentagon Papers. The Pentagon Papers were drawn from secret government documents. They criticized the policies that had led to the war and described how officials had deceived the public about the American role. Daniel Ellsberg, a former Defense Department employee, had given the papers to *The New York Times*. Nixon was outraged by their publication.

Nixon thought he could portray Ellsberg's actions as treason. He recalled his successful prosecution of Alger Hiss in 1948 for spying. But the President was not content to leave Ellsberg to the courts. Nixon's aides recruited a secret group of former CIA employees and others. These men were known as "plumbers" because their job was to plug leaks, such as the Pentagon Papers, that might hurt the White House. Searching for information that would damage Ellsberg's reputation, the plumbers ransacked his psychiatrist's office. They found nothing that could be used against Ellsberg. The plumbers' next mission involved them in the upcoming presidential election.

THE 1972 ELECTION 5B

Nixon was concerned about his chances for re-election in 1972. His advisers believed Senator Edmund Muskie of Maine would be the strongest Democratic candidate. Hoping to eliminate Muskie from competition, the plumbers began to play a series of "dirty tricks." They issued phony state-

George McGovern, the Democratic candidate for President in 1972, campaigns with Spanish-speaking members of the United Farm Workers union. **POLITICS** What factors hampered McGovern's chances in the 1972 election? 5B

Photo Caption Answer
His choice of a running mate became an issue. Nixon raised millions of dollars in illegal campaign funds and announced that peace in Vietnam was at hand.

ments in Muskie's name and fed false rumors about him to the press. Finally, they sent a fake letter to a New Hampshire newspaper accusing Muskie of making ugly remarks about people of French Canadian ancestry. These strategies helped Nixon's aides cripple Muskie's campaign.

In the end, the Democratic nomination went to George McGovern, a liberal senator from South Dakota. His supporters included many people who had supported the civil rights, antiwar, and environmental movements of the 1960s. McGovern had fought to make the nomination process more open and democratic. Congress had also passed the 26th Amendment to the Constitution allowing eighteen-year-olds to vote. As a result, the 1972 Democratic Convention was the first to include large numbers of women, minorities, and young people among the delegates.

McGovern's campaign ran into trouble early. The press revealed that his running mate, Thomas Eagleton, had once received psychiatric treatment. First McGovern stood by Eagleton. Then he abandoned him, picking a different running mate. In addition, many Democratic voters—particularly in the South—were attracted to Nixon because of his conservative positions on the Vietnam War and on law enforcement.

Meanwhile, Nixon's campaign sailed smoothly along, aided by millions of dollars in funds. Nixon campaign officials collected much of the money illegally. Major corporations were told to contribute at least $100,000 each. The collectors made it clear that the donations could buy the companies influence with the White House. Many large corporations went along. As shipbuilding tycoon (and future New York Yankees owner) George Steinbrenner put it, "It was a shakedown. A plain old-fashioned shakedown."

The final blow to McGovern's chances came just days before the election, when Kissinger announced that peace was at hand in Vietnam (page 560). McGovern had made his political reputation as a critic of the war, and the announcement took the wind out of his sails. Nixon scored an enormous victory. He received over 60 percent of the popular vote and won every state except Massachusetts. Congress, however, remained under Democratic control.

THE WATERGATE SCANDAL UNFOLDS 5D

In January 1973, two months after Nixon had won the presidential election, the misdeeds of Watergate began to surface. The Watergate burglars went on trial in a Washington, D.C., courtroom. James McCord, one of the burglars, gave shocking evidence. A former CIA agent who had led the Bay of Pigs invasion of Cuba in 1961, McCord worked for the Nixon re-election campaign. McCord testified that people in high office had paid "hush money" to the five burglars. In return, the burglars were supposed to conceal White House involvement in the crime.

Investigations soon revealed that the break-in had been approved by the Attorney General, John Mitchell. Although Mitchell was one of his most trusted advisers, President Nixon denied knowing anything about the break-in or the cover-up that followed it. The nation would later learn that the President had not told the truth.

President Nixon, it was later learned, had ordered his aides to block the investigators. According to John Dean, the President's lawyer, the White House strategy called for "a public posture of full cooperation but a private attempt to . . . make it as difficult as possible to get information and witnesses."

The White House tried to stop the investigation by arguing that it would uncover national secrets. Nixon also refused to appear before a congressional committee, arguing that forcing the President to testify before Congress would violate the separation of powers. This idea—known as executive privilege—does not appear in the Constitution. It is a tradition that has developed over the years to protect the presidency. Critics complained that Nixon was misusing executive privilege to hide his own crimes.

When it was no longer possible to protect White House staff members, the President fired them. In April 1973, Nixon demanded the resignations of two of his top aides, Bob Haldeman and John Ehrlichman, because they were about to be charged with Watergate crimes. Along with Attorney General Mitchell (who had resigned office in 1972 to lead Nixon's re-election campaign), they were later convicted of conspiracy, obstruction of justice, and perjury.

Background At first, the trail led only to the Committee to Re-Elect the President (CREEP), of which former Attorney General John Mitchell was head. Many of the actions on the part of the Nixon administration were designed to limit the blame to CREEP.

With McCord's testimony, and the subsequent defection of Dean, this strategy failed.

For what crimes were Nixon and his staff responsible? (Illegal break-ins, illegal bugging and wiretapping, illegal solicitation of campaign contributions, harassment of political enemies, sabotage of opposing political campaign, and a cover-up that included perjury and obstruction of justice.)

Developing the Lesson
After students have read the section, you may want to consider the following activities:

Ethics
What "dirty tricks" did the plumbers use against Nixon opponents? (They broke into Daniel Ellsberg's psychiatrist's office, issued phony statements in Edmund Muskie's name, fed the press false rumors about Muskie, and faked a letter claiming Muskie had insulted French Canadians.) *How might President Nixon and his advisers have justified these actions?* (His re-election was more important than moral behavior; the end justifies the means.) *How would you respond to those justifications?*

Participating in Government
Emphasize to students that Nixon won a huge victory in 1972 in spite of the fact that criminal activities on the part of the Committee to Re-Elect the President had already begun to be reported. *In view of this, what responsibilities do voters have in assessing the way candidates conduct their campaigns?* (Voters need to be critical of candidates' ethics and hold them accountable for ethical and honest campaign practices.) Ask students if they think political campaigns today are more ethical than those in the early 1970s.

Senate committee head Sam Ervin (center) and ranking Republican Howard Baker (left) led the 1973 hearings on the Watergate scandal.
CONSTITUTIONAL HERITAGE If the President authorizes illegal actions, should he be subject to trial? If members of his administration act illegally without his knowledge, how much responsibility should the President take? 5D

THE SENATE WATERGATE HEARINGS 7A

In May 1973, millions of Americans watched in fascination as the Senate investigation of the Watergate scandal appeared on television. Many viewers found the broadcasts more gripping than any soap opera—with just as many characters and unbelievable twists of plot.

The Senate committee was headed by Sam Ervin. This grandfatherly, conservative North Carolinian won the trust of most Americans. He made people feel confident that Congress would uphold the law and protect the Constitution.

Ervin posed a critical question: Was the President above the law? Could he, for instance, order the break-in of a person's home? The idea that there are limits to a leader's power has been a central part of Western political tradition, Ervin noted. In his words:

> The concept embodied in the phrase "Every man's home is his castle" represents the realization of one of the most ancient and universal hungers of the human heart. One of the prophets described the mountain of the Lord as being a place where every man might dwell under his own vine and fig tree with none to make him afraid. . . .
> And [as] William Pitt the Elder . . . said, "The poorest man in his cottage may bid defiance to all the forces of the crown. It

may be frail, its roof may shake, the wind may blow through it, the storm may enter, the rain may enter, but the King of England cannot enter. All his force dares not cross the threshold of the ruined tenements."

And yet we are told here today that what the King of England can't do, the President of the United States can.

As the days passed, the focus of the inquiry turned increasingly toward the President's role. The ranking Republican, Howard Baker, repeatedly asked witnesses, "What did the President know and when did he know it?" Most witnesses tried to protect President Nixon. But late in the hearings, it became clear that the nation might learn exactly what the President had done. A minor official revealed that President Nixon had secretly tape-recorded all conversations in the Oval Office. Nixon had hoped these tapes would one day be used by historians to document the triumphs of his presidency. Instead, they were used to prove his guilt.

"**W**hat did the President know and when did he know it?"
—*Senator Howard Baker*

The Senate committee asked for the tapes. So did Archibald Cox, the special prosecutor whom Attorney General Elliot Richardson had appointed. The President refused to release the tapes, claiming that executive privilege gave him the right to keep his records private. The issue went to court.

AGNEW RESIGNS 7A

Before the question of the tapes could be decided, a fresh scandal broke out. Vice President Agnew was charged with income tax evasion. The Vice President was also accused of accepting bribes in exchange for political favors. Agnew agreed not to fight the tax evasion charge if the other charges were dropped. In October 1973 the Vice President resigned in disgrace.

Although the Agnew scandal was unconnected with Watergate, it dealt another blow to President Nixon's image. Nixon nominated Gerald Ford, the Republican leader in the House of Representatives, to replace Agnew. Ford was a solid choice with many friends in Congress. But he could do little to salvage the President's reputation.

THE SATURDAY NIGHT MASSACRE

Two days after Agnew's resignation, a federal court ordered Nixon to turn over his secret tapes. Nixon refused, and when Cox insisted, the President ordered Attorney General Richardson to fire Cox. Richardson admired Cox, who had been his professor in law school. He had also promised Cox and the Senate not to interfere with the special prosecutor's work. Richardson refused Nixon's order and then resigned. President Nixon then ordered the Deputy Attorney General to fire Cox. The Deputy also refused. Nixon then turned to the Solicitor General, Robert Bork. On Saturday night, October 20, 1973, Bork agreed to fire Cox.

This event became known as the Saturday Night Massacre. Many Americans saw President Nixon's effort to block the judicial process as convincing proof of his guilt. Citizens flooded Congress with telegrams urging that it begin impeachment proceedings against the President. Within a few days the House Judiciary Committee did just that.

CALLS FOR IMPEACHMENT 7I

President Nixon maintained that he had done nothing criminal. At a press conference in November 1973, he proclaimed defiantly, "I am not a crook." As he fielded questions, however, he seemed agitated and confused. Many people who watched the press conference on television sensed that the President was in deep trouble.

An Internal Revenue Service employee soon uncovered more information damaging to the President. It was revealed that Nixon had paid only about $800 per year in taxes in 1970 and 1971. During that time he had earned about $500,000. The nation also learned that Nixon had spent millions of dollars in public money to fix up his private estates in Florida and California.

Nixon still refused to release all the Watergate tapes. Then, in April 1974, Nixon released transcripts of most of the tapes. Although he had edited the transcripts in a way that seemed to lessen his guilt, the tapes still damaged his cause.

By July the Committee voted to bring impeachment charges (called "articles") against the President. The first article asserted that the President had knowingly obstructed justice in his cover-up of the Watergate affair. The second accused him of using government agencies to violate the constitutional rights of citizens. The third article called for impeachment because the President had illegally withheld evidence from Congress.

Many House members believed that Nixon's actions represented a grave threat to the Constitution. Barbara Jordan, a representative from Texas, put it most forcefully:

> My faith in the Constitution is whole, it is complete, it is total. I am not going to sit here and be an idle spectator to the diminution, the subversion, the destruction of the Constitution.

> "I am not going to sit here and be an idle spectator to . . . the destruction of the Constitution."
>
> —*Congresswoman Barbara Jordan*

Background Impeachment, provided for in the Constitution, is the first part of the process of removing the President from office. The House of Representatives serves as a kind of grand jury determining whether to indict—impeach—by hearing charges and then voting on these articles. The trial of an impeached President is held before the Senate, which determines whether to remove the President from office. President Andrew Johnson was impeached by the House in 1868, but he was acquitted by the Senate.

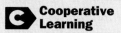
585

NIXON RESIGNS 7A

After the House committee voted to impeach the President, the matter went to the full House for a final decision. At this point, Nixon could still count on the backing of loyal supporters across the nation. They believed that his guilt had not been fully established.

The crucial evidence emerged just days after the committee vote. The Supreme Court ruled, in a unanimous decision, that the President must finally release the complete Watergate tapes. Nixon had no choice but to comply. The most important tape dated from June 23, 1972, just six days after the Watergate break-in. On the tape, President Nixon was heard telling his advisers to keep the FBI from investigating the crime. "Don't go any further into this case, period," Nixon had insisted. Indeed, the FBI and CIA had cooperated in the illegal burglaries and wiretapping that the President and his aides had ordered. Other tapes gave concrete proof that the President had approved more than $400,000 in hush money to cover up the Watergate crimes.

President Nixon had long claimed that he had not known about the cover-up until told about it by John Dean on March 21, 1973. The tapes, however, left little doubt. Not only had the President known about the cover-up, *he had ordered it.* It was now inevitable that the House and Senate

Richard Nixon bids farewell to his staff as he leaves the White House after resigning as President in 1974. Top Republican leaders had told Nixon they would no longer support him. **POLITICS** What would have happened to President Nixon if he had not resigned? 7A, 9A

would vote to convict Nixon of misdeeds in office. A small group of Republican leaders met with Nixon to convince him to resign. Two days later, on August 9, 1974, Richard Nixon became the first President in American history to resign.

CAUSE AND EFFECT: THE WATERGATE SCANDAL

Causes
- Nixon desire to discredit opponents of Vietnam War
- Nixon push for re-election in 1972

The Watergate Scandal (1972–1974)

Effects
- Ford replaces Nixon as President
- Constitutional processes upheld

CHART SKILLS 9E

The illegal activities of the Nixon administration were first revealed by investigative reporters and then probed in depth by Congress. What motivated the administration to commit the crimes that became known as Watergate? **CRITICAL THINKING** What effect did Watergate have on public confidence in government?

Cause and Effect Answers
The desire to discredit opponents of the Vietnam War and remain in office. People lost confidence in the government.

Photo Caption Answer
He might have been impeached and tried before the Senate.

someone is convicted. By pardoning Nixon before a trial, Ford left unanswered the question of Nixon's guilt or innocence. Nixon accepted the pardon and said he had made some "mistakes." But he never apologized or admitted that he had done anything illegal.

Many Americans believed Ford had made a deal with Nixon. Some claimed that Ford had promised, while Vice President, to offer Nixon a pardon if Nixon would resign without fighting impeachment. Ford flatly denied the charge.

An Offer of Amnesty 7C

One week after the pardon, Ford made another attempt to heal some of the nation's wounds. On September 16, 1974, he announced a plan of amnesty to men who had evaded military service in Vietnam. Those who had dodged the draft could regain their rights of citizenship if they performed two years of public service. They also had to take an oath of allegiance to the United States.

Like the presidential pardon, the offer of amnesty did not succeed in reuniting the American people. Those who had supported the war felt that it was unfair to those who had gone to Vietnam. Those who had opposed the war felt that it was too harsh to draft resisters, in light of the treatment President Nixon had just received.

Post-Watergate Politics 5C

Outcry against the pardon slowly died down, and news about Watergate dropped from the front pages, as Ford had hoped. However, opposition to the pardon would hurt his chances for re-election in 1976.

In the aftermath of Watergate, Congress passed laws to clean up elections. The Fair Campaign Practices Act, for example, limited the amount of money individuals and corporations could contribute to political candidates.

However, voter participation declined to an all-time low. In the 1974 congressional elections only 38 percent of eligible voters went to the polls. A bumper sticker of the time said, "DON'T VOTE, IT ONLY ENCOURAGES THEM." In a 1975 survey, more than two-thirds of all Americans agreed that "over the last ten years, this country's leaders have consistently lied to the people."

Vice President Rockefeller 5B

When Ford became President, the office of Vice President became vacant. For Vice President, Ford nominated Nelson A. Rockefeller, the long-time governor of New York. Rockefeller was a moderate Republican, a grandson of John D. Rockefeller and a presidential prospect himself. Ford believed that he would be confirmed easily by Congress.

However, Governor Rockefeller's judgment had been widely questioned in 1971 after he ordered New York security forces to use force to break up a prison strike at Attica State Prison. Congress was also concerned about Rockefeller's use of his vast wealth to advance his political career. But no illegal activity was turned up, and after four months of hearings, Congress confirmed his nomination. It was the only time in American history that neither the President nor the Vice President had been elected to office.

The Mayaguez Incident 1A

In foreign affairs, as in domestic matters, Ford hoped to move beyond the disasters of the recent past. He especially wanted to show that in spite of the loss in Vietnam, the United States remained a powerful nation ready and able to use its strength when necessary.

Henry Kissinger, who remained Secretary of State under Ford, shared this view. In April 1975, Kissinger told a journalist, "The U.S. must carry out some act somewhere in the world which shows its determination to continue to be a world power."

The opportunity for such an act arrived on May 12, 1975, just three weeks after the Communist victories in Vietnam and Cambodia. An American merchant ship, the *Mayaguez*, was seized by Cambodian Communists about 60 miles off the coast of Cambodia.

Ford ordered the marines to free the 39-man crew of the *Mayaguez*. The American people soon heard the good news—the sailors were free. Ford's use of force was widely applauded, as the operation seemed both justifiable and effective. The White House was jubilant.

Months later a government study of the incident cast great doubt on the need for the rescue

Background   As a congressman from Michigan, Ford supported President Johnson's early policies in the Vietnam War. By 1967, however, Ford began to attack United States policy in Vietnam, as a hawk. Ford was President when the Vietnam War ended. Shortly before the Communist takeover, Ford asked Congress to give South Vietnam more than $700 million in emergency military aid. Congress rejected the request.

office.) *Do you think this situation handicapped the effectiveness of the President and Vice President? Explain.* (Students may suggest that neither the people nor the Congress has any particular loyalty to a leader who had not been elected to his or her position.)

Ethics
Review the purpose of Ford's use of military force to gain release of the *Mayaguez* crew. *What facts came to light as a result of a government study of the Mayaguez incident?* (The crew had been released before the marine attack began. Ford knew this but ordered the assault anyway.) Have students suggest reasons why Ford chose to use military force despite the release of the *Mayaguez* crew. (He wanted the U.S. to appear as a strong and active world power, and to renew the confidence of Americans in their military.) *Do you think Ford's actions in ordering the assault were justified?*

Economics
Discuss the Federal Reserve System with the class, making sure that students understand how the Fed can tighten the money supply. You may wish to remind them that the Fed determines interest rates on money it lends to private banks. (By raising interest rates, the Fed makes it more difficult for people and businesses to borrow money, thus tightening the money supply.) Working alone or in pairs, have students create diagrams illustrating how the Fed can lower or raise inflation and unemployment. (Raising interest rates decreases the money supply. Prices go down, because there is less money. Businesses have less money so they lay off workers. Lowering interest rates does the opposite.)

mission. The study revealed that the crew of the *Mayaguez* had been released well before the marine attack began. Ford had received a report of this information but decided to order the assault anyway. The marines attacked a well-defended Cambodian island, believing the *Mayaguez* crew was there. In fact, the crew was already sailing toward the American fleet. Fifteen American servicemen were killed in the mission.

DÉTENTE UNDER ATTACK 1B

In other areas of the world, Ford tried to continue Nixon's policies. With Kissinger acting as the main architect of foreign policy, the United States sought further progress in détente.

At a 1974 meeting in the Soviet city of Vladivostok, Ford and Soviet leader Leonid Brezhnev set the groundwork for a second strategic arms limitation treaty. Another milestone for détente was a meeting in Helsinki, Finland, in 1975. There the two superpowers joined with European nations in accepting the post–World War II borders in Europe. The Soviet Union also pledged to improve its human rights record.

Yet public support for détente was slipping. Liberals complained that Ford's proposals for limiting nuclear weapons did not go far enough. Some conservatives, on the other hand, opposed even talking to the Soviets, much less signing treaties with them. They claimed that Soviet leaders could not be trusted to keep their word.

The right-wing attack on détente became especially intense after the Communist victories in Indochina (Chapter 23). Fearing that the United States was losing ground to communism, conservatives like Ronald Reagan, a former governor of California, gave speech after speech denouncing détente. They claimed that détente was a Soviet attempt to lull the West to sleep while the Soviets expanded throughout the Third World. Meanwhile, the Soviet Union was continuing to expand its military power. The Soviets also remained active in the Third World, helping Communists come to power in the African nation of Angola in 1976.

All these factors pushed Ford into backing away from détente. There would be no major improvement in Soviet-American relations until late in the 1980s.

This magazine cover pictures Ford, a former boxing coach, rolling up his sleeves to get tough with the problem of soaring inflation. Ford labeled inflation "public enemy Number 1." **ECONOMICS** What factors contributed to inflation in the early 1970s? **3E**

STAGFLATION CONTINUES 3E

With United States troops no longer fighting in Vietnam, most Americans focused their attention on problems at home. The economy was their major concern.

Ford inherited a weakened economy. By the end of 1974, the United States had fallen into the worst recession of the post–World War II period. Inflation stood at 13 percent, thanks in part to a staggering 400 percent rise in oil prices. In 1975 unemployment approached 10 percent. People were spending more on everything, yet having a harder time finding good jobs.

The Democrats called for a federal jobs program to bring down unemployment. Ford rejected the plan because he believed that pumping more money into the economy would only increase inflation.

With options for government action against stagflation so limited, Ford asked private citizens to do what they could. He called on the American people to become "inflation fighters and energy savers." Their voluntary actions, he believed, could cure the economy. Ford cheered them on by adopting a snappy slogan—"Whip Inflation Now" (WIN). He urged Americans to turn down their heat, plant vegetable gardens ("WIN gardens"), clean their plates at meals, stop using credit cards, and guard their health. "One of the worst wastes we have in America," Ford said, "is days lost through sickness."

For the most part, these sensible suggestions were ignored or ridiculed. Inflation did drop when the Federal Reserve System tightened the money supply. But this policy also deepened the recession. The Democrats would make the economic problems under Ford a key campaign issue in the 1976 elections.

THE AMERICAN BICENTENNIAL   7B, 7D, 7I, 7K

In 1976 the United States celebrated the bicentennial—200th anniversary—of its Declaration of Independence. Cities and towns around the nation planned special celebrations for the Fourth of July. Yet many feared that the festivities would flop, for there seemed little to celebrate. The nation had just lost a terrible war and endured a major political scandal. It was suffering through an energy crisis and was plagued by serious economic problems.

When the day arrived, however, skeptics were surprised. There was an outpouring of good feeling. At picnics and parades around the nation, people joined together with their friends and neighbors and celebrated. *The New Yorker* wrote:

It had an unplanned, unarranged quality. . . . Government officials took their modest place in the background. . . . People normally drawn to the limelight lay low. And the country's citizens, on their own, took to celebrating a birthday they all shared and suddenly understood. The idea of freedom hung in the air; and the idea of peace. . . . There was little flag-waving, but the flag was once more recognizable and thrilling.

Ford's dream of restoring national pride was partially fulfilled by the bicentennial. Americans had cause to celebrate the survival of the Constitution through the crisis of Watergate. The leadership of the country had passed peacefully from Nixon to Ford. While not a Lincoln, Gerald Ford nonetheless managed to lead the nation through a trying time.

SECTION REVIEW

1. KEY TERMS Fair Campaign Practices Act, *Mayaguez*, bicentennial

2. PEOPLE AND PLACES Nelson A. Rockefeller, Leonid Brezhnev, Helsinki, Vladivostok, Ronald Reagan

3. COMPREHENSION What was the purpose of Ford's pardon of Nixon? What was its effect?

4. COMPREHENSION What criticisms did Americans make of détente? What Soviet actions further damaged détente?

5. CRITICAL THINKING Why, in your opinion, was Ford's call for voluntary actions to help the economy unsuccessful?

CHAPTER 25   A TIME OF DOUBT, 1974–1980   **599**

Section Review Answers

1. *Fair Campaign Practices Act*—Limited the amount of money individuals and corporations could contribute to candidates. *Mayaguez*—American merchant ship seized by Cambodian Communists in 1975. *bicentennial*—200th anniversary of the signing of the Declaration of Independence.

2. *Nelson A. Rockefeller*—Vice President under Gerald Ford. *Leonid Brezhnev*—Soviet leader who met with Ford in 1974. *Helsinki*—City in Finland where superpowers and European nations accepted postwar borders. *Vladivostok*—Site of meeting in eastern Siberia between Ford and Brezhnev to set groundwork for SALT II. *Ronald Reagan*—Conservative who denounced détente.

3. To end public speculation about Nixon's fate, to establish his own identity as President, and to gain support for his own policies. Ford's popularity plunged.

4. Conservative leaders felt the Soviets could not be trusted. Soviets were expanding their military and helping Communist movements in Third World countries.

5. Students may point out that many Americans had little faith in their government, and so were less likely to make personal sacrifices at government suggestion.

Closure

Ask one student to transform the Main Idea of the section into a question, and have other students answer that question. Then have students to read Section 2 for the next class period, noting why women entered the work force in large numbers in the 1970s.

Photo Caption Answer
It celebrated the positive side of the nation's heritage.

2 The Women's Movement

★ Section Focus

Key Terms sexism ■ National Organization for Women ■ *Roe v. Wade*

Main Idea As women entered the work force in great numbers during the 1970s, the women's movement struggled for economic, political, and social equality. Feminists and traditionalists debated the role of women in society.

Objectives As you read, look for answers to these questions:
1. Why did more women go to work in the 1970s?
2. What were the goals of the women's movement?
3. Why was the Equal Rights Amendment defeated?

Section Objective

■ discuss the goals, accomplishments, and failures of the women's movement during the 1970s

Introducing the Section

Connecting with Past Learnings
Trace the changing role of women in the mid-1900s. *Why had many women entered the work force during the early 1940s?* (To take over jobs formerly held by men who went to war.) *What happened to these working women after World War II ended?* (Many returned home to resume traditional roles as housewife and mother.) *What were the values of the 1950s regarding the role of working women?* (Jobs outside the home should not interfere with family life or the economic prospects of men.)

Key Terms
Divide students into three groups. Have members of the first group suggest definitions for the key terms from this section. Have members of the second group revise and clarify definitions. Have members of the third group verify final definitions by looking up the terms in their text. **LEP**

On August 10, 1974, Gerald Ford began his first full day as President by toasting English muffins for his breakfast. The news media portrayed the new leader as an average American, not an imperial President. Without realizing it, perhaps, they also pointed out a change taking place in American society.

A similar scene twenty years earlier would have shown Mrs. Ford serving her husband breakfast. In the average family of the 1950s, it was the woman's job to prepare meals as well as clean house and care for children. A woman's place was in the home; a man's place was at a job.

CHANGES FOR WOMEN 4C
In the 1970s, family roles and responsibilities were not so clearly divided. The traditional family of breadwinner and housewife was no longer the norm, because millions of women had entered the work force. The most dramatic jump occurred among married mothers with young children. In 1950, only 12 percent of this group held jobs; by the end of the 1970s that figure had risen to 40 percent. This sweeping trend affected not only the nation's economy but also its political and social life.

Why did so many women seek jobs? The reasons for this change were many and complex. First among them was economic need. Divorce rates soared during the 1960s and 1970s, and many women needed to work to support themselves and their children. Inflation rates also rose steeply during those years. Many poor and working-class women had to take jobs in order to make ends

meet. Middle-class women also began to feel the economic pinch, as it became difficult for a family to live on just one salary.

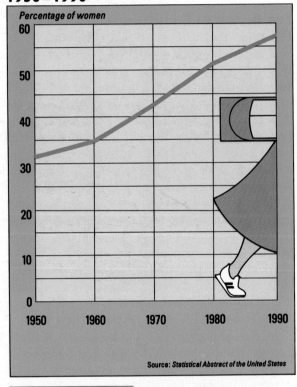

WOMEN WORKING OUTSIDE THE HOME, 1950–1990

Percentage of women

Source: *Statistical Abstract of the United States*

GRAPH SKILLS 9B

This graph shows the increasing number of women in the labor force. When did the number of working women first top 50 percent? **CRITICAL THINKING** Do you think the percentage of women in the work force will continue to rise? Why or why not?

SUPPORTING THE SECTION

Reinforcement Workbook: Worksheet 97
Reteaching Resources: Worksheet 97
Enrichment and Extension Resources: Primary Source Worksheet 50
Teaching Transparencies: Transparency 97

Graph Skills Answers
About 1978. Some students may say that the trend suggests that the percentage will continue to rise. Others may argue that factors fueling the entry of women into the work force may decline.

The entry of large numbers of women into the work force is one of the most important recent changes in American society. Although some women, such as the state trooper at right, have gained admittance to traditionally male fields, progress in breaking out of traditional "women's jobs"—such as nursing, office work, and teaching—has been slow. During the 1970s, women made up about 98 percent of all clerical workers, such as those pictured at left. **NATIONAL IDENTITY** What factors caused so many women to enter the work force? **3E**

Changes in birth rates and life expectancy also made it possible for more women to work. By the end of the 1960s, women were having fewer children and living longer. The average woman who reached adulthood in the 1960s had only one or two children. New methods of birth control allowed her to plan her family and thus have more control over her life. A woman of this generation could also expect to live into her eighties. Raising young children thus occupied a smaller portion of her life. More and more women came to believe that being a mother was only one of many roles they might have in a full and long life.

Yet staying at home was all that many women

BIOGRAPHY 4C

BETTY FRIEDAN (1921–   ), a psychologist and political activist, is considered the founder of the women's movement. In *The Feminine Mystique,* Friedan argued that women required opportunities for fulfillment in addition to those provided by marriage and motherhood. In 1966, Friedan helped found the National Organization for Women (NOW). Some feminists criticized her later writings, saying that they called for a return to traditional roles for women.

saw in their future, and it upset them. In a pioneering book entitled *The Feminine Mystique* (1963), Betty Friedan examined the isolation, boredom, and lack of fulfillment that many housewives felt. In search of a deeper sense of self-worth and a chance to learn new skills, many women took jobs outside the home.

Changes in the labor market created more jobs for them to fill. As the American economy turned away from manufacturing and toward service and sales, employers began seeking women employees to fill the new jobs.

NEW JOBS, NEW PROBLEMS 4D

Working outside the home brought women more money but also new problems. Some of these were practical issues, such as finding and paying for child care. Other issues were philosophical. Was it harmful for children to have working mothers? And now that women were helping earn money, should men help with household chores?

Another problem was the nature of the jobs themselves. Many were in areas like secretarial work, which had long been viewed as the domain of women. These "pink collar" jobs, as they came to be known, paid low wages and offered few chances for advancement. While they brought women into the work force, they were also often a dead end.

Even where women were able to enter new

Focus
Have students create a chart on the board comparing the role of women in American society in the 1950s and in the 1970s. Call on students to list characteristics on the chart. Then ask volunteers to role play "typical" American women of the 1950s and of the 1970s. Be sure students understand that they are stereotyping and generalizing, but that the attitudes they portray reflect changes in American society.

What were the goals of the women's movement of the 1970s? (To oppose sexism and gain equality.) *How successful was the women's movement in achieving these goals in the 1970s?* (Women won some legal victories and made social and economic gains. However, ERA was defeated and issues of equal pay and shared responsibilities at home remained unresolved.)

Developing the Lesson
After students have read the section, you may want to consider the following activities:

Economics
How did sexism affect professional opportunities for women? (Working women faced discrimination from men. Many faced difficulty in advancement.) *How did sexism affect earning power?* (Women generally earned only about 60 percent of what men earned for comparable jobs.) Have students examine the graph on page 600 and consider the effect on the economy of the influx of women workers.

Photo Caption Answer
Rising costs of living, higher divorce rates, and fewer children.

Biography
Discuss with students whether they agree with the thesis of *The Feminine Mystique.* Ask them to consider why Friedan's later writings called for a return to more traditional roles.

Background In 1957 Betty Friedan wrote a questionnaire for her fellow Smith College graduates of 1942. The questionnaire raised the issue of women's role in society, leading to *The Feminine Mystique.*

fields, they faced discrimination from men. During the 1970s, many "blue collar" jobs began to open to women. By the end of the decade, women worked on construction sites, installed and repaired telephones, drove buses, and did many other traditionally male jobs. Yet women in these jobs often reported that they had to work twice as hard to be accepted by their male colleagues.

Women seeking to enter professions did make significant gains. For example, in 1969 only 3 percent of all lawyers were women. By the early 1980s roughly 50 percent of all law school graduates were women. Thousands of women became doctors. Women also entered the top ranks of American business, but at a slower rate. By 1975 slightly more than 5 percent of management jobs went to women. Many women in management positions faced a "glass ceiling," a limit above which they could not rise within a company.

Despite the increase in the number of highly paid professionals, women on the whole earned only about 60 percent of what men made for comparable work. That figure has not changed greatly in the years since.

This difference in earnings was a blatant example of sexism, the idea that one sex is naturally superior to the other. It was said that women lacked the strength, intelligence, and toughness to succeed in the outside world. It took massive ef-

forts from women to show that success depended on training, not biology. Although they outnumbered men, women had to struggle like a minority group to fight discrimination.

1974	Hank Aaron tops Babe Ruth's record for lifetime home runs.
1975	*A Chorus Line* opens on Broadway. By 1983 it becomes longest running musical in Broadway history.
	Russian and U.S. spaceships link up on the *Apollo/Soyuz* space mission.
1978	California's Proposition 13, a tax-cut measure, triggers a taxpayer revolt across the United States.
	Three Americans cross the Atlantic Ocean in a hot-air balloon.
1979	Gasoline prices top $1.00 per gallon for the first time in the United States.
	Chicago elects Jane Byrne its first woman mayor.
	Diana Nyad is the first person to swim from the Bahamas to Florida.

The women's movement promoted a wide-ranging agenda of social reform, including more day-care centers, such as the one pictured here. In the past, many politicians opposed funding day-care programs because they believed they ran counter to traditional child-care arrangements. **ECONOMICS** Why is day care an important issue for so many families? **3E**

THE WOMEN'S MOVEMENT 4C, 4D

Groups of women who organized to work for equality became an important social movement in the 1970s. Like all movements, the women's movement contained a wide range of viewpoints. A few radicals wanted nothing to do with men or with childbirth. Most feminists, however, were more interested in a truly equal partnership with men in both private and public life, based on the sharing of responsibilities.

The women's movement addressed a number of women's practical needs. At the grassroots level, local women's groups took on dozens of projects. These included day-care centers, women's newspapers, food cooperatives, and women's health groups.

The new feminists took part in political campaigns, backing candidates whose positions they supported. As a result, more women were elected to Congress and to positions in state and local government. A major breakthrough came in 1974 when Ella Grasso of Connecticut became the first woman governor who had not succeeded her husband.

Some women worked to remove sexist language from school textbooks and to include study of women at all levels of education. They had good reason to protest. For example, most high school history textbooks published before the mid-1970s included only a very few references to women. Protest brought change. Textbooks began to include women, and universities began to establish women's studies programs.

Many of the ideas and issues of the women's movement of the 1970s had been raised during the 1800s. Early feminists had worked for property rights, better education, and the right to vote. As you read in Chapter 9, these early feminists also had strong ties to the abolitionist movement.

The link between civil rights for blacks and for women could also be seen in the Civil Rights Act of 1964. Part of that bill, Title VII, was intended to prevent employment discrimination on the basis of "race, color, religion, or national origin." As Title VII was being debated, Congressman Howard Smith of Virginia proposed that the word "sex" be added. Smith actually opposed the bill. He inserted the word as a joke, hoping it would make the legislation look so ridiculous it would be voted down. Smith's joke backfired, and the bill was accepted with his amendment in place.

The government was not eager to enforce Title VII as it applied to women. Employers were still allowed to advertise jobs separately by sex. Newspapers still ran listings that read "Help Wanted—Male" and "Help Wanted—Female." How, women asked, was that any different from listing jobs by race, such as "Help Wanted—White"?

Social changes in the 1960s and 1970s helped some American men and women go beyond the traditional division of labor. As large numbers of women entered the work force, some fathers began sharing child-care responsibilities—an experience many found liberating. ISSUES Should men and women have different work roles? Explain your answer. 6C

Addressing Individual Needs

Guided/ Independent Practice

Have students complete **Reinforcement Workbook** Worksheet 97, which helps them interpret a graph showing changes in the labor force.

Reteaching/Correctives

Have students develop timelines of important events of the women's movement during the past three decades. Students should begin by reviewing the section and listing the events they think should be included in their timeline.

Assign **Reteaching Resources** Worksheet 97. This worksheet helps students recognize cause-and-effect relationships between events and trends, and the women's movement of the 1970s.

Enrichment/Extension

Instruct students to complete **Enrichment and Extension Resources** Primary Source Worksheet 50, which analyzes excerpts from *The Feminine Mystique*.

Assessment

You may wish to use the Section 2 Review, page 605, to see how well your students understand the main points in this lesson.

Section Review Answers

1. *sexism*—Idea that one sex is inherently superior to the other. *National Organization for Women*— Formed in 1966 to bring women into full participation in the mainstream of American society. *Roe v. Wade*— Supreme Court decision in 1973 giving women the right to obtain an abortion during the first three months of pregnancy.

THE NATIONAL ORGANIZATION FOR WOMEN

In 1966 the National Organization for Women (NOW) was formed to pressure the government to enforce Title VII. Composed mostly of middle-class professional women, NOW elected Betty Friedan as its first president. Its goal was "to bring women into full participation in the mainstream of American society *now*." NOW pursued that goal by working for equal opportunity in employment. It encouraged protests and other actions in which women could voice their demands for equal rights.

Not all women supported the women's movement and NOW. Many believed that women's traditional role as wife and mother was the best way to preserve social order. They saw women's liberation as a dangerous threat not only to the family but also to the American way of life.

Nevertheless, the women's movement continued to grow, and NOW became its major organization. Starting with just 300 members in 1966, it expanded to 50,000 by the mid-1970s. In its struggle for equal rights for women, NOW won a number of legal victories. One was a Supreme Court decision that forbade references to gender in "help wanted" ads.

ROE V. WADE 4D, 7E, 7F

Another Supreme Court victory for feminists was the case of *Roe v. Wade*. In 1973 the Court declared that a woman had the right to obtain an abortion during the first three months of pregnancy. Before this decision, most states had laws prohibiting or strongly limiting abortion.

Throughout the 1960s feminists had called for laws allowing abortion. They argued that while abortion was unfortunate, it was better than bringing an unwanted child into the world. Legalized abortion would be far safer for women than the dangerous, illegal operations that took the lives of 10,000 women each year. Most of all, the women's movement insisted that the decision whether to have an abortion should be made by the individual woman, not the government.

The *Roe* decision sparked one of the hottest debates of recent times. Opponents began a strong lobbying effort to have the decision overturned. Led by the National Right to Life Committee, they argued that abortion was morally the same as murder and should be outlawed.

Though the *Roe* decision remained in place, it has been challenged and modified. In 1977 the Supreme Court upheld a decision by Congress to ban the use of federal funds to pay for abortions. (Medicaid funds had paid for 300,000 abortions a year.) This decision severely limited the ability of poor women to obtain safe abortions. Encouraged by this victory, abortion opponents vowed not to rest until all abortions had been banned.

THE EQUAL RIGHTS AMENDMENT 4D, 7E

Next to abortion, the Equal Rights Amendment (ERA) was perhaps the most widely debated feminist issue of the 1970s. First proposed to Congress in 1923 (page 219), the ERA aimed to strengthen the position of women as wage earners and to remove limits on women's property rights during and after marriage.

Opponents of the women's movement made defeating the ERA a prime task. Leaders like Phyllis Schlafly rallied both men and women to speak out against the amendment. These opponents thought that the ERA would challenge traditional gender roles and ruin the stability of the family. They maintained that the ERA was unnecessary because women's rights were already protected. They also claimed that the ERA would lead to a draft of women into the military, abolish separate-sex public restrooms, and end alimony payments to divorced women.

In the view of ERA opponents, if men and women were equal in the eyes of the law, women would be as responsible as men for the support of the family. Therefore, a husband could not be held fully responsible for support of his wife and children. An anti-ERA group stated:

> [We believe in] the right of a woman to be a full-time wife and mother, and to have this right recognized by laws that obligate her husband to provide the primary financial support and a home for her and their children, both during their marriage and when she is a widow.

In 1972 Congress passed the Equal Rights Amendment. To become law, it had to be accepted

604 UNIT 9 TOWARD A NEW CENTURY

Background The ERA, like most proposed amendments, included a requirement that ratification must occur within seven years. In 1978, Congress voted to extend the 1979 deadline to June 30, 1982. The amendment's exact wording was: "Equality of rights under the law shall not be denied or abridged by the United States or any state on account of sex."

Supporters of the Equal Rights Amendment (ERA) demonstrate in 1978. The ERA would have rendered unconstitutional all laws that give men and women different rights. **CONSTITUTIONAL HERITAGE** Describe the process by which an amendment to the Constitution becomes law. Why did the ERA fail to become law? **7I**

Phyllis Schlafly, editor of an influential conservative newsletter, led the stop-ERA movement. Schlafly argued that inequality between men and women is biologically determined and cannot be changed, and that the ERA would have a negative effect on families. **ISSUES** Do you support or oppose the ERA? Explain. **6A, 6C**

by three-fourths of the state legislatures. When the time limit for consideration ended in 1982, 35 states had ratified the ERA—three short of the number required.

THE CONTINUING CHALLENGE 7F

Although the ERA was defeated, women were more vocal and more visible in the 1970s than ever before. Economic trends and the women's movement opened new jobs to women. Women moved toward greater social equality and were having a stronger political impact.

Yet there were issues still unresolved. At work, women's earnings still did not match men's. At home, women faced an additional workload. Surveys revealed that most working women with families still did more housework than their husbands and bore more responsibility for raising the children. As one working mother put it, "In the early 1970s, the women's movement told me I could have it all. By the end of the 1970s, I realized I'd been stuck with it all."

SECTION REVIEW

1. KEY TERMS sexism, National Organization for Women, *Roe v. Wade*

2. PEOPLE Betty Friedan, Phyllis Schlafly

3. COMPREHENSION What factors contributed to the entry of millions of women into the work force in the 1970s?

4. COMPREHENSION What objections did people raise to the Equal Rights Amendment?

5. CRITICAL THINKING How successful has the women's movement been in achieving its goals? To what do you attribute its success or failure?

2. *Betty Friedan*—Author of *The Feminine Mystique* and first president of NOW. *Phyllis Schlafly*—Opposed ERA as a challenge to traditional gender roles and the stability of the family.

3. Economic need, changes in birth rates and life expectancy, search for a deeper sense of self-worth, and changes in the job market.

4. It challenged traditional roles and family stability; it was unnecessary because women's rights were already protected; it would lead to a draft of women into the military and end alimony payments to divorced women.

5. Students may point out that women have made social, economic, and political gains as a result of the women's movement, though women's earnings still do not match men's and most working women still have primary responsibility for housework and children. Economic pressures for women to enter the work force and the enormous size of the women's movement's constituency helped in its successes. Its failures are connected to the deep-rooted nature of problems and the lack of agreement on goals.

Closure

Use the Chapter Review Summary for Section 2 (p. 616) to synthesize the important elements in the section. Then have students read Section 3 for the next class period. Ask them to note similarities and differences between Presidents Ford and Carter.

Photo Caption Answers
(Left) An amendment needs to be approved by two-thirds of the House and the Senate and then ratified by three-fourths of the state legislatures. The ERA fell three states short of the three-fourths required for ratification. (Right) Some students may argue that uniform assurances are needed to protect women's rights. Others may argue that women's rights are already protected and the law would weaken the family structure.

3 Jimmy Carter and the Crisis of Confidence

Section Focus

Key Terms Department of Energy ■ National Energy Act ■ meltdown

Main Idea During his presidency, Jimmy Carter faced serious domestic problems—double-digit inflation, a mounting energy crisis, and a lack of public confidence.

Objectives As you read, look for answers to these questions:
1. Why did voters choose Carter over Ford in 1976?
2. What domestic problems did Carter face?
3. How did Carter deal with the energy crisis?

If I'm elected, at the end of four years [as President] I hope people will say: "You know, Jimmy Carter made a lot of mistakes, but he never told me a lie."
—*Jimmy Carter, May 6, 1976*

"Jimmy who?" said many Americans in 1975 when asked their opinion of Jimmy Carter, the ever-smiling candidate for President. Only 2 out of every 100 Americans even recognized Carter's name when he began his long-shot bid for the White House. But just a year later the one-time peanut farmer from Plains, Georgia (population 600), pulled away from a pack of other Democratic contenders and went on to defeat President Ford. It was one of the most unexpected campaign victories in American history.

Americans were enthusiastic about the new President. They were excited to see Carter and his wife Rosalynn walking down Pennsylvania Avenue after the inauguration. This openness was bold and refreshing, a sign that Carter intended to be a people's President.

> "**I**f I ever tell a lie, I want you to come and take me out of the White House."
> —*Jimmy Carter, 1976*

THE ELECTION OF 1976 5B
Carter's skill at winning the trust of American voters was the key factor in his successful campaign. He did so by promising, over and over, to tell the truth. "If I ever tell a lie, I want you to

come and take me out of the White House," he said in almost every speech. In the years after Vietnam and Watergate, Americans craved an honest President, and Carter was brilliant at appealing to that need.

A former governor of Georgia, Carter presented himself as an outsider uncorrupted by the world of

Jimmy Carter, holding a Bible, goes to church with his family. Carter, a born-again Baptist, was Georgia's governor before running for President. **RELIGION** What factors may have contributed to the revival of "born-again" Christianity in the 1970s? 4G, 6A

4 World Affairs in the Carter Years

★ **Section Focus**

★ **Key Terms** Panama Canal Treaty ■ Camp David Accords ■ SALT II ■ deterrence

★ **Main Idea** In foreign affairs Carter had notable successes in Latin America and the Middle East. A hostage crisis in Iran, however, left his presidency in ruins.

Objectives As you read, look for answers to these questions:
1. Why did Carter negotiate a new treaty over the Panama Canal?
2. How was Carter able to ease tensions in the Middle East?
3. How did a crisis develop in Iran?

"We cannot look away when a government tortures people, or jails them for their beliefs or denies minorities fair treatment." With those words Jimmy Carter summed up his call for a foreign policy dedicated to the promotion of human rights.

Carter wanted to make a sharp break from the realpolitik that had guided diplomacy under Nixon and Ford. In those years, Carter argued, American leaders were guided solely by questions of power. The United States had supported virtually any friendly regime, no matter how brutally it treated its own people. Carter said the United States must use its diplomatic and economic power to pressure other nations into behaving more humanely.

Carter's intentions were honorable. His idealism recalled Woodrow Wilson's search for a new world order, based on principle rather than power. Yet Carter found it difficult to translate ideals into practical policies.

Carter's foreign policy, like his economic program, often seemed inconsistent. For example, he cut foreign aid to dictators in nations that were not strategically located—Uruguay and Argentina, for example. Yet he continued to support dictators in South Korea and the Philippines, nations whose backing the United States needed. Both liberals and conservatives accused Carter of hypocrisy.

THE PANAMA CANAL TREATY 1A, 1B

Carter wanted to improve American relations with smaller nations by treating them with more respect. Panama was one example. Panamanians had long accused the United States of forcing an

unfair canal treaty on them in 1903 (Chapter 12). American ownership of the Panama Canal Zone seemed to Panamanians an example of American imperialism.

To satisfy Panamanian demands, the United States signed in 1977 a set of treaty agreements that would gradually give control of the Canal Zone to Panama. The Panama Canal Treaty required the canal to remain neutral and open to all nations. The United States also claimed the right to defend the canal with force if necessary.

The treaty met deep-seated opposition among many conservatives. Ronald Reagan, for example, insisted that the treaty was a "giveaway" of legally purchased territory. Opponents also argued that because the Panama Canal was so important to American security, the United States needed to retain direct control. Many Americans were persuaded by such arguments, and polls indicated that a majority opposed the treaty.

A young woman holds a sign protesting President Carter's treaty giving control of the Panama Canal Zone to Panama. Carter gradually built support for the treaty, which was ratified in 1978. **PATTERNS IN HISTORY** Describe the history of U.S.-Panama relations. 2E

SUPPORTING THE SECTION

Reinforcement Workbook: Worksheet 99
Reteaching Resources: Worksheet 99
Teaching Transparencies: Transparency 99

Photo Caption Answer
The United States helped create Panama by instigating a revolt against Colombia. It occupied the country militarily during the early 1900s and in 1989.

SECTION 4

World Affairs in the Carter Years
(pp. 611–615)

Section Objective
■ describe Carter's successes and failures in foreign affairs

Introducing the Section

Connecting with Past Learnings
Ask students to define and explain the term *realpolitik*. (Policy that the United States should base its foreign policy on power considerations, not ethics.)
Why had Nixon and Ford based diplomacy on realpolitik? (Both Presidents relied on Secretary of State Henry Kissinger who was committed to practical solutions rather than idealism.)

Key Terms
Write the terms from this section on the board. Call on volunteers to write a definition next to each term. Then have students write a paragraph using all the terms. **LEP**

Focus
List the following on the board: *Panama Canal Treaty, Camp David Accords, SALT II, plans for MX, support of Shah of Iran.* Create two columns next to the list, one labeled *Successes* and the other labeled *Failures*. Call on volunteers to enter a tally mark in the success column or the failure column for each of the listed items. Then ask students to play the role of Carter writing his memoirs. Have them describe the high

611

How did the hostage crisis destroy Carter's presidency? (He lost public support because he was unable to do anything to end it.)

Developing the Lesson
After students have read the section, you may want to consider the following activities:

Ethics
Ask students to describe the basis of Carter's foreign policy. (He wanted to support nations who respected human rights.) **Is human rights a sound principle for diplomatic relations? Why or why not?** (Some students may argue in favor of idealism; others may argue that realism demands making allies of nations who can benefit the United States regardless of their form of government.)

Do you think U.S. foreign policy today is guided more by realpolitik or concern for human rights? Have students give specific examples supporting their opinions.

Analyzing Controversial Issues
Divide students into two teams to present opposing views of the Panama Canal Treaty. **What were the arguments in favor of the treaty?** (It would promote good will between the United States and Panama; the canal would remain neutral; the United States could defend the canal if attacked.) **What were the arguments opposing the treaty?** (Giving the canal to Panama would threaten American security and would give away legally purchased territory.) **Looking back, do you think the United States was right to sign the treaty?**

The treaty's backers claimed that it protected American interests and would improve relations with Panama. They also argued that the treaty would prove to Latin American nations that the United States had abandoned the "big stick" policies of the past. Supporters of the treaty received a boost when John Wayne, a movie star and hero to conservatives, publicly supported the treaty. By 1978 public opinion had swung toward the treaty, and the Senate ratified it with the necessary two-thirds vote.

TOWARD PEACE IN THE MIDDLE EAST 1A
Carter's efforts for peace in the Middle East were far less controversial. The peace treaty he helped arrange between Israel and Egypt was the greatest diplomatic success of his presidency.

Conflict between Israel and its Arab neighbors had been so heated over the years that no Arab leader had ever visited Israel. In fact, none had even formally recognized Israel's existence. Thus when Egypt's president, Anwar Sadat, decided to visit Jerusalem in 1977, the world was stunned. Sadat met with Israeli prime minister Menachem Begin and called for a peace treaty between the two nations.

Peace talks soon stalled. Carter stepped in and invited the two leaders to a summit conference at Camp David, the presidential retreat outside Washington, D.C. The offer was widely seen as a huge risk for Carter. Achieving peace between the Arab nations and Israel seemed an impossible task. Yet Carter had now put his own prestige—and that of the presidency—on the line to reach an agreement. Failure at Camp David, coupled with Carter's problems in domestic affairs, could wreck his presidency.

For two weeks in September 1978 Carter went back and forth between Sadat and Begin negotiating an agreement. Eventually they reached an understanding that became known as the Camp David Accords. Under this peace treaty, Israel agreed to withdraw from Egyptian land it had seized in 1967. Egypt, in turn, formally recognized Israel's right to exist.

RELATIONS WITH THE SOVIET UNION 1A, 1B
Improving the prospects for peace was also a theme of Carter's dealings with the Soviet Union. He canceled plans to build a new bomber, the B-1. He also halted development of a nuclear weapon called the neutron bomb, which was designed to kill people but not destroy property. Finally, he moved ahead in the area of arms limitation, sign-

President Carter is flanked by Israeli Prime Minister Menachem Begin (right) and Egyptian President Anwar Sadat at the signing of the Camp David Accords. Carter successfully negotiated a peace treaty between Israel and Egypt—two historical enemies. POLITICS Why might Carter have wanted to promote peace in the Middle East? 7C

612 UNIT 9 TOWARD A NEW CENTURY

Photo Caption Answer
To reduce superpower tensions and to stabilize a region strategically important because of its energy resources and location. Carter's Christian beliefs may have also been a factor.

ing the SALT II agreement with Brezhnev in 1979. This agreement placed new limits on the nuclear strength of the superpowers.

The treaty still needed to be ratified by the Senate, and it promised to be a tough fight. Many conservatives saw SALT II as a fatal weakening of American military strength.

The nuclear balance became the focus of the debate over SALT II. The United States had three kinds of nuclear forces—land-based missiles, submarine-based missiles, and bombers. These three kinds of systems made up what was called a "triad." The idea behind the triad was that while the Soviets might figure out how to wipe out one or even two "legs" of the triad, they would never be able to destroy all three. Thus, the United States would always be able to retaliate after a surprise Soviet attack. This ability to strike back lay at the heart of deterrence—the prevention of nuclear war through the threat of retaliation.

Conservatives believed that new Soviet missiles could destroy American land-based missiles in their silos. This made the land-based leg of the American triad vulnerable. And by canceling the B-1 bomber, critics argued, Carter was weakening the air-based leg as well. They opposed SALT II in part because it did not force the Soviets to scrap their missiles that threatened the American missile force.

Carter tried to appease his critics by backing a new missile system, called the MX. These missiles were to be shuttled from one place to another in underground tunnels so the Soviets would never know where they were. Under SALT II, the United States retained the right to build the MX.

The administration hoped that the MX would help win Senate approval of SALT II. But the treaty's chances collapsed in December 1979 when the Soviet Union invaded Afghanistan to prop up a new Communist government there. Carter knew that Congress, furious over the invasion, was in no mood to ratify SALT II. He shelved the treaty. Carter also declared an embargo on grain exports to the Soviet Union. Finally, he called for a boycott of the 1980 Olympics in Moscow. But as critics pointed out, none of these actions would force the Soviets out of Afghanistan. And the loss of SALT II was a severe blow to Carter's presidency.

THE FALL OF THE SHAH 1A, 1B

On New Year's Eve 1977, President Carter attended a state dinner in Iran's capital, Tehran. He toasted the long-time American ally, Reza Shah Pahlavi. "Because of the great leadership of the Shah," Carter proclaimed, "Iran is an island of stability in a turbulent corner of the world."

Not for long. Just a few months later, angry crowds of Iranians flooded the streets in protests against the Shah. One of their slogans was, "The Shah is Carter's dog." To American leaders, the Shah seemed a shining example of pro-Western modernization. To Iranians, however, he was a brutal, corrupt pawn of the United States.

Iranians had not forgotten that the United States had returned the Shah to power in 1953 (page 475). Nor would they forget that he ruled with an iron fist, using his secret police to torture and murder his opponents. The Shah's economic policies were also unpopular. Even as many Iranians were battling poverty, the Shah was shopping for modern weapons. He spent $15 billion on American arms between 1974 and 1978.

Iranian demonstrators demand that the United States return the deposed Shah for trial. The Shah was undergoing medical treatment in America at the time. HISTORY Describe the connection between popular discontent with the Shah and anti-American feelings among Iranians. 9A

Science and Technology
Ask a volunteer to draw a diagram of the nuclear defense triad on the board. (Nuclear missiles and bombs were carried by submarines in the sea and by bombers in the air; stored in silos on land.) Underneath each part of the triad, have other volunteers list the appropriate weapons systems mentioned. (Bombers—B-1; land-based missiles—MX.)

How did technology affect the nuclear arms race in the 1970s? (United States had the capability of developing the neutron bomb and MX. Carter halted work on the neutron bomb, but supported the MX to appease critics who felt the Soviets had aggressive intentions.)

History
Ask students to interview their parents or other people who remember the Iranian hostage crisis. Tell students to focus on how the crisis influenced the way these people felt about the United States and the President. If students were able to record these recollections, have the class create an audio history of the crisis. If students took written notes, have them create a written history, which they can illustrate.

C Cooperative Learning

Divide the class into small groups. Instruct each group to list ways in which the United States can exert influence on other governments. Then have members of each group decide which methods are ethical. Ask one member of each group to report the results of the discussion. LEP

The revolution to oust the Shah won the support of a broad spectrum of the urban classes—workers, intellectuals, and merchants. Their massive protest demonstrations finally forced the Shah into exile in January 1979. With his departure, Islamic fundamentalists led by the Ayatollah Khomeini (koh–MAY–nee) seized control of the revolution. Under Khomeini, Iran returned to a non-Western, strictly Islamic way of life. Khomeini did not, however, renounce the harsh rule that had marked the Shah's reign. Tolerating no opposition, the Ayatollah had thousands of Iranians imprisoned or executed.

THE HOSTAGE CRISIS 1A, 1B
In October 1979, President Carter allowed the Shah to come to New York for treatment of cancer. In Tehran, demonstrators marched in fury at Carter's aid to the hated Shah. On November 4, 1979, armed Islamic revolutionaries stormed the United States embassy and took 66 Americans hostage. Khomeini insisted that the hostages would not be released until Carter returned the Shah and all of his wealth.

The hostages were paraded, bound and gagged, before screaming crowds of anti-American demonstrators. Television audiences around the world watched Iranians burning American flags and effigies of Jimmy Carter.

Such scenes only made Americans even more determined not to give in. Carter refused to hand over the Shah. He ordered American banks to deny the Iranian government access to its money in those banks. Still, Carter rejected a military rescue. The Iranian guards had pledged to kill the hostages if any such mission were launched.

As the crisis dragged on, Americans grew more restless. Anti-Iranian rallies took place around the nation. TV anchorman Walter Cronkite began counting the days of the hostage crisis in his newscast. In 1968, Cronkite's public statements about the Vietnam War had helped convince Lyndon Johnson that he had lost public support. Now, Cronkite's daily reminders of the hostage crisis symbolized American impatience with the situation. It seemed that Carter, and in fact the entire nation, was being held hostage.

Under unbearable pressure to do *something*, Carter ordered a military rescue mission in April 1980. However, the mission was ill-conceived and poorly executed. When several rescue helicopters broke down in the desert hundreds of miles from Tehran, the mission was aborted. Eight servicemen died in a collision in the desert.

The tangled wreck of U.S. military helicopters in the Iranian desert symbolized the disappointing failure of Carter's foreign policy goals. Coming on top of the Soviet invasion of Afghanistan, the disastrous mission spelled the end of Carter's political career. **HISTORY** How was the Iranian hostage crisis finally resolved? **1A**

Photo Caption Answer
An agreement was made for their release in exchange for the release of Iranian assets in the United States.

Background Secretary of State Cyrus Vance, who had opposed the hostage rescue attempt, resigned after the armed mission failed. Carter named Senator Edmund Muskie of Maine as Vance's successor.

The continuing hostage crisis, along with the failed rescue mission, dimmed Carter's hopes for re-election. The energy crisis and soaring inflation of 1979–1980 also made Carter seem weak and incompetent. The champion of conservatives, Ronald Reagan, would capitalize on Carter's failures to assure himself victory in the 1980 election.

When the Shah died in July 1980, secret talks with the Iranians began to show results. The Iranians agreed to release the hostages if Carter would release the frozen Iranian assets. The complex talks continued throughout the last months of Carter's presidency.

On Inauguration Day, January 20, 1981, the final arrangements for the hostage release were completed. Carter had spent virtually every minute of his last three days as President working on the hostage issue. Sleepless, he sat with his aides waiting for word that the airplane loaded with hostages had left Tehran. The news did not arrive, and the exhausted President had to leave the Oval Office to meet the man who would replace him. Several minutes after Ronald Reagan was sworn in as President, the hostages departed Iran. It was the end to what some have called the "decade of doubt."

THE CARTER YEARS IN PERSPECTIVE 7A

Was Jimmy Carter simply a bad President? Many Americans certainly felt so in 1980. His defenders claim, however, that Carter's reputation will improve in the future. They argue that he was blamed for a series of problems over which he had no control. They further state that he had the courage to undertake policies with long-term, rather than short-term, benefits. And they praise other Carter actions, in areas such as the environment, that received little notice while he was in office.

On the other hand, more than a decade after he left office, Jimmy Carter is still identified with the sense of frustration and helplessness the nation felt while he was in office. OPEC raised prices, Iranians took Americans hostage, the economy went nowhere—and it seemed that Carter could do nothing about any of it. Americans, used to believing that anything is possible, did not accept the idea that the nation had entered an era of limitations on its power. They turned instead to Ronald Reagan, who promised that the only limits are those of the imagination.

SECTION REVIEW

1. KEY TERMS Panama Canal Treaty, Camp David Accords, SALT II, deterrence

2. PEOPLE AND PLACES Anwar Sadat, Menachem Begin, Afghanistan, Ayatollah Khomeini

3. COMPREHENSION What arguments were raised supporting the Panama Canal Treaty? What arguments were raised against it?

4. COMPREHENSION What role did Carter play in bringing about the Camp David Accords?

5. CRITICAL THINKING Should Carter have given in to Iranian demands and returned the Shah and his wealth? Why or why not?

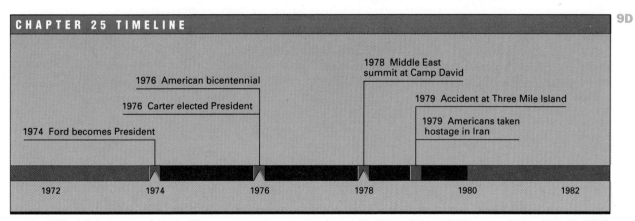

CHAPTER 25 TIMELINE

9D

1978 Middle East summit at Camp David

1976 American bicentennial

1979 Accident at Three Mile Island

1976 Carter elected President

1979 Americans taken hostage in Iran

1974 Ford becomes President

1972   1974   1976   1978   1980   1982

CHAPTER 25   A TIME OF DOUBT, 1974–1980   **615**

2. *Anwar Sadat*—Egyptian president who became first Arab leader to visit Israel. *Menachem Begin*—Israeli prime minister who signed a peace treaty with Sadat. *Afghanistan*—Southwest Asian nation whose invasion by the Soviet Union in 1979 caused the United States to shelve SALT II. *Ayatollah Khomeini*—Leader of Islamic fundamentalists who seized control of Iran in 1979.

3. Supporters said it protected American interests, would improve relations with Panama, and would prove to other Latin American countries that the U.S. was no longer following a "big stick" policy. Opponents felt it gave away territory that legally belonged to the U.S. and was vital to American security.

4. He put his prestige, and that of the presidency, on the line to move along stalled peace negotiations between Egypt and Israel.

5. Students who feel Carter should have returned the Shah may point to the importance of freeing Americans. Students who support Carter's unwillingness to return the Shah should note that the U.S. would appear weak and untrustworthy if it gave in to demands and returned a former ally, and that such action might encourage the taking of more hostages.

Closure
Remind students of the pre-reading objectives in the section opener. Pose one or all of these questions again. Then have students read Section 1 of Chapter 26 for the next class period and contrast the philosophies of Presidents Carter and Reagan.

Chapter 25 Review Answers

Key Terms
1. Fair Campaign Practices Act
2. meltdown
3. *Roe v. Wade*
4. *Mayaguez*
5. deterrence

People to Identify
1. Ayatollah Khomeini
2. Nelson A. Rockefeller
3. Betty Friedan
4. Phyllis Schlafly
5. Menachem Begin

Places to Locate
1. A   4. C
2. B   5. D
3. E

Reviewing the Facts
1. Ford pardoned Nixon in an attempt to end Watergate. Public response was divided and Ford's popularity plunged.

2. Ford called on citizens to voluntarily conserve energy and food and to stop using credit cards. The program was ridiculed and ineffectual.

3. Families needed double incomes to meet inflation, divorce forced many women to support children, smaller families allowed more time for careers. Women faced discrimination, preventing them from earning promotions and higher pay.

4. Equal partnership with men in both private and public life was a general goal. Civil rights legislation protected women and blacks against employment discrimination.

5. The ERA banned discrimination on the basis of sex. Proponents felt it was needed to protect women's rights. Opponents believed those rights were already protected and that it would weaken family structure. The ERA fell three states short of ratification.

CHAPTER 25 SUMMARY

SECTION 1: President Ford worked to restore Americans' confidence in the presidency and in their country.

■ In an attempt to end domestic divisions, Ford pardoned ex-President Nixon and issued an amnesty plan for draft dodgers from the Vietnam era.

■ Ford tried to continue Nixon's pursuit of détente but was criticized by opponents on both left and right.

■ Economic problems grew worse during Ford's presidency, with both inflation and unemployment increasing.

SECTION 2: Women entered the labor force in large numbers during the 1970s, causing vast social and economic changes.

■ Economic need, changes in birth rates and life expectancy, and changes in the job market all drew women into the labor force.

■ The demand for equal treatment in all areas of life led to the expansion of the women's movement.

■ The women's movement scored a major victory in 1973 with the Supreme Court's controversial decision to legalize abortion.

■ The Equal Rights Amendment, also controversial, failed to get the necessary votes for ratification.

SECTION 3: A host of economic problems damaged Jimmy Carter's presidency.

■ Carter, elected as an "outsider" to Washington, had no clear plan for governing and lacked experience in working with Congress.

■ Carter was unable to deal with double-digit inflation, high unemployment, and economic stagnation.

■ Attempting to cut energy consumption, Carter called on the country to conserve fuel. In 1979 oil prices jumped again, harming the economy and Carter's popularity.

SECTION 4: Carter's foreign policy successes were overshadowed by a hostage crisis in Iran.

■ Carter was committed to making human rights the basis of American foreign policy.

■ Carter arranged for Panama eventually to take control of the Panama Canal. He also helped to negotiate a historic peace agreement between Israel and Egypt.

■ Carter continued détente with the Soviet Union, but in 1979 he changed his policies in response to the Soviet invasion of Afghanistan.

■ Carter's inability to resolve the Iran hostage crisis doomed his 1980 re-election campaign.

KEY TERMS ●

Use the following terms to complete the sentences below.

deterrence
Fair Campaign Practices Act
Mayaguez
meltdown
Roe v. Wade

1. The ____ was a post-Watergate reform of the election process.
2. The accident at Three Mile Island raised fears of a nuclear ____ .
3. The ____ decision sparked a debate about abortion that has continued to this day.
4. The capture of the ____ by Cambodians led to an American rescue mission in 1975.
5. Carter's critics warned that his defense policies would weaken ____ .

PEOPLE TO IDENTIFY ●

Match each of the following people with the correct description.

Menachem Begin
Betty Friedan
Ayatollah Khomeini
Nelson A. Rockefeller
Phyllis Schlafly

1. Islamic fundamentalist who came to power in Iran in 1979.
2. Ford's Vice President.
3. Author of *The Feminine Mystique*.
4. Leader of anti-ERA forces.
5. Israeli leader who made peace with Egypt in 1979.

6. Carter appeared honest and uncorrupted. His lack of experience limited his ability to work with Congress.

7. Stagflation and an energy crisis. Carter reduced federal spending, established voluntary wage and price guidelines, created the Department of Energy, and promoted tax incentives for fuel conservation.

616

Match each of the letters on the map with the places that are listed below.

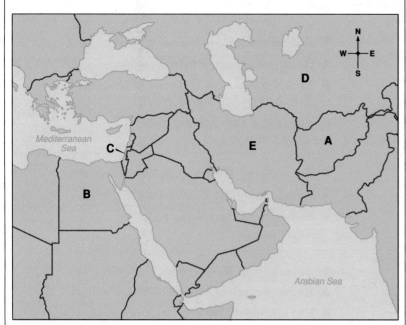

1. Afghanistan
2. Egypt
3. Iran
4. Israel
5. Soviet Union

REVIEWING THE FACTS ▲

1. How did Ford attempt to put Watergate in the past? What was the public reaction?
2. What steps did Ford take to improve the economy? How effective were they?
3. Why did many women enter the labor force in the 1970s? What problems did they face?
4. What were some of the goals of the women's movement? How was the movement connected to the civil rights movement?
5. What was the Equal Rights Amendment? What arguments were made for and against it? What happened to it?

6. What qualities made Jimmy Carter attractive to the American people in 1976? How did these qualities serve him in the presidency?
7. What problems did Carter face domestically? What steps did he take to address them?
8. Why was the Panama Canal Treaty controversial? Why did Carter support it?
9. How did Carter approach relations with the Soviet Union? What changes did he make in his policies?
10. What was the background of the Iran hostage crisis? What steps did Carter take to resolve the crisis?

CRITICAL THINKING SKILLS ▲

1. STATING BOTH SIDES OF AN ISSUE State both sides of the controversy regarding the pardon of Richard Nixon.

2. MAKING JUDGMENTS How did Presidents Ford and Carter try to encourage energy conservation? If you had been President, what energy conservation policy would you have recommended?

3. RECOGNIZING A FRAME OF REFERENCE How did American and Iranian views of the Shah reveal the different perspectives of the two nations?

WRITING ABOUT TOPICS IN AMERICAN HISTORY ■

1. CONNECTING WITH LITERATURE A selection from *On Wings of Eagles* by Ken Follett appears on pages 817–819. Read it and answer the questions. Then answer the following question: What evidence of Western influence in Iran can be seen in this selection?

2. APPLYING THEMES: EXPANDING DEMOCRACY Write a brief history of the Equal Rights Amendment. Note the constitutional process by which an amendment becomes law, the leaders of the debate, and attempts by supporters to restart the adoption process.

3. SCIENCE AND TECHNOLOGY Find out more about the accident at Three Mile Island and its effect on attitudes toward nuclear power in the United States. Write a report to deliver to the class.

10. The exiled Shah went to New York for cancer treatment. Iranians overran the U.S. embassy, taking Americans hostage. Carter attempted diplomatic negotiations and ordered a military rescue operation, which failed.

Critical Thinking Skills
1. Support—it was the best way to end the Watergate affair. Against—it unfairly protected Nixon and left open the question of his guilt.
2. Both promoted voluntary conservation efforts. Carter also established tax incentives for conservation, deregulated natural gas, and created the Department of Energy. Students may support Carter's forcefulness, or feel that Ford was correct in leaving it to individual citizens.
3. The Shah's pro-Western modernization made him seem a sensible leader to Americans. Iranians saw him as harsh and many were unhappy with his pro-Western attitude.

Writing About Topics in American History
1. Students might mention technology such as cars and telephones as well as the American T-shirt worn by a child and the Hyatt Hotel.
2. Students' research should be as up to date as possible. Newspapers, magazines, and books would be good sources.
3. Students may review the debate over opening nuclear plants and attempts at closing operating ones.

8. Some Americans believed the treaty gave away strategic territory, while others felt it protected U.S. interests. Carter supported it, hoping to improve relations with smaller nations.

9. Carter strove for better relations and an arms treaty. After the Soviets invaded Afghanistan, he shelved the treaty, imposed an embargo on grain, and boycotted the Moscow Olympics.

Chapter Review exercises are keyed for student abilities:
● = Basic
▲ = Average
■ = Average/Advanced

Chapter 26 ■ Reagan and the 1980s

	SECTION OBJECTIVES	SECTION RESOURCES
Section 1 **The Reagan Revolution**	■ identify the shift in American politics illustrated by the 1980 elections ■ describe Ronald Reagan's political philosophy and how it affected the economic policies of his first administration	● **Reteaching Resources:** Worksheet 100 ▲ **Reinforcement Workbook:** Worksheet 100 ■ **Enrichment and Extension Resources:** Primary Source Worksheet 51 ▲ **Teaching Transparencies:** Transparency 100
Section 2 **Foreign Affairs, 1981–1984**	■ describe American foreign policy during Reagan's first term of office	● **Reteaching Resources:** Worksheet 101 ▲ **Reinforcement Workbook:** Worksheet 101 ▲ **Teaching Transparencies:** Transparency 101
Section 3 **Life in the 1980s**	■ identify the domestic trends and problems of the 1980s	● **Reteaching Resources:** Worksheet 102 ▲ **Reinforcement Workbook:** Worksheet 102 ■ **Enrichment and Extension Resources:** Historian Worksheet 11 ▲ **Teaching Transparencies:** Transparency 102
Section 4 **Reagan's Second Term**	■ describe the high and low points of Reagan's second term	● **Reteaching Resources:** Worksheet 103 ▲ **Reinforcement Workbook:** Worksheet 103 ■ **Enrichment and Extension Resources:** Primary Source Worksheet 52 ▲ **Teaching Transparencies:** Transparency 103

The list below shows Essential Elements relevant to this chapter. (The complete list of Essential Elements appears in the introductory pages of this Teacher's Edition.)

Section 1: 3E, 3F, 3G, 4G, 5B, 5C, 6C, 8B, 8D, 8F, 8H, 9A, 9B
Section 2: 1A, 1B, 4C, 5B, 6A, 7F, 7H
Section 3: 2B, 2C, 3E, 3F, 4F, 7E, 7F, 7H, 8A, 8D, 8H, 9G
Section 4: 1A, 1B, 3E, 4C, 5B, 7F, 7H, 8E, 9A, 9B, 9D, 9E

Section Resources are keyed for student abilities:
● = Basic
▲ = Average
■ = Average/Advanced

CHAPTER RESOURCES

Geography Resources: Worksheets 51, 52
Tests: Chapter 26 Test

Chapter Project: Constitutional Government

Have students analyze several of Reagan's speeches given between 1980 and 1989. Students may focus on the following questions: What images does Reagan use in his speeches? How do his speeches reflect the times? What do his speeches reveal about Reagan's personality?

Homework Options

Each section contains activities labeled "Addressing Individual Needs." You may wish to choose from among these activities when assigning homework.

> **Provisions for Limited English Proficiency (LEP)**
> Several suggested activities may be particularly helpful for teachers of students with limited English proficiency. These activities have been marked throughout the Teacher's Annotated Edition with the symbol **LEP** .

BIBLIOGRAPHY AND AUDIOVISUAL AIDS

Teacher Bibliography

Correspondents of the New York Times. *Reagan, the Man, the President*. Pergamon, 1981.

McNeil, Frank. *Reality or Illusion: War and Peace in Central America*. Scribners, 1988.

Stockman, David. *The Triumph of Politics: The Inside Story of the Reagan Revolution*. Avon, 1987.

Student Bibliography

Fox, Mary V. *Mister President: The Story of Ronald Reagan*. Enslow, 1986.

Kronenwetter, Michael. *Politics and the Press*. Watts, 1988.

Peirce, Neal R., and Jerry Hagstrom. *The Book of America: Inside 50 States Today*. Norton, 1983.

Woods, Harold. *Equal Justice: A Biography of Sandra Day O'Connor*. Dillon, 1985. Traces the life of the first woman on the Supreme Court.

Literature

Kingston, Maxine Hong. *The Woman Warrior*. Knopf, 1976. The memoir of a Chinese American who grows up caught between two cultures: that of a Chinese village of the recent past and present-day California.

Morrison, Toni. *Beloved*. Knopf, 1987. An escaped slave is haunted by the spirit of the two-year-old daughter she had killed when threatened with recapture.

Stone, Robert. *The Flag for Sunrise*. Ballantine, 1982. A novel about the staff of a Roman Catholic mission who refuse to leave a Central American country.

Welty, Eudora. *One Writer's Beginnings*. G. K. Hall, 1985.

Wolfe, Tom. *Bonfire of the Vanities*. Farrar, Straus and Giroux, 1987. A bitter, satiric novel about a successful Wall Street bond trader.

Films and Videotapes*

America in Search of Itself. 43 min. FI. Social and political reasons for Ronald Reagan's election.

America Works When America Works. 78 min. FI. The effects of industrial change in the 1980's on the American work force and economy.

The Disillusionment of David Stockman. 58 min. PBS. Interview with former Reagan Budget Director reveals how an economic policy doubled the national debt.

In Our Defense. 26 min. FI. Raises questions on the search for security through stockpiling nuclear weapons.

Moyers: The Secret Government: Constitution in Crisis. 90 min. PAT. Historical review of the Iran-Contra controversy.

Computer Software*

On the Campaign Trail: Issues and Images in a Presidential Election (1 disk, Apple II, IBM-PC, or Tandy 1000). TS. This simulation introduces contemporary domestic and foreign policy issues in the context of a presidential election.

*For a complete guide to audiovisual sources, see the introduction to this book (page Txx).

Chapter 26

Reagan and the 1980s
(pp. 618–641)

This chapter examines the changes in American politics and society that occurred in the 1980s. It discusses the influence of President Ronald Reagan's philosophy on American domestic and foreign policies during the decade.

 Themes in American History

- Global interactions
- Economic development
- American culture

Chapter Objectives

After students complete this chapter, they will be able to:

1. Identify the shift in American politics illustrated by the 1980 elections.

2. Describe Ronald Reagan's political philosophy and how it affected the economic policies of his first administration.

3. Describe American foreign policy during Reagan's first term of office.

4. Identify the domestic trends and problems of the 1980s.

5. Describe the high and low points of Reagan's second term.

Chapter Opener Art
Martha Washington Quilters' Guild, *J. C. Penney Celebrates American Style,* 1986.

A *resurgence of patriotism marked the United States during the 1980s. Images on this quilt, designed to commemorate the one-hundredth anniversary of the completion of the Statue of Liberty, reflect the nation's upbeat mood.*

CHAPTER SUPPORT MATERIAL

Reinforcement Workbook: Worksheets 100–103
Reteaching Resources: Worksheets 100–103
Enrichment and Extension Resources: Primary Source Worksheets 51, 52; Historian Worksheet 11
Geography Resources: Worksheets 51, 52
Teaching Transparencies: Transparencies 100–103
Tests: Chapter 26 Test

26 Reagan and the 1980s
(1980–1989)

3E, 3F, 3G, 4G, 5B, 5C, 6C, 8B, 8D, 8F, 8H, 9A, 9B

1 The Reagan Revolution

Section Focus

Key Terms New Right ■ Moral Majority ■ supply-side economics ■ Reaganomics

Main Idea Ronald Reagan led the most conservative administration since the 1920s. He tried to reduce the role of the federal government in American life by cutting taxes and social welfare programs.

Objectives As you read, look for answers to these questions:
1. What factors led to Reagan's election victory in 1980?
2. What was Reagan's philosophy of government?
3. How did the economy perform during the early 1980s?

January 28, 1981. Headline news—"THE HOSTAGES ARE HOME." After 444 days, the 52 American hostages were released from Iran. Their homecoming sparked a wave of public celebration, with flags flying everywhere as symbols of renewed national pride. Whatever their political beliefs, Americans welcomed the chance to celebrate some good news.

The timing was perfect, for the hostages left Iran on the same day that the new President was inaugurated. Thus the new presidency began on an upbeat note. This was just what Americans needed after more than a year of humiliation over the hostage crisis and nearly a decade of inflation. In his Inaugural Address, Ronald Reagan told Americans what they wanted to hear. "Let us begin an era of national renewal," he said. "Let us renew our faith and hope. We have every right to dream heroic dreams."

> "**W**e have every right to dream heroic dreams."
>
> —*Ronald Reagan, 1981*

Flag-waving Americans turned out in force to celebrate the return of the hostages from Iran in January 1981. The hostages' release gave the nation a boost of confidence. POLITICS How did the timing of the hostages' release help Ronald Reagan politically? 9A

Section Objectives
■ identify the shift in American politics illustrated by the 1980 elections
■ describe Ronald Reagan's political philosophy and how it affected the economic policies of his first administration

Introducing the Section

Connecting with Past Learnings
Ask students to recall American society and politics in the 1920s. *How active a role did the federal government play in the lives of most Americans?* (The government felt little or no responsibility to solve social problems.) *How did that role change during Roosevelt's New Deal and Johnson's Great Society?* (The federal government became involved in caring for the elderly, poor, homeless, unemployed, and in protecting the rights of minorities.)

Key Terms
Write the key terms on the board. Have students find the terms in their texts and suggest definitions for them. Have the class agree upon the most precise definition for each. Point out the identical ending of the last two terms and discuss the reason for this similarity. **LEP**

SUPPORTING THE SECTION

Reinforcement Workbook: Worksheet 100
Reteaching Resources: Worksheet 100
Enrichment and Extension Resources: Primary Source Worksheet 51
Teaching Transparencies: Transparency 100

Photo Caption Answer
Their release came on the day of his inauguration and started his presidency on an upbeat note.

RONALD REAGAN 5B

Reagan radiated friendliness, warmth, and traditional values. His ability to inspire Americans' faith in themselves and their nation made him the most appealing candidate in 1980. His life seemed to be a dream come true—a small-town boy from a family of modest means grows up to be President.

Born in Illinois, Reagan graduated from Eureka College. Then he went to Iowa to become a radio sports announcer. Discovered by a talent scout, he moved to Hollywood in 1937 to start a successful career in movies. Reagan began a second career, in politics, when he was elected governor of California in 1966; he won re-election in 1970. He tried for the Republican nomination for President in 1968 and 1976. By 1980 his conservative views were more in line with the times, and he captured the nomination.

Reagan had been politically active throughout his show business career. In the 1930s and 1940s, he supported liberal Democrats. However, over time, Reagan moved sharply to the right. In 1954, General Electric hired him to give morale-boosting speeches to its workers. At hundreds of dinners, Reagan praised capitalism and denounced New Deal liberalism. He said the federal government could not fix social problems and should stop trying. Business should be unregulated, taxes should be lowered, and the government should concentrate on matters of national defense. These were the same ideas that Reagan took on the campaign trail in 1980.

THE ELECTION OF 1980 5B

For his running mate, Reagan chose George Bush, a former congressman, ambassador, and director of the CIA. In their platform they promised to cut taxes, balance the budget, and increase defense spending.

Carter's failure to control inflation and his handling of foreign relations made him an easy target for the Republicans. Carter also faced a Democratic challenge from Edward Kennedy. Kennedy was a liberal senator from Massachusetts and the younger brother of John and Robert Kennedy. Carter took the Democratic nomination. However, the struggle left the Democrats divided and weakened.

Without solid Democratic support and unable to turn around the economy or the hostage crisis, Carter faced an uphill battle. He tried to portray Reagan as a dangerous right-winger who might lead the United States into war. Carter also argued that Reagan's economic proposals would hurt the poor and increase racial tension. But Reagan's sunny personality made it difficult to ac-

Ronald Reagan, a former actor and governor of California, ran for President in 1980. Reagan's personal charm helped him win over crowds such as the one at left. Together with Vice President Bush (below), Reagan scored a decisive election victory. **POLITICS** What problems did Reagan's opponent, Jimmy Carter, face in 1980? 3F

cuse him of being mean-spirited. Instead, Carter lost support for attacking Reagan.

Reagan's backing surged when he asked voters some simple questions: "Are you better off now than you were four years ago? Is it easier for you to go and buy things? . . . Do you feel as safe?" On Election Day, 43 million Americans answered no by voting for Reagan. Carter lost by 8 million votes and won only 5 states.

> "**A**re you better off now than you were four years ago?"
> —*Ronald Reagan, 1980 presidential campaign*

CONSERVATIVES SPEAK UP 4G, 5C, 6C

Ronald Reagan was the most conservative President since the 1920s. During the 1980 campaign, conservative Americans emerged as more articulate and better-organized than at any time in recent history. Where did they get their new strength?

Some of the new energy came from former Democrats who believed their party no longer spoke for their interests. Many working-class voters believed the Democrats had stopped fighting for decent jobs and better pay. In their view, the Democrats spent too much time catering to special interests (like minority groups). They also found the Democrats' stands on social issues—abortion, for example—too liberal.

Some of these unhappy Democrats simply stopped voting. Others joined conservative groups and began to vote Republican. These people became known as the New Right. The New Right focused its energy on controversial social issues, opposing abortion, the ERA, and court-ordered school busing. It also called for a return to school prayer, which had been outlawed by the Supreme Court in 1962. To members of the New Right, liberal positions on all these issues represented an assault on traditional values.

Religion, especially evangelical Christianity, played a key part in the growing strength of conservatism. The 1970s brought a huge religious revival, especially among fundamentalist sects. In 1963 about one-fourth of Americans described themselves as "born-again" Christians. By 1980 that percentage had almost doubled. Each week about 100 million Americans watched television evangelists or listened to them on radio.

Two of the most influential "televangelists" were Jerry Falwell and Pat Robertson. Falwell formed an organization called the Moral Majority to support conservative causes. Falwell and other televangelists backed specific candidates, almost always Republican conservatives. They urged their followers to oppose liberal policies.

Conservatives also opened research centers like the Heritage Foundation and launched massive direct-mail fund-raising projects. These efforts provided the money and talent to support strong political campaigns. In 1980 these campaigns defeated seven of the Senate's most liberal members. For the first time since 1952, Republicans gained control of the Senate. And while Democrats still held a majority in the House, liberalism was clearly on the defensive.

Jerry Falwell, a Baptist minister from Virginia, gathered a large audience for his televised sermons. He encouraged his followers to support conservative causes such as school prayer, banning of abortion, and military spending. RELIGION What role, if any, do you think religious leaders should take in politics? 4G

Patterns in History
How was the New Right different from traditional political conservatives? (Traditional conservatives were usually most interested in preventing government involvement in the economy, while the New Right wanted government involvement in social issues which threatened traditional values.) Ask students to list social issues important to the New Right. (Abortion, ERA, school busing, school prayer.) Have them assess the status of these issues today. *Has the New Right been successful in achieving its goals?*

Religion
What role did religion play in the 1980 elections? (Many televangelists opposed liberal policies and supported conservative Republicans.) *Why did the religious revival of the 1970s strengthen conservatism?* (Religious fundamentalists have traditional values which are often at odds with more liberal stands on social issues.) *In what other ways might the religious revival have affected American society in the 1980s?*

Photo Caption Answer
Some students may argue that the principle of the separation of church and state greatly restricts the involvement of church leaders in politics. Others may believe that religious leaders bring much-needed moral authority to politics.

Background The terms "right" and "right wing" as descriptions of conservatives derive from the French National Assembly of 1789. Nobles, the most conservative members of the Assembly, sat on the king's right.

5B

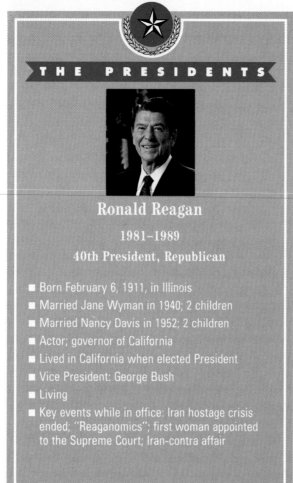

THE PRESIDENTS

Ronald Reagan

1981–1989
40th President, Republican

- Born February 6, 1911, in Illinois
- Married Jane Wyman in 1940; 2 children
- Married Nancy Davis in 1952; 2 children
- Actor; governor of California
- Lived in California when elected President
- Vice President: George Bush
- Living
- Key events while in office: Iran hostage crisis ended; "Reaganomics"; first woman appointed to the Supreme Court; Iran-contra affair

3F, 8B, 8F, 8H

"GOVERNMENT IS THE PROBLEM"

"Government is not the solution to our problem. Government is the problem." This slogan was the heart of Reagan's political creed. He believed that "big government" was the main cause of almost every national problem, including poverty, inflation, and low productivity.

> "**G**overnment is not the solution to our problem. Government is the problem."
> —*Ronald Reagan*

In Reagan's view, raising productivity (the rate of output of production) was the key to building a healthy economy. To spur production of goods and services, Reagan wanted to limit regulations on business and cut both taxes and government spending. This would increase the amount of money that corporations and individuals could save. These savings, in turn, would become available for investment in new and more efficient factories and equipment. Such equipment would turn out more products more cheaply than before. Unemployment would drop. Inflation would ease. These ideas make up a theory called supply-side economics.

By cutting government spending, Reagan had more in mind than simply saving money. He believed that social concerns should be handled by state and local government and by private charities. The federal government should only provide a "safety net" for the truly needy. These ideas reversed the philosophy that had shaped the New Deal and the Great Society. Since the Progressive Era, liberalism had held to the belief that the federal government has a duty to improve society and the lives of its citizens. Reagan, on the other hand, said government handouts robbed people of the incentive to work hard.

Reagan's faith in private enterprise recalled the Republican Presidents of the 1920s. Like Reagan, they believed in the ability of private business to do what was best for the country. As if to underscore this belief, on his first day in office Reagan replaced a portrait of Harry Truman with one of Calvin Coolidge. He might have adopted Coolidge's slogan too—"The business of America is business." Under Reagan, private industry, not the federal government, was to be the agent of change in improving the nation's economy. This radical shift in the role of government became known as the "Reagan Revolution."

To achieve his goals, Reagan would need strong public and congressional support. His election victory gave him a strong start. A near-tragedy gave him an unexpected boost just two months after his inauguration. Outside a Washington hotel, a would-be assassin shot Reagan through the chest. Reagan was 69 years old, the oldest man ever elected President. Yet he made a rapid recovery. Reagan's courage and good humor throughout the ordeal reassured the public and won him much sympathy.

Ronald and Nancy Reagan posed for this photograph while the President was recovering from a 1981 assassination attempt. In a line that might have come from one of his war movies, the 69-year-old Reagan joked to his wife, "Honey, I forgot to duck!" **PATTERNS IN HISTORY** What were some of the similarities between Reagan's political beliefs and those of Republican Presidents during the 1920s? **5B**

REAGAN'S ECONOMIC POLICIES 3F, 8F, 8H

New Presidents usually enjoy a short "honeymoon" of popular support. During this period they have a good chance of convincing Congress to pass their proposals. Reagan's honeymoon lasted almost a year. During this time, Congress passed a sweeping package of new economic policies. These economic changes, dubbed Reaganomics, were made up of three parts: budget cuts, tax cuts, and increased defense spending. They marked the most extreme shift in economic policy since the New Deal.

A major reason for cutting the federal budget was to lower the budget deficit. For years, the government had been spending more than it had collected in taxes. These annual budget deficits fueled inflation and worsened the national debt. By the time Reagan took office the national debt was $1 trillion ($1,000 billion). Reagan had pledged to balance the budget by 1984. Government, he said, simply had to spend less money.

As he had promised, most of Reagan's budget cuts came from social welfare programs. Following the advice of Budget Director David Stockman, Congress in 1981 agreed to cut $500 billion in social programs over a five-year period. As a result, the number of people receiving food stamps fell from about 17 million people to 8 million during Reagan's first term. At least a million people were dropped from welfare and Medicaid. Several job training programs were canceled.

Congress also passed a $750 billion tax cut, lowering rates for individuals and corporations. The richest Americans had once paid 70 percent of their income in taxes. Their tax rate dropped first to 50 percent. Then it fell to 33 percent. In the short run, the tax cut only worsened the budget deficit, since the government was taking in less money than before. But according to supply-side economics, the tax cut would eventually pay for

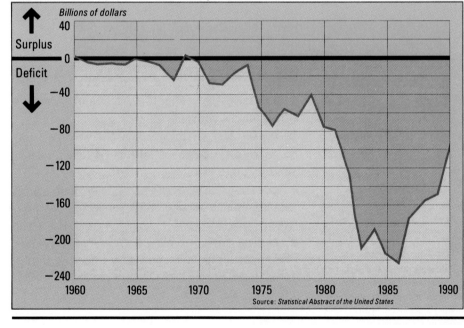

FEDERAL SURPLUS OR DEFICIT, 1960–1990

Billions of dollars

Surplus

Deficit

Source: *Statistical Abstract of the United States*

GRAPH SKILLS 9A, 9B

Despite his promise to balance the federal budget, deficits skyrocketed during the Reagan administration. Explain what is meant by a deficit. What was the deficit level in 1980? **CRITICAL THINKING** How did Reagan's economic policies contribute to the budget deficit?

Photo Caption Answer
He advocated private enterprise rather than the federal government as an agent of economic improvement.

Graph Skills Answers
A deficit occurs when more money is spent than is brought in. About $78 billion. He cut taxes for businesses and the wealthiest Americans while introducing the largest peacetime military buildup in American history.

C Cooperative Learning

Divide the class into small groups. Have each group create a poster on one of the major points of the Reagan Revolution. Groups should present their information from a particular point of view. Have groups display and explain their posters to the rest of the class. **LEP**

Addressing Individual Needs

Guided/ Independent Practice
Instruct students to complete **Reinforcement Workbook** Worksheet 100. Students will analyze a political cartoon on supply-side economics.

Reteaching/Correctives
With the class, create a "web" on the board of the kind used for brainstorming activities. In the central circle write "Reagan Revolution." Have students review the section and add topics that stem out from this center. Students may include items branching out from these topics too.

Have students complete **Reteaching Resources** Worksheet 100, which helps students explain the main ideas of the section.

Enrichment/Extension
Have students complete **Enrichment and Extension Resources** Primary Source Worksheet 51, in which they analyze planks of the Republican Party Platform of 1980.

Assessment

You may wish to use the Section 1 Review, page 624, to see how well your students understand the main points of this lesson.

Section Review Answers

1. *New Right*—Resurgence of conservative movement in the 1980s. *Moral Majority*—

623

itself. The economic growth that the tax cut was supposed to generate would, in theory, bring the government more tax revenue than ever before.

The third element in Reagan's 1981 package concerned military spending. True to his campaign pledge, Reagan introduced the largest peacetime military buildup in American history. Congress approved the buildup. Over a five-year period, the nation spent $1.5 trillion on defense.

RECESSION AND RECOVERY 3E, 3F, 3G

While Reagan was charting a new course for the American economy, the economy itself was sinking into recession. Lasting from July 1981 until November 1982, it was the longest and most severe recession since the Great Depression. Unemployment topped 10 percent. Especially hard hit were the old "smokestack" industries like steel and textiles. These industries, hurt by foreign competition, laid off thousands of workers. And due to federal budget cuts, fewer than half of those who lost jobs received unemployment pay-

This picture shows housing built in California during the period of economic recovery that followed the recession of 1981–1982.
ECONOMICS Why might economists consider construction of new housing a useful indicator of the country's economic health? 8D

ments. By the middle of 1982 almost one-fifth of blue-collar workers were jobless. Each week 450 businesses went bankrupt, the highest rate since the 1930s.

The recession was caused in part by high interest rates. The Federal Reserve Board had raised interest rates in 1981 to cool down inflation. This policy, combined with a drop in the price of oil and other imports, eventually brought inflation down. Then the Federal Reserve began lowering interest rates, and investments increased.

In 1983 the economy began to recover. Inflation and unemployment dropped below 10 percent, and consumer spending jumped. The housing and automobile industries, once stagnant, started to thrive. According to historian William Chafe, by 1984 America had "the most vibrant economy since the early 1960s." People started to gain faith in Reaganomics.

The economic recovery would be crucial in gaining Reagan a second term as President. But beneath the surface of renewed prosperity lay problems which would continue to plague the economy. Tax cuts had helped the rich, while social welfare cuts had hurt the poor. Despite large reductions in parts of the budget, federal spending still outstripped federal revenue. Budget deficits were growing. Even though Reagan asked for and got new taxes in 1982, they were not enough to balance the budget. By the end of his first term, the national debt had almost doubled.

SECTION REVIEW

1. KEY TERMS New Right, Moral Majority, supply-side economics, Reaganomics

2. PEOPLE Jerry Falwell, David Stockman

3. COMPREHENSION Why did Ronald Reagan defeat Jimmy Carter in 1980?

4. COMPREHENSION Why was the economic picture brighter in 1983 than a year earlier? What problems remained?

5. CRITICAL THINKING Why, in your opinion, might it be more difficult to pursue a policy of limited government in the 1980s than was the case in the 1920s?

Photo Caption Answers
The demand for new housing
is related to how much money
people have to spend. Also,
the construction industry uses
raw materials from a range of
other industries and provides
employment for a large
number of workers.

2 Foreign Affairs, 1981–1984

★ ## Section Focus

★ **Key Terms** contra ■ Strategic Defense Initiative

★ **Main Idea** During his first term, Reagan sought to assert American power in many places throughout the world. The United States launched a massive military buildup, and tension with the Soviet Union increased.

★ **Objectives** As you read, look for answers to these questions:
1. What were Reagan's policies toward Central America?
2. What role did the United States play in events in Lebanon?
3. How and why did Reagan increase American defense capability?

"I believe that communism is another sad, bizarre chapter in human history whose last pages are even now being written," Ronald Reagan told a group of evangelicals in March 1983. The President wanted the United States to take the lead in writing those pages. To Reagan, communism was the "focus of evil in the modern world." The Soviet Union, he said, was an "evil empire" with "aggressive impulses." He was convinced that Soviet power was increasing in the Western Hemisphere, especially in Central America.

1B
FIGHTING COMMUNISM IN CENTRAL AMERICA

"Central America is the most important place in the world for the United States today," announced Jeane Kirkpatrick in 1981. Reagan had appointed her to be United States ambassador to the United Nations, the first woman named to that post. A staunch anti-Communist, Kirkpatrick agreed with Reagan that fighting communism was the United States' prime challenge in Central America.

The tiny nation of El Salvador was of particular concern to American leaders. Since 1979, Communist-led rebels had been battling the government in a bloody civil war. Reagan responded by persuading Congress to send aid to the anti-Communist government.

American officials believed that the Salvadoran guerrillas were getting arms from neighboring Nicaragua. In 1979 a revolution had overthrown the Nicaraguan dictator, Anastasio Somoza (page 395). Once they were in power, the rebels—who called themselves Sandinistas—began to nationalize

BIOGRAPHY
JEANE KIRKPATRICK (1926–) held several important positions in the Democratic Party, but grew critical of President Carter's foreign policy emphasis on human rights. Kirkpatrick argued that the United States should support all governments that fought communism even if they were repressive dictatorships. Under President Reagan, Kirkpatrick served as U.S. ambassador to the United Nations, becoming the first woman to do so. 4C

CIA-sponsored contras, shown here in a training camp, disrupted Nicaragua's economy and killed many civilians in their fight against the revolutionary Sandinista government. **HISTORY** Describe the history of U.S.-Nicaraguan relations. 1A, 1B

CHAPTER 26   REAGAN AND THE 1980s, 1980–1989   **625**

Biography
Ask students if they agree with Kirkpatrick's theory of supporting all governments that fight communism.

Photo Caption Answer
The U.S. supported Somoza's takeover and the assassination of Sandino.

SECTION 2

Foreign Affairs, 1981–1984
(pp. 625–628)

Section Objective
■ describe American foreign policy during Reagan's first term of office

Introducing the Section

Connecting with Past Learnings
Have the class recall United States foreign policy toward Latin America since World War II. *How did the U.S. work against the spread of communism in Latin America?* (Supported leaders who were against communism; worked against leaders who leaned toward communism.)

Key Terms
Write the key terms on the board. Ask students to define each one of the three words used in the last term. Refer them to the dictionary if necessary. Then ask volunteers to suggest meanings for each term. **LEP**

Focus
Using a classroom map, or the map of the world at the back of the book, have students note countries affected by Reagan's foreign policy. (El Salvador—U.S. supported it in its fight with Communist rebels. Nicaragua—supported contras in their fight against Nicaragua's pro-Communist government. Lebanon—Marines sent in to maintain peace, but left after 241 were killed. Grenada—U.S. troops sent in to overthrow Marxist government. Soviet Union,

625

Nicaragua's industries. They also welcomed aid from the Soviet Union and Cuba.

Reagan warned that Nicaragua was becoming a springboard for other leftist revolutions in Central America. In 1981 he approved a secret CIA plan to arm, train, and support a group of anti-Sandinista Nicaraguans known as contras. (*Contra* is short for "counter-revolutionary.") The contras did not have enough popular support to base themselves inside Nicaragua. Instead, they camped across the border in Honduras and Costa Rica. From there they launched attacks into Nicaragua. By 1984 the contras had recruited an army of some 15,000 soldiers.

OPPOSITION TO AMERICAN POLICY 1A, 6A
The administration had hoped the CIA's role in helping the contras would remain secret, but in 1982 *Newsweek* magazine ran a cover story called "America's Secret War—Target Nicaragua." When Congress began to ask questions, Reagan insisted that the United States was not trying to overthrow the Sandinistas. He claimed that the contras were merely trying to stop the Sandinistas from sending arms and supplies to rebels in El Salvador.

Congress agreed to fund the contras—with one key condition. The money was to be used simply to stop the flow of arms to Salvadoran rebels, not to wage war against the government of Nicaragua. This condition was called the Boland Amendment.

In 1984 the CIA helped plant mines in Nicaraguan harbors to disrupt the Nicaraguan economy. When the mining was reported, it met with international outrage. The World Court, the judicial branch of the United Nations, condemned the action. It called on Reagan to "cease and desist" all military operations against Nicaragua. Congress responded by cutting aid to the contras.

Nor could Reagan count on much public support. A disturbing number of Americans did not even know which side their government was backing in El Salvador and Nicaragua. Many of those who did know had serious doubts about American policy. The American-backed government in El Salvador had links to "death squads" accused of killing more than 40,000 civilians. Among those

murdered were the archbishop of San Salvador and three American nuns. The Nicaraguan contras likewise had a poor human rights record. Many Americans were haunted by bitter memories of Vietnam. They worried that once again the United States was backing groups that did not represent the will of the people.

THE MIDDLE EAST 1A
Reagan's willingness to use American power abroad was also evident in the Middle East. In June 1982, Israel invaded Lebanon. Its goal was to drive out forces of the Palestine Liberation Organization (PLO). The PLO, formed in 1964, aimed to create an independent Palestinian state in Israel. From bases in southern Lebanon, the PLO had made terrorist raids across the border into Israel.

Marines in Beirut, Lebanon, work to rescue comrades from the rubble of their headquarters. A bomb explosion killed 241 of the marines President Reagan had sent to Lebanon. **POLITICS** How did public opinion concerning the attack affect Reagan's policy in the Middle East? **7F**

Many world leaders condemned the Israeli invasion. As civilian casualties mounted, Reagan also became upset. He called Israeli leader Menachem Begin and said, "I want it stopped and I want it stopped now." Within five days a ceasefire was worked out between Israel and the PLO.

American involvement deepened later in 1982, when Reagan ordered several thousand marines into Lebanon. They remained in Lebanon while the United States tried to work out a lasting peace for that nation. Then, on October 23, 1983, while most of the marines were asleep, a truck came screaming through the entrance to the marine headquarters in the city of Beirut. The truck, loaded with explosives, crashed into the main building, killing 241 marines.

Americans received the news with horror. Reagan came under great pressure to explain American policy in Lebanon. Many critics said the marines had been put in a vulnerable position, like sitting ducks. Most Americans concluded that the marines could not be effective peacekeepers in Lebanon. With little public support for continued American involvement, Reagan pulled out the marines in February 1984.

THE INVASION OF GRENADA 1A

On October 25, 1983, shortly after the marines were killed in Beirut, the United States launched a surprise invasion of Grenada, a tiny Caribbean island. The invasion was not planned to distract public attention from the disaster in Lebanon. However, it certainly had that effect. That is one reason historians have called Reagan one of the luckiest Presidents in history.

A radical Marxist government had just come to power in Grenada. In a bloody coup, it had overthrown a more moderate Socialist government. About 600 American medical students were on the island at the time. To protect them, Reagan sent in 1,900 American troops. However, it soon became clear that the soldiers had a larger mission. They had orders to oust the Grenadian government and gain control of the island. Reagan claimed that Grenada was "a Soviet-Cuban colony being readied as a major military bastion to export terror."

Critics challenged the right of the United States to overthrow a foreign government. European allies also opposed the American use of force. For the most part, though, Americans approved the Grenada invasion, probably because it was a decisive victory. American forces occupied the island for about a year. Elections were held, and a pro-American government took office. Throughout the rest of his presidency, Reagan would point to Grenada as a great victory that had helped restore American pride.

A RENEWED COLD WAR 1B

The new assertiveness by the United States helped heighten Soviet-American tension during the 1980s. Actions by the Soviet Union also led to what was called the revival of the cold war. The brutal war in Afghanistan dragged on, as Soviet troops tried to prop up the Communist government of Afghanistan and anti-Communist rebels tried to overthrow it. The Soviets held the major cities, but could not force the rebels out of their positions in the countryside. Some commentators began to dub the war "Russia's Vietnam."

The Soviets also moved to bolster the Communist government in Poland. Repression and a

Polish workers such as the ones below formed a trade union organization known as Solidarity. Solidarity became the first such organization to operate independently of Poland's Communist government. **POLITICS** How did President Reagan respond to the declaration of martial law in Poland? 7H

Assessment

You may wish to use the Section 2 Review, on this page, to see how well your students understand the main points in this lesson.

Section Review Answers

1. *contra*—Member of a group of anti-Sandinista Nicaraguans. *Strategic Defense Initiative*—Armed space satellites.

2. *Jeane Kirkpatrick*—United States ambassador to the UN under Reagan. *El Salvador*—Central American nation whose government was fighting Communist guerrillas. *Nicaragua*—Central American country led by pro-Communist Sandinistas. *Lebanon*—Middle Eastern country torn by war. *Grenada*—Small Caribbean island, site of United States invasion in 1983.

3. Reagan fought communism in Central America by supporting the government of El Salvador against Communist rebels and helping anti-Communist contras fight the Sandinista government of Nicaragua.

4. The bombing of marine headquarters in Beirut, which killed 241 marines.

5. Previous Presidents believed the United States was strong enough to disarm. Because Reagan felt the U.S. was not militarily equal to the Soviet Union, he was opposed to arms control.

Closure

Use the Chapter Review Summary for Section 2 (p. 640) to synthesize the important elements in the section. Then have students read Section 3 for the next class period, noting the positive and negative changes that marked life in the 1980s in the United States.

stagnant economy there had produced one of the most important democratic uprisings of the twentieth century, the Solidarity labor movement. In 1981, under threat of direct Soviet intervention, the Polish government declared martial law. It outlawed Solidarity and forced the labor movement underground. Reagan responded with new trade restrictions against the Soviet Union and Poland.

Superpower tension was inflamed again in September 1983. A Soviet fighter plane shot down a Korean airliner that had strayed over Soviet airspace. All 269 civilian passengers were killed, including 61 Americans, among them a member of Congress. The American government accused the Soviets of cold-blooded murder. When the Soviets refused to make reparations, relations with the United States grew even worse.

THE ARMS RACE 1B

Compounding these tensions was another round of the nuclear arms race. Presidents Nixon, Ford, and Carter had all worked for arms control agreements with the Soviets. Reagan would not consider arms reductions until he was convinced that the United States was at least equal to the Soviet Union in military power. He came to office claiming that the United States had fallen behind the Soviets. As part of his military buildup, Reagan renewed work on the B-1 bomber and the neutron bomb, both of which Carter had canceled.

Reagan also proceeded with plans to deploy new nuclear missiles in Western Europe. These missiles were intended to balance the Soviet missiles based in Eastern Europe. (During the 1970s the Soviets had greatly expanded their missile force in Europe.) Most NATO leaders supported the deployment of the new missiles. But millions of European citizens protested. They did not want to become the battleground for a Soviet-American war.

American antinuclear groups also protested. They called on both superpowers to seek an agreement to halt the production of nuclear weapons. This "freeze movement" gained widespread support. In 1982 and 1983 the House of Representatives passed resolutions calling for a nuclear freeze. However, the Republican-dominated Sen-

ate rejected the freeze. So did Reagan. He argued that the Soviets could not be trusted to halt nuclear production. The plan to deploy the missiles in Western Europe went forward.

THE DEBATE OVER "STAR WARS" 5B

Critics charged that Reagan's military policies made nuclear war more likely. The President, however, had his own plan to guard against nuclear war. In 1983 he announced a huge new research program called the Strategic Defense Initiative (SDI). The purpose of SDI was to build a defense against nuclear missiles. The new weapons would be space satellites armed with lasers. The lasers would knock down enemy missiles before they reached their target. Because the plan seemed so futuristic, so space-age, it was nicknamed "Star Wars" after a popular science-fiction movie.

Reagan hoped that SDI would make nuclear weapons obsolete by preventing them from reaching their targets. If this were possible, the United States could abandon its policy of deterrence. Rather than simply threaten to retaliate after a Soviet attack, the United States would be able to ward off the Soviet attack. Defense, Reagan argued, was a more moral policy than retaliation.

One crucial question remained: Would SDI work? No one knew whether strategic defense was possible. Congress approved funds to begin SDI research, while scientists and politicians debated the merits of the program.

SECTION REVIEW

1. KEY TERMS contra, Strategic Defense Initiative

2. PEOPLE AND PLACES Jeane Kirkpatrick, El Salvador, Nicaragua, Lebanon, Grenada

3. COMPREHENSION What was the general aim of Reagan's policy in Central America? How did he implement it?

4. COMPREHENSION What event prompted the withdrawal of marines from Lebanon?

5. CRITICAL THINKING Compare President Reagan's attitude toward arms control with that of Presidents who preceded him.

3 Life in the 1980s

Section Focus

Key Term yuppie

Main Idea The 1980s was marked by a surge of patriotism and prosperity. However, beneath the surface lay serious problems of growing poverty, homelessness, and environmental damage.

Objectives As you read, look for answers to these questions:
1. What caused the new prosperity?
2. What were the exceptions to the prosperity?
3. What policies did Reagan follow on the environment?

"U.S.A.! U.S.A.! U.S.A.!" the crowds chanted wildly at the 1984 Summer Olympic Games in Los Angeles. With American athletes winning most of

Bruce Springsteen's high-energy songs about the struggles and dreams of ordinary Americans made him a hero to millions. Springsteen's lyrics spoke with sympathy of unemployed workers and veterans of the Vietnam War. **CULTURE** Which music stars do you admire? Why? **4F, 9G**

the medals, it was a time of celebration and flag-waving for American fans. Many people pointed to the Olympics as an example of a "new patriotism" abroad in the land. During the Reagan years, the new patriotism reflected a widespread yearning to feel proud of the United States.

THE NEW PATRIOTISM 7F, 7H

Advertisers always know which way the wind is blowing. They are paid to pick slogans that appeal to the current public mood. Some of the most memorable ad campaigns of the 1980s featured slogans like "The Pride is Back" and "The Heartbeat of America." The message was clear—it was good to be an American again.

This message also showed up in movies. *Top Gun* portrayed fighter pilots as skillful, daring heroes. Sylvester Stallone played a macho Vietnam veteran named "Rambo" in a popular series of films.

Some forms of the new patriotism expressed a commitment not simply to celebrate the United States but to improve it. Rock star Bruce Springsteen's famous hit "Born in the U.S.A." went beyond pride in being an American. It described the hardships faced by a Vietnam veteran in a declining factory town. Springsteen often raised money at his concerts to help unemployed workers.

However, the most important forms of patriotism were not those offered up by Madison Avenue or celebrities. Instead, they were the quiet efforts of millions of ordinary Americans to make their communities cleaner, healthier, and more generous. This sort of activism was not new in the 1980s. But it was especially important because it came at a time of widespread selfishness.

CHAPTER 26 REAGAN AND THE 1980s, 1980–1989 **629**

Photo Caption Answer
While answers may vary, students should be able to identify what aspect of the music most intrigues them.

A CULTURE OF CONSUMPTION 8A, 8D, 8H

The writer Tom Wolfe once described the 1970s as the "Me Decade." He pointed out that many Americans had turned away from the political commitments of the 1960s and focused on their own desires. Yet it is a label that more accurately describes the 1980s. As in the 1890s, 1920s, and 1950s, American culture seemed to celebrate the pursuit of wealth. Titles of popular songs reflected the mood—"Material Girl," "It's Money That Matters."

Americans went on a buying spree of consumer goods. New technology and a rebounding economy lured consumers to buy video cassette recorders (VCRs), personal computers, designer blue jeans, food processors, and many more items.

Leading the pack of active consumers was a group the media called yuppies—an acronym for "young urban professionals." Typical yuppies were doctors, lawyers, or bankers with driving ambition and high salaries. They worked hard, played hard, and measured their success by what they owned. Yuppies made up only a small portion of the population. The desire for consumption, however, seemed widespread, perhaps as a reaction to the lean years of the 1970s.

All this buying was good for business. But behind this display of prosperity there were problems. Because many of the consumer goods came from other countries, the foreign trade deficit rose to $250 billion in 1984. Once a creditor nation, the United States had become the largest debtor nation in the world.

Moreover, Americans were making more and more of their purchases with credit cards. They, like their government, were spending more than they were making. Personal savings dropped to an all-time low, which meant that there was less money available for businesses to invest. Productivity, which supply-side economics had hoped to improve, grew only slowly.

THE WIDENING INCOME GAP 3E

For many Americans the 1980s was a boom time. Taxes had come down. Inflation was low. Many businesses were thriving. But for those at the bottom of the economic ladder, the decade was one of growing frustration and hardship. In 1986 the journalist (and former Carter aide) Hodding Carter wrote, "The evidence grows steadily stronger that we are building a class-ridden society of ever-sharper contrasts between haves and have-nots."

By the mid-1980s roughly 35 million Americans lived below the official poverty line ($10,600 per year for a family of four). The percentage of poor people had increased from roughly 11.5 percent in the 1970s to 15 percent in the 1980s. Meanwhile, the richest Americans were gaining a larger share of the nation's wealth. And the middle class had to run harder just to stay in place, as living expenses rose more quickly than incomes.

Many factors accounted for this widening gap. One was the skyrocketing number of single-parent families. Such families tended to be poor because they had only one wage-earner. Between 1979 and 1987, the number of single-parent families below the poverty line rose 46 percent. Another factor was the tightening squeeze on low-income workers. A larger labor force increased competition for jobs, and cheap imports forced industries to cut wages.

THE HOMELESS 3E, 3F

Most poor people remained largely invisible to prosperous Americans. Still, it was hard to ignore the growing number of homeless people in American cities. The homeless became, according to one writer, "the cities' symbol of the decade just as surely as civil rights marches were in the sixties." No one knows how many homeless people there were. However, most experts agree that by the late 1980s the figure included between 2 and 3 million people.

Average Americans had an image of homeless people as bums—mainly older men with drinking problems who slept in doorways. But by the 1980s a growing portion were women, children, and families.

Perhaps one-third of the homeless had once been patients in mental hospitals. In the 1970s, there was a movement to re-integrate into society those people who were not severely handicapped. The goal was to give these people more fulfilling lives. However, many were unable to find housing and ended up on the street.

A young family waits for soup at a homeless shelter in Ohio. America's homeless population has been growing rapidly since the mid-1970s. Economic weaknesses and cuts in federal programs for the poor contributed to the increase in homelessness. ECONOMICS What are some other causes of homelessness? 3E

They were joined by a growing number of people forced from their homes by rising housing prices. The federal government was cutting back on its support of low-cost housing. (It was later revealed that corrupt officials at HUD had stolen or squandered millions of dollars of funds meant to provide low-cost housing.) At the same time, real estate developers were buying up rooming houses and apartment buildings and turning them into luxury condominiums. More and more hardworking families simply could not meet skyrocketing rent payments.

As the problem of homelessness gained attention, thousands of Americans pitched in to provide food and shelter. Their efforts inspired Congress to pass the 1987 Emergency Homeless Act, providing almost a billion dollars for relief programs. Homeless shelters were a crucial first step toward solving the problem. However, the challenge remained to find permanent homes and jobs for the nation's poor.

THE ENVIRONMENT 2B, 2C, 7E, 7F, 7H

Many people wanted the federal government to do more to help the homeless. Voices calling for more federal action to protect the environment were also raised. During the 1970s the federal government had taken steps to control air and water pol-

lution and hazardous wastes. There was some progress in solving these problems, but much work remained to be done.

While campaigning for President, Reagan insisted that the problem of pollution had been exaggerated. He also believed that environmental regulations placed too heavy a burden on industry, raising costs and lowering productivity. Reagan argued that the United States could become less dependent on foreign sources of energy. One way, he said, was to give industry greater freedom to mine and drill in federally owned lands.

Reagan's first Secretary of the Interior, James Watt, shared this belief. He came to Washington with the slogan "Open the Wilderness," declaring that Americans "will mine more, drill more, cut more timber to use our resources rather than simply keep them locked up." Under Watt, the federal government sold off some forest lands to lumber companies. It also leased the mineral rights of federal lands to coal and oil companies.

Reagan appointed Anne Burford to head the Environmental Protection Agency. An advocate of reducing the role of the federal government, Burford believed in letting local governments make environmental decisions. She also relaxed some pollution standards. Federal budget cuts reduced the EPA budget by one-third. As a result, the EPA lacked the money to enforce its pollution regulations or carry on new research. After a scandal forced Burford to resign, new leadership at EPA brought some new policies in the late 1980s. However, the nation had yet to confront fully the growing problems of air, water, and soil pollution.

SECTION REVIEW

1. KEY TERM yuppie

2. PEOPLE James Watt, Anne Burford

3. COMPREHENSION Why did homelessness become such a problem in the 1980s?

4. COMPREHENSION Why did Reagan favor fewer environmental regulations?

5. CRITICAL THINKING Compare the prosperity of the 1980s with that of the 1920s.

Photo Caption Answer
Lack of affordable housing, lack of care for the mentally ill, corruption at HUD, the practice of converting cheap rooming houses into luxury condominiums.

Have students complete **Reteaching Resources** Worksheet 102, which asks them to summarize information from the section.

Enrichment/Extension
Assign students to complete **Enrichment and Extension Resources** Historian Worksheet 11.

Assessment
You may wish to use the Section 3 Review, on this page, to see how well your students understand the main points in this lesson.

Section Review Answers
1. *yuppie*—Acronym for young urban professional.
2. *James Watt*—Reagan's first Secretary of Interior. *Ann Burford*—Head of the Environmental Protection Agency.
3. Many of the homeless were mentally-ill people who had been released from hospitals and had problems finding housing. Federal cuts in low-cost housing and the conversion of rooming houses and apartment buildings into luxury condominiums made housing unaffordable for poorer families.
4. He felt that too much control was bad for productivity, the problem of pollution had been exaggerated, and that the U.S. needed to exploit its own natural resources.
5. Both were marked by high consumer spending and optimism, and materialism. The gap between the rich and poor increased during both decades.

Closure
Remind students of the pre-reading objectives in the section opener. Pose one or all of these questions again. Then have students read Section 4 for the next class period, noting the important events characterizing Reagan's second term.

SECTION 4

Reagan's Second Term
(pp. 632–637)

Section Objective

■ describe the high and low points of Reagan's second term

Introducing the Section

Connecting with Past Learnings

Have students recall the election of 1980. *Upon what planks was Reagan's campaign based?* (Tax and budget cuts; increased defense; restoring American pride.) *How successful during his first term was he in implementing his program?* (Cut taxes and some social spending, but deficit rose; successful in increasing defense spending and restoring pride.)

Key Terms

List key terms on the board. Have students identify and then locate in the text the terms that deal with U.S.-Soviet relations. Ask volunteers to suggest definitions for these terms and have the class agree upon a definition for each. Write that definition beside each term. Treat the remaining key term in the same way. **LEP**

4 Reagan's Second Term

★ Section Focus

Key Terms *glasnost* ■ *perestroika* ■ INF Treaty ■ Iran-contra affair

Main Idea Ronald Reagan's second term in office included a major scandal and a great triumph. While the Iran-contra affair threatened to ruin his presidency, Reagan won acclaim for negotiating an arms control agreement with the Soviet Union.

Objectives As you read, look for answers to these questions:
1. How did Reagan win re-election in 1984?
2. What scandal erupted over relations with Iran?
3. How did relations with the Soviet Union improve?

Congresswoman Patricia Schroeder of Colorado nicknamed Reagan "the Teflon President." No criticism seemed to stick to the President. The public forgave or ignored his mistakes.

Much of Reagan's popularity came from his style of leadership. Although he did not always handle specific questions well, he was a master at expressing general themes. Even those who disagreed with him liked him. He moved people and made them feel confident. For this skill, he was often referred to as the "Great Communicator."

Walter Mondale, shown here addressing students in San Francisco, made history by nominating Representative Geraldine Ferraro (seated) for Vice President. Mondale supported liberal positions on civil rights, consumer protection, and education reform. POLITICS What were Reagan's advantages in 1984? 5B

THE DEMOCRATIC CHALLENGE 4C, 5B

The Democrats hoped to defeat the "Great Communicator" in 1984 with Walter Mondale, a former senator from Minnesota and Carter's Vice President. Mondale won the nomination over six other serious contenders. One was the Reverend Jesse Jackson. The first major African American candidate for President, Jackson sought to build a "rainbow coalition" of minorities, women, and working people. A dynamic campaigner with a gift for public speaking, Jackson brought thousands of new voters into the political process.

Knowing that Reagan would be tough to beat, Mondale made a bold decision. He surprised the nation by nominating Geraldine Ferraro as his running mate. The first woman ever nominated for the vice presidency by a major party, Ferraro was a third-term congresswoman from New York and the daughter of Italian immigrants.

REAGAN WINS RE-ELECTION 5B

The scene begins with a misty morning shot of a small American town with green lawns and white picket fences. A voice softly says, "It's morning in America. . . . Just about every place you look things are looking up. Life is better—America is back—and people have a sense of pride they never thought they'd feel again." This was President Reagan's major television ad for re-election.

> "It's morning in America."
> —*1984 Republican campaign slogan*

SUPPORTING THE SECTION

Reinforcement Workbook: Worksheet 103
Reteaching Resources: Worksheet 103
Enrichment and Extension Resources: Primary Source Worksheet 52
Teaching Transparencies: Transparency 103

Photo Caption Answer
Reagan enjoyed great popularity and the public readily forgave or ignored his mistakes. The economy also seemed to be improving under his policies.

The theme worked. When Mondale tried to challenge this rosy view, the Republicans accused him of being negative about the United States. They said that the "D" in Democrat had come to stand for "doubt, decline, and defeatism."

Perhaps no Democratic strategy could have defeated Reagan. Always popular, he had the added advantage of a recovering economy. Mondale tried to persuade the public that the recovery had been built on a mountain of debt. He also insisted that taxes would have to be raised to bring the budget deficit under control. These were messages few voters wanted to hear.

Election Day held no surprises. Reagan and Bush won in a landslide. Reagan carried 59 percent of the vote and won 525 out of 538 electoral votes, the highest number in history.

ENTERING A SECOND TERM 5B

Reagan's second term was quite unlike his first. No longer an outsider leading a revolution in government, Reagan was by this point a part of government. Between 1985 and 1989 he used the power of the presidency to help secure his place in history. A changed Supreme Court and improved superpower ties were his most notable achievements. But as President, Reagan was responsible for the failures of government as well as its successes. Nagging economic problems and a scandal over hostages tarnished the President's image.

REDIRECTING THE SUPREME COURT 4C

Reagan had more impact on the Supreme Court than most Presidents. In 1981 he fulfilled a campaign promise by appointing the first woman to the Supreme Court—Sandra Day O'Connor. A conservative Republican from Arizona, O'Connor had little trouble winning congressional approval. Reagan also named Justice William Rehnquist to replace Chief Justice Warren Burger. Reagan filled Rehnquist's seat with Antonin Scalia of New Jersey and another vacancy with Anthony Kennedy of California.

These three appointments to the Court may prove to be among President Reagan's most enduring legacies. The justices were conservative, relatively young, and likely to rule on many sensitive issues in the 1990s.

A THAW IN SUPERPOWER RELATIONS 1B

The dominant foreign policy issue during Reagan's second term was the improving Soviet-American relationship. Reagan's approach to the Soviet Union changed dramatically in those years. For almost five years in office Reagan had not met with a Soviet leader. And his anti-Soviet speeches gave little hope of improved relations. Yet by the end of 1985 he was off to Geneva, Switzerland, to talk to a new Soviet leader with startling new ideas.

Mikhail Gorbachev, who became the Soviet leader in March 1985, inherited a host of problems. Many of them revolved around the stagnant Soviet economy. But in fact the entire Soviet system suffered from inefficiency. Gorbachev called for changes in Soviet society that were the most significant since the Bolshevik Revolution of 1917. His first effort was to introduce *glasnost* (Russian for "openness") to Soviet life. Gorbachev allowed open criticism of the Soviet government and even took some steps toward freedom of the press.

In 1987 Gorbachev outlined his plans for *perestroika* (payr–es–TROY–kuh), a restructuring of Soviet society. He called for less government control of the economy, the introduction of some private enterprise, and steps toward establishing democracy. The Soviet people, he said in an extraordinary statement, need "to teach and to learn democracy."

Mikhail Gorbachev, shown here with President Reagan in Moscow's Red Square, became leader of the Soviet Union in 1985. The INF Treaty signed by the two leaders was the first treaty to require that existing nuclear forces be destroyed. ECONOMICS What factors contributed to Gorbachev's policy of *perestroika*? 1B

Gorbachev's openness to Western ideas paved the way for improved Soviet-American relations. During his second term, Reagan had four summit conferences with Gorbachev. In 1987 the two leaders made an agreement to eliminate all of their intermediate-range nuclear forces (INF). These were the European-based missiles that had aroused such controversy in the early 1980s. The INF Treaty only eliminated 5 percent of the total superpower nuclear stockpile. However, it was a crucial first step toward reductions on long-range missiles—the next hurdle in Soviet-American negotiations.

At a final summit in Moscow, where the INF Treaty was signed, an American journalist asked Reagan if he still thought the Soviet Union was an evil empire. The President smiled, saying that had been "another time, another era."

CONTINUING ECONOMIC PROBLEMS 3E

In his second term Reagan made little progress with the nation's growing debt. Each year the government had to pay $150 billion in interest alone on the national debt. By the time Reagan left office, the national debt was approaching $3 trillion. Also, the budget deficit remained huge. In 1985 Congress had passed the Gramm-Rudman-Hollings Act. It provided for automatic reductions in the deficit over a several-year period. Still, progress in lowering the deficit was slow and painful.

American farms were among the most troubled parts of the economy in the 1980s. Declining land values and falling exports left thousands of farmers in debt. By 1985 scores of farmers—especially on small family farms—had gone bankrupt and lost their land. Reagan, worried about raising the budget deficit, wanted to limit federal aid to farmers. However, with public concern mounting, Congress passed a bill in 1985 that increased payments to farmers.

Startling proof of the nation's economic troubles came on October 19, 1987, when the stock market plunged 508 points in a single day's trading. Unlike the Crash of 1929, this downturn did not lead to a depression, and the market soon recovered. But it did remind the nation that the economy rested on shaky ground.

American farmers faced a severe farm debt crisis in the early 1980s. High interest rates and lower worldwide demand for American farm products left farmers unable to pay back loans. Many were forced to sell their family farms. Control of more of the nation's farmland fell to huge corporations known collectively as agribusiness. ECONOMICS What are these farmers protesting?

7F, 7H, 8E

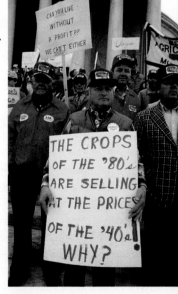

For the labor movement the 1980s were a disaster. Unionized workers made up only 17.5 percent of the labor force, the lowest level in 50 years. Part of this decline resulted from the general trend away from manufacturing and toward sales and service. But unions also faced strong opposition from business leaders. Many industries fought attempts by unions to organize workers. Reagan, too, showed an interest in limiting the power of unions. In 1981 he fired 11,345 air-traffic controllers after they illegally went out on strike.

TRADING FOR HOSTAGES 1A, 1B

In 1981, the release of hostages from Iran had brought Ronald Reagan into the White House on a high tide of popularity. That tide ebbed to its lowest point in 1986, when the public learned of secret dealings with Iran for other hostages.

During the 1980s, Islamic terrorists from the Middle East had carried on a brutal campaign. They took hostages, murdered civilians, hijacked a ship and airplanes. Many of these acts involved United States citizens. These acts were aimed to protest American policy in the Middle East, especially American support of Israel.

Reagan had long taken a hard line against terrorism. In 1985 he declared that "America will never make concessions to terrorists." Americans were shocked to learn late in 1986 that President Reagan had approved the sale of weapons to Iran. Iran needed the weapons for a war it was fighting against Iraq. In exchange for arms sales, Iran promised to win the release of seven American hostages held in Lebanon by pro-Iranian terrorists.

The arms deal was a complicated affair. Oliver North, assistant to the President's National Security Adviser, made arrangements with private arms dealers. They sold American weapons to Israel, and Israel, in turn, sold arms to Iran. In 1985 and 1986 Iran received about 1,500 anti-tank missiles. However, only three hostages were released. Meanwhile, three more hostages were captured in Lebanon.

While the deal failed to bring home all the hostages, it did produce big profits—about $16 million. This money was piling up in secret Swiss bank accounts. North got what he later called a

1981	Sandra Day O'Connor becomes the first woman on the U.S. Supreme Court.
	U.S. Census reveals that over half of the American population lives west of the Mississippi River.
1982	Dr. Barney Clark is the first human to have an artificial heart.
1983	Sally Ride becomes the first American woman in space.
1984	Democrat Geraldine Ferraro becomes the first female vice-presidential candidate to run on a major ticket.
1986	The space shuttle *Challenger* explodes, killing all seven crew members, including Christa McAuliffe, the first citizen observer to ride the shuttle (Jan. 28).
1987	The first human test of an AIDS vaccine is conducted.
1988	Boy Scouts admit first women leaders.

"neat idea." He arranged to send the money to the Nicaraguan contras to help them fight the Sandinista government. With the Boland Amendment (page 626) in effect, the White House could not legally send military aid to the contras. But Reagan had urged his staff to find some way to help the contras, whom he called "brave freedom fighters" and "the moral equivalent of our Founding Fathers."

In November 1986 the whole thing unraveled. First news of the arms deal with Iran, then the diversion of money to the contras, became public. The tangle of shady dealings became known as the Iran-contra affair.

COVER-UPS AND INVESTIGATIONS 1B

During the next two years, a series of investigations into the Iran-contra affair uncovered the worst political scandal since Watergate. In the days after the story first broke, Oliver North, his boss John Poindexter, and former National Security Adviser Robert McFarlane destroyed evidence. They also altered documents and invented

Ethics
Have the class create a diagram illustrating the trades involved in the Iran-contra affair. (American weapons were sold to Israel, which sold the weapons to Iran. Three hostages were released. Money from the arms sale went to a Swiss bank account. The money was taken out of the account and sent to the contras.) *What event in the affair was illegal?* (Sending secret aid to the contras violated the Boland Amendment.) *What event could be considered unethical?* (Reagan said he would not deal with terrorists who kidnapped Americans, but then the U.S. sold arms to free hostages.) *Do you think Reagan was right to do everything possible to release the hostages?*

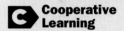

Cooperative Learning

Divide the class into small groups. Have each group evaluate Reagan's legacy as President. Then have each group write a paragraph about Reagan's presidency from the point of view of a historian living 100 years from now. Have them pay particular attention to how the Reagan years changed America. Each group member must contribute at least one idea to the paragraph. **LEP**

Famous Firsts
Ask students to discuss which of the firsts is the most significant today and which first may be considered the most significant in fifty years.

Background Air-traffic controllers are employees of the Federal Aviation Administration. They went on strike for higher wages and better working conditions on August 3, 1981, in violation of federal law. President Reagan refused to negotiate with their union while the strike was on and sought to have it decertified and its leaders jailed.

stories to conceal the truth. Their cover-up actions made it impossible for investigators to learn the whole story.

President Reagan fired North, whom he nonetheless called an "American hero," and accepted Poindexter's resignation. He also appointed a commission headed by Senator John Tower of Texas to get the facts of the case. The Tower Report, published in February 1987, found that the President had not meant to mislead the American public. Reagan, it said, had been led astray by his advisers. North and others had probably violated congressional limits on aid to the contras.

During the summer of 1987, a congressional

During the Iran-contra hearings, Lt. Col. Oliver North admitted to lying to Congress, violating the Boland Amendment, and destroying evidence. Nevertheless, many Americans saw him as a patriotic hero. **HISTORY** Why did the Reagan administration sell missiles to Iran? What did it use the profits for? **9A**

committee investigated the scandal in televised hearings. Oliver North described his actions in patriotic terms, saying he had acted for the good of the country. Many viewers across the nation agreed. But the committee was not convinced. It called the scandal "an evasion of the Constitution's most basic check on executive action—the power of Congress to grant or deny funding for government programs."

The Iran-contra affair seriously tainted Reagan's reputation. He had clearly supported policies that stretched the power of the executive branch beyond its constitutional boundaries. Reagan was never shown to have committed a crime, for it could not be proven that he knew about the diversion of funds to the contras. Yet the committee placed the ultimate responsibility for the Iran-contra affair on Reagan. It said, "If the President did not know what his National Security Advisers were doing, he should have."

After the hearings, North was tried and found guilty of taking part in the cover-up. He was sentenced to pay a stiff fine and perform community service. Yet Congress did not press Reagan on the affair, perhaps because he was nearing the end of his presidency.

THE IMPACT OF THE REAGAN YEARS 5B
Despite the Iran-contra affair, Reagan left office as one of the most popular Presidents of this century. His leadership had restored Americans' faith in their government, their nation, and their economy. He had slowed the growth of the federal government and helped reshape the Supreme Court.

Reagan left his successor many thorny problems. Among them were environmental damage, homelessness, and the growing national debt. But he also left behind a greater optimism about solving national problems than had the Presidents of the 1970s. As columnist George F. Will wrote, "Reagan's greatest gift to his country has been his soaring sense of possibilities." He knew how to move the nation with friendliness, warmth, and optimism. He became a major force in American politics because he projected the image of a dynamic, strong leader—a man with clear answers to hard questions.

However, Reagan's personality and style of lead-

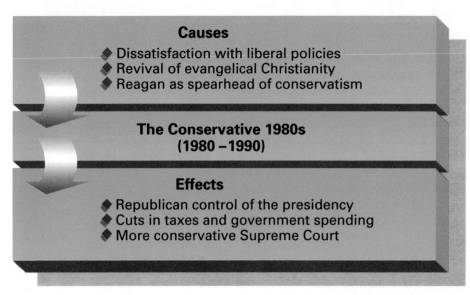

Causes

◆ Dissatisfaction with liberal policies
◆ Revival of evangelical Christianity
◆ Reagan as spearhead of conservatism

The Conservative 1980s
(1980 – 1990)

Effects

◆ Republican control of the presidency
◆ Cuts in taxes and government spending
◆ More conservative Supreme Court

CHART SKILLS 9B, 9E

Conservatives dominated the political agenda of the 1980s. Ronald Reagan's three appointees to the Supreme Court will almost certainly carry that impact into future decades. What factors contributed to conservative victories? **CRITICAL THINKING** What political changes, if any, would you predict for the 1990s? Explain your answer.

ership pose puzzles for historians. The memoirs of a number of Reagan's close associates paint a quite different picture of him. Unlike the friendly public man, they describe him as not at all warm in private. From these accounts he appears as an aloof, hands-off President who delegated his work. He seems uninterested in details and unaware of complexities.

Could a President be so in control of things in public and so out of touch in private? Was Reagan truly an effective leader? Because the events of the Reagan years are so recent, it is difficult to reconcile the conflicting stories. As more information comes to light, historians will be better able to analyze how the Reagan presidency really worked.

SECTION REVIEW

1. KEY TERMS *glasnost, perestroika,* INF Treaty, Iran-contra affair

2. PEOPLE Walter Mondale, Jesse Jackson, Geraldine Ferraro, Sandra Day O'Connor, Oliver North, Mikhail Gorbachev

3. COMPREHENSION How did Mondale's position on the economy differ from Reagan's in the 1984 campaign?

4. COMPREHENSION What shifts in foreign policy did Reagan make toward the Soviet Union?

5. CRITICAL THINKING What constitutional issues did the Iran-contra affair raise?

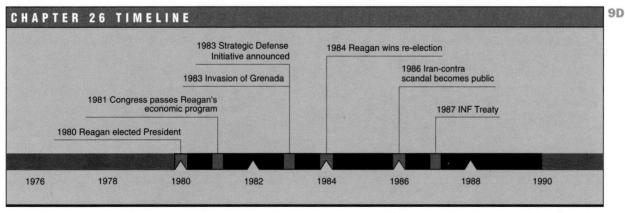

CHAPTER 26 TIMELINE 9D

1983 Strategic Defense Initiative announced

1984 Reagan wins re-election

1983 Invasion of Grenada

1986 Iran-contra scandal becomes public

1981 Congress passes Reagan's economic program

1987 INF Treaty

1980 Reagan elected President

1976   1978   1980   1982   1984   1986   1988   1990

Cause and Effect Answers
Dissatisfaction with liberal policies, revival of religious fundamentalism, and the popularity of President Reagan, who served as a symbol of the movement. Students may predict that conservative trends will continue, or suggest that people are ready for a change to more liberal politics.

Iran, then using accrued money to secretly fund contras.

2. *Walter Mondale*—Democratic presidential candidate, 1984. *Jesse Jackson*—First major black candidate for President. *Geraldine Ferraro*—First woman nominated by a major party for Vice President, Democratic candidate in 1984. *Sandra Day O'Connor*—First woman appointed to the Supreme Court. *Oliver North*—Marine lieutenant colonel involved in Iran-contra affair. *Mikhail Gorbachev*—New Soviet premier, favored more open government.

3. Reagan contended that life was better and things were looking up. Republicans accused Mondale of being negative when he tried to persuade the public that recovery had been built on a mountain of debt and when he insisted that taxes would have to be raised to get the economy back under control.

4. Reagan had four summit conferences with Gorbachev, and he signed the INF Treaty.

5. The affair flaunted the system of checks and balances between executive and legislative branches by circumventing the Boland Amendment; employees of the executive branch who had not been elected wielded enormous power and acted as if they were above the law.

Closure

Use the Chapter Review Summary for Section 4 (p. 640) to synthesize the important elements in the section. Then have students read Section 1 of Chapter 27 for the next class period, noting the important issues of the 1988 elections.

Technology and Everyday Language

Introducing the Feature

Have students consider the importance of technology in their lives. ***What machines do you use on an almost daily basis?*** (Possible answers include cars, telephones, televisions, radios, tape players, computers in one form or another.) Point out that high school students of 100 years ago would be unfamiliar with machines such as televisions, radios, and computers and would most likely have little access to cars and telephones. Have them consider how the introduction of modern technology has affected the language they use today.

You may want to have students copy down a typical conversation between friends, and have them consider if a high school student of 100 years ago would understand the conversation.

Teaching the Expressions

Radar: A number of other terms have been formed in this way, including *laser* (*l*ight *a*mplification by *s*timulated *e*mission of *r*adiation.), *sonar* (*so*und *na*vigation *r*anging), and *quasar* (*quas*i-stell*ar*). Discuss the use of acronyms in creating words, especially from long scientific and organizational names. Ask them to suggest other commonly used acronyms. (OSHA, MADD, NOW, etc.)

Technology and Everyday Language

The late twentieth century has been called the Atomic Age and the Space Age. More recently, it has been the Computer Age. All these important themes have something in common—technology. Today even small children know technical terms that would have meant nothing to their parents at the same age. Much scientific "jargon," in fact, has moved into everyday language.

The Atomic Age began in 1945. Two years later, a daring new style in swimsuits was popular on the beaches of France. It had such a stunning effect on fashion that it was named after the tiny Pacific island where atomic bombs were being tested—**bikini.**

Once the Atomic Age began, terms from nuclear physics moved into everyday speech. There can be **fallout** (though not the radioactive kind) from any important decision. Many things can cause a **chain reaction,** a series of happenings one after another. When things really get out of hand, they can reach **critical mass** or **meltdown.**

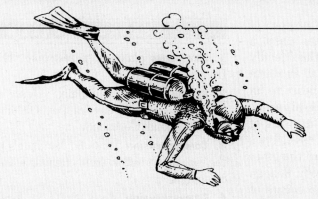

Some familiar words are actually short forms of complicated technical descriptions. **Radar,** for instance, is "*r*adio *d*etecting *a*nd *r*anging." Scuba divers are using "*s*elf-*c*ontained *u*nderwater *b*reathing *a*pparatus."

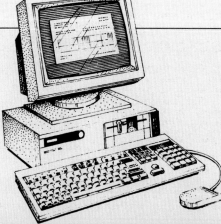

From the language of computers come a number of handy terms, particularly **glitch,** an error somewhere in the system—or any small mistake—and **user-friendly,** meaning "easy to operate or get along with."

Some old words have gained new meanings in "computerese." When your grandparents bought **hardware,** they got hammers, nails, and similar tools—not computer equipment. And to most people, **digital** referred to fingers, not watches.

In 1920 a playwright in Czechoslovakia first used the word **robot** for a machine that did the work of humans (the Czech word meant "forced labor"). From science fiction, we now know many other types of **bionic** beings, who combine human and electronic characteristics. R2D2 and Commander Data, for example, are **androids.** This word sounds new but was first used in 1727 for a "machine that looks or acts like a human."

Aeronautics and the space program have given us many new words, including a variety of ways to start something: **blast-off, lift-off, take-off,** and **launch** (which was borrowed from sailing). And almost any event can be preceded by a **countdown.**

Astronauts comes from two ancient Greek roots, as old as mythology. Together they mean "sailor among the stars."

Politicians also borrowed from scientists. A person's stand on a single crucial issue was termed a **litmus test**—the chemical test that tells, in one reaction, acids and bases.

A group of scientific prefixes found their way out of the laboratory and quickly gave us new ways of saying "big" and "little": **mega-, maxi-, mini-, micro-.** Starting with megaton, maxiskirt, macrobiotic, miniseries, and microdot, what other combinations can you think of for each of these prefixes?

Glitch: The generally accepted source for *glitch* is the Yiddish *glitschen,* meaning "to slip." According to word expert John Ciardi, *glitch* as a mistake or error was used in pre-computer urban slang. Ask students to suggest other computer terms that are older terms with new meanings. (Some examples: *crash*—to stop functioning; *boot up*—to start a computer, from the term "to pull up by one's bootstraps.")

Point out that *computer* is a word from the 1600s, and that it used to mean "someone who calculates or computes." You might note another word that shifted from meaning a person to describing a machine— *typewriter.* At the turn of this century, a *typewriter* was a person who used a *typing machine.* You might have students consider what these shifts say about the relationship between machines and their operators.

Android: R2D2 and Commander Data were important characters in the movie "Star Wars."

Astronaut: Help students break down the word into its components, *astro* ("star") and *naut* ("sailor"). Ask them to identify other words with these roots. (Astrology, astronomy, nautical, nautilus, for example.) Students familiar with mythology may recall the story of Jason and the Argonauts.

Prefixes: Technically, *mega-* means both "million" and "very large." *Micro-* means "one-millionth" and "very small."

Chapter 26 REVIEW

CHAPTER 26 SUMMARY

SECTION 1: During Ronald Reagan's first term as President, an effort was made to reverse the trend toward government growth.

■ Reagan, a staunch conservative, was part of a revival of conservative strength in the United States. He promised to reduce the size and cost of government and bolster national defense.

■ Believing that increased productivity would solve most of the nation's economic and social problems, Reagan asked for tax cuts and less government regulation of business. He attempted to cut government spending by cutting back social programs.

■ Though the nation was in a recession during 1981 and 1982, by 1983 the economy had begun a dramatic recovery.

SECTION 2: In foreign policy, Reagan took a hard line in the cold war and launched a massive military buildup.

■ Reagan aided anti-Communist forces in Central America.

■ In a reversal of policy since Vietnam, Reagan proved willing to use troops to achieve American goals in the world.

■ Believing that the United States had fallen dangerously behind the Soviet Union in military strength, Reagan asked for large increases in the military budget.

SECTION 3: The 1980s was a time of patriotism and prosperity, but underlying problems remained.

■ Enjoying their prosperity, Americans went on a buying spree during the 1980s.

■ Economic problems remained below the surface: national debt, credit buying, homelessness, and a widening gap between rich and poor.

■ Reagan reduced environmental regulations in order to promote business expansion and energy research.

SECTION 4: Reagan's second term brought both successes and failures.

■ Reagan easily won re-election in 1984 on the strength of his personal popularity and a robust economy.

■ The federal debt and a farm crisis were important economic problems during the 1980s.

■ The Iran-contra scandal plagued Reagan during his second term, but improved relations with the Soviet Union and an arms-reduction agreement were a triumph for his foreign policy.

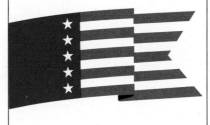

KEY TERMS ●

Define the terms in each of the following pairs.

1. contra; Iran-contra affair
2. *glasnost*; *perestroika*
3. INF treaty; Strategic Defense Initiative
4. supply-side economics; Reaganomics
5. New Right; Moral Majority

PEOPLE TO IDENTIFY ●

Use the following names to complete the sentences below.

Geraldine Ferraro
Mikhail Gorbachev
Jesse Jackson
Jeane Kirkpatrick
Walter Mondale
Sandra Day O'Connor

1. _____ became the leader of the Soviet Union in 1985 and called for many changes in Soviet society.
2. The first woman to run for Vice President on a major-party ticket was_____ .
3. The Democrat who ran against Ronald Reagan in the 1984 election—and lost by a landslide—was _____ .
4. Reagan's first ambassador to the United Nations was _____ .
5. The first woman to be appointed a Supreme Court justice was _____ .
6. The first major black candidate for President was _____ .

PLACES TO LOCATE ●

Match each of the letters on the map with the places that are listed below.

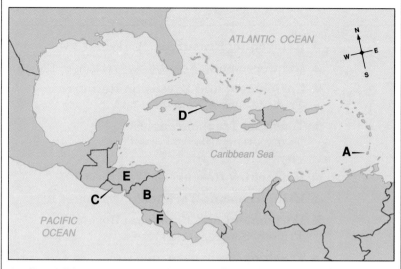

1. Costa Rica
2. Cuba
3. El Salvador
4. Grenada
5. Honduras
6. Nicaragua

REVIEWING THE FACTS ▲

1. Describe the candidates, issues, and outcome of the 1980 presidential election.
2. How was Reagan's philosophy of government different from that of other Presidents since 1945?
3. Describe Reagan's policies in El Salvador, Nicaragua, and Grenada. Why were they controversial?
4. Explain the events leading up to the stationing of American troops in Lebanon in 1982.
5. What were some of the issues that heightened cold war tensions during the early 1980s?

6. What were some of the factors that contributed to rising homelessness during the 1980s? What efforts were made to deal with the problem?
7. Describe the environmental policy of the Reagan administration.
8. What strengths did Reagan have in the 1984 election campaign?
9. What was the Iran-contra affair, and why did it cause a scandal?
10. How did relations between the United States and the Soviet Union change during Reagan's second term? Why did they change?

CRITICAL THINKING SKILLS ▲

1. **FORMING A HYPOTHESIS** How do high popularity ratings help a President to get legislation passed in Congress?

2. **MAKING A JUDGMENT** In your opinion, was President Reagan right to use force in Grenada? Why or why not?

3. **RECOGNIZING A FRAME OF REFERENCE** In this chapter you have read about a "new patriotism" during the Reagan era. What had happened to the "old patriotism"?

4. **MAKING A GENERALIZATION** Why might a widening gap between the richest and poorest citizens of a country be a cause for concern about that country's future?

WRITING ABOUT TOPICS IN AMERICAN HISTORY ■

1. **CONNECTING WITH LITERATURE** A selection from *Love Medicine* by Louise Erdrich appears on pages 819–822. Read it and answer the questions. Then answer the following question: How do Albertine and her family combine white and Indian culture in the way they live?

2. **APPLYING THEMES: AMERICAN CULTURE** Pretend you are a speechwriter for one of the presidential candidates in the 1980 or 1984 election. Write an effective campaign speech based on what you know of the mood of the country and the issues of the day.

8. Reagan's popular style of leadership, his optimistic outlook, and a rebounding economy helped him win re-election.

9. It was an attempt by the Reagan administration to secretly trade arms to Iran in return for U.S. hostages, and use the money to fund the contras. The affair represented an abuse of executive power.

10. Relations became warmer, leading to the INF treaty. Gorbachev's openness to Western ideas paved the way.

Critical Thinking Skills
1. Congressional leaders are sensitive to the feelings of their constituency.

2. Some students may argue that American lives were at stake. Others may argue that the U.S. had no right to use force to intervene.

3. The Vietnam War and Watergate had shaken patriotic beliefs.

4. Great disparities in wealth have led to social unrest and the overthrow of governments.

Writing About Topics in American History
1. Students should note that the family still owns its allotment, that they pick and preserve the local berries and fruits, while at the same time they drive cars, live in town, and are educated away from their traditional lands.

2 Students should consider a speech that is optimitstic, patriotic, and has a clear vision.

5. U.S. assertiveness in Central America and the Middle East; the Soviet Union's war in Afghanistan and intervention in Poland, coupled with the shooting down of a Korean airliner over Soviet airspace.

6. Attempts to re-integrate into society patients from mental hospitals and rising housing prices. The Emergency Homeless Act and charitable groups established temporary shelters and relief programs.

7. Reagan lowered pollution standards and opened federal lands to industry.

Chapter Review exercises are keyed for student abilities:
● = Basic
▲ = Average
■ = Average/Advanced

Chapter 27 ▪ Toward the Year 2000

	SECTION OBJECTIVES	SECTION RESOURCES
Section 1 **The Bush** **Presidency**	▪ identify the issues and strategies of the 1988 presidential campaign ▪ discuss the major domestic challenges of the Bush presidency	● **Reteaching Resources:** Worksheet 104 ▲ **Reinforcement Workbook:** Worksheet 104 ■ **Enrichment and Extension Resources:** Primary Source Worksheet 53 ▲ **Teaching Transparencies:** Transparency 104
Section 2 **Toward a Post–Cold** **War World**	▪ identify trends in international relations at the end of the century	● **Reteaching Resources:** Worksheet 105 ▲ **Reinforcement Workbook:** Worksheet 105 ■ **Enrichment and Extension Resources:** Primary Source Worksheet 54 ▲ **Teaching Transparencies:** Transparency 105
Section 3 **The Impact** **of Science** **and Technology**	▪ describe threats to the environment and efforts to overcome them ▪ identify advantages and disadvantages of the space program	● **Reteaching Resources:** Worksheet 106 ▲ **Reinforcement Workbook:** Worksheet 106 ■ **Enrichment and Extension Resources:** Primary Source Worksheet 55 ▲ **Teaching Transparencies:** Transparency 106

The list below shows Essential Elements relevant to this chapter. (The complete list of Essential Elements appears in the introductory pages of this Teacher's Edition.)

Section 1: 3E, 4C, 4D, 5B, 5D, 7C, 7D, 7E, 7F, 7H, 7I, 7J, 7K, 8C, 9A, 9B, 9G
Section 2: 1A, 1B, 1C, 2D, 3B, 4B, 4C, 6A, 6C, 7F, 8F, 8G, 9A, 9B
Section 3: 2B, 2C, 3A, 4E, 5B, 5E, 6A, 6C, 9D

Section Resources are keyed for student abilities:
● = Basic
▲ = Average
■ = Average/Advanced

CHAPTER RESOURCES

Geography Resources: Worksheets 53, 54
Tests: Chapter 27 Test

Chapter Project: Geography

Have students focus on an environmental project at the local level. Suggestions include: an explanation of how the community handles solid wastes; a report on recycling efforts; a history of the pollution of local waterways; a study of your community's major air pollutants; or a diagram of the different environmental laws that are in effect in your community.

Homework Options

Each section contains activities labeled "Addressing Individual Needs." You may wish to choose from among these activities when assigning homework.

> **Provisions for Limited English Proficiency (LEP)**
> Several suggested activities may be particularly helpful for teachers of students with limited English proficiency. These activities have been marked throughout the Teacher's Annotated Edition with the symbol **LEP** .

BIBLIOGRAPHY AND AUDIOVISUAL AIDS

Teacher Bibliography

Fallows, James. *More Like Us: An American Plan for American Recovery.* Houghton Mifflin, 1989. A comparison of Japanese and American societies.

Kidder, Tracy. *Among Schoolchildren.* Houghton Mifflin, 1989. The American education system, through the experiences of one elementary school teacher.

Meltzer, Milton. *Poverty in America.* Morrow, 1986.

Schlesinger, Arthur. *The Cycles of American History.* Houghton Mifflin, 1987.

Takaki, Ronald. *Strangers from a Different Shore: A History of Asian Americans.* Little, Brown, 1989.

Student Bibliography

Kosof, Anna. *Homeless in America.* Watts, 1988.

Martin, David C. *Best Laid Plans: The Inside Story of America's War Against Terrorism.* Harper and Row, 1988.

Pringle, Laurence P. *Rain of Troubles: The Science and Politics of Acid Rain.* Macmillan, 1988.

Films and Videotapes*

AIDS and the Future. 33 min. FI. Explores historical attitudes toward the disease, introducing the concept of law versus personal responsibility and revealing the terrible effects AIDS has had on our society.

Earth Colonies in Space: "The Society." 20 min. LUCERNE. Examines plans for humanity's future in space and the increasing competition for a foothold in this new frontier of power, profits, and politics.

The Last Empire: Intervention and Nuclear War. 30 min. CDF. Explores the relationship between U.S. foreign policy and the potential for nuclear war.

The New Pilgrim. 25 min. FI. Examines recent trends in United States immigration and the changing make-up of the country.

The Territory Ahead (Spaceflight Series). 60 min. PBS. Current and future directions in space. Explores the possibilities of space stations, colonies, and traveling to the stars.

Computer Software*

Balance of Power (1 disk, Apple II, IBM-PC, Macintosh). MIND. Simulation of the nuclear age where students, assuming positions as either the U.S. President or the Soviet General Secretary, make decisions that may have worldwide consequences.

Simplicon (1 disk, Apple II). CCS. The complex problems of national economic development. Students create and maintain a stable, secure country with a well-balanced economy, while at the same time limiting pollution and preparing for disasters and military conflicts.

*For a complete guide to audiovisual sources, see the introduction to this book (page Txx).

Chapter 27

Toward the Year 2000

(pp. 642–671)

This chapter describes the 1988 presidential campaign and the highlights of the Bush presidency. It identifies major environmental and political challenges facing the United States and the world near the end of the twentieth century, and discusses the continuing advances in technology and space exploration.

Themes in American History

- Global interactions
- Economic development
- Pluralistic society
- American culture

Chapter Objectives

After students complete this chapter, they will be able to:

1. Identify the issues and strategies of the 1988 presidential campaign.

2. Discuss the major domestic challenges of the Bush presidency.

3. Identify trends in international relations at the end of the century.

4. Describe threats to the environment and efforts to overcome them.

5. Identify advantages and disadvantages of the space program.

Modern technology has profoundly changed the way we view our world, as in this three-dimensional computer image. Advances in computer design are only one example of today's quickening pace of technological change.

CHAPTER SUPPORT MATERIAL	
	Reinforcement Workbook: Worksheets 104–106
	Reteaching Resources: Worksheets 104–106
	Enrichment and Extension Resources: Primary Source Worksheets 53–55
	Geography Resources: Worksheets 53, 54
	Teaching Transparencies: Transparencies 104–106
	Tests: Chapter 27 Test

KEY EVENTS

1988	Bush elected President
1989	Communism collapses in Eastern Europe
1990	American troops sent to Middle East
1991	200th anniversary of Bill of Rights
1992	500th anniversary of Columbus's journey to Americas

SECTION 1

The Bush Presidency
(pp. 643–651)

3E, 4C, 4D, 5B, 5D, 7C, 7D, 7E, 7F, 7H, 7I, 7J, 7K, 8C, 9A, 9B, 9G

1 The Bush Presidency

Section Focus

Key Term Savings and Loan crisis

Main Idea Following Ronald Reagan's eight years as President, George Bush's election extended Republican control of the White House. The nation's domestic challenges included the war on drugs, the AIDS epidemic, and economic uncertainty.

Objectives As you read, look for answers to these questions:
1. How did the two major parties select their candidates for the 1988 election?
2. How did Bush come from behind to win the election?
3. What issues dominated the Bush presidency?

It was September 1988. In just a few weeks the American people would choose the next President, and the campaigns of the two major parties were in high gear. Here was Republican George Bush, demonstrating his patriotism by visiting a New Jersey flag factory. There was Democrat Michael Dukakis, showing his toughness by riding around in the army's newest tank.

In 1960, John F. Kennedy's understanding of the power of television had helped him win the presidential debates and hence the election. In 1980 and 1984, Ronald Reagan had made masterful use of television to score landslide victories. Now, in 1988, Bush and Dukakis both tried to use television to project a favorable image to the American people. Critics charged that this was a campaign of style over substance. The American people may have agreed: only slightly more than half of those eligible to vote bothered to do so.

THE REPUBLICANS CHOOSE BUSH 5B

George Bush was the obvious Republican candidate for President. After all, he had been the Vice President of a popular President for eight years. He had held several top positions before

that. He had shrewd and experienced advisers. And two years before the election he already had a campaign fund of more than $12 million.

In the photograph below, George and Barbara Bush attend a rally during the 1988 presidential campaign. NATIONAL IDENTITY Why, do you think, is the American flag such a potent image in political campaigns? 7I, 9A

SECTION 1

The Bush Presidency
(pp. 643–651)

Section Objectives
■ identify the issues and strategies of the 1988 presidential campaign
■ discuss the major domestic challenges of the Bush presidency

Introducing the Section

Connecting with Past Learnings
Review the political shifts of the 1980s with the class. *What was the Reagan Revolution?* (Surge of popularity for political conservatism; decrease in government involvement in social welfare; pro-business attitude; increase in patriotism and national pride.)

Key Term
Write the key term on the board and have students identify what a Savings and Loan is. (A kind of bank.) Then have a volunteer define the term. **LEP**

SUPPORTING THE SECTION

Reinforcement Workbook: Worksheet 104
Reteaching Resources: Worksheet 104
Enrichment and Extension Resources: Primary Source Worksheet 53
Teaching Transparencies: Transparency 104

Photo Caption Answer
The flag symbolizes tradition and patriotism, two qualities likely to build popular support for a candidate.

Focus
On one side of the board, have students list the issues of the 1988 presidential campaign. (Tax increases; a less selfish America; economic growth; control of the deficit; the candidates' personalities; crime; patriotism.) On the other side of the board, list the issues mentioned in the section that the Bush administration faces. (Supreme Court decisions on the death penalty, abortion, and flag-burning; war on drugs; AIDS epidemic; Savings and Loan crisis; deficit.)

Have students compare the lists, noting how many issues are found on both lists.

Yet Bush's nomination was far from guaranteed. For all of his experience, he still lacked a clear political identity. No one questioned his physical courage. Bush had been a decorated World War II bomber pilot. But many believed that he waffled in his views and lacked the courage to take firm positions. In fact, early in the campaign even some Republicans called Bush a "wimp." A graduate of a private boarding school and Yale University, Bush also had to struggle against an image as an overprivileged "preppie."

Believing that Bush was beatable, five other Republicans jumped into the race. As the favorite, Bush faced criticism from all sides. He was helped by his association with Reagan, though at first his connection to the President backfired.

The Iran-contra scandal was unfolding, and people wondered where Bush had been when the decision was made to sell arms for hostages. As one of his opponents, Alexander Haig, asked Bush during a debate, "Were you in the cockpit, or were you . . . in the back of the plane?"

Bush refused to answer. He said his advice to the President about the affair was given in confidence and would remain secret. His firmness in refusing to answer these questions left doubts about his role as Vice President. Yet it also helped overcome his image of weakness.

Bush's main challenge came from the Senate Minority Leader, Robert Dole of Kansas. Dole scored an early victory over Bush in the Iowa caucuses in February 1988. However, when Bush won a huge victory in the crucial New Hampshire primary a week later, his opponents fell far behind. The key to Bush's New Hampshire victory was a simple pledge not to raise taxes. Since Dole had not made the same iron-clad pledge, Bush charged that Dole would raise taxes.

The tactic worked and Bush stuck with it. In speech after speech he said that if Congress ever asked him for a tax increase he would simply say, "Read my lips—no new taxes."

> "**R**ead my lips—no new taxes."
>
> —*George Bush, 1988 campaign*

Bush's other positions were less clear. While he favored continuing most of Reagan's policies, Bush had a response to those who accused Reagan of promoting selfishness and greed. Accepting his party's nomination, Bush called for a "kinder, gentler America." That would be achieved, he said, through the efforts of volunteers—"a thousand points of light," he called them.

Bush's most unexpected campaign decision was his choice of a running mate. He selected Dan Quayle, a young and little-known senator from Indiana. Republicans and Democrats alike questioned whether Quayle had the talent and experience to be second-in-command. Some believed the choice might cost Bush the election.

Dan Quayle, the Republican candidate for Vice President, shakes hands with supporters during the 1988 campaign. Bush's choice of Quayle as his running mate was highly controversial.
CIVIC VALUES Why might shaking hands be considered an old-fashioned way of campaigning? Why is it still popular?

MICHAEL DUKAKIS AND THE DEMOCRATIC NOMINATION 5B

After the terrible defeats of 1980 and 1984, the Democrats looked to 1988 as a do-or-die election. The early favorite for the party's nomination was Senator Gary Hart of Colorado. But Hart's campaign collapsed when questions were raised about his personal life. Hart's downfall disappointed many who believed he could bring a positive new image to the party.

Photo Caption Answers
More modern methods of campaigning, such as television commercials, can reach many more people than hand-shaking. Still, many candidates use a handshake to portray themselves as approachable and responsive.

Along with Hart, the best-known Democratic candidate was Jesse Jackson, who had also run in 1984. In 1988, as in 1984, the bulk of Jackson's support came from African Americans. Yet in 1988 Jackson made significant strides in broadening his "rainbow coalition" to include farmers, blue-collar workers, and women of all races. Jackson finished first in a number of state primaries and second in many others.

Some people said that if Jackson were white he would have won the Democratic nomination in a landslide. Others said that because he had never been elected to public office, he could not have won, whatever his race. Still others claimed that his views were too liberal to be accepted by most Americans.

The rest of the Democratic field had to struggle just to get their names on the evening news. The press belittled them as "the seven dwarfs" because they were not well known nationally. However, Michael Dukakis, the governor of Massachusetts, soon proved himself the candidate to beat. The Massachusetts economy had outpaced much of the nation, and Dukakis claimed he could create similar growth nationwide. Dukakis was also known as a frugal person, which suggested that he could get the federal budget under control. Though some complained that he was humorless and stern, Dukakis impressed many as an intelli-gent and honest man.

Dukakis officially won the nomination at the 1988 Democratic convention in Atlanta. It was the high point of his campaign. Polls showed him lead-ing Bush by as many as 17 points. Dukakis's choice of Lloyd Bentsen as a running mate was also wide-ly applauded. Democrats had high hopes that Bentsen, a respected senator from Texas, would help Dukakis in the South and among conservative Democrats.

Democratic presidential nomi-nee Michael Dukakis, with pho-tographs of himself and his running mate Lloyd Bentsen dis-played behind him, delivers a speech to a Chicago audience. POLITICS What qualities should a good running mate possess? How, if at all, do those qualities differ from those that make a good office-holder? 9A

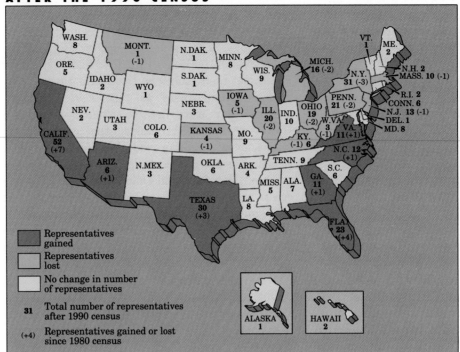

CHANGES IN CONGRESSIONAL REPRESENTATION AFTER THE 1990 CENSUS

MAP SKILLS 9B

Population shifts revealed in the 1990 census will change the number of representatives that many states send to Congress. This map shows the likely outcome of those changes.

CRITICAL THINKING According to the map, which areas of the country will gain representatives? Which areas will lose representatives?

BUSH'S COME-FROM-BEHIND VICTORY 5B

Trailing badly in the polls, Bush went on the attack. This decision produced what journalists Jack Germond and Jules Witcover called "the most mean-spirited and negative campaign in modern-day American political history." Bush's main strategy was to paint Dukakis as an ultra-liberal whose views were "outside the mainstream" of American values. In particular, Bush suggested that Dukakis was soft on crime and unpatriotic.

Bush told his audiences that Dukakis had supported a policy that gave weekend furloughs to first-degree murderers. During one of those weekend leaves, a prisoner had committed rape. Telling the story to a Texas crowd, Bush contrasted Dukakis with the law-and-order movie character "Dirty Harry." Dirty Harry told criminals, "Go ahead, make my day" (an invitation to a shoot-out). "But," joked Bush, "Dukakis says, 'Go ahead, have a nice weekend.'"

Dukakis could not shake off the charge. He correctly pointed out that the furlough policy had been started by a Republican governor and that it was not very different from policies in other states (including California when Reagan was governor). However, the damage had been done. The issue put Dukakis on the defensive, and his inability to counterattack raised doubts among many voters.

Bush also criticized Dukakis's veto of a Massachusetts bill requiring students to recite the "Pledge of Allegiance." Dukakis pointed out that the Supreme Court had struck down a similar law. Bush, again on the attack, called Dukakis's position unpatriotic.

In the final weeks Dukakis struck back. He called Bush's charges "political garbage" and claimed that Bush was the candidate of the rich. "I'm on your side," he told working people. But it was too late. On Election Day, Bush won 40 states and 426 out of 538 electoral votes. Bush's victory marked the first time since the 1940s that either party had held power for three straight terms of office. It also underscored the Republican dominance of the presidency in modern times. Since 1969, Republicans have occupied the White House for all but four years.

Map Skills Answers
The South and West will gain.
The North and East will lose.

LEGAL ISSUES UNDER BUSH 5D, 7D, 7E, 7F

Republican control of the presidency has resulted in a more conservative Supreme Court. In 1989, for instance, the Court toughened laws dealing with capital punishment. In one case, the Court found that the constitutional ban on "cruel and unusual punishment" does not rule out the execution of 16- and 17-year-olds convicted of murder. In a related case, the Court decided to permit the execution of mentally retarded criminals.

The Court also began to reconsider abortion. In *Webster v. Reproductive Health Services* (1989), a 5–4 majority tightened the abortion rights granted by *Roe v. Wade*, the landmark 1973 decision that legalized abortion. Webster did not overturn *Roe v. Wade*. Still, it gave states a good deal of power to restrict the situations in which women could receive abortions.

One key decision went against the wishes of the Bush administration. The Court stirred controversy when it ruled in favor of a Texas man who was arrested for burning an American flag as a political protest. The decision stated that flag-burning is protected by the First Amendment right to free expression.

Appalled by the decision, President Bush called for a constitutional amendment to outlaw the destruction of the American flag. If the flag, he said, "is not defended, it is defamed." Initially, opinion polls showed wide support for the President's position. But legal experts in and out of Congress warned that any attempt to prohibit this form of expression would endanger the entire principle of free speech. Others began to raise the question of what was more important—the flag itself or what the flag stood for.

Both sides of the heated debate over abortion can be seen in this photograph of demonstrators outside the Supreme Court building in Washington, D.C. CONSTITUTIONAL HERITAGE Why is the Supreme Court at the center of the abortion debate? 7H

Cutting drug consumption is one of the biggest challenges facing the United States. Above, President Bush poses with a group of Delaware police officers as part of that state's antidrug efforts. At right, customs agents examine bags of cocaine seized in a freighter off Miami, Florida. GEOGRAPHY Why is Florida an especially important state in the war on drugs? 4D

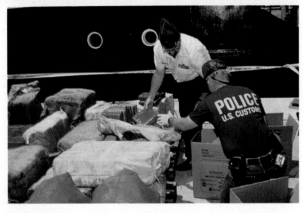

In 1990, Bush had his first chance to nominate a new member to the Supreme Court when justice William Brennan retired. A champion of civil rights and individual liberties, Brennan and Justice Thurgood Marshall were the last liberal links to the Warren Court of the 1950s and 1960s (pages 508–509).

Bush's choice to replace Brennan was David Souter, from New Hampshire. Though known as a conservative, Souter won the Senate's confirmation without revealing the details of his legal views. Many liberals were relieved when he claimed to have an open mind on such controversial issues as abortion and affirmative action. Many conservatives were puzzled by Souter's moving tribute to his predecessor. William Brennan, he said, was "one of the most fearlessly principled guardians of the American Constitution that it has ever had or ever will have." Still, Souter's presence on the Court should strengthen the conservative majority that has prevailed since the Reagan years.

THE WAR ON DRUGS 7K

Two other national issues during the Bush years raised important legal questions. One was the use of illegal drugs. In his Inaugural Address,

President Bush pledged to fight the "scourge" of illegal drugs. Soon after taking office, he unveiled a $6 billion antidrug program. Support for an all-out war on drugs had been building for years. In public-opinion polls a majority of Americans identified drugs as the nation's most urgent domestic problem.

By 1990 Americans were spending $100 billion per year on illegal drugs, consuming 60 percent of the world's supply. Cocaine was one of the most widespread and dangerous of these drugs, especially in a concentrated form known as crack. Most of the cocaine was produced in South America and then smuggled into the United States. Efforts to halt the smuggling failed. The supply of cocaine in the United States tripled in the 1980s, and its street price dropped by half.

Of special concern was the use of cocaine among the urban poor. As one journalist wrote, "Cocaine, once popular in Hollywood and on Wall Street, is fast becoming the narcotic of the ghetto." Drug use has many victims—not only the users but all of society. A congressional study estimated that 70 percent of all violent crimes in the United States are committed by people on drugs or in pursuit of drugs.

Part of Bush's war on drugs involved combating the flow of drugs into the United States. The American government sent military aid to Latin American governments battling rich and powerful drug lords. The Colombia-based Medellín (meh–deh–YEEN) drug cartel, for example, was a target of the Bush administration. So too was Panamanian strongman Manuel Noriega, indicted by a U.S. court on charges of drug trafficking. In 1989 Bush sent U.S. troops to Panama. The invaders overthrew Noriega, who was brought to Miami to stand trial.

Bush's antidrug plan also sought to beef up local enforcement of drug laws. In addition, some extra money was earmarked for drug treatment and education. Some people felt that even more money would have to be spent on the war on drugs if the United States is to win it. However, with the federal debt at $3 trillion, finding the money to pay for that war will not be easy.

Nor will it be easy to deal with the complicated legal issues that have arisen over the drug issue. Some companies, arguing that drug use endangers workers' safety, require drug testing of their employees. Critics of drug testing claim that such tests invade workers' privacy. They also worry that drug testing violates a central belief of the American judicial system, that a person is innocent until proven guilty. Another legal issue deals with the use of drugs by pregnant women. If an unborn child is harmed by its mother's drug use, can the mother be charged with a crime? Issues such as these are sure to spark debate in the years to come.

THE AIDS EPIDEMIC 7C, 7J

A devastating health threat that first appeared in the early 1980s is AIDS—acquired immune deficiency syndrome. AIDS is caused by a virus, called HIV, that eliminates the body's ability to fight diseases and infections. HIV can live in a person for

A quilt in memory of AIDS victims is displayed near the Washington Monument in Washington, D.C. Friends and relatives of AIDS victims made the patches that comprise the quilt. **PARTICIPATION** Why, do you think, would people be eager to participate in constructing such a quilt? 9G

years before he or she shows signs of illness. A carrier of the AIDS virus *cannot* infect someone through ordinary activities. However, the virus *can* be transmitted through direct sexual contact or the sharing of needles. Infected mothers can also pass on HIV to their babies during pregnancy or childbirth.

Scientists continue to investigate treatments and possible cures for AIDS. Meanwhile, the disease is spreading. By the end of 1992, some experts predicted, more than a million Americans would be infected with AIDS. They believe that by that time, some 200,000 Americans may already have died of AIDS.

Legal issues raised by the AIDS crisis, like those raised by the war on drugs, focus on the rights of the individual versus those of society. Should people be forced to undergo testing for AIDS? Should they be forced to reveal the names of persons they might have infected? Who is entitled to see information about people's test results—their employers, their families, the government? The need to balance individual and social rights is still a challenge today, as it has been throughout the history of the United States.

ECONOMIC WOES 7J, 8C

As America entered the 1990s, the federal deficit soared to over $3 trillion, increasing at a rate of $240,000 per minute. A *Washington Post* editorial blamed the President: "The White House has shown an inability to lead the nation on the major issue of the Bush presidency—the budget deficiency." Others blamed Congress. In truth, both branches of government had failed for an entire decade to act on a terrible problem. Making matters worse was the onset in 1990 of an economic recession. Paying off the nation's debt would be all the more difficult in a sluggish economy with rising unemployment.

The failure of hundreds of banks in the late 1980s led to the Savings and Loan crisis. This cartoon compares the crisis to an oil spill. ECONOMICS Do you think the comparison between an oil spill and the S&L crisis is a good one? Why or why not? 9B

Conrad. ©The Los Angeles Times

A key factor in the economic downturn was the Savings and Loan crisis, brought on by the worst string of bank failures since the Great Depression. Savings and Loan banks had once been considered safe family banks that made cautious loans to home buyers and watched over the modest savings of ordinary people. Beginning in the late 1980s, however, hundreds of these "S&L's" went bankrupt, and the federal government stepped in to save them. This bank bailout—rescue from financial problems—may cost American taxpayers close to $500 billion.

The crisis was caused by bankers who made risky loans and investments in hopes of making huge profits in the free-wheeling economy of the 1980s. Such wild speculation was more possible then than in previous decades because the federal government under Reagan stopped regulating many banking practices.

The S&L crisis exposed numerous examples of greed, corruption, and outright law-breaking. Many Americans concluded from this that the economic fate of the entire nation had been compromised by a small class of selfish speculators. Sociologist Ralph Whitehead has called this group the "overclass." By this he meant not just corrupt S&L bankers but also those who gambled in the high-stakes world of corporate takeovers, real estate deals, and risky junk bonds. This overclass, many believe, simply enriched themselves while plunging the rest of the nation further into debt.

NEW TAXES 3E, 7C

In his 1988 campaign, President Bush had given a solemn pledge not to raise taxes. Two years later he insisted that new taxes were needed to help reduce the runaway federal deficit. The deficit, he said, is like "a cancer eating away at our nation's health. . . . Year after year it mortgages the future of our children." Many voters felt betrayed by Bush's flip-flop on taxes. Even those who shared his view that new taxes were necessary complained that he should have realized it in 1988 when the debt was already close to $3 trillion. Administration supporters answered that the Constitution gives Congress the responsibility for checking, altering, and passing the President's budget bill. It was Congress's inability, they con-

Photo Caption Answer
Students may agree with the cartoonist, pointing out that an oil spill and the bank crisis are both examples of private industry ignoring the public good. Those who disagree may note that the oil spill cleanup was mostly paid for by private industry, while the government is paying for the S&L crisis.

During the Persian Gulf crisis, American tanks in Saudi Arabia prepare to battle Iraqi forces. **GLOBAL AWARENESS** How did the end of the cold war affect the international response to the crisis? 1B

Divide the class into small groups and assign each group one of the following issues: immigration to the United States, migration in the United States, the Soviet Union, Eastern Europe, U.S.-Communist relations, international trade, South Africa, the Persian Gulf. Ask each group to write a report, create a collage, or design a poster illustrating the past and future of the issue. Have the groups present their creations to the class. LEP

Though months passed without a shot fired, tensions were raised by Iraq's holding of thousands of hostages, many of them Americans. Selected hostages were held as "shields" at probable targets of attack within Kuwait and Iraq. Hussein finally did release the hostages, but their tales of Iraqi brutality hardened Americans' resolve to force Iraq out of Kuwait. With few prospects for a diplomatic solution, the likelihood of armed conflict seemed inevitable.

One unique aspect of the Persian Gulf crisis was the cooperation between the United States and Soviet Union. In September 1990 President Bush and Soviet President Gorbachev issued a joint statement:

> We are united in the belief that Iraq's aggression must not be tolerated. No peaceful international order is possible if larger states can devour other smaller neighbors. . . . We once again call upon the government of Iraq to withdraw unconditionally from Kuwait. . . .

Iraq refused to budge, despite repeated warnings by President Bush that he would force Iraqi troops out of Kuwait. On January 16, 1991, Americans learned that the United States and its allies had launched a massive assault on Iraqi forces. In a campaign dubbed "Operation Desert Storm," allied planes rained down bombs on Iraq and its positions in Kuwait, destroying vital communications centers, supply routes, and weapons. Iraq was able to fire Scud missiles at Saudi Arabia and Israel, but damage was light. On February 23, after weeks of intense bombing, allied forces unleashed a ground assault. Within days Kuwait was liberated and the war was over.

Photo Caption Answer
The Soviet Union supported United States efforts to force Iraq out of Kuwait, leading to a far more united effort.

Instruct students to complete **Reinforcement Workbook** Worksheet 105, which asks them to identify places discussed in the section.

Reteaching/Correctives
Provide students with a world map or have them trace the map on pages 848–849. Have students review the section. Then on their maps, have them identify areas of the world which present challenges to the United States. Students should write a sentence of explanation for each pinpointed area.

Have students complete **Reteaching Resources** Worksheet 105, in which they identify important places and terms in international affairs.

Enrichment/Extension
Have students complete **Enrichment and Extension Resources** Primary Source Worksheet 54, which presents an argument by a United States representative in favor of economic sanctions against South Africa.

The Geographic Perspective: Trade and the Pacific Rim

Where was your family's TV set made? Your family car? Your sneakers? It is likely that one of these came from Japan or another Asian country. The number of Asian-made goods in American society reflects important new trade patterns.

GROWTH IN PACIFIC TRADE
In 1900 more than 50 percent of American imports came from Europe; 75 percent of American exports went to Europe. By mid-century most of American trade was with the Western Hemisphere. The Western Hemisphere remains important. In fact, Canada is the United States' most important trading partner. In recent decades, however, trade has steadily grown with Asian Pacific Rim nations. Today these nations account for more than 25 percent of U.S. exports and about 40 percent of U.S. imports.

This change partly reflects efforts by the Asian Pacific Rim nations to boost economic growth through exports. Since World War II, these nations have used several methods to make their products competitive on world markets. These include high rates of savings and investment, technological advances, efficient industry, and technical training.

EFFECTS OF TRADE
Increased trade with the Pacific Rim has brought prosperity to West Coast ports. Shipping has steadily increased at such ports as Long Beach, Los Angeles, Portland, Seattle, and Tacoma.

Increased contacts have also produced cultural and political change. For instance, about 40 percent of all foreign students in the United States are Asians. On returning home, such students have worked to promote democracy in Asia. Both South Korea and the Philippines have recently become more democratic.

China, the largest of the Pacific Rim nations, has learned that no nation can let in some ideas and keep out others. Eager to modernize its economy, China sent as many as 30,000 students a year to the United States. They returned home with advanced knowledge—and with the desire for more freedom. In the summer of 1989, Chinese students spearheaded a massive demonstration for democracy, but the government brutally repressed such hopes.

It wanted only economic change, not political change.

A negative result of rising Pacific Rim trade has been a larger American trade deficit. U.S. imports from Asian Pacific Rim nations have increased much faster than U.S. exports to those nations. The trade deficit with Japan alone reached a whopping $52 billion for 1988. Then it began to decline.

This improvement may reflect some government success in encouraging American exports and in pressuring Japan to open up markets for U.S. products. The restoration of balanced trade is a major economic challenge of the 1990s.

1C, 8F, 8G

CRITICAL THINKING QUESTIONS
1. Why might a nation try to restrict imports? What are the drawbacks of such a move?
2. How might the rising importance of Pacific Rim trade affect American foreign policy?

PACIFIC RIM TRADE

SCALE 0 1000 mi / 0 1000 km

ALASKA

SOUTH KOREA

CHINA — JAPAN

TAIWAN — Hong Kong

PHILIPPINES

THAILAND — MALAYSIA

SINGAPORE

INDONESIA

AUSTRALIA

NEW ZEALAND

CANADA

Seattle • UNITED STATES • San Francisco • Los Angeles • New York

$67 billion

$172 billion

HAWAII

PACIFIC OCEAN

MEXICO

Equator

⬅ U.S. exports, 1987
➡ U.S. imports, 1987

MERCATOR PROJECTION

The Geographic Perspective Answers
1. To protect its industries from foreign competition. Other nations might retaliate by restricting imports as well.

2. The United States will have to work more closely with Pacific Rim nations to ensure the continuation of free trade.

Geographic Themes
Geographic themes covered on this page:
_____ Location
_____ Place
_____ Interactions
✔ Movement
✔ Regions

COMPETITION IN TRADE 8F

"Made in Japan." In the 1950s, Americans associated that label with cheap, poorly manufactured products. By the 1970s, it was seen as a badge of quality. Japan had become one of the world's greatest economic powers. Its success spread throughout East Asia. Some experts claimed that the center of the world economy had shifted to the Pacific Rim—the nations bordering the Pacific Ocean.

By many measures, the United States entered the 1990s as the world's most dynamic economy. But its position in relation to other nations had certainly declined. Many American products did not compete well in the world market. For example, a 1989 poll found that only 6 percent of West Germans thought "Made in America" was a mark of quality. Moreover, a serious trade imbalance developed. The United States began to import far more products than it exported.

What worried many Americans was the economic strength of Japan. A growing number viewed the island nation as a disloyal ally that competed unfairly. The major complaint was that Japan used high tariffs or other means to block American imports. Further hostility stemmed from the fact that the United States paid for much of Japan's national defense. Some polls suggested

U.S. FOREIGN TRADE, 1950–1990

Value
Billions of dollars

Imports

Exports

Source: *Historical Statistics of the United States*

GRAPH SKILLS 1C, 9B

The values of American imports and exports are compared in this graph. Which has increased more over the entire period shown, imports or exports? **CRITICAL THINKING** What are the dangers of a trade deficit?

Canada, which lies on the Pacific Rim, is the United States' largest trading partner. Trade, however, is only one of many areas of cooperation between the two nations. American and Canadian military forces work together to guard North American shores and airspace against possible attack. The two governments are exploring ways to combat such problems as acid rain. Here, President Bush and Prime Minister Brian Mulroney meet for talks in Ottawa. **GLOBAL AWARENESS** What factors have helped build lasting friendship between the two nations? 1B

CHAPTER 27   TOWARD THE YEAR 2000, 1988–2000   **661**

Assessment

You may wish to use the Section 2 Review, page 662, to see how well your students understand the main points in the lesson.

Section Review Answers

1. *political prisoner*—Someone confined because of his or her opposition to the government. *protectionism*—Government efforts to protect certain businesses by raising tariffs on imported products.

2. *Mikhail Gorbachev*—Soviet leader responsible for an increased openness and many reforms in Soviet society. *Deng Xiaoping*—China's leader, responsible for repression of pro-democracy movement. *Nelson Mandela*—Black South African leader. *Iraq*—Nation in the Middle East that invaded Kuwait in 1990. *Saddam Hussein*—Iraqi dictator who ordered the invasion of Kuwait. *Pacific Rim*—Economic region of nations bordering the Pacific Ocean.

Photo Caption Answer

Factors include ethnic and economic ties and a common commitment to democracy.

Graph Skills Answers

Imports. A trade deficit can hurt domestic industry, increase foreign debt, and weaken a nation in its dealings with other nations.

662

3. Latin America and Asia.

4. Economic crises and growing public discontent in several Communist countries led to reforms in the late 1980s. The increased friendliness between the United States and the USSR led to the INF Treaty and plans for limitation of long-range missiles.

5. Increase in trade will mean an increase in interaction between people from different countries and cultures, which might increase international understanding. Dependence on foreign trade will also increase the incentive to keep the peace so that trade will not be disrupted. If increased trade means increased unemployment in some countries, however, anger at more successful countries may increase international tensions.

Closure

Ask one student to transform the Main Idea of the section into a question, and have other students answer that question. Then have students read Section 3, noting the pluses and minuses of our increasing dependence on technology.

In 1990 President Carlos Salinas of Mexico and U.S. President George Bush discussed lowering trade barriers between their countries. **ECONOMICS** How might increased trade benefit both countries? **8F**

that most Americans viewed Japan as a greater threat than the Soviet Union. "As fears of the Soviet Union diminish," reported *Newsweek* magazine, "Japan is fast emerging as a new bogeyman." These attitudes built some support for protectionism—government efforts to protect certain businesses by raising tariffs on imported products.

NEW PATTERNS OF TRADE 1C

The formation of regional trading blocs may bring about greater protectionism. The best example is in Europe, which in 1992 will take a giant step toward the creation of a single integrated economy. Similarly, the Asian Pacific Rim nations will soon be trading more among themselves than with Western nations. There has been talk of linking the Canadian, American, and Mexican economies more closely as well. A 1988 trade agreement between the United States and Canada marked a step in this direction. (Canada was already the United States' largest trading partner.)

Regional trading blocs are designed to lower trade barriers among members of the bloc. Trade within each bloc should therefore rise. But, some economists warn, trade among different blocs may suffer if tariffs are not lowered for non-members as well. Free trade, instead of extending across the globe, would be confined to trade within these blocs.

Other economists argue, on the other hand, that the real forces in trade will not be nations or blocs, but rather huge international corporations. Most large companies already engage in countless projects abroad. For example, many cars are no longer truly "Japanese" or "American," but both. More and more products can only be described as international—built with parts from one nation, by workers in another nation, to be sold in yet another nation. The largest corporations, with wealth and power comparable to those of many governments, are sure to affect future decisions regarding world trade.

SECTION REVIEW

1. KEY TERMS political prisoner, protectionism

2. PEOPLE AND PLACES Mikhail Gorbachev, Deng Xiaoping, Nelson Mandela, Iraq, Saddam Hussein, Pacific Rim

3. COMPREHENSION From what parts of the world do most of the recent American immigrants come?

4. COMPREHENSION Why did several Communist nations begin to institute reforms in the late 1980s? How did reforms in the Soviet Union affect Soviet-American relations?

5. CRITICAL THINKING How might the growth of trade among nations of the world reduce international tensions? How, on the other hand, might it increase those tensions?

Photo Caption Answer
It would provide large markets for the goods and services produced by both countries.

3 The Impact of Science and Technology

Section Focus

Key Terms genetic engineering ■ global warming ■ deforestation ■ acid rain ■ NASA

Main Idea New developments in science and technology will affect the lives of all Americans.

Objectives As you read, look for answers to these questions:
1. What is the current state of scientific and technological change?
2. What are some serious environmental problems facing the nation?
3. How has the American space program evolved in recent years?

In his classic work *Democracy in America*, Alexis de Tocqueville remarked that "America is a land of wonders, in which everything is in constant motion and every change seems an improvement." This belief in the value of innovation is one reason why the United States has taken the lead in so many areas of scientific and technological change. The ever-expanding frontiers of science and technology will play an important role in the lives of the American people.

THE WORLD OF TECHNOLOGY 3A, 4E

Of course, technological change is hardly a new story. But the pace of change during this century has been remarkable. A person born in 1900 has lived through the invention of the airplane, mass-produced automobile, penicillin, atomic bomb, computer, and television, to name just a few. These and other developments have transformed not just the world of science but the lives of common people as well.

The future may bring computers that think like people, and superconductors that conduct energy with almost no friction. "Spaceplanes" that can fly at speeds as high as 8,000 miles per hour could bring about a new era in long-distance travel.

An even more revolutionary scientific feat is genetic engineering—altering the genetic makeup of a living organism. Genetic engineering may one day give human beings undreamed-of power. Better crops and livestock have already been produced. Creating specific traits in humans is also theoretically possible, an idea that terrifies many observers. Few would argue against the use of genetic engineering to cure diseases. However,

many people would object to the use of this new technology to alter people's appearance or behavior. Genetic engineering is therefore sure to raise controversial questions in the years to come.

Technological change is so embedded in the modern world that we take it for granted. We expect our children to live longer and more comfortably than earlier generations. Yet technology cannot solve all the world's problems. As the case of genetic engineering suggests, technology often raises troubling moral questions. Sometimes technology is itself a problem. For example, even as we look to new technology to deal with the world's environmental troubles, we must not forget that technology helped create those troubles.

> "**M**ost of the great environmental struggles will be won or lost in the 1990s."
>
> —*Thomas Lovejoy,*
> *Smithsonian Institution*

ENVIRONMENTAL CHALLENGES 2B, 2C

"Most of the great environmental struggles will be either won or lost in the 1990s. By the next century it will be too late." This frightening opinion was offered by Thomas Lovejoy, a biologist at the Smithsonian Institution. Three problems in particular stand out:

(1) Global warming. One of the greatest long-range threats is global warming. Six of the ten

SUPPORTING THE SECTION

Reinforcement Workbook: Worksheet 106
Reteaching Resources: Worksheet 106
Enrichment and Extension Resources: Primary Source Worksheet 55
Teaching Transparencies: Transparency 106

SECTION 3

The Impact of Science and Technology
(pp. 663–667)

Section Objectives
- describe threats to the environment and efforts to overcome them
- identify advantages and disadvantages of the space program

Introducing the Section

Connecting with Past Learnings
Discuss the origins of the United States space program. *What event triggered the establishment of an American space program?* (The Soviet launch of *Sputnik*.) *What was its initial goal?* (To put an American on the moon.)

Key Terms
Help students identify the key terms by finding their definitions in context, and have them write definitions for the terms in their own words. Discuss relationships between terms, noting how acid rain leads to deforestation, which leads to global warming. **LEP**

Focus
Create a scorecard for technology by asking students to list positive and negative effects of technological advances. (Positives—faster transportation, medical advances, better crops and livestock, machines that make life easier, increased knowledge of space. Negatives—ethical questions, global warming, deforestation, high costs and risks of space exploration, pollution.)
On balance, do you think technology has been helpful or harmful to humans?

663

Developing the Lesson

After students have read the section, you may want to consider the following activities:

Ethics

What ethical issues does genetic engineering raise? (The question of whether it should be used to alter humans.) Have students discuss the ethics of genetic engineering by asking: *Should genetic engineering be used to help someone recover from a disease or deficiency? To prevent someone from getting a disease or deficiency? To produce people who are immune to disease or deficiency?* Have students explain their answers.

Impact of Geography

Have students look at an elevation map of the world to determine which areas would be most affected by the melting of the polar ice caps. *Which coast of the United States would be in greater danger? Why?* (East Coast; its coastal plain is broad and low, while the West Coast rises to higher ground before many population centers appear.)

Environment

Working in pairs or small groups, have students create plans for conservation and recycling in the following areas: plastics, use of electric and gas power, use of paper products, use of toxic products, and consumerism in general.

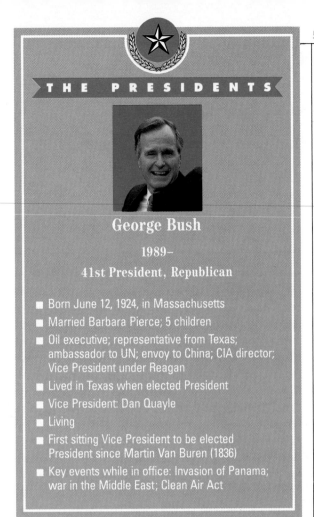

THE PRESIDENTS

George Bush

1989–
41st President, Republican

- Born June 12, 1924, in Massachusetts
- Married Barbara Pierce; 5 children
- Oil executive; representative from Texas; ambassador to UN; envoy to China; CIA director; Vice President under Reagan
- Lived in Texas when elected President
- Vice President: Dan Quayle
- Living
- First sitting Vice President to be elected President since Martin Van Buren (1836)
- Key events while in office: Invasion of Panama; war in the Middle East; Clean Air Act

warmest years in the twentieth century occurred in the 1980s. So far the earth's average temperature has increased less than one degree since 1900. But many scientists expect it to increase 1.5 to 5 degrees by the year 2030.

While that does not sound like a great increase, even small changes in temperature have a great impact. For example, scientists believe that the last Ice Age was ended by a mere five-degree rise in the average temperature. A similar increase today would destroy thousands of species. It could also melt enough ice to flood many of the world's low-lying regions. These include many parts of the coastal United States. Some scientists, however, disagree with these conclusions. They argue that global warming will not be so severe and may actually do some good by extending the growing season in colder regions.

664 UNIT 9 TOWARD A NEW CENTURY

Global warming is caused primarily by the burning of oil, gasoline, and coal. Cars and power plants spew into the atmosphere large amounts—millions of tons—of carbon dioxide. This gas acts as a blanket around the earth, trapping heat that would otherwise escape into space. This is called the "greenhouse effect."

(2) Deforestation. The threat of global warming is worsened by deforestation, the destruction of the world's forests. Trees cleanse air of carbon dioxide and turn it into oxygen. However, many of the earth's most important forests are being destroyed to make way for farming, mining, and grazing. Tropical rain forests are shrinking by 25 million acres a year.

Deforestation may contribute to global warming in two ways. First, it leaves fewer trees to absorb carbon dioxide from the air. Second, the burning of trees to clear land sends even more carbon dioxide into the atmosphere.

(3) Acid rain. Burning fossil fuels has produced not only global warming but also acid rain. This is rain poisoned by acids, including sulfuric acid. Acid rain has destroyed thousands of lakes in Canada and the eastern United States. A major source of acid rain is sulfur dioxide released through the smokestacks of coal-burning industries. Throughout the 1980s, the Canadian govern-

While deforestation is a worldwide concern, its effects are especially devastating in Brazil's Amazon region. In this photograph, trees are being burned to clear land. **ENVIRONMENT** Why does deforestation in Brazil concern people in other nations? **2C**

The Presidents
Have students list the major accomplishments and failures of President Bush. Then ask volunteers to present and explain their lists to the class.

Photo Caption Answer
Deforestation anywhere in the world increases the danger of global warming, which affects the entire earth's climate.

Bare skeletons are all that remain of these once-healthy trees on North Carolina's Mount Mitchell. Acid rain has ruined this and other forests in the eastern United States and Canada. **ECONOMICS** Who should pay to clean up acid rain damage? The polluting states? The entire nation? Explain your answer. 2C

ment and lawmakers from eastern states pushed for stricter regulations against such industrial pollution.

Fighting Pollution 2B

In November 1990 President Bush signed a new Clean Air Act that aimed to reduce industrial and auto pollution as well as urban smog. The act called for a 50 percent reduction in the release of sulfur dioxide by the year 2000. Some environmentalists thought Bush's plan did not go far enough. Yet almost everyone agreed that the new controls would help. Before the Clean Air Act, the United States polluted the air with 2.7 billion pounds of toxic chemicals every year.

Laws against pollution can make a difference. For example, after leaded gasoline was outlawed in 1975, the amount of lead in the atmosphere dropped by 90 percent. Other dangerous substances—mercury, DDT, and PCBs—have also been reduced dramatically through government bans. Tougher laws against water pollution have also brought improvements. In the 1960s, for example, Lake Erie was so contaminated it was pronounced "dead." It is now showing encouraging signs of life.

However, environmental victories are still outweighed by defeats. Full and lasting solutions will require far greater effort. Conservation must be practiced more widely. Reforestation (planting trees) must begin on a massive scale. Clean and renewable sources of energy must be developed. New ways must be found to limit the pollution produced by automobiles, airplanes, and factories. Technology will have an important role to play in these efforts.

The American Space Program 3A, 4E

One of the most stirring examples of the uses of modern technology is the space program, run by NASA—the National Aeronautics and Space Administration. In the early 1970s, following the Apollo moon landings, NASA made the space shuttle the centerpiece of the American space program. The shuttle resembled a huge airplane. After being rocketed into space, it could glide back to earth and be used again. The shuttle's developers hoped to put it to both military and commercial uses. By dropping off satellites and other spacebound merchandise for a fee, NASA believed, the shuttle would soon pay for itself.

After the first flight in 1981, the shuttle missions grew more frequent. However, they were never routine enough to make the shuttle a successful business venture. Since the program relied on funding from Congress, NASA began public relations efforts to promote the shuttle. A part of this campaign involved asking civilians to fly with the shuttle crew. Two members of Congress took part in shuttle missions. NASA then held a nationwide search for a teacher who wanted to fly on the shuttle. It picked a New Hampshire social studies teacher named Christa McAuliffe.

McAuliffe and the six other members of the *Challenger* crew died on January 28, 1986, when one of their solid rocket boosters ignited the fuel tank. It was a horrible moment, even more distressing because millions of students were watching on television. The accident made many people wonder whether space travel was simply too dangerous for humans.

Photo Caption Answer
Students should recognize that public support for cleanup programs may be more easily obtained if the entire nation shares the cost.

In a stirring address to the nation, President Reagan saluted the bravery of the *Challenger* crew. He also appointed a commission to investigate the disaster. Its report was shocking. NASA, the commission learned, had ignored safety warnings in order to keep to its launch schedule. **5E**

> ★ **Historical Documents**
>
> For an excerpt from President Reagan's speech after the *Challenger* disaster, see page 729 of this book.

Public scrutiny had a positive impact on NASA. Safety standards were greatly improved and morale rebounded. In September 1988 the shuttle program resumed with the successful launch of *Columbia*. Yet major questions remain about the value of the shuttle. Even after the successful return to space, *Time* magazine wrote:

> The shuttle was touted in the early 1970s as a cheap, reliable space truck. But 15 years and at least $50 billion later, it is neither cheap nor reliable. It's still an experiment.

TO THE EDGE OF THE SOLAR SYSTEM **4E**
There is another NASA project, however, that has generated almost nothing but praise. In 1977 an unmanned spacecraft named *Voyager 2* was launched on a twelve-year mission to the outer edge of the solar system. Using radio signals, *Voyager 2* sent back thousands of photographs during its 4-billion-mile journey.

At a cost of over $300 million—less than the space shuttle budget for one year—*Voyager 2* provided scientists with reams of new information. Some scientists believe that *Voyager 2* may provide crucial clues to the origins of our solar system.

A somewhat less scientific benefit of the *Voyager* photographs is to give humans a vivid sense of the sheer vastness of space. For instance, they revealed a hurricane as large as the earth moving like a small marble across the surface of Neptune. The winds of the hurricane were estimated at 400 miles per hour.

The *Voyager* mission, along with the revival of the space shuttle program, has sparked renewed enthusiasm for space exploration. Some people continue to argue that the United States should concentrate on unmanned missions. President Bush, on the other hand, has called for a long-term program to send astronauts to Mars. Americans will continue to debate the cost and purpose of such a mission. One factor that must be considered is the effect of space on our national imagination.

F. Scott Fitzgerald ends his novel *The Great Gatsby* by "brooding on the old, unknown world." The novel's narrator, Nick Carraway, tries to imagine what European sailors must have felt when they first set eyes on America. It must have been an "enchanted moment," Carraway thinks; perhaps the "last time in history" when people came "face to face" with a world that matched the human "capacity for wonder."

The exploration of space may give us similar enchanted moments. Yet its ultimate promise is not so much to give us a new world to conquer, although it may do that. More important, it may give us the perspective and the will to see, to cherish, and to protect our own world.

This *Time* magazine cover from the fall of 1988 expresses the nation's relief at the successful launch of the space shuttle *Columbia*. The 1986 accident that destroyed the shuttle *Challenger* had raised serious doubts about the future of the shuttle program. **TECHNOLOGY** Why is space travel so dangerous? **3A, 4E**

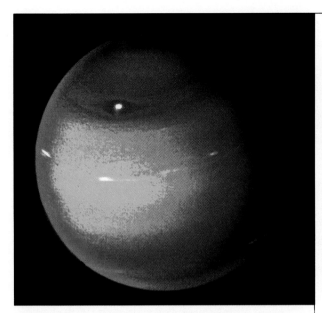

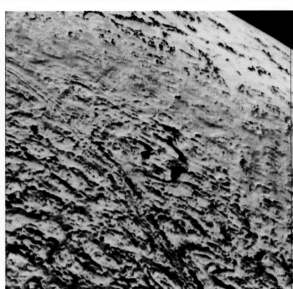

Here are two of the stunning photographs sent back by *Voyager 2* on its journey through the solar system. Both are of the planet Neptune, the second-most-distant planet in the solar system. At left is Neptune from a distance. At right is a close-up of the planet's rocky surface. NATIONAL IDENTITY **What does the act of exploring signify about a nation?** 3A, 4E

In particular, we may learn how to fulfill the promise of America. That promise, expressed countless ways and in countless languages, is of a place where all can enjoy life, liberty, and the pursuit of happiness. The United States has taken great strides toward meeting that promise. In doing so, it has also become in every respect a mighty nation. But much remains to be done—not only to preserve what has been accomplished but also to extend it. Those are the challenges facing the Americans of tomorrow.

SECTION REVIEW

1. KEY TERMS genetic engineering, global warming, deforestation, acid rain, NASA

2. PEOPLE Christa McAuliffe

3. COMPREHENSION Why is genetic engineering a source of controversy?

4. COMPREHENSION What problems are created by global warming? Deforestation? Acid rain?

5. CRITICAL THINKING Some people argue that it is not right to spend money on space exploration when so many people here on earth lack the necessities of life. What are the arguments for and against this position?

---

2. *Christa McAuliffe*—New Hampshire teacher killed in the *Challenger* disaster.

3. The possibility that genetic engineering may be used to control people's appearance or behavior has raised questions about its applications.

4. Global warming causes climate changes and the melting of polar ice caps, resulting in flooding of coastal areas and destruction of thousands of species. Deforestation contributes to global warming by leaving fewer trees to absorb carbon dioxide and, through the burning of trees, by sending even more carbon dioxide into the atmosphere. Acid rain destroys lakes and forests with poisonous acids, killing many animal and plant species.

5. Some students may take the position that exploration should take place only when problems on earth have been solved. Others may suggest that there are far more wasteful expenditures which could be cut to provide more for those in need, and that space exploration may help solve problems on earth by discovering planets that can be colonized or materials that will solve shortages on earth.

Closure

Call students' attention to the beige boxed quotation (p. 663). Ask them to relate this quotation to the main idea of the section.

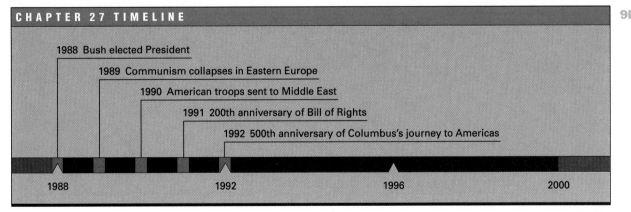

CHAPTER 27 TIMELINE   9D

1988 Bush elected President

1989 Communism collapses in Eastern Europe

1990 American troops sent to Middle East

1991 200th anniversary of Bill of Rights

1992 500th anniversary of Columbus's journey to Americas

1988   1992   1996   2000

Photo Caption Answer
Wealth and technological sophistication, as well as curiosity and a commitment to the future.

Continental United States in 1990

Background

This map is a visual summary of some of the activities, resources, and ways of life in the contiguous United States near the close of the twentieth century. Because of issues of scale, it has not always been possible to place symbols in precise locations. For reasons of space and consistency, Alaska and Hawaii have not been included. The projection, developed for this map by its cartographer, Howard S. Friedman, is based on an oblique view of a polyconic projection. (Other illustrated maps are found on pages 20–21 and 220–221.)

Examining the Map for Content

Review the labeled symbols on the map with the class. Help students identify symbols that have not been labeled by having them find the two dams shown on the map. (In Arizona and South Carolina.) *What does the existence of dams imply about the geography of the areas?* (Presence of large rivers. Also, dams create lakes.)

Ask students to locate the carved faces that represent Mt. Rushmore and then find the symbols that represent some major national parks. Challenge them to identify those parks. (Grand Canyon, Old Faithful in Yellowstone National Park, Yosemite National Park in California.)

Have students refer to the political map of the United States at the back of the book to find the symbols on this map which show the cities of Detroit, Michigan; Chicago, Illinois; Dallas and Houston, Texas; Phoenix, Arizona.

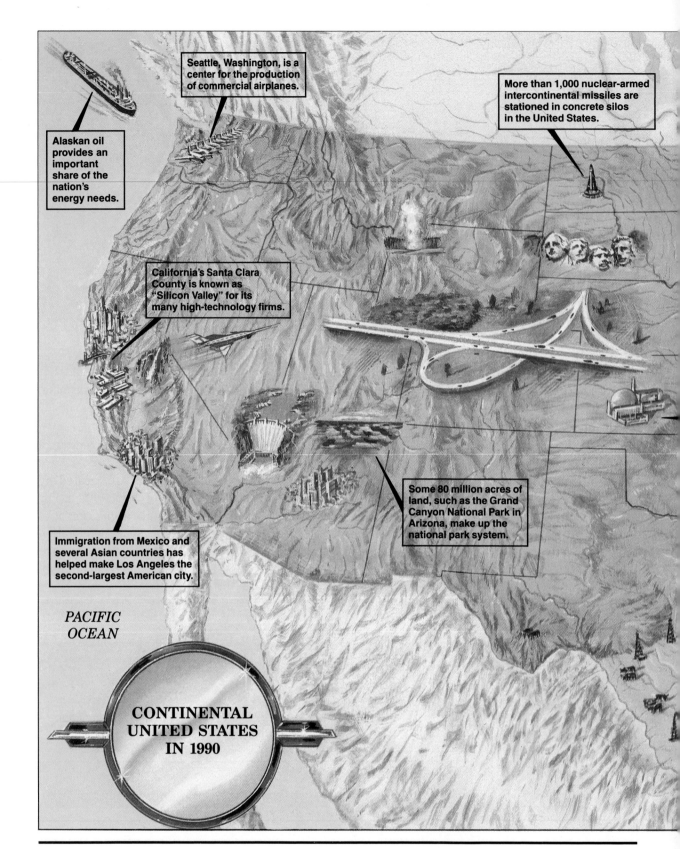

Seattle, Washington, is a center for the production of commercial airplanes.

More than 1,000 nuclear-armed intercontinental missiles are stationed in concrete silos in the United States.

Alaskan oil provides an important share of the nation's energy needs.

California's Santa Clara County is known as "Silicon Valley" for its many high-technology firms.

Some 80 million acres of land, such as the Grand Canyon National Park in Arizona, make up the national park system.

Immigration from Mexico and several Asian countries has helped make Los Angeles the second-largest American city.

PACIFIC OCEAN

CONTINENTAL UNITED STATES IN 1990

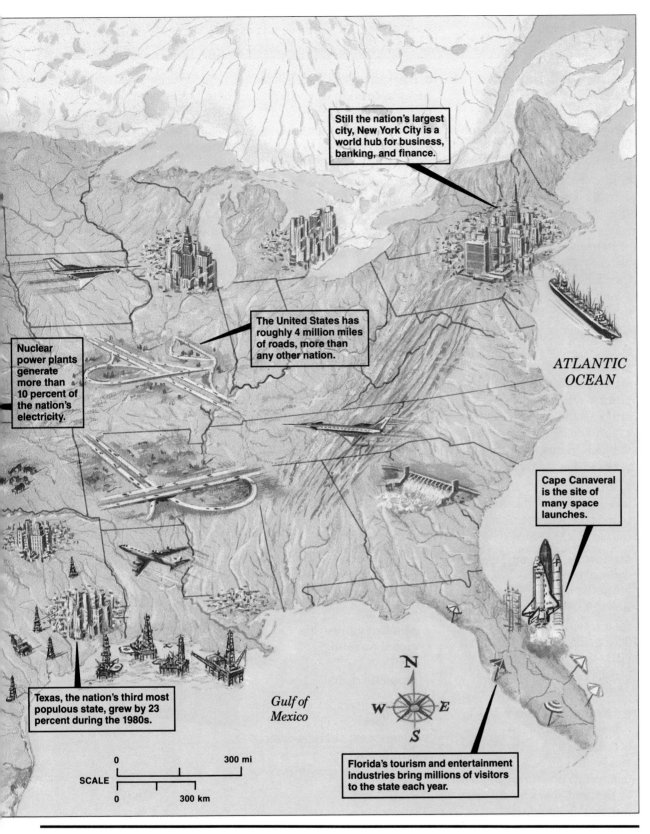

Still the nation's largest city, New York City is a world hub for business, banking, and finance.

The United States has roughly 4 million miles of roads, more than any other nation.

Nuclear power plants generate more than 10 percent of the nation's electricity.

Cape Canaveral is the site of many space launches.

Texas, the nation's third most populous state, grew by 23 percent during the 1980s.

Florida's tourism and entertainment industries bring millions of visitors to the state each year.

ATLANTIC OCEAN

Gulf of Mexico

N
W   E
S

SCALE
0   300 mi
0   300 km

What forms of transportation are shown on this map? (Ships, airplanes, rockets, major highways.)

Connecting Geography with History

Ask students to note the proximity of natural resources to cities in the West. Refer students to the physical map of the United States at the back of the book and ask: **What geographic feature connects the Hoover Dam and the Grand Canyon?** (Colorado River.) Discuss the importance of rivers and water in the settlement of the West.

Have students consider the different forms of energy represented on this map. (Oil, nuclear power, hydroelectric.) Ask them if they think all these energy sources will be on a map of the United States in 2090. **Which energy sources will decrease in importance during the next century? Which will increase?**

Have the class compare this map with the one of the United States in 1790 on pages 20–21 and with the map of the United States in 1900 on pages 220–221. Discuss what the maps show about changes in the following: transportation, technology, natural resources, ways of living, and the economy.

Ask students to devise their own symbols and create a map of what they think the United States will be like in the year 2090.

Chapter 27 Review Answers

Key Terms
1. global warming
2. protectionism
3. genetic engineering
4. NASA
5. acid rain

People to Identify
1. Lloyd Bentsen
2. Dan Quayle
3. Christa McAuliffe
4. Mikhail Gorbachev
5. Michael Dukakis
6. Deng Xiaoping

Places to Locate
1. E   4. D
2. A   5. B
3. C

Reviewing the Facts
1. Bush criticized Dukakis's support for a program that issued weekend furloughs to convicted criminals and his veto of a bill that required students to recite the Pledge of Allegiance.

2. Supreme Court rulings allowed the execution of minors and the mentally retarded, tightened abortion rights, and stated that flag-burning is constitutionally protected.

3. Attempts to fight illegal drugs raised the question of the legality of mandatory drug tests and the criminality of harming an unborn baby through a mother's drug use. The AIDS crisis raised questions over whether AIDS testing should be mandatory and who should know the results.

4. Bankers made risky loans and investments, hoping to make large profits. Instead, many went bankrupt. The federal government had to spend billions bailing out those banks.

5. The sunbelt, especially Florida, Texas, and California.

6. The Soviet Union relaxed foreign policy, withdrew from Afghanistan, and allowed the Communist regimes of Eastern Europe greater sovereignty, which greatly improved Soviet-American relations.

7. Other Eastern European nations, inspired by the expansion of political freedom in the Soviet Union, followed suit. Poland's elections were opened to non-Communist opposition. The Chinese democracy movement ended when the military crushed nonviolent protests.

8. Because U.S. goods had trouble competing with foreign-made goods.

CHAPTER 27 SUMMARY

SECTION 1: George Bush followed Ronald Reagan in office and continued many of his policies.

■ Bush beat Democratic candidate Michael Dukakis in the 1988 presidential race. Bush painted Dukakis as a liberal out of step with the views of the majority. Dukakis called Bush the candidate of the rich. From a campaign widely criticized as mean-spirited, Bush emerged a clear winner.

■ Legal issues such as abortion and free speech gained national attention during Bush's first years in office. His war on drugs sought to reduce both supply and demand. Efforts to fight AIDS raised controversy over victims' rights.

■ A government bailout of failed Savings and Loans added to the economic problems caused by the federal deficit.

SECTION 2: Fast-moving international changes are affecting life in the United States.

■ A new immigration policy in the United States opened the door to more newcomers from Latin America and Asia, making the American population even more diverse.

■ Dramatic reforms in the Communist world have led to better relations between East and West. In China, however, a democratic uprising of students in 1989 ended in a brutal government crackdown.

■ Blacks and whites in South Africa seemed to be making progress toward a freer and less segregated society.

■ An Iraqi invasion and occupation of Kuwait drew United States troops into warfare in the Middle East.

■ Economic competition with Japan led to calls for protectionism in the United States.

SECTION 3: Scientific and technological change continues at a rapid pace.

■ New inventions may improve people's quality of life in the near future.

■ Pollution poses dangers to the entire world. New ways must be found to deal with environmental problems.

■ The space program, though slowed by the *Challenger* tragedy, rebounded with the *Voyager* mission through the solar system.

KEY TERMS ●

Match each of the following terms with its correct definition.

acid rain
genetic engineering
global warming
NASA
protectionism

1. Another name for the "greenhouse effect."
2. Government barriers against free trade.
3. Changing the genetic makeup of a living organism.
4. Government agency in charge of the space program.
5. Cause of damage to lakes in Canada and the eastern United States.

PEOPLE TO IDENTIFY ●

Match each of the following people with the correct description.

Lloyd Bentsen
Deng Xiaoping
Michael Dukakis
Mikhail Gorbachev
Christa McAuliffe
Dan Quayle

1. Democratic vice-presidential candidate in 1988.
2. Republican vice-presidential candidate in 1988.
3. Teacher killed in *Challenger* disaster.
4. Soviet leader who presided over *perestroika*.
5. Democratic presidential candidate in 1988.
6. Chinese leader who ordered the 1989 crackdown on demonstrators.

670

PLACES TO LOCATE ●

Match each of the letters on the map with the places that are listed below.

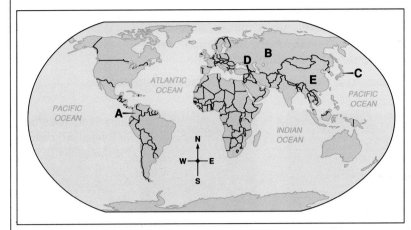

1. China
2. Colombia
3. Japan
4. Iraq
5. Soviet Union

REVIEWING THE FACTS ▲

1. What actions taken by Michael Dukakis did George Bush criticize during the 1988 campaign?
2. What controversial decisions did the Supreme Court make during the late 1980s?
3. What legal questions were raised by the issue of illegal drugs? What issues arose over the AIDS crisis?
4. Why was there a Savings & Loan crisis?
5. What areas of the United States gained most in population during the 1970s and 1980s?

6. What changes swept the Soviet Union under Mikhail Gorbachev? How did these changes affect relations between the United States and the Soviet Union?
7. How did the Soviet example affect other Communist nations? What reforms took place in Poland? How did the Chinese democracy movement end?
8. Why did support for protectionism rise in the United States?
9. How does the burning of fossil fuels harm the environment?
10. Why did the *Challenger* shuttle disaster threaten to cripple the American space program? What was the mission of *Voyager 2*?

CRITICAL THINKING SKILLS ▲

1. **MAKING A HYPOTHESIS** What factors might tend to make one American presidential campaign more negative than others?

2. **MAKING JUDGMENTS** Why did most people in the West assume until recently that no Communist nation would ever be allowed to return to a non-Communist government or a capitalist economy?

3. **PREDICTING OUTCOMES AND CONSEQUENCES** Many people now say that the cold war has officially ended. If that is the case, what are the possible consequences for the United States?

WRITING ABOUT TOPICS IN AMERICAN HISTORY ■

1. **CONNECTING WITH LITERATURE** A selection from *The Joy Luck Club* by Amy Tan appears on pages 822–824. Read it and answer the questions. Then answer the following question: How do the thoughts and actions of both Waverly and Lindo Jong reflect the cultures in which they grew up?

2. **APPLYING THEMES: GLOBAL INTERACTIONS** Examine selected newspapers and news magazines from the last year to find out the state of communism in the Soviet Union, Eastern Europe, and China over the course of the year. Then write a summary of the present political situation in those countries. Has Communist strength increased, decreased, or remained about the same in the last year?

Critical Thinking Skills
1. Campaigns that dwell on the shortcomings of opponents are more negative than those that establish a candidate's credibility and philosophy.
2. Many felt that Communist leaders would not allow the people to challenge or diminish their dictatorial powers.
3. New markets and travel opportunities may be opened. Scientific and technological exchanges may combine the assets of both countries to overcome world problems. The United States might be able to cut its defense budget and build fewer nuclear weapons.

Writing About Topics in American History
1. Students should note the ways that Lindo Jong, who grew up in China, reflects Chinese traditions: being careful about showing her feelings, for example, and being respectful and hardworking. Waverly, on the other hand, reflects the impatience, sense of freedom, and belief in self-expression of American society.
2. Students may do research on how Communist leaders are dealing with the democratization of their countries and how other parties have affected the political situation.

---

9. Burning fossil fuels creates carbon dioxide, which leads to global warming. These fuels also release particles of sulfur that combine with moisture to create acid rain.

10. The *Challenger* disaster caused a re-evaluation of the space program, exposed serious problems in NASA's operation, and challenged established beliefs concerning humans and space travel. The mission of *Voyager 2* was to chart the outer reaches of our solar system.

Chapter Review exercises are keyed for student abilities:
● = Basic
▲ = Average
■ = Average/Advanced

UNIT 9: American Mosaic

★ *A Multicultural Perspective* ★

The population of the United States is now more diverse than ever. African Americans, Hispanic Americans, Asian Americans, and Arab Americans are among the many increasingly visible cultural groups that make up a nation of immigrants.

Philip Habib (right), the son of Lebanese grocery-store owners, grew up in Brooklyn, New York. After joining the Army in World War II, he began a long diplomatic career. Habib's greatest success came when he helped President Carter negotiate the Camp David Accords between Egypt and Israel in 1977.

Cuban-born **Roberto Goizueta** (left) came to the United States in 1950 at age eighteen. After receiving a degree in chemical engineering, he went to work for the Coca Cola corporation. For the next 26 years, Goizueta climbed Coke's corporate ladder and in 1980 became the company's chairman and chief executive. Goizueta's bilingualism and Hispanic background proved to be an asset in a company that does two-thirds of its business outside the United States.

A native of India, **Ved Mehta** (right) became blind from meningitis when he was three years old. He attended a school for blind children in Bombay, but in 1947 war came and Mehta's family lost their home and had to flee for their lives. Mehta traveled to the Arkansas School for the Blind in Little Rock and later attended college in California. In 1957 he published an autobiography and later joined the *New Yorker* magazine as a writer. Since then, Mehta has published many works which tell of his experiences of loss of sight, of family and country, and of the new home he found in the United States.

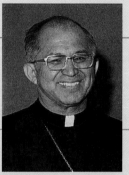

Patrick Flores (right) grew up in a family of nine children who worked alongside their parents as migrant farm laborers in South Texas. When the family settled in Pearland, Flores became involved in a fight led by a Hispanic priest to integrate the town's schools. This experience helped convince Flores to become a priest and fight for social justice. In 1970 he became the first Mexican American bishop, and was later named Archbishop of San Antonio.

In 1986 **Ben Nighthorse Campbell** (left) of the North Cheyenne tribe became the eighth Native American to serve in Congress. As a representative from Colorado, Campbell worked to keep scarce water resources available. Campbell's varied interests include horse breeding and judo, for which he won an Olympic gold medal in 1964.

Maya Ying Lin (right), a Chinese American architecture student, gained national attention after she won a contest to design a memorial to veterans of the Vietnam War. Despite controversy over the design, the Vietnam Memorial is now considered one of the most moving monuments in the nation. Lin later designed a highly regarded memorial to the civil rights movement which stands in front of the Southern Poverty Law Center in Montgomery, Alabama.

Marva Collins (left) became America's best-known teacher in the early 1980s for her work with some of the nation's least privileged students. Collins founded her own school, where she worked with children from Chicago's inner city. Chiefly through her own forceful personality, she improved their reading skills and interested them in classics of literature. According to Collins, "When I see children who are going to fail, when I see a sixteen-year-old kid who can't read . . . those things make me unhappy. I'm not really in this life to buy a lot of things for myself. I ask the children, 'If you died, what would you like the newspapers to say?'"

Luis Valdez (left) changed schools often as his family moved around California in search of farm work. One thing that remained constant was Valdez's love of theater. In the 1960s, he began writing plays whose themes included civil rights issues. Valdez organized a theater group called El Teatro Campesino that performed on college campuses and helped the cause of Cesar Chavez and the United Farm Workers. Valdez later directed *La Bamba,* a 1987 film about Mexican American rock star Ritchie Valens.

The diversity of her influences is one factor that has helped propel singer **Linda Ronstadt** (above) to the top of the music world. Her records include songs from the worlds of folk, country, rock, and gospel music. Ronstadt, who is of Mexican and German descent, grew up in a musical household. Her mother played the ukulele and her father sang Mexican folk songs. Later in her career, she returned to her roots and recorded a highly successful album of songs in Spanish, *Canciones de mi Padre* (Songs of My Father).

In the years between 1980 and 1990 almost half of all legal immigrants to the United States—45 percent—came from Asia. Latin American immigrants made up 35 percent, Europeans and Canadians were 14 percent, and Africans and others were 4 percent of the flood of 5.7 million immigrants who arrived in the decade.

(A Hispanic priest who led a fight to integrate the schools in Flores's community.) *In what way did Luis Valdez use drama to express the aspirations of the Mexican American community?* (He wrote plays with civil rights themes; he organized El Teatro Campesino, which lent support to Cesar Chavez and the United Farm Workers; and he directed the film *La Bamba.*)

Connecting with Art
Tell students that a sculpture of soldiers of various backgrounds was added to the Vietnam Memorial site to answer criticism that the monument itself was too stark and abstract. Ask students who may have visited the memorial to describe their response to it.

Have interested students design a memorial to their community's Vietnam veterans. Monuments should take into account the diverse backgrounds of the soldiers and nurses who participated in the war. **LEP**

Background
Discuss with students the qualities that make a teacher truly great. Have them consider how Marva Collins reflects those qualities. (Students should consider her forceful personality; her high expectations for children; her ability to encourage self-esteem in her students; and her emphasis on the value of knowledge for its own sake, rather than for the sake of material goals.)

Geographic Themes: Movement
Have students make a bar graph of immigration to the United States, showing the country of origin of the 5.7 million immigrants to the country between the years 1980 and 1990. The graph should show the percentage of immigrants from Asia, Latin America, Europe and Canada, and other countries.

Discuss with students whether immigration quotas based on country of origin are necessary or appropriate. Students might suggest how the United States can continue to welcome people who bring fresh ideas and vitality to American society while still maintaining a high standard of living for all U.S. citizens.

Historians' Corner

Vocabulary Preview

Be sure students understand the following terms: *proscribed*—Prohibited. *decibel*—Unit used to describe noise levels. *scope*—Area covered by a subject.

Analyzing Historical Issues

In these selections, two historians probe for the reality behind the American ideal of equality. Ronald Takaki points out that nonwhites have, in the past, been denied the right to immigrate, become citizens, or vote. John Hope Franklin addresses the problem of nonwhite Americans in assimilating and achieving economic advancement.

What social problems might these historians foresee for the United States in the 1990s?

Critical Thinking Answers

1. Nonwhites have received unequal treatment, especially Mexican Americans, Native Americans, African Americans, and Puerto Ricans.

2. Takaki challenges the idea that America's doors are open to all.

3. Naturalization laws allowed Europeans to become citizens easily but denied citizenship to other races. Even when nonwhites could become citizens, they were often denied the right to vote.

4. Differences in physical appearance, language, religion, and social values.

HISTORIANS' CORNER

Perspectives on Pluralism

Many historians agree that since the 1960s, Americans have become more conscious of their distinctive racial, cultural, and ethnic backgrounds. This awareness, along with increased immigration, has raised new questions about diversity and equality, and about ethnic and racial patterns in American history. These excerpts present some of these points of view about our pluralistic society.

Ronald Takaki

Study of the history of citizenship and suffrage disclosed a racial and exclusionist pattern. For 162 years the Naturalization Law, while allowing various European or "white" ethnic groups to enter the United States and acquire citizenship, specifically denied citizenship to other groups on a racial basis. . . .

But what happened to nonwhite citizens? Did they have "equal" rights, particularly the right of suffrage? Citizenship did not necessarily carry this right, for states determined the requirements for voting. A review of this history reveals a basic political inequality between white citizens and nonwhite citizens. . . .

This difference . . . may . . . be seen in the experiences of Native Americans. While the Treaty of Guadalupe-Hidalgo had offered United States citizenship to Mexicans living within its acquired territories, the 1849 Constitution of California granted the right of suffrage only to every "white" male citizen of the United States and only to every "white" male citizen of Mexico who had elected to become a United States citizen.

A color line, in short, had been drawn for the granting of suffrage to American citizens in California. Native Americans were also proscribed politically in other states.

From Ronald Takaki, "Reflections on Racial Patterns in America: An Historical Perspective" from *Ethnicity and Public Policy*, edited by Winston A. Van Horne and Thomas V. Tonneson. Copyright © 1982 by the Board of Regents, University of Wisconsin System. Reprinted by permission of the University of Wisconsin System Ethnic Studies Coordinating Committee.

John Hope Franklin

It has become fashionable in the past three or four decades for various hyphenated Americans [white ethnic groups, such as Irish-Americans] to emphasize the distinctive aspects of their respective cultures—as though these groups have been so successfully and securely assimilated that they can afford to look back to their origins and pay homage to their languages, histories, and the special features of their culture. This new way of looking at themselves and their past has become a luxury no less important than their expensive homes and automobiles.

These same decades witnessed a . . . rise in the decibels of protest and in the crusade for Native Americans, black Americans, Puerto Ricans, and Mexican Americans. It was as though this was *not* the land of room enough and that the assimilation of the others had been accomplished at their expense. These cries of anguish and these demands for attention to their problems serve as a reminder that the very term *assimilability* is one that suggests there are problems that lie outside its scope. These are the problems of those who have not been assimilated.

From John Hope Franklin, "The Land of Room Enough." Reprinted by permission of *Daedalus*, Journal of the American Academy of Arts and Sciences, Spring, 1981, Cambridge, Massachusetts.

Critical Thinking

1. According to both these historians, what groups have received unequal treatment in American society?

2. What assumptions about the acceptance of new groups into American society does Takaki challenge?

3. What contradictory American attitudes does Takaki identify?

4. What factors, do you think, might make it harder for one group to be "assimilated" than another?

Ronald Takaki   (1939–   ) is a social historian who teaches ethnic studies at the University of California, Berkeley.

John Hope Franklin (1915–   ) taught at Duke University and served as a member of the research team whose work led to *Brown v. Board of Education*.

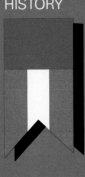

History of the United States in Perspective

At the beginning of *History of the United States*, the authors introduced you to the book's themes—seven key stories that have unfolded over the course of American history. Throughout your study of American history, you have encountered these themes again and again. Now it is time to review the themes. The following pages contain brief essays and timelines charting the progression of each theme. They will help you review some of the material you covered during the course of the year. They can also serve as starting points for you to consider the United States' future. For one of the chief values of studying history is to understand how the past shapes the future—*your* future.

CONTENTS

675

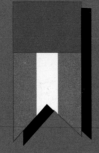

Global Interactions

The United States has always been influenced by events beyond its borders. The American people themselves are the best proof of this. Americans of every ethnic and racial group can point to ancestors who came from other lands. The nation they built reflects this diversity—not merely in its culture, but in the values and political ideas on which it is based.

Still, the American people have been ambivalent about the outside world. George Washington, fearful for the survival of the young republic, urged Americans to pursue economic relations with other nations but to limit political ties. This advice set the tone for American foreign policy for 150 years. Yet even during those years of what some called "isolation," American economic expansion led to political entanglements. (Latin America is one example.) And in the 1900s the United States has twice entered world wars as part of an alliance. American goals in these wars included not just self-defense but also the spread of freedom abroad.

The United States of the 1990s is a global power, with countless ties to other nations. Current world trends suggest that these ties will only increase. But will the United States continue its role of world leadership, promoting the spread of its values around the world? Or will it concentrate on narrower issues of self-interest? These questions, as old as this nation, must be faced by every new generation of Americans.

1492	Christopher Columbus reaches the Americas
1775	American Revolution begins
1823	Monroe Doctrine issued
1846	War with Mexico begins
1898	Spanish-American War
1899	Open Door Policy proposed
1917	United States enters World War I
1919	Senate rejects Treaty of Versailles
1941	United States enters World War II
1945	United States joins United Nations
1947	Truman Doctrine and Marshall Plan announced
1949	United States joins NATO
1950	Korean War begins
1961	Peace Corps founded
1965	Buildup of American troops in Vietnam
1972	Détente with China and Soviet Union
1973	American withdrawal from Vietnam
1983	United States invades Grenada
1988	U.S.-Canada trade pact signed
1989	Reform movements sweep through Eastern Europe
1990	Buildup of American forces in Middle East

Constitutional Government

The American system of government, a blend of political theory and experience, is both stable and flexible. The ideas underlying American democracy were born in Europe. They gained strength in the American colonies, eventually producing a revolution in the name of self-government. The Articles of Confederation proved unable to cope with the nation's problems. In 1787 the Constitutional Convention was called in Philadelphia to set forth the form of government the United States enjoys today.

Over the past two centuries the federal government has grown tremendously in size and power. This growth reflects the nation's expansion and a broadened concept of the role of government. It also shows one effect of major crises. The Civil War, both world wars, and the Great Depression posed challenges that were met by increased federal power.

While new times have produced new changes, the nation's stability depends on a balance among the parts of government. Power remains divided between the federal and state governments. Power within the federal government is divided among its three branches. Maintaining this balance in the midst of rapid change is difficult. How can we ensure the health of state government at a time when so many issues can be handled only by the federal government? How do we keep the President from gaining a monopoly over foreign policy, or the courts from becoming lawmakers instead of judges? Finally, how do we prevent the government from becoming so balanced that it cannot act decisively? Such questions have no easy answers—not in Philadelphia in 1787, and not today.

1619 House of Burgesses assembles

1639 Fundamental Orders of Connecticut written

1774 First Continental Congress meets

1776 Declaration of Independence

1781 Articles of Confederation

1787 Constitutional Convention meets

1788 Constitution ratified

1791 Bill of Rights amends Constitution

1803 *Marbury v. Madison* establishes judicial review

1865 Union victory in Civil War asserts power of federal government

1913 Sixteenth Amendment establishes income tax

1919 Prohibition amendment ratified

1933 New Deal expands role of federal government

1937 Roosevelt's court-packing scheme rejected

1953 Earl Warren named Chief Justice; Supreme Court takes active role

1954 Senate censures Joseph McCarthy

1974 Watergate scandal leads to Nixon resignation

1986 Iran-contra affair

1989 Bush proposes constitutional amendment banning flag-burning

Expanding Democracy

Throughout American history—and world history, to some extent—the definition of liberty has steadily broadened. In England, a historic step toward liberty was taken with the signing of the Magna Carta in 1215. Parliament solidified its power over the monarchy in the Glorious Revolution of 1688.

American colonists shared this tradition of limits on government power. Conditions in America, such as the abundance of land on the frontier, encouraged the ideas of equality and self-government. The Great Awakening of the 1740s reinforced the notion of religious liberty.

The Bill of Rights laid out the fundamental rights of American citizens. But many Americans were denied such rights. Black slaves, for example, had no rights at all. The struggle for equal rights for black Americans began with the abolitionist movement. It continued through the Civil War and Reconstruction, and reached a partial triumph with the civil rights movement of the 1960s. Women too had long been denied political rights. They won the vote in 1920 and, following World War II, gained new economic power and independence. The ending of property qualifications for voting and, later, the lowering of the voting age through the 26th Amendment further expanded voting rights.

The United States has also witnessed an enduring conflict between the rights of the individual and those of society. Freedom of speech in particular has sparked controversies throughout American history, in peacetime as well as during war. This basic conflict is bound to continue, as will the efforts of various groups to overcome discrimination.

1620	Mayflower Compact
1791	Bill of Rights amends Constitution
1848	Women's rights convention at Seneca Falls
1863	Emancipation Proclamation
1865	Thirteenth Amendment abolishes slavery
1868	Fourteenth Amendment defines citizenship
1870	Fifteenth Amendment grants voting rights to black men
1920	Nineteenth Amendment gives women the vote
1924	American Indians gain citizenship
1964	Civil Rights Act of 1964
1964	24th Amendment prohibits poll tax
1965	Voting Rights Act of 1965
1971	26th Amendment lowers voting age to 18
1984	Geraldine Ferraro becomes first female member of major-party ticket

Economic Development

Economic success has played a critical role in American history. The promise of land and trade drew many early settlers to the American colonies. The robust economic health of those colonies strengthened American assertiveness, leading to disagreement with Great Britain over tax policy. Both of these helped cause the American Revolution.

During the 1800s, economic motives lay at the heart of the United States' westward expansion. The 1800s was also a time of dramatic economic changes. The Industrial Revolution, begun in Britain, spread through the United States during the second half of the nineteenth century. These decades saw the rise of such industries as steel and railroads. Federal and state governments aided the growth of industry. Later they started to regulate industry to protect small businesses and consumers.

By 1945 the United States was far and away the world's greatest economic power. Inventions, an abundance of natural resources, and the spirit of free enterprise had all played a role. But problems were to come. Stagflation during the 1970s was followed by skyrocketing budget and trade deficits in the 1980s. Millions were trapped in poverty, seemingly without hope of escape. Can the United States survive as a democratic nation if the promise of economic success dies? That question, asked seriously during the Great Depression, may return to haunt American leaders.

1606	The Virginia Company receives charter to build settlement at Jamestown
1612	First tobacco planted in Virginia
1776	Book by Adam Smith supports private enterprise
1793	Eli Whitney invents cotton gin
1849	Gold rush in California
c. 1850	Bessemer process discovered
1863	National Banking Act
1867	National Grange founded
1869	First transcontinental railroad completed
1883	Brooklyn Bridge completed
1887	Interstate Commerce Act
1890	Sherman Antitrust Act
1901	United States Steel Corporation formed
1913	Henry Ford produces cars on assembly line
1929	Great Depression begins
1933	Roosevelt's New Deal passed by Congress
1947	Marshall Plan announced
1964	Johnson launches Great Society
1981	Congress passes Reagan's economic program
1989	Savings and Loan crisis brought on by widespread bank failures

Teaching the Themes: Economic Development

The following list provides chapter and page references for each of the events listed under the theme of economic development. It may prove helpful for teachers wishing to emphasize this theme in classroom discussion.

Pluralistic Society

The United States is, in John F. Kennedy's words, a "nation of immigrants." From the beginning of the nation's history, people have come to its shores from distant lands. The result has been a nation distinguished by its diverse population.

But diversity requires tolerance, and the United States has not always been a tolerant land. Slavery was not ended until 1865, and many decades passed before blacks were guaranteed political equality. Social equality remains elusive. Anti-immigrant feeling—a result of racism and fear of competition from immigrant labor—has also surfaced in the United States.

Nevertheless, the United States is still a haven for people from all corners of the world. The Statue of Liberty remains a potent symbol, of economic opportunity as well as liberty. Preserving the promise of economic opportunity will be a challenge for American society. The United States is no longer an undeveloped land with an open frontier, but a mature society where success depends more and more on advanced skills and training. Therefore, making a pluralistic society work will require a common effort by government and citizens. We must ensure that all Americans receive equal protection under the laws, and that all Americans have an equal chance of sharing in the nation's prosperity.

1619	Dutch bring first Africans to American mainland
1654	First Jews settle in New York
1865	Slavery abolished
1882	Chinese Exclusion Act
1887	Dawes Act passed
1892	Immigration center opens on Ellis Island
1909	NAACP formed
1917	Espionage Act enforces loyalty
1924	Johnson-Reed Act limits immigration
1942	Internment of Japanese Americans begins
1948	Truman bans segregation in armed forces
1954	Supreme Court outlaws public school segregation
1962	Cesar Chavez begins organizing farm workers
1965	Immigration quota system ended
1968	Kerner Commission warns of social inequalities
1968	Violence mars Democratic National Convention in Chicago
1986	Immigration Reform and Control Act passed
1987	Emergency Homeless Act passed
1989	First Cuban American elected to Congress
1989	Virginia elects nation's first African American governor

American Culture

The culture of the United States, like that of every nation, mirrors the social and political forces that have shaped the nation. American culture reflects both the pluralism of its society and the democratic values of its system of government.

An important part of American pluralism has been the many different religious beliefs that have coexisted in this nation. Religion has aided the development of the United States in countless ways. It provided a structure and purpose for Puritan society. It energized reform movements, from abolitionism to temperance to civil rights. It was for immigrants both a source of security and a family value that could be transplanted to America.

Another sign of this nation's pluralistic culture is the variety of its artistic achievement. Such variety reflects not only ethnic diversity but also the individual liberty that American artists enjoy.

The American commitment to individual liberty has influenced American culture in other ways. One is this nation's rich tradition of statements on liberty—the Declaration of Independence, the Emancipation Proclamation, the speeches of Martin Luther King, Jr. Another is the importance Americans have placed on education, the foundation of a lasting democracy. Education strengthens pluralism by transmitting shared ideals; it strengthens democracy by helping young Americans understand their duties as citizens of a free society.

c. 1740	First Great Awakening
c. 1800	Second Great Awakening
1814	Francis Scott Key writes "The Star-Spangled Banner"
1876	*The Adventures of Tom Sawyer* published
1881	Tuskegee Institute established
1886	Statue of Liberty dedicated
1893	Turner thesis published
1893	Chicago World's Fair
1902	*The Virginian* published
1903	First World Series played
1904	*The Shame of the Cities* published
1920	First radio station goes on the air
1925	*The Great Gatsby* published
1927	First movie with sound
1954	Movie *The Wild One* portrays rebellious youth
1963	Martin Luther King, Jr.'s, "I Have a Dream" speech
1969	Woodstock Festival
c. 1980	"Televangelism" achieves new prominence
1987	Bicentennial of the Constitution

Geography

Teaching the Themes: Geography

The following list provides chapter and page references for each of the events listed under the theme of geography. It may prove helpful for teachers wishing to emphasize this theme in classroom discussion.

The land and its resources have always played a pivotal role in American history. They not only drew immigrants to the United States but also provided a focus for American energies. Throughout the 1800s, the acquisition, exploration, and settlement of the western frontier were important stories. Westward expansion affected the rest of the nation as well. The land supplied food to the nation's cities and yielded raw materials for its factories.

Before the 1800s were over, concern had already begun to grow over the need to protect the land. In 1872 Congress made Yellowstone the first national park. This was only a beginning. Encouraged by the efforts of conservationists such as John Muir, Theodore Roosevelt set aside millions of acres of federal land. He also used the presidency to make conservation a national issue. Later, federally funded programs, such as the Tennessee Valley Authority, also became involved in conservation efforts.

Pollution is the dominant environmental issue currently facing the United States. Automobiles and heavy industry are largely to blame, though practically all Americans have become careless and wasteful. The creation of the Environmental Protection Agency in 1970 marked the federal government's commitment to dealing with pollution. But that commitment was weakened during the 1980s. Meanwhile, problems like the greenhouse effect only make the situation worse. All Americans must come to realize that protecting their nation's natural beauty is a necessity, not a luxury.

1492	Columbus reaches the Americas
1803	Louisiana Purchase
1804	Lewis and Clark expedition
1825	Erie Canal completed
1848	Mexico cedes territories to United States
1867	Alaska purchased from Russia
1872	Yellowstone named first national park
1891	Forest Reserve Act passed
1892	John Muir establishes Sierra Club
1898	Hawaii annexed
1916	National Park Service created
1933	Tennessee Valley Authority created
c. 1935	Dust Bowl ravages Plains
1942	Grand Coulee Dam completed
1956	Highway Act of 1956 finances building of highway system
1970	Environmental Protection Agency created
1970	First Earth Day
1979	Nuclear accident at Three Mile Island
1990	Bush signs new Clean Air Act

Reference Section

683

Government and Citizenship

684

Civics Handbook

"Proclaim liberty throughout the land unto all the inhabitants thereof." This inscription on the Liberty Bell in Philadelphia is an enduring reminder of the American belief in the right of free people to govern themselves. The Constitution of the United States expresses this belief in the language of government—in its powers, in its laws, and in the rights it guarantees. The following pages will help you learn more about the American system of government, and about the rights and responsibilities of citizens of our nation.

Learning how their government operates is a critical task for young Americans—tomorrow's voters and leaders. **CONSTITUTIONAL HERITAGE** Why is it especially important for citizens of a free society to understand the workings of their government?

CIVICS HANDBOOK **685**

CIVICS HANDBOOK
Introduction
In recent years, Americans from all walks of life have expressed dismay at the state of civic literacy among the nation's students. How serious a problem this is becomes clear in "A Generation Adrift," a 1990 publication of the Foundation for Teaching Economics and the Constitutional Rights Foundation. This article details the scope of civic ignorance among America's children and the potential dangers this presents for our future. To address this problem, the above foundations are encouraging the development and teaching of a curriculum designed "to prepare students for full civic participation in the world of the twenty-first century."

How do we prepare students for the next century? According to "A Generation Adrift," we need to help students understand government at all levels; we need to help students look at civic issues from a global perspective; we need to make the civics curriculum relevant to a changing student population; and we need to use the technological innovations available to us in ways that will increase civic understanding and participation. It is with these goals in mind that this Civics Handbook has been developed. The teaching strategies you will find in the margins are designed to augment and promote these civic literacy goals.

For a copy of "A Generation Adrift," write to the Foundation for Teaching Economics, 55 Kearny Street, Suite 1000, San Francisco, CA 94108, or write the Constitutional Rights Foundation, 601 S. Kingsley Drive, Los Angeles, CA 90005.

Who Is an American Citizen?

The richness of American life is due in large part to the different peoples who make up this nation's citizenry. Since the arrival of Europeans and Africans in the sixteenth century, millions more have come from all over the world to help America grow and prosper. All citizens enjoy the special privileges of living in a nation whose government and society is based on democratic principles. In return, citizens must take responsibility for preserving these principles through such means as paying taxes, serving on juries, and voting.

Defining Citizenship

The Fourteenth Amendment, ratified in 1868, gave America its first definition of citizenship: "All persons born or naturalized in the United States, and subject to the juris-diction thereof, are citizens of the United States and of the State wherein they reside." This means that anyone born or naturalized in the United States is an American citizen. In other words, if you were born in any of the 50 states or in any United States territory, you are a citizen. You are also a citizen if you were born in a foreign country but both your parents were American citizens.

Naturalization

Those who do not become citizens by birth may gain citizenship through a process called **naturalization**. The requirements are five years of residence in the United States (three years if married to an American citizen), the ability to read, write, and speak English, and an understanding of American government and history.

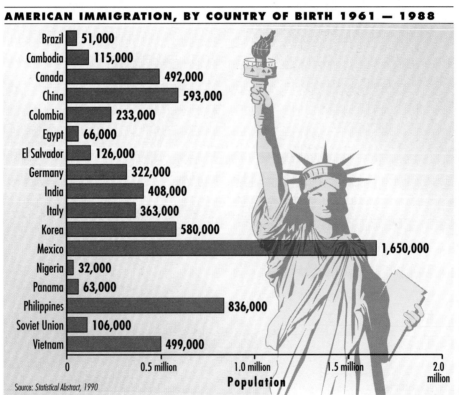

AMERICAN IMMIGRATION, BY COUNTRY OF BIRTH 1961 — 1988

Brazil	51,000
Cambodia	115,000
Canada	492,000
China	593,000
Colombia	233,000
Egypt	66,000
El Salvador	126,000
Germany	322,000
India	408,000
Italy	363,000
Korea	580,000
Mexico	1,650,000
Nigeria	32,000
Panama	63,000
Philippines	836,000
Soviet Union	106,000
Vietnam	499,000

Population (0 — 2.0 million)

Source: *Statistical Abstract, 1990*

CHART SKILLS

This chart shows, for the years 1961–1988, the number of immigrants to the United States from various nations. From which nation did the greatest number of immigrants come? Once they have arrived in the United States, immigrants gain citizenship through the process of naturalization. **CRITICAL THINKING** Why are non-citizens required to have an understanding of American government and history before gaining citizenship?

686 CIVICS HANDBOOK

Rights and Responsibilities of Citizens

The American government guarantees its citizens fundamental rights. These guarantees are found in the Constitution, the Bill of Rights, and other amendments to the Constitution. Along with these rights, however, come responsibilities. When Americans carry out their responsibilities, they help to preserve their freedom and the American system of government.

The rights and responsibilities of citizenship unite Americans of all ages and backgrounds. Citizens' basic rights include freedom of speech, freedom of assembly, and freedom of religion. **CITIZENSHIP** What are some of Americans' basic responsibilities?

The Rights of Citizens

Every member of society is entitled to **civil rights**—the rights of a citizen. The Constitution and laws passed by Congress spell out many of these rights. They include freedom of speech, freedom of assembly (the right to meet with others peacefully for political or other purposes), freedom of the press, and freedom of religion. Others include the right to a fair trial and protection against illegal searches.

Civil rights also means that citizens are equal under the law. That is, each person's vote counts equally, and the government does not discriminate against certain individuals or groups. In a broader sense, citizens are also entitled to equal opportunity. That is, each citizen has an equal chance to develop his or her capabilities without discrimination.

Responsibilities of a Good Citizen

In addition to rights, citizens also have responsibilities. There are certain responsibilities that the government requires from each citizen. These include paying taxes, defending the country, and obeying the laws.

A good citizen has many other duties. One of these is participating in government. There are many ways to participate. One of the most important ways is by voting. When you turn eighteen, you will be given that right. Until then, there are many other ways you can effectively participate in government. Working for a political party, or writing your member of Congress are good examples.

Voting is the most obvious way for citizens to participate in the process of government. Americans over the age of eighteen are entitled to vote. HISTORY How have the rules regarding voter eligibility changed over the course of American history?

What are some other characteristics of a good citizen? One is to be well-informed on important issues. This can be accomplished by regularly reading a newspaper or watching the news on television. Another is to respect people who may have a different way of life than you. Our nation is filled with citizens who have grown up in different cultures and who speak different languages. Understanding that there is no one "correct" cultural background is the mark of a good citizen. A third characteristic is helping your community. Examples include recycling paper and other products or volunteering at a local hospital. There are many other qualities of citizenship that may come to your mind. By training to be an effective citizen, you will help to maintain the democratic values that this country is based upon.

Good citizens make an effort to keep up with the fast pace of events in their community and around the world. Newspapers and television are popular means of getting the news. GLOBAL AWARENESS What have been some of the biggest headlines in world events during the past year?

688 CIVICS HANDBOOK

Volunteering For a Cause

Suppose for a moment that you played basketball for your junior high school. A month before school was to begin, the school superintendent announced that the only way the school could afford to keep its sports programs would be if the people of the community donated a total of $10,000. Can you picture *yourself* volunteering, that is, working for no pay, to help raise the money? Would you sign a petition supporting the cause? Would you write letters to other citizens asking for their help? Would you go door-to-door to raise funds?

These are questions that may not be easy to answer without actually being in that type of situation. They may, however, help you to understand how and why many citizens become involved with community issues.

Small Volunteer Groups

There are thousands of small volunteer groups in the United States. Sometimes they have been in existence for years; other times they are formed for a specific purpose, such as in the example above. Examples of small groups include volunteer firefighters, hospital volunteers, and crossing-guard volunteers. Newspapers or your city hall are good sources of information about such local groups.

Large Volunteer Groups

Large national volunteer organizations are plentiful as well. They include groups ranging from the American Red Cross to the Little League. Other well-known groups include the League of Women Voters, the American Society for the Prevention of Cruelty to Animals, and the Girl Scouts. Your school or local library has information on those groups.

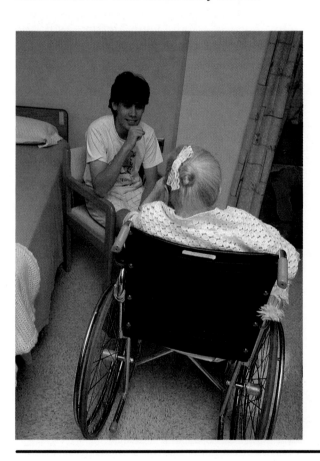

Hospitals benefit greatly from the dedication of volunteer workers. At left, a volunteer chats with a patient. Above, volunteers known as candy stripers (because of their colorful uniforms) help with office tasks. **PARTICIPATION** How do volunteers benefit from their efforts?

Expressing Your Political Opinions

One morning while listening to the news on the radio, you hear your member of Congress speaking in support of a bill that would cut one half of the summer jobs in your community. After a minute you realize that the job you had lined up for the summer could be included in those cuts! You decide at that moment to let your representative know that you oppose the bill. How should you go about voicing your opposition?

Writing an Opinion Letter

The right to express your opinion about local, state, or national issues is one of the important rights you have as a citizen of a democracy. One of the ways to do this is by writing an opinion letter to a public official. The official may be the mayor of your town or your member of Congress. These officials welcome opinion letters, for it allows them to remain in touch with those they represent.

Some Writing Guidelines

There are a few things to keep in mind when writing to a public official:

- **Be sure of what you want to say.** Look into the issue thoroughly and state your opinion thoughtfully.

- **Write your opinions briefly and clearly.** Three or four well-written paragraphs are more effective than several long pages that make the same point.

- **Write your letter in the correct format.** It should follow the format of a proper business letter. Guidelines for business letters can be found in your school or local library.

A letter following these guidelines will help you clearly state your point. It will also help ensure that your letter will be read—and that your opinion will be heard.

Kika de la Garza, a member of the House of Representatives, reads through his mail in his Washington, D.C., office. Elected officials pay careful attention to letters written by the people they represent. POLITICS Why might letters to public officials not always give an accurate picture of public attitudes?

Photo Caption Answer
Often, only those people who feel very strongly about an issue write letters about that issue. On other occasions, special interest groups may orchestrate the writing of large numbers of letters.

Voter's Handbook

When you turn 18 you become entitled to one of the great privileges and responsibilities of American citizenship—the right to vote.

Voting allows you to participate in American government. It gives you a voice in determining the kind of city, county, state, and nation you live in.

This *Voter's Handbook* gives you the information you need to be ready to vote on the next election day.

Participating in Government
Ask students to interview four adults of voting age to find out why they think voting is or is not important. Have students summarize their findings and present them to the class. Encourage students to look for any trends or patterns which may appear in the responses.

Constitutional Heritage

Remind students that the 26th Amendment is not the only amendment that deals with voting rights. Tell them that the 15th, 19th, 23rd, and 24th Amendments increased the number of Americans who were eligible to vote. *How did each of these amendments expand voting rights?* (The 15th Amendment gave African Americans the right to vote; the 19th Amendment gave women the right to vote; the 23rd Amendment gave the residents of Washington, D.C., the right to vote for President and Vice President; the 24th Amendment abolished poll taxes.)

Analyzing Controversial Issues

Tell students that some people have suggested making voting mandatory in order to increase voter turnout. Those who do not vote would be fined. Divide the class into two groups to debate this issue.

Who Can Vote?

To vote in the United States, you must be:
1. an American citizen
2. at least 18 years old

If you meet these two requirements (and are not a convicted felon or legally insane), your right to vote cannot be taken away, regardless of your race, sex, religion, national origin, or income. The 26th Amendment, ratified in 1971, lowered the voting age to 18 in both federal and state elections.

Are you eligible to vote now?

When will you be?

GRAPH SKILLS This graph shows that younger American voters have a lower turnout at the polls than all eligible voters. **CRITICAL THINKING** What factors might explain this?

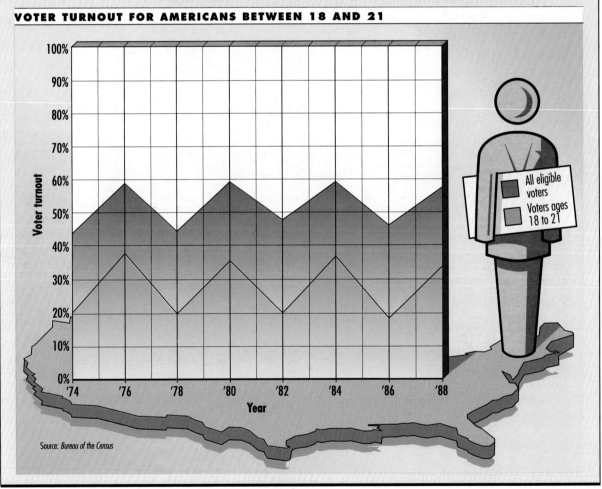

VOTER TURNOUT FOR AMERICANS BETWEEN 18 AND 21

All eligible voters

Voters ages 18 to 21

Source: *Bureau of the Census*

Graph Skills Answer
One possible factor is that young people tend to be more mobile and may therefore fail to meet residency requirements.

How Do You Register to Vote?

In every state except North Dakota you must register to vote. Registration is a simple procedure intended to ensure honest elections. Registration forms are easy to fill out. You usually need to provide little more than your name and address. Some states ask you to declare which political party you belong to.

In most states you can register at a nearby government office, such as a town or municipal hall. Sometimes registration booths are set up in public places such as shopping centers and supermarkets. Some states allow you to register by mail. Be prepared to show proof of your age (such as a birth certificate) and your address.

The detailed requirements for registering to vote vary considerably from state to state. In most states you must register a certain number of days before the election is held. To ensure that voters are knowledgeable about local issues, many states have a minimum residency requirement, usually around 30 days. (The details for registering to vote in each state are shown in the table on the next page.)

Where can you register to vote?

A SAMPLE VOTER REGISTRATION FORM In areas where more than 10 percent of voters speak a language other than English, election materials are printed in several languages.

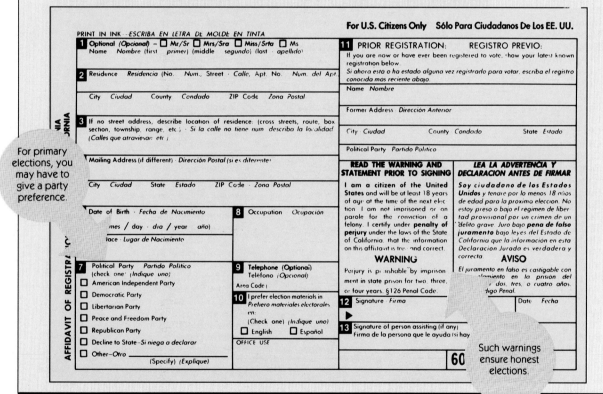

For primary elections, you may have to give a party preference.

Such warnings ensure honest elections.

Civic Values

Tell students that after the 1984 election, 31 percent of those who did not vote gave "not registered" as the reason, according to a public opinion poll. Some people believe that the government should take the initiative by sending workers door-to-door to register voters. Others believe that more people would register if the requirements for registration were eased. For example, they recommend allowing voters in all states to register by mail. *What are the advantages and disadvantages of each of these proposals?* (Advantages include more people registered and more likely to vote; by allowing people to register by mail, fewer registration workers would be needed. Disadvantages include the cost of door-to-door registration and registration by mail could result in voter fraud.) *Which groups of voters would benefit the most from these proposals?* (People who are home-bound such as the elderly or the handicapped; people who work during the hours the registration facilities are open; people who lack the transportation to get to a registration facility.)

Participating in Government

Have students call their local Board of Elections to find out where citizens in their area must go to register to vote and when the registration facility is open.

What Are the Requirements for Registration?

STATE	How long before the election must I register?	What is the residency requirement?	Must I declare party preference for the primaries?[1]	Is there registration by mail?
Alabama	10 days	none	yes; at the polls	no
Alaska	30 days	30 days	no; blanket primary	yes
Arizona	50 days	50 days	yes; at registration	no
Arkansas	20 days	none	yes; at the polls	no
California	29 days	none	yes; at registration	yes
Colorado	25 days	32 days	yes; at registration	no
Connecticut	21 days/14 days[2]	none	yes; at registration	yes
Delaware	21 days[3]	none	yes; at registration	no
Florida	30 days	none	yes; at registration	no
Georgia	30 days	none	yes; at the polls	no
Hawaii	30 days	none	yes; at the polls	yes
Idaho	10 days[4]	30 days	yes; at the polls	no
Illinois	28 days	30 days	yes; at the polls	no
Indiana	29 days	30 days	yes; at the polls	no
Iowa	10 days	none	yes; at the polls	yes
Kansas	20 days	20 days	yes; at the polls	yes
Kentucky	30 days	30 days	yes; at registration	yes
Louisiana	24 days/30 days[2]	none	no; blanket primary	no
Maine	election day	none	yes; at the polls	yes
Maryland	29 days	none	yes; at registration	yes
Massachusetts	28 days	none	yes; at the polls	no
Michigan	30 days	30 days	yes; at the polls	no
Minnesota	election day	20 days	yes; at the polls	yes
Mississippi	30 days	30 days	yes; at the polls	no
Missouri	28 days	none	yes; at the polls	yes
Montana	30 days	30 days	yes; at the polls	yes
Nebraska	10 days	none	yes; at registration	no
Nevada	30 days	30 days	yes; at registration	no
New Hampshire	10 days	10 days	yes; at registration	no
New Jersey	30 days	30 days	yes; at the polls	yes
New Mexico	28 days	none	yes; at registration	no
New York	30 days	30 days	yes; at registration	yes
North Carolina	21 business days	30 days	yes; at registration	no
North Dakota	no registration	none	yes; at the polls	—
Ohio	30 days	30 days	yes; at the polls	yes
Oklahoma	10 days	none	yes; at registration	no
Oregon	20 days	20 days	yes; at registration	yes
Pennsylvania	30 days	30 days	yes; at registration	yes
Rhode Island	30 days	30 days	yes; at the polls	no
South Carolina	30 days	none	yes; at the polls	yes
South Dakota	15 days	none	yes; at registration	yes
Tennessee	30 days	20 days	yes; at the polls	yes
Texas	30 days	none	yes; at the polls	yes
Utah	20 days	30 days	yes; at the polls	yes
Vermont	17 days	none	yes; at the polls	no
Virginia	31 days	none	yes; at the polls	no
Washington	30 days	30 days	no; blanket primary	no
West Virginia	30 days	30 days	yes; at registration	yes
Wisconsin	election day	10 days	yes; at the polls	yes
Wyoming	30 days	none	yes; at the polls	no
District of Columbia	30 days	none	yes; at registration	yes
Puerto Rico	50 days	none	yes; at the polls	yes
Virgin Islands	45 days	45 days	yes; 30 days in advance	no

1. for first-time voters   2. general election/primary election   3. for primary election, before 3rd Saturday in October for general election
4. with country clerk; 17 days with precinct registrar.

694 CIVICS HANDBOOK

Participating in Government

Tell students that the states of Wisconsin, Maine, Minnesota, and Oregon have higher voter turnouts on election days than the other states. *What might be the cause of higher voter turnouts in these states?* (Those states do not have lengthy registration requirements. Citizens can register on the day of the election in those states.)

Local History

Have interested students call the local Board of Elections to find out how voting registration requirements have changed in your state over time. Also have students inquire about how voter turnout has changed during that same period. Ask students to report their findings to the class.

When and Where Are Elections Held?

When Do You Vote?

National elections are held on the Tuesday following the first Monday in November of even-numbered years. Elections for House of Representatives and one-third of the Senate seats are held every two years. Presidential elections are held every four years. Election day in 1992 is November 3; in 1994, November 8.

Elections for state and local offices are often held on the same day as the national elections. However, states may call their own elections at any time they wish. Voters may also be asked to vote "Yes" or "No" on ballot measures such as bond issues and referendums.

A preliminary round of elections, called primary elections, usually precedes the general elections. The primaries decide which candidates' names will go on the ballot in November. The dates of primary elections differ from state to state.

Election judges are allowed to assist voters with disabilities, helping to ensure that everyone will have the chance to vote.

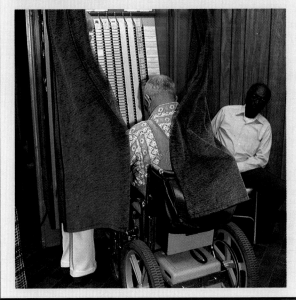

Where Do You Vote?

Based on your home address, you will be assigned to the polling place in your precinct. Although voting hours vary from place to place, polls are generally open from 7 A.M. to 7 P.M.

Before the day of the election, find where your polling place is located and how to get there. If your polling place is not within walking distance of your home, make travel arrangments in advance. Make sure to plan on getting to the polls during voting hours.

At the poll, the names of all registered voters appear on a list. (A few states allow you to register at the polling place on election day.) When you arrive, tell the election officials your name. A judge will check your name off the list, hand you a ballot or punch card (if you need one), and direct you to a voting booth. If you have questions about voting procedures, don't hesitate to ask one of the officials.

You cast your vote in secret, in a private booth behind a closed curtain. Take your ballot or card with you into the voting booth and close the curtain behind you. Now you are free to vote as you choose, without fear or intimidation or pressure. Take your time, read the ballot carefully, and then cast your vote.

Do you know the date of the next election in your state? How can you find out?

Comparing Political Systems

Tell students that other nations do not use calendar-determined elections. Great Britain, for example, can call an election whenever an issue of crucial political importance emerges. As an illustration, if the government began to involve the nation in an unpopular war, an election could be called to let the British people decide whose policies they support and who should lead them. *What are the advantages and disadvantages of such a system?* (Advantages: more issue-oriented campaigns and a government more responsive to the will of the people; disadvantages: could lead to unstable or unproductive government if the leadership was constantly changing hands; a calendar-determined system gives a leader time to see if his or her program works.) *Should the United States consider changing from a calendar-determined system? Why or why not?*

Geographic Themes: Location

Have students contact their local Board of Elections or the League of Women Voters to obtain a map of the voting precincts in your town or city. Ask them to outline the borders of their voting precinct and mark the location of their polling place. Then post the map on a bulletin board. **LEP**

How Do You Read the Ballot?

Two kinds of ballots are most common in the United States. They are illustrated and explained on this page.

The Office-Group Ballot
The office-group (or "Massachusetts") ballot lists candidates together by the office they are seeking. Their party affiliation is listed beside their name.

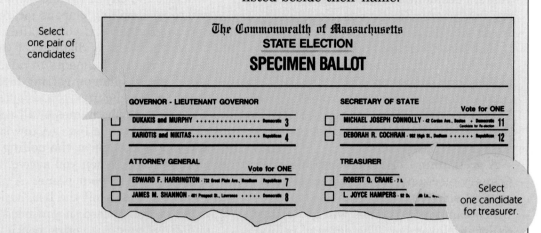

The Party-Column Ballot
The party-column (or "Indiana") ballot lists all the candidates from each party in a single row or column. The parties are identified by symbols at the top of the column. You may vote for one party's entire slate of candidates or office by office, selecting candidates from any party.

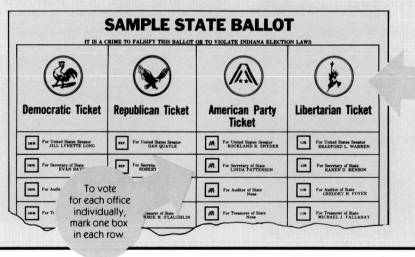

696 CIVICS HANDBOOK

How Do You Use a Voting Machine?

If your polling place uses paper ballots, simply mark your choices directly on the ballot with a pencil in the secrecy of the voting booth. Follow the ballot instructions for marking inside the squares. When you are through, fold your ballot and deposit it in the locked ballot box.

Many polling places now use voting machines to count ballots more quickly and accurately. The most common are the lever and punch-card machines, illustrated on this page.

The Lever Machine

The lever machine is both the ballot and the voting booth. Enter the booth and pull the large lever to one side, which closes a curtain around you. Next, turn down the small levers by the names of candidates you prefer. On a lever machine, you can reset the levers and change your vote up to the last moment. Once you are sure you have turned all the levers you want, a second pull on the large lever records your vote, opens the curtain, and resets the machine for the next voter.

The Punch-Card Machine

In some states, you will be handed a punch-card to use as your ballot. Once you are inside the private booth, insert your card in the voting machine. This lines up the card with the names of the candidates. To vote, use the stylus provided to punch holes at the appropriate places on the ballot. Once you have punched the card, your vote is final. Place your completed card in its envelope and give it to the election judge, who puts it in the ballot box. Your votes will later be counted electronically.

The United States was the first country to use voting machines in elections. The lever machine (below) and punch-card machine (bottom) both have improved the accuracy and lowered the cost of administering elections.

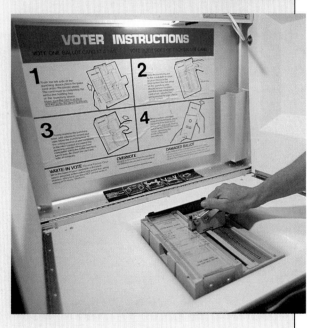

Civic Values
Discuss the differences between the lever machine and punch-card machine with students. *What advantage does the lever machine have over the punch-card machine?* (With the lever machine, you can change your vote up to the last moment. With the punch-card machine, once you have punched a hole, you cannot change your vote.)

Participating in Government
Have students contact the local Board of Elections or League of Women Voters to find out what kind of voting method is used at their polling place.

CIVICS HANDBOOK **697**

How Do You Decide How to Vote?

Your first important voting decision should be *deciding to vote*. Then, to vote intelligently, you must keep informed. This means reading the newspaper, learning about the candidates and the issues, and discussing the election with friends, family, and others. You can get information from the media, from candidates' headquarters, and nonpartisan organizations like the League of Women Voters. The ultimate decision on how you vote, however, is your own.

Most states provide sample ballots well before the elections are held. These give you a chance to become familiar with the candidates and the issues. (Usually you can take your sample ballot into the voting booth.) Before you enter the voting booth, you should know what your choices are. And you should have the information that will help you choose wisely when you finally cast your vote.

> Make sure you know the answer to all of these questions before election day.

★ Voter's Checklist

- Do you know the date of the next primary election in your state?
- The date of the next general election?
- Do you know the requirements for registering in your state?
- Do you know where you can register?
- Are you registered to vote?
- Do you know where your polling place is?
- Do you know when the polls are open?
- Do you know what kind of voting method is used at your polling place?
- Do you know who the candidates are and where they stand on issues you care about?
- Are there any other questions (such as a referendum) on the ballot?
- Do you know where to get more information if you need it?
- Have you carefully read and understood the sample ballot?

698 CIVICS HANDBOOK

698

Great Words in American History

Americans are proud of their great nation and of the freedom for which it stands. Throughout the nation's history, that pride has been expressed in solemn pledges, memorable speeches, and rousing anthems, all of which celebrate freedom and express love of country.

The Pledge of Allegiance

I pledge allegiance to the flag of the United States of America and to the republic for which it stands; one nation under God, indivisible, with liberty and justice for all.

"America the Beautiful"

Oh beautiful for spacious skies, for amber
  waves of grain
For purple mountains majesties above the
  fruited plain
America! America! God shed his grace on
  thee
And crown thy good with brotherhood from
  sea to shining sea

"My Country 'Tis of Thee"

My country 'tis of thee, sweet land of liberty,
  of thee I sing.
Land where my fathers died, land of the
  pilgrims pride,
From every mountainside, let freedom ring.

"God Bless America"

God bless America, land that I love,
Stand beside her and guide her through the
  night with a light from above;
From the mountains, to the prairies to the
  oceans white with foam,
God bless America, my home sweet home.

Great Americans on Patriotism

God grants liberty only to those who live it, and are always ready to guard and defend it.
Daniel Webster
1782–1852

Our country, right or wrong. When right, to be kept right; when wrong, to be put right.
Carl Schurz
1829–1906

There are no days of special patriotism. There are no days when you should be more patriotic than on other days, and I ask you to wear every day in your heart our flag of the Union.
Woodrow Wilson
1856–1924

Ask not what your country can do for you—ask what you can do for your country.
John F. Kennedy
1917–1963

A nation is formed by the willingness of each of us to share in the responsibility for upholding the common good.
Barbara Jordan
1936–

In this two-hundredth anniversary year of our Constitution, you and I stand on the shoulders of giants—men whose words and deeds put wind in the sails of freedom . . . We will be guided tonight by their acts, and we will be guided forever by their words.
Ronald Reagan
1911–

History

Have students skim their history textbooks for other examples of memorable speeches or quotations that celebrate freedom and express love of country. Ask students to identify the person being quoted and the event or events that inspired the quotation.

Patterns in History

Discuss with the class the characteristics that make a person a patriot. *Which Americans that you have learned about would you describe as great patriots? Why?* (Answers will vary but may include George Washington, Abraham Lincoln, and Dwight D. Eisenhower. These Americans fought for and/or spent their lives working for their country.) *Which Americans would you describe as great patriots today? Why?* (Answers will vary but may include astronauts, members of the military, members of Congress, or environmentalists. These people risk their lives for their country or work to promote their nation's welfare.)

Have students make a list on the board of other symbols of our nation. *What other symbols of our nation can you think of in addition to the ones described on pages 700 and 701? What do these symbols represent?* (Answers will vary but may include the Capitol, the Lincoln Memorial, and the American flag. The Capitol is a symbol of our democratic government, the Lincoln Memorial is a symbol of equality, freedom, and preservation of the union, and the flag is a symbol of our independence.) Have students find out more about the symbols they mention by doing research in the library. Ask them to report their findings to the class in the form of an oral report. Also have the students draw pictures of these symbols and organize them into a bulletin board display.

Analyzing Controversial Issues
Tell students that in 1989 the Supreme Court overturned a Texas law that made it a crime to burn the American flag. According to the justices, burning the flag is a form of free speech that is protected by the First Amendment of the Constitution. Discuss with the class whether they agree or disagree with the court's opinion. Also tell students that after this decision some Americans, including President Bush, supported an effort to add an amendment to the Constitution. The proposed amendment would have allowed the states to outlaw flag-burning. Discuss with students why they would support or oppose such an amendment.

Symbols of Our Nation

The Liberty Bell

The Liberty Bell is one of America's most enduring symbols of freedom. It was rung on July 8, 1776, to celebrate Congress's adoption of the Declaration of Independence. It is inscribed with the words from the Bible, "Proclaim Liberty throughout all the land unto all the inhabitants thereof."

The Liberty Bell, first cast in England and weighing over 2,000 pounds, was shipped to Pennsylvania in 1752. Following 1776, the Liberty Bell rang on each anniversary of the adoption of the Declaration until 1835. In that year, the bell received its famous crack while being rung during the funeral of John Marshall, the first Chief Justice of the United States.

The Liberty Bell is now rung only on special occasions. On display in Philadelphia, it attracts thousands of visitors every year.

The Great Seal of the United States

Throughout history, governments have used official seals to signify that documents are authentic. The United States, wanting to show its equal rank with the governments of Europe, adopted the Great Seal in 1782. Both sides of the seal can be found on the back of a one dollar bill.

The face of the seal shows an American bald eagle with a shield on its breast. There are thirteen stripes to represent the thirteen original states. The thirteen leaves and olives in one claw and the thirteen arrows in the other symbolize the nation's desire for peace but its ability to wage war. The words *E pluribus unum* are Latin for "One [nation] out of many [states]."

The reverse side of the seal shows a pyramid with thirteen layers, representing the Union. The Eye of Providence guards the pyramid. The Latin motto *Annuit coeptis* means "He [God] has favored our undertakings." The motto *Novus ordo seclorum* means "New order of the ages."

The Bald Eagle

The bald eagle is one of America's best-known symbols. It became the national bird of the United States in 1782, and appears on the face of the Great Seal. The eagle has been used as a symbol of strength and bravery dating back to Roman times.

The bald eagle is found only in North America. The eagle is not really bald, but has that appearance because white feathers cover its head. Bald eagles are protected by federal law.

Statue of Liberty

The Statue of Liberty has become a symbol of the United States and a symbol of freedom to people all over the world. It stands on Liberty Island at the entrance of New York Harbor. The statue, one of the largest ever built, shows a proud woman in flowing robes holding a torch in her uplifted right hand. Her left hand holds a tablet with the date of the Declaration of Independence in Roman

700 CIVICS HANDBOOK

numerals. At her feet lies the broken chain of tyranny, or unjust rule. On her head rests a crown.

The Statue of Liberty was given to the United States by the people of France in 1884 as a symbol of the friendship between the two nations. The statue, which stands on a large concrete pedestal, rises over 150 feet high and is made of 300 copper sheets fastened together. A spiral staircase brings visitors up from the base of the statue to the crown. Windows in the crown give people an unforgettable view of the harbor.

Millions of immigrants passed the statue upon entering the United States. A poem by American poet Emma Lazarus is inscribed on a plaque on the pedestal. Its well-known lines, "Give me your tired, your poor, Your huddled masses yearning to breathe free," symbolize the nation's dedication to freedom.

Mount Rushmore

The Black Hills of South Dakota are home to a spectacular memorial. Carved into a granite cliff are the heads of George Washington, Thomas Jefferson, Theodore Roosevelt, and Abraham Lincoln, four of America's greatest Presidents. They were chosen to represent,

respectively, the nation's founding, philosophy, expansion, and unity.

The sculptures are approximately 60 feet high, and are situated 5,725 feet above sea level. On a clear day, they can be seen from over 60 miles away.

Gutzon Borglum designed and supervised construction of the Mount Rushmore memorial, which was completed in 1941. The figures were cut from the stone by using drills and dynamite.

Uncle Sam

The figure of Uncle Sam is a well-known patriotic symbol in the United States. He is generally shown as a tall figure with long white hair and a white beard. His costume is red, white, and blue, and decorated with stars and stripes.

Although the exact origin is unclear, the name "Uncle Sam" is thought to have originated with Samuel "Uncle Sam" Wilson, a resident of Troy, New York, who supplied the army with barrels of food stamped with the initials "U.S." Workers joked that the initials stood for Wilson's nickname, "Uncle Sam."

Following the Civil War, the cartoonist Thomas Nast began to draw Uncle Sam as he is pictured today. The symbol soon became widely known, and was heavily used on recruiting posters during World Wars I and II. In 1961 Congress officially recognized Samuel "Uncle Sam" Wilson as being the source of this patriotic symbol.

Participating in Government
Tell students that some of the symbols of our nation are in serious states of disrepair. While federal and private funds were raised to restore the Statue of Liberty in time for its 100th birthday in 1986, other symbolic structures have not been so fortunate. Independence Hall in Philadelphia, for example, has been closed to the public because of roofing problems. The federal government lacks the funds to do all the work necessary to preserve all of our national symbols. Discuss with students why it is important to preserve these symbols and what they can do to help preserve them. Encourage them to act on their ideas. You may also wish to have some students write to the National Trust for Historic Preservation to learn more about the problem and what citizens can do to help. The address is 1785 Massachusetts Avenue, N.W., Washington, D.C. 20036.

Participating in Government

Ask students to make a chart of their representatives and senators. Have students list the lawmaker's name, the political party he or she belongs to, and when the term of office expires. Tell students that this information can be found in a current almanac.

Politics

Ask students to find out which party is the majority party in each house of Congress today. Then have them identify the Speaker of the House and the Senate Majority Leader. Tell students that a current almanac will have this information.

Citizenship

Have students find out how many committees the Senate and House of Representatives have. Then ask them to find out if their representatives and senators lead any of these committees. A current almanac will have this information.

Ⓒ Cooperative Learning

Divide the class into groups and have each group keep track of a bill that is currently making its way through Congress. Tell the groups to find out the following information: which legislator or legislators introduced the bill, what interest groups support and oppose the bill, and what progress the bill is making through Congress. Have each group illustrate the progress of the bill by drawing a chart. Advise the groups that newspapers and magazines will be valuable sources of information in this activity. **LEP**

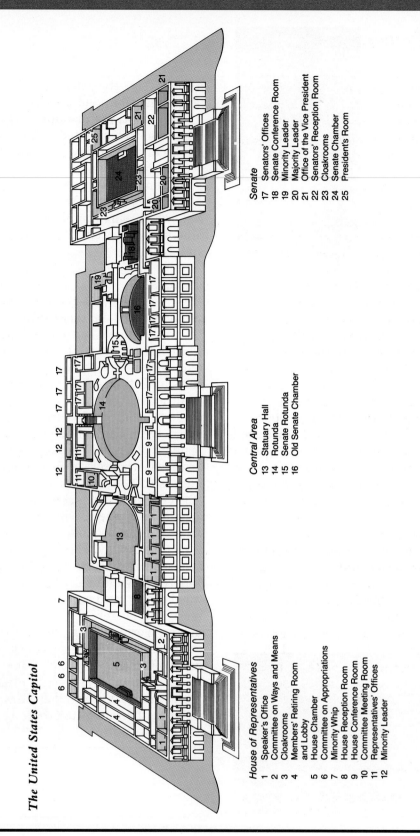

The United States Capitol

House of Representatives
1 Speaker's Office
2 Committee on Ways and Means
3 Cloakrooms
4 Members' Retiring Room and Lobby
5 House Chamber
6 Committee on Appropriations
7 Minority Whip
8 House Reception Room
9 House Conference Room
10 Committee Meeting Room
11 Representatives' Offices
12 Minority Leader

Central Area
13 Statuary Hall
14 Rotunda
15 Senate Rotunda
16 Old Senate Chamber

Senate
17 Senators' Offices
18 Senate Conference Room
19 Minority Leader
20 Majority Leader
21 Office of the Vice President
22 Senators' Reception Room
23 Cloakrooms
24 Senate Chamber
25 Presidents Room

National Government: The Congress

The framers of the Constitution divided the national government into three separate branches. The **legislative branch** is the lawmaking branch of government. The framers believed that Congress, the lawmaking body, should play the leading role because its members are closer to the people.

The Two Houses of Congress

Congress is the lawmaking body of the national government. It is a bicameral, or two house, legislature. Each house acts as a check on the other, so that laws are not passed without the consent of the people.

The lower house is called the **House of Representatives**. Its 435 members are known as representatives, or, more commonly, as congressmen or congresswomen. The number of seats each state has is based on the size of its population. Representatives are elected from congressional districts that are roughly equal in population. Representatives serve two-year terms.

The upper house is called the **Senate**. Its members are known as senators. Membership in the Senate is not based on population; rather, there are two senators from each of the 50 states, for a total of 100. Senators serve six-year terms. Each senator represents his or her whole state.

Who Are Members of Congress?

The Constitution does set up a few qualifications for representatives and senators. Representatives must have been United States citizens for seven years and must be at least 25 years old when taking office; senators must be 30 years old and citizens for nine years.

The Capitol (at left) is where Congress meets to debate the issues of the day. **CONSTITUTIONAL HERITAGE** Why did the framers want Congress to play the leading role in government?

How Is Congress Organized?

With rare exception, members of Congress today belong to either the Democratic or Republican party. In each house of Congress, the party with more members is known as the **majority party**. The one with fewer members is known as the **minority party**.

The majority party in the House chooses one of its members to be the Speaker, the most powerful member of the House. The House Majority Leader is the second most powerful officer. In the Senate, the Majority Leader is most powerful. Other floor leaders in the House and Senate include the Minority Leader and assistant floor leaders known as whips. They help to push through legislation that is favorable to their party.

Committees help Congress deal with the thousands of bills that are introduced every year. They are small groups of members, each group with a specific area of expertise, that gather and study information about proposed legislation.

Congress Has Many Powers

The Constitution gives Congress the lawmaking power of the national government. Those powers specifically granted to Congress are known as the **delegated powers**. These include maintaining an armed force, raising money through taxation, and regulating trade. The **implied powers**, on the other hand, are not listed in the Constitution. However, Congress has the power to make all laws that are "necessary and proper" for carrying out the delegated powers. This clause, known as the **elastic clause**, has allowed the national government to stretch its powers into other areas.

Participating in Government
Tell students that most senators and representatives publish newsletters to inform their constituents about the work they are doing in Washington. Have students write to their representatives and senators asking for copies of their newsletters. After students receive the newsletters, discuss with the class what the concerns and interests of their representatives are and what their positions are on these issues. Ask the class whether they agree or disagree with these positions. Addresses for representatives and senators can be found in the telephone book, usually under United States Government listings.

Constitutional Heritage
Refer students to Article I, Section 8 of the Constitution (pages 743–745). *What other important powers does Congress have in addition to the ones mentioned on this page?* (To borrow money, to coin money, to establish a post office, to declare war, among others.)

Photo Caption Answer
Its members are elected directly by the people, unlike the other two branches.

Constitutional Heritage

Refer students to the Twenty-fifth Amendment to the Constitution. *If a President dies or resigns from office, who becomes the President?* (The Vice President.) *Who assumes the office of the Vice President?* (The new President nominates a Vice President subject to confirmation by Congress.) *What happens if a President becomes unable to perform his or her duties while in office?* (The Vice President assumes the powers of the President until the President notifies Congress that he or she is no longer disabled.)

Cultural Pluralism

Discuss with students possible reasons why the United States has never elected a woman or member of an ethnic minority to the office of President. (Answers will vary but may include prejudice and the inability to attract the money it takes to run a successful campaign.)

Analyzing Controversial Issues

Tell students that many people have criticized the Electoral College system. Some do not like it because it is a winner-take-all system. In other words, the presidential candidate who wins the most votes in each state receives all of the electoral votes of that state. Under this system, a President could win an election with less than a majority of the popular vote. This happened in 1888, when Grover Cleveland won the popular vote but lost the electoral vote to Benjamin Harrison. Another criticism of the system is that it encourages candidates to concentrate their efforts on the states with the largest number of electoral votes, such as California, New York, and Texas. Discuss with students the advantages and disadvantages of changing the current system to one where the President is directly elected by the voters.

704

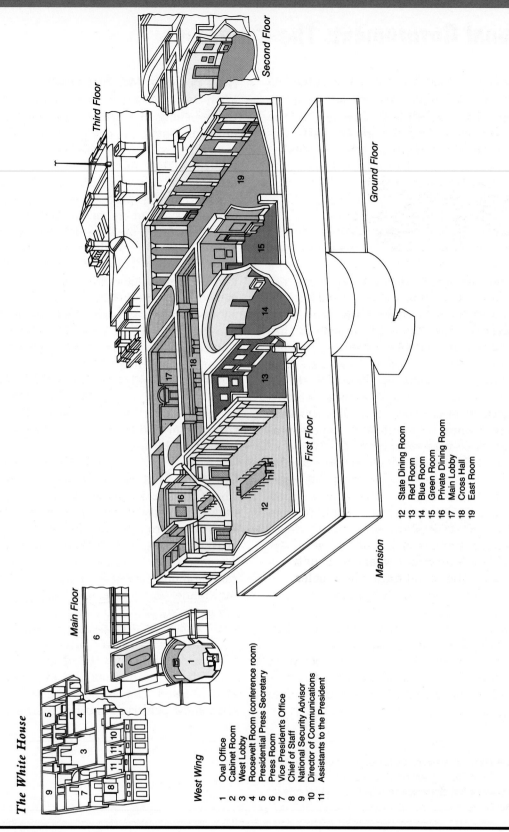

The White House

West Wing

1 Oval Office
2 Cabinet Room
3 West Lobby
4 Roosevelt Room (conference room)
5 Presidential Press Secretary
6 Press Room
7 Vice President's Office
8 Chief of Staff
9 National Security Advisor
10 Director of Communications
11 Assistants to the President

Mansion

12 State Dining Room
13 Red Room
14 Blue Room
15 Green Room
16 Private Dining Room
17 Main Lobby
18 Cross Hall
19 East Room

Main Floor

Second Floor

Third Floor

Ground Floor

First Floor

National Government: The Presidency

The President of the United States heads the executive branch of the federal government, which carries out the laws. The framers of the Constitution wanted a strong leader as Chief Executive, but they did not want a monarchy. Therefore, the President is given enormous powers by the Constitution, but is checked by the other two branches.

Qualifications and Term of Office

There are three qualifications that the Constitution establishes for a President. First, the President must be a natural-born citizen, that is, born on United States territory. Second, the President must be at least 35 years old. Third, the President must have lived in the United States for 14 years.

The President is elected to a four-year term. In 1951, the 22nd Amendment was ratified, which limited the number of terms a President could serve to two. The Constitution does allow a President to be impeached—charged with wrongdoing—and removed from office. Only one President, Andrew Johnson, has ever been impeached. He was found not guilty, however.

Electing the President

The political parties nominate a candidate for President every four years at a national convention. The candidate then selects a vice-presidential candidate, and the two begin a long and expensive campaign that takes them to every part of the nation. The election takes place in November.

The President is not directly elected by popular vote but by an **Electoral College** made up of 538 electors. The winning candidate begins a four-year term in January.

The Office of the President

The President heads the executive branch of government. The branch consists of the presidential staff, independent agencies, and fourteen executive departments. The heads of these fourteen departments make up the Cabinet, which assists the President in making decisions.

The Powers of the President

The President is the Chief Executive of the nation. In this role, the President (1) develops federal policies; (2) enforces the law; (3) appoints federal officials; and (4) prepares the national budget. The President influences legislation by suggesting or recommending laws to Congress. The President delivers a more formal message to Congress through the **State of the Union Address,** which is given yearly at the beginning of each session of Congress. The President can also **veto,** or reject, any bill passed by Congress.

As Chief Executive, the President is responsible for the nation's foreign policy. The Constitution gives the President the power to make treaties, appoint ambassadors, and receive foreign diplomats. The President is also commander-in-chief, which gives the President additional power in foreign affairs. In this role, the President has supreme power over the armed forces. The President defends the country during wartime and keeps it strong during peacetime.

The President is also Chief of State, that is, the symbolic leader of the nation. In that role, the President awards medals to military heroes, dedicates monuments and parks, and performs other ceremonial duties that show pride in American achievements.

The White House (at left) is the official residence of the President of the United States. The President both lives and works in the stately mansion. NATIONAL IDENTITY Why might the White House symbolize world leadership?

Citizenship
Ask students to find out what the fourteen executive departments are and who heads each department. Tell students that a current almanac should contain this information. Then tell students that in 1975 there were 11 Cabinet departments, in 1980 there were 13 Cabinet departments, and in 1990 there were 14. *What are the advantages and disadvantages of letting the executive branch grow in this way?* (Advantages include that the President can get better advice by having more professionals around him or her; disadvantages include the growth in the size and expense of government.)

Comparing Political Systems
Have students compare the term of office and powers of our President with those of other nations. Assign each student a nation and have him or her research the nation's government by using library resources. Then ask students to put the information they have gathered on a bulletin board chart. The chart should contain headings for the name of the nation, the head of the government, the term of office, and the powers given to that official.

Photo Caption Answer
In recent years, the President of the United States has become one of the most powerful figures in the world.

Citizenship

Have students gather information about the current members of the Supreme Court. Tell students to find out the names, ages, and dates of appointment of the associate justices and Chief Justice.

Participating in Government

Have students follow news coverage of a case that is currently before the Supreme Court. Suggest that students consult newspapers and magazines for more in-depth information about the case. After the Court has issued its decision, ask students to write a brief report identifying the events surrounding the case, the arguments presented by each side, and the Supreme Court's decision.

Constitutional Heritage

Discuss with students the advantages and disadvantages of appointing justices for life. *What might be some possible drawbacks to appointing Supreme Court justices for life?* (Students may suggest that age may interfere with the justices' ability to perform their duties; also, their philosophies are those of the Presidents who appointed them, not necessarily those of the majority of Americans today.)

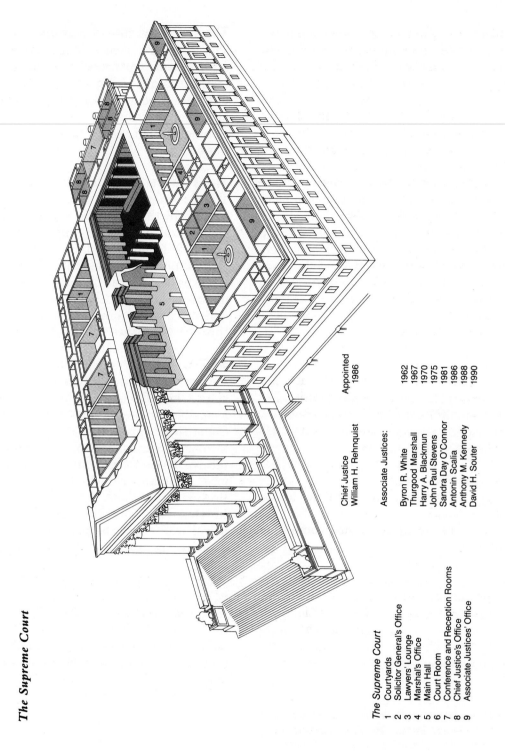

The Supreme Court

	Appointed
Chief Justice	1986
William H. Rehnquist	
Associate Justices:	
Byron R. White	1962
Thurgood Marshall	1967
Harry A. Blackmun	1970
John Paul Stevens	1975
Sandra Day O'Connor	1981
Antonin Scalia	1986
Anthony M. Kennedy	1988
David H. Souter	1990

The Supreme Court
1 Courtyards
2 Solicitor General's Office
3 Lawyers' Lounge
4 Marshal's Office
5 Main Hall
6 Court Room
7 Conference and Reception Rooms
8 Chief Justice's Office
9 Associate Justices' Office

Background In 1984, 5,006 cases came before the Supreme Court. Of that number only 175 were argued before the Court. Most of the others were denied review.

National Government: The Supreme Court

The **judicial branch** of the federal government interprets the nation's laws. The Supreme Court heads the judicial branch and is the highest court in the land.

Membership of the Supreme Court

The Supreme Court has nine members—a Chief Justice and eight associate justices. The justices are appointed by the President, but those nominated must be approved by the Senate. Although there are no constitutional qualifications, most have been well-known lawyers, judges, law professors, or government officials.

Justices are appointed for life, which ensures that they will not be politically controlled by another branch of government. They may be removed for wrongdoing but this has never happened.

Selecting Supreme Court Cases

The Constitution gives the Court authority to hear cases arising from the Constitution, federal laws, treaties, or disputes between states. Its most important power is known as **judicial review**. This allows the Court to decide if a federal or state law, or an action by the President, is constitutional. If it is declared unconstitutional, the law is no longer in force.

Most cases heard by the Court come from its power to review decisions made by lower courts. The Supreme Court itself decides what cases it wants to hear. Certain guidelines apply; in general, the Court will only hear cases involving important national or constitutional questions. Although the Court reviews only a small percentage of the applications it receives, the amount of work it deals with is large.

The Supreme Court building, completed in 1935, has been home to some of the greatest judicial decisions in American history. **CONSTITUTIONAL HERITAGE** What cases does the Court generally hear?

The Supreme Court in Action

After a case is accepted, lawyers for each side file **briefs**, written arguments that support their case. After studying the briefs, the justices hear each side present its case during oral arguments. The justices then meet in private to discuss and vote on the case. Cases are decided by majority vote.

One justice is then selected to write the majority opinion of the case, which becomes the "law of the land." This opinion explains the reasons behind the majority decision in the case and must be followed by all lower courts. A justice has the option to write a concurring opinion, agreeing with the majority decision, but for different reasons. A dissenting opinion is written when a justice disagrees with a majority decision. All opinions are made public.

Influences on Supreme Court Decisions

One of the most important legal principles affecting judicial decisions is *stare decisis,* a Latin term meaning "to let the decision stand." According to this principle, previous Court rulings are used as precedents, or models, for future decisions. However, justices will sometimes depart from *stare decisis* if they feel that the precedent is no longer correct.

Two major philosophies play a role in how a justice will rule. Those who follow **judicial restraint** believe that justices should not contradict the wishes of elected members of government unless the Constitution has clearly been violated. Supporters of **judicial activism** have a different view. They believe that justices should play an active role in policymaking, not simply follow the desires of elected officials.

Tell students that some people have suggested expanding the size of the Supreme Court to deal with its large and growing load of cases. *Is expanding the size of the Supreme Court a good idea? Why or why not?* (Answers will vary but may include yes, because it will allow more cases to be heard and it would prevent the current justices from being overworked; no, because it will not achieve that much more efficiency since all the justices will still have to be consulted before a decision is made.)

History
Have students consult the index to locate important legal cases that were heard before the Supreme Court during our nation's history. Then ask students to identify the national or constitutional question that the Court decided in each case. *How does the Supreme Court seem to have changed over the course of history?* (Answers will vary but may include that the Court has changed from being a protector of established interests to being a guardian of freedom and the disadvantaged.)

Photo Caption Answer
The court generally restricts itself to cases involving important national or constitutional questions.

Facts About the States

State	Admitted to Union	Population	State Capital	Nickname
Alabama	Dec. 14, 1819	3,984,000	Montgomery	Yellowhammer State
Alaska	Jan. 3, 1959	546,000	Juneau	Land of the Midnight Sun
Arizona	Feb. 14, 1912	3,619,000	Phoenix	Grand Canyon State
Arkansas	June 15, 1836	2,337,000	Little Rock	Land of Oppotunity
California	Sept. 9, 1850	29,279,000	Sacramento	Golden State
Colorado	Aug. 1, 1876	3,272,000	Denver	Centennial State
Connecticut	Jan. 9, 1788	3,227,000	Hartford	Nutmeg State
Delaware	Dec. 7, 1787	658,000	Dover	Diamond State
Florida	March 3, 1845	12,775,000	Tallahassee	Sunshine State
Georgia	Jan. 2, 1788	6,387,000	Atlanta	Peach State
Hawaii	Aug. 21, 1959	1,095,000	Honolulu	Aloha State
Idaho	July 3, 1890	1,004,000	Boise	Gem State
Illinois	Dec. 3, 1818	11,325,000	Springfield	Prairie State
Indiana	Dec. 11, 1816	5,499,000	Indianapolis	Hoosier State
Iowa	Dec. 28, 1816	2,767,000	Des Moines	Hawkeye State
Kansas	Jan. 29, 1861	2,468,000	Topeka	Sunflower State
Kentucky	June 1, 1792	3,665,000	Frankfort	Bluegrass State
Louisiana	April 30, 1812	4,181,000	Baton Rouge	Pelican State
Maine	March 15, 1820	1,218,000	Augusta	Pine Tree State
Maryland	April 28, 1788	4,733,000	Annapolis	Free State
Massachusetts	Feb. 6, 1788	5,928,000	Boston	Bay State
Michigan	Jan. 26, 1837	9,180,000	Lansing	Wolverine State
Minnesota	May 11, 1858	4,359,000	St. Paul	North Star State
Mississippi	Dec. 10, 1817	2,535,000	Jackson	Magnolia State
Missouri	Aug. 10, 1821	5,079,000	Jefferson City	Show-Me State

708 CIVICS HANDBOOK

State	Admitted to Union	Population	State Capital	Nickname
Montana	Nov. 8, 1889	794,000	Helena	Treasure State
Nebraska	March 1, 1867	1,573,000	Lincoln	Cornhusker State
Nevada	Oct. 31, 1864	1,193,000	Carson City	Silver State
New Hampshire	June 21, 1788	1,103,000	Concord	Granite State
New Jersey	Dec. 18, 1787	7,617,000	Trenton	Garden State
New Mexico	Jan. 6, 1912	1,490,000	Santa Fe	Land of Enchantment
New York	July 26, 1788	17,627,000	Albany	Empire State
North Carolina	Nov. 21, 1789	6,553,000	Raleigh	Tar Heel State
North Dakota	Nov. 2, 1889	634,000	Bismarck	Sioux State
Ohio	March 1, 1803	10,778,000	Columbus	Buckeye State
Oklahoma	Nov. 16, 1907	3,124,000	Oklahoma City	Sooner State
Oregon	Feb. 14, 1859	2,828,000	Salem	Beaver State
Pennsylvania	Dec. 12, 1787	11,764,000	Harrisburg	Keystone State
Rhode Island	May 29, 1790	989,000	Providence	Ocean State
South Carolina	May 23, 1788	3,407,000	Columbia	Palmetto State
South Dakota	Nov. 2, 1889	693,000	Pierre	Coyote State
Tennessee	June 1, 1796	4,822,000	Nashville	Volunteer State
Texas	Dec. 29, 1845	16,825,000	Austin	Lone Star State
Utah	Jan. 4, 1896	1,711,000	Salt Lake City	Beehive State
Vermont	March 4, 1791	560,000	Montpelier	Green Mountain State
Virginia	June 25, 1788	6,128,000	Richmond	The Old Dominion
Washington	Nov. 11, 1889	4,827,000	Olympia	Evergreen State
West Virginia	June 20, 1863	1,783,000	Charleston	Mountain State
Wisconsin	May 29, 1848	4,870,000	Madison	Badger State
Wyoming	July 10, 1890	450,000	Cheyenne	Equality State

Flags of Our Nation

Flags that have flown over the United States are shown to the left and below. Patriot forces fought under the Grand Union flag during the first days of the Revolution. In 1777 Congress approved a new flag, with 13 stripes and 13 stars. After independence was won, an additional stripe and star were added each time a state entered the Union. In 1818 Congress decided to set the number of stripes at 13 and to add a star for each new state. That practice has been followed ever since.

The American Flag

The Grand Union Flag

The First Stars and Stripes

The Flag of 1818

Alabama

Alaska

Arizona

Arkansas

California

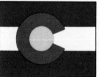

Colorado

Connecticut

Delaware

Florida

Georgia

Hawaii

Idaho

Illinois

Indiana

Iowa

710 CIVICS HANDBOOK

Kansas

Kentucky

Louisiana

Maine

Maryland

Massachusetts

Michigan

Minnesota

Mississippi

Missouri

Montana

Nebraska

Nevada

New Hampshire

New Jersey

New Mexico

New York

North Carolina

North Dakota

Ohio

Oklahoma

Oregon

Pennsylvania

Rhode Island

South Carolina

South Dakota

Tennessee

Texas

Utah

Vermont

Virginia

Washington

West Virginia

Wisconsin

Wyoming

Local History
Ask interested students to find out who designed your state's flag and how the design was arrived at. Have them also find out what the symbols on their flag stand for. Then ask them to present their findings to the class in an oral report. Discuss with the class what new symbols might be appropriate on your state flag if it were being redesigned today.

Local Government

Think about one of your typical mornings. Do you wake up and take a shower? How did that water get to your house? Did you put out the trash in the morning? Who picked up the garbage? The answer to both of the above is your local government. Good local governments protect citizens and improve the quality of life in a community.

Local Governments Provide Needed Services

Protecting citizens is an important role for all local governments. One way this is accomplished is through a local police force. Police provide three basic services: preventing crime, enforcing the laws, and controlling traffic. Fire protection is another important service provided by local governments. Firefighters may be full-time or volunteer. Finally, local governments protect the public health. This is achieved by such means as providing clean drinking water and maintaining hospitals.

Improving citizens' lives is the other main goal of local governments. Many governments help the needy through cash assistance, free medical clinics, homeless shelters, and volunteer programs. Some communities provide public housing developments for low-income families. Improving transportation and offering cultural and recreation activities also help to improve the quality of life in a community.

County Governments

Most states are divided into sections called **counties**, which are the basic unit of local government. They vary widely in size and number. For example, Los Angeles County in California has about 8.6 million people while Loving County in Texas has only about 100.

County governments are responsible for carrying out state government policies. At the head of the county sits an elected board or committee, which oversees the operation of the county. Officials, such as a sheriff and

Here Kathryn Whitmire, the mayor of Houston, Texas, helps assemble a podium for a political rally. Mayors, like other local officials, deal with many different issues that affect the day-to-day lives of people in their communities. **POLITICS** What are some of the qualities that make a local politician successful?

Photo Caption Answer
A knowledge of the community's needs, beliefs, and values.

THREE LAYERS OF GOVERNMENT

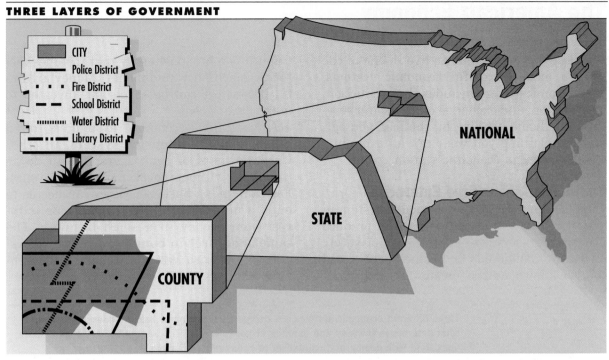

CITY
Police District
Fire District
School District
Water District
Library District

NATIONAL

STATE

COUNTY

CHART SKILLS This chart shows the different levels of government in the United States. Most public services are handled at the local level. **CRITICAL THINKING** Name one advantage and one disadvantage of local control over public services.

treasurer, carry out the county's functions. Some of the services that counties provide are supervising elections, keeping records, and maintaining jails.

Towns, Townships, and Districts

The town is the most important form of government in some states. This form of government began in New England and still plays an important role there. One significant feature of towns is the **town meeting**. Once a year, and sometimes more frequently, the citizens of a town meet to decide the town's policies. Because each citizen has a direct vote, it is the best example of direct democracy in the United States today.

Townships are still common in the Middle Atlantic and Midwestern states. Some are nothing more than lines on a map, while others function much as county governments. Districts serve a more specialized function. School districts are a common example. Most

school districts are governed by an elected school board that determines school policies, such as hiring teachers.

City Government

Because about three-fourths of Americans now live in urban areas, city governments are an important local unit of government. Cities provide many of the necessary services, such as sewage treatment and police protection, that keep the lives of its citizens safe and enjoyable.

There are three main types of city government. The **mayor-council form** has a mayor as the chief executive and an elected council to perform legislative duties. The **council-manager form** of government runs a city more like a business might. An appointed city manager oversees the city's operations. Under the **commission form** of government, a commission of five to nine members is elected to run the city.

CIVICS HANDBOOK **713**

Economics
Tell students that although our economic system is called free enterprise, business owners are not completely free from government interference. Have students talk to a local business owner and ask him or her to describe the ways in which the business is affected by government regulations. Ask students to report their findings to the class.

Global Awareness
Discuss with the class countries that have command economies. ***Which nations of the world have command economies today?*** (Answers may include China, Cuba, and North Korea.) ***Has the number of nations with command economies been increasing or decreasing in recent times? Why?*** (Decreasing; many command economies were plagued by shortages of goods that consumers wanted. When the governments of these countries were replaced, so was the economic system.) ***What are the advantages and disadvantages of a command economy?*** (If planners focus on the people's needs, then a command economy can ensure that all people are adequately housed, fed, and clothed. But when planners do not focus on the people's needs, the goods being produced are not always what the people want.)

The American Economy

Americans are fortunate to live in one of the world's most successful economic systems. An economic system includes the production, distribution, and exchange of goods and services. The home you live in, the food you eat, and the clothing you wear are all a product of the American economic system.

Capitalism Means Free Enterprise

Capitalism describes an economic system in which anything that can be used to produce goods and services—capital—is privately owned by individuals or businesses. Capital is also known as the means of production. Capital is a broad category that includes factories, machinery, and money. Money is capital because it can be saved and invested to make other goods.

A capitalist economic system is often called a **free enterprise system**. In other words, owners of capital are free to do as they like without government interference. For example, a business owner can decide to build a new factory, or you can decide to invest your money in a small business. The same is not true in **command** economic systems. These are systems where the government controls the four factors of production:

CHART SKILLS **Three different economic systems are compared in the chart below. Under capitalism, what determines the kind and quantity of goods sold? CRITICAL THINKING Which is more consistent with democracy, capitalism or communism? Explain.**

COMPARATIVE ECONOMIC SYSTEMS

	Capitalism (market economy)	Socialism (mixed market economy)	Communism (command economy)
Ownership and Control	▶ Means of production owned by individuals and businesses ▶ Market determines what goods will be sold and in what quantity	▶ Basic means of production owned and managed by government ▶ Private ownership, with regulation, of many businesses	▶ Government owns means of production ▶ Government determines what goods will be sold and in what quantity
Competition and Efficiency	▶ Freedom to compete helps to keep prices low and quality high ▶ Desire for profits encourages efficiency	▶ Cooperation stressed over competition ▶ Central planning by government can hinder efficiency of market	▶ Government control over economic decisions hinders efficiency; market not allowed to work ▶ Lack of competition hurts quality of goods
Standard of Living	▶ Goals are high standard of living and economic security ▶ Individuals free to earn profits, but may risk losses	▶ Goals are high standard of living and economic security ▶ High taxes provide free health care and free education	▶ Goals are full employment and income equality ▶ Individual efforts are not rewarded; workers work for nation ▶ Low standard of living with few luxuries

Chart Skills Answers
The market determines the kind and quality of goods sold. Capitalism is, because it encourages individual freedom just as democracy does.

A free enterprise system, such as that in the United States, is powered by the work and imagination of individuals. In recent years, barriers to women and minority groups have been lowered. This trend should bring new prosperity to these groups and new energy to the American economy. **ECONOMICS** In what ways besides preventing discrimination does the government influence the economy?

land, labor, capital, and management. Individuals are not allowed the freedom to make their own economic decisions.

Capitalism is based on the following four principles:

1. Freedom to own—every person has the right to own things, such as land or personal belongings, for themselves.

2. Freedom of choice—individuals are free to choose where they live and work, while business owners can produce the product of their choice.

3. Freedom to compete—businesses compete with one another for customers and for profits, the income left after expenses are paid.

4. Freedom to earn a living—people have the right to better themselves, whether through school, changing their job, or starting their own business.

Government Policy

Government policy influences the nation's economy in a number of ways. For example, it acts to ensure the safety of workers, prevent discrimination in hiring, and reduce pollution from factories. American citizens also expect their government to provide them with an education, defense against attack, care for the needy, and many other goods and services. The government annually spends more than $1.2 trillion providing such services.

To pay for the benefits that government brings, citizens must pay taxes. A tax is a payment from an individual or a business to the government. Paying taxes is a duty required by law. There are many types of taxes—income, property, and sales, to name a few. The largest source of income for the government is income taxes. This is a tax based on how much money a person earns.

The amount of money the government takes in ideally should match the amount of money it spends. When this happens, the government's budget, or plan for raising and spending money, is said to be balanced. However, in recent decades, the government has spent more that it has earned. This results in a deficit, which can lead to problems in the economy.

Photo Caption Answer
It protects workers and provides for education, defense, and care for the needy.

Managing Your Money

You may have heard the expression, "Money makes the world go 'round." In fact, there's some truth to this statement. Money is the means of exchange between buyers and sellers. Without money, the economy would screech to a halt. The kind of money you are most familiar with, bills and coins, is called **currency**. The federal government issues currency and guarantees its value.

Money and Credit

Most Americans make greater use of other kinds of money, especially for larger purchases. They write checks—a written order telling a bank to withdraw money from a checking account and give it to someone else. Credit is another popular means of exchange between buyers and sellers. Credit allows a person to buy something now in return for the promise to pay later. One example is credit cards. If you purchase something with a credit card, you promise to pay back at least part of the purchase every month. Loans are yet another form of credit. A car loan, for example, would allow you to buy a new car by paying a monthly installment with interest until the loan is paid off.

Saving and Investing

Saving money helps both the American economy and you. It helps the economy by making more money available for businesses; it helps you by allowing you to save for long-term spending goals. Your savings should be invested to earn interest, such as in a bank, and not be set aside in a jar at home.

People save their money in a number of ways. Some of the more popular ways include contributing to bank savings accounts, buying bonds from the government, and buying stock in corporations.

HOW SAVING HELPS THE AMERICAN ECONOMY

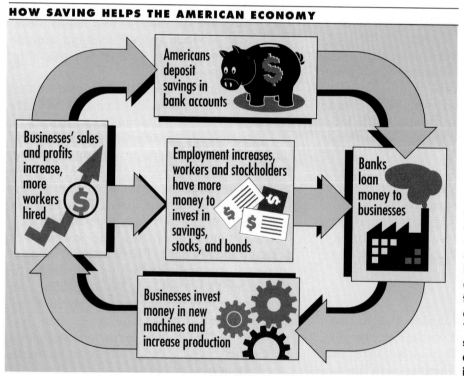

Americans deposit savings in bank accounts

Businesses' sales and profits increase, more workers hired

Employment increases, workers and stockholders have more money to invest in savings, stocks, and bonds

Banks loan money to businesses

Businesses invest money in new machines and increase production

CHART SKILLS

Money that individuals and businesses deposit in banks does not gather dust. It circulates through the economy, spurring economic growth. **CRITICAL THINKING** Using each of the steps outlined in the chart, explain the effects of a drop in savings.

Thinking About Careers

American citizens are fortunate to live in a society with thousands of different career paths. Although many people think of a career as a specific job, it actually involves all the jobs you may hold until your retirement. By making thoughtful decisions as to what career path you choose, you can help yourself build the life you desire.

Learning About Yourself

Before you begin your career exploration, there are some basic things you should think about. Most people will be happiest in jobs that fit their (1) values, (2) interests, and (3) abilities. By addressing these areas, you will learn more about the careers that fit you best.

Values are those things that people believe to be most important in their life. They are thus the goals one usually seeks in a career. Do you want to be famous? Is helping others most important? Do you want to be wealthy? Answering questions such as these will help you learn about your values.

Interests are a reflection of your values. Are you happier working alone or in groups? Are you an artistic person? Athletic? Scientific? Pursuing your main interests will help you to narrow down your career choices.

Abilities, or aptitudes, is another area to examine. For example, if you have artistic ability you might look at careers in the arts. People with mechanical ability, who can construct or repair machines with great skill, might be happy in a training program for automobile or computer repair.

The Importance of Education

Getting the best education you can will help you to reach your career goals. Graduating from high school is an important step in the process. By getting your high school diploma,

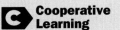

The skyrocketing popularity of computers in recent years has created many new jobs for computer programmers and operators. Like most careers, those dealing with computers require education. **EDUCATION** How does a college degree help a person in the search for a job?

Photo Caption Answer
A college degree gives a person access to more and better-paying jobs.

PROJECTED JOB GROWTH, 1988 — 2000 (Numbers in thousands)

Occupation	1988	Projected, 2000	Percent change
▶ Accountants and auditors	963	1,174	22.0
▶ Clergy	185	199	7.2
▶ Computer programmers	519	769	48.1
▶ General managers and top executives	3,030	3,509	15.8
▶ Mail clerks	136	137	1.2
▶ Lawyers	582	763	31.0
▶ Registered nurses	1,577	2,190	38.8
▶ Salespersons, retail	3,834	4,564	19.0
▶ Secretaries	3,373	3,944	16.9
▶ Teachers, secondary school	1,164	1,388	19.3
▶ Truckdrivers	2,641	3,024	14.5
▶ Waiters and Waitresses	1,786	2,337	30.9

Source: U.S. Department of Labor

CHART SKILLS This chart projects the number of new positions that will be created in various occupations in the near future. What two occupations are expected to grow the most? **CRITICAL THINKING** What other factors should people consider when choosing an occupation?

you will be qualified for a number of occupations. However, more opportunities will be available to you with a college degree. Studies show that persons with a college degree also earn close to 50 percent more than those who have only finished high school.

The World of Work

Occupations can be classified into four major groups, based on the activities of each group. These are (1) white collar, (2) blue collar, (3) farm, and (4) service.

White collar work mainly involves dealing with people and ideas. Managers, salespeople, and clerical workers are examples. Most blue collar occupations, on the other hand, involve working with things. Examples include construction, assembly-line work, and truck driving. Farm workers include anyone who owns, manages, or works on a farm. Service jobs involve providing the public with protective, health, personal, and educational assistance.

Information About Careers

There is a plentiful amount of source material to help you on your career search. Your library and guidance office are two good places to start your search. Both have books, magazines, and other literature describing different careers and giving answers to commonly asked questions. The Department of Labor publishes the popular *Dictionary of Occupational Titles*, which describes over 20,000 jobs. Interviewing people about their jobs and working or volunteering part-time are two other excellent ways to find out more about the world of work.

718 CIVICS HANDBOOK

Historical Documents

The Mayflower Compact (1620)

In 1620, shortly before they landed at Plymouth, 41 of the colonists aboard the *Mayflower* drew up the Mayflower Compact. Under this written agreement, the colonists provided for self-government under majority rule of the male voters.

We, whose names are underwritten, ... having undertaken for the glory of God, and advancement of the Christian faith, and the honor of our King and country, a voyage to plant the first colony in the northern parts of Virginia, do by these presents, solemnly and mutually in the presence of God and one another, covenant and combine ourselves together into a civil body politic, for our better ordering and preservation, and furtherance of the ends aforesaid; And by virtue hereof do enact, constitute, and frame such just and equal laws, ordinances, acts, constitutions, and offices from time to time as shall be thought most [proper] and convenient for the general good of the colony unto which we promise all due submission and obedience. In witness whereof we have hereunto subscribed our names at Cape Cod the eleventh of November, in the year of our sovereign lord King James of England ... anno domini 1620.

From B. P. Poore, ed., *The Federal and State Constitutions*, Part I, p. 931.

The Federalist, No. 10 (1787)

The basis of American government is representative government, rather than direct democracy. In *The Federalist, No. 10*, James Madison put forth his arguments in support of electing representatives to Congress.

The two great points of difference between a democracy and a republic are: first, the delegation of the government, in the latter, to a small number of citizens selected by the rest; secondly, the greater number of citizens and greater sphere of country, over which the latter may be extended.

The effect of the first difference is, on the one hand, to refine and enlarge the public views, by passing them through the medium of a chosen body of citizens, whose wisdom may best discern the true interest of their country and whose patriotism and love of justice will be least likely to sacrifice it to temporary or partial considerations. ...

By enlarging too much the number of electors, you render the representative too little acquainted with all their local circumstances and lesser interests; as by reducing it too much, you render him unduly attached to these, and too little fit to comprehend and pursue great and national objects. ...

Extend the sphere and you take in a greater variety of parties and interests; you make it less probable that a majority of the whole will have a common motive to invade the rights of other citizens.

From J. and A. McLean, eds., *The Federalist: A Collection of Essays*, Vol. I, No. 10.

The Monroe Doctrine (1823)

President Monroe's message to Congress in 1823, later to be called the Monroe Doctrine, proclaimed the pre-eminence of the United States in the Western Hemisphere. The Monroe Doctrine has continued to influence American foreign policy to the present day.

The American continents, by the free and independent condition which they have assumed and maintain, are henceforth not to be

719

Historical Documents

The Mayflower Compact

Analyzing Historical Documents

1. Ask students to explain in their own words what a colonist was agreeing to when he signed the Mayflower Compact. (He agreed to obey laws enacted by the group.)

2. *Why was such a compact deemed necessary?* (Students may suggest that the colonists believed unity was necessary to overcome difficulties and establish a prosperous settlement.)

3. *What is the document's historical significance?* (It provides for government by the consent of the governed which became a fundamental principle of American government.)

The Federalist, No. 10

Analyzing Historical Documents

1. *Which form of government does James Madison prefer, a democracy or a republic? What reasons does he give for his choice?* (He preferred a republic because he believed that a democracy would have too many electors whose local interests would dominate politics.)

2. *Which body in our present-day government corresponds to Madison's "chosen body of citizens"?* (Congress.)

3. *What counter-arguments could be made against Madison's position?* (Madison's faith in wise, selfless, justice-loving representatives may have taken too much for granted.)

The Monroe Doctrine

Analyzing Historical Documents

1. *What position does the Monroe Doctrine take regarding European political influence in the Western Hemisphere?* (European influence should be kept out.)

719

The Seneca Falls Declaration of Sentiments

Analyzing Historical Documents

1. What are some of Elizabeth Cady Stanton's goals for women? (Voting rights, social and religious equality.)

2. What arguments does Stanton make in favor of women's rights? Do you agree or disagree? Why? (Men and women are created equal and should have equal rights.)

3. Why did Stanton choose to model the Seneca Falls Declaration on the Declaration of Independence? (To make people more sympathetic to the cause of women's rights. Like the colonists, Stanton is rebelling against a political order that she sees as oppressive.)

The Emancipation Proclamation

Analyzing Historical Documents

1. By what authority does President Lincoln claim to be freeing the slaves? (As commander-in-chief of the armed forces.)

2. Why did the Emancipation Proclamation specify freedom for slaves in areas "in rebellion against the United States"? (Lincoln had no power to free slaves in the border states, but his role as commander-in-chief allowed him to free Confederate slaves as a military measure.)

---

considered as subject for future colonization by any European powers. . . .

The political system of the [European] powers is essentially different . . . from that of America. . . . We owe it, therefore, to candor . . . to declare that we should consider any attempt on their part to extend their system to any portion of this hemisphere as dangerous to our peace and safety. . . .

Our policy in regard to Europe, which was adopted [many years ago], nevertheless remains the same, which is, not to interfere in the internal concerns of any of its powers.

From J. D. Richardson, ed., *A Compilation of the Messages and Papers of the Presidents*, Vol. II, p. 207.

The Seneca Falls Declaration of Sentiments (1848)

For her opening address at the Seneca Falls Convention, Elizabeth Cady Stanton prepared a "Declaration of Sentiments." She modeled this appeal for women's rights on the Declaration of Independence.

When in the course of human events, it becomes necessary for one portion of the family of man to assume among the people of the earth a position different from that which they have hitherto occupied, but one to which the laws of nature and nature's God entitle them, a decent respect to the opinion of mankind requires that they should declare the causes that impel them to such a course.

We hold these truths to be self-evident: that all men and women are created equal; that they are endowed by their Creator with certain inalienable rights . . . that to secure these rights governments are instituted, deriving their just powers from the consent of the governed. . . .

The history of mankind is a history of repeated injuries and usurpations on the part of man toward woman, having in direct object the establishment of an absolute tyranny over her. . . .

Now, in view of not allowing one half the people of this country to vote, of their social

---

and religious degradation . . . and because women do feel themselves aggrieved, oppressed, and fraudulently deprived of their most sacred rights, we insist that they have immediate admission to all the rights and privileges which belong to them as citizens of the United States.

In entering upon the great work before us, we anticipate mistaken ideas, misrepresentations, and ridicule; but we shall make every effort within our power to secure our object.

From E. C. Stanton, S. B. Anthony, and M. J. Gage, ed., *The History of Woman Suffrage*, Vol. I, p. 70.

The Emancipation Proclamation (1863)

On January 1, 1863, President Lincoln proclaimed the freedom of all slaves in states in rebellion against the United States.

Whereas, on the twenty-second day of September, in the year of our Lord one thousand eight hundred and sixty-two, a proclamation was issued by the President of the United States containing among other things the following, to wit:

"That on the first day of January, in the year of our Lord one thousand eight hundred sixty-three, all persons held as slaves within any State, or designated part of a State, the people whereof shall then be in rebellion against the United States, shall be then, thenceforth and forever free; and the Executive Government of the United States, including the military and naval authorities thereof will recognize and maintain the freedom of such persons, and will do no act or acts to repress such persons, or any of them, in any efforts they may make for their actual freedom.

That the Executive will, on the first day, designate the States and parts of States, if any, in which the people therein respectively shall then be in rebellion against the United States, and the fact that any State . . . shall on that day be in good faith represented in the Congress of the United States by members chosen thereto . . . shall, in the absence of strong counter-

---

At the top left margin:

2. What justification does it offer for this position? (Europe's political system is different.)

3. Ask students to explain the significance of the third paragraph. (Students may suggest that it implies a link between Europe's non-intervention in the Western Hemisphere and American non-intervention in the internal affairs of European nations.)

vailing testimony, be deemed conclusive evidence that such State and the people thereof are not then in rebellion against the United States."

Now, therefore, I, Abraham Lincoln, President of the United States, by virtue of the power in me vested as Commander-in-Chief of the Army and Navy of the United States in time of actual armed rebellion against the authority and Government of the United States, and as a fit and necessary war measure for suppressing said rebellion, do, on this first day of January, in the year of our Lord one thousand eight hundred and sixty-three . . . designate, as the States and parts of States wherein the people thereof . . . are this day in rebellion against the United States, the following, to wit: Arkansas, Texas, Louisiana (except the parishes of St. Bernard, Plaquemines, Jefferson, St. John, St. Charles, St. James, Ascension, Assumption, Terre Bonne, Lafourche St. Mary, St. Martin, and Orleans, including the City of New Orleans), Alabama, Florida, Georgia, South Carolina, North Carolina, and Virginia (except the forty-eight counties designated as West Virginia and also the counties of Berkeley, Accomac, Northampton, Elizabeth City, York, Princess Ann, and Norfolk, including the cities of Norfolk and Portsmouth). . . .

And, by virtue of the power and for the purpose aforesaid, I do order and declare that all persons held as slaves within these said designated States and parts of States are, and henceforward shall be free; and that the Executive Government of the United States, including the military and naval authorities thereof, will recognize and maintain the freedom of said persons.

And I hereby enjoin [urge] upon the people so declared to be free, to abstain from all violence, unless in necessary self-defense, and I recommend to them, that in all cases, when allowed, they labor faithfully for reasonable wages.

And I further declare and make known that such persons of suitable condition will be received into the armed service of the United States to garrison forts, positions, stations, and other places, and to man vessels of all sorts in said service.

And, upon this, sincerely believed to be an act of justice, warranted by the Constitution, upon military necessity, I invoke the considerate judgment of mankind and the gracious favor of Almighty God.

From *United States Statutes at Large*, Vol. XII, p. 1268.

The Gettysburg Address (1863)

President Lincoln presented his memorable Gettysburg Address on November 19, 1863, at the dedication of a national cemetery on the battlefield of Gettysburg. His eloquent words express his hopes for a war-torn nation.

Four score and seven years ago our fathers brought forth on this continent, a new nation, conceived in liberty, and dedicated to the proposition that all men are created equal.

Now we are engaged in a great civil war, testing whether that nation or any nation so conceived and so dedicated, can long endure. We are met on a great battlefield of that war. We have come to dedicate a portion of that field, as a final resting place for those who here gave their lives that that nation might live. It is altogether fitting and proper that we should do this.

But, in a larger sense, we cannot dedicate—we cannot consecrate—we cannot hallow—this ground. The brave men, living and dead, who struggled here, have consecrated it, far above our poor power to add or detract. The world will little note, nor long remember what we say here, but it can never forget what they did here. It is for us the living, rather, to be dedicated here to the unfinished work which they who fought here have thus far so nobly advanced. It is rather for us to be here dedicated to the great task remaining before us—that from these honored dead we take increased devotion to that cause for which they gave the last full measure of devotion—that we here highly resolve that these dead shall not

721

Abraham Lincoln's Second Inaugural Address

Analyzing Historical Documents

1. *According to President Lincoln, what was the Civil War's main cause?* (He implies that the South caused the war by trying to dissolve the Union.)

2. *What does Lincoln say about each side's expectations as the war began?* (Each side thought it would win easily. Both sides underestimated the duration and destructiveness of the war.)

3. *What does the Inaugural Address suggest about the kind of policy Lincoln wanted to follow after the war?* (Lincoln wanted to bind up the wounds of war and make the nation whole. He would probably have tried to pursue policies beneficial to the South.)

For additional teaching strategy, see **History,** page 65.

Theodore Roosevelt on Conservation

Analyzing Historical Documents

1. *What does President Theodore Roosevelt mean by "the conservation of our natural resources"?* (Not using up resources too quickly or letting them go to waste.)

2. *What arguments does Roosevelt make in support of conservation?* (Without conservation the future generations will be robbed of their rightful inheritance.)

3. Ask students to give examples of government policies that support conservation. Also ask what policies individual citizens can practice. (Government policies: laws favoring renewable sources of energy and energy-efficiency, laws against pollution and destruction of land, protection of important

have died in vain—that this nation, under God, shall have a new birth of freedom—and that government of the people, by the people, for the people, shall not perish from the earth.

From *The Writings of Abraham Lincoln*, Constitutional ed., Vol. VIII, p. 20.

Abraham Lincoln's Second Inaugural Address (1865)

Lincoln delivered his second inaugural address just prior to the end of the Civil War. In it he recalls the circumstances which led the nation to war and his hope for the restoration of peace and unity.

Fellow Countrymen: At this second appearing to take the oath of the presidential office there is less occasion for an extended address than there was at the first. Then a statement of a course to be pursued seemed fitting and proper. Now, at the expiration of four years, during which public declarations have been constantly called forth on every point and phase of the great contest which still absorbs the attention and engrosses the energies of the nation, little that is new could be presented. The progress of our arms, upon which all else chiefly depends, is as well known to the public as to myself, and it is, I trust, reasonably satisfactory and encouraging to all. With high hope for the future, no prediction in regard to it is ventured.

On the occasion corresponding to this four years ago, all thoughts were anxiously directed to an impending civil war. All dreaded it, all sought to avert it. While the inaugural address was being delivered from this place, . . . insurgent agents were in the city seeking to destroy it without war—seeking to dissolve the Union. Both parties [disapproved of] war, but one of them would make war rather than let the nation survive, and the other would accept war rather than let it perish, and the war came.

One eighth of the whole population was colored slaves, not distributed generally over the Union, but localized in the southern part of it. These slaves constituted a peculiar and

powerful interest. All knew that this interest was somehow the cause of the war. To strengthen, perpetuate, and extend this interest was the object for which the rebels would tear the Union even by war, while the government claimed no right to do more than to restrict the territorial enlargement of it. Neither party expected for the war the magnitude or the duration which it has already attained. Neither anticipated that the cause of the conflict itself should cease. Each looked for an easier triumph, and a result less fundamental and astounding. . . . Fondly do we hope, fervently do we pray, that this mighty scourge of war may speedily pass away. Yet, if God wills that it continue until all the wealth piled by the slaves' two hundred and fifty years of unpaid toil shall be sunk, and until every drop of blood drawn with the lash shall be paid by another drawn with the sword. . . .

With malice toward none, with charity for all, with firmness in the right as God gives us to see the right, let us strive on to finish the work we are in, to bind up the nation's wounds, to care for him who shall have borne the battle and for his widow and his orphan—to do all which may achieve and cherish a just and a lasting peace among ourselves and with all nations.

From J. D. Richardson, ed., *A Compilation of the Messages and Papers of the Presidents*, Vol. VI, p. 276.

Theodore Roosevelt on Conservation (1907)

Until Theodore Roosevelt drew the nation's attention to the need for conservation, there was no real government commitment to protect what most people assumed was an endless supply of resources. In his Seventh Annual Message to Congress, Roosevelt outlined an ambitious conservation program.

The conservation of our natural resources and their proper use constitute the fundamental problem which underlies almost every other problem of our national life. . . . But there must be the look ahead, there must be a realization of the fact that to waste, to destroy our natural resources, to skin and exhaust the land instead of using it so as to increase its usefulness, will result in undermining in the days of our children the very prosperity which we ought by right to hand down to them amplified and developed. . . . Optimism is a good characteristic, but if carried to an excess it becomes foolishness. We are prone to speak of the resources of this country as inexhaustible; this is not so. The mineral wealth of this country, the coal, iron, oil, gas, and the like, does not reproduce itself, and therefore is certain to be exhausted ultimately; and wastefulness in dealing with it today means that our descendants will feel the exhaustion a generation or two before they otherwise would.

From *The Works of Theodore Roosevelt*, Vol. XV, p. 443.

The Fourteen Points (1918)

Nine months after the United States entered World War I, President Wilson delivered to Congress a statement of war aims that became known as the "Fourteen Points." In the speech, the main parts of which are summarized below, the President set forth fourteen "points" or proposals for helping to reduce the risk of war in the future.

Open covenants of peace, openly arrived at, after which there shall be no private international understandings of any kind, but diplomacy shall proceed always frankly and in public view.

Absolute freedom of navigation upon the seas . . . in peace and in war. . . .

The removal, so far as possible, of all economic barriers and the establishment of an equality of trade conditions among all the nations. . . .

Adequate guarantees given and taken that national armaments will be reduced. . . .

A free, open-minded, and absolutely impartial adjustment of all colonial claims, based upon . . .

the principle that . . . the interests of the populations concerned must have equal weight with the . . . claims of the government whose title is to be determined.

A general association of nations must be formed under specific covenants for the purpose of affording mutual guarantees of political independence and territorial integrity to great and small states alike.

From *Supplement to the Messages and Papers of the Presidents Covering the Second Administration of Woodrow Wilson.*

Franklin D. Roosevelt's First Inaugural Address (1933)

Taking office in the depths of the Great Depression, President Roosevelt sought in his first inaugural address to restore the public's confidence. His words electrified the nation and had the desired effect of boosting morale.

This is pre-eminently the time to speak the truth, the whole truth, frankly and boldly. Nor need we shrink from honestly facing conditions in our country today. This great nation will endure as it has endured, will revive and will prosper.

So first of all let me assert my firm belief that the only thing we have to fear is fear itself—nameless, unreasoning, unjustified terror which paralyzes needed efforts to convert retreat into advance. . . .

Our greatest primary task is to put people to work. This is no unsolvable problem if we face it wisely and courageously.

It can be accomplished in part by direct recruiting by the government itself, treating the task as we would treat the emergency of a war, but at the same time, through this employment, accomplishing greatly needed projects to stimulate and reorganize the use of our national resources. . . .

I am prepared under my constitutional duty to recommend the measures that a stricken nation in the midst of a stricken world may require.

723

areas of land and water. Individuals: Conserving electricity and heat at home, car-pooling, recycling.)

The Fourteen Points

Analyzing Historical Documents

1. Ask students to rephrase the first point in their own words. (Students should note that Wilson called for agreements between nations to be made public, with no secret treaties or alliances.)

2. *Why did President Wilson believe this first point would contribute to world peace?* (Wilson believed that secret military alliances had contributed to World War I.)

3. *What institution grew out of Wilson's final point?* (The League of Nations.)

For additional teaching strategy, see **Focus,** page 304.

Franklin D. Roosevelt's First Inaugural Address

Analyzing Historical Documents

1. *What did President Franklin Roosevelt believe was the most important challenge facing the nation when he took office?* (Unemployment.)

2. *What role did Roosevelt propose for the federal government in dealing with this problem?* (The government should create jobs through public works projects.)

3. *How did Roosevelt's proposals differ from the policies of the previous administration?* (The Hoover Administration had refused to intervene directly in the unemployment problem.)

1. *What were the stated goals of President Franklin Roosevelt's proposal for the federal judiciary? What were his actual goals?* (Stated: improve the courts' efficiency. Actual: appoint judges sympathetic to his programs.)

2. *How, according to the Senate Judiciary Committee, could Roosevelt's proposal affect the nation's judicial system?* (It would increase the power of the executive and legislative branches at the expense of the independent judiciary and threaten the separation of powers.)

3. Ask students to summarize the meaning of the next-to-last paragraph. (Students should emphasize the argument that the independence of the judiciary would be compromised if the President or Congress were granted the power to interpret the Constitution's guidelines for judicial appointments.)

For additional teaching strategy, see **Constitutional Heritage,** page 373.

★ HISTORICAL DOCUMENTS ★

These measures, or such other measures as the congress may build out of its experience and wisdom, I shall seek, within my constitutional authority, to bring to speedy adoption.

From *The Public Papers and Addresses of Franklin D. Roosevelt,* Vol. I.

Senate Judiciary Committee on FDR's Court Reform Plan (1937)

Franklin Roosevelt began his second term as President by asking Congress to redesign the federal judiciary. He claimed there were too few federal judges, resulting in long delays before cases could be heard. As for the Supreme Court, he proposed that not only more, but also younger, justices be appointed. The proposal shocked many Americans, who believed it threatened the independence of the judiciary system. The rejection of the proposal by the Senate Judiciary Committee and, soon thereafter, by the full Senate, marked a major defeat for the President.

The Committee on the Judiciary, to whom was referred the bill to reorganize the judicial branch of the Government, after full consideration, having unanimously amended the measure, hereby report the bill adversely with the recommendation that it do not pass. . . .

Inconvenience and even delay in the enactment of legislation is not a heavy price to pay for our system. Constitutional democracy moves forward with certainty rather than with speed. The safety and the permanence of the progressive march of our civilization are far more important to us than the enactment now of any particular law. The Constitution of the United States provides ample opportunity for the expression of popular will to bring about such reforms and changes as the people may deem essential to their present and future welfare. It is the people's charter of the powers granted those who govern them. . . .

We recommend the rejection of this bill as a needless, futile, and utterly dangerous abandonment of constitutional principle.

It was presented to the Congress in a most intricate form and for reasons that obscured its real purpose. . . .

It is a proposal without precedent and without justification.

It would subjugate the courts to the will of Congress and the President and thereby destroy the independence of the judiciary, the only certain shield of individual rights.

It contains the germ of centralized administration of law that would enable an executive so minded to send his judges into every judicial district in the land to sit in judgment on controversies between the Government and the citizen.

It points the way to the evasion of the Constitution and establishes the method whereby the people may be deprived of their right to pass upon all amendments of the fundamental law.

It stands now before the country acknowledged by its proponents as a plan to force judicial interpretation of the Constitution, a proposal that violates every sacred tradition of American democracy.

Under the form of the Constitution it seeks to do that which is unconstitutional.

Its ultimate operation would be to make this Government one of men rather than one of law, and its practical operation would be to make the Constitution what the executive or legislative branches of the Government choose to say it is—an interpretation to be changed with each change of administration.

It is a measure which should be so emphatically rejected that its parallel will never again be presented to the free representatives of the free people of America.

From Henry Steele Commager, *Documents of American History: Volume II—Since 1898* (Prentice-Hall: Englewood Cliffs, N.J., 1973), p. 387.

Roosevelt's War Message to Congress (1941)

On December 7, 1941, Japanese bombers attacked the American fleet at Pearl Harbor. The next day President Roosevelt asked Congress to declare war on Japan.

Yesterday, December 7, 1941—a date which will live in infamy—the United States was suddenly and deliberately attacked by naval and air forces of the Empire of Japan. . . .

The attack yesterday on the Hawaiian Islands has caused severe damage to American naval and military forces. Very many American lives have been lost. In addition American ships have been reported torpedoed on the high seas between San Francisco and Honolulu.

Yesterday the Japanese Government also launched an attack against Malaya. Last night Japanese forces attacked Hong Kong. Last night Japanese forces attacked Guam. Last night Japanese forces attacked the Philippine Islands. Last night the Japanese attacked Wake Island. This morning the Japanese attacked Midway Island.

Japan has, therefore, undertaken a surprise offensive extending throughout the Pacific area. The facts of yesterday speak for themselves. The people of the United States have already formed their opinion and well understand the implications to the very life and safety of our nation.

As Commander-in-Chief of the Army and Navy, I have directed that all measures be taken for our defense. . . .

No matter how long it may take us to overcome this premeditated invasion, the American people in their righteous might will win through to absolute victory. . . .

I ask that the Congress declare that since the unprovoked and dastardly attack by Japan on Sunday, December seventh, a state of war has existed between the United States and the Japanese Empire.

From *The Public Papers and Addresses of Franklin D. Roosevelt*, Vol. 10, p. 514.

Churchill's Iron Curtain Speech (1946)

Shortly after the end of World War II, Winston Churchill spoke at Westminster College in Fulton, Missouri. He warned of new dangers in the form of Communist totalitarianism and the need for a policy of strength in dealing with the Soviet Union.

A shadow has fallen upon the scenes so lately lighted by the Allied victory. Nobody knows what Soviet Russia and its Communist international organization intends to do in the immediate future, or what are the limits, if any, to their expansive . . . tendencies. . . . We understand the Russian need to be secure on her western frontiers by the removal of all possibility of German aggression. We welcome Russia to her rightful place among the leading nations of the world. We welcome her flag upon the seas. Above all, we welcome constant, frequent, and growing contacts between the Russian people and our own people on both sides of the Atlantic. It is my duty however . . . to place before you certain facts about the present position in Europe.

From Stettin in the Baltic to Trieste in the Adriatic, an iron curtain has descended across the continent. Behind that line lie all the capitals of the ancient states of Central and Eastern Europe. Warsaw, Berlin, Prague, Vienna, Budapest, Belgrade, Bucharest, and Sofia, all of these famous cities and the populations around them lie in what I must call the Soviet sphere, and all are subject in one form or another, not only to Soviet influence but to a very high, and in many cases, increasing measure of control from Moscow. . . . The Communist parties, which were very small in all these Eastern states of Europe, have been raised to pre-eminence and power far beyond their numbers and are seeking everywhere to obtain totalitarian control. Police governments are prevailing in nearly every case, and so far, . . . there is no true democracy. . . .

I repulse the idea that a new war is inevitable; still more that it is imminent. It is because I am sure that our fortunes are still in

Roosevelt's War Message to Congress

Analyzing Historical Documents

1. *What justifications does President Franklin Roosevelt give for the declaration of war against Japan?* (The attack on the U.S. military forces in Hawaii and the Japanese offensive in the Pacific.)

2. *Which branch of government has the power to declare war?* (Legislative.)

3. *What claim does Roosevelt make about public opinion?* (Americans understand that the threat to the nation's security requires a declaration of war.)

For additional teaching strategy, see **National Identity,** page 406.

Churchill's Iron Curtain Speech

Analyzing Historical Documents

1. Ask students whether Winston Churchill believed Soviet policies in Europe were primarily aggressive or defensive. Ask them to cite passages from the speech to support their answers. (Aggressive. Cited passages should include "seeking everywhere to obtain totalitarian control," and "indefinite expansion of their power and doctrines.")

2. *How does Churchill propose that western democracies respond to the situation?* (They should stand together and remain strong militarily.)

3. *What evidence does Churchill present to support his position? Do you find it convincing? Why or why not?* (Churchill cites Soviet influence in Central and Eastern Europe and his observations of the Soviet Union during World War II.)

For additional teaching strategy, see **Geographic Themes: Regions,** page 452.

1. *How does President Truman define the Truman Doctrine?* (United States security is involved when an aggressive threat to peace occurs anywhere in the world.)

2. Have students explain Truman's argument that events in Greece threatened American security. (Truman cites American ideals of support for freedom and the negative effect of inaction on the morale of U.S. allies in Europe and Asia.)

3. *What criticisms might an opponent of the Truman Doctrine make?* (Critics might object that it is simplistic to assume that threats to peace are always the fault of one side, and that the Truman Doctrine commits the United States to intervene in conflicts where its own security is not actually involved.)

★ **HISTORICAL DOCUMENTS** ★

our own hands and that we hold the power to save the future, that I feel the duty to speak out now. . . . I do not believe that Soviet Russia desires war. What they desire is the fruits of war and the indefinite expansion of their power and doctrines. But what we have to consider here today, while time remains, is the permanent prevention of war and the establishment of conditions of freedom and democracy as rapidly as possible in all countries. Our difficulties and dangers will not be removed by closing our eyes to them. They will not be removed by mere waiting to see what happens; not will they be removed by a policy of appeasement. What is needed is a settlement, and the longer this is delayed, the more difficult it will be and the greater our dangers will become.

From what I have seen of our Russian friends and allies during the war, I am convinced that there is nothing they admire so much as strength, and there is nothing for which they have less respect than for weakness, especially military weakness. For that reason the old doctrine of a balance of power is unsound. We cannot afford . . . to work on narrow margins, offering temptations to a trial of strength. If the Western democracies stand together in strict adherence to the principles of the United Nations Charter, their influence for furthering those principles will be immense and no one is likely to molest them. If however they become divided or falter in their duty and if these all-important years are allowed to slip away then indeed catastrophe may overwhelm us all.

From address by Winston Churchill, March 5, 1946, *Vital Speeches*, Vol. 12.

The Truman Doctrine (1947)

In February 1947, with the Greek government under attack by Communist rebels, President Truman announced that the United States would support not only Greece but free people anywhere in the world who were facing subversion. Thus was born the Truman Doctrine.

Greece needed aid, and needed it quickly and in substantial amounts. The alternative was the loss of Greece and the extension of the iron curtain across the eastern Mediterranean. . . .

But the situation had even wider implications. Poland, Rumania, and the other satellite nations of Eastern Europe had been turned into Communist camps because, in the course of the war, they had been occupied by the Russian Army. We had tried, vainly, to persuade the Soviets to permit political freedom in these countries, but we had no means to compel them to relinquish their control, unless we were prepared to wage war.

Greece and Turkey were still free countries being challenged by Communist threats both from within and without. These free peoples were not engaged in a valiant struggle to preserve their liberties and their independence.

America could not, and should not, let these free countries stand unaided. To do so would carry the clearest implications in the Middle East and in Italy, Germany, and France. The ideals and the traditions of our nations demanded that we come to the aid of Greece and Turkey and that we put the world on notice that it would be our policy to support the cause of freedom wherever it was threatened. . . .

On Wednesday, March 12, 1947, at one o'clock in the afternoon, I stepped to the rostrum in the hall of the House of Representatives and addressed a joint session of the Congress. I had asked the senators and representatives to meet together so that I might place before them what I believed was an extremely critical situation.

To cope with this situation, I recommended immediate action by the Congress. But I also wished to state, for all the world to know, what the position of the United States was in the face of the new totalitarian challenge. This declaration of policy soon began to be referred to as the "Truman Doctrine." This was, I believe, the turning point in America's foreign policy, which now declared that wherever aggression, direct or indirect, threatened the peace, the security of the United States was involved.

From Harry S. Truman, *Memoirs of Harry S. Truman: Years of Trial and Hope*, Doubleday & Co., Inc., Publishers, 1956, by permission of Margaret Truman Daniel.

Margaret Chase Smith's "Declaration of Conscience" (1950)

Margaret Chase Smith of Maine was the first Republican senator to speak out against McCarthyism. The following passages are taken from her address to the Senate on June 1, 1950.

Mr. President [of the Senate], I would like to speak briefly and simply about a serious national condition. It is a national feeling of fear and frustration that could result in national suicide and the end of everything that we Americans hold dear. It is a condition that comes from the lack of effective leadership either in the legislative branch or the executive branch of the government. . . .

Mr. President, I speak as a Republican. I speak as a woman. I speak as a United States senator. I speak as an American.

The United States Senate has long enjoyed worldwide respect as the greatest deliberative body in the world. But recently that deliberative character has too often been debased to the level of a forum of hate and character assassination sheltered by the shield of congressional immunity. . . .

I think that it is high time for the United States Senate and its members to do some real soul-searching and to weigh our consciences as to the manner in which we are performing our duty to the people of America and the manner in which we are using or abusing our individual powers and privileges.

I think it is high time that we remembered that we have sworn to uphold and defend the Constitution. I think it is high time that we remembered that the Constitution, as amended, speaks not only of the freedom of speech but also of trial by jury instead of trial by accusation. . . .

Those of us who shout the loudest about Americanism in making character assassinations are all to frequently those who, by our own words and acts, ignore some of the basic principles of Americanism—

The right to criticize.
The right to hold unpopular beliefs.
The right to protest.
The right of independent thought.

The exercise of these rights should not cost one single American citizen his reputation or his right to a livelihood nor should he be in danger of losing his reputation or livelihood merely because he happens to know someone who holds unpopular beliefs. . . .

The American people are sick and tired of being afraid to speak their minds lest they be politically smeared as Communists or Fascists by their opponents. Freedom of speech is not what it used to be in America. It has been so abused by some that it is not exercised by others. . . .

As a United States senator, I am not proud of the way in which the Senate has been made a publicity platform for irresponsible sensationalism. . . .

As an American, I condemn a Republican Fascist just as much as I condemn a Democrat Communist. I condemn a Democrat Fascist just as much as I condemn a Republican Communist. They are equally dangerous to you and me and to our country. As an American, I want to see our nation recapture the strength and unity it once had when we fought the enemy instead of ourselves.

From speech by Margaret Chase Smith, *Congressional Record*, 81st Congress, 2nd Session (June 1, 1950).

Brown v. Board of Education (1954)

In the years following the the Supreme Court decision in *Plessy v. Ferguson*, many areas of the nation maintained "separate-but-equal" educational systems for whites and blacks. Then, in 1954, the Court set aside the 1896 decision when it unani-

★ HISTORICAL DOCUMENTS ★

727

Margaret Chase Smith's "Declaration of Conscience"

Analyzing Historical Documents

1. *What constitutional principles does Senator Margaret Chase Smith say McCarthyism ignores?* (Freedom of speech and freedom of conscience.)

2. *What, according to Smith, is responsible for the nation's condition?* (Lack of effective government leadership.)

3. *How might Senator Joseph McCarthy have responded to Senator Smith's speech?* (He might have claimed that the Communist threat justified the harsh measures taken to uncover it.)

For additional teaching strategy, see **Analyzing Controversial Issues,** page 471.

Brown v. Board of Education

Analyzing Historical Documents

1. *Why, do you think, does the Court stress education's importance in our democratic society?* (To show the important implications for American society if education is not made available on equal terms.)

2. *Were physical facilities really equal in segregated public schools?* (Students should suggest that they were not.)

3. Ask students to explain the Court's argument that even if identical schools existed, "separate educational facilities are inherently unequal." (The condition of being separate carries the implication of inferiority, even if facilities were physically comparable.)

For additional teaching strategy, see **Constitutional Heritage,** page 517.

John F. Kennedy's Inaugural Address

Analyzing Historical Documents

1. **What similarities did President Kennedy see between the United States in 1961 and conditions 175 years earlier? What differences did he see?** (Similarities: belief in the ideals of individual liberty. Differences: powerful technology.)

2. **Against what "common enemies of man" did Kennedy urge Americans to struggle?** (Tyranny, poverty, disease, and war.)

3. **Judging by his Inaugural Address, how do you think Kennedy viewed the Truman Doctrine? Cite passages from the speech to support your answer.** (Students may suggest that Kennedy supported the Truman Doctrine, citing his pledge to "support any friend or oppose any foe in order to assure the survival and success of liberty.")

For additional teaching strategy, see **Civic Values, page 497.**

mously ruled against school segregation in *Brown v. Board of Education.*

Today, education is perhaps the most important function of state and local governments. Compulsory school attendance laws and the great expenditures for education both demonstrate our recognition of the importance of education to our democratic society. It is required in the performance of our most basic public responsibilities, even service in the armed forces. It is the very foundation of good citizenship. Today it is a principal instrument in awakening the child to cultural values, in preparing him for later professional training, and in helping him to adjust normally to his environment. In these days, it is doubtful that any child may reasonably be expected to succeed in life if he is denied the opportunity of an education. Such an opportunity, where the state has undertaken to provide it, is a right which must be made available to all on equal terms.

We come then to the question presented: Does segregation of children in public schools solely on the basis of race, even though the physical facilities and other "tangible" factors may be equal, deprive the children of the minority group of equal educational opportunities? We believe that it does. . . .

We conclude that in the field of public education the doctrine of "separate but equal" has no place. Separate educational facilities are inherently unequal. Therefore, we hold that the plaintiffs and others similarly situated for whom the actions have been brought are, by reason of the segregation complained of, deprived of the equal protection of the laws guaranteed by the Fourteenth Amendment.

From *Brown v. Board of Education of Topeka, United States Report,* Vol. 347 (Washington, D.C., 1954).

John F. Kennedy's Inaugural Address (1961)

President Kennedy's inauguration on January 20, 1961, set the tone for his administration. In his inaugural address, he stirred the nation by asking Americans to serve their country and their fellow human beings.

We observe today not a victory of party but a celebration of freedom—symbolizing an end as well as a beginning—signifying renewal as well as change. For I have sworn before you and Almighty God the same solemn oath our forebears prescribed nearly a century and three quarters ago.

The world is very different now. For man holds in his mortal hands the power to abolish all form of human poverty and to abolish all form of human life. And, yet, the same revolutionary beliefs for which our forebears fought are still at issue around the globe—the belief that the rights of man come not from the generosity of the state but from the hand of God.

We dare not forget today that we are the heirs of that first revolution. Let the word go forth from this time and place, to friend and foe alike, that the torch has been passed to a new generation of Americans—born in this century, tempered by war, disciplined by a cold and bitter peace, proud of our ancient heritage—and unwilling to witness or permit the slow undoing of those human rights to which this nation has always been committed, and to which we are committed today.

Let every nation know, whether it wish us well or ill, that we shall pay any price, bear any burden, meet any hardship, support any friend or oppose any foe in order to assure the survival and success of liberty.

This much we pledge—and more. . . .

In your hands, my fellow citizens, more than in mine, will rest the final success or failure of our course. Since this country was founded, each generation has been summoned to give testimony to its national loyalty. The graves of young Americans who answered the call encircle the globe.

Now the trumpet summons us again—not as a call to bear arms, though arms we need—not as a call to battle, though embattled we are—but a call to bear the burden of a long twilight struggle, year in and year out, "rejoicing in hope, patient in tribulation"—a struggle against the common enemies of man: tyranny, poverty, disease, and war itself. . . .

And so, my fellow Americans: Ask not what your country can do for you—ask what you can do for your country.

My fellow citizens of the world: Ask not what America will do for you, but what together we can do for the freedom of man.

From John F. Kennedy, Inaugural Address, *Department of State Bulletin* (February 6, 1961).

Martin Luther King, Jr.'s, "I Have a Dream" Speech (1963)

In August 1963, while Congress debated civil rights legislation, Martin Luther King led a quarter of a million demonstrators on a March on Washington. On the steps of the Lincoln Memorial he gave a stirring speech in which he told of his dream for America.

I say to you today, my friends, that in spite of the difficulties and frustrations of the moment, I still have a dream. It is a dream deeply rooted in the American dream. I have a dream that one day this nation will rise up and live out the true meaning of its creed: "We hold these truths to be self-evident: that all men are created equal. . . ."

I have a dream that one day on the red hills of Georgia the sons of former slaves and the sons of former slaveowners will be able to sit down together at the table of brotherhood. . . .

I have a dream that my four children will one day live in a nation where they will not be judged by the color of their skin but by the content of their character. I have a dream today.

I have a dream today. . . .

From every mountainside, let freedom ring. And when we allow freedom to ring, when we let it ring from every village, from every hamlet, from every state and every city, we will be able to speed up the day when all God's children, black men and white men, Jews and Gentiles, Protestants and Catholics, will be able

to join hands and sing in the word of the old Negro spiritual: "Free at last! Free at last! Thank God almighty, we are free at last!"

From *I Have a Dream* by Martin Luther King, Jr. Copyright © 1963 by Martin Luther King, Jr. Reprinted by permission of Joan Daves.

A *Challenger* Crew Memorial (1986)

The explosion of the space shuttle *Challenger* on January 28, 1986, shocked Americans. President Reagan delivered the following speech at a memorial service for the seven *Challenger* crew members who died in the accident.

The sacrifice of [the seven astronauts] has stirred the soul of our nation and through the pain our hearts have been opened to a profound truth: The future is not free; the story of all human progress is one of a struggle against all odds. . . . This America . . . was built by men and women like our seven star voyagers, who answered a call beyond duty, who gave more than was expected or required. . . .

We think back to the pioneers of an earlier century . . . who . . . set out into the frontier of the American West. Often they met with terrible hardship. . . . But grief only steeled them to the journey ahead. . . .

Man will continue his conquest of space. To reach out for new goals and ever greater achievements—that is the way we shall commemorate our seven *Challenger* heroes. . . .

From speech by President Ronald Reagan, *The New York Times*, February 1, 1986.

Martin Luther King, Jr.'s, "I Have a Dream" Speech

Analyzing Historical Documents

1. Ask students to describe Martin Luther King, Jr.'s dream for America. Ask what they think is necessary for this vision to come about. (King dreamt of a world without racial prejudice.)

2. Ask students to rephrase the third paragraph in their own words. (King hopes that his children will be seen and judged for who they are as people, rather than as members of a particular race.)

3. *Why did King make a connection between civil rights for black Americans and freedom for all people?* (As long as part of a society is deprived of its rights, the society as a whole is not free.)

For additional teaching strategy, see **Religion**, page 524.

A *Challenger* Crew Memorial

Analyzing Historical Documents

1. Ask students to summarize the point of the memorial speech in their own words. (It emphasizes that the costs of exploration may be heavy, but are worth the price.)

2. *What parallel does President Reagan draw between the astronauts and the settlers of the American West? Do you consider the parallel valid? Why or why not?* (Both groups went to the frontier and met with hardship.)

3. *How does Reagan propose to commemorate the astronauts?* (By continuing their achievements in space exploration.)

For additional teaching strategy, see **Patterns in History**, page 665.

The Declaration of Independence

The first paragraph, known as the Preamble, explains why the American colonists thought it necessary to make a political break with Great Britain.

When in the Course of human events, it becomes necessary for one people to dissolve the political bands which have connected them with another, and to assume among the powers of the earth, the separate and equal station to which the Laws of Nature and of Nature's God entitle them, a decent respect to the opinions of mankind requires that they should declare the causes which impel them to the separation.*

[THE RIGHT OF THE PEOPLE TO CONTROL THEIR GOVERNMENT]

This paragraph states that all people are born with certain God-given rights that are "unalienable." In other words, these rights cannot be given away or taken away by any government. Governments get their authority from the "consent" or approval of the people they govern. If a government lacks the consent of the people, then the people have a right to change or dissolve it. The people should, however, only resort to such change when the existing government has abused its powers.

endowed provided
usurpations wrongful uses of authority
Despotism unlimited power
Tyranny unjust use of power
candid fair

We hold these truths to be self-evident, that all men are created equal, that they are endowed by their Creator with certain unalienable Rights, that among these are Life, Liberty and the pursuit of Happiness. That to secure these rights, Governments are instituted among Men, deriving their just powers from the consent of the governed, That whenever any Form of Government becomes destructive of these ends, it is the Right of the People to alter or to abolish it, and to institute new Government, laying its foundation on such principles and organizing its powers in such form, as to them shall seem most likely to effect their Safety and Happiness. Prudence, indeed, will dictate that Governments long established should not be changed for light and transient causes; and accordingly all experience hath shown, that mankind are more disposed to suffer, while evils are sufferable, than to right themselves by abolishing the forms to which they are accustomed. But when a long train of abuses and usurpations, pursuing invariably the same Object evinces a design to reduce them under absolute Despotism, it is their right, it is their duty, to throw off such Government, and to provide new Guards for their future security. Such has been the patient sufferance of these Colonies; and such is now the necessity which constrains them to alter their former Systems of Government. The history of the present King of Great Britain is a history of repeated injuries and usurpations, all having in direct object the establishment of an absolute Tyranny over these States. To prove this, let Facts be submitted to a candid world.

[TYRANNICAL ACTS OF THE BRITISH KING]

This section lists the colonial grievances against George III and his government. Each of these 27 British offenses occurred

He has refused his Assent to Laws, the most wholesome and necessary for the public good.

He has forbidden his Governors to pass Laws of immediate and

---

*In punctuation and capitalization, the text of the Declaration follows accepted sources.

Assent approval
relinquish give up
inestimable too valuable to be measured
formidable causing fear
fatiguing tiring
Annihilation destruction
convulsions violent disturbances
Naturalization the process of becoming a citizen
tenure term

pressing importance, unless suspended in their operation till his Assent should be obtained; and when so suspended, he has utterly neglected to attend to them.

He has refused to pass other Laws for the accommodation of large districts of people, unless those people would relinquish the right of Representation in the Legislature, a right inestimable to them and formidable to tyrants only.

He has called together legislative bodies at places unusual, uncomfortable, and distant from the depository of their Public Records, for the sole purpose of fatiguing them into compliance with his measures.

He has dissolved Representative Houses repeatedly, for opposing with manly firmness his invasions on the rights of the people.

He has refused for a long time, after such dissolutions, to cause others to be elected; whereby the Legislative powers, incapable of Annihilation, have returned to the People at large for their exercise; the State remaining in the mean time exposed to all the dangers of invasion from without, and convulsions within.

He has endeavoured to prevent the population of these States; for that purpose obstructing the Laws for Naturalization of Foreigners; refusing to pass others to encourage their migrations hither, and raising the conditions of new Appropriations of Lands.

He has obstructed the Administration of Justice, by refusing his Assent to Laws for establishing Judiciary powers.

He has made Judges dependent on his Will alone, for the tenure of their offices, and the amount and payment of their salaries.

He has erected a multitude of New Offices, and sent hither swarms of Officers to harass our People, and eat out their substance.

He has kept among us, in times of peace, Standing Armies without the Consent of our legislatures.

He has affected to render the military independent of and superior to the Civil power.

He has combined with others to subject us to a jurisdiction foreign to our constitution, and unacknowledged by our laws; giving his Assent to their Acts of pretended Legislation:

For quartering large bodies of armed troops among us:

For protecting them, by a mock Trial, from Punishment for any Murders which they should commit on the Inhabitants of these States:

For cutting off our Trade with all parts of the world:

For imposing Taxes on us without our Consent:

For depriving us in many cases, of the benefits of Trial by Jury:

For transporting us beyond Seas to be tried for pretended offences:

For abolishing the free System of English Laws in a neighboring

DECLARATION OF INDEPENDENCE

731

Arbitrary tyrannical
abdicated given up
ravaged destroyed
perfidy treachery
constrained forced
insurrections rebellions

Province, establishing therein an Arbitrary government, and enlarging its Boundaries so as to render it at once an example and fit instrument for introducing the same absolute rule into these Colonies:

For taking away our Charters, abolishing our most valuable Laws, and altering fundamentally the Forms of our Governments:

For suspending our own Legislatures, and declaring themselves invested with power to legislate for us in all cases whatsoever.

He has abdicated Government here, by declaring us out of his Protection and waging War against us.

He has plundered our seas, ravaged our Coasts, burnt our towns, and destroyed the lives of our people.

He is at this time transporting large Armies of foreign Mercenaries to compleat the works of death, desolation and tyranny, already begun with circumstances of Cruelty and perfidy scarcely paralleled in the most barbarous ages, and totally unworthy the Head of a civilized nation.

He has constrained our fellow Citizens taken Captive on the high Seas to bear Arms against their Country, to become the executioners of their friends and Brethren, or to fall themselves by their Hands.

He has excited domestic insurrections amongst us, and has endeavoured to bring on the inhabitants of our frontiers, the merciless Indian Savages, whose known rule of warfare, is an undistinguished destruction of all ages, sexes and conditions.

[EFFORTS OF THE COLONIES TO AVOID SEPARATION]

This section states that the colonists tried, without success, to settle their grievances with the king. George III ignored the colonists' repeated petitions for change. The British people, too, failed to listen to the colonists' pleas. The colonists must now look on them as enemies in war and friends in peace.

Oppressions unjust uses of power
Petitioned for Redress asked for the correction of wrongs
unwarrantable jurisdiction unjust control
magnanimity generous nature
consanguinity blood relationship
acquiesce accept

In every stage of these Oppressions We have Petitioned for Redress in the most humble terms: Our repeated Petitions have been answered only by repeated injury. A Prince, whose character is thus marked by every act which may define a Tyrant, is unfit to be the ruler of a free people.

Nor have we been wanting in attentions to our British brethren. We have warned them from time to time of attempts by their legislature to extend an unwarrantable jurisdiction over us. We have reminded them of the circumstances of our emigration and settlement here. We have appealed to their native justice and magnanimity, and we have conjured them by the ties of our common kindred to disavow these usurpations, which, would inevitably interrupt our connections and correspondence. They too have been deaf to the voice of justice and of consanguinity. We must, therefore, acquiesce in the necessity, which denounces our Separation, and hold them, as we hold the rest of mankind, Enemies in War, in Peace Friends.

[THE COLONIES ARE DECLARED FREE AND INDEPENDENT]

The final paragraph states that the colonies are now free and independent states. All political ties between the United States of America and Great Britain are broken. The United States now has the power to declare war, make peace treaties, form political alliances, and establish trade. In the last sentence, the delegates (signers) pledge their support of the Declaration of Independence. They express their reliance on the protection of God.

rectitude honesty
Absolved freed
divine Providence God's guidance

We, therefore, the Representatives of the United States of America, in General Congress, Assembled, appealing to the Supreme Judge of the world for the rectitude of our intentions, do, in the Name, and by Authority of the good People of these Colonies, solemnly publish and declare, That these United Colonies are, and of Right ought to be Free and Independent States; that they are Absolved from all Allegiance to the British Crown, and that all political connection between them and the State of Great Britain, is and ought to be totally dissolved; and that as Free and Independent States, they have full Power to Levy War, conclude Peace, contract Alliances, establish Commerce, and to do all other Acts and Things which Independent States may of right do. And for the support of this Declaration, with a firm reliance on the protection of divine Providence, we mutually pledge to each other our Lives, our Fortunes and our sacred Honor.

Signers of the Declaration

NEW HAMPSHIRE
Josiah Bartlett
William Whipple
Matthew Thornton

MASSACHUSETTS
John Hancock
Samuel Adams
John Adams
Robert Treat Paine
Elbridge Gerry

RHODE ISLAND
Stephen Hopkins
William Ellery

CONNECTICUT
Roger Sherman
Samuel Huntington
William Williams
Oliver Wolcott

NEW YORK
William Floyd
Philip Livingston
Francis Lewis
Lewis Morris

NEW JERSEY
Richard Stockton
John Witherspoon
Francis Hopkinson
John Hart
Abraham Clark

PENNSYLVANIA
Robert Morris
Benjamin Rush
Benjamin Franklin
John Morton
George Clymer
James Smith
George Taylor
James Wilson
George Ross

DELAWARE
Caesar Rodney
George Read
Thomas McKean

MARYLAND
Samuel Chase
William Paca
Thomas Stone
Charles Carroll of Carrollton

VIRGINIA
George Wythe
Richard Henry Lee
Thomas Jefferson
Benjamin Harrison
Thomas Nelson, Jr.
Francis Lightfoot Lee
Carter Braxton

NORTH CAROLINA
William Hooper
Joseph Hewes
John Penn

SOUTH CAROLINA
Edward Rutledge
Thomas Heyward, Jr.
Thomas Lynch, Jr.
Arthur Middleton

GEORGIA
Button Gwinnett
Lyman Hall
George Walton

Constitution Handbook

The framers of the Constitution wanted to create a government powerful enough to protect the rights of citizens and defend the country against its enemies. It did not want a government, however, so powerful that it could become a tyranny. As James Madison observed, "In framing a government . . . the great difficulty lies in this: you must first enable the government to control the governed; and in the next place oblige it to control itself." As you study the Constitution, you will discover the many ways the framers sought to balance these diverse goals.

PRINCIPLES OF THE AMERICAN SYSTEM OF GOVERNMENT

The United States is dedicated to the proposition that people have the capacity to make wise decisions and govern themselves. Our country is a *republic* because we choose representatives to act for us in governing. It is also a democracy because all qualified citizens have the privilege of voting and therefore determining the kind of government we have. French historian Alexis de Tocqueville studied systems of government in the 1830s. Compared to other forms of government, Tocqueville concluded, republics "will be less brilliant, less glorious, and perhaps less strong, but the majority of the citizens will enjoy a greater degree of prosperity, and the people will remain quiet . . . because it is conscious of the advantages of its condition."

What are some features of our form of government? Under the Constitution, states share power with the federal (national) government. Some powers are given only to the federal government; others belong to the states; some are held jointly. This division of powers, known as federalism, encourages each side to protect its special powers against intrusion by the other.

The Constitution provides for separation of powers within the federal government as well. Only the legislative branch of the government can make laws. The executive branch administers them. The judicial branch interprets laws when disagreements arise over their meanings.

In order to guard against any one branch of the federal government becoming too powerful, the Constitution specifies a system of checks and balances. Each branch of government possesses the power to check, or limit the actions of, the other two branches.

THIRTEEN ENDURING CONSTITUTIONAL ISSUES

Our Constitution is the world's oldest written constitution. In the two centuries since its ratification, the Constitution has been changed through custom and through amendment, though these changes have been remarkably few. Arguments over how to interpret the language of the document, however, have been continual. When disputes over the Constitution's meaning arise, the Supreme Court interprets and decides the issue. Supreme Court interpretations have changed over the years, and many unresolved issues remain. The following thirteen issues have been sources of ongoing debates among legislators, legal scholars, and concerned citizens. The course of these debates shapes our system of government and the society in which we live.

1. National Power

The framers of the Constitution carefully limited the power of the federal government. However, over time, the government has expanded its authority at the expense of sectional interests. In the course of the nation's expansion, the federal government has also taken possession of territories such as Puerto Rico, the Panama Canal, the Philippines and other Pacific islands, and land belonging to American Indian tribes. During national emergencies, the government has tried to take over some businesses and forced others to close. Has the expansion of federal power gone too far? Or is the federal government too weak to deal effectively with complex problems that the nation faces as it nears the twenty-first century?

2. Federalism

The framers of the Constitution divided power between the state governments and the federal government to avoid the dangers of centralized authority. In doing so, however, they created what John Quincy Adams called "the most complicated government on the face of the earth."

The boundaries between state and federal power have been the subject of many lawsuits. Supporters of states' rights argue that state governments should have final authority within their state. Federalists believe that many state policies and laws involve national issues and should be under the authority of the federal government. The Supreme Court has claimed the power to declare state laws unconstitutional.

In addition, the federal government controls most tax revenues. State governments depend on federal aid to carry out many of the powers reserved to them in the Constitution. The federal government has used the threat of withholding this aid to change state policies. Is the increased power of the federal government necessary to enforce justice throughout the nation? Or does it endanger our liberties by destroying the balance of power in the federal system?

3. The Judiciary

The Supreme Court is unique because it decides fundamental social and political questions. These include the boundaries between church and state, between legislative and executive power, and even between racial groups. The Court has the power to declare the acts of governors, Congress, or the President to be unconstitutional. Tocqueville called this power of judicial review "one of the most powerful barriers that have ever been devised against the tyranny of political assemblies." But its opponents have challenged judicial review repeatedly since *Marbury v. Madison* established it in 1803.

In the twentieth century, Supreme Court decisions have helped shape government policies in controversial ,areas such as desegregation and abortion. Some scholars believe it is the Court's responsibility to act when Congress or the state legislatures do not. Others support "judicial self-restraint," claiming that the activism of the unelected federal judiciary represents a threat to the separation of powers and to democracy itself.

4. Civil Liberties

The first ten amendments to the Constitution are known as the Bill of Rights. The First Amendment guarantees individual liberties such as freedom of speech, religion, and assembly. Questions of limits on these individual liberties have been frequently and heatedly debated. For example, should the First Amendment right to freedom of speech prevail if it offends the values of the majority? What if it is racist speech? To what extent should human and civil rights be limited in the name of national security?

5. Suspects' Rights

How can the government balance the rights of persons accused of crimes and the public's right to safety? For example, some believe the courts should allow guilty persons to go free if crucial evidence against them has been obtained without a warrant, or if they were not specifically informed of their constitutional rights. Others argue that these restrictions on law-enforcement needlessly endanger the rest of the community.

Another area of debate concerns the widespread practice of "plea-bargaining" in criminal cases. In order to avoid costly trials, should prosecutors permit accused persons to plead guilty to lesser crimes? Or does this allow the guilty to escape the punishment they deserve?

6. Equality

In what ways are all Americans equal? The Constitution guarantees equality before the law, as well as equal political rights. Traditionally, discriminatory political and legal practices have thwarted these goals. Today, many people believe that the government should actively promote a more equal distribution of economic resources and benefits among citizens. For example, affirmative action programs require employers to promote a racial and sexual balance in the work force by favoring minority and female applicants. Supporters contend that without government intervention, the injustices of the past will continue to plague minorities. Opponents argue that affirmative action is a misguided attempt to guarantee equality of result rather than equality of opportunity.

7. Women's Rights

Does the Constitution adequately protect the rights of women? The document does not mention women, but neither does its use of the terms "person" and "citizen" exclude women. In recent years the nation has debated the merits of the Equal Rights Amendment. Is such an amendment necessary? Is it desirable? Short of a constitutional amendment, how can women be assured that they will not suffer from discrimination in the work force and other areas? How do Supreme Court decisions on reproductive issues affect women's rights?

8. Minority Rights

Slaves had no vote or other rights under the Constitution until passage of the Fourteenth Amendment in 1868. After World War II, the federal government took a larger role in protecting minority groups from discrimination. In *Brown v. Board of Education of Topeka* (1954), the Supreme Court redefined racial boundaries by outlawing school segregation. Often, government decisions involving minority rights met fierce resistance from people who felt that their own rights and the principle of majority rule were threatened. Then, in the 1980s, there appeared to be a reversal of government policy. Critics of Supreme Court decisions argued that minority gains from earlier decades were fast being eroded. Despite some gains, many minorities still suffer from discrimination. What is the federal government's role in protecting minority rights? What is the proper balance between majority rule and minority rights?

9. Foreign Policy

Under the Constitution, Congress alone has the power to declare war, but the President is commander-in-chief of the armed forces. How should the government handle the conduct of war and foreign policy? Should the President have the power to send troops into combat without a declaration of war, as was done in Korea and Vietnam? Some people argue that the President needs to be able to act decisively to protect national security interests. Others take the view that without popular support, in the form of a congressional vote, military actions are misguided and illegitimate. In passing the War Powers Act of 1973, which limited the President's ability to use military power, did Congress unconstitutionally infringe on presidential power?

10. Separation of Powers

Does the separation of powers make the federal government too inefficient to meet modern-day challenges? The framers deliberately pitted the branches of government against one another and, in effect, lessened their efficiency in order to guard against abuses. Some critics argue that these safeguards are not worth the price we pay for them in governmental inefficiency and delay. Others contend that the history of abuse of governmental power proves the worth of the system of checks and balances.

11. Representation

Our government is based on a system of representation. Does our current system of government provide fair and effective representation of our citizenry? The twentieth century has seen the growth of thousands of special interest groups, which often have political clout beyond the size of their memberships. Do these groups protect the rights of minorities? Or are they unacceptable limitations of democracy?

12. Government and the Economy

Does the Constitution's encouragement of business and commerce help all Americans, or does it favor the interests of the wealthy? In the twentieth century, reformers have urged the government to limit the exercise of free enterprise in order to protect the public from a variety of abuses. These abuses include unfair pricing, unsafe products, and environmental destruction.

13. Constitutional Change

How flexible is the Constitution? The framers included Article V so that the Constitution could be revised to suit future conditions. However, they deliberately made the amendment process difficult so that the Constitution would be more than temporary law. Does the requirement of a two-thirds vote of Congress or a three-quarters vote of the state legislatures or state conventions benefit the nation by making its political system more stable? Or does it harm America by preventing the Constitution from adapting to changing times? If, in accordance with Article V, the states called a second constitutional convention, would the delegates have the right to frame an entirely new constitution?

STUDYING THE CONSTITUTION

These thirteen enduring issues involve basic questions of law and policy. It is useful to keep them in mind as you study the Constitution, since they demonstrate the document's importance in the lives of American citizens.

The complete text of the Constitution of the United States begins on the next page. The actual text of the Constitution appears in the inside column on each page, while the other column explains specific parts or provisions.

Headings and subheadings have been added to the Constitution to help you find specific topics. Those parts of the Constitution that are no longer in effect are in lighter type. Some spellings and punctuation have been modified for modern readers.

A Directory of the Constitution

The Constitution of the United States

The Preamble states the purposes for which the Constitution was written: (1) to form a union of states that will benefit all, (2) to make laws and establish courts that are fair, (3) to maintain peace within the country, (4) to defend the nation against attack, (5) to ensure people's general well-being, and (6) to make sure that this nation's people and their descendants remain free.

The opening words of the Constitution make clear that it is the people themselves who have the power to establish a government or change it.

The first branch described is the legislative, or law-making, branch. Congress is made up of two houses—the Senate and the House of Representatives.

Section 2
Note that the states establish qualifications for voting. Any person who has the right to vote for representatives to the state legislature has the right to vote for the state's representatives in the House of Representatives. This is the only qualification for voting listed in the original Constitution. It made sure that the House would be elected by the people themselves.

Preamble

*W*e the people of the United States, in order to form a more perfect union, establish justice, insure domestic tranquility, provide for the common defense, promote the general welfare, and secure the blessings of liberty to ourselves and our posterity, do ordain and establish this Constitution for the United States of America.

ARTICLE I   Legislative Branch

SECTION 1   Congress

All legislative powers herein granted shall be vested in a Congress of the United States, which shall consist of a Senate and House of Representatives.

SECTION 2   The House of Representatives

Clause 1. Election and term of members   The House of Representatives shall be composed of members chosen every second year by the people of the several states, and the electors in each state shall have the qualifications requisite for electors of the most numerous branch of the state legislature.

Clause 2. Qualification of members   No person shall be a representative who shall not have attained to the age of twenty-five years, and been seven years a citizen of the United States, and who shall not, when elected, be an inhabitant of that state in which he shall be chosen.

Clause 3. Appointment of representatives and direct taxes Representatives [and direct taxes] shall be apportioned among the several states which may be included within this Union, according to their respective numbers, [which shall be determined by adding to the whole number of free persons, including those bound to service for a term of years, and excluding Indians not taxed, three-fifths of all other persons]. The actual enumeration shall be made within three years after the first meeting of the Congress of the United States, and within every subsequent term of ten years, in such manner as they shall by law direct. The number of representatives shall not exceed one for every thirty thousand, but each state shall have at least one representative; [and until such enumeration shall be made, the State of New Hampshire shall be entitled to choose three; Massachusetts, eight; Rhode Island and Providence Plantations, one; Connecticut, five; New York, six; New Jersey, four; Pennsylvania, eight; Delaware, one; Maryland, six; Virginia, ten; North Carolina, five; South Carolina, five; and Georgia, three].

Clause 4. Filling vacancies When vacancies happen in the representation from any state, the executive authority thereof shall issue writs of election to fill such vacancies.

Clause 5. Officers; impeachment The House of Representatives shall choose their Speaker and other officers; and shall have the sole power of impeachment.

SECTION 3 The Senate

Clause 1. Number and election of members The Senate of the United States shall be composed of two senators from each state, chosen [by the legislature thereof,] for six years; and each senator shall have one vote.

Clause 3
Several amendments have changed these provisions. All the people of a state are now counted in determining the number of representatives a state shall have, based on a census taken every ten years. The House of Representatives cannot have more than one member for every 30,000 persons in the nation. But each state is entitled to one representative, no matter how small its population. In 1910 Congress limited the number of representatives to 435.

Amendment 16 made the income tax an exception to the rule against direct taxes not based on population.

Clause 4
When a state does not have all the representatives to which it is entitled—for example, when a representative resigns or dies—the governor of the state may call an election to fill the vacancy.

Clause 5
Only the House can impeach, that is, bring charges of misbehavior in office against a U.S. official.

Section 3
Senators are no longer chosen by state legislatures but elected by the people (Amendment 17).

Senators in the 1st Congress were divided into three groups so that their terms would not all end at the same time. Today all senators are elected for six-year terms, but only one-third are elected in any election year.

A bird's-eye view of the nation's capital in 1880, when the Washington Monument was still being built.

Daniel Webster in a tense Senate debate, 1850.

Clause 2. Choosing senators   Immediately after they shall be assembled in consequence of the first election, they shall be divided as equally as may be into three classes. [The seats of the senators of the first class shall be vacated at the expiration of the second year, of the second class at the expiration of the fourth year, and of the third class at the expiration of the sixth year,] so that one-third may be chosen every second year; [and if vacancies happen by resignation, or otherwise, during the recess of the legislature of any state, the executive thereof may make temporary appointments until the next meeting of the legislature, which shall then fill such vacancies.]

Clause 3. Qualifications of members   No person shall be a senator who shall not have attained to the age of thirty years, and been nine years a citizen of the United States, and who shall not, when elected, be an inhabitant of that state for which he shall be chosen.

Clause 4. Senate President   The Vice President of the United States shall be President of the Senate, but shall have no vote, unless they be equally divided.

Clause 5. Other officers   The Senate shall choose their own officers, and also a President pro tempore, in the absence of the Vice President, or when he shall exercise the office of President of the United States.

Clauses 6 and 7
The Senate tries the case when a federal official is impeached by the House of Representatives. The Senators must formally declare that they will be honest and just. If the President of the United States is on trial, the Chief Justice presides over the Senate. Two-thirds of the senators present must agree that the charge is true for the impeached person to be found guilty.

If the Senate finds an impeached official guilty, the only punishment is removal from office and disqualification for ever holding a government job again. Once out of office, however, the former official may be tried in a regular court and, if found guilty, punished like any other person.

Clause 6. Impeachment trials   The Senate shall have the sole power to try all impeachments. When sitting for that purpose, they shall be on oath or affirmation. When the President of the United States is tried, the Chief Justice shall preside; and no person shall be convicted without the concurrence of two-thirds of the members present.

Clause 7. Impeachment convictions   Judgment in cases of impeachment shall not exceed further than to removal from office, and disqualification to hold and enjoy any office of honor, trust, or profit under the United States; but the party convicted shall nevertheless be liable and subject to indictment, trial, judgment, and punishment, according to law.

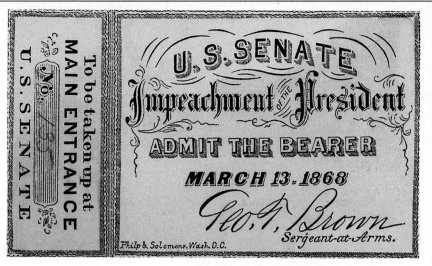

A visitor's ticket to the Senate gallery for the 1868 impeachment trial that acquitted President Johnson.

SECTION 4 Congressional Elections and Meetings

Clause 1. Elections The times, places, and manner of holding elections for senators and representatives shall be prescribed in each state by the legislature thereof; but the Congress may at any time by law make or alter such regulations, [except as to the places of choosing senators.]

Clause 2. Meetings of Congress The Congress shall assemble at least once in every year, [and such meeting shall be on the first Monday in December, unless they shall by law appoint a different day.]

SECTION 5 Organization and Rules

Clause 1. Organization Each house shall be the judge of the elections, returns, and qualifications of its own members, and a majority of each shall constitute a quorum to do business; but a smaller number may adjourn from day to day, and may be authorized to compel the attendance of absent members, in such manner, and under such penalties as each house may provide.

Clause 2. Rules Each house may determine the rules of its proceedings, punish its members for disorderly behavior, and with the concurrence of two-thirds, expel a member.

Clause 3. Journal Each house shall keep a journal of its proceedings, and from time to time publish the same, excepting such parts as may in their judgment require secrecy; and the yeas and nays of the members of either house on any question shall, at the desire of one-fifth of those present, be entered on the journal.

Section 4
The legislature of each state has the right to determine how, when, and where senators and representatives are elected, but Congress may pass election laws that the states must follow. For example, a federal law requires that secret ballots be used. Congress must meet at least once a year. Amendment 20 made January 3 the day for beginning a regular session of Congress.

Andrew Johnson, the only U.S. President impeached.

Clause 3
Each house of Congress keeps and publishes a record of what goes on at its meetings. The *Congressional Record* is issued daily during sessions of Congress. Parts of the record that the members of Congress believe should be kept secret may be withheld. How members of either house vote on a question may be entered in the record if one-fifth of those present wish it.

Clause 4

When Congress is meeting, neither house may stop work for more than three days without the consent of the other house. Neither house may meet in another city without the consent of the other house.

Section 6

Senators and representatives are paid out of the United States Treasury and have a number of other privileges.

Until their terms have ended, senators or representatives may not hold offices created by the Congress of which they are members. The same restriction applies to jobs for which Congress has voted increased pay. No person may be a member of Congress without first giving up any other federal office he or she may hold.

Section 7

Bills for raising money for the federal government must start in the House of Representatives, but the Senate may make changes in such bills. Actually, the Senate now has as much influence over revenue bills as does the House. Other bills may start in either the Senate or the House of Representatives. However, exactly the same bill must be passed by a majority vote in both houses of Congress.

President Gerald Ford signs a tax bill into law.

Clause 4. Adjournment Neither house, during the session of Congress, shall without the consent of the other adjourn for more than three days, nor to any other place than that in which the two houses shall be sitting.

SECTION 6 Privileges and Restrictions

Clause 1. Pay; Congressional immunity The senators and representatives shall receive a compensation for their services, to be ascertained by law, and paid out of the Treasury of the United States. They shall in all cases, except treason, felony, and breach of the peace, be privileged from arrest during their attendance at the session of their respective houses and in going to and returning from the same; and for any speech or debate in either house, they shall not be questioned in any other place.

Clause 2. Restrictions No senator or representative shall, during the time for which he was elected, be appointed to any civil office under the authority of the United States which shall have been created, or the emoluments whereof shall have been increased during such time; and no person holding any office under the United States shall be a member of either house during his continuance in office.

SECTION 7 Method of Passing Laws

Clause 1. Revenue bills All bills for raising revenue shall originate in the House of Representatives; but the Senate may propose or concur with amendments as on other bills.

Clause 2. How bills become law Every bill which shall have passed the House of Representatives and the Senate shall, before it become a law, be presented to the President of the United States; if he approves he shall sign it, but if not he shall return it, with his objections, to that house in which it shall have originated, who shall enter the objections at large on their journal, and proceed to reconsider it. If after such reconsideration two-thirds of that house shall agree to pass the bill, it shall be sent, together with the objections, to the other house, by which it shall likewise be reconsidered, and if approved by two-thirds of that house, it shall become a law. But in all such cases the votes of both houses shall be determined by yeas and nays, and the names of the persons voting for and against the bill shall be entered on the journal of each house respectively. If any bill shall not be returned by the President within ten days (Sundays excepted) after it shall have been presented to him, the same shall be a law, in like manner as if he had signed it, unless the Congress by their adjournment prevent its return, in which case it shall not be a law.

person have a majority, then from the five highest on the list the said house shall in like manner choose the President. But in choosing the President the votes shall be taken by states, the representation from each state having one vote; a quorum for this purpose shall consist of a member or members from two-thirds of the states, and a majority of all the states shall be necessary to a choice. In every case, after the choice of the President, the person having the greatest number of votes of the electors shall be the Vice President. But if there should remain two or more who have equal votes, the Senate shall choose from them by ballot the Vice President.]

Clause 3. Time of elections The Congress may determine the time of choosing the electors, and the day on which they shall give their votes; which day shall be the same throughout the United States.

Clause 4. Qualifications for President No person except a natural-born citizen, [or a citizen of the United States, at the time of the adoption of this Constitution] shall be eligible to the office of President; neither shall any person be eligible to that office who shall not have attained the age of thirty-five years, and been fourteen years a resident within the United States.

Clause 5. Succession In case of the removal of the President from office or of his death, resignation, or inability to discharge the powers and duties of the said office, the same shall devolve on the Vice President; and the Congress may by law provide for the case of removal, death, resignation, or inability, both of the President and Vice President, declaring what officer shall then act as President; and such officer shall act accordingly, until the disability be removed or a President shall be elected.

An 1860 poster for candidates Lincoln and Hannibal Hamlin.

Clause 3
Congress determines when electors are chosen and when they vote. The day is the same throughout the United States. The popular vote for electors takes place on the Tuesday after the first Monday of November every four years. In mid-December the electors meet in their state capitals and cast their electoral votes.

Clause 5
If the presidency becomes vacant, the Vice President becomes the President of the United States. If neither the President nor the Vice President is able to serve, Congress has the right to decide which government official shall act as President. Amendment 25 practically assures that there always will be a Vice President to succeed to the presidency.

The White House — the presidential mansion — in 1848.

★ CONSTITUTION ★

747

Section 2
Presidential powers are described very generally (unlike those of Congress).

Clause 1
The President is commander-in-chief of the armed forces and of the militia when it is called out by the national government. This is another provision to ensure civilian control of the military. No provision is made in the Constitution for the Cabinet or for Cabinet meetings, but the existence of executive departments is implied in this clause.

Clause 2
The President is the nation's chief diplomat, with the power to make treaties. All treaties must be approved in the Senate by a two-thirds vote of the senators present. The President also can appoint important government officials, who must be approved in the Senate by a majority.

Past and future Presidents and their families at the inauguration of John F. Kennedy. (The front row includes the Eisenhowers, Lady Bird Johnson, Jacqueline Kennedy, Lyndon Johnson, Richard Nixon, and the Trumans.)

Clause 6. Salary The President shall, at stated times, receive for his services a compensation, which shall neither be increased nor diminished during the period for which he shall have been elected, and he shall not receive within that period any other emolument from the United States, or any of them.

Clause 7. Oath of office Before he enter on the execution of his office, he shall take the following oath or affirmation: "I do solemnly swear (or affirm) that I will faithfully execute the office of President of the United States, and will to the best of my ability, preserve, protect, and defend the Constitution of the United States."

SECTION 2 Powers of the President

Clause 1. Military powers; Cabinet; pardons The President shall be Commander-in-Chief of the Army and Navy of the United States, and of the militia of the several states, when called into the actual service of the United States. He may require the opinion, in writing, of the principal officer in each of the executive departments, upon any subject relating to the duties of their respective offices, and he shall have power to grant reprieves and pardons for offenses against the United States, except in cases of impeachment.

Clause 2. Diplomatic powers; appointments He shall have power, by and with the advice and consent of the Senate, to make treaties, provided two-thirds of the senators present concur; and he shall nominate and, by and with the advice and consent of the Senate, shall appoint ambassadors, other public ministers and consuls, judges of the Supreme Court, and all other officers of the United States, whose appointments are not herein otherwise provided for, and which shall be established by law; but the Congress may by law vest the appointment of such inferior officers as they think proper in the President alone, in the courts of law, or in the heads of departments.

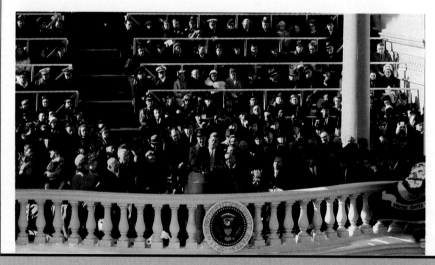

748

Clause 3. Filling vacancies The President shall have power to fill up all vacancies that may happen during the recess of the Senate, by granting commissions which shall expire at the end of their next session.

SECTION 3   Duties of the President

He shall from time to time give to the Congress information of the state of the Union, and recommend to their consideration such measures as he shall judge necessary and expedient; he may, on extraordinary occasions, convene both houses, or either of them, and in case of disagreement between them with respect to the time of adjournment he may adjourn them to such time as he shall think proper; he shall receive ambassadors and other public ministers; he shall take care that the laws be faithfully executed, and shall commission all the officers of the United States.

SECTION 4   Impeachment

The President, Vice-President, and all civil officers of the United States shall be removed from office on impeachment for, and conviction of, treason, bribery, or other high crimes and misdemeanors.

Clause 3
If the Senate is not meeting, the President may make temporary appointments to fill vacancies.

Section 3
The Constitution imposes only a few specific duties on the President. One is to give a "State of the Union" message, which Presidents now deliver once a year.

Section 4
This section makes all Federal officials subject to the impeachment process described in Article I.

The Supreme Court held its first two sessions in this New York building, known as the Exchange.

ARTICLE III   Judicial Branch

SECTION 1   The Federal Courts

The judicial power of the United States shall be vested in one Supreme Court and in such inferior courts as the Congress may from time to time ordain and establish. The judges, both of the Supreme and inferior courts, shall hold their offices during good behavior and shall, at stated times, receive for their services a compensation which shall not be diminished during their continuance in office.

Article III gives the power to interpret the laws of the United States to the third branch, the judicial, which includes the Supreme Court and the other federal courts established by Congress. District courts and courts of appeal are now part of the regular court system. Federal judges are appointed by the President with the approval of the Senate.

Section 2

The federal courts have jurisdiction in certain kinds of cases.

Roger B. Taney, Chief Justice of the United States in the crucial years between 1836 and 1864.

Section 3

The Constitution defines treason and places limits on how it can be punished.

The Supreme Court building today.

SECTION 2   Federal Court Jurisdiction

Clause 1. Federal cases   The judicial power shall extend to all cases, in law and equity, arising under this Constitution, the laws of the United States, and treaties made, or which shall be made, under their authority; to all cases affecting ambassadors, other public ministers, and consuls; to all cases of admiralty and maritime jurisdiction; to controversies to which the United States shall be a party; to controversies between two or more states; [between a state and citizens of another state;] between citizens of different states; between citizens of the same state claiming lands under grants of different states, and between a state, or the citizens thereof, and foreign states, citizens, or subjects.

Clause 2. Supreme Court jurisdiction   In all cases affecting ambassadors, other public ministers, and consuls, and those in which a state be a party, the Supreme Court shall have original jurisdiction. In all the other cases before mentioned, the Supreme Court shall have appellate jurisdiction, both as to law and fact, with such exceptions and under such regulations as the Congress shall make.

Clause 3. Trial rules   The trial of all crimes, except in cases of impeachment, shall be by jury; and such trial shall be held in the state where the said crimes shall have been committed; but when not committed within any state, the trial shall be at such place or places as the Congress may by law have directed.

SECTION 3   Treason

Clause 1. Definition   Treason against the United States shall consist only in levying war against them or in adhering to their enemies, giving them aid and comfort. No person shall be convicted of treason unless on the testimony of two witnesses to the same overt act, or on confession in open court.

Clause 2. Punishment   The Congress shall have power to declare the punishment of treason, but no attainder of treason shall work corruption of blood, or forfeiture except during the life of the person attainted.

ARTICLE IV The States and the Federal Government

SECTION 1 State Records

Full faith and credit shall be given in each state to the public acts, records, and judicial proceedings of every other state. And the Congress may by general laws prescribe the manner in which such acts, records, and proceedings shall be proved, and the effect thereof.

SECTION 2 Rights of Citizens

Clause 1. Privileges and immunities The citizens of each state shall be entitled to all privileges and immunities of citizens in the several states.

Clause 2. Extradition A person charged in any state with treason, felony, or other crime who shall flee from justice and be found in another state shall, on demand of the executive authority of the state from which he fled, be delivered up, to be removed to the state having jurisdiction of the crime.

[**Clause 3. Fugitive workers** No person held to service or labor in one state, under the laws thereof, escaping into another shall, in consequence of any law or regulation therein, be discharged from such service or labor, but shall be delivered upon claim of the party to whom such service or labor may be due.]

SECTION 3 New States and Territories

Clause 1. Admission of new states New states may be admitted by the Congress into this Union; but no new state shall be formed or erected within the jurisdiction of any other state; nor any state be formed by the junction of two or more states, or parts of states, without the consent of the legislatures of the states concerned, as well as of the Congress.

Clause 2. Federal territory The Congress shall have power to dispose of and make all needful rules and regulations respecting the territory or other property belonging to the United States; and nothing in this Constitution shall be so construed as to prejudice any claims of the United States, or of any particular state.

SECTION 4 Federal Duties to the States

The United States shall guarantee to every state in this Union a republican form of government, and shall protect each of them against invasion; and on application of the legislature, or of the executive (whom the legislature cannot be convened), against domestic violence.

Article IV sets out many of the principles of the federal system, describing relations among the states and between the national government and the states. Section 3 tells how new states may be admitted to the Union. Section 4 outlines the national government's duties to the states.

Section 2
The provisions of this section extend most privileges of state citizenship to *all* citizens. (Some exceptions are made.) It also establishes the extradition process.

Clause 3
Amendment 13 abolished slavery and made this clause obsolete.

Dakota Territory applying to Uncle Sam for statehood, in an 1880's cartoon.

Article V sets up two ways of amending the Constitution and two ways of ratifying amendments.

ARTICLE V Amending the Constitution

The Congress, whenever two-thirds of both houses shall deem it necessary, shall propose amendments to this Constitution, or, on the application of the legislatures of two-thirds of the several states, shall call a convention for proposing amendments, which, in either case, shall be valid to all intents and purposes, as part of this Constitution, when ratified by the legislatures of three-fourths of the several states or by conventions in three-fourths thereof, as the one or the other mode of ratification may be proposed by the Congress; provided that [no amendments which may be made prior to the year one thousand eight hundred and eight shall in any manner affect the first and fourth clauses in the ninth section of the first article; and that] no state, without its consent, shall be deprived of its equal suffrage in the Senate.

Article VI makes the Constitution the "supreme law of the land." If state law is in conflict with national law, it is the national law that must be obeyed.

Clause 1
The framers of the Constitution agreed that the United States would be responsible for all debts contracted by the government under the Articles of Confederation.

ARTICLE VI Supremacy of National Law

Clause 1. Public debt All debts contracted and engagements entered into, before the adoption of this Constitution, shall be as valid against the United States under this Constitution as under the Confederation.

Clause 2. Supreme law of the land This Constitution, and the laws of the United States which shall be made in pursuance thereof, and all treaties made, or which shall be made, under the authority of the United States, shall be the supreme law of the land; and the judges in every state shall be bound thereby, anything in the Constitution or laws of any state to the contrary notwithstanding.

Clause 3. Oath of office The senators and representatives before mentioned, and the members of the several state legislatures, and all executive and judicial officers, both of the United States and of the several states, shall be bound by oath or affirmation to support this Constitution; but no religious test shall ever be required as a qualification to any office or public trust under the United States.

Present-day courtroom, Newport, Rhode Island.

The signing of the Constitution, September 17, 1787.

ARTICLE VII Ratification of the Constitution

The ratification of the conventions of nine states shall be sufficient for the establishment of this Constitution between the states so ratifying the same.

Article VII established that the Constitution would go into effect when nine states voted to accept it. This occurred on June 21, 1788, with New Hampshire's ratification.

George Washington —
   President and
   delegate
   from Virginia

New Hampshire
John Langdon
Nicholas Gilman

Massachusetts
Nathaniel Gorham
Rufus King

Connecticut
William Samuel
   Johnson
Roger Sherman

New York
Alexander Hamilton

New Jersey
William Livingston
David Brearley
William Paterson
Jonathan Dayton

Pennsylvania
Benjamin Franklin
Thomas Mifflin
Robert Morris
George Clymer
Thomas FitzSimons
Jared Ingersoll
James Wilson
Gouverneur Morris

Delaware
George Reed
Gunning Bedford, Junior
John Dickinson
Richard Bassett
Jacob Broom

Maryland
James McHenry
Daniel of St. Thomas
   Jenifer
Daniel Carroll

Virginia
John Blair
James Madison, Junior

North Carolina
William Blount
Richard Dobbs
   Spaight
Hugh Williamson

South Carolina
John Rutledge
Charles Cotesworth
   Pinckney
Charles Pinckney
Pierce Butler

Georgia
William Few
Abraham Baldwin

753

AMENDMENTS to the Constitution

Amendments 1–10 make up the Bill of Rights.

Amendment 1 protects citizens from government interference with their freedoms of religion, speech, press, assembly, and petition. These are the basic civil liberties.

AMENDMENT 1   Freedom of Religion, Speech, Press, Assembly, and Petition (1791)

Congress shall make no law respecting an establishment of religion or prohibiting the free exercise thereof; or abridging the freedom of speech, or of the press; or the right of the people peaceably to assemble, and to petition the government for a redress of grievances.

Amendment 2 guarantees that the federal government cannot deny states the right to enlist citizens in the militia and to provide them with training in the use of weapons.

AMENDMENT 2   Right to Bear Arms (1791)

A well-regulated militia being necessary to the security of a free state, the right of the people to keep and bear arms shall not be infringed.

Amendment 3 was included because of the troubles caused when the British sought to quarter and supply their troops in colonists' homes. The amendment guarantees that in time of peace the federal government may not force people to have soldiers live in their homes. Even in time of war, people cannot be compelled to do this unless Congress passes a law requiring it.

AMENDMENT 3   Quartering of Soldiers (1791)

No soldier shall, in time of peace, be quartered in any house without the consent of the owner, nor in time of war, but in a manner to be prescribed by law.

Amendment 4 extends the people's right to privacy and security by setting limits on authorities' power to search property and seize evidence.

AMENDMENT 4   Search and Seizure (1791)

The right of the people to be secure in their persons, houses, papers, and effects, against unreasonable searches and seizures, shall not be violated, and no warrants shall issue but upon probable cause, supported by oath or affirmation and particularly describing the place to be searched and the persons or things to be seized.

★ CONSTITUTION ★

754

AMENDMENT 5   Rights of the Accused (1791)

No person shall be held to answer for a capital or otherwise infamous crime, unless on a presentment or indictment of a grand jury, except in cases arising in the land or naval forces, or in the militia, when in actual service in time of war or public danger; nor shall any person be subject for the same offense to be twice put in jeopardy of life or limb; nor shall be compelled in any criminal case to be a witness against himself, nor be deprived of life, liberty, or property, without due process of law; nor shall private property be taken for public use without just compensation.

Amendment 5 ensures certain rights for people accused of crimes. It says that no person may be tried in a federal court unless a grand jury decides that the person ought to be tried. (Members of the armed forces may be tried in military court under military law.) Other provisions guarantee due process of law. Finally, a person's private property may not be taken for public use without a fair price being paid for it.

AMENDMENT 6   Requirements for Jury Trial (1791)

In all criminal prosecutions, the accused shall enjoy the right to a speedy and public trial by an impartial jury of the state and district wherein the crime shall have been committed, which districts shall have been previously ascertained by law, and to be informed of the nature and cause of the accusation; to be confronted with the witnesses against him; to have compulsory process for obtaining witnesses in his favor; and to have the assistance of counsel for his defense.

Amendment 6 lists additional rights of an individual accused of a crime. A person accused of a crime is entitled to a prompt public trial before an impartial jury. The trial is held in the district where the crime took place. The accused must be told what the charge is. The accused must be present when witnesses give their testimony. The government must help the accused bring into court friendly witnesses. The accused must be provided with legal counsel.

AMENDMENT 7   Rules of Common Law (1791)

In suits at common law, where the value in controversy shall exceed twenty dollars, the right of trial by jury shall be preserved, and no fact tried by a jury shall be otherwise reexamined in any court of the United States than according to the rules of common law.

Amendment 7 is somewhat out of date. Today, cases involving lawsuits are not tried before federal courts unless large sums of money are involved.

The draft of the Bill of Rights — twelve amendments sent to the states in 1789 — only ten of which were approved.

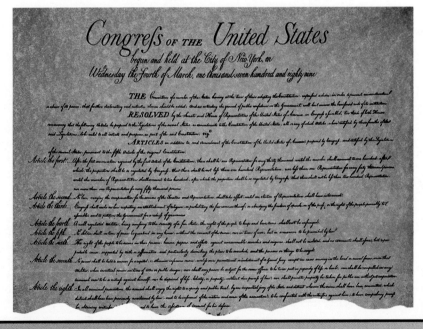

755

Amendment 8 provides that persons accused of crimes may in most cases be released from jail if they or someone else posts bail. Bail, fines, and punishments must be reasonable.

AMENDMENT 8   Limits on Criminal Punishments (1791)

Excessive bail shall not be required, nor excessive fines imposed, nor cruel and unusual punishments inflicted.

Amendment 9 was included because of the impossibility of listing in the Constitution all the rights of the people. The mention of certain rights does not mean that people do not have other fundamental rights, which the government must respect. These include the right to privacy.

AMENDMENT 9   Rights Kept by the People (1791)

The enumeration in the Constitution of certain rights shall not be construed to deny or disparage others retained by the people.

Amendment 10 establishes the reserved powers. It states that the powers that the Constitution does not give to the United States and does not deny to the states belong to the states and to the people.

AMENDMENT 10   Powers of the States and the People (1791)

The powers not delegated to the United States by the Constitution, nor prohibited by it to the states, are reserved to the states respectively, or to the people.

This amendment was the first that was enacted to override a Supreme Court decision. It confirms that no federal court may try a case in which a state is being sued by a citizen of another state or of a foreign country. Amendment 11 changes a provision of Article III, Section 2.

AMENDMENT 11   Lawsuits Against a State (1798)

The judicial power of the United States shall not be construed to extend to any suit in law or equity commenced or prosecuted against one of the United States by citizens of another state or by citizens or subjects of any foreign state.

A southern jury in 1867 included blacks who, for the first time, had the rights of citizens.

AMENDMENT 12 Election of President and Vice President (1804)

The electors shall meet in their respective states and vote by ballot for President and Vice President, one of whom, at least, shall not be an inhabitant of the same state with themselves; they shall name in their ballots the person voted for as President, and in distinct ballots the person voted for as Vice President, and they shall make distinct lists of all persons voted for as President, and of all persons voted for as Vice President, and of the number of votes for each, which lists they shall sign and certify, and transmit sealed to the seat of the government of the United States, directed to the President of the Senate; the President of the Senate shall, in the presence of the Senate and House of Representatives, open all the certificates and the votes shall then be counted; the person having the greatest number of votes for President shall be the President, if such number be a majority of the whole number of electors appointed; and if no person have such majority, then from the persons having the highest numbers not exceeding three on the list of those voted for as President, the House of Representatives shall choose immediately, by ballot, the President. But in choosing the President, the votes shall be taken by states, the representation from each state having one vote; a quorum for this purpose shall consist of a member or members from two-thirds of the states, and a majority of all the states shall be necessary to a choice. And if the House of Representatives shall not choose a President whenever the right of choice shall devolve upon them, [before the fourth day of March next following] then the Vice President shall act as President, as in the case of the death or constitutional disability of the President. The person having the greatest number of votes as Vice President shall be the Vice President, if such number be a majority of the whole number of electors appointed, and if no person have a majority, then from the two highest numbers on the list, the Senate shall choose the Vice President; a quorum for the purpose shall consist of two-thirds of the whole number of senators, and a majority of the whole number shall be necessary to a choice. But no person constitutionally ineligible to the office of President shall be eligible to that of Vice President of the United States.

Amendment 12 changed the Electoral College procedure for choosing a President. The most important change made by this amendment was that the presidential electors would vote for President and Vice President on separate ballots. In 1800, when only one ballot was used, Thomas Jefferson and Aaron Burr received the same number of votes, and the election had to be decided by the House of Representatives. To guard against this possibility in the future, Amendment 12 calls for separate ballots.

Thomas Jefferson, third President of the United States.

AMENDMENT 13 Slavery Abolished (1865)

Section 1. Abolition of slavery Neither slavery nor involuntary servitude, except as a punishment for crime whereof the party shall have been duly convicted, shall exist within the United States or any place subject to their jurisdiction.

Section 2. Enforcement Congress shall have the power to enforce this article by appropriate legislation.

Amendment 13 is the first of three amendments that were a consequence of the Civil War. It states that slavery must end in the United States and its territories.

Congress may pass whatever laws are necessary to enforce Amendment 13. This statement, called an *enabling act*, is now commonly included in amendments.

By the definition of citizenship in Amendment 14, black Americans were granted citizenship. The first section provides that all persons born or naturalized in the United States and subject to this country's laws are citizens of the United States and of the state in which they live. State governments may not deprive anyone of due process of law or equal protection.

This section abolished the provision in Article 1, Section 2, which said that only three-fifths of the slaves should be counted as population.

Section 3 was designed to bar former leaders of the Confederacy from holding federal office.

Following emancipation, most Southern blacks became sharecroppers, working land owned by others.

AMENDMENT 14 Civil Rights Guaranteed (1868)

Section 1. Definition of citizenship All persons born or naturalized in the United States, and subject to the jurisdiction thereof, are citizens of the United States and of the state wherein they reside. No state shall make or enforce any law which shall abridge the privileges or immunities of citizens of the United States; nor shall any state deprive any person of life, liberty, or property, without due process of law; nor deny to any person within its jurisdiction the equal protection of the laws.

Section 2. Apportionment of representatives Representatives shall be apportioned among the several states according to their respective numbers, counting the whole number of persons in each state, [excluding Indians not taxed.] But when the right to vote at any election for the choice of electors for President and Vice President of the United States, representatives in Congress, the executive and judicial officers of a state, or the members of the legislature thereof, is denied to any of the [male] inhabitants of such state, [being twenty-one years of age] and citizens of the United States, or in any way abridged, except for participation in rebellion, or other crime, the basis of representation therein shall be reduced in the proportion which the number of such [male] citizens shall bear to the whole number of [male] citizens [twenty-one years of age] in such state.

Section 3. Restrictions on holding office No person shall be a senator or representative in Congress, or elector of President and Vice President, or hold any office, civil or military, under the United States, or under any state, who, having previously taken an oath as a member of Congress, or as an officer of the United States, or as a member of any state legislature, or as an executive or judicial officer of any state, to support the Constitution of the United States, shall have engaged in insurrection or rebellion against the same, or given aid or comfort to the enemies thereof. But Congress may by vote of two-thirds of each house remove such disability.

Black members of Congress elected after the Civil War.

Section 4. Valid public debts of the United States The validity of the public debt of the United States, authorized by law, including debts incurred for payment of pensions and bounties for services in suppressing insurrection or rebellion, shall not be questioned. But neither the United States nor any state shall assume or pay any debt or obligation incurred in aid of insurrection or rebellion against the United States, or any claim for the loss or emancipation of any slave; but all such debts, obligations, and claims shall be held illegal and void.

This section was included to settle the question of debts incurred during the Civil War. All debts contracted by the United States were to be paid. Neither the United States nor any state government, however, was to pay the debts of the Confederacy. Moreover, no payment was to be made to former slave owners as compensation for slaves who were set free.

Section 5. Enforcement The Congress shall have power to enforce by appropriate legislation the provisions of this article.

AMENDMENT 15   Black Voting Rights (1870)

Section 1. The right of citizens of the United States to vote shall not be denied or abridged by the United States or by any state on account of race, color, or previous condition of servitude.

Amendment 15 sought to protect the right of citizens, particularly former slaves, to vote in federal and state elections.

Section 2. The Congress shall have power to enforce this article by appropriate legislation.

AMENDMENT 16   Income Tax (1913)

The Congress shall have power to lay and collect taxes on incomes, from whatever source derived, without apportionment among the several states and without regard to any census or enumeration.

Amendment 16 authorizes Congress to tax incomes. An amendment was necessary because in 1895 the Supreme Court had decided that an income tax law, passed by Congress a year earlier, was unconstitutional.

759

Amendment 17 changed Article I, Section 3, to allow the direct election of senators by popular vote. Anyone qualified to vote for a state representative may vote for United States senators.

AMENDMENT 17   Direct Election of Senators (1913)

Section 1. Election by the people   The Senate of the United States shall be composed of two senators from each state, elected by the people thereof, for six years; and each senator shall have one vote. The electors in each state shall have the qualifications requisite for electors of the most numerous branch of the state legislatures.

Section 2. Senate vacancies   When vacancies happen in the representation of any state in the Senate, the executive authority of such state shall issue writs of election to fill such vacancies: provided that the legislature of any state may empower the executive thereof to make temporary appointments until the people fill the vacancies by election as the legislature may direct.

Section 3. Effective date   This amendment shall not be so construed as to affect the election or term of any senator chosen before it becomes valid as part of the Constitution.

AMENDMENT 18   Prohibition (1919)

Amendment 18 forbade the manufacture, sale, or shipment of alcoholic beverages within the United States. Importing and exporting such beverages was also forbidden. Amendment 18 was later repealed by Amendment 21.

[Section 1.   After one year from the ratification of this article the manufacture, sale, or transportation of intoxicating liquors within, the importation thereof into, or the exportation thereof from the United States and all territory subject to the jurisdiction thereof for beverage purposes is hereby prohibited.

Section 2.   The Congress and the several states shall have concurrent power to enforce this article by appropriate legislation.

Section 3.   This article shall be inoperative unless it shall have been ratified as an amendment to the Constitution by the legislatures of the several states, as provided in the Constitution, within seven years from the date of the submission hereof to the states by the Congress.]

Federal agents destroying a still to enforce Prohibition.

AMENDMENT 19   Women's Voting Rights (1920)

Section 1.   The right of citizens of the United States to vote shall not be denied or abridged by the United States or by any state on account of sex.

Section 2.   The Congress shall have power to enforce this article by appropriate legislation.

AMENDMENT 20   Terms of Office and Presidential Succession (1933)

Section 1. Terms of office   The terms of the President and Vice President shall end at noon on the 20th day of January, and the terms of senators and representatives at noon on the 3rd day of January, of the years in which such terms would have ended if this article had not been ratified; and the terms of their successors shall then begin.

Section 2. Sessions of Congress   The Congress shall assemble at least once in every year, and such meeting shall begin at noon on the 3rd day of January, unless they shall by law appoint a different day.

Section 3. Presidential succession   If, at the time fixed for the beginning of the term of the President, the President-elect shall have died, the Vice President-elect shall become President. If a President shall not have been chosen before the time fixed for the beginning of his term, or if the President-elect shall have failed to qualify, then the Vice President-elect shall act as President until a President shall have qualified; and the Congress may by law provide for the case wherein neither a President-elect nor a Vice President-elect shall have qualified, declaring who shall then act as President, or the manner in which one who is to act shall be selected, and such person shall act accordingly until a President or a Vice President shall have qualified.

Section 4. House election of President   The Congress may by law provide for the case of the death of any of the persons from whom the House of Representatives may choose a President whenever the right of choice shall have devolved upon them, and for the case of the death of any of the persons from whom the Senate may choose a Vice President whenever the right of choice shall have devolved upon them.

Section 5. Effective date   Sections 1 and 2 shall take effect on the fifteenth day of October following the ratification of this article.

[**Section 6. Ratification**   This article shall be inoperative unless it shall have been ratified as an amendment to the Constitution by the legislatures of three-fourths of the several states within seven years from the date of its submission.]

Amendment 19 provides that women citizens may not be denied the right to vote in a federal or state election.

A suffragist rally.

When the Constitution was written, transportation and communication were slow. There was a long period, therefore, between the President's election (November) and inauguration (March). One purpose of Amendment 20 was to shorten that waiting period. The amendment established that the terms of the President and Vice President end at noon on January 20 following a presidential election. The terms of one-third of the senators and of all representatives, meanwhile, end at noon on January 3 in years ending in odd numbers. The new terms begin when the old terms end.

Section 2 provides that Congress must meet at least once a year, with the regular session beginning on January 3 unless Congress sets a different day.

Section 3 provides ways of filling the office of President in several emergencies.

Because the House of Representatives chooses the President if no candidate receives a majority of the electoral votes, Section 4 also gives Congress power to make a law to decide what to do if one of the candidates dies.

Amendment 21 repealed Amendment 18, putting an end to Prohibition. It was the only amendment submitted to special ratifying conventions instead of state legislatures.

Section 2 allows states or local governments to continue prohibition if they wish.

Amendment 22 set limits on the time a President may serve. No person may be elected President more than twice. A person who has served more than two years in the place of an elected President may be elected President only once. This limitation did not apply to President Truman, who was in office when Amendment 22 was proposed.

Presidents Washington, Jefferson, and Madison set the pattern of serving only two terms in office. Although Ulysses S. Grant and Theodore Roosevelt sought third terms, the precedent of serving only two terms was not broken until 1940, when Franklin D. Roosevelt was elected for a third term.

A victorious Franklin D. Roosevelt with congratulatory mail after his sweeping 1936 election victory.

AMENDMENT 21   Repeal of Prohibition (1933)

Section 1.   The eighteenth article of amendment to the Constitution of the United States is hereby repealed.

Section 2. State laws.   The transportation or importation into any state, territory, or possession of the United States for delivery or use therein of intoxicating liquors, in violation of the laws thereof, is hereby prohibited.

[**Section 3.**   This article shall be inoperative unless it shall have been ratified as an amendment to the Constitution by conventions in the several states, as provided in the Constitution, within seven years from the date of the submission hereof to the states by the Congress.]

AMENDMENT 22   Limits on Presidential Terms (1951)

Section 1.   No person shall be elected to the office of the President more than twice, and no person who has held the office of President, or acted as President, for more than two years of a term to which some other person was elected President shall be elected to the office of the President more than once. But this article shall not apply to any person holding the office of President when this article was proposed by the Congress, and shall not prevent any person who may be holding the office of President, or acting as President, during the term within which this article becomes operative from holding the office of President, or acting as President during the remainder of such term.

[**Section 2.**   This article shall be inoperative unless it shall have been ratified as an amendment to the Constitution by the legislatures of three-fourths of the several states within seven years from the date of its submission to the states by the Congress.]

Celebrating the bicentennial of the Constitution, 1987.

AMENDMENT 23 Voting in the District of Columbia (1961)

Section 1. The District constituting the seat of government of the United States shall appoint, in such manner as the Congress may direct:

A number of electors of President and Vice President equal to the whole number of senators and representatives in Congress to which the District would be entitled if it were a state, but in no event more than the least populous state; they shall be in addition to those appointed by the states, but they shall be considered, for the purposes of the election of President and Vice President, to be electors appointed by a state; and they shall meet in the District and perform such duties as provided by the twelfth article of amendment.

Section 2. The Congress shall have power to enforce this article by appropriate legislation.

This amendment gave the residents of the District of Columbia the right to vote in presidential elections. Before Amendment 23 was adopted, residents of the District of Columbia had not voted for President and Vice President because the Constitution provided that only states should choose presidential electors.

AMENDMENT 24 Poll Tax Illegal (1964)

Section 1. The right of citizens of the United States to vote in any primary or other election for President or Vice President, for electors for President or Vice President, or for senator or representative in Congress, shall not be denied or abridged by the United States or any state by reason of failure to pay any poll tax or other tax.

Section 2. The Congress shall have power to enforce this article by appropriate legislation.

Amendment 24 prohibited using the poll tax to deny voting rights in federal elections. (The poll tax was a device used in some southern states to keep black voters from the polls.) In 1966, the Supreme Court ruled that payment of poll taxes was also an unconstitutional precondition for voting in state and local elections.

AMENDMENT 25 Presidential Disability (1967)

Section 1. Vice President In case of the removal of the President from office or of his death or resignation, the Vice President shall become President.

Amendment 25 clarifies Article 2, Section 1, which deals with filling vacancies in the presidency. It also establishes procedures to follow when the President is too ill to serve and when there is a vacancy in the office of Vice President.

CONSTITUTION

With ratification of the 26th Amendment, the voting age was lowered to eighteen years.

Section 2. Replacing the Vice President Whenever there is a vacancy in the office of the Vice President, the President shall nominate a Vice President who shall take office upon confirmation by a majority vote of both Houses of Congress.

Section 3. Presidential inability to act Whenever the President transmits to the President pro tempore of the Senate and the Speaker of the House of Representatives his written declaration that he is unable to discharge the powers and duties of his office, and until he transmits to them a written declaration to the contrary, such powers and duties shall be discharged by the Vice President as Acting President.

Section 4. Determining presidential disability Whenever the Vice President and a majority of either the principal officers of the executive departments or of such other body as Congress may by law provide, transmit to the President pro tempore of the Senate and the Speaker of the House of Representatives their written declaration that the President is unable to discharge the powers and duties of his office, the Vice President shall immediately assume the powers and duties of the office as Acting President.

Thereafter, when the President transmits to the President pro tempore of the Senate and the Speaker of the House of Representatives his written declaration that no inability exists, he shall resume the powers and duties of his office unless the Vice President and a majority of either the principal officers of the executive department or of such other body as Congress may by law provide, transmit within four days to the President pro tempore of the Senate and the Speaker of the House of Representatives their written declaration that the President is unable to discharge the powers and duties of his office. Thereupon, Congress shall decide the issue, assembling within forty-eight hours for that purpose, if not in session. If the Congress, within twenty-one days after receipt of the latter written declaration, or, if Congress is not in session, within twenty-one days after Congress is required to assemble, determines by two-thirds vote of both Houses that the President is unable to discharge the powers and duties of his office, the Vice President shall continue to discharge the same as Acting President; otherwise, the President shall resume the powers and duties of his office.

AMENDMENT 26 Voting Age (1971)

Section 1. The right of citizens of the United States who are eighteen years of age or older to vote shall not be denied or abridged by the United States or by any state on account of age.

Section 2. The Congress shall have power to enforce this article by appropriate legislation.

Review of the Constitution

KEY TERMS ●

Match the following words with the numbered definitions below: *ratification, impeachment, appropriation, jurisdiction, judicial review, democracy, Bill of Rights.*

1. Charges of crimes or misdeeds in office brought against a government official.
2. Money granted by a legislature to be used for a specific purpose.
3. The first ten amendments to the Constitution.
4. System in which people elect the government either directly or through representatives.
5. The act of giving approval to a document such as a treaty.
6. The limits within which a government body (such as a court) may act and make decisions.
7. The power of the court system to decide whether laws are constitutional.

REVIEWING THE FACTS ●

1. Who holds the office of President of the Senate? When can the President of the Senate cast a vote? Which house of Congress introduces bills needed to raise money for the government?
2. Name six of the specific powers given to Congress by the Constitution. What is the "elastic clause"?
3. According to Article 2, what happens if the President dies in office? How did the Twenty-fifth Amendment provide additional measures in case of this event?
4. How are federal judges chosen? For how long do they hold office?
5. What freedoms are guaranteed by the First Amendment?
6. Under what circumstances may the Constitution be amended?
7. How does the Constitution limit the President's power to make treaties?
8. What three constitutional amendments were passed soon after the Civil War? What issues caused these amendments to be added?
9. Which branch of government has the power to declare war?

CRITICAL THINKING SKILLS ▲

1. **MAKING JUDGMENTS** The Founding Fathers sought both to create and to limit government power. Is this a contradiction in terms? Did they achieve their goal? Explain your answer.

2. **STATING BOTH SIDES OF AN ISSUE** How would you respond to someone who said, "Only the President has the information required to make decisions about war. Often he receives this information in secret. Therefore, we should not question his actions"?

3. **MAKING JUDGMENTS** Supporters of constitutional protections for criminal suspects claim that it is better if some guilty people go free than if innocent people are convicted. Do you agree or disagree? Explain your reasons.

4. **FORMING A HYPOTHESIS** Does testing for drug use and AIDS violate Fourth Amendment restrictions on search and seizure? How might a lawyer make a case in favor of these tests?

WRITING ABOUT THEMES IN AMERICAN HISTORY ■

1. **ISSUES** Find out what constitutional amendments are currently under consideration. Write a report explaining the arguments both for and against two of the proposed amendments.

2. **PARTICIPATION** Research the following Supreme Court decisions on civil rights: *Dred Scott v. Sanford* (1857), *Plessy v. Ferguson* (1896), *Brown v. Board of Education of Topeka* (1954). Write a report describing how constitutional interpretation changed in each case.

3. **CONSTITUTIONAL HERITAGE** Research the history of the War Powers Act (1973). How does it illustrate the tension between the executive branch and the legislative branch under the separation of powers?

Review of the Constitution Answers

Key Terms
1. impeachment
2. appropriation
3. Bill of Rights
4. democracy
5. ratification
6. jurisdiction
7. judicial review

Reviewing the Facts
1. The Vice President of the United States. When there is a tie vote. The House of Representatives.

2. These powers are listed in Section 8 of Article I. The last clause of Article I, Section 8 allows the national government to expand its powers beyond those specifically mentioned.

3. The Vice President becomes President. It provides for replacement of the Vice President.

4. Federal judges are appointed by the President with the approval of the Senate. For life.

5. Free exercise of religion; freedom of speech and the press; right to assemble peacefully to petition the government.

6. Amendments require the approval of two-thirds of both houses of Congress and three-quarters of the states. Two-thirds of the states may also call a constitutional convention.

7. Treaties must have the approval of two-thirds of the Senate.

8. Amendments 13, 14, and 15. The abolition of slavery and civil rights for black Americans.

9. The legislative branch.

Critical Thinking Skills
1. Students may refer to the separation of powers and the system of checks and balances.

2. That threats to society as a whole outweigh individual rights to privacy.

3. Agree: safeguards are necessary to prevent unjust convictions. Disagree: protections for suspects hamper law enforcement.

4. Claiming to act in the nation's security interests does not relieve the executive branch of accountability to the people.

Writing About Themes in American History
1. Students may want to use pertinent Supreme Court decisions in their arguments.

2. Students should be specific when noting how interpretation has changed.

3. Students should be sure to understand the concept of separation of powers and how the two branches may interpret it differently.

The Presidents

	President	Dates	Years in Office	Party	Elected From
1	George Washington	1732–1799	1789–1797	None	Virginia
2	John Adams	1735–1826	1797–1801	Federalist	Massachusetts
3	Thomas Jefferson	1743–1826	1801–1809	Democratic–Republican	Virginia
4	James Madison	1751–1836	1809–1817	Democratic–Republican	Virginia
5	James Monroe	1758–1831	1817–1825	Democratic–Republican	Virginia
6	John Quincy Adams	1767–1848	1825–1829	National Republican	Massachusetts
7	Andrew Jackson	1767–1845	1829–1837	Democratic	Tennessee
8	Martin Van Buren	1782–1862	1837–1841	Democratic	New York
9	William H. Harrison	1773–1841	1841	Whig	Ohio
10	John Tyler	1790–1862	1841–1845	Whig	Virginia
11	James K. Polk	1795–1849	1845–1849	Democratic	Tennessee
12	Zachary Taylor	1784–1850	1849–1850	Whig	Louisiana
13	Millard Fillmore	1800–1874	1850–1853	Whig	New York
14	Franklin Pierce	1804–1869	1853–1857	Democratic	New Hampshire
15	James Buchanan	1791–1868	1857–1861	Democratic	Pennsylvania
16	Abraham Lincoln	1809–1865	1861–1865	Republican	Illinois
17	Andrew Johnson	1808–1875	1865–1869	National Unionist/Democrat	Tennessee
18	Ulysses S. Grant	1822–1885	1869–1877	Republican	Illinois
19	Rutherford B. Hayes	1822–1893	1877–1881	Republican	Ohio
20	James A. Garfield	1831–1881	1881	Republican	Ohio
21	Chester A. Arthur	1830–1886	1881–1885	Republican	New York
22	Grover Cleveland	1837–1908	1885–1889	Democratic	New York
23	Benjamin Harrison	1833–1901	1889–1893	Republican	Indiana
24	Grover Cleveland	1837–1908	1893–1897	Democratic	New York
25	William McKinley	1843–1901	1897–1901	Republican	Ohio
26	Theodore Roosevelt	1858–1919	1901–1909	Republican	New York
27	William H. Taft	1857–1930	1909–1913	Republican	Ohio
28	Woodrow Wilson	1856–1924	1913–1921	Democratic	New Jersey
29	Warren G. Harding	1865–1923	1921–1923	Republican	Ohio
30	Calvin Coolidge	1872–1933	1923–1929	Republican	Massachusetts
31	Herbert Hoover	1874–1964	1929–1933	Republican	California
32	Franklin D. Roosevelt	1882–1945	1933–1945	Democratic	New York
33	Harry S. Truman	1884–1972	1945–1953	Democratic	Missouri
34	Dwight D. Eisenhower	1890–1969	1953–1961	Republican	New York
35	John F. Kennedy	1917–1963	1961–1963	Democratic	Massachusetts
36	Lyndon B. Johnson	1908–1973	1963–1969	Democratic	Texas
37	Richard M. Nixon	1913–	1969–1974	Republican	New York
38	Gerald R. Ford	1913–	1974–1977	Republican	Michigan
39	Jimmy Carter	1924–	1977–1981	Democratic	Georgia
40	Ronald Reagan	1911–	1981–1989	Republican	California
41	George Bush	1924–	1989–	Republican	Texas

The States

State Name	Date of Admission	Population	Number of Representatives	Capital
1 Delaware	1787	658,000	1	Dover
2 Pennsylvania	1787	11,764,000	21	Harrisburg
3 New Jersey	1787	7,617,000	13	Trenton
4 Georgia	1788	6,387,000	11	Atlanta
5 Connecticut	1788	3,227,000	6	Hartford
6 Massachusetts	1788	5,928,000	10	Boston
7 Maryland	1788	4,733,000	8	Annapolis
8 South Carolina	1788	3,407,000	6	Columbia
9 New Hampshire	1788	1,103,000	2	Concord
10 Virginia	1788	6,128,000	11	Richmond
11 New York	1788	17,627,000	31	Albany
12 North Carolina	1789	6,553,000	12	Raleigh
13 Rhode Island	1790	989,000	2	Providence
14 Vermont	1791	560,000	1	Montpelier
15 Kentucky	1792	3,665,000	6	Frankfort
16 Tennessee	1796	4,822,000	9	Nashville
17 Ohio	1803	10,778,000	19	Columbus
18 Louisiana	1812	4,181,000	8	Baton Rouge
19 Indiana	1816	5,499,000	10	Indianapolis
20 Mississippi	1817	2,535,000	5	Jackson
21 Illinois	1818	11,325,000	20	Springfield
22 Alabama	1819	3,984,000	7	Montgomery
23 Maine	1820	1,218,000	2	Augusta
24 Missouri	1821	5,079,000	9	Jefferson City
25 Arkansas	1836	2,337,000	4	Little Rock
26 Michigan	1837	9,180,000	16	Lansing
27 Florida	1845	12,775,000	23	Tallahassee
28 Texas	1845	16,825,000	30	Austin
29 Iowa	1846	2,767,000	5	Des Moines
30 Wisconsin	1848	4,870,000	9	Madison
31 California	1850	29,279,000	52	Sacramento
32 Minnesota	1858	4,359,000	8	St. Paul
33 Oregon	1859	2,828,000	5	Salem
34 Kansas	1861	2,468,000	4	Topeka
35 West Virginia	1863	1,783,000	3	Charleston
36 Nevada	1864	1,193,000	2	Carson City
37 Nebraska	1867	1,573,000	3	Lincoln
38 Colorado	1876	3,272,000	6	Denver
39 North Dakota	1889	634,000	1	Bismarck
40 South Dakota	1889	693,000	1	Pierre
41 Montana	1889	794,000	1	Helena
42 Washington	1889	4,827,000	8	Olympia
43 Idaho	1890	1,004,000	2	Boise
44 Wyoming	1890	450,000	1	Cheyenne
45 Utah	1896	1,711,000	3	Salt Lake City
46 Oklahoma	1907	3,124,000	6	Oklahoma City
47 New Mexico	1912	1,490,000	3	Santa Fe
48 Arizona	1912	3,619,000	6	Phoenix
49 Alaska	1959	546,000	1	Juneau
50 Hawaii	1959	1,095,000	2	Honolulu
District of Columbia		638,000	1 (non-voting)	
			435	

Important Dates in American History

Here is a list of benchmark dates in American history. All of these events had ramifications that remain with us today. Study the list. Think about the effects each event has had and how it still affects our lives.

1492	Columbus reaches Americas
1607	Jamestown settled
1620	Pilgrims settle Plymouth
1775–1783	American Revolution
1789	Constitution ratified
1861–1865	Civil War
1877	Reconstruction ends
1890	Indian wars end Census declares end of frontier; all areas settled
1898	Spanish-American War
1914–1918	World War I
1929	Great Depression begins
1939–1945	World War II
1964	Civil Rights Act
1969	American astronauts land on the moon
1973	Last American troops leave Vietnam
1989–1990	Collapse of communism in Eastern Europe; cold war relationships altered

American Literature

769

★ AMERICAN LITERATURE ★

CHAPTER 1
The Ordways

WILLIAM HUMPHREY

The setting for the start of William Humphrey's novel The Ordways *is Texas in the 1930s. The family whose story it tells are great-ly influenced by their past, especially by the events of the Civil War. Tom, the narrator, has grown up hearing family legends about how his great-grandpar-ents, Thomas and Ella Ordway, moved to Texas after Thomas was injured at the Battle of Shiloh.*

To grow up a boy in Clarksville, Texas, in my time was to be a double dreamer. For there where the woods joined the prairie was the frontier where two legends met. At one's back one heard the music of a banjo and the strains of "Dixie," the tramp of marching men, the roll of drums and bugle calls, the rattle of musketry, the thunder of cannonades. A boy gazing in that direction saw proud, tattered ensigns stream-ing above the haze of battle; saw burst from the clouds of gunsmoke gray-uniformed figures waving sabers and long horsepistols, shouting the rebel yell, grinning at death, glory-bent and beckoning him to follow. Those wooded hills rang all the way back with the names of Jeb Stuart and Stonewall Jackson and Texas's own Albert Sidney Johnston and the hapless but courageous John Bell Hood, and the sonorous Miltonic roll of place names where battles were fought: First Manassas, Antietam, The Wilder-ness, Chickamauga, Chattanooga, Shiloh.

In the other direction stretched Blossom Prairie, the vastness alone of which would have drawn out the soul in vague yearnings, even if beyond it had not lain a place already fabled as a land of romance and the home of heroes. What the ocean is in that once-famous picture

of the boy Raleigh shown sitting on the shore with his knees drawn up to his chin and his eyes fixed on strange distant lands below the horizon, my prairie was to me. Except that I knew what lay beyond my ken. Just beyond the range of my vision the prairie became the plains, and there another world commenced. It was a new world, and in it a new man had come into being, the most picturesque the world has ever produced: the cowboy. There was no place there for old men or for women. Life was spiced with danger there. A man wore his law strapped round his waist out there. Strong, fearless, taciturn, the cowboy was a natural aristocrat, chivalrous towards women, loyal to his friends unto death, reserved towards strangers, relentless towards his enemies, a man who lived by a code as rigid and elaborate as a medieval knight's. The cowboy was a man whose daily occupation was an adventure, whose work clothes a sultan might have envied. A man lifted above the plodding pedestrian world: a horseman—just the best ever known. On that wind which blew in my face off Blossom Prairie I seemed to catch the lowing of vast herds of cattle and the strumming of a guitar to the tune of "The Old Chisholm Trail," and along that flat rim where the earth met the sky there would sometimes appear in silhouette a lone rider sitting tall in the saddle, wearing a broad-brimmed sombrero and chaps, a bandanna knotted round his throat, the sunlight glinting on the pearl handle of the pistol slung low on his thigh.

Lee surrendered to Grant on April 9, 1865. The news was two months reaching Texas. I did not hear about it until 1931. I learned by reading on to the end of my school history book. Before that time I had sensed that we were in for a long struggle, but I had no idea that things were going that bad. We had suffered setbacks—that was war; but we had given as good as we had gotten, and no one having told me any different, I supposed that the fighting was still going on. Suddenly at the age of ten I not only had snatched away from me any chance ever to avenge my great-grandfather and redeem our losses and cover myself with glory on my country's battlefields, I had to swallow down my pride and learn to live with the chronic dyspepsia [indigestion] of defeat.

Nothing had prepared me for this. My knowledge of American history up to that point had conditioned me to the habit of success and leadership. I had theretofore identified myself with my country's eminence and expansion, and as a Southerner I had belonged to the dominant party. The founding fathers, the early generals, the great presidents, were Southerners. In the War, as presented to me, we had fought the better fight. At the point at which the account of it had always previously left off, we were winning. Now all of a sudden it was over, and we had lost. For me, a Texan (which is just another word for "proud"), this was even harder to accept than for most Southerners.

I say that, yet is it true? The moment when he discovers that the Civil War is lost comes to every Southern boy, and proud Texan though I was, it was perhaps less shattering for me than for most. I had, right on my doorstep, another myth to turn to. When the last bugle call went echoing off into eternity and the muskets were stacked and the banners lowered and that star-crossed flag hauled down—in short, when Appomattox came to me and I was demobilized and disarmed and returned home, filled with wounded pride and impatient with peacetime life—like many another veteran—I began to face about and look the other way, towards Blossom Prairie, where the range was open and the fancy free to roam. In my fashion I was repeating not only the history of my family, but of the country. For the West provided America with an escape from the memory of the Civil War.

From *The Ordways* by William Humphrey. Copyright ©1964 by William Humphrey. Reprinted by permission of the author.

Critical Thinking

1. For Tom, the narrator, what two American legends met at his boyhood home in Texas?
2. What was young Tom's mental image of the Civil War?

3. When Tom was young, what earlier events in American history led him to assume that the South had won or was winning the Civil War?
4. According to the narrator, was it easier or harder for Texans to get over their sense of defeat in the Civil War than for other southerners? Why?

■■■ ★ ■■■

CHAPTER 2

Jubilee

MARGARET WALKER

The Civil War inspired much literature, but for many years these books dealt mainly with the lives of white Americans in the North and South. Margaret Walker's exciting novel Jubilee *focuses on a cast of characters—black and white—who live on a Georgia plantation before and during the Civil War. The main character is Vyry, a slave who is the daughter of an African American slave and the plantation owner, "Marse John" Dutton. Randall Ware, a free black man, tries to win Vyry's freedom. In this excerpt, Ware, whose status as a free man is no longer safe in Georgia, has headed north.*

Randall Ware was walking up a dusty road barefooted. Footsore and weary, he was longing for a place to stop and rest, a chance to soak himself in a big wooden tub or tank of water and wishing, too, for some work along the way to replenish his dwindling stock of gold. Three times he had already met the rebuffs of northern white villagers. Once, when he knocked on a back door, the woman screamed and her husband came running with his shotgun. Another time, the dogs ran him away, and once when he was taken in, he slipped away in the night following his unerring instinct that told him he

771

Introducing the Chapter 2 Selection

Jubilee was a milestone when it was published in the mid-1960s—the first full-scale historical novel of the Civil War told from the point of view of a slave. Vyry, the central character, is based on the story of the author's own great-grandmother. For its sweeping story and rich cast of characters, the book has been compared to *Gone With the Wind*. Besides Vyry and her husband Randall Ware (who appears in the excerpt), major characters include "Marse John" Dutton, the plantation owner who is also Vyry's father; Salina Dutton, the strong-willed woman (known as "Big Missy") who controls the plantation; and the Duttons' daughter Lillian.

About the Author

Margaret Walker (1915–) has been a teacher and a poet for most of her career. Born in Birmingham, Alabama, she graduated from Northwestern University and later studied at the Writer's Workshop at the University of Iowa. She taught at several southern colleges and became known as a poet. *For My People,* a protest poem, won the Yale Younger Poets award in 1942. For her writing and her work in black education, Walker has won numerous fellowships and awards. *Jubilee,* published in 1965, is her only novel; it has been translated into several languages.

Vocabulary Preview

Be sure students understand the following terms: *mottled*—Spotted, patterned. *livery stable*—Stable that rents horses and carriages. *crossties*—Wooden crossbars on railroad tracks. *sundry*—Various. *nonplussed*—Confused, baffled. *Shady*—Civil War-era nickname for a black man.

Critical Thinking Answers

1. The heroism of the Confederacy in the Civil War and the myth of the cowboy.
2. He had a romantic image: soldiers emerging from the haze giving the rebel yell, bands playing "Dixie," etc.

3. The first Presidents, founders, and statesmen had been southerners; he assumed they remained the dominant region.

4. Easier, because they had the equally powerful myth of the frontier and the cowboy to turn to.

Other Books by William Humphrey

The Last Husband and Other Stories, 1953.
Home from the Hill, 1958.
A Time and a Place: Stories, 1968.
Farther Off from Heaven, 1977 (memoir).

Connecting with American History

Help students understand the ambiguous and dangerous position of free blacks (such as Randall Ware) in the Civil War period. *What were the fugitive slave laws, and why were they dangerous even to free blacks?* (Laws that allowed slave catchers to "reclaim" runaway slaves and return them to their owners for a reward; slave catchers, however, also frequently kidnapped free blacks, who had little chance of proving they were really free.) *What was the attitude of the U.S. Army toward black volunteers? How did this change during the course of the war?* (The army at first turned down black soldiers; later there were black regiments, but they were paid less than white soldiers for most of the war.)

Have students write an imaginary letter from Randall Ware to a black friend in the South, telling of his experiences in the North.

was not among friends, but they were merely detaining him until they could turn him over to the slave-catchers. He learned to be wary.

A little white boy sitting on a fence was watching him intently. He was barefoot, too, and had on a faded and ragged pair of blue cotton pants held up with sagging suspenders. His short-sleeved shirt had only one button and his old straw hat sat back on his fiery red hair, while his face was mottled with freckles like a child with the measles. His blue eyes were friendly when he spoke.

"Howdy, who are you?"

"Howdy yourself. I'm a stranger man. I'm tired and I'm hungry and I'm looking for work. Where's your father?"

"Are you the same color all over?"

"Are you?"

"I guess."

"Well, so am I. Didn't you never see a black man before?"

"Naw."

"Well, you see one now. I asked you for your father."

"I'll call him."

The man looked as surprised to see Randall Ware as the boy. But he gave him work. And the woman gave him food to eat in the barn. He stayed there and slept in the barn for a week before moving on. For five days the boy followed him around. They made friends, and when he left the youngster held out his hand to say goodbye. But Randall Ware did not like farm work. He was not really a hired man, but he could do most things from chopping and hauling wood to cutting corn stalks and picking cotton. He liked work in the small towns best when he could work at a livery stable shoeing horses. Twice he ventured into the big cities. In Ohio he was tempted to stay in the city of Cincinnati where work was plentiful and he could make more than ten dollars a month, even sometimes as much as a dollar a day. He did stay six months, and then he went wandering through the surrounding Ohio country before going back to Cincinnati for another half-year of odd jobs.

He was in Ohio when the war came. The Union sentiment there was very strong and all the people talked about putting down the Rebellion. He heard many snatches of conversation while he was shoeing horses. Much of what he heard startled him and he came up with strange conclusions.

"Anything those southern rebels don't like they declare on their sacred honor is wrong, and then they start hunting Scripture [the Bible] to prove their interpretation is the only one that can be morally right."

"They're so all-fired twisted in their thinking, they don't know right from wrong."

"Wa'al now I'll tell you, I think it's mostly a war for the [blacks], and I say let the [blacks] . . . do the fighting and the dying. It's a rich man's war, and a poor man's fight, and I don't fancy dying for the [black]."

Randall Ware discovered the painful fact that in the North his status was little better than in the slave-South. He felt free to walk the streets and that was all. He was an experienced blacksmith with his own smithy in Georgia, but here he was lucky if he worked for a journeyman's wages, and then mostly at odd jobs. He longed for his own anvil, to hear the ring of his hammer and watch the sparks fly around him while he forged. But he had been forced to leave because of the hated system and now he wondered who in the country hated colored people more, the slavers, the poor whites, or those northern white people who were not abolitionists.

One good thing about a blacksmith, he kept remembering, *he can always make his own tools.* He managed to hang on to his bellows even when he knew he could not carry most of his tools with him. His hammer was too big. But then he could always make pinchers, and files and the crowbar tool he used for leverage. It was not easy to adjust to another man's hammer, but it wasn't impossible. And he had hardly needed his forging tools because most of the time he was just shoeing horses.

Hearing that the Union Army headquarters in the West were at Cairo, Illinois, he made his way back to the Missouri River and across to St. Louis, then back to East St. Louis and up to Cairo, working all the while at his trade. He was about to leave and head back toward Cincinnati, disappointed because his services as a soldier were rejected by the Union Army, when he heard that the Army was looking for common laborers as well as skilled blacksmiths to work on the railroads leading from Alabama into Tennessee. Blacksmiths were greatly needed as well as sawmill workers to make rails and crossties and repair the roads. General Dodge was recruiting workers, but Randall Ware did not know where to find Dodge. When he inquired, he was given sundry directions, many misleading, but he had found a purpose. Now perhaps there would be a place for him in this conflict. He was determined to find Dodge.

General Dodge was an engineer and a professional railroad man. He had been hired by General U. S. Grant, who was now in command of all the Union Armies in the West, to repair the road from Stevenson, Alabama, into Chattanooga, Tennessee. Although there were blacksmith shops along the way, they were in the hands of the enemy, and all the sawmills likewise were on enemy property. He was, therefore, forced to set up shop in the field and fight his way through the countryside. He captured the necessary shops and sometimes took the men working. If they objected to working for the Union, they were automatically prisoners anyway. These shops had to be brought up to the lines for their protection and this made long, slow, and complicated work.

Many of the workers available were runaway slaves eager to work for Uncle Sam's armies but often not skilled. They could cut down trees, saw wood, and split logs, but most of them were not equipped for the more important jobs.

Randall Ware caught up with Dodge's army camp after five days of traveling from Missouri. While he was traveling through southern territory he had to be as careful as he was when he was running from Georgia. Negroes falling in the hands of the Confederates were frequently killed since the rebels would take no Negroes as prisoners.

"Halt! Who goes there?"

Randall Ware had been watching the soldier walking sentry duty for a long time before he approached the camp. He sat in the tall grass and chewed the sour stalks of sheep sorrel, trying to make up his mind whether to go forward. He thought of St. Louis when he first heard about the war and went there to enlist. He thought about his feelings when he heard the Union Army didn't want [black] soldiers. He heard they were turning them back to the slave-catchers in some places, holding them as contraband of war in others, or putting them to work, but not in uniform. He didn't want anybody treating him like dirt. But he did want to get into this war for freedom.

"Halt! I say, who goes there?"

"Open up, soldier, for Shady. I'm one of Old Ride-up's Boys."

The soldier, nonplussed at first, watched Randall Ware rise up from the tall grass and then rested his gun. The black man moving toward him was ragged and dusty. His feet were bare and the thick hair on his face and head were only slightly darker than his skin. He had a croker sack tied with rope which he carried on his back, and to the soldier's amazement the sack was full of iron tools. The broad back of this Shady was wide as a barn door and under thick beetle brows his eyes peered with a cool and searching gaze at the soldier.

"What you want, Shady?"

"Wanta see the boss-man. Who's in command here?"

"General G. M. Dodge is in command here, but you better have urgent business to see the general."

"Take me to him, soldier, and let him decide how urgent my business is."

He found the General eating his supper in a tent which served as his temporary headquarters.

"What do you want, Shady?"

"Sir, I come all the way from Missouri, mostly crawling on my hands and knees, to

Analysis
How does Margaret Walker use dialogue and action to show the character of Randall Ware? Explain the impressions of Ware that you get from this passage. What kind of man is he?

774

get here and offer my services to you."

"What can you do?"

"I'm a blacksmith, sir, had my own smithy before the war but the rebels ran me away."

"Can you forge?"

"Sir, I just told you I had my own anvil. You wanta see me forge?"

"You can show us bright and early in the morning. Now tell the quartermaster to find you a place to sleep and have the cook feed you. You look as if you did crawl all the way!"

"Thankye sir. I'll prove myself in the morning."

And he did. Happily he watched the sparks fly from the anvil while he lifted his powerful hammer and beat the red hot iron, forging the metal into rails. At last he was in the war, doing what he liked best, and striking a powerful blow for the freedom of the blacks.

From *Jubilee* by Margaret Walker. Copyright ©1966 by Margaret Walker Alexander. Reprinted by permission of Houghton Mifflin Co.

Critical Thinking

1. What problems does Ware encounter because of his race, even though he was a free man?

2. What groups of people does Ware think are his enemies?

3. Why do you think building a railroad in the Southeast was so important for the Union Army?

4. For what reason did Ware want to take an active part in the war? How did he succeed in doing so?

5. What details in *Jubilee* show you that both blacks and whites were poor as a result of the Civil War?

Critical Thinking Answers

1. Even in the North, people were suspicious or frightened; some were hostile and likely to turn him over to slave catchers; he had to work as an ordinary laborer even though he was a craftsman; the army rejected black volunteers.

2. The groups he fears are "the slavers, the poor whites, or those northern white people who were not abolitionists."

3. To transport troops and supplies across the South to headquarters in Illinois.

4. He wanted "to get into this war for freedom." He forged rails for Union trains.

5. Students may suggest the condition of the farmboy's clothes, and the conversation referring to a "rich man's war, and a poor man's fight."

Other Books by Margaret Walker

For My People (poems), 1942.
Ballad of the Free, 1966.
Prophets for a New Day, 1970.
October Journey, 1973.

CHAPTER 3

The Deliverance

ELLEN GLASGOW

Ellen Glasgow's realistic novels about the postwar South reflect the changes she witnessed while growing up in Virginia during this period. The changes included new styles in politics, the loss of family lands and fortunes, and rivalries between social classes. In her book The Deliverance *(1904), the Civil War has ruined the Blake family. The former overseer now owns the family mansion, while Christopher Blake is a laborer in the tobacco fields his family once owned. In this scene, Guy Carraway, a lawyer, discovers that Blake's elderly mother, now blind, is unaware of these momentous changes.*

From a rear chimney a dark streak of smoke was rising, but the front of the house gave no outward sign of life, and as there came no answer to his insistent knocks he [Carraway] at last ventured to open the door and pass into the narrow hall. From the first room on the right a voice spoke at his entrance, and following the sound he found himself face to face with Mrs. Blake in her massive Elizabethan chair.

"There is a stranger in the room," she said rigidly, turning her sightless eyes; "speak at once."

"I beg pardon most humbly for my intrusion," replied Carraway, conscious of stammering like an offending schoolboy, "but as no one answered my knock, I committed the indiscretion of opening a closed door."

Awed as much by the stricken pallor of her appearance as by the inappropriate grandeur of her black brocade and her thread lace cap, he advanced slowly and stood awaiting his dismissal.

"What door?" she demanded sharply, much to his surprise.

Introducing the Chapter 3 Selection

The Deliverance, published in 1904, was one of a series of early novels that Ellen Glasgow planned as a social history of Virginia from 1850 onward. Her models were

"Yours, madam."

"Not answer your knock?" she pursued, with indignation. "So that was the noise I heard, and no wonder that you entered. Why, what is the matter with the place? Where are the servants?"

He humbly replied that he had seen none, to be taken up with her accustomed quickness of touch.

"Seen none! Why, there are three hundred of them, sir. . . .

I don't think I ever had the pleasure of meeting a Carraway before."

"That is more than probable, ma'am, but I have the advantage of you, since, as a child, I was once taken out upon the street corner merely to see you go by on your way to a fancy ball, where you appeared as Diana." . . .

"It was more than fifty years ago," murmured the old lady. . . . "The present is a very little part of life, sir; it's the past in which we store our treasures."

"You're right, you're right," replied Carraway, drawing his chair nearer the embroidered ottoman and leaning over to stroke the yellow cat; "and I'm glad to hear so cheerful a philosophy from your lips."

"It is based on a cheerful experience—I've been as you see me now only twenty years."

Only twenty years! He looked mutely round the soiled whitewashed walls, where hung a noble gathering of Blake portraits in massive old gilt frames. . . .

"Life has its trials, of course," pursued Mrs. Blake, as if speaking to herself. "I can't look out upon the June flowers, you know, and though the pink crape-myrtle at my window is in full bloom I cannot see it."

Following her gesture, Carraway glanced out into the little yard; no myrtle was there, but he remembered vaguely that he had seen one in blossom at the Hall.

"You keep flowers about you, though," he said, alluding to the scattered vases of June roses.

"Not my crape-myrtle. I planted it myself when I first came home with Mr. Blake, and I have never allowed so much as a spray of it to be plucked."

. . . Recalling herself suddenly, her tone took on a sprightliness like that of youth.

"It's not often that we have the pleasure of entertaining a stranger in our out-of-the-way house, sir—so may I ask where you are staying—or perhaps you will do us the honour to sleep beneath our roof. It has had the privilege of sheltering General Washington."

"You are very kind," replied Carraway . . . "but to tell the truth, I feel that I am sailing under false colours. The real object of my visit is to ask a business interview with your son. I bring what seems to me a very fair offer for the place."

Grasping the carved arms of her chair, Mrs. Blake turned the wonder in her blind eyes upon him.

"An offer for the place! Why, you must be dreaming, sir! A Blake owned it more than a hundred years before the Revolution."

At the instant, understanding broke upon Carraway like a thundercloud, and as he rose from his seat it seemed to him that he had missed by a single step the yawning gulf before him . . . he looked up to meet, from the threshold of the adjoining room, the enraged flash of Christopher's eyes. So tempestuous was the glance that Carraway . . . squared himself to receive a physical blow; but the young man . . . came in quietly and took his stand behind the Elizabethan chair.

"Why, what a joke, mother," he said, laughing; "he means the old Weatherby farm, of course. The one I wanted to sell last year, you know."

"I thought you'd sold it to the Weatherbys, Christopher."

"Not a bit of it—they backed out at the last; but don't begin to bother your head about such things; they aren't worth it. And now, sir," he turned upon Carraway, "since your business is with me, perhaps you will have the goodness to step outside."

With the feeling that he was asked out for a beating, Carraway turned for a farewell with Mrs. Blake. . . .

"Business may come later, my son," she said, detaining them by a gesture of her heavily

775

earlier realistic novelists, George Eliot in particular. Despite Glasgow's somewhat sheltered upbringing, she intended her books to give a serious and uncompromisingly real picture of the South, both "old" and new. She once said, "By temperament I was on the side of the disinherited," yet she showed families such as the Blakes with irony as well as sympathy. These ironies are clear in this selection; for instance, the once-wealthy Blakes live in the rundown cottage of the overseer, and Christopher Blake is a day laborer in the tobacco fields.

About the Author
Ellen Glasgow (1873–1945) was one of the first realist writers of the South. Brought up as a "southern belle" in a prominent Rich-

mond family, she wrote about southern society with wit and irony mixed with affection. "We live where we are born," she said in an interview, but did not like to be seen as simply a regionalist. Critics did not take Glasgow seriously until *Barren Ground,* published in 1925 when she was past 50. Her other novels of the 1920s were also popular. Her last book, *In This Our Life,* received the Pulitzer Prize in 1941.

Vocabulary Preview
Be sure students understand the following terms:
pallor—Extreme paleness.
sprightliness—Liveliness.
malignant—Intending hatred or evil. *chaff*—Husks of grain blown away during threshing.

Connecting with American History
Help students understand the past in which old Mrs. Blake still lives and the changes that have occurred in her way of life. *What was life like for wealthy plantation owners before the Civil War?* (Slaves—perhaps several hundred—did the work in both the house and the fields. The plantation families had rich clothing; there were balls and parties; women such as Mrs. Blake were accustomed to being waited on.) *How did the war end this way of life?* (Plantations and houses were burned; possessions, clothes, silver, and other treasures were destroyed or carried away by soldiers. Opportunists—such as the Blake's overseer— took advantage of the situation to acquire land cheaply.) *What were conditions like for others in the postwar South?* (Freed blacks also faced poverty and hunger; though they wanted land of their own, they often became tenants or sharecroppers.)

Analysis
How does Glasgow use "fore-shadowing" to alert the reader to Mrs. Blake's state of mind? Does the reader understand the situation before Carraway does?

Analysis
How does Glasgow use "fore-shadowing" to alert the reader to Mrs. Blake's state of mind? Does the reader understand the situation before Carraway does?

Critical Thinking Answers
1. Mrs. Blake's brocade dress, lace cap, rings; the family portraits; references to 300 servants; a house where Washington had slept; the fact that she had been a "southern belle."
2. The time before the Confederate states seceded.
3. She believed that the Confederacy still existed, with new presidents chosen regularly.

**Other Books
by Ellen Glasgow**
The Voice of the People, 1900.
The Battle-Ground, 1902.
Barren Ground, 1925.
The Romantic Comedians,
    1926.
They Stooped to Folly, 1929.
The Sheltered Life, 1932.
Vein of Iron, 1935.

---

ringed hand. "After dinner you may take Mr. Carraway with you into the library . . . ; meanwhile, he and I will resume our very pleasant talk which you interrupted. He remembers seeing me in the old days when we were all in the United States, my dear."

Christopher's brow grew black, and he threw a sharp and malignant glance of sullen suspicion at Carraway, who summoned to meet it his most frank and open look. . . .

"You may assure yourself," he [said] softly, "that I have her welfare very decidedly at heart."

At this Christopher smiled back at him. . . .

"Well, take care, sir," he answered and went out . . . while Carraway applied himself to a determined entertaining of Mrs. Blake.

To accomplish this he found that he had only to leave her free, guiding her thoughts with his lightest touch into newer channels. . . . Everywhere he felt her wonderful keenness of perception—that intuitive understanding of men and manners which had kept her for so long the reigning belle among her younger rivals.

As she went on he found that her world was as different from his own as if she dwelt upon some undiscovered planet. . . . She lived upon lies, he saw, and thrived upon the sweetness she extracted from them. For her the Confederacy had never fallen, the quiet of her dreamland had been disturbed by no invading army, and the three hundred slaves, who had in reality scattered like chaff before the wind, she still saw in her cheerful visions tilling her familiar fields. It was as if she had fallen asleep with the great blow that had wrecked her body, and had dreamed on steadily throughout the years. . . . In her memory there was no Appomattox, news of the death of Lincoln had never reached her ears, and president had peacefully succeeded president in the secure Confederacy in which she lived. Wonderful as it all was, to Carraway the most wonderful thing was the intricate tissue of lies woven around her chair. Lies—lies—there had been nothing but lies spoken within her hearing for twenty years.

From *The Deliverance* by Ellen Glasgow (Doubleday, Page & Co., 1904).

Critical Thinking
1. What clues does the author give to show the Blake family's former wealth?
2. What does Mrs. Blake mean when she refers to "the old days when we were all in the United States"?
3. What does Mrs. Blake believe was the outcome of the Civil War?

■■■ ★ ■■■

CHAPTER 4
1876

GORE VIDAL

Rapid industrialization produced dramatic changes in America during the late 1800s. In 1876, Americans celebrated the nation's centennial with a huge exposition highlighting science and technology. In Gore Vidal's historical novel 1876, *Charles Schermerhorn Schuyler, a writer who has been living in Europe, comes home with his daughter Emma to write about the celebrations. Here Schuyler reacts to the "modern" New York of 1875.*

At this moment—midnight, December 4, 1875—I am somewhat staggered at the prospect of trying in some way to encompass with words this new world until now known to me only at the farthest remove. I can of course go on and on about the past, write to order of old things by the yard; and happily there is, according to my publisher, Mr. E. P. Dutton, a considerable market for my wares whenever I am in the reminiscent mood. But the real challenge, of course, is to get the sense of the country as it is today—two, three, four times more populous than it was when I left in 1837. Yet, contemplating what I saw of New York this afternoon, I

**Introducing the
Chapter 4 Selection**
1876 is one in Gore Vidal's continuing series of brilliant and entertaining historical novels considered an "American chronicle." The first novel, *Burr,* introduced Charles Schermerhorn

begin only now to get the range as I sit, perspiring, in the parlour of our hotel suite while dry heated air comes through metal pipes in sudden blasts like an African sirocco.

None of the Americans I have met in Europe over the past four decades saw fit to prepare me for the opulence, the grandeur, the vulgarity, the poverty, the elegance, the awful crowded abundance of this city, which, when I last saw it, was a minor seaport with such small pretensions that a mansion was a house like Madame Jumel's property on the Haarlem—no, Harlem—no, *Washington* Heights—a building that might just fill the ballroom of one of those palaces the rich are building on what is called Fifth Avenue, in my day a country road wandering through the farms north of Potter's Field, later to be known as the Parade Ground, and later still as Washington Square Park, now lined with rows of "old" houses containing the heirs of the New York gentry of my youth.

In those days, of course, the burghers [wealthy townsfolk] lived at the south end of the island between the Battery and Broadway where now all is commercial, or worse. I can recall when St. Mark's Place was as far north as anyone would want to live. Now, I am told, a rich woman has built herself a cream-coloured French palace on *Fifty-seventh Street!* opposite the newly completed Central Park (how does one "complete" a park?). . . .

Amongst the thousand and one bits of information I have in the last few hours received: more than half the city's population of a million is foreign-born. Most are from Ireland (as in my day) and Germany. But representatives of the other countries are to be found in ever-increasing numbers. Whole districts of the lower island are devoted to Italians, Poles, Hebrews, Greeks, while the once charming Mott and Pell streets are now entirely occupied by *Chinese!* I cannot wait to explore this new world, more like a city from the *Arabian Nights* than that small staid English-Dutch town or village of my youth.

As the victoria [carriage] left the pier and entered Orton Street, John Apgar indicated tattered beggars, holding out their hands. "We are

known as the almshouse of Europe." He spoke with a mechanical bitterness, no longer even hearing the phrase on his own tongue, for everyone, I gather, uses it.

I suppose to the native New Yorker so many newcomers must be disturbing, particularly when there is not much work for them since the panic of '73, obliging them to turn to—what else? crime. But for the old New Yorkers with money this constant supply of cheap labour must be a singular joy. One can hire an excellent cook for eighteen dollars a month; a lady's maid for twelve dollars. Emma and I have been debating whether or not to indulge her in a lady's maid. Apparently we are the only occupants of a suite in the Fifth Avenue Hotel without personal servants.

The drive from the pier to the hotel was—well, Rip Van Winkle-ish. I have run out of epithets; and must remember not to use to death that hackneyed image.

I asked the driver to take us through Washington Square Park and then up the celebrated Fifth Avenue.

"You will doubtless find the avenue much changed." John's politeness is pleasing, but his gift for saying only the obvious makes him something less than the perfect companion. As a son-in-law, however, he has possibilities. . . .

"Properly speaking, there was no Fifth Avenue in my day. A few brave souls were building houses north of the Parade Ground, as we called Washington Square. But they were thought eccentric, unduly fearful of the summer cholera, of smallpox in the lower island." I spoke without interest in what I was saying; looked this way and that; could hardly take it all in.

A white sun made vivid each detail of this new city, but gave no warmth. Beside me, Emma shivered beneath the fur rug, as enthralled as I.

Everywhere crowds of vehicles—carts, barouches, victorias, brightly painted horsecars, not to mention other and more sinister kinds of transport: when we crossed Sixth Avenue at Cornelia Street, I gasped and Emma gave a cry, as a train of cars drawn by a steam

his first book, *Williwaw*, while overseas in World War II. For a time he wrote plays for television and the stage, including *The Best Man* and *Visit to a Small Planet.*

Vocabulary Preview
Be sure students understand the following terms: *sirocco*—Dry desert wind. *almshouse*—Public home for the very poor. *epithet*—Descriptive nickname. *hackneyed*—Overused, worn-out. *barouche, victoria*—Types of horse-drawn carriages.

Connecting with American History
Help students recall the changes that happened as America industrialized after the Civil War. *What were the major trends or changes in the United States in the late 1800s?* (Expansion of industry, settling of the West, growth of cities.) *How did immigration influence American cities and industry in the late 1800s?* (Immigration from Europe and Asia increased, bringing farmers for the West, supplying laborers for industry, turning New York into a cosmopolitan center.)

Have students write a short description of everyday life in an American city in the period from 1880–1890.

Analysis
What picture do you get of Charles Schuyler from his observations of things and people? Would you like to know him? Find clues in his narrative that tell you what he is like.

777

Schuyler as a much younger man; here he returns to the United States calling himself a "Rip Van Winkle." The focus of *1876* is on the crucial presidential election, which Schuyler believes that Tilden cannot lose. Throughout this series,

Vidal re-creates authentic political history with his distinctive style and wit.

About the Author
Gore Vidal (1925–) is one of the nation's most skillful novelists and essayists. Vidal comes from a political

family, and he has been active in politics. Many of his major novels focus on turning points in American political history; written with wit and humor, they give entertaining insights into events and characters. Vidal wrote

★ AMERICAN LITERATURE ★

engine hurtled with deafening sound *over* our heads at thirty miles an hour!

The horses shied, whinnied; the driver swore. Like a dark rain, ashes fell from the elevated railway above our heads. Emma's cheek was smudged. Happily, we were not set afire by the bright coals that erupted from the steam engine, falling like miniature comets to the dark avenue below.

Then the cars were gone. The nervous horses were persuaded to cross the avenue and enter the quiet precinct of Washington Square Park.

"My God!" Emma put handkerchief to cheek; did not care to refine her language for Mr. John Day Apgar, who was more thrilled than not by our adventure.

"I'm sorry. I ought to have warned you. There's really nothing like it in the world, is there?"

"I'm happy to say, no, there is not." Emma's colour was now high; she looked uncommonly youthful—the sudden fright, the cold wind.

I did not repeat my now constant and, even to me, interminable refrain: How things have changed. Yet in my time (was ever any time mine?) Sixth Avenue was just a name to describe a country road that crossed isolated farms and thick marshes, where my father once took me duck shooting. . . .

From *1876: A Novel* by Gore Vidal. Copyright ©1976 by Gore Vidal. Reprinted by permission of the William Morris Agency.

Critical Thinking

1. According to Schuyler, how has the population of New York changed while he has been away?
2. What changes in transportation and technology does Schuyler notice in the city?
3. What was New York like when Schuyler lived there as a young man?
4. What events in United States history have taken place since Schuyler moved to Europe?

■■■■ ★ ■■■■

Black Elk Speaks

JOHN G. NEIHARDT

Black Elk was an Oglala Sioux whose life spanned the last days of Indian freedom on the Great Plains. A cousin of Crazy Horse, he was also a holy man wise in the ceremonies and visions of Indian religion. In 1930, then an old man, Black Elk shared his memories and visions with a Nebraska poet, John Neihardt. The resulting book became an underground classic, gaining new popularity in the 1970s as American Indians looked into the sources of their heritage.

It was the next summer, when I was 11 years old (1874), that the first sign of a new trouble came to us. Our band had been camping on Split-Toe Creek in the Black Hills, and from there we moved to Spring Creek, then to Rapid Creek where it comes out into the prairie. That evening just before sunset, a big thunder cloud came up from the west, and just before the wind struck, there were clouds of split-tail swallows flying all around above us. It was like part of my vision, and it made me feel queer. The boys tried to hit the swallows with stones and it hurt me to see them doing this, but I could not tell them. I got a stone and acted as though I were going to throw, but I did not. The swallows seemed holy. Nobody hit one, and when I thought about this I knew that of course they could not.

The next day some of the people were building a sweat tepee for a medicine man by the name of Chips, who was going to perform a ceremony and had to be purified first. They say he was the first man who made a sacred ornament for our great chief, Crazy Horse. While they were heating the stones for the sweat tepee, some boys asked me to go with them to shoot squirrels. We went out, and when I was about

Black Elk Speaks is a unique record of Native American thought and culture. While Black Elk remembered much real history, his concern was to "save his Great

to shoot at one, I felt very uneasy all at once. So I sat down, feeling queer, and wondered about it. While I sat there I heard a voice that said: "Go at once! Go home!" I told the boys we must go home at once, and we all hurried. When we got back, everybody was excited, breaking camp, catching the ponies and loading the drags; and I heard that while Chips was in the sweat tepee a voice had told him that the band must flee at once because something was going to happen there.

It was nearly sundown when we started, and we fled all that night on the back trail toward Spring Creek, then down that creek to the south fork of the Good River. I rode most of the night in a pony drag because I got too sleepy to stay on a horse. We camped at Good River in the morning, but we stayed only long enough to eat. Then we fled again, upstream, all day long until we reached the mouth of Horse Creek. We were going to stay there, but scouts came to us and said that many soldiers had come into the Black Hills; and that was what Chips saw while he was in the sweat tepee. So we hurried on in the night towards Smoky Earth River (the White), and when we got there, I woke up and it was daybreak. We camped a while to eat, and then went up the Smoky Earth, two camps, to Robinson, for we were afraid of the soldiers up there.

Afterward I learned that it was Pahuska ["Long Hair," Gen. Custer] who had led his soldiers into the Black Hills that summer to see what he could find. He had no right to go in there, because all that country was ours. Also the Wasichus [non-Indians] had made a treaty with Red Cloud (1868) that said it would be ours as long as grass should grow and water flow. Later I learned too that Pahuska had found there much of the yellow metal that makes the Wasichus crazy; and that is what made the bad trouble, just as it did before, when the hundred were rubbed out.

Our people knew there was yellow metal in little chunks up there; but they did not bother with it, because it was not good for anything.

We stayed all winter at the Soldiers' Town, and all the while the bad trouble was coming fast; for in the fall we heard that some Wasichus had come from the Missouri River to dig in the Black Hills for the yellow metal, because Pahuska had told about it with a voice that went everywhere. Later he got rubbed out for doing that.

The people talked about this all winter. Crazy Horse was in the Powder River country and Sitting Bull was somewhere north of the Hills. Our people at the Soldiers' Town thought we ought to get together and do something. Red Cloud's people said that the soldiers had gone in there to keep the diggers out, but we, who were only visiting, did not believe it. We called Red Cloud's people "Hangs-Around-The-Fort," and our people said they were standing up for the Wasichus, and if we did not do something we should lose the Black Hills.

In the spring when I was twelve years old (1875), more soldiers with many wagons came up from the Soldiers' Town at the mouth of the Laramie River and went into the Hills.

There was much talk all summer, and in the Moon of Making Fat (June) there was a sun dance there at the Soldiers' Town to give the people strength, but not many took part; maybe because everybody was so excited talking about the Black Hills. . . .

In the Moon When the Calves Grow Hair (September) there was a big council with the Wasichus on the Smoky Earth River at the mouth of White Clay Creek. I can remember the council, but I did not understand much of it then. Many of the Lakotas were there, also Shyelas [Cheyenne] and Blue Clouds [Arapaho]; but Crazy Horse and Sitting Bull stayed away. In the middle of the circle there was a shade made of canvas. Under this the councilors sat and talked, and all around them there was a crowd of people on foot and horseback. They talked and talked for days, but it was just like wind blowing in the end. I asked my father what they were talking about in there, and he told me that the Grandfather at Washington wanted to lease the Black Hills so that the Wasichus could dig yellow metal, and that the chief of the soldiers had said if we did not do this, the Black Hills would be just like melting snow

many honors; he was poet laureate of Nebraska.

Vocabulary Preview
Be sure students understand the following terms: *drags*—Frames drawn by ponies to carry goods and supplies. *yellow metal*—Gold. *Soldiers' Town*—American army post or fort. *Grandfather at Washington*—President of the United States.

Connecting with American History
Help students remember the historical events in which Black Elk took part. *After the California Gold Rush, what other parts of the West drew prospectors?* (Colorado, Nevada, Montana, South Dakota.) *How did the discovery of gold in the West increase conflicts betweens whites and the Plains Indians?* (The government tried to limit Indian hunting boundaries; prospectors did not respect Indians' territory; roads were built across Indian lands; miners in the Black Hills crossed sacred Sioux lands.) *What battle resulted from the failure of the council that Black Elk observed?* (Little Bighorn, in June 1876, between the Sioux and Custer's forces.)

Have students write an imaginary dialogue between the Sioux representatives and the army officials at the council about the Black Hills.

Analysis
Have students find ways in which Neihardt's translation retains the flavor of spoken dialogue and of the Indian way of speaking.

Vision for men" and pass his insights along. John Neihardt—called "Flaming Rainbow" by the Indians—had spent much of his own life immersed in Indian life and was the first person to whom Black Elk believed he could entrust the vision.

Black Elk spoke in Sioux, his son translated, and Neihardt, a poet and university lecturer, re-created it in English. *Black Elk Speaks* had only a tiny, scholarly audience in the 1930s but became a best-seller in the 1970s.

About the Author
Black Elk (1863–193?) was a holy man of the Ogalala Sioux, a cousin of the famous leader Crazy Horse. In the early 1930s, he told his story to John G. Neihardt (1881–1973). For his own poetic work, Neihardt received

Critical Thinking Answers

1. Gold had been discovered in the Black Hills. The leader was General Custer.

2. The Indians believed the land was all theirs; in addition, the government had made a treaty with Red Cloud promising them perpetual rights to it.

3. The council was supposedly to negotiate a lease for the Black Hills, but gold miners were already flocking into the region. Black Elk realized that the council was useless from the Indians' viewpoint.

4. Black Elk believed that Crazy Horse had had a vision of the spirit world, which gave him strength when he needed it. The Indians regarded Crazy Horse as a strange man but a great leader.

★ AMERICAN LITERATURE ★

held in our hands, because the Wasichus would take that country anyway.

It made me sad to hear this. It was such a good place to play and the people were always happy in that country. Also I thought of my vision, and of how the spirits took me there to the center of the world.

After the council we heard that creeks of Wasichus were flowing into the Hills and becoming rivers, and that they were already making towns up there. It looked like bad trouble coming, so our band broke camp and started out to join Crazy Horse on Powder River. . . .

The nights were sharp now, but the days were clear and still; and while we were camping there I went up into the Hills alone and sat a long while under a tree. I thought maybe my vision would come back and tell me how I could save that country for my people, but I could not see anything clear. . . .

Afterwhile we came to the village on Powder River and went into camp at the downstream end. I was anxious to see my cousin, Crazy Horse, again, for now that it began to look like bad trouble coming, everybody talked about him more than ever and he seemed greater than before. Also I was getting older.

Of course I had seen him now and then ever since I could remember, and had heard stories of the brave things he did. . . . And the people told stories of when he was a boy and used to be around with the older Hump all the time. Hump was not young any more at the time, and he was a very great warrior, maybe the greatest we ever had until then. They say people used to wonder at the boy and the old man always being together; but I think Hump knew Crazy Horse would be a great man and wanted to teach him everything.

Crazy Horse's father was my father's cousin, and there were no chiefs in our family before Crazy Horse; but there were holy men; and he became a chief because of the power he got in a vision when he was a boy. When I was a man, my father told me something about that vision. Of course he did not know all of it; but he said that Crazy Horse dreamed and went into the world where there is nothing but the spirits of

all things. That is the real world that is behind this one, and everything we see here is something like a shadow from that world. He was on his horse in that world, and the horse and himself on it and the trees and the grass and the stones and everything were made of spirit, and nothing was hard, and everything seemed to float. His horse was standing still there, and yet it danced around like a horse made only of shadow, and that is how he got his name, which does not mean that his horse was crazy or wild, but that in his vision it danced around in that queer way.

It was this vision that gave him his great power, for when he went into a fight, he had only to think of that world to be in it again, so that he could go through anything and not be hurt. . . . He was a queer man. Maybe he was always part way into that world of his vision. He was a very great man, and I think if the Wasichus had not murdered him down there, maybe we should still have the Black Hills and be happy. They could not have killed him in battle. They had to lie to him and murder him. And he was only about thirty years old when he died.

Critical Thinking

1. What was the reason that so many "Wasichus" came into the Black Hills in 1874–1875? Who was their leader?

2. How did the Sioux regard the territory in the Black Hills?

3. For what reason did the September council between the Indians and the army officials take place? Why does Black Elk say that it was finally "just like wind blowing"?

4. What did Black Elk believe was the source of Crazy Horse's power? How did he and the other Sioux regard Crazy Horse?

 ★

CHAPTER 6
"An Unfinished Story"

O. HENRY

O. Henry (the pen name of William Sidney Porter) was among the first American writers to focus on ordinary people in urban America. His career was short, but in the early 1900s he was the country's most popular storyteller. O. Henry often wrote about young working women— typists, store clerks, or seamstresses. Readers particularly loved the twist at the end of an O. Henry story, which sometimes brought a surprise happy ending. This excerpt features a typical heroine.

Dulcie worked in a department store. She sold Hamburg edging [lace], or stuffed peppers, or automobiles, or other little trinkets such as they keep in department stores. Of what she earned, Dulcie received six dollars per week. . . .

During her first year in the store, Dulcie was paid five dollars per week. It would be instructive to know how she lived on that amount. Don't care? Very well; probably you are interested in larger amounts. Six dollars is a larger amount. I will tell you how she lived on six dollars per week.

One afternoon at six, when Dulcie was sticking her hat pin within an eighth of an inch of her [scalp], she said to her chum, Sadie. . . .

"Say, Sade, I made a date for dinner this evening with Piggy."

"You never did!" exclaimed Sadie, admiringly. "Well, ain't you the lucky one? Piggy's an awful swell; and he always takes a girl to swell places. He took Blanche up to the Hoffman House one evening, where they have swell music, and you see a lot of swells. You'll have a swell time, Dulce."

Dulcie hurried homeward. Her eyes were shining, and her cheeks showed the delicate pink of life's—real life's—approaching dawn. It was Friday; and she had fifty cents left of her last week's wages.

The streets were filled with the rush-hour floods of people. The electric lights of Broadway were glowing—calling moths from miles, from leagues, from hundreds of leagues out of darkness around to come in and attend the singeing school. Men in accurate clothes, with faces like those carved on cherry stones by the old salts in sailors' homes, turned and stared at Dulcie as she sped, unheeding, past them. Manhattan, the night-blooming cereus, was beginning to unfold its dead-white, heavy-odored petals.

Dulcie stopped in a store where goods were cheap and bought an imitation lace collar with her fifty cents. That money was to have been spent otherwise—fifteen cents for supper, ten cents for breakfast, ten cents for lunch. Another dime was to be added to her small store of savings; and five cents was to be squandered for licorice drops. . . . The licorice was an extravagance—almost a carouse—but what is life without pleasures?

Dulcie lived in a furnished room. There is this difference between a furnished room and a boarding-house. In a furnished room, other people do not know it when you go hungry.

Dulcie went up to her room—the third-floor-back in a West Side brownstone-front. She lit the gas. . . .

In its one-fourth-candlepower glow we will observe the room.

Couch-bed, dresser, table, washstand, chair— of this much the landlady was guilty. The rest was Dulcie's. On the dresser were her treasures—a gilt china vase presented to her by Sadie, a calendar issued by a pickle works, a book on the divination of dreams, some rice [face] powder in a glass dish, and a cluster of artificial cherries tied with a pink ribbon.

Against the wrinkly mirror stood pictures of General Kitchener, William Muldoon, the Duchess of Marlborough, and Benvenuto Cellini. Against one wall was a plaster of Paris plaque of an O'Callahan [policeman] in a Roman helmet. Near it was a violent oleograph [print]

★ AMERICAN LITERATURE ★

Introducing the Chapter 6 Selection

Some of the best-known and best-loved short stories in American literature—"The Gift of the Magi," and "The Ransom of Red Chief"—were written by O. Henry during his brief career. Although his stories sometimes depend too much on coincidence and the surprise "twist" ending, the plots are skillful and the picture of turn-of-the-century city life is colorful and authentic. Very popular in the early 1900s, O. Henry is still read and enjoyed today. (Appropriately, a major literary award for short story writing is named for him.)

Vocabulary Preview

Be sure students understand the following terms: *league*—Measure of distance (about 3 miles). *cereus*—A fragrant flower. *stigma*— Mark of shame. *connoisseur*— Knowledgeable expert. *spurious*—False, fake.

Connecting with American History

Help students understand the setting and background of this story. *How did technology change the look of American cities and help them grow?* (Steel construction for skyscrapers; elevators; mass transit such as trolleys and streetcars; better sanitation systems.) *Why did businesses start to advertise in the later 1800s?* (Because more consumer goods were being made; because there were new popular media to carry advertising, such as magazines and billboards.) *In what other ways did buying and selling consumer goods change?* (The beginning of chain stores, large department stores, mail order catalogs.)

Have students imagine Dulcie as a "time traveler" to a modern city. What would surprise her? What would she recognize as familiar? Have them write her experiences as a journal entry.

782

Analysis

O. Henry's short stories are famous for their surprise endings. Have students suggest what kind of a twist this story might take at the end. Then have several students read the actual story; they can read it to the class or make a report.

Critical Thinking Answers

1. Students may suggest department stores and other shops, automobiles, crowds of people at rush hour, electric lights on Broadway, elegant restaurants, gaslights in homes. The fact that Dulcie is living alone and working shows changes in society.

2. Their wages were barely enough to rent a room and eat very cheaply; there was almost nothing left for clothes or entertainment unless they skipped meals or were invited out.

3. She has a single furnished room in a brownstone; it is lit with gas that she also uses for cooking. For decoration, she has a china vase, a give-away calendar, cheap prints and photographs of celebrities she admires.

★ AMERICAN LITERATURE ★

of a lemon-colored child assaulting an inflammatory butterfly. This was Dulcie's final judgment in art; but it had never been upset. . . .

Piggy was to call for her at seven. While she swiftly makes ready, let us discreetly face the other way and gossip.

For the room, Dulcie paid two dollars per week. On week-days her breakfast cost ten cents; she made coffee and cooked an egg over the gaslight while she was dressing. On Sunday mornings she feasted royally on veal chops and pineapple fritters at "Billy's" restaurant, at a cost of twenty-five cents—and tipped the waitress ten cents. New York presents so many temptations for one to run into extravagance. She had her lunches in the department-store restaurant at a cost of sixty cents for the week; dinners were $1.05. The evening papers—show me a New Yorker going without his daily paper!—came to six cents; and two Sunday papers—one for the personal column and the other to read—were ten cents. The total amounts to $4.76. Now, one has to buy clothes, and—

I give it up. I hear of wonderful bargains in fabrics, and of miracles performed with needle and thread; but I am in doubt. I hold my pen poised in vain when I would add to Dulcie's life some of those joys that belong to woman. . . . Twice she had been to Coney Island and had ridden the hobby-horses [merry-go-round]. 'Tis a weary thing to count your pleasures by summers instead of by hours.

Piggy needs but a word. When the girls named him, an undeserving stigma was cast upon the noble family of swine. The words-of-three-letters lesson in the old blue spelling book begins with Piggy's biography. He was fat; he had the soul of a rat, the habits of a bat, and the magnanimity of a cat. . . . He wore expensive clothes; and was a connoisseur in starvation. He could look at a shop-girl and tell you to an hour how long it had been since she had eaten anything more nourishing than marshmallows and tea. He hung about the shopping districts, and prowled around in department stores with his invitations to dinner. . . .

At ten minutes to seven Dulcie was ready. She looked at herself in the wrinkly mirror. The reflection was satisfactory. The dark blue dress, fitting without a wrinkle, the hat with its jaunty black feather, the but-slightly-soiled gloves—all representing self-denial, even of food itself—were vastly becoming.

Dulcie forgot everything else for a moment except that she was beautiful, and that life was about to lift a corner of its mysterious veil for her to observe its wonders. No gentleman had ever asked her out before. Now she was going for a brief moment into the glitter and exalted show.

The girls said that Piggy was a "spender." There would be a grand dinner, and music, and splendidly dressed ladies to look at and things to eat. . . . No doubt she would be asked out again. . . .

Somebody knocked at the door. Dulcie opened it. The landlady stood there with a spurious smile, sniffing for cooking by stolen gas.

"A gentleman's downstairs to see you," she said. "Name is Mr. Wiggins."

By such epithet was Piggy known to unfortunate ones who had to take him seriously.

From "An Unfinished Story" in *The Four Million* by O. Henry (1906), reprinted in *The Complete Works of O. Henry* (Doubleday, 1917).

Critical Thinking

1. What things does O. Henry mention in his description of New York that show it as a "modern" big city?
2. What do Dulcie's earnings and expenses show about the way young working women lived in this era?
3. How does Dulcie's room reflect the technology and taste of the times?

■■■■ ★ ■■■■

CHAPTER 7
The House of Mirth

EDITH WHARTON

Some of the best portraits of the Gilded Age come from the writings of Edith Wharton and Henry James. Wharton grew up in New York City high society, but she could still view it with both humor and pity.

In The House of Mirth *(1905) Lily Bart, a young woman with little money, struggles to find a place in high society. In this scene, Lily meets a more practical friend and explains her situation.*

The walk up Fifth Avenue, unfolding before her, in the brilliance of the hard winter sunlight, an interminable procession of fastidiously-equipped carriages . . . this glimpse of the ever-revolving wheels of the great social machine made Lily more than ever conscious of the steepness and narrowness of Gerty's stairs, and of the cramped blind-alley of life to which they led. Dull stairs destined to be mounted by dull people: how many thousands of insignificant figures were going up and down such stairs all over the world at that very moment—figures as shabby and uninteresting as that of the middle-aged lady in limp black who descended Gerty's flight as Lily climbed to it!

"That was poor Miss Jane Silverton—she came to talk things over with me: she and her sister want to do something to support themselves," Gerty explained, as Lily followed her into the sitting-room.

"To support themselves? Are they so hard up?" Miss Bart asked with a touch of irritation: she had not come to listen to the woes of other people.

"I'm afraid they have nothing left. Ned's debts have swallowed up everything. They had such hopes, you know, when he broke away

from Carry Fisher; they thought Bertha Dorset would be such a good influence, because she doesn't care for cards, and—well, she talked quite beautifully to poor Miss Jane about feeling as if Ned were her younger brother, and wanting to carry him off on the yacht, so that he might have a chance to drop cards and racing, and take up his literary work again."

Miss Farish paused with a sigh which reflected the perplexity of her departing visitor. "But that isn't all; it isn't even the worst. It seems that Ned has quarrelled with the Dorsets; or at least Bertha won't allow him to see her, and he is so unhappy about it that he has taken to gambling again. . . . You can fancy how poor Miss Jane felt—she came to me at once, and seemed to think that if I could get her something to do she could earn enough to pay Ned's debts and send him away—I'm afraid she has no idea how long it would take her to pay for one of his evenings at bridge. And he was horribly in debt when he came back from the cruise—I can't see why he should have spent so much more money under Bertha's influence than Carry's: can you?"

Lily met this query with an impatient gesture. "My dear Gerty, I always understand how people can spend much more money—never how they can spend any less!"

She loosened her furs and settled herself in Gerty's easy-chair, while her friend busied herself with the tea-cups.

"But what can they do—the Miss Silvertons? How do they mean to support themselves?" she asked, conscious that the note of irritation still persisted in her voice. It was the very last topic she had meant to discuss—it really did not interest her in the least—but she was seized by a sudden perverse curiosity to know how the two colourless shrinking victims of young Silverton's sentimental experiments meant to cope with the grim necessity which lurked so close to her own threshold.

"I don't know—I am trying to find something for them. Miss Jane reads aloud very nicely—but it's so hard to find any one who is willing to be read to. And Miss Annie paints a little—"

"Oh, I know—apple-blossoms on blotting paper; just the kind of thing I shall be doing myself before long!" exclaimed Lily, starting up with a vehemence of movement that threatened destruction to Miss Farish's fragile tea-table.

Lily bent over to steady the cups; then she sank back into her seat. "I'd forgotten there was no room to dash about in—how beautifully one does have to behave in a small flat! Oh, Gerty, I wasn't meant to be good," she sighed out incoherently.

Gerty lifted an apprehensive look to her pale face, in which the eyes shone with a peculiar sleepless lustre.

"You look horribly tired, Lily; take your tea, and let me give you this cushion to lean against."

Miss Bart accepted the cup of tea, but put back the cushion with an impatient hand.

"Don't give me that! I don't want to lean back—I shall go to sleep if I do."

"Well, why not, dear? I'll be as quiet as a mouse," Gerty urged affectionately.

"No—no; don't be quiet; talk to me—keep me awake! I don't sleep at night, and in the afternoon a dreadful drowsiness creeps over me. . . ."

"But you look so tired: I'm sure you must be ill—"

Miss Bart set down her cup with a start. "Do I look ill? Does my face show it?" She rose and walked quickly toward the little mirror above the writing-table. "What a horrid looking-glass—it's all blotched and discoloured. Anyone would look ghastly in it!" She turned back, fixing her plaintive eyes on Gerty. "You stupid dear, why do you say such odious things to me? It's enough to make one ill to be told one looks so! And looking ill means looking ugly." She caught Gerty's wrists, and drew her close to the window. "After all I'd rather know the truth. Look me straight in the face, Gerty, and tell me: am I perfectly frightful?"

"You're perfectly beautiful now, Lily: your eyes are shining, and your cheeks have grown so pink all of a sudden—"

"Ah, they were pale, then—ghastly pale, when I came in? Why don't you tell me frankly that I'm a wreck? My eyes are bright now because I'm so nervous—but in the mornings they look like lead. And I can see the lines coming in my face—the lines of worry and disappointment and failure! Every sleepless night leaves a new one—and how can I sleep, when I have such dreadful things to think about?"

"Dreadful things—what things?" asked Gerty, gently detaching her wrists from her friend's feverish fingers.

"What things? Well, poverty, for one—and I don't know any that's more dreadful." Lily turned away and sank with sudden weariness into the easy-chair near the tea-table. "You asked me just now if I could understand why Ned Silverton spent so much money. Of course I understand—he spends it on living with the rich. You think we live *on* the rich, rather than with them: and so we do, in a sense—but it's a privilege we have to pay for! We eat their dinners, and drink their wine, and smoke their cigarettes, and use their carriages and their opera-boxes and their private cars—yes, but there's a tax to pay on every one of those luxuries. The man pays it by big tips to the servants, by playing cards beyond his means, by flowers and presents—and—and—lots of other things that cost; the girl pays it by tips and cards too—oh, yes, I've had to take up bridge again—and by going to the best dress-makers, and having just the right dress for every occasion, and always keeping herself fresh and exquisite and amusing!"

She leaned back for a moment, closing her eyes, and as she sat there, her pale lips slightly parted, and the lids dropped above her flagged brilliant gaze, Gerty had a startled perception of the change in her face—of the way in which an ashen daylight seemed suddenly to extinguish its artificial brightness. She looked up, and the vision vanished.

"It doesn't sound very amusing, does it? And it isn't—I'm sick to death of it! And yet the thought of giving it all up nearly kills me—it's what keeps me awake at night, and makes me so crazy for your strong tea. For I can't go on in this way much longer, you know—I'm nearly at the end of my tether. And then what can I do—

how on earth am I to keep myself alive? I see myself reduced to the fate of that poor Silverton woman—slinking about to employment agencies, and trying to sell painted blotting-pads to Women's Exchanges! And there are thousands and thousands of women trying to do the same thing already, and not one of the number who has less idea how to earn a dollar than I have!"

She rose again with a hurried glance at the clock. "It's late, and I must be off. . . . Don't look so worried, you dear thing—don't think too much about the nonsense I've been talking." She was before the mirror again, adjusting her hair with a light hand, drawing down her veil, and giving a dexterous touch to her furs. "Of course, you know, it hasn't come to the employment agencies and the painted blotting-pads yet, but I'm rather hard-up just for the moment, and if I could find something to do—notes to write and visiting-lists to make up, or that kind of thing—it would tide me over till the legacy is paid. And Carry has promised to find somebody who wants a kind of social secretary—you know she makes a specialty of the helpless rich."

From *The House of Mirth* by Edith Wharton. Published by Bantam Books, Inc., 1984.

Critical Thinking

1. What does Lily Bart's situation reveal about the education and expectations for young women in the 1890s?
2. What options for making a living did women like Lily and the Silverton sisters have in this period?
3. According to Lily, why was it so costly for people with less money to keep up with their richer friends?

★

CHAPTER 8
Two Poems
PAUL LAURENCE DUNBAR

In the decades after the Civil War, some reform-minded Americans—both black and white—spread the knowledge that there was a distinctive African American culture, particularly in music, dance, and literature. The poet Paul Laurence Dunbar, born in 1872, was one of the earliest voices of modern black literature. His parents had been slaves who had escaped through the Underground Railroad. Dunbar first became popular for his poems in black rural dialect. His later poems expressed some of the sorrows experienced by African Americans. These are two of the most famous.

Sympathy

I know what the caged bird feels, alas!
When the sun is bright on the upland slopes;
When the wind stirs soft through the springing
    grass
And the river flows like a stream of glass;
When the first bird sings and the first bud
    opes,
And the faint perfume from its chalice steals—
I know what the caged bird feels!

I know why the caged bird beats his wing
Till its blood is red on the cruel bars;
For he must fly back to his perch and cling
When he fain would be on the bough a-swing;
And a pain still throbs in the old, old scars
And they pulse again with a keener sting—
I know why he beats his wing!

I know why the caged bird sings, ah me,
When his wing is bruised and his bosom sore,—
When he beats his bars and would be free;
It is not a carol of joy or glee,

785

Have students write a short poem or story that uses informal speech or slang, or a dialect that they commonly use.

Analysis
Have students read some of Dunbar's other poems and discuss them from a modern-day point of view. Is the use of black dialect offensive to present-day African Americans?

Critical Thinking Answers
1. One interpretation is that African Americans are still imprisoned by their past, by the old wounds and the years of hardship and slavery. Their "song" is not one of joy but a prayer for true freedom and release from pain.

2. The wounds—physical and spiritual—that African Americans suffered as slaves.

3. Interpretations may vary. Dunbar implies that there is a strong undercurrent of pain and anger that blacks are not free to express in white society, which expects them to be cheerful and grateful for their freedom.

But a prayer that he sends from his heart's
    deep core,
But a plea, that upward to Heaven he flings—
I know why the caged bird sings!

We Wear the Mask

We wear the mask that grins and lies,
It hides our cheeks and shades our eyes,—
This debt we pay to human guile;
With torn and bleeding hearts we smile,
And mouth with myriad subtleties.

Why should the world be over-wise,
In counting all our tears and sighs?
Nay, let them only see us, while
    We wear the mask.

We smile, but, O great Christ, our cries
To thee from tortured souls arise.
We sing, but oh the clay is vile
Beneath our feet, and long the mile;
But let the world dream otherwise,
    We wear the mask.

"Sympathy" and "We Wear the Mask" from *The Complete Poems of Paul Laurence Dunbar* by Paul Laurence Dunbar. Published by Dodd, Mead & Co.

Critical Thinking

1. According to Dunbar's metaphor, how are African Americans like a "caged bird" even though they are no longer slaves? Why *does* the caged bird sing?

2. In the poem "Sympathy," what are the "old, old scars" the poet refers to?

3. What kind of "mask" do you think African Americans had to wear in the first decades following the Civil War?

━━━━ ★ ━━━━

CHAPTER 9
"Boy on Horseback"
LINCOLN STEFFENS

Lincoln Steffens was one of the Progressive era's best known investigative journalists—the writers whom Theodore Roosevelt called "muckrakers." As an editor and reporter, he uncovered political corruption and worked actively for reform. Steffens's autobiography (1931) recounts his long and influential career. The first section, "Boy on Horseback," tells about his childhood in Sacramento, California. This excerpt describes how Steffens, as a teenager in the 1880s, first became aware of politics when his friend Charlie Marple got a job as a page in the California Legislature.

I wish I could recall all that I went through that winter. It was a revelation; it was a revolution to me. Charlie was appointed a page; we all went to the opening session, where, with a formal front, the Speaker was elected (just as if it had not been "fixed"), speeches made (just as if spontaneously), and the committees and the whole organization read off (just as if it had not been "settled" days and nights before). Then I saw why Charlie wasn't interested in his salary: he got none of it; it all went home [to his family]; and he had no more money in his pocket than I had in mine. But also I saw that the Legislature wasn't what my father, my teachers, and the grown-ups thought; it wasn't even what my histories and the other books said. There was some mystery about it as there was about art, as there was about everything. Nothing was what it was supposed to be. And Charlie took it as it was; my father took it as it seemed to be; I couldn't take it at all. What troubled me most, however, was that they none of them had any strong feeling about the con-

---

Introducing the Chapter 9 Selection
Lincoln Steffens is still considered one of America's greatest journalists—a man who not only reported history but took part in making it. About his famous *Autobiography*, one critic said:

"More than the story of one remarkable man, this is a portrait of an entire era." The section on Steffens' boyhood, published separately as *Boy on Horseback*, is a delightful and classic recollection about growing up in America.

flict of the two pictures. I had. I remember how I suffered; I wanted, I needed, to adjust the difference between what was and what seemed to be. There was something wrong somewhere, and I could not get it right. And nobody would help me.

Charlie was forever for getting away from the Capitol. So were the legislators. They kept adjourning, over every holiday, over Sundays, over Saturdays and Sundays, over Saturdays, Sundays, and Mondays. We could ride, therefore, and we did. We made long trips out to the ranches, up and down and across the rivers. . . . I enjoyed our many, many days of free play.

But I enjoyed also the sessions of the House when Charlie had to be on the floor. He found me a seat just back of the rail where I could sit and watch him and the other pages running about among the legislators in their seats. Charlie used to stand beside me, he and the other small pages, between calls, and we learned the procedure. We became expert on the rules. The practices of debate, quite aside from the legislation under consideration, fascinated me. I wished it were real. It was beautiful enough to be true. But no, speeches were made on important subjects with hardly anyone present but the Speaker, the clerks, and us boys. Where were the absent members? I did not ask that question often; not out loud. The pages laughed; everybody laughed. Charlie explained.

"The members are out where the fate of the measure debated here is being settled," and he took me to committee rooms and hotel apartments where, with the drinks and cigars, members were playing poker with the lobbyists and leaders. "The members against the bill are allowed to win the price agreed on to buy their vote."

Bribery! I might as well have been shot. Somewhere in my head or my heart I was wounded deeply.

Once, when the Speaker was not in the chair and many members were in their seats, when there was a dead debate in an atmosphere of great tension, I was taken down a corridor to the closed door of a committee room. There stood reporters and a small crowd of others watching outside. We waited awhile till, at last, the Speaker came out, said something, and hurried with the crowd back to the Assembly. Charlie held me back to point out to me "the big bosses" who had come "up the river" to "force that bill through"; they had "put on the screws." I was struck by the observation that one of the bosses was blind. We went back to the House, and quickly, after a very ordinary debate of hours, the bill was passed on the third reading and sent to the Senate, where in due course it was approved. It was a "rotten deal," the boys said, and I remember my father shook his head over it. "The rascals," he muttered.

And that, so far as I could make out from him and from all witnesses—that was the explanation. The Legislature, government—everything was "all right," only there were some "bad men" who spoiled things—now and then. "Politicians" they were called, those bad men. How I hated them, in the abstract. In the concrete—I saw Charlie Prodger often in the lobby of the Legislature, and I remember that someone said he was "one of them," a "politician." But I knew Charlie Prodger, and I knew he was not a "bad man."

And the sergeant-at-arms, who was called "bad"—one of the San Francisco gang—he was one of the kindest, easiest-going men I ever met. He looked out for me; he took care of all the boys. Many a time he let Charlie Marple off to have a free day with me. And there were others: every "crook" I met seemed to me to belong in a class with . . . all the other grown men and women who "understood a fellow"— did not stick at rules; did not laugh at everything a boy said and frown at every little thing he did.

When the Legislature closed and Charlie Marple went home, I was left to ride around the country alone, thinking, thinking. I asked questions, of course; I could not think out alone all that I had been learning that winter; I could not easily drop the problem of government and the goodness and badness of men. But I did not

About the Author
Lincoln Steffens (1866–1936) was not only a crusading journalist but also one of the nation's leading progressive thinkers. Starting as a local reporter, he worked on several newspapers, then in 1901 became editor of *McClure's*, a magazine known for investigative reporting. Steffens' well-documented series on political corruption in American city government was published in book form. He was also a popular lecturer. Later he studied and wrote about revolutionary politics in Mexico and Russia.

Vocabulary Preview
Be sure students understand the following terms: *revelation*—Surprising disclosure. *adjourning*—Ending a meeting until another time. *defiance*—Opposition to authority.

★ AMERICAN LITERATURE ★

Connecting with American History

Help students recall some milestones of the Progressive movement. *What were the goals of muckraking journalists like Steffens?* (Exposing crime, graft, and corruption in government; revealing the anti-competitive tactics and sharp practices of big business.) *What kinds of legislation resulted from the work of the progressives?* (Business regulation to protect workers and consumers; constitutional amendments for the income tax, direct election of senators, women's suffrage.) *Why was young Lincoln Steffens so impressed with the actions of the Johnsons?*

Have students write a short essay about some incident in which their own perception of things was changed by someone's courage.

Analysis

Explore with students the development of young Steffens's awareness of what is going on in the legislature and his ways of looking at it. What qualities and traits did he already have that would later make him a great investigative journalist?

Critical Thinking Answers

1. He has expected legislators to be dedicated, hardworking, and honest; to discuss issues seriously and make big decisions. Instead he finds laws being made in "backroom deals" and legislators absent much of the time. He is surprised that this doesn't seem to bother anybody.

2. Some of the people who are classed as "politicians" are the ones who are the most friendly, pleasant, and easy-going to Steffens and his friends.

3. Hiram Johnson, presumably inspired by his father's crusading actions, became a reform politician; Steffens himself became a reforming journalist.

---

draw from my friends any answers that cleared my darkness. The bridge-tender said that all Legislatures were like that. . . .

But there was an answer of a sort about that time, an answer to one of my questions: Why didn't somebody challenge the rascals—if they were so bad? The boss of Sacramento, Frank Rhodes, the gambler, was having one of his conventions of the local ringleaders in a room under his gambling-house. It was at night. There were no outsiders present, none wanted, and the insiders were fighting, shooting men. During the meeting Grove L. Johnson, a well-known attorney in the town, walked in with his two sons, Albert and Hiram, both little more than boys, and both carrying revolvers. They went up to the front, and with one of his boys on one side of him, the other on the other, Mr. Johnson told those crooks all about themselves and what they were doing. He was bitter, fearless, free-spoken; he insulted, he defied those politicians; he called upon the town to clean them out and predicted that their power would be broken some day. There was no answer. When he had finished, he and his sons walked out.

Something in me responded to that proceeding. It was one way to solve my problem. There was no other response, so far as I could see or hear. People said unpleasant things about Grove L. Johnson, and the Rhodes ring went right on governing the town. Later, much later, the boss disappeared, and still later Grove L. Johnson himself was one of the bosses of the Legislature. Albert Johnson died. But Hiram Johnson became a reform Governor of California and a United States Senator.

What struck and stunned me at the time was that this courageous attack by the Johnsons—especially by the boys—had no effect upon the people I knew. I was trying to see the Legislature and the government as Mr. Marple [Charlie's father, a painter] saw the sunset through the brush in the river bottom; not the mud but—the gold, the Indians—some beauty in them. The painter said there always was something beautiful to see. Well, Mr. Johnson and his two boys—their defiance was beautiful; wasn't

it? I thought so, and yet nobody else did. Why? I gave it up, or, better, I laid the question aside. I had other things to think of, wonderful things, things more in my line.

From *Boy on Horseback* by Lincoln Steffens. Copyright 1931, 1935 by Harcourt, Brace and Company. Reprinted by permission of Harcourt Brace Jovanovich Inc.

Critical Thinking

1. What ideals about government did young Steffens hold? How did his first encounters with politics shake them?

2. What problem did Steffens have with the difference between his abstract dislike of politicians as "bad men" and his feelings for the real people he met?

3. How did the political situation in Sacramento help inspire the careers of both Steffens and Hiram Johnson?

■■■■ ★ ■■■■

CHAPTER 10

Ragtime

E. L. DOCTOROW

Historical novelists often invent fictional characters as the focus of their stories, then involve them with real events and real-life characters. E. L. Doctorow's novel Ragtime *is set in the early 1900s. Its fictional characters encounter such historical figures as J. P. Morgan, Harry Houdini, Emma Goldman, and Booker T. Washington. Here "Tateh," a Russian Jewish immigrant artist, and his young daughter are caught up in labor violence.*

This same winter [1909] found Tateh and his daughter in the mill town of Lawrence, Massachusetts. They had come there the previous autumn, having heard there were jobs. Tateh

Other Books by Lincoln Steffens

The Shame of the Cities, 1904.

The Autobiography of Lincoln Steffens, 1931.

The World of Lincoln Steffens, 1962 (collected essays and memoirs).

stood in front of a loom for fifty-six hours a week. His pay was just under six dollars. The family lived in a wooden tenement on a hill. They had no heat. They occupied one room overlooking an alley in which residents customarily dumped their garbage. He feared she would fall victim to the low-class elements of the neighborhood. He refused to enroll her in school—it was easier here than in New York to avoid the authorities—and made her stay home when he was not there to go out with her. After work he'd walk with her for an hour through the dark streets. She became thoughtful. She held her shoulders straight and walked like a woman. . . .

The dismal wooden tenements lay in endless rows. Everyone from Europe was there—the Italians, the Poles, the Belgians, the Russian Jews. The feeling was not good between the different groups. One day the biggest of the mills, American Woolen Company, gave out envelopes with short pay, and a tremor went through the workers in the plant. Several Italian workers left their machines. They ran through the mill calling for a strike. They pulled out wires and threw lumps of coal through the windows. Others followed them. The anger spread. Throughout the city people left their machines. Those who couldn't make up their minds were carried along in the momentum. In three days every textile mill in Lawrence was virtually shut down.

Tateh was overjoyed. We were going to starve to death or freeze to death, he told his daughter. Now we'll be shot to death. But people from the I.W.W. [Industrial Workers of the World] who knew how to run a strike quickly came up from New York and organized things. A strike committee was formed with every one of the races represented and the message went out to the workers: no violence. Taking the girl with him Tateh joined the thousands of pickets encircling the mill, a massive brick building that went on for blocks. They trudged under the cold gray sky. Trolley cars came down the street, the drivers peering at the sight of thousands of marchers moving silently through the snow. Overhead the telephone and telegraph wires drooped with ice. Militia with rifles nervously guarded the mill gates. The militia all had overcoats.

There were many incidents. A woman worker was shot in the street. The only ones with guns were the police and the militia, but the two strike leaders, Ettor and Giovanetti, were arrested for complicity in the shooting. They were put in jail pending their trial. Something of the sort had been expected. Tateh went down to the train station to be on hand for the arrival in Lawrence of replacements for Ettor and Giovanetti. There was an immense crowd. Out of the train stepped Big Bill Haywood, the most famous Wobbly [nickname for the IWW] of them all. He was a Westerner and wore a stetson which he now removed and waved. A cheer went up. Haywood raised his hands for quiet. He spoke. His voice was magnificent. There is no foreigner here except the capitalists, he said. The place went wild. Afterward everyone marched through the streets and sang the *Internationale*. The girl had never seen her Tateh [father] so inflamed. She liked the strike because it got her out of the room. She held his hand.

But the battle went on week after week. Relief committees had set up kitchens in every neighborhood. It's not charity, a woman told Tateh when, after the child received her portion, he refused his. The bosses want you weak, therefore you have to be strong. The people who help us today will need our help tomorrow. On the picket line each cold day they wrapped their scarves around their necks and stamped their feet in the cold snow. The girl's little cloak was threadbare. Tateh volunteered for service on the strike display committee and got them off the cold streets by designing posters. The posters were very beautiful. But the man in charge told him they were not right. We don't want art, the man said. We want something to stir the anger. We want to keep the fires stoked. Tateh had drawn pickets, stark figures with their feet in snow. He had drawn families huddled in their tenements. He switched to lettering. All for one and one for all. He felt better. At night he took home scraps of paper, oak

★ AMERICAN LITERATURE ★

789

Introducing the Chapter 10 Selection

E. L. Doctorow writes a different kind of imaginative historical novel, in which real figures from history meet and interact with memorable but eccentric fictional characters. Doctorow does not try to re-create the details of a historical time (as Gore Vidal does) but the atmosphere—the sights, sounds, smells, and emotions of a particular era, from the old West to the gangster era of the 1920s. *Ragtime* begins in 1902 and ends in 1915, weaving together stories of three different families: affluent middle-class whites, black revolutionaries, Jewish Socialist immigrants from Russia. Critics praised the way it caught the spirit of what makes America truly "American."

About the Author
Edgar Laurence Doctorow (1931–   ), grew up in New York during the Depression, the background for his novel *World's Fair*. He was educated at Kenyon College and Columbia University and worked in motion pictures and book publishing while writing his early novels. Doctorow's novels are an imaginative blend of historical fact and colorful fiction, creating memorable (if unbelievable) characters and a rich, detailed picture of people's lives and emotions. His books have won many awards.

Vocabulary Preview
Be sure students understand the following terms:
tenements—Run-down apartment buildings. *tremor*—Mood of tension, a shiver. *militia*—State military force. *complicity*—Involvement in wrongdoing. *stetson*—Western-style hat. *children's crusade*—Reference to one of the medieval Crusades.

789

★ AMERICAN LITERATURE ★

tag, pens and India ink, and to take the child's mind off their troubles he began to entertain her with silhouette drawings. . . .

Meanwhile the strike had become famous. Reporters arrived daily from all over the country. Support was coming in from other cities. But there was a growing weakness in the unity of the strike front. A man with children found it difficult to keep his courage and resolve. A plan was put into effect whereby children of strikers were to be sent to other cities to board with families in sympathy with the strike. Hundreds of families in Boston and New York and Philadelphia offered to take them in. Others sent money. Every family was carefully checked by the strike committee. The parents of the children had to sign permission forms. The experiment began. Wealthy women came up from New York to escort the first hundred on the train. Each child had had a medical examination and wore a new outfit of clothes. They arrived at Grand Central Station in New York like a religious army. A crowd met them and for a moment everyone held the picture of the children hand in hand staring resolutely ahead as if toward the awful fate industrial America had prepared for them. The press coverage was enormous. The mill owners in Lawrence realized that of all the stratagems devised by the workers this one, the children's crusade, was the most damaging. If it was allowed to go on, national sentiment would swing to the workingmen and the owners would have to give in. This would mean an increase in wages that would bring some workers up to eight dollars a week. They would get extra pay for overtime and for machine speed-ups. They would get off without any punishment for their strike. It was unthinkable. The mill owners knew who were the stewards of civilization and the source of progress and prosperity in the city of Lawrence. For the good of the country and the American democratic system they resolved there would be no more children's crusades.

In the meantime Tateh debated with himself: Clearly the best thing for his girl would be to have a place for a few weeks with a settled family. She would be properly fed, she would be warm, and she would get a taste of a normal home life. But he couldn't bear to part from her. The thought gave him forebodings. He went down to the relief committee, a storefront not far from the mill, and talked to one of the women there. She assured him they had more good working-class families who had volunteered to board a child than they knew what to do with. Jewish? Tateh said. You name it we got it, the woman said. But he couldn't bring himself to sign the papers. Every family is investigated, the woman told him. Could we be careless about such things? I've been a socialist all my life, Tateh assured her. Of course, the woman said. A doctor will listen to her chest. For that alone it's worthwhile. She'll eat hot meals and know her father has friends in the world. But no one's pushing you. Look, look at the line behind you, plenty of customers.

Tateh thought Here I am in the middle of brotherhood in action and I'm thinking like some bourgeois from the *shtetl* [Russian Jewish village]. He signed the permission papers.

From *Ragtime* by E. L. Doctorow. Copyright ©1974, 1975 by E. L. Doctorow. Reprinted by permission of Random House, Inc.

Critical Thinking

1. What working conditions led to the textile-mill strike in Lawrence? What Progressive-era legislation was intended to improve conditions such as these?

2. What immigrant groups made up the labor force in the textile mills?

3. Why did people in other cities volunteer to help the children of the strikers?

4. How does Doctorow portray the mill owners' attitude toward the strike and the strikers?

■■■■■■ ★ ■■■■■■

Other Books by E. L. Doctorow

The Book of Daniel, 1971.
Loon Lake, 1980.
Lives of the Poets, 1984 .
World's Fair, 1985.
Billy Bathgate, 1989.

CHAPTER 11
"Versos Sencillos"
JOSÉ MARTÍ

José Martí was a hero to Cuban patriots in the late 1800s and a voice of the independence movement. His poems, such as "Versos Sencillos (Simple Poetry)," spoke of justice and liberty. Martí was killed during Cuba's 1895 revolution against Spain.

Yo soy un hombre sincero
De donde crece la palma,
Y antes morirme quiero
Echar mis versos del alma.

Con los pobres de la tierra
Quiero yo mi suerte echar:
El arroyo de la sierra
Me complace más que el mar.

Mi verso al valiente agrada:
Mi verso, breve y sincero,
Es del vigor del acero
Con que se funde la espada.

I am an honest man
From where the palms grow;
Before I die I want my soul
To shed its poetry.

I want to cast my lot
With the humble of this world;
A mountain brook means more to me
Than does the sea.

My poems please the valiant;
Sincere and brief, my poetry
Is rugged as the steel they use
To forge a sword.

From "Versos Sencillos (Simple Poetry)" in *José Martí: Major Poems A Bilingual Edition*, edited by Philip S. Foner, English translation by Elinor Randall. Copyright ©1982 by Holmes & Meier Publishers, Inc. Reprinted by permission.

Critical Thinking

1. Martí spent much of his life in exile from Cuba. How is this reflected in his poetry?
2. Why does Martí say "my poetry is rugged as the steel they use to forge a sword"?
3. From this poem, what can you tell about the kind of people in Cuba who most strongly wanted independence from Spain?

━━━━━ ★ ━━━━━

CHAPTER 12
Complete Book of Marvels
RICHARD HALLIBURTON

By the turn of the century, Latin America held many attractions for North Americans. Though right next door, it still seemed to be an exotic land of tropical jungles, ancient ruins, and colorful animals, with the promise of great wealth in gold and minerals. It drew not only politicians and business people but also travelers and adventurers. One of the latter was the American writer Richard Halliburton. Born in 1900, he traveled widely and wrote of his daring adventures in several popular books. Here Halliburton describes swimming the Panama Canal in 1928.

From Haiti we are going, on our quest for marvels, straight to Panama. For here we'll find another world-wonder—the Panama Canal.

For me this canal has always held a special charm. Long before I ever saw it I had read the story of the Isthmus it crosses; of the battles for gold, of the pirates and their plunder, that have crowded Panama with drama; of Columbus and Balboa who explored there; of all the colorful villains and heroes who have died there.

791

Connecting with American History
Help students understand the origin of the American connection with Cuba. *What prompted rebellion in Cuba in the 1890s?* (Harsh Spanish policies, economic problems.) *What aroused American interest in the Cuban rebellion?* (Reports from Cuba, competition for readers by "yellow journalist" newspapers; the sinking of the *Maine*.)

Analysis
How does Martí use images of nature and the outdoors to convey the idea of freedom?

Critical Thinking Answers
1. The verses seem to reflect homesickness for the landscape of Cuba.
2. It will be long-lasting.
3. Seemingly the poor and underprivileged.

Introducing the Chapter 12 Selection
Richard Halliburton's romantic enthusiasm for travel and adventure made his books best-sellers both for adults and for younger readers growing up in the late 1930s and early 1940s. Halliburton, unlike many travel writers, actually lived the adventures he wrote about—in addition to swimming the Panama Canal, he scaled the Matterhorn and rode an elephant to retrace Hannibal's journey over the Alps into Italy.

About the Author
After graduating from Princeton, Richard Halliburton (1900–1939) went to sea and roamed the world. He soon became a popular speaker; his first book was a best-seller. On one of his many real-life adventures he retraced the voyage of Ulysses through the Greek islands. He also flew his own small plane, "The Flying Carpet." In March 1939 Halliburton left Hong Kong in a 75-foot Chinese junk, heading

Introducing the Chapter 11 Selection
For Cuban patriots in the late 1800s, the writer and revolutionary poet José Martí was a symbol and a spokesman for the freedom they wanted. Most Americans know Martí's poetry, however, from the 1960s folksong "Guantanamera." Early in the 1960s, a young Cuban in the United States, Hector Angulo, set some of Martí's verses to a traditional Cuban folk tune. Arranged and sung by folk singer Pete Seeger, the song quickly became a favorite. The verses of "Guantanamera" came from some of the last poems Martí wrote before he was killed in the revolution in 1895.

Vocabulary Preview
Be sure students understand the following terms: *isthmus*—Narrow neck of land connecting two larger areas. *scourge*—Deadly, painful affliction. *futile*—Useless, hopeless.

Connecting with American History
Help students recall the background of the building of the Panama Canal. *What was the Clayton-Bulwer Treaty?* (An agreement in 1850 between the U.S. and Britain promising political neutrality for any canal in Central America.) *What effect did the Spanish-American War have on plans for a canal?* (It became strategically important to be able to move ships quickly from the Pacific to the Atlantic.) *What did the United States do to obtain the territory in Panama?* (It encouraged a Panamanian rebellion against Colombia.)

Have students think of a place in history that has caught their imagination. Have them write a description of what it would be like to visit there.

Analysis
What tone and techniques does Halliburton use to involve the reader in his adventure? Have students locate places where the author tries to make the reader feel "You are there."

★ AMERICAN LITERATURE ★

As a boy I followed with eager interest the construction of the Canal across this romantic country. What a thrill I felt when the first ship passed through!

As a young man I made a long-awaited trip to see it, and was so enchanted by the sight of this engineering miracle and by the history behind it, that I obeyed an impulse to swim it from end to end. I dived into its waters on the Atlantic side, and, by daily stages, swam to the Pacific—locks, lake, and all—fifty miles.

So I like to think that I know the Panama Canal as well as anyone, and will make a good guide.

For four hundred years people had been thinking about a canal across the Isthmus, and about the ten-thousand-mile voyage around the tip of South America it would save. Soon after Balboa's discovery of the "South Sea" (as he called the Pacific), the Spanish conquerors proposed to the King of Spain that a canal be cut through Panama, to join the oceans. But the King thought the project too expensive, and dismissed it.

As the centuries passed, other schemes for a canal were born and faded. It was not until 1881 that a French company, headed by the famous French engineer, De Lesseps, began to dig.

Twelve years before, De Lesseps had successfully completed the hundred-mile Suez Canal from the Mediterranean to the Red Sea. But his attempt to repeat that success in Panama was one of the greatest tragedies of engineering history. The company had plenty of money, machinery, skill. However, they had not reckoned with the mosquito, or with the deadly fever germs this insect carries.

Hardly was the work begun before malaria and yellow fever descended upon the labor camps. Nobody knows exactly how many the fever killed, but the total was certainly not less than twenty thousand. The construction company dug more graves than canal. Unable to control the terrible scourge of fever, De Lesseps, after heroic but futile labor, had to abandon his dream. He left behind hundreds of railroad engines, thousands of derricks and dredges and freight-cars, to be engulfed by the jungle. The French company had spent $325,000,000. The total cost of the entire canal which the Americans built was $375,000,000—only $50,000,000 more than the French spent. But for *their* vast outlay of money, the French gained nothing but jungle-covered graves and broken hearts.

In 1903 the Americans took over the work. They had learned by now of the mosquito's deadly character. So before a single spadeful of earth was turned, war was waged against the tiny pests. By 1906, the mosquito had been driven from the Canal Zone, and work could start.

Steam shovels began to dig from the Atlantic side and from the Pacific side at the same time. Across the pathway of the Canal stretched a ridge 660 feet high, called Gold Hill. This too the engineers attacked, and through its center they carved out Culebra Cut, the biggest ditch ever dug. A great artificial lake was dammed up to cover more than half the route with water, and huge locks were constructed to lift ships up to this lake and drop them down again.

As the man-made canyon deepened in Gold Hill, the lake rose to meet it. In January, 1914, the locks were finished, and a ship sailed through from ocean to ocean. That was one of the greatest days in the history of geography.

Aboard our own ship we reach the Atlantic entrance of the Canal. Ahead of us and behind are dozens of other ships that have collected here from a thousand ports and a hundred nations—battleships, tankers, tramps, long liners, sailboats, tugboats, freight boats—every flag, every color, an endless parade steaming up the channel through the tropical sunshine, on toward the magic water-steps—the most romantic journey granted the ships of the sea.

I remember this entrance to the Canal particularly well. As I swam across the outer harbor, everybody said I'd be eaten by sharks and barracudas. Because of these savage fish few people ever swam here. And likewise I remember the inner channel too, since the current from the emptying locks was so strong it took me seven hours to swim three miles. . . .

We reach the first of the mighty locks. The double steel gates, as high as a seven-story building, fold back soundlessly. . . . We are towed into the thousand-foot concrete chamber by electric "mules." The gates close behind, and the water-level in our lock begins to rise, as the water, flowing down from the lock above, rushes through the intake tubes. There are dozens of these tubes and each one is as large as a railroad tunnel. Our ship is lifted thirty feet. Now the gates ahead swing open, and we are towed on into the next lock—the second step in these giant stairs. Again the gates close after us. We are raised another thirty feet, as the water boils up beneath. Then through still another lock we climb, before we steam out into Gatun Lake, ninety feet above the level of the sea.

As a swimmer, I found it fun being locked through just as if I were a ship. . . . When I reached the end of the third lock the official in charge asked me how I intended to pay for the nine million cubic feet of water . . . that had been used to raise me the ninety feet from ocean level to Gatun Lake.

I answered that I was the *S.S. Richard Halliburton* and would pay toll just like all the other ships—according to my tonnage. So I was put on the scales and found to weigh one-thirteenth of one ton. The charge was thirty-six cents, the smallest toll ever paid by any ship in the history of the Canal.

From *Richard Halliburton's Complete Book of Marvels* by Richard Halliburton. Copyright ©1941, 1960 by The Bobbs-Merrill Company and renewed by the Macmillan Publishing Company. Reprinted by permission of the Macmillan Publishing Company.

Critical Thinking

1. When was the idea of a canal across Panama first suggested?
2. What prevented De Lesseps and the French from completing the canal?
3. When and why did the author of this selection first become interested in the Canal?
4. What problems in geography and technology did the builders of the Canal have to overcome? What were the solutions?

—————— ★ ——————

CHAPTER 13

Three Soldiers

JOHN DOS PASSOS

The high death tolls and grim devastation of World War I created a mood of futility and hopelessness among many American writers. John Dos Passos had been an ambulance driver in France during the war. He began his writing career in 1921 with the realistic war novel Three Soldiers. *In this scene, Dan Fuselli and his company get ready to ship out.*

The stars were very bright when Fuselli, eyes stinging with sleep, stumbled out of the barracks. They trembled like bits of brilliant jelly in the black velvet of the sky, just as something inside him trembled with excitement.

"Anybody know where the electricity turns on?" asked the sergeant in a good-humored voice. "Here it is." The light over the door of the barracks snapped on, revealing a rotund cheerful man with a little yellow mustache and an unlit cigarette dangling out of the corner of his mouth. Grouped about him, in overcoats and caps, the men of the company rested their packs against their knees.

"All right; line up, men."

Eyes looked curiously at Fuselli as he lined up with the rest. He had been transferred into the company the night before.

"Attenshun," shouted the sergeant. Then he wrinkled up his eyes and grinned hard at the slip of paper he had in his hand, while the men of his company watched him affectionately.

"Answer 'Here' when your name is called. Allan, B.C."

"Yo!" came a shrill voice from the end of the line.

"Anspach."

"Here."

Meanwhile outside the other barracks other companies could be heard calling the roll. Somewhere from the end of the street came a cheer.

"Well, I guess I can tell you now, fellers," said the sergeant with his air of quiet omniscience, when he had called the last name. "We're going overseas."

Everybody cheered.

"Shut up, you don't want the Huns to hear us, do you?"

The company laughed, and there was a broad grin on the sergeant's round face.

"Seem to have a pretty decent top-kicker," whispered Fuselli to the man next to him.

"You bet yer, kid, he's a peach," said the other man in a voice full of devotion. "This is some company, I can tell you that."

"You bet it is," said the next man along. "The corporal's in the Red Sox outfield."

The lieutenant appeared suddenly in the area of light in front of the barracks. He was a pink-faced boy. His trench coat, a little too large, was very new and stuck out stiffly from his legs.

"Everything all right, sergeant? Everything all right?" he asked several times, shifting his weight from one foot to the other.

"All ready for entrainment, sir," said the sergeant heartily.

"Very good, I'll let you know the order of march in a minute."

Fuselli's ears pounded with strange excitement. These phrases, "entrainment," "order of march," had a businesslike sound. He suddenly started to wonder how it would feel to be under fire. Memories of movies flickered in his mind.

"Gawd, ain't I glad to git out o' this hell-hole," he said to the man next him.

"The next one may be more of a hell-hole yet, buddy," said the sergeant striding up and down with his important confident walk.

Everybody laughed.

"He's some sergeant, our sergeant is," said the man next to Fuselli. "He's got brains in his head, that boy has."

"All right, break ranks," said the sergeant, "But if anybody moves away from this bar-racks, I'll put him in K.P. till—till he'll be able to peel spuds in his sleep."

The company laughed again. Fuselli noticed with displeasure that the tall man with the shrill voice whose name had been called first on the roll did not laugh but spat disgustedly out of the corner of his mouth.

"Well, there are bad eggs in every good bunch," thought Fuselli.

It gradually grew grey with dawn. Fuselli's legs were tired from standing so long. Outside all the barracks, as far as he could see up the street, men stood in ragged lines waiting.

The sun rose hot on a cloudless day. A few sparrows twittered about the tin roof of the barracks.

"Well, we're not goin' this day."

"Why?" asked somebody savagely.

"Troops always leaves at night. . . . Here comes Sarge."

Everybody craned their necks in the direction pointed out.

The sergeant strolled up with a mysterious smile on his face.

"Put away your overcoats and get out your mess kits."

Mess kits clattered and gleamed in the slanting rays of the sun. They marched to the mess hall and back again, lined up again with packs and waited some more.

Everybody began to get tired and peevish. Fuselli wondered where his old friends of the other company were. They were good kids too, Chris and that educated fellow, Andrews. Tough luck they couldn't have come along.

The sun rose higher. Men sneaked into the barracks one by one and lay down on the bare cots.

"What you want to bet we won't leave this camp for a week yet?" asked someone.

At noon they lined up for mess again, ate dismally and hurriedly. As Fuselli was leaving the mess hall tapping a tattoo on his kit with two dirty fingernails, the corporal spoke to him in a low voice.

"Be sure to wash yer kit, buddy. We may have pack inspection."

The corporal was a slim yellow-faced man

with a wrinkled skin, though he was still young, and an arrow-shaped mouth that opened and shut like the paper mouths children make.

"All right, corporal," Fuselli answered cheerfully. He wanted to make a good impression. "Fellers'll be sayin' 'All right, corporal,' to me soon," he thought. An idea that he repelled came into his mind. The corporal didn't look strong. He wouldn't last long overseas. And he pictured Mabe [Mabel] writing Corporal Dan Fuselli, O.A.R.D.5.

At the end of the afternoon, the lieutenant appeared suddenly, his face flushed, his trench coat stiffer than ever.

"All right, sergeant; line up your men," he said in a breathless voice.

All down the camp street companies were forming. One by one they marched out in columns of fours and halted with their packs on. The day was getting amber with sunset. Retreat sounded.

Fuselli's mind had suddenly become very active. The notes of the bugle and of the band playing "The Star-Spangled Banner" sifted into his consciousness through a dream of what it would be like over there. He was in a place like the Exposition ground, full of old men and women in peasant costume, like in the song, "When It's Apple Blossom Time in Normandy." Men in spiked helmets who looked like firemen kept charging through, like the Ku-Klux Klan in the movies, jumping from their horses and setting fire to buildings with strange outlandish gestures, spitting [spearing] babies on their long swords. Those were the Huns. Then there were flags blowing very hard in the wind, and the sound of a band. The Yanks were coming. Everything was lost in a scene from a movie in which khaki-clad regiments marched fast, fast across the scene. The memory of the shouting that always accompanied it drowned out the picture. "The guns must make a racket, though," he added as an after-thought.

"Atten-shun!

"Forwa-ard, march!"

The long street of the camp was full of the tramping of feet. They were off. As they passed through the gate Fuselli caught a glimpse of Chris standing with his arm about Andrews's shoulders. They both waved. Fuselli grinned and expanded his chest. They were just rookies still. He was going overseas.

The weight of the pack tugged at his shoulders and made his feet heavy as if they were charged with lead. The sweat ran down his close-clipped head under the overseas cap and streamed into his eyes and down the sides of his nose. Through the tramp of feet he heard confusedly cheering from the sidewalk. In front of him the backs of heads and the swaying packs got smaller, rank by rank up the street. Above them flags dangled from windows, flags leisurely swaying in the twilight. But the weight of the pack, as the column marched under arc lights glaring through the afterglow, inevitably forced his head to droop forward. The soles of boots and legs wrapped in puttees and the bottom strap of the pack of the man ahead of him were all he could see. The pack seemed heavy enough to push him through the asphalt pavement. And all about him was the faint jingle of equipment and the tramp of feet. Every part of him was full of sweat. He could feel vaguely the steam of sweat that rose from the ranks of struggling bodies about him. But gradually he forgot everything but the pack tugging at his shoulders, weighing down his thighs and ankles and feet, and the monotonous rhythm of his feet striking the pavement and of the other feet, in front of him, behind him, beside him, crunching, crunching.

From *Three Soldiers* by John Dos Passos. Copyright ©1921, 1949 by John Dos Passos. Reprinted by permission of Elizabeth H. Dos Passos.

Critical Thinking

1. Who were the "Huns"? What is the historical reference for this nickname?
2. Where did Fuselli get most of his ideas for imagining the war in Europe?
3. What is Fuselli's attitude toward being in the army? Do you think this was typical of World War I soldiers?

━━━━━ ★ ━━━━━

Analysis

Have students pick out the concrete details that contribute to the realistic picture of how the camp and his fellow soldiers look to Fuselli. How does this realistic picture become more "impressionistic" as the troops start to move out?

Critical Thinking Answers

1. "Huns" was the World War I nickname for the Germans; it derives from the barbaric tribes of central Asia that invaded central Europe beginning in the fourth century, known for their destructiveness.
2. From the movies.
3. He finds much of the atmosphere exciting; he imagines he is going to do well and become a hero. Probably many American soldiers thought that going to war was a chance for adventure. Opinions may vary, however.

Other Books by John Dos Passos

One Man's Initiation, 1919.
Manhattan Transfer, 1925.
U.S.A.:
  The 42nd Parallel (1930),
  Nineteen-Nineteen (1931),
  The Big Money (1936).
District of Columbia
  (trilogy), 1952.

CHAPTER 14

The Great Gatsby

F. SCOTT FITZGERALD

F. Scott Fitzgerald's stories of "the rich and famous" of the Jazz Age did more than describe the era—they helped create its ideal lifestyle. Fitzgerald's novel The Great Gatsby *(1925) tells the story of a self-made millionaire with a mysterious past. In this scene, Nick Carraway (the book's narrator) and Daisy Buchanan visit Jay Gatsby's Long Island mansion.*

"My house looks well, doesn't it?" he [Gatsby] demanded. "See how the whole front of it catches the light."

I agreed that it was splendid.

"Yes." His eyes went over it, every arched door and square tower. "It took me just three years to earn the money that bought it."

"I thought you inherited your money."

"I did, old sport," he said automatically, "but I lost most of it in the big panic—the panic of the war."

I think he hardly knew what he was saying, for when I asked him what business he was in he answered: "That's my affair," before he realized that it wasn't an appropriate reply.

"Oh, I've been in several things," he corrected himself. "I was in the drug business and then I was in the oil business. But I'm not in either one now." He looked at me with more attention. "Do you mean you've been thinking over what I proposed the other night?"

Before I could answer, Daisy came out of the house and two rows of brass buttons on her dress gleamed in the sunlight.

"That huge place *there?*" she cried pointing.

"Do you like it?"

"I love it, but I don't see how you live there all alone."

"I keep it always full of interesting people, night and day. People who do interesting things. Celebrated people."

Instead of taking the short cut along the Sound we went down to the road and entered by the big postern. With enchanting murmurs Daisy admired this aspect or that of the feudal silhouette against the sky, admired the gardens, the sparkling odor of jonquils and the frothy odor of hawthorn and plum blossoms and the pale gold odor of kiss-me-at-the-gate. It was strange to reach the marble steps and find no stir of bright dresses in and out of the door, and hear no sound but bird voices in the trees.

And inside, as we wandered through Marie Antoinette music-rooms and Restoration salons, I felt that there were guests concealed behind every couch and table, under orders to be breathlessly silent until we had passed through. As Gatsby closed the door of "the Merton College Library" I could have sworn I heard the owl-eyed man break into ghostly laughter.

We went upstairs, through period bedrooms swathed in rose and lavender silk and vivid with new flowers, through dressing-rooms and poolrooms, and bathrooms, with sunken baths—intruding into one chamber where a dishevelled man in pajamas was doing liver exercises on the floor. It was Mr. Klipspringer, the "boarder." I had seen him wandering hungrily about the beach that morning. Finally we came to Gatsby's own apartment, a bedroom and a bath, and an Adam study, where we sat down and drank a glass of some Chartreuse he took from a cupboard in the wall.

He hadn't once ceased looking at Daisy, and I think he revalued everything in his house according to the measure of response it drew from her well-loved eyes. Sometimes, too, he stared around at his possessions in a dazed way, as though in her actual and astounding presence none of it was any longer real. Once he nearly toppled down a flight of stairs.

His bedroom was the simplest room of all—except where the dresser was garnished with a toilet set [comb, brush, mirror] of pure dull gold. Daisy took the brush with delight and smoothed her hair, whereupon Gatsby sat

automobile industry and related fields. Buying on credit increased.) *In what ways is Gatsby a typical figure of the 1920s?* (He lives well and is impressed by his material possessions.)

Analysis

Have students note how Fitzgerald uses sensory details—color, odor, texture—to create an atmosphere that seems luxurious. Have them pick out individual phrases and adjectives (e.g., "pale gold odor").

down and shaded his eyes and began to laugh.

"It's the funniest thing, old sport," he said hilariously. "I can't—when I try to—"

He had passed visibly through two states and was entering upon a third. After his embarrassment and his unreasoning joy he was consumed with wonder at her presence. He had been full of the idea so long, dreamed it right through to the end, waited with his teeth set, so to speak, at an inconceivable pitch of intensity. Now, in the reaction, he was running down like an overwound clock.

Recovering himself in a minute he opened for us two hulking patent cabinets which held his massed suits and dressing-gowns and ties, and his shirts, piled like bricks in stacks a dozen high.

"I've got a man in England who buys me clothes. He sends over a selection of things at the beginning of each season, spring and fall."

He took out a pile of shirts and began throwing them, one by one, before us, shirts of sheer linen and thick silk and fine flannel, which lost their folds as they fell and covered the table in many-colored disarray. While we admired he brought more and the soft rich heap mounted higher—shirts with stripes and scrolls and plaids in coral and apple-green and lavender and faint orange, with monograms of India blue. Suddenly, with a strained sound, Daisy bent her head into the shirts and began to cry stormily.

"They're such beautiful shirts," she sobbed, her voice muffled in the thick folds. "It makes me sad because I've never seen such—such beautiful shirts before."

After the house, we were to see the grounds and the swimming pool, and the hydroplane and the mid-summer flowers—but outside Gatsby's window it began to rain again, so we stood in a row looking at the corrugated surface of the Sound.

"If it wasn't for the mist we could see your home across the bay," said Gatsby. "You always have a green light that burns all night at the end of your dock."

Daisy put her arm through his abruptly, but he seemed absorbed in what he had just said.

Possibly it had occurred to him that the colossal significance of that light had now vanished forever. Compared to the great distance that had separated him from Daisy it had seemed very near to her, almost touching her. It had seemed as close as a star to the moon. Now it was again a green light on a dock. His count of enchanted objects had diminished by one.

Critical Thinking

1. How does Gatsby's way of life reflect the prosperity of the 1920s?
2. According to what Gatsby says here, how did historical events affect the ups and downs of his fortune?
3. How does Gatsby's behavior show that he is not yet completely used to being rich?
4. How are Gatsby's wealth and lifestyle different from affluent lifestyles in the "Gilded Age" of the 1880s and 1890s?

■■■■ ★ ■■■■

CHAPTER 15

Their Eyes Were Watching God

ZORA NEALE HURSTON

For some black writers of the Harlem Renaissance, the Depression years were a time of hardship and bitterness. Although Zora Neale Hurston also faced hard times in the 1930s, her writing had a different feeling: love for the African American traditions of rural Florida. In this scene

Critical Thinking Answers

1. His mansion is decorated in opulent "period" styles; it has grounds, a garden, and a swimming pool. Gatsby's possessions are luxurious and he entertains lavishly.

2. Gatsby says he inherited money, lost it in the wartime economic panic, then made it back quickly.

3. He is self-conscious and tends to show off his possessions, trying to impress Daisy.

4. Gatsby is a self-made millionaire; he does not have "old money" or belong to an upper-class family, as was necessary to be part of society in the 1890s.

Other Books by F. Scott Fitzgerald
This Side of Paradise, 1920.
Tales of the Jazz Age, 1922 (short stories).
The Beautiful and Damned, 1922.
Tender Is the Night, 1934.
The Last Tycoon, started 1939 (unfinished).

Introducing the Chapter 15 Selection
When *Their Eyes Were Watching God* was published in the mid-1930s, novelist Richard Wright, a powerful voice in black literature, said that it had "no theme and no message." This was typical of the criticism that the book and its author received from the almost exclusively male writers of the Harlem Renaissance. Decades ahead of her time, Zora Neale Hurston had written a novel about another strong-willed woman—Janie Crawford—and her search for self-fulfillment. Although it took several decades, the civil rights movement, and the women's movement, Hurston has now been rediscovered as a major American writer as well as an early feminist voice.

★ AMERICAN LITERATURE ★

from Their Eyes Were Watching God *(1937), Janie Crawford reacts to the death of her husband Joe (Jody) Starks, mayor of their small Florida town.*

"Dis sittin' in de rulin' chair is been hard on Jody," she muttered out loud. She was full of pity for the first time in years. Jody had been hard on her and others but life had mishandled him too. Poor Joe! Maybe if she had known some other way to try, she might have made his face different. But what that other way could be, she had no idea. She thought back and forth about what had happened in the making of a voice out of a man. Then thought about herself. Years ago, she had told her girl self to wait for her in the looking glass. It had been a long time since she had remembered. Perhaps she'd better look. She went over to the dresser and looked hard at her skin and features. The young girl was gone, but a handsome woman had taken her place. She tore off the kerchief from her head and let down her plentiful hair. The weight, the length, the glory was there. She took careful stock of herself, then combed her hair and tied it back up again. Then she starched and ironed her face, forming it into just what people wanted to see, and opened up the window and cried, "Come heah people! Jody is dead. Mah husband is gone from me."

Joe's funeral was the finest thing Orange County had ever seen with Negro eyes. The motor hearse, the Cadillac and Buick carriages; Dr. Henderson there in his Lincoln; the hosts from far and wide. Then again the gold and red and purple, the gloat and glamour of the secret orders, each with its insinuations of power and glory, undreamed of by the uninitiated. People on farm horses and mules; babies riding astride of brothers' and sisters' backs. The Elks band ranked at the church door and playing "Safe in the Arms of Jesus" with such a dominant drum rhythm that it could be stepped off smartly by the long line as it filed inside. The Little Emperor of the cross-roads was leaving Orange County as he had come—with the outstretched hand of power.

Janie starched and ironed her face and came set in the funeral behind her veil. It was like a wall of stone and steel. The funeral was going on outside. All things concerning death and burial were said and done. Finish. End. Nevermore. Darkness. Deep hole. Dissolution. Eternity. Weeping and wailing outside. Inside the expensive black folds were resurrection and life. She did not reach outside for anything, nor did the things of death reach inside to disturb her calm. She sent her face to Joe's funeral, and herself went rollicking with the springtime across the world. After a while the people finished their celebration and Janie went on home.

Before she slept that night she burnt up every one of her head rags and went about the house the next morning with her hair in one thick braid swinging well below her waist. That was the only change people saw in her. She kept the store in the same way except of evenings she sat on the porch and listened and sent Hezekiah in to wait on late custom [customers]. She saw no reason to rush at changing things around. She would have the rest of her life to do as she pleased.

Most of the day she was at the store, but at night she was there in the big house and sometimes it creaked and cried all night under the weight of lonesomeness. Then she'd lie awake in bed asking lonesomeness some questions. She asked if she wanted to leave and go back to where she had come from and try to find her mother. Maybe tend her grandmother's grave. Sort of look over the old stamping ground generally. Digging around inside of herself like that she found that she had no interest in that seldom-seen mother at all. She hated her grandmother and had hidden it from herself all these years under a cloak of pity. She had been getting ready for her great journey to the horizons in search of *people*; it was important to all the world that she should find them and they find her. But she had been whipped like a cur dog and run off down a back road after *things*.

It was all according to the way you see things. Some people could look at a mud-puddle and see an ocean with ships. But Nanny [her grandmother] belonged to that other kind that loved to deal in scraps. Here Nanny had taken the biggest thing God ever made, the horizon—for no matter how far a person can go the horizon is still way beyond you—and pinched it in to such a little bit of a thing that she could tie it about her granddaughter's neck tight enough to choke her. She hated the old woman who had twisted her so in the name of love. . . .

Janie found out very soon that her widowhood and property was a great challenge in South Florida. Before Jody had been dead a month, she noticed how often men who had never been intimates of Joe drove considerable distances to ask after her welfare and offer their services as advisor.

"Uh woman by herself is uh pitiful thing," she was told over and again. "Dey needs aid and assistance. God never meant 'em tuh try tuh stand by theirselves. You ain't been used tuh knockin' round and doin' fuh yo'self, Mis' Starks. You been well taken keer of, you needs uh man."

Janie laughed at all these well-wishers because she knew that they knew plenty of women alone; that she was not the first one they had ever seen. But most of the others were poor. Besides, she liked being lonesome for a change. This freedom feeling was fine.

From *Their Eyes Were Watching God* by Zora Neale Hurston. Copyright ©1937 by J. B. Lippincott Company; copyright © renewed 1965 by John C. Hurston and Joel Hurston. Reprinted by permission of HarperCollins Publishers and J. M. Dent & Sons, Ltd.

Critical Thinking

1. Why might life during the Depression have been better for blacks in small towns like this one than it was for blacks in cities?
2. From the funeral and the description "Little Emperor," what picture do you get of Joe Starks? Of the social structure of the town?
3. What do the other men's attitudes toward Janie as a widow show about the status of women at this time? What does Janie herself feel about being on her own?

■■■ ★ ■■■

CHAPTER 16

Point of No Return

JOHN P. MARQUAND

The stock market crash of 1929 was one of those milestone events that people remembered long afterward—where they were when they heard the news, how the events affected them and the people around them. Many writers of the 1930s and 1940s used the stock market crash as a turning point in their novels and short stories. This excerpt from John P. Marquand's 1949 novel Point of No Return *describes events in the life of Charles Grey at the time of the stock market crash.*

During all of his [Charles's] later business experience, many otherwise reasonable people kept resurrecting the details of the crash of 1929. They discussed it, apparently, for the same reason that old ladies enjoyed describing surgical operations and sessions with their dentists. There was a snob value in boasting of old pain. Instead of wishing to forget, they kept struggling to remember. The older men would talk about Black Friday in the nineties [1890s] and the more technical panic of 1907 as though all these debacles were just alike. . . . There were even people, who should have known better, who seemed to be imbued with the fixed idea that the crash of 1929 caused the depression. They could no longer see it as a symptom or as an extreme example of mass hysteria. Only unattractively strong individuals should have been allowed to dabble in that market.

Most people never seemed to see what Charles saw in the crash—a sordidly ugly exhibition of the basest of human fears. They had forgotten the desperation that made cowards and thieves out of previously respectable people, and the fear evolved from greed which had no decency or dignity. Instead, they always harked back to the spectacular—the confusion, the lights in downtown New York burning night after night while clerks were struggling to balance the brokerage accounts; and sooner or later they always asked Charles where he

★ AMERICAN LITERATURE ★

John P. Marquand, a writer in the tradition of Edith Wharton and John Cheever, wrote about the lives of affluent families in the Northeast. The protagonist of *Point of No Return,* Charles Grey, was deeply affected by the suicide of his father after the 1929 Crash. The novel satirizes the business and consumer-oriented society of the mid-1900s.

About the Author

John Phillips Marquand (1893–1960) was born in Wilmington, Delaware, but spent most of his adult life in New England, first as as student at Harvard University, and then as a reporter for the *Boston Transcript.* He was a successful short story writer before publishing his serious novels, one of which, *The Late George Apley,* won a Pulitzer Prize in 1938. He also wrote a popular detective series which described the adventures of a secret agent, Mr. Moto.

Critical Thinking Answers

1. They were more self-sufficient and less affected by the national economic situation; they depended on local farmers, the local economy, and each other.
2. It is an all-black town, led by the men who own the stores and belong to the "secret orders." Joe, as a prosperous store owner, was proud of his prominent social and political position.
3. They believed that women needed to be looked after, that Janie would not be able to manage without a man. Janie enjoys the feeling of freedom and self-determination.

Other Books by Zora Neale Hurston

Jonah's Gourd Vine, 1934.
Mules and Men, 1935.
Moses: Man of the Mountain, 1939.

Vocabulary Preview
Be sure students understand the following terms:
imbued—Filled. *sordidly*—Dirtily. *basest*—Most evil. *phenomenally*—Unusual. *ominous*—Threatening. *composure*—Self-control.

Connecting with American History
Review the events of the stock market crash of 1929 with the class. **What was the general attitude toward the stock market in September 1929?** (People believed prosperity would continue, and stock prices would stay high.) **Why did the market crash?** (Stocks were overvalued, illegal market practices, overspeculation.)

How did Gray's memories of the Crash differ from the memories of others he describes? (Their memories are all of the excitement and confusion of the time, while he remembers it as a time of mass hysteria, when people acted badly.) **Whose point of view is probably more accurate?**

Analysis
Have students write short essays recalling their personal memories surrounding an important event that happened when they were younger.

had been working then and whether he too had been long on the market on that particular day in October. He had learned long ago to answer accurately, with only part of the truth. He always said that he had been in Boston with E. P. Rush & Company and nothing much had happened to him. He had made some money out of the market the year before and had put it into government bonds. . . .

He never told the whole truth to anyone, except to Nancy and to Arthur Slade, and Arthur Slade may have told some of it to Tony Burton at the Stuyvesant Bank but Charles was never sure. . . . There were some things which were better not told, and there was no use digging up what was so completely finished. His own illusions and everything he had planned had crashed in that common crash, but then millions of lives and plans had been crashing ever since. It did no good to imagine what he might have done to have prevented it. Actually he could have done nothing. Everything was what Mr. Lovell would have called an accomplished fact before Charles had been permitted to face it. He was always glad he did not have to blame himself, at least not very much.

When the drop occurred in September, that minor break which nearly everyone considered a normal readjustment considering the market's phenomenally unbroken rise, he had seen it for what it was—the first rumblings of a landslide, an ominous shift of stress and strain that would never strike a balance until the whole structure broke. He knew this was the beginning of a greater break even before Mr. Rush, after a partners' meeting, called him in to help compose a letter advising customers of Rush & Company to sell their holdings of common stocks. . . .

The day when the market first broke in October must have started for everyone the way it did for Charles, as a part of the ordinary routine of living. He remembered reading later, in a brochure published by a banking house: "In years to come the 1929 crash will doubtless be remembered merely as a summer thundershower." When this was written prosperity was still just around the corner and happy days like those old happy ones would be here again if you were not a bear on the United States. When the storm did break, in a cloudless sky, work went on that first day without much interruption in conservative offices like Rush & Company. It was only when the drop went on the next day and the next and when the tickers lagged further and further behind the trading that Charles began to observe that all the faces in the office were stamped with an expression that began to erase individuality.

Jessica had come to Boston on the morning of the break and they were to have had lunch together but he had called her up at her aunt's house to say that, although it had nothing to do with his own department, he felt he had better stay at the office on general principles. Yet at home for the first day or so he could not notice any change and there seemed to be no more connection between home and E. P. Rush & Company than there ever had been. Back in Clyde [a fictional Boston suburb] he could forget the crowd around the board and those sickly individual attempts at indifference and composure.

That first evening before supper, his father said it would be nice if Axel were to mix some Martini cocktails because it had been quite a day in Boston and Dorothea and Elbridge were coming to dinner. Elbridge had something particular to tell them and he hoped that Elbridge had not been monkeying with the market. It was impossible to read anything on his father's face but as soon as they had a moment alone together Charles asked him if everything was all right, and his father looked very cheerful.

"I wish you wouldn't try to look like a doctor," he said, "and I wish you wouldn't think of me as a widow or an orphan. Hasn't everybody been expecting this? Of course I'm all right."

He was like all the rest of them. They were already beginning to say that they had seen it coming, but Charles felt deeply relieved. His father drank two Martinis, which was unusual for him, but he did not speak again about the market. . . .

Critical Thinking

1. To what earlier economic problems do the older men compare the stock market crash of 1929?
2. What current events does the author incorporate into this section of the novel?
3. What does Charles see as the cause of the stock market crash?

━━━━ ★ ━━━━

CHAPTER 17
Babbitt

SINCLAIR LEWIS

For many Americans, the years after World War I were a time of isolationism from European affairs and "normalcy" at home. Many writers, however, criticized what they saw as the narrow outlook of middle-class, small-town America. In this excerpt from Babbitt *(1922) by Sinclair Lewis, George Babbitt, a "typical American business man," makes a speech in his home town of Zenith.*

This autumn a Mr. W. G. Harding, of Marion, Ohio, was appointed President of the United States, but Zenith was less interested in the national campaign than in the local election. Seneca Doane . . . was candidate for mayor of Zenith on an alarming labor ticket. To oppose him the Democrats and Republicans united on Lucas Prout, a mattress-manufacturer with a perfect record for sanity. Mr. Prout was supported by the banks, the Chamber of Commerce, all the decent newspapers, and George F. Babbitt.

Babbitt was precinct-leader on Floral Heights, but his district was safe and he longed for stouter battling. His convention paper had given him the beginning of a reputation for oratory, so the Republican-Democratic Central Committee sent him to the Seventh Ward and South Zenith, to address small audiences of workmen and clerks, and wives uneasy with their new votes. He acquired a fame enduring for weeks. Now and then a reporter was present at one of his meetings, and the headlines (though they were not very large) indicated that George F. Babbitt had addressed Cheering Throng, and Distinguished Man of Affairs had pointed out the Fallacies of Doane. . . .

His reputation for oratory established, at the dinner of the Zenith Real Estate Board he made the Annual Address. The *Advocate-Times* reported this speech with unusual fullness:

. . ."Gentlemen, it strikes me that each year at this annual occasion when friend and foe get together and lay down the battle-ax and let the waves of good-fellowship waft them up the flowery slopes of amity, it behooves us, standing together eye to eye and shoulder to shoulder as fellow-citizens of the best city in the world, to consider where we are both as regards ourselves and the common weal. . . .

"It may be true that New York, Chicago, and Philadelphia will continue to keep ahead of us in size. But aside from these three cities, . . . it's evident to any one with a head for facts that Zenith is the finest example of American life and prosperity to be found anywhere.

"I don't mean to say we're perfect. We've got a lot to do in the way of extending the paving of motor boulevards, for, believe me, it's the fellow with four to ten thousand a year, say, and an automobile and a nice little family in a bungalow on the edge of town, that makes the wheels of progress go round!

"That's the type of fellow that's ruling America to-day; in fact, it's the ideal type to which the entire world must tend, if there's to be a decent, well-balanced, Christian, go-ahead future for this little old planet! Once in a while I just naturally sit back and size up this Solid American Citizen, with a whale of a lot of satisfaction. . . .

"With all modesty, I want to stand up here as a representative business man and gently whis-

★ AMERICAN LITERATURE ★

Introducing the Chapter 17 Selection

Only a few fictional characters are so memorable that their names become synonyms for a type: one of those is George F. Babbitt. Sinclair Lewis's devastating satire of the narrow-minded, small-town, Midwestern businessman created an unforgettable portrait—and gave the language the term "babbitry" for the kind of false, bombastic patriotism that Babbitt represents and that Lewis despised.

About the Author

Sinclair Lewis (1885–1951), novelist and journalist, was a critic of post-World War I society and the first American to win the Nobel Prize for Literature (1930). Born in Sauk Centre, Minnesota, Lewis was especially critical of small-town midwestern values and attitudes. Other targets for his satire were the medical profession and religious hypocrites. His later novels showed concern with the rise of fascism in Europe and race relations in the United States.

Vocabulary Preview

Be sure students understand the following terms:
fallacies—Mistaken or illogical ideas.
amity—Friendship.
burgs—Towns (slang).
shekels—Money (slang).

Critical Thinking Answers
1. "Black Friday" in the 1890s and the Panic of 1907.

2. He recounts scenes in New York at the time of the Crash; mentions reactions to the first drop of the market in September; then the growing effects on people in his own office after the October crash.

3. Greed and an unhealthy economy.

Other Books by John P. Marquand
H. M. Pulham, Esq., 1941.
Stopover: Tokyo, 1957.
Wickford Point, 1939.

per, 'Here's our kind of folks! Here's the specifications of the Standardized American Citizen! Here's the new generation of Americans: fellows with hair on their chests and smiles in their eyes and adding machines in their offices. . . .'

"So! In my clumsy way I have tried to sketch the Real He-man, the fellow with Zip and Bang. And it's because Zenith has so large a proportion of such men that it's the most stable, the greatest of our cities. New York also has its thousands of Real Folks, but New York is cursed with unnumbered foreigners. So are Chicago and San Francisco. . . .

"But it's here in Zenith, the home for manly men and womanly women and bright kids, that you find the largest proportion of these Regular Guys, and that's what sets it in a class by itself; that's why Zenith will be remembered in history as having set the pace for a civilization that shall endure when the old time-killing ways are gone forever and the day of earnest efficient endeavor shall have dawned all round the world!

"Some time I hope folks will quit handing all the credit to a lot of moth-eaten, mildewed, out-of-date, old, European dumps, and give proper credit to the famous Zenith spirit, that clean fighting determination to win Success that has made the little old Zip City celebrated in every land and clime, wherever condensed milk and pasteboard cartons are known! Believe me, the world has fallen too long for these worn-out countries that aren't producing anything but bootblacks and scenery and booze, that haven't got one bathroom per hundred people, and that don't know a loose-leaf ledger from a slip-cover; and it's just about time for some Zenithite to get his back up and holler for a show-down!

"I tell you, Zenith and her sister-cities are producing a new type of civilization. There are many resemblances between Zenith and these other burgs, and I'm darn glad of it! The extraordinary, growing, and sane standardization of stores, offices, streets, hotels, clothes, and newspapers throughout the United States shows how strong and enduring a type is ours. . . .

"The American business man is generous to a fault, but one thing he does demand of all teachers and lecturers and journalists: if we're going to pay them our good money, they've got to help us by selling efficiency and whooping it up for rational prosperity! And when it comes to these blab-mouth, fault-finding, pessimistic cynical University teachers, let me tell you that during this golden coming year it's just as much our duty to bring influence to have those cusses fired as it is to sell all the real estate and gather in all the good shekels we can.

"Not till that is done will our sons and daughters see that the ideal of American manhood and culture isn't a lot of cranks sitting around chewing the rag about their Rights and their Wrongs, but a God-fearing, hustling, successful, two-fisted Regular Guy, who belongs to some church with pep and piety to it, who belongs to the Boosters or the Rotarians or the Kiwanis, to the Elks or Moose or Red Men or Knights of Columbus or any one of a score of organizations of good, jolly, kidding, laughing, sweating, upstanding, lend-a-handing Royal Good Fellows, who plays hard and works hard, and whose answer to his critics is a square-toed boot that'll teach the grouches and smart alecks to respect the He-Man and get out and root for Uncle Samuel, U.S.A.!"

Critical Thinking

1. How does George Babbitt view Europe and European culture?
2. What does Babbitt think about the American trend to mass-production?
3. How did attitudes like Babbitt's influence American government policies in the 1920s and 1930s?

━━━━ ★ ━━━━

802

CHAPTER 18
The Wall

JOHN HERSEY

The rise of European dictatorships cast a shadow over the literature of the late 1930s. Some American writers voiced their admiration of fascism, while others condemned it.

The war itself inspired powerful literature. John Hersey wrote several novels showing the impact of war on civilians in Europe and Asia. The Wall is written as the fictional journal of Noach (NO–ahk) Levinson. Read to find out how some Jews of the Warsaw ghetto resisted German efforts to destroy them.

EVENTS SEPTEMBER 5–12, 1942. ENTRY SEPTEMBER 14, 1942. N. L. [Noach Levinson] We are calling this horrible experience "the Kettle." The Germans' purpose seems to have been to disrupt our order completely—moving us from our homes, invalidating our previous system of working cards, and thereby shaking out all those who had managed before those days improperly to evade deportation. They shut us up in a manageable area—the "Kettle"—and combed through our helpless crowd. According to the best estimate I can make, we numbered about 120,000 when the "Kettle" was put on the stove, so to speak. The German figures on deportation for the six days are 47,791 Jews taken. On one day, September 8, they took 13,596—the worst day we have had. It may be that this was the worst day in all of Jewish history—up to now, at any rate. There are today perhaps 70,000 of us left here in the ghetto, where once half a million Jews were crowded together.

Our first warning of the "Kettle" came when the Germans put up posters. . . .

EVENTS SEPTEMBER 4, 1942. ENTRY DITTO. N. L. Berson and I were walking in the streets together when we saw the first poster.

N. L., after I had read only a few words: "The noose is tightening."

The poster commanded that by ten o'clock tomorrow morning all Jews remaining within the Large Ghetto are to gather *for registration purposes*. . . . They are directed to bring food for two days and drinking utensils, and to leave their apartments unlocked. Anyone found outside the designated area six city blocks by two, to contain more than a hundred thousand Jews, will be shot.

Berson, with earnest expression: "Soon we must choose: either die fighting or die like sheep in a shambles." I think he is right, but how could we ever make such a choice?

EVENTS SEPTEMBER 5–10, 1942. ENTRY SEPTEMBER 11, 1942. FROM DOLEK BERSON. . . . For a time Berson and Rachel let themselves be pushed and carried by the crowd now half a block toward Zamenhofa Street, now back a few yards toward Lubetzkiego, purposelessly. At the sound of a shot down the street to the eastward, part of the mob recoiled and with a violent surge broke through into Ostrowska Street, which was itself crowded, and there the meaningless undulations began again. Nothing seemed to be happening. Berson and Rachel exchanged only brief mutterings. Berson says he was impatient with Rachel. He felt as if he were in the grip of a bad dream; he had the sensation of struggling to wake up and being unable to. The crowd pushed and pulled.

It was late afternoon before Berson recovered from his dazed, dreamlike state. Suddenly once he looked down and saw and felt Rachel beating on his chest with her fists, crying: "Do something! Do something!" They came to a place where the mob was, if possible, thicker than elsewhere. Berson lifted Rachel up above the heads of the people to see what she could see. She told him that a huge selection was taking place at the street corner. Berson eased her

★ AMERICAN LITERATURE ★

down and said: "Why should we go to them? Let them come and get us!"

Most of the houses and courtyards were barricaded or guarded, but Berson and Rachel found one into which the mob had broken, and they went inside and climbed a staircase and with many others jumped from a second-story window into the next courtyard and broke through a fence behind that into still another and climbed high in a building and got out onto some roofs (by this time the sky was darkening) and crossed the roofs until they found a skylight, which they broke (now there were fewer people, perhaps a score; the group had scattered on the roofs) and they let themselves down into an empty apartment house and went into one of them and threw themselves on the beds and lay there through the night, hearing shots and screams all night near by and naturally not sleeping, and stayed there half the next day until curiosity and fear made them go out and down the stairs of the apartment to the street level, but when they saw, in the courtyard, a pile of perhaps thirty bloody Jewish corpses, newly executed, they drew back and climbed again into the same apartment, this time taking the precaution, however, of observing and preparing three different escape routes downstairs into some cellars and out an areaway; up through the skylight; and, as a third choice, out into the courtyard past the corpses and directly into the street—and during the second night they had occasion to be thankful for this foresight, because at a late hour they heard footsteps and the shouts of German hunters, and escaping by the skylight, they spent the hot night shivering on the roofs, listening to shots and screams below, and in the soft dawn they returned yet once more to the same apartment, on the theory that the chances of its being searched again immediately were slight. . . .

And thus, in what seemed a scarcely punctuated continuity of terror, movement, vigilance, hunger, filth, and bare survival, returning again and again to the same apartment, Berson and Rachel passed six days without facing the peripatetic selections. At the end of six days it was

over. A few of the former tenants of the apartment came home and said it was over. The Germans . . . had left the "registration area." Berson and Rachel went through hushed and dreary streets to Pavel's shop.

From *The Wall* by John Hersey. Copyright 1950 by John Hersey. Reprinted by permission of Random House, Inc.

Critical Thinking

1. Describe the different reactions of Jews in the Warsaw ghetto to German efforts to destroy them.
2. What do the first few sentences tell you about the restrictions imposed on Jews in the ghetto even before the Nazis stepped up the persecutions?
3. What does Berson conclude is the real aim of the "registration" order?

■■■■ ★ ■■■■

CHAPTER 19
Maud Martha
GWENDOLYN BROOKS

Despite the social changes brought by World War II, black and white Americans in the postwar years still lived in very separate worlds. In 1950 Gwendolyn Brooks became the first African American to win the Pulitzer Prize for poetry (Annie Allen). *Brooks's only novel,* Maud Martha *(1953), tells of a young woman trying to keep her dignity and pride amidst racial prejudice. In this chapter, titled "we're the only colored people here," Maud Martha and her husband go to the movies and encounter the invisible wall between blacks and whites in late-1940s Chicago.*

When they went out to the car there were just the very finest bits of white powder coming down with an almost comical little ethereal hauteur, to add themselves to the really important, piled-up masses of their kind.

And it wasn't cold.

Maud Martha laughed happily to herself. It was pleasant out, and tonight she and Paul were very close to each other.

He held the door open for her—instead of going on around to the driving side, getting in, and leaving her to get in at her side as best she might. When he took this way of calling her "lady" and informing her of his love she felt precious, protected, delicious. She gave him an excited look of gratitude. He smiled indulgently.

"Want it to be the Owl again?"

"Oh, no no, Paul. Let's not go there tonight. I feel too good inside for that. Let's go downtown?"

She had to suggest that with a question mark at the end, always. He usually had three protests. Too hard to park. Too much money. Too many white folks. And tonight she could almost certainly expect a no, she feared, because he had come out in his blue work shirt. There was a spot of apricot juice on the collar, too. His shoes were not shined. . . . But he nodded!

"We've never been to the World Playhouse," she said cautiously. "They have a good picture. I'd feel rich in there."

"You really wanta?"

"Please?"

"Sure."

It wasn't like other movie houses. People from the Studebaker Theatre which, as Maud Martha whispered to Paul, was "all-locked-arms" with the World Playhouse, were strolling up and down the lobby, laughing softly, smoking with gentle grace.

"There must be a play going on in there and this is probably an intermission," Maud Martha whispered again.

"I don't know why you feel you got to whisper," whispered Paul. "Nobody else is whispering in here." He looked around, resentfully, wanting to see a few, just a few, colored faces. There were only their own.

Maud Martha laughed a nervous defiant little laugh; and spoke loudly. "There certainly isn't any reason to whisper. Silly, huh."

The strolling women were cleverly gowned. Some of them had flowers or flashers in their hair. They looked—cooked. Well cared-for. And as though they had never seen a roach or a rat in their lives. Or gone without heat for a week. And the men had even edges. They were men, Maud Martha thought, who wouldn't stoop to fret over less than a thousand dollars.

"We're the only colored people here," said Paul.

"There's the box office. Go on up."

He went on up. It was closed.

"Well," sighed Maud Martha, "I guess the picture has started already. But we can't have missed much. Go on up to that girl at the candy counter and ask her where we should pay our money."

He didn't want to do that. The girl was lovely and blonde and cold-eyed, and her arms were akimbo, and the set of her head was eloquent. No one else was at the counter.

"Well. We'll wait a minute. And see—"

Maud Martha hated him again. Coward. She ought to flounce over to the girl herself—show him up. . . .

The people in the lobby tried to avoid looking curiously at two shy Negroes wanting desperately not to seem shy. The white women looked at the Negro woman in her outfit with which no special fault could be found, but which made them think, somehow, of close rooms, and wee, close lives. They looked at her hair. They liked to see a dark colored girl with long, long hair. They were always slightly surprised, but agreeably so, when they did. They supposed it was the hair that had got her that yellowish, good-looking Negro man.

The white men tried not to look at the Negro man in the blue work shirt, the Negro man without a tie.

An usher opened a door of the World Playhouse part and ran quickly down the few steps that led from it to the lobby. Paul opened his mouth.

"Say, fella. Where do we get the tickets for the movie?"

The usher glanced at Paul's feet before answering. Then he said coolly, but not unpleasantly, "I'll take the money."

805

About the Author

Gwendolyn Brooks (1917–) has used poetry to portray her long-time friends and neighbors in the black community of Chicago, where she has lived most of her life. When *Annie Allen*, a long narrative poem about a young woman growing up in Chicago, received the Pulitzer Prize for poetry in 1950, Brooks became the first African American Pulitzer Prize winner. *In the Mecca* focused on ghetto life in a huge apartment building on Chicago's South Side. Brooks has taught writing at several Chicago-area colleges; in 1968 she was named poet laureate of Illinois, succeeding Carl Sandburg.

Vocabulary Preview

Be sure students understand the following terms:
ethereal—Light, heavenly.
hauteur—Haughtiness.
[arms] akimbo—Hands on hips, with bent elbows.
Marshall Field's—Large Chicago department store.

Connecting with American History

Help students recall the background of the late 1940s, the Truman era. *What happened in the American economy at the end of World War II?* (Demand for consumer goods brought inflation and high prices; workers struck for higher wages.) *What steps toward giving blacks their civil rights were taken after World War II?* (Truman spoke out against job discrimination and violence against blacks, but his civil rights proposals mainly failed in Congress. He ended segregation in the military by executive order.) *How could Truman's Fair Deal programs have helped Maud Martha have the kind of home and life she wanted?*

Have students write a description of a society in which everybody does have a "Fair Deal."

They were able to go in.

And the picture! Maud Martha was so glad that they had not gone to the Owl! Here was technicolor, and the love story was sweet. And there was classical music that silvered its way into you and made your back cold. And the theater itself! It was no palace, no such Great Shakes as the Tivoli out south, for instance (where many colored people went every night). But you felt good sitting there, yes, good, and as if, when you left it, you would be going home to a sweet-smelling apartment with flowers on little gleaming tables; and wonderful silver on night-blue velvet, in chests; and crackly sheets; and lace spreads on such beds as you saw at Marshall Field's. Instead of back to your kit'n't apt. [kitchenette apartment], with the garbage of your floor's families in a big can just outside your door, and the gray sound of little gray feet scratching away from it as you drag up those flights of narrow complaining stairs.

Paul pressed her hand. Paul said, "We oughta do this more often."

And again. "We'll have to do this more often. And go to plays, too. I mean at that Blackstone, and Studebaker."

She pressed back, smiling beautifully to herself in the darkness. Though she knew that once the spell was over it would be a year, two years, more, before he would return to the World Playhouse. And he might never go to a real play. But she was learning to love moments. To love moments for themselves.

When the picture was over, and the lights revealed them for what they were, the Negroes stood up among the furs and good cloth and faint perfume, looked about them eagerly. They hoped they would meet no cruel eyes. They hoped no one would look intruded upon. They had enjoyed the picture so, they were so happy, they wanted to laugh, to say warmly to the other outgoers, "Good, huh? Wasn't it swell?"

This, of course, they could not do. But if only no one would look intruded upon. . . .

From *Maud Martha* by Gwendolyn Brooks. Copyright ©1951 by the Curtis Publishing Company; copyright ©1953 by Gwendolyn Brooks Blakely. Reprinted by permission of HarperCollins Publishers.

■■■■ ★ ■■■■

CHAPTER 20
Chicano
RICHARD VASQUEZ

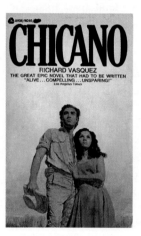

The Eisenhower years were years of peace at home, with prosperity and suburban domestic life the national ideal. Not everyone had a share in this "American dream," however. Richard Vasquez's novel Chicano traces the successes and tragedies of the Sandoval family from the time of their arrival in the
United States from Mexico up through the 1960s. In this scene set in the early 1950s, the Sandovals' twin children, Sammy and Mariana, start school in Los Angeles.

On the first day of the new semester Mrs. Eva Weimer sat at her desk in the elementary school in East Los Angeles and waited for the classroom to fill. She was heavy, with a sagging, bulgy face, and wisps of red hair testified that she had not always been gray. She looked out through thick spectacles as one little dark head after another protruded into the room from the hall, looking this way and that.

"Come in, find a seat," she would call out pleasantly in Spanish. Her grammar and syntax were perfect, but in the dozens of years she had spoken Spanish she had found it impossible to master the flat *e*, the lightning trill of the double *r*, or even the flick of the single *r*. She had given up on accent, but found solace in the ability to carry on a conversation in Spanish at any pace, and say anything in that language as well as it could be said.

Soon all the seats were taken and Mrs. Weimer stood up and confronted the class.

"Buenos días, niños, Me llamo Señora Weimer." Good morning, children. My name is Mrs. Weimer.

From the class came a half-hearted attempt at coordinating the sentence, "Buenos días, señora."

The children were seven years old, and even at this age they understood that the gringos who spoke Spanish fluently but with a poor accent were usually the kinds of persons who went out of their way to be helpful.

"This is our first day in second grade," Mrs. Weimer told them in Spanish. "And this year we are *all* going to learn to work in English. Can anyone here tell us why we must learn to work in English?" She looked out over the dark eager faces and felt the children's trust in her. One large, homely boy raised his hand and she nodded to him.

"Because we live in the United States," he said matter-of-factly in Spanish, and quickly sat down. She noticed he glanced around for signs of approval or disapproval among his peers.

"Yes," Mrs. Weimer continued. "We all live in a country called the United States, or America. And in the United States most people speak English. But there are many other languages spoken here, too. Here in Los Angeles many of us speak Spanish. Can someone tell us what other language is spoken here?"

A girl's hand went up and Mrs. Weimer gave consent. The girl stood up.

"Japanese," she said and quickly sat down. Another hand went up and Mrs. Weimer

nodded. The boy stood up and announced:

"They had to lock all the Japanese up because they were spies, but they're out now."

Mrs. Weimer listened with warmhearted amusement as the children named the various languages they'd heard spoken. One boy rose and said, "My father says we aren't Spanish, we're Mexican, so why do we speak Spanish?"

"We do speak Mexican," another volunteered.

Mrs. Weimer sighed a little. It was too early in their lives to go into the differentiation between Spanish, Mexican, English, Mexican-American, and American. They were not ready for any attempt to crystallize the opaque walls of their little world. She knew her job this semester was to get these youngsters communicating in English as well as possible. She opposed this rule—at least so far as youngsters this age were concerned—but she had no choice but to comply. The board had run into too much criticism by graduating teenagers unable to speak or read English.

"All right, now," she still spoke in Spanish. "We live in America, which is an English-speaking nation. Some of us speak Spanish. Now, tell the truth. Everyone who can speak English raise your hand." She raised hers to start them off.

A few hands shot up quickly, others slowly, and then more slowly yet the remaining hands went up. There was no child present who did not hold up his hand. Mrs. Weimer smiled and slightly shook her head.

"All right," she said warmly. "Hands down. Now, we'll start in this row here, and I want each one in turn to rise and say something in English." It was the only way she could think of to find out for sure. "Please rise, say your name, and say something in English." She didn't want them to feel pressure. "Say anything you want."

The first boy stood up. "My name ees Jorge Alesandro," he said fairly clearly in English. He paused, and Mrs. Weimer could hardly refrain from laughing as she saw him wrinkle his brow, racking his mind for something to say. "I have two dogs at home with fleas," he finally said, then sat down and twisted so that he

★ AMERICAN LITERATURE ★

the rise of the family fortunes through two world wars, but ends in tragedy when both Maria and Sammy are defeated— in different ways—in their encounters with society outside their family.

About the Author
Richard Vasquez drew on his own background in the *barrio* to write one of the first major novels centering on a Chicano family and Chicano life. Vasquez has been a newspaperman for both Spanish- and English-language papers, as well as a publicist and screenwriter. He lives in California.

Vocabulary Preview
Be sure students understand the following terms: *protruded*—Pushed forward. *solace*—Comfort. *gringos*—Hispanic term for non-Hispanics. *sibling*—Referring to brothers and sisters. (The dialogue in Spanish is translated within the selection.)

Connecting with American History
Help students understand the background for the cultural problems encountered by Chicanos in mainstream American society. *What events in Mexico led many Mexicans to move to the United States in the early 1900s?* (The Mexican Revolution, continuing political turmoil, lack of jobs at home.) *In general, what were relationships between Chicanos and non-Hispanic Americans in the 1940s and 1950s?* (Students should be aware of the tensions and violence in the 1940s, discrimination against Hispanics in jobs and housing in the 1950s; resentment of immigrants.) *Why do you think so few of the children in this school speak English?*

808

Have students write a thoughtful essay (or prepare a debate) on the question of bilingual education in school districts where a majority of students speak a language other than English.

Analysis

Have students look at the way the author uses dialogue to point up the differences between the teacher and the Hispanic students and among the students themselves.

Critical Thinking Answers

1. The school and neighborhood are both predominantly Mexican and Spanish-speaking.

2. They refer to the wartime internment of Japanese Americans, which left the impression that "all Japanese were spies."

3. The better English speakers have an advantage socially and economically; teachers in school will tend to favor them.

★ AMERICAN LITERATURE ★

might watch the child behind perform.

"My name is John Garza. John is the English word for Juan."

Next a little girl stood up. "My name is Alicia Herrera. I live with my mother and father in East Los Angeles and have three sisters and five brothers." Mrs. Weimer nodded approval. . . .

The next child rose and said, "Maria Torrez. Ice cream, candy, doughnuts." It was obviously the extent of her English vocabulary.

The next girl caught the eye of Mrs. Weimer. What would some day be breath-taking beauty, she thought, was already firmly started. She must not favor this child, for already, because of her childish beauty, she received special attention wherever she went. Already, this child had an image of herself as something special. It could be damaging. The girl stood up.

"My name is Mariana Sandoval," she said in a clear and exuberant voice. "I live with my mother and father and my brother. He's right here. His name's Sammy." Mariana turned to Sammy, seated directly behind her.

Sammy rose. "I'm Sammy Sandoval," he mumbled awkwardly. "She's my sister." Mrs. Weimer sensed Sammy was aware how Mariana outshone him. Although they were obviously twins, the girl was much more advanced. Mrs. Weimer knew how shattering it could be for one sibling to be overshadowed completely, at this age. This is where the tendencies began. She guessed his poor English, as compared to hers, was the result of lack of confidence in himself, a lack caused by her irresistible dainty charm and bright manner.

By the time each child in the class had given his name and talked, Mrs. Weimer knew that less than half could converse in English, a dozen or so could recognize many words, and a half dozen knew either no words or a little profanity. Among the first things she did was have Mariana and Sammy sit as far apart as possible to eliminate sibling comparison, if not rivalry, in the classroom.

By the time for the first recess she had them seated the way she wanted. She carefully explained how long the recess would be and that

they should be back in their seats promptly at the end of recess.

She watched as they got up when the bell rang. She saw those who were advanced seeking one another out cautiously, while those who spoke no English quickly formed a league and felt much more at ease together. She sighed.

From *Chicano* by Richard Vasquez. Copyright ©1970 by Richard Vasquez.

Critical Thinking

1. From this scene, what can you tell about the ethnic make-up of this school and of East Los Angeles at this time?

2. What reference do the children make to World War II? What is their cultural stereotype of Japanese people?

3. Why is speaking English a factor that divides the children into groups or cliques?

━━━━ ★ ━━━━

CHAPTER 21

The Mambo Kings Play Songs of Love

OSCAR HIJUELOS

The revolution in Cuba led by Fidel Castro brought a wide range of reactions in the United States, especially among Cuban Americans. Oscar Hijuelos's novel The Mambo Kings Play Songs of Love *tells the story of the brothers Nestor and Cesar Castillo, Cuban musicians—the Mambo Kings—who have been in New York since 1949. The high point of their memories is an appearance on the "I Love Lucy" show. Here is how the turmoil in Cuba affected Cesar Castillo.*

Introducing the Chapter 21 Selection

In the opening scene of *The Mambo Kings Play Songs of Love* (the title of the Castillo brothers' best-known record), the narrator is watching a rerun of the 1950s episode of "I Love Lucy" that

Of course, it was a pleasure to perform for the people again. Got his mind off things. And it always made him happy when someone would come along and ask him for an autograph ("*Ciertamente!*"). It felt good when he'd go walking along the 125th Street markets on a Sunday afternoon and some guy in a sleeveless T-shirt would call out to him from a window, "Hey! Mambo King, how's it going?"

Still he felt his sadness. Sometimes when he played those jobs with Manny, he would get a ride back home. But most often he rode the subways, as he didn't like to drive at night anymore. . . .

Anonymous in a pair of sunglasses and with his hat pulled low over his brow, guitar or trumpet case wedged between his knees, the Mambo King traveled to his jobs around the city. It was easy to get home when he worked restaurants in the Village or Madison Avenue bars, where he would serenade the Fred Mac-Murray-looking executives and their companions ("Now, girls, sing after me, Babaloooooo!"), as those jobs usually ended around eleven at night. But when he'd play small clubs and dance halls out on the edges of Brooklyn and the Bronx, he'd get home at four-thirty, five in the morning. Spending many a night riding the trains by himself, he'd read *La Prensa* or *El Diario* or the *Daily News*.

He made lots of friends on the trains; he knew the flamenco guitarist from Toledo, Spain, a fellow named Eloy García, who played in the Café Madrid; an accordionist with a tango orchestra in Greenwich Village, named Macedonio, a roly-poly fellow who'd go to work in a gaucho hat. . . . He knew Estela and Nilda, two *zarzuela* singers who would pass through matronhood with wilting carnations in their hair. He knew a black three-man dance team with conk hairdos, friendly and hopeful fellows, resplendent in white tuxedos and spats, who were always heading out to do auditions. ("These days we're hoping to get on the Ed Sullivan show.") Then there were the Mexicans with their over-sized guitars, trumpets, and an accordion that resembled an altar, its fingerboard shiny with hammer-flattened religious medals. . . . The men wore big sombreros and trousers that jangled with bells, and high, thin-heeled cowboy boots, leather-etched with swirly flowers, and traveled with a woman and a little girl. The woman wore a mantilla and a frilly dress made of Aztec-looking fabric; the little girl wore a red dress and played a tambourine on which an enamel likeness of John the Baptist had been painted. She'd sit restlessly, unhappily during the rides, while Cesar would lean forward and speak quietly to her mother. ("How is it going with you today?" "Slow lately, the best time is during Christmas, and then everybody gives.") They'd ride to the last stop downtown, to the Staten Island Ferry terminal, where they would play *bambas, corridos, huapangos,* and *rancheras* for the waiting passengers.

"*Que Dios te bendiga.* God bless you."

"The same to you."

There were others, a lot of Latin musicians like himself on their way to weary late-night jobs in the deepest reaches of Brooklyn and the Bronx. Some were young and didn't know the name Cesar Castillo, but the old-timers, the musicians who had been kicking around in New York since the forties, they knew him. Trumpet players, guitarists, and drummers would come over and sit with the Mambo King.

Still there were the tunnels, the darkness, the dense solitude of a station at four in the morning, and the Mambo King daydreaming about Cuba.

It made a big difference to him that he just couldn't get on an airplane and fly down to Havana to see his daughter or to visit the family in Las Piñas.

Who would ever have dreamed that would be so? That Cuba would be chums with Russia?

It was all a new kind of sadness.

Sitting in his room in the Hotel Splendour . . . the Mambo King preferred not to think about the revolution in Cuba. What . . . had he ever cared about Cuban politics in the old days, except for when he might play a political rally in the provinces for some local crooked politician? What . . . had he cared when the consensus among his musician pals was that it wouldn't

featured his father, Nestor Castillo (now dead), and his uncle Cesar. The rest of the novel skips forward and backward in time, looking at events mainly through the memories of the aging Cesar Castillo. For both of his novels, which focus on Cuban Americans in New York, critics have called Oscar Hijuelos an "urban poet."

About the Author
Oscar Hijuelos (1951–   ), born in New York, has used his background and his sense of "being Cuban" in all his writing. He worked in advertising and wrote short stories before publishing his first novel (1983), about a Cuban family in New York in the 1940s. The author feels that his work—like that of some Latin American writers—combines realism with touches of "magic" or the surreal. *The Mambo Kings Play Songs of Love* won the Pulitzer Prize.

Vocabulary Preview
Be sure students understand the following terms: *La Prensa, El Diario*—Spanish-language New York newspapers. *zarzuela*—Mexican/Spanish popular musical play. *resplendent*—Splendid, shining brilliantly. *spats*—Small covering for the ankle and upper shoe, worn with formal clothes.

Connecting with American History

Help students recall the background of the revolution in Cuba. *What kind of government did Cuba have before 1959?* (A harsh dictatorship led by Batista.) *Why did official American support for Fidel Castro come to an end?* (Castro declared he was a Communist and signed a treaty with the Soviet Union. His regime suppressed opposition and persecuted political opponents.) *Why did the Bay of Pigs invasion fail?* (There was no popular support for the invasion; the invaders appeared badly prepared.)

Have students write a newspaper editorial that either supports or rejects the Castro regime.

Analysis

This novel is written in the third person but still gives insights into the thoughts and feelings of Cesar Castillo. What techniques does Hijuelos use to show Cesar's character? Ask students to tell what kind of person Cesar seems to be.

★ AMERICAN LITERATURE ★

make any difference who came to power, until Fidel. What could he have done about it, anyway? Things must have been pretty bad. The orchestra leader René Touzet had fled to Miami with his sons, playing the big hotels there and concerts for the Cubans. Then came the grand master of Cuban music, Ernesto Lecuona, arriving in Miami distraught and in a state of creative torpor, unable to play a note on his piano and ending up in Puerto Rico, "bitter and disenchanted," before he died, he'd heard some people say. Bitter because his Cuba no longer existed.

God, all the Cubans were worked up. Even that *compañero*—who never forgot the family—Desi Arnaz had scribbled a little extra message on one of his Christmas cards: "We Cubans should stick together in these troubled times."

What had a friend called the revolution? "The rose that sprouted a thorn."

The great Celia Cruz would come to the States, too, in 1967. (On the other hand, Pala de Nieve—the musician "Snowball"—and the singer Elena Burke chose to remain behind.)

When his mother had died in 1962, the news came in a telegram from Eduardo [another brother, still in Cuba], and a funny thing, too, because he had been thinking about her a lot that week, almost a soft pulsing in his heart, and his head filled with memories. And when he first read the line "I have bad news," he instantly thought "No." After reading the telegram, all he could do for hours was to . . . remember how she would take him into the yard as a child and wash his hair in a tub, again and again and again, her soft hands that smelled of rose water scrubbing his head and touching his face, the sun down through the treetops, her hair swirling with curls of light. . . .

The man cried for hours, until his eyelids were swollen, and he fell asleep with his head against the worktable.

Wished he had seen her one more time. Told himself that he would have gone back the previous year, when he'd first heard that she had gotten sick, if it hadn't been for Castro.

Sometimes he got into big arguments with Ana Maria's husband, Raúl, about the situation down there. A long-time union man, Raúl kept himself busy organizing union shops in factories in the West Twenties, where most of the workers were immigrants from Central America and Puerto Rico. They were still friends, despite their differences of opinion. But Raúl kept trying to persuade the Mambo King about Castro. On a Friday night he went so far as to bring him down to a club on 14th Street where old Spanish and Portuguese leftists held meetings. He sat in the back listening as the old Spaniards, their expressions and politics shaped by beatings and jail terms in Franco's Spain, gave long, heartfelt speeches about "what must be done," which always came down to "*Viva el socialismo!*" and "Viva Fidel!"

Nothing wrong with doing away with the world's evils. He had seen a lot of that. In Cuba there had been rotting sheds made of cardboard and crates, skeleton children and dying dogs. A funeral procession in a small town called Minas. On the side of the plain pine coffin, a sign: "*Muerto de hambre.*" ["Died of hunger."] On the street corners where the handsome *suavecitos* hung out talking, some guy who'd lost a limb while working at the sugar mill, in the *calderas*, begging. . . .

He had no argument with wanting to help others, Raúl. Back in Cuba, the people took care of their own. Families giving clothing, food, money, and, sometimes, a job in the household or in a business.

"My own mother, Raúl, listen to me. My own mother was always giving money to the poor, even when we didn't have very much. What more could anyone ask?"

"More."

"Raúl, you're my friend. I don't want to argue with you, but the people are leaving because they can't bear it."

From *The Mambo Kings Play Songs of Love* by Oscar Hijuelos. Copyright ©1989 by Oscar Hijuelos. Reprinted by permission of Farrar Straus & Giroux Inc.

810

1. What are some of the different cultures represented among the New Yorkers that Cesar knows?

2. How has the revolution in Cuba affected Cesar personally?

3. What viewpoint among Cuban Americans does Raúl represent? How does Cesar answer his arguments?

4. How do memories of the Spanish Civil War influence some of the older Spanish people?

★

CHAPTER 22
The Women of Brewster Place

GLORIA NAYLOR

The civil rights movement of the 1960s helped literature about the African American experience become part of mainstream American culture. In her novel The Women of Brewster Place *(1982), Gloria Naylor wove together stories about the people of a dead-end urban neighborhood. In this excerpt, Kiswana Browne, who lives in Brewster Place, argues with her mother over differences within the black community.*

"I don't care. I still think it's downright selfish of you to be sitting over here with no phone, and sometimes we don't hear from you in two weeks—anything could happen—especially living among these people."

Kiswana snapped her head up. "What do you mean, *these people*. They're my people and yours, too, Mama—we're all black. But maybe you've forgotten that over in Linden Hills."

"That's not what I'm talking about, and you know it. These streets—this building—it's so shabby and rundown. Honey, you don't have to live like this."

"Well, this is how poor people live."

"Melanie, you're not poor."

"No, Mama, *you're* not poor. And what you have and I have are two totally different things. I don't have a husband in real estate with a five-figure income and a home in Linden Hills—*you* do. What I have is a weekly unemployment check and an overdrawn checking account at United Federal. So this studio on Brewster is all I can afford."

"Well, you could afford a lot better," Mrs. Browne snapped, "if you hadn't dropped out of college and had to resort to these dead-end clerical jobs."

"Uh-huh, I knew you'd get around to that before long." Kiswana could feel the rings of anger begin to tighten around her lower backbone, and they sent her forward onto the couch. "You'll never understand, will you? Those bourgie schools were counterrevolutionary. My place was in the streets with my people, fighting for equality and a better community."

"Counterrevolutionary!" Mrs. Browne was raising her voice. "Where's your revolution now, Melanie? Where are all those black revolutionaries who were shouting and demonstrating and kicking up a lot of dust with you on that campus? Huh? They're sitting in wood-paneled offices with their degrees in mahogany frames, and they won't even drive their cars past this street because the city doesn't fix potholes in this part of town."

"Mama," she said, shaking her head slowly in disbelief, "how can you—a black woman—sit there and tell me that what we fought for during the Movement wasn't important just because some people sold out?"

"Melanie, I'm not saying it wasn't important. It was . . . important to stand up and say that you were proud of what you were and to get the vote and other social opportunities for every person in this country who had it due. But you kids thought you were going to turn the world upside down, and it just wasn't so. When all the smoke had cleared, you found yourself with a fistful of new federal laws and a

★ AMERICAN LITERATURE ★

★ AMERICAN LITERATURE ★

country still full of obstacles for black people to fight their way over—just because they're black. There was no revolution, Melanie, and there will be no revolution. . . .

"You don't have to live in a slum to be concerned about social conditions, Melanie. Your father and I have been charter members of the NAACP for the last twenty-five years." . . .

Kiswana threw her head back in exaggerated disgust. "That's being concerned? That middle-of-the-road, Uncle Tom dumping ground for black Republicans!"

"You can sneer all you want, young lady, but that organization has been working for black people since the turn of the century, and it's still working for them. Where are all those radical groups of yours that were going to put a Cadillac in every garage and Dick Gregory in the White House? I'll tell you where."

I knew you would, Kiswana thought angrily.

"They burned themselves out because they wanted too much too fast. Their goals weren't grounded in reality. And that's always been your problem." . . .

Kiswana jumped up from the couch. "Oh, God, I can't take this anymore. . . . Trying to be proud of my heritage and the fact that I was of African descent. If that's being what I'm not, then I say fine. But I'd rather be dead than be like you. . . !"

Kiswana saw streaks of gold and ebony light follow her mother's flying body out of the chair. She was swung around by the shoulders and made to face the deadly stillness in the angry woman's eyes. . . . And she listened in that stillness to a story she had heard from a child.

"My grandmother," Mrs. Browne began slowly in a whisper, "was a full-blooded Iroquois, and my grandfather a free black from a long line of journeymen who had lived in Connecticut since the establishment of the colonies. And my father was a Bajan who came to this country as a cabin boy on a merchant mariner."

"I know all that," Kiswana said, trying to keep her lips from trembling.

"Then, know this. . . . I am alive because of the blood of proud people who never scraped or begged or apologized for what they were. They

lived asking only one thing of this world—to be allowed to be. And I learned through the blood of these people that black isn't beautiful and it isn't ugly—black is! It's not kinky hair and it's not straight hair—it just is.

"It broke my heart when you changed your name. I gave you my grandmother's name, a woman who bore nine children and educated them all, who held off six white men with a shotgun when they tried to drag one of her sons to jail for 'not knowing his place.' Yet you needed to reach into an African dictionary to find a name to make you proud.

"When I brought my babies home from the hospital, my ebony son and my golden daughter, I swore before whatever gods would listen—those of my mother's people or those of my father's people—that I would use everything I had and could ever get to see that my children were prepared to meet this world on its own terms, so that no one could sell them short and make them ashamed of what they were or how they looked—whatever they were or however they looked. And Melanie, that's not being white or red or black—that's being a mother."

Critical Thinking

1. Why did Kiswana drop out of college?
2. What does Mrs. Browne see as the successes of the civil rights movement? How does she believe it failed?
3. What is the NAACP? Why does Kiswana criticize her mother for belonging to it?
4. What did the name "Kiswana" mean to each of these women?

■■■■■ ★ ■■■■■

CHAPTER 23
Going After Cacciato
TIM O'BRIEN

The controversies and doubts that surrounded the Vietnam War are reflected in the literature about that war. Tim O'Brien's novel Going After Cacciato *is the story of what happened to one squad of soldiers, combined with one man's dreams about what* might *have happened. As the book begins, Cacciato, a young soldier, has walked away from camp, telling his friends he is going to walk from Vietnam to Paris, 8,600 miles away. The squad is ordered to follow Cacciato as he travels across the mountains.*

"I just hope Cacciato keeps moving," Paul Berlin whispered. "That's all. I hope he uses his head and keeps moving."

"It won't get him anywhere."

"Get him to Paris, maybe."

"Maybe," Doc sighed, turning onto his side, "and where is he then?"

"In Paris."

"Nope. I dig adventure, too, but you can't get to Paris from here. Just can't."

"No?"

"No way. None of the roads lead to Paris."

The lieutenant finished his cigarette and lay back. His breath came hard, as if the air were too heavy or thick for him, and for a long time he twisted restlessly from side to side.

"Maybe we better light a Sterno," Doc said gently. "I'm pretty cold myself."

"No."

"Just for a few minutes maybe."

"No," the lieutenant said. "It's still a war, isn't it?"

"I guess."

"There you have it. It's still a lousy war."

There was thunder. Then lightning lighted the valley deep below, then more thunder, then the rain resumed.

They lay quietly and listened.

Where was it going, where would it end? Paul Berlin was suddenly struck between the eyes by a vision of murder. . . . It scared him. He sat up, searched for his cigarettes. He wondered where the image had come from. Cacciato's skull exploding like a bag of helium: boom. So simple, the logical circuit-stopper. No one gets away with gross stupidity forever. Not in a war. Boom, and that always ended it.

What could you do? It was sad. It was sad, and it was still a war. The old man was right about that.

Pitying Cacciato with wee-hour tenderness, pitying himself, Paul Berlin couldn't help hoping for a miracle. The whole idea was crazy of course, but that didn't make it impossible. A lot of crazy things were possible. Billy Boy, for example. Dead of fright. Billy and Sidney Martin and Buff and Pederson. He was tired of it. Not scared—not just then—and not awed or overcome or crushed or defeated, just tired. He smiled, thinking of some of the nutty things Cacciato used to do. Dumb things. But brave things, too. . . .

They spent the fourth night in a gully beside the trail, then in the morning continued west. There were no signs of Cacciato.

For most of the day the trail ran parallel to a small hidden stream. . . . It was wilderness now. Jagged, beautiful, lasting country. Things grew as they grew, unchanging. And there was always the next mountain.

Twice during the day there were brief, violent showers, but afterward the sky seemed to lift and lighten, and they marched without stopping. Stink Harris stayed at point, then the lieutenant, then Oscar, then Harold Murphy and Eddie, then Doc, then Paul Berlin at the rear. Sometimes Eddie would sing as he marched. It was a good, rich voice, and the songs were always familiar, and Doc and Harold Murphy would sometimes come in on the chorus. Paul Berlin just climbed. . . .

★ AMERICAN LITERATURE ★

Introducing the Chapter 23 Selection

Going After Cacciato is as unique among war novels as the Vietnam War was unique among military conflicts. One reviewer said, "To call *Going After Cacciato* a novel about war is like calling *Moby Dick* a novel about whales. . . ." Mixing dream-fantasy and reality, the book tells the story of Cacciato—a private who decides to walk away from the war and hike 8,600 miles to Paris—and the squad who are ordered to follow him, through both real terrain and the landscape of dreams and "magic realism." The author, Tim O'Brien, was a foot soldier in Vietnam; his book won the National Book Award in 1979.

About the Author
Tim O'Brien (1946–   ) grew up in rural Minnesota and attended Macalester College and Harvard before becoming a writer. He was a reporter for the *Washington Post,* then was drafted in 1968 and went to Vietnam, eventually becoming a sergeant. Most of O'Brien's works, fiction and nonfiction, reflect his experiences in Vietnam.

Vocabulary Preview
Be sure students understand the following terms: *Sterno*—Solid fuel in small cans, used for portable stoves. *gulling*—Tricking, cheating. *klick*—Kilometer.

Connecting with American History

Help students set the historical background for this selection. *What was the background for American involvement in Vietnam?* (U.S. backing for the government of South Vietnam after the fall of French colonial rule; increasing U.S. aid and military advisers, leading to the sending of troops and planes.) *What American Presidents backed giving support to the South Vietnamese government?* (Eisenhower, Kennedy, Johnson, Nixon.)

Have students write a letter home telling about how Cacciato has walked away from the war. Is Cacciato's behavior smart, stupid, a reasonable reaction?

Analysis

Have students notice the concrete details that the author uses to make this sequence seem real even though its premise is dream or fantasy. For example, what clues does Cacciato leave behind?

Critical Thinking Answers

1. There seems to be a lull in the fighting, but several men from the group have died or been killed. There do not seem to be any enemy troops or any civilians around. As they follow Cacciato, they get out of range of radio and artillery.

2. The land is "jagged," with mountains and valleys crossed by streams. The author describes it as unchanging, despite the war.

3. Laos. U.S. troops were not supposed to cross the border.

Other Books by Tim O'Brien

Northern Lights, 1975.
If I Die in a Combat Zone (Box Me Up and Ship Me Home), 1973 (personal narrative).
The Nuclear Age, 1987.
The Things They Carried, 1990.

An hour before dusk the trail twisted up through a stand of dwarf pines, leveled off, then opened into a large clearing. Oscar Johnson found the second map.

The red dotted line crossed the border into Laos.

Farther ahead they found Cacciato's armored vest and bayonet, then his ammo pouch, then his entrenching tool and ID card.

"Why?" the lieutenant muttered.

"Sir?"

"Why? Tell me why." The old man was speaking to a small pine. "Why the clues? Why don't he just leave the trail? Lose us, leave us behind. . . . Tell me why."

"A rockhead," said Stink Harris. "That's why."

Liquid and shiny, a mix of rain and clay, the trail took them higher. Out of radio range, beyond the reach of artillery.

Cacciato eluded them but he left behind the wastes of his march: empty ration cans, bits of bread, a belt of gold-cased ammo dangling from a shrub, a leaking canteen, candy wrappers, worn rope. Hints that kept them going. Luring them on, gulling them. Once they spotted him far below, plodding along the bed of a valley; once they saw his fire on a distant hill. Straight ahead was the frontier.

"He makes it that far," Doc said on the morning of the sixth day, pointing to the next line of mountains, "and he's gone, we can't touch him. He makes the border and it's bye-bye Cacciato."

"How far?"

Doc shrugged. "A klick, two klicks. Not far."

"Then he's made it," Paul Berlin said.

"Maybe so."

"By God he has!"

"Maybe."

"By God! Lunch at Maxim's!"

"What?"

"A cafeteria deluxe. My old man ate there once . . . truffles heaped on chipped beef and toast."

"Maybe."

The trail narrowed, then climbed, and a half hour later Stink spotted him.

He stood at the top of a small grassy hill, two hundred meters ahead. Loose and at ease, smiling, Cacciato already had the look of a civilian. Hands in his pockets, patient, serene, not at all frightened. He might have been waiting for a bus.

Critical Thinking

1. What is the war like, at this time, for this group of soldiers?
2. How does the author describe the Vietnamese countryside?
3. What country lies across the border? Why will Cacciato be safe when he reaches there?

■ ★ ■

CHAPTER 24

"Saturday Belongs to the Palomía"

DANIEL GARZA

Daniel Garza, a Texas-born writer of Mexican descent, published this short story in 1962. It describes how everyday life changed for Mexican American residents of a small Texas town when the migrant cotton pickers, the palomía, *came to town.*

Every year, in the month of September, the cotton pickers come up from the Valley, and the braceros come from Mexico itself. They come to the town in Texas where I live, all of them, the whole *palomía*. "Palomía" is what we say: it is slang among my people, and I do not know how to translate it exactly. It means . . . the cotton pickers when they come. You call the whole bunch of them the *palomía*, but one by one they are cotton pickers, *pizcadores*.

Not many of them have traveled so far north before, and for the ones who have not it is a

814

Introducing the Chapter 24 Selection

Daniel Garza, a Texan of Mexican descent, writes in both Spanish and English. His short stories reflect his own youth growing up as a Mexican American in a predominantly "gringo" (non-Hispanic) town in Texas. According to Garza, "I wrote Palomía in Spanish and then translated it into English, trying to keep the flavor of the language. . . ."

great experience. And it is an opportunity to know other kinds of people, for the young ones. For the older ones it is only a chance to make some money picking cotton. Some years the cotton around my town is not so good, and then the *pizcadores* have to go farther north, and we see them less.

But when they come, they come in full force to my little town that is full of gringos. Only a few of us live there who speak Spanish among ourselves, and whose parents maybe came up like the *pizcadores* a long time ago. It is not like the border country where there are many of both kinds of people; it is gringo country mostly, and most of the time we and the gringos live there together without worrying much about such matters.

In September and October in my town, Saturdays belong to the *pizcadores*. During the week they are in the fields moving up and down the long cotton rows with big sacks and sweating frightfully, but making *centavitos* [small change] to spend on Saturday at the movie, or on clothes, or on food. The gringos come to town during the week to buy their merchandise and groceries, but finally Saturday arrives, and the *pizcadores* climb aboard their trucks on the cotton farms, and the trucks all come to town. It is the day of the *palomía*, and most of the gringos stay home.

"*Ay, qué gringos!*" the *pizcadores* say. "What a people to hide themselves like that. But such is life. . . ."

For Saturday the *pizcadores* dress themselves in a special and classy style. The girls comb their black hair, put on new bright dresses and low-heeled shoes, and the color they wear on their lips is, the way we say it, enough. The boys dress up in black pants and shoes with taps on the heels and toes. They open their shirts two or three buttons to show their chests and their Saint Christophers [medals]; then at the last they put a great deal of grease on their long hair and comb it with care. The old men, the *viejos*, shave and put on clean plain clothes, and the old women put on a tunic and comb their hair and make sure the little ones are clean, and all of them come to town.

They come early, and they arrive with a frightful hunger. The town, being small, has only a few restaurants. The *pizcadores*—the young ones and the ones who have not been up from Mexico before—go into one of the restaurants, and the owner looks at them.

One who speaks a little English says they want some *desayuno*, some breakfast.

He looks at them still. He says: "Sorry. We don't serve Meskins."

Maybe then one of the *pachuco* types with the long hair and the Saint Christopher says something ugly to him in Spanish, maybe not. Anyhow the others do not, but leave sadly, and outside the old men who did not go in nod among themselves, because they knew already. Then maybe, standing on the sidewalk, they see a gringo go into the restaurant. He needs a shave and is dirty and smells of sweat, and before the door closes they hear the owner say: "What say, Blacky? What'll it be this morning?"

The little ones who have understood nothing begin to holler about the way their stomachs feel, and the *papás* go to the market to buy some food there.

I am in the grocery store, me and a few gringos and many of the *palomía*. I have come to buy flour for my mother. I pass a *pizcador*, a father who is busy keeping his little ones from knocking cans down out of the big piles, and he smiles to me and says: "*¿Que tal, amigo?*"

"*Pues, así no más,*" I answer.

He looks at me again. He asks in a quick voice, "You are a Chicano?"

"*Sí.*"

"How is it that you have missed the sun in your face, *muchacho*?" he says. "A big hat, maybe?"

"No, señor," I answer, "I live here."

"You have luck."

And I think to myself, yes, I have luck; it is good to live in one place. And all of a sudden the *pizcador* and I have less to say to each other, and he says adiós and gathers up his flow of little ones and goes out to the square where the boys and girls of the *palomía* are walking together.

On the square too there is usually a little lady

★ AMERICAN LITERATURE ★

selling hot tamales. She is dressed simply, and her white hair is in a bun, and she has a table with a big can of tamales on it which the *palomía* buy while they are still hot from the stove at the little lady's home.

"*Mamacita, mamacita,*" the little ones shout at their mothers. "Doña Petra is here. Will you buy me some tamalitos?"

Doña Petra lives there in the town, and the mothers in the *palomía* are her friends because of her delicious tamales and because they go to her house to talk of the cotton picking, of children, and maybe of the fact that in the north of Texas it takes somebody like Doña Petra to find good *masa* for tamales and tortillas. Away from home as the *pizcadores* are, it is good to find persons of the race in a gringo town.

On the street walk three *pachucos*, seventeen or eighteen years old. They talk *pachuco* talk. One says: "Listen, *chabos*, let's go to the good movie."

"O.K.," another one answers. "Let's go flutter the good eyelids."

They go inside a movie house. Inside, on a Saturday, there are no gringos, only the *palomía*. The *pachucos* find three girls, and sit down with them. The movie is in English, and they do not understand much of it, but they laugh with the girls and make the *viejos* angry, and anyhow the cartoon—the mono, they call it—is funny by itself, without the need for English.

Other *pachucos* walk in gangs through the streets of the town, looking for something to do. One of them looks into the window of Mr. Jones' barber shop and tells the others that he thinks he will get a haircut. They laugh, because haircuts are something that *pachucos* do not get, but one of them dares him. "It will be like the restaurant," he says. "Gringo scissors do not cut Chicano hair."

So he has to go in, and Mr. Jones looks at him as the restaurant man looked at the others in the morning. But he is a nicer man, and what he says is that he has to go to lunch when he has finished with the customers who are waiting. "There is a Mexican barber across the square," he says. "On Walnut Street. You go there."

The *pachuco* tells him a very ugly thing to do and then combs his long hair in the mirror and then goes outside again, and on the sidewalk he and his friends say bad things about Mr. Jones for a while until they get tired of it, and move on. The gringo customers in the barber shop rattle the magazines they are holding in their laps, and one of them says a thing about cotton pickers, and later in the day it is something that the town talks about, gringos and *pizcadores* and those of my people who live there, all of them. I hear about it, but forget, because September in my town is full of such things, and in the afternoon I go to the barbershop for a haircut the way I do on Saturdays all year long.

Mr. Jones is embarrassed when he sees me. "You hear about that?" he says. "That kid this morning?"

I remember then, and I say yes, I heard.

"I'm sorry, Johnny," he says. "Doggone it. You know I'm not. . . ."

"I know," I say.

"The trouble is, if they start coming, they start bringing the whole . . . family, and then your regular customers get mad," he says.

"I know," I say, and I do. There is no use in saying that I don't, because I live in the town for the other ten or eleven months of the year when the *palomía* is not here but in Mexico and the Valley. I know the gringos of the town and what they are like, and they are many different ways. So I tell Mr. Jones that I know what he means.

"Get in the chair," he says. "You want it short or medium this time?"

And I think about the *pizcador* in the grocery store and what he said about my having luck, and I think again it is good to live in one place and not to have to travel in trucks to where the cotton is.

At about six in the afternoon all the families begin to congregate at what they call the *campo*. *Campo* means camp or country, but this *campo* is an area with a big tin shed that the State Unemployment Commission puts up where the farmers who have cotton to be picked can come and find the *pizcadores* who have not yet found a place to work. But on Saturday nights in September the *campo* does not have anything to do with work. The families come, bringing tacos to eat and maybe a little beer if they have it. After it is dark, two or three of the men bring out guitars, and some others have concertinas. They play the fast, twisty *mariachi* music of the places they come from, and someone always sings. The songs are about women and love and sometimes about a town that the song says is a fine town, even if there is no work there for *pizcadores*. All the young people begin to dance, and the old people sit around making certain that the *pachucos* do not get off into the dark with their daughters. They talk, and they eat, and they drink a little beer, and then at twelve o'clock it is all over.

The end of Saturday has come. The old men gather up their sons and daughters, and the mothers carry the sleeping little ones like small sacks of cotton to the trucks, and the whole *palomía* returns to the country to work for another week, and to earn more *centavitos* with which, the Saturday that comes after the week, to go to the movies, and buy groceries, and pay for tamalitos of Dona Petra and maybe a little beer for the dance at the *campo*. And the mothers will visit with Dona Petra, and the *pachucos* will walk the streets, and the other things will happen, all through September and October, each Saturday the same, until finally, early in November, the cotton harvest is over, and the *pizcadores* go back to their homes in the Valley or in Mexico.

The streets of my town are empty then, on Saturdays. It does not have many people, most of the year. On Saturday mornings you see a few gringo children waiting for the movie to open, and not much else. The streets are empty, and the gringos sit in the restaurant and the barber shop and talk about the money they made or lost on the cotton crop that fall.

"Saturday Belongs to the Palomía" by Daniel Garza, reprinted in *The Chicanos: Mexican-American Voices*, edited by Ed Ludwig and James Santibañez. Copyright 1962 by *Harper's Magazine, Inc.*; copyright © renewed by Daniel Garza. Reprinted by permission of the author.

Critical Thinking

1. How do the "gringo" townspeople treat the migrant workers differently from the Chicanos who live there year round? Why do you think this is true?
2. How might the farm workers' movement have helped the *pizcadores* described in this story?
3. What kinds of ties does the narrator feel—and not feel—to the *pizcadores*?
4. Does the narrator think he should have taken the migrants' part against Mr. Jones the barber? What does he mean when he says, "I know the gringos of the town . . . and they are many different ways"?

━━━ ★ ━━━

CHAPTER 25
On Wings of Eagles
KEN FOLLETT

By the late 1970s, terrorism and hostage-taking appeared frequently in newspaper headlines. During the Islamic revolution in Iran, the Shah's officials detained two American businessmen in jail. The head of their company, Texas businessman Ross Perot, first tried to negotiate their freedom, then sent in an undercover rescue team. The dramatic escape inspired Ken Follett to retell the true story. In this scene, revolutionaries have wrecked the jail, and the two Americans are now fugitives in the city of Tehran.

Paul and Bill stood at the foot of the prison wall and looked around.

The scene in the street reminded Paul of a New York parade. In the apartment buildings across from the jail everyone was at the windows, cheering and applauding as they watched

817

Critical Thinking Answers
1. The gringos actually avoid the migrants; in town they discriminate against them more, refuse to give them haircuts or serve them in restaurants. The Chicanos in town are familiar; the two groups are used to each other.
2. It could have changed living conditions and improved their pay.
3. He understands their culture and why they behave as they do; on the other hand, he prefers his own life and the acceptance of the gringo townspeople.
4. He feels slightly guilty because he thoroughly understands the gringo point of view. He knows that some of the non-Hispanic townspeople are very prejudiced and some are not.

Introducing the Chapter 25 Selection
On Wings of Eagles is a thriller that happens to be true. While the book has all the elements of one of the author's best-selling novels of adventure and espionage, Follett points out in the preface that this story is entirely true: a retired Green Beret colonel did in fact train a group of computer executives as a commando team to rescue two Americans from an Iranian jail—and the mission succeeded. Intrigued by these real-life heroes, Follett spent two years writing the book, taping hours of interviews and talking to everyone involved. Every event in the book really happened; the main characters read Follett's manuscript to ensure accuracy.

the prisoners escape. At the streetcorner a
vendor was selling fruit from a stall. There was
gunfire not far away, but in the immediate
vicinity nobody was shooting. Then, as if to remind Paul and Bill that they were not yet out of
danger, a car full of revolutionaries raced by
with guns sticking out of every window.
   "Let's get out of here," said Paul.
   "Where do we go? The U.S. Embassy? The
French Embassy?"
   "The Hyatt."
   Paul started walking, heading north. Bill
walked a little behind him, with his coat collar
turned up and his head bent to hide his pale
American face. They came to an intersection. It
was deserted: no cars, no people. They started
across. A shot rang out.
   Both of them ducked and ran back the way
they had come.
   It was not going to be easy.
   "How are you doing?" said Paul.
   "Still alive."
   They walked back past the prison. The scene
was the same: at least the authorities had not
yet got organized enough to start rounding up
the escapers.
   Paul headed south and east through the
streets, hoping to circle around until he could
go north again. Everywhere there were boys,
some only thirteen or fourteen, with automatic
rifles. On every corner was a sandbagged
bunker, as if the streets were divided up into
tribal territories. Farther on they had to push
their way through a crowd of yelling, chanting,
almost hysterical people: Paul carefully avoided
meeting people's eyes, for he did not want them
to notice him, let alone speak to him—if they
were to learn there were two Americans in
their midst they might turn ugly.
   The rioting was patchy. It was like New
York, where you had only to walk a few steps
and turn a corner to find the character of the
district completely changed. Paul and Bill went
through a quiet area for half a mile, then ran
into a battle. There was a barricade of overturned cars across the road and a bunch of
youngsters with rifles shooting across the barricade toward what looked like a military in-

stallation. Paul turned away quickly, fearful of
being hit by a stray bullet.
   Each time he tried to turn north he ran into
some obstruction. They were now farther from
the Hyatt than they had been when they start-
ed. They were moving south, and the fighting
was always worse in the south.
   They stopped outside an unfinished building.
"We could duck in there and hide until nightfall," Paul said. "After dark nobody will notice
that you're American."
   "We might get shot for being out after curfew."
   "You think there's still a curfew?"
   Bill shrugged.
   "We're doing all right so far," Paul said.
"Let's go on a little longer."
   They went on.
   It was two hours—two hours of crowds and
street battles and stray sniper fire—before at
last they could turn north. Then the scene
changed. The gunfire receded, and they found
themselves in a relatively affluent area of
pleasant villas. They saw a child on a bicycle,
wearing a T-shirt that said something about
southern California.
   Paul was tired. He had been in jail for forty-
five days, and during most of that time he had
been sick: he was no longer strong enough to
walk for hours. "What do you say we hitch-
hike?" he asked Bill.
   "Let's give it a try."
   Paul stood at the roadside and waved at the
next car that came along. (He remembered not
to stick out his thumb the American way—this
was an obscene gesture in Iran.) The car
stopped. There were two Iranian men in it.
Paul and Bill got in the back.
   Paul decided not to mention the name of the
hotel. "We're going to Tajrish," he said. That
was a bazaar area to the north of the city.
   "We can take you part of the way," said the
driver.
   "Thanks." Paul offered them cigarettes, then
sat back gratefully and lit one for himself.
   The Iranians dropped them off at Kurosh-e-
Kabir, several miles south of Tajrish, not far
from where Paul had lived. They were in a

818

main street, with plenty of traffic and a lot more people around. Paul decided not to make himself conspicuous by hitchhiking here.

"We could take refuge in the Catholic Mission," Bill suggested.

Paul considered. The authorities presumably knew that Father Williams had visited them in Gasr Prison just two days ago. "The Mission might be the first place Dadgar [the Iranian judge] looks for us."

"Maybe."

"We should go to the Hyatt."

"The guys [from their company] may not be there any longer."

"But there'll be phones, some way to get plane tickets. . . ."

"And hot showers."

"Right."

They walked on.

Suddenly a voice called: "Mr. Paul! Mr. Bill!"

Paul's heart stopped. He looked around. He saw a car full of people moving slowly along the road beside him. He recognized one of the passengers: it was a guard from the Gasr Prison.

The guard had changed into civilian clothes, and looked as if he had joined the revolution. His big smile seemed to say: don't tell who I am, and I won't tell who you are.

He waved, then the car gathered speed and passed on.

Paul and Bill laughed with a mixture of amusement and relief.

From *On Wings of Eagles* by Ken Follett. Copyright © by Ken Follett. Reprinted by arrangement with New American Library, a division of Penguin Books USA Inc.

Critical Thinking

1. At this time, were Paul and Bill, the two Americans, in more danger from Iranian officials or from the revolutionaries? Why?
2. On which side do most of the people of Tehran appear to be?
3. Were most Iranians hostile toward Americans at this time? Explain.

Love Medicine

LOUISE ERDRICH

During the Reagan era, many American writers were concerned with those who were not part of the surface prosperity. Instead they looked at other kinds of lives: rural families, ethnic and cultural minorities, the urban poor. Novelist Louise Erdrich, whose heritage is part Chippewa Indian, drew on her background for a series of novels about interwoven families in North Dakota. In this scene from Love Medicine, *Albertine, home from nursing school, observes the members of her family.*

All along the highway that early summer the land was beautiful. The sky stretched bare. Tattered silver windbreaks bounded flat, plowed fields that the government had paid to lie fallow. Everything else was dull tan—the dry ditches, the dying crops, the buildings of farms and towns. Rain would come just in time that year. Driving north, I could see the earth lifting. The wind was hot and smelled of tar and the moving dust.

At the end of the big farms and the blowing fields was the reservation. I always knew it was coming a long way off. Even in the distance you sense hills from their opposites—pits, dried sloughs, ditches of cattails, potholes. And then the water. There would be water in the hills when there wasn't any on the plains, because the hollows saved it, collected runoff from the low slopes, and the dense trees held it, too. I thought of water in the roots of trees, brown and bark smelling, cold.

The highway narrowed off and tangled, then turned to gravel with ruts, holes, and tall blue alfalfa bunching in the ditches. Small hills reared up. Dogs leaped from nowhere and ran themselves out fiercely. The dust hung thick.

★ AMERICAN LITERATURE ★

819

Introducing the Chapter 26 Selection

Love Medicine is one of three novels by Erdrich which trace several generations of Chippewa Indians in South Dakota from the early 1900s to the present. Each chapter of the novel is narrated by a different character. Critics have praised Erdrich's lyrical style and distinctive, often eccentric characters.

About the Author

Louise Erdrich (1954–) is part Chippewa Indian, and her Native American heritage is reflected in her writing. Author of short stories, novels, and poetry, she was, as of 1989, one of only three women poets to be included in the *Norton Anthology of Poetry.* Erdrich writes in collaboration with her novelist-professor husband Michael Dorris. Though their books are published under the only one of their names, each work is a joint effort.

Critical Thinking Answers
1. Probably from Iranian officials; because it was the government that had held them in jail and was now looking for them. The revolutionaries were more interested in the revolution.

2. The side of the revolution.
3. Not completely hostile, because people gave them rides and the guard waved. They were afraid the crowd might turn ugly if they were recognized as Americans, though.

Other Books by Ken Follett
Eye of the Needle, 1978.
The Key to Rebecca, 1980.
The Man from St. Petersburg, 1982.
Lie Down with Lions, 1986.
Pillars of the Earth, 1989.

My mother lives just on the very edge of the
reservation with her new husband, Bjornson,
who owns a solid wheat farm. She's lived there
about a year. I grew up with her in an aqua-
and-silver trailer, set next to the old house on
the land my great-grandparents were allotted
when the government decided to turn Indians
into farmers.

The policy of allotment was a joke. As I was
driving toward the land, looking around, I saw
as usual how much of the reservation was sold
to whites and lost forever. Just three miles, and
I was driving down the rutted dirt road, home.

The main house, where all of my aunts and
uncles grew up, is one big square room with a
cooking shack tacked onto it. The house is a
light peeling lavender now, the color of a pale
petunia, but it was never painted while I lived
there. My mother had it painted for Grandma
as an anniversary present one year. Soon after
the paint job the two old ones moved into town
where things were livelier and they didn't have
to drive so far to church. Luckily, as it happened, the color suited my Aunt Aurelia, because she moved into the house and has taken
care of it since.

Driving up to the house I saw that her brown
car and my mother's creamy yellow one were
parked in the yard. I got out. They were indoors, baking. I heard their voices from the
steps and smelled the rich and browning
piecrusts. But when I walked into the dim,
warm kitchen they hardly acknowledged me,
they were so involved in their talk.

"She sure *was* good-looking," Aurelia argued,
hands buried in a dishpan of potato salad.

"Some people use spoons to mix." My mother
held out a heavy tin one from the drawer and
screwed her lips up like a coin purse to kiss me.
She lit her eyes and widened them. "I was only
saying she had seen a few hard times. . . ."

She puffed her cheeks out in concentration,
patting and crimping the edges of the pies.
They were beautiful pies—rhubarb, wild
Juneberry, apple, and gooseberry, all fruits pre-
served by Grandma Kashpaw or my mother or
Aurelia.

"I suppose you washed your hands before you
put them in that salad," she said to Aurelia.

Aurelia squeezed her face into crescents of
patient exasperation. "Now Zelda," she said,
"Your girl's going to think you still treat me
like your baby sister."

"Well you are aren't you? Can't change that."

"I'm back," I said.

They looked at me as if I had, at that very
moment, walked in the door.

"Albertine's home," observed Aurelia. "My
hands are full or I'd hug you."

"Here," said Mama, setting down a jar of
pickles near me. "Aren't you dressed nice. Did
you get your top in Fargo? Was the drive
good?"

I said yes.

"Dice these pickles up." She handed me a
bowl and knife. . . .

After a while we heard the car from the main
road as it slowed for the turn. It would be
June's son, King, his wife, Lynette, and King
Junior. They drove up to the front steps in their
brand-new sportscar. King Junior was bundled
in the front seat and both Grandma and Grandpa Kashpaw were stuffed, incredibly, into the
tiny backseat.

"There's that white girl." Mama peeked out
the window.

"Oh, for gosh sakes." Aurelia gave her heady
snort again, and this time did not hold her
tongue. "What about your Swedish boy?"

"Learnt my lesson," Mama wiped firmly
around the edges of Aurelia's dishpan. "Never
marry a Swedish is my rule."

Grandma Kashpaw's rolled-down nylons and
brown support shoes appeared first, then her
head in its iron-gray pageboy. Last of all the
entire rest of her squeezed through the door,
swathed in acres of tiny black sprigged flowers.
When I was very young she always seemed the
same size to me as the rock cairns [mounds]
commemorating Indian defeats around here.
But every time I saw her now I realized that
she wasn't so large, it was just that her figure
was weathered and massive as a statue
roughed out in rock. She never changed much,

at least not so much as Grandpa. Since I'd left home, gone to school, he'd turned into an old man. Age had come upon him suddenly, like a storm in fall, shaking yellow leaves down overnight, and now his winter, deep and quiet, was on him. As Grandma shook out her dress and pulled bundles through the back window, Grandpa sat quietly in the car. He hadn't noticed that it had stopped. . . .

He turned to the open door and stared at his house.

"This reminds me of something," he said.

"Well it should. It's your house!" Mama barreled out the door, grabbed both of his hands, and pulled him out of the little backseat.

"You have your granddaughter here, Daddy!" Zelda shrieked carefully into Grandpa's face. "Zelda's daughter. She came all the way up here to visit from school."

"Zelda . . . born September fourteenth, nineteen forty-one. . . ."

"No, Daddy. This here is my daughter, Albertine. Your granddaughter."

I took his hand.

Dates, numbers, figures stuck with Grandpa since he strayed, and not the tiring collection of his spawn, proliferating [increasing] beyond those numbers into nowhere. He took my hand and went along, trusting me whoever I was.

Whenever he came out to the home place now, Grandpa had to get reacquainted with the yard of stunted oaks, marigold beds, the rusted car that had been his children's playhouse and mine, the few hills of potatoes and stalks of rhubarb that Aurelia still grew. She worked nights, managing a bar called the So Long, and couldn't keep the place as nicely as Grandpa always had. Walking him slowly across the lawn, I sidestepped prickers. The hollyhocks were choked with pigweed, and the stones that lined the driveway, always painted white or blue, were flaking back to gray. So was the flat boulder under the clothesline—once my favorite cool place to sit doing nothing while the clothes dried, hiding me.

This land had been allotted to Grandpa's mother, old Rushes Bear, who had married the original Kashpaw. When allotments were handed out all of her eighteen children except the youngest—twins, Nector and Eli—had been old enough to register for their own. But because there was no room for them in the North Dakota wheatlands, most were deeded less-desirable parcels far off, in Montana, and had to move there or sell. The older children left, but the twin brothers still lived on opposite ends of Rushes Bear's land.

She had let the government put Nector in school, but hidden Eli, the one she couldn't part with, in the root cellar dug beneath her floor. In that way she gained a son on either side of the line. Nector came home from boarding school knowing white reading and writing, while Eli knew the woods. Now, these many years later, hard to tell why or how, my Great-uncle Eli was still sharp, while Grandpa's mind had left us, gone wary and wild. When I walked with him I could feel how strange it was. His thoughts swam between us, hidden under rocks, disappearing in weeds, and I was fishing for them, dangling my own words like baits and lures.

I wanted him to tell me about things that happened before my time, things I'd been too young to understand. The politics, for instance. What had gone on? He'd been an astute political dealer, people said, horse-trading with the government for bits and shreds. Somehow he'd gotten a school built, a factory too, and he'd kept the land from losing its special Indian status under that policy called termination. I wanted to know it all. I kept asking questions as we walked along, as if he'd take the hook by miracle and blurt the memory out right there.

"Remember how you testified. . . ? What was it like . . . the old schools . . . Washington?"

Elusive, pregnant with history, his thoughts finned off and vanished. The same color as water. Grandpa shook his head, remembering dates with no events to go with them, names without faces, things that happened out of place and time.

From *Love Medicine* by Louise Erdrich. Copyright ©1984 by Louise Erdrich. Reprinted by permission of Henry Holt & Co.

★ AMERICAN LITERATURE ★

Analysis
Have students identify the similes and metaphors Erdrich uses in this excerpt. Discuss how these images reinforce the relationship between the characters and nature.

Introducing the Chapter 27 Selection

The 1980s and 1990s were decades in which Asian Americans became a more prominent part of American life and society—as outstanding scientists, students, business leaders, performing artists, and writers. The interlocked stories of *The Joy Luck Club* introduce four mother-daughter pairs caught up in these changes—the mothers raised in traditional China, the daughters in contemporary America. One reviewer noted that the book shows the "persistent tensions and powerful bonds" between generations and cultures.

Critical Thinking

1. What had been the federal government's land policy for Indians in this area? What results does Albertine see?
2. What did it mean for Nector and Eli's mother to have "a son on either side of the line"? Which "side of the line" was Albertine's grandfather on?
3. How had Nector Kashpaw been successful as an Indian politician?

■ ★ ■

CHAPTER 27
The Joy Luck Club
AMY TAN

Amy Tan's 1989 novel The Joy Luck Club *tells the interwoven stories of four pairs of mothers and daughters. The mothers, all brought up in China, came to the United States at the time of the 1949 revolution to begin new lives. They find, however, that the strength of traditional Chinese culture ties them to the past. In flashbacks, each character tells her own story—the daughters about growing up in two cultures, the mothers about changing cultures.*

My daughter wanted to go to China for her second honeymoon, but now she is afraid.

"What if I blend in so well they think I'm one of them?" Waverly asked me. "What if they don't let me come back to the United States?"

"When you go to China," I told her, "you don't even need to open your mouth. They already know you are an outsider."

"What are you talking about?" she asked. My daughter likes to speak back. She likes to question what I say.

"Aii-ya," I said. "Even if you put on their clothes, even if you take off your makeup and hide your fancy jewelry, they know. They know just watching the way you walk, the way you carry your face. They know you do not belong."

My daughter did not look pleased when I told her this, that she didn't look Chinese. She had a sour American look on her face. Oh, maybe ten years ago, she would have clapped her hands—hurray!—as if this were good news. But now she wants to be Chinese, it is so fashionable. And I know it is too late. All those years I tried to teach her! She followed my Chinese ways only until she learned how to walk out the door by herself and go to school. So now the only Chinese words she can say are *houche, chr fan,* and *gwan deng shweijyau.* How can she talk to people in China with these words? Choo-choo train, eat, close light sleep. How can she think she can blend in? Only her skin and her hair are Chinese. Inside—she is all American-made.

It's my fault she is this way. I wanted my children to have the best combination: American circumstances and Chinese character. How could I know these two things do not mix?

I taught her how American circumstances work. If you are born poor here, it's no lasting shame. You are first in line for a scholarship. If the roof crashes on your head, no need to cry over this bad luck. You can sue anybody, make the landlord fix it. You do not have to sit like a Buddha under a tree letting pigeons drop their dirty business on your head. You can buy an umbrella. Or go inside a Catholic church. In America, nobody says you have to keep the circumstances somebody else gives you.

She learned these things, but I couldn't teach her about Chinese character. How to obey parents and listen to your mother's mind. How not to show your own thoughts, to put your feelings behind your face so you can take advantage of hidden opportunities. Why easy things are not worth pursuing. How to know your own worth and polish it, never flashing it around like a cheap ring. Why Chinese thinking is best.

No, this kind of thinking didn't stick to her. She was too busy chewing gum, blowing bubbles bigger than her cheeks. Only that kind of thinking stuck.

"Finish your coffee," I told her yesterday. "Don't throw your blessings away."

"Don't be so old-fashioned, Ma," she told me, finishing her coffee down the sink. "I'm my own person."

And I think, How can she be her own person? When did I give her up? . . .

It's hard to keep your Chinese face in America. At the beginning, before I even arrived, I had to hide my true self. I paid an American-raised Chinese girl in Peking to show me how.

"In America," she said, "you cannot say you want to live there forever. If you are Chinese, you must say you admire their schools, their ways of thinking. You must say you want to be a scholar and come back to teach Chinese people what you have learned."

"What should I say I want to learn?" I asked. "If they ask me questions, if I cannot answer. . . ."

"Religion, you must say you want to study religion," said this smart girl. "Americans all have different ideas about religion, so there are no right and wrong answers. Say to them, I'm going for God's sake, and they will respect you."

For another sum of money, this girl gave me a form filled out with English words. I had to copy these words over and over again as if they were English words formed from my own head. Next to the word NAME, I wrote *Lindo Sun.* Next to the word BIRTHDATE, I wrote May 11, 1918, which this girl insisted was the same as three months after the Chinese lunar new year. Next to the word BIRTHPLACE, I put down *Taiyuan, China.* And next to the word OCCUPATION, I wrote *student of theology.*

I gave the girl even more money for a list of addresses in San Francisco, people with big connections. And finally, this girl gave me, free of charge, instructions for changing my circumstances. "First," she said, "you must find a husband. An American citizen is best."

She saw my surprise and quickly added, "Chinese! Of course, he must be Chinese. 'Citizen' does not mean Caucasian. But if he is not a citizen, you should immediately do number two. See here, you should have a baby. Boy or girl, it doesn't matter in the United States. Neither will take care of you in your old age, isn't that true?" And we both laughed.

"Be careful, though," she said. "The authorities there will ask you if you have children now or if you are thinking of having some. You must say no. You should look sincere and say you are not married, you are religious, you know it is wrong to have a baby."

I must have looked puzzled, because she explained further: "Look here now, how can an unborn baby know what it is not supposed to do? And once it has arrived, it is an American citizen and can do anything it wants. It can ask its mother to stay. Isn't that true?"

But that is not the reason I was puzzled. I wondered why she said I should look sincere. How could I look any other way when telling the truth?

See how truthful my face still looks. Why didn't I give this look to you? Why do you always tell your friends that I arrived in the United States on a slow boat from China? This is not true. I was not that poor. I took a plane. I had saved the money my first husband's family gave me when they sent me away. And I had saved money from my twelve years' work as a telephone operator. But it is true I did not take the fastest plane. The plane took three weeks. It stopped everywhere: Hong Kong, Vietnam, the Philippines, Hawaii. So by the time I arrived, I did not look sincerely glad to be here.

Why do you always tell people that I met your father in the Cathay House, that I broke open a fortune cookie and it said I would marry a dark, handsome stranger, and that when I looked up, there he was, the waiter, your father. Why do you make this joke? This is not sincere. This was not true! Your father was not a waiter, I never ate in that restaurant. The Cathay House had a sign that said "Chinese Food," so only Americans went there before it was torn

823

About the Author
Amy Tan (1952–) was born in Oakland, California, less than three years after her parents came to the United States. A writer's workshop gave her the encouragement to begin writing fiction. *The Joy Luck Club* got its start as a series of magazine short stories. After visiting China for the first time in 1987, Tan said, "As soon as my feet touched China, I became Chinese."

Vocabulary Preview
Be sure students understand the following terms:
lunar new year—Referring to the first day of the Chinese calendar, which is based on cycles of the moon.
theology—Study of religion.

Connecting with American History
Help students understand the increasing pluralism in American society. *How is the population of the United States today different from that of the 1940s?* (A new wave of immigrants, mainly Asian and Hispanic rather than European; a population shift to the South and West; easier immigration laws since 1965.) *In what other ways have Asia and the people of Asia influenced the United States in the 1990s?* (Through trade with the "Pacific Rim" nations; an increase in Asian products bought and used; closer political and diplomatic relations with Japan because of its economic importance.)

Have students write a short essay describing any cultural clashes in their own families that they are willing to share.

Analysis
Have students note how the author uses first-person narration to show Lindo's style and character. Ask them to give their impressions (from this narration) of the kind of person she is.

1. Having an "ethnic identity" has become fashionable for Waverly's generation; she is no longer ashamed of having a Chinese background.

2. She had to claim to be a temporary student, intending to go back to China to teach; she was told she would have to marry an American citizen in order to stay in the United States permanently.

3. According to Waverly, her mother was a poor immigrant who came on "a slow boat from China," read a fortune cookie predicting she would meet a handsome man, and married a waiter from a Chinese restaurant.

★ AMERICAN LITERATURE ★

down. Now it is a McDonald's restaurant with a big Chinese sign that says *mai dong lou*—"wheat," "east," "building." All nonsense. Why are you attracted only to Chinese nonsense? You must understand my real circumstances, how I arrived, how I married, how I lost my Chinese face, why you are the way you are.

From *The Joy Luck Club* by Amy Tan. Copyright ©1989 by Amy Tan. Reprinted by permission of The Putnam Publishing Group.

Critical Thinking

1. Why does Lindo Jong's daughter, Waverly, now want to be thought of as "really" Chinese when she visits China? Why has she changed her mind about her heritage?

2. Why was the immigration process for Lindo more difficult than it would be for present-day immigrants?

3. According to Lindo, what stereotypes does her daughter use in telling people about her mother's background and history?

Skill Review

Skill Review

From Study Skills Through Critical Thinking

History of the United States (Volume 2) takes you on a journey from early times to the present day. Along the way you encounter many events, issues, and political figures that may be new to you. At times the people and events may seem so remote that it is hard for you to grasp their importance. To help you understand American history and remember it clearly, there are certain skills that you can use. For the purposes of this review, the skills are divided into two groups: Study Skills and Critical Thinking Skills.

Study Skills

Study skills can help you locate, gather, and organize information. They will make it possible for you to learn more effectively and efficiently. This review covers the following study skills: building vocabulary, understanding charts, reading graphs, using the library, writing an outline, taking notes, writing reports, and taking tests.

STUDY SKILL 1

Building Vocabulary

A good vocabulary makes it easier to learn American history or any other subject. If you can grasp the meaning of unusual words, you will finish your reading more quickly, and it will stay with you longer.

Your vocabulary will grow larger naturally if you read a wide range of books. You should also make an effort to learn and use the new words you come across. Here is one method for adding words to your vocabulary:

- As you read, be aware of words you do not understand. Pay close attention to the words that are somewhat familiar but that you cannot define exactly. These words are easiest to learn.

- Make a list of the words you want to learn and on what page you found them. When you have finished reading, make an index card for each word on your list.

- Look up each word in a dictionary. On the front of the index card, write down the pronunciation of the word. (It is easier to use and remember words that you know how to say.) On the back of the card, write down the word's meaning.

- Study your cards from time to time until you have mastered the words. If possible, work them into your assignments so that you become comfortable using them.

Context clues. When you lack the time or the opportunity to look up an unfamiliar word in the dictionary, you can often figure out its meaning from the *context*—the setting in which it appears. Search the context for clues that help you understand the word. For example, on page 322 of Chapter 14, under the subheading "Political Scandals," you will find this sentence:

"The Secretary of the Interior, Albert B. Fall, was found to have leased government oil reserves—including one in Teapot Dome, Wyoming—to oilmen who paid him kickbacks worth hundreds of thousands of dollars."

★ SKILLS ★

Notice the word *kickbacks*. There are clues in the passage to its meaning. The passage is about scandals and illegal actions. You know that the kickbacks were made in return for oil leases and that they were "worth hundreds of thousands of dollars." These clues indicate that kickbacks are illegal payments made to someone who controls a possible source of income.

Examples. An example can explain an unfamiliar word by showing what kinds of things the word refers to. In the chapter quoted from above, the following passage appears:

> "The economic growth of the 1920s led to a greater demand for white-collar workers. More and more people were needed for sales and management."

If the term *white-collar* is unfamiliar, you can figure out that sales representatives and managers are examples of white-collar workers. Therefore *white-collar* probably refers to workers who do not perform physical labor.

Synonyms. Sometimes an unfamiliar word will be restated or defined. If you know the meaning of the second word, you can figure out the meaning of the unknown word. On page 305, under the subheading "The Treaty in the Senate," you will see this sentence:

> They opposed one article of its covenant, or charter, which called for members of the League to defend one another's territory against aggression.

Practicing Skills

1. What words are easiest to learn? Why is it helpful to learn how to pronounce a new word?
2. Reread a section of this book that you have studied recently. List at least five unfamiliar words. Try using context clues, examples, and synonyms to figure out the meaning of each word. Then compare your definitions with those given in a dictionary.

★ SKILLS ★

STUDY SKILL 2

Understanding Charts

Charts are a good way to summarize information. They can present a clear visual outline of a complex idea. Two kinds of charts that you will encounter while studying American history are organization charts and flow charts.

A **flow chart** shows a process, or how things happen. Flow charts are useful for outlining or simplifying the steps in a procedure. The cause and effect chart on page 58 is an example of a flow chart.

An **organization chart** shows the inner workings of a particular organization. For example, if the chart describes a government agency, it will briefly explain the duties of each official and show who has authority over whom. The chart found on this page is an example of an organization chart.

Organization of the United Nations

Secretariat
Under leadership of Secretary General

Security Council
Five permanent and ten non-permanent members

International Court of Justice (World Court)
Fifteen judges

General Assembly
All member nations represented

Trusteeship Council
Five members

Economic and Social Council
Fifty-four members

★ SKILLS ★

You will be able to use a chart with confidence if you can recognize and understand all its parts. The first thing you should look for on a chart is the **title.** Locate the title of the chart on the previous page. It tells you the subject and purpose of the chart.

Next, read all the **labels** on the chart. Labels identify the different sections of a chart. In an organization chart, the labels show the major units of the organization. In a flow chart, labels identify the major steps in a process.

Lines and arrows are important symbols in both organization charts and flow charts. In an organization chart, lines or arrows show the links between units. Arrows connect the different parts of a flow chart and show the order of steps in a process.

Practicing Skills

1. What kind of chart is best for showing the steps in a procedure? What kind of chart is best for showing the structure of a branch of government?

2. Read the title of the chart on the previous page. What is this chart about?

3. What is the central unit of the organization represented on the previous page?

4. Draw an organization chart of a real or fictional club. Show the officers or leaders, committees, and ordinary members.

5. Think of a procedure you go through often, like studying for a test. Make a flow chart showing the important steps.

STUDY SKILL 3

Reading Graphs

The ability to compare statistics is another useful skill for students of American history. Graphs present numerical data in a way that has visual impact and is easy to understand. They make it possible for students to grasp the meaning of statistics without being overwhelmed by them.

The most commonly used types of graphs are the line graph and the bar graph. On a **line graph,** such as the one shown at the right, information is plotted by dots, which are then connected by a line. A line graph is good for showing trends, or how things change over time. A **bar graph** (like the one on page 308) shows information in bars or columns. Bar graphs are often used to compare quantities or amounts.

In order to read a graph, you need to understand its parts:

- The title of a graph tells you what the graph is about.

- The **horizontal axis** runs along the bottom of the graph. On graphs that show a trend,

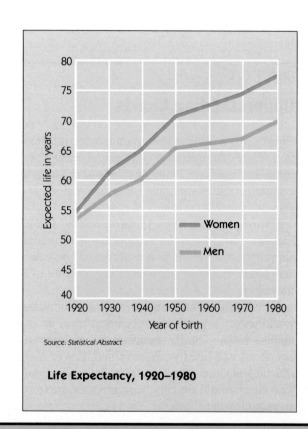

Life Expectancy, 1920–1980

Source: *Statistical Abstract*

the horizontal axis often shows the time period—days, months, or years. Look for the horizontal label that explains the purpose of the axis.

- The **vertical axis** runs up one side of the graph. It often shows statistical information such as quantities or prices. Like the horizontal axis, the vertical axis has a label that explains its purpose.
- Graphs sometimes show two or more lines or types of bars in order to make comparisons. When that happens, the lines or bars are usually identified by labels or in a key.
- The **source line,** sometimes found at the bottom of the graph, tells you where the information was found.

Another kind of graph used in this book is a **circle graph,** often called a **pie graph** because it is cut into sections like a pie. Each "slice" represents a percentage of the whole. Circle graphs are especially useful for showing at a glance how something is divided. For example, the lower-left circle graph on page 44 shows how manufacturing plants in the United States in 1860 were divided between the North and the South.

Practicing Skills

1. Study the graph on the facing page. What is the subject of the graph?

2. (a) What does the horizontal axis show? (b) The vertical axis? (c) What does each line stand for? (d) What overall trend does this graph show? (e) What comparison can be made?

3. Look at the pie graph on page 44 labeled "Population." (a) What does the whole pie represent? (b) What do the slices show? (c) Which slice is the biggest? (d) About how much does it stand for?

STUDY SKILL 4

Using the Library

There may be times when you need or want more information about a topic than you can find in the textbook. If you know what sources the library has available, you can locate the information you need without wasting your time and effort.

Locating information. Books of fiction are usually alphabetized on library shelves, using the last names of authors. To arrange books of nonfiction, some libraries use the **Dewey decimal system.** Under this system, subjects are organized in ten categories that are numbered from 000 to 999. The categories are subdivided so that every subject has its own number. In the 700's, for example, 720 is the number for architecture and 720.793 is the number for American architecture.

Some libraries use the **Library of Congress system** rather than the Dewey decimal system. The Library of Congress system uses 21 lettered classifications.

The **card catalog** lists all the books in the library. Books are listed in three ways: by author, by title, and by subject. If you know exactly which book you want, look up either the author's name or the title. If you are not sure which book you want, use the card catalog to look up subjects that interest you.

For easier access, many libraries have put their card catalogs on computer. Each entry that appears on the computer screen represents a "card."

Any of the cards (author, title, or subject) will tell where you can find a book in the library. In the upper left-hand corner of the card (next page), is the book's **call number.** This number will be either under the Dewey decimal system or the Library of Congress system.

829

```
Ref
E
176.1
.B683
1984
        Boller, Paul F.
           Presidential campaigns / Paul F.
        Boller, Jr. -- New York : Oxford
        University Press, 1984.
           xii, 420 p. ; 25 cm.
           Includes bibliographical references
        and index.
           ISBN 0-19-503420-1


           1. Presidents--United States--
        Election--History--Anecdotes, facetiae,
        satire, etc. 2. United States--
        Politics and government--Anecdotes,
        facetiae, satire, etc. I. Title

        06 MAY 87   10207716  HMCCat      83-25047
```

★ SKILLS ★

Another important source for locating books is the librarian. Librarians will help you understand the card catalog and find other sources that may be useful to you.

Using reference books. A great deal of information is readily available in the reference section of the library. Reference books are designed to make facts easy to find.

Dictionaries. **Dictionaries** are not new to you, but you may not be aware that many libraries have dictionaries on specialized subjects such as geography, biography, and jazz. A biographical dictionary, for instance, will contain basic information on many people not important enough to be listed in an encyclopedia.

Encyclopedias. You probably know that in an **encyclopedia** you will find articles arranged alphabetically by subject. You should also become familiar with using the index (a separate volume) for a set of encyclopedias. The index helps you locate articles quickly.

Atlases and gazetteers. **Atlases** are books of maps. Not all atlases contain the same information. Some may concentrate on *political* maps, which show political areas such as countries, states, provinces, and cities. Other atlases may specialize in *physical* maps, which depict geographical features such as rivers, lakes, and mountain ranges.

Gazetteers are dictionaries that list the names of geographical features as well as political place names. Gazetteers give the location of a place, the pronunciation of its name, and other pertinent information, such as population and area.

Almanacs and yearbooks. These reference books are published yearly, and they give up-to-date facts on many subjects. Almanacs such as the *Information Please Almanac* are loaded with statistics. You can find information on American sports, on former Presidents, on crime and divorce rates, on Supreme Court justices, and on every state and territory in the United States. Almanacs also give information on every country of the world, including units of money, population, capital, political leaders, and recent history.

Yearbooks, such as *The Statesman's Year-Book*, give the latest information on science, economics, the arts, and the events of the world. The *World Book Year-Book* is organized like an encyclopedia. It lists developments in places all over the world during a single year. For example, if you look under *Canada* in the *Year-Book* for 1990, you will find an account of significant events in Canada during that year.

Periodical indexes. The *Readers' Guide to Periodical Literature* lists articles that have

830

appeared in nearly two hundred periodicals (magazines and newspapers). The *Readers' Guide* is issued several times a year and is compiled into an annual single-volume edition. It is the best source to use when you want to find the most recent information on a given subject. The librarian can help you to request the periodicals that are listed in the guide.

Most libraries also have *The New York Times Index*, which lists articles that have appeared in *The New York Times*. Articles are listed in this index by subject. The newspaper you want will often be stored on microfilm.

Practicing Skills

1. What kind of reference book would you use to find out about (a) the major tributaries of the Mississippi River? (b) The mayors of the 50 largest cities in the United States?

2. What is a periodical? What kind of information can periodicals help you find?

3. What is the call number of the book listed on the card on the facing page? Under what other headings would you find this book listed in the card catalog?

STUDY SKILL 5

Writing an Outline

A good way to organize information you have read is to write an **outline**. Outlining can help you to remember the most important facts in a chapter. It is also a useful method of organizing information for an essay or report.

The first step in writing an outline is to classify all the information in the material you are reading. Look for main themes, or ideas, and separate them from the details that support these ideas. The main themes will become the main headings in your outline. The supporting details will become your subheadings.

Suppose you wanted to write an outline for the topic "Presidential Administrations of the 1920s." Your outline might look like this:

I. Warren G. Harding
  A. Election victory in 1920
    1. Return to normalcy
    2. Calvin Coolidge as Vice President
  B. Laissez faire economic policy
  C. Political scandals
II. Calvin Coolidge
  A. Took office after Harding's death in 1923
  B. Election victory in 1924
  C. Pro-business economic policy

III. Herbert Hoover
  A. Election victory in 1928
  B. Response to the Crash
    1. Call for individual initiative
    2. Laissez faire economic policy

Notice that each main heading comes after a roman numeral (I, II, III). Each subheading starts with a capital letter, and supporting details are numbered. For additional subheadings, you can use lower-case letters (a, b, c . . .), then lower-case roman numerals (i, ii, iii . . .).

Practicing Skills

1. What are two uses of outlining?

2. Read pages 318–319 of Chapter 14. Beginning with the heading, *I. The Red Scare*, complete an outline of these pages with subheadings and supporting details.

3. Imagine that you are writing a paper on the three branches of government. Write an outline for your paper, using each branch as a main heading. Use subheadings to give enough supporting detail so that it is clear what each branch does.

★ SKILLS ★

831

Taking Notes/Writing Reports

Note-taking is one of the most important study skills you can master. Taking notes will help you get the most out of assigned reading and classroom lectures. It is also an invaluable skill for doing research papers and writing reports.

Taking notes. Taking notes helps you identify and remember main ideas. The following suggestions will help you take notes efficiently:

- *Finish reading each passage before making any notes.* It is usually necessary to read a complete paragraph, for instance, before you can determine its main idea.
- *Use abbreviations and symbols.* These can help you take notes more rapidly. Examples of abbreviations are *HR* for House of Representatives and *gov't* for government. Some commonly used symbols are & (and), *w/* (with), and *w/o* (without).
- *Write down only the main ideas and the most important information.* Note-taking is a process of picking out the main ideas from the supporting details. Watch for words that signal main points, such as *first, finally,* or *most important.* Also pay attention to words in **boldface type** and *italic type.*
- *Review your notes.* As soon as possible after taking notes, reread them. Correct any words you cannot read and fill in any spaces you may have left blank. Reviewing your notes will reinforce and help you remember what you have just read or heard.

Writing reports. When you research a topic and write a report, the ability to take good notes will come in handy. Though a research paper may seem like a daunting task, it is easier to do when you divide the task into steps.

Begin by choosing a subject that fits your assignment and that interests you. Narrow your topic to something that you can describe fully in the allotted number of words or pages. For example, a topic like "Civil Rights Legislation" may be too broad for a three-page paper. A

Hardy, <u>Gov't in America,</u> pp.63-64

Separation of powers— 3 branches of gov't to keep any 1 group from having too much power. (idea of Montesquieu)

<u>legislative</u> branch— Congress— Sen. + HR— makes laws

<u>executive</u> branch— Pres.—carries out laws
<u>judicial</u> branch— S.C.—interprets laws

topic like "The Voting Rights Act of 1965" would be easier to cover.

Use the suggestions in Study Skill 4 to find sources of information about your topic. Keep good records about each source you find. For books, write down the author's name, the title, the publisher, and the city and year of publication. For magazine articles, list the author's name, the title, the name and date of the magazine, and the page numbers. You will need this information when you prepare the bibliography for your report or for writing footnotes.

Using the hints explained above, take notes as you read your sources. Many students find it convenient to make notes on index cards, like the one shown on this page, using a different card for each topic. On each card, make sure to record the author and page number of the source at the top. If you find a passage you might want to quote in your report, write it down exactly as it appears.

When you feel you have taken enough notes, organize the information on your cards. Separate them into stacks that contain similar ideas. Then read through the notes in each stack and write a sentence or phrase that identifies the main point of each stack. Arrange your main points in a logical order to make an outline for your report. Look through the cards in each stack again, picking out key phrases and ideas to provide supporting details.

Follow your outline and, referring to your notes when necessary, write a first draft. After you have finished the first draft, revise your report. Make sure that your main points are clear and that your paper moves smoothly from topic to topic. Each paragraph should present a single idea, and every sentence should make sense. Before you write or type your final copy, correct all spelling, punctuation, and grammar. At the end of your report, include a bibliography. The bibliography should list, in alphabetical order (by author's last name), all the sources you used.

Practicing Skills

1. What are four points to remember about taking notes? Why should you review your notes while the lecture or reading assignment is still fresh in your memory?
2. What are five steps involved in writing a report?

Taking Tests

Good study habits will improve your test results. Information you have memorized over a period of days will stay with you longer than material you tried to learn all at once on the night before a test.

Reading your assignments carefully and taking notes as you read will reduce the amount of work required to prepare for a test. If you have kept up with daily assignments, getting ready for a test is merely reviewing material that you already know.

When the day of the test arrives, remember the first rule of test-taking: "Follow directions." Read the test instructions carefully.

When you get the test, skim through it quickly to decide how much time you can spend on each part. If you cannot answer a question, go on to the next one so that you get credit for all the questions you can answer. When you have been through all the questions, then go back to the ones you skipped and work on them.

The most common kinds of questions on American history tests are multiple-choice, matching, and essay questions.

A **multiple-choice** question asks you to choose the correct answer from three or four possible answers. Read the question carefully and try to answer it before looking at the choices. If you are not certain of the right answer, eliminate those that you know are wrong. Then pick the best remaining answer.

In **matching** questions, you must match items in one column with items in a second column. Match first those items that you know with certainty. Then look for clues to the remaining answers.

An **essay** question requires you to write a short composition in a limited time. Read the question carefully so that you will know exactly what you are being asked to do: *list*, *discuss*, *compare*, *contrast*, or *summarize*. If you are asked to describe the similarities between a capitalist and socialist economy, for instance, do not waste time by listing the differences. On scratch paper, jot down the facts required in your answer and arrange them in appropriate order. Write an outline if you have time, listing main points and supporting details.

Be specific in your essay. An answer that is brief, detailed, and well-organized will receive more points than a long, rambling essay. After you have finished writing your essay, reread it and correct any errors in grammar, spelling, or punctuation.

Practicing Skills

1. What is the first thing you should do when you take a test?
2. What should you do if you are not certain of the answer to a multiple-choice question?

★ SKILLS ★

Study Skill 6 Answers
1. Finish reading each passage before making any notes; use abbreviations and symbols; write down only the main ideas; review your notes. If you review your notes soon after taking them, you will reinforce the information contained in them and ensure they will be readable later.
2. Choosing a subject, finding sources of information, taking notes, making an outline, and writing the report.

Study Skill 7 Answers
1. Skim through the test to determine how much time you can spend on each part.
2. Eliminate the answers that you know are wrong and then pick the best remaining answer.

833

Critical Thinking Skills

You need to bring more to the study of history than just a good memory for facts and dates. The ability to memorize is useful, but you must also be able to *think* effectively. If you can look critically at the events of other times, you will be able to make sense of today's world.

Critical thinking skills help you look below the surface of American history. They make the study of history more interesting, because they enable *you* to become the historian.

★ SKILLS ★

CRITICAL THINKING SKILL 1

Interpretation

Interpretation is the attempt to identify a relationship between facts, ideas, or values. In the study of history, it often means offering an opinion on why something happened. You may be asked to use the skill of interpretation in the ways described below.

Determining cause-and-effect relationships. An action that produces an event is a *cause.* The development produced by an action is an *effect.* Identifying causes helps us determine what made certain things happen and what kept others from happening.

During the 1920s, for example, the United States experienced a boom in productivity due to technological advances and a larger labor force. This led to the growth of advertising, as companies sought to convince Americans to buy the products they were turning out so fast. The growth of advertising led, in turn, to the expansion of credit. Credit was one method advertisers used to promote their products.

Look at the cause-and-effect relationship in the following diagram:

Boom in productivity (Cause) ⟶ Growth of advertising (Effect)

Sometimes an effect becomes the cause of another effect. This kind of cause-and-effect relationship is shown below:

Boom in productivity (Cause) ⟶ Growth of advertising (Effect/Cause) ⟶ Expansion of credit (Effect)

Some cause-and-effect relationships may not be clear until many years after the events took place. Historians may find after studying an event that several causes led to an effect or that one cause was responsible for many effects.

Make it a habit to note the various effects of certain causes, which of those effects in turn became new causes, and whether multiple causes or multiple effects were involved.

Making and supporting generalizations. Generalizations are brief summaries or conclusions based on facts. You may often recognize them as topic sentences, which express the main idea of a paragraph.

In Chapter 14, page 321, for example, you will note the topic sentence, "With the approval of the federal government, the owners of industry stepped up their opposition to labor unions." The paragraph gives facts that support this generalization. It tells you that employers refused to deal with unions. They tried to break unions by firing workers who went on strike.

Keep in mind that generalizations are general. They are used to make broad statements such as the example given above: the owners of industry stepped up their opposition to labor unions. Do not assume that labor unions were stamped out in every industry or that every single employer opposed unions.

Inferring and drawing conclusions. These skills require you to make up your mind about something you read. **Inferring** is getting more information from reading than is specifically stated. It might be described as reading be-

834

tween the lines. In Chapter 10 on page 225, for instance, you learn that Theodore Roosevelt was a sickly child who was determined to grow stronger. Later you are told that he made the boxing team at Harvard University. From this you can infer that Roosevelt overcame his ill health. When you infer, you make an assumption based on what you read.

When you draw **conclusions,** you make a judgment about what you have read. Read this paragraph about Roosevelt's Square Deal from page 228:

Roosevelt's policy toward trusts was based on the principle of fairness. As he saw it, only firms that were behaving unfairly should be broken up. This same principle was applied to disputes between companies and their workers. Here too Roosevelt looked for a fair solution—a Square Deal.

From this you can conclude that Roosevelt believed labor disputes should be resolved on a case-by-case basis. His policy was to give equal access to both sides.

Recognizing points of view. A point of view reflects an opinion, attitude, belief, or feeling. A

useful skill in studying history is the ability to recognize a point of view for what it is.

Detecting bias. Look carefully for **bias**—personal preference—on the part of the person whose views are being presented. If a writer or politician wants to persuade people to act, he or she will usually try to appeal to people's emotions. Many famous historical figures had strong opinions that show up in their writings and speeches. These views should be examined critically. Just because a person is famous does not mean that you must agree with his or her opinions. A good student will detect bias and opinion when examining documents of the past or reading articles today.

Practicing Skills

1. Read the material on page 344 of Chapter 15. What were the multiple causes of the Crash? How did the effects of the Crash in turn become new causes?
2. Why do generalizations make good topic sentences?
3. What is the difference between drawing a conclusion and offering an opinion?

★ SKILLS ★

CRITICAL THINKING SKILL 2

Analysis

The purpose of **analyzing** is to show that you understand what you read. When you analyze information, you do three things:

1. Break the information down into its different parts.
2. Recognize the relationship between parts.
3. Understand why the material has been organized as it has.

Analysis can be applied to chapters, single paragraphs or even sentences.

Look at Chapter 22, page 517. Read the paragraphs under the subheadings "Crusading Lawyers" and "A Historic Decision." What is

the relationship between these two parts? Why has the author chosen this method to discuss the legal battles of the civil rights movement?

If you look closely at "Crusading Lawyers," you will see that it gives background information on the training of civil rights lawyers. It also explains the legal obstacles that the civil rights movement sought to overcome. "A Historic Decision" describes the Supreme Court decision that outlawed racial segregation in the schools. You can conclude that the author wanted to describe the history of the struggle for desegregation before telling you how the Supreme Court ruled on the matter in the 1950s.

Critical Thinking
Skill 2 Answers

1. While concrete figures are used and the information can be checked for accuracy, the statement is a prediction and therefore an educated opinion. The author's belief that everyone "ought to be rich" is a value statement.

2. The cartoonist wants to point out how heated the debate in Congress became over the issue of escalation in Vietnam.

★ SKILLS ★

Distinguishing facts, opinions, and values. **Facts** are those things that are known to be true or to have happened. Facts are based on information that can be checked for accuracy. **Opinions** express how people feel about something, what their beliefs are, and what attitudes they take. **Values** are opinions that often involve the standards of right and wrong. All values are opinions, but not all opinions are values. You may express an opinion on a subject you know little about. You may also express an opinion about what you think will happen in a certain situation. In either example, your opinion may prove to be a fact. Values are never facts. You may believe in them so strongly that they seem like facts. If they cannot be proven to be true, however, they are not facts.

Even though opinions are not always based on fact, and values cannot be proven to be true, you can still learn from them. You can learn how people felt at a certain time, what they considered important, and what they thought about. You cannot always learn what really happened or what the facts were.

Certain words give clues that opinions are being presented—"It is my belief" or "in my view" are lead-ins to what somebody thinks. Not all opinions are easily recognized. You need to read carefully to identify what you read as fact or opinion.

Analyzing political cartoons. Political cartoons are an effective way to express opinions and points of view. Political cartoons often use symbols to get their point across. The United States, for example, is often depicted as Uncle Sam or as an American eagle, while the Soviet Union is frequently shown as a bear. The ele-

from THE HERBLOCK GALLERY (Simon and Schuster, 1964).

ESCALATION

phant and the donkey are used to represent the Republican and Democratic parties.

Political cartoons usually deal with contemporary issues or events. The cartoons used in this textbook were contemporary when they were first drawn. Some call attention to an important debate. Others convey the cartoonist's opinion.

Practicing Skills

1. Read the primary source document in Chapter 15 on page 341. What can you identify as a fact? What can you identify as an opinion? Do you recognize any value statements?
2. Look at the political cartoon on this page. What point is the cartoonist making?

CRITICAL THINKING SKILL 3

Translating and Synthesizing

Translating and synthesizing are skills that require you to play an active role in the process of studying history.

Translating. Translating is presenting infor-

mation in a form that is different from the way you receive it. If you tell a classmate something you read, you are translating from the written to the oral form. You might make a chart or draw a picture instead of giving the information orally. That too would be translating.

Historians must translate in order to write histories. They gather as much information as they can about a historical period, including sources such as paintings, photographs, and oral histories. They must then find a way of conveying in their writing what impression these things give about the time period they describe. Look at the photograph of textile workers on page 213. What impression does it give you of conditions in the mill?

Synthesizing. Synthesizing enables you to explain events of history and to determine what might have happened. When you synthesize, you create a different approach to looking at a subject. In order to do this effectively, you need to use what knowledge you already have of a historical event.

Take the Civil War as an example. You could synthesize by writing a diary of a young northern soldier in a Confederate prison, based on research about what prisoners-of-war actually experienced in the South. You might also write a one-act play that provides details of the conversation between General Grant and General Lee at Appomattox.

In this type of synthesis, you should not alter known events. You should merely add to the information, using what you know about the geography of the area and the customs of the period.

Predicting events. Predicting can be sepa-

rated into two categories. The first of these asks you to speculate about what might have happened if something else had not. Suppose, for example, that the Soviets had refused to back down during the Cuban missile crisis in 1962 (pages 499–500). How would the United States have reacted? How might the course of history have been altered?

The other form of predicting asks you to suggest the outcome of an event that is not yet resolved. Again, your prediction should be based on solid evidence and should not be guesswork. News commentators often utilize this skill when they examine recent events. For example, they may report a minor controversy in a political campaign and then predict its effect on the election.

Practicing Skills

1. Why is the ability to translate information important to a historian?
2. Choose an important event, such as a battle, an inauguration, a debate in Congress, or a political rally, in a section of this book you have recently read. Write an account of the event as it would be given by a first-hand observer.
3. Consider the present justices of the Supreme Court. Predict how vacancies and new appointments might change the character of the Court. What important laws might change if the Court changes?

CRITICAL THINKING SKILL 4

Problem Solving

When you try to solve a problem, you draw on previous experiences and on knowledge you already have. The solution you offer is your creation, and it may or may not solve the problem. When you participate in problem solving, you are expected to come up with an answer to a problem for which no answer yet exists.

Problem solving involves making choices or

making decisions. With difficult problems, there are steps that can be taken to help you make the right decision.

1. Clearly identify the problem.
2. Consider the various alternatives.
3. Consider the consequences and merits of each of the alternatives.
4. Make a decision.

837

★ SKILLS ★

Throughout history people have been faced with solving problems, some of which have affected the lives of thousands or even millions of people. For instance, Franklin Roosevelt, President of the United States from 1933 to 1945, wanted to bring the nation out of the Great Depression. To achieve this goal, Roosevelt had to solve several serious problems. The first step was to identify and list the problems.

1. How to stabilize the banking system.
2. How to combat falling prices.
3. How to revive agriculture.
4. How to put Americans back to work.

After President Roosevelt had identified the problems, he then had to consider various approaches to solving them. When he had decided on what course to take, he put a plan of action into effect.

When the problems are of the size and scope of those facing Roosevelt, the results of a plan of action may not be known for many years. Americans still argue over whether Roosevelt's New Deal ended the Great Depression.

Practicing Skills

1. What is the first step in the process of making a decision?
2. Read the description of Roosevelt's Second New Deal on pages 370–373 of Chapter 16. What problems did he face when he formulated this plan? How did he hope to solve them?

CRITICAL THINKING SKILL 5

Forming Hypotheses

Many people think that history consists of the dates and descriptions of important events, such as political rallies, financial panics, elections, revolutions, and assassinations. They assume that a history book can tell them all there is to know about events like these. That is partly true. Clear records do exist of many important events, particularly in American history, which has lasted only a few hundred years. But these records do not tell the whole story. How can you know, for instance, how a nation was affected by a political assassination? How can a historian explain what suddenly caused a country to decline economically?

These are matters that can never be known for sure, but that does not mean they are not of interest to the historian. Like archeologists and scientists, historians piece together the bits of information they acquire in order to answer a puzzling question. When they feel they may know what caused something or what occurred in a given situation, they form a **hypothesis**—a theory based on evidence. Hypotheses are not proven facts. They might rather be called "educated guesses."

After doing research on the Great Depression, for example, a historian might form this hypothesis: the New Deal restored American confidence and paved the way for economic recovery. The historian would explain why the morale of the country had improved and offer evidence to link this improvement with economic recovery.

Historians often use each other's hypotheses as the basis for further discussion. They may put forward new evidence that proves an old hypothesis correct. Or, if new evidence seems to prove the hypothesis incorrect, they may propose a new hypothesis to replace it.

Practicing Skills

1. What kinds of questions are historians unable to solve with certainty? How do historians address these "unknowns?"
2. Turn to a chapter you have recently read and form a hypothesis about an event in that chapter. List evidence to back up your hypothesis.

CRITICAL THINKING SKILL 6

Evaluation

When you **evaluate** you are making a judgment. It may be a judgment about an event or something you have read. You should not make a judgment without first thinking it through. You need to provide reasons that explain why you have judged something as you have.

Developing criteria for making judgments. When you evaluate for the purpose of making a judgment, you need to do two things:

1. Set standards. That is, determine the purpose of the evaluation.
2. Decide how well your standards are met. In judging material, you might question how accurate, adequate, or biased it is.

Suppose you were asked to identify which American Presidents were good leaders and which were poor leaders. When you are faced with making that judgment, you need first to establish what constitutes a good leader. You might list such considerations as:

1. Brought prosperity to the country.
2. Suggested just and useful laws.
3. Managed foreign affairs successfully.
4. Gained the confidence of the people.

Once you have decided what qualities a good President should have, you can judge how well various Presidents measure up to your standards.

Evaluating historical sources. Different historical sources often provide varying accounts of the same event. When this happens, you need to evaluate the accuracy and fairness of these differing views.

When you evaluate historical documents, consider the following questions:

1. *Is the information from primary or secondary sources?* It is important to know whether the material is a **primary source,** written at the time the event happened, or a **secondary source,** written long after the event occurred. Primary sources are records from the past such as newspapers, diaries, letters, and government documents. Secondary sources are written by people who were not witnesses to or participants in the events they write about. Sometimes secondary sources may be more useful than primary sources even though they were written by people who did not witness the events. Secondary sources may be more accurate, more objective, and more complete. This textbook, for example, is a secondary source.

2. *Is the material fact or opinion?* As you know, most historical evidence includes statements of both fact and opinion.

3. *Is the information accurate?* A good way to check accuracy is to see how the information is presented in other sources. If you find that different sources give different data, you may wonder where your source got the information. You may also begin to question its accuracy. On the other hand, if you find that different sources give the same basic information, you may be fairly certain the material is accurate. Determining a writer's credentials is another way to check accuracy. What makes this person qualified to write about this subject?

The skills described in this Skill Review will benefit you not only in history courses but in other subjects that you study. Many of them are also known as life skills because you will use them throughout your life.

Practicing Skills

1. What is a primary source? What is a secondary source?
2. What methods can you use to determine whether information is accurate?
3. Choose an American President and consider the goals that he outlined at the beginning of his administration. Set standards for judging those goals and decide how close he came to meeting them.

★ S K I L L S ★

Atlas, Gazetteer, and Reference

The United States

CITES AND STATES

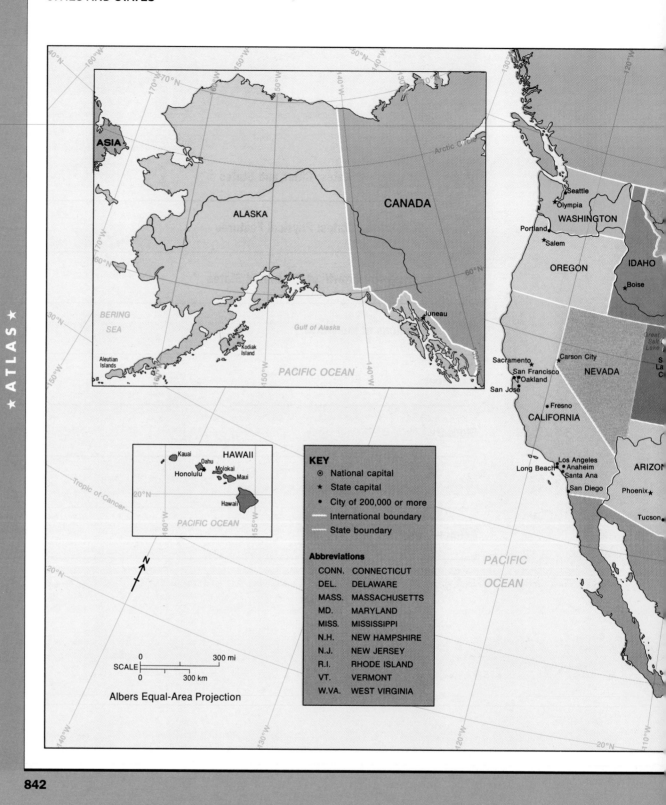

KEY
⊙ National capital
★ State capital
• City of 200,000 or more
━━ International boundary
━━ State boundary

Abbreviations

CONN.	CONNECTICUT
DEL.	DELAWARE
MASS.	MASSACHUSETTS
MD.	MARYLAND
MISS.	MISSISSIPPI
N.H.	NEW HAMPSHIRE
N.J.	NEW JERSEY
R.I.	RHODE ISLAND
VT.	VERMONT
W.VA.	WEST VIRGINIA

SCALE
0 — 300 mi
0 — 300 km

Albers Equal-Area Projection

★ ATLAS ★

CANADA

Hudson Bay

MONTANA
Helena

NORTH DAKOTA
Bismarck

MINNESOTA
Minneapolis ★ St. Paul

WISCONSIN
Madison
Milwaukee

Lake Superior

MICHIGAN

Lake Michigan
Lake Huron

MAINE
Augusta

Montpelier ★ N.H.
NEW VT.
YORK Concord
Albany Boston
Rochester MASS.
Hartford Providence
Buffalo R.I.
CONN.

WYOMING

SOUTH DAKOTA
Pierre

IOWA
Des Moines

NEBRASKA
Omaha
Lincoln

Lansing
Detroit
Chicago
Toledo Cleveland Akron
Pittsburgh

PENNSYLVANIA
Harrisburg

Jersey City New York
Trenton
Philadelphia
N.J.
Dover
DEL.

Cheyenne

UTAH

COLORADO
Denver
Colorado
Springs

KANSAS
Topeka
Kansas
City

MISSOURI
Jefferson
City
St.
Louis

Wichita

ILLINOIS
Springfield
Indianapolis

INDIANA
OHIO
Columbus
Dayton
Cincinnati

Louisville
Frankfort
Lexington

KENTUCKY

W.VA.
Charleston

Baltimore
Washington, D.C.
Annapolis
MD.

Richmond

VIRGINIA

Norfolk
Virginia
Beach

ATLANTIC

OCEAN

Santa Fe
Albuquerque

NEW MEXICO

El Paso

Tulsa

Oklahoma
City

OKLAHOMA

ARKANSAS
Little
Rock

Memphis

Nashville

TENNESSEE

NORTH CAROLINA
Charlotte

Raleigh

SOUTH
CAROLINA
Columbia

Birmingham

MISS.
Jackson

ALABAMA
Montgomery

GEORGIA
Atlanta

Fort Worth Dallas
Arlington
Shreveport

Baton
Rouge

TEXAS

Austin

San Antonio

Houston

LOUISIANA
New Orleans

Mobile

Tallahassee

Jacksonville

FLORIDA
Tampa
St. Petersburg

Miami

Corpus Christi

MEXICO

Gulf of Mexico

Tropic of Cancer

BAHAMAS

CUBA

843

The United States

PHYSICAL FEATURES

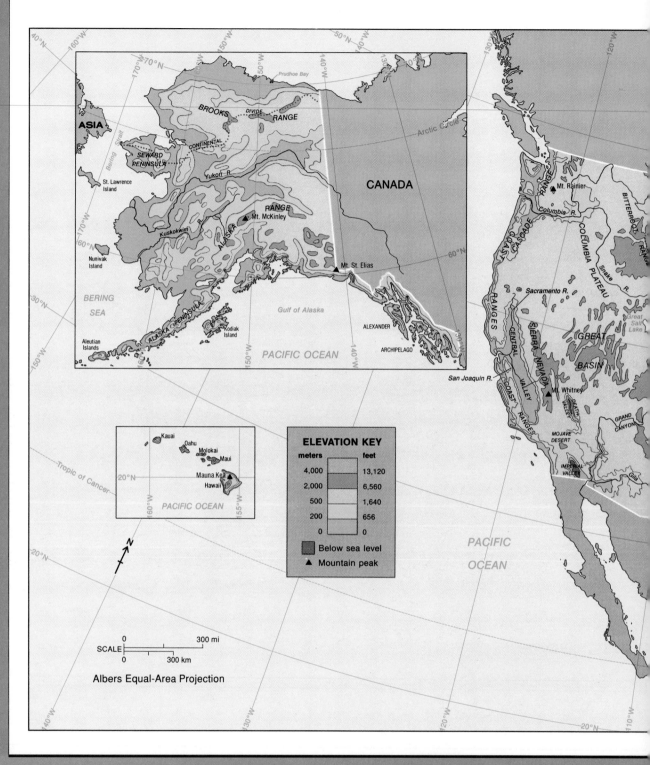

ELEVATION KEY

meters		feet
4,000		13,120
2,000		6,560
500		1,640
200		656
0		0

Below sea level
▲ Mountain peak

SCALE
0 — 300 mi
0 — 300 km

Albers Equal-Area Projection

CANADA

Hudson Bay

MEXICO

Gulf of Mexico

Tropic of Cancer

CUBA

BAHAMAS

ATLANTIC
OCEAN

ROCKY

GREAT

PLAINS

MOUNTAINS

CONTINENTAL

DIVIDE

Missouri R.

Yellowstone R.

BLACK
HILLS

Platte R.

Mt. Elbert

Pikes Peak

Colorado

COLORADO
PLATEAU

LLANO
ESTACADO

Pecos R.

EDWARDS
PLATEAU

Rio Grande

Nieces R.

Brazos R.

Red R.

Arkansas R.

OUACHITA MTS.

OZARK PLATEAU

INTERIOR

PLAINS

MESABI
RANGE

Lake Superior

Lake Michigan

Lake Huron

Lake Erie

Lake Ontario

Mississippi R.

Missouri R.

Wabash R.

Ohio R.

Cumberland R.

Tennessee R.

Mississippi R.

Pearl R.

GULF

COASTAL

PLAIN

MISSISSIPPI
DELTA

Alabama R.

Chattahoochee R.

ATLANTIC COASTAL PLAIN

APPALACHIAN

BLUE RIDGE MTS.

CUMBERLAND PLATEAU

MOUNTAINS

St. Lawrence R.

ADIRONDACK
MTS.

Mohawk R.

CATSKILL
MTS.

WHITE
MTS.

GREEN MTS.

Connecticut R.

Hudson R.

Susquehanna R.

Delaware R.

Potomac R.

James R.

Savannah R.

Appalachicola R.

CAPE
CANAVERAL

EVERGLADES

FLORIDA KEYS

CAPE COD

Long Island

CAPE
HATTERAS

845

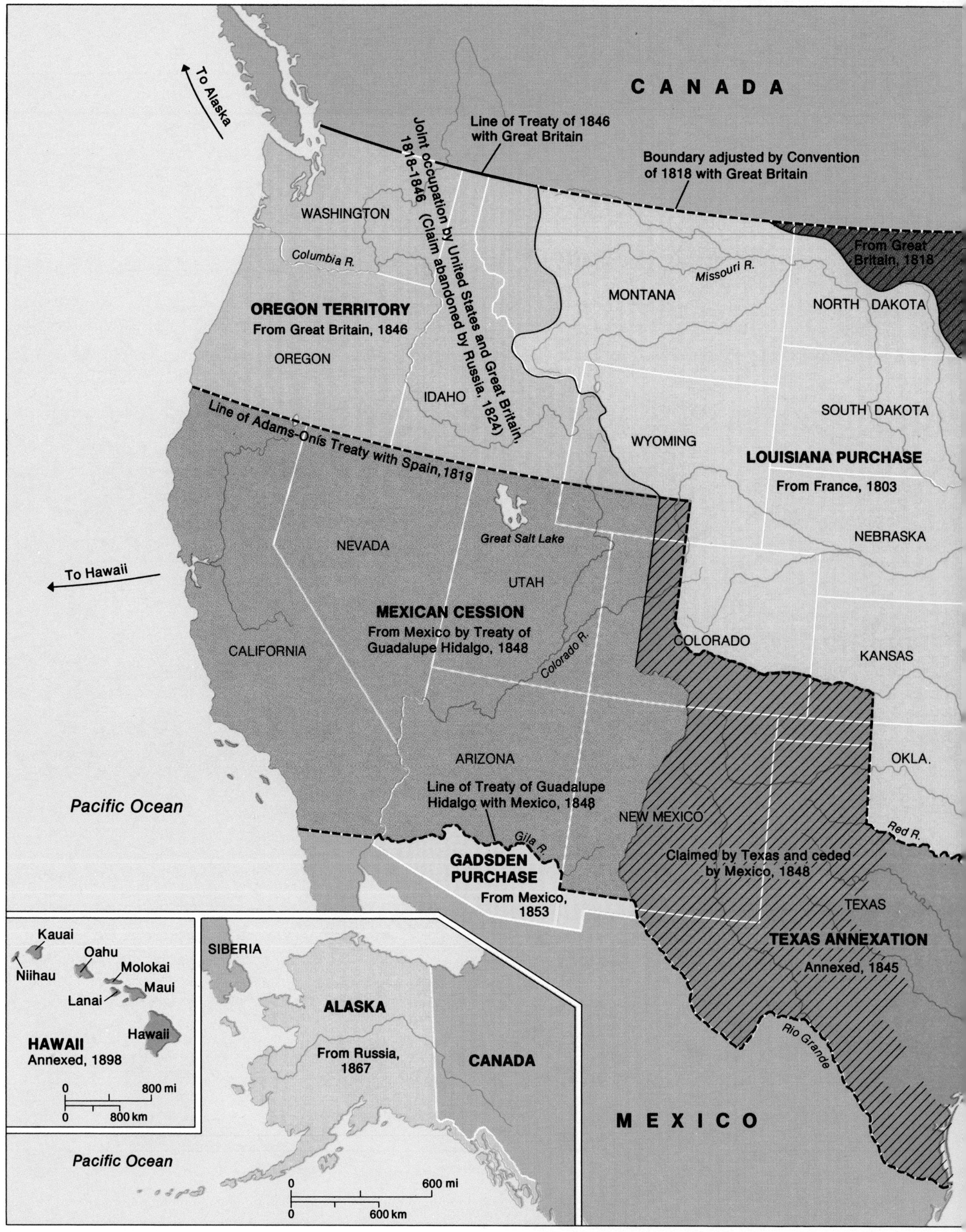

C A N A D A

To Alaska

Line of Treaty of 1846
with Great Britain

Boundary adjusted by Convention
of 1818 with Great Britain

Joint occupation by United States and Great Britain,
1818-1846 (Claim abandoned by Russia, 1824)

WASHINGTON

Columbia R.

From Great
Britain, 1818

MONTANA

Missouri R.

NORTH DAKOTA

OREGON TERRITORY
From Great Britain, 1846

OREGON

IDAHO

SOUTH DAKOTA

WYOMING

Line of Adams-Onis Treaty with Spain, 1819

LOUISIANA PURCHASE
From France, 1803

NEBRASKA

NEVADA

Great Salt Lake

UTAH

To Hawaii

MEXICAN CESSION
From Mexico by Treaty of
Guadalupe Hidalgo, 1848

CALIFORNIA

COLORADO

KANSAS

Colorado R.

ARIZONA

Line of Treaty of Guadalupe
Hidalgo with Mexico, 1848

NEW MEXICO

OKLA.

Red R.

Pacific Ocean

Gila R.

**GADSDEN
PURCHASE**
From Mexico,
1853

Claimed by Texas and ceded
by Mexico, 1848

TEXAS

TEXAS ANNEXATION
Annexed, 1845

Kauai

Oahu

Niihau

Molokai

Lanai

Maui

SIBERIA

ALASKA
From Russia,
1867

CANADA

HAWAII
Annexed, 1898

Hawaii

0   800 mi

0   800 km

Rio Grande

M E X I C O

Pacific Ocean

0   600 mi

0   600 km

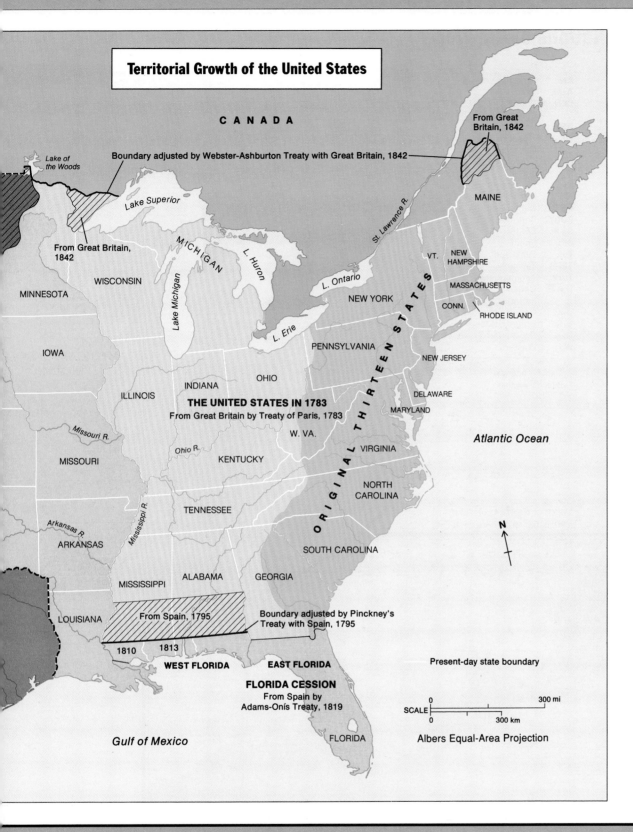

Territorial Growth of the United States

CANADA

Boundary adjusted by Webster-Ashburton Treaty with Great Britain, 1842

From Great Britain, 1842

From Great Britain, 1842

Lake of the Woods

MAINE

Lake Superior

L. Huron

MICHIGAN

MINNESOTA

WISCONSIN

L. Michigan

St. Lawrence R.

VT.

NEW HAMPSHIRE

L. Ontario

NEW YORK

MASSACHUSETTS

CONN.

RHODE ISLAND

IOWA

L. Erie

PENNSYLVANIA

NEW JERSEY

ILLINOIS

INDIANA

OHIO

DELAWARE

MARYLAND

THE UNITED STATES IN 1783
From Great Britain by Treaty of Paris, 1783

Missouri R.

Ohio R.

W. VA.

VIRGINIA

Atlantic Ocean

MISSOURI

KENTUCKY

ORIGINAL THIRTEEN STATES

NORTH CAROLINA

Arkansas R.

TENNESSEE

ARKANSAS

Mississippi R.

N

SOUTH CAROLINA

MISSISSIPPI

ALABAMA

GEORGIA

LOUISIANA

From Spain, 1795

Boundary adjusted by Pinckney's Treaty with Spain, 1795

1810   1813

WEST FLORIDA   **EAST FLORIDA**

Present-day state boundary

FLORIDA CESSION
From Spain by
Adams-Onís Treaty, 1819

SCALE

0   300 mi

0   300 km

Gulf of Mexico

FLORIDA

Albers Equal-Area Projection

Nations of the World

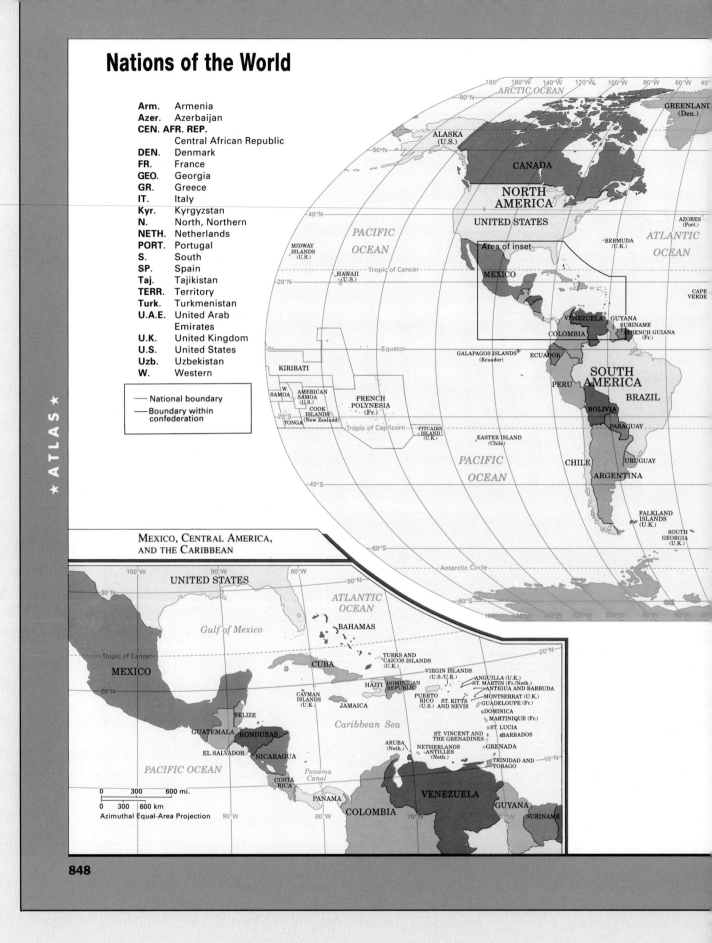

Arm.   Armenia
Azer.   Azerbaijan
CEN. AFR. REP.
            Central African Republic
DEN.   Denmark
FR.   France
GEO.   Georgia
GR.   Greece
IT.   Italy
Kyr.   Kyrgyzstan
N.   North, Northern
NETH.   Netherlands
PORT.   Portugal
S.   South
SP.   Spain
Taj.   Tajikistan
TERR.   Territory
Turk.   Turkmenistan
U.A.E.   United Arab
            Emirates
U.K.   United Kingdom
U.S.   United States
Uzb.   Uzbekistan
W.   Western

— National boundary
— Boundary within
  confederation

MEXICO, CENTRAL AMERICA,
AND THE CARIBBEAN

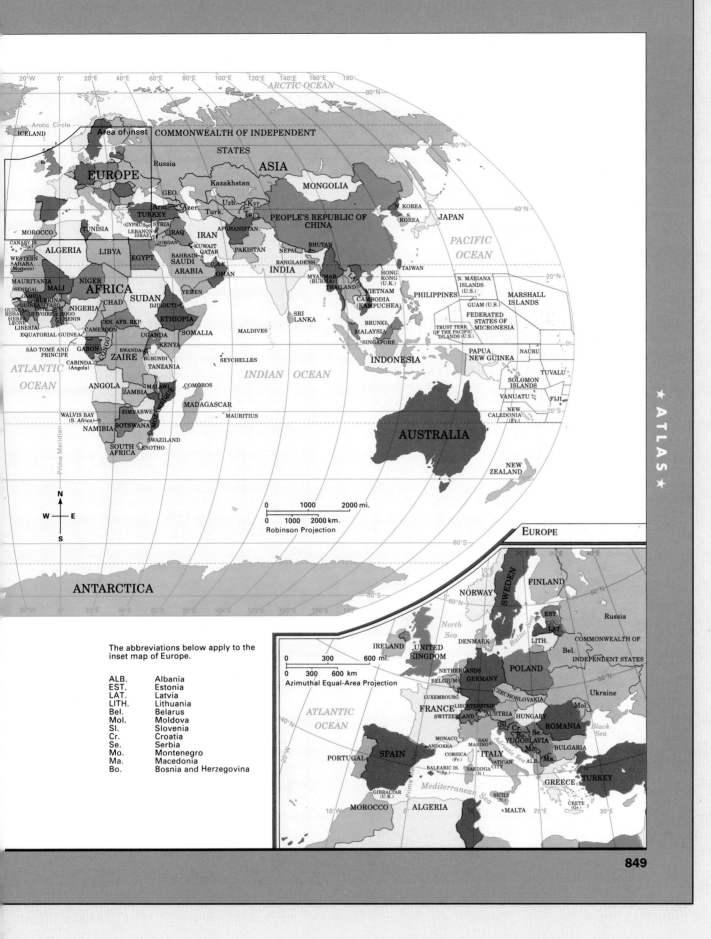

ARCTIC OCEAN

ICELAND

COMMONWEALTH OF INDEPENDENT
STATES

EUROPE

Russia

ASIA

Kazakhstan

GEO.
Arm. Azer.
TURKEY
Uzb. Kyr.
Turk. Taj.

MONGOLIA

N. KOREA
S. KOREA

JAPAN

CYPRUS
LEBANON
ISRAEL
SYRIA
JORDAN
IRAQ

MOROCCO

TUNISIA

IRAN

AFGHANISTAN

PEOPLE'S REPUBLIC OF
CHINA

PACIFIC
OCEAN

CANARY IS.
(Sp.)

ALGERIA

LIBYA

EGYPT

KUWAIT
QATAR
BAHRAIN
SAUDI
ARABIA
U.A.E.
OMAN

PAKISTAN

NEPAL

BHUTAN

TAIWAN

WESTERN
SAHARA
(Morocco)

MAURITANIA

NIGER

CHAD

SUDAN

YEMEN

INDIA

BANGLADESH

MYAN-MAR
(BURMA)
THAILAND

HONG
KONG
(U.K.)

N. MARIANA
ISLANDS
(U.S.)

MARSHALL
ISLANDS

GUAM (U.S.)

MALI

AFRICA

DJIBOUTI

VIETNAM
CAMBODIA
(KAMPUCHEA)

PHILIPPINES

SENEGAL
GAMBIA
GUINEA
BISSAU
GUINEA
SIERRA
LEONE
LIBERIA
BURKINA
FASO
CÔTE
D'IVOIRE
TOGO
BENIN
NIGERIA

CEN. AFR. REP.

ETHIOPIA

SRI
LANKA

BRUNEI

FEDERATED
STATES OF
MICRONESIA

EQUATORIAL GUINEA
CAMEROON

UGANDA

SOMALIA

MALDIVES

MALAYSIA

TRUST TERR.
OF THE PACIFIC
ISLANDS (U.S.)

SINGAPORE

SÃO TOMÉ AND
PRINCIPE
GABON
CONGO
RWANDA
ZAIRE
BURUNDI

KENYA

TANZANIA

SEYCHELLES

INDONESIA

PAPUA
NEW GUINEA

NAURU

ATLANTIC
OCEAN

CABINDA
(Angola)

INDIAN OCEAN

TUVALU

ANGOLA

ZAMBIA

MALAWI

COMOROS

SOLOMON
ISLANDS

MOZAMBIQUE

MADAGASCAR

MAURITIUS

VANUATU

NEW
CALEDONIA
(Fr.)

FIJI

WALVIS BAY
(S. Africa)

ZIMBABWE

NAMIBIA

BOTSWANA

SOUTH
AFRICA

SWAZILAND

LESOTHO

AUSTRALIA

N
W   E
S

NEW
ZEALAND

0   1000   2000 mi.
0   1000   2000 km.
Robinson Projection

ANTARCTICA

★ A T L A S ★

EUROPE

The abbreviations below apply to the
inset map of Europe.

ALB.	Albania
EST.	Estonia
LAT.	Latvia
LITH.	Lithuania
Bel.	Belarus
Mol.	Moldova
Sl.	Slovenia
Cr.	Croatia
Se.	Serbia
Mo.	Montenegro
Ma.	Macedonia
Bo.	Bosnia and Herzegovina

SWEDEN

FINLAND

NORWAY

EST.
LAT.

Russia

IRELAND

UNITED
KINGDOM

North
Sea

DENMARK

LITH.

COMMONWEALTH OF
INDEPENDENT STATES

Bel.

0   300   600 mi.
0   300   600 km.
Azimuthal Equal-Area Projection

NETHERLANDS
BELGIUM
GERMANY

POLAND

LUXEMBOURG
CZECHOSLOVAKIA
Mol.

Ukraine

ATLANTIC
OCEAN

FRANCE
SWITZERLAND
LIECHTENSTEIN
AUSTRIA
HUNGARY

ROMANIA

Black
Sea

Sl.
Cr.
Bo.
Se.
YUGOSLAVIA
Mo.

MONACO
SAN
MARINO

BULGARIA

PORTUGAL

SPAIN

ANDORRA

CORSICA
(Fr.)

ITALY

VATICAN
CITY

ALB.

Ma.

GREECE

TURKEY

BALEARIC IS.
(Sp.)

SARDINIA
(It.)

GIBRALTAR
(U.K.)

MOROCCO

ALGERIA

Mediterranean Sea

SICILY
(It.)

MALTA

CRETE
(Gr.)

849

Gazetteer

The gazetteer provides information about important places and geographical features in this book. Entries include a short description, a reference to the text page on which the entry is discussed, and a reference to the map page on which the place appears. Latitudes and longitudes are approximate, and for large areas (countries, for example) they are generally a central point.

A

Abilene cow town in Kansas that was the first cattle railhead. (39°N 97°W) *page 118; map, page 118*

Afghanistan Southwest Asian nation whose invasion by the Soviet Union caused the United States to shelve the SALT II treaty. (34°N 66°E) *page 613; map, page 579*

Alabama 22nd state, from Indian tribe *Alibamu*, meaning "I clear the thicket," known as the Heart of Dixie. Capital city: Montgomery (32°N 86°W) *map, page 843*

Alaska largest state in the United States, bought from Russia for $7,200,000, or about two cents per acre. Capital city: Juneau (58°N 134°W) *map, page 842*

Antietam site of bloodiest one-day battle of Civil War, which halted the southern offensive in 1862 and led to the Emancipation Proclamation. (39°N 77°W) *page 52; map, page 50*

Appomattox Courthouse site of Lee's surrender to Grant. (37°N 79°W) *page 58; map, page 57*

Ardennes Forest Belgian site of the Battle of the Bulge. (51°N 5°E) *page 427; map, page 424*

Arizona 48th state, from Indian word *arizonac*, probably meaning "little spring," nicknamed the Grand Canyon State. Capital city: Phoenix (33°N 112°W) *map, pages 842–843*

Arkansas part of territory acquired from France in 1803 in Louisiana Purchase. Capital city: Little Rock (34°N 92°W) *map, page 843*

B

Baltimore largest city in Maryland (39°N 76°W) *page 44; map, page 50*

Beijing capital of China. (40°N 117°E) *page 265; map, page 265*

Belgium neutral European nation, whose invasion by Germany brought Great Britain into World War I. (51°N 5°E) *page 289; map, page 296*

Birmingham city in Alabama that is known as the Pittsburgh of the South for its large steel industry (33°N 86°W) *page 91; map, page 843*

Boston capital and chief port city of Massachusetts. (42°N 71°W) *page 135; map, page 94*

Buffalo city in New York State, on Lake Erie. (43°N 79°W) *page 145; map, page 94*

C

California third largest state in the U.S., the "Golden State" has more people than any other. Capital city: Sacramento (38°N 121°W) *map, page 842*

Cambodia (Kampuchea) border nation to Vietnam, invaded in 1970 in hopes of shortening the war. (12°N 105°E) *page 558; map, page 539*

Canada nation on the northern border of the United States. Capital city: Ottawa (45°N 76°W) *page 850; map, page 848*

Casablanca Moroccan city, site of conference between FDR and Churchill in 1943. (33°N 7°W) *page 423; map, page 424*

Château-Thierry town in France where Allies stopped German advance in World War I. (49°N 3°E) *page 295; map, page 296*

Chicago city in Illinois, on Lake Michigan; boomed as a transportation center linking east and west. (42°N 87°W) *page 136; map, page 94*

Cleveland city in Ohio, on Lake Erie; a center of steel production, and also the birthplace of the Standard Oil Company. (41°N 81°W) *page 91; map, page 94*

Colombia Panama was part of this South American nation prior to a revolution in 1903. (5°N 74°W) *page 276; map, page 282*

Colorado the "Centennial State," Colorado joined the Union in 1876, the centennial of the Declaration of Independence. Capital city: Denver (39°N 105°W) *map, page 843*

Confederate States of America new nation formed by eleven southern states in 1861. Capital city: Richmond (37°N 77°W) *page 40; map, page 41*

Connecticut as colony, this state was governed under the Fundamental Orders, the first written constitution. Capital city: Hartford (41°N 72°W) *map, page 843*

Costa Rica Central American nation. (10°N 84°W) *page 271; map, page 282*

Cuba Caribbean nation; as Spanish colony, revolt there led to Spanish-American War. (22°N 82°W) *page 257; map, page 259*

D

Dallas second largest city in Texas; site of President Kennedy's assassination in 1963. (32°N 96°W) *page 504; map, page 94*

Deadwood Gulch town in the Dakota Territory created by a gold rush in 1876. (44°N 103°W) *page 125; map, page 125*

Delaware first state to approve the United States Constitution, on December 7, 1787. Capital city: Dover (39°N 75°W) *map, page 843*

Detroit important auto-producing city in Michigan. (42°N 83°W) *page 91; map, page 136*

Dominican Republic Caribbean nation occupied by the United States from 1916 to 1924. (18°N 71°W) *page 279; map, page 282*

Dunkirk port in France from which Allied troops escaped in 1940. (51°N 2°E) *page 404; map, page 405*

E

Elbe River German river where Soviet and American troops met in World War II. (51°N 13°E) *page 428; map, page 424*

El Salvador Central American nation whose government fought Communist guerrillas be-

ginning in 1979. (14°N 89°W) *page 625; map, page 275*

English Channel water separating France and England, crossed by Allied forces on D-Day. (50°N 3°W) *page 426; map, page 426*

F

Florida obtained from Spain in 1821, became the 27th state in 1845. Capital city: Tallahassee (30°N 84°W) *map, page 843*

Fort Sumter United States fort in Charleston harbor attacked by Confederates, beginning Civil War. (33°N 80°W) *page 42; map, page 57*

G

Galveston Texas city on the Gulf Coast that created the first commission form of city government after a devastating hurricane in 1900. (29°N 95°W) *page 210; map, page 50*

Georgia last of the thirteen colonies, it was named for England's King George II. Capital city: Atlanta (33°N 84°W) *map, page 843*

Gettysburg site of Pennsylvania battle at which Union forces halted invasion of North; also where Lincoln delivered the Gettysburg Address. (40°N 77°W) *page 54; map, page 55*

Great Plains region stretching from the Rocky Mountains to the Mississippi River. *page 350; map, page 845*

Grenada small Caribbean island invaded by the United States in 1983. (12°N 61°W) *page 627; map, page 848*

Guadalcanal one of the Solomon islands, where the first Allied offensive in the Pacific took place during World War II. (9°S 160°E) *page 417; map, page 431*

H

Haiti Caribbean nation occupied by United States troops in 1915. (18°N 73°W) *page 280; map, page 282*

Harlem New York City neighborhood that was home to many black artists in the 1920s. (40°N 74°W) *page 331; map, page 94*

Harpers Ferry site of United States arsenal in western Virginia attacked by abolitionist John Brown in 1859. (39°N 78°W) *page 38; map, page 50*

Hawaii the 50th state and the only state not on mainland North America. Capital city: Honolulu (21°N 157°W) *map, page 842*

Hiroshima Japanese city, target of first atomic bomb attack in 1945. (34°N 132°E) *page 432; map, page 431*

Honduras Central American nation, once part of the United Provinces of Central America. (15°N 87°W) *page 271; map, page 275*

Hué ancient city of Vietnam, destroyed during Tet Offensive in 1968. (16°N 107°E) *page 552; map, page 552*

I

Idaho famous for its potatoes, Idaho became the 43rd state in 1890. Capital city: Boise (43°N 116°W) *map, pages 842–843*

Illinois the "Land of Lincoln," where the 16th President lived most of his life. Capital city: Springfield (39°N 89°W) *map, page 843*

Inchon South Korean city, site of General MacArthur's daring landing during Korean War. (37°N 126°E) *page 460; map, page 462*

Indiana the "Crossroads of America," it lay on the path of westward movement in the 1800s. Capital city: Indianapolis (39°N 86°W) *map, page 843*

Indochina nations of Vietnam, Laos, and Cambodia. (15°N 106°E) *page 538; map, page 539*

Iowa farms make up about 93 percent of the state's area, its chief crops being corn and soybeans. Capital city: Des Moines (41°N 93°W) *map, page 843*

Iran oil-rich country in the Middle East. (30°N 54°E) *page 449; map, page 579*

Iraq Middle Eastern country, invaded Kuwait in 1990. (33°N 44°E) *page 657; map, page 579*

Israel country in Middle East, created to be a Jewish homeland. (31°N 35°E) *page 474; map, page 579*

Iwo Jima Pacific island near Japan; site of an American World War II victory. (24°N 141°E) *page 430; map, page 431*

J

Jacksonville Florida city that was the site of yellow fever epidemic in 1888. (30°N 81°W) *pages 137–138; map, page 55*

K

Kansas state lying midway between the Atlantic and Pacific oceans, it is known as Midway, U.S.A. Capital city: Topeka (39°N 95°W) *map, page 843*

Kansas Territory battleground over slavery in the mid-1850s, includes modern-day Kansas and part of Colorado. (38°N 98°W) *page 35; map, page 35*

Kentucky birthplace of Abraham Lincoln and Jefferson Davis, opposing Presidents in the Civil War. Capital city: Frankfort (38°N 85°W) *map, page 843*

L

Laos Asian nation through which the Ho Chi Minh Trail ran during the Vietnam War. (20°N 102°E) *page 546; map, page 539*

Lebanon Middle Eastern country torn by a long civil war. (34°N 36°E) *page 626; map, page 579*

Leningrad northwestern Soviet city, site of fierce fighting in World War II. (60°N 30°E) *page 413; map, page 424*

Leyte Gulf Philippine site of the largest naval engagement in history, during World War II. (11°N 126°E) *page 429; map, page 431*

Little Bighorn river in Montana, site of "Custer's Last Stand." (45°N 107°W) *page 113; map, page 113*

Louisiana a mixture of many cultures, representative of early French and Spanish influence. Capital city: Baton Rouge (30°N 91°W) *map, page 843*

M

Maine the easternmost state, an important farming and fishing state. Capital city: Augusta (44°N 70°W) *map, page 843*

Manassas Junction site of the Battle of Bull Run. (39°N 78°W) *page 47; map, page 50*

Manchuria large, mineral-rich territory in northeastern China. (46°N 127°E) *page 267; map, page 265*

Maryland site of Fort McHenry, where a War of 1812 battle inspired Francis Scott Key to write "The Star-Spangled Banner." Capital city: Annapolis (39°N 76°W) *map, page 843*

Massachusetts the Bay State, it is the birthplace of four American Presidents. Capital city: Boston (42°N 71°W) *map, page 843*

Mexico nation on the southern border of the United States. Capital city: Mexico City (19°N 100°W) *page 281; map, page 282*

Michigan the Wolverine State, it is a leader in the production of automobiles and steel. Capital city: Lansing (42°N 85°W) *map, page 843*

Midway island site of a World War II battle that marked the turning point of the war in the Pacific. (28°N 177°W) *page 416; map, page 431*

Minneapolis river port in Minnesota, also the flour mill center of the Midwest. (45°N 93°W) *page 135; map, page 136*

Minnesota the largest of the midwestern states, it entered the Union in 1858. Capital city: St. Paul (45°N 93°W) *map, page 843*

Mississippi state named for the river that forms most of its western border. Capital city: Jackson (32°N 90°W) *map, page 843*

Missouri state containing the nation's two longest rivers, the Missouri and the Mississippi. Capital city: Jefferson City (38°N 92°W) *map, page 843*

Montana site of 1862 gold rush, the Treasure State has a great wealth of gold and silver mines. Capital city: Helena (46°N 112°W) *map, pages 842–843*

N

Nagasaki city in Japan where second atomic bomb was dropped in 1945. (32°N 129°E) *page 432; map, page 431*

Nashville city in Tennessee; first Confederate city to fall to the North. (36°N 86°W) *page 49; map, page 50*

Nebraska devoting 95 percent of its area to farming, the Cornhusker State is a leading corn producer. Capital city: Lincoln (40°N 96°W) *map, page 843*

Nevada a mining state rich in gold, silver, and petroleum. Capital city: Carson City (39°N 119°W) *map, page 842*

New Hampshire first of the original thirteen colonies to adopt its own constitution, on January 5, 1776. Capital city: Concord (43°N 71°W) *map, page 843*

New Jersey the most densely populated state, it gained statehood in 1787. Capital city: Trenton (40°N 74°W) *map, page 843*

New Mexico the first atomic bomb was built and exploded in this state in 1945. Capital city: Santa Fe (35°N 106°W) *map, page 843*

New Orleans Louisiana port city at the mouth of the Mississippi River. (30°N 90°W) *page 51; map, page 94*

New York 11th state, New York is second only to California in population. Capital city: Albany (43°N 74°W) *map, page 843*

New York City since 1800, the most populous American city. (41°N 74°W) *page 89; map, page 94*

Nicaragua Central American nation where American-backed rebels fought to overthrow the government in the 1980s. (13°N 85°W) *page 271; map, page 275*

Normandy its beaches were the site of the Allied invasion of France on D-Day in 1944. (49°N 2°W) *page 426; map, page 424*

North Carolina 12th state, it is the leading producer of tobacco products. Capital city: Raleigh (35°N 78°W) *map, page 843*

North Dakota the geographic center of North America is near the city of Rugby in this state. Capital city: Bismarck (47°N 100°W) *map, page 843*

O

Ohio first state formed out of the Northwest Territory in 1803. Capital city: Columbus (40°N 83°W) *map, page 843*

Okinawa island site of the bloodiest battle of the Pacific war. (26°N 127°E) *page 430; map, page 431*

Oklahoma obtained in the Louisiana Purchase from France, it became a state in 1907. Capital city: Oklahoma City (35°N 97°W) *map, page 843*

Omaha Nebraska city on the Missouri River; starting point of first transcontinental railroad. (41°N 96°W) *page 92; map, page 94*

Oregon this northwestern state leads the United States in production of lumber. Capital city: Salem (45°N 123°W) *map, page 842*

★ G A Z E T T E E R ★

★ GAZETTEER ★

P

Pacific Rim economic region of nations bordering the Pacific Ocean. *page 660; map, page 660*

Panama Central American nation, site of canal connecting Caribbean Sea with the Pacific Ocean. (8°N 82°W) *page 273; map, page 275*

Panmunjom village where armistice ending the Korean War was signed. (38°N 126°E) *page 469; map, page 462*

Pearl Harbor American naval base attacked by Japan on December 7, 1941. (21°N 158°W) *page 408; map, page 408*

Pennsylvania known as the Keystone State because of its central position in the "arch" of the original thirteen states. Capital city: Harrisburg (40°N 77°W) *map, page 843*

Petrified Forest National Park in northeast Arizona, protected under the Antiquities Act of 1906. (35°N 111°W) *page 242; map, page 244*

Philippine Islands once controlled by Spain, this Pacific island group was captured by United States forces during the Spanish-American War. (12°N 123°W) *page 258; map, page 259*

Pittsburgh major steel-producing city in Pennsylvania, located at junction of three rivers: the Allegheny, Monongahela, and Ohio. (40°N 80°W) *page 91; map, page 94*

Promontory settlement in Utah where Central Pacific and Union Pacific railroads met. (41°N 112°W) *page 106; map, page 94*

Puerto Rico Caribbean island transferred to United States as a result of the Spanish-American War. (18°N 66°W) *page 260; map, page 259*

Pusan city on southern tip of Korean peninsula. (35°N 129°E) *page 460; map, page 462*

R

Rhineland area near France militarized by Hitler in 1936. (49°N 7°E) *page 403; map, page 405*

Rhode Island the smallest state, it covers only 1,210 square miles. Capital city: Providence (42°N 71°W) *map, page 843*

Richmond city in Virginia that was the capital of the Confederacy. (37°N 77°W) *page 43; map, page 50*

S

Samoa island nation in South Pacific that was divided between the United States and Germany in 1899. (15°S 172°W) *page 255; map, page 259*

Sand Creek Colorado site of massacre of Cheyenne Indians. (38°N 103°W) *page 112; map, page 113*

San Francisco cultural and financial center of the Far West; also site of devastating 1906 earthquake. (38°N 122°W) *page 211; map, page 94*

Santiago port city in Cuba, site of hardest fighting in Spanish-American War. (20°N 75°W) *page 259; map, page 259*

Sarajevo city in Bosnia where Franz Ferdinand was killed, an immediate cause of World War I. (44°N 18°E) *page 287; map, page 296*

Sharpsburg site, in Maryland, of the Battle of Antietam, fought during the Civil War. (39°N 77°W) *page 52; map, page 50*

Shiloh name of a church near site of Union victory in Tennessee during Civil War. (35°N 88°W) *page 49; map, page 50*

Sicily Italian island; first place Allies invaded in Europe in 1943. (37°N 14°E) *page 425; map, page 296*

South Carolina 8th state, it was the first to secede from the Union before the Civil War. Capital city: Columbia (34°N 81°W) *map, page 843*

South Dakota primarily a farming state, the geographic center of the United States is near the city of Castle Rock. Capital city: Pierre (44°N 100°W) *map, page 843*

Stalingrad Soviet city; site of World War II battle marking the turning point of war on Russian front. (48°N 44°E) *page 414; map, page 424*

Suez Canal in Egypt, key route for shipping oil from the Middle East to Europe. (30°N 32°E) *page 273; map, page 579*

T

Taiwan island nation ruled by Chinese who fled the mainland when the Communists came to power. (23°N 121°E) *page 454; map, page 408*

Tennessee last Confederate state to leave the Union and first to return. Capital city: Nashville (36°N 87°W) *map, page 843*

Texas second-largest state; originally part of Mexico, it joined the Union in 1845. Capital city: Austin (30°N 97°W) *map, page 843*

Thailand East Asian nation bordering Laos and Cambodia. (15°N 103°E) *map, page 539*

U

Utah first white settlers in this state were Mormon pioneers led by Brigham Young; Utah became the 45th state in 1896. Capital city: Salt Lake City (40°N 112°W) *map, pages 842–843*

V

Venezuela oil-rich South American nation. (8°N 65°W) *page 278; map, page 282*

Vermont the first state admitted to the Union after the original thirteen colonies, in March 1791. Capital city: Montpelier (44°N 72°W) *map, page 843*

Vichy city in southern France where a Nazi-backed puppet government was established in 1940. (46°N 3°E) *page 404; map, page 405*

Vicksburg site of Civil War battle in Mississippi that gave the Union complete control of the Mississippi River. (32°N 91°W) *page 51; map, page 50*

Virginia birthplace of eight American Presidents, including four of the first five; also site of first permanent English settlement, at Jamestown. Capital city: Richmond (37°N 77°W) *map, page 843*

Virginia City mining town near the Comstock Lode in Nevada. (39°N 119°W) *page 125; map, page 125*

W

Washington 42nd state, it is the only one named in honor of a United States President.

Capital city: Olympia (47°N 123°W) *map, page 842*

Washington, D.C. capital of the United States since 1800. (39°N 77°W) *page 43; map, page 94*

Watts neighborhood in Los Angeles where race riots erupted in the summer of 1965. (34°N 118°W) *page 528; map, page 94*

West Virginia part of Virginia until the Civil War, it broke away and remained loyal to the Union, becoming a state on its own in 1863. Capital city: Charleston (38°N 81°W) *map, page 843*

Wisconsin the nation's leading milk producer, also birthplace of progressivism in the early 1900s. Capital city: Madison (43°N 89°W) *map, page 843*

Wounded Knee South Dakota site of 1890 Indian massacre. (43°N 102°W) *page 114; map, page 113*

Wyoming known as the Equality State, Wyoming women were the first to vote, hold public office, and serve on juries. Capital city: Cheyenne (41°N 105°W) *map, page 843*

Y

Yalta Soviet resort on the Black Sea where Churchill, Stalin, and Roosevelt met to discuss the postwar world. (44°N 34°E) *page 427; map, page 424*

Yalu River border between North Korea and China. *page 461;* (41°N 126°E) *map, page 462*

Yellowstone Park first national park, located mainly in northwestern Wyoming. (45°N 110°W) *page 130; map, page 244*

Ypres city in Belgium near which Allies stabilized Western Front in World War I. (51°N 3°E) *page 289; map, page 296*

★ GAZETTEER ★

Glossary

The glossary defines important words and terms in this book. Remember that many words have more than one meaning. The definitions given here are the ones that will be most helpful in your reading of this book. The page number in parentheses after each definiton refers to the page on which each word or term is first used in the textbook.

A

abolitionist a person who worked in the movement to do away with slavery. *(page 27)*

acid rain rain poisoned by acids created in the burning of fossil fuels. *(page 664)*

affirmative action the policy of giving preference to women or minority members who apply for jobs or for admission to schools. *(page 532)*

Alliance for Progress an aid program for Latin America proposed by President Kennedy in 1961. *(page 497)*

Allies the World War I alliance of France, Russia, and Great Britain *(page 289)*; during World War II, all of the countries that opposed the Axis Powers, primarily the United States, Great Britain, and the Soviet Union. *(page 413)*

American Expeditionary Forces the American troops sent to Europe during World War I. *(page 294)*

American Indian Movement (AIM) an organization formed in the 1960s to fight for better treatment for Indians. *(page 569)*

American Liberty League a group of Republicans and conservative Democrats who defended the laissez-faire theory of government and opposed the New Deal. *(page 367)*

American Plan a policy used by employers in the 1920s to break labor unions. *(page 321)*

amnesty a general pardon by a government for political offenses. *(page 65)*

anarchist a person who favors abolishing all forms of government. *(page 184)*

anesthetic a pain-killer. *(page 46)*

Anti-Imperialist League an organization founded in 1898 to oppose the possession of colonies by the United States. *(page 262)*

anti-Semitism prejudice against Jews. *(page 399)*

antiseptic a germ-killing substance. *(page 46)*

appeasement a policy of granting concessions to a potential enemy in order to maintain peace. *(page 403)*

Army-McCarthy hearings the televised investigations in 1954 of alleged Communist influence in the army. *(page 470)*

Army of the Republic of Vietnam (ARVN) the South Vietnamese army. *(page 546)*

Articles of Confederation the plan, ratified by the states in 1781, that established a national Congress with limited powers. *(page 14)*

assimilate to absorb. *(page 116)*

Atlantic Charter the 1941 agreement between Roosevelt and Churchill that outlined their ideas for a postwar world. *(page 407)*

attrition a military strategy aimed at killing so many of the enemy that they no longer have the ability or the will to fight. *(page 549)*

automation the use of machines rather than human labor to perform tasks. *(page 480)*

Axis Powers the World War II alliance of Germany, Italy, and Japan. *(page 413)*

B

baby boom the rapid population increase during the 1950s, caused by a rising birth rate. *(page 480)*

Balfour Declaration a statement issued by Great Britain in 1917 supporting the establishment of a national homeland for Jews in Palestine. *(page 306)*

Bataan Death March the brutal forced march of Allied prisoners after the surrender of the Philippines in World War II. *(page 416)*

Battle of Antietam a Civil War battle near Sharpsburg, Maryland, resulting in a military draw but a political victory for the North. *(page 52)*

Battle of the Atlantic the Allies' successful effort during World War II to protect the shipping lanes between North America and Europe. *(page 423)*

Battle of Britain Germany's World War II air offensive against Britain, repulsed by British pilots. *(page 406)*

Battle of the Bulge the last major German offensive of World War II, which temporarily forced back the Allies in the Ardennes Forest in Belgium. *(page 427)*

Battle of Bull Run the first major clash of the Civil War, resulting in a Confederate victory. *(page 48)*

Battle of El Alamein a decisive British victory over Germany in North Africa in World War II. *(page 414)*

Battle of Gettysburg the greatest single battle of the Civil War, won by the Union in 1863. *(page 55)*

Battle of Iwo Jima the American invasion and conquest of the island of Iwo Jima in World War II. *(page 430)*

Battle of Leyte Gulf an American naval victory over Japan in World War II that led to the recapture of the Philippines. *(page 429)*

Battle of Midway the turning point in the Pacific during World War II, in which the Allies repulsed a Japanese invasion of the Midway Islands. *(page 416)*

Battle of Okinawa the American invasion and conquest of the island of Okinawa in World War II. *(page 430)*

Battle of Shiloh a Civil War battle near Pittsburg Landing, Tennessee, resulting in a Union victory. *(page 49)*

Battle of Stalingrad the decisive World War II battle in which Soviet troops halted the German advance into the Soviet Union. *(page 414)*

Battle of Vicksburg the Union capture of Vicksburg, Mississippi, in the Civil War, giving the North complete control of the Mississippi River. *(page 56)*

Berlin blockade the Soviet blockade of the western-occupied section of Berlin during 1948–1949. *(page 452)*

Berlin Wall a wall separating East and West Berlin built by East Germany to keep citizens from escaping to the West. *(page 499)*

Bessemer process a process for removing impurities from iron that made it possible to manufacture steel in large quantities. *(page 91)*

bicentennial a 200th anniversary. *(page 599)*

Bill of Rights the first ten amendments to the Constitution, which guarantee the basic rights of American citizens. *(page 18)*

black Cabinet name given to those black Americans whom Franklin Roosevelt placed in significant federal positions. *(page 377)*

black codes laws passed by southern states after the Civil War to stop the movement of freedmen and to return them to plantation labor. *(page 66)*

blacklist a list of people or organizations to be boycotted for acts of disloyalty. *(page 186)*

black power a 1960s movement by black Americans to organize politically and to foster cultural pride. *(page 530)*

black separatism the belief that black Americans could only improve their lives by forming a separate society. *(page 529)*

Black Thursday October 24, 1929, when the stock market's downward slide caused panic. *(page 343)*

bonanza farm a large, productive farm of the late 1800s financed by outside capital. *(page 123)*

Bonus Army a group of World War I veterans who marched on Washington in 1932, demanding immediate payment of a promised bonus. *(page 354)*

Boxer Rebellion a violent, unsuccessful attempt by some Chinese in 1900 to drive foreigners from China. *(page 265)*

Brown v. Board of Education of Topeka the 1954 Supreme Court decision that declared racial segregation in public schools to be unconstitutional. *(page 517)*

Bull Moose Party another name for the Progressive Party formed by Theodore Roosevelt during the 1912 presidential election. *(page 234)*

Bureau of Indian Affairs a government agency established in 1824 to deal with issues affecting American Indians. *(page 115)*

business cycle the regular pattern of a nation's economy, in which times of prosperity alternate with downturns. *(page 182)*

C

Camp David Accords a peace agreement between Egypt and Israel, negotiated with the help of Jimmy Carter. *(page 612)*

capitalism an economic system based on private ownership and free competition. *(page 19)*

carpetbagger a term of insult applied to northerners who moved to the South during Reconstruction. *(page 70)*

caudillo a Latin American dictator. *(page 271)*

censure an expression of disapproval; in Congress, official condemnation of a member's behavior. *(page 471)*

Central Powers the World War I alliance of Germany, Austria-Hungary, and the Ottoman Empire. *(page 289)*

charter a written grant, issued by a government or other authority, giving the holder the right to establish a colony, corporation, or other organization. *(page 5)*

checks and balances a government structure designed to keep any one branch of the federal government from gaining too much power. *(page 17)*

Chinese Exclusion Act an act passed in 1882 suspending all immigration from China for ten years. *(page 264)*

Civil Rights Act of 1964 an act that prohibited an employer from denying someone a job because of race, sex, or religion, and that gave the government the power to desegregate public places. *(page 507)*

Civil Service Act of 1883 an act establishing a commission to develop examinations for entry into government service. *(page 170)*

city commission a board elected by voters to run a city. *(page 210)*

city manager an individual hired by a city council or commission to run a city. *(page 210)*

Clayton Antitrust Act a law passed in 1914 that strengthened the Sherman Antitrust Act by defining unfair business practices. *(page 238)*

Clayton-Bulwer Treaty an 1850 agreement between the United States and Britain in which the two nations agreed that any Central American canal would be politically neutral. *(page 273)*

closed shop a place of employment in which only union members are hired. *(page 185)*

coalition a temporary alliance to promote a common cause. *(page 73)*

cold war the uneasy peace after World War II, marked by a rivalry between the United States and the Soviet Union. *(page 449)*

collective bargaining direct talks between organized workers and their employer. *(page 185)*

Columbian exchange the transfer of plants, animals, and diseases between Europe and the Americas that took place after Columbus reached the Americas. *(page 3)*

community chest a welfare fund that is financed by private contributions and is used for the benefit of charitable organizations. *(page 352)*

Compromise of 1850 a congressional agreement on slavery including resolutions to admit California as a free state, not to restrict slavery in New Mexico or Utah, to abolish the slave trade in Washington, D.C., and to pass a stricter fugitive slave law. *(page 34)*

Compromise of 1877 the compromise which gave Rutherford B. Hayes the presidency in return for the ending of Reconstruction in the South. *(page 75)*

Confederate States of America the nation, which lasted from 1861 to 1865, made up of states seceding from the United States. *(page 40)*

conflict of interest the practice of mixing one's personal occupation with his or her public responsibilities. *(page 168)*

conglomerate a corporation made up of companies in widely different fields. *(page 480)*

consensus a general agreement or a general opinion reached by a group. *(page 204)*

conservation the preservation and wise use of natural resources. *(page 131)*

conspicuous consumption the extravagant display of riches. *(page 160)*

containment the postwar American foreign policy that sought to check the expansion of the Soviet Union through diplomatic, economic, and military means. *(page 450)*

contra a Nicaraguan rebel, backed by the United States, who opposed the Sandinista government. *(page 626)*

convoy a group of ships traveling together for protection. *(page 294)*

cooperative a business owned and operated by its workers. *(page 182)*

Copperhead a northerner who called for peace and a compromise with the South during the Civil War. *(page 54)*

corporation a business chartered by a state and owned by shareholding investors. *(page 97)*

counterculture a group whose values are opposed to those of the established culture. *(page 571)*

coup an overthrow of a government. *(page 544)*

Coxey's Army a group of several hundred people, led by Jacob Coxey, who marched from Ohio to Washington, D.C., to protest unemployment during the Depression of 1893. *(page 194)*

D

Dawes Act a law abolishing tribal organizations, dividing reservations into tracts to be given to Indian families, and providing that proceeds from the sale of reservation lands would go to Indian education. *(page 116)*

Dawes Plan a 1924 American plan to ease Germany's repayment schedule for war reparations. *(page 393)*

D-Day the Allied invasion of German-occupied France on June 6, 1944, during World War II. *(page 425)*

Declaration of Independence the document adopted by the Continental Congress on July 4, 1776, establishing the United States as a nation independent from Great Britain. *(page 13)*

deficit spending spending more money than is raised from taxes. *(page 382)*

deflation falling prices. *(page 192)*

deforestation the destruction of forests. *(page 664)*

demobilization a reduction in the size of the armed forces. *(page 445)*

Department of Energy an agency of the federal government created in 1977. *(page 609)*

depression a period of drastic decline in business activity accompanied by high unemployment. *(page 182)*

détente a relaxing of tensions between two nations. *(page 578)*

deterrence the prevention of nuclear war through the threat of retaliation. *(page 613)*

dime novel a cheap and plentiful piece of popular fiction written after the Civil War. *(page 128)*

disenfranchisement exclusion from voting privileges. *(page 68)*

dividend the portion of a corporation's profits that is paid to each shareholder. *(page 97)*

Dixiecrat a member of a dissenting group of southern Democrats who formed the States' Rights Party in 1948. *(page 447)*

doctrine of nullification a doctrine asserting that a state could declare a federal law null and void within its borders. *(page 28)*

dollar diplomacy a policy of the United States, begun under President Taft, that aimed to encourage American investment in Latin America. *(page 280)*

domino theory the belief that a Communist victory in one nation will lead to Communist victories in neighboring nations. *(page 542)*

dove during the Vietnam War, someone opposed to American involvement in the war. *(page 553)*

Dow Jones Industrial Average the average value of stocks from 30 of the nation's largest firms. *(page 343)*

Dred Scott case the 1857 Supreme Court case that decided that slaves did not have the rights of citizens and that Congress could not forbid slavery in the territories. *(page 37)*

dry farming a method of farming in arid areas without irrigation. *(page 121)*

Dust Bowl areas in the Great Plains that suffered a severe drought in the 1930s. *(page 350)*

dynamo an electric generator. *(page 95)*

E

economies of scale a theory stating that the more units of a product a company makes, the less it costs to make each unit. *(page 97)*

Emancipation Proclamation the announcement on January 1, 1863, by President Lincoln that all slaves in Confederate territory would be considered free. *(page 53)*

embargo a ban. *(page 580)*

End Poverty in California (EPIC) Upton Sinclair's 1934 plan to revive the California economy. *(page 369)*

Environmental Protection Agency (EPA) a federal government agency established in 1970. *(page 575)*

escalation an increase. *(page 546)*

Espionage Act a law passed during World War I forbidding actions that hindered the war effort. *(page 301)*

Exoduster a black southerner who migrated to the Plains states in the 1870s to claim land for farming. *(page 120)*

F

Fair Campaign Practices Act a 1970s law that limited the amount of money individuals or corporations could contribute to political candidates. *(page 597)*

Fair Deal President Truman's domestic program, emphasizing job creation, public housing, and the ending of job discrimination against blacks. *(page 446)*

federalism the distribution of power between a central government and its political subdivisions. *(page 17)*

Federal Reserve Act the law passed in 1913 establishing the Federal Reserve Bank system. *(page 237)*

Federal Trade Commission a commission created by Congress in 1914 to ensure that corporations obey antitrust laws. *(page 238)*

Fifteenth Amendment an 1870 constitutional amendment declaring that the right to vote should not be denied "on account of race, color, or previous condition of servitude." *(page 71)*

fireside chat one of a series of radio talks given by Franklin Roosevelt to explain his policies. *(page 362)*

flapper a term used to describe young women of the 1920s who behaved or dressed in an unconventional way. *(page 328)*

flexible response John Kennedy's policy of seeking a range of options from which to choose in dealing with international crises. *(page 497)*

Fourteenth Amendment an 1868 constitutional amendment declaring that all native-born or naturalized persons were citizens and had the same rights as citizens. *(page 69)*

Freedmen's Bureau a federal agency set up after the Civil War to distribute clothing, food, and fuel to the poor of the South. *(page 67)*

freedom riders protesters who rode buses and trains throughout the South to call attention to discrimination in transportation. *(page 522)*

Freedom Summer a 1964 private effort to recruit and register black voters in Mississippi. *(page 527)*

French and Indian War a conflict between France and Britain in North America fought between 1754 and 1763. *(page 10)*

G

genetic engineering altering the genetic makeup of a living organism. *(page 663)*

genocide the systematic destruction of an entire people. *(page 307)*

Gentlemen's Agreement an agreement signed between the United States and Japan in 1907–1908 that restricted Japanese immigration to the United States. *(page 266)*

GI Bill of Rights a 1944 law providing financial aid to veterans entering college or starting businesses. *(page 435)*

Gilded Age the late 1800s, a period characterized by great wealth, corruption, and inequality. *(page 159)*

glasnost Gorbachev's policy of encouraging freedom of expression in the Soviet Union. *(page 633)*

global warming an increase in the earth's temperature as a result of the burning of fossil fuels. *(page 663)*

Glorious Revolution the 1688 overthrow of England's King James II by Parliament. *(page 7)*

gold standard a policy in which the value of a nation's currency is based on the value of gold. *(page 193)*

Good Neighbor Policy the policy announced by Franklin Roosevelt in 1933 that aimed to improve relations between the United States and Latin America. *(page 395)*

Great Compromise a plan providing for a two-house Congress in which the people would be represented in a House of Representatives and the states in a Senate. *(page 16)*

Great Depression a period of severe economic hardship lasting from 1929 to World War II. *(page 344)*

Great Migration the emigration to America by English Puritans during the 1630s. *(page 5)*

Great Society Lyndon Johnson's 1964 program to end poverty and racial injustice. *(page 509)*

gross national product (GNP) the total value of all goods and services produced by a nation in a year. *(page 480)*

Gulf of Tonkin Resolution the resolution passed by Congress in 1964 that authorized President Johnson to increase American military involvement in Vietnam. *(page 545)*

★ G L O S S A R Y ★

H

Harlem Renaissance a 1920s literary movement by black poets and novelists living in Harlem. *(page 331)*

hawk during the Vietnam War, a person who supported American involvement in the war. *(page 552)*

Haymarket Riot a violent confrontation in Chicago in 1886 between workers and police. *(page 184)*

Hay-Pauncefote Treaty the 1901 agreement between the United States and Britain which granted the United States the sole right to build a canal in Central America. *(page 274)*

Highway Act of 1956 a law committing $32 billion to the construction of 41,000 miles of highways. *(page 480)*

Ho Chi Minh Trail the system of roads and trails used to supply rebels in South Vietnam during the Vietnam War. *(page 546)*

Holocaust Nazi Germany's systematic murder of millions of European Jews. *(page 434)*

Homestead Act an 1862 law that offered free western land for settlement. *(page 121)*

Homestead Strike a bloody union strike at the Carnegie Steel Company in 1892. *(page 187)*

Hooverville a shantytown built by the homeless from cartons and crates during the early years of the Great Depression. *(page 348)*

horizontal integration expanding in one area of production, such as steelmaking or shipping. *(page 99)*

House of Burgesses the Virginia legislature, founded in 1619, which served as an early step toward the establishment of representative government in America. *(page 5)*

House Committee on Un-American Activities (HUAC) a committee in the House of Representatives created to expose Communist subversion in American society. *(page 455)*

hydrogen bomb the nuclear bomb developed in the 1950s whose power came from atomic fusion. *(page 471)*

I

imperialism establishing political or economic control over other countries. *(page 255)*

Industrial Revolution the period of rapid industrial growth that began in Britain in the 1700s and then spread to other nations. *(page 24)*

INF Treaty a 1987 agreement between the Soviet Union and the United States calling for the elimination of all intermediate-range nuclear forces in Europe. *(page 634)*

initiative a process by which citizens propose legislation or constitutional amendments. *(page 212)*

installment plan a plan whereby a consumer buys a product by paying a small sum of money over several months. *(page 101)*

institutional investor a company, such as an insurance firm, that buys and sells stocks in large volumes. *(page 343)*

internment imprisonment. *(page 418)*

interstate commerce the transaction of business across state lines. *(page 104)*

Interstate Commerce Act an 1887 law establishing a commission to oversee rate-setting by the railroads. *(page 107)*

Iran-contra affair a scandal uncovered in 1986 that involved a secret arms deal with Iran and the diversion of money to support Nicaraguan rebels. *(page 635)*

iron curtain a phrase used by Winston Churchill in 1946 to describe the postwar division of Europe. *(page 450)*

island-hopping the American strategy to win World War II in the Pacific by capturing a few strategic Japanese-held islands and isolating the rest. *(page 429)*

isolationism the policy of avoiding involvement in world affairs. *(page 391)*

J

Jacksonian democracy the emerging democratic spirit in the United States that existed after Andrew Jackson's election as President in 1828. *(page 26)*

Jim Crow laws laws introduced in southern states following Reconstruction that segregated schools, railway cars, and eventually all public facilities. *(page 76)*

judicial activism the making, as opposed to interpreting, of laws. *(page 509)*

K

kamikaze a Japanese suicide pilot. *(page 429)*

Kansas-Nebraska Act an 1854 law that repealed the Missouri Compromise and declared that the issue of slavery in the Kansas and Nebraska territories would be left up to the residents. *(page 35)*

Kellogg-Briand Pact a 1928 treaty, signed by many nations, that outlawed war. *(page 392)*

Kerner Commission the commission appointed by Lyndon Johnson to study the causes of the urban riots of the 1960s. *(page 531)*

Khmer Rouge a group of Cambodian Communists, led by Pol Pot, who ruled Cambodia from 1975 to 1979. *(page 562)*

L

laissez faire the theory that government should not interfere in economic affairs. *(page 102)*

League of Nations an organization of nations established at the end of World War I to maintain world stability. *(page 303)*

Lend-Lease Act a 1941 act allowing the President to sell, lease, or lend defense equipment to nations whose defense the President deemed vital to American security. *(page 407)*

★ GLOSSARY ★

Liberty Loan a form of long-term bond sold to the American public to help finance World War I. *(page 300)*

limited liability the fact that stockholders in a corporation are only liable for the total amount of their investment in the corporation. *(page 97)*

limited war a war fought for limited goals or with limited means. *(page 461)*

log drive a method in lumber production whereby felled trees are floated downstream to a sawmill. *(page 126)*

logrolling the practice by which legislators exchange favors by supporting one another's bills. *(page 173)*

long drive the herding of cattle from Texas to railroad towns farther north. *(page 118)*

Lost Generation group of 1920s writers who wrote about disillusionment with American society. *(page 331)*

M

McCarthyism unfairly accusing others of disloyalty and subversion. *(page 457)*

mandate a region administered by another country until it is judged ready for independence. *(page 304)*

Manhattan Project the code name for the top-secret project to design the atomic bomb. *(page 431)*

March on Washington an August 1963 civil rights rally in Washington, D.C. *(page 526)*

margin buying buying stocks by paying only a fraction of the price and borrowing the remainder from a broker. *(page 344)*

Marshall Plan a massive American aid program announced in 1947 to help European nations recover economically from World War II. *(page 451)*

massive retaliation the Eisenhower administration's threat of swift, all-out military action against a nation committing aggression. *(page 473)*

mass transit transporting large numbers of people at one time. *(page 137)*

Mayaguez an American merchant ship seized by Cambodia in 1975 off the coast of Cambodia. *(page 597)*

Mayflower Compact an agreement signed by the male passengers aboard the *Mayflower* to respect laws agreed upon for the general good of the colony. *(page 5)*

Medicare a program under the Social Security Administration that provides medical care for the aged. *(page 510)*

meltdown the melting of a nuclear reactor's core. *(page 609)*

mercantilism an economic policy based on state monopoly of trade and an attempt to transfer wealth from colonies to the parent country. *(page 4)*

Mexican War a war between Mexico and the United States fought from 1846 to 1848 and ending in a United States victory. *(page 29)*

military-industrial complex the close ties between the armed forces and the corporations that build and sell weapons. *(page 487)*

Mississippi Plan a strategy developed by Mississippi Democrats during Reconstruction to force all whites into the Democratic Party and intimidate black voters. *(page 74)*

Missouri Compromise an act of Congress in 1820 whereby Missouri was admitted as a slave state, Maine was admitted as a free state, and slavery was forbidden north of the parallel 36°30'. *(page 28)*

modern Republicanism the term used to describe the Eisenhower administration's belief that the federal government has some responsibility for the well-being of the people. *(page 479)*

money formula the belief that a candidate's ability to win office hinges on the amount of money he or she spends on the campaign. *(page 168)*

Montgomery bus boycott the 1955–1956 boycott by black citizens of the Montgomery, Alabama, bus system to protest segregated seating. *(page 519)*

Moral Majority an organization formed by televangelist Jerry Falwell in 1979 to promote conservative causes. *(page 621)*

Morrill Act an 1862 law granting land to each state to be used for establishing colleges offering courses of study in agriculture and mechanical arts. *(page 104)*

Morrill Tariff a tariff designed to increase federal revenues during the Civil War. *(page 103)*

mortgage a pledge of property to a lender as security for a loan. *(page 190)*

muckraker a writer during the Progressive Era who exposed social and political evils. *(page 204)*

Mugwump a Reform Republican who in 1884 supported Grover Cleveland rather than James Blaine for President. *(page 170)*

Munich Conference a 1938 conference between Britain, France, Germany, and Italy at which Germany was allowed to occupy part of Czechoslovakia. *(page 403)*

My Lai massacre the 1968 slaughter of unarmed Vietnamese civilians by American soldiers in the Vietnamese village of My Lai. *(page 558)*

N

National Aeronautics and Space Administration (NASA) the federal agency that runs the United States space program. *(page 665)*

National Association for the Advancement of Colored People (NAACP) an organization established in 1909 to secure the legal rights of black Americans. *(page 240)*

National Banking Act an 1863 law that created a system of federally licensed banks. *(page 103)*

★ GLOSSARY ★

861

National Energy Act a 1978 law that created new economic incentives for fuel conservation. *(page 609)*

nationalize to convert from private to governmental control. *(page 475)*

National Labor Relations Act a 1935 law that reaffirmed the right of labor to organize and gave enforcement powers to the National Labor Relations Board. *(page 374)*

National Organization for Women (NOW) an organization formed in 1966 to push for women's rights. *(page 604)*

National Park Service a federal agency established in 1916 to maintain and protect the United States' national parks. *(page 130)*

National Park Service Act the 1916 law that created the National Park Service. *(page 245)*

National Reclamation Act a 1902 law permitting the use of proceeds from the sale of federal lands in the West to build dams and irrigation projects. *(page 242)*

nativism hostility toward immigrants. *(page 144)*

natural selection Charles Darwin's philosophy that focuses on the importance of competition and evolution in the development of species. *(page 160)*

Nazi Party Germany's National Socialist German Workers' Party, formed after World War I. *(page 398)*

New Deal Franklin Roosevelt's program to end the Great Depression. *(page 363)*

New Freedom Woodrow Wilson's reform program announced during the 1912 presidential campaign. *(page 234)*

New Frontier John Kennedy's reform program introduced in the early 1960s. *(page 502)*

new immigration the wave of immigration beginning in the 1880s, when large numbers of people arrived in the United States from southern and eastern Europe. *(page 141)*

New Nationalism President Theodore Roosevelt's plan for economic and social reforms. *(page 233)*

New Right the organizations and lobbying groups that supported conservative causes during the 1970s and 1980s. *(page 621)*

nonaggression pact an agreement whereby two or more nations agree not to attack one another. *(page 404)*

North Atlantic Treaty Organization (NATO) an alliance formed in 1949 by the United States, a group of European nations, and Canada to provide mutual aid in the event of armed attack. *(page 453)*

Nuclear Test-Ban Treaty a 1963 agreement between the United States, Great Britain, and the Soviet Union to stop all nuclear weapons' tests in the air and under water. *(page 500)*

Nuremberg Trials the post-World War II trials of Nazi leaders for war crimes. *(page 434)*

O

Occupational Safety and Health Administration (OSHA) a federal agency established in 1970 to maintain safe conditions in the workplace. *(page 575)*

Office of Economic Opportunity (OEO) the federal agency created in 1964 to direct President Johnson's war on poverty. *(page 507)*

Ohio Gang a group of political friends whom Warren Harding appointed to high government posts. *(page 322)*

Okie a migrant farm worker who moved west in search of work during the 1930s. *(page 351)*

old immigration the period from 1800 to 1880, during which large numbers of people arrived in the United States from western and northern Europe. *(page 140)*

Open Door Policy a policy set forth by Secretary of State John Hay in 1899, advocating equal commercial opportunity for all nations

dealing with China. *(page 264)*

Organization of Petroleum Exporting Countries (OPEC) an organization of major oil-producing nations formed in 1960 to set oil prices and production levels. *(page 580)*

P

Palmer raids 1919–1920 raids authorized by Attorney General A. Mitchell Palmer against thousands of suspected Communists. *(page 318)*

Panama Canal Treaty the treaty between the United States and Panama, ratified in 1978, calling for the gradual turnover of the Panama Canal to Panama. *(page 611)*

parochial school a school run by a religious group. *(page 143)*

patent war a legal battle over ownership of the patents for a given product. *(page 101)*

Peace Corps a volunteer organization formed by the Kennedy administration in 1961 to provide help to developing countries. *(page 497)*

Pentagon Papers a history of American involvement in Vietnam drawn from secret government documents. *(page 582)*

perestroika Gorbachev's plan for restructuring Soviet society. *(page 633)*

perjury lying under oath. *(page 456)*

placer mining mining the deposits of a stream bed. *(page 124)*

Platt Amendment an agreement between the United States and Cuba that gave the United States the right to intervene in Cuban affairs and forced Cuba to lease harbors to the United States for naval stations. *(page 262)*

Plessy v. Ferguson an 1896 Supreme Court decision upholding segregation. *(page 78)*

political machine an organization created by public officials to maintain and extend their power. *(page 143)*

political prisoner someone confined simply because of his or her opposition to the state. *(page 656)*

pool an agreement among several firms to control their output and divide up the market. *(page 106)*

primary system a system whereby party members choose their party's candidate for public office. *(page 212)*

productivity the rate of output of production. *(page 90)*

progressive tax a tax that assigns higher tax rates to people with higher incomes. *(page 215)*

progressivism a movement beginning around 1900 that aimed at solving political, economic, and social problems. *(page 203)*

prohibition a ban on the manufacture and sale of alcoholic beverages. *(page 216)*

promotion a gimmick designed to increase sales. *(page 100)*

protectionism governmental policies that protect domestic businesses against foreign competition. *(page 662)*

protectorate a nation that is formally independent but whose policies are guided by an outside power. *(page 255)*

Pullman Strike an 1894 strike by railroad employees against the Pullman Company. *(page 188)*

puppet state a country controlled by an outside power. *(page 401)*

Pure Food and Drug Act a 1906 law designed to eliminate abuses in food processing and the manufacturing of patent medicines. *(page 230)*

Q

quartz mining a mining process whereby rock is blasted from a mountainside and then crushed to separate the gold. *(page 126)*

R

railhead a shipping station set up along a railroad line. *(page 118)*

Reaganomics the Reagan administration's economic policies of budget cuts, tax cuts, and increased defense spending. *(page 623)*

realpolitik "practical politics," in which success matters more than legality or idealism. *(page 576)*

recall the procedure by which a public official may be voted out of office before the next election. *(page 212)*

recession a moderate slump in the economy. *(page 182)*

Reconstruction the federal government's plan to rebuild and reestablish the states of the former Confederacy. *(page 63)*

Red Scare the 1919–1920 panic over socialism and communism in the United States. *(page 318)*

referendum a process by which the people vote directly on proposed legislation. *(page 212)*

reparations payments required from a defeated nation for war damages. *(page 265)*

republic a form of government controlled by the people through elected representatives. *(page 14)*

reverse discrimination discrimination against members of a dominant group. *(page 532)*

rock 'n' roll a popular style of music that emerged during the 1950s, combining elements of rhythm and blues, country, and gospel music. *(page 485)*

Roe v. Wade the 1973 Supreme Court decision declaring that women had the right to obtain an abortion during the first three months of pregnancy. *(page 604)*

rollback the Republican Party's call during the 1950s for the liberation of nations under Communist rule. *(page 473)*

Rome-Berlin Axis an alliance between Italy and Germany, signed in 1936. *(page 402)*

Roosevelt Corollary a 1904 corollary to the Monroe Doctrine in which the United States claimed the right to intervene in the affairs of other nations of the Western Hemisphere. *(page 278)*

Russo-Japanese War the war between Russia and Japan that began in 1904 over Asian territo-

ries and ended in 1905 with a Japanese victory. *(page 267)*

S

Salary Grab Act an 1873 law granting Congress a 50 percent salary increase effective two years earlier. *(page 167)*

SALT II signed in 1979, the second strategic arms limitation treaty, limiting the number, type, and deployment of intercontinental ballistic weapons. *(page 613)*

satellite a nation that is formally independent but dominated by another power. *(page 450)*

Saturday Night Massacre during the Watergate affair, the firing of Special Prosecutor Cox, which led to the resignation of Attorney General Richardson and calls for President Nixon's impeachment. *(page 585)*

Savings and Loan crisis starting in the late 1980s, a string of bank failures that called for a huge government bailout. *(page 650)*

scalawag a southern white who supported Radical Reconstruction and who joined with blacks in reconstruction legislatures. *(page 70)*

Second New Deal the additional reform legislation that Congress passed in the summer of 1935 to supplement the New Deal. *(page 372)*

Sedition Act a law passed during World War I that prohibited any disloyal speech about the government, flag, Constitution, or armed forces. *(page 301)*

Selective Service Act the military draft enacted in 1917, requiring all men between ages 21 and 30 to sign up for military service. *(page 298)*

Selective Training and Service Act a 1940 law marking the first American peacetime military draft. *(page 406)*

settlement house an urban center providing various social services to the poor. *(page 164)*

Seven Days' Battle a series of Civil War battles in Virginia in 1862,

863

resulting in Confederate victories. *(page 52)*

sexism discrimination based on sex. *(page 602)*

Share-Our-Wealth program a 1934 program proposed by Huey Long to redistribute wealth. *(page 368)*

share tenantry an arrangement in which a farmer and his family work a plot of land in exchange for part of the crop. *(page 75)*

Sherman Antitrust Act an 1890 law that made it illegal for businesses to set up monopolies. *(page 107)*

sit-in a method of nonviolent protest whereby people sit down in a public place and refuse to move. *(page 522)*

Smoot-Hawley Tariff high tariff rates enacted by Congress in 1930. *(page 346)*

Social Darwinism Herbert Spencer's application of Charles Darwin's natural selection philosophy to the development of society. *(page 160)*

Social Gospel the view that churches should work to fulfill Christian ideals in society. *(page 165)*

Social Security Act a 1935 law that used a tax levied on employers to provide compensation and protection for Americans unable to support themselves. *(page 372)*

sod blocks of thickly matted soil. *(page 122)*

solid South an expression coined around 1900 to denote the Democratic Party's control of southern politics. *(page 78)*

Southern Manifesto a document signed by southern representatives declaring that *Brown v. Board of Education of Topeka* unfairly increased federal powers at the expense of states' rights. *(page 518)*

Spanish-American War the 1898 war between Spain and the United States, won by the United States. *(page 257)*

Spanish Civil War the struggle between 1936 and 1939 in which Fascists gained control of Spain. *(page 402)*

sphere of influence a section of one country in which another country has special influence. *(page 264)*

spoils system the giving of government jobs to party supporters after an election victory. *(page 27)*

Sputnik the world's first space satellite, launched by the Soviet Union in 1957. *(page 486)*

Square Deal President Theodore Roosevelt's goal of fairness and justice for the American people. *(page 227)*

stagflation a combination of high unemployment and rising inflation. *(page 568)*

Stamp Act a 1765 British decree taxing all legal papers issued in the colonies. *(page 11)*

standard gauge the common distance between the rails of a railroad track. *(page 91)*

standpatter in the years following the Civil War, a politician who resisted change. *(page 170)*

steerage the lowest deck on a ship. *(page 141)*

stock pool a practice whereby a group of investors collaborate to drive up the price of a stock and then sell the stock all at once for a large profit. *(page 344)*

Strategic Arms Limitations Talks (SALT) Soviet-American discussions begun in 1969 to establish limits on the number of strategic nuclear weapons held by both sides. *(page 578)*

Strategic Defense Initiative (SDI) President Reagan's 1983 proposal for a research program to devise a defense against nuclear attack. *(page 628)*

subsidy financial assistance given by the government. *(page 105)*

suffrage the right to vote. *(page 214)*

superpower a nation that combines huge military might and international influence. *(page 436)*

supply-side economics the belief that a reduction in taxes will stimulate investment and productivity. *(page 622)*

Sussex Pledge Germany's promise in 1916 not to sink unarmed ships without warning. *(page 293)*

sweatshop a workplace with extremely poor working conditions. *(page 163)*

T

Taft-Hartley Act a 1947 law that imposed certain restrictions on the activities of labor unions. *(page 447)*

Teapot Dome scandal the secret, illegal leasing of government oil reserves to private oil companies during the Harding administration. *(page 322)*

Teller Amendment an amendment to the declaration of war on Spain in 1898, stating that the United States would let the Cuban people rule themselves. *(page 258)*

tenement a multi-family building constructed to house large numbers of people as cheaply as possible. *(page 162)*

Tet Offensive the January 1968 attack by Vietcong and North Vietnamese forces on more than 100 cities and towns throughout South Vietnam. *(page 551)*

Third World underdeveloped or developing countries not aligned with the Communist or non-Communist blocs. *(page 474)*

Thirteenth Amendment an 1865 constitutional amendment that abolished slavery in the United States. *(page 66)*

total war a war aiming at the total destruction of the enemy. *(page 56)*

Townsend Plan a plan proposed by Francis Townsend to help the elderly and lift the economy out of the Great Depression. *(page 369)*

Trading with the Enemy Act a law passed during World War I that gave the Postmaster General the power to censor any publications exchanged with other countries. *(page 301)*

Treaty of Brest-Litovsk the 1918 treaty between Germany and Russia that took Russia out of World War I and gave much of its western territory to Germany. *(page 295)*

Treaty of Versailles the peace agreement that formally ended World War I. *(page 304)*

Triple Alliance the alliance between Germany, Austria-Hungary, and Italy before World War I. *(page 288)*

Triple Entente the alliance between France, Russia, and Great Britain before World War I. *(page 288)*

Truman Doctrine Harry Truman's 1947 promise that the United States would defend free peoples from subversion or outside pressure. *(page 450)*

trust a group of companies whose stock is controlled by a central board of directors. *(page 106)*

trustbusting breaking up trusts. *(page 227)*

Turner thesis Frederick Jackson Turner's 1893 claim that the American frontier played a major role in molding American institutions and beliefs. *(page 128)*

Tweed Ring a political machine that dominated New York City politics during the late 1800s. *(page 166)*

U

U-2 incident the shooting down over the USSR of an American U-2 spy plane in 1960. *(page 478)*

U-boat a German submarine. *(page 291)*

unconditional surrender surrender without any limitations. *(page 423)*

Underwood Tariff a 1913 law that lowered tariffs on hundreds of items. *(page 237)*

union contract written agreement between an employer and a union. *(page 187)*

United Nations an international organization founded in 1945 to promote world peace and progress. *(page 436)*

urban renewal federally sponsored programs to rebuild run-down parts of cities. *(page 502)*

V

vertical integration gaining control of all the steps involved in turning a raw material into a finished product. *(page 97)*

Vietcong during the Vietnam War, southern revolutionaries who formed the National Liberation Front and fought for the reunification of Vietnam. *(page 543)*

Vietminh the League of Independence of Vietnam formed by Ho Chi Minh in 1941. *(page 539)*

Vietnamization the Nixon administration's policy of building up South Vietnamese forces while gradually withdrawing American troops. *(page 558)*

Vietnam War the conflict in Vietnam between 1946 and 1975 in which the Vietnamese overthrew French rule, followed by the conquest of South Vietnam by North Vietnam. *(page 537)*

Volstead Act the 1919 act enforcing the prohibition of alcoholic beverages. *(page 336)*

Voting Rights Act of 1965 a law that expanded the federal government's powers to eliminate discrimination in voting. *(page 528)*

W

War Industries Board an agency created by Woodrow Wilson during World War I to regulate the supply of raw materials to manufacturers and the delivery of finished products. *(page 299)*

War Powers Act a 1973 act of Congress requiring the President to inform Congress within two days of any use of American troops in a foreign country and to withdraw the troops within 60 days if Congress does not support their deployment. *(page 562)*

War Production Board (WPB) an agency created by Franklin Roosevelt in 1942 to organize the shift of the economy to wartime production. *(page 420)*

Warren Commission a panel headed by Chief Justice Earl Warren that investigated the assassination of President Kennedy. *(page 504)*

Watergate scandal the public exposure of a burglary and its cover-up by the Nixon administration that eventually led to Nixon's resignation in 1974. *(page 582)*

Weimar Republic the republican government of Germany between the end of World War I and the rise of nazism in 1933. *(page 307)*

welfare state a social system in which the government assumes a responsibility for the economic security of its people. *(page 383)*

white backlash in the 1960s, white Americans' growing opposition to black demands. *(page 531)*

White Citizens Council groups of whites organized throughout the South in the 1950s to oppose integration. *(page 519)*

Wisconsin Idea a program of progressive reforms in Wisconsin in the early 1900s. *(page 209)*

workmen's compensation a state-run insurance program that supports workers injured on the job. *(page 208)*

World War I a global conflict between 1914 and 1918 in which the Allied Powers defeated the Central Powers. *(page 287)*

World War II a global conflict between 1939 and 1945 in which the Allies defeated the Axis Powers. *(page 404)*

★ GLOSSARY ★

Y

Yalta Conference a meeting of Churchill, Roosevelt, and Stalin in 1945 to plan for the post–World War II world. *(page 427)*

yellow dog contract an agreement in which an employee pledges that he or she is not a union member and will never join a union. *(page 214)*

yellow journalism journalism that exploits, distorts, or exaggerates events in order to attract readers. *(page 150)*

yuppie a young urban professional. *(page 630)*

Z

Zimmermann Note a secret message sent to Mexico in 1917 by the German foreign minister, proposing an alliance between Germany and Mexico if Germany and the United States went to war. *(page 294)*

Index

The purpose of the index is to help you quickly locate information on any topic in this book. The index includes references not only to the text but to maps, pictures, and charts as well. A page number with *m* before it, such as *m143*, refers to a map. Page numbers with *p* and *c* before them refer to pictures and charts.

★ I N D E X ★

869

INDEX

INDEX

★ INDEX ★

★ INDEX ★

INDEX

★ I N D E X ★

Acknowledgments

Text Credits

Grateful acknowledgment is made to authors, publishers, and other copyright holders for permission to reprint (and in some cases to adapt slightly) copyright material listed below.

16 From *James Madison* by Robert A. Rutland. Library of Congress, 1981. **42** Arthur M. Schlesinger, Jr., in *The Causes of the Civil War* edited by Kenneth M. Stampp. Prentice-Hall, 1959. **56** From *The Blue and the Gray: The Story of the Civil War as Told by Participants* edited by Henry Steele Commager. Bobbs-Merrill, 1950. **59** From *Battle Cry of Freedom: The Civil War Era* by David M. McPherson. Ballantine, 1988. **63** From *Lay My Burden Down: A Folk History of Slavery* edited by B. A. Botkin. University of Chicago Press, 1945. **65** From *Reconstruction: America's Unfinished Revolution, 1863–1877* by Eric Foner. Harper & Row, 1988. **70** From *Ordeal by Fire: The Civil War and Reconstruction* by James M. McPherson. Knopf, 1982. **72** From *The Trouble They Seen: Black People Tell the Story of Reconstruction* edited by Dorothy Sterling. Doubleday and Company, 1976. **76** From *The American Heritage History of the Confident Years* by Charles Nordhoff. Bonanza, 1987. **100** From *The Cornflake Crusade* by Gerard Carson. Ayer Company Publishers, 1976. **111** From *Morrow Book of Quotations in American History* by Joseph R. Conlin. Morrow, 1984. **138** From *An American Primer* edited by Daniel Boorstin. Merrill, 1968. **140** From *The Promised Land* by Mary Antin. Houghton Mifflin Company, 1912. **142** From *From Immigrant to Inventor* by Michael Pupin. Charles Scribner's Sons, 1950. **143** From "Mr. Richard Croker and Greater New York" by William Stead, *Review of Reviews*, October, 1897. **149** From *The New York Times*, January 2, 1887. **150** From *The New York Times*, December 31, 1886. **160** From *Acres of Diamonds* by Russell H. Conwell. Harper & Brothers, 1915. **165** From "Salvation Army Work in the Slums" by Maud Billington Booth, *Scribner's Magazine*, January, 1895. **182** From *Sidney Hillman* by Matthew Josephson. Doubleday & Company, Inc., 1952. **189** From "The Populist Uprising" by Elizabeth N. Barr, in *History of Kansas, State and People, Vol. 2* edited by W.E. Connelly. American Historical Society, 1928. **214** From *The President's Annual Message* by Carrie Chapman Catt. National American Woman Suffrage Association, 1902. **219** From *A Pictorial History of Women in America* by Ruth Warren. Crown Publishers, 1975. **259** From *The American Reader* edited by Paul Angle. Rand McNally & Company, 1968. **261** From "To the Person Sitting in Darkness" by Mark Twain, *North American Review*, February, 1901. **264** From "Some Reasons for Chinese Exclusion" by the American Federation of Labor in *Senate Documents*, Vol. XIII. Government Printing Office, 1902. **276** From *Panama: La Création, La Destruction, La Résurrection*, by Phillipe Bunau-Varilla. Plon-Nourrit, 1913. **276** From *The New York Times*, March 25, 1911. **276** From *The New York Tribune*, February 4, 1904. **277** From *The Path Between the Seas* by David McCullough. Simon and Schuster, 1977. **283** From *Some Memories of a Soldier* by Hugh L. Scott. The Century Company, 1928. **289** From *American Heritage History of World War I* by S.L.A. Marshall. American Heritage Publishing Co., Inc., 1964. **290** From *World War I* by Robert Hoare. Macdonald and Company, Ltd., 1973. **297** From *Dear Bess: The Letters of Harry to Bess Truman, 1910–1959* edited by Robert H. Ferrell. Norton, 1983. **297** From *World War I: An Illustrated History* by Susanne Everett. Rand, McNally & Company, 1989. **299** From *American Pageant* by Thomas A. Bailey and David M. Kennedy. D.C. Heath and Company, 1979. **301** From *Over Here* by David M. Kennedy. Oxford University Press, 1980. **307** From *Armenia: Cradle of Civilization* by David Marshall Lang. Allen and Unwin, 1978. **320** From H. L. Mencken in *The Baltimore Evening Sun*, October 18, 1920. **332** "Harlem," by Langston Hughes reprinted by permission of Harold Ober Associates Incorporated. **349** From *Redeeming the Time* by Page Smith. McGraw-Hill Book Company, 1987. **349** From *Movin' On Up* by Mahalia Jackson. E.P. Dutton, 1966. **417** From *The Glory and the Dream* by William Manchester. Little, Brown and Company, 1974. **422, 439** From *"The Good War": An Oral History of World War Two* by Studs Terkel. Copyright © 1984 by Studs Terkel. Reprinted by permission of Pantheon Books, a division of Random House, Inc. **426** From *V Was for Victory* by John Morton Blum. Harcourt Brace Jovanovich, 1977. **426** From *War and Society* by Richard Polenberg. Lippencott, 1972. **458** From *War In Korea* by Marguerite Higgins. Time Inc., 1951. **467** From *Eisenhower, Vol. 1*, by Stephen Ambrose. Simon and Schuster, 1983. **516** From *The Southern Case for School Segregation* by James J. Kilpatrick. Copyright © 1962 by Crowell-Collier Publishers. Reprinted with permission of Collier Books, an imprint of Macmillan Publishing Company. **525** From "Letter from a Birmingham Jail" in *Why We Can't Wait* by Martin Luther King, Jr. Copyright © 1963, 1964 by Martin Luther King, Jr. Reprinted by permission of Joan Daves. **537** "Eve of Destruction" by P. F. Sloane. Copyright © 1965 by MCA Music Publishing, a division of MCA, Inc. Used by permission. **539** From *Vietnam: Anthology and Guide* by Steven Cohen. Knopf, 1983. **540** From *Winners and Losers* by Gloria Emerson. Penguin, 1985. **548** From *And A Hard Rain Fell* by John Ketwig. Macmillan, 1985. **552** From *The Road From War* by Robert Shaplen. Harper & Row, 1971. **563** From *The Bad War* by Kim Willenson. New American Library, 1987. **570** From *Robert Kennedy and His Times* by Arthur M. Schlesinger, Jr. Houghton Mifflin Company, 1978. **573** "Pollution" by Tom Lehrer. Copyright © 1965 by Tom Lehrer. Used by permission of the author. **584** From *Breach of Faith: The Fall of Richard Nixon* by Theodore H. White. Copyright © 1975 by Theodore H. White. Reprinted with permission of Atheneum Publishers, an imprint of Macmillan Publishing Company. **599** From *The New Yorker*, July 19, 1976. **604** From *Hearts of Men* by Barbara Ehrenreich. Doubleday, 1983. **808** From *Chicano* by Richard Vasquez. Extensive efforts to locate the rights holder were unsuccessful. If the rights holder sees this notice, he or she should contact the School Division Permissions Department, Houghton Mifflin Company, 1 Beacon Street, Boston, MA 02108.

Art Credits

Cover design: James Stockton and Associates.
Cover image: (front) ©Bob Daemmrich Photos; (back) © David Muench.
Text design: James Stockton and Associates.
Text maps: Richard Sanderson; map p. G2, Precision Graphics; maps pp. G3, 842–849, RR Donnelley and Sons, Cartographic Services; maps pp. 20–21, 220–221, 668–669, Howard S. Friedman; map, p. 840, Map of North and South America, 1596 (detail), by Theodore de Bry. Coll: National Map Collection, Ottawa.
Text charts and graphs: Dave Fischer.
Cause and Effect charts: Precision Graphics.
Civics Handbook charts: Neil Pinchin Design.
Illustrations: pp. 20–21, 220–221, 668–669, Chris Costello.
Photo Research: Linda Rill.

Positions are shown in abbreviated form as follows: **T**–top; **B**–bottom; **C**–center; **L**–left; **R**–right

Key: BA–Bettmann Archive. GC–Granger Collection. LC–Library of Congress. PR–Photo Researchers.

Table of Contents and Unit Opener photos credited within text. **2** Keller and Peet Associates; **4** Archivo Fotographico/Ampliaciones Reproducciones MAS; **6** "Departure of the East Indiaman" by Willaerts/National Maritime Museum, London; **7** "The Rice Hope Plantation" by Charles Fraser. Carolina Art Association, Gibbes Art Gallery; **11** "The Deerfield Massacre, 1704" by Brooks and Pitman/Fruitlands Museum, Harvard, MA; **12** GC; **13** "Washington Crossing the Delaware" by Emanuel Gottlieb Leutze. Oil on canvas. H. 149 in. W. 255 in. Metropolitan Museum of Art. Gift of John Stewart Kennedy, 1897; **18** © 1983 Robert J. Quataert/Folio, Inc.; **22 TL** The Thomas Gilcrease Institute of American History and Art, Tulsa, Oklahoma; **22 TR** Missouri Historical Society, Neg. CT. LA 109; **22 B** Smithsonian Institution, Neg. #83–7221; **23** "Dolley Madison" by Bass Otis. Courtesy of The New-York Historical Society, New York City; **24** Yale University Art Gallery, The Mabel Brady Garvan Collection; **25** "Junction of the Erie and Northern Canals" by John Hill. Courtesy of The New-York Historical Society, New York City; **26 T** GC; **26 R** LC; **27 T** Philadelphia Museum of Art; **27 B** New Bedford Whaling Museum; **29** "Fall of the Alamo" by Robert Onderdonk. Friends of the Governor's Mansion, Austin; **32** Private Collection/Laura Platt Winfrey, Inc.; **34 B** BA; **T** National Portrait Gallery, Smithsonian Institution; **36 TL, BL** Copyrighted by The White House Historical Association, photograph by The National Geographic Society; **TR, BR** National Portrait Gallery, Smithsonian Institution; **38** GC; **39** Courtesy of the Illinois State Historical Library; **40 BL** LC; **BR** Smithsonian Institution, Division of Numismatics; **46 TL** LC; **BR** GC; **48** © Sam Abell; **51** LC; **53 B** Chicago Historical Society; **T** Sophia Smith Collection, Smith College; **56** Copyrighted by The White House Historical Association, photograph by The National Geographic Society; **57** LC; **62** Bradley Smith; **64 TL** Winslow Homer, "Sunday Morning in Virginia." Cincinnati Art Museum; **BL** GC; **65** From the Collections of the South Carolina Historical Society; **67** Copyrighted by The White House Historical Association, photograph by The National Geographic Society; **68** LC; **71** Missouri Historical Society; **72** Copyrighted by The White House Historical Association, photograph by The National Geographic Society; **73** LC; **74** GC; **75 T** Copyrighted by The White House Historical Association, photograph by The National Geographic Society; **76** Cook Collection, The Valentine Museum; **79** BA; **82 TL** Sonoma Valley Historical Society; **TR** BA; **CL** Courtesy Museum of New Mexico, Neg. #146695; **BR** BA; **83 B** The Trustees of Amherst College, Amherst MA; **CL** University of Oklahoma Library, Western Collection. Rose Collection Neg. #16; **TR** The Kansas State Historical Society; **86** John Ferguson Weir, "The Gun Foundry," Putnam County Historical Society, Cold Spring, NY; **88** Culver Pictures, Inc.; **89** LC; **92** The Oakland Museum; **93 L** The Oakland Museum; **R** Union Pacific Railroad Company; **95 BL** LC; Culver Pictures, Inc.; **98** The Newberry Library, Chicago; **99** GC; **100** Photo Courtesy of Kellogg Company; **101** BA; **103** LC; **104 BR** Michigan State University, Public Relations Office; **105** Culver Pictures, Inc.; **110** California Historical Society; **114 T** From "A Pictographic History of the Oglala Sioux," by Amos Bad Heart Bull, plate no. 147. Courtesy University of Nebraska Press; **BL** National Portrait Gallery, Smithsonian Institution; **115 T** Smithsonian Institution; **BR** Culver Pictures, Inc.; **116** LC; **119** LC; **121** Solomon D. Butcher Collection, Nebraska State Historical Society; **122** Culver Pictures, Inc.; **123** New-York Historical Society; **125** Levi Strauss & Company; **127** LC; **129 TL** Denver Public Library, Western History Department, photo by David F. Barry; **BR** LC; **130** National Museum of American Art, Smithsonian Institution, lent by the U.S. Department of the Interior, Office of the Secretary; **134** George Wesley Bellows, "New York," National Gallery of Art, Washington, Collection of Mr. and Mrs. Paul Mellon; **137** Culver Pictures, Inc.; **138** The Los Angeles County Museum of Art, Los Angeles County Funds. "Cliff Dwellers," by George Wesley Bellows. Copyright © 1989 Museum Associates, Los Angeles County Museum of Art; **141** Museum of the City of New York; **143** LC; **144 TL** Culver Pictures, Inc.; **TR** Seaver Center for Western History Research, Natural History Museum of Los Angeles County; **145** AP/Wide World Photos; **146–147** George Ulrich; **149 TL** Chicago Historical Society; **CR, BR** Smithsonian Institution, Warshaw Collection, **CL** Courtesy the Coca Cola Company; **150** Smithsonian Institution, Warshaw Collection; **151** by Jacob A. Riis, the Jacob A. Riis Collection, Museum of the City of New York; **152** Metropolitan Life Insurance Company Archives; **153 T** Museum of the City of New York; **BR** National Archives; **154 TL** LC; **BR** National Portrait Gallery, Smithsonian Institution; **155** Philadelphia Museum of Art: the W. P. Wilstach Collection; **158** GC; **TL** The Preservation Society of Newport County, photo by Richard

892

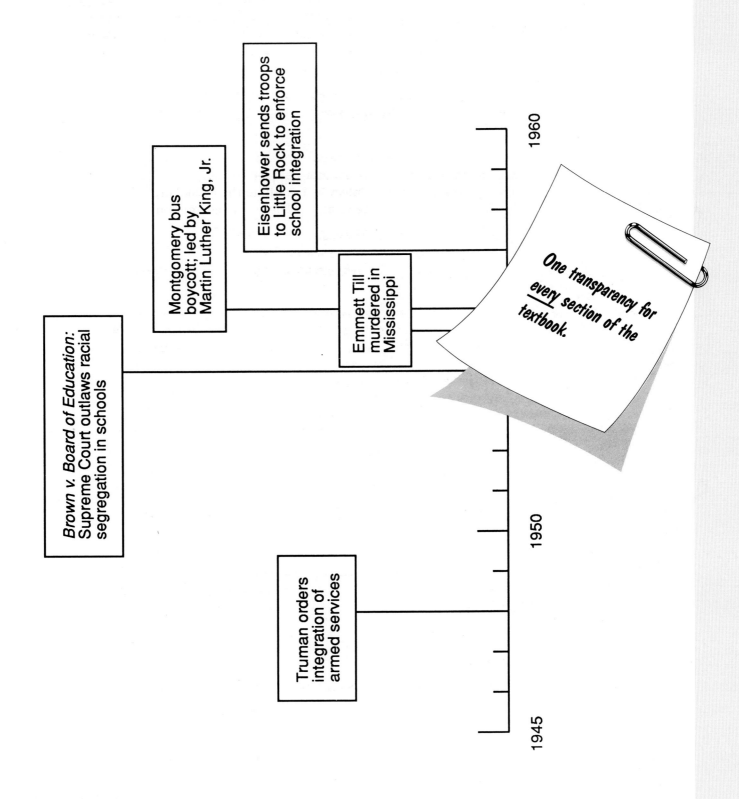

Brown v. Board of Education: Supreme Court outlaws racial segregation in schools

Montgomery bus boycott; led by Martin Luther King, Jr.

Eisenhower sends troops to Little Rock to enforce school integration

Emmett Till murdered in Mississippi

Truman orders integration of armed services

1945

1950

1960

One transparency for *every* section of the textbook.

Name _____   Date _____

(Use with Section 1, textbook pages 515–521.)

Find the name of the person in the second column that best matches
the description in the first column. Write the letter of your answer in
the blank.

_____ **1.** Victim of lynching in Mississippi

_____ **2.** Law professor at Howard University

_____ **3.** First black justice on the Supreme Court

_____ **4.** Kansas student named in a landmark civil rights
lawsuit

_____ **5.** Chief Justice who wrote key civil rights
decisions

A. Charles Houston

B. Emmett Till

C. Earl Warren

D. Linda Brown

E. Thurgood Marshall

Form D of the Tests
consists of section
quizzes—for more
frequent evaluation.

SECTION 2
Freedom Now
(Textbook pages 521–526)

The worksheets, transparency, and quiz for this section follow on pages S10–S13.

CHAPTER 22
(Use with Section 2, textbook pages 521–526.)

Reinforcement Worksheet 85
Observing for Details

A. Five main factors gave hope to the civil rights movement after World
War II. List those factors.

_____

_____

_____

_____

_____

B. Answer the questions below to explain how those factors influenced the
civil rights movement.

  1. Why was the civil rights movement strongest in southern cities? _____

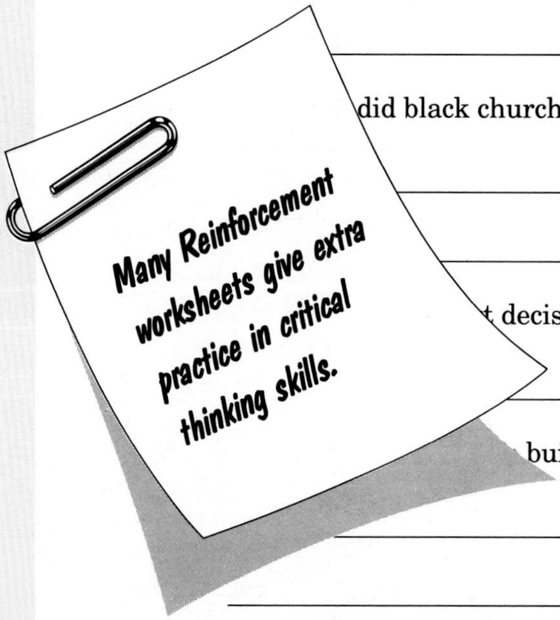

_____

_____

  did black churches play in the civil rights movement? _____

_____

_____

Many Reinforcement
worksheets give extra
practice in critical
thinking skills.

  t decision strengthened blacks' belief that their protests were justified?

_____

  build white support for civil rights? _____

_____

_____

  5. How did African independence movements affect black Americans? _____

_____

_____

CHAPTER 22
(Use with Section 2, textbook pages 521–526.)

Reteaching Worksheet 85
Sequencing Historical Events

A. Using the blank in front of each event, list the following events in the order in which they occurred. Then, in the blank following each event, identify one result of each event.

1. _____ About 250,000 people take part in the March on Washington. _____

_____

2. _____ Freedom riders travel on buses in the South. _____

_____

3. _____ Governor Barnett refuses to obey a court order admitting James Meredith to University of Mississippi. _____

_____

4. _____ Martin Luther King, Jr., and the SCLC begin demonstrations in Birmingham.

_____

5. _____ Students stage sit-ins in Greensboro and Nashville. _____

_____

B. List and briefly explain the five main factors that gave rise to the civil rights movement after World War II.

_____

_____

_____

_____

_____

_____

_____

Reteaching worksheets help students grasp the main idea.

CHAPTER 22   The Civil Rights Movement

Test: Form D

(Use with Section 2, textbook pages 521–526.)

Section 2 Quiz

Fill in the blanks with the correct answers. Answers may require
more than one word.

1. _____ at lunch counters were an early protest against Jim
   Crow laws.

2. _____ were people who traveled across the South to protest
   segregation on interstate trains and buses.

3. American blacks were inspired when _____ won independence in the 1950s.

4. _____ became the NAACP's first field director in Mississippi
   and helped a black student gain admission to the University of Mississippi.

5. The Civil Rights Act of 1964 put an end to _____ laws in the
   South.

SECTION 3
High Hopes and Tragic Setbacks
(Textbook pages 527–533)

The worksheets, transparency, and quiz for this section follow on pages S15–S19.

CHAPTER 22
(Use with Section 3, textbook pages 527–533.)

Reinforcement Worksheet 86
Comparing Points of View

Martin Luther King, Jr., and Malcolm X had very different points of view. Using information from your textbook, write answers to the following questions to reflect the attitudes of each of these leaders.

1. What is your attitude toward white people?

    a. Martin Luther King, Jr.: _____

    _____

    _____

    b. Malcolm X: _____

    _____

    _____

Motivating Reinforcement activities make review interesting—not just a rehash!

2. What are your goals for American society?

    a. Martin Luther King, Jr.: _____

    _____

    _____

    b. Malcolm X: _____

    _____

    _____

3. What methods should blacks use to achieve their goals?

    a. Martin Luther King, Jr.: _____

    _____

    _____

    b. Malcolm X: _____

    _____

    _____

CHAPTER 22
(Use with Section 3, textbook pages 527–533.)

Reteaching Worksheet 86
Finding the Main Idea

A. Give a brief definition of each of the items listed below. Then list one positive effect and one negative effect of that item.

1. Freedom Summer

   Definition: _____

   Positive: _____

   Negative: _____

2. March from Selma to Montgomery

   Definition: _____

   Positive: _____

   N~~egat~~ive: _____

   ~~ver~~ movement

   _____

   _____

   _____

Three to five worksheets per chapter—106 in all!

   _____

   _____

   Negative: _____

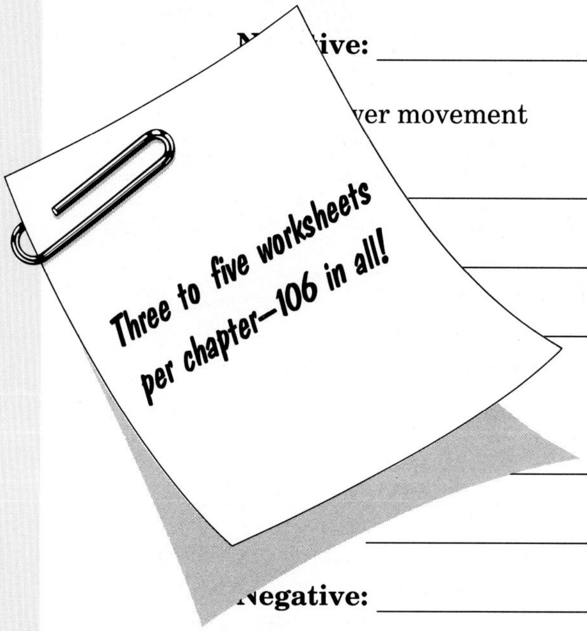

B. Explain how economic issues affected the civil rights movement.

   _____

   _____

   _____

   _____

   _____

CHAPTER 22
Robert F. Kennedy on Martin Luther King, Jr.'s, Death
(Use with Section 3, textbook pages 527–533.)

**Primary Source
Worksheet 44**

Martin Luther King, Jr., was killed by an assassin's bullet on April 4, 1968. That same night, Robert Kennedy broke the news to a crowd in Indiana where he was campaigning for President. Read the excerpts below from his speech.

Martin Luther King dedicated his life to love and to justice for his fellow human beings, and he died because of that effort.

In this difficult day, in this difficult time for the United States, it is perhaps well to ask what kind of a nation we are and what direction we want to move in. For those of you who are black . . . you can be filled with bitterness, with hatred, and a desire for revenge. We can move in that direction as a country, in great polarization—black people amongst black, white people amongst white, filled with hatred toward one another.

Or we can make an effort, as Martin Luther King did, to understand and to comprehend, and to replace that violence, that stain of bloodshed that has spread across our land, with . . . compassion and love.

For those of you who are black and are tempted to be filled hatred and distrust at the injustice of such an act, against all white pe ple, I can only say that I feel in my own heart the same kind of feelin I had a member of my family killed. . . . But we have to make an ef . . . to go beyond these rather difficult times.

We can do well in this country. We will have difficult times. We've had difficult times in the past. We will have difficult times in the future. . . .

But the vast majority of white people and the vast majority of black people in this country want to live together, want to improve the quality of our life, and want justice for all human beings who abide in our land. . . .

In addition to primary sources, eleven readings from noted historians enrich students' study of American history.

From a statement by Senator Robert F. Kennedy on the death of the Reverend Martin Luther King, at a campaign rally in Indianapolis, Indiana, April 4, 1968.

Comprehension

1. According to Kennedy, what choices did the nation have?
2. Why was Kennedy able to identify with blacks' feelings of hatred and distrust at the injustice of King's assassination?
3. Why was Kennedy optimistic about the future despite his sense that there would be difficult times ahead?

Critical Thinking

4. Do you agree or disagree that events in the civil rights movement following King's death bore out Kennedy's optimism?

Cause and Effect: The Civil Rights Movement

Transparency 86

Causes

- Black urbanization
- Religious faith
- Demand for constitutional rights
- Greater media coverage of protests
- Success of African independence movements

The Civil Rights Movement (1954 – 1968)

Effects

- Elimination of legal segregation
- Civil Rights Acts of 1964 and 1968
- Voting Rights Act of 1965
- Creation of affirmative action programs
- Example for other minority groups

A User's Guide provides background information and teaching strategies for each transparency.

Name _____   Date _____

CHAPTER 22   The Civil Rights Movement

(Use with Section 3, textbook pages 527–533.)

Test: Form D
Section 3 Quiz

Write **T** in the blank if the statement is true. If the statement is
false, write **F** in the blank and the corrected statement on the lines
below.

1. _____   The project through which college students from the North spent the summer in
Mississippi registering black voters was called affirmative action.

_____

_____

_____

2. _____   Medgar Evers, a minister of the Black Muslims, advocated black separatism.

_____

_____

3. _____   The Kerner Commission warned that the United States was becoming two
societies—one black, one white.

_____

_____

4. _____   Critics of white backlash believed it was reverse discrimination.

_____

_____

5. _____   Martin Luther King, Jr., campaigned for economic justice as well as civil rights.

_____

_____

_____

CHAPTER MATERIALS

(Textbook pages 515–533)

The following tests and geography worksheets (pages S21–S30) cover material from all three sections of the chapter.

CHAPTER 22   The Civil Rights Movement   **Test: Form A**

Choose the best answer for each item. Completely fill the circle for that answer in the answer column.

Answer Column

1. (A) (B) (C) (D)

2. (A) (B) (C) (D)

3. (A) (B) (C) (D)

4. (A) (B) (C) (D)

5. (A)   (D)

6. (A)

7.

1. Why did blacks in the South feel like second-class citizens during the 1950s? **(A)** Blacks needed passes to cross state lines. **(B)** Federal laws prohibited blacks from voting. **(C)** State laws prohibited blacks from owning land. **(D)** Public facilities were segregated by law.

2. What made segregation legal and established the "separate-but-equal" doctrine in 1896? **(A)** Jim Crow laws **(B)** *Plessy v. Ferguson* **(C)** *Brown v. Board of Education* **(D)** Southern Manifesto

3. Who led legal attacks against segregation with his students from Howard University? **(A)** Emmett Till **(B)** Charles Houston **(C)** Martin Luther King, Jr. **(D)** Medgar Evers

4. What precedent did *Brown v. Board of Education* establish? **(A)** Public facilities could no longer be legally segregated. **(B)** Public schools could no longer be legally segregated. **(C)** Black teachers could not teach in public schools. **(D)** White children could not be bused to school.

5. In the 1950s the White Citizens Council was formed to **(A)** help end the Montgomery bus boycott, **(B)** ease racial tension, **(C)** oppose integration, **(D)** oust Orval Faubus.

6. The law that Rosa Parks challenged required blacks to **(A)** go to segregated schools, **(B)** ride blacks-only buses, **(C)** give up bus seats to whites, **(D)** not assemble on city streets in groups.

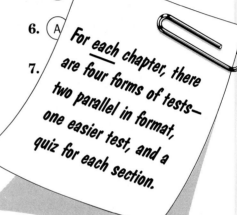

For each chapter, there are four forms of tests— two parallel in format, one easier test, and a quiz for each section.

7. Which letter on the map shows the location of the state where blacks staged a year-long bus boycott as a form of social protest?

8. Which letter on the map shows the location of the state where Roy Bryant was found innocent of killing Emmett Till?

9. Which letter on the map shows the location of the state where Orval Faubus challenged a city law requiring schools to integrate?

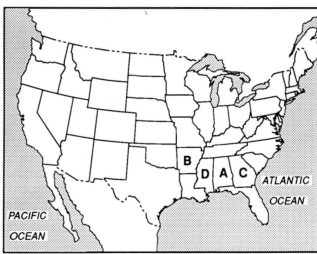

10. How did President Eisenhower respond when Orval Faubus opposed Little Rock's school integration plan? **(A)** He had the state's National Guard surround the public schools. **(B)** He sent federal troops to enforce the law. **(C)** He arrested Governor Faubus. **(D)** He let the state settle the dispute.

11. Why was SNCC formed?   **(A)** to organize the sit-in movement **(B)** to demonstrate more actively for civil rights   **(C)** to oppose integration   **(D)** to promote black separatism

11. (A) (B) (C) (D)

12. All of the following gave hope to the civil rights movement in the years after World War II *except*   **(A)** television coverage of the unfair treatment of blacks,   **(B)** the unity that was possible among blacks in urban areas,   **(C)** the absence of segregationist politicians in the South,   **(D)** religious faith in equality before God.

12. (A) (B) (C) (D)

13. (A) (B) (C) (D)

13. Which of these people opposed segregation?   **(A)** Eugene "Bull" Connor   **(B)** Ross Barnett   **(C)** Medgar Evers   **(D)** George Wallace

14. (A) (B) (C) (D)

15. (A) (B) (C) (D)

14. The purpose of the March on Washington was to   **(A)** demand public housing,   **(B)** urge Congress to pass a civil rights bill, **(C)** protest discrimination in interstate transportation, **(D)** protest welfare cuts.

16. (A) (B) (C) (D)

17. (A) (B) (C) (D)

15. Where did the SCLC launch an all-out nonviolent challenge to segregation in April 1963?   **(A)** Money, Mississippi   **(B)** Little Rock, Arkansas   **(C)** Birmingham, Alabama   **(D)** Washington, D.C.

18. (A) (B) (C) (D)

19. (A) (B) (C) (D)

16. In the summer of 1964, white college students traveled south to **(A)** build public housing,   **(B)** take part in the Kerner Commission,   **(C)** support school segregationists,   **(D)** register black voters.

20. (A) (B) (C) (D)

17. In 1965, the National Guard was called to Watts in order to **(A)** protect black voters,   **(B)** put down a race riot,   **(C)** arrest civil rights marchers,   **(D)** enforce integration in public housing.

18. In 1963 Malcolm X advocated   **(A)** interracial harmony, **(B)** black separatism,   **(C)** white backlash,   **(D)** affirmative action.

19. White backlash in America was a response to all of the following *except*   **(A)** affirmative action,   **(B)** urban riots,   **(C)** segregation,   **(D)** black separatism.

20. The black leader who addressed poverty as a roadblock to freedom for whites as well as blacks was   **(A)** Stokely Carmichael, **(B)** Martin Luther King, Jr.,   **(C)** Malcolm X,   **(D)** Elijah Muhammad.

Essay Questions

Write your essays on a separate sheet of paper.

1. What were some of the inequalities black leaders worked to correct in the 1950s and 1960s? What methods did activists use?

2. Choose two of the black leaders who had an impact in the 1960s. Tell about their ideas and what they accomplished.

Name _____ Date _____

Choose the best answer for each item. Completely fill the circle for
that answer in the answer column.

1. Which of the following was *not* among the goals of American
   blacks in the 1950s?   **(A)** an end to slavery   **(B)** the opportunity
   to vote   **(C)** equal opportunity in employment   **(D)** an end to
   segregated public facilities

2. *Plessy v. Ferguson* made   **(A)** Jim Crow laws illegal,   **(B)** segregation illegal,   **(C)** bus boycotts legal,   **(D)** segregation legal.

3. In the first half of this century, battles to overturn segregation
   laws in the South were fought by   **(A)** Emmett Till,   **(B)** the
   ACLU,   **(C)** the NAACP,   **(D)** Jim Crow.

4. The Supreme Court ruling that public schools could not segre-
   gate by race was known as   **(A)** *Brown v. Board of Education,*
   (B) *Plessy v. Ferguson,*   **(C)** the Southern Manifesto,
   (D) *Eckford v. Faubus.*

5. In the 1950s, what was organized to oppose integration?
   (A) the March on Washington   **(B)** freedom rides   **(C)** the
   Montgomery bus boycott   **(D)** the White Citizens Council

6. Rosa Parks' actions led to the   **(A)** school desegregation movement,   **(B)** founding of the White Citizens Council,   **(C)** March
   on Washington,   **(D)** Montgomery bus boycott.

Each item in Form B tests the same content as the corresponding item in Form A.

1. (A) (B) (C) (D)
2. (A) (B) (C) (D)
3. (A) (B) (C) (D)
4. (A)
5. (A)
6.
10. (A) (B) (C) (D)

7. Which letter on the map shows the
   location of the state where blacks, as
   a form of social protest, did not use
   public transportation in 1955 and
   1956?

8. Which letter on the map shows the
   location of the state where Emmett
   Till was murdered?

9. Which letter on the map shows
   the location of the state where
   President Eisenhower ordered
   federal troops to enforce school
   desegregation?

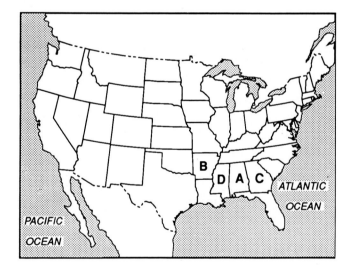

10. Who was Orval Faubus?
    (A) leader of the Montgomery bus boycott   **(B)** first black
    student to attend Little Rock public school   **(C)** Arkansas gover-
    nor who opposed school integration   **(D)** Alabama senator who
    supported civil rights

Answer Column

11. What civil rights group was formed in 1960 to take the nonviolent movement into the streets?   **(A)** Black Panthers
(B) NAACP   **(C)** SNCC   **(D)** SCLC

11. (A) (B) (C) (D)

12. Which of the following gave hope to the civil rights movement in
the years after World War II?   **(A)** the repeal of Jim Crow laws
(B) the conviction of James Meredith   **(C)** the teachings of Ross
Barnett   **(D)** the African independence movement

12. (A) (B) (C) (D)

13. Who worked for the admission of a black student to the University of Mississippi?   **(A)** Medgar Evers   **(B)** Eugene "Bull"
Connor   **(C)** Ross Barnett   **(D)** George Wallace

13. (A) (B) (C) (D)

14. Where was the site of a massive rally in 1963 to urge Congress to
pass a strong civil rights bill?   **(A)** Washington, D.C.
(B) Birmingham   **(C)** New York City   **(D)** Nashville

14. (A) (B) (C) (D)

15. The purpose of the April 1963 civil rights campaign in Birmingham, Alabama, was to   **(A)** promote school busing,   **(B)** urge
Congress to pass civil rights legislation,   **(C)** protest welfare
cuts,   **(D)** launch an all-out nonviolent challenge to segregation.

15. (A) (B) (C) (D)

16. Registering black voters in the Deep South was a task under-
taken by   **(A)** the Democratic Party of Mississippi,   **(B)** the
White Citizens Council,   **(C)** white college students and SNCC,
(D) the Black Panthers.

16. (A) (B) (C) (D)

17. What happened in Watts in 1965?   **(A)** Martin Luther King, Jr.,
delivered his "I Have a Dream" speech.   **(B)** College students
from the North registered black voters.   **(C)** The SNCC organized massive sit-ins.   **(D)** Race riots ravaged the Los Angeles
neighborhood.

17. (A) (B) (C) (D)

18. Malcolm X first attracted attention in the early 1960s as a
spokesman for   **(A)** affirmative action,   **(B)** passive resistance,
(C) white backlash,   **(D)** black separatism.

18. (A) (B) (C) (D)

19. Critics of affirmative action believed it was   **(A)** reverse discrimination,   **(B)** illegal under the Voting Rights Act of 1965,
(C) a result of the black separatists' demands,   **(D)** in conflict
with the recommendations of the Kerner Report.

19. (A) (B) (C) (D)

20. By 1967 Martin Luther King, Jr., was convinced that the major
roadblock to genuine freedom was   **(A)** black separatism,
(B) black power,   **(C)** poverty,   **(D)** reverse discrimination.

20. (A) (B) (C) (D)

Essay Questions

Write your essays on a separate sheet of paper.

1. What were some of the inequalities that black leaders tried to correct in the 1950s and
1960s? What methods did they use?

2. Describe the work of two black leaders in the 1960s. What were their ideas and
accomplishments?

Name _____   Date _____

CHAPTER 22   The Civil Rights Movement   **Test: Form C**

Choose the best answer for each item. Circle the appropriate letter.

1. What made segregation legal and established the "separate-but-equal" doctrine in 1896?
   A *Brown v. Board of Education*
   B Southern Manifesto
   C *Plessy v. Ferguson*
   D White Citizens Council

2. What precedent did *Brown v. Board of Education* establish?
   A Discrimination in housing was illegal.
   B Public schools could no longer be legally segregated.
   C The *Plessy v. Ferguson* ruling was reinforced.
   D White children could no longer be bused to school.

3. Rosa Parks challenged the law that required blacks to
   A remain indoors after dark.
   B ride blacks-only buses.
   C give up bus seats to whites.
   D attend segregated schools.

4. Which letter on the map shows the location of the state in which blacks boycotted city buses as a form of social protest?   **A**   **B**   **C**   **D**

5. Which letter on the map shows the location of the state in which Governor Orval Faubus prevented black students from entering the public school?   **A**   **B**   **C**   **D**

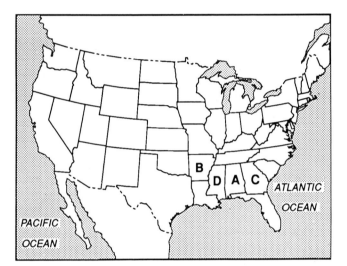

6. SNCC was formed in order to
   A organize the sit-in movement.
   B oppose integration.
   C conduct more visible civil rights demonstrations.
   D promote black separatism.

7. Which of these people opposed segregation?
   A Ross Barnett
   B Bull Connor
   C Medgar Evers
   D George Wallace

8. Malcolm X first became known as a spokesman for
   A civil rights.
   B interracial harmony.
   C passive resistance.
   D black separatism.

Form C is an easier version that allows students to grasp basic concepts.

9. White backlash was a reaction to all of the following *except*
   A affirmative action.
   B reverse discrimination.
   C segregation.
   D urban riots.

10. The black leader who spoke of poverty as a roadblock to freedom for whites and blacks alike was
    A Martin Luther King, Jr.
    B Stokely Carmichael.
    C Malcolm X.
    D Elijah Muhammad.

Essay Questions

1. What were some of the inequalities that civil rights leaders tried to correct in the 1950s and

   1960s? What were some of their social protest tactics?_____

   _____

   _____

   _____

   _____

   _____

   _____

   _____

2. Describe the ideas of Martin Luther King, Jr. What is he remembered for today?_____

   _____

   _____

   _____

   _____

   _____

   _____

   _____

CHAPTER 22
The Civil Rights Movement

Map Practice
Geography Worksheet 43

A. Use the map of United States cities and states on pages 842–843 to locate
the following states and cities. Label these features on the Outline Map on the
back of this page.

States	Mississippi	*Cities*	Atlanta
Kansas	Louisiana	Topeka	Washington, D.C.
Alabama	Virginia	Montgomery	Los Angeles
Arkansas	Florida	Birmingham	New York
North Carolina	California	Little Rock	Baton Rouge
Tennessee	New York	Memphis	Richmond
Georgia	Illinois	Nashville	Chicago

B. Use the Outline Map and the text of Chapter 22 to answer the following
questions.

1. Many historians consider a famous bus boycott to be the beginning of the activist phase of

   the civil rights movement. Where did this boycott take place? _____

2. In which city and state was Dr. Martin Luther King, Jr., born? Where was he
   during a violent response by police to a sit-in? Where was he assassinated w
   a group of striking garbage collectors?

   _____

   _____

3. In which state was there a conflict over integration of the state

   voter registration drive known as "Freedom Summer"? _____

4. In which city did the challenge to segregation lead to a landmark Supreme

   ing for integration of public schools? _____

5. In which city did the Freedom Riders win a major victory when the mayor admitted that it

   was wrong to discriminate against people on the basis of color? _____

6. In which city was black leader Malcolm X assassinated? _____

7. In which community of a large West Coast city did a major riot break out in 1965?

   _____

8. In which state did civil rights marchers walk from one city to the capital to protest denial of

   voting rights? Which cities were they? _____

Map practice for every chapter builds basic map skills.

CHAPTER 22: Outline Map

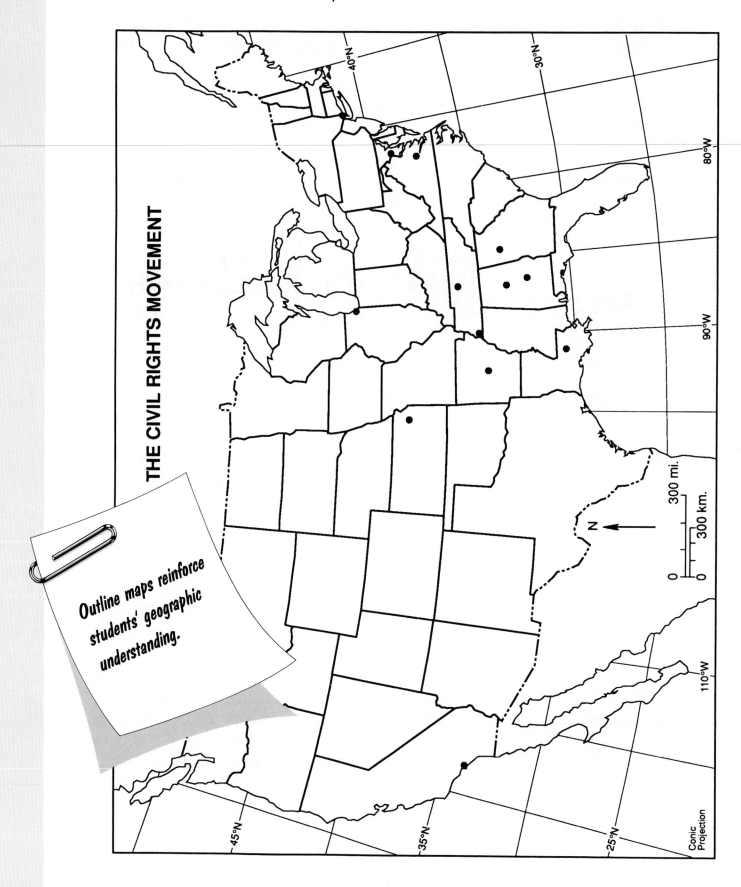

THE CIVIL RIGHTS MOVEMENT

Outline maps reinforce students' geographic understanding.

Name _____   Date _____

CHAPTER 22
School Integration, 1954–1960

In 1954, after years of legal action, the Supreme Court ruled that the "separate but equal" doctrine that underlay racial segregation in the schools was unconstitutional. The Court called for integration "with all deliberate speed." Study the map and answer the questions that follow.

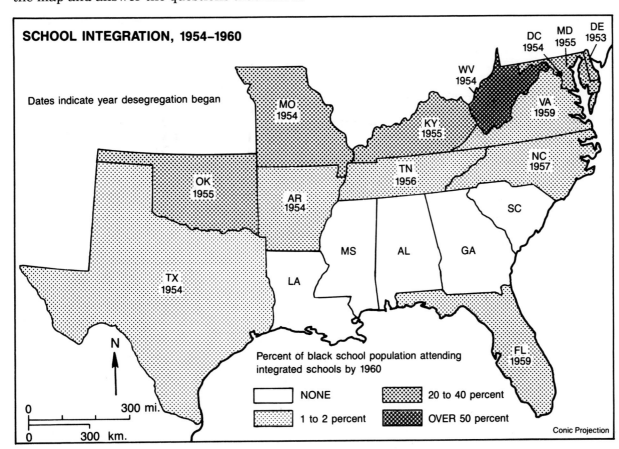

1. Which state on the map had begun to integrate its public schools before the Supreme Court ruling in 1954? In what year did this happen? _____

_____

2. Of the states that integrated their schools before 1960, which were the first following the Court's decision? Which were the last? _____

_____

_____

One Geography Challenge worksheet for every chapter!

3. Which other location, not a state, also began integration in 1954? _____

_____

4. Which states still had not begun to integrate their school systems by 1960? _____

_____

5. Which states had integrated from 20 to 40 percent of their schoolchildren by 1960?

_____

_____

6. What percentage of integration had been achieved by West Virginia by 1960? _____

_____

7. Geographic Theme: Regions   Which states resisted school integration most strongly? Where are these states located? How did the economic and social history of this region influence the practice of segregation?

_____

_____

_____

_____

_____

_____

_____

_____

Challenge activities focus on the five geographic themes.

About the Test Generator

This computerized testing program, offering great flexibility in testing, is fast, easy, and convenient to use. It is available in separate IBM and Macintosh versions.

Among its appealing features are the following:

- *FLEXIBILITY.* The **Test Generator** offers a minimum of 50 test items for each chapter of *History of the United States (Volume 2).* The user may choose the items to include in a test or let the computer randomly select the items.

- *COVERAGE.* The **Test Generator** offers a comprehensive evaluation program for use with *History of the United States (Volume 2).* Test items focus on understanding the content of each chapter and are correlated with the chapter learning objectives listed in the **Teacher's Annotated Edition.**

- *CUSTOMIZATION.* Tests can easily be altered to suit particular classroom needs and objectives. Not only can teachers use existing test items, but they can create their own items or edit existing items, expanding and customizing the Test Bank according to individual needs.

- *PRINTED TEST BANK.* Users can preview all test items in the **Test Generator** by referring to the **Test Bank,** printed pages containing all the test items.

- *EASE OF USE.* No knowledge of computer language or programming skill is necessary to use the **Test Generator.** Full instructions are provided in a **User's Guide.**

A demonstration disk of the **Test Generator** is available. The demonstration disk illustrates the full capabilities of the complete package.

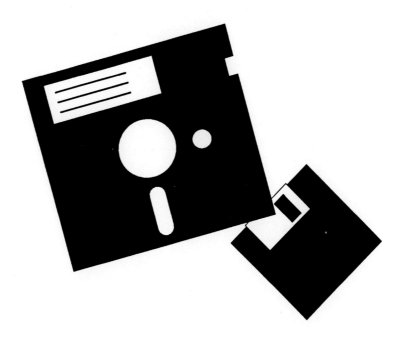